Teacher's Edition

HOLT McDOUGAL

Western World

Christopher L. Salter

HISTORY™

HOLT McDOUGAL

HOUGHTON MIFFLIN HARCOURT

Author

Dr. Christopher L. Salter

Dr. Christopher L. "Kit" Salter is Professor Emeritus of geography and former Chair of the Department of Geography at the University of Missouri. He did his undergraduate work at Oberlin College and received both his M.A. and Ph.D. degrees in geography from the University of California at Berkeley.

Dr. Salter is one of the country's leading figures in geography education. In the 1980s he helped found the national Geographic Alliance network to promote geography education in all 50 states. In the 1990s Dr. Salter was Co-Chair of the National Geography Standards Project, a group of distinguished geographers who created *Geography for Life* in 1994, the document outlining national standards in geography. In 1990 Dr. Salter received the National Geographic Society's first-ever Distinguished Geography Educator Award. In 1992 he received the George Miller Award for distinguished service in geography education from the National Council for Geographic Education. In 2006 Dr. Salter was awarded *Lifetime Achievement Honors* by the Association of American Geographers for his transformation of geography education.

Over the years, Dr. Salter has written or edited more than 150 articles and books on cultural geography, China, field work, and geography education. His primary interests lie in the study of the human and physical forces that create the cultural landscape, both nationally and globally.

ISBN-13 978-0-547-48587-4

1 2 3 4 5 6 7 8 9 10 0914 19 18 17 16 15 14 13 12 11 10

4500264427   ^ B C D E F G

Reviewers

Academic Reviewers

Elizabeth Chako, Ph.D.
Department of Geography
The George Washington University

Altha J. Cravey, Ph.D.
Department of Geography
University of North Carolina

Eugene Cruz-Uribe, Ph.D.
Department of History
Northern Arizona University

Toyin Falola, Ph.D.
Department of History
University of Texas

Sandy Freitag, Ph.D.
Director, Monterey Bay History
    and Cultures Project
Division of Social Sciences
University of California,
    Santa Cruz

Oliver Froehling, Ph.D.
Department of Geography
University of Kentucky

Reuel Hanks, Ph.D.
Department of Geography
Oklahoma State University

Phil Klein, Ph.D.
Department of Geography
University of Northern Colorado

B. Ikubolajeh Logan, Ph.D.
Department of Geography
Pennsylvania State University

Marc Van De Mieroop, Ph.D.
Department of History
Columbia University
New York, New York

Christopher Merrett, Ph.D.
Department of History
Western Illinois University

Thomas R. Paradise, Ph.D.
Department of Geosciences
University of Arkansas

Jesse P. H. Poon, Ph.D.
Department of Geography
University at Buffalo–SUNY

Robert Schoch, Ph.D.
CGS Division of Natural Science
Boston University

Derek Shanahan, Ph.D.
Department of Geography
Millersville University
Millersville, Pennsylvania

David Shoenbrun, Ph.D.
Department of History
Northwestern University
Evanston, Illinois

Sean Terry, Ph.D.
Department of Interdisciplinary
    Studies, Geography and
    Environmental Studies
Drury University
Springfield, Missouri

Educational Reviewers

Dennis Neel Durbin
Dyersburg High School
Dyersburg, Tennessee

Carla Freel
Hoover Middle School
Merced, California

Tina Nelson
Deer Park Middle School
Randallstown, Maryland

Don Polston
Lebanon Middle School
Lebanon, Indiana

Robert Valdez
Pioneer Middle School
Tustin, California

Teacher Review Panel

Heather Green
LaVergne Middle School
LaVergne, Tennessee

John Griffin
Wilbur Middle School
Wichita, Kansas

Rosemary Hall
Derby Middle School
Birmingham, Michigan

Rose King
Yeatman-Liddell School
St. Louis, Missouri

Mary Liebl
Wichita Public Schools USD 259
Wichita, Kansas

Jennifer Smith
Lake Wood Middle School
Overland Park, Kansas

Melinda Stephani
Wake County Schools
Raleigh, North Carolina

Contents

UNIT 1 Introduction to Geography

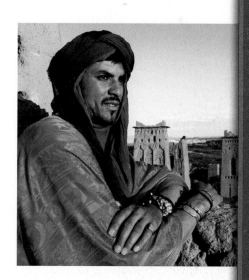

VIDEO
HISTORY **Tornado Alley Twister**

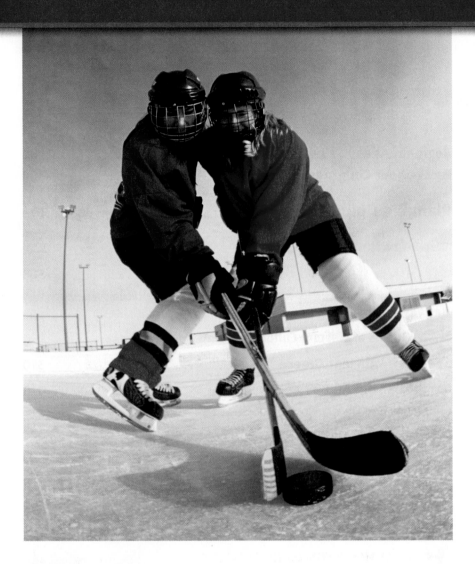

![HISTORY] **VIDEO**
Tech of the Ice Road

VIDEO
Winston Churchill

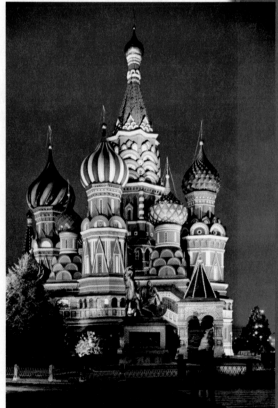

References

Available @

↗ hmhsocialstudies.com

- Facts About the World
- Regions of the World Handbook
- Standardized Test-Taking Strategies
- Economics Handbook

The Idea Book for Educators

classroom resources that
bring the past to life

Live webcasts

HISTORY Take a Veteran to School Day

In addition to premium video-based resources, **HISTORY** has extensive offerings for teachers, parents, and students to use in the classroom and in their in-home educational activities, including:

▶ *The Idea Book for Educators* is a biannual teacher's magazine, featuring guides and info on the latest happenings in history education to help keep teachers on the cutting edge.

▶ **HISTORY Classroom (www.history.com/classroom)** is an interactive website that serves as a portal for history educators nationwide. Streaming videos on topics ranging from the Roman aqueducts to the civil rights movement connect with classroom curricula.

▶ **HISTORY email newsletters** feature updates and supplements to our award-winning programming relevant to the classroom with links to teaching guides and video clips on a variety of topics, special offers, and more.

▶ **Live webcasts** are featured each year as schools tune in via streaming video.

▶ **HISTORY Take a Veteran to School Day** connects veterans with young people in our schools and communities nationwide.

In addition to **HOUGHTON MIFFLIN HARCOURT**, our partners include the *Library of Congress*, the *Smithsonian Institution*, *National History Day*, *The Gilder Lehrman Institute of American History*, the *Organization of American Historians*, and many more. HISTORY video is also featured in museums throughout America and in over 70 other historic sites worldwide.

Inspire students with the story...

HISTORY™ **video** and **interactive games** transport students into what they are studying, providing them with an unforgettable virtual experience.

Essential Question What are the major physical, cultural, and economic features of Mexico?

The **Essential Question,** at the beginning of each chapter, engages students by connecting people, places and events and setting the main purpose for reading.

Compelling stories told with dynamic visuals bring people, places and events to life, grabbing students' interest to stimulate and encourage learning.

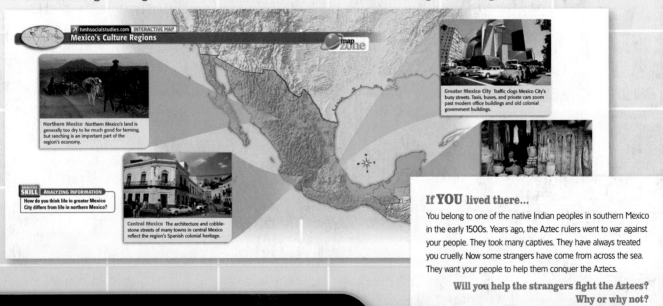

Northern Mexico Northern Mexico's land is generally too dry to be much good for farming, but ranching is an important part of the region's economy.

ANALYSIS SKILL ANALYZING INFORMATION
How do you think life in greater Mexico City differs from life in northern Mexico?

Central Mexico The architecture and cobblestone streets of many towns in central Mexico reflect the region's Spanish colonial heritage.

Greater Mexico City Traffic clogs Mexico City's busy streets. Taxis, buses, and private cars zoom past modern office buildings and old colonial government buildings.

If YOU lived there...
You belong to one of the native Indian peoples in southern Mexico in the early 1500s. Years ago, the Aztec rulers went to war against your people. They took many captives. They have always treated you cruelly. Now some strangers have come from across the sea. They want your people to help them conquer the Aztecs.

Will you help the strangers fight the Aztecs? Why or why not?

HOLT McDOUGAL

Connect to 21st century learners...

Holt McDougal Social Studies programs are organized to help students connect to the content and develop skills. The Student Editions are designed with:

- **Main Ideas, Big Idea, Key Terms and People,** and **Taking Notes** that prepare students to learn with focused success

- **Section sub-headings** tied to the Main Ideas that provide an outline for reading

- **Maps, visuals, charts,** and **documents** that make content accessible to all students

- **21st Century Skills** that require students to apply what they know

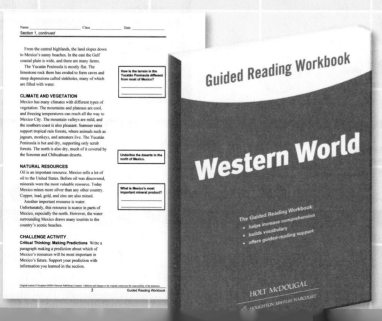

Guided Reading Workbooks (English and Spanish) help guide students as they read, take notes while reading adapted-level summaries, practice skills with an activity, and assess their understanding of content.

Experience
engaging interactive multimedia...

Multimedia Connections, developed in partnership with HISTORY™, provide in-depth coverage of key concepts brought to life in the **Interactive Online Edition** with interactive features, video, primary source documents, and engaging activities.

Power Presentations with Media Gallery DVD-ROM allows teachers to show, edit, and create dynamic multimedia presentations using interactive maps, informative graphics, and fine art and engages students with games and puzzles.

Imagine

easy-to-access, digital content...

The **Interactive Online Edition** is an interactive textbook that links the content of the Student Edition with the world of enhanced features such as activities, interactive maps, and assessments.

Premium Interactive Online Edition contains everything included in the Interactive Online Edition and:

- Additional chapter-based, interactive **Multimedia Connections** with HISTORY™ video, primary sources and maps for both the teacher and the student.

- **eReader files** of the Student Edition are also included for download to any mobile device.

The **Teacher One Stop** includes everything you need to plan, present, and assess—all on one convenient DVD. Easy to use, editable resources include:

- Reading Support
- Assessment
- Teacher Resources
- Chapter Resource Files
- Lesson Plans
- Videos
- Interactive Teacher's Edition
- Enrichment Activities
- Skill Development Activities
- Examview Assessment Suite
- MindPoint Quiz Show
- Calendar Planner
- PuzzleMaker
- State Specific Resources

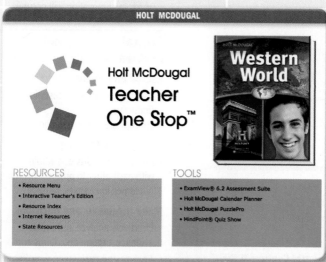

HOLT McDOUGAL

Holt McDougal
Teacher One Stop™

Western World

RESOURCES
- Resource Menu
- Interactive Teacher's Edition
- Resource Index
- Internet Resources
- State Resources

TOOLS
- ExamView® 6.2 Assessment Suite
- Holt McDougal Calendar Planner
- Holt McDougal PuzzlePro
- MindPoint® Quiz Show

HOLT McDOUGAL

Partnership for 21st Century Skills

The Partnership for 21st Century Skills is the leading advocacy organization focused on infusing 21st century skills into education. The organization brings together the business community, education leaders, and policy makers to define a powerful vision for 21st century education to ensure every child's success as citizens and workers in the 21st century by providing tools and resources to help facilitate and drive change.

A listing of the 21st century skills (P21) outlined by the Partnership is provided here. As an Affiliate of the Partnership, Houghton Mifflin Harcourt helps support the teaching of these skills.

Throughout this book skills lessons that can be used to support the instruction of the P21 framework are indicated by this logo.

For more information about the Partnership for 21st Century Skills, visit www.p21.org

Learning and Innovation Skills

Learning and innovation skills increasingly are being recognized as those that separate students who are prepared for a more and more complex life and work environments in the 21st century, and those who are not. A focus on creativity, critical thinking, communication and collaboration is essential to prepare students for the future.

Creativity and Innovation

Think Creatively

- Use a wide range of idea creation techniques (such as brainstorming)
- Create new and worthwhile ideas (both incremental and radical concepts)
- Elaborate, refine, analyze and evaluate their own ideas in order to improve and maximize creative efforts

Work Creatively with Others

- Develop, implement and communicate new ideas to others effectively
- Be open and responsive to new and diverse perspectives; incorporate group input and feedback into the work
- Demonstrate originality and inventiveness in work and understand the real world limits to adopting new ideas
- View failure as an opportunity to learn; understand that creativity and innovation is a long-term, cyclical process of small successes and frequent mistakes

Implement Innovations

- Act on creative ideas to make a tangible and useful contribution to the field in which the innovation will occur

Critical Thinking and Problem Solving

Reason Effectively

- Use various types of reasoning (inductive, deductive, etc.) as appropriate to the situation

Use Systems Thinking

- Analyze how parts of a whole interact with each other to produce overall outcomes in complex systems

Make Judgments and Decisions

- Effectively analyze and evaluate evidence, arguments, claims and beliefs
- Analyze and evaluate major alternative points of view
- Synthesize and make connections between information and arguments

- Interpret information and draw conclusions based on the best analysis
- Reflect critically on learning experiences and processes

Solve Problems

- Solve different kinds of non-familiar problems in both conventional and innovative ways
- Identify and ask significant questions that clarify various points of view and lead to better solutions

Communication and Collaboration

Communicate Clearly

- Articulate thoughts and ideas effectively using oral, written and nonverbal communication skills in a variety of forms and contexts
- Listen effectively to decipher meaning, including knowledge, values, attitudes and intentions
- Use communication for a range of purposes (e.g. to inform, instruct, motivate and persuade)
- Utilize multiple media and technologies, and know how to judge their effectiveness a priori as well as assess their impact
- Communicate effectively in diverse environments (including multi-lingual)

Collaborate with Others

- Demonstrate ability to work effectively and respectfully with diverse teams
- Exercise flexibility and willingness to be helpful in making necessary compromises to accomplish a common goal
- Assume shared responsibility for collaborative work, and value the individual contributions made by each team member

Information, Media and Technology Skills

People in the 21st century live in a technology and media-suffused environment, marked by various characteristics, including: 1) access to an abundance of information, 2) rapid changes in technology tools, and 3) the ability to collaborate and make individual contributions on an unprecedented scale. To be effective in the 21st century, citizens and workers must be able to exhibit a range of functional and critical thinking skills related to information, media and technology.

Information Literacy

Access and Evaluate Information

- Access information efficiently (time) and effectively (sources)
- Evaluate information critically and competently

Use and Manage Information

- Use information accurately and creatively for the issue or problem at hand
- Manage the flow of information from a wide variety of sources
- Apply a fundamental understanding of the ethical/legal issues surrounding the access and use of information

Media Literacy

Analyze Media

- Understand both how and why media messages are constructed, and for what purposes
- Examine how individuals interpret messages differently, how values and points of view are included or excluded, and how media can influence beliefs and behaviors
- Apply a fundamental understanding of the ethical/legal issues surrounding the access and use of media

Create Media Products

- Understand and utilize the most appropriate media creation tools, characteristics and conventions
- Understand and effectively utilize the most appropriate expressions and interpretations in diverse, multi-cultural environments

ICT (Information, Communications and Technology) Literacy

Apply Technology Effectively

- Use technology as a tool to research, organize, evaluate and communicate information
- Use digital technologies (computers, PDAs, media players, GPS, etc.), communication/networking tools and social networks appropriately to access, manage, integrate, evaluate and create information to successfully function in a knowledge economy
- Apply a fundamental understanding of the ethical/legal issues surrounding the access and use of information technologies

Life and Career Skills

Today's life and work environments require far more than thinking skills and content knowledge. The ability to navigate the complex life and work environments in the globally competitive information age requires students to pay rigorous attention to developing adequate life and career skills.

Flexibility and Adaptability

Adapt to Change

- Adapt to varied roles, job responsibilities, schedules and contexts
- Work effectively in a climate of ambiguity and changing priorities

Be Flexible

- Incorporate feedback effectively
- Deal positively with praise, setbacks and criticism
- Understand, negotiate and balance diverse views and beliefs to reach workable solutions, particularly in multi-cultural environments

Initiative and Self-Direction

Manage Goals and Time

- Set goals with tangible and intangible success criteria
- Balance tactical (short-term) and strategic (long-term) goals
- Utilize time and manage workload efficiently

Work Independently

- Monitor, define, prioritize and complete tasks without direct oversight

Be Self-directed Learners

- Go beyond basic mastery of skills and/or curriculum to explore and expand one's own learning and opportunities to gain expertise
- Demonstrate initiative to advance skill levels towards a professional level
- Demonstrate commitment to learning as a lifelong process
- Reflect critically on past experiences in order to inform future progress

Social and Cross-Cultural Skills

Interact Effectively with Others

- Know when it is appropriate to listen and when to speak
- Conduct themselves in a respectable, professional manner

Work Effectively in Diverse Teams

- Respect cultural differences and work effectively with people from a range of social and cultural backgrounds
- Respond open-mindedly to different ideas and values
- Leverage social and cultural differences to create new ideas and increase both innovation and quality of work

Productivity and Accountability

Manage Projects

- Set and meet goals, even in the face of obstacles and competing pressures
- Prioritize, plan and manage work to achieve the intended result

Produce Results

- Demonstrate additional attributes associated with producing high quality products including the abilities to:
  - Work positively and ethically
  - Manage time and projects effectively
  - Multi-task
  - Participate actively, as well as be reliable and punctual
  - Present oneself professionally and with proper etiquette
  - Collaborate and cooperate effectively with teams
  - Respect and appreciate team diversity
  - Be accountable for results

Leadership and Responsibility

Guide and Lead Others

- Use interpersonal and problem-solving skills to influence and guide others toward a goal
- Leverage strengths of others to accomplish a common goal
- Inspire others to reach their very best via example and selflessness
- Demonstrate integrity and ethical behavior in using influence and power

Be Responsible to Others

- Act responsibly with the interests of the larger community in mind

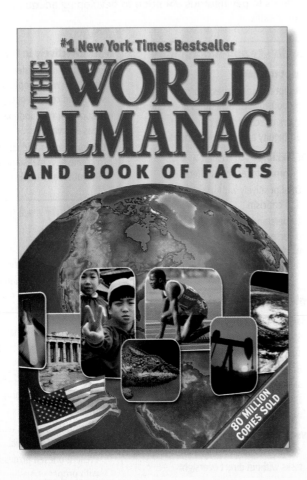

Teaching Readers About Our World Since 1868

The World Almanac® and Book of Facts has been delivering information about our world since the presidency of Johnson—Andrew Johnson! Today, The World Almanac continues this tradition, using its expertise to compile, authenticate, and distribute information in award-winning reference texts.

The World Almanac & World Almanac for Kids

Of course, The World Almanac's reputation is based on *The World Almanac and Book of Facts*. First published in 1868, *The World Almanac and Book of Facts* is America's all-time best-selling reference book, with more than 80 million copies sold. Many middle schoolers also enjoy the colorful, fun *World Almanac for Kids*. Updated annually, these trusted reference sources present valuable geographic and social studies data in an engaging, easy-to-read format that will inspire your students to inquire about the world around them.

On-line Databases

Facts On File delivers award-winning online subscription databases. These easy-to-use, accessible from anywhere databases teach kids about current events, topical issues, and science news. For a free trial visit: www.infobasepublishing. com. Teachers also love the *Issues & Controversies Yearbooks*, which give students a quick understanding of more than 60 of the year's most talked-about topics.

WORLD ALMANAC

The World Almanac and Your Student Edition

Throughout the *Student Edition*, you'll find dozens of tables compiled by the editors of The World Almanac. Drawing on only the most authoritative sources, these tables teach students about the key elements of geography:

- natural resources
- ethnicity
- immigration
- urban and rural areas
- wealth and poverty
- demographics
- climate
- topography
- natural disasters
- religion
- economics and trade
- languages

Students will learn to understand and evaluate graphical and tabular materials. The pictorial presentation will appeal to many students who may be more comfortable learning in this way. These data tables will help all students understand a little better what life might be like in places few of us will ever have the opportunity to visit.

These graphics are also available at **hmhsocialstudies.com**, where they will be updated annually. If you have any suggestions or questions about the tables, please e-mail us at worldalmanac@factsonfile.com.

THE WORLD ALMANAC Facts about the World — Major Eruptions in the Ring of Fire

Volcano	Year
Tambora, Indonesia	1815
Krakatau, Indonesia	1883
Mount Saint Helens, United States	**1980**
Nevado del Ruiz, Colombia	1985
Mount Pinatubo, Philippines	1991

hmhsocialstudies.com

THE WORLD ALMANAC — Facts about the World

World Energy Production

Energy Production (quadrillion Btu)

Legend:
- Coal
- Oil
- Natural gas
- Nuclear power
- Renewable energy

Regions: Asia, Europe*, Middle East, North America, South America, Africa

*includes the former Soviet Union

All countries need energy. Yet, energy resources are not evenly spread across Earth. As a result, energy production differs by region. For example, the Middle East has rich oil deposits. For this reason, the Middle East leads the world in oil production.

Interpreting Graphs
Which world region has the most balanced production of different types of energy?

hmhsocialstudies.com

The Importance of a Geographic Perspective

By Dr. Christopher L. Salter

Dr. Christopher L. Salter is one of the country's leading figures in Geography Education. In the 1980s, he helped found the National Geographic Alliance network to promote Geography Education. In the 1990s, Dr. Salter was Co-Chair of the National Geography Standards Project, a group of distinguished geographers who created Geography for Life in 1994, the document outlining national standards in geography. In 2006 Dr. Salter was awarded Lifetime Achievement Honors by the Association of American Geographers for his transformation of geography education.

Geography is often simply defined as "location, location, location." Geography—and a geographic perspective of the world—deals with far more, however. A geographic perspective is a way of looking at the world that blends an understanding of location, resources use, landscape change, and human use of the world into a way of thinking—a way of seeing how Earth is, how it has been shaped, and why it matters to people. A geographic perspective also provides ideas about how future landscapes should be modified and maintained.

Having a geographic perspective is important for many reasons. For example, a geographic perspective helps us understand the spatial character-istics of the world around us. At the personal and local level, something as basic as finding a good parking spot requires a solid spatial knowledge of a neighborhood. If you know a neighborhood's street network, traffic patterns, and parking laws, you will have a major advantage in finding a great parking space. At the global level, understanding spatial characteristics such as the patterns of human migration and the locations of resources can help leaders and societies make better decisions for the future. As geographers know, societies must not only think in terms of the immediate consequences of our human transformation of the world and its landscapes. They must also look well down the road and think about what might be around each turn.

A geographic perspective can help us better understand how human settlement and patterns of human migration shape the world around us. The engine of such migrations is a blend of human perceptions of place and the human fascination with moving to new places, seeking new futures. For thousands of years, people have been curious about what might exist just over the next mountain or across the seas or beyond a nearby border. Human migration patterns are not driven just by people's objective knowledge. The images people have of various places are shaped by many factors—stories they hear, information from TV, or impressions from exposure to all sorts of media. These varied and often random bits of information help make up people's 'mental maps' of places they may never have seen. People rely on their stored database of knowledge when undertaking the difficult process of migration. Such movement leads to geographic change both at the origin and destination of such geographic shifts. Understanding the origin and significance of our powerful mental maps is also part of a geographic perspective.

Likewise, a geographic perspective can help us think about resources and the location and nature of environmental features that are likely to be modified by human actions. The resources we depend on—that is, the various elements essential for life—are all geography. From the most basic resources of water and farmland to the more complex goods that we associate with city centers, malls, or technology (computers, new medicines, mountain bicycles), all are part of the power of geography. Consider where we get the vital raw materials for energy and the manufacturing of important goods. In the process from the discovery of resources to the final production and selling of goods, the geography of location, transportation, human settlements, population, and popular culture are all at steady interplay.

For example, look at the country-of-origin label (e.g, "Made in China") on your clothes, computer, or cell phone. The distance from your home to the place where those things were manufactured had to be overcome by transport, by international agreements, by some sort of advertising that caused you—or someone—to decide which specific item to buy. Geographic influences were at work throughout every aspect of the creation, shipping, and marketing of those goods. At the same time, geographic images of other places likely stimulated people living in the countryside in places such as China, India, or Mexico to move from rural areas to cities to seek jobs in the very factories that made those goods. Furthermore, American companies often increase their profits by using global trade networks to have goods such as cell phones or T-shirts manufactured by foreign companies. The geographic impact of such decisions might be felt negatively in the United States if factories close and felt positively in places where global trade is booming.

In this textbook, the Five Fundamental Themes and the Six Essential Elements of Geography all work together to influence, shape, and teach us how to understand, maintain—and one hopes, improve—the human, cultural, and geographic landscape. We are all responsible for the intelligent management of the environment and the broader cultural landscapes around us. If you utilize a geographic perspective that focuses on the ways in which humans transform and manage Earth, you will be making a productive use of geography.

A Geographic Perspective

- is a way of looking at the world that blends an understanding of location, resource use, landscape change, and human use of the world.

- is a way of seeing how Earth is, how it has been shaped, and why it matters to people.

- provides ideas about how future landscapes should be modified and maintained.

Geography and Map Skills Handbook

Contents

Throughout this textbook, you will be studying the world's people, places, and landscapes. One of the main tools you will use is the map—the primary tool of geographers. To help you begin your studies, this Geography and Map Skills Handbook explains some of the basic features of maps. For example, it explains how maps are made, how to read them, and how they can show the round surface of Earth on a flat piece of paper. This handbook will also introduce you to some of the types of maps you will study later in this book. In addition, you will learn about the different kinds of features on Earth and about how geographers use themes and elements to study the world.

 hmhsocialstudies.com | INTERACTIVE MAPS

Geography Skills With map zone geography skills, you can go online to find interactive versions of the key maps in this book. Explore these interactive maps to learn and practice important map skills and bring geography to life.

You can access all of the interactive maps in this book through the Interactive Student Edition at

hmhsocialstudies.com

Mapping the Earth
Using Latitude and Longitude

GEOGRAPHY AND MAP SKILLS

A **globe** is a scale model of the Earth. It is useful for showing the entire Earth or studying large areas of Earth's surface.

To study the world, geographers use a pattern of imaginary lines that circles the globe in east-west and north-south directions. It is called a **grid**. The intersection of these imaginary lines helps us find places on Earth.

The east-west lines in the grid are lines of **latitude**, which you can see on the diagram. Lines of latitude are called **parallels** because they are always parallel to each other. These imaginary lines measure distance north and south of the **equator**. The equator is an imaginary line that circles the globe halfway between the North and South Poles. Parallels measure distance from the equator in **degrees**. The symbol for degrees is °. Degrees are further divided into **minutes**. The symbol for minutes is ´. There are 60 minutes in a degree. Parallels north of the equator are labeled with an N. Those south of the equator are labeled with an S.

The north-south imaginary lines are lines of **longitude**. Lines of longitude are called **meridians**. These imaginary lines pass through the poles. They measure distance east and west of the **prime meridian**. The prime meridian is an imaginary line that runs through Greenwich, England. It represents 0° longitude.

Lines of latitude range from 0°, for locations on the equator, to 90°N or 90°S, for locations at the poles. Lines of longitude range from 0° on the prime meridian to 180° on a meridian in the mid-Pacific Ocean. Meridians west of the prime meridian to 180° are labeled with a W. Those east of the prime meridian to 180° are labeled with an E. Using latitude and longitude, geographers can identify the exact location of any place on Earth.

Lines of Latitude

Lines of Longitude

Northern Hemisphere

The equator divides the globe into two halves, called **hemispheres**. The half north of the equator is the Northern Hemisphere. The southern half is the Southern Hemisphere. The prime meridian and the 180° meridian divide the world into the Eastern Hemisphere and the Western Hemisphere. Look at the diagrams on this page. They show each of these four hemispheres.

Earth's land surface is divided into seven large landmasses, called **continents**. These continents are also shown on the diagrams on this page. Landmasses smaller than continents and completely surrounded by water are called **islands**.

Geographers organize Earth's water surface into major regions too. The largest is the world ocean. Geographers divide the world ocean into the Pacific Ocean, the Atlantic Ocean, the Indian Ocean, and the Arctic Ocean. Lakes and seas are smaller bodies of water.

Southern Hemisphere

Western Hemisphere

Eastern Hemisphere

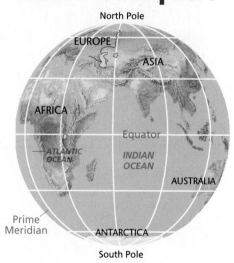

Mapmaking
Understanding Map Projections

A **map** is a flat diagram of all or part of Earth's surface. Mapmakers have created different ways of showing our round planet on flat maps. These different ways are called **map projections**. Because Earth is round, there is no way to show it accurately on a flat map. All flat maps are distorted in some way. Mapmakers must choose the type of map projection that is best for their purposes. Many map projections are one of three kinds: cylindrical, conic, or flat-plane.

Paper cylinder

Cylindrical Projections

Cylindrical projections are based on a cylinder wrapped around the globe. The cylinder touches the globe only at the equator. The meridians are pulled apart and are parallel to each other instead of meeting at the poles. This causes landmasses near the poles to appear larger than they really are. The map below is a Mercator projection, one type of cylindrical projection. The Mercator projection is useful for navigators because it shows true direction and shape. However, it distorts the size of land areas near the poles.

Mercator projection

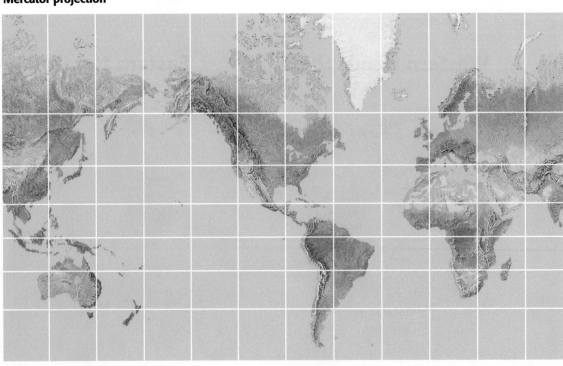

Conic Projections

Conic projections are based on a cone placed over the globe. A conic projection is most accurate along the lines of latitude where it touches the globe. It retains almost true shape and size. Conic projections are most useful for showing areas that have long east-west dimensions, such as the United States.

Paper cone

Conic projection

Flat-plane Projections

Flat-plane projections are based on a plane touching the globe at one point, such as at the North Pole or South Pole. A flat-plane projection is useful for showing true direction for airplane pilots and ship navigators. It also shows true area. However, it distorts the true shapes of landmasses.

Flat-plane projection

Flat plane

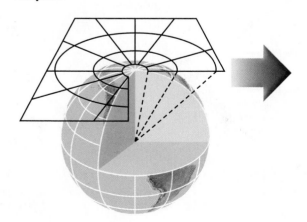

Map Essentials
How to Read a Map

Maps are like messages sent out in code. To help us translate the code, mapmakers provide certain features. These features help us understand the message they are presenting about a particular part of the world. Of these features, almost all maps have a title, a compass rose, a scale, and a legend. The map below has these four features, plus a fifth—a locator map.

❶ Title

A map's **title** shows what the subject of the map is. The map title is usually the first thing you should look at when studying a map, because it tells you what the map is trying to show.

The First Crusade, 1096

North Sea
ENGLAND
HOLY ROMAN EMPIRE
Regensburg
Vienna
ATLANTIC OCEAN
FRANCE
Lyon
Trieste
Genoa
Zadar
Corsica
Rome
Black Sea
Sardinia
Constantinople
SELJUK TURKS
40°N
Mediterranean Sea
Sicily
BYZANTINE EMPIRE
Edessa
Crete
Antioch
Tripoli
HOLY LAND
Acre
Jerusalem

Christian lands, 1095
Muslim lands, 1095
First Crusade, 1096–1099
0   100   200 Miles
0   100   200 Kilometers
Projection: Azimuthal Equal Area

❷ Compass Rose

A directional indicator shows which way north, south, east, and west lie on the map. Some mapmakers use a "north arrow," which points toward the North Pole. Remember, "north" is not always at the top of a map. The way a map is drawn and the location of directions on that map depend on the perspective of the mapmaker. Most maps in this textbook indicate direction by using a compass rose. A **compass rose** has arrows that point to all four principal directions.

❸ Scale

Mapmakers use scales to represent the distances between points on a map. Scales may appear on maps in several different forms. The maps in this textbook provide a **bar scale**. Scales give distances in miles and kilometers.

To find the distance between two points on the map, place a piece of paper so that the edge connects the two points. Mark the location of each point on the paper with a line or dot. Then, compare the distance between the two dots with the map's bar scale. The number on the top of the scale gives the distance in miles. The number on the bottom gives the distance in kilometers. Because the distances are given in large intervals, you may have to approximate the actual distance on the scale.

❹ Legend

The **legend**, or key, explains what the symbols on the map represent. Point symbols are used to specify the location of things, such as cities, that do not take up much space on the map. Some legends show colors that represent certain features like empires or other regions. Other maps might have legends with symbols or colors that represent features such as roads. Legends can also show economic resources, land use, population density, and climate.

❺ Locator Map

A **locator map** shows where in the world the area on the map is located. The area shown on the main map is shown in red on the locator map. The locator map also shows surrounding areas so the map reader can see how the information on the map relates to neighboring lands.

Working with Maps
Using Different Kinds of Maps

As you study the world's regions and countries, you will use a variety of maps. Political maps and physical maps are two of the most common types of maps you will study. In addition, you will use special-purpose maps. These maps might show climate, population, resources, ancient empires, or other topics.

Political Maps

Political maps show the major political features of a region. These features include country borders, capital cities, and other places. Political maps use different colors to represent countries, and capital cities are often shown with a special star symbol.

Caribbean South America: Political

ATLANTIC OCEAN

PACIFIC OCEAN

Barranquilla
Cartagena
Maracaibo
Caracas
Valencia
TRINIDAD AND TOBAGO
Lake Maracaibo
PANAMA
Orinoco River
VENEZUELA
Georgetown
Medellín
GUYANA
Paramaribo
Cayenne
Bogotá
SURINAME
FRENCH GUIANA (FRANCE)
Cali
COLOMBIA
Orinoco River
Magdalena River
Cauca River
ECUADOR
Putumayo River
Río Negro
BR
PERU
Amazon River

⊕ National capital
★ Other capitals
● Other cities

0   100   200 Miles
0 100 200 Kilometers
Projection: Azimuthal Equal-Area

The Indian Subcontinent: Physical

K2
28,251 ft
(8,611 m)

Hindu Kush

Karakoram Range

IRAN

AFGHANISTAN

CHINA

HIMALAYAS

Mount
Everest
29,035 ft
(8,850 m)

PAKISTAN

Chenab River

Sutlej R.

Indus River

NEPAL

BHUTAN

Thar
Desert

Yamuna R.

Gangetic Plain

Tarai

Indus
River
Valley

Chambal R.

Ganges

Brahmaputra River

Tropic of Cancer

BANGLADESH

MYANMAR

Narmada River

Ganges
Delta

INDIA

Gulf of
Khambhat

Godavari River

Ghats

Arabian Sea

Deccan
Plateau

Krishna River

Bay of
Bengal

Western Ghats

Eastern Ghats

Coromandel Coast

Malabar Coast

10°N

ELEVATION

Feet	Meters
13,120	4,000
6,560	2,000
1,640	500
656	200
(Sea level) 0	0 (Sea level)
Below sea level	Below sea level

Gulf of
Mannar

SRI LANKA

INDIAN OCEAN

0   250   500 Miles

0   250   500 Kilometers

MALDIVES

Projection: Albers Equal-Area

Physical Maps

Physical maps show the major physical features of a region. These features may include mountain ranges, rivers, oceans, islands, deserts, and plains. Often, these maps use different colors to represent different elevations of land. As a result, the map reader can easily see which areas are high elevations, like mountains, and which areas are lower.

Special-Purpose Maps

Special-purpose maps focus on one special topic, such as climate, resources, or population. These maps present information on the topic that is particularly important in the region. Depending on the type of special-purpose map, the information may be shown with different colors, arrows, dots, or other symbols.

West Africa: Climate

MAURITANIA

MALI

NIGER

CHAD

SENEGAL

GAMBIA

Niger River

GUINEA

BURKINA FASO

BENIN

NIGERIA

GUINEA-BISSAU

CÔTE D'IVOIRE

SIERRA LEONE

LIBERIA

GHANA

TOGO

Gulf of
Guinea

Equator

ATLANTIC
OCEAN

Climate Types

■ Humid tropical	■ Desert
□ Tropical savanna	■ Steppe

0   400   800 Miles

0   400   800 Kilometers

Projection: Azimuthal Equal-Area

Using Maps in Geography The different kinds of maps in this textbook will help you study and understand geography. By working with these maps, you will see what the physical geography of places is like, where people live, and how the world has changed over time.

Geographic Dictionary

OCEAN
a large body of water

CORAL REEF
an ocean ridge made up of
skeletal remains of tiny sea animals

GULF
a large part of
the ocean that
extends into land

PENINSULA
an area of land that sticks
out into a lake or ocean

BAY
part of a large
body of water
that is smaller
than a gulf

ISLAND
an area of land
surrounded entirely
by water

ISTHMUS
a narrow piece of land
connecting two larger
land areas

DELTA
an area where a
river deposits soil
into the ocean

STRAIT
a narrow body of
water connecting two
larger bodies of water

SINKHOLE
a circular depression
formed when the roof
of a cave collapses

WETLAND
an area of land
covered by
shallow water

RIVER
a natural flow of
water that runs
through the land

LAKE
an inland body
of water

FOREST
an area of densely
wooded land

COAST
an area of land near the ocean

MOUNTAIN
an area of rugged land that generally rises higher than 2,000 feet

VALLEY
an area of low land between hills or mountains

GLACIER
a large area of slow-moving ice

VOLCANO
an opening in Earth's crust where lava, ash, and gases erupt

CANYON
a deep, narrow valley with steep walls

HILL
a rounded, elevated area of land smaller than a mountain

PLAIN
a nearly flat area

DUNE
a hill of sand shaped by wind

OASIS
an area in the desert with a water source

DESERT
an extremely dry area with little water and few plants

PLATEAU
a large, flat, elevated area of land

Themes and Essential Elements of Geography

by Dr. Christopher L. Salter

To study the world, geographers have identified 5 key themes, 6 essential elements, and 18 geography standards.

"How should we teach and learn about geography?" Professional geographers have worked hard over the years to answer this important question.

In 1984 a group of geographers identified the 5 Themes of Geography. These themes did a wonderful job of laying the groundwork for good classroom geography. Teachers used the 5 Themes in class, and geographers taught workshops on how to apply them in the world.

By the early 1990s, however, some geographers felt the 5 Themes were too broad. They created the 18 Geography Standards and the 6 Essential Elements. The 18 Geography Standards include more detailed information about what geography is, and the 6 Essential Elements are like a bridge between the 5 Themes and 18 Standards.

Look at the chart to the right. It shows how each of the 5 Themes connects to the Essential Elements and Standards. For example, the theme of Location is related to The World in Spatial Terms and the first three Standards. Study the chart carefully to see how the other themes, elements, and Standards are related.

The last Essential Element and the last two Standards cover The Uses of Geography. These key parts of geography were not covered by the 5 Themes. They will help you see how geography has influenced the past, present, and future.

5 Themes of Geography

Location The theme of location describes where something is.

Place Place describes the features that make a site unique.

Regions Regions are areas that share common characteristics.

Movement This theme looks at how and why people and things move.

Human-Environment Interaction People interact with their environment in many ways.

6 Essential Elements

18 Geography Standards

1. How to use maps and other tools
2. How to use mental maps to organize information
3. How to analyze the spatial organization of people, places, and environments

I. The World in Spatial Terms

4. The physical and human characteristics of places
5. How people create regions to interpret Earth
6. How culture and experience influence people's perceptions of places and regions

II. Places and Regions

7. The physical processes that shape Earth's surface
8. The distribution of ecosystems on Earth

9. The characteristics, distribution, and migration of human populations
10. The complexity of Earth's cultural mosaics
11. The patterns and networks of economic interdependence on Earth
12. The patterns of human settlement
13. The forces of cooperation and conflict

III. Physical Systems

IV. Human Systems

14. How human actions modify the physical environment
15. How physical systems affect human systems
16. The distribution and meaning of resources

V. Environment and Society

17. How to apply geography to interpret the past
18. How to apply geography to interpret the present and plan for the future

VI. The Uses of Geography

Become an Active Reader

Did you ever think you would begin reading your social studies book by reading about *reading*? Actually, it makes better sense than you might think. You would probably make sure you knew some soccer skills and strategies before playing in a game. Similarly, you need to know something about reading skills and strategies before reading your social studies book. In other words, you need to make sure you know whatever you need to know in order to read this book successfully.

Tip #1

Read Everything on the Page!

You can't follow the directions on the cake-mix box if you don't know where the directions are! Cake-mix boxes always have directions on them telling you how many eggs to add or how long to bake the cake. But, if you can't find that information, it doesn't matter that it is there.

Likewise, this book is filled with information that will help you understand what you are reading. If you don't study that information, however, it might as well not be there. Let's take a look at some of the places where you'll find important information in this book.

The Chapter Opener
The chapter opener gives you a brief overview of what you will learn in the chapter. You can use this information to prepare to read the chapter.

The Section Openers
Before you begin to read each section, preview the information under What You Will Learn. There you'll find the main ideas of the section and key terms that are important in it. Knowing what you are looking for before you start reading can improve your understanding.

Boldfaced Words
Those words are important and are defined somewhere on the page where they appear—either right there in the sentence or over in the side margin.

Maps, Charts, and Artwork
These things are not there just to take up space or look good! Study them and read the information beside them. It will help you understand the information in the chapter.

Questions at the End of Sections
At the end of each section, you will find questions that will help you decide whether you need to go back and re-read any parts before moving on. If you can't answer a question, that is your cue to go back and re-read.

Questions at the End of the Chapter
Answer the questions at the end of each chapter, even if your teacher doesn't ask you to. These questions are there to help you figure out what you need to review.

Tip #2

Use the Reading Skills and Strategies in Your Textbook

Good readers use a number of skills and strategies to make sure they understand what they are reading. In this textbook you will find help with important reading skills and strategies such as "Using Prior Knowledge," and "Understanding Main Ideas."

We teach the reading skills and strategies in several ways. Use these activities and lessons and you will become a better reader.

- First, on the opening page of every chapter we identify and explain the reading skill or strategy you will focus on as you work through the chapter. In fact, these activities are called "Focus on Reading."

- Second, as you can see in the example at right, we tell you where to go for more help. The back of the book has a reading handbook with a full-page practice lesson to match the reading skill or strategy in every chapter.

- Third, we give you short practice activities and examples as you read the chapter. These activities and examples show up in the margin of your book. Again, look for the words, "Focus on Reading."

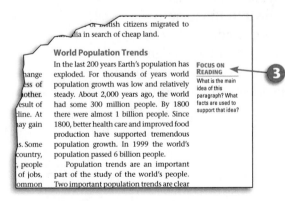

- Finally, we provide another practice activity in the Chapter Review at the end of every chapter. That activity gives you one more chance to make sure you know how to use the reading skill or strategy.

Focus on Reading and Writing

Understanding Main Ideas *Read the paragraph in question 15 below. Then, write out the main idea of the paragraph.*

15. The ancient Greeks were the first to practice democracy. Since then many countries have adopted democratic government. The United Kingdom, South Korea, and Ghana all practice democracy. Democracy is the most widely used government in the world today.

16. **Creating a Poster** Review your notes about the world's cultures, populations, governments, and economies. Then, select a topic for your poster. On large sheet of paper, write a title that identifies your topic. Illustrate your poster with images that support your topic. Write a short caption explaining each image.

Tip #3

Pay Attention to Vocabulary

It is no fun to read something when you don't know what the words mean, but you can't learn new words if you only use or read the words you already know. In this book, we know we have probably used some words you don't know. But, we have followed a pattern as we have used more difficult words.

- First, at the beginning of each section you will find a list of key terms that you will need to know. Be on the lookout for those words as you read through the section. You will find that we have defined those words right there in the paragraph where they are used. Look for a word that is in boldface with its definition highlighted in yellow.

- Second, when we use a word that is important in all classes, not just social studies, we define it in the margin under the heading Academic Vocabulary. You will run into these academic words in other textbooks, so you should learn what they mean while reading this book.

Tip #4

Read Like a Skilled Reader

You won't be able to climb to the top of Mount Everest if you do not train! If you want to make it to the top of Mount Everest then you must start training to climb that huge mountain.

Training is also necessary to become a good reader. You will never get better at reading your social studies book—or any book for that matter—unless you spend some time thinking about how to be a better reader.

Skilled readers do the following:

1. They preview what they are supposed to read before they actually begin reading. When previewing, they look for vocabulary words, titles of sections, information in the margin, or maps or charts they should study.

2. They get ready to take some notes while reading by dividing their notebook paper into two parts. They title one side "Notes from the Chapter" and the other side "Questions or Comments I Have."

3. As they read, they complete their notes.

4. They read like **active readers**. The Active Reading list below shows you what that means.

5. Finally, they use clues in the text to help them figure out where the text is going. The best clues are called signal words. These are words that help you identify chronological order, causes and effects, or comparisons and contrasts.

Chronological Order Signal Words: *first, second, third, before, after, later, next, following that, earlier, subsequently, finally*

Cause and Effect Signal Words: *because of, due to, as a result of, the reason for, therefore, consequently, so, basis for*

Comparison/Contrast Signal Words: *likewise, also, as well as, similarly, on the other hand*

Active Reading

There are three ways to read a book: You can be a turn-the-pages-no-matter-what type of reader. These readers just keep on turning pages whether or not they understand what they are reading. Or, you can be a stop-watch-and-listen kind of reader. These readers know that if they wait long enough, someone will tell them what they need to know. Or, you can be an active reader. These readers know that it is up to them to figure out what the text means. Active readers do the following as they read:

Predict what will happen next based on what has already happened. When your predictions don't match what happens in the text, re-read the confusing parts.

Question what is happening as you read. Constantly ask yourself why things have happened, what things mean, and what caused certain events. Jot down notes about the questions you can't answer.

Summarize what you are reading frequently. Do not try to summarize the entire chapter! Read a bit and then summarize it. Then read on.

Connect what is happening in the section you're reading to what you have already read.

Clarify your understanding. Be sure that you understand what you are reading by stopping occasionally to ask yourself whether you are confused by anything. Sometimes you might need to re-read to clarify. Other times you might need to read further and collect more information before you can understand. Still other times you might need to ask the teacher to help you with what is confusing you.

Visualize what is happening in the text. In other words, try to see the events or places in your mind. It might help you to draw maps, make charts, or jot down notes about what you are reading as you try to visualize the action in the text.

Social Studies Words

As you read this textbook, you will be more successful if you learn the meanings of the words on this page. You will come across these words many times in your social studies classes, like geography and history. Read through these words now to become familiar with them before you begin your studies.

Social Studies Words

WORDS ABOUT TIME

AD	refers to dates after the birth of Jesus
BC	refers to dates before Jesus's birth
BCE	refers to dates before Jesus's birth, stands for "before the common era"
CE	refers to dates after Jesus's birth, stands for "common era"
century	a period of 100 years
decade	a period of 10 years
era	a period of time
millennium	a period of 1,000 years

WORDS ABOUT THE WORLD

climate	the weather conditions in a certain area over a long period of time
geography	the study of the world's people, places, and landscapes
physical features	features on Earth's surface, such as mountains and rivers
region	an area with one or more features that make it different from surrounding areas
resources	materials found on Earth that people need and value

WORDS ABOUT PEOPLE

anthropology	the study of people and cultures
archaeology	the study of the past based on what people left behind
citizen	a person who lives under the control of a government
civilization	the way of life of people in a particular place or time
culture	the knowledge, beliefs, customs, and values of a group of people
custom	a repeated practice or tradition
economics	the study of the production and use of goods and services
economy	any system in which people make and exchange goods and services
government	the body of officials and groups that run an area
history	the study of the past
politics	the process of running a government
religion	a system of beliefs in one or more gods or spirits
society	a group of people who share common traditions
trade	the exchange of goods or services

Academic Words

What are academic words? They are important words used in all of your classes, not just social studies. You will see these words in other textbooks, so you should learn what they mean while reading this book. Review this list now. You will use these words again in the chapters of this book.

Academic Words

advocate	to plead in favor of
affect	to change or influence
agreement	a decision reached by two or more people or groups
aspects	parts
cause	to make something happen
consequences	the effects of a particular event or events
contemporary	modern
contract	a binding legal agreement
development	the process of growing or improving
distinct	clearly different and separate
element	part
establish	to set up or create
facilitate	to make easier
factor	cause
features	characteristics
function	use or purpose
implications	consequences
incentive	something that leads people to follow a certain course of action
influence	change or have an effect on
innovation	a new idea or way of doing something
logical	reasoned, well thought out
neutral	unbiased, not favoring either side in a conflict
policy	rule, course of action
primary	main, most important
process	a series of steps by which a task is accomplished
purpose	the reason something is done
reaction	a response to something
rebel	to fight against authority
strategy	a plan for fighting a battle or war
structure	the way something is set up or organized
traditional	customary, time-honored
vary	to be different

Making This Book Work for You

Studying geography will be easy for you with this textbook. Take a few minutes now to become familiar with the easy-to-use structure and special features of your book. See how it will make geography come alive for you!

Unit

Each unit begins with a satellite image, a regional atlas, and a table with facts about each country. Use these pages to get an overview of the region you will study.

Regional Atlas

The maps in the regional atlas show some of the key physical and human features of the region.

Facts about Countries See which countries are included in each region and learn some important facts about them with these helpful tables.

Chapter

Each regional chapter begins with a preview of what you will learn and a map of the region. Special instruction is also given in reading and skills.

Reading Social Studies

Chapter reading lessons give you skills and practice to help you read the textbook. More help with each lesson can be found in the back of the book. Margin notes and questions in the chapter make sure you understand the reading skill.

Social Studies Skills

The Social Studies Skills lessons give you an opportunity to learn, practice, and apply an important skill. Chapter Review questions then follow up on what you learned.

Section

The section opener pages include Main Ideas, an overarching Big Idea, and Key Terms and Places. In addition, each section includes these special features:

If YOU Lived There . . . Each section begins with a situation for you to respond to, placing you in a place that relates to the content you will be studying in the section.

Building Background Building Background connects what will be covered in each section with what you already know.

Short Sections of Content The information in each section is organized into small chunks of text that you can easily understand.

Taking Notes Suggested online graphic organizers help you read and take notes on the important ideas in the section.

SECTION **2**

History and Culture

What You Will Learn...

Main Ideas

1. Early cultures of Mexico included the Olmec, the Maya, and the Aztec.
2. Mexico's period as a Spanish colony and its struggles since independence have shaped its culture.
3. Spanish and native cultures have influenced Mexico's customs and traditions today.

The Big Idea

Native American cultures and Spanish colonization shaped Mexican history and culture.

Key Terms

empire, p. 147
mestizos, p. 148
missions, p. 148
haciendas, p. 148

hmhsocialstudies.com
TAKING NOTES

Use the graphic organizer online to organize your notes on Mexico's history and culture.

If YOU lived there...

You belong to one of the native Indian peoples in southern Mexico in the early 1500s. Years ago, the Aztec rulers went to war against your people. They took many captives. They have always treated you cruelly. Now some strangers have come from across the sea. They want your people to help them conquer the Aztecs.

Will you help the strangers fight the Aztecs? Why or why not?

BUILDING BACKGROUND Mexico was home to several of the earliest advanced cultures in the Americas. Early farmers there developed crops that became staples in much of North America. Mexico also has valuable minerals, which drew Spanish conquerors and colonists. Spanish culture blended with native Mexican cultures.

Early Cultures

People first came to Mexico many thousands of years ago. As early as 5,000 years ago, they were growing beans, peppers, and squash. They also domesticated an early form of corn. Farming allowed these people to build the first permanent settlements in the Americas.

Early Cultures of Mexico

hmhsocialstudies.com
ANIMATED GEOGRAPHY

Olmec

- The Olmec made sculptures of giant stone heads.
- The heads may have represented rulers or gods.

ACADEMIC VOCABULARY
affect to change or influence

Northern Mexico's closeness to the border has **affected** the region's culture as well as its economy. American television, music, and other forms of entertainment are popular there. Many Mexicans cross the border to shop, work, or live in the United States. While many people cross the border legally, the U.S. government tries to prevent Mexicans and others from crossing the border illegally.

Southern Mexico

Southern Mexico is the least populated and industrialized region of the country. Many people in this region speak Indian languages and practice traditional ways of life. Subsistence farming and slash-and-burn agriculture are common.

FOCUS ON READING
What do you think makes southern Mexico vital to the country's economy?

However, southern Mexico is vital to the country's economy. Sugarcane and coffee, two major export crops, grow well in the region's warm, humid climate. Also, oil production along the Gulf coast has increased in recent years. The oil business has brought more industry and population growth to this coastal area of southern Mexico.

Another place in southern Mexico that has grown in recent years is the Yucatán Peninsula. Maya ruins, beautiful sunny beaches, and clear blue water have made tourism a major industry in this area. Many cities that were just tiny fishing villages only 20 years ago are now booming with new construction for the tourist industry.

Mexico will continue to change in the future. Changes are likely to bring more development. However, maintaining the country's unique regional cultures may be a challenge as those changes take place.

READING CHECK Comparing and Contrasting What similarities and differences exist between greater Mexico City and southern Mexico?

SUMMARY AND PREVIEW Mexico has a democratic government and a growing economy. It also has distinct regions with different cultures, economies, and environments. In the next chapter you will learn about the countries to the south of Mexico.

Section 3 Assessment

hmhsocialstudies.com
ONLINE QUIZ

Reviewing Ideas, Terms, and Places

1. **a. Define** What is the term for the practice of burning forest in order to clear land for planting?
   b. Compare and Contrast How is Mexico's government similar to and different from the government of the United States?
2. **a. Identify** What is an environmental problem found in **Mexico City**?
   b. Make Inferences What conditions in Mexico lead some Mexicans to cross the border into the United States?
   c. Develop If you were to start a business in Mexico, what type of business would you start and where would you start it? Explain your decisions.

Critical Thinking

3. **Finding Main Ideas** Review your notes on Mexico's economy. Then use a chart like this one to show what parts of the economy are important in each region.

Greater Mexico City	Central Mexico	Northern Mexico	Southern Mexico

FOCUS ON WRITING

4. **Describing Mexico Today** Write some details about the four culture regions of Mexico. Which details will you include in your poem?

Reading Check Questions end each section of content so you can check to make sure you understand what you just studied.

Summary and Preview The Summary and Preview connects what you studied in the section to what you will study in the next section.

Section Assessment Finally, the section assessment boxes make sure that you understand the main ideas of the section. We also provide assessment practice online!

Features

Your book includes many features that will help you learn about geography, such as Close-up and Satellite View.

Satellite View
See and explore the world through satellite images.

Satellite View

Close-up
A Market in Guatemala

Villages in Guatemala and all over Central America hold weekly markets. On market day, people come from all around to buy and sell food and other items. The market is also an important gathering spot for the community. Scenes like this one are typical in the region.

The Catholic church is a major influence in most towns.

Patterns on women's clothing are unique to the village where the woman lives.

People often spend all day at the market and need to eat lunch there.

Tourists contribute to the local economy when they buy crafts.

168 CHAPTER 7

Close-up These features help you see how people live and what places look like around the world.

Venice

Venice, in northeastern Italy, is one of the country's most visited tourist attractions. Look at the image of Venice above, taken by an orbiting satellite. Does it look like other cities you have seen? What may not be obvious is that the paths that wind their way through the city are not roads, but canals. In fact, Venice has very few roads. This is because the city was built on islands—118 of them! People move about the city on boats that navigate along the canals. Every year, millions of tourists travel to Venice to see the sights as they are rowed along the scenic waterways.

Contrasting How is Venice unlike other cities you have studied?

Chapter Review

At the end of each chapter, the Chapter Review will help you review key concepts, analyze information critically, complete activities, and show what you have learned.

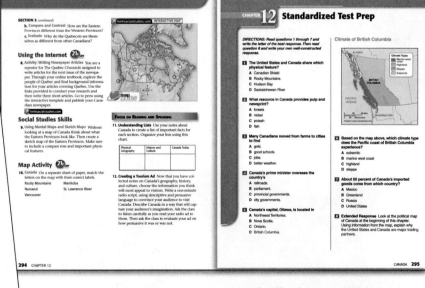

Standardized Test Practice Practice for standardized tests with the last page of each chapter before moving on to another region of the world!

Scavenger Hunt

Are you ready to explore the world of geography? *Holt McDougal: Western World* is your ticket to this exciting world. Before you begin your journey, complete this scavenger hunt to get to know your book and discover what's inside.

On a separate sheet of paper, fill in the blanks to complete each sentence below. In each answer, one letter will be in a yellow box. When you have answered every question, copy these letters in order to reveal the answer to the question at the bottom of the page.

1 According to the Table of Contents, Section 2 of Chapter 18 is called The B r i t i s h Isles. What else does the Table of Contents show?
chapter titles, page numbers

2 The first term listed in the English and Spanish Glossary is a b s o l u t e location. What does this term mean?
a specific description of where a place is located

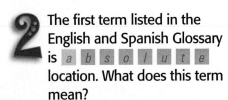

3 The first word of the first Main Idea on page 248 is m a j o r.

4 The first entry listed under "B" in the Index is B a h a m a s.

5 Page 29 includes a Focus on Culture feature called The Midnight S u n. What other features can you find in this book?
Case Study, Geography and History, Close-up, Satellite View

6 Page 549 of the Atlas shows a map of E u r o p e.

7 The Social Studies Skill lesson on page 180 will teach you to interpret a c l i m a t e   g r a p h.

Fact!

One of the most popular foods in the United States was named after a German city. What city was it?

H a m b u r g

Introduction to Geography

Introduce the Unit

Share the information in the chapter overviews with students.

Chapter 1 Geography is the study of the world's people and places. Geographers use many tools to study the main branches of geography—human and physical. They organize their studies by using the five themes and the six essential elements of geography.

Chapter 2 Solar energy, water, and landforms are all part of life on Earth. Life depends on solar energy and on water. The sun's position and movement create the seasons. Processes below and on Earth's surface shape landforms.

Chapter 3 Weather and climate are affected by various forces, including sun, location, wind, water, and mountains. Earth has five major climate zones. Living things and the environment are connected, but changes can upset the balance in an ecosystem. Earth's natural resources have many uses.

Chapter 4 The world's people have many cultures, which differ from place to place and change over time. Geographers study population patterns. They also study the world's governments and economies. Around the world, people are linked by culture and trade in a global community.

Deserts
Huge deserts, such as the Sahara in North Africa, are visible from space and appear yellow and brown.

Oceans
About 71 percent of Earth's surface is covered by vast amounts of salt water, which form the world's oceans.

B INTRODUCTION TO GEOGRAPHY

Unit Resources

Planning

- Differentiated Instruction Teacher Management System: Pacing Guide
- TOS Calendar Planner
- Power Presentations with Media Gallery

Differentiating Instruction

- Differentiated Instruction Teacher Management System: Lesson Plans for Differentiated Instruction
- Differentiated Instruction Modified Worksheets and Tests CD-ROM

Enrichment

- RF: Interdisciplinary Projects
  - A Geographer's World
  Map Your Neighborhood: Forecast the Weather
  - Climate, Environment, and Resources: Diagram an Ecosystem
  - The World's People
  World Governments: Poster Presentation
- Geography, Science, and Culture Activities with Answer Key

Assessment

- PASS: Unit Test
- TOS ExamView Test Generator: Unit Test
- Holt Online Assessment Program, in the Premier Online Student Edition
- Alternative Assessment Handbook

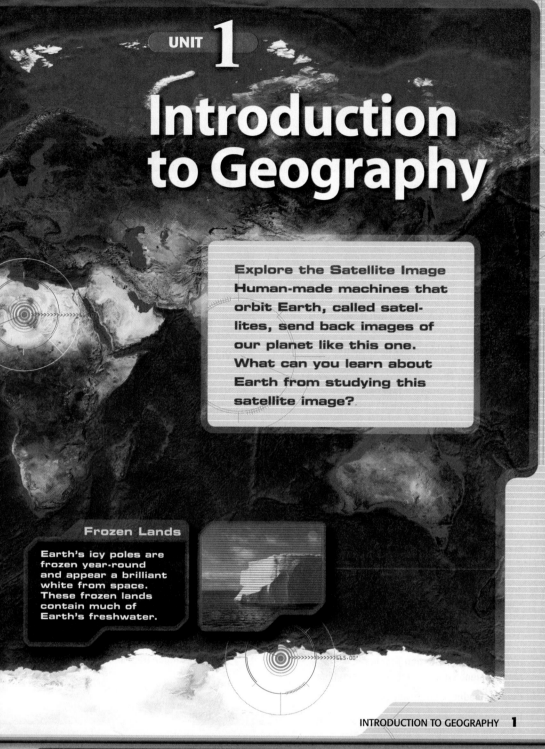

Introduction to Geography

Explore the Satellite Image
Human-made machines that orbit Earth, called satellites, send back images of our planet like this one. What can you learn about Earth from studying this satellite image?

Frozen Lands
Earth's icy poles are frozen year-round and appear a brilliant white from space. These frozen lands contain much of Earth's freshwater.

INTRODUCTION TO GEOGRAPHY **1**

Unit Preview

Explore the Pictures
Point out that the photographs and satellite image show some of Earth's major contrasts—ice and water, desert and forest. Ask students where they think most people on Earth live, and why. *(possible answer—in the temperate regions, where the weather is mild and where there is water and vegetation)*

Connect to the Unit
Activity Hold a Job Fair Have students imagine that they are planning a career in geography. Assign small groups various career options for geographers and have students research the qualifications and possible projects that geographers in each field might work on. Students might find information on the Internet or by interviewing a geographer about his or her work.

Then hold a class job fair. Have students in each group present information about each field of geography. Ask students to narrow down their choices. What aspect of geography interests them the most? Are they more interested in studying human or physical geography? Would they prefer to work in a laboratory, office, or in the field? Would they like to teach geography?

During their study of the unit, have students reconsider their choices, asking themselves whether their preferences or interests have shifted, and if so, to what. **LS Interpersonal**

📝 Alternative Assessment Handbook, Rubric 11: Discussions

Critical Thinking: Interpreting Maps

At Level

Analyze Satellite Technology

1. Point out the relative size of Antarctica compared to the rest of Earth as pictured in this satellite image. Then ask students to find Antarctica on a globe and on a world map. How is Antarctica represented in these sources? Which gives the most accurate representation of the continent?

2. Have students research satellite images of the poles over the last 30 years or so. One source for these images is the Web site of the U.S. Geological Survey. Ask students to write a report based on their findings, including conclusions drawn by scientists about the causes of the shrinking polar ice caps.

3. Have students speculate about what other long-term changes might be tracked by satellites (e.g., urban growth, deforestation, and desertification). Discuss the potential impact of satellite imagery on public policy debates. **LS Visual/Spatial, Verbal/Linguistic**

📝 Alternative Assessment Handbook, Rubrics 21: Map Reading; and 42: Writing to Inform

Answers

Explore the Satellite Image *possible answers—types of landforms, such as deserts, mountains, and plains; distribution of vegetation; proportion of water to land; depth of oceans; extent of ice packs; the fact that there is less vegetation at the equator and none at the poles; the lands between those regions generally have more temperate climates*

1

Chapter 1 Planning Guide

A Geographer's World

Overview	Instructional Resources	
CHAPTER 1 **Essential Question:** How does geography help us understand our world? **Focus on the Essential Question Podcast**	**TOS** **Differentiated Instruction Teacher Management System:** • Instructional Pacing Guides • Lesson Plans for Differentiated Instruction **Guided Reading Workbook** **Resource File:** • Chapter Review • Focus on Reading: Using Prior Knowledge • Focus on Writing: Writing a Job Description • Social Studies Skills: Analyzing Satellite Images **Experiencing World History and Geography**	**TOS** **Calendar Planner** **Power Presentations with Media Gallery** **Differentiated Instruction Modified Worksheets and Tests CD-ROM** **Interactive Skills Tutor CD-ROM** **Student Edition on Audio CD-ROM** **The World's Music Audio Program** **World Outline Maps: Transparencies and Activities** **Video:** Satellites
Section 1: **Studying Geography** **The Big Idea:** The study of geography and the use of geographic tools help us view the world in new ways.	**TOS** **Differentiated Instruction Teacher Management System:** Section 1 Lesson Plan **Guided Reading Workbook:** Section 1 **Resource File:** • Vocabulary Builder: Section 1 • Biography: Claudius Ptolemy • Critical Thinking: The Importance of Geography • Interdisciplinary Project: Map Your Neighborhood	**Daily Bellringer Transparency:** Section 1 **Map Zone Transparency:** High School Soccer Participation
Section 2: **Geography Themes and Essential Elements** **The Big Idea:** Geographers have created two different but related systems for organizing geographic studies.	**TOS** **Differentiated Instruction Teacher Management System:** Section 2 Lesson Plan **Guided Reading Workbook:** Section 2 **Resource File:** • Vocabulary Builder: Section 2 • Geography and History: Migration of Early Humans • Geography for Life: Spatial Perspective	**Daily Bellringer Transparency:** Section 2 **Map Zone Transparency:** The Five Themes of Geography **Map Zone Transparency:** Satellite Images of Italy
Section 3: **The Branches of Geography** **The Big Idea:** Geography is divided into two main branches—physical and human geography.	**TOS** **Differentiated Instruction Teacher Management System:** Section 3 Lesson Plan **Guided Reading Workbook:** Section 3 **Resource File:** • Vocabulary Builder: Section 3 • Literature: *The Wind Makes Dust* by Carl Sagan • Biography: Ellen Churchill Semple • Primary Source: *The Travels of Marco Polo* by Marco Polo • Interdisciplinary Project: Forecast the Weather	**Daily Bellringer Transparency:** Section 3

Review, Assessment, Intervention

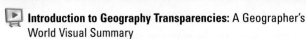 **Introduction to Geography Transparencies:** A Geographer's World Visual Summary

 Spanish Chapter Summaries Audio CD

 Progress Assessment Support System (PASS): Chapter Test

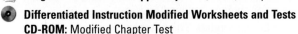 **Differentiated Instruction Modified Worksheets and Tests CD-ROM:** Modified Chapter Test

TOS **ExamView® Assessment Suite (English/Spanish)**

 Alternative Assessment Handbook

 Online Assessment Program, in the Interactive Student Edition

---

 PASS: Section 1 Quiz

 Online Quiz: Section 1

 Alternative Assessment Handbook

 PASS: Section 2 Quiz

 Online Quiz: Section 2

 Alternative Assessment Handbook

PASS: Section 3 Quiz

Online Quiz: Section 3

Alternative Assessment Handbook

Supporting Resources

GLOBAL HISTORY
TEACHER'S GUIDE

HISTORY.

• Multimedia Classroom Global History Series
• Global History Teacher's Guide

Maps and Globes Level F

• Student Workbook
• Teacher's Guide

Social Studies Trade Library Collections

• World Regions Trade Collection
• NCSS Middle School Trade Collection

Geography's Impact

Geography's Impact Video Program

• **Impact of Studying Geography**

For more information or to purchase go to **hmhsocialstudies.com**

Power Presentations with Media Gallery

Power Presentations with Media Gallery are visual presentations of each chapter's main ideas. Presentations can be customized by including Quick Facts charts, images from the text, and video clips.

CHAPTER 1 PLANNING GUIDE

Differentiating Instruction

How do I address the needs of varied learners?
The Target Resource acts as your primary strategy for differentiated instruction.

ENGLISH-LANGUAGE LEARNERS & STRUGGLING READERS

TARGET RESOURCE

Graphic Organizer Transparencies with Support for Reading and Writing

Spanish Resources

Spanish Chapter Summaries Audio CD Program

Teacher One Stop:
- ExamView Assessment Suite, Spanish
- PuzzleView, Spanish

English-Language Learner Strategies and Activities

Additional Resources

Differentiated Instruction Teacher Management System: Lesson Plans for Differentiated Instruction

Resource File:
- Vocabulary Builder Activities
- Social Studies Skills: Analyzing Satellite Images

Introduction to Geography Transparencies:
- A Geographer's World Visual Summary

Student Edition on Audio CD Program

Interactive Skills Tutor CD-ROM

Spanish/English Guided Reading Workbook

SPECIAL NEEDS LEARNERS

TARGET RESOURCE

Differentiated Instruction Modified Worksheets and Tests CD-ROM
- Vocabulary Flash Cards
- Modified Vocabulary Builder Activities
- Modified Chapter Review Activity
- Modified Chapter Test

Additional Resources

Differentiated Instruction Teacher Management System: Lesson Plans for Differentiated Instruction

Guided Reading Workbook

Resource File: Social Studies Skills: Analyzing Satellite Images

Student Edition on Audio CD Program

Interactive Skills Tutor CD-ROM

Graphic Organizer Transparencies with Support for Reading and Writing

ADVANCED/GIFTED AND TALENTED STUDENTS

TARGET RESOURCE

Resource File

The Resource File activities allow students to extend their knowledge of chapter-related places and people and to practice geography skills.
- Focus on Reading: Using Prior Knowledge
- Focus on Writing: Writing a Job Description
- Literature: *The Wind Makes Dust* by Carl Sagan

Additional Resources

Differentiated Instruction Teacher Management System: Lesson Plans for Differentiated Instruction

World History and Geography Document-Based Questions Activities

Geography, Science, and Cultures Activities

Experiencing World History and Geography

Differentiated Activities in the Teacher's Edition

- Using a Graphic Organizer, p. 5
- Describe Pictures, p. 11
- Analyzing Malawi Image, p. 17
- Using Food to Understand Culture, p. 18
- Identifying Main Idea, p. 19

Teacher One Stop™

How can I manage the lesson plans and support materials for differentiated instruction?

With the Teacher One Stop, you can easily organize and print lesson plans, planning guides, and instructional materials for all learners. The Teacher One Stop includes the following materials to help you differentiate instruction:

- **· Interactive Teacher's Edition**
- **· Calendar Planner and pacing guides**
- **· Editable lesson plans**
- **· All reproducible ancillaries in Adobe Acrobat (PDF) format**
- **· ExamView Assessment Suite (English & Spanish)**
- **· Transparency and video previews**

Differentiated Activities in the Teacher's Edition

- Describing Fruit, p. 7
- Creating a Geography Puzzle, p. 9

Interactive Student Edition

Complete online student edition with interactive multimedia support for chapter content assessment and reporting

- Interactive Maps and Notebook
- Standardized Test Prep
- Online Homework Practice and Research Activities
- Current Events
- Chapter-based Internet Activities
- Animated Geography Activities

Differentiated Activities in the Teacher's Edition

- Researching the Channel Tunnel, p. 7
- Compare Monuments, p. 11
- Examine Eratosthenes's Process, p. 18

Essential Question

Introduce the Essential Question

- Tell students that geography is the study of the world, its people, and the landscapes they create. To help us better understand how the world works, geographers study the various human and physical features that make places unique.

- Explain that geographers often use five main themes and six essential elements to identify the most important ideas in the study of geography.

- Describe the differences between physical and human geography. Tell students that other key fields of geography include cartography, hydrology, and meteorology. Challenge students to identify what geographers in each of those fields do.

Focus on Reading and Writing

Reading The Resource File provides a worksheet to help students practice using prior knowledge.

📄 **RF:** Focus on Reading, Using Prior Knowledge

Writing The Resource File provides a worksheet to help students organize and write their job description.

📄 **RF:** Focus on Writing, Writing a Job Description

Key to Differentiating Instruction

Below Level

Basic-level activities designed for all students encountering new material

At Level

Intermediate-level activities designed for average students

Above Level

Challenging activities designed for honors and gifted and talented students

Standard English Mastery

Activities designed to improve standard English usage

LS Learning Styles

CHAPTER 1

A Geographer's World

Essential Question How does geography help us understand our world?

❓ What You Will Learn...

In this chapter you will learn about the field of geography, the study of the world's people and places. You will also learn why people study geography and how they organize their studies.

SECTION 1: Studying Geography 4

The Big Idea The study of geography and the use of geographic tools helps us view the world in new ways.

SECTION 2: Geography Themes and Essential Elements.................................10

The Big Idea Geographers have created two different but related systems for organizing geographic studies.

SECTION 3: The Branches of Geography 16

The Big Idea Geography is divided into two main branches—physical and human geography.

FOCUS ON READING AND WRITING

Using Prior Knowledge Prior knowledge is what you already know about a subject. Before you read a chapter, review the chapter and section titles. Then make a list of what you already know. Later, you can compare your prior knowledge with what you learned from the chapter. **See the lesson, Using Prior Knowledge, on page 516.**

Writing a Job Description Geographers are people who study geography, but what is it exactly that they do? As you read this chapter, you will learn about the work that geographers do. Then you will write a job description that could be included in a career-planning guide.

Studying the World Exploring the world takes people to exciting and interesting places.

2 CHAPTER 1

Introduce the Chapter

At Level

Through a Geographer's Eyes

1. Ask students to imagine that they are geographers studying the area in which they live. Have them write down several things they think a geographer would want to learn about and the methods and tools they might use.

2. Ask volunteers to state a topic or method they wrote down, and why they think it is important to their area. Write the answers on the board or a flip chart.

3. After the answers are written down, ask students if they see any patterns in the kinds of things geographers might be interested in studying.

4. Explain that geography looks at physical and human features, in regions large and small, using specific methods and tools. Encourage students to think about how they might adapt or expand the list as they learn.

LS Verbal/Linguistic, Visual/Spatial

📄 Alternative Assessment Handbook, Rubric 11: Discussions

HISTORY Satellites

↗ hmhsocialstudies.com **VIDEO**

Explore the Pictures

Nepal Some of the world's highest mountains, part of the Himalayas, lie within or border Nepal. Strong rivers run from these mountains to create lush valleys. But clearing mountain lands for new fields or wood for fuel has led to serious problems with erosion.

Analyzing Visuals

What do the girl's clothes tell you about the climate in her country? *The climate is cool—at least for part of the year.*

↗ hmhsocialstudies.com
Teacher Resources

ANALYSIS SKILL **ANALYZING VISUALS**

This village is in the country of Nepal. It rests high in the Himalayas, the highest mountains in the world.

What is the land around the village like? How can you tell that people live in this area?

Human Geography Geography is also the study of people. It asks where people live, what they eat, what they wear, and even what kinds of animals they keep.

Physical Geography Geography is the study of the world's land features, such as this windswept rock formation in Arizona.

3

Critical Thinking: Comparing and Contrasting   At Level

Understanding Location

1. Bring a globe to the front of the class. Ask for a volunteer to locate Nepal, Greenland, and Indonesia. Discuss where each country is in relation to the equator and what the climate might be like there.

2. Ask students to discuss how people's lives might be similar or different in each place due to location. Discuss how features such as mountains and bodies of water might affect people's lives.

3. Organize students into small groups of mixed ability. Have groups discuss the similarities and differences between the climate and features of your home state and those of Nepal, Greenland, and Indonesia.

4. As a class, go over the group's findings.
   LS **Verbal/Linguistic, Visual/Spatial**

   Alternative Assessment Handbook, Rubrics 9: Comparing and Contrasting; and 11: Discussions

Answers

Analyzing Visuals *Answers will vary but may note the snow-capped mountains and terraced landscape; the houses, walkways, and gardens are signs that people live in this area.*

Bellringer

If YOU lived there. . . Use the **Daily Bellringer Transparency** to help students answer the question.

▶ Daily Bellringer Transparency, Section 1

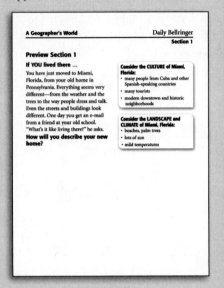

Key Terms and Places

📖 **RF:** Vocabulary Builder, Section 1

Taking Notes

Have students use the graphic organizer online to take notes on the section. This activity will prepare students for the Section Assessment, in which they will complete a graphic organizer that builds on the information using the Critical Thinking Skill: Summarizing.

SECTION 1

Studying Geography

What You Will Learn...

Main Ideas

1. Geography is the study of the world, its people, and the landscapes they create.
2. Geographers look at the world in many different ways.
3. Maps and other tools help geographers study the planet.

The Big Idea

The study of geography and the use of geographic tools helps us view the world in new ways.

Key Terms

geography, *p. 4*
landscape, *p. 4*
social science, *p. 5*
region, *p. 6*
map, *p. 8*
globe, *p. 8*

🔗 hmhsocialstudies.com
TAKING NOTES

Use the graphic organizer online to record details about geography and what geographers do.

If YOU lived there...

You have just moved to Miami, Florida, from your old home in Pennsylvania. Everything seems very different—from the weather and the trees to the way people dress and talk. Even the streets and buildings look different. One day you get an e-mail from a friend at your old school. "What's it like living there?" he asks.

How will you describe your new home?

> **BUILDING BACKGROUND** Often, when you are telling someone about a place they have never been, what you are describing is the place's geography. What the place looks like, what kind of weather it has, and how people live there are all parts of its geography.

What Is Geography?

Think about the place where you live. What does the land look like? Are there tall mountains nearby, or is the land so flat that you can see for miles? Is the ground covered with bright green grass and trees, or is the area part of a sandy desert?

Now think about the weather in your area. What is it like? Does it get really hot in the summer? Do you see snow every winter? How much does it rain? Do tornadoes ever strike?

Finally, think about the people who live in your town or city. Do they live mostly in apartments or houses? Do most people own cars, or do they get around town on buses or trains? What kinds of jobs do adults in your town have? Were most of the people you know born in your town, or did they move there?

The things that you have been thinking about are part of your area's geography. **Geography** is the study of the world, its people, and the landscapes they create. To a geographer, a place's **landscape** is all the human and physical features that make it unique. When they study the world's landscapes, geographers ask questions much like the ones you just asked yourself.

Teach the Big Idea

At Level

Studying Geography

1. **Teach** Ask students the questions in the Main Idea boxes under Direct Teach.

2. **Apply** Have students work in small groups to create a poster describing their community for a geographer who will be studying it. The group should agree on labels for physical and human characteristics. For each label, students should provide visual or written information, indicate known regional or global connections (such as the names of rivers or immigrant groups), and suggest a method of study (make observations).

3. **Review** Have each group present its poster to the class.

4. **Practice/Homework** Have students draw a map of their neighborhood. Tell students to include a compass rose and a legend.
   LS Verbal/Linguistic, Visual/Spatial

📝 Alternative Assessment Handbook, Rubrics 20: Map Creation; and 28: Posters

Geography as a Science

Many of the questions that geographers ask deal with how the world works. They want to know what causes mountains to form and what creates tornadoes. To answer questions like these, geographers have to think and act like scientists.

As scientists, geographers look at data, or information, that they gather about places. Gathering data can sometimes lead geographers to fascinating places. They might have to crawl deep into caves or climb tall mountains to make observations and take measurements. At other times, geographers study sets of images collected by satellites orbiting high above Earth.

However geographers gather their data, they have to study it carefully. Like other scientists, geographers must examine their findings in great detail before they can learn what all the information means.

Geography as a Social Science

Not everything that geographers study can be measured in numbers, however. Some geographers study people and their lives. For example, they may ask why countries change their governments or why people in a place speak a certain language. This kind of information cannot be measured.

Because it deals with people and how they live, geography is sometimes called a social science. A **social science** is a field that studies people and the relationships among them.

The geographers who study people do not dig in caves or climb mountains. Instead, they visit places and talk to the people who live there. They want to learn about people's lives and communities.

READING CHECK Analyzing In what ways is geography both a science and a social science?

What Is Geography?

Geography is the study of the world, its people, and the landscapes they create. To study a place's geography, we look at its physical and human features.

The physical features of Algeria include huge deserts full of tall sand dunes.

Many Algerians live in small villages like this one. The village is one of Algeria's human features.

Together, Algeria's physical and human features create the country's landscape.

ANALYSIS SKILL ANALYZING VISUALS
What is the landscape of this part of Algeria like?

A GEOGRAPHER'S WORLD 5

Differentiating Instruction

At Level

Struggling Readers

1. To help students understand that geography is both a science and a social science, draw the graphic organizer for students to see. Omit the blue, italicized answers.

2. Have each student copy and complete the graphic organizer. When students are finished, review the answers with the group.
LS Verbal/Linguistic, Visual/Spatial
Alternative Assessment Handbook, Rubric 13: Graphic Organizers

Geography

Science — Social Science

Observe | Measure | View satellite images | Visit places people live | Talk to people

Direct Teach

Main Idea

1 **What Is Geography?**
Geography is the study of the world, its people, and the landscapes they create.

Identify What are three ways that geographers can gather scientific data about places? *make observations, take measurements, study satellite images*

Explain Why is geography sometimes called a social science? *It deals with people and how they live.*

Summarize What are some types of work a geographer might do? *study places close-up, such as caves and mountains; study the earth using images taken from a distance; study the lives of people in a certain place*

Predict In what ways could studying geography be useful? *help communities plan change; learn how people protect themselves from weather; see how world regions affect each other*

Connect to English/Language Arts

Geography The word *geography* comes from the Greek *geographein*, meaning "to describe the earth's surface"; "ge" means "earth" and "graphein" means "to write." Can you think of another type of study of the earth that begins with "geo"? *geology*

Answers

Reading Check *Like scientists, geographers gather and study data. Geographers also study people and how they live, like social scientists.*

Analyzing Visuals *small village, huge desert, tall sand dunes*

5

Direct Teach

❷ Looking at the World

Geographers look at the world in many different ways.

Recall What two types of characteristics can define a region? *physical, human*

Contrast What might a geographer study at the local, regional, and global levels? *local—how people in a community or town live; regional—how the landscape affects people's lives, how people in the region interact; global—how people interact all over the world, how people's actions in one place affect other parts of the world*

Identify Cause and Effect What do you think will happen as communication and transportation systems improve? *global relationships will become more common*

 RF: Biography, Claudius Ptolemy

 RF: Teacher's Interdisciplinary Project, Map Your Neighborhood

Looking at the World

Whether they study volcanoes and storms or people and cities, geographers have to look carefully at the world around them. To fully understand how the world works, geographers often look at places at three different levels.

Local Level

Some geographers study issues at a local level. They ask the same types of questions we asked at the beginning of this chapter: How do people in a town or community live? What is the local government like? How do the people who live there get around? What do they eat?

By asking these questions, geographers can figure out why people live and work the way they do. They can also help people improve their lives. For example, they can help town leaders figure out the best place to build new schools, shopping centers, or sports complexes. They can also help the people who live in the city or town plan for future changes.

Regional Level

Sometimes, though, geographers want to study a bigger chunk of the world. To do this, they divide the world into regions. A **region** is a part of the world that has one or more common features that distinguish it from surrounding areas.

Some regions are defined by physical characteristics such as mountain ranges, climates, or plants native to the area. As a result, these types of regions are often easy to identify. The Rocky Mountains of the western United States, for example, make up a physical region. Another example of this kind of region is the Sahara, a huge desert in northern Africa.

Other regions may not be so easy to define, however. These regions are based on the human characteristics of a place, such as language, religion, or history. A place in which most people share these kinds of characteristics can also be seen as a region. For example, most people in Scandinavia, a region in northern Europe, speak similar languages and practice the same religion.

Looking at the World

Geographers look at the world at many levels. At each level, they ask different questions and discover different types of information. By putting information gathered at different levels together, geographers can better understand a place and its role in the world.

ANALYZING VISUALS Based on these photos, what are some questions a geographer might ask about London?

Local Level This busy neighborhood in London, England, is a local area. A geographer here might study local foods, housing, or clothing.

6 CHAPTER 1

Critical Thinking: Identifying Frame of Reference

Using a Globe

1. Bring a globe to the front of the class. Ask students what *global* means. Be sure they understand it refers to the whole planet.

2. Ask what *local* means. Ask for a volunteer to point on the globe to their town or city. Ask the class if everyone agrees this location is correct.

3. Ask what *regional* means. Ask a volunteer to show the region the school community is part of (for example, surrounding cities or states). Have the student explain why this is a region (for example, shared land features). You

may want to have other volunteers cite other shared features.

4. Ask volunteers to show on the globe the local and regional locations for cities in other countries.

5. Lastly, name some physical and human characteristics. Then ask for volunteers to identify a region on the globe that shares those characteristics.

🅛🅢 Verbal/Linguistic, Visual/Spatial

Alternative Assessment Handbook, Rubric 9: Comparing and Contrasting

Answers

Analyzing Visuals *Students' questions should focus on images that refer to the local, regional, and global levels of London.*

Regions come in all shapes and sizes. Some are small, like the neighborhood called Chinatown in San Francisco. Other regions are huge, like the Americas. This huge region includes two continents, North America and South America. The size of the area does not matter, as long as the area shares some characteristics. These shared characteristics define the region.

Geographers divide the world into regions for many reasons. The world is a huge place and home to billions of people. Studying so large an area can be extremely difficult. Dividing the world into regions makes it easier to study. A small area is much easier to examine than a large area.

Other geographers study regions to see how people interact with one another. For example, they may study a city such as London, England, to learn how the city's people govern themselves. Then they can compare what they learn about one region to what they learn about another region. In this way, they can learn more about life and landscapes in both places.

Global Level

Sometimes geographers do not want to study the world just at a regional level. Instead they want to learn how people interact globally, or around the world. To do so, geographers ask how events and ideas from one region of the world affect people in other regions. In other words, they study the world on a global level.

Geographers who study the world on a global level try to find relationships among people who live far apart. They may, for example, examine the products that a country exports to see how those products are used in other countries.

In recent decades, worldwide trade and communication have increased. As a result, we need to understand how our actions affect people around the world. Through their studies, geographers provide us with information that helps us figure out how to live in a rapidly changing world.

READING CHECK **Finding Main Ideas** At what levels do geographers study the world?

Regional Level As a major city, London is also a region. At this level, a geographer might study the city's population or transportation systems.

. London

Global Level London is one of the world's main financial centers. Here a geographer might study how London's economy affects the world.

A GEOGRAPHER'S WORLD **7**

7

Direct Teach

Main Idea

❸ The Geographer's Tools

Maps and other tools help geographers study the planet.

List What are some reasons that geographers might make maps? *show land use and cities; show information such as languages, where ancestors came from, people's activities*

Explain Why are maps not completely accurate in how they show Earth? *not possible to show a round, 3-D area (Earth) perfectly on a flat surface (map)*

Infer What tool would be best for seeing how the sizes of Earth's continents compare to each other? *globe*

▶ Map Zone Transparency: The Geographer's Tools

Info to Know

Modern Mapping *Internet mapping* can mean many things–using software to create and update maps and graphs; gathering data from the Internet to make maps; and using road maps and other kinds of maps found on the Internet to make decisions in daily life. For example, "real time" maps may show wildfire locations in an area so residents can stay updated. Other real time maps may show the flow of traffic or approaching storms, so that commuters can choose routes.

Answers

Analyzing Visuals *the location of a place and the activities of people who live there*

Focus on Reading *Responses will vary, but may include how maps are used on trips.*

The Geographer's Tools

Geographers use many tools to study the world. Each tool provides part of the information a geographer needs to learn what a place is like.

ANALYZING VISUALS What information could you learn from each of these tools?

A geographer can use a globe to see where a place, such as the United States, is located.

High School Soccer Participation

Participation in High School Soccer
- More than 9%
- 5–9%
- 3–5%
- Fewer than 3%
- Data not available

Maps usually give geographers more information about a place than globes do. This map, for example, shows rates of soccer participation in the United States.

The Geographer's Tools

Have you ever seen a carpenter building or repairing a house? If so, you know that builders need many tools to do their jobs correctly. In the same way, geographers need many tools to study the world.

Maps and Globes

FOCUS ON READING
What do you already know about maps and globes?

The tools that geographers use most often in their work are maps and globes. A **map** is a flat drawing that shows all or part of Earth's surface. A **globe** is a spherical, or ball-shaped, model of the entire planet.

Both maps and globes show what the world looks like. They can show where mountains, deserts, and oceans are. They can also identify and describe the world's countries and major cities.

There are, however, major differences between maps and globes. Because a globe is spherical like Earth, it can show the world as it really is.

A map, though, is flat. It is not possible to show a spherical area perfectly on a flat surface. To understand what this means, think about an orange. If you took the peel off of an orange, could you make it lie completely flat? No, you could not, unless you stretched or tore the peel first.

The same principle is true with maps. To draw Earth on a flat surface, people have to distort, or alter, some details. For example, places on a map might look to be farther apart than they really are, or their shapes or sizes might be changed slightly.

Still, maps have many advantages over globes. Flat maps are easier to work with than globes. Also, it is easier to show small areas like cities on maps than on globes.

In addition, maps usually show more information than globes. Because globes are more expensive to make, they do not usually show anything more than where places are and what features they have.

8 CHAPTER 1

Critical Thinking: Interpreting Charts

At Level

Using Charts to Understand Geography

1. Have students copy the chart, then circle one item in each of the first three columns.

2. In the "Example" column, have them write a specific topic of study that incorporates the circled items. For example, a student who circles *science*, *local*, and *map*, might give an example of mapping local wetland areas that are threatened by development.

3. Ask volunteers to share their examples.
   LS Verbal/Linguistic, Visual/Spatial

Alternative Assessment Handbook, Rubric 7: Charts

Causes	Level	Effects	Example
Science	Local	Map	*Example for Science, Local, and Map:*
Social Science	Regional	Globe	
	Global	Satellite image	*Mapping wetland areas in the community that need to be protected from development*
		Computer program	
		Measuring device	
		Notebook	
		Tape recorder	

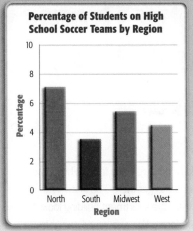

Percentage of Students on High School Soccer Teams by Region

Charts and graphs are also tools geographers can use to study information. They are often used when geographers want to compare numbers, such as the number of students who play soccer in each region of the country.

Maps, on the other hand, can show all sorts of information. Besides showing land use and cities, maps can include a great deal of information about a place. A map might show what languages people speak or where their ancestors came from. Maps like the one on the opposite page can even show how many students in an area play soccer.

Satellite Images

Maps and globes are not the only tools that geographers use in their work. As you have already read, many geographers study information gathered by satellites.

Much of the information gathered by these satellites is in the form of images. Geographers can study these images to see what an area looks like from above Earth. Satellites also collect information that we cannot see from the planet's surface. The information gathered by satellites helps geographers make accurate maps.

Other Tools

Geographers also use many other tools. For example, they use computer programs to create, update, and compare maps. They also use measuring devices to record data. In some cases, the best tools a geographer can use are a notebook and tape recorder to take notes while talking to people. Armed with the proper tools, geographers learn about the world's people and places.

READING CHECK **Summarizing** What are some of the geographer's basic tools?

SUMMARY AND PREVIEW Geography is the study of the world, its people, and its landscapes. In the next section, you will learn about two systems geographers use to organize their studies.

Section 1 Assessment

hmhsocialstudies.com
ONLINE QUIZ

Reviewing Ideas, Terms, and Places

1. **a. Define** What is **geography**?
   b. Explain Why is geography considered a science?
2. **a. Identify** What is a **region**? Give two examples.
   b. Elaborate What global issues do geographers study?
3. **a. Describe** How do geographers use satellite images?
   b. Compare and Contrast How are maps and globes similar? How are they different?

Critical Thinking

4. **Summarizing** Draw three ovals like the ones shown here. Use your notes to fill the ovals with information about geography, geographers, and their tools.

What Geography Is → What Geographers Study → The Geographer's Tools

FOCUS ON WRITING

5. **Describing a Field** Based on what you have learned, what might attract people to work in geography? In your notebook, list some details about geography that might make people interested in working in the field.

Direct Teach

Info to Know

GIS and GPS A computer system that gathers and stores geographic information according to location is called a Geographic Information System (GIS). Maps are one type of information stored on GIS systems. A GIS can also take digital satellite images and other data and turn them into maps.

Another system that helps geographers make maps is the Global Positioning System (GPS). This is a set of satellites orbiting above Earth. With the information from these satellites, people around the world can determine their position 24 hours a day. GPS technology is also used for exploration, navigation, and surveying.

Review & Assess

Close

Ask students how geography's methods and tools can increase understanding of other places.

Review

 Online Quiz, Section 1

Assess

SE Section 1 Assessment
  PASS: Section 1 Quiz
  Alternative Assessment Handbook

Reteach/Classroom Intervention

  Guided Reading Workbook, Section 1

Section 1 Assessment Answers

1. **a.** the study of the world, its people, and the landscapes they create
   b. It involves gathering and studying data.
2. **a.** a part of the world that has common features; Rocky Mountains and Sahara
   b. how people interact all over the world; how actions in one place affect other places
3. **a.** to see what land in an area looks like from above Earth; to make accurate maps
   b. Both show what the world looks like: globes are spheres, like the planet, and can show Earth as it really is; maps are flat, easier to work with, and better for showing small areas.
4. Students' responses should reflect their understanding of section content.
5. possible response—Working in geography might attract people who want to study how the world works and how people live, and who want to help improve human-environment interaction.

Answers

Reading Check *maps, globes, satellite images, computer programs, measuring devices, notebooks, and tape recorders*

Bellringer

If YOU lived there. . . Use the **Daily Bellringer Transparency** to help students answer the question.

▶ Daily Bellringer Transparency, Section 2

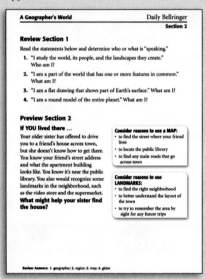

Key Terms and Places

Review with students the high-use academic term in this section.

element part (p. 13)

📖 **RF:** Vocabulary Builder, Section 2

Taking Notes

Have students use the graphic organizer online to take notes on the section. This activity will prepare students for the Section Assessment, in which they will complete a table that builds on the information using the Critical Thinking Skill: Categorizing.

Geography Themes and Essential Elements

What You Will Learn...

Main Ideas

1. The five themes of geography help us organize our studies of the world.
2. The six essential elements of geography highlight some of the subject's most important ideas.

The Big Idea

Geographers have created two different but related systems for organizing geographic studies.

Key Terms

absolute location, *p. 12*
relative location, *p. 12*
environment, *p. 12*

hmhsocialstudies.com
TAKING NOTES

Use the graphic organizer online to take notes on the five themes and six essential elements of geography.

If YOU lived there...

Your older sister has offered to drive you to a friend's house across town, but she doesn't know how to get there. You know your friend's street address and what the apartment building looks like. You know it's near the public library. You also would recognize some landmarks in the neighborhood, such as the video store and the supermarket.

What might help your sister find the house?

> **BUILDING BACKGROUND** Like drivers, geographers have to know where places are in order to study them. An area's location is only one of the aspects that geographers study, though. In fact, it is only one of the five themes that geographers use to describe a place.

The Five Themes of Geography

Have you ever gone to a Fourth of July party with a patriotic theme? If so, you probably noticed that almost everything at the party was related to that theme. For example, you may have seen American flags and decorations based on the flag's stars and stripes. You may have seen clothes that were red, white, and blue or heard patriotic music being played. Chances are that almost everything at the party reflected the theme of patriotism.

Like party planners, geographers use themes in their work. Geographers do not study parties, of course, but they do note common themes in their studies. Just as a party's theme is reflected in nearly every aspect of the party, these geography themes can be applied to nearly everything that geographers study. The five major themes of geography are Location, Place, Human-Environment Interaction, Movement, and Regions.

Teach the Big Idea   At Level

Geography Themes and Essential Elements

1. **Teach** Ask students the questions in the Main Idea boxes under Direct Teach.

2. **Apply** Organize students into groups. Each group will create a brochure introducing the school's buildings and grounds to a new student. Have groups organize their brochures by geography theme and write or draw information about the school related to that theme. Then have students review the essential elements. If an element relates to a theme, students should add that information to their brochures.

3. **Review** Discuss how this project illustrates the "Uses of Geography" element. Display the brochures in the classroom.

4. **Practice/Homework** Have students repeat this project using as a subject their home, yard, or another place of their choosing. **LS Verbal/Linguistic, Visual/Spatial**

   📖 Alternative Assessment Handbook, Rubric 14: Group Activity

The Five Themes of Geography

Geographers use five major themes, or ideas, to organize and guide their studies.

Location The theme of location describes where something is. The mountain shown above, Mount Rainier, is in west-central Washington.

Place Place describes the features that make a site unique. For example, Washington, D.C., is our nation's capital and has many great monuments.

UNITED STATES

Regions Regions are areas that share common characteristics. The Mojave Desert, shown here, is defined by its distinctive climate and plant life.

Human-Environment Interaction People interact with their environments in many ways. Some, like this man in Florida, use the land to grow crops.

Movement This theme looks at how and why people and things move. Airports like this one in Dallas, Texas, help people move around the world.

ANALYSIS SKILL | **ANALYZING VISUALS**
Which of the five themes deals with the relationships between people and their surroundings?

A GEOGRAPHER'S WORLD **11**

Main Idea

❶ **The Five Themes of Geography**

The five themes of geography help us organize our studies of the world.

Explain How are the five themes of geography helpful to geographers? *can be applied to nearly everything geographers study; helps geographers organize their work*

Identify What are some common interactions between people and their environments? *agriculture, fishing, building a place to live*

Analyze Which one of the following does not belong: location, place, human-environment interaction, language, movement, regions? *language—the others are the five themes of geography*

Elaborate Why do you think it is helpful to use themes for studying geography? *possible answer—helps you remember to consider all important aspects; helps to compare and contrast studies of different places by looking at the same topics*

▶ Map Zone Transparency: The Five Themes of Geography

Did you know. . .

The story of the Lincoln Memorial (shown at left in the picture of Washington, D.C.) gives us a window into other places and times. The memorial was built to resemble an ancient Greek temple. It has 36 columns, one for each state at the time of Lincoln's death.

Differentiating Instruction

English-Language Learners
At Level

1. To help students apply their understanding of the themes, have students read a picture caption aloud and describe it.

2. Then ask each student to write two paragraphs, the first starting with, "In this picture you see . . ." and the second starting with "The geography theme this picture shows is . . ." Students should give a reason that links the theme and the picture.
LS Verbal/Linguistic, Visual/Spatial

📖 Alternative Assessment Handbook, Rubric 40: Writing to Describe

Advanced/Gifted and Talented
Above Level
Research Required

1. Have students research a building or monument in Washington, D.C., and one in ancient Greece, Egypt, or Rome. How are they alike? Different?

2. Have students use their research to create a presentation, including artwork, on their findings.

3. Ask students to make a presentation to the class. Have their classmates offer constructive feedback. **LS Verbal/Linguistic, Visual/Spatial**

📖 Alternative Assessment Handbook, Rubric 29: Presentations

Answers
Analyzing Visuals *Human-environment interaction deals most directly with this theme.*

11

① The Five Themes of Geography, *continued*

The five themes of geography help us organize our studies of the world.

Identify Give an example of absolute location. *a street address*

Define What is relative location? *expressing location in general terms, such as the U.S. being south of Canada*

Identify Cause and Effect What are two examples of people's actions that are an effect of their environment? *wearing heavy clothing in cold areas, finding ways to protect homes from river or ocean flooding*

📋 **RF:** Geography and History, Migration of Early Humans

Info to Know

Lots of Land? According to "The World Factbook" at the CIA Web site, the total land area of the world is 148.94 million square kilometers (km). Of that land, only 10.73% is arable (fit for or used for growing crops).

Connect to Math

How Much Land? One kilometer is equal to about 0.62 miles. How many square miles is the total land area of the world? How many square miles of arable land are there? *about 57.5 million square miles of total land; about 6.17 million square miles of arable land*

Answers

Focus on Reading *Students' responses should reflect their understanding of Earth's land, water, climate, plants, and animals.*

Reading Check *location, place, human-environment interaction, movement, regions*

Analyzing Visuals *Students' responses will vary but may include all elements except for The World in Spatial Terms.*

Location

Every point on Earth has a location, a description of where it is. This location can be expressed in many ways. Sometimes a site's location is expressed in specific, or absolute, terms, such as an address. For example, the White House is located at 1600 Pennsylvania Avenue in the city of Washington, D.C. A specific description like this one is called an **absolute location**. Other times, the site's location is expressed in general terms. For example, Canada is north of the United States. This general description of where a place lies is called its **relative location**.

Place

Another theme, Place, is closely related to Location. However, Place does not refer simply to where an area is. It refers to the area's landscape, the features that define the area and make it different from other places. Such features could include land, climate, and people. Together, they give a place its own character.

Human-Environment Interaction

FOCUS ON READING
What do you know about environments?

In addition to looking at the features of places, geographers examine how those features interact. In particular, they want to understand how people interact with their environment—how people and their physical environment affect each other. An area's **environment** includes its land, water, climate, plants, and animals.

People interact with their environment every day in all sorts of ways. They clear forests to plant crops, level fields to build cities, and dam rivers to prevent floods. At the same time, physical environments affect how people live. People in cold areas, for example, build houses with thick walls and wear heavy clothing to keep warm. People who live near oceans look for ways to protect themselves from storms.

12 CHAPTER 1

Movement

People are constantly moving. They move within cities, between cities, and between countries. Geographers want to know why and how people move. For example, they ask if people are moving to find work or to live in a more pleasant area. Geographers also study the roads and routes that make movement so common.

Regions

You have already learned how geographers divide the world into many regions to help the study of geography. Creating regions also makes it easier to compare places. Comparisons help geographers learn why each place has developed the way it has.

READING CHECK **Finding Main Ideas** What are the five themes of geography?

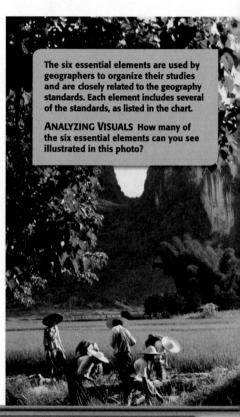

The six essential elements are used by geographers to organize their studies and are closely related to the geography standards. Each element includes several of the standards, as listed in the chart.

ANALYZING VISUALS How many of the six essential elements can you see illustrated in this photo?

Point of View

Standard English Mastery

1. Review with students the five themes of geography and the kind of information each theme helps you learn.

2. Ask students to imagine that they lived in your area several hundred years ago and have somehow ended up in that same spot today. Brainstorm with students about what might seem different.

3. Have each student use standard English to write a journal entry as if they were such a person, describing one day from start to finish. Journal entries should include observations related to each of the five

themes. Encourage students to describe what the person might feel, how he or she might try to make sense of the changes, and possible conflicts or funny situations.

4. Ask for volunteers to read their entries aloud. For each entry, discuss what information relates to each theme. As a class, discuss any necessary corrections to the sentences to align them with standard English usage.

LS **Verbal/Linguistic**

📝 Alternative Assessment Handbook, Rubric 39: Writing to Create

The Six Essential Elements

The five themes of geography are not the only system geographers use to study the world. They also use a system of standards and essential **elements**. Together, these standards and essential elements identify the most important ideas in the study of geography. These ideas are expressed in two lists.

The first list is the national geography standards. This is a list of 18 basic ideas that are central to the study of geography. These standards are listed in black type on the chart below.

The essential elements are based on the geography standards. Each element is a big idea that links several standards together. The six essential elements are The World in Spatial Terms, Places and Regions, Physical Systems, Human Systems, Environment and Society, and The Uses of Geography. On the chart, they are shown in purple.

Read through that list again. Do you see any similarities between geography's six essential elements and its five themes? You probably do. The two systems are very similar because the six essential elements build on the five themes.

The Essential Elements and Geography Standards

The World in Spatial Terms

- How to use maps and other geographic representations, tools, and technologies to acquire, process, and report information from a spatial perspective
- How to use mental maps to organize information about people, places, and environments in a spatial context
- How to analyze the spatial organization of people, places, and environments on Earth's surface

Places and Regions

- The physical and human characteristics of places
- How people create regions to interpret Earth's complexity
- How culture and experience influence people's perceptions of places and regions

Physical Systems

- The physical processes that shape the patterns of Earth's surface
- The characteristics and spatial distribution of ecosystems on Earth's surface

Human Systems

- The characteristics, distributions, and migration of human populations on Earth's surface
- The characteristics, distribution, and complexity of Earth's cultural mosaics
- The patterns and networks of economic interdependence on Earth's surface
- The processes, patterns, and functions of human settlement
- How the forces of cooperation and conflict among people influence the division and control of Earth's surface

Environment and Society

- How human actions modify the physical environment
- How physical systems affect human systems
- Changes that occur in the meaning, use, distribution, and importance of resources

The Uses of Geography

- How to apply geography to interpret the past
- How to apply geography to interpret the present and plan for the future

A GEOGRAPHER'S WORLD **13**

Primary Source

Geography for Life

Recall Where were the six elements of geography first outlined? *in a book called* Geography for Life

Compare What are some ways that the six elements of geography build on the five themes? *The element Places and Regions combines the Place theme and the Regions theme; the element Environment and Society deals with similar issues as the Human-Environment Interaction theme.*

Analyze If a local committee were planning a new park, which theme or element of geography would apply most directly? *the element Uses of Geography*

Review & Assess

Close

Have each student make a bookmark that lists the themes and elements of geography.

Review

↗ Online Quiz, Section 2

Assess

SE Section 2 Assessment

🖺 PASS: Section 2 Quiz

🖺 Alternative Assessment Handbook

Reteach/Classroom Intervention

🖺 Guided Reading Workbook, Section 2

💿 Interactive Skills Tutor CD-ROM

Answers

Analyzing Primary Sources *to find answers to questions about the world, make wiser decisions, solve issues at local and global levels*

Reading Check *world in spatial terms, places and regions, physical systems, human systems, environment and society, uses of geography*

Primary Source

BOOK
Geography for Life

The six essential elements were first outlined in a book called Geography for Life. *In that book, the authors—a diverse group of geographers and teachers from around the United States—explained why the study of geography is important.*

❝Geography *is* for life in every sense of that expression: lifelong, life-sustaining, and life-enhancing. Geography is a field of study that enables us to find answers to questions about the world around us—about where things are and how and why they got there.❞

❝Geography focuses attention on exciting and interesting things, on fascinating people and places, on things worth knowing because they are absorbing and because knowing about them lets humans make better-informed and, therefore, wiser decisions.❞

❝With a strong grasp of geography, people are better equipped to solve issues at not only the local level but also the global level.❞

–from *Geography for Life*,
by the Geography Education Standards Project

ANALYSIS SKILL **ANALYZING PRIMARY SOURCES**

Why do the authors of these passages think that people should study geography?

For example, the element Places and Regions combines two of the five themes of geography—Place and Regions. Also, the element called Environment and Society deals with many of the same issues as the theme Human-Environment Interaction.

There are also some basic differences between the essential elements and the themes. For example, the last element, The Uses of Geography, deals with issues not covered in the five themes. This element examines how people can use geography to plan the landscapes in which they live.

Throughout this book, you will notice references to both the themes and the essential elements. As you read, use these themes and elements to help you organize your own study of geography.

READING CHECK **Summarizing** What are the six essential elements of geography?

SUMMARY AND PREVIEW You have just learned about the themes and elements of geography. Next, you will explore the branches into which the field is divided.

Section 2 Assessment

hmhsocialstudies.com
ONLINE QUIZ

Reviewing Ideas, Terms, and Places

1. **a. Define** What is the difference between a place's **absolute location** and its **relative location**? Give one example of each type of location.
   b. Contrast How are the themes of Location and Place different?
   c. Elaborate How does using the five themes help geographers understand the places they study?
2. **a. Identify** Which of the five themes of geography is associated with airports, highways, and the migration of people from one place to another?
   b. Explain How are the geography standards and the six essential elements related?
   c. Compare How are the six essential elements similar to the five themes of geography?

Critical Thinking

3. **Categorizing** Draw a chart like the one below. Use your notes to list the five themes of geography, explain each of the themes, and list one feature of your city or town that relates to each.

Theme					
Explanation					
Feature					

FOCUS ON WRITING

4. **Including Themes and Essential Elements** The five themes and six essential elements are central to a geographer's job. How will you mention them in your job description? Write down some ideas.

14 CHAPTER 1

Section 2 Assessment Answers

1. **a.** Absolute location is a specific description, such as an address. A relative location describes one place by its relation to another. For example, the U.S. is south of Canada.
   b. location—description of where a point on Earth is; place—physical and human features that define an area/its character
   c. possible answer—It lets them study a place from many points of view and compare it to other places using the same system.

2. **a.** movement

   b. The elements build on the five themes but also expand upon them.
   c. Both are systems geographers use to study the world.

3. Students' charts will vary but should show that they can apply knowledge of each theme to their city or town's characteristics.

4. Student responses should reflect an understanding of each theme and element. Students may mention knowledge of maps and other geographers' tools.

Social Studies Skills

| Chart and Graph | Critical Thinking | Geography | Study |

Analyzing Satellite Images

Learn

In addition to maps and globes, satellite images are among the geographer's most valuable tools. Geographers use two basic types of these images. The first type is called true color. These images are like photographs taken from high above Earth's surface. The colors in these images are similar to what you would see from the ground. Vegetation, for example, appears green.

The other type of satellite image is called an infrared image. Infrared images are taken using a special type of light. These images are based on heat patterns, and so the colors on them are not what we might expect. Bodies of water appear black, for example, since they give off little heat.

Practice

Use the satellite images on this page to answer the following questions.

❶ On which image is vegetation red?

❷ Which image do you think probably looks more like Italy does from the ground?

Vegetation appears green.

Water appears blue.

True color satellite image of Italy

Vegetation appears red.

Water appears black.

Infrared satellite image of Italy

Apply

Search the Internet to find a satellite image of your state or region. Determine whether the image is true color or infrared. Then write three statements that describe what you see on the image.

A GEOGRAPHER'S WORLD **15**

Social Studies Skills Activity: Analyzing Satellite Images

The Many Uses of Satellite Images

`At Level` `Research Required`

1. Review with students why satellite images are useful for geographers. *to make accurate maps, to show changes to regions, to show effects of climate changes*

2. Ask students to brainstorm other possible uses for satellite images. *to predict weather, to track hurricanes, for military purposes* List these on a chart or on the board.

3. Divide students into pairs. Have each pair research one of the uses listed or choose another use with your approval. Students'

research should determine exactly how satellite images are used, their importance, and other significant details.

4. Students should report their findings to the class and include artwork or actual satellite images, if possible.
   LS Visual/Spatial, Verbal/Linguistic
   📋 Alternative Assessment Handbook, Rubric 24: Oral Presentations

Social Studies Skills

Analyzing Satellite Images

Activity Comparing Satellite Images to a Map, Atlas, and Globe

Materials: satellite images of your region (the National Oceanic & Atmospheric Administration Web site— www.noaa.gov/satellites.html—has up-to-date satellite images you or your students can print or view on screen), map(s), atlas(es), and globe(s)

1. Ask students to view the satellite images and to identify as many specific places or features as they can.

2. Have students compare the satellite images to a map and a globe.

3. Ask students to explain how each geographic tool is alike and how each is different. You may want to encourage them to use a chart or other graphic organizer for this step.

4. Have students compare their results with their classmates. Then review the results as a class.
   LS Visual/Spatial, Verbal/Linguistic
   📋 RF: Social Studies Skills, Analyzing Satellite Images
   📋 Alternative Assessment Handbook, Rubric 9: Comparing and Contrasting
   💽 Interactive Skills Tutor CD-ROM, Lesson 6: Interpret Maps, Graphs, Charts, Visuals, and Political Cartoons

Answers

Practice 1. *infrared satellite image;* **2.** *true color satellite image*

Apply *Students' statements should accurately describe the satellite image they chose.*

15

Bellringer

If YOU lived there... Use the **Daily Bellringer Transparency** to help students answer the question.

▶ Daily Bellringer Transparency, Section 3

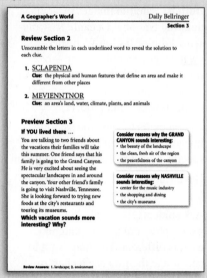

Key Terms and Places

📖 **RF:** Vocabulary Builder, Section 3

Taking Notes

Have students use the graphic organizer online to take notes on the section. This activity will prepare students for the Section Assessment, in which they will complete a graphic organizer that builds on the information using the Critical Thinking Skill: Comparing and Contrasting.

The Branches of Geography

What You Will Learn...

Main Ideas

1. Physical geography is the study of landforms, water bodies, and other physical features.
2. Human geography focuses on people, their cultures, and the landscapes they create.
3. Other branches of geography examine specific aspects of the physical or human world.

The Big Idea

Geography is divided into two main branches—physical and human geography.

Key Terms

physical geography, *p. 16*
human geography, *p. 18*
cartography, *p. 19*
meteorology, *p. 20*

hmhsocialstudies.com
TAKING NOTES

Use the graphic organizer online to take notes on the branches of geography.

If YOU lived there...

You are talking to two friends about the vacations their families will take this summer. One friend says that his family is going to the Grand Canyon. He is very excited about seeing the spectacular landscapes in and around the canyon. Your other friend's family is going to visit Nashville, Tennessee. She is looking forward to trying new foods at the city's restaurants and touring its museums.

Which vacation sounds more interesting? Why?

BUILDING BACKGROUND Geography is the study of the world and its features. Some features are physical, like the Grand Canyon. Others are human, like restaurants and museums. The main branches of geography focus on these types of features.

Physical Geography

Think about a jigsaw puzzle. Seen as a whole, the puzzle shows a pretty or interesting picture. To see that picture, though, you have to put all the puzzle pieces together. Before you assemble them, the pieces do not give you a clear idea of what the puzzle will look like when it is assembled. After all, each piece contains only a tiny portion of the overall image.

In many ways, geography is like a huge puzzle. It is made up of many branches, or divisions. Each of these branches focuses on a single part of the world. Viewed separately, none of these branches shows us the whole world. Together, however, the many branches of geography improve our understanding of our planet and its people.

Geography's two main branches are physical geography and human geography. The first branch, **physical geography**, is the study of the world's physical features—its landforms, bodies of water, climates, soils, and plants. Every place in the world has its own unique combination of these features.

Teach the Big Idea

At Level

The Branches of Geography

1. **Teach** Ask students the questions in the Main Idea boxes under Direct Teach.

2. **Apply** Have students draw or write a detailed depiction of a feature—physical or human—of the town or city where the school is located. Have each student show or read his or her work to the class.

3. **Review** As a class, create a collage of all the works. Decide on the collage design as a class. For example, you could arrange the pictures according to location.

4. **Practice/Homework** Have students write from an ant's eye view about a baseball field or other spot with physical and human features. Tell students to include details about how the ant puts the pieces of the "big picture" together as it travels over the area.
   🔲 **Verbal/Linguistic, Visual/Spatial**

   📋 Alternative Assessment Handbook, Rubrics 8: Collages; and 40: Writing to Describe

Physical Geography	Human Geography
The study of Earth's physical features, including rivers, mountains, oceans, weather, and other features, such as Victoria Falls in southern Africa	The study of Earth's people, including their ways of life, homes, cities, beliefs, and customs, like those of these children in Malawi, a country in central Africa

Geography

The study of Earth's physical and cultural features

The Physical World

What does it mean to say that physical geography is the study of physical features? Physical geographers want to know all about the different features found on our planet. They want to know where plains and mountain ranges are, how rivers flow across the landscape, and why different amounts of rain fall from place to place.

More importantly, however, physical geographers want to know what causes the different shapes on Earth. They want to know why mountain ranges rise up where they do and what causes rivers to flow in certain directions. They also want to know why various parts of the world have very different weather and climate patterns.

To answer these questions, physical geographers take detailed measurements. They study the heights of mountains and the temperatures of places. To track any changes that occur over time, physical geographers keep careful records of all the information they collect.

Uses of Physical Geography

Earth is made up of hundreds of types of physical features. Without a complete understanding of what these features are and the effect they have on the world's people and landscapes, we cannot fully understand our world. This is the major reason that geographers study the physical world—to learn how it works.

There are also other, more specific reasons for studying physical geography, though. Studying the changes that take place on our planet can help us prepare to live with those changes. For example, knowing what causes volcanoes to erupt can help us predict eruptions. Knowing what causes terrible storms can help us prepare for them. In this way, the work of physical geographers helps us adjust to the dangers and changes of our world.

READING CHECK **Analyzing** What are some features in your area that a physical geographer might study?

A GEOGRAPHER'S WORLD **17**

Main Idea

❶ Physical Geography

Physical geography is the study of landforms, water bodies, and other physical features.

Compare How is the study of geography similar to pieces of a jigsaw puzzle? *Viewed separately, no branch shows the whole world; viewed together, the different branches improve understanding of the planet and its people.*

Recall What might geographers measure to learn about the world? Name two elements or features. *mountain heights, temperatures*

Infer How could the study of physical geography help people who live in an area at risk for tsunamis? *understand what conditions may cause them, recognize the signs that one is coming, make changes and plans to minimize its effects*

📖 RF: Literature, *The Wind Makes Dust* by Carl Sagan

Did you know. . .

Victoria Falls, on the Zambezi River bordering Zambia and Zimbabwe, is one of the seven natural wonders of the world. It is the largest known "curtain of water." Here, the mild river, about 2 km (1.2 miles) wide, plummets into a narrow gorge about 100 m (328 feet) deep, causing a thunderous roar and a towering spray. In the 1850s, Scottish missionary and physician David Livingstone reported the falls to the outside world. He named them for Queen Victoria. The local people call the falls "Mosi-oa-Tunya" which means "smoke that thunders."

Answers

Reading Check *Answers will vary, but should include features related to land, soils or plants, weather or climate, and any bodies of water in your area.*

❷ Human Geography

Human geography focuses on people, their cultures, and the landscapes they create.

Recall What are some needs common to all people? *food, water, shelter, dealing with others*

Draw Conclusions Why do human geographers often specialize in a smaller area of study? *People's lives are so different that no one can study every aspect.*

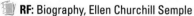 **RF:** Biography, Ellen Churchill Semple

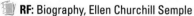 **RF:** Primary Source, *The Travels of Marco Polo*

Linking to Today

Helping Others The work of Heifer International (www.heifer.org), an organization whose mission is to end hunger, is an example of human geography in practice. The organization donates animals so that people can work the land and improve their situation. "Heifer's Cornerstones" include: the community deciding together what animals and help they want, training people to feed and shelter the animals, and having people pass on offspring of animals so others can benefit.

Answers

Biography *He made many contributions to the field, including being the first to use the term* geography.

Reading Check *people, communities, and landscapes*

18

Eratosthenes
(c. 276–c. 194 BC)

Did you know that geography is over 2,000 years old? Actually, the study of the world is even older than that, but the first person ever to use the word *geography* lived then. His name was Eratosthenes (er-uh-TAHS-thuh-neez), and he was a Greek scientist and librarian. With no modern instruments of any kind, Eratosthenes figured out how large Earth is. He also drew a map that showed all of the lands that the Greeks knew about. Because of his many contributions to the field, Eratosthenes has been called the Father of Geography.

Generalizing Why is Eratosthenes called the Father of Geography?

Human Geography

The physical world is only one part of the puzzle of geography. People are also part of the world. **Human geography** is the study of the world's people, communities, and landscapes. It is the second major branch of geography.

The Human World

Put simply, human geographers study the world's people, past and present. They look at where people live and why. They ask why some parts of the world have more people than others, and why some places have almost no people at all.

Human geographers also study what people do. What jobs do people have? What crops do they grow? What makes them move from place to place? These are the types of questions that geographers ask about people around the world.

Because people's lives are so different around the world, no one can study every aspect of human geography. As a result, human geographers often specialize in a smaller area of study. Some may choose to study only the people and landscapes in a certain region. For example, a geographer may study only the lives of people who live in West Africa.

Other geographers choose not to limit their studies to one place. Instead, they may choose to examine only one aspect of people's lives. For example, a geographer could study only economics, politics, or city life. However, that geographer may compare economic patterns in various parts of the world to see how they differ.

Uses of Human Geography

Although every culture is different, people around the world have some common needs. All people need food and water. All people need shelter. All people need to deal with other people in order to survive.

Human geographers study how people in various places address their needs. They look at the foods people eat and the types of governments they form. The knowledge they gather can help us better understand people in other cultures. Sometimes this type of understanding can help people improve their landscapes and situations.

On a smaller scale, human geographers can help people design their cities and towns. By understanding where people go and what they need, geographers can help city planners place roads, shopping malls, and schools. Geographers also study the effect people have on the world. As a result, they often work with private groups and government agencies who want to protect the environment.

READING CHECK **Summarizing** What do human geographers study?

Differentiating Instruction

English-Language Learners
At Level
Standard English Mastery

1. Explain that studying what people eat can help us understand other people and cultures.

2. On the board, make four columns: *animal*, *vegetable*, *fruit*, and *grain*. Ask volunteers to tell one food they ate the day before and which category that food fits.

3. Have students use standard English to write two sentences explaining how the foods tell about their own cultures.
LS Verbal/Linguistic

Alternative Assessment Handbook, Rubric 38: Writing to Classify

Advanced/Gifted and Talented
Above Level
Research Required

1. Have students do Internet or library research to learn how Eratosthenes determined Earth's size. Ask them to organize their findings about his process using a graphic organizer or chart.

2. Have students create a labeled poster or 3-D display to explain the process Eratosthenes used. **LS Logical/Mathematical, Verbal/Linguistic**

Alternative Assessment Handbook, Rubrics 28: Posters, and 30: Research

Other Fields of Geography

Physical geography and human geography are the two largest branches of the subject, but they are not the only ones. Many other fields of geography exist, each one devoted to studying one aspect of the world.

Most of these fields are smaller, more specialized areas of either physical or human geography. For example, economic geography—the study of how people make and spend money—is a branch of human geography. Another specialized branch of human geography is urban geography, the study of cities and how people live in them. Physical geography also includes many fields, such as the study of climates. Other fields of physical geography are the studies of soils and plants.

Cartography

One key field of geography is **cartography**, the science of making maps. You have already seen how important maps are to the study of geography. Without maps, geographers would not be able to study where things are in the world.

In the past, maps were always drawn by hand. Many were not very accurate. Today, though, most maps are made using computers and satellite images. Through advances in mapmaking, we can make accurate maps on almost any scale, from the whole world to a single neighborhood, and keep them up to date. These maps are not only used by geographers. For example, road maps are used by people who are planning long trips.

CONNECTING TO Technology

Computer Mapping

In the past, maps were drawn by hand. Making a map was a slow process. Even the simplest map took a long time to make. Today, however, cartographers have access to tools people in the past—even people who lived just 50 years ago—never imagined. The most important of these tools are computers.

Computers allow us to make maps quickly and easily. In addition, they let us make new types of maps that people could not make in the past.

The map shown here, for example, was drawn on a computer. It shows the number of computer users in the United States who were connected to the Internet on a particular day. Each of the lines that rises off of the map represents a city in which people were using the Internet. The color of the line indicates the number of computer users in that city. As you can see, this data resulted in a very complex map.

Making such a map required cartographers to sort through huge amounts of complex data. Such sorting would not have been possible without computers.

Contrasting How are today's maps different from those created in the past?

Connect to History

Telegraph The invention of the telegraph (a system of sending coded messages over wires using electricity) in the 19th century was important in the development of the field of meteorology. People had been observing and recording the weather long before the telegraph's invention (in daily farm journals, for example). But the telegraph enabled collecting, plotting, and analyzing weather observations from different places in a more timely manner. Today's computers have made this process even faster and more accurate, but the basic process is still the same—collecting weather data and analyzing it to make predictions.

Close

Ask students to suggest a local example of each branch of geography discussed in this section.

Review

↗ Online Quiz, Section 3

Assess

SE Section 3 Assessment
PASS: Section 3 Quiz
Alternative Assessment Handbook

Reteach/Classroom Intervention

Guided Reading Workbook, Section 3
Interactive Skills Tutor CD-ROM

Answers

Focus on Reading *Students' responses should reflect their understanding of the qualities that make water potable.*
Reading Check *The two main branches are physical and human, with some major branches including cartography, hydrology, and meteorology.*

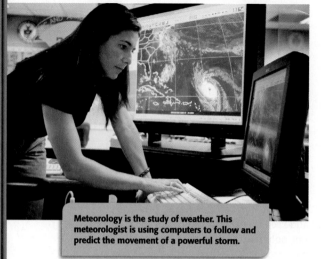

Meteorology is the study of weather. This meteorologist is using computers to follow and predict the movement of a powerful storm.

Meteorology

Have you ever seen the weather report on television? If so, you have seen the results of another branch of geography. This branch is called **meteorology**, the study of weather and what causes it.

Meteorologists study weather patterns in a particular area. Then they use the information to predict what the weather will be like in the coming days. Their work helps people plan what to wear and what to do on any given day. At the same time, their work can save lives by predicting the arrival of terrible storms. These predictions are among the most visible ways in which the work of geographers affects our lives every day.

READING CHECK Finding Main Ideas What are some major branches of geography?

SUMMARY AND PREVIEW In this section, you learned about two main branches of geography, physical and human. In the next chapter, you will learn more about the physical features that surround us and the processes that create them.

Hydrology

FOCUS ON READING
What do you already know about drinking water?

Another important branch of geography is hydrology, the study of water on Earth. Geographers in this field study the world's river systems and rainfall patterns. They study what causes droughts and floods and how people in cities can get safe drinking water. They also work to measure and protect the world's supply of water.

Section 3 Assessment

↗ hmhsocialstudies.com
ONLINE QUIZ

Reviewing Ideas, Terms, and Places

1. **a. Define** What is **physical geography**?
   b. Explain Why do we study physical geography?
2. **a. Identify** What are some things that people study as part of **human geography**?
   b. Summarize What are some ways in which the study of human geography can influence our lives?
   c. Evaluate Which do you think would be more interesting to study, physical geography or human geography? Why?
3. **a. Identify** What are two specialized fields of geography?
   b. Analyze How do cartographers contribute to the work of other geographers?

Critical Thinking

4. **Comparing and Contrasting** Draw a diagram like the one shown here. In the left circle, list three features of physical geography from your notes. In the right circle, list three features of human geography. Where the circles overlap, list one feature they share.

   Physical   Human

FOCUS ON WRITING

5. **Choosing a Branch** Your job description should point out to people that there are many branches of geography. How will you note that?

Section 3 Assessment Answers

1. **a.** study of world's landforms, water bodies, other physical features
   b. to learn how physical world works, help us prepare for and adapt to changes

2. **a.** people past or present, where they live and why, their jobs/crops/movements
   b. better understand other cultures, improve landscapes, design cities and towns, protect environments
   c. possible response—physical, because you learn about why features are the way they are; human, because you understand people better

3. **a.** cartography, meteorology
   b. They make maps that other geographers use to study different aspects of the world.

4. possible response: physical—landforms, water, climate; human—people, communities, landscape; both—help us understand world better

5. Student responses should include a reasonable explanation, such as including some of the branches in the "areas of responsibilities" section of the job description.

Chapter Review

Geography's Impact
video series
Review the video to answer the closing question:
Why do you think it might be valuable to know the absolute location of a place?

Visual Summary

Use the visual summary below to help you review the main ideas of the chapter.

QUICK FACTS

Physical geography—the study of the world's physical features—is one main branch of geography.

Human geography—the study of the world's people and how they live—is the second main branch.

Geographers use many tools to study the world. The most valuable of these tools are maps.

Reviewing Vocabulary, Terms, and Places

Match the words in the columns with the correct definitions listed below.

1. geography
2. physical geography
3. human geography
4. element
5. meteorology
6. region
7. cartography
8. map
9. landscape
10. globe

a. a part of the world that has one or more common features that make it different from surrounding areas
b. a flat drawing of part of Earth's surface
c. a part
d. a spherical model of the planet
e. the study of the world's physical features
f. the study of weather and what causes it
g. the study of the world, its people, and the landscapes they create
h. the science of making maps
i. the physical and human features that define an area and make it different from other places
j. the study of people and communities

Comprehension and Critical Thinking

SECTION 1 *(Pages 4–9)*

11. a. **Identify** What are three levels at which a geographer might study the world? Which of these levels covers the largest area?

    b. **Compare and Contrast** How are maps and globes similar? How are they different?

    c. **Elaborate** How might satellite images and computers help geographers improve their knowledge of the world?

Answers

Visual Summary

Review and Inquiry Have students use the visual summary to discuss details related to the study of geography.

 Quick Facts Transparency: A Geographer's World Visual Summary

Reviewing Vocabulary, Terms, and Places

1. g	**6.** a
2. e	**7.** h
3. j	**8.** b
4. c	**9.** i
5. f	**10.** d

Comprehension and Critical Thinking

11. a. levels—local, regional, global; largest—global

b. possible response: similar—Both generally show what world looks like. different—Globes are round and show world as it really appears. Maps are flat but easier to work with and can show smaller areas, such as cities.

c. possible response—They allow geographers to analyze more data at once and to get updates more often to track changes, so information is more accurate.

Review and Assessment Resources

Review and Reinforce

- **SE** Chapter Review
- **RF:** Chapter Review
- Quick Facts Transparency: A Geographer's World Visual Summary
- Spanish Chapter Summaries Audio CD Program
- **TOS** Holt McDougal PuzzleView®; Quiz Show for ExamView
- Quiz Game CD-ROM

Assess

- **SE** Standardized Test Practice
- PASS: Chapter Test, Forms A and B
- Alternative Assessment Handbook
- **TOS** ExamView Test Generator, Chapter Test
- Differentiated Instruction Modified Worksheets and Tests CD-ROM: Chapter Test
- Online Assessment Program, in the Interactive Student Edition

Reteach/Intervene

- Guided Reading Workbook
- Differentiated Instruction Teacher Management System: Lesson Plans
- Differentiated Instruction Modified Worksheets and Tests CD-ROM
- Interactive Skills Tutor CD-ROM

hmhsocialstudies.com
Chapter Resources

12. a. They mean the physical and human features that define an area and make it different from other places.

b. so people can use them to organize and guide their study of geography

c. possible response—as a study guide, helping to understand all aspects of places and people that are important to know

13. a. physical—landforms, bodies of water, other physical features; human—world's people and their cultures

b. It helps them make predictions and preparations.

c. possible response—because studying each part helps give a better understanding of Earth and its people

Using the Internet

14. Go to to access a rubric for this activity.

Social Studies Skills

15. true-color

16. light blue

17. to improve accuracy

Map Activity

18. Students' maps should clearly show where the school is and include major streets or roads and other features, such as stores.

Focus on Reading and Writing

19. Students' charts should clearly list prior knowledge, information learned in terms of the main ideas in each section, and questions or topics they would like to learn more about.

📝 **RF:** Focus on Reading, Using Prior Knowledge

20. Rubric Students' job descriptions should:

• give reasons why the job is important

• list the job's major tasks and responsibilities

• include characteristics needed to do the job well

📝 **RF:** Focus on Writing, Writing a Job Description

SECTION 2 *(Pages 10–14)*

12. a. Define What do geographers mean when they discuss an area's landscape?

b. Explain Why did geographers create the five themes and the six essential elements?

c. Predict How might the five themes and six essential elements help you in your study of geography?

SECTION 3 *(Pages 16–20)*

13. a. Identify What are the two main branches of geography? What does each include?

b. Summarize How can physical geography help people adjust to the dangers of the world?

c. Elaborate Why do geographers study both physical and human characteristics of places?

Using the Internet 21ST CENTURY

14. Activity: Using Maps Through your online textbook, explore how maps can help you understand your community and learn about its features. Then search the Internet to find a map of your community. Use the map to find the locations of at least five important features. For example, you might locate your school, the library, a park, or major highways. Be creative and find other places you think your classmates should be aware of.

↗ hmhsocialstudies.com

Social Studies Skills

Analyzing Satellite Images *Use the satellite images of Italy from the Social Studies Skills lesson in this chapter to answer the following questions.*

15. On which image do forests appear more clearly, the true-color or the infrared image?

16. What color do you think represents mountains on the infrared satellite image?

17. Why might geographers use satellite images like these while making maps of Italy?

Map Activity

18. Sketch Map Draw a map of your school and the surrounding neighborhood. Your map should include major features like streets and buildings. Use the map shown here as an example.

FOCUS ON READING AND WRITING

19. Using Prior Knowledge Create a chart with three columns. In the first column, list what you knew about geography before you read the chapter. In the second column, list what you learned in the chapter. In the third column, list questions that you now have about geography.

20. Writing Your Job Description Review your notes on the different jobs geographers do. Then write your job description. You should begin your description by explaining why the job is important. Then identify the job's tasks and responsibilities. Finally, tell what kind of person might do well as a geographer.

Standardized Test Prep

Standardized Test Prep

DIRECTIONS: Read questions 1 through 7 and write the letter of the best response. Then read question 8 and write your own well-constructed response.

1 Which of the following subjects would a human geographer study the most?

  A mountains

  B populations

  C rivers

  D volcanoes

2 The study of weather is called

  A meteorology.

  B hydrology.

  C social science.

  D cartography.

3 A region is an area that has

  A one or more common features.

  B no people living in it.

  C few physical features.

  D set physical boundaries.

4 How many essential elements of geography have geographers identified?

  A two

  B four

  C six

  D eight

5 The physical and human characteristics that define an area are its

  A landscape.

  B location.

  C region.

  D science.

The United States

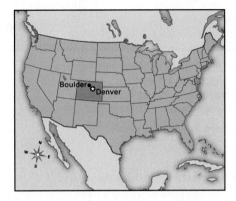

6 Which of the five themes of geography would a geographer most likely study using this map?

  A movement

  B location

  C human-environment interaction

  D landscape

7 The smallest level at which a geographer might study a place is

  A microscopic.

  B local.

  C regional.

  D global.

8 **Extended Response** Look at the map of the United States above. Do you think this map is more likely to be used by a physical geographer or by a human geographer? Give two reasons for your answer. Then write two statements about what a geographer could find on this map.

A GEOGRAPHER'S WORLD **23**

1. B
Break Down the Question This question requires students to eliminate answer choices a physical geographer would study.

2. A
Break Down the Question This question requires students to recall factual information. Refer students who miss it to Section 3.

3. A
Break Down the Question This question requires students to recall factual information. Refer students who miss it to Section 1.

4. C
Break Down the Question Suggest that students try to picture the elements chart in their mind to recall the correct number. Refer students who miss it to Section 2.

5. A
Break Down the Question This question requires students to recall factual information. Refer students who miss it to Section 1.

6. B
Break Down the Question Students can eliminate movement, since the map does not show this theme.

7. B
Break Down the Question Students can eliminate "microscopic" because it is not one of the three levels geographers use.

8. Extended Response Possible response—by a physical geographer, because it can be used to understand the relative locations of two cities within Colorado and within the United States; A geographer could find the state boundaries of the United States and the capital of Colorado.

Reteach/Intervention Resources

Reproducible

🗐 Guided Reading Workbook

🗐 Differentiated Instruction Teacher Management System: Lesson Plans

Technology

▶️ Quick Facts Transparency: A Geographer's World Visual Summary

💿 Differentiated Instruction Modified Worksheets and Tests CD-ROM

💿 Interactive Skills Tutor CD-ROM

Tips for Test Taking

Anticipate the Answers Give students this important tip: Before you read the answer choices, answer the question yourself. Then, read the choices. If the answer you gave is among the choices listed, it is probably correct!

Planet Earth

Overview	Instructional Resources	
CHAPTER 2 **Essential Question:** How do physical processes and features shape life on Earth? 🔊 **Focus on the Essential Question Podcast**	**TOS Differentiated Instruction Teacher Management System:** • Instructional Pacing Guides • Lesson Plans for Differentiated Instruction 📑 **Guided Reading Workbook** 📑 **Resource File:** • Chapter Review • Focus on Reading: Using Word Parts • Focus on Writing: Writing a Haiku • Social Studies Skills: Using a Physical Map 📑 **Experiencing World History and Geography**	**TOS Calendar Planner** 💿 **Power Presentations with Media Gallery** 💿 **Differentiated Instruction Modified Worksheets and Tests CD-ROM** 💿 **Interactive Skills Tutor CD-ROM** 🔊 **Student Edition on Audio CD-ROM** 🔊 **The World's Music Audio Program** ▶️ **World Outline Maps: Transparencies and Activities** Ⓗ **Video:** How the Earth Was Made
Section 1: **Earth and the Sun's Energy** **The Big Idea:** Earth's movement and the sun's energy interact to create day and night, temperature changes, and the seasons.	**TOS Differentiated Instruction Teacher Management System:** Section 1 Lesson Plan 📑 **Guided Reading Workbook:** Section 1 📑 **Resource File:** • Vocabulary Builder: Section 1 • Literature: *Julie of the Wolves* by Jean Craighead George	▶️ **Daily Bellringer Transparency:** Section 1 ▶️ **Map Zone Transparency:** The Seasons: Northern Hemisphere ↗️ **Internet Activity:** Diagram of Earth, the Sun, and the Moon Ⓗ **Video:** Secrets of the Sun
Section 2: **Water on Earth** **The Big Idea:** Water is a dominant feature on Earth's surface and is essential for life.	**TOS Differentiated Instruction Teacher Management System:** Section 2 Lesson Plan 📑 **Guided Reading Workbook:** Section 2 📑 **Resource File:** • Vocabulary Builder: Section 2 • Biography: Robert D. Ballard • Geography for Life: Ocean Currents	▶️ **Daily Bellringer Transparency:** Section 2
Section 3: **The Land** **The Big Idea:** Processes below and on Earth's surface shape the planet's physical features.	**TOS Differentiated Instruction Teacher Management System:** Section 3 Lesson Plan 📑 **Guided Reading Workbook:** Section 3 📑 **Resource File:** • Vocabulary Builder: Section 3 • Biography: Georgia O'Keeffe • Primary Source: Survivors of Krakatau • Geography and History: The California Gold Rush • Critical Thinking: Volcanoes	▶️ **Daily Bellringer Transparency:** Section 3 ▶️ **Map Zone Transparency:** Earth's Plates ▶️ **Map Zone Transparency:** Ring of Fire ▶️ **Map Zone Transparency:** India: Physical ↗️ **Internet Activity:** Continental Drift in the Future ↗️ **Animated Geography:** Earth's Plates Ⓗ **Video:** Earthquakes

Chart Key:

 SE Student Edition   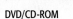 Presentation Resource   MP3 Audio

TOS Teacher One Stop   DVD/CD-ROM   HISTORY™

Printable Resource

Program Resources available on **TOS** and @ hmhsocialstudies.com

Review, Assessment, Intervention

Introduction to Geography Transparencies: Planet Earth Visual Summary

Spanish Chapter Summaries Audio CD

Progress Assessment Support System (PASS): Chapter Test

Differentiated Instruction Modified Worksheets CD-ROM: Modified Chapter Test

TOS **ExamView® Assessment Suite (English/Spanish)**

Alternative Assessment Handbook

Online Assessment Program, in the Interactive Student Edition

---

PASS: Section 1 Quiz

Online Quiz: Section 1

Alternative Assessment Handbook

PASS: Section 2 Quiz

Online Quiz: Section 2

Alternative Assessment Handbook

PASS: Section 3 Quiz

Online Quiz: Section 3

Alternative Assessment Handbook

Supporting Resources

HISTORY.

• Multimedia Classroom Global History Series
• Global History Teacher's Guide

Maps Globes Graphs Level F

• Student Workbook
• Teacher's Guide

Social Studies Trade Library Collections

• World Regions Trade Collection
• NCSS Middle School Trade Collection

Geography's Impact

Geography's Impact Video Program

• **Impact of Water on Earth**

For more information or to purchase go to 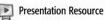 hmhsocialstudies.com

Power Presentations with Media Gallery

Power Presentations with Media Gallery are visual presentations of each chapter's main ideas. Presentations can be customized by including Quick Facts charts, images from the text, and video clips.

CHAPTER 2 PLANNING GUIDE

Differentiating Instruction

How do I address the needs of varied learners?
The Target Resource acts as your primary strategy for differentiated instruction.

ENGLISH-LANGUAGE LEARNERS & STRUGGLING READERS

Spanish/English Guided Reading Workbook

The activities in the Spanish/English Guided Reading Workbook engage students with questions while presenting summaries of chapter content and provide opportunities for students to practice critical thinking skills.

Additional Resources

Differentiated Instruction Teacher Management System: Lesson Plans for Differentiated Instruction

Resource File:
- Vocabulary Builder Activities
- Social Studies Skills: Using a Physical Map

Introduction to Geography Transparencies:
- Planet Earth Visual Summary

Student Edition on Audio CD Program

Spanish Chapter Summaries Audio CD Program

Teacher One Stop:
- ExamView Assessment Suite, Spanish
- PuzzleView, Spanish

English-Language Learner Strategies and Activities

SPECIAL NEEDS LEARNERS

Differentiated Instruction Teacher Management System

Lesson Plans for Differentiated Instruction provide teachers with strategies to help plan instruction for all learners.

Additional Resources

Guided Reading Workbook

Resource File: Social Studies Skills: Using a Physical Map

Student Edition on Audio CD Program

Interactive Skills Tutor CD-ROM

Graphic Organizer Transparencies with Support for Reading and Writing

ADVANCED/GIFTED AND TALENTED STUDENTS

Resource File

The Resource File activities allow students to extend their knowledge of chapter-related places and people and to practice geography skills.
- Focus on Reading: Using Word Parts
- Focus on Writing: Writing a Haiku
- Literature: *Julie of the Wolves* by Jean Craighead George

Additional Resources

Differentiated Instruction Teacher Management System: Lesson Plans for Differentiated Instruction

World History and Geography Document-Based Questions Activities

Geography, Science, and Cultures Activities

Experiencing World History and Geography

Differentiated Activities in the Teacher's Edition

- Writing a Letter, p. 31
- Learning from Visuals, p. 38

Teacher One Stop™

How can I manage the lesson plans and support materials for differentiated instruction?

With the Teacher One Stop, you can easily organize and print lesson plans, planning guides, and instructional materials for all learners. The Teacher One Stop includes the following materials to help you differentiate instruction:

- **· Interactive Teacher's Edition**
- **· Calendar Planner and pacing guides**
- **· Editable lesson plans**
- **· All reproducible ancillaries in Adobe Acrobat (PDF) format**
- **· ExamView Assessment Suite (English & Spanish)**
- **· Transparency and video previews**

Differentiated Activities in the Teacher's Edition

- Demonstrating Rotation and Revolution, p. 27
- Making a Collage, p. 38

Interactive Student Edition

Complete online student edition with interactive multimedia support for chapter content assessment and reporting

- Interactive Maps and Notebook
- Standardized Test Prep
- Online Homework Practice and Research Activities
- Current Events
- Chapter-based Internet Activities
- Animated Geography Activities

Differentiated Activities in the Teacher's Edition

- Understanding Gravity, p. 27
- Drawing a Diagram, p. 31
- Evaluating Information, p. 39

Essential Question

Introduce the Essential Question

- Ask students how seasons affect their lives. Explain that seasons are a result of Earth's tilt on its axis and its rotation around the sun. Places tilting toward the sun at any given time during the year receive more solar energy and experience warmer temperatures.

- Point out that water is a physical feature that also shapes life on Earth. Remind students that water is not only crucial to survival but provides other benefits, such as food, power, and recreation.

- Ask students what they know about volcanoes and earthquakes. Use their responses to introduce natural forces that shape Earth's landforms, which in turn affect where and how people live.

Focus on Reading and Writing

Reading The Resource File provides a worksheet to help students practice using word parts.

📝 **RF: Focus on Reading: Using Word Parts**

Writing The Resource File provides a worksheet to help students organize and write their haikus.

📝 **RF: Focus on Writing: Writing a Haiku**

Key to Differentiating Instruction

Below Level

Basic-level activities designed for all students encountering new material

At Level

Intermediate-level activities designed for average students

Above Level

Challenging activities designed for honors and gifted and talented students

Standard English Mastery

Activities designed to improve standard English usage

LS Learning Styles

CHAPTER **2**

Planet Earth

Essential Question How do physical processes and features shape life on Earth?

What You Will Learn...

In this chapter you will learn about important processes on planet Earth. You will discover how Earth's movements affect the energy we receive from the sun, how water affects life, and how Earth's landforms were made.

FOCUS ON READING AND WRITING

Using Word Parts Sometimes you can figure out the meaning of a word by looking at its parts. A root is the base of the word. A prefix attaches to the beginning, and a suffix attaches to the ending. When you come across a word you don't know, check to see whether you recognize its parts. **See the lesson, Using Word Parts, on page 517.**

Writing a Haiku Join the poets who have celebrated our planet for centuries. Write a haiku, a short poem, about planet Earth. As you read the chapter, gather information about changes in the sun's energy, Earth's water supply, and shapes on the land. Then choose the most intriguing information to include in your haiku.

Energy from the Sun The planet's movement creates differences in the amount of energy Earth receives from the sun.

24 CHAPTER 2

Introduce the Chapter

At Level

Solar Energy, Water, and Land

1. Tell students that they are going to learn about the relationship between Earth and the sun and how it influences human activities, the part that water plays in sustaining life, and the variety of landforms on Earth and how they were shaped.

2. Explain that various regions have different climates and different landforms. Ask: Which parts of the United States are desert? Mountains? Plains? Where is it coldest in winter and warmest in summer? Where is the most water found?

3. Have students work in pairs to examine the chapter's photos, maps, and graphics. Encourage them to make a list of questions they would like to have answered as they read the chapter. **LS** **Visual/Spatial, Interpersonal**

📝 Alternative Assessment Handbook, Rubric 1: Acquiring Information

HISTORY
How the Earth Was Made

⇗ hmhsocialstudies.com VIDEO

ANALYSIS SKILL ANALYZING VISUALS

Many of Earth's features are visible from space. This photo, taken from a satellite orbiting the planet, shows part of the North American continent.

Which of Earth's features are visible in this photo?

Land Forces on and under Earth's surface have shaped the different landforms on our planet. Geographers study how mountains and other landforms were made.

Water on Earth Water is essential for life on Earth. Much of the planet's water supply is stored in Earth's oceans and ice caps.

25

• Chapter Preview •

Explore the Pictures

Earth As the photograph shows, the planet is made up of land and water. Landforms and seasons vary greatly from one region to another.

Energy from the Sun Have students identify what season is likely shown in the photo. Ask them to describe other seasons. Do all places have varied seasons? Explain that in some places, such as southern California, the differences between the seasons are less obvious. Ask students to speculate about why this might be so.

Land This photo was taken in the American Southwest, where the temperature is warm and dry most of the year. Discuss with students how they think this landform was created. Ask them how it is different from other mountains they might have seen.

Water on Earth Icebergs are solid forms of water found near the poles. Ask students why they think the icebergs can stay solid.

⇗ hmhsocialstudies.com
Teacher Resources

Writing a Poem   Standard English Mastery

1. Have students study the photographs in the chapter opener and throughout the chapter. Have them find additional photographs of Earth from space and of the planet's landforms, either on the Internet or in the library.

2. Have them list several words that describe each image. Suggest that they think of words that appeal to the senses of sight, sound, touch, hearing, and taste. Encourage students to use a thesaurus to find words that are interesting and descriptive.

3. Next, have students write a poem from the point of view of a traveler approaching Earth for the first time. As the traveler comes closer to the surface of the planet, have students imagine his or her reaction and write a description of what the traveler might see.

4. Have volunteers read their poems aloud.
   LS Verbal/Linguistic, Visual/Spatial

   Alternative Assessment Handbook, Rubrics 26: Poems and Songs; and 39: Writing to Create

Answers

Analyzing Visuals *land, mountains, lakes, ocean*

25

Earth and the Sun's Energy

Preteach

Bellringer

If YOU lived there. . . Use the **Daily Bellringer Transparency** to help students answer the question.

▶ Daily Bellringer Transparency, Section 1

Academic Vocabulary

Review with students the high-use academic term in this section.

factor cause (p. 27)

RF: Vocabulary Builder, Section 1

Taking Notes

Have students use the graphic organizer online to take notes on the section. This activity will prepare students for the Section Assessment, in which they will complete a graphic organizer that builds on the information using the Critical Thinking Skill: Identifying Cause and Effect.

What You Will Learn...

Main Ideas

1. Earth's movement affects the amount of energy we receive from the sun.
2. Earth's seasons are caused by the planet's tilt.

The Big Idea

Earth's movement and the sun's energy interact to create day and night, temperature changes, and the seasons.

Key Terms

solar energy, *p. 26*
rotation, *p. 26*
revolution, *p. 27*
latitude, *p. 27*
tropics, *p. 29*

hmhsocialstudies.com
TAKING NOTES

Use the graphic organizer online to take notes on Earth's movement and the seasons.

If YOU lived there...

You live in Chicago and have just won an exciting prize—a trip to Australia during winter vacation in January. As you prepare for the trip, your mother reminds you to pack shorts and a swimsuit. You are confused. In January you usually wear winter sweaters and a heavy jacket.

Why is the weather so different in Australia?

BUILDING BACKGROUND Seasonal differences in weather are an important result of Earth's constant movement. As the planet moves, we experience changes in the amount of energy we receive from the sun. Geographers study and explain why different places on Earth receive differing amounts of energy from the sun.

Earth's Movement

Energy from the sun helps crops grow, provides light, and warms Earth. It even influences the clothes we wear, the foods we eat, and the sports we play. All life on Earth requires **solar energy**, or energy from the sun, to survive. The amount of solar energy places on Earth receive changes constantly. Earth's rotation, revolution, and tilt, as well as latitude, all affect the amount of solar energy parts of the planet receive from the sun.

Rotation

Imagine that Earth has a rod running through it from the North Pole to the South Pole. This rod represents Earth's axis—an imaginary line around which a planet turns. As Earth spins on its axis, different parts of the planet face the sun. It takes Earth 24 hours, or one day, to complete this rotation. A **rotation** is one complete spin of Earth on its axis. As Earth rotates during this 24-hour period, it appears to us that the sun moves across the sky. The sun seems to rise in the east and set in the west. The

---

Teach the Big Idea

At Level

Earth and the Sun's Energy

1. **Teach** Ask students the questions in the Main Idea boxes under Direct Teach.

2. **Apply** Organize students into small groups. Have half of the groups plan presentations about Earth's rotation and the other half plan presentations about the revolution of Earth around the sun. Encourage students to incorporate key terms from the section and extend their presentations with illustrations, drawings, and/or models.

3. **Review** Ask students to give their presentations as a review of the section.

4. **Practice/Homework** Have each group come up with five questions about the topic and then quiz each member of their group.
   LS Interpersonal, Verbal/Linguistic

   Alternative Assessment Handbook, Rubrics 14: Group Activity; and 24: Oral Presentations

---

Solar Energy

Earth's tilt and rotation cause changes in the amount of energy we receive from the sun. As Earth rotates on its axis, energy from the sun creates periods of day and night. Earth's tilt causes some locations, especially those close to the equator, to receive more direct solar energy than others.

23.5°

North Pole

Equator

Sun's Rays

South Pole

HISTORY VIDEO
Secrets of the Sun

hmhsocialstudies.com

ANALYSIS SKILL ANALYZING VISUALS

Is the region north or south of the equator receiving more solar energy? How can you tell?

---

sun, however, does not move. It is actually Earth's rotation that creates the sense of the sun's movement.

Earth's rotation also explains why day changes to night. As you can see in the illustration, solar energy strikes only the half of Earth facing the sun. Warmth and light from the sun create daytime. At the same time, the half of the planet facing away from the sun experiences the cooler temperatures and darkness of night. Earth's rotation causes regular shifts from day to night. As a result, levels of solar energy on Earth constantly change.

Revolution

As Earth spins on its axis, it also follows a path, or orbit, around the sun. Earth's orbit around the sun is not a perfect circle. Sometimes the orbit takes Earth closer to the sun, and at other times the orbit takes it farther away. It takes 365¼ days for Earth to complete one **revolution**, or trip around the sun. We base our calendar year on the time it takes Earth to complete its orbit around the sun. To allow for the fraction of a day, we add an extra day—February 29—to our calendar every four years.

Tilt and Latitude

Another **factor** affecting the amount of solar energy we receive is the planet's tilt. As the illustration shows, Earth's axis is not straight up and down. It is actually tilted at an angle of 23½ degrees from vertical. At any given time of year, some locations on Earth are tilting away from the sun, and others are tilting toward it. Places tilting toward the sun receive more solar energy and experience warmer temperatures. Those tilting away from the sun receive less solar energy and experience cooler temperatures.

A location's **latitude**, the distance north or south of Earth's equator, also affects the amount of solar energy it receives. Low-latitude areas, those near the equator like Hawaii, receive direct rays from the sun all year. These direct rays are more intense and produce warmer temperatures. Regions with high latitudes, like Antarctica, are farther from the equator. As a result, they receive indirect rays from the sun and have colder temperatures.

READING CHECK **Finding Main Ideas** What factors affect the solar energy Earth receives?

ACADEMIC VOCABULARY

factor cause

Main Idea

❶ Earth's Movement

Earth's movement affects the amount of energy we receive from the sun.

Explain How does rotation explain why day changes into night? *It takes 24 hours for Earth to spin on its axis. The half of the planet that faces the sun during this period experiences daytime, and it experiences night when it turns away from the sun.*

Make Judgments Would you rather live at high or low latitudes? Why? *Students' answers should reflect an understanding of the section's content. Low latitudes are warmer, with more direct sunlight; high latitudes have cooler temperatures and less sunlight.*

Did you know. . .

On its year-long trip around the sun, Earth travels more than 1,500,000 miles per day.

MISCONCEPTION ALERT

An Illusion? The sun only appears to rise and set. The same is true of the moon. The moon's rotation as it revolves around Earth keeps the same side of the moon always in view. The moon "rises" and "sets" as it revolves around Earth.

hmhsocialstudies.com

Online Resources
Activity: Diagram of Earth, the Sun, and the Moon

Differentiating Instruction

Special Needs Learners
Below Level

Provide student pairs with a ball. Have one student observe while the other rotates the ball in front of a light source. They should identify daytime and nighttime from the ball's position. Next, have one student represent the sun while the other orbits him or her carrying the ball. Have students identify the seasons from the position of the sun and Earth.

LS Kinesthetic, Visual/Spatial

Alternative Assessment Handbook, Rubric 14: Group Activity

Advanced/Gifted and Talented
Above Level
Research Required

Have students research the effect of gravity on Earth's rotation and on its revolution around the sun. They might also investigate how gravity influences the moon and the tides. Have them write a brief report explaining what they have learned. Encourage students to illustrate their reports in order to clarify difficult concepts.

LS Verbal/Linguistic

Alternative Assessment Handbook, Rubrics 30: Research; and 42: Writing to Inform

Answers

Analyzing Visuals *North; tilted toward the sun*

Reading Check *rotation, revolution, tilt, and latitude*

❷ The Seasons

Earth's seasons are caused by the planet's tilt.

Explain When is it summer in South America? *when the South Pole is tilted toward the sun*

Describe What are monsoons? Where do they take place? *seasonal winds that bring heavy rainfall; in the tropics*

Predict What would happen if Earth's axis did not tilt but pointed straight up and down? *There would be no seasons.*

📖 **RF:** Literature, *Julie of The Wolves* by Jean Craighead George

Info to Know

Little Free Flier NASA engineers have developed a mini-satellite camera, nicknamed "Little Free Flier," for use in future space missions. The camera is less than eight inches in diameter. It gives views that aren't possible with fixed cameras on robotic arms. The mini-satellite camera can monitor the outside of a spacecraft for problems—thus astronauts may not have to risk leaving the spacecraft in order to inspect it while in space. To learn more, visit www.nasa.gov.

Did you know. . .

Eileen M. Collins was the first female space shuttle commander, leading *Columbia* in July 1999. One of her mission's duties was to record images of Earth's moon, Mercury, Venus, and Jupiter in order to study their atmospheres and surfaces.

Answers

Focus on Reading *half of a sphere, or half of Earth*

Analyzing Visuals *summer*

The Seasons

FOCUS ON READING
The prefix *hemi-* means half. What does the word *hemisphere* mean?

Does the thought of snow in July or 100-degree temperatures in January seem odd to you? It might if you live in the Northern Hemisphere, where cold temperatures are common in January, not July. The planet's changing seasons explain why we often connect certain weather with specific times of the year, like snow in January. Seasons are periods during the year that are known for a particular type of weather. Many places on Earth experience four seasons—winter, spring, summer, and fall. These seasons are based on temperature and length of day. In some parts of the world, however, seasons are based on the amount of rainfall.

Winter and Summer

The change in seasons is created by Earth's tilt. As you can see in the illustration below, while one of Earth's poles tilts away from the sun, the other tilts toward it. During winter part of Earth is tilted away from the sun, causing less direct solar energy, cool temperatures, and less daylight. Summer occurs when part of Earth is tilted toward the sun. This creates more direct solar energy, warmer temperatures, and longer periods of daylight.

Because of Earth's tilt, the Northern and Southern hemispheres experience opposite seasons. As the North Pole tilts toward the sun in summer, the South Pole tilts away

The Seasons: Northern Hemisphere

As Earth orbits the sun, the tilt of its axis toward and away from the sun causes the seasons to change. Seasons in the Northern Hemisphere change at about the same time every year.

ANALYZING VISUALS As the Northern Hemisphere experiences winter, what season is it in the Southern Hemisphere?

Winter and Spring The North Pole tilts away from the sun in winter, causing cooler temperatures. In the spring, temperatures gradually rise as the North Pole begins to point toward the sun.

March 21
SPRING

December 21
WINTER

June 21
SUMMER

Summer and Fall Summer's warm temperatures are the result of the North Pole's tilt toward the sun. As we move away from the sun in the fall, temperatures slowly decline.

North Pole

Tropic of Cancer
Equator
Tropic of Capricorn

South Pole

September 22
FALL

28 CHAPTER 2

Critical Thinking: Understanding Cause and Effect
At Level

Writing a Letter to the Editor
Research Required

1. Have students research global warming on the Internet or at the library. Ask them to look for answers to these questions: What is global warming? Why does it occur? What effects has it had on the continents and oceans? What effects do scientists predict it will have in the future? What can be done to stop global warming?

2. Have students write letters to the editor explaining what they have learned about global warming and what they think should be done about the problem. Encourage them to include interesting quotes they found in their research.

3. Have volunteers read their letters and discuss their conclusions. Encourage students to submit their letters to the local newspaper.

LS Verbal/Linguistic

📝 Alternative Assessment Handbook, Rubrics 17: Letters to Editors; and 43: Writing to Persuade from it. As a result, the Southern Hemisphere experiences winter. Likewise, when it is spring in the Northern Hemisphere, it is fall in the Southern Hemisphere.

Spring and Fall

As Earth orbits the sun, there are periods when the poles tilt neither toward nor away from the sun. These periods mark spring and fall. During the spring, as part of Earth begins to tilt toward the sun, solar energy increases. Temperatures slowly start to rise, and days grow longer. In the fall the opposite occurs as winter approaches. Solar energy begins to decrease, causing cooler temperatures and shorter days.

Rainfall and Seasons

Some regions on Earth have seasons marked by rainfall rather than temperature. This is true in the **tropics**, regions close to the equator. At certain times of year, winds bring either dry or moist air to the tropics, creating wet and dry seasons. In India, for example, seasonal winds called monsoons bring heavy rains from June to October and dry air from November to January.

READING CHECK Identifying Cause and Effect What causes the seasons to change?

FOCUS ON CULTURE

The Midnight Sun

Can you imagine going to sleep late at night with the sun shining in the sky? People who live near the Arctic and Antarctic circles experience this every summer, when they can receive up to 24 hours of sunlight a day. The time-lapse photo below shows a typical sunset during this period—except the sun never really sets! This phenomenon is known as the midnight sun. For locations like Tromso, Norway, this means up to two months of constant daylight each summer. People living near Earth's poles often use the long daylight hours to work on outdoor projects in preparation for winter, when they can receive 24 hours of darkness a day.

Predicting How might people's daily lives be affected by the midnight sun?

SUMMARY AND PREVIEW Solar energy is crucial for all life on the planet. Earth's position and movements affect the amount of energy we receive from the sun and determine our seasons. Next, you will learn about Earth's water supply and its importance to us.

Section 1 Assessment

hmhsocialstudies.com
ONLINE QUIZ

Reviewing Ideas, Terms, and Places

1. **a. Identify** What is **solar energy**, and how does it affect Earth?
   b. Analyze How do **rotation** and tilt each affect the amount of solar energy that different parts of Earth receive?
   c. Predict What might happen if Earth received less solar energy than it currently does?
2. **a. Describe** Name and describe Earth's seasons.
   b. Contrast How are seasons different in the Northern and Southern hemispheres?
   c. Elaborate How might the seasons affect human activities?

Critical Thinking

3. **Identifying Cause and Effect** Use your notes and the diagram to identify the causes of seasons.

FOCUS ON WRITING

4. **Describing the Seasons** What are the seasons like where you live? In your notebook, jot down a few notes that describe the changing seasons.

Bellringer

If YOU lived there. . . Use the **Daily Bellringer Transparency** to help students answer the question.

▶ Daily Bellringer Transparency, Section 2

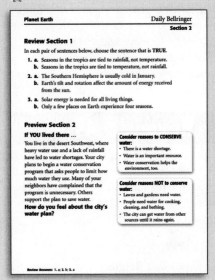

Planet Earth   Daily Bellringer
                                         Section 2

Review Section 1

In each pair of sentences below, choose the sentence that is TRUE.

1. **a.** Seasons in the tropics are tied to rainfall, not temperature.
   b. Seasons in the tropics are tied to temperature, not rainfall.
2. **a.** The Southern Hemisphere is usually cold in January.
   b. Earth's tilt and rotation affect the amount of energy received from the sun.
3. **a.** Solar energy is needed for all living things.
   b. Only a few places on Earth experience four seasons.

Preview Section 2

If YOU lived there ...
You live in the desert Southwest, where heavy water use and a lack of rainfall have led to water shortages. Your city plans to begin a water conservation program that asks people to limit how much water they use. Many of your neighbors have complained that the program is unnecessary. Others support the plan to save water. **How do you feel about the city's water plan?**

Consider reasons to CONSERVE water:
• There is a water shortage.
• Water is an important resource.
• Water conservation helps the environment, too.

Consider reasons NOT to conserve water:
• Lawns and gardens need water.
• People need water for cooking, cleaning, and bathing.
• The city can get water from other sources until it rains again.

Review Answers: 1. a; 2. b; 3. a

Key Terms and Places

📝 **RF:** Vocabulary Builder, Section 2

Taking Notes

Have students use the graphic organizer online to take notes on the section. This activity will prepare students for the Section Assessment, in which they will complete a graphic organizer that builds on the information using the Critical Thinking Skill: Sequencing.

SECTION 2

Water on Earth

Main Ideas

1. Salt water and freshwater make up Earth's water supply.
2. In the water cycle, water circulates from Earth's surface to the atmosphere and back again.
3. Water plays an important role in people's lives.

The Big Idea

Water is a dominant feature on Earth's surface and is essential for life.

Key Terms

freshwater, *p. 31*
glaciers, *p. 31*
surface water, *p. 31*
precipitation, *p. 31*
groundwater, *p. 32*
water vapor, *p. 32*
water cycle, *p. 33*

hmhsocialstudies.com
TAKING NOTES

Use the graphic organizer online to take notes on Earth's water.

If YOU lived there...

You live in the desert Southwest, where heavy water use and a lack of rainfall have led to water shortages. Your city plans to begin a water conservation program that asks people to limit how much water they use. Many of your neighbors have complained that the program is unnecessary. Others support the plan to save water.

How do you feel about the city's water plan?

BUILDING BACKGROUND Although water covers much of Earth's surface, water shortages, like those in the American Southwest, are common all over the planet. Because water is vital to the survival of all living things, geographers study Earth's water supply.

Earth's Water Supply

Think of the different uses for water. We use water to cook and clean, we drink it, and we grow crops with it. Water is used for recreation, to generate electricity, and even to travel from place to place. Water is perhaps the most important and abundant resource on Earth. In fact, water covers some two-thirds of the planet. Understanding Earth's water supply and how it affects our lives is an important part of geography.

Earth's Distribution of Water

Earth's water supply is divided into two main types—salt water and freshwater. Humans, plants, and animals rely on Earth's freshwater supply for survival.

Teach the Big Idea

At Level | Standard English Mastery

Water on Earth

1. **Teach** Ask students the questions in the Main Idea boxes under Direct Teach.

2. **Apply** Ask students to imagine that they will interview a geographer about water on Earth. Have them use standard English to write a list of interview questions about the material in the chapter. They should write at least three questions about the information under each major heading.

3. **Review** Have students take turns interviewing each other and answering the questions.

4. **Practice/Homework** Have students write the answers next to their interview questions. Then have them work to come up with more questions. **LS Verbal/Linguistic**

📝 Alternative Assessment Handbook, Rubrics 1: Acquiring Information; and 11: Discussions

Salt Water

Although water covers much of the planet, we cannot use most of it. About 97 percent of the Earth's water is salt water. Because salt water contains high levels of salt and other minerals, it is unsafe to drink.

In general, salt water is found in Earth's oceans. Oceans are vast bodies of water covering some 71 percent of the planet's surface. Earth's oceans are made up of smaller bodies of water such as seas, gulfs, bays, and straits. Altogether, Earth's oceans cover some 139 million square miles (360 million square km) of the planet's surface.

Some of Earth's lakes contain salt water. The Great Salt Lake in Utah, for example, is a saltwater lake. As salt and other minerals have collected in the lake, which has no outlet, the water has become salty.

Freshwater

Since the water in Earth's oceans is too salty to use, we must rely on other sources for freshwater. **Freshwater**, or water without salt, makes up only about 3 percent of our total water supply. Much of that freshwater is locked in Earth's **glaciers**, large areas of slow-moving ice, and in the ice of the Antarctic and Arctic regions. Most of the freshwater we use everyday is found in lakes, in rivers, and under Earth's surface.

One form of freshwater is surface water. **Surface water** is water that is found in Earth's streams, rivers, and lakes. It may seem that there is a great deal of water in our lakes and rivers, but only a tiny amount of Earth's water supply—less than 1 percent—comes from surface water.

Streams and rivers are a common source of surface water. Streams form when precipitation collects in a narrow channel and flows toward the ocean. **Precipitation** is water that falls to Earth's surface as rain, snow, sleet, or hail. In turn, streams join together to form rivers. Any smaller stream or river that flows into a larger stream or river is called a tributary. For example, the Missouri River is the largest tributary of the Mississippi River.

Lakes are another important source of surface water. Some lakes were formed as rivers filled low-lying areas with water. Other lakes, like the Great Lakes along the U.S.–Canada border, were formed when glaciers carved deep holes in Earth's surface and deposited water as they melted.

Most of Earth's available freshwater is stored underground. As precipitation falls to Earth, much of it is absorbed into the ground, filling spaces in the soil and rock.

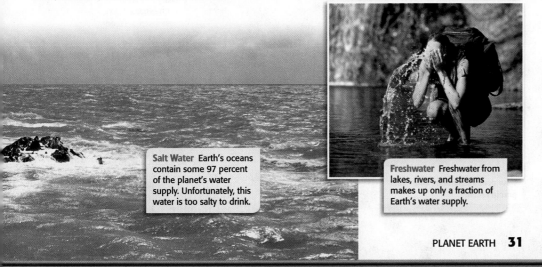

Salt Water Earth's oceans contain some 97 percent of the planet's water supply. Unfortunately, this water is too salty to drink.

Freshwater Freshwater from lakes, rivers, and streams makes up only a fraction of Earth's water supply.

Main Idea

❷ The Water Cycle

In the water cycle, water circulates from Earth's surface to the atmosphere and back again.

Recall What forms does water take? *solid (snow, ice), liquid (rain, oceans, rivers), gas (water vapor)*

Describe What happens to precipitation during the water cycle? *Some is absorbed into the soil as groundwater; runoff collects in streams, rivers, and oceans.*

Activity **Diagram** Have students make a poster with a detailed diagram of the water cycle. Students should write captions explaining each element of the diagram.

LS **Visual-Spatial/Verbal-Linguistic**

📝 Alternative Assessment Handbook, Rubric 3: Artwork

Connect to Science

Recycling Water in Space Whether on a space shuttle or the International Space Station, astronauts need to recycle water. Using new technologies developed by NASA, astronauts' wastewater is collected, cleaned, and then reused. New recycling technologies are in development, including new ways of making water cleaner using bacteria. Perhaps more importantly, NASA's water recycling technologies may be useful elsewhere—on Earth.

Answers

Reading Check *Freshwater is suitable for drinking. It is locked in glaciers or stored as groundwater or surface water, whereas salt water is found in oceans and some lakes and is not suitable for drinking.*

Analyzing Visuals *Evaporation occurs when water turns from liquid to gas; precipitation is water that falls to Earth from condensed water vapor.*

Water found below Earth's surface is called **groundwater**. In some places on Earth, groundwater naturally bubbles from the ground as a spring. More often, however, people obtain groundwater by digging wells, or deep holes dug into the ground to reach the water.

READING CHECK **Contrasting** How is salt water different from freshwater?

↗ hmhsocialstudies.com **INTERACTIVE ART**
Close-up

The Water Cycle

Energy from the sun drives the water cycle. Surface water evaporates into Earth's atmosphere, where it condenses, then falls back to Earth as precipitation. This cycle repeats continuously, providing us with a fairly constant water supply.

Condensation occurs when water vapor cools and forms clouds.

When the droplets in clouds become too heavy, they fall to Earth as precipitation.

Runoff is excess precipitation that flows over land into rivers, streams, and oceans.

ANALYSIS SKILL **ANALYZING VISUALS**
How does evaporation differ from precipitation?

32 CHAPTER 2

The Water Cycle

When you think of water, you probably visualize a liquid—a flowing stream, a glass of ice-cold water, or a wave hitting the beach. But did you know that water is the only substance on Earth that occurs naturally as a solid, a liquid, and a gas? We see water as a solid in snow and ice and as a liquid in oceans and rivers. Water also occurs in the air as an invisible gas called **water vapor**.

Water is always moving. As water heats up and cools down, it moves from the planet's surface to the atmosphere, or the mass of air that surrounds Earth. One of the most important processes in nature

---

Critical Thinking: Evaluating Information   **Above Level**

Creating a Public Service Announcement   **Research Required**

1. Have students write a script for a public service announcement about keeping groundwater free of pesticides.

2. Have them begin by exploring government or nonprofit Web sites. They should find out where pesticides come from, how they enter the water cycle, and how they affect the environment.

3. Before they begin writing, have students evaluate the information and draw conclusions. Some students might argue

that the benefits of pesticides outweigh any harmful effects. Students might write announcements expressing different opinions.

4. Have students read their announcements aloud to the class. Ask listeners to comment or ask questions about information that they found particularly interesting or surprising.

LS **Verbal/Linguistic**

📝 Alternative Assessment Handbook, Rubrics 16: Judging Information; and 29: Presentations is the water cycle. The **water cycle** is the movement of water from Earth's surface to the atmosphere and back.

The sun's energy drives the water cycle. As the sun heats water on Earth's surface, some of that water evaporates, or turns from liquid to gas, or water vapor. Water vapor then rises into the air. As the vapor rises, it cools. The cooling causes the water vapor to condense, or change from a vapor into tiny liquid droplets. These droplets join together to form clouds. If the droplets become heavy enough, precipitation occurs—that is, the water falls back to Earth as rain, snow, sleet, or hail.

When that precipitation falls back to Earth's surface, some of the water is absorbed into the soil as groundwater. Excess water, called runoff, flows over land and collects in streams, rivers, and oceans. Because the water cycle is constantly repeating, it allows us to maintain a fairly constant supply of water on Earth.

READING CHECK **Finding Main Ideas** What is the water cycle?

As energy from the sun heats water on Earth's surface, the water evaporates, or turns to water vapor, and rises to the atmosphere.

Water and People

How many times a day do you think about water? Many of us rarely give it a second thought, yet water is crucial for survival. Water problems such as the lack of water, polluted water, and flooding are concerns for people all around the world. Water also provides us with <u>countless</u> benefits, such as energy and recreation.

Water Problems

One of the greatest water problems people face is a lack of available freshwater. Many places face water shortages as a result of droughts, or long periods of lower-than-normal precipitation. Another cause of water shortages is overuse. In places like the southwestern United States, where the population has grown rapidly, the heavy demand for water has led to shortages.

Even where water is plentiful, it may not be clean enough to use. If chemicals and household wastes make their way into streams and rivers, they can contaminate the water supply. Polluted water can carry diseases. These diseases may harm humans, plants, and animals.

Flooding is another water problem that affects people around the world. Heavy rains often lead to flooding, which can damage property and threaten lives. One example of dangerous flooding occurred in Bangladesh in 2004. Severe floods there destroyed roads and schools, affecting about 25 million people.

Water's Benefits

Water does more than just quench our thirst. It provides us with many benefits, such as food, power, and even recreation.

Water's most important benefit is that it provides us with food to eat. Everything we eat depends on water. For example, fruits and vegetables need water to grow.

FOCUS ON READING

Look at the word *countless* in this paragraph. The suffix *-less* means unable to. What does *countless* mean?

Main Idea

❸ Water and People

Water plays an important role in people's lives.

Explain Why is water necessary for survival? *People need water to drink and to produce food.*

Identify Cause and Effect What problems can be caused by too much or too little water? *too much—flooding; too little—drought*

Collaborative Learning

At Level

Making a Chart

Research Required

1. Organize the class into small groups. Have each group find out about your community's water supply. Ask them to brainstorm a list of questions they would like to have answered.

2. Next, have students look for answers by going to the library or using the Internet, or by contacting the local water department.

3. Have groups organize their findings in a chart, such as the one shown here:

Our Community's Water Supply

Question	Answer
Where does our water come from?	
How is drinking water treated?	
How much water does our community need?	

4. Have groups display their charts and discuss their findings.

LS **Verbal/Linguistic, Visual/Spatial**

Alternative Assessment Handbook, Rubrics 7: Charts; and 30: Research

Answers

Reading Check *the circulation of water from Earth's surface to the atmosphere and back*

Focus on Reading *unable to be counted*

The Benefits of Water
Many people take advantage of the recreational and agricultural benefits that water provides.

Animals also need water to live and grow. As a result, we use water to farm and raise animals so that we will have food to eat.

Water is also an important source of energy. Using dams, we harness the power of moving water to produce electricity. Electricity provides power to air-condition or heat our homes, to run our washers and dryers, and to keep our food cold.

Water also provides us with recreation. Rivers, lakes, and oceans make it possible for us to swim, to fish, to surf, or to sail a boat. Although recreation is not critical for our survival, it does make our lives richer and more enjoyable.

READING CHECK Summarizing How does water affect people's lives?

SUMMARY AND PREVIEW In this section you learned that water is essential for life on Earth. Next, you will learn about the shapes on Earth's surface.

Section 2 Assessment

hmhsocialstudies.com
ONLINE QUIZ

Reviewing Ideas, Terms, and Places
1. **a. Describe** Name and describe the different types of water that make up Earth's water supply.
   b. Analyze Why is only a small percentage of Earth's **freshwater** available to us?
   c. Elaborate In your opinion, which is more important—**surface water** or **groundwater**? Why?
2. **a. Recall** What drives the **water cycle**?
   b. Make Inferences From what bodies of water do you think most evaporation occurs? Why?
3. **a. Define** What is a drought?
   b. Analyze How does water support life on Earth?
   c. Evaluate What water problem do you think is most critical in your community? Why?

Critical Thinking
4. **Sequencing** Draw the graphic organizer at right. Then use your notes and the graphic organizer to identify the stages in Earth's water cycle.

FOCUS ON WRITING

5. **Learning about Water** Consider what you have learned about water in this section. How might you describe water in your haiku? What words might you use to describe Earth's water supply?

Heat from the sun evaporates water on Earth.
↓
↓
↓
↓
The water cycle repeats.

Section 2 Assessment Answers

1. **a.** freshwater—suitable for drinking, makes up 3 percent of Earth's water supply; salt water—unsafe to drink, makes up 97 percent of Earth's water supply, mainly found in oceans
   b. Most freshwater is stored underground or locked in glaciers.
   c. Answers will vary, but should reflect section content. surface water—more accessible; groundwater—abundant
2. **a.** evaporation and precipitation
   b. oceans and lakes because of size
3. **a.** a long period of lower-than-normal precipitation

   b. We depend on it for drinking, food, energy, and recreation.
   c. Answers will vary. Students may note pollution, lack of water, or flooding.
4. The water vapor cools and forms clouds. Droplets in the clouds become too heavy, causing precipitation. Runoff flows over land into rivers, streams, and oceans.
5. Students' word choices will vary but may include precious, vital, and cool.

The Land

If YOU lived there...

You live in the state of Washington. All your life, you have looked out at the beautiful, cone-shaped peaks of nearby mountains. One of them is Mount Saint Helens, an active volcano. You know that in 1980 it erupted violently, blowing a hole in the mountain and throwing ash and rock into the sky. Since then, scientists have watched the mountain carefully.

How do you feel about living near a volcano?

> **BUILDING BACKGROUND** Over billions of years, many different forces have changed Earth's surface. Processes deep underground have built up landforms and even shifted the position of continents. Wind, water, and ice have also shaped the planet's landforms. Changes in Earth's surface continue to take place.

Landforms

Do you know the difference between a valley and a volcano? Can you tell a peninsula from a plateau? If you answered yes, then you are familiar with some of Earth's many landforms. **Landforms** are shapes on the planet's surface, such as hills or mountains. Landforms make up the landscapes that surround us, whether it's the rugged mountains of central Colorado or the flat plains of Oklahoma.

Earth's surface is covered with landforms of many different shapes and sizes. Some important landforms include:

- mountains, land that rises higher than 2,000 feet (610 m)
- valleys, areas of low land located between mountains or hills
- plains, stretches of mostly flat land
- islands, areas of land completely surrounded by water
- peninsulas, land surrounded by water on three sides

Because landforms play an important role in geography, many scientists study how landforms are made and how they affect human activity.

> **READING CHECK** Summarizing What are some common landforms?

What You Will Learn...

Main Ideas
1. Earth's surface is covered by many different landforms.
2. Forces below Earth's surface build up our landforms.
3. Forces on the planet's surface shape Earth's landforms.
4. Landforms influence people's lives and culture.

The Big Idea
Processes below and on Earth's surface shape the planet's physical features.

Key Terms
landforms, *p. 35*
continents, *p. 36*
plate tectonics, *p. 36*
lava, *p. 37*
earthquakes, *p. 38*
weathering, *p. 39*
erosion, *p. 39*

hmhsocialstudies.com
TAKING NOTES

Use the graphic organizer online to take notes on Earth's landforms.

Teach the Big Idea

The Land

1. **Teach** Ask students the questions in the Main Idea boxes under Direct Teach.

2. **Apply** Have each student create a chart with three columns. In the first column have them list what they know about landforms. In the second column, have students write questions about landforms. Finally, have students look through the chapter to see if they can find answers to their questions in the illustrations, captions, headings, and terms. Have them write the answers in the third column.

3. **Review** Have students quiz a partner by asking the questions in the second column and checking them against their answers in the third column.

4. **Practice/Homework** Have students create five multiple-choice questions about the section. Remind them to provide an answer key. **LS Verbal/Linguistic**

   Alternative Assessment Handbook, Rubric 37: Writing Assignments

---

Bellringer

If YOU lived there. . . Use the **Daily Bellringer Transparency** to help students answer the question.

▶ Daily Bellringer Transparency, Section 3

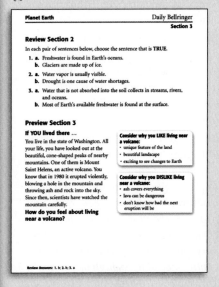

Academic Vocabulary

Review with students the high-use academic term in this section.

structure the way something is set up or organized (p. 36)

📝 **RF:** Vocabulary Builder, Section 3

Main Idea

❶ Landforms

Earth's surface is covered by many different landforms.

Define What is a landform? *a shape on Earth's surface*

Taking Notes

Have students use the graphic organizer online to take notes on the section. This activity will prepare students for the Section Assessment, in which they will complete a graphic organizer that builds on the information using the Critical Thinking Skill: Analyzing.

Answers

Reading Check *mountains, valleys, plains, islands, and peninsulas*

❷ Forces below Earth's Surface

Forces below Earth's surface build up our landforms.

Define What is plate tectonics? *A theory to explain how landforms are formed; Earth's crust has several plates that create landforms when they collide, separate, or slide past each other.*

Summarize What are the two types of tectonic plates? *ocean plates and continental plates* What three types of plate collisions are there, and what landforms result from these collisions? *two ocean plates—ocean trenches; ocean plates and continental plates—mountain ranges near the ocean; two continental plates—high mountains*

▶ Map Zone Transparency: Earth's Plates

Did you know. . .

Alfred Wegener called the original "supercontinent" Pangaea, which in Greek means "all the land" or "all earth." A South African geologist named Alexander L. Du Toit suggested an alternative theory in 1937—that there were originally two continents: Gond wanaland in the south and Laurasia in the north.

Did you know. . .

Many facts support the theory of continental drift. One of them is the similarity in rock formations along the coasts of South America and Africa.

↗ hmhsocialstudies.com

Online Resources
Activity: Continental Drift in the Future

Forces below Earth's Surface

Geographers often study how landforms are made. One explanation for how landforms have been shaped involves forces below Earth's surface.

Earth's Plates

ACADEMIC VOCABULARY
structure the way something is set up or organized

To understand how these forces work, we must examine Earth's **structure**. The planet is made up of three layers. A solid inner core is surrounded by a liquid layer, or mantle. The solid outer layer of Earth is called the crust. The planet's **continents**, or large landmasses, are part of Earth's crust.

Geographers use the theory of plate tectonics to explain how forces below Earth's surface have shaped our landforms. The theory of **plate tectonics** suggests that Earth's surface is divided into a dozen or so slow-moving plates, or pieces of Earth's crust. As you can see in the image below,

some plates, like the Pacific plate, are quite large. Others, like the Nazca plate, are much smaller. These plates cover Earth's entire surface. Some plates are under the ocean. These are known as ocean plates. Other plates, known as continental plates, are under Earth's continents.

Why do these plates move? Energy deep inside the planet puts pressure on Earth's crust. As this pressure builds up, it forces the plates to shift. Earth's tectonic plates all move. However, they move in different directions and at different speeds.

The Movement of Continents

Earth's tectonic plates move slowly—up to several inches per year. The continents, which are part of Earth's plates, shift as the plates move. If we could look back some 200 million years, we would see that the continents have traveled great distances. This idea is known as continental drift.

Earth's Plates

↗ hmhsocialstudies.com
ANIMATED GEOGRAPHY

map zone

- North American plate
- Eurasian plate
- Indian plate
- Pacific plate
- African plate
- Nazca plate
- South American plate
- Australian plate
- Antarctic plate

Collaborative Learning

Above Level

Designing a Slide Show Presentation

1. Organize students in pairs or small groups. Ask them to imagine that they are park rangers at a national park in a region where landforms were formed by colliding continents.

2. Have students work together to design a slide show presentation about plate tectonics, to be shown to park visitors. They should include maps, photographs, and/or drawings to illustrate the information.

3. Have students write the commentary on the slide show. Finally, have them present the slide show to the class, having one student show the images while another reads the commentary. Encourage listeners to ask questions about the material.
   LS Interpersonal, Verbal/Linguistic

   Alternative Assessment Handbook, Rubrics 14: Group Activity; and 22: Multimedia Presentations

The theory of continental drift, first developed by Alfred Wegener, states that the continents were once united in a single supercontinent. According to this theory, Earth's plates shifted over millions of years. As a result, the continents slowly separated and moved to their present positions.

Earth's continents are still moving. Some plates move toward each other and collide. Other plates separate and move apart. Still others slide past one another. Over time, colliding, separating, and sliding plates have shaped Earth's landforms.

Plates Collide

As plates collide, the energy created from their collision produces distinct landforms. The collision of different types of plates creates different shapes on Earth's surface. Ocean trenches and mountain ranges are two examples of landforms produced by the collision of tectonic plates.

BIOGRAPHY

Alfred Wegener
(1880–1930)

German scientist Alfred Wegener's fascination with the similarities between the western coast of Africa and the eastern coast of South America led to his theory of continental drift. Wegener argued that the two continents had once been joined together. Years of plate movement broke the continents apart and moved them to their current locations. It was only after Wegener's death that his ideas became a central part of the theory of plate tectonics.

The theory of plate tectonics suggests that the plates that make up Earth's crust are moving, usually only a few inches per year. As Earth's plates collide, separate, and slide past each other, they create forces great enough to shape many of Earth's landforms.

ANALYZING VISUALS Looking at the map, what evidence indicates that plates have collided or separated?

When two ocean plates collide, one plate pushes under the other. This process creates ocean trenches. Ocean trenches are deep valleys in the ocean floor. Near Japan, for example, the Pacific plate is slowly moving under other plates. This collision has created several deep ocean trenches, including the world's deepest trench, the Mariana Trench.

Ocean plates and continental plates can also collide. When this occurs, the ocean plate drops beneath the continental plate. This action forces the land above to crumple and form a mountain range. The Andes in South America, for example, were formed when the South American and Nazca plates collided.

The collision of two continental plates also results in mountain-building. When continental plates collide, the land pushes up, sometimes to great heights. The world's highest mountain range, the Himalayas, formed when the Indian plate crashed into the Eurasian plate. In fact, the Himalayas are still growing as the two plates continue to crash into each other.

Plates Separate

A second type of plate movement causes plates to separate. As plates move apart, gaps between the plates allow magma, a liquid rock from the planet's interior, to rise to Earth's crust. **Lava**, or magma that reaches Earth's surface, emerges from the gap that has formed. As the lava cools, it builds a mid-ocean ridge, or underwater mountain. For example, the separation of the North American and Eurasian plates formed the largest underwater mountain, the Mid-Atlantic Ridge. If these mid-ocean ridges grow high enough, they can rise above the surface of the ocean, forming volcanic islands. Iceland, on the boundary of the Eurasian and North American plates, is an example of such an island.

FOCUS ON READING
The suffix –sion means the act of. What does the word collision mean?

Critical Thinking: Understanding Cause and Effect

Cause-and-Effect Chart

1. Have students reread the material under the Plates Collide heading on this page. Ask them if they can identify the main idea of each paragraph. Point out that the second, third, and fourth paragraphs each begin with a topic sentence that contains the main idea.

2. Ask students to identify the main ideas in the Plates Separate paragraphs and Plates Slide paragraphs on the following page. Help them see that each type of

plate movement results in a different kind of landform by making cause-and-effect charts to clarify this information.

Cause	Effect
colliding	ocean trenches mountains
separating	mid-ocean ridge (underwater mountains) volcanic islands
sliding	earthquakes

3. Ask volunteers to share their charts and get feedback. Have the class discuss examples of landforms they are familiar with that were caused by plate movement.

LS Visual/Spatial, Verbal/Linguistic

Alternative Assessment Handbook, Rubrics 6: Cause and Effect; and 7: Charts

Info to Know

Quake Force Powerful earthquakes have caused huge death tolls and devastation throughout the world. Of the nine most destructive earthquakes in the twentieth century, four occurred in China. In 1976 the town of Tangshan, China, was hit with an earthquake that killed approximately 240,000 people. About 500,000 were estimated to have been wounded.

In the United States, the largest magnitude earthquakes have taken place in Alaska. On the mainland, most of the high-magnitude earthquakes have occurred in California. A number of earthquake faults, particularly in California, are closely watched by geologists. The San Andreas fault system runs about 800 miles north to south through the state. At its widest point, the fault is a few hundred feet wide.

 RF: Critical Thinking, Volcanoes

Teaching Tip

Help students navigate this page by discussing each pair of visuals and captions separately. Explain that the illustration on the left of each pair of visuals shows the process, and the photograph on the right shows the result of the process. Have students reread the text about the separation of plates and the collision of continental plates.

Plates Slide

Tectonic plates also slide past each other. As plates pass by one another, they sometimes grind together. This grinding produces **earthquakes**—sudden, violent movements of Earth's crust. Earthquakes often take place along faults, or breaks in Earth's crust where movement occurs. In California, for example, the Pacific plate is sliding by the edge of the North American plate. This has created the San Andreas Fault zone, an area where earthquakes are quite common.

The San Andreas Fault zone is one of many areas that lie along the boundaries of the Pacific plate. The frequent movement of this plate produces many earthquakes and volcanic eruptions along its edges. In fact, the region around the Pacific plate, called the Ring of Fire, is home to most of the world's earthquakes and volcanoes.

HISTORY
VIDEO
Earthquakes
hmhsocialstudies.com

READING CHECK Finding Main Ideas What forces below Earth's surface shape landforms?

Plate Movement

The movement of tectonic plates has produced many of Earth's landforms. Volcanoes, islands, and mountains often result from the separation or collision of Earth's plates.

ANALYZING VISUALS What type of landform is created by the collision of two continental plates?

Plate A
magma
Plate B

The separation of plates can allow magma to rise up and create volcanic islands like Surtsey Island, near Iceland.

Plate A
Plate B

The Himalayas in South Asia resulted from the collision of two massive continental plates.

Answers

Reading Check *Energy in Earth's core and mantle creates pressure against the crust. This pressure can force tectonic plates to move. When these plates collide or separate, they can form volcanoes, ocean trenches, mid-ocean ridges, and mountains. Sliding plates can also cause earthquakes and volcanic eruptions.*

Analyzing Visuals *mountains*

38

Differentiating Instruction

Below Level

Struggling Readers

To help struggling readers, have them study each photo and then match the text to the photo. Have students discuss what they see, and read the introduction and the captions aloud. Remind them to look for illustrations and captions throughout the book. **LS** Visual/Spatial, Verbal/Linguistic

Alternative Assessment Handbook, Rubric 1: Acquiring Information

Special Needs Learners

Provide images of mountains and volcanoes from magazines and the Internet and have students make collages. Challenge them to distinguish volcanoes and other kinds of mountains. Point out that volcanoes are made when plates pull apart and that mountains are made when plates crash into each other. **LS** Visual/Spatial

Alternative Assessment Handbook, Rubric 8: Collages

Forces on Earth's Surface

For millions of years, the movement of Earth's tectonic plates has been building up landforms on Earth's surface. At the same time, other forces are working to change those very same landforms.

Imagine a small pile of dirt and rock on a table. If you poured water on the pile, it would move the dirt and rock from one place to another. Likewise, if you were to blow at the pile, the rock and dirt would also move. The same process happens in nature. Weather, water, and other forces change Earth's landforms by wearing them away or reshaping them.

Weathering

One force that wears away landforms is weathering. **Weathering** is the process by which rock is broken down into smaller pieces. Several factors cause rock to break down. In desert areas, daytime heating and nighttime cooling can cause rocks to crack. Water may get into cracks in rocks and freeze. The ice then expands with a force great enough to break the rock. Even the roots of trees can pry rocks apart.

Regardless of which weathering process is at work, rocks eventually break down. These small pieces of rock are known as sediment. Once weathering has taken place, wind, ice, and water often move sediment from one place to another.

Erosion

Another force that changes landforms is the process of erosion. **Erosion** is the movement of sediment from one location to another. Erosion can wear away or build up landforms. Wind, ice, and water all cause erosion.

Powerful winds often cause erosion. Winds lift sediment into the air and carry it across great distances. On beaches and in deserts, wind can deposit large amounts of sand to form dunes. Blowing sand can also wear down rock. The sand acts like sandpaper to polish and wear away at rocks. As you can see in the photo below, wind can have a dramatic effect on landforms.

Earth's glaciers also have the power to cause massive erosion. Glaciers, or large, slow-moving sheets of ice, build up when winter snows do not melt the following summer. Glaciers can be huge. Glaciers in Greenland and Antarctica, for example, are great sheets of ice up to two miles (3 km) thick. Some glaciers flow slowly downhill like rivers of ice. As they do so, they erode the land by carving large U-shaped valleys and sharp mountain peaks. As the ice flows downhill, it crushes rock into sediment and can move huge rocks long distances.

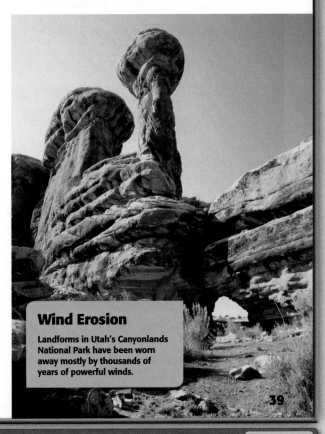

Wind Erosion
Landforms in Utah's Canyonlands National Park have been worn away mostly by thousands of years of powerful winds.

39

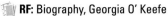

Direct Teach

Main Idea

❸ Forces on Earth's Surface

Forces on the planet's surface shape Earth's landforms.

Describe What is weathering? *the process of breaking rock into smaller pieces* What are the causes of erosion? *wind, ice, water* What landforms are shaped by liquid water? *coastlines, canyons, floodplains, deltas*

Explain How does wind erode some landforms? *It can lift soil and move it from place to place, form dunes by depositing sand, and wear down rocks with blowing sand.*

📖 **RF:** Biography, Georgia O' Keefe

Connect to Science

The Living Dirt of the Canyonlands
Located in Utah, Canyonlands National Park preserves a unique desert ecosystem. The Canyonlands was largely formed out of sedimentary rock deposits from the Colorado River and its tributaries. Continual erosion still shapes life in the Canyonlands today. For example, a layer of dirt, or soil crust, called *Biological Soil Crust* lies over much of the Canyonlands area. This crust includes algae, lichens, and bacteria—and serves as a living, but secure, foundation for desert plants.

Critical Thinking: Acquiring Information

Above Level

Advanced/Gifted and Talented

Research Required

1. Have students study (in small groups or pairs) how erosion affects their neighborhood or community. Ask them to begin by finding and observing examples of erosion.

2. As they record their observations, have them answer questions such as the following: What kind of erosion do you observe (wind, water, soil, etc.)? What is causing the erosion? Where is the material (soil, sand, etc.) going? What effect does the erosion have? Can you think of a way to stop the erosion?

3. Ask students to write a report about what they have learned. Have them read the reports aloud.

4. Lead a discussion about which form of erosion students think is the biggest problem, and why. **LS Verbal/Linguistic**

📖 Alternative Assessment Handbook, Rubrics 1: Acquiring Information; and 40: Writing to Describe

4 Landforms Influence Life

Landforms influence people's lives and culture.

Recall Where was the first civilization built? *in the valley of the Tigris and Euphrates rivers*

Explain How did the location help the civilization thrive? *People had plenty of water for crops and could use the rivers for trade.*

Analyze How do the landforms in your area influence your daily life? *Answers will vary. Students should identify the landforms in their region and tell how these landforms affect them.*

📄 **RF:** Geography and History, The California Gold Rush

Connect to History

The Hoover Dam A National Historic Landmark located on the Nevada-Arizona border, the Hoover Dam was built in five years—in a harsh, barren desert—during the Great Depression. Although people lived along the Colorado River for thousands of years, the dam changed the area and how people lived there. For the first time ever, the Hoover Dam allowed the Colorado River to be controlled, providing dependable water supplies for millions of people in Nevada, Arizona, and California. To learn more about the Hoover Dam, visit www.usbr.gov/lc/hooverdam.

Answers

Reading Check *similar—both cause rock to break up; water contributes to both; different—weathering occurs when, as a result of weather factors, rocks crack and break; erosion occurs when ice, wind, and water cause rocky materials to move from one location to another.*

Water is the most common cause of erosion. Waves in oceans and lakes can wear away the shore, creating jagged coastlines, like those on the coast of Oregon. Rivers also cause erosion. Over many years, the flowing water can cut through rock, forming canyons, or narrow areas with steep walls. Arizona's Horseshoe Bend and Grand Canyon are examples of canyons created in this way.

Flowing water shapes other landforms as well. When water deposits sediment in new locations, it creates new landforms. For example, rivers create floodplains when they flood their banks and deposit sediment along the banks. Sediment that is carried by a river all the way out to sea creates a delta. The sediment settles to the bottom, where the river meets the sea. The Nile and Mississippi rivers have created two of the world's largest river deltas.

READING CHECK **Comparing** How are weathering and erosion similar?

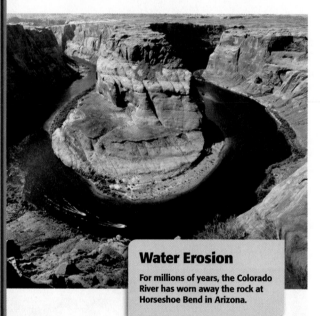

Water Erosion

For millions of years, the Colorado River has worn away the rock at Horseshoe Bend in Arizona.

Landforms Influence Life

Why do you live where you do? Perhaps your family moved to the desert to avoid harsh winter weather. Or possibly one of your ancestors settled near a river delta because its fertile soil was ideal for growing crops. Maybe your family wanted to live near the ocean to start a fishing business. As these examples show, landforms exert a strong influence on people's lives. Earth's landforms affect our settlements and our culture. At the same time, we affect the landforms around us.

Earth's landforms can influence where people settle. People sometimes settle near certain landforms and avoid others. For example, many settlements are built near fertile river valleys or deltas. The earliest urban civilization, for example, was built in the valley between the Tigris and Euphrates rivers. Other times, landforms discourage people from settling in a certain place. Tall, rugged mountains, like the Himalayas, and harsh desert climates, like the Sahara, do not usually attract large settlements.

Landforms affect our culture in ways that we may not have noticed. Landforms often influence what jobs are available in a region. For example, rich mineral deposits in the mountains of Colorado led to the development of a mining industry there. Landforms even affect language. On the island of New Guinea in Southeast Asia, rugged mountains have kept the people so isolated that more than 700 languages are spoken on the island today.

People sometimes change landforms to suit their needs. People may choose to modify landforms in order to improve their lives. For example, engineers built the Panama Canal to make travel from the Atlantic Ocean to the Pacific Ocean easier. In Southeast Asia, people who farm on steep hillsides cut terraces into the slope to

---

Critical Thinking: Drawing Conclusions

Writing a Persuasive Letter

1. Ask students to imagine that they are early settlers in the United States and that they are trying to find the best location to live. Have them explore the advantages and disadvantages of living in certain locations, based on the information in the section as well as their previous knowledge.

2. Have them write a persuasive letter to a friend or family member, urging them to settle in the location they have chosen. In the letter, have students give reasons why the location

they have chosen is the best for their needs. If they wish, they can include a drawing of the location.

3. Have students share their letters and illustrations with the class and discuss which letters are most persuasive. **LS Verbal/Linguistic**

📄 Alternate Assessment Handbook, Rubrics 9: Comparing and Contrasting; 25: Personal Letters; and 43: Writing to Persuade

Living with Landforms

The people of Rio de Janeiro, Brazil, have learned to adapt to the mountains and bays that dominate their landscape.

ANALYZING VISUALS How have people in Rio de Janiero adapted to their landscape?

create more level space to grow their crops. People have even built huge dams along rivers to divert water for use in nearby towns or farms.

READING CHECK **Analyzing** What are some examples of humans adjusting to and changing landforms?

SUMMARY AND PREVIEW Landforms are created by actions deep within the planet's surface, and they are changed by forces on Earth's surface, like weathering and erosion. In the next chapter you will learn how other forces, like weather and climate, affect Earth's people.

Section 3 Assessment

hmhsocialstudies.com
ONLINE QUIZ

Reviewing Ideas, Terms, and Places

1. **a. Describe** What are some common **landforms**?
   b. Analyze Why do geographers study landforms?
2. **a. Identify** What is the theory of **plate tectonics**?
   b. Compare and Contrast How are the effects of colliding plates and separating plates similar and different?
   c. Predict How might Earth's surface change as tectonic plates continue to move?
3. **a. Recall** What is the process of **weathering**?
   b. Elaborate How does water affect sediment?
4. **a. Recall** How do landforms affect life on Earth?
   b. Predict How might people adapt to life in an area with steep mountains?

Critical Thinking

5. **Analyzing** Use your notes and the chart below to identify the different factors that alter Earth's landforms and the changes that they produce.

Factor	Change in Landform

FOCUS ON WRITING

6. **Writing about Earth's Land** Think of some vivid words you could use to describe Earth's landforms. As you think of them, add them to your notebook.

PLANET EARTH **41**

Section 3 Assessment Answers

1. **a.** mountains, valleys, plains, islands
   b. to learn how they are made and how they affect human activity
2. **a.** It explains landforms through movement of pieces of Earth's crust, or plates.
   b. both form landforms; colliding—form ocean trenches, mountains; separating—form ocean ridges, volcanic islands
   c. create new landforms, change existing ones
3. **a.** breaking of rock into smaller pieces
   b. It moves sediment from one place to another, creating new landforms.

4. **a.** possible answer—People settle in certain areas because of landforms. Landforms also affect what kinds of jobs are available in an area.
   b. They might cut terraces to grow crops and build roads for transportation.
5. possible answer—movement of plates: creates ocean trenches and mountains; weathering: wears down landforms; erosion: moves sediment
6. Descriptions will vary, but may include dramatic, spectacular, and weathered.

Case Study

Case Study

Essential Elements

The World in Spatial Terms
Places and Regions
Physical Systems
Human Systems
Environment and Society
The Uses of Geography

The Ring of Fire

Info to Know

Recovering from a Volcanic Eruption

The eruption of Mount Saint Helens was devastating. A 230 square mile blast zone was a wasteland of ash, lava, and dead trees. It was hard to believe that the area could ever recover, that plants and animals could regain their former numbers. But more than 25 years after the eruption, many species have returned, including birds, mammals, flowers, and trees. Elk herds have grown, and numerous black-tailed deer now live in the area. In the absence of future eruptions, scientists expect that the area will continue to recover.

Map Zone Transparency: Ring of Fire

Did you know. . .

The eruption of Mount Saint Helens had 500 times the force of the atomic blast at Hiroshima.

Background Does "the Ring of Fire" sound like the title of a fantasy novel? It's actually the name of a region that circles the Pacific Ocean known for its fiery volcanoes and powerful earthquakes. The Ring of Fire stretches from the tip of South America all the way up to Alaska, and from Japan down to the islands east of Australia. Along this belt, the Pacific plate moves against several other tectonic plates. As a result, thousands of earthquakes occur there every year, and dozens of volcanoes erupt.

The Eruption of Mount Saint Helens One of the best-known volcanoes in the Ring of Fire is Mount Saint Helens in Washington State. Mount Saint Helens had been dormant, or quiet, since 1857. Then in March 1980, it began spitting out puffs of steam and ash. Officials warned people to leave the area. Scientists brought in equipment to measure the growing bulge in the mountainside. Everyone feared the volcano might erupt at any moment.

On May 18, after a sudden earthquake, Mount Saint Helens let loose a massive explosion of rock and lava. Heat from the blast melted snow on the mountain, which

Ring of Fire

map zone

Asia
North America
PACIFIC OCEAN
South America
Australia
Antarctica

- ▬ Plate boundary line
- ⋰ Earthquakes
- ▲ Active volcanoes

THE WORLD ALMANAC Facts about the World	**Major Eruptions in the Ring of Fire**	
Volcano		**Year**
Tambora, Indonesia		1815
Krakatau, Indonesia		1883
Mount Saint Helens, United States		**1980**
Nevado del Ruiz, Colombia		1985
Mount Pinatubo, Philippines		1991
⊿ hmhsocialstudies.com		

42 CHAPTER 2

Critical Thinking: Interpreting Maps

At Level

Making a Map of the Ring of Fire

Research Required

1. Have students use an atlas and other sources from the Internet or library to research the Ring of Fire. Have them draw a map showing the perimeter of the Ring of Fire, labeling continents and bodies of water. Then have them add symbols showing where volcanoes and earthquake faults can be found within the area covered by the map. Encourage students to annotate the maps with information about specific volcanoes, faults, and earthquakes.

2. Have students display their maps. Have them compare their maps with political maps of the region and note how close the earthquake faults and volcanoes are to centers of population. **LS** **Visual/Spatial**

   Alternative Assessment Handbook, Rubric 20: Map Creation

Mount Saint Helens, 1980
The 1980 eruption of Mount Saint Helens blew ash and hot gases miles into the air. Today, scientists study the volcano to learn more about predicting eruptions.

mixed with ash to create deadly mudflows. As the mud quickly poured downhill, it flattened forests, swept away cars, and destroyed buildings. Clouds of ash covered the land, killing crops, clogging waterways, and blanketing towns as far as 200 miles (330 km) away. When the volcano finally quieted down, 57 people had died. Damage totaled nearly $1 billion. If it were not for the early evacuation of the area, the destruction could have been much worse.

What It Means By studying Mount Saint Helens, scientists learned a great deal about stratovolcanoes. These are tall, steep, cone-shaped volcanoes that have violent eruptions. Stratovolcanoes often form in areas where tectonic plates collide.

Because stratovolcanoes often produce deadly eruptions, scientists try to predict when they might erupt. The lessons learned from Mount Saint Helens helped scientists

warn people about another stratovolcano, Mount Pinatubo in the Philippines. That eruption in 1991 was the second-largest of the 1900s. It was far from the deadliest, however. Careful observation and timely warnings saved thousands of lives.

The Ring of Fire will always remain a threat. However, the better we understand its volcanoes, the better prepared we'll be when they erupt.

Geography for Life Activity

1. How did the eruption of Mount Saint Helens affect the surrounding area?

2. Why do scientists monitor volcanic activity?

3. **Investigating the Effects of Volcanoes** Some volcanic eruptions affect environmental conditions around the world. Research the eruption of either Mount Saint Helens or the Philippines' Mount Pinatubo to find out how its eruption affected the global environment.

PLANET EARTH   **43**

Cross-Discipline Activity: English/Language Arts   `At Level`

Writing a Story

1. Have students research and write an eyewitness account of the eruption of Mount Saint Helens, Mount Vesuvius, Krakatau, or another volcano.

2. Ask them to imagine that they were living in or visiting the area near the volcano when it erupted. Using the information they gather as well as their imagination and prior knowledge, have them write a short story about the eruption and the events that preceded and followed the disaster.

Encourage students to include vivid images and details of the experience in their stories.

3. Finally, have students read their short stories aloud. Encourage class members to ask questions about the information.

LS **Verbal/Linguistic**

Alternative Assessment Handbook, Rubrics 1: Acquiring Information; and 40: Writing to Describe

Answers

Geography for Life **1.** *It flattened forests, killed crops, clogged waterways, and destroyed buildings;* **2.** *to try to predict when volcanoes might erupt so they can warn people;* **3.** *Students should find in their research that the amount of sulfur released into the atmosphere by the volcanic eruptions caused a decrease in worldwide temperatures.*

Social Studies Skills

Using a Physical Map

Materials: a physical map of your region to print or copy for students

1. Provide students with a physical map of your region.

2. Tell students that they will use the map to plan a sightseeing tour of physical features in your area.

3. Have students identify places they would like to visit and mark them on the map.

4. Have students plan their route. They should label their start and end points and the routes they will take to get from one place to another.

5. When they have finished, have students share their plans with the class. They should tell whether they will be travelling by foot, bicycle, or another means of transportation. They should also use the scale of miles to estimate how long their trip will take.

LS Visual/Spatial, Verbal/Linguistic

RF: Social Studies Skills, Using a Physical Map

Alternative Assessment Handbook, Rubric 24: Oral Presentations

Map Zone Transparency: India: Physical

Interactive Skills Tutor CD-ROM, Lesson 6: Interpret Maps, Graphs, Charts, Visuals, and Political Cartoons

Using a Physical Map

Learn

Physical maps show important physical features, like oceans and mountains, in a particular area. They also indicate an area's elevation, or the height of the land in relation to sea level.

When you use a physical map, there are important pieces of information you should always examine.

- Identify physical features. Natural features, such as mountains, rivers, and lakes, are labeled on physical maps. Read the labels carefully to identify what physical features are present.

- Read the legend. On physical maps, the legend indicates scale as well as elevation. The different colors in the elevation key indicate how far above or below sea level a place is.

Practice

Use the physical map of India at right to answer the questions below.

1. What landforms and bodies of water are indicated on the map?

2. What is the highest elevation in India? Where is it located?

India: Physical

Apply

Locate the physical map of Africa in the atlas in the back of the book. Use the map to answer the questions below.

1. Which region has the highest elevation?

2. What bodies of water surround Africa?

3. What large island is located off the east coast of Africa?

Social Studies Skill Activity: Using a Physical Map **At Level**

Describe Physical Features **Research Required**

1. Divide students into small groups and assign each group a different region of the world.

2. Have students locate physical maps of their region using atlases or other library or Internet resources.

3. Students should use the maps to identify important physical features of their region. Then have them conduct further research to find out more about each feature.

4. When they have finished, have each group present their findings to the class.

LS Visual/Spatial, Verbal/Linguistic

Alternative Assessment Handbook, Rubric 24: Oral Presentations

Answers

Practice 1. mountain, desert, delta, plateau, river, bay, ocean, sea; **2.** 28,208 ft., Himalayas

Apply 1. the eastern region, Mount Kilimanjaro, Tanzania; **2.** Indian Ocean, Atlantic Ocean, Red Sea, Mediterranean Sea; **3.** Madagascar

Chapter Review

Geography's Impact
video series
Review the video to answer the closing question:
What are some reasons for water shortages, and what can be done to solve this problem?

Visual Summary

Use the visual summary below to help you review the main ideas of the chapter.

QUICK FACTS

The amount of solar energy Earth receives changes based on Earth's movement and position.

Water is crucial to life on Earth. Our abundant water supply is stored in oceans, in lakes, and underground.

Earth's various landforms are shaped by complex processes both under and on the planet's surface.

Reviewing Vocabulary, Terms, and Places

For each statement below, write T if it is true and F if it is false. If the statement is false, write the correct term that would make the sentence a true statement.

1. **Weathering** is the movement of sediment from one location to another.

2. Because high **latitude** areas receive indirect rays from the sun, they have cooler temperatures.

3. Most of our **groundwater** is stored in Earth's streams, rivers, and lakes.

4. It takes 365¼ days for Earth to complete one **rotation** around the sun.

5. Streams are formed when **precipitation** collects in narrow channels.

6. **Earthquakes** cause erosion as they flow downhill, carving valleys and mountain peaks.

7. The planet's tilt affects the amount of **erosion** Earth receives from the sun.

Comprehension and Critical Thinking

SECTION 1 *(Pages 26–29)*

8. **a. Identify** What factors influence the amount of energy that different places on Earth receive from the sun?

   b. Analyze Why do the Northern and Southern hemispheres experience opposite seasons?

   c. Predict What might happen to the amount of solar energy we receive if Earth's axis were straight up and down?

SECTION 2 *(Pages 30–34)*

9. **a. Describe** What different sources of water are available on Earth?

   b. Draw Conclusions How does the water cycle keep Earth's water supply relatively constant?

   c. Elaborate What water problems affect people around the world? What solutions can you think of for one of those problems?

PLANET EARTH **45**

10. **a.** a shape on a planet's surface; hills, mountains
b. because they rest on tectonic plates, which are moving
c. possible response—valleys, which are good for farming and raising livestock

Using the Internet

11. Go to ⬀ hmhsocialstudies.com to access a rubric for this activity.

Social Studies Skills

12. Gulf Coastal Plain

13. Rocky Mountains

14. Death Valley, Imperial Valley

Map Activity

15. C

16. A

17. B

18. F

19. E

20. D

Focus on Reading and Writing

21. not visible; not active

22. the action or process of moving

📓 **RF:** Focus on Reading, Using Word Parts

23. **Rubric** Students' haikus should
- be short
- either be traditional with three lines and 17 syllables or have a nontraditional form
- use descriptive words
- describe an aspect of Earth

📓 **RF:** Focus on Writing, Writing a Haiku

SECTION 3 *(Pages 35–41)*

10. **a. Define** What is a landform? What are some common types of landforms?
b. Analyze Why are Earth's landforms still changing?
c. Elaborate What physical features dominate the landscape in your community? How do they affect life there?

Using the Internet

11. **Activity: Researching Earth's Seasons** Earth's seasons not only affect temperatures, they also affect how much daylight is available during specific times of the year. Through your online textbook, research Earth's seasons and view animations to see how seasons change. Then use the interactive worksheet to answer some questions about what you learned.

⬀ hmhsocialstudies.com

Social Studies Skills

Using a Physical Map *Examine the physical map of the United States in the back of this book. Use it to answer the questions below.*

12. What physical feature extends along the Gulf of Mexico?

13. What mountain range in the West lies above 6,560 feet?

14. Where does the elevation drop below sea level?

Map Activity

Physical Map *Use the map on the right to answer the questions that follow.*

15. Which letter indicates a river?

16. Which letter on the map indicates the highest elevation?

17. The lowest elevation on the map is indicated by which letter?

18. An island is indicated by which letter?

19. Which letter indicates a large body of water?

20. Which letter indicates an area of land between 1,640 feet and 6,560 feet above sea level?

⬀ hmhsocialstudies.com **INTERACTIVE MAP**

map zone

MONGOLIA

CHINA

ELEVATION

Feet		Meters
13,120		4,000
6,560		2,000
1,640		500
656		200
(Sea level) 0		0 (Sea level)
Below sea level		Below sea level

0   250   500   750 Miles

0   250   500   750 Kilometers

Projection: Two-Point Equidistant

FOCUS ON READING AND WRITING

Using Word Parts *Use what you learned about prefixes, suffixes, and word roots to answer the questions below.*

21. The prefix *in-* means not. What do the words *invisible* and *inactive* mean?

22. The suffix *-ment* means action or process. What does the word *movement* mean?"

23. **Writing a Haiku** Look back through your notes about Earth. Choose one aspect of Earth to describe in a haiku. A haiku is a three-line poem that consists of 17 syllables—five in the first line, seven in the second line, and five in the third line. Be sure to use descriptive words to paint a picture of planet Earth.

Standardized Test Prep

DIRECTIONS: Read questions 1 through 7 and write the letter of the best response. Then read question 8 and write your own well-constructed response.

1 Which regions on Earth have seasons tied to the amount of rainfall?

A polar regions

B the tropics

C the Northern Hemisphere

D high latitudes

2 Most of Earth's water supply is made up of

A groundwater.

B water vapor.

C freshwater.

D salt water.

3 The theory of continental drift explains how

A Earth's continents have moved thousands of miles.

B Earth's axis has moved to its current position.

C mountains and valleys are formed.

D sediment moves from one place to another.

4 Which of the following is a cause of erosion?

A evaporation

B ice

C plate collisions

D Earth's tilt

5 Changes in solar energy that create day and night are a result of

A the movement of tectonic plates.

B Earth's rotation.

C the revolution of Earth around the sun.

D Earth's tilt.

The Water Cycle

6 In the illustration above, which letter *best* reflects the process of evaporation?

A W

B X

C Y

D Z

7 Which of the following is *most likely* a cause of water pollution?

A River water is used to produce electricity.

B Heavy rainfall causes a river to overflow its banks.

C Chemicals from a factory seep into the local water supply.

D Groundwater is used faster than it can be replaced.

8 **Extended Response Question** Use the water cycle diagram above to explain how Earth's water cycle affects our water supply.

Reteach/Intervention Resources

Reproducible

Guided Reading Workbook

Differentiated Instruction Teacher Management System: Lesson Plans

Technology

Quick Facts Transparency: Planet Earth Visual Summary

Differentiated Instruction Modified Worksheets and Tests CD-ROM

Interactive Skills Tutor CD-ROM

Tips for Test Taking

How Much Do I Write? Point out to students that if a writing question contains any of the following terms, they will need to write several sentences for a complete answer: *describe, justify, why, explain,* or *elaborate.* These are not the only words, however, that may indicate several sentences are required.

Answers

Standardized Test Prep

1. B
Break Down the Question This question requires students to recall factual information. Refer students who miss it to Section 1.

2. D
Break Down the Question Remind students not to confuse Earth's water supply, or the total water on the planet, with water available to people. Refer students who miss it to Section 2.

3. A
Break Down the Question This question requires students to recall factual information. Refer students who miss it to Section 3.

4. B
Break Down the Question Suggest that students try to recall the three causes of erosion. This will allow them to eliminate all choices except for B. Refer students who miss it to Section 3.

5. B
Break Down the Question This question requires students to recall factual information. Refer students who miss it to Section 1.

6. C
Break Down the Question Remind students that evaporation is when water on Earth turns to water vapor and rises to the atmosphere.

7. C
Break Down the Question Remind students to focus on the term "most likely" to come up with the correct answer.

8. Extended Response Possible answer—Surface water evaporates into the atmosphere, condenses, then falls back to Earth as precipitation. This cycle helps keep the water supply fairly constant.

Chapter 3 Planning Guide

Climate, Environment, and Resources

Overview	Instructional Resources	
CHAPTER 3 **Essential Question:** What factors shape Earth's different environments? 🔊 **Focus on the Essential Question Podcast**	**TOS** **Differentiated Instruction Teacher Management System:** • Instructional Pacing Guides • Lesson Plans for Differentiated Instruction 📄 **Guided Reading Workbook** 📄 **Resource File:** • Chapter Review • Focus on Reading: Understanding Cause and Effect • Focus on Viewing: Presenting and Viewing a Weather Report • Social Studies Skills: Analyzing a Bar Graph 📄 **Experiencing World History and Geography**	**TOS** **Calendar Planner** 💿 **Power Presentations with Media Gallery** 💿 **Differentiated Instruction Modified Worksheets and Tests CD-ROM** 💿 **Interactive Skills Tutor CD-ROM** 🔊 **Student Edition on Audio CD-ROM** 🔊 **The World's Music Audio Program** ▶️ **World Outline Maps: Transparencies and Activities** 📺 **Video:** Tornado Alley Twister
Section 1: **Weather and Climate** **The Big Idea:** The sun, location, wind, water, and mountains affect weather and climate.	**TOS** **Differentiated Instruction Teacher Management System:** Section 1 Lesson Plan 📄 **Guided Reading Workbook:** Section 1 📄 **Resource File:** • Vocabulary Builder: Section 1 • Biography: Edward Lorenz • Geography for Life: Hurricane Season	▶️ **Daily Bellringer Transparency:** Section 1 ▶️ **Map Zone Transparency:** Global Wind Systems ▶️ **Map Zone Transparency:** Major Ocean Currents ↗️ **Internet Activity:** Solar Energy ↗️ **Internet Activity:** Experiencing Extremes
Section 2: **World Climates** **The Big Idea:** Earth's five major climate zones are identified by temperature, precipitation, and plant life.	**TOS** **Differentiated Instruction Teacher Management System:** Section 2 Lesson Plan 📄 **Guided Reading Workbook:** Section 2 📄 **Resource File:** • Vocabulary Builder: Section 2 • Literature: "To Build a Fire" by Jack London	▶️ **Daily Bellringer Transparency:** Section 2 ▶️ **Map Zone Transparency:** World Climate Regions
Section 3: **Natural Environments** **The Big Idea:** Plants, animals, and the environment, including soil, interact and affect one another.	**TOS** **Differentiated Instruction Teacher Management System:** Section 3 Lesson Plan 📄 **Guided Reading Workbook:** Section 3 📄 **Resource File:** • Vocabulary Builder: Section 3 • Biography: Jane Goodall • Primary Source: *Protection of Game in Yellowstone National Park* • Critical Thinking: Geography from Trees • Interdisciplinary Project: Diagram an Ecosystem	▶️ **Daily Bellringer Transparency:** Section 3 ▶️ **Map Zone Transparency:** North America in the Dinosaur Age 📺 **Video:** Future Chill
Section 4: **Natural Resources** **The Big Idea:** Earth's natural resources have many valuable uses, and their availability affects people in many ways.	**TOS** **Differentiated Instruction Teacher Management System:** Section 4 Lesson Plan 📄 **Guided Reading Workbook:** Section 4 📄 **Resource File:** • Vocabulary Builder: Section 4	▶️ **Daily Bellringer Transparency:** Section 4

Chart Key:

SE Student Edition   Presentation Resource   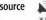 MP3 Audio

TOS Teacher One Stop   DVD/CD-ROM   HISTORY™

 Printable Resource

Program Resources available on **TOS** and @ hmhsocialstudies.com

Review, Assessment, Intervention

 Introduction to Geography Transparencies: Climate, Environment, and Resources Visual Summary

 Spanish Chapter Summaries Audio CD

 Progress Assessment Support System (PASS): Chapter Test

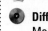 **Differentiated Instruction Modified Worksheets CD-ROM:** Modified Chapter Test

TOS **ExamView® Assessment Suite (English/Spanish)**

 Alternative Assessment Handbook

 Online Assessment Program, in the Interactive Student Edition

 PASS: Section 1 Quiz

 Online Quiz: Section 1

 Alternative Assessment Handbook

 PASS: Section 2 Quiz

 Online Quiz: Section 2

 Alternative Assessment Handbook

 PASS: Section 3 Quiz

 Online Quiz: Section 3

 Alternative Assessment Handbook

 PASS: Section 4 Quiz

 Online Quiz: Section 4

 Alternative Assessment Handbook

Supporting Resources

HISTORY.

- Multimedia Classroom Global History Series
- Global History Teacher's Guide

Maps Globes Graphs Level F

- Student Workbook
- Teacher's Guide

Social Studies Trade Library Collections

- World Regions Trade Collection
- NCSS Middle School Trade Collection

Geography's Impact

Introduction to Geography's Impact Video Program

- **Impact of Weather**

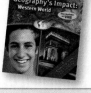

For more information or to purchase go to hmhsocialstudies.com

Power Presentations with Media Gallery

Power Presentations with Media Gallery are visual presentations of each chapter's main ideas. Presentations can be customized by including Quick Facts charts, images from the text, and video clips.

Differentiating Instruction

How do I address the needs of varied learners?
The Target Resource acts as your primary strategy for differentiated instruction.

ENGLISH-LANGUAGE LEARNERS & STRUGGLING READERS

Resource File

The Resource File activities allow students to extend their knowledge of chapter-related places and people and to practice geography skills.

- Vocabulary Builder Activities
- Social Studies Skills: Analyzing a Bar Graph

Additional Resources

Differentiated Instruction Teacher Management System: Lesson Plans for Differentiated Instruction

Introduction to Geography Transparencies:
- Climate, Environment, and Resources Visual Summary

Student Edition on Audio CD Program

Interactive Skills Tutor CD-ROM

Spanish Chapter Summaries Audio CD Program

Teacher One Stop:
- ExamView Assessment Suite, Spanish
- PuzzleView, Spanish
- PuzzlePro, Spanish

English-Language Learner Strategies and Activities

Spanish/English Guided Reading Workbook

SPECIAL NEEDS LEARNERS

Differentiated Instruction Modified Worksheets and Tests CD-ROM

- Vocabulary Flash Cards
- Modified Vocabulary Builder Activities
- Modified Chapter Review Activity
- Modified Chapter Test

Additional Resources

Differentiated Instruction Teacher Management System: Lesson Plans for Differentiated Instruction

Guided Reading Workbook

Resource File: Social Studies Skills: Analyzing a Bar Graph

Student Edition on Audio CD Program

Guided Reading Workbook

Graphic Organizer Transparencies with Support for Reading and Writing

ADVANCED/GIFTED AND TALENTED STUDENTS

Differentiated Instruction Teacher Management System

Lesson Plans for Differentiated Instruction provide teachers with strategies to help plan instruction for all learners.

Additional Resources

Resource File:
- Focus on Reading: Understanding Cause and Effect
- Focus on Viewing: Presenting and Viewing a Weather Report
- Literature: "To Build a Fire" by Jack London

World History and Geography Document-Based Questions Activities

Geography, Science, and Cultures Activities

Experiencing World History and Geography

Teacher One Stop™

How can I manage the lesson plans and support materials for differentiated instruction?

With the Teacher One Stop, you can easily organize and print lesson plans, planning guides, and instructional materials for all learners. The Teacher One Stop includes the following materials to help you differentiate instruction:

- **Interactive Teacher's Edition**
- **Calendar Planner and pacing guides**
- **Editable lesson plans**
- **All reproducible ancillaries in Adobe Acrobat (PDF) format**
- **ExamView Assessment Suite (English & Spanish)**
- **Transparency and video previews**

Interactive Student Edition

Complete online student edition with interactive multimedia support for chapter content assessment and reporting

- Interactive Maps and Notebook
- Standardized Test Prep
- Online Homework Practice and Research Activities
- Current Events
- Chapter-based Internet Activities
- Animated Geography Activities

DIFFERENTIATED INSTRUCTION PLANNING GUIDE

Essential Question

Introduce the Essential Question

- Explain that weather is a short-term change in the air, while climate is a region's average weather conditions over a long period. Solicit from students examples of how climate can affect people's lives and the kinds of work they do.

- Variations in temperature, precipitation, and plant life let geographers identify five climate zones—tropical, temperate, polar, dry, and highland. Have students infer why people in different climate zones develop different ways of life.

- Discuss how living things and their environments are connected and affect each other.

- Tell students that the availability of natural resources can affect people's lifestyles and needs.

Focus on Reading and Viewing

Reading The Resource File provides a worksheet to help students practice understanding cause and effect.

📑 **RF:** Focus on Reading, Understanding Cause and Effect

Viewing The Resource File provides a worksheet to help students create and view a weather report.

📑 **RF:** Focus on Viewing, Creating and Viewing a Weather Report

Key to Differentiating Instruction

Below Level

Basic-level activities designed for all students encountering new material

At Level

Intermediate-level activities designed for average students

Above Level

Challenging activities designed for honors and gifted and talented students

Standard English Mastery

Activities designed to improve standard English usage

📑 **LS** Learning Styles

CHAPTER 3

Climate, Environment, and Resources

Essential Question What factors shape Earth's different environments?

 What You Will Learn...
In this chapter you will learn about weather and climate. You will also learn about how living things and the environment are connected and about natural resources.

FOCUS ON READING AND VIEWING

Understanding Cause and Effect A cause makes something happen. An effect is the result of a cause. Words such as *because*, *result*, *since*, and *therefore* can signal causes or effects. As you read, look for causes and effects to understand how things relate. **See the lesson, Understanding Cause and Effect, on page 518.**

Writing a Weather Report You have likely seen a TV weather report, which tells the current weather conditions and predicts future conditions. After reading this chapter, prepare a weather report for a reason and place of your choosing. Present your report to the class and then view your classmates' reports.

Climate Earth has many climates, such as the dry climate of the region shown here.

Introduce the Chapter
At Level

The World Around Us

1. Draw three large bubbles on the board in a triangular pattern, and label them *Climate, Environment,* and *Resources*. Ask students to suggest words or short phrases that belong inside each bubble. Write down all appropriate suggestions, emphasizing words that also appear as key terms in the chapter. Help students write a definition for each term based as much as possible on the words or short phrases they originally suggested.

2. Ask students to look for connections from bubble to bubble. For example, *forest* under *Resources* could be connected to *rainfall* under *Climate* and *habitat* under *Environment*.

3. After enough connections have been established, point out to students that almost everything in the world around us is connected to everything else.
📑 **LS** Verbal/Linguistic, Visual/Spatial

📑 Alternative Assessment Handbook, Rubric 14: Group Activity

ANALYSIS SKILL ANALYZING VISUALS

This photo shows a severe thunderstorm. These storms produce violent weather, such as heavy rainfall and strong winds, which affects people's lives.

How do you think this storm might have affected the people who lived in this area?

Environments Living things, such as this koala, depend on their surroundings.

Natural Resources Earth provides many valuable and useful natural resources, such as oil.

49

• Chapter Preview •

Explore the Picture

Severe Thunderstorms Violent storms often occur when hot and cold air masses come together. Often, temperatures drop dramatically after such storms pass. This type of storm can also produce a tornado. More tornadoes strike the United States than any other country.

Analyzing Visuals Ask students to name regions with dry climates. Have them describe what they think a dry climate is like. Then have them name other types of climates, where they occur, and what they might be like.

Have students think about how plants and animals survive in different environments. For example, koalas in eastern Australia depend on the eucalyptus trees there for food and shelter. Ask students to explain how other animals depend on their surroundings.

⬀ hmhsocialstudies.com
Teacher Resources

Collaborative Learning

At Level

Ways Resources Are Recycled

1. Divide students into four groups and assign each group one of the following: paper, glass, plastics, and metals. Have students use the Internet to identify ways each material is recycled.

2. Students should make a list of five ways their material can be reused or recycled. For example, a fleece garment can be made out of 12 two-liter plastic bottles. Students should also list three ways that their assigned material can be recycled at home or at school. For example, students can print only necessary pages when doing research.

3. Have students write their lists on a poster, then share their posters with the other three groups.

4. Display the posters around the school to teach others how resources are recycled.
   LS Verbal/Linguistic
   Alternative Assessment Handbook, Rubrics 30: Research; and 28: Posters

Answers

Analyzing Visuals *possible answer— People probably had to stop any outdoor activities and take shelter.*

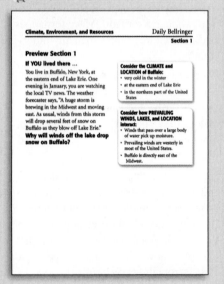

SECTION 1

Weather and Climate

What You Will Learn...

Main Ideas

1. While weather is short term, climate is a region's average weather over a long period.
2. The amount of sun at a given location is affected by Earth's tilt, movement, and shape.
3. Wind and water move heat around Earth, affecting how warm or wet a place is.
4. Mountains influence temperature and precipitation.

The Big Idea

The sun, location, wind, water, and mountains affect weather and climate.

Key Terms

weather, *p. 50*
climate, *p. 50*
prevailing winds, *p. 51*
ocean currents, *p. 52*
front, *p. 53*

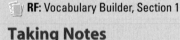

hmhsocialstudies.com
TAKING NOTES

Use the graphic organizer online to take notes on the factors that affect weather and climate.

50 CHAPTER 3

If YOU lived there...

You live in Buffalo, New York, at the eastern end of Lake Erie. One evening in January, you are watching the local TV news. The weather forecaster says, "A huge storm is brewing in the Midwest and moving east. As usual, winds from this storm will drop several feet of snow on Buffalo as they blow off Lake Erie."

Why will winds off the lake drop snow on Buffalo?

BUILDING BACKGROUND All life on Earth depends on the sun's energy and on the cycle of water from the land to the air and back again. In addition, sun and water work with other forces, such as wind, to create global patterns of weather and climate.

Understanding Weather and Climate

"Climate is what you expect; weather is what you get."
—Robert Heinlein, from *Time Enough for Love*

What is it like outside right now where you live? Is it hot, sunny, wet, cold? Is this what it is usually like outside for this time of year? The first two questions are about **weather**, the short-term changes in the air for a given place and time. The last question is about **climate**, a region's average weather conditions over a long period.

Weather is the temperature and precipitation from hour to hour or day to day. "Today is sunny, but tomorrow it might rain" is a statement about weather. Climate is the expected weather for a place based on data and experience. "Summer here is usually hot and muggy" is a statement about climate. The factors that shape weather and climate include the sun, location on Earth, wind, water, and mountains.

READING CHECK **Finding Main Ideas** How are weather and climate different from each other?

Teach the Big Idea

At Level

Weather and Climate

1. **Teach** Ask students the questions in the Main Idea boxes under Direct Teach.

2. **Apply** Distribute one flashcard-sized strip of cardboard or paper to each student. Ask students to write one of these words or phrases on their strip: *altitude, large body of water, high pressure, low pressure, latitude, ocean current, westerly wind, doldrums, moisture, cold air mass, warm air mass, precipitation, desert, hurricane, rain shadow, front, wind, tornado, hurricane, moderate temperatures.*

Have a student hold up a card, and ask others to also hold up their cards if their term is related. Have them explain how their term is related.

3. **Review** Ask students to define their term and to tell if it applies to weather, climate, or both.

4. **Practice/Homework** Have students write ten true statements, each of which uses at least two of the terms in the list.
   LS Verbal/Linguistic

   📑 Alternative Assessment Handbook, Rubric 40, Writing to Describe

Sun and Location

Energy from the sun heats the planet. Different locations receive different amounts of sunlight, though. Thus, some locations are warmer than others. The differences are due to Earth's tilt, movement, and shape.

You have learned that Earth is tilted on its axis. The part of Earth tilted toward the sun receives more solar energy than the part tilted away from the sun. As the Earth revolves around the sun, the part of Earth that is tilted toward the sun changes during the year. This process creates the seasons. In general, temperatures in summer are warmer than in winter.

Earth's shape also affects the amount of sunlight different locations receive. Because Earth is a sphere, its surface is rounded. Therefore, solar rays are more direct and concentrated near the equator. Nearer the poles, the sun's rays are less direct and more spread out.

As a result, areas near the equator, called the lower latitudes, are mainly hot year-round. Areas near the poles, called the higher latitudes, are cold year-round. Areas about halfway between the equator and poles have more seasonal change. In general, the farther from the equator, or the higher the latitude, the colder the climate.

READING CHECK **Summarizing** How does Earth's tilt on its axis affect climate?

Wind and Water

Heat from the sun moves across Earth's surface. The reason is that air and water warmed by the sun are constantly on the move. You might have seen a gust of wind or a stream of water carrying dust or dirt. In a similar way, wind and water carry heat from place to place. As a result, they make different areas of Earth warmer or cooler.

Global Wind Systems

Prevailing winds blow in circular belts across Earth. These belts occur at about every 30° of latitude.

ANALYZING VISUALS Which direction do the prevailing winds blow across the United States?

NORTH POLE
90°N
Polar easterlies
60°N
Westerlies
30°N
Trade winds
0° Equator   Doldrums
Tradewinds
30°S
Westerlies
60°S
Polar easterlies
90°S
SOUTH POLE

→ Cool air
→ Warm air
→ Wind direction

Global Winds

Wind, or the sideways movement of air, blows in great streams around the planet. **Prevailing winds** are winds that blow in the same direction over large areas of Earth. The diagram above shows the patterns of Earth's prevailing winds.

To understand Earth's wind patterns, you need to think about the weight of air. Although you cannot feel it, air has weight. This weight changes with the temperature. Cold air is heavier than warm air. For this reason, when air cools, it gets heavier and sinks. When air warms, it gets lighter and rises. As warm air rises, cooler air moves in to take its place, creating wind.

Main Idea

❸ **Wind and Water**

Wind and water move heat around Earth, affecting how warm or wet a place is.

Recall In which direction do the prevailing winds blow in the middle latitudes? *westerly*

Explain What effect does a large body of water have on a region or climate? *It helps to moderate temperatures.*

Draw Conclusions Why is it a good idea to check a weather forecast when a front moves through your area? *The front may bring severe weather.*

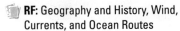 Map Zone Transparency: Major Ocean Currents

 RF: Geography and History, Wind, Currents, and Ocean Routes

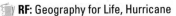 **RF:** Geography for Life, Hurricane

Info to Know

Temperature Scales In the United States, most people use the Fahrenheit scale to measure temperature. Water freezes at 32°F and boils at 212°F.

Many people use the Celsius system. Water freezes at 0°C and boils at 100°C.

Here are some equivalent values:

Fahrenheit	Celsius
32	0
50	10
68	20
86	30
104	40
212	100

Answers

Map Zone 1. *cold;* **2.** *When warm water currents flow to colder areas, the air is heated above the currents, then the warmer air is blown by westerly winds.*

Focus on Reading *Prevailing winds curve east or west instead of in a straight line north or south.*

Major Ocean Currents

← Warm current
← Cold current

Arctic Ocean
NORTH AMERICA
EUROPE
ASIA
North Pacific Ocean
North Atlantic Ocean
AFRICA
SOUTH AMERICA
Equator
Indian Ocean
South Pacific Ocean
South Atlantic Ocean
AUSTRALIA
ANTARCTICA

Geography Skills

Movement Ocean currents carry warm water from the equator toward the poles and cold water from the poles toward the equator. The currents affect temperature.

1. **Use the Map** Does a warm or cold ocean current flow along the lower west coast of North America?
2. **Explain** How do ocean currents move heat between warmer and colder areas of Earth?

FOCUS ON READING
What is the effect of Earth's rotation on prevailing winds?

On a global scale, this rising, sinking, and flowing of air creates Earth's prevailing wind patterns. At the equator, hot air rises and flows toward the poles. At the poles, cold air sinks and flows toward the equator. Meanwhile, Earth is rotating. Earth's rotation causes prevailing winds to curve east or west rather than flowing directly north or south.

Depending on their source, prevailing winds make a region warmer or colder. In addition, the source of the winds can make a region drier or wetter. Winds that form from warm air or pass over lots of water often carry moisture. In contrast, winds that form from cold air or pass over lots of land often are dry.

Ocean Currents

Like wind, **ocean currents**—large streams of surface seawater—move heat around Earth. Winds drive these currents. The map above shows how Earth's ocean currents carry warm or cool water to different areas. The water's temperature affects air temperature near it. Warm currents raise temperatures; cold currents lower them.

The Gulf Stream is a warm current that flows north along the U.S. East Coast. It then flows east across the Atlantic to become the North Atlantic Drift. As the warm current flows along northwestern Europe, it heats the air. Westerlies blow the warmed air across Europe. This process makes Europe warmer than it otherwise would be.

Critical Thinking: Draw Conclusions

At Level

Oceans and Climate

Research Required

1. Using an almanac or the Internet, have students find the monthly average high and low temperatures for San Francisco and St. Louis.

2. Have students draw a 2-column table and record the high and low temperatures for each city in the first four rows. Have them fill in the next two rows with the differences between the highs and lows for each month.

3. Remind students that San Francisco is on the ocean, and St. Louis is located inland. Ask

students to explain the temperature patterns for each city. Call attention to the data for January and July.

4. Have students find monthly temperature data for other cities around the world. Invite them to predict where these cities are located and then check their conclusions by finding the cities on a map. **LS Logical/Mathematical**

Alternative Assessment Handbook, Rubric 7: Charts

Large Bodies of Water

Large bodies of water, such as an ocean or sea, also affect climate. Water heats and cools more slowly than land does. For this reason, large bodies of water make the temperature of the land nearby milder. Thus, coastal areas, such as the California coast, usually do not have as wide temperature ranges as inland areas.

As an example, the state of Michigan is largely surrounded by the Great Lakes. The lakes make temperatures in the state milder than other places as far north.

Wind, Water, and Storms

If you watch weather reports, you will hear about storms moving across the United States. Tracking storms is important to us because the United States has so many of them. As you will see, some areas of the world have more storms than others do.

Most storms occur when two air masses collide. An air mass is a large body of air. The place where two air masses of different temperatures or moisture content meet is a **front**. Air masses frequently collide in regions like the United States, where the westerlies meet the polar easterlies.

Fronts can produce rain or snow as well as severe weather such as thunderstorms and icy blizzards. Thunderstorms produce rain, lightning, and thunder. In the United States, they are most common in spring and summer. Blizzards produce strong winds and large amounts of snow and are most common during winter.

Thunderstorms and blizzards can also produce tornadoes, another type of severe storm. A tornado is a small, rapidly twisting funnel of air that touches the ground. Tornadoes usually affect a limited area and last only a few minutes. However, they can be highly destructive, uprooting trees and tossing large vehicles through the air. Tornadoes can be extremely deadly as well.

In 1925 a tornado that crossed Missouri, Illinois, and Indiana left 695 people dead. It is the deadliest U.S. tornado on record.

The largest and most destructive storms, however, are hurricanes. These large, rotating storms form over tropical waters in the Atlantic Ocean, usually from late summer to fall. Did you know that hurricanes and typhoons are the same? Typhoons are just hurricanes that form in the Pacific Ocean.

Extreme Weather

Severe weather is often dangerous and destructive. In the top photo, rescuers search for people during a flood in Yardley, Pennsylvania. Below, a tornado races across a wheat field.

53

Rain Shadow Effect

Most of the moisture in the ocean air falls on the mountainside facing the wind. Little moisture remains to fall on the other side, creating a rain shadow.

Hurricanes produce drenching rain and strong winds that can reach speeds of 155 miles per hour (250 kph) or more. This is more than twice as fast as most people drive on highways. In addition, hurricanes form tall walls of water called storm surges. When a storm surge smashes into land, it can wipe out an entire coastal area.

READING CHECK **Analyzing** Why do coastal areas have milder climates than inland areas?

Mountains

Mountains can influence an area's climate by affecting both temperature and precipitation. Many high mountains are located in warm areas yet have snow at the top all year. How can this be? The reason is that temperature decreases with elevation—the height on Earth's surface above sea level.

Mountains also create wet and dry areas. Look at the diagram at left. A mountain forces air blowing against it to rise. As it rises, the air cools and precipitation falls as rain or snow. Thus, the side of the mountain facing the wind is often green and lush. However, little moisture remains for the other side. This effect creates a rain shadow, a dry area on the mountainside facing away from the direction of the wind.

READING CHECK **Finding Main Ideas** How does temperature change with elevation?

SUMMARY AND PREVIEW As you can see, the sun, location on Earth, wind, water, and mountains affect weather and climate. In the next section you will learn what the world's different climate regions are like.

Section 1 Assessment

hmhsocialstudies.com
ONLINE QUIZ

Reviewing Ideas, Terms, and Places

1. **a. Recall** What shapes **weather** and **climate**?
   b. Contrast How do weather and climate differ?
2. **a. Identify** What parts of Earth receive the most heat from the sun?
   b. Explain Why do the poles receive less solar energy than the equator does?
3. **a. Describe** What creates wind?
   b. Summarize How do **ocean currents** and large bodies of water affect climate?
4. **a. Define** What is a rain shadow?
   b. Explain Why might a mountaintop and a nearby valley have widely different temperatures?

Critical Thinking

5. **Identifying Cause and Effect** Draw a chart like this one. Use your notes to explain how each factor affects climate.

	Effect on Climate
Sun and Location	
Wind	
Water	
Mountains	

Focus on Viewing

6. **Writing about Weather and Climate** Jot down information to include in your weather report. For example, you might want to include a term such as fronts or describe certain types of storms such as hurricanes or tornadoes.

54 CHAPTER 3

World Climates

If YOU lived there...

You live in Colorado and are on your first serious hike in the Rocky Mountains. Since it is July, it is hot in the campground in the valley. But your guide insists that you bring a heavy fleece jacket. By noon, you have climbed to 11,000 feet. You are surprised to see patches of snow in shady spots. Suddenly, you are very happy that you brought your jacket!

Why does it get colder as you climb higher?

BUILDING BACKGROUND While weather is the day-to-day changes in a certain area, climate is the average weather conditions over a long period. Earth's different climates depend partly on the amount of sunlight a region receives. Differences in climate also depend on factors such as wind, water, and elevation.

Major Climate Zones

In January, how will you dress for the weekend? In some places, you might get dressed to go skiing. In other places, you might head out in a swimsuit to go to the beach. What the seasons are like where you live depends on climate.

Earth is a patchwork of climates. Geographers identify these climates by looking at temperature, precipitation, and native plant life. Using these items, we can divide Earth into five general climate zones—tropical, temperate, polar, dry, and highland.

The first three climate zones relate to latitude. Tropical climates occur near the equator, in the low latitudes. Temperate climates occur about halfway between the equator and the poles, in the middle latitudes. Polar climates occur near the poles, in the high latitudes. The last two climate zones occur at many different latitudes. In addition, geographers divide some climate zones into more specific climate regions. The chart and map on the next two pages describe the world's climate regions.

READING CHECK Drawing Inferences Why do you think geographers consider native plant life when categorizing climates?

What You Will Learn...

Main Ideas

1. Geographers use temperature, precipitation, and plant life to identify climate zones.
2. Tropical climates are wet and warm, while dry climates receive little or no rain.
3. Temperate climates have the most seasonal change.
4. Polar climates are cold and dry, while highland climates change with elevation.

The Big Idea

Earth's five major climate zones are identified by temperature, precipitation, and plant life.

Key Terms

monsoons, *p. 58*
savannas, *p. 58*
steppes, *p. 59*
permafrost, *p. 61*

hmhsocialstudies.com
TAKING NOTES

Use the graphic organizer online to take notes on Earth's major climate zones.

55

Preteach

Bellringer

If YOU lived there. . . Use the **Daily Bellringer Transparency** to help students answer the question.

▶ Daily Bellringer Transparency, Section 2

Academic Vocabulary

Review with students the high-use academic term in this section.

distinct clearly different and separate (p. 60)

RF: Vocabulary Builder, Section 2

Taking Notes

Have students use the graphic organizer online to take notes on the section. This activity will prepare students for the Section Assessment, in which they will complete a graphic organizer that builds on the information using the Critical Thinking Skill: Categorizing.

...ach the Big Idea

At Level

...rld Climate

Teach Ask students the questions in the Main Idea boxes under Direct Teach.

Apply Have each student select a location and write and illustrate a travel brochure about it. Each brochure should include a cover drawing, information about what the climate is like at different times of year, what kind of recreation is available, and what a traveler should pack for the trip. The brochure can have small spot drawings wherever needed.

3. **Review** Have each student present a short "sales pitch" for their travel destination to the class.

4. **Practice/Homework** Have students select the three locations they would like to travel to in March, August, and December. Have them write a paragraph explaining each choice. **LS Visual/Spatial, Verbal/Linguistic**

   Alternative Assessment Handbook, Rubric 40: Writing to Describe

Answers

Reading Check *Certain plants only thrive under specific climate conditions.*

55

Main Idea

❶ Major Climate Zones

Geographers use temperature, precipitation, and plant life to identify climate zones.

Recall In which climate zone is the tundra located? *polar*

Explain Why are there different weather patterns in highland areas? *Weather patterns depend on elevation and location.*

Draw Conclusions Can native animal life be used to help identify climate zones? Explain your answer. *Yes. For example, some animals have thick fur for cold weather or can survive only in wet climates.*

Info to Know

Ice Ages Many people in the United States live in areas that were covered by ice until about 10,000 years ago. Glaciers more than one mile thick extended across most of the northern United States. Water from the melting glaciers formed the Great Lakes.

Generally, ice ages have come about every 40,000 to 100,000 years. No one knows how or when another ice age will begin. But our knowledge of ice ages reminds us that climate zones can and do change over time.

↗ hmhsocialstudies.com **INTERACTIVE MAP**

World Climate Regions

To explore the world's climate regions, start with the chart below. After reading about each climate region, locate the places on the map that have that climate. As you locate climates, look for patterns. For example, places near the equator tend to have warmer climates than places near the poles. See if you can identify some other climate patterns.

Tropical climate

	Climate	Where is it?	What is it like?	Plants
Tropical	HUMID TROPICAL	On and near the equator	Warm with high amounts of rain year-round; in a few places, monsoons create extreme wet seasons	Tropical rain forest
	TROPICAL SAVANNA	Higher latitudes in the tropics	Warm all year; distinct rainy and dry seasons; at least 20 inches (50 cm) of rain during the summer	Tall grasses and scattered trees
Dry	DESERT	Mainly center on 30° latitude; also in middle of continents, on west coasts, or in rain shadows	Sunny and dry; less than 10 inches (25 cm) of rain a year; hot in the tropics; cooler with wide daytime temperature ranges in middle latitudes	A few hardy plants, such as cacti
	STEPPE	Mainly bordering deserts and interiors of large continents	About 10–20 inches (25–50 cm) of precipitation a year; hot summers and cooler winters with wide temperature ranges during the day	Shorter grasses; some trees and shrubs by water
Temperate	MEDITERRANEAN	West coasts in middle latitudes	Dry, sunny, warm summers; mild, wetter winters; rain averages 15–20 inches (30–50 cm) a year	Scrub woodland and grassland
	HUMID SUBTROPICAL	East coasts in middle latitudes	Humid with hot summers and mild winters; rain year-round; in paths of hurricanes and typhoons	Mixed forest
	MARINE WEST COAST	West coasts in the upper-middle latitudes	Cloudy, mild summers and cool, rainy winters; strong ocean influence	Evergreen forests
	HUMID CONTINENTAL	East coasts and interiors of upper-middle latitudes	Four distinct seasons; long, cold winters and short, warm summers; average precipitation varies	Mixed forest

56 CHAPTER 3

Collaborative Learning

At Level

Give a Weather Forecast

1. Have students work with a partner. Assign one of the climate regions to each pair.

2. Have each pair use the world climate regions map to find a place where their assigned climate region exists. Have them look on a political world map or globe and identify a city in that climate region.

3. Have students present a television news-style weather forecast for their city. Have them use the information in the climate region table to

guide them as to what a reasonable forecast would be for the city they selected.

4. Encourage students to add visuals to their presentations such as weather maps, pictures of rain clouds, snowflakes, and so on.

LS Interpersonal

Alternative Assessment Handbook, Rubric 29: Presentations

Polar climate

Dry climate

Climate		Where is it?	What is it like?	Plants
Polar	SUBARCTIC	Higher latitudes of the interior and east coasts of continents	Extremes of temperature; long, cold winters and short, warm summers; little precipitation	Northern evergreen forests
	TUNDRA	Coasts in high latitudes	Cold all year; very long, cold winters and very short, cool summers; little precipitation; permafrost	Moss, lichens, low shrubs
	ICE CAP	Polar regions	Freezing cold; snow and ice; little precipitation	No vegetation
Highland	HIGHLAND	High mountain regions	Wide range of temperatures and precipitation amounts, depending on elevation and location	Ranges from forest to tundra

Geography Skills

Regions Note how Earth's climate regions relate to different locations.

1. **Locate** Which climates are found mainly in the Northern Hemisphere?

2. **Identify** What climate does most of northern Africa have?

3. **Make Generalizations** Where are many of the world's driest climates found on Earth?

4. **Interpreting Charts** Examine the chart. Which two climates have the least amount of vegetation?

🔼 hmhsocialstudies.com

CLIMATE, ENVIRONMENT, AND RESOURCES **57**

Main Idea

❷ Tropical and Dry Climates

Tropical climates are wet and warm, while dry climates receive little or no rain.

Define What is a monsoon? *prevailing winds that change direction, creating wet and dry seasons*

Contrast How much rain falls in a desert compared to a humid tropical region? *desert: less than 10 inches per year; humid tropical regions: 70–450 inches per year*

Identify Cause and Effect What causes rapid cooling at night in the desert? *dry air and clear skies*

Info to Know

The Blooming Sahara? The Sahara in northern Africa is the world's largest desert, roughly the size of the entire United States. Like most places on Earth, the Sahara has had different climates at different times. As recently as about 5,000 years ago, the great Sahara Desert enjoyed a period of wetter climate, with far more vegetation than we see today.

Answers

Focus on Culture *They raise camels and wear veils to protect against windblown dust.*

FOCUS ON CULTURE

The Tuareg of the Sahara.

In the Sahara, the world's largest desert, temperatures can top 130°F (54°C). Yet the Tuareg (TWAH-reg) of North and West Africa call the Sahara home—and prefer it. The Tuareg have raised camels and other animals in the Sahara for more than 1,000 years. The animals graze on sparse desert plants. When the plants are gone, the Tuareg move on.

In camp, Tuareg families live in tents made from animal skins. Some wealthier Tuareg live in adobe homes. The men traditionally wear blue veils wrapped around their face and head. The veils help protect against windblown desert dust.

Summarizing How have the Tuareg adapted to life in a desert?

Tropical and Dry Climates

Are you the type of person who likes to go to extremes? Then tropical and dry climates might be for you. These climates include the wettest, driest, and hottest places on Earth.

Tropical Climates

Our tour of Earth's climates starts at the equator, in the heart of the tropics. This region extends from the Tropic of Cancer to the Tropic of Capricorn. Look back at the map to locate this region.

Humid Tropical Climate At the equator, the hot, damp air hangs like a thick, wet blanket. Sweat quickly coats your body.

Welcome to the humid tropical climate. This climate is warm, muggy, and rainy year-round. Temperatures average about 80°F (26°C). Showers or storms occur almost daily, and rainfall ranges from 70 to more than 450 inches (180 to 1,140 cm) a year. In comparison, only a few parts of the United States average more than 70 inches (180 cm) of rain a year.

Some places with a humid tropical climate have **monsoons**, seasonal winds that bring either dry or moist air. During one part of the year, a moist ocean wind creates an extreme wet season. The winds then shift direction, and a dry land wind creates a dry season. Monsoons affect several parts of Asia. For example, the town of Mawsynram, India, receives on average more than 450 inches (1,140 cm) of rain a year—all in about six months! That is about 37 feet (11 m) of rain. As you can imagine, flooding during wet seasons is common and can be severe.

The humid tropical climate's warm temperatures and heavy rainfall support tropical rain forests. These lush forests contain more types of plants and animals than anywhere else on Earth. The world's largest rain forest is in the Amazon River basin in South America. There you can find more than 50,000 species, including giant lily pads, poisonous tree frogs, and toucans.

Tropical Savanna Climate Moving north and south away from the equator, we find the tropical savanna climate. This climate has a long, hot, dry season followed by short periods of rain. Rainfall is much lower than at the equator but still high. Temperatures are hot in the summer, often as high as 90°F (32°C). Winters are cooler but rarely get cold.

This climate does not receive enough rainfall to support dense forests. Instead, it supports **savannas**—areas of tall grasses and scattered trees and shrubs.

58 CHAPTER 3

Differentiating Instruction

Struggling Readers

1. Ask students to select one of the tropical or dry climates and draw a picture showing how people adapt to it.

2. Remind students that temperature, precipitation, and native plant life help geographers identify climates. Have them include examples of each in their drawings.

3. Have students use standard English to write a short paragraph on a separate sheet of paper identifying the type of climate and describing specifically what the people in the drawing are doing to adapt to it.

4. Have students present their drawings to the class and read their descriptive paragraphs. As a class, discuss any necessary corrections to the sentences to align them with standard English usage.

LS Visual/Spatial, Verbal/Linguistic

Alternative Assessment Handbook, Rubric 3: Artwork

Dry Climates

Leaving Earth's wettest places, we head to its driest. These climates are found in a number of locations on the planet.

Desert Climate Picture the sun baking down on a barren wasteland. This is the desert, Earth's hottest and driest climate. Deserts receive less than 10 inches (25 cm) of rain a year. Dry air and clear skies produce high daytime temperatures and rapid cooling at night. In some deserts, highs can top 130°F (54°C)! Under such conditions, only very hardy plants and animals can live. Many plants grow far apart so as not to compete for water. Others, such as cacti, store water in fleshy stems and leaves.

Steppe Climate Semidry grasslands or prairies—called **steppes** (STEPS)—often border deserts. Steppes receive slightly more rain than deserts do. Short grasses are the most common plants, but shrubs and trees grow along streams and rivers.

> **READING CHECK** **Contrasting** What are some ways in which tropical and dry climates differ?

Temperate Climates

If you enjoy hot, sunny days as much as chilly, rainy ones, then temperate climates are for you. *Temperate* means "moderate" or "mild." These mild climates tend to have four seasons, with warm or hot summers and cool or cold winters.

Temperate climates occur in the middle latitudes, the regions halfway between the equator and the poles. Air masses from the tropics and the poles often meet in these regions, which creates a number of different temperate climates. You very likely live in one, because most Americans do.

Mediterranean Climate Named for the region of the Mediterranean Sea, this sunny, pleasant climate is found in many popular vacation areas. In a Mediterranean climate, summers are hot, dry, and sunny. Winters are mild and somewhat wet. Plant life includes shrubs and short trees with scattered larger trees. The Mediterranean climate occurs mainly in coastal areas. In the United States, much of California has this climate.

Mediterranean Climate

The climate graph shows average temperatures and precipitation for Nice (NEECE), France, which has a Mediterranean climate.

ANALYZING GRAPHS During which month is precipitation lowest?

FRANCE
Nice

Climate Graph for Nice, France

Source: The Weather Channel Interactive, Inc.

CLIMATE, ENVIRONMENT, AND RESOURCES **59**

59

Info to Know

Seattle's Marine West Coast Climate

Seattle, Washington, is a good example of the marine west coast climate. Temperatures are moderate, and ocean moisture produces 226 cloudy days per year. However, in Puget Sound, not far from Seattle, the island town of Friday Harbor has a very different climate. Located in the rain shadow of the Olympic Mountains, Friday Harbor has only 118 cloudy days per year.

Did you know. . .

Eastern Siberia is neither the hottest nor the coldest place on Earth, but it does hold the record for the greatest temperature range. The town of Verhoyansk, near the Arctic Circle, is a fur-collecting depot in a reindeer-raising area. It has recorded a high of 98°F and a low of 90° below 0° F. This produces an astounding temperature range of 188°F.

Highland Climates

Mount Kilimanjaro is the tallest mountain in Africa. Although Kilimanjaro is only about 200 miles (320 km) south of the equator, snow blankets its highest peak.

Kilimanjaro rises to 19,341 ft (5,895 m). The snow-covered summit has an ice cap climate.

Climate and plant life ranges from rain forest, to steppe, to desert, to tundra.

A tropical savanna climate is found around the base of Mount Kilimanjaro.

ANALYSIS SKILL **ANALYZING VISUALS**
Which type of tropical climate is found on Mount Kilimanjaro?

Humid Subtropical Climate The southeastern United States is an example of the humid subtropical climate. This climate occurs along east coasts near the tropics. In these areas, warm, moist air blows in from the ocean. Summers are hot and muggy. Winters are mild, with occasional frost and snow. Storms occur year-round. In addition, hurricanes can strike, bringing violent winds, heavy rain, and high seas.

A humid subtropical climate supports mixed forests. These forests include both deciduous trees, which lose their leaves each fall, and coniferous trees, which are green year-round. Coniferous trees are also known as evergreens.

Marine West Coast Climate Parts of North America's Pacific coast and of western Europe have a marine west coast climate. This climate occurs on west coasts where winds carry moisture in from the seas.

ACADEMIC VOCABULARY

distinct
clearly different and separate

The moist air keeps temperatures mild year-round. Winters are foggy, cloudy, and rainy, while summers can be warm and sunny. Dense evergreen forests thrive in this climate.

Humid Continental Climate Closer to the poles, in the upper–middle latitudes, many inland and east coast areas have a humid continental climate. This climate has four **distinct** seasons. Summers are short and hot. Spring and fall are mild, and winters are long, cold, and in general, snowy.

This climate's rainfall supports vast grasslands and forests. Grasses can grow very tall, such as in parts of the American Great Plains. Forests contain both deciduous and coniferous trees, with coniferous forests occurring in the colder areas.

READING CHECK **Categorizing** Which of the temperate climates is too dry to support forests?

60 CHAPTER 3

Critical Thinking: Making Predictions   At Level

Climate in Hawaii

1. Have students collect the following data for each of the Hawaiian Islands: all-time lowest recorded temperature and average year-round temperature.

2. Point out to students that each of the islands has a similar climate. We know this because each island's average year-round temperature is similar. Have students study the all-time lowest recorded temperatures. Make sure they notice that some islands have much lower all-time low temperatures than others.

3. Remind students that temperatures decrease at higher altitudes. Have them predict which of the Hawaiian Islands have tall volcanic peaks, based on analysis of the low temperature data.

4. Have students look up the highest elevation for each of the Hawaiian Islands. Ask them if their predictions were confirmed by these data. **LS** **Logical/Mathematical**

 Alternative Assessment Handbook, Rubric 30: Research

Polar and Highland Climates

Get ready to feel the chill as we end our tour in the polar and highland climates. The three polar climates are found in the high latitudes near the poles. The varied highland climate is found on mountains.

Subarctic Climate The subarctic climate and the tundra climate described below occur mainly in the Northern Hemisphere south of the Arctic Ocean. In the subarctic climate, winters are long and bitterly cold. Summers are short and cool. Temperatures stay below freezing for about half the year. The climate's moderate rainfall supports vast evergreen forests called taiga (TY-guh).

Tundra Climate The tundra climate occurs in coastal areas along the Arctic Ocean. As in the subarctic climate, winters are long and bitterly cold. Temperatures rise above freezing only during the short summer. Rainfall is light, and only plants such as mosses, lichens, and small shrubs grow.

In parts of the tundra, soil layers stay frozen all year. Permanently frozen layers of soil are called **permafrost**. Frozen earth absorbs water poorly, which creates ponds and marshes in summer. This moisture causes plants to burst forth in bloom.

Ice Cap Climate The harshest places on Earth may be the North and South poles. These regions have an ice cap climate. Temperatures are bone-numbingly cold, and lows of more than –120°F (–84°C) have been recorded. Snow and ice remain year-round, but precipitation is light. Not surprisingly, no vegetation grows. However, mammals such as penguins and polar bears thrive.

Highland Climates The highland climate includes polar climates plus others. In fact, this mountain climate is actually several climates in one. As you go up a mountain, the climate changes. Temperatures drop, and plant life grows sparser. Going up a mountain can be like going from the tropics to the poles. On very tall mountains, ice coats the summit year-round.

FOCUS ON READING
What is the effect of elevation on climate?

READING CHECK Comparing How are polar and highland climates similar?

SUMMARY AND PREVIEW As you can see, Earth has many climates, which we identify based on temperature, precipitation, and native plant life. In the next section you will read about how nature and all living things are connected.

Section 2 Assessment

Reviewing Ideas, Terms, and Places

1. **a. Recall** Which three major climate zones occur at certain latitudes?
   b. Summarize How do geographers categorize Earth's different climates?
2. **a. Define** What are **monsoons**?
   b. Make Inferences In which type of dry climate do you think the fewest people live, and why?
3. **a. Identify** What are the four temperate climates?
   b. Draw Conclusions Why are places with a Mediterranean climate popular vacation spots?
4. **a. Describe** What are some effects of **permafrost**?
   b. Explain How are highland climates unique?

Critical Thinking

5. **Categorizing** Create a chart like the one below for each climate region. Then use your notes to describe each climate region's average temperatures, precipitation, and native plant life.

Climate Region	→	Temperature	Precipitation	Plant Life

FOCUS ON VIEWING

6. **Discussing World Climates** Add information about the climate of the place you have selected, such as average temperature and precipitation.

CLIMATE, ENVIRONMENT, AND RESOURCES **61**

Direct Teach

Main Idea

❹ **Polar and Highland Climates**

Polar climates are cold and dry, while highland climates change with elevation.

Explain Where in a highland climate might you go to enter a polar climate? *the top of a tall mountain*

Identify What are subarctic evergreen forests called? *taiga*

Interpret Why does the climate change as you go up a mountain? *The air gets colder.*

📖 **RF:** Literature, "To Build a Fire" by Jack London

Review & Assess

Close

Ask students to identify the climate that is most different from their own and explain how it is different.

Review

↗ Online Quiz, Section 2

Assess

SE Section 2 Assessment
📋 PASS: Section 2 Quiz
📋 Alternative Assessment Handbook

Reteach/Classroom Intervention

📋 Guided Reading Workbook, Section 2
💿 Interactive Skills Tutor CD-ROM

Section 2 Assessment Answers

1. **a.** tropical (in low latitudes), temperate (midway between the equator and the poles), and polar (in high latitudes)
   b. They categorize climates on temperature, precipitation, and native plant life.
2. **a.** seasonal winds that bring either dry or moist air
   b. desert, because it has little water
3. **a.** Mediterranean, humid subtropical, marine west coast, and humid continental
   b. Summers are hot, dry, and sunny, making these places attractive to vacationers.
4. **a.** Because frozen earth absorbs water poorly, marshes form in summer. The moisture makes plants bloom.
   b. Highland climates are made up of several other climates.
5. Answers should include temperature, precipitation, and plant life for all climates within the five major climate zones.
6. Information should include details from Section 2.

Answers

Focus on Reading *As elevation increases, temperature decreases, and climate changes.*

Reading Check *In the highland climate, the tops of mountains are often cold enough for glaciers, just like at the poles.*

61

Bellringer

If YOU lived there. . . Use the **Daily Bellringer Transparency** to help students answer the question.

▶ Daily Bellringer Transparency, Section 3

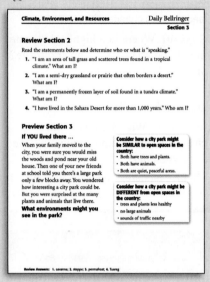

Academic Vocabulary

consequences the effects of a particular event or events (p. 64)

📝 **RF:** Vocabulary Builder, Section 3

Taking Notes

Have students use the graphic organizer online to take notes on the section. This activity will prepare students for the Section Assessment, in which they will complete a graphic organizer that builds on the information using the Critical Thinking Skill: Identifying Cause and Effect

---

SECTION 3

What You Will Learn...

Main Ideas

1. The environment and life are interconnected and exist in a fragile balance.
2. Soils play an important role in the environment.

The Big Idea

Plants, animals, and the environment, including soil, interact and affect one another.

Key Terms

environment, *p. 62*
ecosystem, *p. 63*
habitat, *p. 64*
extinct, *p. 64*
humus, *p. 65*
desertification, *p. 65*

↗ **hmhsocialstudies.com**
 TAKING NOTES

Use the graphic organizer online to take notes on Earth's natural environments.

Natural Environments

If YOU lived there...

When your family moved to the city, you were sure you would miss the woods and pond near your old house. Then one of your new friends at school told you there's a large park only a few blocks away. You wondered how interesting a city park could be. But you were surprised at the many plants and animals that live there.

What environments might you see in the park?

BUILDING BACKGROUND No matter where you live, you are part of a natural environment. From a desert to a rain forest to a city park, every environment is home to a unique community of plant and animal life. These plants and animals live in balance with nature.

The Environment and Life

If you saw a wild polar bear outside your school, you would likely be shocked. In most parts of the United States, polar bears live only in zoos. This is because plants and animals must live where they are suited to the **environment**, or surroundings. Polar bears are suited to very cold places with lots of ice, water, and fish. As you will see, living things and their environments are connected and affect each other in many ways.

Limits on Life

The environment limits life. As our tour of the world's climates showed, factors such as temperature, rainfall, and soil conditions limit where plants and animals can live. Palm trees cannot survive at the frigid North Pole. Ferns will quickly wilt and die in deserts, but they thrive in tropical rain forests.

At the same time, all plants and animals are adapted to specific environments. For example, kangaroo rats are adapted to dry desert environments. These small rodents can get all the water they need from food, so they seldom have to drink water.

62 CHAPTER 3

Natural Environments

1. Teach Ask students the questions in the Main Idea boxes under Direct Teach.

2. Apply Have students outline the section, then ask them to write two or three paragraphs summarizing it. Tell students they must include all of the section's key terms in their paragraphs. Have them underline the key terms.

3. Review Go through the list of key terms and have students read the sentence they wrote using that term to the class.

4. Practice/Homework Have students write five multiple-choice questions based on their section summaries. **LS Verbal/Linguistic**

📝 Alternative Assessment Handbook, Rubric 42: Writing to Inform

Connections in Nature

The interconnections between living things and the environment form ecosystems. An **ecosystem** is a group of plants and animals that depend on each other for survival and the environment in which they live. Ecosystems can be any size and can occur wherever air, water, and soil support life. A garden pond, a city park, a prairie, and a rain forest are all examples of ecosystems.

The diagram below shows a forest ecosystem. Each part of this ecosystem fills a certain role. The sun provides energy to the plants, which use the energy to make their own food. The plants then serve as food, either directly or indirectly, for all other life in the forest. When the plants and animals die, their remains break down and provide nutrients for the soil and new plant growth. Thus, the cycle continues.

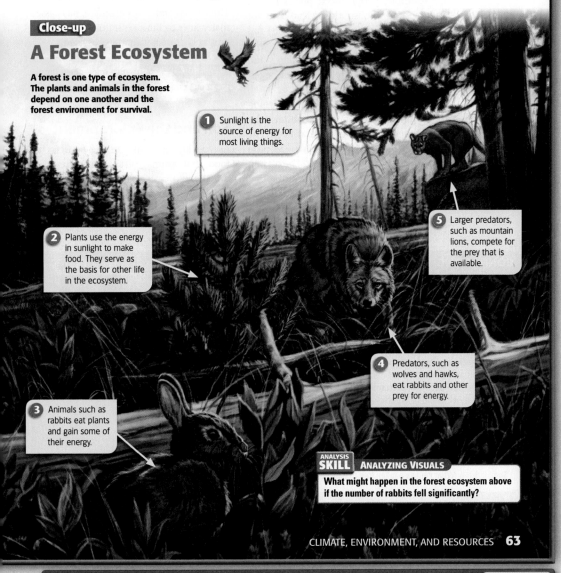

Close-up

A Forest Ecosystem

A forest is one type of ecosystem. The plants and animals in the forest depend on one another and the forest environment for survival.

1. Sunlight is the source of energy for most living things.

2. Plants use the energy in sunlight to make food. They serve as the basis for other life in the ecosystem.

3. Animals such as rabbits eat plants and gain some of their energy.

4. Predators, such as wolves and hawks, eat rabbits and other prey for energy.

5. Larger predators, such as mountain lions, compete for the prey that is available.

ANALYSIS SKILL **ANALYZING VISUALS**

What might happen in the forest ecosystem above if the number of rabbits fell significantly?

CLIMATE, ENVIRONMENT, AND RESOURCES **63**

Collaborative Learning

Above Level

Your Local Ecosystem

1. Have students draw a two-column, five-row table on a sheet of paper. Have them label the first column *Forest* and the second column *Our Ecosystem*. Have students number the rows 1 through 5.

2. Review with students the *Close-up: A Forest Ecosystem* graphic. As a class, have them fill in the key terms for each numbered text box on the graphic, and put them in the *Forest* column of the table. For example, keywords for the first row might be "sunlight" and "energy."

3. Have students work in small groups to fill in equivalent keywords for a local ecosystem. Have them brainstorm the plants and animals they have seen near the school, at local parks, in their backyards, and so on.

4. Compile a composite list of each group's results on the board. **LS** **Visual/Spatial**

   Alternative Assessment Handbook, Rubric 14: Group Activity

63

❷ Soil and the Environment

Soils play an important role in the environment.

Recall Why is soil important to human life? *Soil supports plant life, which is where humans get much of their food.*

Explain Where do fertile soils get their humus? *decayed plant or animal matter*

Draw Conclusions If there was no soil for growing food, what could we eat? *fish, other seafood, seaweed*

RF: Interdisciplinary Project, Diagram an Ecosystem

Did you know. . .

- As many as 10 million bacteria can live in one gram of soil.
- More than one thousand animal species live in soil, including worms, ants, pill bugs, and millipedes.
- In the temperate Midwest, soil accumulates at about four inches per 1,000 years.
- Soil can be as much as 100 feet thick in tropical regions.
- The United States has lost an estimated 35 percent of its topsoil since 1776.

Answers

Focus on Reading *clearing land, pollution*

Reading Check *Living things and the environment are interconnected.*

Connecting to Science *The decaying tree turns into a blend of organic material called humus, which mixes with soil and adds nutrients to it.*

64

Changes to Environments

The interconnected parts of an ecosystem exist in a fragile balance. For this reason, a small change to one part can affect the whole system. A lack of rain in the forest ecosystem could kill off many of the plants that feed the rabbits. If the rabbits die, there will be less food for the wolves and mountain lions. Then they too may die.

Many actions can affect ecosystems. For example, people need places to live and food to eat, so they clear land for homes and farms. Clearing land has **consequences**, however. It can cause the soil to erode. In addition, the plants and animals that live in the area might be left without food and shelter.

Actions such as clearing land and polluting can destroy habitats. A **habitat** is the place where a plant or animal lives. The most diverse habitats on Earth are tropical rain forests. People are clearing Earth's rain forests for farmland, lumber, and other reasons, though. As a result, these diverse habitats are being lost.

ACADEMIC VOCABULARY

consequences the effects of a particular event or events

FOCUS ON READING

What are some causes of habitat destruction?

Extreme changes in ecosystems can cause species to die out, or become **extinct**. As an example, flightless birds called dodos once lived on Mauritius (maw-RI-shuhs), an island in the Indian Ocean. When people began settling on the island, their actions harmed the dodos' habitat. First seen in 1507, dodos were extinct by 1681.

Recognizing these problems, many countries are working to balance people's needs with the needs of the environment. The United States, for example, has passed many laws to limit pollution, manage forests, and protect valuable ecosystems.

READING CHECK **Drawing Inferences** How might one change affect an entire ecosystem?

Soil and the Environment

As you know, plants are the basis for all food that animals eat. Soils help determine what plants will grow and how well. Because soils support plant life, they play an important role in the environment.

CONNECTING TO Science

Soil Factory

The next time you see a fallen tree in the forest, do not think of it as a dead log. Think of it as a soil factory. A fallen tree is buzzing with the activity of countless insects, bacteria, and other organisms. These organisms invade the fallen log and start to break the wood down.

As the tree decays and crumbles, it turns into humus. Humus is a rich blend of organic material. The humus mixes with the soil and broken rock material. These added nutrients then enrich the soil, making it possible for new trees and plants to grow. Fallen trees provide as much as one-third of the organic material in forest soil.

Summarizing What causes a fallen tree to change into soil?

64 CHAPTER 3

Differentiating Instruction

At Level | Standard English Mastery

English-Language Learners

1. Have students make a list of all unfamiliar words in *Soil Factory*. The list may include words such as *activity, bacteria, organism, invade, decay, organic,* or *nutrients*.

2. Compile a composite list of each student's results on the board. Assign a word to each student to look up in the dictionary. One by one, have students write their definitions on the board.

3. Definitions should include part of speech, language origin, and the correct meaning (if multiple definitions are included).

4. Have another student write a sentence on the board using the defined word.

LS **Verbal/Linguistic**

Alternative Assessment Handbook, Rubric 30: Research

Fertile soils are rich in minerals and **humus** (HYOO-muhs), decayed plant or animal matter. These soils can support abundant plant life. Like air and water, fertile soil is essential for life. Without it, we could not grow much of the food we eat.

Soils can lose fertility in several ways. Erosion from wind or water can sweep topsoil away. Planting the same crops over and over can also rob soil of its fertility. When soil becomes worn out, it cannot support as many plants. In fragile dry environments this can lead to the spread of desertlike conditions, or **desertification**. The spread of desertlike conditions is a serious problem in many parts of the world.

READING CHECK Analyzing What do fertile soils contain, and why are these soils important?

SUMMARY AND PREVIEW Living things and the environment are connected, but changes can easily upset the balance in an ecosystem. Because they support plant life, soils are important parts of ecosystems. In the next section you will learn about Earth's many resources.

Soil Layers

The three layers of soil are the topsoil, subsoil, and broken rock. The thickness of each layer depends on the conditions in a specific location.

ANALYZING VISUALS In which layer of soil are most plant roots and insects found?

Topsoil

Subsoil

Broken Rock

Solid Rock

Section 3 Assessment

hmhsocialstudies.com
ONLINE QUIZ

Reviewing Ideas, Terms, and Places

1. **a. Define** What is an **ecosystem**, and what are two examples of ecosystems?
   b. Summarize How do nature and people change ecosystems?
   c. Elaborate Why can plants and animals not live everywhere?

2. **a. Recall** What is **humus**, and why is it important to soil?
   b. Identify Cause and Effect What actions can cause **desertification**, and what might be some possible effects?
   c. Elaborate Why it is important for geographers and scientists to study soils?

Critical Thinking

3. **Identifying Cause and Effect** Review your notes. Then use a chart like this one to identify some of the causes and effects of changes to ecosystems.

FOCUS ON VIEWING

4. **Writing about Natural Environments** Jot down ideas about how different types of weather might affect the environment of the place you chose. For example, how might lack of rain affect the area?

Info to Know

Soil Erosion Erosion is a natural process that only becomes a problem when it happens too quickly. As long as soil is replaced as fast as it erodes, balance is maintained. Unfortunately, in many areas, human activity has upset the balance. Farming and cattle grazing are two activities that have caused a lot of soil erosion. Trees, wetlands, and plant cover all help to slow down erosion and maintain the balance.

Review & Assess

Close

Have students define an ecosystem and discuss the importance of connections and interactions among species.

Review

↗ Online Quiz, Section 3

Assess

SE Section 3 Assessment
📋 PASS: Section 3 Quiz
📋 Alternative Assessment Handbook

Reteach/Classroom Intervention

📋 Guided Reading Workbook, Section 3
💿 Interactive Skills Tutor CD-ROM

Section 3 Assessment Answers

1. **a.** A place where living things depend on each other and the environment for survival. Possible examples: a river and a meadow
   b. through small changes that affect the system, such as drought or clearing land
   c. They are adapted to specific environments.

2. **a.** decayed plants and animals, helps make soil fertile
   b. erosion or planting the same crops over and over again; The soil could not support plant life.
   c. Soils determine which plants can grow, and plants are the basis for all animal food.

3. Possible answers: Cause—clearing of land, drought; effect—Plants disappear, causing

small animals to lose food supply and die, resulting in large animals losing food supply. Cause—extinction of species; effect—Predators of extinct species lose food supply and die. Cause—pollution; effect—Habitats are destroyed, causing animals to die or move away.

4. Ideas should reflect an understanding of information in this section. Possible answer: Lack of rain may kill off plants that certain animals depend on for food.

Answers

Analyzing Visuals *topsoil*
Reading Check *humus, minerals; They can support abundant life.*

Connect to Science

Extinction Theories Paleontologists and historians have come up with several theories explaining the disappearance of dinosaurs. Below are four of the most popular theories.

Asteroid Perhaps the most common extinction theory is that an asteroid about six miles wide hit Earth at the tip of the Yucatán Peninsula in Mexico. Upon impact, the asteroid could have sent dust and steam into the atmosphere, causing forest fires, tidal waves, severe storms, and eliminating all sunlight for six months.

Climate Change Some scientists believe that at the end of the Cretaceous period, world temperatures dropped. This could have caused many plants to die. Plant-eating dinosaurs would have then died. If the plant-eaters died, then the meat-eaters would die out, too.

Volcanoes Major volcanic eruptions could have made the air nearly impossible to breathe and changed the world's climates. The ground would also have been covered with layers of molten rock, killing plants that dinosaurs relied upon for food.

Disease Toward the end of the Cretaceous period, the oceans started to dry up. The dinosaurs could have walked across the land bridges that appeared. As they searched for food, they would have encountered unfamiliar dinosaurs. This contact could have then spread fatal diseases.

Geography and History

Earth's Changing Environments

hmhsocialstudies.com
ANIMATED GEOGRAPHY

PANGAEA

Pangaea About 250 million years ago, all of Earth's continents were connected, forming one giant landmass called Pangaea.

What was North America like 74 million years ago, when dinosaurs roamed Earth? You might be surprised to learn that it was a very different place. Earth's environments are always changing. The map at right shows North America in the age of dinosaurs. Back then, the climate was warm and humid, and large inland seas covered much of the land. The region's plants and animals were completely different. Slowly, however, things changed. Some major event, possibly an asteroid impact, wiped out the dinosaurs. Over time, North America's environments changed into the ones that exist today.

HISTORY
VIDEO
Future Chill
hmhsocialstudies.com

What Survived Dinosaurs, such as the plant-eating ceratopsian at left, are long gone. But insects, such as cockroaches and dragonflies, are still around.

66

Critical Thinking: Understanding Cause and Effect　　At Level

What Happened to the Dinosaurs?　　Research Required

1. Lead a class discussion about common extinction theories. Then have students choose which theory makes the most sense to them. Make a tally on the board or a chart of the students' choices.

2. Have students use the Internet or library resources to gather more information about the theory they selected.

3. Students should then write a brief, persuasive essay explaining the theory they selected and

why they think that theory best explains the extinction of dinosaurs.

4. Ask volunteers to share their essays with the class. After hearing the persuasive essays, take another tally to see how many students now support each theory. Did the numbers change based on the persuasive essays?
LS Verbal/Linguistic

Alternative Assessment Handbook, Rubric 43: Writing to Persuade

North America in the Dinosaur Age Over time, Earth's continents slowly moved apart. About 74 million years ago, North America looked like the map at left. Inland seas covered parts of the continent. The map below shows North America today.

NORTH AMERICA TODAY

ANALYSIS SKILL **ANALYZING VISUALS**

1. **Name** What mountain ranges covered parts of North America 74 million years ago?
2. **Contrast** Based on the maps above, how has North America changed since the dinosaur age?

67

Did you know. . .

Earth's continents are constantly moving and shifting. Scientists measure these usually small movements. Based on their findings, they predict that over time the Atlantic Ocean will get bigger, while the Pacific Ocean will shrink. The Mediterranean Sea will dry up, connecting Europe and Africa. India will push farther into Asia, causing the Himalayas to grow even higher. Los Angeles will continue to move north toward San Francisco. Of course, continental drift is so slow that these changes won't likely occur for several million years!

MISCONCEPTION ALERT

Humans and Dinosaurs Many people believe that humans and dinosaurs co-existed. Perhaps they have read stories or seen movies of humans with spears, attacking or defending themselves against various dinosaurs. According to scientific evidence, however, the last dinosaurs died out about 62 million years *before* the first human walked the earth.

Differentiating Instruction

Struggling Readers   Below Level

Have students use books and Internet sources to identify and label each of the dinosaurs pictured in the feature. Students should also label each dinosaur as a plant-eater (herbivore) or a meat-eater (carnivore). Students might also enjoy researching the types of dinosaurs that lived in your state or region.

LS **Verbal/Linguistic, Visual/Spatial**

Alternative Assessment Handbook, Rubrics 30: Research; and 38: Writing to Classify

Advanced/Gifted and Talented   Above Level

Have students research major climate changes in Earth's history. Students could investigate the Ice Ages or recent trends in global warming. Ask students to organize their information and present what they learn using graphic organizers and other visuals.

LS **Verbal/Linguistic, Visual/Spatial**

Alternative Assessment Handbook, Rubrics 6: Cause and Effect; and 30: Research

Answers

Analyzing Visuals 1. *Appalachian Mountains, Rocky Mountains, Coast Mountains, and Sierra Madre Occidental;* **2.** *It has changed shape, and the inland seas dried up.*

Preteach

Preteach

Preteach

Bellringer

If YOU lived there. . . Use the **Daily Bellringer Transparency** to help students answer the question.

▶ Daily Bellringer Transparency, Section 4

Climate, Environment, and Resources   Daily Bellringer
Section 4

Review Section 3

Match the sets of letters to the correct vocabulary term.

1. EN __ __ __ ONMENT   TIN
2. EC __ __ __ STEM   VIR
3. H __ __ __ S   BIT
4. EX __ __ CT   OSY
5. HA __ __ __ AT   UMU

Preview Section 4

If YOU lived there ...
You live in Southern California, where the climate is warm and dry. Every week, you water the grass around your house to keep it green. Now the city has declared a "drought emergency" because of a lack of rain. City officials have put limits on watering lawns and on other uses of water.
How can you help conserve scarce water?

Consider USES of water:
• watering lawns
• taking showers
• washing dishes

Consider how to USE LESS water:
• water lawn less often, early or late in the day
• take shorter showers
• soak dishes

Review Answers: 1. VIR, environment; 2. OSY, ecosystem; 3. UMU, humus; 4. TIN, extinct; 5. BIT, habitat

Key Terms and Places

📝 **RF:** Vocabulary Builder, Section 4

Taking Notes

Have students use the graphic organizer online to take notes on the section. This activity will prepare students for the Section Assessment, in which they will complete a graphic organizer that builds on the information using the Critical Thinking Skill: Categorizing.

Natural Resources

What You Will Learn...

Main Ideas

1. Earth provides valuable resources for our use.
2. Energy resources provide fuel, heat, and electricity.
3. Mineral resources include metals, rocks, and salt.
4. Resources shape people's lives and countries' wealth.

The Big Idea

Earth's natural resources have many valuable uses, and their availability affects people in many ways.

Key Terms

natural resource, *p. 68*
renewable resources, *p. 69*
nonrenewable resources, *p. 69*
deforestation, *p. 69*
reforestation, *p. 69*
fossil fuels, *p. 69*
hydroelectric power, *p. 70*

hmhsocialstudies.com
TAKING NOTES

Use the graphic organizer online to take notes on Earth's resources.

If YOU lived there...

You live in Southern California, where the climate is warm and dry. Every week, you water the grass around your house to keep it green. Now the city has declared a "drought emergency" because of a lack of rain. City officials have put limits on watering lawns and on other uses of water.

How can you help conserve scarce water?

BUILDING BACKGROUND In addition to plant and animal life, other resources in the environment greatly influence people. In fact, certain vital resources, such as water, soils, and minerals, may determine whether people choose to live in a place or how wealthy people are.

Earth's Valuable Resources

Think about the materials in nature that you use. You have learned about the many ways we use sun, water, and land. They are just a start, though. Look at the human-made products around you. They all required the use of natural materials in some way. We use trees to make paper for books. We use petroleum, or oil, to make plastics for cell phones. We use metals to make machines, which we then use to make many items. Without these materials, our lives would change drastically.

Using Natural Resources

Trees, oil, and metals are all examples of natural resources. A **natural resource** is any material in nature that people use and value. Earth's most important natural resources include air, water, soils, forests, and minerals.

Understanding how and why people use natural resources is an important part of geography. We use some natural resources just as they are, such as wind. Usually, though, we change natural resources to make something new. For example, we change metals to make products such as bicycles and watches. Thus, most natural resources are raw materials for other products.

Teach the Big Idea

At Level

Using Resources around Us

1. **Teach** Ask students the questions in the Main Idea boxes under Direct Teach.

2. **Apply** Have students make a two-column table. Have them go through the entire section and list all of the resources mentioned in this section in the left column. Then have students list in the right column how often they use that resource.

3. **Review** Ask volunteers to share their ideas and write them on the board. If necessary,

have students explain the use of a resource (Example: Paper comes from the forest.)

4. **Practice/Homework** For homework, have students rank all the resources discussed in class in order of importance. Ask them to explain their rankings.
   LS Verbal/Linguistic

📝 Alternative Assessment Handbook, Rubric 42: Writing to Inform

Reforestation

Members of the Green Belt Movement plant trees in Kenya. Although trees are a renewable resource, some forests are being cut down faster than new trees can replace them. Reforestation helps protect Earth's valuable forestlands.

ANALYZING VISUALS How does reforestation help the environment?

BIOGRAPHY

Wangari Maathai
(1940–)

Can planting a tree improve people's lives? Wangari Maathai thinks so. Born in Kenya in East Africa, Maathai wanted to help people in her country, many of whom were poor. She asked herself what Kenyans could do to improve their lives. "Planting a tree was the best idea that I had," she says. In 1977 Maathai founded the Green Belt Movement to plant trees and protect forestland. The group has now planted more than 30 million trees across Kenya! These trees provide wood and prevent soil erosion. In 2004 Maathai was awarded the Nobel Peace Prize. She is the first African woman to receive this famous award.

Types of Natural Resources

We group natural resources into two types, those we can replace and those we cannot. **Renewable resources** are resources Earth replaces naturally. For example, when we cut down a tree, another tree can grow in its place. Renewable resources include water, soil, trees, plants, and animals. These resources can last forever if used wisely.

Other natural resources will run out one day. These **nonrenewable resources** are resources that cannot be replaced. For example, coal formed over millions of years. Once we use the coal up, it is gone.

Managing Natural Resources

People need to manage natural resources to protect them for the future. Consider how your life might change if we ran out of forests, for example. Although forests are renewable, we can cut down trees far faster than they can grow. The result is the clearing of trees, or **deforestation**.

By managing resources, however, we can repair and prevent resource loss. For example, some groups are engaged in **reforestation**, planting trees to replace lost forestland.

READING CHECK Contrasting How do renewable and nonrenewable resources differ?

Energy Resources

Every day you use plants and animals from the dinosaur age—in the form of energy resources. These resources power vehicles, produce heat, and generate electricity. They are some of our most important and valuable natural resources.

Nonrenewable Energy Resources

Most of the energy we use comes from **fossil fuels**, nonrenewable resources that formed from the remains of ancient plants and animals. The most important fossil fuels are coal, petroleum, and natural gas.

Coal has long been a reliable energy source for heat. However, burning coal causes some problems. It pollutes the air and can harm the land. For these reasons, people have used coal less as other fuel options became available.

CLIMATE, ENVIRONMENT, AND RESOURCES **69**

Main Idea

❷ Energy Resources

Energy resources provide fuel, heat, and electricity.

Recall What are some nonrenewable energy resources? *coal, natural gas, petroleum or oil, all of the fossil fuels*

Draw Conclusions What is a disadvantage of wind power? *When the wind does not blow, it provides no power.*

Contrast What are the advantages and disadvantages of coal? *Advantages—It can provide both heat and electricity; it is plentiful. Disadvantages—It creates pollution; it will run out some day.*

Info to Know

Future Energy Use Today all countries rely on energy from nonrenewable resources such as coal and oil. The more developed countries use huge amounts of these resources. As the world's population grows, the need for energy will grow. However, people will not be able to rely on these same resources. Their use causes pollution, and eventually nonrenewable resources will run out. More people around the world will have to develop cleaner, renewable sources of energy.

Answers

Focus on Reading *coal is plentiful; looking for cleaner ways to burn it*
Interpreting Graphs *North America*

Today we use coal mainly to create electricity at power plants, not to heat single buildings. Because coal is plentiful, people are looking for cleaner ways to burn it.

Petroleum, or oil, is a dark liquid used to make fuels and other products. When first removed from the ground, petroleum is called crude oil. This oil is shipped or piped to refineries, factories that process the crude oil to make products. Fuels made from oil include gasoline, diesel fuel, and jet fuel. Oil is also used to make petrochemicals, which are processed to make products such as plastics and cosmetics.

As with coal, burning oil-based fuels can pollute the air and land. In addition, oil spills can harm wildlife. Because we are so dependent on oil for energy, however, it is an extremely valuable resource.

The cleanest-burning fossil fuel is natural gas. We use it mainly for heating and cooking. For example, your kitchen stove may use natural gas. Some vehicles run on natural gas as well. These vehicles cause less pollution than those that run on gasoline.

Renewable Energy Resources

Unlike fossil fuels, renewable energy resources will not run out. They also are generally better for the environment. On the other hand, they are not available everywhere and can be costly.

The main alternative to fossil fuels is **hydroelectric power**—the production of electricity from waterpower. We obtain energy from moving water by damming rivers. The dams harness the power of moving water to generate electricity.

Hydroelectric power has both pros and cons. On the positive side, it produces power without polluting and lessens our use of fossil fuels. On the negative side, dams create lakes that replace existing resources, such as farmland, and disrupt wildlife habitats.

Another renewable energy source is wind. People have long used wind to power windmills. Today we use wind to power wind turbines, a type of modern windmill. At wind farms, hundreds of turbines create electricity in windy places.

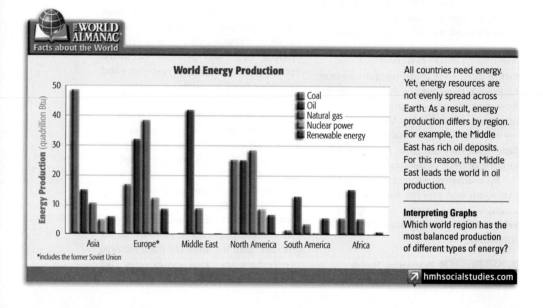

THE WORLD ALMANAC Facts about the World

World Energy Production

All countries need energy. Yet, energy resources are not evenly spread across Earth. As a result, energy production differs by region. For example, the Middle East has rich oil deposits. For this reason, the Middle East leads the world in oil production.

Interpreting Graphs
Which world region has the most balanced production of different types of energy?

hmhsocialstudies.com

Critical Thinking: Drawing Conclusions

Above Level

World Energy Consumption

Research Required

1. Review with students the World Energy Production chart. Point out that an area might produce more energy than it uses and that some places use more energy than they produce.

2. Have students use an almanac or the Internet to find energy production and consumption data, by country. Ask them to make a chart of the top ten producers and the top ten consumers.

3. Have students find countries in each of three categories: those that consume more than they produce (example: Japan), those that produce more than they consume (example: Norway), those that consume about the same as they produce (example: United Kingdom).

4. Have students write a short essay exploring what impact a consumption/production imbalance might have on a country's economy as well as on the future spatial organization of Earth. **LS Verbal/Linguistic**

Alternative Assessment Handbook, Rubric 30: Research

A third source of renewable energy is heat from the sun and Earth. We can use solar power, or power from the sun, to heat water or homes. Using special solar panels, we turn solar energy into electricity. We can also use geothermal energy, or heat from within Earth. Geothermal power plants use steam and hot water located within Earth to create electricity.

Nuclear Energy

A final energy source is nuclear energy. We obtain this energy by splitting atoms, small particles of matter. This process uses the metal uranium, so some people consider nuclear energy a nonrenewable resource. Nuclear power does not pollute the air, but it does produce dangerous wastes. These wastes must be stored for thousands of years before they are safe. In addition, an accident at a nuclear power plant can have terrible effects.

READING CHECK Drawing Inferences Why might people look for alternatives to fossil fuels?

Mineral Resources

Like energy resources, mineral resources can be quite valuable. These resources include metals, salt, rocks, and gemstones. Minerals fulfill countless needs. Look around you to see a few. Your school building likely includes steel, made from iron. The outer walls might be granite or limestone. The window glass is made from quartz, a mineral in sand. From staples to jewelry to coins, metals are everywhere.

Minerals are nonrenewable, so we need to conserve them. Recycling items such as aluminum cans will make the supply of these valuable resources last longer.

READING CHECK Categorizing What are the major types of mineral resources?

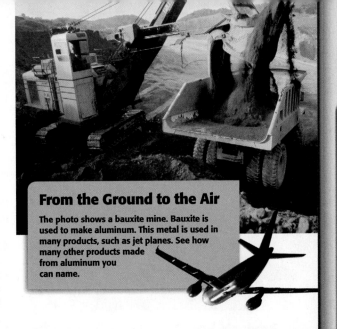

From the Ground to the Air

The photo shows a bauxite mine. Bauxite is used to make aluminum. This metal is used in many products, such as jet planes. See how many other products made from aluminum you can name.

Resources and People

Natural resources vary from place to place. The resources available in a region can shape life and wealth for the people there.

Resources and Daily Life

The natural resources available to people affect their lifestyles and needs. In the United States we have many different kinds of natural resources. We can choose among many different ways to dress, eat, live, travel, and entertain ourselves. People in places with fewer natural resources will likely have fewer choices and different needs than Americans.

For example, people who live in remote rain forests depend on forest resources for most of their needs. These people may craft containers by weaving plant fibers together. They may make canoes by hollowing out tree trunks. Instead of being concerned about money, they might be more concerned about food.

CLIMATE, ENVIRONMENT, AND RESOURCES **71**

Direct Teach

Main Idea

④ Resources and People

Resources shape people's lives and countries' wealth.

Identify Name some natural resources found in the United States. *fertile farmland, forests, oil*

Draw Conclusions If people do not have a resource, what can they do? *Trade something else for it, find a substitute for it, or do without it.*

Review & Assess

Close

Have students discuss ways to conserve resources and why it is important.

Review

Online Quiz, Section 4

Assess

SE Section 4 Assessment

PASS: Section 4 Quiz

Alternative Assessment Handbook

Reteach/Classroom Intervention

Guided Reading Workbook, Section 4

Interactive Skills Tutor CD-ROM

Products from Petroleum

This Ohio family shows some common products made from petroleum, or oil.

ANALYZING VISUALS What petroleum-based products can you identify in this photo?

Resources and Wealth

The availability of natural resources affects countries' economies as well. For example, the many natural resources available in the United States have helped it become one of the world's wealthiest countries. In contrast, countries with few natural resources often have weak economies.

Some countries have one or two valuable resources but few others. For example, Saudi Arabia is rich in oil but lacks water for growing food. As a result, Saudi Arabia must use its oil profits to import food.

READING CHECK Identifying Cause and Effect How can having few natural resources affect life and wealth in a region or country?

SUMMARY AND PREVIEW You can see that Earth's natural resources have many uses. Important natural resources include air, water, soils, forests, fuels, and minerals. In the next chapter you will read about the world's people and cultures.

Section 4 Assessment

hmhsocialstudies.com
ONLINE QUIZ

Reviewing Ideas, Terms, and Places

1. a. Define What are **renewable resources** and **nonrenewable resources**?
b. Explain Why is it important for people to manage Earth's natural resources?
c. Develop What are some things you can do to help manage and conserve natural resources?
2. a. Define What are **fossil fuels**, and why are they significant?
b. Summarize What are three examples of renewable energy resources?
c. Predict How do you think life might change as we begin to run out of petroleum?
3. a. Recall What are the main types of mineral resources?
b. Analyze What are some products that we get from mineral resources?

4. a. Describe How do resources affect people?
b. Make Inferences How might a country with only one valuable resource develop its economy?

Critical Thinking

5. Categorizing
Draw a chart like this one. Use your notes to identify and evaluate each energy resource.

Fossil Fuels	Renewable Energy	Nuclear Energy
Pros	Pros	Pros
Cons	Cons	Cons

FOCUS ON VIEWING

6. Noting Details about Natural Resources What natural resources does the place you chose have? Note ways to refer to some of these resources (or the lack of them) in your weather report.

Section 4 Assessment Answers

1. a. renewable—resources that are replaced naturally; nonrenewable—resources that cannot be replaced
b. They could easily disappear in the future.
c. Possible answers include recycling materials, turning lights off, and watering the lawn sparingly.
2. a. They are nonrenewable resources formed from remains of living things. They are energy resources.
b. hydroelectric, wind, solar, geothermal, and nuclear power
c. People will have to conserve energy and depend more on renewable energy sources.

3. a. metals, salt, rocks
b. Possible answers include coins, glass, and cans.
4. a. They are the source of the energy and products people use.
b. It could trade with other countries.
5. Charts should reflect details from the section.
6. Answers will vary depending on the places students chose.

Answers

Analyzing Visuals *Responses should indicate students' understanding of the petroleum content in plastic, vinyl, synthetic fibers, adhesive, and other materials.*

Reading Check *Regions or countries with few natural resources often have weak economies and different concerns than regions or countries with abundant resources.*

from
The River

by Gary Paulsen

About the Reading *In the novel* The River, *a teenager named Brian has already proven his ability to survive in the wilderness. On this trip into the wilderness, he is accompanied by a man who wants to learn survival skills from him. With only a pocket knife and a transistor radio as tools, the two men meet challenges that at first appear too difficult to overcome. In the following passage from the novel, the men have just arrived in the wilderness.*

AS YOU READ Notice how Brian uses his senses to predict how some natural resources can help him survive.

He didn't just hear birds singing, not just a background sound of birds, but each bird. He listened to each bird. Located it, knew where it was by the sound, listened for the sound of alarm. He didn't just see clouds, but light clouds, scout clouds that came before the heavier clouds that could mean rain and maybe wind. ❶ The clouds were coming out of the northwest, and that meant that weather would come with them. Not could, but would. There would be rain. Tonight, late, there would be rain.

His eyes swept the clearing. . . There was a stump there that probably held grubs; hardwood there for a bow, and willows there for arrows; a game trail, . . . porcupines, raccoons, bear, wolves, moose, skunk would be moving on the trail and into the clearing. ❷ He flared his nostrils, smelled the air, pulled the air along the sides of his tongue in a hissing sound and tasted it, but there was nothing. Just summer smells. The tang of pines, soft air, some mustiness from rotting vegetation. No animals. ❸

GUIDED READING

WORD HELP

grubs soft, thick wormlike forms of insects
flared widened
tang sharp, biting smell
mustiness damp, stale smell

❶ Scout clouds are clouds that appear to be searching for other clouds to come.

❷ Brian notes that the stump likely holds grubs. He can eat the grubs for food.

❸ Brian does not smell any animals nearby.

Why might Brian want to know if animals are around?

Connecting Literature to Geography

1. **Predicting** Brian observes the clouds and can tell from their appearance and movement that rain is coming. What might be some ways that he can use his environment to prepare for the rain?

2. **Finding Main Ideas** The environment provides many resources that we can use, from wood to plants to animals. What resources does Brian identify around him that he can use to survive?

73

Cross-Discipline Activity: Literature

At Level

Writing a Journal

1. Tell students that hikers often keep journals in which they record what they see during their journeys. Ask students what Brian may have written in a journal, based on the passage.

2. Invite students to pretend they are accompanying Brian on a wilderness trip. Ask them to write entries into their own journal, including things that they experience by using their senses. For example, students might hear a babbling brook, indicating that water

is nearby, or they might see a lightning bolt in the distance, indicating an oncoming storm.

3. Invite volunteers to share their journals with the class. **LS** **Verbal/Linguistic**

📓 Alternative Assessment Handbook, Rubrics 15: Journals; and 24: Oral Presentations

Literature

The River

As You Read Have students think about how they use their senses when they are outdoors. Invite them to make a list of things they see, hear, feel, smell, and taste when they are at a park, field, or playground. Discuss with students how their senses connect them with their environment.

Meet the Writer

Gary Paulsen Born in 1939, Gary Paulsen has written many books for children and young adults. Paulsen took up dogsled racing when he lived in Minnesota and entered the Iditarod in 1983. His books have achieved popular and critical success, and three of his novels are Newbery Honor Books.

Did you know. . .

The way birds learn to sing is similar to the development of human speech. When birds are young, they listen to adult birds sing, then copy the song and practice it until it is perfect.

Answers

Guided Reading *Brian might have to hide if any dangerous animals were around.*

Connecting Literature to Geography 1. *Possible answers include looking for a cave or another form of shelter that will keep them dry;* **2.** *birds, a tree stump and trees, a game trail, the air*

Analyzing a Bar Graph

Activity Create and Compare Bar Graphs

Materials: Almanac, art paper, colored pencils

1. Tell students that they are going to use information from an almanac to create bar graphs.

2. Find data about the highest elevations of each state in feet. Have students get together in groups of four, and give each group four elevations to use for their bar graphs. Make sure every group has different states.

3. Students should use the art supplies to create their bar graphs. Ask them to show the states in alphabetical order across the bottom. Also help students to figure out which interval of feet works best along the left side. Encourage them to color each bar differently.

4. As a class, compare the bar graphs. Ask volunteers which states have the highest and lowest elevations at their respective high points.

LS Verbal/Linguistic

Alternative Assessment Handbook, Rubric 7: Charts

Interactive Skills Tutor CD-ROM, Lesson 6: Interpreting Graphs

RF: Social Studies Skills, Analyzing a Bar Graph

Analyzing a Bar Graph

Learn

Bar graphs are drawings that use bars to show data in a clear, visual format. Use these guidelines to analyze bar graphs.

- Read the title to identify the graph's subject and purpose.

- Read the graph's other labels. Note what the graph is measuring and the units of measurement being used. For example, this bar graph is measuring precipitation by climate. The unit of measurement is inches. If the graph uses colors, note their purpose.

- Analyze and compare the data. As you do, note any increases or decreases and look for trends or changes over time.

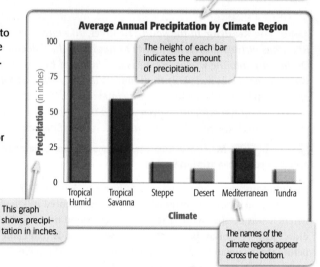

This bar graph compares the average annual precipitation of six climate regions.

Average Annual Precipitation by Climate Region

The height of each bar indicates the amount of precipitation.

This graph shows precipitation in inches.

The names of the climate regions appear across the bottom.

Practice

1. On the bar graph above, which climate region has the highest average annual precipitation?

2. Which two climate regions have about the same amount?

3. Which climate region receives an average of between 50 and 75 inches of precipitation each year?

Apply

Examine the World Energy Production Today bar graph in Section 4. Then use the graph to answer the following questions.

1. Which region produces the most oil?

2. Which three regions produce little or no nuclear power?

3. Based on the graph, what type of energy resource do most Asian countries likely use?

74 CHAPTER 3

Social Studies Skills Activity: Analyzing a Bar Graph   At Level

Bar Graph Quiz

1. Have each student create a four-question quiz based on the bar graph on this page.

2. Allow students to make separate answer keys for their quizzes.

3. Invite pairs of students to exchange quizzes, then answer the questions before exchanging them back for grading.

4. Students should then summarize the information shown in the bar graph. Allow volunteers to read their summaries to the class. **LS Visual/Spatial**

Alternative Assessment Handbook, Rubric 7: Charts

Answers

Practice 1. *tropical humid;* **2.** *tundra and desert;* **3.** *tropical savanna*

Apply 1. *Middle East;* **2.** *Africa, Middle East, and South America;* **3.** *coal*

Chapter Review

Geography's Impact
video series
Review the video to answer the
closing question:
*How are climate and weather
different, and how does the
influence they have differ?*

Visual Summary

Use the visual summary below to help you review the main ideas of the chapter.

QUICK FACTS

Earth has a wide range of climates, which we identify by precipitation, temperature, and native plant life.

Plants, animals, and the environment are interconnected and affect one another in many ways.

Earth's valuable natural resources, such as air, water, forests, and minerals, have many uses and affect people's lives.

Reviewing Vocabulary, Terms, and Places

Unscramble each group of letters below to spell a term that matches the given definition.

1. **usumh**—decayed plant or animal matter
2. **tahrewe**—changes or conditions in the air at a certain time and place
3. **netorietfaosr**—planting trees where forests were
4. **neticxt**—completely died out
5. **estpep**—semidry grassland or prairie
6. **sifeticatorined**—spread of desertlike conditions
7. **laitemc**—an area's weather patterns over a long period of time
8. **arsmofrtpe**—permanently frozen layers of soil
9. **snonomo**—winds that change direction with the seasons and create wet and dry periods
10. **vansanas**—areas of tall grasses and scattered shrubs and trees

Comprehension and Critical Thinking

SECTION 1 *(Pages 50–54)*

11. **a. Identify** What five factors affect climate?

   b. Analyze Is average annual precipitation an example of weather or climate?

   c. Evaluate Of the five factors that affect climate, which one do you think is the most important? Why?

SECTION 2 *(Pages 55–61)*

12. **a. Recall** What are the five major climate zones?

   b. Explain How does latitude relate to climate?

   c. Elaborate Why do you think the study of climate is important in geography?

SECTION 3 *(Pages 62–65)*

13. **a. Define** What is an ecosystem, and why does it exist in a fragile balance?

CLIMATE, ENVIRONMENT, AND RESOURCES **75**

Visual Summary

Review and Inquiry Have students use the visual summary to provide details about Earth's climates, environments, and resources.

▶ Quick Facts Transparency: Climate, Environment, and Resources Visual Summary

Reviewing Vocabulary, Terms, and Places

1. humus
2. weather
3. reforestation
4. extinct
5. steppe
6. desertification
7. climate
8. permafrost
9. monsoon
10. savanna

Comprehension and Critical Thinking

11. **a.** sun, location, wind, water, and mountains
   b. climate
   c. Students' responses will vary. Possible response—The sun is most important because its energy provides heat and light.

12. **a.** tropical, temperate, polar, dry, and highland
   b. Generally, the higher the latitude is, the colder the climate.
   c. possible answer—Climate affects all living things.

13. **a.** An ecosystem is a group of plants and animals that depend on each other for survival. If part of the ecosystem changes, it affects the entire system.

Review and Assessment Resources

Review and Reinforce

SE Chapter 3 Review

RF: Chapter Review

▶ Quick Facts Transparency: Climate, Environment, and Resources Summary

🔊 Spanish Chapter Summaries Audio CD Program

TOS Holt McDougal PuzzleView, Quiz Show for ExamView

💿 Quiz Game CD-ROM

Assess

SE Standardized Test Practice

PASS: Chapter Test, Forms A and B

Alternative Assessment Handbook

TOS ExamView Test Generator, Chapter Test

💿 Differentiated Instruction Modified Worksheets and Tests CD-ROM: Chapter Test

↗ Online Assessment Program, in the Interactive Student Edition

Reteach/Intervene

Guided Reading Workbook

Differentiated Instruction Teacher Management System: Lesson Plans

💿 Differentiated Instruction Modified Worksheets and Tests CD-ROM

💿 Interactive Skills Tutor CD-ROM

↗ hmhsocialstudies.com

Chapter Resources

13. b. Plants are the foundation for all food eaten by animals.

c. Possible answer: Plants could no longer grow, forcing animals to leave the area.

14. a. Minerals are nonrenewable resources that come from Earth.

b. Nonrenewable resources cannot be replaced. Earth replaces renewable resources naturally.

c. It would require people to rely on fewer resources or to trade for the resources they need.

Using the Internet

15. Go to [hmhsocialstudies.com] to access a rubric for this activity.

Social Studies Skills

16. tropical humid

17. Mediterranean

18. 75 inches

Map Activity

19. A. westerly
B. trade wind
C. equator
D. North Pole
E. South Pole

Focus on Reading and Viewing

20. erosion, growing the same crops over and over

21. Abundant resources can lead to a strong economy.

RF: Focus on Reading, Understanding Cause and Effect

22. Rubric Students' weather reports should:

- include a description of the current weather, as well as the extended forecast for the chosen area based on typical weather for the given season

- make a connection between the weather and the local environment or resources, if applicable

RF: Focus on Viewing, Creating and Viewing a Weather Report

SECTION 3 (continued)

b. Explain Why are plants an important part of the environment?

c. Predict What might be some results of desertification?

SECTION 4 (Pages 68–72)

14. a. Define What are minerals?

b. Contrast How do nonrenewable resources and renewable resources differ?

c. Elaborate How might a scarcity of natural resources affect life in a region?

Using the Internet

15. Activity: Experiencing Extremes Could you live in a place where for part of the year it is always dark and temperatures plummet to −104°F? What if you had to live in a place where it is always wet and stormy? Through your online textbook, learn more about some of the world's extreme climates. Then create a poster that describes some of those climates and the people, animals, and plants that live in them.

[hmhsocialstudies.com]

Social Studies Skills

Analyzing a Bar Graph *Examine the bar graph titled Average Annual Precipitation by Climate Region in the Social Studies Skills for this chapter. Then use the bar graph to answer the following questions.*

16. Which climate region receives an average of 100 inches of precipitation a year?

17. Which climate region receives an average of 25 inches of precipitation a year?

18. What is the difference in average annual precipitation between tropical humid climates and Mediterranean climates?

Map Activity

19. Prevailing Winds On a separate sheet of paper, match the letters on the map with their correct labels.

equator	South Pole	westerly
North Pole	trade wind	

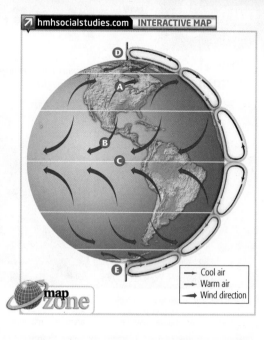

hmhsocialstudies.com **INTERACTIVE MAP**

→ Cool air
→ Warm air
➡ Wind direction

FOCUS ON READING AND VIEWING

Understanding Cause and Effect *Answer the following questions about causes and effects.*

20. What causes desertification?

21. What are the effects of abundant natural resources on a country's economy?

22. Presenting and Viewing a Weather Report Select a place and a season to write a weather report about. Describe the weather and predict upcoming weather. Present your report to your class. Use a professional, friendly tone of voice and make frequent eye contact with your audience. Then view your classmates' weather reports. Be prepared to give feedback on the content and their presentation techniques.

Standardized Test Prep

DIRECTIONS: *Read questions 1 through 7 and write the letter of the best response. Then read question 8 and write your own well-constructed response.*

1 The cold winds that flow away from the North and South poles are the

A doldrums.

B polar easterlies.

C trade winds.

D westerlies.

2 Which climate zone occurs only in the upper latitudes?

A highland

B temperate

C tropical

D polar

3 Where are the most diverse habitats on Earth found?

A steppe

B tropical rain forest

C tropical savanna

D tundra

4 What is the cleanest burning fossil fuel?

A coal

B natural gas

C oil

D petroleum

5 Which renewable energy source uses the heat of Earth's interior to generate power?

A geothermal energy

B hydroelectric energy

C nuclear energy

D solar energy

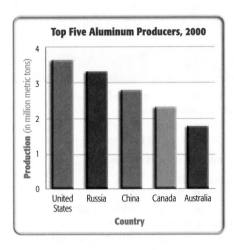

Top Five Aluminum Producers, 2000

Production (in million metric tons) / Country: United States, Russia, China, Canada, Australia

6 Based on the graph above, which country produced about 2.8 million tons of aluminum in 2000?

A Australia

B China

C Russia

D United States

7 Which of the following form over tropical waters and are Earth's largest and most destructive storms?

A blizzards

B hurricanes

C thunderstorms

D tornadoes

8 **Extended Response** Forces such as the sun, latitude, wind, and water shape climate. Examine the World Climate Regions map in Section 2. Describe two climate patterns that you see on the map and explain how various forces combine to create the two patterns.

CLIMATE, ENVIRONMENT, AND RESOURCES **77**

1. B
Break Down the Question This question requires students to recall factual information. Refer students who miss it to Section 1.

2. D
Break Down the Question This question requires students to recall factual information. Refer students who miss it to Section 2.

3. B
Break Down the Question The steppe and tropical savanna have some shrubs, trees, and grasses, while the tundra has little vegetation.

4. B
Break Down the Question This question requires students to recall factual information. Refer students who miss it to Section 4.

5. A
Break Down the Question The prefix *geo* means "earth," and *thermal* refers to heat.

6. B
Break Down the Question This question requires students to be able to read bar graphs. Refer students who miss it to the Social Studies Skills feature in this section.

7. B
Break Down the Question This question requires students to recall factual information. Refer students who miss it to Section 1.

8. Extended Response Possible response—Humid tropical climates are found on or near the equator. Because of their location, the climate is warm, muggy, and rainy year round. Mediterranean climates are on the west coasts in the middle latitudes. These locations mean summers are dry, sunny, and warm while winters are mild and wet.

Intervention Resources

Reproducible

📖 Guided Reading Workbook

📖 Differentiated Instruction Teacher Management System: Lesson Plans

Technology

▶️ Quick Facts Transparency: Climate, Environment, and Resources Visual Summary

💿 Differentiated Instruction Modified Worksheets and Tests CD-ROM

💿 Interactive Skills Tutor CD-ROM

Tips for Test Taking

When a question refers to a graph, such as Question 6 above, encourage students to first study the data plotted on the graph, as well as any headings and labels, before answering the question.

The World's People

Overview	Instructional Resources

CHAPTER 4

Essential Question: What concepts help geographers understand the world's people?

🔊 **Focus on the Essential Question Podcast**

TOS Differentiated Instruction Teacher Management System:
- Instructional Pacing Guides
- Lesson Plans for Differentiated Instruction

📝 **Guided Reading Workbook**

📝 **Resource File:**
- Chapter Review
- Focus on Reading: Understanding Main Ideas
- Focus on Writing: Creating a Poster
- Social Studies Skills: Organizing Information

📝 **Experiencing World History and Geography**

TOS Calendar Planner

💿 **Power Presentations with Media Gallery**

💿 **Differentiated Instruction Modified Worksheets and Tests CD-ROM**

💿 **Interactive Skills Tutor CD-ROM**

🔊 **Student Edition on Audio CD-ROM**

🔊 **The World's Music Audio Program**

▶️ **World Outline Maps: Transparencies and Activities**

Section 1:

Culture

The Big Idea: Culture, a group's shared practices and beliefs, differs from group to group and changes over time.

TOS Differentiated Instruction Teacher Management System: Section 1 Lesson Plan

📝 **Guided Reading Workbook:** Section 1

📝 **Resource File:**
- Vocabulary Builder: Section 1
- Biography: Margaret Mead
- Geography and History: Cultural Diversity in America

▶️ **Daily Bellringer Transparency:** Section 1

▶️ **Map Zone Transparency:** Arab Culture Region

▶️ **Map Zone Transparency:** Cultural Diffusion of Baseball

Section 2:

Population

The Big Idea: Population studies are an important part of geography.

TOS Differentiated Instruction Teacher Management System: Section 2 Lesson Plan

📝 **Guided Reading Workbook:** Section 2

📝 **Resource File:**
- Vocabulary Builder: Section 2
- Literature: *Cry, the Beloved Country* by Alan Paton
- Primary Source: "The New Colossus" by Emma Lazarus
- Critical Thinking: Wheat and the World

▶️ **Daily Bellringer Transparency:** Section 2

▶️ **Map Zone Transparency:** World Population Density

📱 **Internet Activity:** World Monuments

📱 **Animated Geography:** Earth at Night

Section 3:

Government and Economy

The Big Idea: The world's countries have different governments and levels of economic development.

TOS Differentiated Instruction Teacher Management System: Section 3 Lesson Plan

📝 **Guided Reading Workbook:** Section 3

📝 **Resource File:**
- Vocabulary Builder: Section 3
- Geography for Life: Shopping Rules!
- Interdisciplinary Project: World Governments: Poster Presentation

▶️ **Daily Bellringer Transparency:** Section 3

▶️ **Map Zone Transparency:** World Population Density

Section 4:

Global Connections

The Big Idea: Fast, easy global connections have made cultural exchange, trade, and a cooperative world community possible.

TOS Differentiated Instruction Teacher Management System: Section 4 Lesson Plan

📝 **Guided Reading Workbook:** Section 4

📝 **Resource File:**
- Vocabulary Builder: Section 4
- Biography: Kofi Annan

▶️ **Daily Bellringer Transparency:** Section 4

📱 **Internet Activity:** The Global Economy

Chart Key:

SE Student Edition
 Presentation Resource
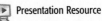 MP3 Audio

TOS Teacher One Stop
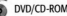 DVD/CD-ROM
HISTORY™

Printable Resource

Program Resources available on **TOS** and @ hmhsocialstudies.com

Review, Assessment, Intervention

 Introduction to Geography Transparencies: Climate, Environment, and Resources Visual Summary

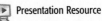 **Spanish Chapter Summaries Audio CD**

Progress Assessment Support System (PASS): Chapter Test

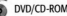 **Differentiated Instruction Modified Worksheets CD-ROM:** Modified Chapter Test

TOS ExamView® Assessment Suite (English/Spanish)

Alternative Assessment Handbook

Online Assessment Program, in the Interactive Student Edition

---

PASS: Section 1 Quiz

Online Quiz: Section 1

Alternative Assessment Handbook

PASS: Section 2 Quiz

Online Quiz: Section 2

Alternative Assessment Handbook

PASS: Section 3 Quiz

Online Quiz: Section 3

Alternative Assessment Handbook

PASS: Section 4 Quiz

Online Quiz: Section 4

Alternative Assessment Handbook

Supporting Resources

HISTORY™

- Multimedia Classroom Global History Series
- Global History Teacher's Guide

Maps Globes Graphs Level F

- Student Workbook
- Teacher's Guide

Social Studies Trade Library Collections

- World Regions Trade Collection
- NCSS Middle School Trade Collection

Geography's Impact

Geography's Impact Video Program

- **Impact of Culture**

For more information or to purchase go to hmhsocialstudies.com

Power Presentations with Media Gallery

Power Presentations with Media Gallery are visual presentations of each chapter's main ideas. Presentations can be customized by including Quick Facts charts, images from the text, and video clips.

Differentiating Instruction

How do I address the needs of varied learners?

The Target Resource acts as your primary strategy for differentiated instruction.

ENGLISH-LANGUAGE LEARNERS & STRUGGLING READERS

TARGET RESOURCE

Graphic Organizer Transparencies with Support for Reading and Writing

Spanish Resources

Spanish Chapter Summaries Audio CD Program

Teacher One Stop:
- ExamView Assessment Suite, Spanish
- PuzzleView, Spanish

English-Language Learner Strategies and Activities

Additional Resources

Differentiated Instruction Teacher Management System: Lesson Plans for Differentiated Instruction

Resource File:
- Vocabulary Builder Activities
- Social Studies Skills: Organizing Information

Introduction to Geography Transparencies:
- The World's People Visual Summary

Student Edition on Audio CD Program

Interactive Skills Tutor CD-ROM

Spanish/English Guided Reading Workbook

SPECIAL NEEDS LEARNERS

TARGET RESOURCE

Differentiated Instruction Modified Worksheets and Tests CD-ROM

- Vocabulary Flash Cards
- Modified Vocabulary Builder Activities
- Modified Chapter Review Activity
- Modified Chapter Test

Additional Resources

Differentiated Instruction Teacher Management System: Lesson Plans for Differentiated Instruction

Guided Reading Workbook

Resource File: Social Studies Skills: Organizing Information

Student Edition on Audio CD Program

Interactive Skills Tutor CD-ROM

Graphic Organizer Transparencies with Support for Reading and Writing

ADVANCED/GIFTED AND TALENTED STUDENTS

TARGET RESOURCE

Resource File

The Resource File activities allow students to extend their knowledge of chapter-related places and people and to practice geography skills.

- Focus on Reading Activity: Understanding Main Ideas
- Focus on Writing: Creating a Poster
- Literature: *Cry, the Beloved Country* by Alan Paton

Additional Resources

Differentiated Instruction Teacher Management System: Lesson Plans for Differentiated Instruction

World History and Geography Document-Based Questions Activities

Geography, Science, and Cultures Activities

Experiencing World History and Geography

Differentiated Activities in the Teacher's Edition

- Researching School Experiences, p. 79
- Illustrating Population Density, p. 87
- Completing a Population Chart, p. 89
- Listing Economic Activities, p. 93
- Researching Team Cultures, p. 98

Differentiated Activities in the Teacher's Edition

- Analyzing Sports Diffusion, p. 84

Differentiated Activities in the Teacher's Edition

- Researching Sports Diffusion, p. 84
- Reporting on Tertiary Industries, p. 93
- Researching Product Sales, p. 98

Teacher One Stop™

How can I manage the lesson plans and support materials for differentiated instruction?

With the Teacher One Stop, you can easily organize and print lesson plans, planning guides, and instructional materials for all learners. The Teacher One Stop includes the following materials to help you differentiate instruction:

- **Interactive Teacher's Edition**
- **Calendar Planner and pacing guides**
- **Editable lesson plans**
- **All reproducible ancillaries in Adobe Acrobat (PDF) format**
- **ExamView Assessment Suite (English & Spanish)**
- **Transparency and video previews**

Interactive Student Edition

Complete online student edition with interactive multimedia support for chapter content assessment and reporting

- Interactive Maps and Notebook
- Standardized Test Prep
- Online Homework Practice and Research Activities
- Current Events
- Chapter-based Internet Activities
- Animated Geography Activities

DIFFERENTIATED INSTRUCTION PLANNING GUIDE

Essential Question

Introduce the Essential Question

- Explain that geographers understand the world's people by studying their cultures. A culture is a set of beliefs, values, and practices that a group of people has in common.

- Point out that geographers study population—where people live, how many people live there, and the effects those people have on the environment. Geographers track population changes and study the reasons for those changes.

- Discuss how studying different systems of government and different economic systems help geographers understand the world's people.

- Tell students that countries are increasingly linked to each other through culture and trade. Ask students why they think some people call our world a global village.

Focus on Reading and Writing

Reading The Resource File provides a worksheet to help students practice understanding main ideas.

📓 **RF:** Focus on Reading, Understanding Main Ideas

Writing The Resource File provides a worksheet to help students organize and create their posters.

📓 **RF:** Focus on Writing, Creating a Poster

Key to Differentiating Instruction

Below Level

Basic-level activities designed for all students encountering new material

At Level

Intermediate-level activities designed for average students

Above Level

Challenging activities designed for honors and gifted and talented students

Standard English Mastery

Activities designed to improve standard English usage

LS **Learning Styles**

CHAPTER **4**

The World's People

Essential Question What concepts help geographers understand the world's people?

What You Will Learn...

In this chapter you will learn what culture is and how it changes over time. You will also learn about population, different types of governments and economic systems, and globalization.

FOCUS ON READING AND WRITING

Understanding Main Ideas A main idea is the central idea around which a paragraph or passage is organized. As you read, ask yourself what each paragraph is about. Look for a sentence or two that summarizes the main point of the entire paragraph. **See the lesson, Understanding Main Ideas, on page 519.**

Creating a Poster Think of some great posters you have seen at the movies, in bus stations, or in the halls of your school. They likely all had a colorful image that captured your attention and a few words that explained the main idea. Read this chapter about the world's people. Then create a poster that includes words and images that summarize the chapter's main ideas.

78 CHAPTER 4

Culture Thousands of different cultures make up our world. Clothing, language, and music are just some parts of culture.

Introduce the Chapter

At Level | **Prep Required**

Learning About a Country

Materials: a world almanac

1. Using a map, have students select a country (not the U.S.). Ask them to imagine a boy and girl their age and describe how they are dressed, what their favorite foods are, music they might enjoy, and so on. Explain that all of these things are part of culture.

2. Ask students to guess the population of the country. Look up the population in the almanac and explain that geographers study population to learn more about an area and its people.

3. Have students tell what they know about the country's government and economy. Explain that these vary in different countries.

4. Ask students how they might get in touch with a boy or girl from that country. Discuss with them how it is easier today than ever before to communicate with people across the world. **LS** **Visual/Spatial, Verbal/Linguistic**

📝 Alternative Assessment Handbook, Rubric 11: Discussions

Explore the Pictures

The Olympics The opening and closing ceremonies of the Olympics allow athletes from around the world to march together. Events such as the Olympics can help promote global connections, allowing people to learn about many different cultures.

Analyzing Visuals What unique things about the picture of the woman making music can you see? *her clothing, jewelry, instrument* Explain to students that these items are all parts of what make up a person's culture.

How can we study why people live where they do, such as the people shown in India? *possible answer—using geography to study human populations*

What kinds of technology let people communicate with each other? *possible answers—telephones, cell phones, the Internet, air travel*

↗ hmhsocialstudies.com

Teacher Resources

Did you know. . .

The Olympic games began as a festival by Greek city-states in 776 BC. They lasted about 400 years. In 1896 the games were started again with the hope that they would help create a more peaceful world.

ANALYSIS SKILL | **ANALYZING VISUALS**

Many of the world's people come together every four years to compete in the Olympics.

What indicates that some of the people in this photo are from different parts of the world?

Population Geographers study human populations like this one in India to learn where and why people live in certain places.

Global Connections Technology allows people in remote places around the world to communicate.

79

Differentiating Instruction

At Level | Standard English Mastery

English-Language Learners

Research Required

1. Explain what *socialization* means (how people learn the rules of society). Discuss how people become socialized—for example, through family members, neighbors, their community, the workplace, and schools.

2. Discuss how socialization differs, depending on the time and place. As an example, you may want to compare and contrast urban schools and rural schools in the United States.

3. Direct students to pair up and research school experiences from two different time periods and places (such as Ancient Greece and

colonial America). Have them determine how they were alike and how they differed.

4. Guide students in finding reliable information from library and Internet resources and in taking notes.

5. Have students use Standard English to present their findings to the class. Then discuss how students' school experiences are similar to and different from those researched.

LS Verbal/Linguistic

📖 Alternative Assessment Handbook, Rubrics 11: Discussions; and 24: Oral Presentations

Answers

Analyzing Visuals *different flags and clothing styles*

Bellringer

If YOU lived there. . . Use the **Daily Bellringer Transparency** to help students answer the question.

▶ Daily Bellringer Transparency, Section 1

The World's People | Daily Bellringer
Section 1

Preview Section 1

If YOU lived there ...
You live in New York City, and your young cousin from out of state has come to visit. As you take her on a tour of the city, you point out the different cultural neighborhoods, like Chinatown, Little Italy, Spanish Harlem, and Koreatown. Your cousin isn't quite sure what culture means or why these neighborhoods are so different.

How can you explain what culture is?

Consider the FOOD in each neighborhood:
· menus in the restaurants
· items sold in markets
· food in farmer's markets, festivals

Consider the LANGUAGES in each neighborhood:
· native languages spoken
· amount of English spoken
· language in signs, posters, leaflets

Academic Vocabulary

Preteach or review the following term:
innovation a new idea or way of doing something (p. 84)

▧ RF: Vocabulary Builder, Section 1

Taking Notes

Have students use the graphic organizer online to take notes on the section. This activity will prepare students for the Section Assessment, in which they will complete a graphic organizer that builds on the information using the Critical Thinking Skill: Finding Main Ideas.

SECTION 1

Culture

What You Will Learn...

Main Ideas

1. Culture is the set of beliefs, goals, and practices that a group of people share.
2. The world includes many different culture groups.
3. New ideas and events lead to changes in culture.

The Big Idea

Culture, a group's shared practices and beliefs, differs from group to group and changes over time.

Key Terms

culture, *p. 80*
culture trait, *p. 81*
culture region, *p. 82*
ethnic group, *p. 83*
cultural diversity, *p. 83*
cultural diffusion, *p. 85*

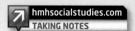
hmhsocialstudies.com
TAKING NOTES

Use the graphic organizer online to take notes on culture.

If **YOU** lived there...

You live in New York City, and your young cousin from out of state has come to visit. As you take her on a tour of the city, you point out the different cultural neighborhoods, like Chinatown, Little Italy, Spanish Harlem, and Koreatown. Your cousin isn't quite sure what culture means or why these neighborhoods are so different.

How can you explain what culture is?

BUILDING BACKGROUND For hundreds of years, immigrants from around the world have moved to the United States to make a new home here. They have brought with them all the things that make up culture—language, religion, beliefs, traditions, and more. As a result, the United States has one of the most diverse cultures in the world.

What Is Culture?

If you traveled around the world, you would experience many different sights and sounds. You would probably hear unique music, eat a variety of foods, listen to different languages, see distinctive landscapes, and learn new customs. You would see and take part in the variety of cultures that exist in our world.

A Way of Life

What exactly is culture? **Culture** is the set of beliefs, values, and practices that a group of people has in common. Culture includes many aspects of life, such as language and religion, that we may share with people around us. Everything in your day-to-day life is part of your culture, from the clothes you wear to the music you hear to the foods you eat.

On your world travels, you might notice that all societies share certain cultural features. All people have some kind of government, educate their children in some way, and create some type of art or music. However, not all societies practice their culture in the same way. For example, in Japan the school year begins in the spring, and students wear school uniforms. In the United States, however, the school year begins in the late

---

Teach the Big Idea

At Level

Culture

1. **Teach** Ask students the questions in the Main Idea boxes under Direct Teach.

2. **Apply** Write three headings on the board: Culture, Culture Groups, and Culture Change. Call on students to add words or phrases under each to describe the United States. Challenge students to provide examples under each from countries other than the United States. **LS Verbal/Linguistic**

3. **Review** Ask each student to write on a piece of paper one culture that was either mentioned in the text or that they know about. They

should list some culture traits, and how that culture has changed. Call on students to share what they have written.

4. **Practice/Homework** Ask students to discuss their own culture with a parent and make a list of some favorite culture traits. They can also discuss and list how their culture is changing. **LS Verbal/Linguistic, Interpersonal, Intrapersonal**

📑 Alternative Assessment Handbook, Rubric 11: Discussions

Culture Traits

These students in Japan and Kenya have some culture traits in common, like eating lunch at school. Other culture traits are different.

ANALYZING VISUALS What culture traits do these students share? Which are different?

summer, and ~~most schools do not require~~ uniforms. Differences like these are what make each culture unique.

NOT SO

Culture Traits

Cultural features like starting the school year in the spring or wearing uniforms are types of culture traits. A **culture trait** is an activity or behavior in which people often take part. The language you speak and the sports you play are some of your culture traits. Sometimes a culture trait is shared by people around the world. For example, all around the globe people participate in the game of soccer. In places as different as Germany, Nigeria, and Saudi Arabia, many people enjoy playing and watching soccer.

While some culture traits are shared around the world, others change from place to place. One example of this is how people around the world eat. In China most people use chopsticks to eat their food. In Europe, however, people use forks and spoons. In Ethiopia, many people use bread or their fingers to scoop their food.

Development of Culture

How do cultures develop? Culture traits are often learned or passed down from one generation to the next. Most culture traits develop within families as traditions, foods, or holiday customs are handed down over the years. Laws and moral codes are also passed down within societies. Many laws in the United States, for example, can be traced back to England in the 1600s and were brought by colonists to America.

Cultures also develop as people learn new culture traits. Immigrants who move to a new country, for example, might learn to speak the language or eat the foods of their adopted country.

Other factors, such as history and the environment, also affect how cultures develop. For example, historical events changed the language and religion of much of Central and South America. In the 1500s, when the Spanish conquered the region, they introduced their language and Roman Catholic faith. The environment in which we live can also shape culture.

FOCUS ON READING

What is the main idea of this paragraph?

THE WORLD'S PEOPLE **81**

Direct Teach

Main Idea

❶ What Is Culture?

Culture is the set of beliefs, goals, and practices that a group of people share.

Describe What role do families play in the development of culture? *pass down traditions such as foods, holiday customs, and so on.*

Identify What is one culture trait you share with many other people around the world? What is one that is not shared by many other cultures? *possible answers: shared—love of soccer, movies, computers; not shared—particular holiday customs, education, clothing style, and so on*

Make Generalizations What are some culture traits that immigrants to your area have adopted from the United States? *possible answers— language, style of dress, educational system, foods, involvement in government, and so on*

📰 **RF:** Biography, Margaret Mead

Did you know. . .

Food is a unique part of a people's culture. Certain fish eggs, called caviar, have been a favorite in Russia for centuries, while in Japan, some types of raw fish, called sushi, have been popular for a long time. In France, geese were specially raised and overfed so their livers would taste a certain way. Today, all of these foods are enjoyed in the United States and many other parts of the world.

Critical Thinking: Comparing and Contrasting   **At Level**

Ethnic Groups in Different Countries   **Research Required**

1. Organize the class into pairs.

2. Have each pair select two countries (not the United States). Each student will research one of the countries to determine the different ethnic groups living there, population in each group, how people in the group distinguish themselves from others (by religion, language, and so on), how they came there, and how they have cooperated or come into conflict with others.

3. When the research is complete, have each pair prepare a chart with two columns that summarizes the information for the two countries. Ask each pair to compare and contrast the ethnic groups in each country.

4. Ask volunteers to share their findings with the class. Guide the class in a discussion of these findings. **LS Verbal/Linguistic**

📄 Alternative Assessment Handbook, Rubrics 30: Research; and 11: Discussions

Answers

Analyzing Visuals *Shared traits include eating with friends, western style clothing; different traits include manner of eating and food eaten.*

Focus on Reading *Culture traits are frequently learned or passed down through generations.*

Main Idea

❷ Culture Groups

The world includes many different culture groups.

Identify What is one country with a single central culture? *Japan*

Make Generalizations About how many culture regions are there in Mexico? *two—northern Mexico (more modern) and southern Mexico (more traditional)*

Make Inferences Why is a shared language such an important part of a culture region? *because it allows people to communicate easily*

Linking to Today

Corporate Culture Many students and job seekers assume that one company is just like another. Yet corporate culture—a company's unique set of values, rules, and way of doing business—varies greatly. Corporate culture can affect how many hours employees are expected to work, whether work relationships are formal or casual, and even how employees are expected to dress. When considering careers, experts often advise people to consider how well they will "fit in" with a company's culture—which can be just as important a factor to consider as salary, benefits, and career growth.

Answers

Reading Check *language, religion, clothes, music, food, sports, traditions, laws*

For example, the desert environment of Africa's Sahara influences the way people who live there earn a living. Rather than grow crops, they herd animals that have adapted to the harsh environment. As you can see, history and the environment affect how cultures develop.

READING CHECK **Finding Main Ideas** What practices and customs make up culture?

Culture Groups

Earth is home to thousands of different cultures. People who share similar culture traits are members of the same culture group. Culture groups can be based on a variety of factors, such as age, language, or religion. American teenagers, for example, can be said to form a culture group based on location and age. They share similar tastes in music, clothing, and sports.

Culture Regions

When we refer to culture groups, we are speaking of people who share a common culture. At other times, however, we need to refer to the area, or region, where the culture group is found. A **culture region** is an area in which people have many shared culture traits.

In a specific culture region, people share certain culture traits, such as religious beliefs, language, or lifestyle. One well-known culture region is the Arab world. As you can see at right, an Arab culture region spreads across Southwest Asia and North Africa. In this region, most people write and speak Arabic and are Muslim. They also share other traits, such as foods, music, styles of clothing, and architecture.

Occasionally, a single culture region dominates an entire country. In Japan, for example, one primary culture dominates the country. Nearly everyone in Japan

speaks the same language and follows the same practices. Many Japanese bow to their elders as a sign of respect and remove their shoes when they enter a home.

A single country may also include more than one culture region within its borders. Mexico is one of many countries that is made up of different culture regions. People in northern Mexico and southern Mexico, for example, have different culture traits. The culture of northern Mexico tends to be more modern, while traditional culture remains strong in southern Mexico.

A culture region may also stretch across country borders. As you have already learned, an Arab culture region dominates much of Southwest Asia and North Africa. Another example is the Kurdish culture region, home to the Kurds, a people that live throughout Turkey, Iran, and Iraq.

Arab Culture Region

Culture regions are based on shared culture traits. Southwest Asia and North Africa make up an Arab culture region based on ethnic heritage, a common language, and religion. Most people in this region are Arab, speak and write Arabic, and practice Islam.

Collaborative Learning

At Level

Culture Groups Based on Age

Prep Required

Materials: magazines appealing to different age groups; materials for making a collage

1. Organize the class into four teams. Assign each team an age group: children and teenagers, young adults, older adults, or seniors. Distribute magazines to each team for the age group it was assigned.

2. Have each team discuss the people in the United States in its assigned group and list some culture traits they share. Students may use the magazines to help them determine tastes in food, music, clothing, and so on.

3. Ask each team to construct a collage using magazine ads or articles to illustrate the culture.

4. Have teams display their collages and answer questions about them. Ask each team whether the same age group in other cultures has similar culture traits. **LS** **Visual/Spatial, Interpersonal**

📋 Alternative Assessment Handbook Rubric 8: Collages

Cultural Diversity

As you just learned, countries may contain several culture regions within their borders. Often, these culture regions are based on ethnic groups. An **ethnic group** is a group of people who share a common culture and ancestry. Members of ethnic groups often share certain culture traits such as religion, language, and even special foods.

Some countries are home to a variety of ethnic groups. For example, more than 100 different ethnic groups live in the East African country of Tanzania. Countries with many ethnic groups are culturally diverse. **Cultural diversity** is the state of having a variety of cultures in the same area. While cultural diversity creates an interesting mix of ideas, behaviors, and practices, it can also lead to conflict.

In some countries, ethnic groups have been in conflict. In Canada, for example, some French Canadians want to separate from the rest of Canada to preserve their language and culture. In the 1990s ethnic conflict in the African country of Rwanda led to extreme violence and bloodshed.

Although ethnic groups have clashed in some culturally diverse countries, they have cooperated in others. In the United States, for example, many different ethnic groups live side by side. Cities and towns often celebrate their ethnic heritage with festivals and parades, like the Saint Patrick's Day Parade in Boston or Philadelphia's Puerto Rican Festival.

READING CHECK **Making Inferences** Why might cultural diversity cause conflict?

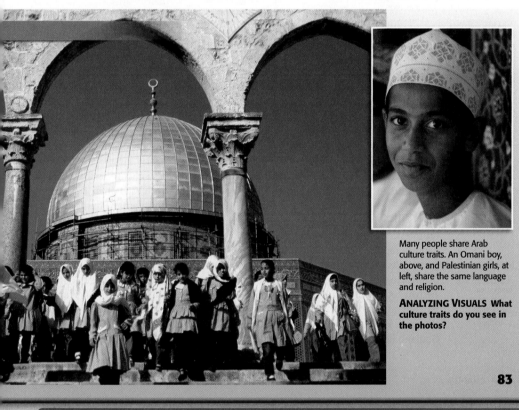

Many people share Arab culture traits. An Omani boy, above, and Palestinian girls, at left, share the same language and religion.

ANALYZING VISUALS What culture traits do you see in the photos?

83

❸ Changes in Culture

New ideas and events lead to changes in culture.

Describe How did the Native American culture change after the Spanish conquered the Americas? How did the Spanish culture change? *started to use horses and firearms; started to use new foods such as potatoes and chocolate*

Analyze How could the Internet encourage cultural diffusion? *allows communication quickly between many people and cultures*

Make Inferences Why have immigrant groups usually adopted the language of their new home? Why have some continued to speak their native language? *to make communication easier and fit in with the culture; to maintain some of their native culture*

📑 **RF:** Critical Thinking, Wheat and the World

Did you know. . .

The Internet was first developed and used by the U.S. military in the 1970s. Today, millions of people worldwide use it. Contact through the Internet may become an important way that cultures change.

Cultural Diffusion of Baseball

Like many other ideas and customs, baseball has spread around the world through the process of cultural diffusion. Since its beginnings in New York in the 1800s, baseball has spread throughout the United States, into Central and South America, and to Asia.

American missionaries introduced baseball to Korea in 1905.

American students first brought baseball to Cuba in the 1800s.

Changes in Culture

You've read books or seen movies set in the time of the Civil War or in the Wild West of the late 1800s. Think about how our culture has changed since then. Clothing, food, music—all have changed drastically. When we study cultural change, we try to find out what caused the changes and how those changes spread from place to place.

How Cultures Change

ACADEMIC VOCABULARY
innovation a new idea or way of doing something

Cultures change constantly. Some changes happen rapidly, while others take many years. What causes cultures to change? **Innovation** and contact with other people are two key causes of cultural change.

New ideas often bring about cultural changes. For example, when Alexander Graham Bell invented the telephone, it changed how people communicate with each other. Other innovations, such as motion pictures, changed how people spend their free time. More recently, the creation of the Internet dramatically altered the way people find information, communicate, and shop.

Cultures also change as societies come into contact with each other. For example, when the Spanish arrived in the Americas, they introduced firearms and horses to the region, changing the lifestyle of some Native American groups. At the same time, the Spaniards learned about new foods like potatoes and chocolate. These foods then became an important part of Europeans' diet. The Chinese had a similar influence on Korea and Japan, where they introduced Buddhism and written language.

84 CHAPTER 4

Differentiating Instruction

Advanced/Gifted and Talented
Above Level
Research Required

Ask students to research the diffusion of a sport, including major sports in the United States such as soccer, basketball, or tennis, or more specialized sports such as curling, sumo wrestling, bocce, or others. Once they have completed their research, have students write a paragraph which describes the cultural diffusion of the sport. Ask students to make a map with arrows that show the paths it traveled. **LS Verbal/Linguistic, Visual/Spatial**

📑 Alternative Assessment Handbook, Rubrics 30: Research; and 20: Map Creation

Special Needs Learners
Below Level
Research Required

Ask students to look in newspapers and magazines for photos of sports played in other countries. Have students choose one photo. Ask them to identify the sport and country in which it is played. Ask students to describe how the picture and media coverage of the sport might encourage cultural diffusion. Students can give their answers in either written or oral form. **LS Visual/Spatial, Verbal/Linguistic**

📑 Alternative Assessment Handbook, Rubrics 19: Magazine; and 23: Newspapers

Organized baseball began in New York around 1845 and quickly spread around the world.

How Ideas Spread

You have probably noticed that a new slang word might spread from teenager to teenager and state to state. In the same way, clothing styles from New York or Paris might become popular all over the world. More serious cultural traits spread as well. Religious beliefs or ideas about government may spread from place to place. The spread of culture traits from one region to another is called **cultural diffusion**.

Cultural diffusion often occurs when people move from one place to another. For example, when Europeans settled in the Americas, they brought their culture along with them. As a result, English, French, Spanish, and Portuguese are all spoken in the Americas. American culture also spread as pioneers moved west, taking with them their form of government, religious beliefs, and customs.

Cultural diffusion also takes place as new ideas spread from place to place. As you can see on the map above, the game of baseball first began in New York, then spread throughout the United States. As

more and more people learned the game, it spread even faster and farther. Baseball eventually spread around the world. Wearing blue jeans became part of our culture in a similar way. Blue jeans originated in the American West in the mid-1800s. They gradually became popular all over the country and the world.

READING CHECK   Finding Main Ideas How do cultures change over time?

SUMMARY AND PREVIEW In this section you learned about the role that culture plays in our lives and how our cultures change. Next, you will learn about human populations and how we keep track of Earth's changing population.

Section 1 Assessment

hmhsocialstudies.com
ONLINE QUIZ

Reviewing Ideas, Terms, and Places

1. **a. Define** What is **culture**?
   b. Analyze What influences the development of culture?
   c. Elaborate How might the world be different if we all shared the same culture?
2. **a. Identify** What are the different types of **culture regions**?
   b. Analyze How does **cultural diversity** affect societies?
3. **a. Describe** How does **cultural diffusion** take place?
   b. Make Inferences How can the spread of new ideas lead to cultural change?
   c. Evaluate Do you think that cultural diffusion has a positive or a negative effect? Explain your answer.

Critical Thinking

4. **Finding Main Ideas** Using your notes and a chart like the one here, explain the main idea of each aspect of culture in your own words.

Culture Traits	Culture Groups	Cultural Change

FOCUS ON WRITING

5. **Writing about Culture** What key words about culture can you include on your poster? What images might you include? Jot down your ideas in your notebook.

THE WORLD'S PEOPLE **85**

Bellringer

If YOU lived there. . . Use the **Daily Bellringer Transparency** to help students answer the question.

▶ Daily Bellringer Transparency, Section 2

Key Terms

📖 **RF:** Vocabulary Builder, Section 2

Taking Notes

Have students use the graphic organizer online to take notes on the section. This activity will prepare students for the Section Assessment, in which they will complete a graphic organizer that builds on the information using the Critical Thinking Skill: Summarizing.

SECTION 2

Population

What You Will Learn...

Main Ideas

1. The study of population patterns helps geographers learn about the world.
2. Population statistics and trends are important measures of population change.

The Big Idea

Population studies are an important part of geography.

Key Terms

population, *p. 86*
population density, *p. 86*
birthrate, *p. 88*
migration, *p. 89*

hmhsocialstudies.com
TAKING NOTES

Use the graphic organizer online to take notes on population.

If **YOU** lived there...

You live in Mexico City, one of the largest and most crowded cities in the world. You realize just how crowded it is whenever you ride the subway at rush hour! You love the excitement of living in a big city. There is always something interesting to do. At the same time, the city has a lot of crime. Heavy traffic pollutes the air.

What do you like and dislike about living in a large city?

BUILDING BACKGROUND An important part of geographers' work is the study of human populations. Many geographers are interested in where people live, how many people live there, and what effects those people have on resources and the environment.

Population Patterns

How many people live in your community? Do you live in a small town, a huge city, or somewhere in between? Your community's **population**, or the total number of people in a given area, determines a great deal about the place in which you live. Population influences the variety of businesses, the types of transportation, and the number of schools in your community.

Because population has a huge impact on our lives, it is an important part of geography. Geographers who study human populations are particularly interested in patterns that emerge over time. They study such information as how many people live in an area, why people live where they do, and how populations change. Population patterns like these can tell us much about our world.

Population Density

Some places on Earth are crowded with people. Others are almost empty. One statistic geographers use to examine populations is **population density**, a measure of the number of people living in an area. Population density is expressed as persons per square mile or square kilometer.

Teach the Big Idea | At Level

Population

1. **Teach** Ask students the questions in the Main Idea boxes under Direct Teach.

2. **Apply** Divide the room into at least three "countries." Assign students randomly to each, creating unequal groups. Ask each group to name its "country," count its citizens for this year, and determine its density according to a random number of square miles you provide. Then tell students it is ten years later and direct some students to "migrate" to different countries. Give students a reason for their migration, such as famine, flood, war, and so on. Ask each group to recalculate its density after the migration is done.

3. **Review** Have each group post its density on the board for each year. Ask students how life in their country might have changed as the population changed.

4. **Practice/Homework** Ask students to create a chart or bar graph that shows the population density for each country for each year. 🔲 **Interpersonal, Visual/Spatial**

📖 Alternative Assessment Handbook, Rubric 7: Charts

World Population Density

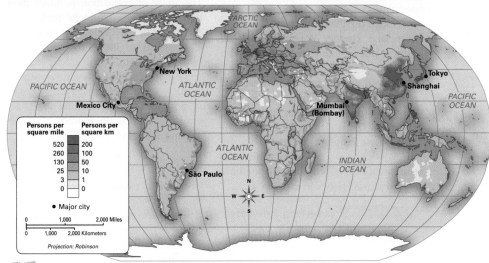

Persons per square mile | **Persons per square km**
520 | 200
260 | 100
130 | 50
25 | 10
3 | 1
0 | 0

● Major city

0   1,000   2,000 Miles
0   1,000   2,000 Kilometers

Projection: Robinson

map zone
Geography Skills

Location While low population densities are common throughout much of the world, South and East Asia are two of the world's most densely populated regions.

1. **Identify** Which continent is the most densely populated? Which is the least densely populated?
2. **Making Inferences** Why might the population density of far North America be so low?

Population density provides us with important information about a place. The more people per square mile in a region, the more crowded, or dense, it is. Japan, for example, has a population density of 880 people per square mile (340 per square km). That is a high population density. In many parts of Japan, people are crowded together in large cities, and space is very limited. In contrast, Australia has a very low population density. Only 6 people per square mile (2 per square km) live there. Australia has many wide-open spaces with very few people.

How do you think population density affects life in a particular place? In places with high population densities, the land is often expensive, roads are crowded, and buildings tend to be taller. On the other hand, places with low population densities tend to have more open spaces, less traffic, and more available land.

Where People Live

Can you tell where most of the world's people live by examining the population density map above? The reds and purples on the map indicate areas of very high population density, while the light yellow areas indicate sparse populations. When an area is thinly populated, it is often because the land does not provide a very good life. These areas may have rugged mountains or harsh deserts where people cannot grow crops. Some areas may be frozen all year long, making survival there very difficult.

↗ hmhsocialstudies.com
ANIMATED GEOGRAPHY
Earth at Night

THE WORLD'S PEOPLE **87**

---

❷ **Population Change**

Population statistics and trends are important measures of population change.

Identify What statistic subtracts from a country's population? *death rate*

Recall Which continents have countries with the lowest rates of natural increase? *Europe and North America*

Summarize How does migration affect the population of the world? *It doesn't affect the total population but affects the population of individual countries.*

📄 **RF:** Primary Source: "The New Colossus" by Emma Lazarus

Connecting to Math
Calculating Population Density

Activity **Calculate Density of the Classroom** Have students calculate the population density of the classroom (persons per square feet) by counting the people and dividing by the (estimated) square feet of the classroom. You may want to provide the estimated square footage of the classroom or have students measure and calculate. **LS** **Logical/Mathematical**

📄 Alternative Assessment Handbook, Rubric 35: Solving Problems

---

Answers

Reading Check *how crowded a place is, possibly the price and availability of land, type of buildings, traffic*

Connecting to Math *2,460 people per square mile*

For these reasons, very few people live in parts of far North America, Greenland, northern Asia, and Australia.

Notice on the map that some areas have large clusters of population. Such clusters can be found in East and South Asia, Europe, and eastern North America. Fertile soil, reliable sources of water, and a good agricultural climate make these good regions for settlement. For example, the North China Plain in East Asia is one of the most densely populated regions in the world. The area's plentiful agricultural land, many rivers, and mild climate have made it an ideal place to settle.

READING CHECK **Generalizing** What types of information can population density provide?

CONNECTING TO Math

Calculating Population Density

Population density measures the number of people living in an area. To calculate population density, divide a place's total population by its area in square miles (or square kilometers). For example, if your city has a population of 100,000 people and an area of 100 square miles, you would divide 100,000 by 100. This would give you a population density of 1,000 people per square mile (100,000 ÷ 100 = 1,000).

Analyzing If a city had a population of 615,000 and a total land area of 250 square miles, what would its population density be?

City	Population	Total Area (square miles)	Population Density (people per square mile)
Adelaide, Australia	1,145,000	336	3,408
Lima, Peru	8,012,000	1,029	7,786
Nairobi, Kenya	3,010,000	266	11,316

Population Change

The study of population is much more important than you might realize. The number of people living in an area affects all elements of life—the availability of housing and jobs, whether hospitals and schools open or close, even the amount of available food. Geographers track changes in populations by examining important statistics, studying the movement of people, and analyzing population trends.

Tracking Population Changes

Geographers examine three key statistics to learn about population changes. These statistics are important for studying a country's population over time.

Three key statistics—birthrate, death rate, and the rate of natural increase—track changes in population. Births add to a population. Deaths subtract from it. The annual number of births per 1,000 people is called the **birthrate**. Similarly, the death rate is the annual number of deaths per 1,000 people. The birthrate minus the death rate equals the percentage of natural increase, or the rate at which a population is changing. For example, Denmark has a rate of natural increase of 0.05%. This means it has slightly more births than deaths and a very slight population increase.

Population growth rates differ from one place to another. In some countries, populations are growing very slowly or even shrinking. Many countries in Europe and North America have very low rates of natural increase. In Russia, for example, the birthrate is about 10.8 and the death rate is 16.1. The result is a negative rate of natural increase and a shrinking population.

In most countries around the world, however, populations are growing. Mali, for example, has a rate of natural increase of about 3.3 percent. While that may sound

---

Critical Thinking: Understanding Cause and Effect **Above Level**

Factors Affecting Death Rates

Prep Required **Research Required**

Materials: a listing of world death rates (available at https://www.cia.gov/cia/publications/factbook/index.html)

1. **Prepare** Select countries to research, such as countries with high and low death rates or those affected by epidemic, drought, tsunami, and so on.

2. **Assign** Divide the class into small groups. Assign a country to each group. Tell students their job is to research factors such as

standard of living, medical care, and natural disasters. Tell students these factors will help explain their country's ranking among other countries in the world.

3. **Assess** Have each group present an oral report listing factors which have affected the death rate in their country in recent years.
LS **Verbal/Linguistic**

📄 Alternative Assessment, Rubric 30: Research

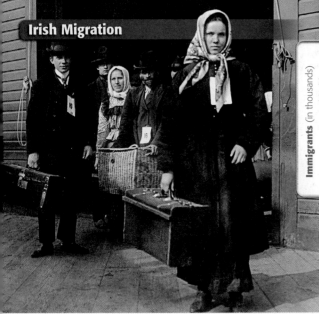
Irish Migration

Irish Migration to the United States, 1845–1855

Immigrants (in thousands) vs *Year*

Source: *Historical Statistics of the United States*

The failure of Ireland's most important food crop, the potato, caused widespead starvation. Disease and high food prices forced many Irish to flee to America in search of a better life.

ANALYZING GRAPHS In what year did Irish migration to the United States peak?

small, it means that Mali's population is expected to double in only 21 years! High population growth rates can pose some challenges, as governments try to provide enough jobs, education, and medical care for their rapidly growing populations.

Migration

A common cause of population change is migration. **Migration** is the process of moving from one place to live in another. As one country loses citizens as a result of migration, its population can decline. At the same time, another country may gain population as people settle there.

People migrate for many reasons. Some factors push people to leave their country, while other factors pull, or attract, people to new countries. Warfare, a lack of jobs, or a lack of good farmland are common push factors. For example, during the Irish potato famine of the mid-1800s, poverty and disease forced some 1.5 million people to leave Ireland. Opportunities for a better life often pull people to new countries. For example, in the 1800s and early 1900s thousands of British citizens migrated to Australia in search of cheap land.

World Population Trends

In the last 200 years Earth's population has exploded. For thousands of years world population growth was low and relatively steady. About 2,000 years ago, the world had some 300 million people. By 1800 there were almost 1 billion people. Since 1800, better health care and improved food production have supported tremendous population growth. In 1999 the world's population passed 6 billion people.

Population trends are an important part of the study of the world's people. Two important population trends are clear today. The first trend indicates that the population growth in some of the more industrialized nations has begun to slow.

FOCUS ON READING
What is the main idea of this paragraph? What facts are used to support that idea?

THE WORLD'S PEOPLE **89**

Direct Teach

Did you know. . .

In the period from AD 1 to about 1800 the world's population grew on average by about 444,000 people per year.

Between 1800 and 2000 it grew by about 25 million people per year, more than 50 times that of the previous period.

In 2005 the U.S. Census Bureau estimated that the world population would grow by about 75 million people, more than 150 times the rate before 1800.

Review & Assess

Close

Briefly review the benefits and methods of studying population and how population affects people's lives.

Review

↗ Online Quiz, Section 2

Assess

SE Section 2 Assessment
PASS: Section 2 Quiz
Alternative Assessment Handbook

Reteach/Classroom Intervention

Guided Reading Workbook, Section 2
Interactive Skills Tutor CD-ROM

Answers

Analyzing Graphs *about five billion*

Reading Check *population change (natural increase) and migration (movement) trends; to understand how population affects the elements of life (jobs, housing, schools, medical care, available food)*

World Population Growth

Advances in food production and health care have dramatically lowered death rates. As a result, the global population has seen incredible growth over the last 200 years.

ANALYZING GRAPHS By how much did the world's population increase between 1800 and 2000?

World Population Growth, 1500–2000

Source: *Atlas of World Population History*

For example, Germany and France have low rates of natural increase. A second trend indicates that less industrialized countries, like Nigeria and Bangladesh, often have high growth rates. These trends affect a country's workforce and government aid.

READING CHECK **Summarizing** What population statistics do geographers study? Why?

SUMMARY AND PREVIEW In this section you have learned where people live, how crowded places are, and how population affects our world. Geographers study past and present population patterns in order to plan for the future. In the next section, you will learn how governments and economies affect people on Earth.

Section 2 Assessment

hmhsocialstudies.com
ONLINE QUIZ

Reviewing Ideas, Terms, and Places

1. **a. Identify** What regions of the world have the highest levels of **population density**?
   b. Draw Conclusions What information can be learned by studying population density?
   c. Evaluate Would you prefer to live in a region with a dense or a sparse population? Why?
2. **a. Describe** What is natural increase? What can it tell us about a country?
   b. Analyze What effect does **migration** have on human populations?
   c. Predict What patterns do you think world population might have in the future?

Critical Thinking

3. **Summarizing** Draw a graphic organizer like the one here. Use your notes to write a sentence that summarizes each aspect of the study of population.

Population Patterns

Population Change

FOCUS ON WRITING

4. **Discussing Population** What effect does population have on our world? Write down some words and phrases that you might use on your poster to explain the importance of population.

90 CHAPTER 4

Section 2 Assessment Answers

1. **a.** East Asia, South Asia, Europe, eastern North America
   b. possible answers—the amount of open space, the price and availability of land, height of buildings, traffic on roads
   c. possible answers—dense, because there are more options for working, shopping, and being around other people; sparse, because there is more open space and less traffic
2. **a.** rate at which a population is changing (yearly birthrate minus the yearly death rate as a percentage); its growth and economic situation

   b. It affects the population of countries.
   c. possible answers—continued rapid growth; slowing of growth as resources diminish
3. possible answers: population patterns—Geographers study how many people live in areas, where they live and why, and how populations change. Population change—They study birthrate, death rate, and rate of natural increase to find population trends.
4. Students' answers should reflect what they learned about population in Section 2, such as population growth resulting in a scarcity of resources.

Government and Economy

If YOU were there...

You live in Raleigh, North Carolina. Your class at school is planning a presentation about life in the United States for a group of visitors from Japan. Your teacher wants you to discuss government and economics in the United States. As you prepare for your speech, you wonder what you should say.

How do government and economics affect your life?

BUILDING BACKGROUND Although you probably don't think about them every day, your country's government and economy have a big influence on your life. That is true in every country in every part of the world. Governments and economic systems affect everything from a person's rights to the type of job he or she has.

Governments of the World

Can you imagine what life would be like if there were no rules? Without ways to establish order and ensure justice, life would be chaotic. That explains why societies have governments. Our governments make and enforce laws, regulate business and trade, and provide aid to people. Governments help shape the culture and economy of a country as well as the daily lives of the people who live there.

Democratic Governments

Many countries—including the United States, Canada, and Mexico—have democratic governments. A **democracy** is a form of government in which the people elect leaders and rule by majority. In most democratic countries, citizens are free to choose representatives to make and enforce the laws. Voters in the United States, for example, elect members of Congress, who make the laws, and the president, who enforces those laws.

What You Will Learn...

Main Ideas

1. The governments of the world include democracy, monarchy, dictatorship, and communism.
2. Different economic activities and systems exist throughout the world.
3. Geographers group the countries of the world based on their level of economic development.

The Big Idea

The world's countries have different governments and levels of economic development.

Key Terms

democracy, *p. 91*
communism, *p. 92*
market economy, *p. 94*
command economy, *p. 94*
gross domestic product (GDP), *p. 95*
developed countries, *p. 95*
developing countries, *p. 95*

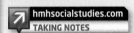

hmhsocialstudies.com
TAKING NOTES

Use the graphic organizer online to take notes on different types of governments and economies.

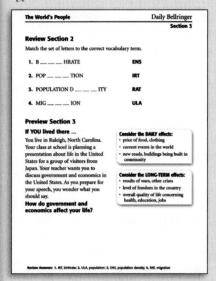

Main Idea

❶ Governments of the World

The governments of the world include democracy, monarchy, dictatorship, and communism.

Describe Why do societies have governments? *to establish order and ensure justice*

Explain How do most dictators rule? *by force*

Contrast How much control over people's lives do democratic countries have compared to Communist countries? *Communist countries have strict control of the economy and daily life, and people have restricted rights and little freedom; democracies do not have complete control over the economy or the daily lives of people, and people usually have many rights and freedoms*

▶️ Map Zone Transparency: Governments of the World

Connect to Civics

Democracy The word *democracy* comes from Greek words that mean "rule by the people." Ancient Greeks were the first known society to practice democracy. Because they were a small society, they practiced direct democracy where all citizens could discuss and vote directly on laws and leaders. Later democracies are indirect, where people vote for representatives who discuss and make the laws.

Answers

Map Zone *North America, South America, Asia, Africa, Europe*

Focus on Reading *the last sentence*

Reading Check *Democracies allow for rights and freedoms; dictatorships restrict rights and freedoms.*

Governments of the World

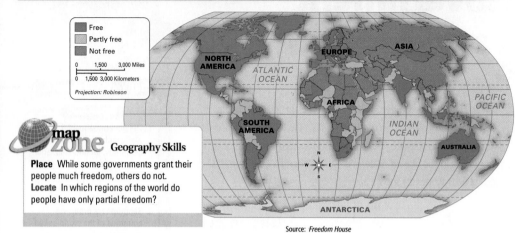

Free
Partly free
Not free

0   1,500   3,000 Miles
0   1,500   3,000 Kilometers
Projection: Robinson

map zone **Geography Skills**

Place While some governments grant their people much freedom, others do not.
Locate In which regions of the world do people have only partial freedom?

Source: Freedom House

FOCUS ON READING

Main ideas are not always stated in the first sentence. Which sentence in this paragraph states the main idea?

Most democratic governments in the world work to protect the freedoms and rights of their people, such as the freedom of speech and the freedom of religion. Other democracies, however, restrict the rights and freedoms of their people. Not all democratic governments in the world are completely free.

Other Types of Government

Not all of the world's countries, however, are democracies. Several other types of government are found in the world today, including monarchies, dictatorships, and Communist states.

Monarchy is one of the oldest types of government in the world. A monarchy is ruled directly by a king or queen, the head of a royal family. Saudi Arabia is an example of a monarchy. The Saudi king has executive, legislative, and judicial powers. In some monarchies, power is in the hands of just one person. As a result, the people have little say in their government. Other monarchies, however, like Norway and Spain, use many democratic practices.

Dictatorship is a type of government in which a single, powerful ruler has total control. This leader, called a dictator, often rules by force. Iraq under Saddam Hussein was an example of a dictatorship. People who live under a dictatorship are not free. They have few rights and no say in their own government.

Yet another form of government is communism. **Communism** is a political system in which the government owns all property and dominates all aspects of life in a country. Leaders of most Communist governments are not elected by citizens. Rather, they are chosen by the Communist Party or by Communist leaders. In most Communist states, like Cuba and North Korea, the government strictly controls the country's economy and the daily life of its people. As a result, people in Communist states often have restricted rights and very little freedom.

READING CHECK **Supporting a Point of View** Why might people prefer to live in a democracy as opposed to a dictatorship?

92 CHAPTER 4

Critical Thinking: Comparing and Contrasting   At Level

Kinds of Government

Ask students to copy the chart to the right (except for blue answers) on a piece of paper and fill in the columns. After they have completed their work, call on volunteers to provide the answers so that you can fill in the chart on the board. Discuss issues or misconceptions along the way. **LS** **Visual/Spatial, Verbal/Linguistic**

📝 Alternative Assessment Handbook, Rubric 7: Charts

	Democracy	Monarchy	Dictatorship	Communism
Leaders take power	Elected	Passed down	Take power by force or are elected	By force or election of party
People's freedoms	Many	Vary	Few	Few
Economic Control	Little government control	Vary	Control by government	Control by government

Economies of the World

One important function of government is to monitor a country's economy. The economy is a system that includes all of the activities that people and businesses do to earn a living. Countries today use a mix of different economic activities and systems.

Economic Activity

Every country has some level of economic activity. Economic activities are ways in which people make a living. Some people farm, others manufacture goods, while still others provide services, such as driving a taxi or designing skyscrapers. Geographers divide these economic activities into four different levels.

The first level of economic activity, the primary industry, uses natural resources or raw materials. People in these industries earn a living by providing raw materials to others. Farming, fishing, and mining are all examples of primary industries. These activities provide raw materials such as grain, seafood, and coal for others to use.

Secondary industries perform the next step. They use natural resources or raw materials to manufacture other products. Manufacturing is the process in which raw materials are changed into finished goods. For example, people who make furniture might take wood and make products such as tables, chairs, or desks. Automobile manufacturers use steel, plastic, glass, and rubber to put together trucks and cars.

In the third level of activity, or tertiary industry, goods and services are exchanged. People in tertiary industries sell the furniture, automobiles, or other products made in secondary industries. Other people, like health care workers or mechanics, provide services rather than goods. Teachers, store clerks, doctors, and TV personalities are all engaged in this level of economic activity.

Economic Activity

Primary Industry

Primary industries use natural resources to make money. Here a farmer sells milk from dairy cows to earn a living.

Secondary Industry

Secondary economic activities use raw materials to produce or manufacture something new. In this case, the milk from dairy cows is used to make cheese.

Tertiary Industry

Tertiary economic activities provide services to people and businesses. This grocer selling cheese in a market is involved in a tertiary activity.

Quaternary Industry

Quaternary industries process and distribute information. Skilled workers research and gather information. Here, inspectors examine and test the quality of cheese.

THE WORLD'S PEOPLE **93**

Direct Teach

Main Idea

2 Economies of the World

Different economic activities and systems exist throughout the world.

Identify Which type of industry are retail stores? *tertiary*

Make Inferences How are primary and secondary industries related? *Primary industries provide raw materials while secondary industries use those materials to manufacture products.*

Make Generalizations What problems might a command economy face? *possible answers—poor decisions on what and how much to produce, high prices for some goods, poor motivation for workers and business people*

RF: Geography for Life: Shopping Rules!

Info to Know

U.S. Economic Activities In the current U.S. economy, nearly every job or industry is connected to a primary, secondary, tertiary, and quaternary industry. For example, computers require raw materials (silicon); manufacturers produce chips, screens, keyboards, and so on; sales and service people sell and fix computers; programmers and others design and engineer computers.

Another example is construction. Raw materials such as wood are required for building; manufacturers create windows, concrete, siding, and so on; sales and services help sell and repair homes; architects and planners design homes, buildings, subdivisions, and so on.

Differentiating Instruction

Advanced/Gifted and Talented
At Level
Research Required

Ask students to identify one tertiary or quaternary industry in the local area and interview a worker for a written report. The report should include the name and type of industry, what services or information it provides, how large it is, the specific job the person does, what training he or she has had, and so on. **LS Verbal/Linguistic**

Alternative Assessment Handbook, Rubric 40: Writing to Describe

English-Language Learners
At Level
Research Required

Ask students to list the four types of economic activities on a sheet of paper and then list one or more companies or people in the local area engaged in each activity. They can use a local telephone book or business directory for assistance. If there are none of a particular type in the local area, identify one or more in the state. **LS Verbal/Linguistic**

Alternative Assessment Handbook, Rubric 38: Writing to Classify

THE WORLD'S PEOPLE **93**

❸ Economic Development

Geographers group the countries of the world based on their level of economic development.

Identify What economic indicators do geographers use to evaluate a country's development? *gross domestic product, per capita GDP, level of industrialization, quality of life*

Make Inferences Why do you think industrialization can help a country develop a strong, wealthy economy? *It allows quicker and easier production in manufacturing so GDP rises and more wealth is available.*

Analyze How do you think a low literacy rate affects economic development? *possible answers—fewer people able to learn and perform complex jobs in other than primary industries; fewer new ideas and ways to improve the economic system*

Connect to Economics

Economic Systems In 1776 a Scotsman, Adam Smith, wrote that private competition without government regulation was the best economic system. He felt that private businesses that followed their own interests in free markets organized the economy in the best way "as if by an invisible hand."

Today's market economies are often called "mixed economies" (rather than "free market economies") because government does regulate many types of business, from interstate commerce to rules governing health and safety of employees and consumers. Capitalism and market economies have become the dominant economic systems in the world.

Answers

Reading Check *traditional, market, and command economies*

Contrasting *lower income, life expectancy, and literacy rate; fewer doctors*

94

The highest level of economic activity, quaternary industry, involves the research and distribution of information. People making a living at this level work with information rather than goods, and often have specialized knowledge and skills. Architects, lawyers, and scientists all work in quaternary industries.

Economic Systems

Just as economic activities are organized into different types, so are our economic systems. Economic systems can be divided into three types: traditional, market, and command. Most countries today use a mix of these economic systems.

One economic system is a **traditional** economy, a system in which people grow their own food and make their own goods. Trade may take place through barter, or the exchange of goods without the use of money. Rural and remote communities often have a mostly traditional economy.

ACADEMIC VOCABULARY
traditional customary, time-honored

The most common economic system used around the world today is a market economy. A **market economy** is a system based on private ownership, free trade, and competition. Individuals and businesses are free to buy and sell what they wish. Prices are determined by the supply and demand for goods. This is sometimes called capitalism. The United States is one of many countries that use this system.

A third system is a **command economy**, a system in which the central government makes all economic decisions. The government decides what goods to produce, how much to produce, and what prices will be. While no country has a purely command economy, the economies of North Korea and Cuba are close to it. The Communist governments of these nations own and control most businesses.

READING CHECK **Summarizing** What economic systems are used in the world today?

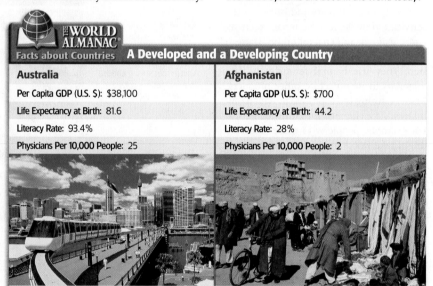

THE WORLD ALMANAC®
Facts about Countries   **A Developed and a Developing Country**

Australia	Afghanistan
Per Capita GDP (U.S. $): $38,100	Per Capita GDP (U.S. $): $700
Life Expectancy at Birth: 81.6	Life Expectancy at Birth: 44.2
Literacy Rate: 93.4%	Literacy Rate: 28%
Physicians Per 10,000 People: 25	Physicians Per 10,000 People: 2

Contrasting How does the quality of life in Afghanistan differ from that in Australia?

↗ hmhsocialstudies.com

94 CHAPTER 4

At Level

Developed and Developing Countries

Research Required

1. Organize the class into pairs.

2. Assign each pair two countries (one developed and one developing). Each student will research one country to locate facts as in "The World Almanac" feature: Per capita GDP, Life Expectancy, Literacy Rate, Physicians Per 10,000 People.

3. Ask pairs to report their findings orally and to classify each country as developed or developing. Ask them why they chose to classify each country as they did.

4. Make two columns on the board and list countries researched as developed or developing. You might discuss what GDP or other standards students might use to classify countries or discuss countries that are closer to the middle. **LS Logical/Mathematical, Verbal/ Linguistic**

Alternative Assessment Handbook, Rubric 30: Research

Economic Development

Economic systems and activities affect a country's economic development, or the level of economic growth and quality of life. Geographers often group countries into two basic categories—developed and developing countries—based on their level of economic development.

Economic Indicators

Geographers use economic indicators, or measures of a country's wealth, to decide if a country is developed or developing. One such measure is gross domestic product. **Gross domestic product (GDP)** is the value of all goods and services produced within a country in a single year. Another indicator is a country's per capita GDP, or the total GDP divided by the number of people in a country. As you can see in the chart, per capita GDP allows us to compare incomes among countries. Other indicators include the level of industrialization and overall quality of life. In other words, we look at the types of industries and technology a country has, in addition to its level of health care and education.

Developed and Developing Countries

Many of the world's wealthiest and most powerful nations are **developed countries**, countries with strong economies and a high quality of life. Developed countries like Germany and the United States have a high per capita GDP and high levels of industrialization. Their health care and education systems are among the best in the world. Many people in developed countries have access to technology.

The world's poorer nations are known as **developing countries**, countries with less productive economies and a lower quality of life. Almost two-thirds of the people in the world live in developing countries. These developing countries have a lower per capita GDP than developed countries. Most of their citizens work in farming or other primary industries. Although these countries typically have large cities, much of their population still lives in rural areas. People in developing countries usually have less access to health care or technology. Guatemala, Nigeria, and Afghanistan are all developing countries.

 READING CHECK **Analyzing** What factors separate developed and developing countries?

SUMMARY AND PREVIEW The world's countries have different governments, economies, and levels of development. Next, you will learn how people are linked in a global community.

Section 3 Assessment

hmhsocialstudies.com
ONLINE QUIZ

Reviewing Ideas, Terms, and Places

1. **a. Identify** What are some different types of government?
   b. Elaborate Under which type of government would you most want to live? Why?
2. **a. Describe** What are the levels of economic activity?
   b. Evaluate Which economic system do you think is best? Explain your answer.
3. **a. Define** What is **gross domestic product**?
   b. Contrast In what ways do **developed countries** differ from **developing countries**?

Critical Thinking

4. **Categorizing** Draw a chart like the one here. Use the chart and your notes to identify the different governments, economies, and levels of economic development in the world today.

Types of Government	Economic Systems	Economic Development

FOCUS ON WRITING

5. **Thinking about Government and Economy** What kinds of images and words could you use to present the main ideas behind the world's governments and economies?

THE WORLD'S PEOPLE **95**

Organizing Information

Learn

Remembering new information is easier if you organize it clearly. As you read and study, try to organize what you are learning. One way to do this is to create a graphic organizer. Follow these steps to create a graphic organizer as you read.

- Identify the main idea of the passage. Write the main idea in a circle at the top of your page.
- As you read, look for subtopics under the main idea. On your paper, draw a row of circles below the main idea, one for each subtopic. Write the subtopics in the circles.
- Below each subtopic, draw a big box. Look for facts and supporting details for each subtopic. List them in the box below the subtopic.

Main Idea → **Subtopic** → **Facts and Details**; **Subtopic** → **Facts and Details**

Practice

Read the passage below carefully. Then use the graphic organizer above to organize the information from the passage.

> Cultures change slowly over time. New ideas and new people can often lead to cultural change.
>
> Cultures often change as new ideas are introduced to a society. New ways of doing things, new inventions, and even new beliefs can all change a culture. One example of this is the spread of computer technology. As people adopted computers, they learned a new language and new work habits.
>
> Cultures also change when new people introduce their culture traits to a society. For example, as immigrants settle in the United States, they add new culture traits, like food, music, and clothing, to American culture.

Apply

Turn to Section 1 and read the passage titled Culture Regions. Draw a graphic organizer like the one above. Then follow the steps to organize the information you have read. The passage will have two or more subtopics. Add additional circles and rectangles for each additional subtopic you find.

Social Studies Skills

Organizing Information

Activity Use of Graphic Organizers

Materials: enough newspaper or magazine articles so that each student has access to one lengthy article

1. Pass out articles. Each student will read the article and create a graphic organizer that organizes the information.

2. When complete, ask volunteers to draw their graphic organizer on the board, including the notes they took. They should then provide a short oral summary of the article.
   LS Verbal/Linguistic, Visual/Spatial

- Alternative Assessment Handbook, Rubric 13: Graphic Organizers
- Interactive Skills Tutor CD-ROM, Lesson 8: Create written, visual, oral presentations
- RF: Social Studies Skills, Organizing Information

Answers

Practice and Apply *Students' graphic organizers will vary but should include the main idea of each passage, at least two subtopics, and facts and supporting details for each subtopic.*

Social Studies Skills Activity: Organizing Information   **Below Level**

Struggling Readers

Materials: copies of a short news article

1. Have students read a news article.

2. Discuss with the group different ways to create graphic organizers. Let them select a way and draw their choice on the board.

3. Go through the article and ask each student to provide a detail. Fill in the organizer on the board and discuss how it can help students remember information. **LS Visual/Spatial**

Alternative Assessment Handbook, Rubric 13: Graphic Organizers

Special Needs Learners

Materials: copies of a graphic organizer and a short news article

1. Pass out the copies of the graphic organizer and the news article.

2. Copy the graphic organizer onto the board.

3. Read the article aloud and ask students to help fill in the organizer after a few sentences. Continue until the article is complete. Discuss the process with the students. **LS Visual/Spatial**

Alternative Assessment Handbook, Rubric 13: Graphic Organizers

Global Connections

If YOU lived there...

You live in Louisville, Kentucky, and you have never traveled out of the United States. However, when you got ready for school this morning, you put on a T-shirt made in Guatemala and jeans made in Malaysia. Your shoes came from China. You rode to school on a bus with parts manufactured in Mexico. At school, your class even took part in a discussion with students in Canada.

What makes your global connections possible?

> **BUILDING BACKGROUND** Trade and technology have turned the world into a "global village." People around the world wear clothes, eat foods, and use goods made in other countries. Global connections are bringing people around the world closer than ever before.

Globalization

In just seconds an e-mail message sent by a teenager in India beams all the way to a friend in London. A band in Seattle releases a song that becomes popular in China. People from New York to Singapore respond to a crisis in Brazil. These are all examples of **globalization**, the process in which countries are increasingly linked to each other through culture and trade.

What caused globalization? Improvements in transportation and communication over the past 100 years have brought the world closer together. Airplanes, telecommunications, and the Internet allow us to communicate and travel the world with ease. As a result, global culture and trade have increased.

Popular Culture

What might you have in common with a teenager in Japan? You probably have more in common than you think. You may use similar technology, wear similar clothes, and watch many of the same movies. You share the same global popular culture.

What You Will Learn...

Main Ideas

1. Globalization links the world's countries together through culture and trade.
2. The world community works together to solve global conflicts and crises.

The Big Idea

Fast, easy global connections have made cultural exchange, trade, and a cooperative world community possible.

Key Terms

globalization, *p. 97*
popular culture, *p. 98*
interdependence, *p. 99*
United Nations (UN), *p. 99*
humanitarian aid, *p. 100*

hmhsocialstudies.com
TAKING NOTES

Use the graphic organizer online to take notes on globalization and the world community.

Direct Teach

Main Idea

1 Globalization

Globalization links the world's countries together through culture and trade.

Describe In what way does improved communication and transportation affect global trade? *It becomes quicker and easier.*

Draw Conclusions How has globalization affected the English language? *commonly used around the world in business, science, and education; added many words from other cultures*

Connect to Economics

The Global Car Since automobiles were invented, foreign cars (cars not produced by a U.S. company) have been available to people in this country. Manufacturers in Italy, Germany, and Japan were producing cars by the 1920s, but most people in the United States purchased cars from American companies such as Ford, Chevrolet, and Chrysler.

In the 1960s and 1970s companies such as Volkswagen, Nissan, Toyota, and Honda found ways to produce dependable cars more cheaply. Although U.S. manufacturers encouraged people to "Buy American," their control of the U.S. market weakened. By the 1990s nearly every major automobile producer in the world was connected to factories and parts from around the world. It is now almost impossible to "Buy American" or to buy a car solely produced in the United States, Japan, Germany, or a single other country.

hmhsocialstudies.com

Online Resources
Activity: The Global Economy

More and more, people around the world are linked through popular culture. **Popular culture** refers to culture traits that are well known and widely accepted. Food, sports, music, and movies are all examples of our popular culture.

The United States has great influence on global popular culture. For example, American soft drinks are sold in almost every country in the world. Many popular American television shows are broadcast internationally. English has become the major global language. One-quarter of the world's people speak English. It has become the main language for international music, business, science, and education.

At the same time, the United States is influenced by global culture. Martial arts movies from Asia attract large audiences in the United States. Radio stations in the United States play music by African, Latin American, and European musicians. We even adopt many foreign words, like *sushi* and *plaza*, into English.

Close-up

A Global Economy

The growth of the global economy has affected many businesses, especially the automobile industry. Automakers can now buy parts from countries all around the world, depending on where they can get the best price.

Many engines are manufactured in the United States and Canada.

Bumpers are often designed and produced in France, Germany, and the United States.

Tires come from a number of countries, including Mexico, South Korea, or Chile.

98 CHAPTER 4

Differentiating Instruction

Advanced/Gifted and Talented
Above Level
Research Required

Ask students to select one American product or brand and determine through research on the Internet or elsewhere the countries in which it is sold. Students can give an oral report when research is complete. **LS Verbal/Linguistic**

Alternative Assessment Handbook, Rubric 30: Research

English-Language Learners
At Level
Research Required

Ask students to select a favorite U.S. sports team and determine how many of its players come from other countries. Students can use the Internet or other resources. Invite students to give an oral report when their work is complete. **LS Verbal/Linguistic**

Alternative Assessment Handbook, Rubric 30: Research

Global Trade

Globalization not only links the world's people, but it also connects businesses and affects trade. For centuries, societies have traded with each other. Improvements in transportation and communication have made global trade quicker and easier. For example, a shoe retailer in Chicago can order the sneakers she needs on a Web site from a company in China. The order can be flown to Chicago the next day and sold to customers that afternoon.

Many cars feature windows manufactured in Venezuela or the United States.

Seats are sometimes assembled in Japan from covers sewn in Mexico.

ANALYSIS SKILL ANALYZING VISUALS

From what different countries do automotive parts often originate?

The expansion of global trade has increased interdependence among the world's countries. **Interdependence** is a relationship between countries in which they rely on one another for resources, goods, or services. Many companies in one country often rely on goods and services produced in another country. For example, automakers in Europe might purchase auto parts made in the United States or Japan. Consumers also rely on goods produced elsewhere. For example, American shoppers buy bananas from Ecuador and tomatoes from Mexico. Global trade gives us access to goods from around the world.

READING CHECK Finding Main Ideas How has globalization affected the world?

A World Community

Some people call our world a global village. What do you think this means? Because of globalization, the world seems smaller. Places are more connected. What happens in one part of the world can affect the entire planet. Because of this, the world community works together to promote cooperation among countries in times of conflict and crisis.

The world community encourages cooperation by working to resolve global conflicts. From time to time, conflicts erupt among the countries of the world. Wars, trade disputes, and political disagreements can threaten the peace. Countries often join together to settle such conflicts. In 1945, for example, 51 nations created the United Nations. The **United Nations (UN)** is an organization of the world's countries that promotes peace and security around the globe.

The world community also promotes cooperation in times of crisis. A disaster may leave thousands of people in need.

FOCUS ON READING
What is the main idea of this paragraph? What facts are used to support that idea?

Direct Teach

Main Idea

❷ A World Community

The world community works together to solve global conflicts and crises.

Identify What kinds of conflicts do world organizations work to solve? *wars, trade disputes, and political disagreements*

Interpret How is today's world more like a village than in earlier times? *possible answers—People are in close contact; a problem in one country affects other countries, much like village neighbors; people share some culture traits like people in a village.*

Summarize How does a large-scale disaster promote cooperation between countries? *possible answers—It may be too big for a single nation to solve; it affects more than one nation.*

RF: Biography, Kofi Annan

Did you know. . .

Popular musicians have often helped the world community solve problems by raising money through benefit concerts. One of the first was the Concert for Bangladesh in 1971, when the new country of Bangladesh was devastated by famine and floods. The concert raised more than $13 million for UNICEF, although legal troubles delayed its use. Many other concerts have followed to benefit world health, world peace, and other causes.

Critical Thinking: Analyzing Information   At Level

World Relief Efforts   Research Required

1. Tell students that they will be responsible for selecting and researching a world problem and a relief organization that helps address the problem. Encourage students to consider areas of interest to them or organizations they may have heard about. Tell them to take notes to prepare an oral presentation.

2. Ask for volunteers to present information on their world problem and relief organization. If there is not enough time for all students to report, ask them to hand in their notes.

3. Discuss as a class ways that individuals or groups might participate in efforts to solve world problems and how they might choose which efforts to support. **Ⓛ Verbal/Linguistic**

Alternative Assessment Handbook, Rubrics 30: Research; and 11: Discussions

Answers

Analyzing Visuals *France, Germany, United States, Canada, Mexico, South Korea, Chile, Venezuela, Japan*

Reading Check *It linked people and businesses around the world and affected trade.*

Focus on Reading *the world community works together to solve conflicts; creation and purpose of UN*

Direct Teach

Info to Know

Origins of the UN The United Nations was created out of the global devastation caused by World War II. However, the idea for an international group that would work to prevent war began in the late 1700s. In the early 1900s the League of Nations was formed after World War I to try to prevent further wars, but it was unsuccessful, partly because the United States decided not to join.

In 1942, during World War II, the leaders of the United States, Britain, and their allies committed to forming an organization to prevent wars. The United Nations has had mixed success in preventing regional wars, but no global wars have occurred since it was founded.

● Review & Assess ●

Close

Briefly review global culture and trade and how they have helped build a world community that works together to solve problems.

Review

 Online Quiz, Section 4

Assess

SE   Section 4 Assessment

PASS: Section 4 Quiz

Alternative Assessment Handbook

Reteach/Classroom Intervention

Guided Reading Workbook, Section 4

 Interactive Skills Tutor CD-ROM

Answers

Analyzing Primary Sources *to prevent war, practice tolerance, promote security, and promote economic and social advancement of all people*

Reading Check *Countries work together to solve problems because a problem in one country often affects many countries.*

100

Primary Source

HISTORIC DOCUMENT
The Charter of the United Nations

Created in 1945, the United Nations is an organization of the world's countries that works to solve global problems. The Charter of the United Nations outlines the goals of the UN, some of which are included here.

We the Peoples of the United Nations Determined ...

to save succeeding generations from the scourge [terror] of war ...

to practice tolerance and live together in peace with one another as good neighbors, and

to unite our strength to maintain international peace and security, and

to ensure ...that armed forces shall not be used, save [except] in the common interest, and

to employ international machinery [systems] for the promotion of the economic and social advancement of all peoples,

Have Resolved to Combine our Efforts to Accomplish these Aims.

—from the Charter of the United Nations

ANALYSIS SKILL   ANALYZING PRIMARY SOURCES

What are some of the goals of the United Nations?

Earthquakes, floods, and drought can cause crises around the world. Groups from many nations often come together to provide **humanitarian aid**, or assistance to people in distress.

Organizations representing countries around the globe work to help in times of crisis. For example, in 2004 a tsunami, or huge tidal wave, devastated parts of Southeast Asia. Many organizations, like the United Nations Children's Fund (UNICEF) and the International Red Cross, stepped in to provide humanitarian aid to the victims of the tsunami. Some groups lend aid to refugees, or people who have been forced to flee their homes. Groups like Doctors Without Borders give medical aid to those in need around the world.

READING CHECK   **Analyzing** How has globalization promoted cooperation?

SUMMARY In this section you learned how globalization links the countries of the world through shared culture and trade. Globalization allows organizations around the world to work together. They often solve conflicts and provide humanitarian aid.

Section 4 Assessment

 hmhsocialstudies.com
ONLINE QUIZ

Reviewing Ideas, Terms, and Places

1. **a. Describe** What is **globalization**?
   b. Make Inferences How has **popular culture** influenced countries around the world?
   c. Evaluate In your opinion, has globalization hurt or helped the people of the world?
2. **a. Define** What is **humanitarian aid**?
   b. Draw Conclusions How has globalization promoted cooperation among countries?
   c. Predict What types of problems might lead to international cooperation?

Critical Thinking

3. **Identifying Cause and Effect** Use your notes and the graphic organizer at right to identify the effects that globalization has on our world.

[Graphic organizer: Globalization → Effects, Effects, Effects]

FOCUS ON WRITING

4. **Writing about Global Connections** What aspects of globalization could you include in your poster? Jot down your ideas in your notebook.

100   CHAPTER 4

Section 4 Assessment Answers

1. **a.** a process in which countries are increasingly linked through culture and trade
   b. It has spread culture traits such as food, music, sports, movies, and language around the world.
   c. possible answers: helped—globalization encourages understanding and cooperation; hurt—destroys some individual culture traits
2. **a.** assistance to people in distress
   b. provides more goods and services to help people, increases and improves communication to identify and relieve distress

   c. possible answers—epidemic, drought, famine, war
3. possible answers—links people in different countries, connects businesses around the world, makes global trade and communication quicker and easier
4. Students' notes should reflect an understanding of globalization, such as how countries are linked through communication.

Geography's Impact
video series
Review the video to answer the closing question:
Why do you think some peoples must work to preserve their cultures in the modern world?

Visual Summary

Use the visual summary below to help you review the main ideas of the chapter.

QUICK FACTS

The world has many different cultures, or shared beliefs and practices.

The world's people practice different economic activities and systems.

Globalization brings people around the world closer than ever before.

Reviewing Vocabulary, Terms, and Places

Choose one word from each word pair to correctly complete each sentence below.

1. Members of a/an _____ often share the same religion, traditions, and language. **(ethnic group/population)**

2. People in a _____ are free to buy and sell goods as they please. **(command economy/market economy)**

3. Organizations like the International Red Cross provide _____ to people in need around the world. **(humanitarian aid/cultural diffusion)**

4. _____, the process of moving from one place to live in another, is a cause of population change. **(Population density/Migration)**

5. A country with a strong economy and a high standard of living is considered a _____. **(developed country/developing country)**

Comprehension and Critical Thinking

SECTION 1 *(Pages 80–85)*

6. **a. Describe** What is cultural diversity?

   b. Analyze What causes cultures to change over time?

   c. Elaborate Describe some of the culture traits practiced by people in your community.

SECTION 2 *(Pages 86–90)*

7. **a. Describe** What does population density tell us about a place?

   b. Draw Conclusions Why do certain areas attract large populations?

   c. Elaborate Why do you think it is important for geographers to study population trends?

SECTION 3 *(Pages 91–95)*

8. **a. Recall** What is a command economy?

THE WORLD'S PEOPLE **101**

Answers

Visual Summary

Review and Inquiry Have students use the visual summary to discuss details related to the world's cultures, population, governments, and economies.

▶ Quick Facts Transparency: The World's People Visual Summary

Reviewing Vocabulary, Terms, and Places

1. ethnic group
2. market economy
3. humanitarian aid
4. Migration
5. developed country

Comprehension and Critical Thinking

6. **a.** a variety of cultures existing in the same area
   b. new ideas and contact with other cultures
   c. Students may mention types of foods, music, holiday traditions, language, religion, and so on.

7. **a.** how crowded a place is, availability of land, type of building, traffic on roads
   b. They may have fertile soil, a source of water, and a favorable climate for agriculture.
   c. possible answers—so that they can solve future problems and understand and address current problems

8. **a.** an economic system in which the government decides what and how much to produce and what the prices will be

---

Review and Assessment Resources

Review and Reinforce

SE Chapter Review

📖 **RF:** Chapter Review

▶ Quick Facts Transparency: The World's People Visual Summary

🔊 Spanish Chapter Summaries Audio CD Program

TOS Holt McDougal PuzzleView®; Quiz Show for ExamView

💿 Quiz Game CD-ROM

Assess

SE Standardized Test Practice

📖 PASS: Chapter Test, Forms A and B

📖 Alternative Assessment Handbook

TOS ExamView Test Generator, Chapter Test

💿 Differentiated Instruction Modified Worksheets and Tests CD-ROM: Chapter Test

🔲 Online Assessment Program, in the Interactive Student Edition

Reteach/Intervene

📖 Guided Reading Workbook

📖 Differentiated Instruction Teacher Management System: Lesson Plans

💿 Differentiated Instruction Modified Worksheets and Tests CD-ROM

💿 Interactive Skills Tutor CD-ROM

🔲 hmhsocialstudies.com
Chapter Resources

8. b. They may not have a developed economy to support services for businesses and consumers or educated workers to develop these systems.

c. possible answers—yes, because of the need for laws, regulation of business and trade, and provision of aid to people

9. a. through technology and communication

b. increased world trade and interdependence, spread of popular culture around the world

c. possible answers—better understanding between people, increased trade, addressing world problems like famine, and so on

Social Studies Skills

10. Students' graphic organizers should reflect an understanding of Section 3.

Using the Internet

11. Go to hmhsocialstudies.com to access a rubric for this activity.

Map Activity

12. A

13. D

14. B

Focus on Reading and Writing

15. Democracy, which is a system of government used around the world today, has been practiced since the time of the ancient Greeks.

📑 **RF:** Focus on Reading, Understanding Main Ideas

16. Rubric Students' posters should

- include a title and a caption for each image

- have illustrations that reflect the main idea

📑 **RF:** Focus on Writing, Creating a Poster

SECTION 3 *(continued)*

b. Make Inferences Why might developing countries have only primary and secondary economic activities?

c. Evaluate Do you think government is important in our everyday lives? Why or why not?

SECTION 4 *(Pages 97–100)*

9. a. Describe How have connections among the world's countries improved?

b. Analyze What impact has globalization had on world trade and culture?

c. Evaluate What do you think has been the most important result of globalization? Why?

Social Studies Skills

10. Organizing Information Practice organizing information by creating a graphic organizer for Section 3. Use the main ideas on the first page of the section for your large circles. Then write the subtopics under each main idea. Finally, identify supporting details for each subtopic.

Using the Internet

11. Activity: Writing a Report Population changes have a huge impact on the world around us. Countries around the world must deal with shrinking populations, growing populations, and other population issues. Through your online textbook, explore the issues surrounding global population. Then imagine you have been asked to report on global population trends to the United Nations. Write a report in which you identify world population trends and their impact on the world today.

↗ hmhsocialstudies.com

Map Activity ⊃21ST CENTURY

Population Density *Use the map to the right to answer the questions that follow.*

12. What letter on the map indicates the least crowded area?

13. What letter on the map indicates the most densely crowded area?

14. Which letter indicates a region with 260–520 people per square mile (100–200 people per square km)?

↗ hmhsocialstudies.com **INTERACTIVE MAP**

Persons per square mile	Persons per square km
520	200
260	100
130	50
25	10
3	1
0	0

0   50   100 Miles
0   50   100 Kilometers
Projection: Albers Equal-Area

FOCUS ON READING AND WRITING

Understanding Main Ideas *Read the paragraph in question 15 below. Then, write out the main idea of the paragraph.*

15. The ancient Greeks were the first to practice democracy. Since then many countries have adopted democratic government. The United Kingdom, South Korea, and Ghana all practice democracy. Democracy is the most widely used government in the world today.

16. Creating a Poster Review your notes about the world's cultures, populations, governments, and economies. Then, select a topic for your poster. On large sheet of paper, write a title that identifies your topic. Illustrate your poster with images that support your topic. Write a short caption explaining each image.

Standardized Test Prep

DIRECTIONS: Read questions 1 through 7 and write the letter of the best response. Then read question 8 and write your own well-constructed response.

1 Which of the following is *most likely* a culture trait?

A religion
B population density
C interdependence
D cultural diffusion

2 What developments led to the rapid increase in world population in the last 200 years?

A a decline in migration
B improvements in technology and communication
C a decrease in standard of living
D improvements in health care and agriculture

3 Which economic system is used in the United States?

A market economy
B command economy
C traditional economy
D domestic economy

4 A government in which a single, powerful ruler exerts complete control is a

A Communist state.
B democracy.
C dictatorship.
D republic.

5 Global connections have improved as a result of

A population growth.
B cultural diversity.
C the spread of democratic government.
D improvements in technology.

Developed and Developing Countries

Country	Per Capita GDP (U.S. $)	Life Expectancy at Birth	TVs per 1,000 People
Cameroon	$2,400	53.0	34
Singapore	$30,900	81.8	341
Ukraine	$7,600	67.9	433
Uruguay	$10,700	76.5	531

6 Which of the countries in the chart above is *most likely* a developed country?

A Cameroon
B Singapore
C Ukraine
D Uruguay

7 Which of the following is an example of economic interdependence?

A Cattle ranchers in Oklahoma sell beef to grocery stores in Maryland.
B Students in Germany use the Internet to communicate with scientists in Brazil.
C Construction companies in Canada build skyscrapers with steel imported from the United States.
D Immigrants from Russia settle in London.

8 **Extended Response** Using the data in the chart above, write a paragraph in which you compare and contrast the standard of living in Ukraine and Singapore.

Answers

Standardized Test Prep

1. A
Break Down the Question Religion relates to a choice for individuals; the other terms describe processes or measures not related to individuals.

2. D
Break Down the Question Migration does not change total population. Technology and communication do not generally affect population growth. A lower standard of living might decrease population.

3. A
Break Down the Question This question requires students to recall factual information. Refer students who miss it to Section 3.

4. C
Break Down the Question A democracy and a republic involve elected leaders who do not have complete control. Communist states do not always have one ruler with complete control.

5. D
Break Down the Question Technology improves communication and contact. The other answer choices do not necessarily improve global connections.

6. B
Break Down the Question Cameroon has a low GDP and life expectancy, and few people own TVs. Ukraine and Uruguay also have low GDPs as compared to Singapore.

7. C
Break Down the Question The other answer choices do not reflect the definition of interdependence. Refer students who miss this question to Section 4.

8. Extended Response Possible answers—Singapore's per capita GDP is more than four times that of Ukraine. Although Ukraine has more TVs per 1,000 people than does Singapore, its people live about 12 years fewer than people in Singapore.

Reteach/Intervention Resources

Reproducible

📝 Guided Reading Workbook
📝 Differentiated Instruction Teacher Management System: Lesson Plans

Technology

▶ Quick Fact Transparency: The World's People Visual Summary
💿 Differentiated Instruction Modified Worksheets and Tests CD-ROM
💿 Interactive Skills Tutor CD-ROM

Tips for Test Taking

Search for Skips and Smudges Remind students that to avoid losing points on a machine-graded test, they should be sure they did not skip any answers, gave only one answer for each question, made the marks dark and within the lines, and erased any smudges. Students should also make sure there are no stray pencil marks, such as from pencil tapping. They should cleanly erase places where they changed their minds.

Bellringer

Motivate Tell students that writing about how something works or how something is developed will help improve their critical thinking abilities. Encourage them to explain the steps in the process in a way that will clearly make sense to their readers.

Prewrite

Organization Some students may struggle with organizing the information they have gathered. Offer them the following tips:

- Review the information and list the steps on a sheet of paper.
- Make sure the steps are in chronological order or order of importance. Redo the list if they are out of order.
- Review each step to determine what facts and details you need to explain that step.
- Find those facts and details in the information you have gathered and add them to the steps on your list.
- Use your list as an outline.

Editing

Activity **Practice Editing** Use portions of two or three students' papers (with student permission) to review editing. Using an overhead projector or computer presentation tool, work with students to revise the sections for content and style. You may also want to review standard editing marks.

Rubric

Students' explanations should

- start with an interesting fact or question.
- clearly identify the big idea.
- provide at least one paragraph for each point that supports the big idea with facts and details.
- follow an organization based on chronological order or order of importance.
- end with a paragraph that summarizes the steps in the process.
- use correct grammar, punctuation, spelling, and capitalization.

104

Explaining a Process

How does soil renewal work? How do cultures change? Often the first question we ask about something is how it works or what process it follows. One way we can answer these questions is by writing an explanation.

Assignment
Write a paper explaining one of these topics:
- how water recycles on Earth
- how agriculture developed

1. Prewrite

Choose a Process
- Choose one of the topics above to write about.
- Turn your topic into a big idea, or thesis. For example, your big idea might be "Water continually circulates from Earth's surface to the atmosphere and back."

> **TIP** **Organizing Information** Explanations should be in a logical order. You should arrange the steps in the process in chronological order, the order in which the steps take place.

Gather and Organize Information
- Look for information about your topic in your textbook, in the library, or on the Internet.
- Start a plan to organize support for your big idea. For example, look for the individual steps of the water cycle.

2. Write

Use a Writer's Framework

A Writer's Framework

Introduction
- Start with an interesting fact or question.
- Identify your big idea.

Body
- Create at least one paragraph for each point supporting the big idea. Add facts and details to explain each point.
- Use chronological order or order of importance.

Conclusion
- Summarize your main points in your final paragraph.

3. Evaluate and Revise

Review and Improve Your Paper
- Re-read your paper and make sure you have followed the framework.
- Make the changes needed to improve your paper.

Evaluation Questions for an Explanation of a Process
1. Do you begin with an interesting fact or question?
2. Does your introduction identify your big idea? Does it provide any background information your readers might need?
3. Do you have at least one paragraph for each point you are using to support the big idea?
4. Do you include facts and details to explain and illustrate each point?
5. Do you use chronological order or order of importance to organize your main points?

4. Proofread and Publish

Give Your Explanation the Finishing Touch
- Make sure you have capitalized the first word in every sentence.
- Check for punctuation at the end of every sentence.
- Think of a way to share your explanation.

5. Practice and Apply

Use the steps and strategies outlined in this workshop to write your explanation. Share your paper with others and find out whether the explanation makes sense to them.

104

Differentiating Instruction

Below Level

Struggling Readers

Discuss chronological order and order of importance with students. Do the following activity with students to help them organize information.

1. Tell students that they are going to describe the process of making lunch. Ask the group to visualize the process of putting together a lunch to bring to school.

2. Have students contribute words that would be helpful in describing the process. Write the words on the board, e.g., *first, next, then, before, after, last, finally*. Ask students what

type of organization would work best to describe the process. *chronological*

3. Write sentences to describe the process. Ask individual students to write sentences on the board—with other students contributing ideas. Decide as a group whether the process is clearly explained and why. **LS Kinesthetic, Verbal/Linguistic**

Alternative Assessment Handbook, Rubric 14: Group Activity

The Americas

Unit Preview

Introduce the Unit

Share the information in the chapter overviews with students.

Chapter 5 Before contact with Europeans, the Americas were home to the Maya, Aztec, and Inca civilizations.

Chapter 6 Mexico has a history of great civilizations, colonialism, and struggles for independence.

Chapter 7 The physical beauty of Central America and the Caribbean is one of the region's greatest resources. Native and colonial influences are strong in the region.

Chapter 8 Colombia, Venezuela, and the Guianas have geographical diversity, European influences, and challenging economies.

Chapter 9 The influence of the history of Brazil, Argentina, Uruguay, and Paraguay is seen in these countries' people and culture.

Chapter 10 The Andes dominate the physical geography of Ecuador, Peru, and Chile. These countries have been shaped by native cultures and Spanish colonization.

Chapter 11 The United States has diverse physical features, resources, and cultures. Its history has helped shape the democratic nation it is today.

Chapter 12 Canada, the United States' northern neighbor, is a country with rich resources. Its culture and history reflect native and European influences.

The Great Lakes

Five huge lakes in North America known as the Great Lakes make up the largest group of fresh water lakes on Earth.

The Andes

Stretching along South America's western coast, the Andes are the longest mountain range in the world.

B THE AMERICAS

Unit Resources

Planning

- Differentiated Instruction Teacher Management System: Pacing Guide
- **TOS** Calendar Planner
- Power Presentations with Media Gallery

Differentiating Instruction

- Differentiated Instruction Teacher Management System: Lesson Plans for Differentiated Instruction
- Differentiated Instruction Modified Worksheets and Tests CD-ROM

Enrichment

- **RF:** Interdisciplinary Projects
  - Mexico: Create a Mural
  - Atlantic South America: Products of the Rain Forest
  - Central America and the Caribbean: Doing Maya Math
  - The United States: Create a Pop-Up Book
- Geography, Science, and Culture Activities with Answer Key

Assessment

- Progress Assessment Support System (PASS): Benchmark Test
- **TOS** ExamView Assessment Suite: Benchmark Test
- Online Assessment Program, in the Interactive Student Edition
- Alternative Assessment Handbook

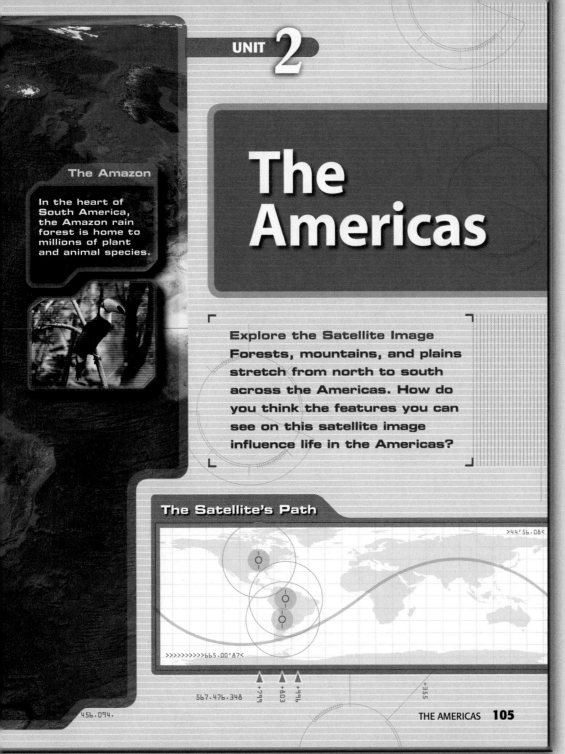

UNIT 2

The Americas

The Amazon

In the heart of South America, the Amazon rain forest is home to millions of plant and animal species.

Explore the Satellite Image
Forests, mountains, and plains stretch from north to south across the Americas. How do you think the features you can see on this satellite image influence life in the Americas?

The Satellite's Path

>44'56.08<

>>>>>>>>>665.00'87<

+799   +803   +999   +355

567.476.348

456.094.

Connect to the Unit

Activity **Physical Geography and Settlement Patterns** Have students study the photographs and satellite image of the region on these pages, as well as the physical and political maps of the Americas in the Regional Atlas. Ask students to describe what they know about where people have settled in the Western Hemisphere.

During study of the Americas, have students work as a class or in small groups to make a collage of urban development in the region. Encourage them to do Internet or library research to show the changes in cities over time—either specific cities or specific kinds of cities. Have them add captions to the collages describing factors affecting urban change, such as colonization and immigration. **LS** **Visual/Spatial, Interpersonal**

Explore the Photographs

Help students identify the location in each photograph and then compare the locations' elevations and features of vegetation. Lead a discussion, based on students' interpretation of the satellite image and the atlas maps, about which of these three areas might be most hospitable to human settlement. *possible answer—the Great Lakes area probably is most populated; it probably does not have the same extremes of temperature (Amazon) or elevation (Andes) and is the best location for food supply and trade.*

Critical Thinking: Making Generalizations

At Level

Analyzing Migration Routes

1. Tell students that every fall, millions of birds migrate along ancient flyways from their breeding grounds in North America to their winter homes in South America. They travel an opposite path in the spring. Other creatures, including monarch butterflies, follow similar routes.

2. Have students work with a partner to find maps of these migratory flyways. Have them compare these maps with the satellite image of the Americas on these pages and in the atlas.

3. Explain that much of the habitat supporting migrating birds, particularly along the Gulf Coast, has been harmed or destroyed. Speculate about causes and the impact on human populations.

4. Help students draw conclusions from their research. You might also want to lead a general discussion about the geographic concepts of movement and human/environment interaction. **LS** **Visual/Spatial**
   📖 Alternative Assessment Handbook, Rubrics 11: Discussions; and 21: Map Reading

Answers

Explore the Satellite Image *possible answer—It is likely that more people live in the areas with plains and forests instead of the mountains.*

105

Direct Teach

Explore the Map

The Americas: Physical As students examine the map on this page, point out the variety of physical features found in this world region.

Name What two major mountain systems are located in the Americas? *Rocky Mountains and Andes Mountains*

Place In which country is the land barrier between the Pacific and Atlantic oceans the narrowest? *Panama*

Location Which country lies directly north of the United States? Which country lies directly south? *Canada; Mexico*

▶ Map Zone Transparency: The Americas: Physical

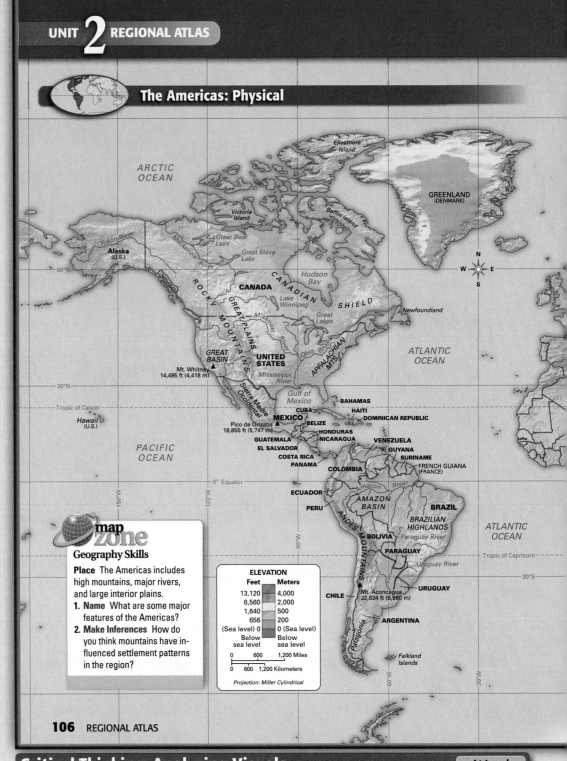

The Americas: Physical

map zone

Geography Skills

Place The Americas includes high mountains, major rivers, and large interior plains.

1. Name What are some major features of the Americas?

2. Make Inferences How do you think mountains have influenced settlement patterns in the region?

ELEVATION

Feet	Meters
13,120	4,000
6,560	2,000
1,640	500
656	200
(Sea level) 0	0 (Sea level)
Below sea level	Below sea level

0   600   1,200 Miles
0   600   1,200 Kilometers

Projection: Miller Cylindrical

Critical Thinking: Analyzing Visuals

At Level

Using the Physical Map

1. Focus students' attention on the physical map of the Americas on this page.

2. Have each student write a sentence that describes a physical feature in terms of its relative location. (Examples: Hudson Bay is in northeastern Canada. The Rocky Mountains are in western North America.)

3. Call on volunteers to read their sentences. Continue until all the major physical features have been located.

📝 Alternative Assessment Handbook, Rubric 21: Map Reading

Answers

Map Zone 1. *Rocky Mountains, Great Basin, Canadian Shield, Hudson Bay, Great Plains, Appalachian Mountains, Gulf of Mexico, Amazon Basin, Brazilian Highlands, Andes Mountains;* **2.** *possible answer—Mountainous regions probably have been less densely settled than other regions because the terrain makes it more difficult to move goods and people.*

106

The Americas

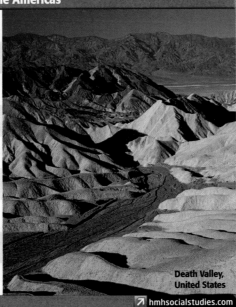

THE WORLD ALMANAC®
Facts about the World **Geographical Extremes: The Americas**

Longest River	Amazon River, Brazil/Peru: 4,000 miles (6,435 km)
Highest Point	Mt. Aconcagua, Argentina: 22,834 feet (6,960 m)
Lowest Point	Death Valley, United States: 282 feet (86 m) below sea level
Highest Recorded Temperature	Death Valley, United States: 134°F (56.6°C)
Lowest Recorded Temperature	Snag, Canada: -81.4°F (-63°C)
Wettest Place	Lloro, Colombia: 523.6 inches (1,329.9 cm) average precipitation per year
Driest Place	Arica, Chile: .03 inches (.08 cm) average precipitation per year
Highest Waterfall	Angel Falls, Venezuela: 3,212 feet (979 m)
Most Tornadoes	United States: More than 1,000 per year

Death Valley, United States

↗ hmhsocialstudies.com

Checking for Understanding

True or False Answer each statement *T* if it is true or *F* if it is false. If false, explain why.

1. The longest river in the Americas is the Mississippi. *F: The Amazon is the longest river in the Americas.*

2. According to the comparison map, the United States is about the same size as Brazil. *T*

Size Comparison: The United States and the Americas

THE AMERICAS **107**

Critical Thinking: Comparing

At Level

Thinking about Geographical Extremes

1. Tell students to examine the list of geographical extremes in the chart on this page. To help students better comprehend the extremes, have them compare the extremes listed in the table with those found in your state or local community.

2. Have students conduct research to identify the highest point in your state, the lowest recorded temperature, the greatest natural disaster, average rainfall, and so on. Encourage students to search for other extremes that may be unique to your state or region.

3. Ask volunteers to share their findings with the class, and record the information in a chart on the board.

📝 Alternative Assessment Handbook, Rubric 1: Acquiring Information

Direct Teach

Explore the Map

North America: Political As students look at the map on this page, point out that the borders between the United States and Canada are often straight lines. Have the students discuss why this might be so.

Region How many countries are located in North America? *22 including the small island nations in the Caribbean Sea*

Place Which river helps form the political boundary between the United States and Mexico? *Rio Grande*

▶ Map Zone Transparency: North America: Political

North America: Political

ARCTIC OCEAN

GREENLAND (DENMARK)

Alaska (U.S.)

CANADA

Vancouver
Calgary
Saskatchewan R.

St. Lawrence River

Montreal
Ottawa
Toronto
Boston

Columbia River

Chicago
New York
Washington, D.C.

UNITED STATES

Los Angeles

Hawaii (U.S.)

PACIFIC OCEAN

Tropic of Cancer

Houston

ATLANTIC OCEAN

⊕ National capital

0   300   600 Miles
0 300 600 Kilometers

Projection:
Lambert Azimuthal Equal-Area

BAHAMAS

Nassau

Monterrey
Havana
CUBA
HAITI
DOMINICAN REPUBLIC

MEXICO
Guadalajara
Santo Domingo
Port-au-Prince

Mexico City

BELIZE
Belmopan
HONDURAS
GUATEMALA
Guatemala City
Tegucigalpa
NICARAGUA
San Salvador
Managua
Panama City
EL SALVADOR
San José
COSTA RICA
PANAMA

SOUTH AMERICA

Caribbean inset:

ATLANTIC OCEAN

DOMINICAN REPUBLIC
VIRGIN IS. (U.S.)
BRITISH VIRGIN IS. (U.K.)
ANGUILLA (U.K.)
ANTIGUA AND BARBUDA
PUERTO RICO (U.S.)
Basseterre
St. John's
MONTSERRAT (U.K.)
ST. KITTS AND NEVIS
GUADELOUPE (FRANCE)
Roseau
DOMINICA
MARTINIQUE (FRANCE)
Castries
ST. LUCIA
Caribbean Sea
Bridgetown
Kingstown
BARBADOS
ST. VINCENT AND THE GRENADINES
St. George's
GRENADA
Port of Spain
TRINIDAD AND TOBAGO

VENEZUELA

map zone
Geography Skills

Place North America includes both large and small countries.
1. Locate Where are North America's smaller countries located?

2. Make Generalizations What are some advantages or disadvantages that countries might face because they are large or small?

108 REGIONAL ATLAS

Answers

Differentiating Instruction

Below Level

Special Needs Learners

1. Make an enlarged copy of the political map on this page or allow students to use a classroom wall map to complete the map activity and answer the questions.

2. As students examine the political map, have them say aloud the name of each country featured on the map. If they have difficulty with pronunciation, have them repeat the country's name after you say it.

3. Have pairs of students take turns quizzing each other on the countries in the region.

   📝 Alternative Assessment Handbook, Rubric 21: Map Reading

The Americas

South America: Political

Cartagena
Caracas
VENEZUELA
Georgetown
GUYANA
Paramaribo
Bogotá
SURINAME
French Guiana
(FRANCE)
COLOMBIA
Quito
ECUADOR
Guayaquil
Manaus
Amazon River
Galápagos
Islands
0° Equator
10°N
PACIFIC
OCEAN
PERU
BRAZIL
Lima
10°S
Salvador
La Paz
Brasília
BOLIVIA
ATLANTIC
OCEAN
Sucre
20°S
Parana River
Tropic of Capricorn
PARAGUAY
Rio de
Janeiro
CHILE
São Paulo
Asunción
Córdoba
30°S
Santiago
URUGUAY
Buenos Aires
Montevideo
ARGENTINA
40°S
50°S
Falkland
Islands
South Georgia
Island

National capital

0   300   600 Miles
0   300   600 Kilometers

Projection:
Lambert Azimuthal Equal-Area

map Zone
Geography Skills

Place South America includes
12 countries and one overseas
department of France.
1. **Name** Which country is by far
the largest in South America?
2. **Compare** Compare this map to
the physical map of the Americas. What physical feature
separates Chile and Argentina?

Direct Teach

Explore the Map

South America: Political As
students look at the map on this page,
have them notice that some countries
do not have an ocean coastline. Ask
them to discuss how this might affect a
country.

Region Which country possesses the
most Pacific Ocean coastline? *Chile*

Location Along which feature are
most of the large cities in Brazil
located? *Atlantic Ocean coast*

▶ Map Zone Transparency: South America:
Political

Critical Thinking: Comparing and Contrasting

At Level

Analyze Maps

1. Have students study the political map on this
page in order to compare and contrast the
countries with one another.

2. Ask students to set up a graphic organizer
on a separate sheet of paper to record their
findings. It can be a three-column chart, a
series of Venn diagrams, a cluster chart, or
another style of graphic organizer.

3. Students should write the name of each
country, then list one way that country is

similar to the other countries in the region,
and one way that country is unique.

4. When complete, draw a graphic organizer on
the board and have students take turns adding
details about the countries in South America.

🗎 Alternative Assessment Handbook, Rubrics 9:
Comparing and Contrasting; and 13: Graphic
Organizers

Answers

Map Zone 1. *Brazil;* **2.** *the Andes
Mountains*

Direct Teach

Explore the Map

The Americas: Population Have students compare the population map on this page with the political map of the same region. Then have students answer the following questions:

Location Which country has the most cities with more than 2 million inhabitants? *The United States*

Place What are the largest cities located south of the equator? *Lima, São Paulo, Santiago, Buenos Aires*

▶ Map Zone Transparency: The Americas: Population

The Americas: Population

ARCTIC OCEAN

60°N

30°N

Tropic of Cancer

PACIFIC OCEAN

0° Equator

Chicago

New York

ATLANTIC OCEAN

Los Angeles

Mexico City

Caracas

Bogotá

Lima

São Paulo

Santiago

Buenos Aires

ATLANTIC OCEAN

Tropic of Capricorn

30°S

Geography Skills

Place Overall, population density in the Americas is not high, but many people live in large cities.

1. **Identify** Which areas of the United States have the highest population density?
2. **Make Inferences** Notice that most large cities in South America are located near the coast. Why do you think that is?

Persons per square mile	Persons per square km
520	200
260	100
130	50
25	10
3	1
0	0

● Major cities over 2 million

0   600   1,200 Miles
0   600   1,200 Kilometers

Projection: Miller Cylindrical

110 REGIONAL ATLAS

Differentiating Instruction

Above Level

Advanced/Gifted and Talented

1. Have students interpret the population statistics shown on the map and compare the data with a current almanac. Then have students create a computer-generated pie chart or bar graph displaying the population density for two countries in the region.

2. Students may wish to create a separate graphic for each country or combine the two countries' data into one chart or graph.

Remind students to use accurate labeling for their charts. If computers are unavailable, students can create the graphics using a ruler and a protractor. Have students display their completed graphs on a bulletin board.

LS Logical/Mathematical, Visual/Spatial

Alternative Assessment Handbook, Rubrics 7: Charts; and 21: Map Reading

Answers

Map Zone 1. *the northeast (including New York), the Great Lakes region (including Chicago), southern California (including Los Angeles);* **2.** *possible answer— Coastal locations facilitate trade on a continent with many obstacles to trade, such as rain forests and mountains.*

The Americas

ARCTIC
OCEAN

ATLANTIC
OCEAN

60°N

30°N

Tropic of Cancer

PACIFIC
OCEAN

0° Equator

ATLANTIC
OCEAN

Tropic of Capricorn

30°S

map zone

Geography Skills

Place The Americas has a huge variety of climates.
1. **Name** What are the main climates in North America and South America?
2. **Compare** Compare this map to the population map. How does climate relate to population distribution?

Climate Types

- Humid tropical
- Tropical savanna
- Desert
- Steppe
- Mediterranean
- Humid subtropical
- Marine west coast
- Humid continental
- Subarctic
- Tundra
- Ice cap
- Highland

0   600   1,200 Miles

0   600   1,200 Kilometers

Projection: Miller Cylindrical

THE AMERICAS **111**

111

World Almanac: Facts about Countries

Identify Which country in the Americas has the largest area? Which has the largest population? *area—Canada; population—United States*

Generalize How do you think Haiti's per capita GDP affects the number of people there who own televisions? *Haiti has a low per capita GDP, which suggests that not many people can afford luxuries like television.*

Evaluate If you were going to move from the United States to one of the other countries listed on this chart, which would you want to move to? Why? *Students' answers will vary but should be supported.*

THE WORLD ALMANAC® Facts about Countries

The Americas

COUNTRY CAPITAL	FLAG	POPULATION	AREA (sq mi)	PER CAPITA GDP (U.S. $)	LIFE EXPECTANCY AT BIRTH	TVS PER 1,000 PEOPLE
Antigua and Barbuda St. John's		85,632	171	$19,600	74.3	493
Argentina Buenos Aires		40.9 million	1,068,302	$14,200	76.5	293
The Bahamas Nassau		309,156	5,382	$29,600	65.8	243
Barbados Bridgetown		284,589	166	$19,100	73.2	290
Belize Belmopan		307,899	8,867	$8,400	68.3	183
Bolivia La Paz, Sucre		9.8 million	424,164	$4,500	66.6	118
Brazil Brasilia		198.7 million	3,286,488	$10,200	71.9	333
Canada Ottawa		33.5 million	3,855,101	$39,100	81.3	709
Chile Santiago		16.6 million	292,260	$14,900	77.3	240
Colombia Bogotá		45.6 million	439,736	$8,800	72.6	279
Costa Rica San José		4.3 million	19,730	$11,500	77.5	229
Cuba Havana		11.5 million	42,803	$9,500	77.3	248
Dominica Roseau		72,660	291	$9,900	75.4	232
Dominican Republic Santo Domingo		9.7 million	18,815	$8,200	73.4	96
Ecuador Quito		14.6 million	109,483	$7,500	76.9	213
United States Washington, D.C.		307.2 million	3,794,083	$46,900	78.2	844

Differentiating Instruction

Below Level

Special Needs Learners

1. Have each student draw a table with four columns titled Less than $5,000; Between $5,000 and $10,000; Between $10,000 and $20,000; and Greater than $20,000.

2. Refer students to the column on the chart titled Per Capita GDP. Instruct students to list each country on their tables under the correct heading.

3. Give each student an outline map of the Americas with the countries labeled.

4. Direct students to color all the countries in the first column of their tables in red, those in the second column in yellow, those in the third column in green, and those in the fourth column in blue.

5. Lead a class discussion about any patterns students might see on their maps. Ask students where the countries with the higher per capita GDPs are located *(north)* and where those with the lowest per capita GDPs are located *(northern South America, Central America, and the Caribbean).* **LS Visual/Spatial**

Alternative Assessment Handbook, Rubrics 11: Discussions, and 20: Map Creation

COUNTRY Capital	FLAG	POPULATION	AREA (sq mi)	PER CAPITA GDP (U.S. $)	LIFE EXPECTANCY AT BIRTH	TVS PER 1,000 PEOPLE
El Salvador San Salvador		7.2 million	8,124	$6,200	72.2	191
Grenada Saint George's		90,739	133	$12,900	65.6	376
Guatemala Guatemala City		13.3 million	42,043	$5,300	70.1	61
Guyana Georgetown		772,298	83,000	$3,800	66.5	70
Haiti Port-au-Prince		9 million	10,714	$1,300	57.6	5
Honduras Tegucigalpa		7.8 million	43,278	$4,100	69.4	95
Jamaica Kingston		2.8 million	4,244	$7,500	73.7	191
Mexico Mexico City		111.2 million	761,606	$14,200	75.9	272
Nicaragua Managua		5.9 million	49,998	$2,900	71.3	69
Panama Panama City		3.4 million	30,193	$11,700	77	192
Paraguay Asunción		7 million	157,047	$4,200	75.7	205
Peru Lima		29.5 million	496,226	$8,500	70.5	147
Saint Kitts and Nevis Basseterre		40,131	101	$19,500	73.1	256
Saint Lucia Castries		160,267	238	$11,100	76.3	368
Saint Vincent and the Grenadines; Kingstown		104,574	150	$10,200	74.4	230
United States Washington, D.C.		307.2 million	3,794,083	$46,900	78.2	844

THE AMERICAS **113**

Direct Teach

World Almanac: Facts about Countries

Activity **Write a Description** Have each student choose one country from the chart and write a detailed description of that country's flag. (Students may wish to use reference books or the Internet to find larger images of their chosen flags.) Once students have finished writing their descriptions, call on volunteers to read their work to the class. Challenge the rest of the class to identify the volunteer's chosen country based on the written description.

Alternative Assessment Handbook, Rubric 40: Writing to Describe

Cross-Discipline Activity: Mathematics

Calculate Population Density

1. Organize the class into five groups and assign each group seven countries from the region.

2. Remind students that population density is calculated by dividing a country's population by its land area. For example, the United States would be determined as follows: 307,200,000 people/3,794,083 sq mi = 79.4 people per square mile.

3. Have students work as groups to calculate the population density for each of their assigned countries.

4. Once students have completed their calculations, have groups compare their results to determine which countries have the highest and lowest population densities in the region. **LS Logical/Mathematical**

Alternative Assessment Handbook, Rubric 14: Group Activity

Direct Teach

Checking for Understanding

True or False Answer each statement *T* if it is true or *F* if it is false. If false, explain why.

1. Two of the five largest cities in the world are in the Americas. *F:*
   Three of the five largest cities are in the Americas: Mexico City, New York City, and São Paulo

2. Venezuela has the highest percentage of urban dwellers in its population. *T*

THE WORLD ALMANAC® Facts about Countries

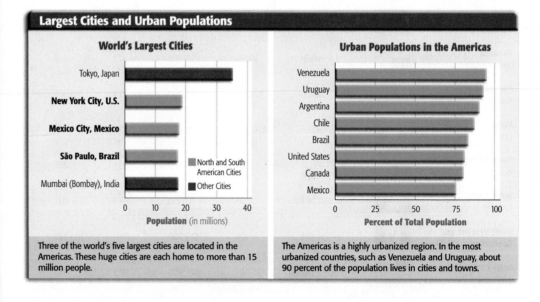

COUNTRY Capital	FLAG	POPULATION	AREA (sq mi)	PER CAPITA GDP (U.S. $)	LIFE EXPECTANCY AT BIRTH	TVS PER 1,000 PEOPLE
Suriname Paramaribo		481,267	63,039	$8,900	73.6	241
Trinidad and Tobago Port-of-Spain		1.2 million	1,980	$23,600	67.1	337
Uruguay Montevideo		3.5 million	68,039	$12,400	76.2	531
Venezuela Caracas		26.8 million	352,144	$13,500	73.6	185
United States Washington, D.C.		307.2 million	3,794,083	$46,900	78.2	844

ANALYSIS SKILL ANALYZING TABLES

1. Compare the information for the United States, Canada, Brazil, and Mexico. How do these four countries compare?
2. Which country has the lowest per capita GDP?

Largest Cities and Urban Populations

World's Largest Cities

Three of the world's five largest cities are located in the Americas. These huge cities are each home to more than 15 million people.

Urban Populations in the Americas

The Americas is a highly urbanized region. In the most urbanized countries, such as Venezuela and Uruguay, about 90 percent of the population lives in cities and towns.

114 FACTS ABOUT COUNTRIES

Collaborative Learning

At Level

Write a Letter

1. Divide students into small groups to write letters to an imaginary pen pal in the capital of a country of the Americas. Assign each group a country.

2. Have groups work together to think of questions they would ask a person their own age who lived in the capital city of the country.

3. Have each group read aloud their letter. Students can also make a display of their questions.

4. Lead a class discussion about what life might be like in the various countries of the Americas. Ask students how life might be similar or different.

   Alternative Assessment Handbook, Rubrics 11: Discussions, and 14: Group Activity

Answers

Map Zone 1. *The United States has the largest population (307.2 million) and Canada has the smallest population (33.5 million). Canada, Brazil, and the United States are the largest in area, while Mexico is the smallest. Per capita GDP is highest in the United States and Canada ($46,900 and $39,100, respectively) and lowest in Brazil and Mexico ($10,200 and $14,200, respectively). The life expectancy at birth is highest in Canada and the United States and lowest in Brazil and Mexico. The United States leads the four countries in the number of TVs per 1,000 people—844. Mexico has the fewest TVs per 1,000 people—272.* **2.** *Haiti ($1,300)*

114

Major Food Exports of the Americas

Coffee Exports

- Brazil 20.5%
- Colombia 8.5%
- Rest of the Americas 15.4%
- Rest of the World 55.6%

Wheat Exports

- United States 18.3%
- Canada 9.9%
- Rest of the Americas 8.4%
- Rest of the World 63.4%

Corn Exports

- Rest of the World 33.4%
- United States 49.1%
- Rest of the Americas 2.7%
- Argentina 14.8%

Banana Exports

- Rest of the World 33.7%
- Ecuador 27.9%
- Costa Rica 10.7%
- Rest of the Americas 18.9%
- Colombia 8.8%

The Americas is a major exporter of some crops, like coffee, wheat, corn, and bananas. While the United States leads in wheat and corn exports, other crops like coffee and bananas are exported from Central and South America.

ANALYSIS SKILL ANALYZING GRAPHS

1. What percentage of the world's corn exports come from the Americas?
2. Which countries in the Americas export the most coffee?

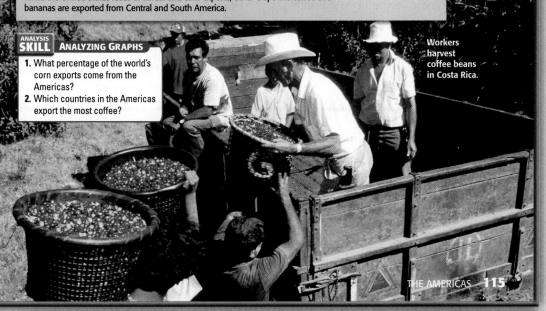

Workers harvest coffee beans in Costa Rica.

THE AMERICAS **115**

115

Chapter 5 Planning Guide

Early History of the Americas

<table>
<tr><th colspan="1">Overview</th><th colspan="2">Instructional Resources</th></tr>
<tr>
<td>

CHAPTER 5

Essential Question: What major civilizations thrived in the Americas prior to the arrival of European explorers?

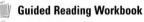 **Focus on the Essential Question Podcast**

</td>
<td>

TOS Differentiated Instruction Teacher Management System:
• Instructional Pacing Guides
• Lesson Plans for Differentiated Instruction

 Guided Reading Workbook

Resource File:
• Chapter Review
• Focus on Reading: Setting a Purpose
• Focus on Writing: Writing a Newspaper Article
• Social Studies Skills: Analyzing Information

Experiencing World History and Geography

</td>
<td>

TOS Calendar Planner

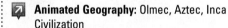 **Power Presentations with Media Gallery**

Differentiated Instruction Modified Worksheets and Tests CD-ROM

Interactive Skills Tutor CD-ROM

Student Edition on Audio CD-ROM

The World's Music Audio Program

Map Zone Transparency: The Americas, 500 BC–AD 1537

World Outline Maps: Transparencies and Activities

Video: Machu Picchu

</td>
</tr>
<tr>
<td>

Section 1:

The Maya

The Big Idea: The Maya developed an advanced civilization that thrived in Mesoamerica from about 250 until the 900s.

</td>
<td>

TOS Differentiated Instruction Teacher Management System: Section 1 Lesson Plan

Guided Reading Workbook: Section 1

Resource File:
• Vocabulary Builder: Section 1
• Biography: Bishop Diego de Landa

</td>
<td>

Daily Bellringer Transparency: Section 1

Map Zone Transparency: Maya Civilization

 Animated Geography: The Maya

Internet Activity: Adding the Maya Way

Video: The Disappearance

</td>
</tr>
<tr>
<td>

Section 2:

The Aztecs

The Big Idea: The strong Aztec Empire, founded in central Mexico in 1325, lasted until the Spanish conquest in 1521.

</td>
<td>

TOS Differentiated Instruction Teacher Management System: Section 2 Lesson Plan

Guided Reading Workbook: Section 2

Resource File:
• Vocabulary Builder: Section 2
• Biography: Moctezuma II
• Biography: Tlacaelel
• Geography and History: The Aztec Empire
• Primary Source: Cortés's First Meeting with Moctezuma (1519)

</td>
<td>

Daily Bellringer Transparency: Section 2

Map Zone Transparency: The Aztec Empire

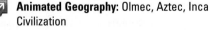 **Animated Geography:** Olmec, Aztec, Inca Civilization

</td>
</tr>
<tr>
<td>

Section 3:

The Incas

The Big Idea: The Incas controlled a huge empire in South America, but it was conquered by the Spanish.

</td>
<td>

TOS Differentiated Instruction Teacher Management System: Section 3 Lesson Plan

Guided Reading Workbook: Section 3

Resource File:
• Vocabulary Builder: Section 3

</td>
<td>

Daily Bellringer Transparency: Section 3

Map Zone Transparency: The Inca Empire

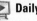 **Internet Activity:** Brochure on Machu Picchu

 Animated Geography: The Inca

 Animated Geography: Olmec, Aztec, Inca Civilization

</td>
</tr>
</table>

CHAPTER 5 PLANNING GUIDE

Chart Key:

SE Student Edition   Presentation Resource   MP3 Audio

TOS Teacher One Stop   DVD/CD-ROM   HISTORY™

 Printable Resource

Program Resources available on **TOS** and @ hmhsocialstudies.com

Review, Assessment, Intervention

 The Americas Transparencies: Early History of the Americas Visual Summary

Spanish Chapter Summaries Audio CD

Progress Assessment Support System (PASS): Chapter Test

Differentiated Instruction Modified Worksheets CD-ROM: Modified Chapter Test

TOS ExamView® Assessment Suite (English/Spanish)

Alternative Assessment Handbook

Online Assessment Program, in the Interactive Student Edition

---

PASS: Section 1 Quiz

Online Quiz: Section 1

Alternative Assessment Handbook

PASS: Section 2 Quiz

Online Quiz: Section 2

Alternative Assessment Handbook

PASS: Section 3 Quiz

Online Quiz: Section 3

Alternative Assessment Handbook

Supporting Resources

HISTORY.

• Multimedia Classroom Global History Series
• Global History Teacher's Guide

Maps Globes Graphs Level F

• Student Workbook
• Teacher's Guide

Social Studies Trade Library Collections

• NCSS Middle School Collection
• Native American Trade Collection
• World Regions Trade Collection

Geography's Impact

Geography's Impact Video Program

• **Impact of Mayan Achievements on Math and Astronomy**

For more information or to purchase go to 🡕 hmhsocialstudies.com

Power Presentations with Media Gallery

Power Presentations with Media Gallery are visual presentations of each chapter's main ideas. Presentations can be customized by including Quick Facts charts, images from the text, and video clips.

Differentiating Instruction

How do I address the needs of varied learners?
The Target Resource acts as your primary strategy for differentiated instruction.

ENGLISH-LANGUAGE LEARNERS & STRUGGLING READERS

Graphic Organizer Transparencies with Support for Reading and Writing

Spanish Resources

Spanish Chapter Summaries Audio CD Program

Teacher One Stop:
• ExamView Assessment Suite, Spanish
• PuzzleView, Spanish

English-Language Learner Strategies and Activities

Additional Resources

Differentiated Instruction Teacher Management System: Lesson Plans for Differentiated Instruction

Resource File:
• Vocabulary Builder Activities
• Social Studies Skills: Analyzing Information

The Americas Transparencies:
• Early History of the Americas Visual Summary

Student Edition on Audio CD Program

Interactive Skills Tutor CD-ROM

Spanish/English Guided Reading Workbook

SPECIAL NEEDS LEARNERS

Differentiated Instruction Modified Worksheets and Tests CD-ROM
• Vocabulary Flash Cards
• Modified Vocabulary Builder Activities
• Modified Chapter Review Activity
• Modified Chapter Test

Additional Resources

Differentiated Instruction Teacher Management System: Lesson Plans for Differentiated Instruction

Guided Reading Workbook

Resource File: Social Studies Skills: Analyzing Information

Student Edition on Audio CD Program

Interactive Skills Tutor CD-ROM

Graphic Organizer Transparencies with Support for Reading and Writing

ADVANCED/GIFTED AND TALENTED STUDENTS

Resource File
The Resource File activities allow students to extend their knowledge of chapter-related places and people and to practice geography skills.

Additional Resources

Differentiated Instruction Teacher Management System: Lesson Plans for Differentiated Instruction

World History and Geography Document-Based Questions Activities

Geography, Science, and Cultures Activities

Experiencing World History and Geography

Differentiated Activities in the Teacher's Edition

- Chart Characteristics, p. 121
- Modeling Maya Artwork, p. 122
- Modeling the Inca Empire, p. 130

Teacher One Stop™

How can I manage the lesson plans and support materials for differentiated instruction?

With the Teacher One Stop, you can easily organize and print lesson plans, planning guides, and instructional materials for all learners. The Teacher One Stop includes the following materials to help you differentiate instruction:

- · **Interactive Teacher's Edition**
- · **Calendar Planner and pacing guides**
- · **Editable lesson plans**
- · **All reproducible ancillaries in Adobe Acrobat (PDF) format**
- · **ExamView Assessment Suite (English & Spanish)**
- · **Transparency and video previews**

Differentiated Activities in the Teacher's Edition

- Factors in Aztec Wealth, p. 125

Interactive Student Edition

Complete online student edition with interactive multimedia support for chapter content assessment and reporting

- Interactive Maps and Notebook
- Standardized Test Prep
- Online Homework Practice and Research Activities
- Current Events
- Chapter-based Internet Activities
- Animated Geography Activities

Differentiated Activities in the Teacher's Edition

- Using a Globe, p. 117
- Step into the Picture, p. 121
- Looking at Inca Religion, p. 131
- Maya Classic Age Recipe, p. 120
- Making More Farmland, p. 126
- The Spanish Conquest, p. 132

Introduce the Essential Question

- Have students identify from the map on pages 116–117 three civilizations that thrived in the Americas prior to 1537. Tell students that the Maya civilization, which included more than 40 large cities, developed systems for writing and measuring time. However, the Maya civilization began to collapse in the AD 900s. Have students speculate why.

- Explain that through war, tribute from conquered enemies, and an elaborate trade system, the Aztecs created a powerful empire. The Aztecs, who valued art and learning, were conquered by the Spanish.

- The Inca Empire in South America established a strong central government and a well-organized economy. Like the Aztecs, the Incas were defeated by the Spanish.

Focus on Reading and Writing

Reading The Resource File provides a worksheet to help students set a purpose for their reading.

📄 **RF: Focus on Reading, Setting a Purpose**

Writing The Resource File provides a worksheet to help students organize and write their newspaper articles.

📄 **RF: Focus on Writing, Writing a Newspaper Article**

Key to Differentiating Instruction

Below Level

Basic-level activities designed for all students encountering new material

At Level

Intermediate-level activities designed for average students

Above Level

Challenging activities designed for honors and gifted and talented students

Standard English Mastery

Activities designed to improve standard English usage

LS Learning Styles

CHAPTER 5

Early History of the Americas
500 BC–AD 1537

Essential Question What major civilizations thrived in the Americas prior to the arrival of European explorers?

What You Will Learn...
In this chapter you will learn about the location, growth, and decline of the Maya, Aztec, and Inca civilizations in the Americas.

FOCUS ON READING AND WRITING

Setting a Purpose Setting a purpose for your reading can help give you a focus. Before you read, look at pictures and headings to find out what the text is about. Then decide what your purpose in reading the text is. Keep your purpose in mind as you read. **See the lesson, Setting a Purpose, on page 520.**

Writing a Newspaper Article You are a writer for a European newspaper who is traveling with some explorers to the Americas. As you read this chapter, you will decide what you want to share with readers in a newspaper article—the land, the people, or the events that occurred after the explorers arrived.

PACIFIC OCEAN

map zone Geography Skills

Regions Three great civilizations existed in North and South America before 1537.
1. **Identify** Which civilization was located in South America?
2. **Make Inferences** What do you think happened when the Spanish arrived in the Americas?

The Maya The Maya traded jade between their cities in Mesoamerica.

Introduce the Chapter

At Level

Lost Cities in the Jungle

1. Ask students to imagine that they are on an archaeological expedition in the jungles of Central America. They hack their way through the growth and, suddenly, there before them is a large, elaborately carved stone. Beyond are other ruins of an ancient lost city.

2. Have students discuss what they might feel at the sight of the ancient ruins. Encourage discussion.

3. Then ask students what they and other scientists might do to find out more about the people who lived in this ancient city. What questions might they ask? What objects might they study?

4. Explain to students that in this chapter they will be learning about the first people who came to the Americas and some of the early civilizations that developed.

LS Intrapersonal, Verbal/Linguistic

📄 Alternative Assessment Handbook, Rubric 11: Discussions

ATLANTIC OCEAN

Maya temple

Tenochtitlán

Palenque

Aztec warrior

HISTORY **Machu Picchu**

hmhsocialstudies.com **VIDEO**

20°N

10°N

Spanish explorers' ship

0° Equator

Inca with llama

Cuzco

10°S

20°S

• Ancient city

0   300   600 Miles

0   300   600 Kilometers

Projection:
Lambert Azimuthal Equal-Area

Tropic of Capricorn

The Aztecs The Aztecs were known for warfare as well as for their arts.

The Incas The Incas built well-crafted stone cities high in the Andes.

117

Chapter Preview

Explore the Map and Pictures

The Americas, 500 BC–AD 1537
Three remarkable and complex civilizations—the Maya, the Aztec, and the Inca—existed in the Americas before the 1500s. This map shows where these civilizations were located in North and South America. The part of the region extending from central Mexico south to the northern border of Central America is known as Mesoamerica. These civilizations are also known as pre–Columbian civilizations because they existed before the arrival of Christopher Columbus in the Americas.

Analyzing Visuals Which civilizations on the map were located in Mesoamerica? *Maya and Aztec civilizations* Why is the photo of the Aztec skull considered to be an example of pre–Columbian art? *It was made before Columbus arrived in the Americas.* What can you tell about these civilizations from the photos? *Trade and religion were important to the Maya; Aztecs were known as warriors and as artists; Incas used llamas to get around in the Andes and were skilled builders.*

▶ Map Zone Transparency: The Americas, 500 BC–AD 1537

↗ hmhsocialstudies.com
Teacher Resources

Differentiating Instruction

Above Level

Advanced/Gifted and Talented
Materials: globe

1. Bring a globe to the front of the class. Ask a volunteer to locate North and South America. Discuss where the Maya, Aztec, and Inca civilizations would be located if they existed today. Ask students where the Aztec city of Tenochtitlán would be located today. *Present-day Mexico City*

2. Have students identify which major physical feature was located in the Inca civilization. *the Andes* What challenges would living there bring? *possible answers—difficult to farm mountainous land, snow, difficult to get around high mountain passes.*

LS Visual/Spatial, Verbal/Linguistic

📖 Alternative Assessment Handbook, Rubric 21: Map Reading

Answers

Map Zone 1. *the Inca civilization;* **2.** *Answers will vary, but students may note that the Spanish would influence life for the Maya, Aztecs, and Incas.*

The Maya

If YOU lived there...

You are a Maya farmer, growing corn in fields outside a city. Often you enter the city to join in religious ceremonies. You watch the king and his priests standing at the top of a tall pyramid. They wear capes of brightly colored feathers and gold ornaments that glitter in the sun. Far below them, thousands of worshippers crowd into the plaza with you to honor the gods.

How do these ceremonies make you feel?

BUILDING BACKGROUND Religion was very important to the Maya, one of the early peoples in the Americas. The Maya believed the gods controlled everything in the world around them.

What You Will Learn...

Main Ideas

1. Geography helped shape the lives of the early Maya.
2. During the Classic Age, the Maya built great cities linked by trade.
3. Maya culture included a strict social structure, a religion with many gods, and achievements in science and the arts.
4. The decline of Maya civilization began in the 900s.

The Big Idea

The Maya developed an advanced civilization that thrived in Mesoamerica from about 250 until the 900s.

Key Terms and Places

maize, *p. 118*
Palenque, *p. 119*
observatories, *p. 122*

hmhsocialstudies.com
TAKING NOTES

Use the graphic organizer online to organize your notes on the Maya.

Geography and the Early Maya

The region known as Mesoamerica stretches from the central part of Mexico south to include the northern part of Central America. It was in this region that a people called the Maya (MY-uh) developed a remarkable civilization.

Around 1000 BC the Maya began settling in the lowlands of what is now northern Guatemala. Thick tropical forests covered most of the land, but the people cleared areas to farm. They grew a variety of crops, including beans, squash, avocados, and **maize**, or corn. The forests provided valuable resources, too. Forest animals such as deer, rabbits, and monkeys were sources of food. In addition, trees and other forest plants made good building materials. For example, some Maya used wooden poles and vines, along with mud, to build their houses.

The early Maya lived in small, isolated villages. Eventually, though, these villages started trading with one another and with other groups in Mesoamerica. As trade increased, the villages grew. By about AD 200, the Maya had begun to build large cities in Mesoamerica.

READING CHECK **Finding Main Ideas** How did the early Maya make use of their physical environment?

The Classic Age

The Maya civilization reached its height between about AD 250 and 900. This time in Maya history is known as the Classic Age. During this time, Maya territory grew to include more than 40 large cities. Each had its own government and its own king. No single ruler united the many cities into one empire.

Instead, the Maya cities were linked through trade. People exchanged goods for products that were not available locally. Look at the trade routes on the map to see the goods that were available in different areas of Maya civilization. For example,

the warm lowlands were good for growing cotton and cacao (kuh-KOW), the source of chocolate. But lowland crops did not grow well in the cool highlands. Instead, the highlands had valuable stones, such as jade and obsidian. People carried these and other products along trade routes.

Through trade, the Maya got supplies for construction. Maya cities had grand buildings, such as palaces decorated with carvings and paintings. The Maya also built stone pyramids topped with temples. Some temples honored local kings. For example, in the city of **Palenque** (pah-LENG-kay), the king Pacal (puh-KAHL) had a temple built to record his achievements.

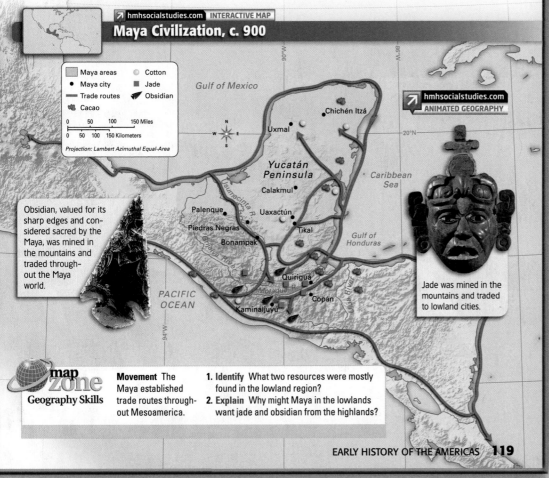

↗ hmhsocialstudies.com INTERACTIVE MAP
Maya Civilization, c. 900

Map Key
- Maya areas
- Maya city
- Trade routes
- Cacao
- Cotton
- Jade
- Obsidian

0   50   100   150 Miles
0   50   100   150 Kilometers
Projection: Lambert Azimuthal Equal-Area

Gulf of Mexico

Chichén Itzá
Uxmal

↗ hmhsocialstudies.com ANIMATED GEOGRAPHY

20°N

Yucatán Peninsula
Calakmul

Caribbean Sea

Palenque
Piedras Negras
Uaxactún
Bonampak
Tikal

Gulf of Honduras

Obsidian, valued for its sharp edges and considered sacred by the Maya, was mined in the mountains and traded throughout the Maya world.

PACIFIC OCEAN

Quiriguá
Copán
Kaminaljuyú

Jade was mined in the mountains and traded to lowland cities.

map Zone Geography Skills

Movement The Maya established trade routes throughout Mesoamerica.

1. **Identify** What two resources were mostly found in the lowland region?
2. **Explain** Why might Maya in the lowlands want jade and obsidian from the highlands?

EARLY HISTORY OF THE AMERICAS **119**

Direct Teach

Main Idea

❶ **Geography and the Early Maya**

Geography helped shape the lives of the early Maya.

Describe How did the Maya adapt to and change their environment? *cleared wooded areas for farmland, used available resources for building materials, traded to obtain resources not available locally*

Make Inferences Why do you think the Maya expanded into the highlands? *needed more space as populations grew, to access resources*

Answers

Map Zone 1. *cacao and cotton;*
2. *They could use jade and obsidian to make tools and create artwork.*

❷ The Classic Age

During the Classic Age, the Maya built great cities linked by trade.

Describe List some nouns and adjectives that describe Maya cities. *Nouns might include temples, palaces, plazas, canals, ball courts; adjectives might include grand, decorated, terraced, and paved.*

Summarize How did the Maya change their environment to improve city life? *terraced land for farming, paved areas for public gatherings, built canals*

▶ Map Zone Transparency: Maya Civilization

Biography

John Lloyd Stephens (1805–1852) In the 1830s John Lloyd Stephens, an American lawyer, was advised to travel for his health. He went to the Middle East and eastern Europe, where he toured ruins and archaeological sites. Having developed a passion for exploration, in 1839 Stephens went to Honduras. He was in search of ancient ruins said to exist deep in the Yucatán jungle. After struggling through dense tropical rain forest, Stephens came upon a magnificent carved stone. He had found the ruins of the ancient Maya city of Palenque. News of the find sparked interest in the Maya and led to modern historical study of Maya civilization. Today scientists and explorers continue to find Maya ruins hidden in the jungle.

Answers

Reading Check *No single ruler united the many city-states into one empire.*

In addition to palaces and temples, the Maya built canals and paved large plazas, or open squares, for public gatherings. Farmers used stone walls to shape hillsides into flat terraces so they could grow crops on them. Almost every Maya city also had a stone court for playing a special ball game. Using only their heads, shoulders, or hips, players tried to bounce a heavy rubber ball through stone rings attached high on the court walls. The winners of these games received jewels and clothing. The losers were often killed.

READING CHECK **Analyzing** Why is Maya civilization not considered an empire?

Maya Culture

In Maya society, people's daily lives were heavily influenced by two main forces. One was the social structure, and the other was religion.

Social Structure

The king held the highest position in Maya society. The Maya believed their kings were related to the gods, so Maya kings had religious as well as political authority. Priests, rich merchants, and noble warriors were also part of the upper class. Together with the king, these people held all the power in Maya society.

Close-up

Palenque

The ancient Maya city of Palenque was a major power on the border between the Maya highlands and lowlands. Its great temples and plazas were typical of the Classic Age of Maya civilization.

Flat terraces made more land usable for farming.

Priests led religious ceremonies from the tops of temples.

120 CHAPTER 5

Critical Thinking: Synthesizing

Above Level

Maya Classic Age Recipe

1. Have students create an imaginary recipe for the Maya Classic Age. The recipe should include a list of ingredients and preparation steps. Students will specify the "dish" they want to make.

2. Explain that the recipe's ingredients should be the defining characteristics of the Maya Classic Age. Ingredient amounts should reflect the importance of each characteristic. Preparation or cooking instructions should be creative or symbolize aspects of the Maya Classic Age. For example, preparation might

require actively beating two ingredients together to symbolize the warfare common to the Maya Classic Age. Or the recipe might include a warning not to overcook the dish to symbolize theories about the decline of the Maya civilization.

3. Encourage students to illustrate or decorate their recipes. **LS Verbal/Linguistic**

📝 Alternative Assessment Handbook, Rubric 37: Writing Assignments

Most Maya, though, belonged to the lower class. This group was made up of farming families who lived outside the cities. The women cared for the children, cooked, made yarn, and wove cloth. The men farmed, hunted, and crafted tools.

Lower-class Maya had to "pay" their rulers by giving the rulers part of their crops and goods such as cloth and salt. They also had to help construct temples and other public buildings. If their city went to war, Maya men had to serve in the army, and if captured in battle, they often became slaves. Slaves carried goods along trade routes or worked for upper-class Maya as servants or farmers.

Religion

The Maya worshipped many gods, such as a creator, a sun god, a moon goddess, and a maize god. Each god was believed to control a different aspect of daily life.

According to Maya beliefs, the gods could be helpful or harmful, so people tried to please the gods to get their help. The Maya believed their gods needed blood to prevent disasters or the end of the world. Every person offered blood to the gods by piercing their tongue or skin. On special occasions, the Maya made human sacrifices. They usually used prisoners captured in battle, offering their hearts to stone carvings of the gods.

Maya temples were shaped like mountains, which the Maya considered sacred because they allowed people to approach the gods.

Maya buildings were covered with stucco and painted in bright colors.

BIOGRAPHY

Pacal
(603–683)
Pacal became king of the Maya city of Palenque when he was just 12 years old. As king, Pacal led many important community events, such as religious dances and public meetings. When he died, he was buried at the bottom of the Temple of the Inscriptions shown to the near left.

ANALYSIS SKILL   ANALYZING VISUALS
In what ways might Palenque's setting have helped the city? In what ways might it have hurt the city?

EARLY HISTORY OF THE AMERICAS   **121**

③ Maya Culture, continued

Maya culture included a strict social structure, a religion with many gods, and achievements in science and the arts.

Summarize What advances did the Maya make in astronomy? *built observatories, developed calendars, determined length of year*

Make Generalizations Why might builders today be impressed with Maya building methods? *The Maya built great cities without metal tools or wheeled vehicles.*

Connect to Science

Maya Astronomy The Maya considered stars and planets to be gods. They watched the stars to predict events on Earth that they believed the gods controlled. The planet Venus was one of the Maya's most important "stars." The Maya determined that Venus took about 584 days to reappear at the same point on the horizon.

⤴ hmhsocialstudies.com
Online Resources
Activity: Adding the Maya Way

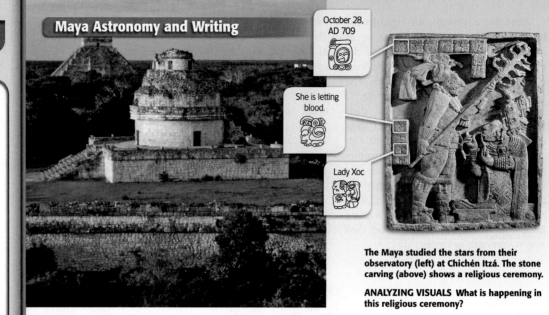

Maya Astronomy and Writing

October 28, AD 709

She is letting blood.

Lady Xoc

The Maya studied the stars from their observatory (left) at Chichén Itzá. The stone carving (above) shows a religious ceremony.

ANALYZING VISUALS What is happening in this religious ceremony?

Achievements

FOCUS ON READING
What will be your purpose in reading about Maya achievements?

The Maya's religious beliefs led them to make impressive advances in science. They built large **observatories**, or buildings from which people could study the sky, so their priests could watch the stars and plan the best times for religious festivals. With the knowledge they gained about astronomy, the Maya developed two calendars. One, with 365 days, guided farming activities, such as planting and harvesting. This calendar was more accurate than the one used in Europe at that time. The Maya also had a separate 260-day calendar that they used for keeping track of religious events.

The Maya were able to measure time accurately partly because they were skilled mathematicians. They created a number system that helped them make complex calculations, and they were among the first people with a symbol for zero. The Maya used their number system to record key dates in their history.

The Maya also developed a writing system. Anthropologists, or scholars who study people and cultures, have figured out that symbols used in Maya writing represented both objects and sounds. The Maya carved these symbols into large stone tablets to record their history. They also wrote in bark-paper books and passed down stories and poems orally.

The Maya created amazing art and architecture as well. Their jade and gold jewelry was exceptional. Also, their huge temple-pyramids were masterfully built. The Maya had neither metal tools for cutting nor wheeled vehicles for carrying heavy supplies. Instead, workers used obsidian tools to cut limestone into blocks. Then workers rolled the giant blocks over logs and lifted them with ropes. The Maya decorated their buildings with paintings.

READING CHECK **Categorizing** What groups made up the different classes in Maya society?

Differentiating Instruction

Below Level

English-Language Learners

Prep Required

Materials: butcher paper, art supplies

1. Ask students to imagine that they are Maya artists during the Classic Age and that the king has asked them to create a mural showing Maya achievements in science, math, writing, and architecture.

2. Organize students into small groups. If possible, place students who are proficient in English in the same groups with English learners.

3. Have students examine the examples of Maya artwork in this section and use the artwork as a model.

4. Then have each group create and display its mural. **LS Interpersonal, Visual/Spatial**

📄 Alternative Assessment Handbook, Rubrics 3: Artwork; and 14: Group Activity

Answers

Analyzing Visuals *possible answer— there is blood letting, which suggests a rite of healing*

Focus on Reading *possible answer— to learn how the Maya influenced civilizations that developed after them*

Reading Check *king, priests, merchants, noble warriors, farmers, and slaves*

Decline of Maya Civilization

Maya civilization began to collapse in the AD 900s. People stopped building temples and other structures. They left the cities and moved back to the countryside. What caused this collapse? Historians are not sure, but they think that a combination of factors was probably responsible.

One factor could have been the burden on the common people. Maya kings forced their subjects to farm for them or work on building projects. Perhaps people didn't want to work for the kings. They might have decided to <u>rebel</u> against their rulers' demands and abandon their cities.

Increased warfare between cities could also have caused the decline. Maya cities had always fought for power. But if battles became more widespread or destructive, they would have disrupted trade and cost many lives. People might have fled from the cities for their safety.

A related theory is that perhaps the Maya could not produce enough food to feed everyone. Growing the same crops year after year would have weakened the soil. In addition, as the population grew, the demand for food would have increased. To meet this demand, cities might have begun competing fiercely for new land. But the resulting battles would have hurt more crops, damaged more farmland, and caused even greater food shortages.

Climate change could have played a role, too. Scientists know that Mesoamerica suffered from droughts during the period when the Maya were leaving their cities. Droughts would have made it hard to grow enough food to feed people in the cities.

Whatever the reasons, the collapse of Maya civilization happened gradually. The Maya scattered after 900, but they did not disappear entirely. In fact, the Maya civilization later revived in the Yucatán

Peninsula. By the time Spanish conquerors reached the Americas in the 1500s, though, Maya power had faded.

READING CHECK **Summarizing** What factors may have caused the end of Maya civilization?

SUMMARY AND PREVIEW The Maya built a civilization that peaked between about 250 and 900 but later collapsed for reasons still unknown. In Section 2 you will learn about another people who lived in Mesoamerica, the Aztecs.

VIDEO
The
Disappearance

hmhsocialstudies.com

ACADEMIC VOCABULARY

rebel to fight against authority

Section 1 Assessment

hmhsocialstudies.com
ONLINE QUIZ

Reviewing Ideas, Terms, and Places

1. **a. Recall** What resources did the Maya get from the forest?
   b. Elaborate How do you think Maya villages grew into large cities?
2. **a. Describe** What features did Maya cities include?
   b. Make Inferences How did trade strengthen the Maya civilization?
3. **a. Identify** Who belonged to the upper class in Maya society?
   b. Explain Why did the Maya build **observatories**?
   c. Rank What do you think was the most impressive cultural achievement of the Maya? Why?
4. **a. Describe** What happened to the Maya after 900?
   b. Evaluate What would you consider to be the key factor in the collapse of Maya civilization? Explain.

Critical Thinking

5. **Evaluating** Draw a diagram like the one to the right. Use your notes to rank Maya achievements, with the most important at the top.

FOCUS ON WRITING

6. **Gathering Information about the Maya** Part of your article will probably be devoted to the Maya. Use the map and pictures in this section to help you decide what to write about. How would you describe the land and the Maya cities? What could you add about the history and culture of the Maya? Take notes on your ideas.

EARLY HISTORY OF THE AMERICAS **123**

• **Direct Teach** •

Main Idea

❹ **Decline of Maya Civilization**

The decline of Maya civilization began in the 900s.

Recall When did the Maya civilization decline, and what resulted? *In the AD 900s; the Maya stopped building temples and other structures, and left their cities.*

Evaluate Which theory do you think best explains why the Maya civilization collapsed, and why? *Answers will vary, but students should accurately describe the theory they choose.*

• **Review & Assess** •

Close

Have students summarize and discuss the different theories for the decline of the Classic Age in Maya civilization.

Review

 Online Quiz, Section 1

Assess

SE Section 1 Assessment

PASS: Section 1 Quiz

Alternative Assessment Handbook

Reteach/Classroom Intervention

Guided Reading Workbook, Section 1

Interactive Skills Tutor CD-ROM

Section 1 Assessment Answers

1. **a.** deer, rabbits, and monkeys for food; wood poles, vines, and mud for building materials
   b. increased food supply and trade
2. **a.** possible answers—temples, pyramids, palaces, plazas, canals, ball courts
   b. brought city-states into contact with each other, provided food and supplies that were not available locally, held civilization together
3. **a.** kings, priests, warriors, merchants
   b. Priests could look at the stars and decide on the best times for religious festivals.

c. Answers will vary, but students should give reasons for the achievement they think is most impressive.

4. **a.** Their civilization began to decline.
   b. possible answers—rebellion, food shortages, warfare, climate change
5. Answers should show Maya achievements in art, math, science, and writing.
6. Students' notes might include a list of some of the cities on the Maya Civilization map and a description of some features of Maya cities that they want to include in their article.

Answers

Reading Check *rebellion by the common people, increased warfare between cities, lack of food, climate change*

123

Bellringer

If YOU lived there. . . Use the **Daily Bellringer Transparency** to help students answer the question.

▶ Daily Bellringer Transparency, Section 2

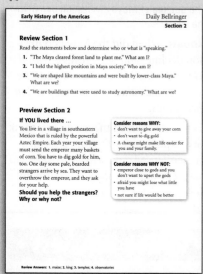

Early History of the Americas — Daily Bellringer
Section 2

Review Section 1

Read the statements below and determine who or what is "speaking."

1. "The Maya cleared forest land to plant me." What am I?
2. "I held the highest position in Maya society." Who am I?
3. "We are shaped like mountains and were built by lower-class Maya." What are we?
4. "We are buildings that were used to study astronomy." What are we?

Preview Section 2

If YOU lived there ...
You live in a village in southeastern Mexico that is ruled by the powerful Aztec Empire. Each year your village must send the emperor many baskets of corn. You have to dig gold for him, too. One day some pale, bearded strangers arrive by sea. They want to overthrow the emperor, and they ask for your help.
Should you help the strangers? Why or why not?

Consider reasons WHY:
- don't want to give away your corn
- don't want to dig gold
- A change might make life easier for you and your family.

Consider reasons WHY NOT:
- emperor close to gods and you don't want to upset the gods
- afraid you might lose what little you have
- not sure if life would be better

Review Answers: 1. maize; 2. king; 3. temples; 4. observatories

Key Terms and Places

📑 **RF:** Vocabulary Builder, Section 2

Taking Notes

Have students use the graphic organizer online to take notes on the section. This activity will prepare students for the Section Assessment, in which they will complete a graphic organizer that builds on the information using the Critical Thinking Skill: Evaluating.

The Aztecs

If **YOU** lived there...

You live in a village in southeastern Mexico that is ruled by the powerful Aztec Empire. Each year your village must send the emperor many baskets of corn. You have to dig gold for him, too. One day some pale, bearded strangers arrive by sea. They want to overthrow the emperor, and they ask for your help.

Should you help the strangers? Why or why not?

What You Will Learn...

Main Ideas

1. The Aztecs built a rich and powerful empire in central Mexico.
2. Social structure, religion, and warfare shaped life in the empire.
3. Hernán Cortés conquered the Aztec Empire in 1521.

The Big Idea

The strong Aztec Empire, founded in central Mexico in 1325, lasted until the Spanish conquest in 1521.

Key Terms and Places

Tenochtitlán, *p. 124*
causeways, *p. 124*
conquistadors, *p. 128*

hmhsocialstudies.com
TAKING NOTES

Use the graphic organizer online to organize your notes on the Aztecs.

BUILDING BACKGROUND The Aztecs ruled a large empire in Mesoamerica. Each village they conquered had to contribute heavily to the Aztec economy. This system helped create a mighty state, but one that did not inspire loyalty.

The Aztecs Build an Empire

The first Aztecs were farmers who migrated from the north to central Mexico. Finding the good farmland already occupied, they settled on a swampy island in the middle of Lake Texcoco (tays-KOH-koh). There, in 1325, they began building their capital and conquering nearby towns.

War was a key factor in the Aztecs' rise to power. The Aztecs fought fiercely and demanded tribute payments from the people they conquered. The cotton, gold, and food that poured in as a result became vital to their economy. The Aztecs also controlled a huge trade network. Merchants carried goods to and from all parts of the empire. Many merchants doubled as spies, keeping the rulers informed about what was happening in their lands.

War, tribute, and trade made the Aztec Empire strong and rich. By the early 1400s the Aztecs ruled the most powerful state in Mesoamerica. Nowhere was the empire's greatness more visible than in its capital, **Tenochtitlán** (tay-nawch-teet-LAHN).

To build this amazing island city, the Aztecs first had to overcome many geographic challenges. One problem was the difficulty getting to and from the city. The Aztecs addressed this challenge by building three wide **causeways**—raised roads across water or wet ground—to connect the island to the lakeshore.

Teach the Big Idea

At Level

The Aztecs

1. **Teach** Ask students the questions in the Main Idea boxes under Direct Teach.
2. **Apply** Create a flowchart for students to see that lists, in order, the major events in Aztec history. The flowchart should have about five or six major events.
3. **Review** Pair students and have them copy the flowchart. One partner teaches the flowchart to the other person. The second person adds additional details.

4. **Practice/Homework** Instruct students to write down one or more causes for each event in the flowchart. *possible answer: "The Aztecs built their capital on an island in Lake Texcoco." cause—"because other tribes had already taken the good farmland in the area."* 🖪 **Verbal/Linguistic, Visual/Spatial**
   📑 Alternative Assessment Handbook, Rubric 6: Cause and Effect

The Aztec Empire, 1519

SIERRA MADRE ORIENTAL

Lerma River

Gulf of Mexico

Tula

Lake Texcoco

Tenochtitlán
Texcoco
Tlacopán
Tlaxcala

Cempoala

20°N

Teotitlán

Balsas River

SIERRA MADRE DEL SUR

Mitla

Isthmus of Tehuantepec

PACIFIC OCEAN

Xoconocho

The Aztecs' magnificent capital, Tenochtitlán, was built on an island in Lake Texcoco.

Aztec Empire
0   50   100 Miles
0   50   100 Kilometers
Projection: Azimuthal Equal-Area

map zone — Geography Skills

Place The Aztecs ruled much of central Mexico.
1. **Identify** Which cities were located on Lake Texcoco?
2. **Make Inferences** Why do you think the area around Tlaxcala was not part of the Aztec Empire?

hmhsocialstudies.com
ANIMATED GEOGRAPHY

They also built canals that crisscrossed the city. The causeways and canals made travel and trade much easier.

Tenochtitlán's island location also limited the amount of land available for farming. To solve this problem, the Aztecs created floating gardens called *chinampas* (chee-NAHM-pahs). They piled soil on top of large rafts, which they anchored to trees that stood in the water.

The Aztecs made Tenochtitlán a truly magnificent city. Home to some 200,000 people at its height, it had huge temples, a busy market, and a grand palace.

READING CHECK **Finding Main Ideas** How did the Aztecs rise to power?

Life in the Empire

The Aztecs' way of life was as distinctive as their capital city. They had a complex social structure, a demanding religion, and a rich culture.

Aztec Society

The Aztec emperor, like the Maya king, was the most important person in society. From his great palace, he attended to law, trade, tribute, and warfare. Trusted nobles helped him as tax collectors, judges, and other government officials. These noble positions were passed down from fathers to sons, and young nobles went to school to learn their responsibilities.

THE IMPACT TODAY

Mexico's capital, Mexico City, is located where Tenochtitlán once stood.

EARLY HISTORY OF THE AMERICAS **125**

Direct Teach

Main Idea

❶ **The Aztecs Build an Empire**

The Aztecs built a rich and powerful empire in central Mexico.

Recall About when did the Aztec Empire become the most powerful state in Mesoamerica? *early 1400s*

Analyze Why do you think merchants would make good spies for the emperor? *The merchants traveled widely and interacted with many different people.*

Identify How did visitors travel to and from Tenochtitlán? *across a causeway*

▶ Map Zone Transparency: The Aztec Empire, 1519

📝 RF: Geography and History, The Aztec Empire

Linking to Today

Mexica and Mexico The Aztecs were also called Mexica, probably from Metzliapán ("Moon Lake"), another name for Lake Texcoco. The name Mexica is the source of the name of the present-day country, Mexico.

Analyzing Maps
The Aztec Empire

Location How far was Tenochtitlán from the Gulf of Mexico? *about 150 miles*

Place What physical features surrounded Lake Texcoco? *mountains or hills*

Differentiating Instruction

Below Level

Special Needs Learners

1. Draw a chart similar to the following for students to see and discuss what it means.

War — Tribute — Trade → Aztec Wealth and Power

2. Explain that *tribute* means what one pays a ruler to show that you recognize his or her power over you, expecting protection in return. Ask what kind of protection those paying tribute to the Aztecs might have expected.

3. Ask students what people might have given as tribute. Also, ask what items might have been traded. **LS Visual/Spatial, Verbal/Linguistic**

📄 Alternative Assessment Handbook, Rubric 12: Drawing Conclusions

Answers

Map Zone 1. *Tenochtitlán, Texcoco, and Tlacopán;* **2.** *possible answer—it was too mountainous to settle*
Reading Check *war, tribute, and trade*

Close-up
Tenochtitlán

Ask students these questions based on the illustration of Tenochtitlán.

Identify What goods were traded at the market? *possible answers—crops, animals, rugs, gold, silver, cloaks, and precious stones*

Analyze How did people travel throughout the city? *by boat*

Draw Conclusions Because the best farmland was already taken when the Aztecs arrived in central Mexico, they had to work hard at making the swampy land usable. How do you think this affected their success? *Answers will vary; often when people must overcome difficulties, they work harder.*

Did you know. . .

A major reason the Aztecs were so prosperous was that they engaged in intensive agriculture. This means that the Aztecs farmed the available land to the greatest possible extent.

About the Illustration

This illustration is an artist's conception based on available resources. However, historians are uncertain exactly what this scene looked like.

Close-up
Tenochtitlán

The Aztecs turned a swampy, uninhabited island into one of the largest and grandest cities in the world. The first Europeans to visit Tenochtitlán were amazed. At the time, the Aztec capital was about five times bigger than London.

The Great Temple stood at the heart of the city. On top of the temple were two shrines—a blue shrine for the rain god and a red shrine for the sun god.

Gold, silver, cloaks, and precious stones were among the many items sold at the market.

A network of canals linked different parts of the city.

Aztec farmers grew crops on floating gardens called *chinampas*.

ANALYSIS SKILL **ANALYZING VISUALS**
What is the most important building in this picture? How can you tell?

126

Critical Thinking: Solving Problems

Above Level

Making More Farmland

1. Organize students into small groups. Ask students to imagine they are Aztecs who have come to build a new home around Lake Texcoco. However, there is not enough farmland.

2. Each group should explore options for creating more farmland, such as building *chinampas*. Encourage students to brainstorm.

3. Once groups have decided how they are going to create additional farmland, have them list necessary materials and processes. For

example: What tools will be needed? If they need rafts, what materials will be required? How will they move soil around?

4. Have students explain how these resources will be used to create more farmland. Ask for volunteers to share their solutions.

LS **Logical/Mathematical, Interpersonal**

Alternative Assessment Handbook, Rubric 14: Group Activity

Answers

Analyzing Visuals *the Great Temple; it is by far the largest building in the city*

Aztec Ceremonial Jewelry

Aztec artists were very skilled. They created detailed and brightly colored items. This double-headed serpent was probably worn during religious ceremonies. The man on the right is wearing it on his chest.

ANALYZING VISUALS What are some features of Aztec art that you can see in these pictures?

Just below the emperor and his nobles was a class of warriors and priests. Aztec warriors were highly respected and had many privileges, but priests were more influential. They led religious ceremonies and, as keepers of the calendars, decided when to plant and harvest.

The next level of Aztec society included merchants and artisans. Below them, in the lower class, were farmers and laborers, who made up the majority of the population. Many didn't own their land, and they paid so much in tribute that they often found it tough to survive. Only slaves, at the very bottom of society, struggled more.

Religion and Warfare

Like the Maya, the Aztecs worshipped many gods whom they believed controlled both nature and human activities. To please the gods, Aztec priests regularly made human sacrifices. Most victims were battle captives or slaves. In bloody ritual ceremonies, priests would slash open their victims' chests to "feed" human hearts and blood to the gods. The Aztecs sacrificed as many as 10,000 people a year. To supply enough victims, Aztec warriors often fought battles with neighboring peoples.

Cultural Achievements

As warlike as the Aztecs were, they also appreciated art and beauty. Architects and sculptors created fine stone pyramids and statues. Artisans used gold, gems, and bright feathers to make jewelry and masks. Women embroidered colorful designs on the cloth they wove.

The Aztecs valued learning as well. They studied astronomy and devised a calendar much like the Maya one. They kept detailed written records of historical and cultural events. They also had a strong oral tradition. Stories about ancestors and the gods were passed from one generation to the next. The Aztecs also enjoyed fine speeches and riddles such as these:

> "What is a little blue-green jar filled with popcorn? Someone is sure to guess our riddle: it is the sky.
> What is a mountainside that has a spring of water in it? Our nose."
> –Bernardino de Sahagún, from Florentine Codex

Knowing the answers to riddles showed that one had paid attention in school.

READING CHECK **Identifying Cause and Effect** How did Aztec religious practices influence warfare?

EARLY HISTORY OF THE AMERICAS **127**

Cross-Discipline Activity: Arts and the Humanities

Aztecs at Work

Prep Required

Materials: examples of Mexican murals, butcher paper, art supplies

1. Display examples from art or history books of murals by great Mexican artists, including Diego Rivera and José Clemente Orozco. Point out that these artists have portrayed aspects of Mexican history in their murals.

2. Organize students into groups of three or four. Have each group conduct additional research on Aztec daily life, especially as it affected the various occupations of the Aztec people.

3. Ask each group to paint a mural, using Rivera or Orozco murals as models, showing the various levels of Aztec society performing the tasks assigned to that group.

4. Display the murals in the classroom.
   LS Visual/Spatial, Interpersonal
   📓 Alternative Assessment Handbook, Rubric 3: Artwork

127

Direct Teach

Main Idea

③ Cortés Conquers the Aztecs

Hernán Cortés conquered the Aztec Empire in 1521.

Identify What were the Spanish soldiers called? *conquistadors*

Evaluate Do you think Moctezuma was too trusting of Cortés and his men? Explain your answer. *Students' answers should reflect the text.*

 RF: Primary Source, Cortés's First Meeting with Moctezuma (1519)

 RF: Biography, Moctezuma II

● Review & Assess ●

Close

Ask students which factors that contributed to the Aztecs' defeat were the most and least important and to defend their choices.

Review

↗ Online Quiz, Section 2

Assess

SE Section 2 Assessment

PASS: Section 2 Quiz

Alternative Assessment Handbook

Reteach/Classroom Intervention

● Guided Reading Workbook, Section 2

● Interactive Skills Tutor CD-ROM

Answers

Focus on Reading *The Spanish conquered the Aztecs.*

Reading Check *alliances with other people in the region, better weapons, horses, disease*

128

Cortés Conquers the Aztecs

FOCUS ON READING If your purpose is to learn about the end of the Aztecs, how will reading about the Spanish help you?

In the late 1400s the Spanish arrived in the Americas, seeking adventure, riches, and converts to Catholicism. One group of **conquistadors** (kahn-KEES-tuh-dohrz), or Spanish conquerors, reached Mexico in 1519. Led by Hernán Cortés (er-NAHN kawr-TEZ), their motives were to find gold, claim land, and convert the native peoples to Christianity.

The Aztec emperor, Moctezuma II (MAWK-tay-SOO-mah), cautiously welcomed the strangers. He believed Cortés to be the god Quetzalcoatl (ket-suhl-kuh-WAH-tuhl), whom the Aztecs believed had left Mexico long ago. According to legend, the god had promised to return in 1519.

Moctezuma gave the Spanish gold and other gifts, but Cortés wanted more. He took the emperor prisoner, enraging the Aztecs, who attacked the Spanish. They managed to drive out the conquistadors, but Moctezuma was killed in the fighting.

Within a year, Cortés and his men came back. This time they had help from other peoples in the region who resented the Aztecs' harsh rule. In addition, the Spanish had better weapons, including armor, cannons, and swords. Furthermore, the Aztecs were terrified of the enemy's big horses—animals they had never seen before. The Spanish had also unknowingly brought diseases such as smallpox to the Americas. Diseases weakened or killed thousands of Aztecs. In 1521 the Aztec Empire came to an end.

READING CHECK **Summarizing** What factors helped the Spanish defeat the Aztecs?

SUMMARY AND PREVIEW The Aztec Empire, made strong by warfare and tribute, fell to the Spanish in 1521. In the next section you will learn about another empire in the Americas, that of the Incas.

Section 2 Assessment

↗ hmhsocialstudies.com
ONLINE QUIZ

Reviewing Ideas, Terms, and Places

1. **a. Recall** Where and when did Aztec civilization develop?
   b. Explain How did the Aztecs in **Tenochtitlán** adapt to their island location?
   c. Elaborate How might Tenochtitlán's location have been both a benefit and a hindrance to the Aztecs?
2. **a. Recall** What did the Aztecs feed their gods?
   b. Rate Consider the roles of the emperor, warriors, priests, and others in Aztec society. Who do you think had the hardest role? Explain.
3. **a. Identify** Who was Moctezuma II?
   b. Make Generalizations Why did allies help Cortés defeat the Aztecs?
   c. Predict The Aztecs vastly outnumbered the **conquistadors**. If the Aztecs had first viewed Cortés as a threat rather than a god, how might history have changed?

Critical Thinking

4. **Evaluating** Draw a diagram like the one shown. Use your notes to identify three factors that contributed to the Aztecs' power. Put the factor you consider most important first and put the least important last. Explain your choices.

1.	2.	3.

FOCUS ON WRITING

5. **Describing the Aztec Empire** Tenochtitlán would certainly be described in your article. Make notes about how you would describe it. Be sure to explain the causeways, chinampas, and other features. What activities went on in the city? Your article should also describe the events that occurred when the Spanish discovered the Aztec capital. Make notes on the fall of the Aztec Empire.

128 CHAPTER 5

Section 2 Assessment Answers

1. **a.** in central Mexico in the early 1300s
   b. built causeways, canals, chinampas
   c. benefit—improved trade; hindrance—limited farmland, made Aztecs vulnerable to isolation
2. **a.** human hearts and blood
   b. possible answer—slaves, because they had to work for other people and could be sacrificed to the Aztec gods
3. **a.** the Aztec emperor conquered by Cortés
   b. They resented the Aztecs' harsh rule.

   c. possible answer—Aztecs might not have been conquered by the Spanish
4. Aztecs were fierce warriors, demanded tribute from conquered people, controlled trade network; order of answers will vary.
5. Responses will vary. Students should use vivid, colorful language to describe Tenochtitlán, chinampas, and other features, as well as the fall of the Aztec Empire.

The Incas

If YOU lived there...

You live in the Andes Mountains, where you raise llamas. You weave their wool into warm cloth. Last year, soldiers from the powerful Inca Empire took over your village. They brought in new leaders, who say you must all learn a new language and send much of your woven cloth to the Inca ruler. They also promise that the government will provide for you in times of trouble.

How do you feel about living in the Inca Empire?

> **BUILDING BACKGROUND** The Incas built their huge empire by taking over village after village in South America. They brought many changes to the people they conquered before they were themselves conquered by the Spanish.

The Incas Create an Empire

While the Aztecs were ruling Mexico, the Inca Empire arose in South America. The Incas began as a small tribe in the Andes. Their capital was **Cuzco** (KOO-skoh) in what is now Peru.

In the mid-1400s a ruler named Pachacuti (pah-chah-KOO-tee) began to expand Inca territory. Later leaders followed his example, and by the early 1500s the Inca Empire was huge. It stretched from what is now Ecuador south to central Chile. It included coastal deserts, snowy mountains, fertile valleys, and thick forests. About 12 million people lived in the empire. To rule effectively, the Incas formed a strong central government.

> The Incas lived in a region of high plains and mountains.

What You Will Learn...

Main Ideas

1. The Incas created an empire with a strong central government in South America.
2. Life in the Inca Empire was influenced by social structure, religion, and the Incas' cultural achievements.
3. Francisco Pizarro conquered the Incas and took control of the region in 1537.

The Big Idea

The Incas controlled a huge empire in South America, but it was conquered by the Spanish.

Key Terms and Places

Cuzco, p. 129
Quechua, p. 130
masonry, p. 131

hmhsocialstudies.com
TAKING NOTES

Use the graphic organizer online to organize your notes on the Inca Empire.

Bellringer

If YOU lived there. . . Use the **Daily Bellringer Transparency** to help students answer the question.

▶ Daily Bellringer Transparency, Section 3

Early History of the Americas	Daily Bellringer
	Section 3

Review Section 2

Unscramble the letters in each underlined word to reveal the solution to each clue.

1. TUMMOCEAZ
   Clue: This Aztec emperor welcomed Cortés and gave the Spanish gold and gifts.

2. SUSEWYAAC
   Clue: These were raised roads across water or wet ground.

3. OQUACDOTNIRSS
   Clue: These Spanish soldiers reached Mexico in 1519.

Preview Section 3

If YOU lived there ...
You live in the Andes Mountains, where you raise llamas. You weave their wool into warm cloth. Last year, soldiers from the powerful Inca Empire took over your village. They brought in new leaders, who say you must all learn a new language and send much of your woven cloth to the Inca ruler. They also promise that the government will provide for you in times of trouble.
How do you feel about living in the Inca Empire?

Consider the PROS of living under the Incas:
• government would help if a natural disaster struck
• living a simple life—own only as much as you need

Consider the CONS of living under the Incas:
• have to learn a new language
• don't want to give away your woven cloth
• don't want to give up much of your culture for new ways

Review Answers: 1. Moctezuma; 2. causeways; 3. conquistadors

Key Terms and Places

📄 **RF:** Vocabulary Builder, Section 3

Taking Notes

Have students use the graphic organizer online to take notes on the section. This activity will prepare students for the Section Assessment, in which they will complete a graphic organizer that builds on the information using the Critical Thinking Skill: Analyzing.

129

Teach the Big Idea

At Level

The Incas

1. **Teach** Ask students the questions in the Main Idea boxes under Direct Teach.

2. **Apply** Create a two-columned chart for students to see. Title the left column *Before the Spanish Arrived* and the right column *After the Spanish Arrived*. Title the whole chart *The Inca Empire*. Have students copy the chart. Call on volunteers to provide key words and phrases to describe the Inca Empire before and after the Spanish arrival. Place those words and phrases on the chart.
   LS Visual/Spatial

3. **Review** Ask students if any characteristics in the *Before* column may have continued after the conquest. *possible answer—aspects of daily life, such as farming techniques, use of llamas*

4. **Practice/Homework** Have each student write a paragraph about how the lives of the Inca people changed after the Spanish conquest. **LS Verbal/Linguistic**

   📄 Alternative Assessment Handbook, Rubric 37: Writing Assignments

Main Idea

❶ The Incas Create an Empire

The Incas created an empire with a strong central government in South America.

Recall What were some of the jobs that Incas performed as part of the *mita? farmed, produced cloth and other goods, mined, served in the army, built roads*

Make Inferences Why were children of conquered leaders used to govern and teach the Inca way of life? *They would have been trusted and respected.*

▶ Map Zone Transparency: The Inca Empire, 1530

Analyzing Maps
The Inca Empire

Regions How do the size, shape, and physical features of the Inca Empire compare to those of the Aztec Empire? *Inca Empire—long and narrow, located along Pacific coast, two major lakes, high mountains; Aztec Empire—coasts on two oceans, more compact, some mountains, Lake Texcoco*

Answers

Map Zone 1. *about 2,400 miles if measured in a straight line, about 2,700 if measured along the Pacific coast;* **2.** *centrally located, mountains provided protection from invaders*

Reading Check *brought in new leaders, educated leaders' children in the capital, established an official religion, established Quechua as the official language, imposed a labor tax, collected and distributed goods*

130

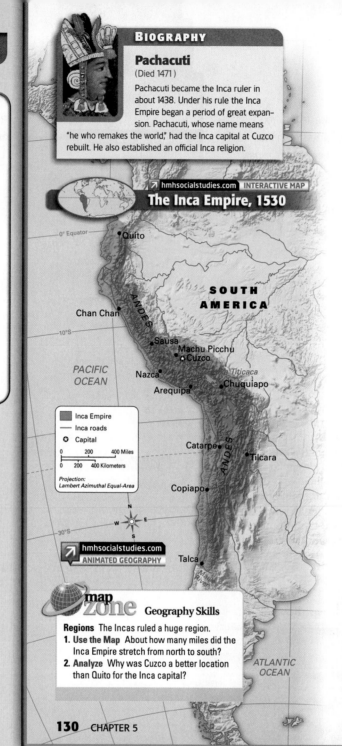

BIOGRAPHY

Pachacuti
(Died 1471)

Pachacuti became the Inca ruler in about 1438. Under his rule the Inca Empire began a period of great expansion. Pachacuti, whose name means "he who remakes the world," had the Inca capital at Cuzco rebuilt. He also established an official Inca religion.

hmhsocialstudies.com **INTERACTIVE MAP**

The Inca Empire, 1530

hmhsocialstudies.com
ANIMATED GEOGRAPHY

map zone Geography Skills

Regions The Incas ruled a huge region.
1. **Use the Map** About how many miles did the Inca Empire stretch from north to south?
2. **Analyze** Why was Cuzco a better location than Quito for the Inca capital?

130 CHAPTER 5

Central Rule

Pachacuti did not want the people he conquered to have too much power. He began a policy of removing local leaders and replacing them with new officials whom he trusted. He also made the children of conquered leaders travel to Cuzco to learn about Inca government and religion. When the children were grown, they were sent back to govern their villages, where they taught their people about the Incas' history, traditions, and way of life.

As another way of unifying the empire, the Incas used an official Inca language, **Quechua** (KE-chuh-wuh). Although people spoke many other languages, all official business had to be done in Quechua. Even today, many people in Peru and the other former Inca lands still speak Quechua.

A Well-Organized Economy

The Inca government strictly controlled the economy and told each household what work to do. Most Incas had to spend time working for the government as well as themselves. Farmers tended government land in addition to their own. Villagers made cloth and other goods for the army. Some Incas served as soldiers, worked in mines, or built roads and bridges. In this way the people paid taxes in the form of labor rather than money. This labor tax system was called the *mita* (MEE-tah).

Another feature of the Inca economy was that there were no merchants or markets. Instead, government officials would distribute goods collected through the *mita*. Leftover goods were stored in the capital for emergencies. If a natural disaster struck, or if people simply could not care for themselves, the government provided supplies to help them.

READING CHECK **Summarizing** How did the Incas control their empire?

Differentiating Instruction

Below Level

Struggling Readers

Prep Required

Materials: heavy string or twine

1. Clear a space in the classroom about 6 feet by 20 feet or secure a space of that size in the hallway.

2. Supply students with heavy string or twine. Have students use the string to create an outline of the Inca Empire. They can position chairs and desks to hold the string in place.

3. Have students determine the locations of major Inca cities and place individuals at those locations.

4. Call on a volunteer to walk from one end of the "empire" to the other. Point out that if the same amount of area was in a different shape, such as a square or circle, the distance from end to end would be much shorter.

5. Ask students how they think the empire's shape affected travel and communication.
   LS Kinesthetic, Visual/Spatial

📋 Alternative Assessment Handbook, Rubric 14: Group Activity

Life in the Inca Empire

Because the rulers controlled Inca society so closely, the common people had little personal freedom. At the same time, the government protected the general welfare of all in the empire. But that did not mean everyone was treated equally.

Social Divisions

Inca society had two main social classes. The emperor, government officials, and priests made up the upper class. Members of this class lived in stone houses in Cuzco and wore the best clothes. They did not have to pay the labor tax, and they enjoyed many other privileges. The Inca rulers, for example, could relax in luxury at Machu Picchu (MAH-choo PEEK-choo). This royal retreat lay nestled high in the Andes.

The people of the lower class in Inca society included farmers, artisans, and servants. There were no slaves, however, because the Incas did not practice slavery. Most Incas were farmers. In the warmer valleys they grew crops such as maize and peanuts. In the cooler mountains they carved terraces into the hillsides and grew potatoes. High in the Andes, people raised llamas—South American animals related to camels—for wool and meat.

Lower-class Incas dressed in plain clothes and lived simply. By law, they could not own more goods than just what they needed to survive. Most of what they made went to the *mita* and the upper class.

Religion

The Inca social structure was partly related to religion. For example, the Incas thought that their rulers were related to the sun god and never really died. As a result, priests brought mummies of former kings to many ceremonies. People gave these royal mummies food and gifts.

Most Incas were farmers. The Incas in this drawing from the mid-1500s are harvesting potatoes.

THE GRANGER COLLECTION, NEW YORK

Inca ceremonies included sacrifices. But unlike the Maya and the Aztecs, the Incas rarely sacrificed humans. They sacrificed llamas, cloth, or food instead.

In addition to practicing the official religion, people outside Cuzco worshipped other gods at local sacred places. The Incas believed certain mountaintops, rocks, and springs had magical powers. Many Incas performed sacrifices at these places as well as at the temple in Cuzco.

Achievements

Inca temples were grand buildings. The Incas were master builders, known for their expert **masonry,** or stonework. They cut stone blocks so precisely that they did not need cement to hold them together. The Incas also built a major network of roads.

The Incas produced works of art as well. Artisans made pottery as well as gold and silver jewelry. They even created a life-sized cornfield of gold and silver, crafting each cob, leaf, and stalk individually. Inca weavers also made some of the finest textiles in the Americas.

FOCUS ON READING
What will be your purpose in reading about Inca achievements?

EARLY HISTORY OF THE AMERICAS **131**

Direct Teach

Main Idea

❷ **Life in the Inca Empire**

Life in the Inca Empire was influenced by social structure, religion, and the Incas' cultural achievements.

Explain Why did the Inca believe their rulers never really died? *They believed rulers were related to the sun god.*

Analyze How do you think lower-class workers felt about having to work long and hard to pay the labor tax? *possible answer—may have felt that the Inca government was taking advantage of them*

Connect to Music
Ancient Instruments of the Andes
Some musical instruments still popular in the Andes today may have been played at Machu Picchu. One example is the *quena*—a flute made from bone or cane. Large and small drums also date back many centuries. When the Spanish arrived, the Andean peoples adapted Spanish instruments. Instead of guitars, the Andean natives made stringed instruments called *charangos* from armadillo shells.

hmhsocialstudies.com

Online Resources
Activity: Brochure on Machu Picchu

Differentiating Instruction

Above Level

Advanced/Gifted and Talented

Research Required

Tell students that the Incas had many gods. Some of the gods were connected to the stars and other heavenly bodies. One god was Virachoca, the creator god. He had many names, including Old Man of the Sky and Lord Instructor of the World. Apu Illapu, the rain god, was believed to cause rain by drawing water from the Milky Way. The Incas also paid close attention to the waxing and waning of the moon when planning events such as religious observances.

1. Ask each student to choose and conduct research on a subject related to Inca religion in which they are interested.

2. Students should prepare brief oral presentations on their chosen subjects. Encourage students to make the presentation entertaining by including interesting myths and using visual aids.

3. Have students give their presentations to the class. **LS Verbal/Linguistic, Visual/Spatial**
   Alternative Assessment Handbook, Rubric 24: Oral Presentations

Answers

Focus on Reading *possible answer— to compare Inca achievements to those of the Maya and the Aztecs*

Direct Teach

Main Idea

❸ Pizarro Conquers the Incas

Francisco Pizarro conquered the Incas and took control of the region in 1537.

Identify Who was the Inca ruler when Pizarro arrived in the empire? *Atahualpa*

Make Inferences Why do you think the Spanish attacked when Atahualpa wouldn't convert to Christianity? *possible answer—The Spanish saw Atahualpa's refusal to convert as an unforgivable insult to Christianity.*

Primary Source

Pizarro In his book *History of the Conquest of Peru*, published in 1847, William H. Prescott quotes Pizarro as saying the following to get his men to leave Panama and head to Peru with him:

"On that side are toil, hunger, nakedness, the drenching storm, desertion, and death; on this side ease and pleasure. There lies Peru with its riches; here, Panama and its poverty. Choose, each man, what best becomes a brave Castilian. For my part, I go to the south."

Interpret Ask students if they think this is an exact quote and to support their opinions. *possible answer—depends on what sources Prescott used*

Answers

Analyzing Visuals *bright colors, intricate detail, gold and silver, animals, and people*

Reading Check *upper class—lived in stone houses, wore the best clothes, did not have to pay labor taxes; lower class—most were farmers, dressed in plain clothes and lived simply, most of what they made went to the labor tax and upper class*

Inca Arts

Inca arts included beautiful textiles and gold and silver objects.

Inca artisans made many silver offerings to the gods.

The Incas are famous for their textiles. Inca weavers made cloth from cotton and from the wool of llamas.

ANALYSIS SKILL **ANALYZING VISUALS**
What are some features of Inca art that you can see in these pictures?

Inca artisans also made many gold objects, such as this mask.

While such artifacts tell us much about the Incas, nothing was written about their empire until the Spanish arrived. Indeed, the Incas had no writing system. Instead, they kept records with knotted cords called *quipus* (KEE-pooz). Knots in the cords stood for numbers. Different colors represented information about crops, land, and other important topics.

The Incas also passed down their stories and history orally. People sang songs and told stories about daily life and military victories. Official "memorizers" learned long poems about Inca legends and history. When the conquistadors arrived, the Inca records were written in Spanish and Quechua. We know about the Incas from these records and from the stories that survive in the songs and religious practices of the people in the region today.

READING CHECK **Contrasting** How did daily life differ for upper- and lower-class Incas?

Pizarro Conquers the Incas

The arrival of conquistadors changed more than how the Incas recorded history. In the late 1520s a civil war began in the Inca Empire after the death of the ruler. Two of the ruler's sons, Atahualpa (ah-tah-WAHL-pah) and Huáscar (WAHS-kahr), fought to claim the throne. Atahualpa won the war in 1532, but fierce fighting had weakened the Inca army.

On his way to be crowned as king, Atahualpa got news that a band of about 180 Spanish soldiers had arrived in the Inca Empire. They were conquistadors led by Francisco Pizarro. When Atahualpa came to meet the group, the Spanish attacked. They were greatly outnumbered, but they caught the unarmed Incas by surprise. They quickly captured Atahualpa and killed thousands of Inca soldiers.

To win his freedom, Atahualpa asked his people to fill a room with gold and silver for Pizarro. Incas brought jewelry,

---

Critical Thinking: Identifying Points of View [Above Level]

The Spanish Conquest

[Research Required]

1. Have students conduct research on the arrival of the Spanish, Atahualpa's meeting with them, and the subsequent Spanish attack.

2. Then have students write two journal entries. The first entry should present the events related to the conquest of the Inca Empire from the point of view of one of Pizarro's men. The second should describe the same events from an Inca point of view.

3. Each account should be written in the first person and begin by describing the author. Encourage students to be as descriptive and detailed as possible.

4. Ask for volunteers to share their journal entries with the class. **LS** **Verbal/Linguistic**
   Alternative Assessment Handbook, Rubric 15: Journals

states, and other valuable items from all parts of the empire. Melted down, the gold and silver may have totaled 24 tons. The precious metals would have been worth millions of dollars today. Despite this huge payment, the Spanish killed Atahualpa. They knew that if they let the Inca ruler live, he might rally his people and defeat the smaller Spanish forces.

Some Incas did fight back after the emperor's death. In 1537, though, Pizarro defeated the last of the Incas. Spain took control over the entire Inca Empire and ruled the region for the next 300 years.

READING CHECK **Identifying Cause and Effect** What events ended the Inca Empire?

SUMMARY AND PREVIEW The Incas built a huge empire in South America. But even with a strong central government, they could not withstand the Spanish conquest in 1537. In the next chapters you will learn about how the Americas have changed since the great civilizations of the Maya, Aztecs, and Incas and what these places are like today.

BIOGRAPHY

Atahualpa
(1502–1533)

Atahualpa was the last Inca emperor. He was a popular ruler, but he didn't rule for long. At his first meeting with Pizarro, he was offered a religious book to convince him to accept Christianity. Atahualpa held the book to his ear and listened. When the book didn't speak, Atahualpa threw it on the ground. The Spanish considered this an insult and a reason to attack.

Identifying Bias How do you think the Spanish viewed non-Christians?

BIOGRAPHY

Francisco Pizarro
(1475–1541)

Francisco Pizarro organized expeditions to explore the west coast of South America. His first two trips were mostly uneventful. But on his third trip, Pizarro met the Incas. With only about 180 men, he conquered the Inca Empire, which had been weakened by disease and civil war. In 1535 Pizarro founded Lima, the capital of modern Peru.

Predicting If Pizarro had not found the Inca Empire, what do you think might have happened?

Section 3 Assessment

hmhsocialstudies.com
ONLINE QUIZ

Reviewing Ideas, Terms, and Places

1. **a. Identify** Where was the Inca Empire located? What kinds of terrain did it include?
   b. Evaluate Do you think the *mita* system was a good government policy? Why or why not?
2. **a. Describe** What was a unique feature of Inca masonry?
   b. Make Inferences How might the Inca road system have helped strengthen the empire?
3. **a. Recall** When did the Spanish defeat the last of the Incas?
   b. Analyze Why do you think Pizarro was able to defeat the much larger forces of the Incas? Name at least two possible reasons.

Critical Thinking

4. **Analyzing** Draw a diagram like the one below. Using your notes, write a sentence in each box about how that topic influenced the next topic.

Geography → Government → Society → Achievements

FOCUS ON WRITING

5. **Adding Information about the Inca Empire** Your article would also describe the Inca Empire. Include some comments about how the Incas' building activities related to their environment. Also, note what happened when the Spanish arrived.

Section 3 Assessment Answers

1. **a.** along the west coast of South America; coastal deserts, snowy mountains, fertile valleys, and thick forests
   b. possible answers: yes—resources distributed effectively; no—limited freedoms
2. **a.** The stone blocks were cut so precisely that cement was not needed.
   b. All parts of the empire were connected, simplifying travel and communication.
3. **a.** 1537
   b. internal problems, leader captured, Spanish advantage with guns and horses, disease

4. possible answer—Fertile valleys existed in much of Inca Empire; government had farmers work the fertile lands; farmers had little wealth while government officials had much wealth; wealth allowed the Incas to build temples
5. Students' responses will vary, but may include adding information about the building of temples and roads, as well as the defeat of the Incas by Pizarro.

Close

Lead a brief discussion about the major events leading to the fall of the Inca Empire. Ask students how these events might have interacted with one another.

Review

Online Quiz, Section 3

Assess

SE Section 3 Assessment
PASS: Section 3 Quiz
Alternative Assessment Handbook

Reteach/Classroom Intervention

Guided Reading Workbook, Section 3
Interactive Skills Tutor CD-ROM

Answers

Biographies *Atahualpa: possible answers—as uncivilized and deserving conquest and death; Pizarro: possible answers—Inca empire would continue to control South America; weakened by civil war, empire might still have collapsed.*

Reading Check *war between Atahualpa and Huáscar, refusal of Atahualpa to convert to Christianity, capture and killing of Atahualpa*

133

Info to Know

Cultivating Crops Some of the first crops cultivated in North America were corn, beans, and squash. The Iroquois called these crops the *Three Sisters* or *Our Supporters*. Corn would soon become central to many diverse Native American peoples. Cultivating corn helped transform some nomadic societies into peoples who settled into communities and evolved complex cultures. Many rituals developed involving corn. The Osage rubbed newborn babies with cornmeal to protect them. Choctaws arranged marriages during corn festivals. The Hopi began each day by spreading cornmeal in the direction of the sun.

Did you know. . .

People living east of the Rocky Mountains in the United States and Canada sometimes feel warm, dry winds blowing from the west called chinook winds. A native term, *chinook* means *snow eater*, and describes how quickly these warm winds melt the winter snow.

Info to Know

Hopi Pueblos In the southwest, the Hopi built homes called pueblos. Pueblos are made from stones set in mud, then plastered with more mud. Trees were rare in the region, so Hopi men traveled great distances to find wood to make beams for the roof. Because pueblos had no windows or doors, the Hopi climbed through openings in the flat roofs. Some pueblos were as high as four or five stories.

▶ Map Zone Transparency: North America's Native Cultures

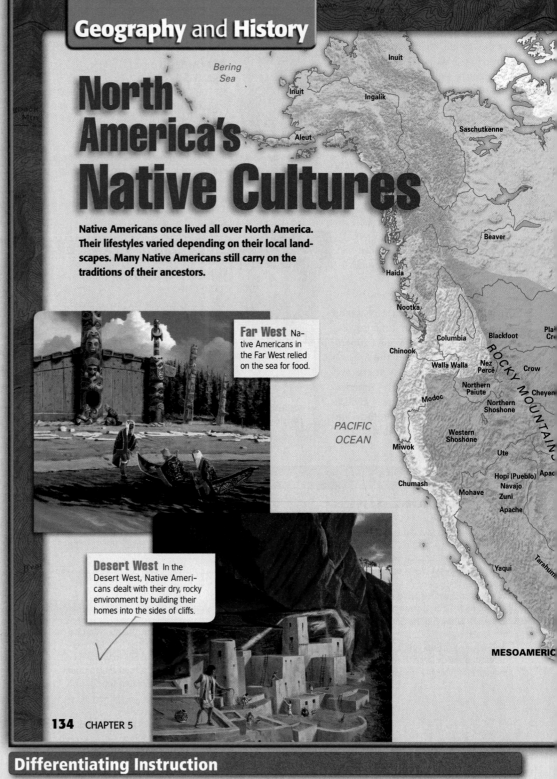

Geography and History

North America's Native Cultures

Native Americans once lived all over North America. Their lifestyles varied depending on their local landscapes. Many Native Americans still carry on the traditions of their ancestors.

Far West Native Americans in the Far West relied on the sea for food.

Desert West In the Desert West, Native Americans dealt with their dry, rocky environment by building their homes into the sides of cliffs.

134 CHAPTER 5

Map labels: Bering Sea, Inuit, Ingalik, Aleut, Saschutkenne, Beaver, Haida, Nootka, Chinook, Columbia, Blackfoot, Walla Walla, Nez Percé, Crow, Northern Paiute, Modoc, Cheyenne, Northern Shoshone, PACIFIC OCEAN, Western Shoshone, Miwok, Ute, Hopi (Pueblo), Apache, Chumash, Navajo, Mohave, Zuni, Apache, Yaqui, Tarahumara, MESOAMERICA, ROCKY MOUNTAINS, Plains Cree

Differentiating Instruction

Struggling Readers
Below Level

To help struggling readers, have them look at the images in the feature. Read aloud the introduction and each caption. As you do, have students talk about what they see in the images and how they correspond to the areas on the map.

LS Verbal/Linguistic

▤ Alternative Assessment Handbook, Rubric 11: Discussions

Special Needs Learners
At Level

Have students discuss how Native Americans depended on natural resources. Have them talk about how difficult it would be to only use materials found where they lived. Suggest that they give several examples of what would have been available to Native Americans living in their region. **LS** Verbal/Linguistic

▤ Alternative Assessment Handbook, Rubric 11: Discussions

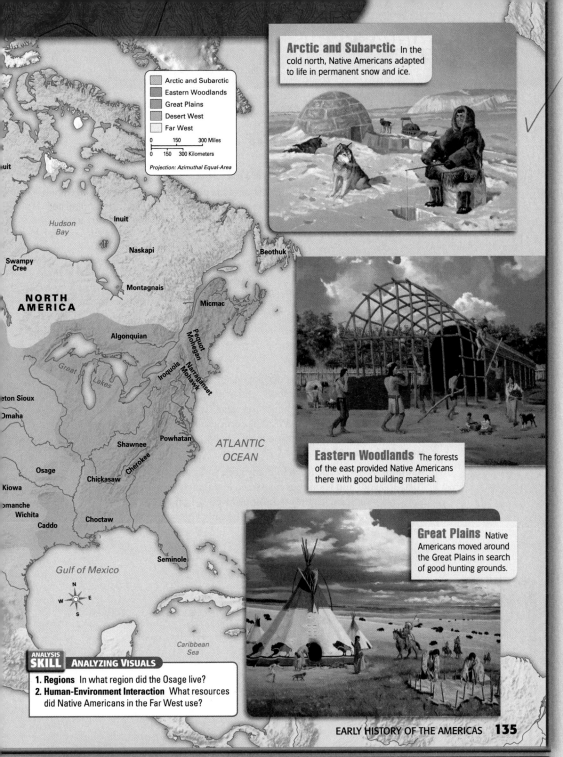

Arctic and Subarctic In the cold north, Native Americans adapted to life in permanent snow and ice.

Eastern Woodlands The forests of the east provided Native Americans there with good building material.

Great Plains Native Americans moved around the Great Plains in search of good hunting grounds.

Arctic and Subarctic
Eastern Woodlands
Great Plains
Desert West
Far West

0   150   300 Miles
0   150   300 Kilometers
Projection: Azimuthal Equal-Area

Hudson Bay

Inuit

Naskapi

Beothuk

Montagnais

Micmac

NORTH AMERICA

Algonquian

Great Lakes

Pequot
Mohegan

Iroquois

Narraganset
Mohawk

eton Sioux

Omaha

Shawnee

Powhatan

ATLANTIC OCEAN

Osage

Chickasaw

Cherokee

Kiowa

omanche

Wichita

Caddo

Choctaw

Seminole

Gulf of Mexico

N
W   E
S

Caribbean Sea

ANALYSIS SKILL   ANALYZING VISUALS

1. **Regions** In what region did the Osage live?
2. **Human-Environment Interaction** What resources did Native Americans in the Far West use?

EARLY HISTORY OF THE AMERICAS **135**

Geography and History

Info to Know

Inuit Igloos The Inuit in the Arctic lived in different kinds of dwellings, including tents, huts, and igloos. Igloos are winter snow houses made from blocks of snow formed in the shape of a dome. A hole in the top of the dome provided ventilation, and the walls were sometimes insulated with animal skins. The only furniture in a traditional igloo was a sleeping platform, a lamp for burning fuel, and a cooking rack and pot. The temperature inside an igloo was usually just above freezing.

Connect to Economics

Trading Currency Early Native Americans and First Nations, as Native Americans in Canada are called, prized wampum beads. Wampum is made from shells found along the Atlantic coast. Native Americans, such as the Algonquian, would grind the raw materials into beads and then string them into belts and bracelets. Wampum became valuable because grinding the shells took a lot of time and labor, and the shells were only available to coastal tribes. Wampum belts were originally used as tribal records, to commemorate special events, or as gifts. In time, wampum became a form of money. The Dutch began to use wampum as currency at their trading stations. They bought wampum from the Algonquians, brought it up the Hudson River, and traded it at fur-trading posts.

Collaborative Learning

At Level

Researching Villages

Research Required

1. Have students work in small groups to research what early Native American villages looked like.

2. Have students begin by looking at the illustrations in their text. Then have each group brainstorm words and phrases that describe the illustrations.

3. Ask students to use Internet or library sources to find out what Native American villages looked like and the ways in which different Native America groups interacted.

4. Have groups report their findings to the entire class. Encourage students to draw or illustrate what different villages may have looked like.

LS Interpersonal, Verbal/Linguistic, Visual/Spatial

Alternative Assessment Handbook, Rubric 30: Research

Answers

Analyzing Visuals 1. *Great Plains;*
2. *the sea, the forest*

135

Social Studies Skills

Analyzing Information
Activity Create an Outline

Materials: one newspaper or magazine article for each student

1. Provide students with a newspaper or magazine article.

2. Tell students that they will create an outline of the article's main idea and supporting details.

3. Have students read the articles. Ask them to write the main idea on a piece of paper in outline form. Under the main idea, ask students to write down all of the details that support the main idea.

4. When they have finished, ask students to swap outlines with one another. Ask them to provide an oral summary of the other student's article based on their partner's outline.
LS Verbal/Linguistic

Alternative Assessment Handbook, Rubrics 24: Oral Presentations

Interactive Skills Tutor CD-ROM, Lesson 14: Identify Main Ideas and Supporting Details

RF: Social Studies Skills, Analyzing Information

Answers

Practice 1. *Main Idea: The Maya developed an advanced form of writing that used many symbols. Supporting details: They recorded information on large stone monuments; the Maya also made books of paper made from the bark of fig trees.* **2.** *Unnecessary information: Our writing system uses 26 letters; some early civilizations drew pictures on cave walls; fig trees need a lot of light.*

Apply 1. *The Maya believed in many gods and goddesses* **2.** *More than 160 gods and goddesses are named in a single Maya manuscript. Among the gods they worshipped were a corn god, a rain god, a sun god, and a moon goddess.* **3.** *The early Greeks also worshipped many gods and goddesses.*

136

Analyzing Information

Learn

An important skill to learn is analyzing information presented in the text you read. One way to do this is to identify main ideas and supporting details. Everything in the paragraph should support the main idea.

After you identify the main idea, watch out for anything that is not related to it or necessary for its understanding. Don't let that extra information distract you from the most important material.

Practice

Look at the paragraph on this page about communication in the Maya civilization. Some unrelated and unnecessary information has been added so that you can learn to identify it. Use the paragraph to answer the questions here.

1 Which sentence expresses the main idea? What details support it?

2 What information is unnecessary or unrelated to the main idea?

> ### The Maya
>
> **Communication** The Maya developed an advanced form of writing that used many symbols. Our writing system uses 26 letters. They recorded information on large stone monuments. Some early civilizations drew pictures on cave walls. The Maya also made books of paper made from the bark of fig trees. Fig trees need a lot of light.
>
> **Religion** The Maya believed in many gods and goddesses. More than 160 gods and goddesses are named in a single Maya manuscript. Among the gods they worshipped were a corn god, a rain god, a sun god, and a moon goddess. The early Greeks also worshipped many gods and goddesses.

Apply

Use the passage on this page about Maya religion to answer the following questions.

1. What is the main idea of the paragraph?
2. What details support the main idea?
3. What information is unnecessary or unrelated?

136 CHAPTER 5

Social Studies Skills Activity: Analyzing Information
Below Level

Struggling Readers

Materials: copies of a short newspaper article

1. Have students read a short newspaper article.

2. Ask students to read the first paragraph of the article. Ask them what the main idea is.

3. Go through the article and ask each student to provide one supporting detail. Continue until they have gone through the entire article.
LS Verbal/Linguistic

Alternative Assessment Handbook, Rubric 16: Judging Information

Special Needs Students

Materials: copies of one short newspaper article

1. Pass out copies of the newspaper article.

2. Draw a large concept map on the board.

3. Read the article aloud and ask students to help fill in the concept map with the main idea in the middle circle and supporting details in the outer circles. Continue until the article is complete. Discuss the process with the students. LS Verbal/Linguistic

Alternative Assessment Handbook, Rubric 16: Judging Information

Chapter Review

Geography's Impact
video series
Review the video to answer the closing question:
How do archaeologists know the Maya built their pyramids without the aid of metal tools?

Visual Summary

Use the visual summary below to help you review the main ideas of the chapter.

QUICK FACTS

The Maya
The Maya traded valuable goods like jade along trade routes that linked their great cities.

The Aztecs
The Aztec capital, Tenochtitlán, was a huge, bustling city. People came to its marketplace from all over the empire.

The Incas
The Incas are known for their organized empire, impressive stonework, and crafts in gold and silver.

Reviewing Vocabulary, Terms, and Places

For each statement below, write T if it is true and F if it is false. If the statement is false, replace the underlined term with one that would make the sentence a true statement.

1. The main crops of the Maya included **maize** and beans.
2. The **Quechua** came to the Americas to find land, gold, and converts to Catholicism.
3. **Palenque**, located on a swampy island, was the capital of the Aztec Empire.
4. Maya priests studied the sun, moon, and stars from stone **observatories**.
5. The official language of the Inca Empire was **Cuzco**.
6. The Aztecs built raised roads called **masonry** to cross from Tenochtitlán to the mainland.
7. **Tenochtitlán** was the Inca capital.
8. Many people in Mesoamerica died at the hands of the **conquistadors**.

Comprehension and Critical Thinking

SECTION 1 *(Pages 118–123)*

9. **a. Recall** Where did the Maya live, and when was their Classic Age?

   b. Analyze What was the connection between Maya religion and astronomy? How do you think this connection influenced Maya achievements?

   c. Elaborate Why did Maya cities trade with each other? Why did they fight?

SECTION 2 *(Pages 124–128)*

10. **a. Describe** What was Tenochtitlán like? Where was it located?

    b. Make Inferences Why do you think warriors had many privileges and were such respected members of Aztec society?

EARLY HISTORY OF THE AMERICAS **137**

Answers

Visual Summary

Review and Inquiry Use the visual summary to review the chapter's main ideas about the Maya, Aztecs, and Incas. Ask students to explain the significance of each main idea.

📺 Quick Facts Transparency: Early History of the Americas Visual Summary

Reviewing Vocabulary, Terms, and Places

1. T
2. F; conquistadors
3. F; Tenochtitlán
4. T
5. F; Quechua
6. F; causeways
7. F; Cuzco
8. T

Comprehension and Critical Thinking

9. **a.** Northern Guatemala and the Yucatán Peninsula; AD 250 to 900
   b. Their priests studied the stars to plan the best times for religious festivals; they used the knowledge they gained about astronomy to develop a calendar that helped guide farming activities.
   c. to get goods not available locally; for power and new farmland

10. **a.** magnificent city with 200,000 people, chinampas, huge temples, a busy market, and a grand palace; on an island in Lake Texcoco
    b. War, tribute, and human sacrifices were important to Aztec power, and warriors were responsible for all these things.

Review and Assessment Resources

Review and Reinforce

SE Chapter Review

📋 **RF:** Chapter Review

📺 Quick Facts Transparency: Early History of the Americas Visual Summary

🔊 Spanish Chapter Summaries Audio CD Program

TOS Holt McDougal PuzzleView®; Quiz Show for ExamView

💿 Quiz Game CD-ROM

Assess

SE Standardized Test Practice

📋 PASS: Chapter Test, Forms A and B

📋 Alternative Assessment Handbook

TOS ExamView Test Generator, Chapter Test

💿 Differentiated Instruction Modified Worksheets and Tests CD-ROM: Chapter Test

🔲 Online Assessment Program, in the Interactive Student Edition

Reteach/Intervene

📋 Guided Reading Workbook

📋 Differentiated Instruction Teacher Management System: Lesson Plans

💿 Differentiated Instruction Modified Worksheets and Tests CD-ROM

💿 Interactive Skills Tutor CD-ROM

🔲 hmhsocialstudies.com
Chapter Resources

10. **c.** possible answers—alliances, weapons and horses, geography, and disease. Students should give reasons for their answers.

11. **a.** Pachacuti—expanded the Inca Empire, rebuilt Cuzco, and established an official Inca religion; Atahualpa—fought Huáscar to claim the throne, was captured and killed by Francisco Pizarro
b. the empire's long, narrow shape, high Andes, coastal deserts, many different peoples and languages within the empire
c. possible answers—appreciated, because they knew the government would take care of them; resented, because they had no freedom

Using the Internet

12. Go to **hmhsocialstudies.com** to access a rubric for this activity.

Social Studies Skills

13. Cacao trees are evergreens.

Map Activity

14. **A.** Palenque
B. Cuzco
C. Tenochtitlán

Focus on Reading and Writing

15. Students' descriptions should reflect an understanding of various aspects of Mayan civilization.

📄 **RF: Focus on Reading, Setting a Purpose**

16. **Rubric** Students' articles should
- specifically describe what travelers to these areas will see and experience
- make a connection between the attractions and the history and culture
- use persuasive language
- talk about attractions related to the Maya, Incas, and Aztecs

📄 **RF: Focus on Writing, Writing a Newspaper Article**

SECTION 2 (continued)
c. Evaluate What factor do you think played the biggest role in the Aztecs' defeat? Defend your answer.

SECTION 3 (Pages 129–133)
11. **a. Identify** Name two Inca leaders and explain their roles in Inca history.
b. Draw Conclusions What geographic and cultural problems did the Incas overcome to rule their empire?
c. Elaborate Do you think most people in the Inca Empire appreciated or resented the *mita* system? Explain your answer.

Using the Internet 🌐

12. **Activity: Making Diagrams** In this chapter you learned about the rise and fall of the Maya, Aztecs, and Incas. Through your online textbook, track the rise and fall of empires in the Americas. Then create a diagram that shows the factors that cause empires to form and the factors that cause empires to fall apart.

 hmhsocialstudies.com

Social Studies Skills

Analyzing Information *In the passage below, the first sentence expresses the main idea. One of the following sentences is nonessential to the main idea. Identify the nonessential sentence.*

13. Cacao beans had great value to the Maya. Cacao trees are evergreens. They were the source of chocolate, known as a favorite food of rulers and the gods. The Maya also used cacao beans as money.

Map Activity 🌐

14. **Early History of the Americas** On a separate sheet of paper, match the letters on the map with their correct labels.

Palenque   Tenochtitlán
Cuzco

↗ **hmhsocialstudies.com** **INTERACTIVE MAP**

map zone

FOCUS ON READING AND WRITING

15. **Setting a Purpose** Look back over the information about the Maya in Section 1. For each blue heading, write down the purpose of reading that text. Then describe how reading the text below each heading achieves your purpose.

16. **Writing Your Article** Now that you have collected information about the Americas, you are ready to write a newspaper article. Your purpose is to inform readers in Europe about these fascinating civilizations. Write a headline or title and a two- or three-sentence introduction to the civilizations. Then write a short paragraph about one aspect of each civilization. Choose the most interesting topic to discuss. For example, you might discuss their religion, their social structure, or their scientific achievements.

DIRECTIONS: Read questions 1 through 6 and write the letter of the best response. Then read question 7 and write your own well-constructed response.

1 Maya, Aztec, and Inca societies were similar in many ways. Which of the following practices was common to all three civilizations?

  A developing calendars

  B keeping written historical records

  C building stone temples

  D practicing slavery

2 Farming was important to the Maya, the Aztecs, and the Incas. Which of the following statements about farming is false?

  A The Maya grew crops on *chinampas*.

  B Farmers in all three civilizations grew maize, but only the Incas raised llamas.

  C Maya farmers might not have been able to produce enough food to feed the entire population.

  D Maya and Aztec priests decided the best times to plant and harvest.

3 Which of the following factors helped the Spanish to conquer the Aztecs and the Incas?

  A a greater number of soldiers

  B superior weapons

  C surprise attacks

  D good knowledge of the land

4 Which of the following was a possible reason for the decline of Maya civilization?

  A increased warfare and lack of good farmland

  B the arrival of Spanish conquistadors and spread of disease

  C the development and misuse of guns

  D floods that destroyed crops and cities

Early Civilizations of the Americas

5 The Aztec and Inca empires are indicated on the map above by

  A X for the Inca and Y for the Aztec.

  B Y for the Aztec and Z for the Inca.

  C Y for the Inca and Z for the Aztec.

  D X for the Aztec and Z for the Inca.

6 Which statement *best* describes the social structure in Maya, Aztec, and Inca civilizations?

  A The ruler held the highest position in society, and merchants held the lowest.

  B The Aztecs had a simpler class structure than the Maya or the Incas.

  C Social divisions were very important to the Maya and the Aztecs, but power and wealth were equally distributed in the Inca Empire.

  D Social class helped shape daily life, with the upper class enjoying special privileges made possible by the labor of the common people.

7 **Extended Response** Use the map above and your knowledge of the Maya and Aztecs to write a brief essay comparing and contrasting the two civilizations. Be sure to discuss the physical geography, achievements, and decline of both civilizations.

EARLY HISTORY OF THE AMERICAS **139**

Standardized Test Prep

1. C
Break Down the Question Point out that the Inca kept no written records and did not practice slavery, and only the Maya developed calendars.

2. A
Break Down the Question This question requires students to recall factual information. Refer students who missed it to Section 2.

3. B
Break Down the Question Point out that all but one of the answers was a factor in the defeat of the Aztecs. There were fewer Spanish soldiers, though, than Aztec soldiers.

4. A
Break Down the Question Refer students who miss the question to coverage of the decline of Maya civilization at the end of Section 1.

5. D
Break Down the Question Refer students who miss the question to the maps in Sections 2 and 3. The area marked Y on the map was the area controlled by the Maya.

6. D
Break Down the Question This question requires students to recall factual information. Refer students who miss the question to coverage of daily life in Sections 1, 2, and 3.

7. Extended Response Students' answers should include the following:

• Maya—central Mexico to northern Central America; Aztecs—central Mexico

• Maya—built grand buildings and pyramids, built canals and terraced land for farming, developed calendars, number systems, and writing systems; Aztecs—built an island city and created floating gardens, built causeways and canals, developed a calendar, kept written records

• Maya civilization may have declined because of rebellion against rulers, increased warfare between cities, lack of food, and climate change; Aztecs fell to the Spanish.

Reteach/Intervention Resources

Reproducible

- Guided Reading Workbook
- Differentiated Instruction Teacher Management System: Lesson Plans

Technology

- Quick Facts Transparency: Early History of the Americas Visual Summary
- Differentiated Instruction Modified Worksheets and Tests CD-ROM
- Interactive Skills Tutor CD-ROM

Tips for Test Taking

I'm Stuck! If students come across a question that stumps them, tell them not to get frustrated or worried. Remind them to master the question to make sure they understand what is being asked. Then instruct students to go through the list of test-taking strategies they have learned. If still stuck, they should practice the 50/50 strategy and make their best educated guess.

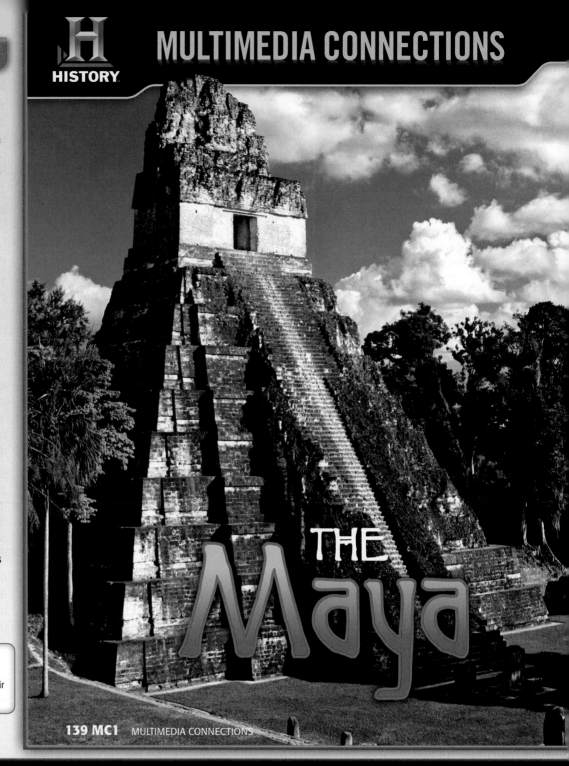

HISTORY MULTIMEDIA CONNECTIONS

THE Maya

The **HISTORY**™ Multimedia **Classroom** is a set of exciting new social studies teaching tools featuring award-winning program content. These comprehensive lesson plans, correlated to individual state and national curriculum standards, are easy to use for both teachers and students.

Each lesson contains the following:
• Short video segments that bring history topics to life
• Maps and visual materials
• Discussion and review questions
• Easily printable primary source documents
• Classroom activities and Internet-based activity links

The Multimedia Classroom has been specially designed to be versatile and easily adaptable to existing courses, lesson plans, and syllabi. Every lesson is designed to offer maximum flexibility. Teachers can select entire plans or only the elements they need, allowing them to individually tailor each lesson. Each multimedia lesson is available in CD-ROM format and is accompanied by full-length award-winning programs on DVD from HISTORY™.

For more information or to purchase go to ⬀ hmhsocialstudies.com

Because some of these lessons may contain video material of a sensitive nature, we recommend that teachers and parents review these materials in their entirety before showing them to students.

The Maya

Resources ⬀ hmhsocialstudies.com

The following resources come with printable introductions, comprehension and critical thinking questions, transcripts, and vocabulary support.

Full Length DVD

The Maya (50 minutes)

Video Clips

• Who Were the Maya People? (1:43)
• The Beginnings of Maya Life (2:29)
• Finding the City of Palenque (2:37)
• The Builders of Palenque (2:38)
• Destroying the Maya's Past (1:47)
• The Mystery in the Temple (3:59)
• Inside King Pakal's Tomb (3:04)
• Tomb of an Unknown Woman (6:12)
• A Civilization Abandoned (3:29)
• Descendants of the Maya (2:09)

Primary Sources

• The Quiche Popol Vuh
• Chumayel Chilam Balam (i)
• Chumayel Chilam Balam (ii)
• Burial Remains from Tikal

The Maya developed one of the most advanced civilizations in the Americas, but their story is shrouded in mystery. Around A.D. 250, the Maya began to build great cities in southern Mexico and Central America. They developed a writing system, practiced astronomy, and built magnificent palaces and pyramids with little more than stone tools. Around A.D. 900, however, the Maya abandoned their cities, leaving their monuments to be reclaimed by the jungle and, for a time, forgotten.

Explore some of the incredible monuments and cultural achievements of the ancient Maya online. You can find a wealth of information, video clips, primary sources, and more at
hmhsocialstudies.com.

"Thus let it be done! Let the emptiness be filled! Let the water recede and make a void, let the earth appear and become solid; let it be done ... "Earth!" they said, and instantly it was made."

The Popol Vuh
Read the document to learn how the Maya believed the world was created.

Destroying the Maya's Past
Watch the video to learn how the actions of one Spanish missionary nearly destroyed the written record of the Maya world.

Finding the City of Palenque
Watch the video to learn about the great Maya city of Palenque and the European discovery of the site in the eighteenth century.

Pakal's Tomb
Watch the video to explore how the discovery of the tomb of a great king helped archaeologists piece together the Maya past.

THE MAYA **139 MC2**

The Popol Vuh

The Popol Vuh tells the Maya creation story. In 1702, the Spanish priest Francisco Ximenez discovered the most complete Popol Vuh manuscript. The text is an invaluable resource for historians and linguists.

Destroying the Maya's Past

The Maya had a sophisticated writing system. However, the language of the Maya fell victim to colonizing forces. Spanish missionaries attempted to put an end to all non-Christian practices of the Maya by destroying all their written documents. Only four Maya manuscripts survived and they have proved invaluable to scholars.

Finding the City of Palenque

The Maya civilization flourished for more than 600 years in the jungles of what are now Mexico, Guatemala, Honduras, Belize, and El Salvador. Yet, at some point around the 10th century, the Maya abandoned their cities. It was not until the late 18th century that Palenque, one of the Maya's most important cities, was rediscovered by archaeologists.

Pakal's Tomb

At Palenque, archaeologist Alberto Ruz Lhuillier and his team discovered an elaborately decorated tomb. At first, they could only guess that the figure buried there was of great importance. Later, they discovered that the figure was Pakal, one of the Maya's greatest kings.

Maps
• Palenque Site Plan

Activities
• At Home in the Rainforest
• Centers of the Maya World
• Opposite Sides of the Globe
• The Measurement of Time

General Review Questions

General Discussion Questions

Web Links

Bibliography

Chapter 6 Planning Guide

Mexico

Overview	Instructional Resources	

CHAPTER 6

Essential Question: What are the major physical, cultural, and economic features of Mexico?

🔊 **Focus on the Essential Question Podcast**

TOS Differentiated Instruction Teacher Management System:
- Instructional Pacing Guides
- Lesson Plans for Differentiated Instruction

Guided Reading Workbook

Resource File:
- Chapter Review
- Focus on Reading: Predicting
- Focus on Writing: Writing an "I Am" Poem
- Social Studies Skills: Taking Notes

Experiencing World History and Geography

TOS Calendar Planner
- **Power Presentations with Media Gallery**
- **Differentiated Instruction Modified Worksheets and Tests CD-ROM**
- **Interactive Skills Tutor CD-ROM**
- **Student Edition on Audio CD-ROM**
- **The World's Music Audio Program**
- **Map Zone Transparency:** Mexico: Political
- **World Outline Maps: Transparencies and Activities**
- **Video:** Mexico's Ancient Civilizations
- **Multimedia Connections** Mexico: Conquest and Courage

Section 1:

Physical Geography

The Big Idea: Mexico is a large country with different natural environments in its northern, central, and southern regions.

TOS Differentiated Instruction Teacher Management System: Section 1 Lesson Plan

Guided Reading Workbook: Section 1

Resource File:
- Vocabulary Builder: Section 1

- **Daily Bellringer Transparency:** Section 1
- **Map Zone Transparency:** Mexico: Physical
- **Map Zone Transparency:** Mexico: Climate

Section 2:

History and Culture

The Big Idea: Native American cultures and Spanish colonization shaped Mexican history and culture.

TOS Differentiated Instruction Teacher Management System: Section 2 Lesson Plan

Guided Reading Workbook: Section 2

Resource File:
- Vocabulary Builder: Section 2
- Biography: Sor Juana Inés de la Cruz
- Biography: Miguel Hidalgo
- Geography and History: Hernán Cortés and the Aztec Empire
- Geography for Life: Female Pioneers
- Interdisciplinary Project: Create a Mural

- **Daily Bellringer Transparency:** Section 2
- **Internet Activity:** Mexican Revolution
- **Animated Geography:** Early Cultures of Mexico
- **Animated Geography:** Chinampas
- **Video:** The Peasant Revolution

Section 3:

Mexico Today

The Big Idea: Mexico has four culture regions that all play a part in the country's government and economy.

TOS Differentiated Instruction Teacher Management System: Section 3 Lesson Plan

Guided Reading Workbook: Section 3

Resource File:
- Vocabulary Builder: Section 3
- Critical Thinking: Mexico's Expanding Capital
- Literature: from *Itinerary* by Octavio Paz
- Primary Source: 1917 Constitution of Mexico

- **Daily Bellringer Transparency:** Section 3
- **Map Zone Transparency:** Mexico's Culture Regions
- **Video:** Mexico in the Modern Era

Chart Key:

 SE Student Edition

 Presentation Resource

 MP3 Audio

TOS Teacher One Stop

 DVD/CD-ROM

HISTORY™

 Printable Resource

Program Resources available on **TOS** and @ **hmhsocialstudies.com**

Review, Assessment, Intervention

 The Americas Transparencies: Mexico Visual Summary

 Spanish Chapter Summaries Audio CD

 Progress Assessment Support System (PASS): Chapter Test

 Differentiated Instruction Modified Worksheets and Tests CD-ROM: Modified Chapter Test

 TOS **ExamView® Assessment Suite (English/Spanish)**

 Alternative Assessment Handbook

 Online Assessment Program, in the Interactive Student Edition

 PASS: Section 1 Quiz

 Online Quiz: Section 1

Alternative Assessment Handbook

 PASS: Section 2 Quiz

 Online Quiz: Section 2

 Alternative Assessment Handbook

 PASS: Section 3 Quiz

 Online Quiz: Section 3

Alternative Assessment Handbook

Supporting Resources

HISTORY.

- Multimedia Classroom Global History Series
- Global History Series Teacher's Guide

Maps Globes Graphs Level F

- Student Workbook
- Teacher's Guide

Social Studies Trade Library Collections

- NCSS Middle School Trade Collection
- Latino Trade Collection

Geography's Impact

The Americas Video Program

- **Impact of Emigration**

For more information or to purchase go to **hmhsocialstudies.com**

Power Presentations with Media Gallery

Power Presentations with Media Gallery are visual presentations of each chapter's main ideas. Presentations can be customized by including Quick Facts charts, images from the text, and video clips.

Differentiating Instruction

How do I address the needs of varied learners?

The Target Resource acts as your primary strategy for differentiated instruction.

ENGLISH-LANGUAGE LEARNERS & STRUGGLING READERS

Interactive Skills Tutor CD-ROM

The Interactive Skills Tutor CD-ROM contains lessons that provide additional practice for 20 different critical thinking skills.

Additional Resources

Differentiated Instruction Teacher Management System: Lesson Plans for Differentiated Instruction

Resource File:
- Vocabulary Builder Activities
- Social Studies Skills: Taking Notes

The Americas Transparencies:
- Mexico Visual Summary

Student Edition on Audio CD Program

Spanish/English Guided Reading Workbook

Spanish Chapter Summaries Audio CD

Teacher's One Stop:
- ExamView Test Generator, Spanish
- PuzzlePro, Spanish

English-Language Learner Strategies and Activities

SPECIAL NEEDS LEARNERS

Differentiated Instruction Teacher Management System

Lesson Plans for Differentiated Instruction provide teachers with strategies to help plan instruction for all learners.

Additional Resources

Guided Reading Workbook

Resource File: Social Studies Skills: Taking Notes

Student Edition on Audio CD Program

Interactive Skills Tutor CD-ROM

Graphic Organizer Transparencies with Support for Reading and Writing

ADVANCED/GIFTED AND TALENTED STUDENTS

Resource File

The Resource File activities allow students to extend their knowledge of chapter-related places and people and to practice geography skills.
- Focus on Reading: Predicting
- Focus on Writing: Writing an "I Am" Poem
- Literature: from *Itinerary* by Octavio Paz

Additional Resources

Differentiated Instruction Teacher Management System: Lesson Plans for Differentiated Instruction

World History and Geography Document-Based Questions Activities

Geography, Science, and Cultures Activities

Experiencing World History and Geography

Differentiated Activities in the Teacher's Edition

- Reading Maps, p. 143
- Using Words and Illustrations to Describe Cultures, p. 147
- Making an Outline, p. 151
- Reading Before Listening, p. 155
- Creating a Poster About a Mexican City, p. 155

Teacher One Stop™

How can I manage the lesson plans and support materials for differentiated instruction?

With the Teacher One Stop, you can easily organize and print lesson plans, planning guides, and instructional materials for all learners. The Teacher One Stop includes the following materials to help you differentiate instruction:

- Interactive Teacher's Edition
- Calendar Planner and pacing guides
- Editable lesson plans
- All reproducible ancillaries in Adobe Acrobat (PDF) format
- ExamView Assessment Suite (English & Spanish)
- Transparency and video previews

Differentiated Activities in the Teacher's Edition

- Analyzing and Describing Murals, p. 148

Interactive Student Edition

Complete online student edition with interactive multimedia support for chapter content assessment and reporting

- Interactive Maps and Notebook
- Standardized Test Prep
- Online Homework Practice and Research Activities
- Current Events
- Chapter-based Internet Activities
- Animated Geography Activities

Differentiated Activities in the Teacher's Edition

- Using Resources, p. 143
- Researching Maquiladoras, p. 155

DIFFERENTIATED INSTRUCTION PLANNING GUIDE

Essential Question

Introduce the Essential Question

- Point out that, because the United States and Mexico share a border, we share some of the same physical environments. Explain that Mexico generally has warmer and more tropical environments than the United States because it is located farther south.

- Ask students what languages are spoken in Mexico. Use their responses to introduce how the country's cultural geography was shaped by Spanish contact.

- Point out that the economies of Mexico and the United States are closely connected. Invite students to give examples of these connections and infer what the connections might indicate about Mexico's economy.

Focus on Reading and Writing

Reading The Resource File provides a worksheet to help students practice predicting.

📄 **RF:** Focus on Reading, Predicting

Writing The Resource File provides a worksheet to help students plan and write their poems.

📄 **RF:** Focus on Writing, Writing an "I am" Poem

Key to Differentiating Instruction

Below Level

Basic-level activities designed for all students encountering new material

At Level

Intermediate-level activities designed for average students

Above Level

Challenging activities designed for honors and gifted and talented students

Standard English Mastery

Activities designed to improve standard English usage

LS Learning Styles

Mexico

Essential Question What are the major physical, cultural, and economic features of Mexico?

❓ What You Will Learn...

In this chapter you will learn about Mexico's physical geography. You will also study the influence of early cultures and Spanish colonial history on Mexico's culture. Today, Mexico is experiencing many changes in its government and economy.

FOCUS ON READING AND WRITING

Predicting Predicting is trying to guess what will happen next. As you read a chapter, stop along the way and consider what you have read. Does the text provide any clues about what will happen next? If it does, see if you can make a prediction about the text. **See the lesson, Predicting, on page 521.**

Writing an "I Am" Poem Countries have stories to tell, just like people do. As you read this chapter, gather details about Mexico—how it looks, what its history was like, and what it is like today. Then write an "I Am" poem from the point of view of Mexico telling what you have learned.

map zone

Geography Skills

Location Mexico is located just south of the United States.

1. **Locate** What is the absolute location of Mexico's capital?
2. **Make Inferences** Do you think Tijuana or Mérida is more influenced by the United States? Why?

Culture Brightly costumed dancers perform a traditional dance in Cancún.

Introduce the Chapter

At Level

Share What You Know

1. Ask students to share what they already know about Mexico from other classes, the news, or other sources. Tell them that this chapter will help them learn more about Mexico.

2. Guide students in an overview of the chapter by looking at the photos and reading the captions as a class. Encourage students to share any additional information that they may have about what they see in the photos or captions. Students may also comment on information that is new to them, that they

find especially interesting, or that they don't understand.

3. Have students keep track of topics in the chapter that are of special interest to them. Encourage them to read other material on these topics outside of class so that they can share what they learned when the topic is covered in class.

LS Verbal/Linguistic, Visual/Spatial

📄 Alternative Assessment Handbook, Rubric 14: Group Activity

↗ hmhsocialstudies.com **VIDEO**

Mexico's Ancient Civilizations

Gulf of Mexico

National capital
Other cities

0   100   300 Miles
0   100   200 Kilometers
Projection: Lambert Conformal Conic

25°N

Tropic of Cancer

UNITED STATES

Ciudad Juárez

hihuahua

Rio Grande

Monterrey

MEXICO

Guadalajara

Rio Lerma

Balsas River

Mexico City
Puebla

Veracruz

Oaxaca

Acapulco

Bay of Campeche

Yucatán Channel

Mérida   Cancún
Cozumel Island

20°N

Caribbean Sea

Usumacinta R.

Grijalva River

Gulf of Tehuantepec

CENTRAL AMERICA

105°W   100°W   M-96

Geography
Much of Mexico's landscape is dry, with high plateaus and mountains.

History The Spanish brought Christianity to Mexico and built churches like this one.

141

Explore the Map and Pictures

Mexico: Political Mexico is bordered by the United States to the north and by Guatemala and Belize to the south. It is a federal republic, with 31 states and one federal district. In 2000, Mexico's population numbered approximately 97.5 million. Its biggest cities are Mexico City, Guadalajara, and Monterrey.

Analyzing Visuals How can you tell from the picture of the church that religion was important to the Spanish? *The churches were very large, elaborate, and probably expensive to build.* What kind of vegetation do you think covers most of Mexico? *plants that need little water to survive, such as cacti and shrubs, since much of Mexico's landscape is dry*

▶ Map Zone Transparency: Mexico: Political

↗ hmhsocialstudies.com
Teacher Resources

Info to Know

History After the conquest of Mexico in 1521, the Spanish destroyed manyIndian temples and, in some cases, used their stones to build Catholic churches. Some churches were even built on top of pyramids, with the pyramids serving as a base. The widest pyramid in the world, the Great Pyramid of Cholula, located near the city of Puebla, has a colonial church at its top.

Other People, Other Places

Mexico's Border Mexico shares a border with these U.S. states: Texas, New Mexico, Arizona, and California. These states, in whole or in part, were part of Mexico until the Mexican-American War, which began in 1846. Mexico lost that war in 1848 and gave up almost half of its land to the United States for a sum of $15 million. This included parts of modern-day Texas, Colorado, Arizona, New Mexico, and Wyoming. It also included the entire states of California, Nevada, and Utah.

Answers

Map Zone 1. *approximately 20° North, 100° West;* **2.** *Tijuana, because it is closer to the United States*

142 CHAPTER 6

Preteach

Bellringer

If YOU lived there. . . Use the **Daily Bellringer Transparency** to help students answer the question.

▶ Daily Bellringer Transparency, Section 1

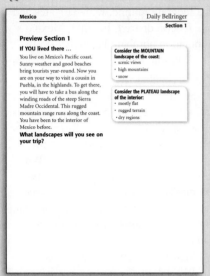

| Mexico | Daily Bellringer Section 1 |

Preview Section 1

If YOU lived there ...

You live on Mexico's Pacific coast. Sunny weather and good beaches bring tourists year-round. Now you are on your way to visit a cousin in Puebla, in the highlands. To get there, you will have to take a bus along the winding roads of the steep Sierra Madre Occidental. This rugged mountain range runs along the coast. You have been to the interior of Mexico before.

What landscapes will you see on your trip?

Consider the MOUNTAIN landscape of the coast:
• scenic views
• high mountains
• snow

Consider the PLATEAU landscape of the interior:
• mostly flat
• rugged terrain
• dry regions

Academic Vocabulary

Review with students the high-use academic term in this section.

vary to be different (p. 144)

📝 RF: Vocabulary Builder, Section 1

Taking Notes

Have students use the graphic organizer online to take notes on the section. This activity will prepare students for the Section Assessment, in which they will complete a graphic organizer that builds on the information using the Critical Thinking Skill: Categorizing.

Physical Geography

What You Will Learn...

Main Ideas

1. Mexico's physical features include plateaus, mountains, and coastal lowlands.
2. Mexico's climate and vegetation include deserts, tropical forests, and cool highlands.
3. Key natural resources in Mexico include oil, silver, gold, and scenic landscapes.

The Big Idea

Mexico is a large country with different natural environments in its northern, central, and southern regions.

Key Terms and Places

Río Bravo (Rio Grande), *p. 142*
peninsula, *p. 142*
Baja California, *p. 142*
Gulf of Mexico, *p. 142*
Yucatán Peninsula, *p. 142*
Sierra Madre, *p. 143*

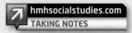

hmhsocialstudies.com
TAKING NOTES

Use the graphic organizer online to organize your notes on Mexico's physical geography.

If **YOU** lived there...

You live on Mexico's Pacific coast. Sunny weather and good beaches bring tourists year-round. Now you are on your way to visit a cousin in Puebla, in the highlands. To get there, you will have to take a bus along the winding roads of the steep Sierra Madre Occidental. This rugged mountain range runs along the coast. You have never been to the interior of Mexico before.

What landscapes will you see on your trip?

BUILDING BACKGROUND Mexico is part of Latin America, a region in the Western Hemisphere where Spanish and Portuguese culture shaped life. Mexico is also part of North America, along with the United States and Canada. Unlike its northern neighbors, Mexico's landscape consists mainly of highlands and coastal plains.

Physical Features

Mexico, our neighbor to the south, shares a long border with the United States. Forming part of this border is one of Mexico's few major rivers, the **Río Bravo**. In the United States this river is called the Rio Grande. At other places along the U.S.–Mexico border it is impossible to tell where one country ends and the other country begins.

Bodies of Water

As you can see on the map, except for its border with the United States, Mexico is mostly surrounded by water. Mexico's border in the west is the Pacific Ocean. Stretching south into the Pacific Ocean from northern Mexico is a narrow **peninsula**, or piece of land surrounded on three sides by water, called **Baja California**. To the east, Mexico's border is the **Gulf of Mexico**. The Gulf of Mexico is separated from the Caribbean Sea by a part of Mexico called the **Yucatán** (yoo-kah-TAHN) **Peninsula**.

142 CHAPTER 6

Teach the Big Idea

Physical Geography

1. **Teach** Ask students the questions in the Main Idea boxes under Direct Teach.

2. **Apply** Have students create a graphic organizer with an oval in the center labeled "Mexico's Physical Geography" and three ovals connected to it—one labeled "northern," one labeled "central," and one labeled "southern." Have students write two questions about each region of Mexico next to the appropriate oval. Tell students to vary their questions so that they cover physical features, climate, vegetation, and natural resources. Have students write the answers to their questions on a separate sheet of paper. **LS Verbal/Linguistic**

3. **Review** Have students exchange graphic organizers to quiz a partner.

4. **Practice/Homework** Have students use their graphic organizers to help them create at least one illustration for every region of Mexico. **LS Visual/Spatial**

📝 Alternative Assessment Handbook, Rubric 13: Graphic Organizers

UNITED STATES

MEXICAN PLATEAU

Gulf of Mexico

YUCATÁN PENINSULA

Cozumel Island

Caribbean Sea

Yucatán Channel

Bay of Campeche

Popocatépetl 17,887 ft (5,452 m) ①

ISTHMUS OF TEHUANTEPEC

Gulf of Tehuantepec

SIERRA MADRE DEL SUR

PACIFIC OCEAN

CENTRAL AMERICA

ELEVATION

Feet	Meters
13,120	4,000
6,560	2,000
1,640	500
656	200
(Sea level) 0	0 (Sea level)
Below sea level	Below sea level

0 150 300 Miles
0 150 300 Kilometers
Projection: Lambert Conformal Conic

map Zone

Geography Skills

Regions The rugged Mexican Plateau covers much of Mexico.

1. Name What feature extends into the Gulf of Mexico?

2. Analyze Where in Mexico would it be easiest to cross from the Pacific Ocean to the Gulf of Mexico?

① Plateaus and mountains cover much of Mexico. Here, the volcano Popocatépetl rises above a mountain valley. Many people live and farm in the mountain valleys.

Plateaus and Mountains

Much of the interior landscape of Mexico consists of a high, mostly rugged region called the Mexican Plateau. The plateau's lowest point is more than a half mile above sea level. Its highest point is close to two miles above sea level. The entire plateau spreads between two mountain ranges that rise still higher. One range, the Sierra Madre Oriental, lies in the east. The other, the Sierra Madre Occidental, lies in the west. Together, these two mountain ranges and another shorter one in southern Mexico make up the **Sierra Madre** (SYER-rah MAH-dray), or "mother range."

Between the two ranges in the south lies the Valley of Mexico. Mexico City, the country's capital, is located there. The mountains south of Mexico City include towering, snowcapped volcanoes. Volcanic eruptions, as well as earthquakes, are a threat there. The volcano Popocatépetl (poh-puh-cah-TE-pet-uhl) near Mexico City has been active as recently as 2010.

FOCUS ON READING

What do you think the text will discuss next?

MEXICO **143**

Direct Teach

Main Idea

❶ **Physical Features**

Mexico's physical features include plateaus, mountains, and coastal lowlands.

Recall What are Mexico's borders on the north, west, and east? *north—Río Bravo (Rio Grande); west—Pacific Ocean; east—Gulf of Mexico*

Identify What does *Sierra Madre* mean? *"mother range"*

Evaluate Why do you think people in the area of Mexico City continue to live there despite the threat of volcanic eruptions and earthquakes? *possible answer—The area is their home, so they don't want to leave it.*

▶ Map Zone Transparency: Mexico: Physical

Connect to History

Site of Mexico City Mexico City was built on a dried-out lake bed, which adds to the instability of the soil beneath it. When the Aztecs founded the city as their capital, Tenochtitlán, in 1345, they built it on a swampy island in a lake. When the Spaniards conquered the Aztecs in 1521, they cut the aqueducts that brought water to the city. Canals that had connected the island to the mainland were filled in with rubble from the Aztec buildings

Differentiating Instruction

Struggling Readers   **Below Level**

1. To help struggling readers, have them find physical features on the map as they are mentioned in the text.

2. To verify students' understanding and strengthen their literacy, call on them to point out the feature and have them reread or paraphrase the information about it.

LS Visual/Spatial, Verbal/Linguistic

🗐 Alternative Assessment Handbook, Rubrics 1: Acquiring Information; and 21: Map Reading

Advanced/Gifted and Talented   **Above Level** **Research Required**

Have students use the library, the Internet, or other resources to find the answers to the following: What is the name of the other volcano close to Mexico City? What legend tells how this volcano and Popocatépetl came to be?

LS Verbal/Linguistic

🗐 Alternative Assessment Handbook, Rubric 30: Research

Answers

Map Zone 1. *Yucatán Peninsula;* **2.** *at the Isthmus of Tehuantepec*

Focus on Reading *Students may say coastal lowlands or climate.*

2 Climate and Vegetation

Mexico's climate and vegetation include deserts, tropical forests, and cool highlands.

Recall What is the reason Mexico has so many different types of vegetation? *great variety of climates*

Describe What is the climate like in the northern part of the Yucatán Peninsula? What kind of vegetation is found there? *hot and dry; scrub forest*

Contrast How is the climate in most of southern Mexico different from that in northern Mexico? *southern Mexico—warm and humid; northern Mexico—hot and dry*

▶ Map Zone Transparency: Mexico: Climate

Did you know. . .

Cactus is a favorite food in Mexico. In the center of the Mexican flag is a picture of an eagle with a snake in its beak, perched on a prickly pear cactus. This cactus, called *nopal* in Spanish, is not just a national symbol—it is also a delicious food used in a variety of Mexican dishes. After the prickly spikes are removed, the juicy, tender *nopales* are served in salads, main courses, and desserts.

↗ **hmhsocialstudies.com**

Online Resources
Activity: Explore
Mexico

Answers

Reading Check *plateaus, mountains, and deserts*

Map Zone 1. *the north;* **2.** *the south (humid tropical climate area)*

144

Coastal Lowlands

From the highlands in central Mexico, the land slopes down to the coasts. Beautiful, sunny beaches stretch all along Mexico's eastern and western coasts. The plain that runs along the west coast is fairly wide in the north. It becomes narrower in the south. On the east side of the country, the Gulf coastal plain is wide and flat. The soils and climate there are good for farming.

ACADEMIC VOCABULARY
vary to be different

The Yucatán Peninsula in the southeast is also mostly flat. Limestone rock underlies much of the area. Erosion there has created caves and sinkholes, steep-sided depressions that form when the roof of a cave collapses. Many of these sinkholes are filled with water.

READING CHECK **Summarizing** What are Mexico's major physical features?

↗ hmhsocialstudies.com **INTERACTIVE MAP**

Mexico: Climate

Climate Types
- Humid tropical
- Tropical savanna
- Desert
- Steppe
- Highland

0 200 400 Miles
0 200 400 Kilometers

Projection: Lambert Conformal Conic

25°N
Tropic of Cancer
Gulf of California
PACIFIC OCEAN
20°N
15°N
Gulf of Mexico

map zone **Geography Skills**

Regions Mexico's climate regions range from dry to tropical.
1. Locate Where is Mexico's desert climate located?
2. Interpret What part of Mexico probably gets the most rain?

144 CHAPTER 6

Climate and Vegetation

From snowcapped mountain peaks to warm, sunny beaches, Mexico has many different climates. You can see Mexico's climate regions on the map below. This great variety of climates results in several different types of vegetation.

In some areas, changes in elevation cause climates to **vary** widely within a short distance. For example, the areas of high elevation on the Mexican Plateau can have surprisingly cool temperatures. At times, freezing temperatures reach as far south as Mexico City—even though it is located in the tropics. Mexico's mountain valleys generally have mild climates, and many people have settled there.

The valleys along Mexico's southern coastal areas also have pleasant climates. Warm temperatures and a summer rainy season support the forests that cover about 25 percent of Mexico's land area. Tropical rain forests provide a home for jaguars, monkeys, anteaters, and other animals.

While most of southern Mexico is warm and humid, the climate in the northern part of the Yucatán Peninsula is hot and dry. The main vegetation there is scrub forest.

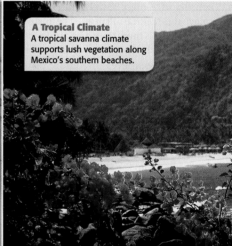

A Tropical Climate
A tropical savanna climate supports lush vegetation along Mexico's southern beaches.

Cross-Discipline Activity: Literature

At Level

Writing a Travelogue

1. Explain to students that a travelogue is a type of writing used to describe a place. Tell them travelogue writers try to make the location come alive by including personal experiences, the more adventurous the better. Point out that travelogues are often written from the first person point of view.

2. Have students write a short travelogue of an imagined trip across Mexico, based on the information in the text. Suggest that they describe such things as snow-capped

volcanoes, lush tropical rain forests, and swift and powerful jaguars. Encourage students to support their descriptions with drawings.

3. Ask volunteers to share their travelogues with the class. **LS Verbal/Linguistic**

📝 Alternative Assessment Handbook, Rubric 40: Writing to Describe

Like the Yucatán Peninsula in the south, most of northern Mexico is dry. The deserts in Baja California and the northern part of the plateau get little rainfall. Desert plants and dry grasslands are common in the north. Cougars, coyotes, and deer live in some areas of the desert.

READING CHECK Analyzing Why does Mexico City sometimes experience freezing temperatures even though it is in the tropics?

Natural Resources

Mexico is rich in natural resources. One of its most important resources is petroleum, or oil. Oil reserves are found mainly under the southern and Gulf coastal plains as well as offshore in the Gulf of Mexico. Mexico sells much of its oil to the United States.

Before oil was discovered in Mexico, minerals were the country's most valuable resource. Some gold and silver mines that were begun many centuries ago are still in operation. In addition, new mines have been developed in Mexico's mountains. Today Mexico's mines produce more silver than any other country in the world. Mexican mines also yield large amounts of copper, gold, lead, and zinc.

Another important resource is water. The refreshing water surrounding Mexico draws many tourists to the country's scenic beaches. Unfortunately, water is limited in many parts of Mexico. Water scarcity is a serious issue.

READING CHECK Finding Main Ideas What is one of Mexico's most important resources?

SUMMARY AND PREVIEW The natural environments of Mexico range from arid plateaus in the north to humid, forested mountains in the south. Next, you will study the history and culture of Mexico.

Section 1 Assessment
hmhsocialstudies.com
ONLINE QUIZ

Reviewing Ideas, Terms, and Places

1. **a. Describe** What is the interior of Mexico like?
   b. Analyze Do you think the **Yucatán Peninsula** is a good place for farming? Explain your answer.
2. **a. Recall** What is the climate like in the northern part of the Yucatán Peninsula?
   b. Explain Why can climates sometimes vary widely within a short distance?
   c. Elaborate How do you think climate and vegetation affect where people live in Mexico?
3. **a. Identify** Where are Mexico's oil reserves located?
   b. Make Inferences What problems might water scarcity cause for Mexican citizens?
   c. Elaborate How are Mexico's location, climate, and physical features also natural resources?

Critical Thinking

4. **Categorizing** Draw a chart like the one here. Using your notes, list the geographical features found in northern Mexico and southern Mexico.

	Geography
Northern Mexico	
Southern Mexico	

FOCUS ON WRITING

5. **Telling What Mexico Looks Like** What features of Mexico's physical geography will you include in your "I Am" poem? Write notes about the physical features, climate and vegetation, and natural resources of Mexico.

Direct Teach

Main Idea

❸ **Natural Resources**

Key natural resources in Mexico include oil, silver, gold, and scenic landscapes.

Identify Which country buys most of Mexico's oil? *the United States*

Recall What mineral does Mexico produce more of than any other country in the world? *silver*

Analyze Why is water scarcity a serious issue, particularly in the north of Mexico? *because of the hot, dry climate*

Review & Assess

Close

Discuss with students the main differences between northern and southern Mexico in terms of physical features, climate, and vegetation.

Review

⬈ Online Quiz, Section 1

Assess

SE Section 1 Assessment
PASS: Section 1 Quiz
Alternative Assessment Handbook

Reteach/Classroom Intervention

Guided Reading Workbook, Section 1
Interactive Skills Tutor CD-ROM

Section 1 Assessment Answers

1. **a.** high, rugged plateau; mountains
   b. No, the limestone, erosion, and climate are not good for farming.
2. **a.** hot and dry
   b. differences in elevation
   c. Fewer people live in the desert, where water and vegetation are scarce. More people live where there is enough rainfall to grow crops.
3. **a.** the southern and Gulf coastal plains and offshore in the Gulf of Mexico
   b. possible answers—Fewer people can live in an area; crops cannot be grown; people

may need to conserve water or bring it in from outside.
   c. Beautiful landscapes, tropical climate, and scenic beaches bring tourists, providing jobs for many.
4. northern Mexico—desert, plateau; southern Mexico—volcanoes, rain forests
5. Student responses will vary, but students' notes should include information about the climate and physical features of the different regions of Mexico. They should also indicate how these features would appeal to tourists.

Answers

Reading Check (left) *It is located at a high elevation.*
Reading Check *petroleum (oil)*

Preteach

Bellringer

If YOU lived there. . . Use the **Daily Bellringer Transparency** to help students answer the question.

▶ Daily Bellringer Transparency, Section 2

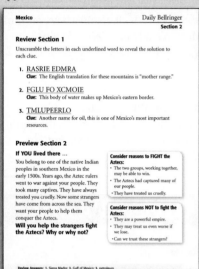

Academic Vocabulary

Review with students the high-use academic term in this section.

influence change or have an effect on (p. 149)

📝 **RF:** Vocabulary Builder, Section 2

Taking Notes

Have students use the graphic organizer online to take notes on the section. This activity will prepare students for the Section Assessment, in which they will complete a graphic organizer that builds on the information using the Critical Thinking Skill: Sequencing.

What You Will Learn...

Main Ideas

1. Early cultures of Mexico included the Olmec, the Maya, and the Aztec.
2. Mexico's period as a Spanish colony and its struggles since independence have shaped its culture.
3. Spanish and native cultures have influenced Mexico's customs and traditions today.

The Big Idea

Native American cultures and Spanish colonization shaped Mexican history and culture.

Key Terms

empire, *p. 147*
mestizos, *p. 148*
missions, *p. 148*
haciendas, *p. 148*

hmhsocialstudies.com
TAKING NOTES

Use the graphic organizer online to organize your notes on Mexico's history and culture.

History and Culture

SECTION 2

If YOU lived there...

You belong to one of the native Indian peoples in southern Mexico in the early 1500s. Years ago, the Aztec rulers went to war against your people. They took many captives. They have always treated you cruelly. Now some strangers have come from across the sea. They want your people to help them conquer the Aztecs.

Will you help the strangers fight the Aztecs? Why or why not?

BUILDING BACKGROUND Mexico was home to several of the earliest advanced cultures in the Americas. Early farmers there developed crops that became staples in much of North America. Mexico also has valuable minerals, which drew Spanish conquerors and colonists. Spanish culture blended with native Mexican cultures.

Early Cultures

People first came to Mexico many thousands of years ago. As early as 5,000 years ago, they were growing beans, peppers, and squash. They also domesticated an early form of corn. Farming allowed these people to build the first permanent settlements in the Americas.

Early Cultures of Mexico

hmhsocialstudies.com
ANIMATED GEOGRAPHY

Olmec

- The Olmec made sculptures of giant stone heads.
- The heads may have represented rulers or gods.

Teach the Big Idea

At Level

History and Culture

1. **Teach** Ask students the questions in the Main Idea boxes under Direct Teach.

2. **Apply** Tell students to draw a time line on their own paper. As they read through the section, have them create an interval for each event discussed. Encourage them to space their intervals appropriately and to label them clearly, giving the year, place, and people involved in the event.

3. **Review** As you review the section's main ideas, have students compare and discuss the events they listed on their time lines. Tell

students to add events to their time lines as necessary, based on the time lines of fellow students.

4. **Practice/Homework** Have students choose one event and write about its immediate and long-term impact on Mexican history and culture.

   LS **Visual/Spatial, Verbal/Linguistic**

   📝 Alternative Assessment Handbook, Rubrics 36: Time Lines; and 37: Writing Assignments

Olmec

By about 1500 BC the Olmec people in Mexico were living in small villages. The Olmec lived on the humid southern coast of the Gulf of Mexico, where they built temples and giant statues. They also traded carved stones like jade and obsidian with other cultures in eastern Mexico.

Maya

A few hundred years later, the Maya built on the achievements of the Olmec. Between about AD 250 and 900, the Maya built large cities in Mexico and Central America. In these cities they built stone temples to worship their gods. They studied the stars and developed a detailed calendar. They also kept written records that scholars still study today to learn about Maya history. However, scholars do not fully understand why Maya civilization suddenly collapsed sometime after 900.

Aztec

After the decline of the Maya civilization, people called the Aztecs moved to central Mexico from the north. In 1325 they built their capital on an island in a lake. Known as Tenochtitlán (tay-nawch-teet-LAHN), this capital grew into one of the largest and most impressive cities of its time.

The Aztecs also built a large, powerful empire. An **empire** is a land with different territories and peoples under a single ruler.

CONNECTING TO Technology

hmhsocialstudies.com
ANIMATED GEOGRAPHY

Chinampas

The Aztecs practiced a form of raised-field farming in the swampy lake areas of central Mexico. They called these raised fields *chinampas*. To make them, Aztec farmers piled earth on rafts anchored to trees in the lake. There they grew the corn, beans, and squash that most people ate.

Analyzing Why do you think the Aztecs decided to build raised fields for their crops?

The Aztecs planted trees in the lake to anchor the rafts.

The Aztecs built their empire through conquest. They defeated their neighboring tribes in war. Then they forced the other people to pay taxes and to provide war captives for sacrifice to the Aztec gods.

READING CHECK Summarizing What were some achievements of Mexico's early cultures?

Maya
- The Maya had a trade network between cities.
- This Maya pyramid stands in Uxmal.

Aztec
- The Aztecs built the first empire in the Americas.
- Aztec artisans made art like this turquoise mask.

MEXICO **147**

Main Idea

❷ Colonial Mexico and Independence

Mexico's period as a Spanish colony and its struggles since independence have shaped its culture.

Describe What were missions and why were they established? *outposts of the Roman Catholic Church; so that priests could learn the languages of the native peoples, teach them Spanish, and convert them to Catholicism*

Recall When did the fight for Mexican independence from Spain begin? When did it end? *1810, 1821*

Make Judgments Which of Mexico's struggles after independence do you think was most difficult for the Mexican people? Why? *possible answer—the war with the United States because Mexico lost nearly half its territory*

📄 **RF:** Biography, Sor Juana Inés de la Cruz

📄 **RF:** Biography, Miguel Hidalgo

📄 **RF:** Geography for Life, Female Pioneers

Did you know. . .

When Hernán Cortés entered the Aztec capital of Tenochtitlán, he was worshipped and welcomed as the great god-king Quetzalcoatl, returning to his people as had been foretold in the Aztec calendar. One of the principal creator deities of Middle American peoples, Quetzalcoatl was represented as a fair-skinned and bearded god who had left his people to go east, promising to return in 1519.

Answers

Focus on Reading *Students may say that the Spanish will colonize the land after defeating the Aztecs.*

Analyzing Visuals *peasants, Indians, soldiers, priests*

148

Colonial Mexico and Independence

FOCUS ON READING
What do you think will happen to the Aztec Empire?

In spite of its great size and power, the Aztec Empire did not last long after the first Europeans landed in Mexico. In 1519 Hernán Cortés, a Spanish soldier, arrived in Mexico with about 600 men. These conquistadors (kahn-KEES-tuh-dawrz), or conquerors, gained allies from other tribes in the region. They also had guns and horses, which the Aztecs had never seen before. The new weapons terrified the Aztecs and gave the Spanish an advantage.

The Spanish also unknowingly brought European diseases such as smallpox. The Aztecs had no resistance to these diseases, so many of them died. Greatly weakened by disease, the Aztecs were defeated. In 1521 Cortés claimed the land for Spain.

Hidalgo Calls for Independence

148 CHAPTER 6

Colonial Times

After the conquest, Spanish and American Indian peoples and cultures mixed. This mixing formed a new Mexican identity. Spaniards called people of mixed European and Indian ancestry **mestizos** (me-STEE-zohs). When Africans were brought to America as slaves, they added to this mix of peoples. The Spaniards called people of mixed European and African ancestry mulattoes (muh-LAH-tohs). Africans and American Indians also intermarried.

Life in colonial Mexico was greatly influenced by the Roman Catholic Church. Large areas of northern Mexico were left to the church to explore and to rule. Church outposts known as **missions** were scattered throughout the area. Priests at the missions learned native languages and taught the Indians Spanish. They also worked to convert the American Indians to Catholicism.

In addition to spreading Christianity, the Spaniards wanted to find gold and silver in Mexico. American Indians and enslaved Africans did most of the hard physical labor in the mines. As a result, many died from disease and overwork.

Like mining, agriculture became an important part of the colonial economy. After the conquest, the Spanish monarch granted **haciendas** (hah-see-EN-duhs), or huge expanses of farm or ranch land, to some favored people of Spanish ancestry. Peasants, usually Indians, lived and worked on these haciendas. The haciendas made their owners very wealthy.

> Miguel Hidalgo (center, in black) calls for independence from Spain in 1810. The famous Mexican painter Juan O'Gorman painted this image.
>
> **ANALYZING VISUALS** What kinds of people joined Hidalgo in his revolt?

Differentiating Instruction

At Level

Special Needs Learners

Prep Required

Materials: several examples of Mexican murals

1. Find books or Web sites showing the works of Mexican muralists and bring in copies of five or six murals for the class. Explain to students that Mexican murals tell a story about history or politics because the muralists wanted all Mexicans, including those who could not read, to know about their past.

2. Display the murals one at a time to the class and ask students to talk generally about the story each mural tells.

3. Divide the class into groups and assign a mural to each group. Ask students to talk more in-depth about the story their mural tells, focusing on such details as characters, objects, colors, proportion, perspective, and so on.

4. Ask each group to present their mural to the class, highlighting details they discussed.

LS Visual/Spatial, Verbal/Linguistic

📄 Alternative Assessment Handbook, Rubrics 3: Artwork; and 6: Oral Presentations

Independence

Spain ruled Mexico for almost 300 years before the people of Mexico demanded independence. The revolt against Spanish rule was led by a Catholic priest named Miguel Hidalgo. In 1810, he gave a famous speech calling for the common people to rise up against the Spanish. Hidalgo was killed in 1811, but fighting continued until Mexico won its independence in 1821.

Later Struggles

Fifteen years after Mexico gained its independence, a large area, Texas, broke away. Eventually, Texas joined the United States. As a result, Mexico and the United States fought over Texas and the location of their shared border. This conflict led to the Mexican-American War, in which Mexico lost nearly half its territory to the United States.

In the mid-1800s, Mexico faced other challenges. During this time, the popular president Benito Juárez helped Mexico survive a French invasion. He also made reforms that reduced the privileges of the church and the army.

In spite of these reforms, in the early 1900s the president helped the hacienda owners take land from peasants. Also, foreign companies owned huge amounts of land in Mexico and, in turn, influenced Mexican politics. Many Mexicans thought the president gave these large landowners too many privileges.

As a result, the Mexican Revolution broke out in 1910. The fighting lasted 10 years. One major result of the Mexican Revolution was land reform. The newly formed government took land from the large landowners and gave it back to the peasant villages.

READING CHECK Sequencing What events occurred after Mexico gained independence?

Culture

Mexico's history has **influenced** its culture. For example, one major influence from history is language. Most Mexicans speak Spanish because of the Spanish influence in colonial times. Another influence from Spain is religion. About 90 percent of all Mexicans are Roman Catholic.

However, Mexico's culture also reflects its American Indian heritage. For example, many people still speak American Indian languages. In Mexico, a person's language is tied to his or her ethnic group. Speaking an American Indian language identifies a person as Indian.

Mexicans also have some unique cultural practices that combine elements of Spanish influence with the influence of Mexican Indians. An example of this combining can be seen in a holiday called Day of the Dead. This holiday is a day to remember and honor dead ancestors.

ACADEMIC VOCABULARY
influence change or have an effect on

VIDEO
The Peasant Revolution

hmhsocialstudies.com

MEXICO **149**

Direct Teach

Main Idea

❸ **Culture**

Spanish and native cultures have influenced Mexico's customs and traditions today.

Recall What identifies a person as Indian in Mexico? *speaking an American Indian language*

Describe How do many Mexican families celebrate Day of the Dead? *They gather in graveyards to clean and decorate graves of their loved ones and set out food and drink.*

Evaluate Why do you think the beliefs of the Mexican Indians survive today? *possible answers—because they were ancient beliefs, deeply rooted in the Indian culture; because many Mexican Indian beliefs have common elements with Christian religion, making it easy for the two to blend*

RF: Interdisciplinary Project, Mexican Artists: Create a Mural

Biography

Emiliano Zapata (c. 1879–1919) A tenant farmer from the south of Mexico, Emiliano Zapata took up arms with a cry of "land and liberty" in 1910. Zapata fought for almost a decade for the simple idea that the land should belong to the people, not a few powerful landowners. He was, and still is, a hero to the native Indian people. Today revolutionaries fighting for land reform in Mexico call themselves *zapatistas.*

hmhsocialstudies.com
Online Resources
Activity: Mexican Revolution

Answers

Reading Check *Texas broke away from Mexico, resulting in a war with the United States; France tried to invade Mexico; the Mexican Revolution*

Biography *He was of Indian heritage, which was a group that had not enjoyed many rights or privileges.*

Cross-Discipline Activity: Language Arts
At Level

Persuasive Writing

1. Review with students the causes of the Mexican Revolution of 1910. Ask students to imagine that they are living in Mexico in 1909. Have them write a letter to President Porfirio Díaz asking the government to treat the peasants more fairly. As an alternative, students may wish to write a political speech.

2. Ask volunteers to read their letters or speeches to the class. Have the rest of the class write down any two- or three-word phrases that they thought were especially persuasive.

3. Help students choose the phrases that were most effective. Have students work in groups to design political posters promoting the revolution that use the most effective phrases chosen by the class. **LS** **Verbal/Linguistic**

   Alternative Assessment Handbook, Rubric 43: Writing to Persuade

Direct Teach

Connect to History

The Virgin of Guadalupe The patron saint of Mexico, the brown-skinned Virgin of Guadalupe, is an example of the combination of the Mexican Indian and Catholic cultures. She is believed by Catholics to have appeared to Juan Diego, a Mexican Indian convert, at the site of a demolished shrine of an Aztec goddess in 1531. Her image is believed to have been miraculously imprinted on Juan Diego's garment, which hangs today in the Basilica de Guadalupe in Mexico City.

Review & Assess

Close

Discuss with students how life changed for the native Indians of Mexico after the Spanish came.

Review

↗ Online Quiz, Section 2

Assess

SE Section 2 Assessment

PASS: Section 2 Quiz

Alternative Assessment Handbook

Reteach/Classroom Intervention

Guided Reading Workbook, Section 2

Interactive Skills Tutor CD-ROM

Answers

Focus on Culture *to remember and honor dead ancestors*

Reading Check *language, Roman Catholic beliefs*

150

FOCUS ON CULTURE

Day of the Dead

Everyone is sad when a loved one dies. But during Day of the Dead, Mexicans celebrate death as part of life. This attitude comes from the Mexican Indian belief that the souls of the dead return every year to visit their living relatives. To prepare for this visit, Mexican families gather in graveyards. They clean up around their loved one's grave and decorate it with flowers and candles. They also set out food and drink for the celebration. Favorite foods often include sugar candy skulls, chocolate coffins, and sweet breads shaped like bones.

Summarizing Why do Mexicans celebrate Day of the Dead?

Mexicans celebrate Day of the Dead on November 1 and 2. These dates are similar to the dates that the Catholic Church honors the dead with All Souls' Day. The holiday also reflects native customs and beliefs about hopes of life after death.

READING CHECK **Categorizing** What aspects of Mexican culture show the influence of Spanish rule?

SUMMARY AND PREVIEW Mexico's early cultures formed great civilizations, but after the conquest of the Aztec Empire, power in Mexico shifted to Spain. Spain ruled Mexico for nearly 300 years before Mexico gained independence. Mexico's history and its mix of Indian and Spanish backgrounds have influenced the country's culture. In the next section you will learn about life in Mexico today.

Section 2 Assessment

↗ hmhsocialstudies.com
ONLINE QUIZ

Reviewing Ideas, Terms, and Places

1. **a. Recall** Where in Mexico did the Olmec live?
   b. Explain How did the Aztecs build and rule their empire?
   c. Elaborate Why do you think scholars are not sure what caused the end of Maya civilization?
2. **a. Identify** Who began the revolt that led to Mexico's independence?
   b. Explain What was Mexico like in colonial times?
   c. Predict How may history have been different if the Aztecs had defeated the Spanish?
3. **a. Identify** What Mexican holiday honors dead ancestors?
   b. Summarize How did Mexico's colonial past shape its culture?

Critical Thinking

4. **Sequencing** Draw a diagram like the one below. Then, using your notes, list the major events in Mexico's history in the order they happened.

FOCUS ON WRITING

5. **Learning about History and Culture** Mexico's history is full of fascinating stories. In your notebook, jot down ideas about people and stories from Mexico's history.

150 CHAPTER 6

Section 2 Assessment Answers

1. **a.** the southern coast of the Gulf of Mexico
   b. warfare, taxes, taking captives for sacrifice to the gods
   c. It collapsed suddenly.
2. **a.** Miguel Hidalgo
   b. People of Spanish ancestry owned most of the land; American Indians and African slaves did the hard work; the Roman Catholic Church converted people and ruled in the north.
   c. The Aztecs may have been able to keep their empire.
3. **a.** Day of the Dead

b. Spanish colonists brought their language, culture, and religious beliefs.

4. 1500 BC—The Olmec arrive in Mexico.
   900—The Maya civilization collapses.
   1325—The Aztec build their capital.
   1521—The Spanish conquer the Aztecs.
   1821—Mexico wins independence from Spain.
   1845—Mexico loses nearly half of its land in war with United States.
   1910—The Mexican Revolution begins.

5. Responses will vary. Students' notes should include information about the history and culture of Mexico.

Social Studies Skills

Taking Notes

Learn

Taking notes can help you remember what you have learned from your textbook or in class. To be effective, your notes must be clear and organized. One good way to organize your notes is in a chart like the one here. Use the following steps to help you take useful notes:

- Before you read: Divide a page in your notebook into two columns as shown.

- While you read: Write down your notes in phrases or sentences in the large column on the right.

- After you read: Review your notes. Then in the small column on the left, jot down ideas, key terms, or questions in your own words based on the notes you took.

Recall	Notes
New Mexican identity	-Spanish and American Indian cultures mixed. -mestizos -Africans came as slaves.
Influence on Catholic Church	-Life in colonial Mexico was influenced by the Roman Catholic Church. -missions -Priests taught Spanish.
Economy: mining and agriculture	-Spaniards were interested in gold and silver. -American Indians and enslaved Africans worked in mines. -Agriculture was important. -haciendas

Practice

Answer the following questions about taking notes.

1 Where should you write your notes while you read or listen in class?

2 How can jotting down key ideas, terms, and questions help you clarify your notes after you take them?

Apply

Look back at Section 1 of this chapter. Divide your paper into two columns and take notes on the section using the suggestions above. Then answer the following questions.

1. What ideas or questions did you write in the Recall column on the left?

2. What are some advantages of taking notes?

MEXICO **151**

Social Studies Skills

Taking Notes

Activity Notes from an Interview
Ask students to interview a family member or someone in the community or at school. Tell them that they can focus their interview on the person's life or achievements or on special knowledge the person has. Have students prepare a list of 5–10 questions to ask. Encourage them to take detailed notes on the answers. If the interviewee allows it, students may want to tape record their interviews and then take notes using the recording. Have students use their notes to write a two-paragraph article about the person they interviewed.

LS Interpersonal, Verbal/Linguistic

- Alternative Assessment Handbook, Rubric 7: Charts
- Interactive Skills Tutor CD-ROM, Lesson 8: Create Written Presentations
- RF: Social Studies Skills, Taking Notes

Social Studies Skills Activity: Taking Notes

Struggling Readers `At Level`

Have students make an outline of a chapter section using the heads in the section. Tell students to copy the section head and all subheads, leaving space between the heads to write notes. Have them write down phrases summarizing important information. Remind students that the beginnings and ends of paragraphs contain key information. **LS Verbal/Linguistic**

- Alternative Assessment Handbook, Rubric 13: Graphic Organizers

English-Language Learners `At Level`

Tell students that becoming familiar with chapter material ahead of time can help them understand discussions during class. Have students read sections of the chapter before you cover them in class and write down ideas or terms that seem important. When the content is covered in class, ask these students to join the class discussion by sharing their notes. **LS Verbal/Linguistic**

- Alternative Assessment Handbook, Rubrics 1: Acquiring Information; and 11: Discussions

Answers

Practice 1. *in the large column on the right;* **2.** *by organizing the notes to remember the most important information*

Apply 1. *Students' ideas or questions should include information about Mexico's physical features, climate and vegetation, and natural resources;* **2.** *remembering what you have learned from a textbook or in class; being better prepared for tests*

Mexico Today

Preteach

Bellringer

If YOU lived there... Use the **Daily Bellringer Transparency** to help students answer the question.

▶ Daily Bellringer Transparency, Section 3

Academic Vocabulary

Review with students the high-use academic term in this section.

affect to change or influence (p. 156)

📝 RF: Vocabulary Builder, Section 3

Taking Notes

Have students use the graphic organizer online to take notes on the section. This activity will prepare students for the Section Assessment, in which they will complete a graphic organizer that builds on the information using the Critical Thinking Skill: Finding Main Ideas.

What You Will Learn...

Main Ideas

1. Government has traditionally played a large role in Mexico's economy.
2. Mexico has four distinct culture regions.

The Big Idea

Mexico has four culture regions that all play a part in the country's government and economy.

Key Terms and Places

inflation, *p. 152*
slash-and-burn agriculture, *p. 153*
cash crop, *p. 153*
Mexico City, *p. 154*
smog, *p. 154*
maquiladoras, *p. 155*

hmhsocialstudies.com
TAKING NOTES

Use the graphic organizer online to take notes on Mexico's government and economy.

If **YOU** lived there...

For many years, your family has lived in a small village in southern Mexico. Jobs are scarce there. Your older brother and sisters talk about moving to a larger city. Big cities may provide some more opportunities, but they can be crowded and noisy. Many people from your village have already gone to the city.

How do you feel about moving to the city?

BUILDING BACKGROUND After Mexico gained independence, many government leaders did not rule democratically. For years the Mexican people had little say in their government. But changes in the 1990s and 2000s led toward more democracy and prosperity.

Government and Economy

Today people in Mexico can vote in certain elections for the first time. People can find jobs in cities and buy their families a home. More children are able to attend school. In recent years, changes in Mexico's government and economy have made improvements like these possible.

Government

Mexico has a democratic government. However, Mexico is not like the United States where different political parties have always competed for power. In Mexico the same political party controlled the government for 71 years. But this control ended in 2000 when Mexicans elected Vicente Fox their president. Fox represented a different political party.

For many years, Mexico's government controlled most of the country's economic activity. Today the government has less control of the economy.

Economy

Mexico is a developing country. It has struggled with debts to foreign banks, unemployment, and inflation. **Inflation** is a rise in prices that occurs when currency loses its buying power.

Teach the Big Idea

At Level

Mexico Today

1. **Teach** Ask students the questions in the Main Idea boxes under Direct Teach.

2. **Apply** Have students create a chart with two columns labeled "Government" and "Economy" and four rows labeled "Greater Mexico City," "Central Mexico," "Northern Mexico," and "Southern Mexico." Have them complete the chart with information on how Mexico's government and economy influence and are influenced by each of its four culture regions. 🅛🅢 **Verbal/Linguistic**

3. **Review** Ask students to exchange their charts with each other to review the section.

4. **Practice/Homework** Have students use the information on their charts to draw sketches of each of the four culture regions.
   🅛🅢 **Visual/Spatial**

   📝 Alternative Assessment Handbook, Rubrics 3: Artwork; and 7: Charts

Although living standards in Mexico are lower than in many other countries, Mexico's economy is growing. The North American Free Trade Agreement (NAFTA), which took effect in 1994, has made trade among Mexico, the United States, and Canada easier. Mexico's agricultural and industrial exports have increased since NAFTA went into effect.

Agriculture Agriculture has long been a key part of the Mexican economy. This is true even though just 13 percent of the land is good for farming. Many farmers in southern Mexico practice **slash-and-burn agriculture**, which is the practice of burning forest in order to clear land for planting.

The high market demand for food in the United States has encouraged many farmers in Mexico to grow cash crops. A **cash crop** is a crop that farmers grow mainly to sell for a profit. Trucks bring cash crops like fruits and vegetables from Mexico to the United States.

Industry Oil is also an important export for Mexico. Many Mexicans work in the oil, mining, and manufacturing industries. These industries are growing.

The fastest-growing industrial centers in Mexico lie along the U.S. border. Because wages are relatively low in Mexico, many U.S. and foreign companies have built factories in Mexico. Mexican workers in these factories assemble goods for export to the United States and other countries. Some Mexican workers also come to the United States to look for jobs that pay more than they can make at home.

Tourism Tourism is another important part of Mexico's economy. Many tourists visit old colonial cities and Maya and Aztec monuments. Coastal cities and resorts such as Cancún and Acapulco are also popular with tourists.

READING CHECK **Summarizing** How is the government's role in the economy changing?

HISTORY
VIDEO
Mexico in the Modern Era
hmhsocialstudies.com

hmhsocialstudies.com
ANIMATED GEOGRAPHY
Resources and Products of Mexico

Satellite View

Many people in Mexico are subsistence farmers. They do not own much land and grow only enough food to feed their families. To gain more land, farmers in southern Mexico burn patches of forest. The fires clear the trees and kill weeds, and ash from the fires fertilizes the soil. However, growing the same crops year after year drains valuable nutrients from the soil. The farmers then have to burn new forest land.

In the satellite image here, agricultural fires appear as red dots. As you can see, the fires create a lot of smoke. Wind then blows the smoke great distances. Every few years, when the conditions are right, smoke from agricultural fires in Mexico reaches as far as the southern United States. The smoke can cause health problems for some people.

Analyzing What direction was the wind blowing in this image?

Smoke

Fire

MEXICO **153**

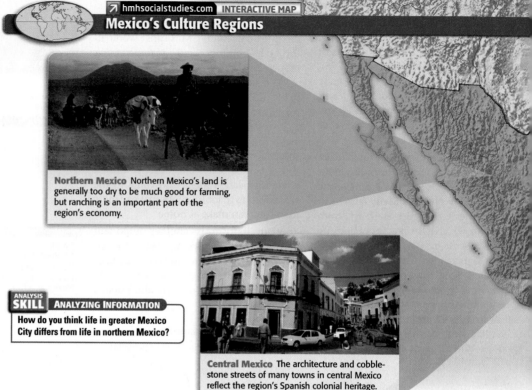

Northern Mexico Northern Mexico's land is generally too dry to be much good for farming, but ranching is an important part of the region's economy.

ANALYSIS SKILL | **ANALYZING INFORMATION**
How do you think life in greater Mexico City differs from life in northern Mexico?

Central Mexico The architecture and cobblestone streets of many towns in central Mexico reflect the region's Spanish colonial heritage.

❷ Mexico's Culture Regions

Mexico has four distinct culture regions.

Compare Where do the poor in Mexico City live? How is this different from where the poor in the United States live? *in large urban slums; The slums are often right next to modern buildings.*

Interpret What are some architectural characteristics of colonial cities and towns? *colonial church, main central square*

Contrast How are northern Mexico and southern Mexico different economically? *northern Mexico—one of country's richest areas, industrialized, has many foreign-owned factories; southern Mexico—has many subsistence farmers, little industrialization, produces oil and agricultural products*

▶ Map Zone Transparency: Mexico's Culture Regions

📝 RF: Critical Thinking, Mexico's Expanding Capital

📝 RF: Literature, *Itinerary* by Octavio Paz

Did you know. . .

Mexico City's main square, known as the *Zócalo*, is the vibrant heart of the city. The second-largest public square in the world (after Red Square in Moscow), it was built on the ruins of the Aztec palaces and temples. Every day, Mexicans from all over the country congregate at the Zócalo for political protests, patriotic or civic celebrations, buying and selling goods, and entertainment by Mexican Indian dancers and musicians.

Answers

Analyzing Information *Answers will vary. Students should discuss how Northern Mexico is dry, and ranching is important, while Greater Mexico City provides job and educational opportunities not found elsewhere in the country. Both regions have advantages and disadvantages.*

154

Mexico's Culture Regions

Although all Mexicans share some cultural characteristics, we can divide Mexico into four regions based on regional differences. These four culture regions differ from each other in their population, resources, climate, and other features.

Greater Mexico City

Greater Mexico City includes the capital and about 50 smaller cities near it. With a population of more than 19 million, **Mexico City** is the world's second-largest city and one of the most densely populated urban areas. Thousands of people move there every year looking for work.

While this region does provide job and educational opportunities not so easily found in the rest of the country, its huge population causes problems. For example, Mexico City is very polluted. Factories and cars release exhaust and other pollutants into the air. The surrounding mountains trap the resulting **smog**—a mixture of smoke, chemicals, and fog. Smog can cause health problems like eye irritation and breathing difficulties.

Another problem that comes from crowding is poverty. Wealth and poverty exist side by side in Mexico City. The city has large urban slums. The slums often exist right next to modern office buildings, apartments, museums, or universities.

154 CHAPTER 6

Critical Thinking: Contrasting

Life in the Big City

1. Divide the class into groups. Ask students to imagine that they are new arrivals to Mexico City from the countryside. Tell students to write descriptions of how a new arrival's life would be different in the city in these three ways: environmentally, socially, and economically.

2. Give the groups time to brainstorm and record their ideas. Encourage them to support their ideas by giving specific examples. For example, they might describe how hard it would be to go from the quiet in villages to the noise and traffic congestion in the city.

3. Have the groups present their descriptions to the class and lead a class discussion on life in Mexico City. Guide the discussion so that students are focusing on the particulars of adapting to life in Mexico City with its congestion, poverty, and pollution—not just making generalizations about differences between urban and rural life.

LS **Interpersonal, Verbal/Linguistic**

📋 Alternative Assessment Handbook, Rubrics 11: Discussions; and 24: Oral Presentations

Greater Mexico City Traffic clogs Mexico City's busy streets. Taxis, buses, and private cars zoom past modern office buildings and old colonial government buildings.

Southern Mexico While poverty is a problem in much of southern Mexico, some people make money selling traditional handicrafts to tourists.

Central Mexico

North of greater Mexico City lies Mexico's central region. Many cities in this region were established as mining or ranching centers during the colonial period. Mexico's colonial heritage can still be seen today in these cities and towns. For example, small towns often have a colonial-style church near a main central square. The central square, or plaza, has served for hundreds of years as a community meeting spot and market area.

In addition to small colonial towns, central Mexico has many fertile valleys and small family farms. Farmers in this region grow vegetables, corn, and wheat for sale, mostly to cities in Mexico.

While central Mexico has always been a mining center, in recent years the region has also attracted new industries from overcrowded Mexico City. As a result, some cities in the region, such as Guadalajara, are growing rapidly.

Northern Mexico

Northern Mexico has become one of the country's richest and most modern areas. Trade with the United States has helped the region's economy grow. Monterrey and Tijuana are now major cities there. Many U.S.- and foreign-owned factories called **maquiladoras** (mah-kee-lah-DORH-ahs) have been built along Mexico's long border with the United States.

MEXICO **155**

MEXICO **155**

156

Direct Teach

Connect to Art

Indian Influences The southern states of Oaxaca and Chiapas are two states in Mexico with a strong Indian influence and presence. Both states have magnificent ruins built by ancient civilizations—the Zapotec and Mixtec in Oaxaca, and the Maya in Chiapas. The descendants of these and other Indian groups still live in the regions, following traditional ways of life. Some make a living by creating intricate textiles, pottery, and other folk art that is becoming increasingly sought after by tourists.

Review & Assess

Close

Discuss with students how the four culture regions of Mexico are distinct from one another.

Review

↗ Online Quiz, Section 3

Assess

SE Section 3 Assessment

PASS: Section 3 Quiz

Alternative Assessment Handbook

Reteach/Classroom Intervention

Guided Reading Workbook, Section 3

● Interactive Skills Tutor CD-ROM

Answers

Focus on Reading *Students may say agriculture, oil production, or tourism.*

Reading Check *similarities—Both are vital to the economy; both have poverty; differences—Mexico City is densely populated and highly industrialized; southern Mexico is the least populated and least industrialized of Mexico's regions.*

ACADEMIC VOCABULARY
affect to change or influence

Northern Mexico's closeness to the border has **affected** the region's culture as well as its economy. American television, music, and other forms of entertainment are popular there. Many Mexicans cross the border to shop, work, or live in the United States. While many people cross the border legally, the U.S. government tries to prevent Mexicans and others from crossing the border illegally.

Southern Mexico

FOCUS ON READING
What do you think makes southern Mexico vital to the country's economy?

Southern Mexico is the least populated and industrialized region of the country. Many people in this region speak Indian languages and practice traditional ways of life. Subsistence farming and slash-and-burn agriculture are common.

However, southern Mexico is vital to the country's economy. Sugarcane and coffee, two major export crops, grow well in the region's warm, humid climate. Also, oil production along the Gulf coast has increased in recent years. The oil business has brought more industry and population growth to this coastal area of southern Mexico.

Another place in southern Mexico that has grown in recent years is the Yucatán Peninsula. Maya ruins, beautiful sunny beaches, and clear blue water have made tourism a major industry in this area. Many cities that were just tiny fishing villages only 20 years ago are now booming with new construction for the tourist industry.

Mexico will continue to change in the future. Changes are likely to bring more development. However, maintaining the country's unique regional cultures may be a challenge as those changes take place.

READING CHECK **Comparing and Contrasting** What similarities and differences exist between greater Mexico City and southern Mexico?

SUMMARY AND PREVIEW Mexico has a democratic government and a growing economy. It also has distinct regions with different cultures, economies, and environments. In the next chapter you will learn about the countries to the south of Mexico.

Section 3 Assessment

↗ hmhsocialstudies.com
ONLINE QUIZ

Reviewing Ideas, Terms, and Places

1. a. Define What is the term for the practice of burning forest in order to clear land for planting?
b. Compare and Contrast How is Mexico's government similar to and different from the government of the United States?
2. a. Identify What is an environmental problem found in **Mexico City**?
b. Make Inferences What conditions in Mexico lead some Mexicans to cross the border into the United States?
c. Develop If you were to start a business in Mexico, what type of business would you start and where would you start it? Explain your decisions.

Critical Thinking

3. Finding Main Ideas Review your notes on Mexico's economy. Then use a chart like this one to show what parts of the economy are important in each region.

Greater Mexico City	Central Mexico	Northern Mexico	Southern Mexico

FOCUS ON WRITING

4. Describing Mexico Today Write some details about the four culture regions of Mexico. Which details will you include in your poem?

Section 3 Assessment Answers

1. a. slash-and-burn agriculture
b. It is similar in that it is a democracy headed by a president. It is different in that Mexico was ruled for 71 years by one political party, and the government controlled the economy.
2. a. pollution
b. poverty and the lack of jobs that pay enough to live
c. Answers will vary but should reflect knowledge of Section 3 content.

3. Greater Mexico City—jobs and education; Central Mexico—farming, mining, industry; Northern Mexico—foreign-owned maquiladoras, modern cities; Southern Mexico—subsistence farming, slash-and-burn agriculture, oil industry, tourism

4. Student responses will vary, but students should list details about the four cultural regions of Mexico.

Chapter Review

Geography's Impact
video series
Review the video to answer the closing question:
Do you think emigration from Mexico to the United States hurts or helps Mexico? Why?

Visual Summary

Use the visual summary below to help you review the main ideas of the chapter.

QUICK FACTS

The physical geography of Mexico includes a high region of plateaus and mountains.

The Spanish conquered the Aztecs and ruled Mexico for about 300 years until the Mexicans gained independence.

Greater Mexico City, one of Mexico's four culture regions, is the center of Mexico's government and economy.

Reviewing Vocabulary, Terms, and Places

Unscramble each group of letters below to spell a term that matches the given definition.

1. **pmreie**—a land with different territories and peoples under a single ruler

2. **tflinnaoi**—a rise in prices that occurs when currency loses its buying power

3. **mogs**—a mixture of smoke, chemicals, and fog

4. **snipluane**—a piece of land surrounded on three sides by water

5. **ztosemsi**—people of mixed European and Indian ancestry

6. **hacs rpoc**—a crop that farmers grow mainly to sell for a profit

7. **ssnmiosi**—church outposts

8. **dqamiuarsloa**—U.S.- and foreign-owned factories in Mexico

9. **ndhceiasa**—expanses of farm or ranch land

Comprehension and Critical Thinking

SECTION 1 *(Pages 143–145)*

10. **a. Define** What is the Mexican Plateau? What forms its edges?

  b. Contrast How does the climate of Mexico City differ from the climate in the south?

  c. Evaluate What do you think would be Mexico's most important resource if it did not have oil? Explain your answer.

SECTION 2 *(Pages 146–150)*

11. **a. Recall** What early civilization did the Spanish conquer when they came to Mexico?

  b. Analyze How did Spanish rule influence Mexico's culture?

  c. Evaluate Which war—the war for independence, the Mexican War, or the Mexican Revolution—do you think changed Mexico the most? Explain your answer.

MEXICO **157**

Answers

Visual Summary

Review and Inquiry Have students use the visual summary to discuss details about the chapter's main ideas.

  Quick Facts Transparency: Mexico Visual Summary

Reviewing Vocabulary, Terms, and Places

  1. empire   6. cash crop
  2. inflation   7. missions
  3. smog   8. maquiladoras
  4. peninsula   9. haciendas
  5. mestizos

Comprehension and Critical Thinking

10. **a.** a high, mostly rugged region in the interior of Mexico; three mountain ranges—one along the east, one along the west, and another one along the south
  b. Mexico City—mild climate with some freezing; south—mostly warm and humid
  c. Answers will vary but students may cite minerals or tourist destinations and should provide an explanation.

11. **a.** Aztec
  b. Spanish rule brought their language, religion, and culture.
  c. possible answers—the war for independence because it created the Mexican nation; the Mexican War because Mexico lost so much of its territory to the United States; the Mexican Revolution because it brought land reform

---

Review and Assessment Resources

Review and Reinforce

SE Chapter Review
RF: Chapter Review
  Quick Facts Transparency: Mexico Visual Summary
  Spanish Chapter Summaries Audio CD Program
TOS Holt McDougal PuzzleView®; Quiz Show for ExamView
  Quiz Game CD-ROM

Assess

SE Standardized Test Practice
  PASS: Chapter Test, Forms A and B
  Alternative Assessment Handbook
TOS ExamView Assessment Suite, Chapter Test
  Differentiated Instruction Modified Worksheets and Tests CD-ROM: Chapter Test
  Online Assessment Program, in the Interactive Student Edition

Reteach/Intervene

  Guided Reading Workbook
  Differentiated Instruction Teacher Management System: Lesson Plans
  Differentiated Instruction Modified Worksheets and Tests CD-ROM
  Interactive Skills Tutor CD-ROM

hmhsocialstudies.com
Chapter Resources

Answers

12. a. Greater Mexico City—world's second-largest urban area, densely populated, polluted, poverty, economy offers job and educational opportunities; central Mexico—colonial heritage, fertile farmland, growing industialization; northern Mexico—industrialized, modern, rich, influenced by U.S. culture and economy; southern Mexico—least populated and industrialized, large Indian population, growing oil production and tourism

b. possible answers—Mexico City because it is the capital and a great city of the world; central Mexico for its history; northern Mexico because it is close to the U.S.; southern Mexico because of its Indian culture and beautiful tourist areas

c. The soil is drained of valuable nutrients; fires create smoke that is harmful to people.

Using the Internet

13. Go to [hmhsocialstudies.com] to access a rubric for this activity.

Social Studies Skills

14. Students' charts should provide information about Mexico today, its government and economy, and its culture regions.

Map Activity

15. A. Yucatán Peninsula
B. Mexico City
C. Baja California
D. Tijuana
E. Gulf of Mexico
F. Río Bravo (Rio Grande)

Focus on Reading and Writing

16. Possible Answer The economy will continue to grow because of NAFTA, industrialization, and the tourist industry. U.S. factories built in Mexico will increase Mexico's economic ties to the United States. Mexican workers will continue to travel to the United States if opportunities for work are greater there than in Mexico.

RF: Focus on Reading, Predicting

---

12. a. Describe What are Mexico's four culture regions? Describe a feature of each.

b. Analyze What regions do you think are the most popular with tourists? Explain your answer.

c. Evaluate What are two major drawbacks of slash-and-burn agriculture?

Using the Internet

13. Activity: Writing a Description Colorful textiles, paintings, and pottery are just some of the many crafts made throughout Mexico. Each region in Mexico has its own style of crafts and folk art. Through your online textbook, visit some of the different regions of Mexico and explore their arts and crafts. Pick a favorite object from each region. Learn about its use, its design, how it was made, and the people who made it. Then write a brief paragraph that describes each object and its unique characteristics.

[hmhsocialstudies.com]

Social Studies Skills

14. Taking Notes Look back at the information in Section 3 about Mexico's government and economy. Then use a chart like this one to take notes on the information in your book.

Recall	Notes

Map Activity

15. Mexico On a separate sheet of paper, match the letters on the map with their correct labels.

Gulf of Mexico   Baja California
Río Bravo (Rio Grande) Tijuana
Yucatán Peninsula   Mexico City

hmhsocialstudies.com   INTERACTIVE MAP

FOCUS ON READING AND WRITING

16. Predicting Now you can use your skills in predicting to think about events that might happen in the future. Reread the text in your book about Mexico's economy. Write three to four sentences about how you think the economy might change in the future.

17. Writing an "I Am" Poem Now it is time to write your poem. Title your poem "I am Mexico" and make it six lines long. Use each line to give details about Mexico, such as "I have towering, snowcapped volcanoes." Make sure at least one line deals with physical geography, one line with history and culture, and one line with Mexico today. Your poem does not need to rhyme, but you should try to use vivid language.

---

17. Rubric Students' "I Am" poems should:

• be six lines long.

• describe a different detail about Mexico in each line.

• include details from all three chapter sections.

RF: Focus on Writing, Writing an "I Am" Poem

Answers

DIRECTIONS: Read questions 1 through 6 and write the letter of the best response. Then read question 7 and write your own well-constructed response.

1 **What physical features make up much of central Mexico?**

A plateaus and mountains

B peninsulas

C beaches and lowlands

D sinkholes

2 **What early culture in Mexico did the Spanish conquer?**

A Olmec

B Maya

C Aztec

D conquistador

3 **Which of the following was a way in which the Spanish affected Mexico during colonial times?**

A granted land to the native people

B set up missions and taught about Christianity

C started the Mexican Revolution

D gave away half of Mexico to the United States

4 **Where are Mexico's fastest-growing industrial centers?**

A on the Gulf coast

B in Mexico City

C on the Yucatán Peninsula

D along the U.S. border

5 **What factor helps classify Mexico as a developing country?**

A high unemployment

B few political parties

C an economy based on oil and tourism

D relatively high living standards

Mexico's Trading Partners

Mexico's Imports

Other 27%

United States 63%

China 4%

Japan 6%

Mexico's Exports

United States 89%

Other 9%

Canada 2%

Source: *World Almanac and Book of Facts,* 2005

6 **Based on the graphs above, which of the following statements is false?**

A The United States is Mexico's biggest trading partner.

B The United States imports 63% of its goods from Mexico.

C 89% of Mexico's exports go to the United States.

D Imports from Japan make up 6% of Mexico's total imports.

7 **Extended Response** Look at the graphs above and the information in Section 3. Then write a brief essay explaining how NAFTA has influenced Mexico.

Answers

Standardized Test Prep

1. A

Break Down the Question This question requires students to recall factual information from Section 1.

2. C

Break Down the Question This question requires students to recall factual information from Section 2.

3. B

Break Down the Question Remind students that during the colonial period, the Spanish took land and rights away from the native people.

4. D

Break Down the Question This question requires students to recall factual information from Section 3.

5. A

Break Down the Question This question requires students to recall information about the characteristics of developing nations from Section 3.

6. B

Break Down the Question This question requires students to carefully read the graphics.

7. Extended Response

Students' essays should point out that after NAFTA went into effect, Mexico's main trading partners are North American countries—the United States and Canada.

Intervention Resources

Reproducible

Guided Reading Workbook

Differentiated Instruction Teacher Management System: Lesson Plans

Technology

Quick Facts Transparency: Mexico Visual Summary

Differentiated Instruction Modified Worksheets and Tests CD-ROM

Interactive Skills Tutor CD-ROM

Tips for Test Taking

Getting the Full Picture When a question refers to a graph or a chart, such as Questions 6 and 7 above, students should carefully read all the information in the graphic, including headings and labels, before answering the question.

HISTORY **MULTIMEDIA CONNECTIONS**

The **HISTORY™ Multimedia Classroom** is a set of exciting new social studies teaching tools featuring award-winning program content. These comprehensive lesson plans, correlated to individual state and national curriculum standards, are easy to use for both teachers and students.

Each lesson contains the following:
• Short video segments that bring history topics to life
• Maps and visual materials
• Discussion and review questions
• Easily printable primary source documents
• Classroom activities and Internet-based activity links

The Multimedia Classroom has been specially designed to be versatile and easily adaptable to existing courses, lesson plans, and syllabi. Every lesson is designed to offer maximum flexibility. Teachers can select entire plans or only the elements they need, allowing them to individually tailor each lesson. Each multimedia lesson is available in CD-ROM format and is accompanied by full-length award-winning programs on DVD from HISTORY™.

For more information or to purchase go to ⟦↗ hmhsocialstudies.com⟧

Because some of these lessons may contain video material of a sensitive nature, we recommend that teachers and parents review these materials in their entirety before screening them to students.

Mexico

Teotihuacán, established around 200 B.C., was the first great civilization of ancient Mexico. At its height around the middle of the first millennium A.D., the "City of the Gods" was one of the largest cities in the world. It covered 12 square miles and was home to some 200,000 people. The Pyramid of the Sun, above, was the largest building in Teotihuacán.

For centuries after the fall of Teotihuacán, present-day Mexico was home to a number of great empires, including the highly sophisticated Aztec civilization. The arrival of the Spanish in the early 1500s forever changed life for Mexico's ancient peoples, and Mexican culture today is dominated by a blend of indigenous and Spanish cultures.

Explore the history of Mexico from ancient to modern times online. You can find a wealth of information, video clips, primary sources, activities, and more at ⟦↗ hmhsocialstudies.com⟧.

159 MC1 MULTIMEDIA CONNECTIONS

Mexico: Courage and Conquest

Resources ⟦↗ hmhsocialstudies.com⟧

The following resources come with printable introductions, comprehension and critical thinking questions, transcripts, and vocabulary support.

▐◼ Full Length DVD

Mexico: Courage and Conquest (3 hrs 20 mins)

▐◼ Video Clips

• Mexico's Ancient Civilizations (3:44)
• The Arrival of the Spanish (3:15)
• Catholicism and the Crown (3:39)
• Miguel Hidalgo's Call to Arms (3:13)
• Independence for Texas (4:36)
• The Mexican-American War (3:42)
• Transforming the Nation (4:44)
• The Peasant Revolution (5:08)
• Power Plays and Politics (3:31)
• Mexico in the Modern Era (2:09)

🌎 Maps

• Site Plan of Tenochtitlán
• Mexico, 1824–1867

💡 Activities

• The Columbian Exchange
• The Struggle for Equality
• Mexico's Reform Movements
• A Hundred Years of Change
• Women and the Revolution
• Comparing Constitutions

The Arrival of the Spanish

Watch the video to learn how the arrival of the conquistadors led to the fall of the Aztec Empire.

Miguel Hidalgo's Call to Arms

Watch the video to learn about Miguel Hidalgo's path from priest to revolutionary leader.

Mexico in the Modern Era

Watch the video to learn about the role of oil in the industrialization of Mexico's economy.

MEXICO **159 MC2**

Mexico's Ancient Civilizations

Watch the video to learn about the great civilizations that arose in ancient Mexico.

Mexico's Ancient Civilizations

The first people to live in what is now Mexico were migratory hunters that eventually settled and established civilizations in the region. Powerful groups came to dominate the area, including the Maya and the Toltecs. The latest arrivals to the region, the Aztecs, would build the greatest empire of ancient Mexico.

The Arrival of the Spanish

Aztec mythology told of the eventual return of the god Quetzalcoatl. When Spanish explorer Hernán Cortés arrived in Mexico in 1519, many believed the prophecy had been fulfilled. Moctezuma II, the Aztec king, first welcomed the newcomers, believing they might be descendants of Quetzalcoatl. Soon after, though, the Aztecs realized the Spanish were in fact a powerful enemy. The conquistadors and their Indian allies overpowered the Aztecs, and Tenochtitlán, the ancient Aztec capital, was destroyed in 1521.

Miguel Hidalgo's Call to Arms

During the Spanish Inquisition, a Catholic priest named Miguel Hidalgo was banished to the city of Dolores for his controversial beliefs that were in opposition to Church doctrine. In Dolores, Hidalgo dedicated himself to helping improve life for Indians and mestizos. On September 16, 1810, he called for revolution against Spanish rule in his "Grito de Dolores." His actions helped spark the independence movement and later earned him the name "Father of the Mexican Revolution."

Mexico in the Modern Era

In the late 1930s, Mexico's Institutional Revolutionary Party, or PRI, nationalized the oil industry. The country prospered from its vast oil deposits. PRI's leaders had promised economic reform and a more equal distribution of wealth. Yet the disparity between Mexico's socioeconomic classes remained virtually unchanged.

Primary Sources

- Pyramid of the Sun
- The Fall of Tenochtitlán
- On Female Education
- Concerning the Caste System
- Observations on Texas, 1827
- Treaty of Guadalupe Hidalgo, 1848
- The Plan of San Luis Potosí
- Photograph of Zapata
- Response to U.S. Intervention, 1915
- Disembarkation at Veracruz

? General Review Questions

? General Discussion Questions

Web Links

Bibliography

Chapter 7 Planning Guide

Central America and the Caribbean

Overview	Instructional Resources

CHAPTER 7

Essential Question: How have Central America and the Caribbean been shaped by geography and history?

 Focus on the Essential Question Podcast

TOS Differentiated Instruction Teacher Management System:
- Instructional Pacing Guides
- Lesson Plans for Differentiated Instruction

Guided Reading Workbook

Resource File:
- Chapter Review
- Focus on Reading: Understanding Comparison-Contrast
- Focus on Writing: Creating a Travel Guide
- Social Studies Skills: Interpreting a Climate Graph

Experiencing World History and Geography

TOS Calendar Planner

Power Presentations with Media Gallery

Differentiated Instruction Modified Worksheets and Tests CD-ROM

Interactive Skills Tutor CD-ROM

Student Edition on Audio CD-ROM

The World's Music Audio Program

Map Zone Transparency: Central America

World Outline Maps: Transparencies and Activities

Video: Panama Canal

Section 1:

Physical Geography

The Big Idea: The physical geography of Central America and the Caribbean islands includes warm coastal lowlands, cooler highlands, and tropical forests.

TOS Differentiated Instruction Teacher Management System: Section 1 Lesson Plan

Guided Reading Workbook: Section 1

Resource File:
- Vocabulary Builder: Section 1
- Social Studies Skills: Interpreting a Climate Graph

Daily Bellringer Transparency: Section 1

Map Zone Transparency: Central America and the Caribbean: Physical

Map Zone Transparency: Volcanic Activity in Central America and the Caribbean

Internet Activity: Panama Canal

Section 2:

Central America

The Big Idea: Central America's native traditions and colonial history have created a mixed culture, unstable governments, and uncertain economies.

TOS Differentiated Instruction Teacher Management System: Section 2 Lesson Plan

Guided Reading Workbook: Section 2

Resource File:
- Vocabulary Builder: Section 2
- Biography: Oscar Arias Sanchez
- Critical Thinking: Civil War in Central America
- Interdisciplinary Project: Doing Maya Math: Create a Poster and a Test
- Literature: *Strong Wind*, from the book by Miguel Ángel Asturias

Daily Bellringer Transparency: Section 2

Internet Activity: Regional Foods

Video: Panama Canal

Section 3:

The Caribbean Islands

The Big Idea: The Caribbean islands have a rich history and culture influenced by European colonization.

TOS Differentiated Instruction Teacher Management System: Section 3 Lesson Plan

Guided Reading Workbook: Section 3

Resource File:
- Vocabulary Builder: Section 3
- Biography: Toussaint L'Ouverture
- Geography and History: The Triangle Trade
- Geography for Life: Planning for Tourism in Dominica
- Interdisciplinary Project: Create a Collage: Illustrate the Economy of a Place
- Primary Source: Christopher Columbus's Letter about the West Indies

Daily Bellringer Transparency: Section 3

Map Zone Transparency: European Colonies in the Caribbean, 1763

Review, Assessment, Intervention

 The Americas Transparencies: Central America and the Caribbean Visual Summary

 Spanish Chapter Summaries Audio CD

 Progress Assessment Support System (PASS): Chapter Test

 Differentiated Instruction Modified Worksheets and Tests CD-ROM: Modified Chapter Test

TOS **ExamView® Assessment Suite (English/Spanish)**

 Alternative Assessment Handbook

 Online Assessment Program, in the Interactive Student Edition

---

 PASS: Section 1 Quiz

 Online Quiz: Section 1

 Alternative Assessment Handbook

 PASS: Section 2 Quiz

 Online Quiz: Section 2

 Alternative Assessment Handbook

PASS: Section 3 Quiz

Online Quiz: Section 3

Alternative Assessment Handbook

Supporting Resources

• Multimedia Classroom Global History Series
• Global History Series Teacher's Guide

Maps Globes Graphs Level F

• Student Workbook
• Teacher's Guide

Social Studies Trade Library Collections

• NCSS Middle School Collection
• African American Trade Collection

Geography's Impact

Geography's Impact Video Program

• **Impact of Tourism**

For more information or to purchase go to hmhsocialstudies.com

Power Presentations with Media Gallery

Power Presentations with Media Gallery are visual presentations of each chapter's main ideas. Presentations can be customized by including Quick Facts charts, images from the text, and video clips.

CHAPTER 7 PLANNING GUIDE

Differentiating Instruction

How do I address the needs of varied learners?
The Target Resource acts as your primary strategy for differentiated instruction.

ENGLISH-LANGUAGE LEARNERS & STRUGGLING READERS

TARGET RESOURCE

Resource File

The Resource File activities allow students to extend their knowledge of chapter-related places and people and to practice geography skills.

- Vocabulary Builder Activities
- Social Studies Skills: Interpreting Graphs

Additional Resources

Differentiated Instruction Teacher Management System: Lesson Plans for Differentiated Instruction

The Americas Transparencies:
- Central America and the Caribbean Visual Summary

Student Edition on Audio CD Program

Interactive Skills Tutor CD-ROM

Spanish Chapter Summaries Audio CD

Teacher One Stop:
- ExamView Assessment Suite, Spanish
- PuzzleView, Spanish

English-Language Learner Strategies and Activities

Spanish/English Guided Reading Workbook

SPECIAL NEEDS LEARNERS

TARGET RESOURCE

Differentiated Instruction Modified Worksheets and Tests CD-ROM

- Vocabulary Flash Cards
- Modified Vocabulary Builder Activities
- Modified Chapter Review
- Modified Chapter Test

Additional Resources

Differentiated Instruction Teacher Management System: Lesson Plans for Differentiated Instruction

Guided Reading Workbook

Resource File: Social Studies Skills: Interpreting a Climate Graph

Student Edition on Audio CD Program

Interactive Skills Tutor CD-ROM

Graphic Organizer Transparencies with Support for Reading and Writing

ADVANCED/GIFTED AND TALENTED STUDENTS

TARGET RESOURCE

Differentiated Instruction Teacher Management System

Lesson Plans for Differentiated Instruction provide teachers with strategies to help plan instruction for all learners.

Additional Resources

Resource File
- Focus on Reading: Understanding Comparison-Contrast
- Focus on Writing: Creating a Travel Guide
- Literature: from *Strong Wind* by Miguel Angel Asturias

World History and Geography Document-Based Questions Activities

Geography, Science, and Cultures Activities

Experiencing World History and Geography

Differentiated Activities in the Teacher's Edition

- Making a Table of Native American and European Items, p. 169
- Discussing a Diagram, p. 172

Teacher One Stop™

How can I manage the lesson plans and support materials for differentiated instruction?

With the Teacher One Stop, you can easily organize and print lesson plans, planning guides, and instructional materials for all learners. The Teacher One Stop includes the following materials to help you differentiate instruction:

- **· Interactive Teacher's Edition**
- **· Calendar Planner and pacing guides**
- **· Editable lesson plans**
- **· All reproducible ancillaries in Adobe Acrobat (PDF) format**
- **· ExamView Assessment Suite (English & Spanish)**
- **· Transparency and video previews**

Differentiated Activities in the Teacher's Edition

- Planning a Trip, p. 163

Interactive Student Edition

Complete online student edition with interactive multimedia support for chapter content assessment and reporting

- Interactive Maps and Notebook
- Standardized Test Prep
- Online Homework Practice and Research Activities
- Current Events
- Chapter-based Internet Activities
- Animated Geography Activities

Differentiated Activities in the Teacher's Edition

- Writing about Cultural Items, p. 169
- Making a Time Line, p. 172

Essential Question

Introduce the Essential Question

- Have students locate Central America and the Caribbean on the map on pages 160–161 and predict climate characteristics for the region. Explain that the region is a popular tourist destination because of its sunny and warm climate.

- Explain that the countries of Central America were once European colonies. Have students infer how that colonial history influences the region today.

- Point out that many Caribbean islands are independent countries, but others are not. While the cultures of the region's islands share a colonial past, diverse economies and governments now encourage different ways of life.

Focus on Reading and Writing

Reading The Resource File provides a worksheet to help students practice comparison and contrast.

📝 **RF:** Focus on Reading, Understanding Comparison-Contrast

Writing The Resource File provides a worksheet to help students organize and write their travel guide.

📝 **RF:** Focus on Writing, Creating a Travel Guide

Key to Differentiating Instruction

Below Level

Basic-level activities designed for all students encountering new material

At Level

Intermediate-level activities designed for average students

Above Level

Challenging activities designed for honors and gifted and talented students

Standard English Mastery

Activities designed to improve standard English usage

LS Learning Styles

CHAPTER 7

Central America and the Caribbean

Gulf of Mexico

Essential Question How have Central America and the Caribbean been shaped by geography and history?

❓ What You Will Learn...

In this chapter you will learn about the beautiful physical landscapes of Central America and the Caribbean. You will also study the history of the region along with the people who live there and the way they live today.

FOCUS ON READING & WRITING

Understanding Comparison-Contrast When you compare, you look for ways in which things are alike. When you contrast, you look for ways in which things are different. As you read the chapter, look for ways you can compare and contrast information. **See the lesson, Understanding Comparison-Contrast, on page 522.**

Creating a Travel Guide People use travel guides to learn more about places they want to visit. As you read about Central America and the Caribbean in this chapter, you will collect information about places tourists might visit. Then you will create your own travel guide for visitors to one of these vacation spots.

MEXICO
Belmopan
BELIZE
GUATEMALA
Guatemala City
HONDURAS
Tegucigalpa
San Salvador
EL SALVADOR
PACIFIC OCEAN
NICARAGUA
Managua
San Juan River
COSTA RICA
San José

⊙ National capital

0   100   200 Miles
0   100   200 Kilometers
Projection: Azimuthal Equal-Area

History The Spanish built forts like this one in Puerto Rico to defend their islands and protect the harbors from pirates.

Introduce the Chapter

At Level

Getting to Know the Region

1. Call on students to share what they know about Central America and the Caribbean region, such as climate, tourist attractions, and music.

2. Point out to students some highlights of the history of this region:

- part of Central America was home to the great Maya civilization;

- San Salvador in the Bahamas was the first land Columbus came upon in 1492;

- colonization and the slave trade produced cultures with a mix of ethnic and racial groups.

3. Have students look at the photos and headings to stimulate discussion about the history and culture of the region. Ask them to share other information they might have, particularly recent events.

LS Verbal/Linguistic, Visual/Spatial

📝 Alternative Assessment Handbook, Rubric 11: Discussions

Central America and the Caribbean: Political

ATLANTIC
OCEAN

map zone

Geography Skills

Location Central America and the Caribbean islands surround the Caribbean Sea.

1. **Identify** Which Central American country has no Caribbean coast?

2. **Analyze** How might geography affect communication in this region?

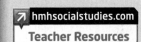

HISTORY Panama Canal

↗ hmhsocialstudies.com VIDEO

UNITED STATES

Nassau

Havana

CUBA

BAHAMAS

Turks and Caicos Islands (U.K.)

Tropic of Cancer

Cayman Islands (U.K.)

HAITI DOMINICAN REPUBLIC

Port-au-Prince

Puerto Rico (U.S.)

British Virgin Islands (U.K.)

Anguilla (U.K.)

St. Martin (FRANCE AND NETHERLANDS)

20°N

Kingston

JAMAICA

Santo Domingo

U.S. Virgin Islands (U.S.)

Basseterre

St. John's

ANTIGUA AND BARBUDA

Montserrat (U.K.)

ST. KITTS AND NEVIS

Guadeloupe (FRANCE)

Roseau DOMINICA

15°N

Martinique (FRANCE)

ST. LUCIA

Castries

ST. VINCENT AND THE GRENADINES

Caribbean Sea

Aruba (NETHERLANDS)

Netherlands Antilles (NETHERLANDS)

Kingstown

BARBADOS

Bridgetown

St. George's GRENADA

Port-of-Spain

TRINIDAD AND TOBAGO

10°N

Panama City

PANAMA

COLOMBIA

VENEZUELA

Geography Beautiful, sandy beaches and tropical forested plains are common in Central America and the Caribbean.

Culture Many people in the region maintain their traditional cultures. These Kuna women are from Panama.

161

Critical Thinking: Analyzing Visuals

At Level

Culture

Research Required

1. Explain to students that many native Indian groups in Central America and the Caribbean islands died out after the Europeans came, as a result of disease and brutal treatment at the hands of their conquerors. However, the Kuna of Panama survived and have kept their traditions intact.

2. Encourage students to do research on the Internet or in the library to learn about the Kuna. Challenge them to come up with

theories, based on what they learn, that would explain why the Kuna were able to survive and maintain their way of life.

LS **Verbal/Linguistic**

Alternative Assessment Handbook, Rubric 30: Research

• **Chapter Preview** •

Explore the Map and Pictures

Central America and the Caribbean: Political Guide students to note the range of countries in Central America and the Caribbean, from tiny islands to larger countries on the isthmus. Ask students to think of one question related to the photographs and captions. *Examples: When and where did the Spanish build forts? What are some other native people in Central America and the Caribbean? How have they maintained their traditions?*

▶ Map Zone Transparency: Central America and the Caribbean: Political

Info to Know

Castillo de San Felipe del Morro
Puerto Rico's best-known fortress, known as El Morro, became a UNESCO World Heritage Site in 1933. It is also a National Historic Site in the U.S. National Park Service. Its foundations were laid in 1539, but it was not completed until 1787. El Morro overlooks the entrance to San Juan Bay. It has borne assaults by many foes, including Sir Francis Drake in 1595 and the U.S. Navy in 1898 during the Spanish-American War.

↗ hmhsocialstudies.com
Teacher Resources

Answers

Map Zone 1. *El Salvador;* **2.** *The sea may make it difficult to communicate because it separates countries from each other.*

Bellringer

If **YOU** lived there. . . Use the **Daily Bellringer Transparency** to help students answer the question.

▶ Daily Bellringer Transparency, Section 1

Key Terms and Places

 RF: Vocabulary Builder, Section 1

Taking Notes

Have students use the graphic organizer online to take notes on the section. This activity will prepare students for the Section Assessment, in which they will complete a graphic organizer that builds on the information using the Critical Thinking Skill: Categorizing.

Physical Geography

What You Will Learn...

Main Ideas

1. Physical features of the region include volcanic highlands and coastal plains.
2. The climate and vegetation of the region include forested highlands, tropical forests, and humid lowlands.
3. Key natural resources in the region include rich soils for agriculture, a few minerals, and beautiful beaches.

The Big Idea

The physical geography of Central America and the Caribbean islands includes warm coastal lowlands, cooler highlands, and tropical forests.

Key Terms and Places

isthmus, p. 162
Caribbean Sea, p. 162
archipelago, p. 163
Greater Antilles, p. 163
Lesser Antilles, p. 163
cloud forest, p. 164

hmhsocialstudies.com
TAKING NOTES

Use the graphic organizer online to take notes on Mexico's physical geography.

If **YOU** lived there...

You live in San José, the capital of Costa Rica. But now you are visiting a tropical forest in one of the country's national parks. You make your way carefully along a swinging rope bridge in the forest canopy—40 feet above the forest floor! You see a huge green iguana making its way along a branch. A brilliantly colored parrot flies past you.

What other creatures might you see in the forest?

BUILDING BACKGROUND Nearly all the countries of Central America and the Caribbean lie in the tropics. That means they generally have warm climates and tropical vegetation. Many people like to visit these countries because of their physical beauty.

Physical Features

Sandy beaches, volcanic mountains, rain forests, clear blue water—these are images many people have of Central America and the Caribbean islands. This region's physical geography is beautiful. This beauty is one of the region's greatest resources.

Central America

The region called Central America is actually the southern part of North America. Seven countries make up this region: Belize, Guatemala, Honduras, El Salvador, Nicaragua, Costa Rica, and Panama. As you can see on the map, Central America is an **isthmus**, or a narrow strip of land that connects two larger land areas. No place on this isthmus is more than about 125 miles (200 km) from either the Pacific Ocean or the **Caribbean Sea**.

A chain of mountains and volcanoes separates the Pacific and Caribbean coastal plains, and only a few short rivers flow through Central America. The ruggedness of the land and the lack of good water routes make travel in the region difficult.

162 CHAPTER 7

Teach the Big Idea

At Level

Physical Geography

Prep Required

1. **Teach** Ask students the questions in the Main Idea boxes under Direct Teach.

2. **Apply** Use a large wall map of the world. Prepare and read a list of all of the countries in Central America and the Caribbean islands one at a time. As you read each country, invite a volunteer to come up to the map and point to the country. Have volunteers add other information they may know about the country. **LS Visual/Spatial**

3. **Review** At the map, review the names of the countries, grouping them into Central America, the Greater Antilles, and the Lesser Antilles.

4. **Practice/Homework** Have students select one country from each group (Central America, Greater Antilles, Lesser Antilles) and write a short paragraph about it.
LS Verbal/Linguistic

📋 Alternative Assessment Handbook, Rubric 21: Map Reading

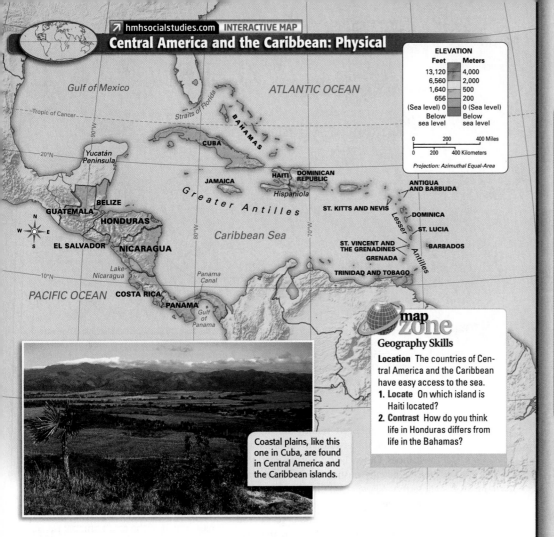

Central America and the Caribbean: Physical

ELEVATION

Feet	Meters
13,120	4,000
6,560	2,000
1,640	500
656	200
(Sea level) 0	0 (Sea level)
Below sea level	Below sea level

0   200   400 Miles
0   200   400 Kilometers
Projection: Azimuthal Equal-Area

Gulf of Mexico

ATLANTIC OCEAN

Tropic of Cancer

Straits of Florida

BAHAMAS

Yucatán Peninsula

CUBA

20°N

HAITI   DOMINICAN REPUBLIC

JAMAICA

Hispaniola

Greater Antilles

ANTIGUA AND BARBUDA

ST. KITTS AND NEVIS

GUATEMALA   BELIZE

DOMINICA

HONDURAS

Caribbean Sea

ST. LUCIA

Lesser Antilles

EL SALVADOR   NICARAGUA

ST. VINCENT AND THE GRENADINES

BARBADOS

GRENADA

Lake Nicaragua

Panama Canal

TRINIDAD AND TOBAGO

10°N

PACIFIC OCEAN   COSTA RICA

PANAMA

Gulf of Panama

map Zone

Geography Skills

Location The countries of Central America and the Caribbean have easy access to the sea.

1. **Locate** On which island is Haiti located?
2. **Contrast** How do you think life in Honduras differs from life in the Bahamas?

Coastal plains, like this one in Cuba, are found in Central America and the Caribbean islands.

The Caribbean Islands

Across the Caribbean Sea from Central America lie hundreds of islands known as the Caribbean islands. They make up an **archipelago** (ahr-kuh-PE-luh-goh), or large group of islands. Arranged in a long curve, the Caribbean islands stretch from the southern tip of Florida to northern South America. They divide the Caribbean Sea from the Atlantic Ocean.

There are two main island groups in the Caribbean. The four large islands of Cuba, Jamaica, Hispaniola, and Puerto Rico make up the **Greater Antilles** (an-TI-leez). Many smaller islands form the **Lesser Antilles**. They stretch from the Virgin Islands to Trinidad and Tobago. A third island group, the Bahamas, lies in the Atlantic Ocean southeast of Florida. It includes nearly 700 islands and thousands of reefs.

FOCUS ON READING

How are the Greater and Lesser Antilles different?

CENTRAL AMERICA AND THE CARIBBEAN **163**

Direct Teach

Main Idea

❶ Physical Features

Physical features of the region include volcanic highlands and coastal plains.

Summarize How would you summarize Central America's main physical features? *an isthmus that contains a central chain of volcanic mountains, with coastal plains on both sides*

Define What is an archipelago? *a large group of islands*

Identify Cause and Effect What happens when tectonic plates shift? *Earthquakes and volcanic eruptions occur.*

▶ Map Zone Transparency: Central America and the Caribbean: Physical

Info to Know

The Bahamas Unlike many other Caribbean islands, the Bahamas originated as coral reefs and are made up mainly of limestone and coral rising from a submarine plateau. The islands are generally low, flat, and swampy. Shoals and coral reefs make navigation around them difficult, and some of the outer islands are uninhabited. Other islands in the group, however, are extremely popular with tourists. Favorite attractions are the brightly colored coral gardens and the great variety of sea life around the islands.

↗ hmhsocialstudies.com

Online Resources
Activity: The Panama Canal

Differentiating Instruction

Below Level

Special Needs Learners

1. Tell students to imagine that they are planning a vacation to Central America and the Caribbean islands. Have students listen to Section 1 of the textbook chapter on audio CD in preparation for their trip, then guide them in a brief discussion about what they heard.

2. Have students cut out pictures of items from magazines and catalogs that they would take with them to one of these destinations: San Pedro, Belize (near coral reefs); Chirripó National Park, Costa Rica (mountainous region); San Juan, Puerto Rico (colonial city with historic fort); St. Thomas, U.S. Virgin Islands (beach resort).

3. Have students write the destination they chose on poster board and paste the pictures of the items they cut out. Ask volunteers to share their posters with the class and explain their choices.

LS Auditory/Musical, Kinesthetic, Visual/Spatial

📝 Alternative Assessment Handbook, Rubrics 18: Listening; and 28: Posters

Answers

Map Zone 1. *Hispaniola;* **2.** *possible answer—Because Honduras is more mountainous and farther away from the U.S., it may have fewer tourists.*

Focus on Reading *The Greater Antilles are made up of four large islands while the Lesser Antilles are made up of many small islands.*

Main Idea

❷ Climate and Vegetation

The climate and vegetation of the region include forested highlands, tropical forests, and humid lowlands.

Identify What has replaced original savanna vegetation on Central America's Pacific coast? *plantations and ranches*

Recall When do hurricanes threaten the Caribbean? *late summer to fall; between June and November*

Make Generalizations What is the climate like in the region? *generally sunny and warm, but more humid in the mountains and along the eastern coast; dry winters and wet summers*

RF: Social Studies Skills, Interpreting a Climate Graph

Map Zone Transparency: Volcanic Activity in Central America and the Caribbean

Did you know. . .

The only tropical rain forest in the United States National Forest System is in Puerto Rico. The Caribbean National Forest, also known as El Yunque, lies less than an hour's drive from Puerto Rico's capital, San Juan. Cool and mountainous, El Yunque has a yearly rainfall of more than 100 billion gallons. It is home to many unique plant and animal species, including the endangered Puerto Rican parrot. According to ancient Indian legend, El Yunque was also home to Yuquiyu, a benevolent god spirit who protected his land and people.

Answers

Map Zone **1.** *Caribbean and Cocos plates;* **2.** *because there are no tectonic plate boundaries in the Caribbean*

Reading Check *mountains, volcanoes, plains, beaches*

164

↗ hmhsocialstudies.com **INTERACTIVE MAP**
Volcanic Activity in Central America and the Caribbean

— Plate boundary
▲ Active volcano
◄— Direction of plate movement

0   200   400 Miles
0   200   400 Kilometers
Projection: Azimuthal Equal-Area

❶ The Santa Ana volcano in El Salvador was formed by tectonic movements.

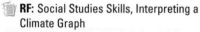
map zone
Geography Skills

Regions Movement of tectonic plates has caused volcanic activity at their boundaries, forming both the highlands of Central America and many Caribbean islands.

1. Use the Map Active volcanoes in Central America mostly occur at the boundary of which two plates?
2. Explain Why are there no volcanoes in the middle of the Caribbean Sea?

Many Caribbean islands are actually the tops of underwater mountains and volcanoes. Others began as coral reefs that were gradually pushed up to become flat limestone islands. Colliding tectonic plates have pushed this region's land up out of the sea over several million years. You can see these tectonic plates on the map above. Notice how the land follows the boundaries of the plates. Earthquakes and volcanic eruptions occur frequently as these plates shift. When such events do occur, they can cause great damage to the region and its people.

READING CHECK **Comparing** What physical features do Central America and the Caribbean islands have in common?

Climate and Vegetation

Central America and the Caribbean islands are generally sunny and warm. Humid tropical and tropical savanna climates are common in the islands and on Central America's coastal plains. On the Pacific coast, much of the area's original savanna vegetation has been cleared. It has been replaced by plantations and ranches. The opposite coast, along the Caribbean, has areas of tropical rain forest.

Inland mountain areas contain cool, humid climates. Some mountainous parts of Central America are covered with dense cloud forest. A **cloud forest** is a moist, high-elevation tropical forest where low clouds are common. These forests are home to numerous plant and animal species.

164 CHAPTER 7

Critical Thinking: Interpreting Maps | **At Level**

More on Tectonic Plates | **Prep Required**

1. Have students use a globe or a world map to predict where else in the world two tectonic plates are colliding. Remind them that tall mountains and volcanoes are found along the boundaries between plates. Point out that earthquakes are another indication of plate boundaries, and have them recall where they have heard of earthquakes happening recently.

2. If available, distribute blackline masters of world maps and have students sketch in their predicted plate boundaries.

3. Using a map showing the tectonic plate boundaries, compare students' predictions to actual data. **LS** **Visual/Spatial**

Alternative Assessment Handbook, Rubric 21: Map Reading

Temperatures in most of Central America and the Caribbean do not change much from day to night or from summer to winter. Instead, the change in seasons is marked by a change in rainfall. Winters in the region are generally dry, while it rains nearly every day during the summers.

From summer to fall, hurricanes are a threat in the region. These tropical storms bring violent winds, heavy rain, and high seas. Most hurricanes occur between June and November. Their winds and flooding can cause destruction and loss of life.

READING CHECK Generalizing Where would one find the coolest temperatures in the region?

Resources

The region's best resources are its land and climate. These factors make tourism an important industry. They also influence agriculture. Agriculture in the region can be profitable where volcanic ash has enriched the soil. Coffee, bananas, sugarcane, and cotton grow well and are major crops. Timber is exported from the rain forests.

Although its land and climate make good agricultural resources, the region has few mineral resources. Energy resources are also limited. Central America and the Caribbean islands must rely on energy imports, which limits their development.

READING CHECK Analyzing Why would having few energy resources limit economic development?

SUMMARY AND PREVIEW Central America and the Caribbean islands share volcanic physical features and a warm, tropical climate good for agriculture. In the next section you will learn about the history and culture of Central America.

Satellite View

Strong hurricane winds spin around a calm center point called the eye.

Hurricane Isabel

Hurricanes are rotating storms that bring heavy rain and winds that can reach speeds higher than 155 miles per hour (249 kph). This image shows Hurricane Isabel sweeping through the Caribbean Sea in 2003. Strong hurricanes like this one can shatter houses and hurl cars through the air.

Analyzing How can you tell the storm is rotating?

Section 1 Assessment

hmhsocialstudies.com
ONLINE QUIZ

Reviewing Ideas, Terms, and Places

1. **a. Define** What is an **isthmus**?
   b. Explain How has tectonic activity affected Central America and the Caribbean islands?
2. **a. Describe** What is a **cloud forest**?
   b. Make Inferences Why do temperatures in the region change little from summer to winter?
3. **a. Recall** What crops grow well in the region?
   b. Evaluate Do you think tourists who want to go to the beach are more likely to visit Guatemala or the Bahamas? Explain your answer.

Critical Thinking

4. **Categorizing** Draw a diagram like the one here. Using your notes, write descriptive phrases about the physical features, climate, and resources of both places.

Central America	Caribbean Islands

FOCUS ON WRITING

5. **Writing about Geography** What information about the physical geography of the region might interest readers of your travel guide? Jot down some ideas.

CENTRAL AMERICA AND THE CARIBBEAN **165**

Section Assessment Answers

1. **a.** a narrow strip of land that connects two larger land areas
   b. caused the mountains and islands to be formed; caused earthquakes and volcanoes; helped form rich volcanic soil
2. **a.** a moist, high-elevation tropical forest where low clouds are common
   b. It is in the tropics.
3. **a.** coffee, bananas, sugarcane, cotton
   b. possible answer—the Bahamas; more beaches on islands

4. Central America—mountain ranges, on an isthmus, has cloud forests; Caribbean—many islands, coral reefs, tops of submerged mountains; both—warm climate, at boundaries of tectonic plates, earthquakes and volcanoes, agriculture, tourism, limited energy resources

5. possible answers—sandy beaches; warm climate; tropical rain forests; dry winters

---

Direct Teach

Main Idea

Resources ❸

Key natural resources in the region include rich soils for agriculture, a few minerals, and beautiful beaches.

Identify What helps to enrich the region's soil? *volcanic ash*

Analyze Which of the region's resources are nonrenewable? *mineral and energy resources*

Review & Assess

Close

Have students look at a globe or world map and find examples of archipelagos around the world.

Review

Online Quiz, Section 1

Assess

SE Section 1 Assessment
PASS: Section 1 Quiz
Alternative Assessment Handbook

Reteach/Classroom Intervention

Guided Reading Workbook, Section 1
Interactive Skills Tutor CD-ROM

Answers

Reading Check (top) *at high elevations*
(bottom) *Most products require energy to be produced.*

Satellite View *The picture shows spinning clouds caused by winds that are spinning.*

Bellringer

If YOU lived there. . . Use the **Daily Bellringer Transparency** to help students answer the question.

▶ Daily Bellringer Transparency, Section 2

Central America and the Caribbean   Daily Bellringer
Section 2

Review Section 1

Read the statements below and determine what is "speaking."

1. "I am an archipelago across the sea from Central America." What am I?
2. "I am made up of the islands of Cuba, Jamaica, Hispaniola, and Puerto Rico." What am I?
3. "I am a humid, tropical forest high in the mountains where low clouds commonly occur." What am I?
4. "I am a narrow strip of land that makes up Central America." What am I?

Preview Section 2

If YOU lived there ...
You live in El Salvador, in a town that is still living with the effects of a civil war 20 years ago. Your parents and your older neighbors still speak about those years with fear. One effect of the war was damage to the economy. Many people have gone to Mexico to try to make a better life. Now your parents are talking about going there to look for work. But you are not sure. **How do you feel about leaving your home?**

Consider the PROS of leaving your town:
- poor economy in El Salvador
- better opportunities in Mexico
- fear of conflicts starting up again

Consider the CONS of leaving your town:
- have to say goodbye to friends
- will need to start at new school
- have to adjust to new culture

Review Answers: 1. Caribbean Islands; 2. Greater Antilles; 3. cloud forest; 4. isthmus

Academic Vocabulary

Review with students the high-use academic term in this section.

traditional   customary, time-honored (p. 169)

📝 RF: Vocabulary Builder, Section 2

Taking Notes

Have students use the graphic organizer online to take notes on the section. This activity will prepare students for the Section Assessment, in which they will complete a graphic organizer that builds on the information using the Critical Thinking Skill: Summarizing.

Central America

What You Will Learn...

Main Ideas

1. The history of Central America was mostly influenced by Spain.
2. The culture of Central America is a mixture of Native American and European traditions.
3. The countries of Central America today have challenges and opportunities.

The Big Idea

Central America's native traditions and colonial history have created a mixed culture, unstable governments, and uncertain economies.

Key Terms and Places

ecotourism, *p. 170*
civil war, *p. 170*
Panama Canal, *p. 171*

hmhsocialstudies.com
TAKING NOTES

Use the graphic organizer online to organize your notes on Central America.

If **YOU** lived there...

You live in El Salvador, in a town that is still living with the effects of a civil war 20 years ago. Your parents and your older neighbors still speak about those years with fear. One effect of the war was damage to the economy. Many people have gone to Mexico to try to make a better life. Now your parents are talking about going there to look for work. But you are not sure.

How do you feel about leaving your home?

BUILDING BACKGROUND All the countries of Central America were once colonies of European nations. Years of colonial rule made it hard for most of these countries to establish strong economies or democratic governments. Today things are slowly improving.

History

Many countries of Central America have a shared history. This shared history has been influenced by the Maya, the Spanish, and the United States.

Early History

In several Central American countries, the Maya were building large cities with pyramids and temples by about AD 250. The Maya abandoned most of their cities around 900, but the ruins of many ancient cities still stand in the region today. People of Maya descent still live in Guatemala and Belize. In fact, many ancient Maya customs still influence modern life there.

Hundreds of years later, in the early 1500s, most of Central America came under European control. Spain claimed most of the region. Britain claimed what is now Belize and also occupied part of Nicaragua's coast. The Spanish established large plantations in their colonies to grow crops like tobacco and sugarcane. They made Central American Indians work on the plantations or in gold mines elsewhere in the Americas. In addition, Europeans brought many enslaved Africans to the region to work on plantations and in mines.

Teach the Big Idea

At Level

Central America

1. **Teach** Ask students the questions in the Main Idea boxes under Direct Teach.

2. **Apply** Point out to students that some Central American countries have been politically unstable, while others have had few problems. Have students discuss what might be the ingredients for political stability. Encourage them to support their ideas with information from the text. **LS Verbal/Linguistic**

3. **Review** Go over some of the more popular ideas that were suggested by students and write them on the board.

4. **Practice/Homework** Have students write a short essay outlining a plan for political stability for Guatemala, Nicaragua, or El Salvador. **LS Verbal/Linguistic**

📝 Alternative Assessment Handbook, Rubric 43: Writing to Persuade

The economies of many Central American countries relied on only one crop—bananas. The U.S.-based United Fruit Company was the biggest banana exporter and the largest employer in the region for many years. The old photo below shows the company's hiring hall in Guatemala.

ANALYZING VISUALS Why do workers place cushions between bananas?

Central America Since Independence

The Spanish colonies of Central America declared independence from Spain in 1821, but much of the region remained joined together as the United Provinces of Central America. The countries of Costa Rica, Nicaragua, Honduras, El Salvador, and Guatemala separated from each other in 1838 to 1839. Panama remained part of Colombia until 1903. Belize did not gain independence from Britain until 1981.

For most countries in Central America, independence brought little change. The Spanish officials left, but wealthy land-owners continued to run the countries and their economies. The plantation crops of bananas and coffee supported Central American economies.

In the early to mid-1900s, one land-owner in particular, the U.S.-based United Fruit Company, controlled most of the banana production in Central America. To help its business, the company developed railroads and port facilities. This kind of development helped transportation and communications in the region.

Many people resented the role of foreign companies, however. They thought it was wrong that only a few people should own so much land while many people struggled to make a living. In the mid- to late 1900s, demands for reforms led to armed struggles in Guatemala, El Salvador, and Nicaragua. Only in recent years have these countries achieved peace.

READING CHECK Evaluating How did Spain influence the region's history?

Direct Teach

❷ Culture

The culture of Central America is a mixture of Native American and European traditions.

Define What is cacao? *the source of chocolate*

Recall What is the official language of Belize? *English*

Draw Conclusions Why do some people in the region still speak Native American languages? *They live in remote highlands or tropical forests, which were difficult for the Europeans to reach.*

📄 **RF:** Biography, Rigoberta Menchú Tum

📄 **RF:** Interdisciplinary Project, Doing Maya Math: Create a Poster and a Test

Connect to History

The Maya in Belize In 2004 archaeologists digging in the Punta Ycacos Lagoon in Belize made a startling underwater discovery about the ancient Maya. A perfectly preserved wooden paddle, dating from AD 680–880, was found. More than two hundred wooden posts from the same period have also been found. Archaeologists believe that the lagoon was a large Maya salt production site with many buildings. The paddle suggests that it was also a distribution center from which salt was paddled up rivers to cities inland.

Culture

Central America's colonial history has influenced its culture. The region's people, languages, religion, and festivals reflect both Spanish and native practices.

People and Languages

Most of the people in Central America are mestizos, or people of mixed European and Indian ancestry. Various Indian peoples descended from the ancient Maya live in places such as the Guatemalan Highlands.

People of African ancestry also make up a significant minority in this region. They live mostly along the Caribbean coast.

In some countries in Central America, many people still speak the native Indian languages. In places that were colonized by England, English is spoken. For example, it is the official language of Belize. In most countries, however, Spanish is the official language. The Spanish colonization of Central America left this lasting mark on the region.

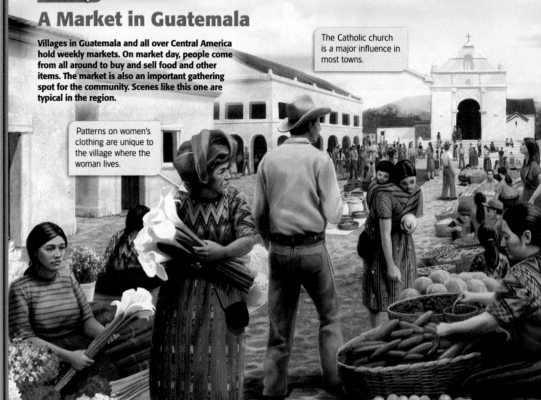

Close-up

A Market in Guatemala

Villages in Guatemala and all over Central America hold weekly markets. On market day, people come from all around to buy and sell food and other items. The market is also an important gathering spot for the community. Scenes like this one are typical in the region.

The Catholic church is a major influence in most towns.

Patterns on women's clothing are unique to the village where the woman lives.

168 CHAPTER 7

Cross-Discipline Activity: Art

At Level

Travel Posters

Research Required

1. Have students select a Central American country and design a travel poster highlighting a famous tourist attraction or an ecotourist destination. Posters should be drawn in pencil on four sheets of copy paper taped together. Their designs should have only a few words (the name of the country and the name of the attraction) and should feature a large drawing. Work with students to help them achieve a pleasing design.

2. Using the best paper and art materials available, have students carefully transfer their poster designs on larger sheets of paper. Emphasize to students that time spent on the design stage will help them to keep from making mistakes on the final product.

🔲 **Visual/Spatial**

📄 Alternative Assessment Handbook, Rubrics 3: Artwork; and 28: Posters

Religion, Festivals, and Food

Many Central Americans practice a religion brought to the region by Europeans. Most people are Roman Catholic because Spanish missionaries taught the Indians about Catholicism. However, Indian traditions have influenced Catholicism in return. Also, Protestant Christians are becoming a large minority in places such as Belize.

Religion has influenced celebrations in towns throughout the region. For example, to celebrate special saints' feast days, some people carry images of the saint in parades through the streets. Easter is a particularly important holiday. Some towns decorate whole streets with designs made of flowers and colorful sawdust.

During festivals, people eat **traditional** foods. Central America shares some of its traditional foods, like corn, with Mexico. The region is also known for tomatoes, hot peppers, and cacao (kuh-KOW), which is the source of chocolate.

READING CHECK **Contrasting** How is Belize culturally different from the rest of the region?

Tourists contribute to the local economy when they buy crafts.

People often spend all day at the market and need to eat lunch there.

ANALYSIS SKILL **ANALYZING VISUALS**

How do the contributions of tourists and Guatemalans affect the local economy differently?

CENTRAL AMERICA AND THE CARIBBEAN **169**

3 Central America Today

The countries of Central America today have challenges and opportunities.

Identify Who ruled Nicaragua in the 1980s? *the Sandinistas*

Define What is ecotourism? *the practice of using an area's natural environment to attract tourists*

Contrast How does Costa Rica differ from many other Central American countries? *It has a history of peace; it has a stable, democratic government; it does not have an army.*

Info to Know

The Sandinistas The Sandinista National Liberation Front, or Sandinistas, formed in Nicaragua in 1962 to oppose dictator Anastasio Somoza Debayle. Somoza's family had controlled Nicaragua since 1937, greatly enriching themselves and their associates. Working with another faction, the Sandinistas toppled the Somoza government in 1979. The Sandinistas took control of the government and took immediate measures to help the poor. The United States was not supportive of the leftist Sandinista government and in 1981 began to finance counter-revolutionary military forces, or contras, to overthrow the Sandinistas.

Ecotourism

A diver practices ecotourism as he explores Belize's coral reefs.

ANALYZING VISUALS What do you think the diver saw in the coral reefs?

Central America Today

The countries of Central America share similar histories and cultures. However, they all face their own economic and political challenges today. In 2005 Costa Rica, the Dominican Republic, El Salvador, Guatemala, Honduras, and Nicaragua signed the Central American Free Trade Agreement (CAFTA) with the United States to help increase trade among the countries.

Guatemala

Guatemala is the most populous country in Central America. More than 13 million people live there. About 60 percent of Guatemalans are mestizo and European. About 40 percent are Central American Indians. Many speak Maya languages.

Most people in Guatemala live in small villages in the highlands. Fighting between rebels and government forces there killed some 200,000 people between 1960 and 1996. Guatemalans are still recovering from this conflict.

Coffee, which grows well in the cool highlands, is Guatemala's most important crop. The country also is a major producer of cardamom, a spice used in Asian foods.

Belize

Belize has the smallest population in Central America. The country does not have much land for agriculture, either. But **ecotourism**—the practice of using an area's natural environment to attract tourists—has become popular lately. Tourists come to see the country's coral reefs, Maya ruins, and coastal resorts.

Honduras

Honduras is a mountainous country. Most people live in mountain valleys and along the northern coast. The rugged land makes transportation difficult and provides little land where crops can grow. However, citrus fruits and bananas are important exports.

El Salvador

In El Salvador, a few rich families own much of the best land while most people live in poverty. These conditions were a reason behind a long civil war in the 1980s. A **civil war** is a conflict between two or more groups within a country. The war killed many people and hurt the economy.

El Salvador's people have been working to rebuild their country since the end of the war in 1992. One advantage they have in this rebuilding effort is the country's fertile soil. People are able to grow and export crops such as coffee and sugarcane.

Nicaragua

Nicaragua has also been rebuilding since the end of a civil war. In 1979, a group called the Sandinistas overthrew a dictator.

170 CHAPTER 7

Critical Thinking: Making Decisions

At Level

Ecotourist Code of Ethics

1. Point out to students that tourists who want to visit unspoiled lands and fragile ecosystems face a dilemma—they must tread lightly and make sure they do no harm.

2. Have students work in small groups to discuss the types of vacation sites in Central America that would attract ecotourists and precautions that should be taken to preserve the sites. Have each group make a poster of their proposed rules and label it *Ecotourist Code of Ethics*.

3. Have each group present to the class.

4. Alternately, have students use the Internet to research commercially-available ecotours to see if they explain how they prevent environmental damage by the tourists they guide. If the Web site posts no policy, suggest that students email the Webmaster for more information. **LS Verbal/Linguistic, Interpersonal**

Alternative Assessment Handbook, Rubics 14: Group Activity; and 28: Posters

Answers

Analyzing Visuals *possible answers—an eel, fish, coral, other sea life*

Many Nicaraguans supported the Sandinistas, but rebel forces aided by the United States fought the Sandinistas for power. The civil war ended in 1990 when elections ended the rule of the Sandinistas. Nicaragua is now a democracy.

Costa Rica

Unlike most other Central American countries, Costa Rica has a history of peace. It also has a stable, democratic government. The country does not even have an army. Peace has helped Costa Rica make progress in reducing poverty.

Agricultural products like coffee and bananas are important to Costa Rica's economy. Also, many tourists visit Costa Rica's rich tropical rain forests.

Panama

Panama is the narrowest, southernmost country of Central America. Most people live in areas near the **Panama Canal**. Canal fees and local industries make the canal area the country's most prosperous region.

The Panama Canal provides a link between the Pacific Ocean, the Caribbean Sea, and the Atlantic Ocean. The United States finished building the canal in 1914. For years the Panama canal played an important role in the economy and politics of the region. The United States controlled the canal until 1999. Then, as agreed to in a treaty, Panama finally gained full control of the canal.

READING CHECK **Drawing Inferences** Why do you think Panama might want control of the canal?

FOCUS ON READING
What word in the paragraphs on Costa Rica signals contrast?

SUMMARY AND PREVIEW Native peoples, European colonizers, and the United States have influenced Central America's history and culture. Today most countries are developing stable governments. Their economies rely on tourism and agriculture. In the next section you will learn about the main influences on the Caribbean islands and life there today.

Section 2 Assessment

hmhsocialstudies.com
ONLINE QUIZ

Reviewing Ideas, Terms, and Places

1. a. Recall What parts of Central America did the British claim?
b. Analyze How did independence affect most Central American countries?
c. Elaborate What benefits and drawbacks might there be to the United Fruit Company's owning so much land?
2. a. Identify What language do most people in Central America speak?
b. Explain How have native cultures influenced cultural practices in the region today?
3. a. Define What is a **civil war**, and where in Central America has a civil war been fought?
b. Explain Why might some people practice **ecotourism**?
c. Elaborate Why is the **Panama Canal** important to Panama? Why is it important to other countries?

Critical Thinking

4. Summarizing Copy the graphic organizer below. Using your notes, write at least one important fact about each Central American country today.

Guatemala	
Belize	
Honduras	
El Salvador	
Nicaragua	
Costa Rica	
Panama	

FOCUS ON WRITING

5. Describing Central America Note details about the history, culture, and life today of people in Central America. Which details will appeal to people who are thinking of visiting the region?

CENTRAL AMERICA AND THE CARIBBEAN **171**

Section 2 Assessment Answers

1. a. Belize; part of Nicaragua's coast
b. Control of the land passed from Spain to a few wealthy landowners.
c. benefits—transportation and communication improved; drawbacks—most people struggled to survive because they didn't own any land.
2. a. Spanish
b. native languages still spoken; Indian beliefs influenced Catholicism; corn part of diet
3. a. a conflict between two or more groups within a country; Guatemala, Nicaragua, El Salvador
b. to see features of a country's natural environment

c. Panama—as a source of income; other countries—to shorten the trip from the Pacific Ocean to the Caribbean Sea and Atlantic Ocean
4. possible answer—Guatemala: most populous country; Belize: supports ecotourism; Honduras: exports fruit; El Salvador: rebuilding after civil war; Nicaragua: a democracy; Costa Rica: has no army; Panama: site of Panama Canal
5. Students' notes should include details that would appeal to tourists.

Geography and History

Did you know...

After gold was discovered in California in 1849, thousands of fortune-seekers from the East Coast rushed to Panama because it was the shortest way to get to the gold fields. They traveled by foot, canoe, and pack animal over treacherous jungle and mountain terrain. The trip could take five to six weeks, but this was a vast improvement over a trip lasting five to six months around the tip of South America. The journey got much easier after 1855, when the Panama Railroad Company finished a rail line across the isthmus. From 1855 until 1869, this railroad carried tens of thousands of gold-seekers bound for California. Its importance diminished once the U.S. transcontinental railroad was completed in 1869.

▶ Map Zone Transparency: Routes Before and After the Panama Canal

The Panama Canal

The Panama Canal links the Atlantic and Pacific oceans. Built in the early 1900s, workers on the canal faced tropical diseases and the dangers of blasting through solid rock. The result of their efforts was an amazing feat of engineering. Today some 13,000 to 14,000 ships pass through the canal each year.

Routes Before and After the Panama Canal

map zone

San Francisco — New York
NORTH AMERICA
ATLANTIC OCEAN
5,200 MILES (8,368 KM)
Panama Canal
PACIFIC OCEAN
13,000 MILES (20,921 KM)
SOUTH AMERICA

— Route around South America
— Route through the Panama Canal

0   750   1,500 Miles
0   750   1,500 Kilometers
Projection: Azimuthal Equal-Area

The Panama Canal shortens a trip from the east coast of the United States to the west coast by about 8,000 miles (15,000 km).

172 CHAPTER 7

Differentiating Instruction

Struggling Readers
Below Level

Have students describe what they see in the diagram. Then read aloud the introduction and each label. Remind students of things they said in their descriptions that are confirmed in the text. Encourage students to point out other parts of the diagram that might have been labeled, such as the maximum size of ships the canal can handle. **LS** Visual/Spatial

📝 Alternative Assessment Handbook, Rubric 11: Discussions

Advanced/Gifted and Talented
Above Level

Research Required

Have students use the Internet or library to research early ideas for a canal in Central America, who proposed them, and what came of them. Have them make a time line showing events leading up to the beginning of construction of the Panama Canal in 1904. **LS** Verbal/Linguistic, Visual/Spatial

📝 Alternative Assessment Handbook, Rubric 36: Time Lines

Crossing a Continent
The Panama Canal takes ships from sea level, across a mountain range, and back to sea level.

Caribbean Sea

Gatún Locks

Pedro Miguel Locks

Miraflores Locks

Gatún Lake

Pacific Ocean

Trains help guide large ships through the canal.

These locks act as doors to different compartments of the canal. Underground pumps raise and lower the water in each compartment like an elevator.

HISTORY VIDEO Panama Canal
hmhsocialstudies.com

ANALYSIS SKILL ANALYZING VISUALS
1. Why was Panama a good location for a canal?
2. Why must ships be raised and lowered in order to get through the canal?

Geography and History

Connect to History

The Panama Canal When the United States turned over control of the Panama Canal to Panama in 1999, some Panamanians worried that their country would fall on hard times. The United States' presence had brought jobs and stability, although it had also been a cause for resentment among Panamanians who viewed the United States as a colonial power. Since regaining control of the canal, Panama has begun turning former military installations into housing, hotels, universities, recreation areas, and other developments.

MISCONCEPTION ALERT

The Canal's Direction When a ship passes through the Panama Canal from the Pacific Ocean to the Caribbean Sea, students may think that it is traveling in an easterly direction. In reality, these ships are traveling in a northwesterly direction, as can be seen by examining a detailed map.

Critical Thinking: Making Predictions

At Level

A Canal Worker's Life

Research Required

1. Ask students to imagine what it was like to be a worker on the Panama Canal. Have them write a description of what they think a typical worker's life was like.

2. Have students use the library or Internet to research the working and living conditions for Panama Canal workers. Ask them to write a description of a typical worker's life based on their research.

3. Call on volunteers to share their descriptions of a worker's life before and after research. Encourage students to discuss facts they learned that were especially surprising or intriguing. **LS Verbal/Linguistic**

Alternative Assessment Handbook, Rubrics 30: Research; and 40: Writing to Describe

Answers

Analyzing Visuals 1. *It contains the narrowest point on the isthmus.* **2**. *to go over mountains*

173

174 CHAPTER 7

Preteach

Bellringer

If YOU lived there. . . Use the **Daily Bellringer Transparency** to help students answer the question.

▶ Daily Bellringer Transparency, Section 3

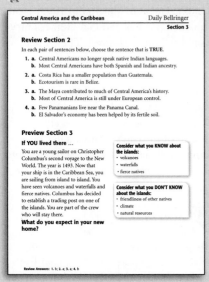

Central America and the Caribbean	Daily Bellringer
	Section 3

Review Section 2

In each pair of sentences below, choose the sentence that is TRUE.

1. **a.** Central Americans no longer speak native Indian languages.
   b. Most Central Americans have both Spanish and Indian ancestry.
2. **a.** Costa Rica has a smaller population than Guatemala.
   b. Ecotourism is rare in Belize.
3. **a.** The Maya contributed to much of Central America's history.
   b. Most of Central America is still under European control.
4. **a.** Few Panamanians live near the Panama Canal.
   b. El Salvador's economy has been helped by its fertile soil.

Preview Section 3

If YOU lived there ...

You are a young sailor on Christopher Columbus's second voyage to the New World. The year is 1493. Now that your ship is in the Caribbean Sea, you are sailing from island to island. You have seen volcanoes and waterfalls and fierce natives. Columbus has decided to establish a trading post on one of the islands. You are part of the crew who will stay there.

What do you expect in your new home?

Consider what you KNOW about the islands:
• volcanoes
• waterfalls
• fierce natives

Consider what you DON'T KNOW about the islands:
• friendliness of other natives
• climate
• natural resources

Review Answers: 1. b; 2. a; 3. a; 4. b

Key Terms and Places

📄 **RF: Vocabulary Builder, Section 3**

Taking Notes

Have students use the graphic organizer online to take notes on the section. This activity will prepare students for the Section Assessment, in which they will complete a graphic organizer that builds on the information using the Critical Thinking Skill: Summarizing.

The Caribbean Islands

What You Will Learn...

Main Ideas

1. The history of the Caribbean islands includes European colonization followed by independence.
2. The culture of the Caribbean islands shows signs of past colonialism and slavery.
3. Today the Caribbean islands have distinctive governments with economies that depend on agriculture and tourism.

The Big Idea

The Caribbean islands have a rich history and culture influenced by European colonization.

Key Terms and Places

dialect, *p. 176*
commonwealth, *p. 177*
refugee, *p. 177*
Havana, *p. 178*
cooperative, *p. 178*

🔲 **hmhsocialstudies.com**
TAKING NOTES

Use the graphic organizer online to organize your notes on the Caribbean islands.

If YOU lived there...

You are a young sailor on Christopher Columbus's second voyage to the New World. The year is 1493. Now that your ship is in the Caribbean Sea, you are sailing from island to island. You have seen volcanoes and waterfalls and fierce natives. Columbus has decided to establish a trading post on one of the islands. You are part of the crew who will stay there.

What do you expect in your new home?

> **BUILDING BACKGROUND** In the late 1400s and early 1500s, European nations began to compete for colonies. Sailing for Spain, Christopher Columbus made four voyages to the Americas. He and his men discovered and explored many islands.

History

When Christopher Columbus discovered America in 1492, he actually discovered the Caribbean islands. These islands now include 13 independent countries. The countries themselves show the influence of those first European explorers.

Early History

Christopher Columbus first sailed into the Caribbean Sea from Spain in 1492. He thought he had reached the Indies, or the islands near India. Therefore, he called the Caribbean islands the West Indies and the people who lived there Indians.

Spain had little interest in the smaller Caribbean islands, but the English, French, Dutch, and Danish did. In the 1600s and 1700s, these countries established colonies on the islands. They built huge sugarcane plantations that required many workers. Most Caribbean Indians had died from disease, so Europeans brought Africans to work as slaves. Soon Africans and people of African descent outnumbered Europeans on many islands.

Teach the Big Idea

At Level

The Caribbean Islands

1. **Teach** Ask students the questions in the Main Idea boxes under Direct Teach.

2. **Apply** Have students use the textbook to compile a list of Caribbean "records," roughly modeled after the *Guinness Book of World Records*. Have students find the largest and smallest islands in the Caribbean, the most and least populous, the first and last to become independent, the island that is the farthest east, west, north, or south, and so on. Students can invent their own categories based on any information they find interesting. 📘 **Verbal/Linguistic**

3. **Review** Have students take turns reading their Caribbean facts and writing the most important or interesting ones on the board.

4. **Practice/Homework** Have students write up a page of their five favorite Caribbean "records." 📘 **Verbal/Linguistic**

📄 Alternative Assessment Handbook, Rubric 9: Comparing and Contrasting

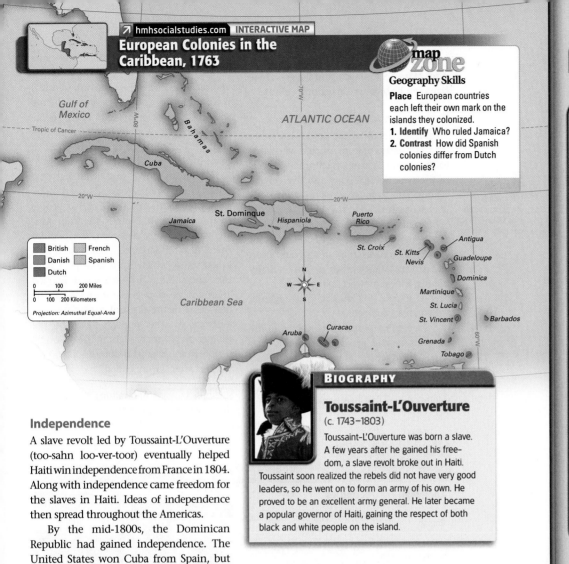

European Colonies in the Caribbean, 1763

map zone

Geography Skills

Place European countries each left their own mark on the islands they colonized.
1. **Identify** Who ruled Jamaica?
2. **Contrast** How did Spanish colonies differ from Dutch colonies?

Gulf of Mexico

ATLANTIC OCEAN

Tropic of Cancer

Bahamas

Cuba

Jamaica · St. Dominque · Hispaniola · Puerto Rico · Antigua · St. Croix · St. Kitts · Nevis · Guadeloupe · Dominica · Martinique · St. Lucia · St. Vincent · Barbados · Grenada · Tobago

Aruba · Curacao

Caribbean Sea

Legend
- British
- Danish
- Dutch
- French
- Spanish

0 100 200 Miles
0 100 200 Kilometers
Projection: Azimuthal Equal-Area

Independence

A slave revolt led by Toussaint-L'Ouverture (too-sahn loo-ver-toor) eventually helped Haiti win independence from France in 1804. Along with independence came freedom for the slaves in Haiti. Ideas of independence then spread throughout the Americas.

By the mid-1800s, the Dominican Republic had gained independence. The United States won Cuba from Spain, but Cuba gained independence in 1902. The other Caribbean countries did not gain independence until more than 40 years later, after World War II. At that time, the Europeans transferred political power peacefully to most of the islands.

Many Caribbean islands still are not independent countries. For example, the islands of Martinique and Guadeloupe are still French possessions. Each has its own elected government and is also represented in the French government. Most people on these islands seem not to wish for independence from their ruling countries.

READING CHECK Identifying Points of View
Why might an island's people not be interested in gaining independence?

BIOGRAPHY

Toussaint-L'Ouverture
(c. 1743–1803)

Toussaint-L'Ouverture was born a slave. A few years after he gained his freedom, a slave revolt broke out in Haiti. Toussaint soon realized the rebels did not have very good leaders, so he went on to form an army of his own. He proved to be an excellent army general. He later became a popular governor of Haiti, gaining the respect of both black and white people on the island.

Direct Teach

Main Idea

① History

The history of the Caribbean islands includes European colonization followed by independence.

Recall How many independent Caribbean island countries are there? *thirteen*

Explain What did Toussaint L'Ouverture do? *helped Haiti gain independence; became governor of Haiti*

Sequence Who has controlled Cuba over the years? *Spain claimed Cuba from the Native Americans; the United States took Cuba from Spain; Cuba gained independence from the United States in 1902.*

- RF: Biography, Toussaint L'Ouverture
- RF: Primary Source, Christopher Columbus's Letter about the West Indies
- RF: Geography and History, The Triangle Trade
- Map Zone Transparency: European Colonies in the Caribbean, 1763

MISCONCEPTION ALERT

Conquest from Cuba Some students may think that the conquests of Mexico and other parts of the Americas were carried out by the Spanish sailing all the way from Spain. In fact, Cuba was a base for many of these expeditions. The island was visited in 1492 by Columbus on his first voyage, and conquered by the Spanish in 1511. It became the headquarters for launching expeditions to the Americas and the assembly point for treasure fleets returning to Spain.

Cross-Discipline Activity: Mathematics

At Level

Colonies in the Caribbean

Research Required

1. Have students use the map from the Chapter Preview to list the political entities that make up the Caribbean islands. For each entity (island or group of islands, such as the U.S. Virgin Islands), have them research the following information: country the entity was first colonized by, current status (independent or not independent), and year independence was gained (if applicable).

2. Have students calculate the percentage of the entities colonized by each European country, and make a bar graph showing this.

3. Have students find which European countries still have colonies, and how many each has. Have them determine if some countries hold on to their colonies more than others, and if so, which ones.

4. If students detect a pattern, invite them to give possible reasons why this is the case.
   LS Logical/Mathematical

   Alternative Assessment Handbook, Rubrics 7: Charts; and 21, Map Reading

Answers

Map Zone 1. *Britain;* **2.** *They were larger because they were on larger islands.*

Reading Check *possible answer— An island may want a larger country's financial support or military protection.*

175

❷ Culture

The culture of the Caribbean islands shows signs of past colonialism and slavery.

Recall What holiday is celebrated right before the Christian season of Lent? *Carnival*

Explain Why do people in Barbados eat souse? *This dish, made of pigs' tails, ears, and snouts, was developed among slaves because slaveholders ate the best parts of the pig and gave the slaves leftovers.*

Summarize What elements of Caribbean culture show mixtures of European and African influences? *people of mixed ancestry; Creole dialects; religious practices like Santería*

Connect to Language Arts

Creole The reggae classic *Sweet and Dandy* by Toots and the Maytals is one of many reggae songs written in the English-based Creole language of Jamaica. The song tells of a couple, getting cold feet just before their wedding, who are being persuaded by family members to go through with the ceremony:

One poun' ten for de weddin' cake,
Twenty bokkle of cola wine,
All di people-dem dress up inna white,
Fi go h'eat off Johnson weddin' cake.
Line 1: One pound, ten shillings was an expensive cake!
Line 2: bokkle = bottle
Line 3: The –dem ending is used as a plural marker, like English –s. Inna = in
Line 4: Fi = To; h'eat = eat

Answers

Focus on Reading *for example, such as, also, another*

Reading Check *Creole languages are influenced by African languages; African religious beliefs influence Santería; some foods come from Africa or from the experiences of Africans during slavery.*

Interpreting Charts *English*

Culture

Today nearly all Caribbean islands show signs of past colonialism and slavery. These signs can be seen in the region's culture.

People, Languages, and Religion

Most islanders today are descended either from Europeans or from Africans who came to the region as slaves, or from a mixture of the two. Some Asians also live on the islands. They came to work on plantations after slavery ended in the region.

Languages spoken in the region reflect a colonial heritage. Spanish, English, or French as well as mixtures of European and African languages are spoken on many islands. For example, Haitians speak French Creole. Creole is a **dialect**, or a regional variety of a language.

The region's past is also reflected in the religions people practice. Former French and Spanish territories have large numbers of Catholics. People also practice a blend of Catholicism and traditional African religions. One blended religion is Santería.

FOCUS ON READING
What words in the paragraph on food signal comparison?

Festivals and Food

People on the Caribbean islands celebrate a variety of holidays. One of the biggest and most widespread is Carnival. Carnival is a time of feasts and celebration before the Christian season of Lent begins. People usually celebrate Carnival with big parades and fancy costumes. Festivals like Carnival often include great music.

Caribbean food and cooking also reflect the region's past. For example, slave ships carried foods as well as people to the Caribbean. Now foods from Africa, such as yams and okra, are popular there. Also, in Barbados, people eat a dish called souse, which is made of pigs' tails, ears, and snouts. This dish was developed among slaves because slaveholders ate the best parts of the pig and gave slaves the leftovers. Another popular flavor on the islands, curry, was brought to the region by people from India who came as plantation workers after slavery ended.

READING CHECK **Generalizing** How does Caribbean culture reflect African influences?

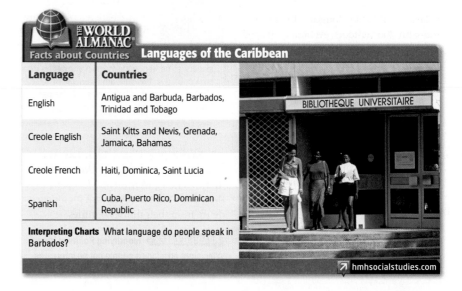

THE WORLD ALMANAC Facts about Countries — Languages of the Caribbean

Language	Countries
English	Antigua and Barbuda, Barbados, Trinidad and Tobago
Creole English	Saint Kitts and Nevis, Grenada, Jamaica, Bahamas
Creole French	Haiti, Dominica, Saint Lucia
Spanish	Cuba, Puerto Rico, Dominican Republic

Interpreting Charts What language do people speak in Barbados?

hmhsocialstudies.com

176 CHAPTER 7

Cross-Discipline Activity: Music

At Level

Caribbean Music

Prep Required

1. Bring in tapes or CDs that contain examples of various types of Caribbean music. Depending on the types of recordings, review with students basic facts about the type of music, island of origin, and languages the songs are sung in.

2. Play a selection, identifying the name of the piece, the artist, country of origin, instruments used, and any other helpful information. Invite students to give their reactions before moving on to the next selection.

3. Since this is lively music, it may be impossible to keep students from dancing. If necessary, push the furniture to the side and let students show off their best moves.

LS Auditory/Musical, Kinesthetic

Alternative Assessment Handbook, Rubric 22: Multimedia Presentations

CONNECTING TO the Arts

Caribbean Music

The Caribbean islands have produced many unique styles of music. For example, Jamaica is famous as the birthplace of reggae. Merengue is the national music and dance of the Dominican Republic. Trinidad and Tobago is the home of steel-drum and calypso music.

Here, a band in the Grenadines performs on steel drums. Steel-drum bands can include as few as 4 or as many as 100 musicians. The instruments are actually metal barrels like the kind used for shipping oil. The end of each drum is hammered into a curved shape with multiple grooves and bumps. Hitting different-sized bumps results in different notes.

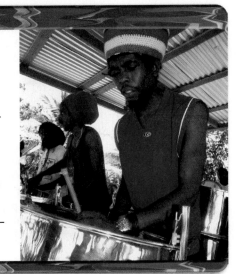

Drawing Inferences What role might trade have played in the development of steel-drum music?

The Caribbean Islands Today

Many Caribbean islands share a similar history. Still, each island has its own economy, government, and culture.

Puerto Rico

Once a Spanish colony, Puerto Rico today is a U.S. commonwealth. A **commonwealth** is a self-governing territory associated with another country. Puerto Ricans are U.S. citizens, but they do not have voting representation in Congress.

Overall, Puerto Rico's economy has benefitted from U.S. aid and investment. Still, wages are lower and unemployment is higher on the island than in the United States. Many Puerto Ricans have moved to the United States for better paying jobs. Today, Puerto Ricans debate whether their island should remain a U.S. commonwealth, become an American state, or become an independent nation.

Haiti

Haiti occupies the western part of the island of Hispaniola. Haiti's capital, Port-au-Prince, is the center of the nation's limited industry. Most Haitians farm small plots. Coffee and sugarcane are among Haiti's main exports.

Haiti is the poorest country in the Americas. Its people have suffered under a string of corrupt governments during the last two centuries. Violence, political unrest, and poverty have created many political refugees. A **refugee** is someone who flees to another country, usually for political or economic reasons. Many Haitian refugees have come to the United States.

On January, 12, 2010, a catastrophic earthquake struck close to Port-au-Prince. The quake devastated Haiti, leaving about 230,000 Haitians dead, 300,000 injured, and over a million homeless. Today, many Haitians continue working to rebuild their lives and nation.

CENTRAL AMERICA AND THE CARIBBEAN **177**

Info to Know

Baseball in the Dominican Republic
Many people in the Caribbean love baseball. Thousands of major league players got started in places like Puerto Rico and Cuba. However, the greatest number of foreign stars have come from the Dominican Republic, especially the city of San Pedro de Macoris. A remarkable number—eleven—of major league All Stars, including Sammy Sosa, came from this relatively small city. The capital, Santo Domingo, had the most (14) but is more than ten times as large!

Connect to History

Teofilo Stevenson Who was the greatest amateur boxer of all time? Some say the Cuban Teofilo Stevenson, who won three consecutive Olympic Gold medals between 1972 and 1980. At the peak of his career he was offered $5 million to leave Cuba and become a professional boxer. He turned the offer down, saying, "What's five million dollars worth, when I have the love of five million Cubans?"

Answers

Analyzing Visuals *possible answer—People seem distressed; they are not in a sturdy boat.*

178

Dominican Republic

The Dominican Republic occupies the eastern part of Hispaniola. The capital is Santo Domingo. Santo Domingo was the first permanent European settlement in the Western Hemisphere.

The Dominican Republic is not a rich country. However, its economy, health care, education, and housing are more developed than Haiti's. Agriculture is the basis of the economy in the Dominican Republic. The country's tourism industry has also grown in recent years. Beach resorts along the coast are popular with many tourists from Central and South America as well as from the United States.

Cuba

Cuba is the largest and most populous country in the Caribbean. It is located just 92 miles (148 km) south of Florida. **Havana**, the capital, is the country's largest and most important city.

Cuba has been run by a Communist government since Fidel Castro came to power in 1959. At that time, the government took over banks, large sugarcane plantations, and other businesses. Many of these businesses were owned by U.S. companies. Because of the takeovers, the U.S. government banned trade with Cuba and restricted travel there by U.S. citizens.

Today the government still controls the economy. Most of Cuba's farms are organized as cooperatives or government-owned plantations. A **cooperative** is an organization owned by its members and operated for their mutual benefit.

Besides controlling the economy, Cuba's government also controls all the newspapers, television, and radio stations. While many Cubans support these policies, others oppose them. Some people who oppose the government have become refugees in the United States. Many Cuban refugees have become U.S. citizens.

Cubans Divided

178 CHAPTER 7

Government-sponsored rallies are a part of Cuban life. Meanwhile, some Cubans try to flee their country on tiny rafts.

ANALYZING VISUALS How can you tell that the people in the raft are trying to flee Cuba?

Critical Thinking: Recognizing Bias

At Level

The Politics of the Caribbean

Research Required

1. Review with students the information in the section about politics in Haiti, Cuba, and Puerto Rico. Using the Internet, find articles and editorials about one of the following:
   • the Castro government of Cuba
   • the regime of Jean-Bertrand Aristide of Haiti
   • the regimes of François and Jean-Claude Duvalier in Haiti
   • the movement for Puerto Rican independence
   Supplement with sources that should be neutral, such as books or online encyclopedias.

2. Divide students into two groups. Have each group examine all sources for bias, focusing on one side of the issue. Have them list a variety of statements showing their point of view. Discuss as a class.

3. On the board, use a three-column table to sort statements as *Biased (Pro)*, *Biased (Con)*, and *Verified Facts.* **LS Verbal/Linguistic, Interpersonal**

   Alternative Assessment Handbook, Rubrics 14: Group Activity; and 16: Judging Information

Other Islands

The rest of the Caribbean islands are small countries. Jamaica is the largest of the remaining Caribbean countries. The smallest country is Saint Kitts and Nevis. It is not even one-tenth the size of Rhode Island, the smallest U.S. state!

A number of Caribbean islands are not independent countries but territories of other countries. These territories include the U.S. and British Virgin Islands. The Netherlands and France also still have some Caribbean territories.

Some of these islands have enough land to grow some coffee, sugarcane, or spices. However, most islands' economies are based on tourism. Hundreds of people on the islands work in restaurants and hotels visited by tourists. While tourism has provided jobs and helped economies, not all of its effects have been positive. For example, new construction sometimes harms the same natural environment tourists come to the islands to enjoy.

READING CHECK **Contrasting** How are the governments of Puerto Rico and Cuba different?

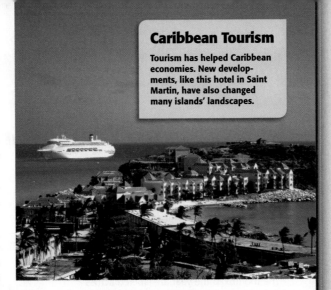

Caribbean Tourism
Tourism has helped Caribbean economies. New developments, like this hotel in Saint Martin, have also changed many islands' landscapes.

SUMMARY AND PREVIEW The Caribbean islands were colonized by European countries, which influenced the culture of the islands. Today the islands have different types of governments but similar economies. Next, you will read about countries in South America that are also located near the Caribbean Sea.

Section 3 Assessment

hmhsocialstudies.com
ONLINE QUIZ

Reviewing Ideas, Terms, and Places

1. a. Describe What crop was the basis of the colonial economy on the Caribbean islands?
b. Make Inferences Why do you think most smaller Caribbean countries were able to gain independence peacefully?

2. a. Define What is a **dialect**?
b. Explain In what ways have African influences shaped Caribbean culture?

3. a. Recall What is a **refugee**, and from what Caribbean countries have refugees come?
b. Make Inferences Why do you think many Cubans support their government's policies?
c. Evaluate What would be the benefits and drawbacks for Puerto Rico if it became a U.S. state?

Critical Thinking

4. Summarizing Look over your notes. Then use a diagram like this one to note specific influences on the region and where they came from in each circle. You may add more circles if you need to.

Caribbean Islands

FOCUS ON WRITING

5. Telling about the Caribbean Islands These islands have a fascinating history and a rich culture. Take notes about them for your travel guide.

CENTRAL AMERICA AND THE CARIBBEAN **179**

Did you know. . .

A centuries-old controversy over the final resting place of Christopher Columbus's bones was finally settled in 2004. Spanish scientists examined bones buried in Seville's cathedral and determined that they were those of Columbus's son Diego, not Christopher's, as had been believed. Columbus is buried in Santo Domingo, the capital of the Dominican Republic. Columbus visited the island of Hispaniola on his first voyage and founded the first European colony there. He, his brother, and his son governed the colony in its early years. Columbus died in Valladolid, Spain in 1506, and his body was moved from Spain to the cathedral in Santo Domingo two decades later.

• Review & Assess •

Close
Discuss with students which Caribbean island they would most like to visit and why.

Review
Online Quiz, Section 3

Assess
SE Section 3 Assessment
PASS: Section 3 Quiz
Alternative Assessment Handbook

Reteach/Classroom Intervention
Guided Reading Workbook, Section 3
Interactive Skills Tutor CD-ROM

Section 3 Assessment Answers

1. a. sugarcane
b. Many islands had few resources, so they were of little value as colonies.

2. a. a regional variety of a language
b. possible answers—African languages influenced Creole; African beliefs mixed with Catholicism in Santería; souse eaten by enslaved Africans; traditional African foods such as okra and yams are popular.

3. a. someone who flees to another country for political or economic reasons; Haiti, Cuba
b. possible answer—They think that the government is working, and they are happy with its current policies.

c. possible answers—benefits: voting representation in the U.S. Congress; drawbacks: loss of some self-government

4. possible answer—Spanish language from Spanish colonization; Santería religion from Catholicism and African religions; foods such as yams and okra brought from Africa

5. Students' notes should include information about the history and culture of the Caribbean islands.

Answers

Reading Check *Cuba has a Communist government, which controls the economy and media; Puerto Rico is a U. S. commonwealth and has an economy and laws similar to those in the U.S.*

Social Studies Skills

Interpreting a Climate Graph

Activity What a Climate Graph Shows

Materials: printouts of climate graphs from the Internet

1. Pass out printouts of climate graphs from the Internet. The graphs should be from different cities or regions and should show some variety in graphics. Include graphs with temperatures in centigrade and with the seasons reversed (summer running from December to March).

2. Have students examine the climate graphs. Ask them to write a brief summary of the information presented. Their summaries should begin with a sentence identifying what the graph shows (average temperature and rainfall) and for what place. The rest of the summary should make generalizations about the climate year-round or during certain seasons. Encourage students to link information about rainfall to information about temperature. For example: *August is very humid, with temperatures averaging in the 90s.*

3. Have students present their graphs and summaries to the class. As students present, compare and contrast the climates in the different places.

LS Verbal/Linguistic

📝 Alternative Assessment Handbook, Rubrics 40: Writing to Describe; and 24: Oral Presentations

📝 **RF:** Social Studies Skills, Interpreting a Climate Graph

---

Interpreting a Climate Graph

Learn

A climate graph is a visual representation of the climate in a certain region. The graph shows the average precipitation and average temperature for each month of the year.

Use the following tips to help you interpret a climate graph:

- The months of the year are labeled across the bottom of the graph.
- The measurements for monthly average temperatures are found on the left side of the graph.
- The measurements for monthly average precipitation are found on the right side of the graph.

Practice

Use the climate graph here to answer the following questions.

❶ What four months get the highest amount of precipitation?

❷ What months get fewer than two inches of precipitation?

❸ What is the average temperature in February?

A line shows the average temperature each month.

Climate Graph: Tegucigalpa, Honduras

Source: The Weather Channel Interactive, Inc.

Bars show the average precipitation each month.

Apply

Using the Internet, an almanac, or a newspaper, look up the monthly average temperatures and precipitation for your home town. Then make your own climate graph using that information.

180 CHAPTER 7

Social Studies Activity: Interpreting Graphs

At Level

Working Backward

1. Have students examine the climate graph on this page. Tell them that they will "work backward" to find and record the information on rainfall and temperature for every month. Choose a month and model this process for students.

2. Ask students to record the information for temperature and rainfall on separate lists. Remind them to include every month.

3. Guide the class in a discussion about climate graphs. Point out that students have recreated

the information from which the climate graph on the page was drawn. Tell them that while graphics and details may vary in climate graphs, they are all built from the following three lists:

- months of the year
- monthly average temperature
- monthly average rainfall

LS Verbal/Linguistic, Logical/Mathematical

📝 Alternative Assessment Handbook, Rubric 11: Discussions

Answers

Practice 1. *May, June, September, October* **2.** *January, February, March, April, November, December* **3.** *about 80°F*

Apply *Students' climate graphs should include monthly average temperatures and precipitation.*

Chapter Review

Geography's Impact
video series
Review the video to answer the closing question:
Why do so many visitors to the Caribbean come from the United States and Canada?

Visual Summary

Use the visual summary below to help you review the main ideas of the chapter.

QUICK FACTS

The region's landscapes include warm coastal lowlands and cool highland regions with tropical forests.

Native cultures still influence Central America. Today governments and economies there are changing.

The Caribbean islands have a history of colonial rule. Today many countries' economies there depend on tourism.

Reviewing Vocabulary, Terms, and Places

Choose one word from each word pair to correctly complete each sentence below.

1. A(n) _____ is a narrow strip of land that connects two larger land areas. **(archipelago/isthmus)**

2. A _____ is a self-governing territory associated with another country. **(commonwealth/cooperative)**

3. A _____ is someone who flees to another country, usually for political or economic reasons. **(traditional/refugee)**

4. The United States controlled the _____ until 1999. **(Caribbean Sea/Panama Canal)**

5. The large islands of Cuba, Jamaica, Hispaniola, and Puerto Rico make up the _____. **(Greater Antilles/Lesser Antilles)**

6. _____ is found in the mountainous part of Central America. **(Cloud forest/Havana)**

Comprehension and Critical Thinking

SECTION 1 *(Pages 162–165)*

7. **a. Describe** What process has formed many of the Caribbean islands? Describe the effect this process has on the region today.

b. Compare and Contrast How are summer and winter similar in Central America and the Caribbean? How are the seasons different?

c. Elaborate What kinds of damage might hurricanes cause? What damage might earthquakes and volcanic eruptions cause?

SECTION 2 *(Pages 166–171)*

8. **a. Identify** In what Central American country is English the official language?

b. Make Inferences Why do you think people of African ancestry live mainly along the coast?

c. Elaborate How might recent political conflict have affected development in some countries?

CENTRAL AMERICA AND THE CARIBBEAN **181**

Answers

Visual Summary

Review and Inquiry Have students use the visual summary to discuss details related to the landscape, history, and culture of Central America and the Caribbean.

▶ Quick Facts Transparency: Central America and the Caribbean Visual Summary

Reviewing Vocabulary, Terms, and Places

1. isthmus
2. commonwealth
3. refugee
4. Panama Canal
5. Greater Antilles
6. Cloud forest

Comprehension and Critical Thinking

7. **a.** volcanoes and the movement of tectonic plates; plenty of rich volcanic soil

b. Temperatures are the same year-round; the seasons are marked by variations in rainfall.

c. hurricanes—flooding and wind damage; earthquakes and volcanic eruptions—damage to land and buildings

8. **a.** Belize

b. because their ancestors were brought from Africa on ships and worked near the coast

c. possible answer—Political conflict may hurt a country's economy by creating a labor shortage if people try to leave as refugees.

Review and Assessment Resources

Review and Reinforce

SE Chapter Review

RF: Chapter Review

▶ Quick Facts Transparency: Central America and the Caribbean Visual Summary

Spanish Chapter Summaries Audio CD Program

TOS Holt McDougal PuzzleView®; Quiz Show for ExamView

Quiz Game CD-ROM

Assess

SE Standardized Test Practice

PASS: Chapter Test, Forms A and B

Alternative Assessment Handbook

TOS ExamView Test Generator, Chapter Test

Differentiated Instruction Modified Worksheets and Tests CD-ROM: Chapter Test

↗ Online Assessment Program, in the Interactive Student Edition

Reteach/Intervene

Guided Reading Workbook

Differentiated Instruction Teacher Management System: Lesson Plans

Differentiated Instruction Modified Worksheets and Tests CD-ROM

Interactive Skills Tutor CD-ROM

↗ hmhsocialstudies.com
Chapter Resources

9. a. Haiti; Toussaint L'Ouverture

b. their main source of income; sometimes causes environmental damage and overcrowding

c. possible answer—benefits: operated for members' benefit; drawbacks: all members affected if crops fail

Social Studies Skills

10. June and September

11. 75°F

Using the Internet

12. Go to hmhsocialstudies.com to access a rubric for this activity.

Map Activity

13. A. Havana, Cuba
   B. Lesser Antilles
   C. Guatemala
   D. Caribbean Sea
   E. Puerto Rico
   F. Panama

Focus on Reading and Writing

14. possible answer—The Caribbean countries are islands in an archipelago, while Central America is an isthmus. Both areas have generally warm, sunny climates, although the more elevated areas of Central America are cool and humid. For both areas, mineral and energy resources are limited, but the soil is rich. The climate is the best resource, as it brings tourists, but the political unrest in Central America limits tourism.

RF: Focus on Reading, Understanding Comparison-Contrast

15. Rubric Students' travel guides should

- have an attractive design
- give information about physical geography, history, and culture
- help visitors decide what time of year they would like to visit
- tell visitors what to expect about life in the place today

RF: Focus on Writing, Creating a Travel Guide

SECTION 3 *(Pages 174–179)*

9. a. Recall What country was the first to gain independence? Who led the revolt that led to independence?

b. Analyze How does tourism impact the smaller islands of the Caribbean?

c. Evaluate What might be some benefits and drawbacks of working for a cooperative?

Social Studies Skills

Interpreting a Climate Graph *Use the climate graph below to answer the questions that follow.*

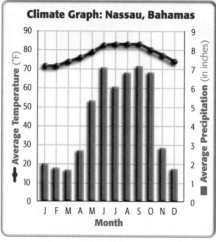

Climate Graph: Nassau, Bahamas

Source: The Weather Channel Interactive, Inc.

10. What two months get the most rainfall?

11. What is the average temperature in December?

Using the Internet

12. Activity: Taking an Ecotour Ecotourism is all about visiting places to appreciate the environment. Through your online textbook, take your own Internet ecotour of Central America and the Caribbean islands. Visit the Web sites to learn more about some of the people and places you have read about in this chapter. Then create a postcard from a place you visited on your trip.

 hmhsocialstudies.com

Map Activity

13. Central America and the Caribbean On a separate sheet of paper, match the letters on the map with their correct labels.

Guatemala   Caribbean Sea
Panama   Puerto Rico
Havana, Cuba   Lesser Antilles

hmhsocialstudies.com **INTERACTIVE MAP**

FOCUS ON READING AND WRITING

14. Understanding Comparison-Contrast Look back over the section on physical geography. Then write a paragraph comparing and contrasting Central America with the Caribbean islands. Consider their physical features, climates, landscapes, and resources.

15. Creating a Travel Guide Choose one place in this region to be the subject of your travel guide. Then look over your notes for facts about that place to interest your reader. Your guide should begin with a paragraph describing the outstanding physical features of the place. Your second paragraph should identify interesting details about its history and culture. End with a sentence that might encourage your readers to visit. Include two images in your guide to show off the features of the place you have chosen.

Standardized Test Prep

DIRECTIONS: Read questions 1 through 7 and write the letter of the best response. Then read question 8 and write your own well-constructed response.

1 Which country is an example of an isthmus?
- **A** Guatemala
- **B** Bahamas
- **C** Panama
- **D** Cuba

2 Which European country established the most colonies in the Greater Antilles?
- **A** France
- **B** Spain
- **C** England
- **D** Netherlands

3 Which country has a Communist government?
- **A** Cuba
- **B** Puerto Rico
- **C** Dominican Republic
- **D** Haiti

4 Which of the following countries has remained at peace since independence?
- **A** Guatemala
- **B** El Salvador
- **C** Nicaragua
- **D** Costa Rica

5 Which of the following sentences about the region's economy is false?
- **A** Coffee and bananas are major export crops.
- **B** The region has good energy resources.
- **C** The region's climate, land, and history attract many tourists.
- **D** Most countries have limited economic development.

Languages of Central America

6 On the map above, which letter represents the country where English is spoken?
- **A** W
- **B** X
- **C** Y
- **D** Z

7 On the map above, which letters represent countries whose people speak either Spanish or a native language?
- **A** W and X
- **B** X and Y
- **C** Y and Z
- **D** X and Z

8 **Extended Response** Using the map above and your knowledge of Central America, write a description of influences on culture in Central America today.

CENTRAL AMERICA AND THE CARIBBEAN **183**

Answers

Standardized Test Prep

1. C
Break Down the Question This question requires students to recall factual information from Section 2.

2. B
Break Down the Question This question requires students to recall factual information from Section 3.

3. A
Break Down the Question This question requires students to recall factual information from Section 3.

4. D
Break Down the Question This question requires students to recall factual information from Section 3.

5. B
Break Down the Question This question requires students to recall factual information from Section 1.

6. A
Break Down the Question This question requires students to accurately read the graphic.

7. D
Break Down the Question This question requires students to accurately read the graphic. Remind students who miss this question to read the question carefully and observe the graphic carefully.

8. Extended Response Answers will vary, but students may describe influences on culture in Central America today, such as the changing geography due to volcanoes and hurricanes or ecotourism. Students should also mention the influence of European colonization on Central America.

Reteach/Intervention Resources

Reproducible
- Guided Reading Workbook
- Differentiated Instruction Teacher Management System: Lesson Plans

Technology
- Quick Facts Transparency: Central America and the Caribbean Visual Summary
- Differentiated Instruction Modified Worksheets and Tests CD-ROM
- Interactive Skills Tutor CD-ROM

Tips for Test Taking

I'm Stuck! If you come across a question that stumps you, don't get frustrated. First, master the question to make sure you understand what is being asked. Then work through the strategies you have already learned. If you are still stuck, circle the question and go on to others. Come back to it later. What if you still have no idea? Practice the 50/50 strategy and make an educated guess.

Chapter 8 Planning Guide

Caribbean South America

Overview	Instructional Resources	
CHAPTER 8 **Essential Question:** What challenges have the countries of Caribbean South America faced since gaining their independence? 🔊 **Focus on the Essential Question Podcast**	**TOS Differentiated Instruction Teacher Management System:** • Instructional Pacing Guides • Lesson Plans for Differentiated Instruction 📄 **Guided Reading Workbook** 📄 **Resource File:** • Chapter Review • Focus on Reading: Identifying Supporting Details • Focus on Writing: Writing a Letter • Social Studies Skills: Using Latitude and Longitude 📄 **Experiencing World History and Geography**	**TOS Calendar Planner** 💿 **Power Presentations with Media Gallery** 💿 **Differentiated Instruction Modified Worksheets and Tests CD-ROM** 💿 **Interactive Skills Tutor CD-ROM** 🔊 **Student Edition on Audio CD-ROM** 🔊 **The World's Music Audio Program** ▶️ **Map Zone Transparency:** Caribbean South America: Political ▶️ **World Outline Maps: Transparencies and Activities**
Section 1: **Physical Geography** **The Big Idea:** Caribbean South America is a region with diverse physical features, wildlife, climates, and resources.	**TOS Differentiated Instruction Teacher Management System:** Section 1 Lesson Plan 📄 **Guided Reading Workbook:** Section 1 📄 **Resource File:** • Vocabulary Builder: Section 1 • Geography and History: History of the Amazon • Geography for Life: Regional Images of the Venezuelan Andes • Primary Source: *Living to Tell the Tale* by Gabriel García Márquez	▶️ **Daily Bellringer Transparency:** Section 1 ▶️ **Map Zone Transparency:** Caribbean South America: Physical 🔗 **Internet Activity:** Volcanoes in the Andes
Section 2: **Colombia** **The Big Idea:** Spanish conquest, valuable resources, and civil war have shaped the history, culture, and economy of Colombia.	**TOS Differentiated Instruction Teacher Management System:** Section 2 Lesson Plan 📄 **Guided Reading Workbook:** Section 2 📄 **Resource File:** • Vocabulary Builder: Section 2 • Biography: Manuel Ancízar • Literature: "Eldorado" by Edgar Allan Poe	▶️ **Daily Bellringer Transparency:** Section 2
Section 3: **Venezuela and the Guianas** **The Big Idea:** European settlement, immigration, and natural resources have greatly influenced the culture and economy of Venezuela and the Guianas.	**TOS Differentiated Instruction Teacher Management System:** Section 3 Lesson Plan 📄 **Guided Reading Workbook:** Section 3 📄 **Resource File:** • Vocabulary Builder: Section 3 • Biography: José Antonio Páez • Critical Thinking: Spanish Towns in the Americas	▶️ **Daily Bellringer Transparency:** Section 3 ▶️ **Map Zone Transparency:** Venezuela's Major Resources ▶️ **Map Zone Transparency:** World: Political 🔗 **Internet Activity:** Exploring Caracas

Chart Key:

SE Student Edition

 Presentation Resource

 MP3 Audio

TOS Teacher One Stop

 DVD/CD-ROM

 HISTORY™

 Printable Resource

Program Resources available on **TOS** and @ **hmhsocialstudies.com**

Review, Assessment, Intervention

 The Americas Transparencies: Caribbean South America Visual Summary

 Spanish Chapter Summaries Audio CD

 Progress Assessment Support System (PASS): Chapter Test

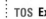 **Differentiated Instruction Modified Worksheets CD-ROM:** Modified Chapter Test

TOS **ExamView® Assessment Suite (English/Spanish)**

 Alternative Assessment Handbook

 Online Assessment Program, in the Interactive Student Edition

---

 PASS: Section 1 Quiz

 Online Quiz: Section 1

Alternative Assessment Handbook

 PASS: Section 2 Quiz

 Online Quiz: Section 2

Alternative Assessment Handbook

 PASS: Section 3 Quiz

 Online Quiz: Section 3

 Alternative Assessment Handbook

Supporting Resources

HISTORY.

- Multimedia Classroom Global History Series
- Global History Teacher's Guide

Maps Globes Graphs Level F

- Student Workbook
- Teacher's Guide

Social Studies Trade Library Collections

- NCSS Middle School Collection
- Latino Trade Collection
- World Regions Trade Collection

Geography's Impact

Geography's Impact Video Program

- **Impact of the Orinoco River**

For more information or to purchase go to **hmhsocialstudies.com**

Power Presentations with Media Gallery

Power Presentations with Media Gallery are visual presentations of each chapter's main ideas. Presentations can be customized by including Quick Facts charts, images from the text, and video clips.

Differentiating Instruction

How do I address the needs of varied learners?
The Target Resource acts as your primary strategy for differentiated instruction.

ENGLISH-LANGUAGE LEARNERS & STRUGGLING READERS

TARGET RESOURCE

Graphic Organizer Transparencies with Support for Reading and Writing

Spanish Resources

Spanish Chapter Summaries Audio CD Program

Teacher One Stop:
- ExamView Assessment Suite, Spanish
- PuzzleView, Spanish

English-Language Learner Strategies and Activities

Additional Resources

Differentiated Instruction Teacher Management System: Lesson Plans for Differentiated Instruction

Resource File:
- Vocabulary Builder Activities
- Social Studies Skills: Using Latitude and Longitude

Quick Facts Transparencies:
- Caribbean South America Visual Summary

Student Edition on Audio CD Program

Interactive Skills Tutor CD-ROM

Spanish/English Guided Reading Workbook

SPECIAL NEEDS LEARNERS

TARGET RESOURCE

Interactive Reader and Study Guide

The activities in the Interactive Reader and Study Guide engage students with questions while presenting summaries of chapter content and provide opportunities for students to practice critical thinking skills.

Additional Resources

Differentiated Instruction Teacher Management System: Lesson Plans for Differentiated Instruction

Resource File: Focus on Reading: Identifying Supporting Details

Student Edition on Audio CD Program

Interactive Skills Tutor CD-ROM

Graphic Organizer Transparencies with Support for Reading and Writing

ADVANCED/GIFTED AND TALENTED STUDENTS

TARGET RESOURCE

Resource File

The Resource File activities allow students to extend their knowledge of chapter-related places and people and to practice geography skills.

- Focus on Reading: Identifying Supporting Details
- Focus on Writing: Writing a Letter
- Literature: "Eldorado" by Edgar Allan Poe

Additional Resources

Differentiated Instruction Teacher Management System: Lesson Plans for Differentiated Instruction

World History and Geography Document-Based Questions Activities

Geography, Science, and Cultures Activities

Experiencing World History and Geography

Differentiated Activities in the Teacher's Edition

- Researching and Presenting Information on Plant and Animal Species, p. 188
- Creating a Map of the Western Hemisphere, p. 191

Teacher One Stop™

How can I manage the lesson plans and support materials for differentiated instruction?

With the Teacher One Stop, you can easily organize and print lesson plans, planning guides, and instructional materials for all learners. The Teacher One Stop includes the following materials to help you differentiate instruction:

- **Interactive Teacher's Edition**
- **Calendar Planner and pacing guides**
- **Editable lesson plans**
- **All reproducible ancillaries in Adobe Acrobat (PDF) format**
- **ExamView Assessment Suite (English & Spanish)**
- **Transparency and video previews**

Differentiated Activities in the Teacher's Edition

- Analyzing Point of View, p. 197

Interactive Student Edition

Complete online student edition with interactive multimedia support for chapter content assessment and reporting

- Interactive Maps and Notebook
- Standardized Test Prep
- Online Homework Practice and Research Activities
- Current Events
- Chapter-based Internet Activities
- Animated Geography Activities

Differentiated Activities in the Teacher's Edition

- Making a Bar Graph, p. 191
- Writing a Report, p. 195

Essential Question

Introduce the Essential Question

- Explain that all five countries that make up the Caribbean South America region border the Caribbean Sea. Huge river systems drain the region's rugged mountains, highlands, and plains. The region's location near the equator and its elevation affect its climate.

- Tell students that Colombia is South America's most populous country. Since gaining its independence from Spain, Colombia has experienced periods of conflict over cultural, economic, and political differences.

- Point out that Venezuela, like Colombia, was once a Spanish colony and that history has shaped Venezuela's culture. The Guianas were colonized by Great Britain, the Netherlands, and France. French Guiana remains a territory of France.

Focus on Reading and Writing

Reading The Resource File provides a worksheet to help students practice Identifying Supporting Details.

📝 **RF:** Focus on Reading, Identifying Supporting Details

Writing The Resource File provides a worksheet to help students organize and write their letters.

📝 **RF:** Focus on Writing, Writing a Letter

Key to Differentiating Instruction

Below Level

Basic-level activities designed for all students encountering new material

At Level

Intermediate-level activities designed for average students

Above Level

Challenging activities designed for honors and gifted and talented students

Standard English Mastery

Activities designed to improve standard English usage

LS Learning Styles

184   CHAPTER 8

CHAPTER **8**

Caribbean South America

Essential Question What challenges have the countries of Caribbean South America faced since gaining their independence?

? What You Will Learn...

In this chapter you will learn about the physical geography, history, and cultures of Colombia, Venezuela, Guyana, Suriname, and French Guiana. These countries make up the region of Caribbean South America.

FOCUS ON READING AND WRITING

Identifying Supporting Details Supporting details are the facts and examples that provide information to support the main ideas of a chapter, section, or paragraph. At the beginning of each section in this book, there is a list of main ideas. As you read this chapter, look for the details that support each section's main ideas. **See the lesson, Identifying Supporting Details, on page 523.**

Writing a Letter You live in a country in Caribbean South America. Your pen pal in the United States has asked you to write a letter telling her about life in your region. As you read this chapter, collect details to include in your letter. Your friend will want to know about your country as well as the whole region.

184   CHAPTER 8

History The architecture of Cartagena, Colombia, reflects the city's Spanish colonial past.

[Map labels: Caribbean Sea, Barranquilla, Cartagena, Maracaibo, Lake Maracaibo, PANAMA, Medellín, Magdalena River, Cauca River, PACIFIC OCEAN, Bogotá, Cali, COLOMBIA, 0° Equator, ECUADOR, Putumayo River, PERU]

Introduce the Chapter

At Level

Sizing Up the Region

1. Ask students what clues they can find in the pictures and map that help them understand the region of Caribbean South America. To get them started, remind them that most areas near the equator are hot, except for the higher elevations.

2. Have students use the map scale to estimate how large the region is. Have them compare that to the area of the United States. Invite a volunteer to draw the Caribbean South America map on the board. For comparison, have them also draw a map of the continental United States to the same scale.

3. Point out to students that while most cities of the region are located near the coastline, Bogotá is an exception. Invite them to guess why. *possible responses: favorable climate, protected, scenic* **LS** Visual/Spatial

📝 Alternative Assessment Handbook, Rubric 21: Map Reading

Caribbean South America: Political

◎ National capital
★ Other capitals
● Other cities

0   100   200 Miles
0   100   200 Kilometers
Projection: Azimuthal Equal-Area

ATLANTIC OCEAN

Caracas
Valencia

TRINIDAD AND TOBAGO

Orinoco River

VENEZUELA

Georgetown

GUYANA

Paramaribo

Cayenne

SURINAME

FRENCH GUIANA (FRANCE)

Orinoco River

Rio Negro

BRAZIL

Amazon River

Culture Cowboys called llaneros work on the plains of Venezuela.

map Zone

Geography Skills

Place Most of Caribbean South America is located on the Caribbean Sea.

1. **Identify** What is the capital of Venezuela?
2. **Contrast** How is Colombia's location different from Venezuela's location?

Geography Dense rain forest covers much of Suriname.

185

Chapter Preview

Explore the Map and Pictures

Caribbean South America: Political
Before the Europeans arrived, Caribbean South America's most advanced civilizations lived in the cool, fertile valleys of the region's tallest mountains, the Andes. The lower Guiana Highlands are located in the east. The lowest land is along the northern coast and the region's major river, the Orinoco. The south is dominated by dense, hot tropical rain forests.

Analyzing Visuals What can you infer about the architecture of Cartagena, Colombia, from the picture? *It likely reflects the influence of Spanish settlers and the city's Spanish colonial past.* What can you infer about the region's geography from the pictures of the cowboy and rain forest? *The region likely has diverse physical features and climates, as evidenced by the plains and rain forest.*

🔼 hmhsocialstudies.com

Teacher Resources

Info to Know

"West" and "East" America? The continents of the western hemisphere are called North and South America, but West and East America would also be accurate names. Look at a globe. As you can see, our eastern capital, Washington, D.C., is actually west of Colombia's capital Bogotá, one of the most westerly cities of Caribbean South America.

Other People, Other Places

The Gauchos of Argentina The American West and the Llanos are not the only places where cowboys ride. In Mexico, cowboys are called *vaqueros*. In Chile, where rodeo is the national sport, they are called *huasos*. In Argentina, cowboys are called *gauchos,* a word that once meant "vagabond." Gauchos travel on horseback with everything they own, wearing their trademark woolen ponchos. They became heroic cultural icons, immortalized in poems, stories, and songs, just like their American counterparts.

Answers

Map Zone 1. *Caracas;* **2.** *Colombia has a long coast on the Pacific Ocean and has a land border with Central America, unlike Venezuela, which has neither.*

Physical Geography

186 CHAPTER 8

Preteach

Bellringer

If YOU lived there. . . Use the **Daily Bellringer Transparency** to help students answer the question.

 Daily Bellringer Transparency, Section 1

Caribbean South America	Daily Bellringer
	Section 1

Preview Section 1

If YOU lived there ...
You live in Caracas, Venezuela, but this is your first visit to the great Orinoco River. You've heard about the fierce creatures that live in the river, so you think your guide is kidding when he says he's going to catch a piranha. You're expecting a monster and are surprised when he pulls up a small orange fish. It has many sharp teeth, but it's only seven inches long!
What other animals might you see in the region?

Consider what might live IN THE RIVER:
• fish
• reptiles
• snails

Consider what might live NEAR THE RIVER:
• birds
• reptiles and mammals
• insects

Key Terms and Places

 RF: Vocabulary Builder, Section 1

Taking Notes

Have students use the graphic organizer online to take notes on the section. This activity will prepare students for the Section Assessment, in which they will complete a graphic organizer that builds on the information using the Critical Thinking Skill: Categorizing.

What You Will Learn...

Main Ideas

1. Caribbean South America has a wide variety of physical features and wildlife.
2. The region's location and elevation both affect its climate and vegetation.
3. Caribbean South America is rich in resources, such as farmland, oil, timber, and rivers for hydroelectric power.

The Big Idea

Caribbean South America is a region with diverse physical features, wildlife, climates, and resources.

Key Terms and Places

Andes, *p. 186*
cordillera, *p. 186*
Guiana Highlands, *p. 187*
Llanos, *p. 187*
Orinoco River, *p. 188*

hmhsocialstudies.com
TAKING NOTES

Use the graphic organizer online to take notes on the physical geography of Caribbean South America.

If YOU lived there...

You live in Caracas, Venezuela, but this is your first visit to the great Orinoco River. You've heard about the fierce creatures that live in the river, so you think your guide is kidding when he says he's going to catch a piranha. You're expecting a monster and are surprised when he pulls up a small orange fish. It has many sharp teeth, but it's only seven inches long!

What other animals might you see in the region?

BUILDING BACKGROUND The narrow Isthmus of Panama joins the continent of South America at its northwestern corner, the country of Colombia. Like the countries of Central America, the five countries in Caribbean South America border the Caribbean Sea. They all vary in landscape, climate, and culture and have large rivers and rugged mountains.

Physical Features and Wildlife

If you were traveling through the region of Caribbean South America, you might see the world's highest waterfall, South America's largest lake, and even the world's largest rodent! As you can see on the map, the geography of this region includes rugged mountains, highlands, and plains drained by huge river systems.

Mountains and Highlands

The highest point in the region is in Colombia, a country larger than California and Texas combined. On the western side of Colombia the **Andes** (AN-deez) reach 18,000 feet (5,490 m). The Andes form a **cordillera** (kawr-duhl-YER-uh), a mountain system made up of roughly parallel ranges. Some of the Andes' snowcapped peaks are active volcanoes. Eruptions and earthquakes shake these mountains frequently.

Teach the Big Idea

At Level

Physical Geography

1. **Teach** Ask students the questions in the Main Idea boxes under Direct Teach.

2. **Apply** Have students make a two-columned table with *Colombia, Venezuela,* and *The Guianas* in the first column. Then have them read through the section and write down related facts in the second column.

3. **Review** Have students share facts they wrote down and ask them to volunteer additional related information they might know.

4. **Practice/Homework** Have students select one of the facts on their sheets to research further. Students should then write one paragraph about the topic. Have volunteers read their paragraphs to the class.
   LS Verbal/Linguistic

   Alternative Assessment Handbook, Rubric 40: Writing to Describe

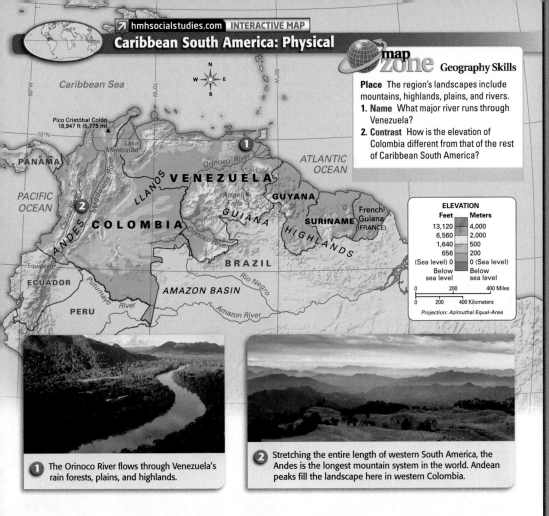

Caribbean South America: Physical

map zone Geography Skills

Place The region's landscapes include mountains, highlands, plains, and rivers.
1. **Name** What major river runs through Venezuela?
2. **Contrast** How is the elevation of Colombia different from that of the rest of Caribbean South America?

ELEVATION

Feet	Meters
13,120	4,000
6,560	2,000
1,640	500
656	200
(Sea level) 0	0 (Sea level)
Below sea level	Below sea level

0   200   400 Miles
0   200   400 Kilometers
Projection: Azimuthal Equal-Area

1 The Orinoco River flows through Venezuela's rain forests, plains, and highlands.

2 Stretching the entire length of western South America, the Andes is the longest mountain system in the world. Andean peaks fill the landscape here in western Colombia.

Lying on the Caribbean coast, Venezuela is located in the middle of the other countries in the region. Venezuela's highest elevation is in the **Guiana Highlands**, which stretch into Guyana and Suriname. For millions of years, wind and rain have eroded these highlands' plateaus. However, some of the steep-sided plateaus are capped by sandstone layers that have resisted erosion. These unusual flat-topped formations are sometimes called *tepuís* (tay-PWEEZ). The *tepuís* create a dramatic landscape as they rise about 3,000 to 6,000 feet (900 to 1,800 m) above the surrounding plains.

Plains, Rivers, and Wildlife

As you look at the map above, notice how much the elevation drops between the highlands and the Andes. This region of plains is known as the **Llanos** (YAH-nohs). The Llanos is mostly grassland with few trees. At a low elevation and not much vegetation, these plains flood easily.

CARIBBEAN SOUTH AMERICA **187**

Main Idea

❷ Climate and Vegetation

The region's location and elevation both affect its climate and vegetation.

Recall What type of climate does the Llanos have? *tropical savanna*

Draw Conclusions Why does the rain forest have more trees than the Llanos? *Rain falls throughout the year in the rain forest, but the Llanos has wet and dry seasons.*

Analyze Why is there snow year-round at the top of the Andes? *Temperatures can drop four degrees every 1000 feet, and the Andes are up to 18,000 feet high.*

📝 **RF:** Geography and History, History of the Amazon

Info to Know

National Bird of Colombia As in the United States, a bird of prey symbolizes freedom for Colombians. The Andean condor, whose wingspan can reach up to 10 feet, is the largest bird of prey in the world. It nests as high as 18,000 feet in the Andes Mountains and is one of the world's highest flying birds. The condor was chosen in 1834 for the Colombian coat of arms as a symbol of liberty.

Answers

Focus on Reading *The Orinoco, Cauca, and Magdalena Rivers flow through Caribbean South America.*

Reading Check *Guiana Highlands, tepuís, Llanos, Orinoco River, Andes*

Analyzing Visuals *beautiful scenery, wildlife, access to natural areas*

188

Flowing for about 1,600 miles (2,575 km), the **Orinoco** (OHR-ee-NOH-koh) **River** is the region's longest river. Snaking its way through Venezuela to the Atlantic Ocean, the Orinoco and its tributaries drain the plains and highlands. Two other important rivers, the Cauca and the Magdalena, drain the Andean region.

Caribbean South America is home to some remarkable wildlife. For example, hundreds of bird species, meat-eating fish called piranhas, and crocodiles live in or around the Orinoco River. Colombia has one of the world's highest concentrations of plant and animal species. The country's wildlife includes jaguars, ocelots, and several species of monkeys.

READING CHECK Summarizing What are the region's major physical features?

Venezuela's Canaima National Park

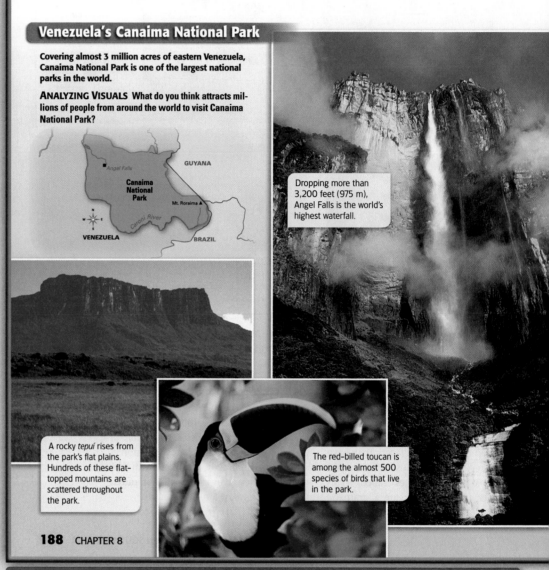

Covering almost 3 million acres of eastern Venezuela, Canaima National Park is one of the largest national parks in the world.

ANALYZING VISUALS What do you think attracts millions of people from around the world to visit Canaima National Park?

Dropping more than 3,200 feet (975 m), Angel Falls is the world's highest waterfall.

A rocky *tepuí* rises from the park's flat plains. Hundreds of these flat-topped mountains are scattered throughout the park.

The red-billed toucan is among the almost 500 species of birds that live in the park.

188 CHAPTER 8

Differentiating Instruction

At Level | Standard English Mastery

English-Language Learners

1. Have students read through the *Plains, Rivers, and Wildlife, Climate and Vegetation,* and *Resources* subheadings and make a list of names of plant and animal species mentioned.

2. Have students research three species and create a mini-poster for each selected species. Each mini-poster should include a drawing of the plant or animal, its English name, its Spanish name, and a few important facts, such as its habitat, what it eats, life expectancy,

endangered status, and so on. Have students use a dictionary to confirm spellings and proper usage of the English names.

3. Have students present their information to each other in small groups.

LS **Verbal/Linguistic, Visual/Spatial**

📝 Alternative Assessment Handbook, Rubrics 28: Posters; and 29: Presentations

Climate and Vegetation

Caribbean South America's location near the equator means that most of the region has warm temperatures year-round. However, temperatures do vary with elevation. For example, in the Andes, as you go up in elevation, the temperature can drop rapidly—about four degrees Fahrenheit every 1,000 feet (305 m).

In contrast, the vast, flat landscape of the Llanos region has a tropical savanna climate. Here, both the wet and dry seasons provide favorable conditions for grasslands to grow.

Rain forests, another type of landscape, thrive in the humid tropical climate of southern Colombia. This area is a part of the Amazon Basin. Here, rain falls throughout the year, watering the forest's huge trees. These trees form a canopy where the vegetation is so dense that sunlight barely shines through to the jungle floor.

READING CHECK Analyzing What causes the region's temperatures to vary?

Resources

Good soil and moderate climates help make most of Caribbean South America a rich agricultural region. Major crops include rice, coffee, bananas, and sugarcane.

In addition, the region has other valuable resources, such as oil, iron ore, and coal. Both Venezuela and Colombia have large oil-rich areas. Forests throughout the region provide timber. While the seas provide plentiful fish and shrimp, the region's major rivers are used to generate hydroelectric power.

READING CHECK Summarizing How do geographic factors affect economic activities in Caribbean South America?

SUMMARY AND PREVIEW In this section you learned that the physical geography of Caribbean South America includes mountains, highlands, plains, and rivers. The region's location near the equator and its elevation affect the region's climate. In the next section you will learn about Colombia's history, people, and economy. You will also learn about the challenges Colombia is facing today, which include a civil war.

Section 1 Assessment

ONLINE QUIZ hmhsocialstudies.com

Reviewing Ideas, Terms, and Places

1. **a. Recall** Where are the **Andes** located?
   b. Explain How are the rock formations called *tepuís* unusual?
   c. Elaborate Why do the **Llanos** in Colombia and Venezuela flood easily?
2. **a. Describe** In the Andes, how does the temperature change with elevation?
   b. Make Inferences How does the region's location near the equator affect its climate?
3. **a. Identify** What is a major resource in both Venezuela and Colombia?
   b. Explain Which resource provides hydroelectric power?

Critical Thinking

4. **Categorizing** Use your notes to identify four types of physical features in the region. Write each type in one of the small circles of the diagram.

FOCUS ON WRITING

5. **Describing Physical Geography** Take notes about the physical features, wildlife, climate, vegetation, and resources of the region. After you decide which country you are living in, collect more details about it.

CARIBBEAN SOUTH AMERICA **189**

Bellringer

If YOU lived there. . . Use the **Daily Bellringer Transparency** to help students answer the question.

▶ Daily Bellringer Transparency, Section 2

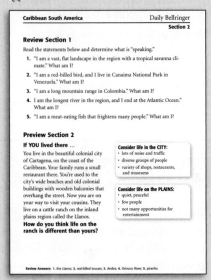

Caribbean South America   Daily Bellringer
                                                    Section 2

Review Section 1

Read the statements below and determine what is "speaking."

1. "I am a vast, flat landscape in the region with a tropical savanna climate." What am I?
2. "I am a red-billed bird, and I live in Canaima National Park in Venezuela." What am I?
3. "I am a long mountain range in Colombia." What am I?
4. "I am the longest river in the region, and I end at the Atlantic Ocean." What am I?
5. "I am a meat-eating fish that frightens many people." What am I?

Preview Section 2

If YOU lived there ...

You live in the beautiful colonial city of Cartagena, on the coast of the Caribbean. Your family runs a small restaurant there. You're used to the city's wide beaches and old colonial buildings with wooden balconies that overhang the street. Now you are on your way to visit your cousins. They live on a cattle ranch on the inland plains region called the Llanos.
How do you think life on the ranch is different than yours?

Consider life in the CITY:
· lots of noise and traffic
· diverse groups of people
· variety of shops, restaurants, and museums

Consider life on the PLAINS:
· quiet, peaceful
· few people
· not many opportunities for entertainment

Review Answers: 1. the Llanos; 2. red-billed toucan; 3. Andes; 4. Orinoco River; 5. piranha

Key Terms and Places

📰 **RF:** Vocabulary Builder, Section 2

Taking Notes

Have students use the graphic organizer online to take notes on the section. This activity will prepare students for the Section Assessment, in which they will complete a graphic organizer that builds on the information using the Critical Thinking Skill: Analyzing.

SECTION 2

Colombia

If YOU lived there...

You live in the beautiful colonial city of Cartagena, on the coast of the Caribbean. Your family runs a small restaurant there. You're used to the city's wide beaches and old colonial buildings with wooden balconies that overhang the street. Now you are on your way to visit your cousins. They live on a cattle ranch on the inland plains region called the Llanos.

How do you think life on the ranch is different from yours?

What You Will Learn...

Main Ideas

1. Native cultures, Spanish conquest, and independence shaped Colombia's history.
2. In Colombia today, the benefits of a rich culture and many natural resources contrast with the effects of a long period of civil war.

The Big Idea

Spanish conquest, valuable resources, and civil war have shaped the history, culture, and economy of Colombia.

Key Terms and Places

Cartagena, *p. 191*
Bogotá, *p. 192*
guerrillas, *p. 193*

hmhsocialstudies.com
TAKING NOTES

Use the graphic organizer online to organize your notes on Colombia.

BUILDING BACKGROUND Like most of the countries of Central and South America, Colombia was once a colony of Spain. Colombians gained their independence from Spain in 1819. The new country was then named after the explorer Christopher Columbus.

Colombia's History

Giant mounds of earth, mysterious statues, and tombs—these are the marks of the people who lived in Colombia more than 1,500 years ago. Colombia's history begins with these people. It also includes conquest by Spain and, later, independence.

The Chibcha

Have you heard of the legend of El Dorado (el duh-RAH-doh), or the Golden One? That legend about

This gold Chibcha artifact represents the ceremonial raft used by their king.

Teach the Big Idea

At Level

Colombia

1. **Teach** Ask students the questions in the Main Idea boxes under Direct Teach.

2. **Apply** Have students imagine they are vacationing in Colombia. Have them write a letter to a friend back home. Letters should include details from all regions of the country with descriptions of the scenery, the weather, historical sites, what they like the most, and so on.

3. **Review** Ask volunteers to read their letter aloud. Then have students discuss what place they liked the most and see if there was a class favorite.

4. **Practice/Homework** Have students list five important facts about Colombia.

   LS Verbal/Linguistic, Intrapersonal

   📰 Alternative Assessment Handbook, Rubric 40: Writing to Describe a land rich in gold was inspired by the Chibcha culture in Colombia. The Chibcha covered their new rulers in gold dust. Then they took each ruler to a lake to wash the gold off. As the new ruler washed, the Chibcha threw gold and emerald objects into the water. A well-developed civilization, they practiced pottery making, weaving, and metalworking. Their gold objects were among the finest in ancient America.

Spanish Conquest

In about 1500 Spanish explorers arrived on the Caribbean coast of South America. The Spaniards wanted to expand Spain's new empire. In doing so, the Spanish conquered the Chibcha and seized much of their treasure. Soon after claiming land for themselves, the Spaniards founded a colony and cities along the Caribbean coast.

One colonial city, **Cartagena**, was a major naval base and commercial port in the Spanish empire. By the 1600s Spaniards and their descendants had set up large estates in Colombia. Spanish estate owners forced South American Indians and enslaved Africans to work the land.

Independence

In the late 1700s people in Central and South America began struggling for independence from Spain. After independence was achieved, the republic of Gran Colombia was created. It included Colombia, Ecuador, Panama, and Venezuela. In 1830 the republic dissolved, and New Granada, which included Colombia and Panama, was created.

After independence, two different groups of Colombians debated over how Colombia should be run. One group wanted the Roman Catholic Church to participate in government and education. On the other hand, another group did not want the church involved in their lives.

CONNECTING TO History

Cartagena's Spanish Fort

Imagine you are a Spanish colonist living in Cartagena, Colombia, in the 1600s. Your city lies on the Caribbean coast and has been attacked by English pirates several times. They have stolen tons of silver and gold that were waiting shipment to Spain. How do you protect your city from these pirates? Build an enormous fort, of course! You make sure to design the fort's walls to deflect the cannonballs that the pirates shoot from their ships. Today this fort still stands on a peninsula outside Cartagena. A statue commemorates one of the heroes that defended the city from attack.

Drawing Conclusions Why did the Spanish want to defend Cartagena from the pirates?

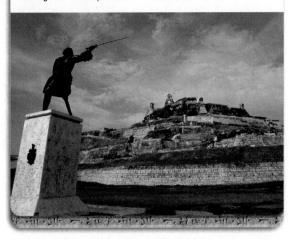

Outbreaks of violence throughout the 1800s and 1900s killed thousands. Part of the problem had to do with the country's rugged geography, which isolated people in one region from those in another region. As a result, they developed separate economies and identities. Uniting these different groups into one country was hard.

READING CHECK **Drawing Conclusions** How did Spanish conquest shape Colombia's history and culture?

CARIBBEAN SOUTH AMERICA **191**

Daily Life in Colombia

Different regions of Colombia are home to diverse ethnic groups.

ANALYZING VISUALS What are some of the goods sold in this market?

Colombians of African descent unload their goods at a local market near the Pacific coast.

Direct Teach

Main Idea

❷ Colombia Today

In Colombia today, the benefits of a rich culture and many natural resources contrast with the effects of a long period of civil war.

Identify What has recently become Colombia's major export? *oil*

Recall Name two of Colombia's export crops. *coffee, flowers, bananas, corn, sugarcane, rice*

Elaborate Why do most Colombians live in the river valleys of the Andes? *Land is good for farming; climate is moderate; rivers provide water and transportation.*

Info to Know

Colombian Coffee Colombia produces 12% of the world's coffee, which is second only to Brazil. Most of it is very good quality because it is grown at high elevations, on the slopes of the Andes Mountains. The coffee grown on the eastern and central cordilleras is better than the coffee grown on the western cordilleras. It takes five years of care for a coffee tree to produce its first beans, and then one tree produces only about a pound of coffee per year.

Colombia Today

Colombia is Caribbean South America's most populous country. The national capital is **Bogotá**, a city located high in the eastern Andes. Although Colombia is rich in culture and resources, more than 40 years of civil war have been destructive to the country's economy.

People and Culture

Most Colombians live in the fertile valleys and river basins among the mountain ranges, where the climate is moderate and good for farming. Rivers, such as the Cauca and the Magdalena, flow down from the Andes to the Caribbean Sea. These rivers provide water and help connect settlements located between the mountains and the coast. Other Colombians live on cattle ranches scattered throughout the Llanos. Few people live in the tropical rainforest regions in the south.

Because the physical geography of Colombia isolates some regions of the country, the people of Colombia are often known by the region where they live. For example, those who live along the Caribbean coast are known for songs and dances influenced by African traditions.

FOCUS ON READING
In the first paragraph under Economy, find at least three details to support the idea stated in the first sentence.

Colombian culture is an interesting mix of influences:

- Music: traditional African songs and dances on the Caribbean coast and South American Indian music in remote areas of the Andes
- Sports: soccer, as well as a traditional Chibcha ring-toss game called *tejo*
- Religion: primarily Roman Catholicism
- Official language: Spanish
- Ethnic groups: 58 percent mestizo; also Spanish, African, and Indian descent

Economy

Colombia's economy relies on several valuable resources. Rich soil, steep slopes, and tall shade trees produce world-famous Colombian coffee. Other major export crops include bananas, sugarcane, and cotton. Many farms in Colombia produce flowers that are exported around the world. In fact, 80 percent of the country's flowers are shipped to the United States.

Colombia's economy depends on the country's valuable natural resources. Recently oil has become Colombia's major export. Other natural resources include iron ore, gold, and coal. Most of the world's emeralds also come from Colombia.

192 CHAPTER 8

Answers

Analyzing Visuals *bananas, squash (gourds), and sugarcane*

Focus on Reading *The resources that Colombia's economy relies on include rich soil, steep slopes, and tall shade trees.*

192

Collaborative Learning

At Level

Cultural Influences

1. Review with students the list describing Colombian cultural influences under the subheading *People and Culture.*

2. Divide the class into five groups and assign one group to each topic: *Music, Sports, Religion, Languages,* and *Ethnic Groups* (**Note:** Use *Languages* instead of *Official Language.*)

3. Have each group brainstorm or research an equivalent list of influences for cultural elements in the United States. Have them

name as many influences as they can and research others.

4. Have each group report to the class. Encourage members of the class to add information the groups may have missed. Write the results on the board under the five headings as the reports are delivered.

LS Verbal/Linguistic, Interpersonal

Alternative Assessment Handbook, Rubrics 9: Comparing and Contrasting; and 14: Group Activity

Students from a school in Colombia's capital, Bogotá, take a break from their classes.

Here in the Andes people travel from town to town on these colorful buses, called *chivas*.

Civil War

Civil war is a major problem in Colombia today. Many different groups have waged war with each other and with Colombia's government. For more than 40 years, these heavily armed militant groups have controlled large areas of the country.

One of these groups is an army of **guerrillas**, or members of an irregular military force. These guerrillas want to overthrow the government. The guerrillas, as well as other militant groups, have forced farmers off their land and caused thousands of Colombians to flee the country. All of these groups are also involved in growing crops of the illegal coca plant. This plant is used to make cocaine, a dangerous drug.

Because of the instability caused by civil war, the future of Colombia is uncertain. However, the Colombian government has passed new laws that make it harder for the guerrillas and other militant groups to operate freely. In addition, the United States provides assistance to Colombia's government. Colombia is one of the top recipients of U.S. foreign aid.

READING CHECK Drawing Conclusions How do you think civil war affects daily life in Colombia?

SUMMARY AND PREVIEW Colombia's history includes the Chibcha, Spanish conquest, and independence. Today, Colombia's people are dealing with a long civil war. Next, you will learn about Colombia's neighbor, Venezuela.

Section 2 Assessment

hmhsocialstudies.com
ONLINE QUIZ

Reviewing Ideas, Terms, and Places

1. **a. Recall** Who were the Chibcha?
   b. Draw Conclusions Why did Spain want land in Colombia?
2. **a. Describe** What factors make Colombia ideal for growing coffee?
   b. Interpret In what part of the country do most Colombians live?
   c. Predict How might Colombia solve the problem of **guerrillas** trying to control the country?

Critical Thinking

3. **Analyzing** Using your notes, write a sentence about the topic of each box in a diagram like this one.

Music	→	
Sports	→	
Religion	→	
Language	→	

FOCUS ON WRITING

4. **Writing about Colombia** What information about the history, culture, and daily life of Colombia might your pen pal like to learn? Add these details to your notes.

CARIBBEAN SOUTH AMERICA **193**

193

Bellringer

If YOU lived there. . . Use the **Daily Bellringer Transparency** to help students answer the question.

▶ Daily Bellringer Transparency, Section 3

Caribbean South America   Daily Bellringer
           Section 3

Review Section 2
In each pair below, select the event that came first.
1. Conquest of the Chibcha **OR** creation of New Granada
2. Civil war between guerillas and the government **OR** enslavement of Africans
3. Independence from Spain **OR** establishment of Cartagena
4. Spanish settlement **OR** creation of Gran Colombia

Preview Section 3

If YOU lived there …
You've come from your home in eastern Venezuela to visit the nearby country of Suriname. Your visit is full of surprises. As you walk along the streets of the country's capital, Paramaribo, people are not speaking Spanish, but Dutch, English, and some languages you don't even recognize. You see Hindu temples and Muslim mosques alongside Christian churches.

Why is Suriname so different from Venezuela?

Consider CULTURE of Venezuela:
- mostly Spanish and Indian descent
- most speak Spanish
- mainly Roman Catholics

Consider CULTURE of Suriname:
- diverse population—many people of Asian and African descent
- many different languages spoken
- Christian, Hindu, and Muslim religions

Review Answers: 1. Conquest of the Chibcha; 2. enslavement of Africans; 3. establishment of Cartagena; 4. Spanish settlement

Academic Vocabulary

Review with students the high-use academic term in this section.

policy rule, course of action (p. 198)

📄 RF: Vocabulary Builder, Section 3

Taking Notes

Have students use the graphic organizer online to take notes on the section. This activity will prepare students for the Section Assessment, in which they will complete a graphic organizer that builds on the information using the Critical Thinking Skill: Identifying Cause and Effect.

Venezuela and the Guianas

What You Will Learn...

Main Ideas

1. Spanish settlement shaped the history and culture of Venezuela.
2. Oil production plays a large role in Venezuela's economy and government today.
3. The Guianas have diverse cultures and plentiful resources.

The Big Idea

European settlement, immigration, and natural resources have greatly influenced the culture and economy of Venezuela and the Guianas.

Key Terms and Places

llaneros, *p. 196*
Lake Maracaibo, *p. 196*
Caracas, *p. 197*
strike, *p. 198*
referendum, *p. 198*

📷 hmhsocialstudies.com
TAKING NOTES

Use the graphic organizer online to organize your notes on Venezuela and the Guianas.

If **YOU** lived there...

You've come from your home in eastern Venezuela to visit the nearby country of Suriname. Your visit is full of surprises. As you walk along the streets of the country's capital, Paramaribo, people are not speaking Spanish, but Dutch, English, and some languages you don't even recognize. You see Hindu temples and Muslim mosques alongside Christian churches.

Why is Suriname so different from Venezuela?

BUILDING BACKGROUND Venezuela, like Colombia, was once a Spanish colony, but the Guianas were colonized by other nations— Great Britain, the Netherlands, and France. When these countries gained independence, British Guiana became Guyana and Dutch Guiana became Suriname.

History and Culture of Venezuela

Venezuela was originally the home of many small tribes of South American Indians. Those groups were conquered by the Spanish in the early 1500s. Though Venezuela became independent from Spain in the early 1800s, those three centuries of Spanish rule shaped the country's history and culture.

Spanish Settlement and Colonial Rule

The Spanish came to Venezuela hoping to find gold and pearls. They forced the native Indians to search for these treasures, but they finally realized there was little gold to be found. Then the Spanish turned to agriculture, once again forcing the Indians to do the work. They grew indigo (IN-di-goh), a plant used to make a deep blue dye. Because the work was very hard, many of the Indians died. Then the Spanish began bringing enslaved Africans to take the Indians' places. Eventually, some of the slaves escaped, settling in remote areas of the country.

Teach the Big Idea   At Level

Venezuela and the Guianas

1. **Teach** Ask students the questions in the Main Idea boxes under Direct Teach.

2. **Apply** Have students scan the section for details about the region. Have them write down at least two details for each of the Guianas and five details for Venezuela. Have them select a city that they would like to visit and explain why they think it might be interesting.

3. **Review** Discuss with students what they think would be the most interesting details to include in describing the city they chose.

4. **Practice/Homework** Have students write the lyrics to a song or a poem about Venezuela and the Guianas, incorporating the details they recorded. **LS** **Verbal/Linguistic**

📄 Alternative Assessment Handbook, Rubric 1: Acquiring Information

Venezuela's Independence

Each year, Venezuelans celebrate Simon Bolívar's efforts in achieving Venezuela's independence. Independence Day is filled with parades and parties.

Independence and Self-Rule

Partly because the colony was so poor, some people in Venezuela revolted against Spain. Simon Bolívar helped lead the fight against Spanish rule. Bolívar is considered a hero in many South American countries because he led wars of independence throughout the region. Bolívar helped win Venezuelan independence from Spain by 1821. However, Venezuela did not officially become independent until 1830.

Throughout the 1800s Venezuelans suffered from dictatorships and civil wars. Venezuela's military leaders ran the country. After oil was discovered in the early 1900s, some leaders kept the country's oil money for themselves. As a result, the people of Venezuela did not benefit from their country's oil wealth.

People and Culture

The people of Venezuela are descended from native Indians, Europeans, and Africans. The majority of Venezuelans are of mixed Indian and European descent. Indians make up only about 2 percent of the population. People of European descent tend to live in the large cities. People of African descent tend to live along the coast. Most Venezuelans are Spanish-speaking Roman Catholics, but the country's Indians speak 25 different languages and follow the religious practices of their ancestors.

Venezuelan culture includes dancing and sports. Venezuela's national dance, the *joropo*, is a lively foot-stomping couples' dance. Large crowds of Venezuelans attend rodeo events. Baseball and soccer are also popular throughout Venezuela.

READING CHECK **Summarizing** How did the Spanish contribute to Venezuela's history?

Main Idea

❷ Venezuela Today

Oil production plays a large role in Venezuela's economy and government today.

Describe What are the slums near Caracas like? *shacks with no running water, sewers, or electricity*

Identify What mineral resources are found in the Guiana Highlands? *gold and iron ore*

Draw Conclusions Even with its oil wealth, why do you think many of Venezuela's people still live in poverty? *possible answer—The money earned with oil sales goes to a few people.*

Info to Know

Bolivarian Revolution When Venezuela's President Hugo Chavez was elected in 1999, he began a set of reforms called the Bolivarian Revolution, named after Simon Bolívar, the hero of his country's independence movement. These reforms called for more equal distribution of income and a renewed fight against corruption. He also pushed for a new Venezuelan constitution, which became law in 2000. The new constitution, for the first time, guarantees all citizens the right to education, health, work, and dignity.

Answers

Focus on Reading *Venezuela earned huge sums of money from oil; these immigrants, like most other Venezuelans, suffered in the 1980s when the price of oil dropped; the Venezuelan economy continues to be based on oil production.*

Focus on Culture *They dress up like devils, wear pig and jaguar masks, dance, beat drums, and shake their maracas to keep evil away.*

196

FOCUS ON READING

In the paragraphs under Venezuela Today, what details support the main idea that oil production plays a large role in Venezuela's economy and government?

Venezuela Today

Many Venezuelans make a living by farming and ranching. However, most wealthy Venezuelans have made money in the country's oil industry. In addition, Venezuela's government has also benefited from oil wealth.

Agriculture and Ranching

Rural areas of Venezuela are dotted by farms and ranches. Northern Venezuela has some small family farms as well as large commercial farms. **Llaneros** (yah-NAY-rohs)—or Venezuelan cowboys—herd cattle on the many ranches of the Llanos region. However, some small communities of Indians practice traditional agriculture.

Economy and Natural Resources

In the 1960s Venezuela began earning huge sums of money from oil production. This wealth allowed part of the population to buy luxuries. However, the vast majority of the population still lived in poverty. Many of Venezuela's poor people moved to the cities to try to find work. Some settled on the outskirts in communities of shacks. They had no running water, sewers, or electricity.

Venezuela's wealth attracted many immigrants from Europe and other South American countries. These immigrants, like most other Venezuelans, suffered in the 1980s when the price of oil dropped sharply. Without the money provided by high oil prices, the economy couldn't support the people. Oil prices recovered in the 1990s, and the Venezuelan economy continues to be based on oil production.

As you can see on the map on the next page, the Orinoco River basin and **Lake Maracaibo** (mah-rah-KY-boh) are rich in oil. Venezuela is the only South American member of the Organization of Petroleum

FOCUS ON CULTURE

The Feast of Corpus Christi

One day each summer, men dressed as devils dance in the streets of the Venezuelan town of San Francisco de Yare. On this day, people here honor the Roman Catholic feast day of Corpus Christi. Spanish settlers brought the tradition of dressing up as devils to Venezuela. This tradition includes the making of elaborate, colorful masks that the dancers wear. These masks usually resemble pigs or jaguars. Dancing through the town's streets to the beat of drums, the dancers shake musical instruments called maracas. They believe their dancing, music, and scary masks will keep evil away from their town.

Summarizing How do some Venezuelans celebrate the Feast of Corpus Christi?

Cross-Discipline Activity: Mathematics

At Level

The Impact of Oil Price Changes

1. Review with students the *World's Top Oil Exporters* chart under the Venezuela Today heading in Section 3. For this activity, use these rounded population figures:

   Saudi Arabia 25,000,000

   Venezuela 25,000,000

   United Arab Emirates 2,500,000

2. Have students compute the economic impact of a $20 per barrel rise or fall in the price of oil for the three countries listed above. Find both daily and yearly figures.

3. Have students compute the economic impact on each citizen (per capita) of the three countries.

4. Record the results on the board and have students decide which country's people would be most affected by oil price fluctuations. Discuss the effects of being so heavily dependent on oil exports.

LS Logical/Mathematical

Alternative Assessment Handbook, Rubric 9: Comparing and Contrasting

Venezuela's Major Resources

World's Top Oil Exporters

	Country	Oil Exports (million barrels per day)
1	Saudi Arabia	7.92
2	Russia	7.00
3	Norway	3.47
4	Iran	2.50
4	United Arab Emirates	2.50
5	Venezuela	2.10

⚲ hmhsocialstudies.com

Oil fields —
Oil pipelines —
Gold
Coal

0   100   200 Miles
0 100 200 Kilometers
Projection: Azimuthal Equal-Area

map zone Geography Skills

Human-Environment Interaction Oil, gold, and coal are Venezuela's major resources.

1. Locate What resource is located near the Orinoco River?

2. Draw Conclusions What resource do you think is the most difficult to transport to port cities?

Exporting Countries (OPEC). The member countries in this organization attempt to control world oil production and keep oil prices from falling too low.

The Guiana Highlands in the southeast are rich in other minerals, such as iron ore for making steel. Gold is also mined in remote areas of the highlands. Dams on tributaries of the Orinoco River produce hydroelectricity.

Caracas (kah-RAH-kahs) is Venezuela's capital and the economic and cultural center of the country. It is a large city with a modern subway system, busy expressways, and tall office buildings. Still, neither Caracas nor Venezuela has escaped poverty.

Caracas is encircled by slums, and many Venezuelans living in the rural areas of the country are also poor.

Government

After years of suffering under military dictatorships, the people of Venezuela elected their first president in 1959. Since then, Venezuela's government has dealt with economic turmoil and political protests.

In 2002 Venezuela's president, Hugo Chavez, started to distribute the country's oil income equally among all Venezuelans. Before Chavez's presidency, only a small percentage of wealthy Venezuelans benefited from the country's oil income.

Info to Know

Organization of Petroleum Exporting Countries Members of OPEC, formed in 1960, account for about 40 percent of the world's oil production. They attempt to control world oil prices by manipulating supply. In 1973 after the Yom Kippur War, OPEC caused a dramatic rise in prices that lasted for about ten years and resulted in economic hardship around the world. Since then OPEC has mostly tried to keep prices moderately high, but stable, making sure its members have profitable markets for their product.

Connect to Literature

Operation Dulcinea In 2005 to mark the 400th anniversary of the publication of Cervantes' *Don Quixote de la Mancha*, President Hugo Chavez gave away one million copies of the novel to the people of Venezuela. "We are all going to read 'Quixote' and feed ourselves once again with that spirit of a fighter who came to undo injustice and fix the world," Chavez said. The effort was called *Operation Dulcinea*, after the woman Don Quixote falls in love with in the book.

▶ Map Zone Transparency: Venezuela's Major Resources

⚲ hmhsocialstudies.com
Online Resources
Activity: Exploring Caracas

Differentiating Instruction

Below Level

Special Needs Learners

Materials: audio tape recorder, cassette tape

1. Divide the class into three groups, making sure that each group has mixed-ability students. Assign each group to role-play Venezuela's government, Venezuela's wealthy people, or Venezuela's poor people.

2. Tell students that a recent rise in oil prices has brought unexpected income into the country. Have each group meet to discuss what they think should be done with the extra money.

3. Ask each group to plan a skit expressing their proposal. Ensure that every group member has an active role or speaking part in the skit.

4. Have students perform their skits for the other groups. Then lead a brief discussion about different points of view. Have students write a paragraph summarizing what they learned from the skits. Special needs and English-language learners can record their paragraphs on audio tape instead of writing them if they choose.

LS Kinesthetic, Interpersonal

📄 Alternative Assessment Handbook, Rubric 33: Skits and Reader's Theater

Answers

Map Zone 1. *oil;* **2.** *gold because it is spread far apart, away from the cities and rivers*

Main Idea

❸ The Guianas

The Guianas have diverse cultures and plentiful resources.

Identify What are Guyana's major agricultural products? *rice and sugar*

Recall Where do nearly half of Suriname's people live? *in the capital city of Paramaribo*

Interpret Why are the Guianas culturally different from the rest of the continent? *The physical environment of the region kept them isolated; they were colonized by countries other than Spain.*

Connect to Literature

Anansi the Spider Stories of the West African hero and trickster, Anansi the Spider, came with enslaved Africans to the Caribbean. In some stories Anansi creates the sun and moon; in others he teaches humans how to sow grain. In Paramaribo, Suriname, the stories are called *Anansi-Tori*. People tell part of the *Anansi-Tori* on the eighth night after someone dies. The stories, they believe, must be told only at night or the dead will overhear them and cause the storyteller to also die.

Caracas, Venezuela

With a population of more than 4 million, Venezuela's capital city, Caracas, is the country's financial and cultural center.

ANALYZING VISUALS Why do you think Caracas is located in this mountain valley?

Millions of Venezuelans went on strike to protest the president's actions. A **strike** is a group of workers stopping work until their demands are met. The strike lasted for about two months. The protestors wanted Chavez to resign, but he refused. As a result of the strike, Venezuela's economy suffered and oil exports fell dramatically.

Many Venezuelans opposed to President Chavez called for a **referendum**, or recall vote. The referendum was defeated. In 2006 about 63 percent of Venezuelans re-elected Chavez president. In his second term, Chavez adopted new **policies** aimed at bringing an end to poverty, illiteracy, and hunger. Chavez has also supported changing his nation's constitution to end presidential term limits. Many Venezuelans fear that Chavez has grown too powerful and might rule indefinitely.

ACADEMIC VOCABULARY
policy rule, course of action

READING CHECK **Identifying Cause and Effect** What effect did the workers' strike have on Venezuela's economy?

The Guianas

The countries of Guyana, Suriname, and French Guiana are together known as the Guianas (gee-AH-nuhz). Dense tropical rain forests cover much of this region, which lies east of Venezuela.

Guyana

Guyana (gy-AH-nuh) comes from a South American Indian word that means "land of waters." About one-third of the country's population lives in Georgetown, the capital. Nearly all of Guyana's agricultural lands are located on the flat, fertile plains along the coast. Guyana's most important agricultural products are rice and sugar.

Guyana's population is diverse. About half of its people are descended from people who migrated to Guyana from India. These immigrants came to Guyana to work on the country's sugar plantations. Most Guyanese today farm small plots of land or run small businesses. About one-third of the population is descended from

Critical Thinking: Comparing and Contrasting

At Level

1. Have students make a three-columned table with the headings *Guyana*, *Suriname*, and *French Guiana*. Have them fill in the table with facts about the three countries.

2. Draw a three-circled Venn diagram on the board and have students write facts in the appropriate segments. For example, "independent country" would go in the *Guyana* and *Suriname* area of the diagram.

3. When finished, have students copy the diagram on their own sheet of paper.
LS Visual/Spatial

Alternative Assessment Handbook, Rubrics 13: Graphic Organizer; and 14: Group Activity

Answers

Analyzing Visuals *possible answers—fertile land may have brought the first settlers to the valley; the mountains provide shelter from storms and other weather.*

Reading Check *Oil exports fell dramatically and its economy suffered.*

former African slaves. These people operate large businesses and hold most of the government positions.

Suriname

The resources and economy of Suriname (soohr-uh-NAHM) are similar to those of Guyana. Like Guyana, Suriname has a diverse population. The country's population includes South Asians, Africans, Chinese, Indonesians, and Creoles—people of mixed heritage. The capital, Paramaribo (pah-rah-MAH-ree-boh), is home to nearly half of the country's people.

French Guiana

French Guiana (gee-A-nuh) is a territory of France and sends representatives to the government in Paris. French Guiana's roughly 200,000 people live mostly in coastal areas. About two-thirds of the people are of African descent. Other groups include Europeans, Asians, and South American Indians. The country depends heavily on imports for its food and energy.

READING CHECK **Contrasting** How is French Guiana different from the rest of the Guianas?

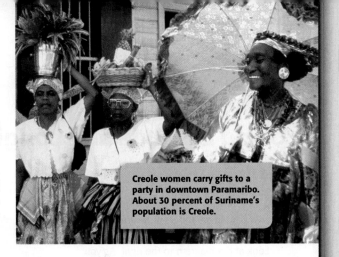

Creole women carry gifts to a party in downtown Paramaribo. About 30 percent of Suriname's population is Creole.

SUMMARY AND PREVIEW In this section, you learned that Venezuela's history was largely shaped by Spanish settlement. Today Venezuela's economy is based on oil. You also learned that to the east, the Guianas are home to a diverse population. In the next chapter, you will learn about the history and people of Atlantic South America.

Direct Teach

Info to Know

Immigrants from India In the 1800s both the British in Guyana and the Dutch in Suriname ended slavery. Both brought in workers from India. However, life for these workers was very different, depending on which of the two countries they immigrated to. In Guyana the British forced everyone to learn English and to convert to Christianity if they wanted to get good jobs. In Suriname the Dutch allowed Indian immigrants to speak their native language of Hindi and practice Hinduism, which they continue to do to this day.

Review & Assess

Close

Have students discuss which country in the region they would most like to live in.

Review

↗ Online Quiz, Section 3

Assess

SE Section 3 Assessment

PASS: Section 3 Quiz

Alternative Assessment Handbook

Reteach/Classroom Intervention

Guided Reading Workbook, Section 3

Interactive Skills Tutor CD-ROM

Section 3 Assessment

 hmhsocialstudies.com
ONLINE QUIZ

Reviewing Ideas, Terms, and Places

1. **a. Recall** What did Spanish settlers hope to find in Venezuela?
   b. Explain Who led Venezuela's revolt against Spain?
2. **a. Describe** What does the landscape of **Caracas** include?
   b. Explain How is oil important to Venezuela's economy?
   c. Elaborate Why did some Venezuelans go on **strike**?
3. **a. Describe** What are Guyana's agricultural lands and products like?
   b. Contrast How is population of the Guianas different from that of Colombia and Venezuela?

Critical Thinking

4. **Identifying Cause and Effect** Using your notes on Venezuela's natural resources and this diagram, list the effects of oil production on Venezuela's people, economy, and government.

Oil Production → People
Oil Production → Economy
Oil Production → Government

FOCUS ON WRITING

5. **Writing about Venezuela and the Guianas** Collect details about Venezuela and the Guianas for your letter. What is interesting about these cultures?

CARIBBEAN SOUTH AMERICA **199**

Section 3 Assessment Answers

1. **a.** gold
   b. Simon Bolívar

2. **a.** a mountain valley
   b. Venezuela's economy is based on oil production.
   c. to protest the actions of President Chavez and a failing economy

3. **a.** flat, fertile plains; rice and sugar
   b. The Guianas are more diverse and have more Asian immigrants, especially from India.

4. possible answers—wealth, immigration, social polarization and conflict, urban development, slums

5. Responses will vary, but should note interesting details about the cultures of Venezuela and the Guianas and be consistent with text content.

Answers

Reading Check *It is not an independent country.*

Using Latitude and Longitude

Activity The Difference Between Latitude and Longitude

1. Point out to students that although latitude and longitude are measured the same way, they do not behave the same way. Lines of latitude are parallel—they never meet. Lines of longitude converge at the poles.

2. Use a peeled orange to illustrate longitude and different-sized plates or disks stacked in a globe shape to illustrate latitude.

3. Use 6,300 miles as a rough estimate for the distance between the equator and the north pole. Have students compute what one degree of latitude is, in miles. *(6,300 divided by 90 = 70 miles per degree of latitude.)* Ask students why the same kind of calculation cannot be made for longitude.

4. Have students draw a diagram illustrating how latitude and longitude are different.
   LS Visual/Spatial

   RF: Social Studies Skills, Using Latitude and Longitude

   Alternative Assessment Handbook, Rubric 21: Map Reading

Using Latitude and Longitude

Learn

The pattern of imaginary lines that circle the globe in east-west and north-south directions is called a grid. Geographers measure the distances between the lines of the grid in degrees.

Look at the diagram to the right. As you can see, lines that run east to west are lines of latitude. These lines measure distance north and south of the equator. Lines that run north to south are lines of longitude. These lines measure distance east and west of the prime meridian.

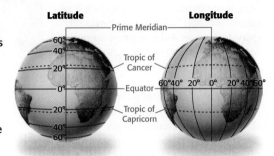

Practice

Look at the world map to the right. Use these guidelines to read latitude and longitude.

1 Pick a city on the map.

2 To find the latitude of the city you picked, first look at the equator. From there, look at the city's location. Then find the closest line of latitude to see how many degrees the city is north or south of the equator.

3 To find the longitude of the city, first look at the prime meridian. Then find the closest line of longitude to see how many degrees the city is east or west of the prime meridian.

World: Political

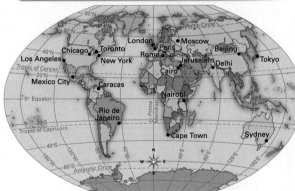

Apply

Using an atlas, find a map of the United States and a map of the world. On the map of the United States, find the line of latitude that is located near your hometown. Then look at a world map and follow this line of latitude across the world. Which countries share the same latitude as your hometown?

Differentiating Instruction

Advanced/Gifted and Talented

Above Level

Research Required

1. Have students research and write one-page reports with illustrations on the following topics:
   • world time zones (their relation to longitude, their average size, why their boundaries are not straight)
   • the Arctic and Antarctic circles and the Tropics of Cancer and Capricorn (what changes when you cross them)
   • the International Date Line and Greenwich Mean Time (what they are used for)
   • the length of daylight in different locations around the world (why Bogotá gets close to twelve hours of sunlight every day while the amount of daily sunlight varies widely with the season in Helsinki, Finland)

2. Have students present their reports.
   LS Verbal/Linguistic

   Alternative Assessment Handbook, Rubric 37: Writing Assignments

---

Answers

Practice and Apply 1. *Students' answers will vary, depending on the city chosen and the location of their hometown.*

200

Geography's Impact
video series
Review the video to answer the closing question:
What are some advantages and disadvantages of industries along the Orinoco River?

Visual Summary

Use the visual summary below to help you review the main ideas of the chapter.

QUICK FACTS

Caribbean South America's physical features include rivers, plains, mountains, and the world's highest waterfall.

A country rich in history and culture, Colombia is enduring a civil war today.

Venezuela is an oil-rich nation that has a population of mostly mixed Indian and European descent.

Reviewing Vocabulary, Terms, and Places

For each statement below, write T if it is true and F if it is false.

1. The Andes is a river system.

2. The Orinoco River flows 1,300 miles (2,100 km) through Venezuela.

3. Caribbean South America's location near the equator means that the region is very cold.

4. The Chibcha were the first people to settle Colombia.

5. Colombian culture includes traditional African songs and dances.

6. Most Venezuelans are of mixed Indian and European descent.

7. Venezuela gained its independence from France.

8. Venezuela's economy depends on oil production.

Comprehension and Critical Thinking

SECTION 1 *(Pages 186–189)*

9. **a. Recall** What is the region's longest river?

   b. Analyze How does the temperature vary in the Andes?

   c. Evaluate Why do you think it would be hard to live in the rain forest of Colombia?

SECTION 2 *(Pages 190–193)*

10. **a. Describe** How did the Chibcha treat their ruler?

    b. Draw Conclusions What created a problem for all Colombians after independence?

    c. Elaborate Why do most Colombians live in fertile valleys and river basins?

SECTION 3 *(Pages 194–199)*

11. **a. Define** What is a strike?

CARIBBEAN SOUTH AMERICA **201**

Answers

Visual Summary

Review and Inquiry Have students use the visual summary to discuss details related to Caribbean South America's physical features, history, and culture.

▶ Quick Facts Transparency: Caribbean South America Visual Summary

Reviewing Vocabulary, Terms, and Places

1. F   5. T
2. T   6. T
3. F   7. F
4. T   8. T

Comprehension and Critical Thinking

9. **a.** Orinoco River

   b. Temperatures drop at higher elevations.

   c. possible answers—Vegetation is dense; there are not many roads or basic services.

10. **a.** They covered the new ruler in gold dust, which he washed off in the river. Then they threw gold and emeralds into the water.

    b. Geographic isolation caused people in different regions to have different economies and cultural identities.

    c. The climate is good for farming, and the rivers provide connections to other settlements.

11. **a.** a group of workers stopping work until their demands are met

---

Review and Assessment Resources

Review and Reinforce

SE Chapter Review

▤ **RF:** Chapter Review

▶ Quick Facts Transparency: Caribbean South America Visual Summary

▶ Spanish Chapter Summaries Audio CD

TOS Holt McDougal PuzzleView®; Quiz Show for ExamView

● Quiz Game CD-ROM

Assess

SE Standardized Test Practice

▤ PASS: Chapter Test Forms A and B

▤ Alternative Assessment Handbook

TOS ExamView Test Generator, Chapter Test

● Differentiated Instruction Modified Worksheets and Tests CD-ROM: Chapter Test

↗ Online Assessment Program, in the Interactive Student Edition

Reteach/Intervene

▤ Guided Reading Workbook

▤ Differentiated Instruction Teacher Management System: Lesson Plans

● Differentiated Instruction Modified Worksheets and Tests CD-ROM

● Interactive Skills Tutor CD-ROM

↗ hmhsocialstudies.com
Chapter Resources

11. b. to work on sugar plantations

c. Answers will vary. Students may say that yes, the government is committed to helping the people as evidenced by policies to end poverty and hunger; no, the government might decide to take over the oil industry and not share the wealth.

Using the Internet

12. Go to to access a rubric for this activity.

Social Studies Skills

13. 10°N; Colombia

Map Activity

14. A. Orinoco River
B. Lake Maracaibo
C. Andes
D. Llanos
E. Guiana Highlands

Focus on Reading and Writing

15. possible answer—The Chibcha made fine gold objects; the Spanish conquered the Chibcha and seized their treasure; the Spanish founded a colony and cities; the Spanish forced the native Indians to work; enslaved Africans were brought in; Colombians gained their independence from Spain; people argued over power, and violence broke out; regions were isolated from each other; civil wars have been destructive; the official language is Spanish; about sixty percent of the people are mestizos; Colombia produces a lot of coffee; oil is Colombia's major export; guerillas control large areas; cultivation of coca is a problem; the United States provides foreign aid.

RF: Focus on Reading, Identifying Supporting Details

SECTION 3 *(continued)*

b. Draw Conclusions Why did people from India immigrate to Guyana?

c. Predict Do you think Venezuela's government will continue to use oil wealth to help the country's people? Explain your answer.

Using the Internet

12. Activity: Writing a Journal Entry Ride with the llaneros! Pack your bags and prepare for a trek through the South American countryside. Explore the vast grasslands, visit villages, and learn about the life and work of the cowboys, or llaneros, of the Venezuelan plains. Through your online textbook, research and take notes that will help you describe your adventure. Use the interactive template to write your journal entry. Describe what you have learned about the people and places you visited.

 hmhsocialstudies.com

Social Studies Skills

13. Using Latitude and Longitude Look at the physical map in Section 1. Find the lines of latitude and longitude. What line of latitude, shown on the map, runs through both Venezuela and Colombia? Which country in Caribbean South America is partly located on the equator?

Map Activity

14. Caribbean South America On a separate sheet of paper, match the letters on the map with their correct labels.

Llanos   Andes
Guiana Highlands   Orinoco River
Lake Maracaibo

hmhsocialstudies.com **INTERACTIVE MAP**

FOCUS ON READING AND WRITING

15. Identifying Supporting Details Look back over Section 2 on Colombia. Then make a list of details you find to support the section's main ideas. Make sure you include details about the Spanish conquest, independence, culture, resources, and civil war.

16. Writing a Letter By now you have information about the region and the country you have chosen to live in. Begin your letter to your pen pal by describing the most interesting physical and cultural features of the whole region. Then write a second paragraph telling your pen pal about the special physical and cultural features of the country you've chosen to live in. Try to keep your pen pal interested in reading by including fascinating details and descriptions.

16. Rubric Students' letters should
- be two paragraphs long
- include interesting details
- tell about all five countries in Caribbean South America

RF: Focus on Writing, Writing a Letter

Standardized Test Prep

DIRECTIONS: Read questions 1 through 7 and write the letter of the best response. Then read question 8 and write your own well-constructed response.

1 Temperatures in Caribbean South America remain warm year-round because of the region's location near the
A equator.
B Caribbean Sea.
C Amazon Basin.
D Tropic of Cancer.

2 What valuable natural resource were the Chibcha known for using?
A silver
B gold
C copper
D iron

3 What Colombian city was a major naval base and commercial port in the Spanish empire?
A Bogotá
B Cali
C Caracas
D Cartagena

4 Venezuela's economy is based on
A oil production.
B flower exports.
C small farms.
D silver mining.

5 Simon Bolívar helped several South American countries gain independence from
A Britain.
B Brazil.
C Spain.
D Mexico.

Volcanoes of Colombia

6 Based on the map above, active volcanoes are located in Colombia's
A rivers.
B mountains.
C plains.
D coastal areas.

7 The physical geography of the Guianas includes
A dense rain forests.
B deserts.
C the Orinoco River.
D the Andes.

8 **Extended Response** Look at the table of the world's oil exporters and the map of Venezuela's major resources in Section 3. Write a paragraph explaining why oil is Venezuela's most important resource. Identify at least two reasons.

Intervention Resources

Reproducible
▤ Guided Reading Workbook
▤ Differentiated Instruction Teacher Management System: Lesson Plans

Technology
▣ Quick Facts Transparency: Caribbean South America Visual Summary
◉ Differentiated Instruction Modified Worksheets and Tests CD-ROM
◉ Interactive Skills Tutor CD-ROM

Tips for Test Taking

Minutes to Go Point out to students that if they are short on time, they should quickly scan the unanswered questions to see which ones they could answer easily. Students should go with their first answers on those questions in order to complete as many questions as possible.

CHAPTER 9 PLANNING GUIDE

Overview	Instructional Resources

CHAPTER 9

Essential Question: How have the nations of Atlantic South America addressed economic and environmental challenges?

🔊 **Focus on the Essential Question Podcast**

TOS Differentiated Instruction Teacher Management System:
- Instructional Pacing Guides
- Lesson Plans for Differentiated Instruction

Guided Reading Workbook

Resource File:
- Chapter Review
- Focus on Reading: Using Context Clues
- Focus on Writing: Creating a Web Site
- Social Studies Skills: Connecting Ideas

Experiencing World History and Geography

TOS Calendar Planner

🔘 **Power Presentations with Media Gallery**

🔘 **Differentiated Instruction Modified Worksheets and Tests CD-ROM**

🔘 **Interactive Skills Tutor CD-ROM**

🔊 **Student Edition on Audio CD-ROM**

🔊 **The World's Music Audio Program**

▶️ **Map Zone Transparency:** Atlantic South America: Political

▶️ **World Outline Maps: Transparencies and Activities**

Section 1:

Physical Geography

The Big Idea: The physical geography of Atlantic South America includes large river systems, plains and plateaus, and the Amazon rain forest.

TOS Differentiated Instruction Teacher Management System: Section 1 Lesson Plan

Guided Reading Workbook: Section 1

Resource File
- Vocabulary Builder: Section 1
- Critical Thinking: Forests at Risk
- Geography and History: Northern Brazil: Rivers Run Through It
- Interdisciplinary Project: Products of the Rain Forest

▶️ **Daily Bellringer Transparency:** Section 1

▶️ **Map Zone Transparency:** Atlantic South America: Physicall

↗️ **Internet Activity:** The Amazon Rain Forest

↗️ **Animated Geography:** Amazon Rain Forest

Section 2:

Brazil

The Big Idea: The influence of Brazil's history can be seen today all over the country in its people and culture.

TOS Differentiated Instruction Teacher Management System: Section 2 Lesson Plan

Guided Reading Workbook: Section 2

Resource File
- Vocabulary Builder: Section 2
- Biography: Dom Pedro II
- Geography for Life: Mapping Wealth and Poverty in Brazil
- Primary Source: Posters from Brazil

▶️ **Daily Bellringer Transparency:** Section 2

↗️ **Animated Geography:** Present-day Brazil

Section 3:

Argentina, Uruguay, and Paraguay

The Big Idea: Argentina, Uruguay, and Paraguay have been influenced by European immigration, a tradition of ranching, and large urban populations.

TOS Differentiated Instruction Teacher Management System: Section 3 Lesson Plan

Guided Reading Workbook: Section 3

Resource File
- Vocabulary Builder: Section 3
- Biography: Agustín Barrios Mangoré
- Literature: *Chúcaro: Wild Pony of the Pampa* by Francis Kalnay

---

▶️ **Daily Bellringer Transparency:** Section 3

▶️ **Map Zone Transparency:** Argentina: Population

▶️ **Map Zone Transparency:** Paraguay and Uruguay

↗️ **Internet Activity:** The Gauchos of Argentina

Chart Key:

SE Student Edition   Presentation Resource   MP3 Audio

TOS Teacher One Stop   DVD/CD-ROM   HISTORY™

Printable Resource

Program Resources available on **TOS** and @ hmhsocialstudies.com

Review, Assessment, Intervention

 The Americas Transparencies: Atlantic South America Visual Summary

 Spanish Chapter Summaries Audio CD

 Progress Assessment Support System (PASS): Chapter Test

 Differentiated Instruction Modified Worksheets and Tests CD-ROM: Modified Chapter Test

TOS **ExamView® Assessment Suite (English/Spanish)**

 Alternative Assessment Handbook

 Online Assessment Program, in the Interactive Student Edition

---

 PASS: Section 1 Quiz

 Online Quiz: Section 1

Alternative Assessment Handbook

 PASS: Section 2 Quiz

 Online Quiz: Section 2

 Alternative Assessment Handbook

 PASS: Section 3 Quiz

 Online Quiz: Section 3

 Alternative Assessment Handbook

Supporting Resources

- Multimedia Classroom Global History Series
- Global History Teacher's Guide

Maps Globes Graphs Level F

- Student Workbook
- Teacher's Guide

Social Studies Trade Library Collections

- NCSS Middle School Collection
- World Regions Trade Collection

Geography's Impact

Geography's Impact Video Program

- **Impact of Deforestation in the Amazon Basin**

For more information or to purchase go to hmhsocialstudies.com

Power Presentations with Media Gallery

Power Presentations with Media Gallery are visual presentations of each chapter's main ideas. Presentations can be customized by including Quick Facts charts, images from the text, and video clips.

Differentiating Instruction

How do I address the needs of varied learners?
The Target Resource acts as your primary strategy for differentiated instruction.

ENGLISH-LANGUAGE LEARNERS & STRUGGLING READERS

TARGET RESOURCE

Interactive Skills Tutor CD-ROM

The Interactive Skills Tutor CD-ROM contains lessons that provide additional practice for 20 different critical thinking skills.

Additional Resources

Differentiated Instruction Teacher Management System: Lesson Plans for Differentiated Instruction

Resource File:
- Vocabulary Builder Activities
- Social Studies Skills: Connecting Ideas

Spanish/English Guided Reading Workbook

Student Edition on Audio CD Program

Interactive Skills Tutor CD-ROM

Spanish Chapter Summaries Audio CD

Teacher One Stop:
- ExamView Assessment Suite, Spanish
- PuzzleView, Spanish

English-Language Learner Strategies and Activities

SPECIAL NEEDS LEARNERS

TARGET RESOURCE

Student Edition on Audio CD Program

Additional Resources

Differentiated Instruction Teacher Management System: Lesson Plans for Differentiated Instruction

Guided Reading Workbook

Resource File: Social Studies Skills: Connecting Ideas

Interactive Skills Tutor CD-ROM

Graphic Organizer Transparencies with Support for Reading and Writing

ADVANCED/GIFTED AND TALENTED STUDENTS

TARGET RESOURCE

Differentiated Instruction Teacher Management System

Lesson Plans for Differentiated Instruction provide teachers with strategies to help plan instruction for all learners.

Additional Resources

Resource File:
- Focus on Reading: Using Context Clues
- Focus on Writing: Creating a Web Site
- Literature: from *Chúcaro: Wild Pony of the Pampa* by Francis Kalnay

World History and Geography Document-Based Questions Activities

Geography, Science, and Cultures Activities

Experiencing World History and Geography

Differentiated Activities in the Teacher's Edition

- Researching Origins of Cultural Traditions, p. 212
- Working with a Graphic Organizer, p. 213
- Building Vocabulary, p. 215
- Learning from Visuals, p. 218
- Categorizing Facts about Argentina, Uruguay, and Paraguay, p. 220
- Illustrating a Scene, p. 222

Differentiated Activities in the Teacher's Edition

- Using Word Webs, p. 215

Differentiated Activities in the Teacher's Edition

- Discussing Population and Economy, p. 218
- Writing a Poem, p. 222

Teacher One Stop™

How can I manage the lesson plans and support materials for differentiated instruction?

With the Teacher One Stop, you can easily organize and print lesson plans, planning guides, and instructional materials for all learners. The Teacher One Stop includes the following materials to help you differentiate instruction:

- **Interactive Teacher's Edition**
- **Calendar Planner and pacing guides**
- **Editable lesson plans**
- **All reproducible ancillaries in Adobe Acrobat (PDF) format**
- **ExamView Assessment Suite (English & Spanish)**
- **Transparency and video previews**

Interactive Student Edition

Complete online student edition with interactive multimedia support for chapter content assessment and reporting

- Interactive Maps and Notebook
- Standardized Test Prep
- Online Homework Practice and Research Activities
- Current Events
- Chapter-based Internet Activities
- Animated Geography Activities

DIFFERENTIATED INSTRUCTION PLANNING GUIDE

Chapter Preview

Essential Question

Introduce the Essential Question

- Tell students that deforestation and soil exhaustion threaten two of the Atlantic South America region's most important resources—the rain forest and the lands used for commercial farming.

- Explain that Brazil is the largest country in South America—both in size and in population—and has the continent's largest economy. Challenge students to predict how Brazil's size creates both opportunities and challenges for its people.

- Point out that the other countries of Atlantic South America have experienced economic crises at various times in the past and continue to search for ways to improve their economies.

Focus on Reading and Writing

Reading The Resource File provides a worksheet to help students practice using context clues.

📄 **RF:** Focus on Reading, Using Context Clues

Writing The Resource File provides a worksheet to help students organize and write their Web sites.

📄 **RF:** Focus on Writing, Creating a Web Site

Key to Differentiating Instruction

Below Level

Basic-level activities designed for all students encountering new material

At Level

Intermediate-level activities designed for average students

Above Level

Challenging activities designed for honors and gifted and talented students

Standard English Mastery

Activities designed to improve standard English usage

LS Learning Styles

CHAPTER 9

Atlantic South America

Essential Question How have the nations of Atlantic South America addressed economic and environmental challenges?

❓ What You Will Learn...

In this chapter you will learn about the plains and rain forest of Atlantic South America. You will also study the histories of the different countries and how different influences have shaped their cultures. In addition, you will learn about life, landscapes, and issues in Brazil, Argentina, Uruguay, and Paraguay today.

FOCUS ON READING AND WRITING

Using Context Clues As you read, you may find some unknown words. You can usually figure out what a word means by using context clues. Look at the words and sentences around the unknown word—its context—to figure out the definition. **See the lesson, Using Context Clues, on page 524.**

Creating a Web Site You are a Web designer at a travel agency. Read this chapter and then use what you learn to create a Web site about Atlantic South America. The goal of your Web site will be to convince viewers to visit the region.

204 CHAPTER 9

PACIFIC OCEAN

○ National capital
● Other cities

0   300   600 Miles
0   300   600 Kilometers

Projection:
Lambert Azimuthal Equal-Area

map zone

Geography Skills

Place Brazil and Argentina are South America's largest countries.
1. **Identify** What city lies on the Amazon River?
2. **Analyze** What would be some benefits of the location of Buenos Aires?

Culture During Carnival, Brazilians celebrate with music, dancing, and costumes.

Introduce the Chapter

At Level

Traveling to Atlantic South America

1. Talk with students about how all regions around the world have unique physical features, history, and cultures.

2. Explain to students that they are going to learn how the physical features and history of the countries in Atlantic South America make that part of the world unique.

3. Ask students to make a list of each major physical feature or natural resource (such as the Amazon Basin) and historical event (such as Brazil's independence in 1822) that they think might influence how people live in that part of the world today. **LS Verbal/Linguistic**

📄 Alternative Assessment Handbook, Rubric 11: Discussions

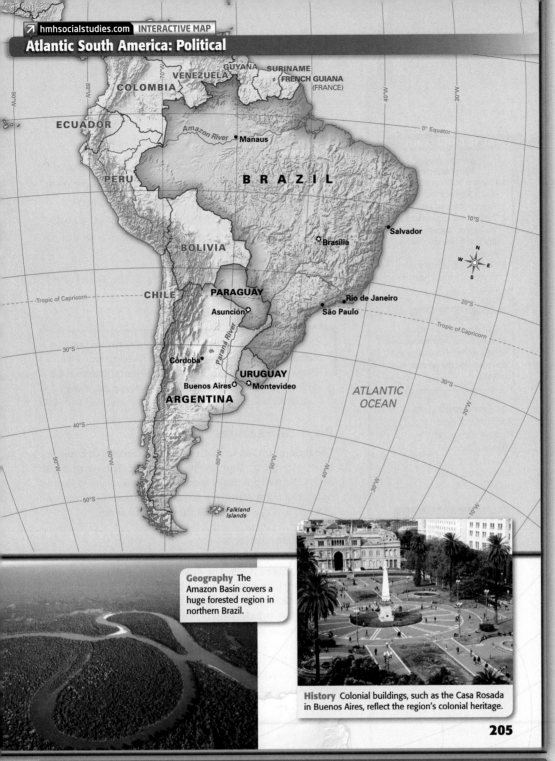

Atlantic South America: Political

VENEZUELA
GUYANA
SURINAME
FRENCH GUIANA
(FRANCE)
COLOMBIA

ECUADOR

Amazon River • Manaus

PERU

B R A Z I L

BOLIVIA

• Salvador
✪ Brasília

CHILE

PARAGUAY
Asunción ✪

• Rio de Janeiro
São Paulo •

Córdoba •

URUGUAY
Buenos Aires ✪ ✪ Montevideo
ARGENTINA

ATLANTIC OCEAN

Falkland Islands

0° Equator

10°S

Tropic of Capricorn

20°S

30°S

40°S

50°S

Tropic of Capricorn

Paraná River

Geography The Amazon Basin covers a huge forested region in northern Brazil.

History Colonial buildings, such as the Casa Rosada in Buenos Aires, reflect the region's colonial heritage.

205

• Chapter Preview •

Explore the Map and Pictures

Atlantic South America: Political
What can you tell about Atlantic South America by looking at this political map? *the locations of countries, cities, and rivers*

Analyzing Visuals Why do you think most cities are located near a body of water? *Water is an important natural resource that can be used for agriculture, travel, and trade.* Which country does not border an ocean? *Paraguay*

▶ Map Zone Transparency: Atlantic South America: Political

↗ hmhsocialstudies.com

Teacher Resources

Critical Thinking: Comparing and Contrasting   [At Level]

1. Explain that the first people to live in Brazil were American Indians. In 1500, Portuguese explorers were the first Europeans to find Brazil. Portuguese settlers moved there for the favorable climate and soil, making Brazil a large sugar-growing colony. Europeans also settled other countries in the Atlantic South America region. These include Argentina, Uruguay, and Paraguay.

2. Tell students they will learn more about the colonization of these four countries. Have students think about how the United States was first colonized and then gained independence. Ask them to look for similarities and differences between the history of the countries in Atlantic South America and the history of the United States.
LS Verbal/Linguistic

Alternative Assessment Handbook, Rubric 9: Comparing and Contrasting

Answers

Map Zone **1.** *Manaus;* **2.** *It is near the ocean and the Paraná River, which makes it an important seaport.*

Preteach

Bellringer

If YOU lived there... Use the **Daily Bellringer Transparency** to help students answer the question.

▶ Daily Bellringer Transparency, Section 1

Atlantic South America	Daily Bellringer
	Section 1

Preview Section 1

If YOU lived there ...
You live on the coast of Brazil, near the mouth of the Amazon River. Now you are taking your first trip up the river deep into the rain forest. The river is amazingly wide and calm. Trees on the riverbanks seem to soar to the sky. Your boat slows as you pass a small village. You notice that all the houses rest on poles that lift them 8 to 10 feet out of the water.
What would it be like to live in the rain forest?

Consider the CLIMATE:
· constant rain
· moist, humid air
· warm temperatures

Consider the ENVIRONMENT:
· wide variety of plants and trees
· many different animals
· wide rivers and flooded land

Key Terms and Places

📖 **RF:** Vocabulary Builder, Section 1

Taking Notes

Have students use the graphic organizer online to take notes on the section. This activity will prepare students for the Section Assessment, in which they will complete a graphic organizer that builds on the information using the Critical Thinking Skill: Categorizing.

Physical Geography

What You Will Learn...

Main Ideas

1. Physical features of Atlantic South America include large rivers, plateaus, and plains.
2. Climate and vegetation in the region range from cool, dry plains to warm, humid forests.
3. The rain forest is a major source of natural resources.

The Big Idea

The physical geography of Atlantic South America includes large river systems, plains and plateaus, and the Amazon rain forest.

Key Terms and Places

Amazon River, *p. 206*
Río de la Plata, *p. 207*
estuary, *p. 207*
Pampas, *p. 207*
deforestation, *p. 209*
soil exhaustion, *p. 209*

↗ **hmhsocialstudies.com**
TAKING NOTES

Use the graphic organizer online to take notes on the physical geography of Atlantic South America.

If YOU lived there...

You live on the coast of Brazil, near the mouth of the Amazon River. Now you are taking your first trip up the river deep into the rain forest. The river is amazingly wide and calm. Trees on the riverbanks seem to soar to the sky. Your boat slows as you pass a small village. You notice that all the houses rest on poles that lift them 8 to 10 feet out of the water.

What would it be like to live in the rain forest?

BUILDING BACKGROUND While rugged mountains and highlands dominate the lansdcape of Caribbean South America, much of the Atlantic region is made up of broad interior plains. Landscapes in this region range from tropical rain forest to temperate, grassy plains.

Physical Features

The region of Atlantic South America includes four countries: Brazil, Argentina, Uruguay, and Paraguay. This large region covers about two-thirds of South America. Brazil alone occupies nearly half of the continent. Most of the physical features found in South America are found in these four countries.

Major River Systems

The world's largest river system, the Amazon, flows eastward across northern Brazil. The **Amazon River** is about 4,000 miles (6,440 km) long. It extends from the Andes Mountains in Peru to the Atlantic Ocean. Hundreds of tributaries flow into it, draining an area that includes parts of most South American countries.

Because of its huge drainage area, the Amazon carries more water than any other river in the world. About 20 percent of the water that runs off Earth's surface flows down the Amazon. Where it meets the Atlantic, this freshwater lowers the salt level of the Atlantic for more than 100 miles (160 km) from shore.

Teach the Big Idea

At Level

Physical Geography

1. **Teach** Ask students the questions in the Main Idea boxes under Direct Teach.

2. **Apply** Ask students to choose one physical feature found in Atlantic South America, such as the Amazon River or the Río de la Plata. Have students write down at least five reasons they think the resource is important to nearby farmers, the community, the economy, and the environment.
   LS Verbal/Linguistic

3. **Review** Have students review their lists and put the reasons in order from most important to least important.

4. **Practice/Homework** Have students research the resource they chose and write a paragraph describing its significance.
   LS Verbal/Linguistic

   📄 Alternative Assessment Handbook, Rubrics 30: Research; and 42: Writing to Inform

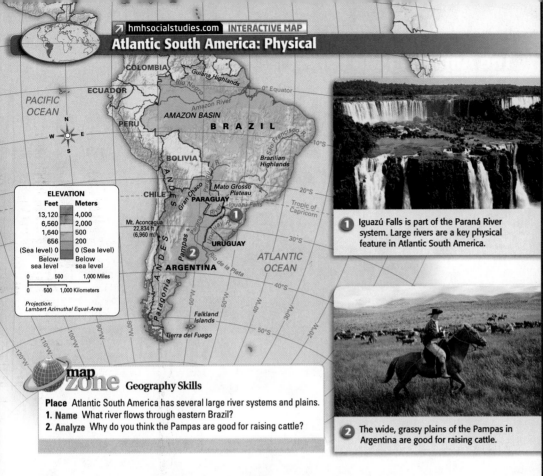

ELEVATION

Feet	Meters
13,120	4,000
6,560	2,000
1,640	500
656	200
(Sea level) 0	0 (Sea level)
Below sea level	Below sea level

0   500   1,000 Miles
0   500   1,000 Kilometers

Projection:
Lambert Azimuthal Equal-Area

Mt. Aconcagua
22,834 ft
(6,960 m)

map Zone Geography Skills

Place Atlantic South America has several large river systems and plains.
1. Name What river flows through eastern Brazil?
2. Analyze Why do you think the Pampas are good for raising cattle?

1 Iguazú Falls is part of the Paraná River system. Large rivers are a key physical feature in Atlantic South America.

2 The wide, grassy plains of the Pampas in Argentina are good for raising cattle.

The Paraná (pah-rah-NAH) River drains much of the central part of South America. Water from the Paraná River eventually flows into the **Río de la Plata** (REE-oh day lah PLAH-tah) and the Atlantic Ocean beyond. The Río de la Plata is an estuary. An **estuary** is a partially enclosed body of water where freshwater mixes with salty seawater.

Plains and Plateaus

As you can see on the map, this region's landforms mainly consist of plains and plateaus. The Amazon Basin in northern Brazil is a giant, flat floodplain. South of the Amazon Basin are the Brazilian Highlands, a rugged region of old, eroded mountains, and another area of high plains called the Mato Grosso Plateau.

Farther south, a low plains region known as the Gran Chaco (grahn CHAH-koh) stretches across parts of Paraguay and northern Argentina. In central Argentina are the wide, grassy plains of the **Pampas**. South of the Pampas is Patagonia—a region of dry plains and plateaus. All of these southern plains rise in the west to form the high Andes Mountains.

FOCUS ON READING
Where can you find the definition of *Pampas*?

READING CHECK Summarizing What are the region's major landforms and rivers?

ATLANTIC SOUTH AMERICA **207**

Main Idea

1 Physical Features

Physical features of Atlantic South America include large rivers, plateaus, and plains.

Identify How long is the Amazon River? *about 4,000 miles long* What is the Río de la Plata? *an estuary where salty seawater mixes with freshwater*

Explain Describe the main landforms of the region of Atlantic South America. *The region's landforms mainly consist of plains and plateaus.*

Summarize Describe the main physical features of the region of Atlantic South America. *The main features include the river systems, plains, and plateaus.*

📑 RF: Geography and History, Northern Brazil: Rivers Run Through It

▶️ Map Zone Transparency: Atlantic South America: Physical

Connect to Geography

One of Earth's Greatest Natural Features The Andes Mountains are a vast series of very high plateaus with some of the world's highest peaks. Many of these peaks are higher than 20,000 feet. The Andes stretch across seven countries: Argentina, Chile, Bolivia, Peru, Ecuador, Colombia, and Venezuela.

Using Natural Resources   **Standard English Mastery**

1. Organize the class into small groups.

2. Have each group imagine they are starting a business somewhere in Atlantic South America. Have students choose a business. Allow students to be creative—they might choose raising cattle, fishing, river tours down the Amazon, or a resort hotel. Once students choose their business, have them plan which area they think would be best to run it. Ask why they think their business would be successful there.

3. Have students use standard English to write a "business proposal." Proposals should be 1–2 paragraphs in length.

4. Call on a volunteer from each group to read the group's proposal. As a class, discuss any necessary corrections to the paragraphs to align them with standard English usage.
LS Verbal/Linguistic

📄 Alternative Assessment Handbook, Rubrics 14: Group Activity; and 43: Writing to Persuade

Answers

Map Zone 1. *Rio São Francisco;*
2. because there is plenty of room for the cattle to roam and plenty of grass for the cattle to eat

Focus on Reading *in the sentence where the word* Pampas *is in boldface*

Reading Check *plains, plateaus, and highlands; the Amazon and Paraná rivers*

Info to Know

The Amazon Rain Forest Tropical rain forests have four distinct layers:

1. The forest floor is almost bare. It is covered with fallen leaves and branches, which rot and provide nutrients for other plants to grow.

2. The understory (also called the lower canopy) is where young trees and shrubs grow. Plants at this level cannot get very big because the upper canopy blocks the sun.

3. The upper canopy is where most of the rain forest animals live.

4. The emergent trees make up the very top of the rain forest. Here some trees poke out of the upper canopy.

Activity Have students create rain forest diagrams, illustrating each of the four layers of a rain forest. For each layer, ask students to write a sentence explaining why the layer is important for the rest of the rain forest's survival.

LS Verbal/Linguistic, Visual/Spatial

Alternative Assessment Handbook, Rubric 3: Artwork

About the Illustration

This illustration is an artist's conception based on available sources.

↗ hmhsocialstudies.com

Online Resources
Activity: The Amazon Rain Forest

Close-up

The Amazon Rain Forest

The Amazon rain forest covers more than one-third of South America. Seen from the air, it looks like a big, green carpet. The top level of tree branches is called the canopy. Most action in the forest takes place in the canopy, but plenty of life also exists below.

↗ hmhsocialstudies.com
ANIMATED GEOGRAPHY

Animals such as monkeys and sloths can spend their entire lives in the canopy.

People have cleared parts of the rain forest for farming, ranching, and logging.

Parts of the forest are flooded for half the year, and trees stand in water up to 40 feet (12 m) deep.

ANALYSIS SKILL **ANALYZING VISUALS**
What kinds of animals could not survive living in the canopy?

208 CHAPTER 9

Critical Thinking: Cause and Effect

Below Level

Interdependence

1. Explain to students that in rain forests, as in most of nature, plants and animals depend on each other to survive. The term for this is *interdependence*. For example, some types of birds can eat only one type of insect. Some insects can only survive in a certain type of tree. If something happens to the tree, the insect is in danger. If something happens to the insects, the birds are in danger.

2. Ask students to consider how clearing the rain forest might affect rain forest life. Then ask the following questions: What might happen to the insects and animals who eat plant life to survive? If the insects die, what other animals and plant life could be affected? How might this affect humans?

3. Have students make posters to illustrate how rain forest plants and animals depend on each other. Ask for student volunteers to present their posters. **LS Verbal/Linguistic, Visual/Spatial**

Alternative Assessment Handbook, Rubric 6: Cause and Effect

Answers

Analyzing Visuals *animals that cannot climb or live in trees*

208

Climate and Vegetation

Atlantic South America has many climates. Generally, cool climates in southern and highland areas give way to tropical, moist climates in northern and coastal areas.

In southern Argentina Patagonia has a cool, desert climate. North of Patagonia, rich soils and a humid subtropical climate make parts of the Pampas good for farming. Farther north in Argentina, the Gran Chaco has a humid tropical climate. There, summer rains can turn some parts of the plains into marshlands.

North of Argentina, in Brazil, a large part of the central region has a tropical savanna climate with warm grasslands. The northeastern part of the country has a hot, dry climate, while the southeast is cooler and more humid.

In northern Brazil the Amazon Basin's humid tropical climate supports the world's largest tropical rain forest. Rain falls almost every day in this region. The Amazon rain forest contains the world's greatest variety of plant and animal life.

READING CHECK Finding Main Ideas What is the climate like in the rain forest?

Natural Resources

The Amazon rain forest is one of the region's greatest natural resources. It provides food, wood, rubber, plants for medicines, and other products. In recent years **deforestation**, or the clearing of trees, has become an issue in the forest.

The region's land is also a resource for commercial farming, which is found near coastal areas of Atlantic South America. In some areas, however, planting the same crop every year has caused **soil exhaustion**, which means the soil is infertile because it has lost nutrients needed by plants.

Atlantic South America also has good mineral and energy resources such as gold, silver, copper, iron, and oil. Dams on some of the region's large rivers also provide hydroelectric power.

READING CHECK Summarizing What resources does the rain forest provide?

SUMMARY AND PREVIEW Physical features of Atlantic South America include great river systems and plains. The Amazon rain forest makes up a huge part of the region. Next you will learn about Brazil, the country of the Amazon.

Section 1 Assessment
hmhsocialstudies.com
ONLINE QUIZ

Reviewing Ideas, Terms, and Places
1. **a. Define** What is an **estuary**?
   b. Explain How does the **Amazon River** affect the Atlantic Ocean at the river's mouth?
   c. Elaborate What benefits do you think the rivers might bring to Atlantic South America?
2. **a. Recall** What kind of climate does Patagonia have?
   b. Make Inferences Why are temperatures in the south generally cooler than temperatures in the north?
3. **a. Identify** What resources does the rain forest provide?
   b. Analyze What is one benefit and one drawback of practicing commercial agriculture in the rain forest?
   c. Elaborate **Soil exhaustion** might lead to what kinds of additional problems?

Critical Thinking
4. **Categorizing** Look back over your notes. Then use a table like this one to organize the physical geography of Atlantic South America by country.

	Geography
Brazil	
Argentina	

FOCUS ON WRITING
5. **Describing Physical Geography** Jot down notes about the physical features, climate and vegetation, landscapes, and resources of this area. Identify one or two images you could use for your Web site.

ATLANTIC SOUTH AMERICA **209**

209

Bellringer

If YOU lived there. . . Use the **Daily Bellringer Transparency** to help students answer the question.

▶ Daily Bellringer Transparency, Section 2

Academic Vocabulary

Review with students the high-use academic term in this section:

aspects parts (p. 12)

RF: Vocabulary Builder Activity, Section 2

Taking Notes

Have students use the graphic organizer online to take notes on the section. This activity will prepare students for the Section Assessment, in which they will complete a graphic organizer that builds on the information using the Critical Thinking Skill: Finding Main Ideas.

SECTION 2

Brazil

What You Will Learn...

Main Ideas

1. Brazil's history has been affected by Brazilian Indians, Portuguese settlers, and enslaved Africans.
2. Brazil's society reflects a mix of people and cultures.
3. Brazil today is experiencing population growth in its cities and new development in rain forest areas.

The Big Idea

The influence of Brazil's history can be seen all over the country in its people and culture.

Key Terms and Places

São Paulo, *p. 212*
megacity, *p. 212*
Rio de Janeiro, *p. 212*
favelas, *p. 213*
Brasília, *p. 213*
Manaus, *p. 213*

hmhsocialstudies.com
TAKING NOTES

Use the graphic organizer online to take notes on Brazil.

If YOU lived there...

You live in Rio de Janeiro, Brazil's second-largest city. For months your friends have been preparing for Carnival, the year's biggest holiday. During Carnival, people perform in glittery costumes and there is dancing all day and all night in the streets. The city is packed with tourists. It can be fun, but it is hectic! Your family is thinking of leaving Rio during Carnival so they can get some peace and quiet, but you may stay in Rio with a friend if you like.

Would you stay for Carnival? Why or why not?

BUILDING BACKGROUND Carnival is a tradition that is not unique to Brazil, but it has come to symbolize certain parts of Brazilian culture. Brazilian culture differs from cultures in the rest of South America in many ways. Brazil's unique history in the region is responsible for most of the cultural differences.

History

Brazil is the largest country in South America. Its population of more than 188 million is larger than the population of all of the other South American countries combined. Most Brazilians are descended from three groups of people who contributed in different ways throughout Brazil's history.

Colonial Brazil

The first people in Brazil were American Indians. They arrived in the region many thousands of years ago and developed a way of life based on hunting, fishing, and small-scale farming.

In 1500 Portuguese explorers became the first Europeans to find Brazil. Soon Portuguese settlers began to move there. Good climates and soils, particularly in the northeast, made Brazil a large sugar-growing colony. Colonists brought a third group of people—Africans—to work as slaves on the plantations. Sugar plantations made Portugal rich, but they also eventually replaced forests along the Atlantic coast.

Teach the Big Idea

At Level

Brazil

1. **Teach** Ask students the questions in the Main Idea boxes under Direct Teach.

2. **Apply** Have students create a three-columned chart on their own paper. In the first column have students write important facts they read. These can include important dates and terms. In the second column, have students write one or two questions for each item in the first column. Last, have students write the answers to their questions in the third column. **LS Verbal/Linguistic**

3. **Review** Pair students and have them ask each other the questions they wrote.

4. **Practice/Homework** Have students choose one of the facts they listed on their charts to learn more about. Have them write 1–2 paragraphs about their subject. Ask volunteers to read their paragraphs to the class. **LS Verbal/Linguistic**

   Alternative Assessment Handbook, Rubric 1: Acquiring Information

Pampas

Other parts of Brazil also contributed to the colonial economy. Inland, many Portuguese settlers created cattle ranches. In the late 1600s and early 1700s, people discovered gold and precious gems in the southeast. A mining boom drew people to Brazil from around the world. Finally, in the late 1800s southeastern Brazil became a major coffee-producing region.

Brazil Since Independence

Brazil gained independence from Portugal without a fight in 1822. However, independence did not change Brazil's economy much. For example, Brazil was the last country in the Americas to end slavery.

Since the end of Portuguese rule, Brazil has been governed at times by dictators and at other times by elected officials. Today the country has an elected president and legislature. Brazilians can participate in politics through voting.

READING CHECK **Summarizing** What was Brazil's colonial economy like?

People and Culture

The people who came to Brazil over the years brought their own traditions. These traditions blended to create a unique Brazilian culture.

People

More than half of Brazilians consider themselves of European descent. These people include descendants of original Portuguese settlers along with descendants of more recent immigrants from Spain, Germany, Italy, and Poland. Nearly 40 percent of Brazil's people are of mixed African and European descent. Brazil also has the largest Japanese population outside of Japan.

Because of its colonial heritage, Brazil's official language is Portuguese. In fact, since Brazil's population is so huge, there are more Portuguese-speakers in South America than there are Spanish-speakers, even though Spanish is spoken in almost every other country on the continent. Other Brazilians speak Spanish, English, French, Japanese, or native languages.

FOCUS ON READING
What context clues in this paragraph help you understand the meaning of *descent*?

FOCUS ON CULTURE

Soccer in Brazil

To Brazilians, soccer is more than a game. It is part of being Brazilian. Professional stars are national heroes. The national team often plays in Rio de Janeiro, home of the world's largest soccer stadium. Some fans beat drums all through the games. But it is not just professional soccer that is popular. People all over Brazil play soccer—in cleared fields, on the beach, or in the street. Here, boys in Rio practice their skills.

Analyzing Why do you think soccer is so popular in Brazil?

ATLANTIC SOUTH AMERICA **211**

Critical Thinking: Comparing and Contrasting   At Level

Brazil's History

1. Review Brazil's history with students. Ask students if they can think of any similarities between how Brazil was colonized and how America was colonized. For example, Europeans began settling in North America in the 1500s, just as they did in Brazil. Colonists brought Africans to Brazil to work as slaves on plantations, just as they did in America.

2. As students discuss the similarities, write them on the board.

3. Have students choose a topic from the board to write an essay. Essays should compare and contrast Brazil's history with United States history.

4. Have students present their essays to the class. **LS** **Verbal/Linguistic**

   Alternative Assessment Handbook, Rubric 9: Comparing and Contrasting

Direct Teach

Main Idea

❶ History

Brazil's history has been affected by Brazilian Indians, Portuguese settlers, and enslaved Africans.

Identify Who were the first people to live in Brazil? *American Indians*

Explain Why did Portuguese settlers move to Brazil in the 1500s? *Good climates and soils made Brazil a large sugar-growing colony. Later, settlers also built cattle ranches, began mining, and produced coffee.*

Summarize How has Brazil changed since it gained independence from Portugal? *The economy stayed the same, but the government has changed from being run by dictators to being run by elected officials.*

📄 RF: Biography, Dom Pedro II

❷ People and Culture

Brazil's society reflects a mix of people and cultures.

Explain What has contributed to Brazil's culture? *People who came to Brazil from other countries brought their own traditions.*

Identify What is Brazil's official language? *Portuguese*

📄 RF: Primary Source, Posters from Brazil

Answers

Reading Check *Brazil's colonial economy included sugar plantations, cattle ranching, mining, and eventually coffee production.*

Focus on Reading *descendants, original Portuguese settlers*

Focus on Culture *Soccer is a fun sport and is an important part of Brazil's history and culture.*

211

Info to Know

Food in Brazil As mentioned in the text, feijoada is a dish that many Brazilians and tourists enjoy eating. There are many other foods that are eaten throughout Brazil. One of these is queijo de minas, which is a type of cheese. Papaya, mango, pineapple, and guava are common fruits. Other ingredients typical of the Brazilian kitchen are beans, root vegetables, coconut, rice, pork, beef, and fish. People across Brazil use some of these ingredients to create their own regional dishes.

Checking for Understanding

Re-read Religion Answer the following questions.

1. What is Macumba? *a religion that combines beliefs and practices of African, Indian, and Catholic religions*
2. What is Carnival? *a celebration that mixes traditions from Africa, Brazil, and Europe*
3. Name two immigrant-influenced foods that are now common Brazilian dishes. *vatapá and feijoada*

Regions of Brazil

Brazil's regions differ from each other in their people, climates, economies, and landscapes.

ANALYZING VISUALS Which region appears to be the wealthiest?

① The southeast has the country's largest cities, such as Rio de Janeiro.

☑ hmhsocialstudies.com
ANIMATED GEOGRAPHY
Present-Day Brazil

ACADEMIC VOCABULARY
aspects parts

Religion

Brazil has the largest population of Roman Catholics of any country in the world. About 75 percent of Brazilians are Catholic. In recent years Protestantism has grown in popularity, particularly among the urban poor. Some Brazilians practice macumba (mah-KOOM-bah), a religion that combines beliefs and practices of African and Indian religions with Christianity.

Festivals and Food

Other **aspects** of Brazilian life also reflect the country's mix of cultures. For example, Brazilians celebrate Carnival before the Christian season of Lent. The celebration mixes traditions from Africa, Brazil, and Europe. During Carnival, Brazilians dance the samba, which was adapted from an African dance.

Immigrant influences can also be found in Brazilian foods. In parts of the country, an African seafood dish called vatapá (vah-tah-PAH) is popular. Many Brazilians also enjoy eating feijoada (fay-ZHWAH-dah), a stew of black beans and meat.

READING CHECK **Analyzing** How has cultural borrowing affected Brazilian culture?

Brazil Today

Brazil's large size creates opportunities and challenges for the country. For example, Brazil has the largest economy in South America and has modern and wealthy areas. However, many Brazilians are poor.

While some of the same issues and characteristics can be found throughout Brazil, other characteristics are unique to a particular region of the country. We can divide Brazil into four regions based on their people, economies, and landscapes.

The Southeast

Most people in Brazil live in the southeast. **São Paulo** is located there. Almost 19 million people live in and around São Paulo. It is the largest urban area in South America and the fourth largest in the world. São Paulo is considered a **megacity**, or a giant urban area that includes surrounding cities and suburbs.

Rio de Janeiro, Brazil's second-largest city, lies northeast of São Paulo. Almost 12 million people live there. The city was the capital of Brazil from 1822 until 1960. Today Rio de Janeiro remains a major port city. Its spectacular setting and exciting culture are popular with tourists.

Differentiating Instruction

Below Level

Struggling Readers

1. Talk with students about how cultural traditions originate. Have students work in pairs to write about a tradition they both celebrate.

2. Have students research the tradition by using primary and secondary sources. For example, students can ask family members about family traditions surrounding the holiday, and they can use the Internet and other sources to learn more about the history of the tradition and where and when it began.

3. Have partners work together to organize the information they find into a class presentation. ⓁⓈ **Verbal/Linguistic**

📖 Alternative Assessment Handbook, Rubrics 29: Presentations; and 14: Group Activity

Answers

Analyzing Visuals *the southeast*
Reading Check *Religion, festivals, and food from other countries are now a part of Brazilian culture.*

② About one third of Brazilians live in the dry northeast, the nation's poorest region.

③ Rivers provide resources and transportation for people living in the Amazon region.

In addition to having the largest cities, the southeast is also Brazil's richest region. It is rich in natural resources and has most of the country's industries and productive farmland. It is one of the major coffee-growing regions of the world.

Although the southeast has a strong economy, it also has poverty. Cities in the region have huge slums called **favelas** (fah-VE-lahz). Many people who live in favelas have come to cities of the southeast from other regions of Brazil in search of jobs.

The Northeast

Immigrants to Brazil's large cities often come from the northeast, which is Brazil's poorest region. Many people there cannot read, and health care is poor. The region often suffers from droughts, which make farming and raising livestock difficult. The northeast has also had difficulty attracting industry. However, the region's beautiful beaches do attract tourists.

Other tourist attractions in northeastern Brazil are the region's many old colonial cities. These cities were built during the days of the sugar industry. They have brightly painted buildings, cobblestone streets, and elaborate Catholic churches.

The Interior

The interior region of Brazil is a frontier land. Its abundant land and mild climate could someday make it an important area for agriculture. For now, few people live in this region, except for those who reside in the country's capital, **Brasília**.

In the mid-1950s government officials hoped that building a new capital city in the Brazilian interior would help develop the region. Brasília has modern buildings and busy highways. More than 2 million people live in Brasília, although it was originally designed for only 500,000.

The Amazon

The Amazon region covers the northern part of Brazil. **Manaus**, which lies 1,000 miles (1,600 km) from the mouth of the Amazon, is a major port and industrial city. More than 1 million people live there. They rely on the river for transportation and communication.

Isolated Indian villages are scattered throughout the region's dense rain forest. Some of Brazil's Indians had little contact with outsiders until recently. Now, logging, mining, and new roads are bringing more people and development to this region.

Main Idea

③ Brazil Today

Brazil today is experiencing population growth in its cities and new development in rain forest areas.

Explain Why does Brazil's large size create opportunities and challenges for the country? *Brazil has the largest economy in South America. The country has modern and wealthy areas, but many Brazilians are poor.*

Identify What are the four regions of Brazil? *the southeast, the northeast, the interior, and the Amazon*

Define What is a megacity? *a giant urban area that includes surrounding cities and suburbs*

📑 **RF:** Geography for Life, Mapping Wealth and Poverty in Brazil

Teaching Tip

Brazil's Regions Have students create their own regional maps of Brazil. Ask students to include facts about each region, using symbols and colors to illustrate their maps. Be sure to have students include major cities as well.

Differentiating Instruction

At Level

English-Language Learners

1. To help students remember the key information about each region, draw the graphic organizer for students to see. Omit the blue, italicized answers.

2. Have students work in pairs to fill out the organizer. When students are finished, review the answers with the class.

LS Verbal/Linguistic, Visual/Spatial

📑 Alternative Assessment Handbook, Rubric 13: Graphic Organizers

Regions of Brazil

The Southwest	The Northeast	The Interior	The Amazon
São Paulo: • *17 million* • *megacity* *Rio de Janeiro:* • *2nd largest city* • *11 million* *Resources:* • *farmland* • *coffee*	*poorest region* *Industry:* • *tourism*	*frontier land* *mild climate* *Brasília:* • *capital* • *2 million*	*rain forest* *Manaus:* • *port* • *industrial city* • *1 million* *Industry:* • *logging* • *mining*

Direct Teach

Linking to Today

Deforestation in the Amazon Many people living in the Amazon and surrounding regions depend on the Amazon rain forest's natural resources to help fuel the economy. But using these resources is leading to deforestation, which in turn threatens the lives of the people who depend on the rain forest's resources. If you were a government official living in the region, what would you do to help preserve the rain forest and the region's economy?

Review & Assess

Close

Briefly review the history of Brazil, Brazil's people and culture, and what Brazil is like today.

Review

 Online Quiz, Section 2

Assess

SE Section 2 Assessment

PASS: Section 2 Quiz

Alternative Assessment Handbook

Reteach/Classroom Intervention

Guided Reading Workbook, Section 2

 Interactive Skills Tutor CD-ROM

Answers

Satellite View *More trees would be cut down to make way for the roads; animals could be hit by cars.*

Reading Check *The northeast is Brazil's poorest region while the southeast is Brazil's richest region.*

214

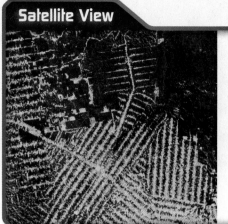

Satellite View

Deforestation in the Amazon

Deforestation is changing the landscape of the Amazon rain forest. This satellite image shows new roads and cleared areas where people have taken resources from the forest.

Many people depend on the industries that result in deforestation. For example, people need wood for building and making paper. Also, farmers, loggers, and miners need to make a living. However, deforestation in the Amazon also threatens the survival of many plant and animal species. It also threatens hundreds of unique ecosystems.

Making Inferences What do you think might be some effects of building roads in the rain forest?

This new development provides needed income for some people. But it destroys large areas of the rain forest. It also creates tensions among the Brazilian Indians, new settlers, miners, and the government.

READING CHECK **Contrasting** How does the northeast of Brazil differ from the southeast?

SUMMARY AND PREVIEW In this section you read about Brazil—a huge country of many contrasts. Brazil reflects the mixing of people and cultures from its history. In the next section you will learn about Brazil's neighbors—Argentina, Uruguay, and Paraguay.

Section 2 Assessment

hmhsocialstudies.com
ONLINE QUIZ

Reviewing Ideas, Terms, and Places

1. **a. Recall** What European country colonized Brazil?
   b. Make Inferences Why did the colonists bring Africans to work on plantations as slaves?
   c. Elaborate Why do you think the main basis of Brazil's colonial economy changed over the years?
2. **a. Identify** What religion is most common in Brazil?
   b. Explain Why is so much of Brazil's culture influenced by African traditions?
3. **a. Define** What is a **megacity**, and what is an example of a megacity in Brazil?
   b. Make Inferences Why might development in the Amazon cause tensions between Brazilian Indians and new settlers?
   c. Elaborate How might life change for a person who moves from the northeast to the southeast?

Critical Thinking

4. **Finding Main Ideas** Review your notes on Brazil. Then, write a main idea statement about each region. Use a graphic organizer like this one.

	Main Idea
The Southeast	
The Northeast	
The Interior	
The Amazon	

FOCUS ON WRITING

5. **Writing about Brazil** What information about the history, people, and culture of Brazil will draw readers to the country? What regions do you think they would like to visit? List details and ideas for possible images for your Web site.

214 CHAPTER 9

Section 2 Assessment Answers

1. **a.** Portugal
   b. for free labor
   c. The economy changed as more resources were discovered.

2. **a.** Roman Catholic
   b. because many Brazilians are of African descent

3. **a.** a giant urban area that includes surrounding cities and suburbs; São Paulo
   b. because they both rely on the rain forest for survival
   c. Life might be better because the southeast is Brazil's richest region.

4. The Southeast has the largest cities and a strong economy; the Northeast is Brazil's poorest region, with tourism as its strongest industry; the Interior is less populated, but has abundant land and a mild climate which could be good for agriculture; the Amazon is in the northern part of Brazil, with logging and mining as its main industries, even though these threaten the rain forest.

5. Tourists may be attracted to the seacoast in the Southeast and old colonial cities in the Northeast. Tourists might also like to attend Carnival and other celebrations.

Connecting Ideas

Learn

You have already used several types of graphic organizers in this book. Graphic organizers are drawings that help you organize information and connect ideas.

One type of graphic organizer is a word web. A word web like the one at right helps you organize specific facts and details around a main topic. Notice that information gets more detailed as it gets farther away from the main topic.

Practice

Use the word web here to answer the following questions. You may also want to look back at the information on Brazilian culture in your textbook.

1 How can a graphic organizer help you connect ideas?

2 What is the main topic of this word web?

3 What three main ideas does this graphic organizer connect?

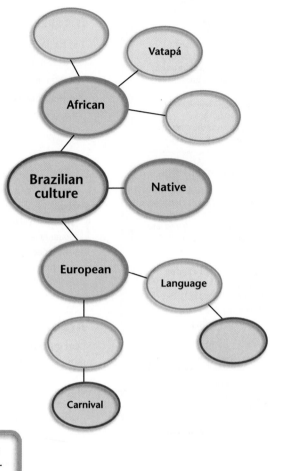

Apply

Copy the graphic organizer shown here in your notebook. Use the information on Brazilian culture in your textbook to fill in the blank circles with additional details about the main topic.

ATLANTIC SOUTH AMERICA **215**

Bellringer

If YOU lived there... Use the **Daily Bellringer Transparency** to help students answer the question.

▶ Daily Bellringer Transparency, Section 3

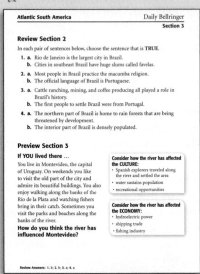

Key Terms and Places

RF: Vocabulary Builder, Section 3

Taking Notes

Have students use the graphic organizer online to take notes on the section. This activity will prepare students for the Section Assessment, in which they will complete a graphic organizer that builds on the information using the Critical Thinking Skill: Comparing and Contrasting.

What You Will Learn...

Main Ideas

1. European immigrants have dominated the history and culture of Argentina.
2. Argentina's capital, Buenos Aires, plays a large role in the country's government and economy today.
3. Uruguay has been influenced by its neighbors.
4. Paraguay is the most rural country in the region.

The Big Idea

Argentina, Uruguay, and Paraguay have been influenced by European immigration, a tradition of ranching, and large urban populations.

Key Terms and Places

gauchos, *p. 217*
Buenos Aires, *p. 218*
Mercosur, *p. 218*
informal economy, *p. 219*
landlocked, *p. 220*

hmhsocialstudies.com
TAKING NOTES

Use the graphic organizer online to organize your notes on Argentina, Uruguay, and Paraguay.

Argentina, Uruguay, and Paraguay

If **YOU** lived there...

You live in Montevideo, the capital of Uruguay. On weekends you like to visit the old part of the city and admire its beautiful buildings. You also enjoy walking along the banks of the Río de la Plata and watching fishers bring in their catch. Sometimes you visit the parks and beaches along the banks of the river.

How do you think the river has influenced Montevideo?

BUILDING BACKGROUND The southern countries of Atlantic South America—Argentina, Uruguay, and Paraguay—have all been influenced by their locations and European culture. Neither Spanish influence nor Indian culture is as strong in the southern part of South America as in other parts of the continent.

Argentina's History and Culture

Like most of South America, Argentina was originally home to groups of Indians. Groups living in the Pampas hunted wild game, while farther north Indians built irrigation systems for farming. However, unlike most of South America, Argentina has very few native peoples remaining. Instead, Argentina's culture has been mostly influenced by Europeans.

Early History

The first Europeans to come to Argentina were the Spanish. In the 1500s Spanish conquerors spread from the northern part of the continent into southern South America in search of silver and gold. They named the region Argentina. *Argentina* means "land of silver" or "silvery one."

216 CHAPTER 9

Argentina, Uruguay, and Paraguay

1. **Teach** Ask students the questions in the Main Idea boxes under Direct Teach.

2. **Apply** Refer students to the chapter opener map to locate Argentina, Uruguay, and Paraguay. Ask students to make their own list of all the clues the map provides to tell them something about each country. For example, does the country have many rivers and lakes? Where are the countries' borders? Have students make a list for each country. **LS Visual/Spatial**

3. **Review** Ask students to exchange their lists with one another to compare what clues they found.

4. **Practice/Homework** Have students research each country, finding five facts about each one. **LS Verbal/Linguistic**

   Alternative Assessment Handbook, Rubrics 30: Research; and 42: Writing to Inform

---

Gauchos on the Pampas

Gauchos were a popular subject in Argentine art. In this painting from 1820, gauchos gather to watch a horse race.

ANALYZING VISUALS Why would horses be important to a gaucho?

The Spanish soon built settlements in Argentina. The Spanish monarch granted land to the colonists, who in turn built the settlements. These landowners were also given the right to force the Indians living there to work.

During the colonial era, the Pampas became an important agricultural region. Argentine cowboys, called **gauchos** (GOW-chohz), herded cattle and horses on the open grasslands. Although agriculture is still important on the Pampas, very few people in Argentina live as gauchos today.

In the early 1800s Argentina fought for independence from Spain. A period of violence and instability followed. Many Indians were killed or driven away by fighting during this time.

Modern Argentina

As the Indians were being killed off, more European influences dominated the region. New immigrants arrived from Italy, Germany, and Spain. Also, the British helped build railroads across the country. Railroads made it easier for Argentina to transport agricultural products for export to Europe. Beef exports, in particular, made the country rich.

Argentina remained one of South America's richest countries throughout the 1900s. However, the country also struggled under dictators and military governments during those years.

Some political leaders, like Eva Perón, were popular. But many leaders abused human rights. During the "Dirty War" in the 1970s, they tortured and killed many accused of disagreeing with the government. Both the country's people and its economy suffered. Finally, in the 1980s, Argentina's last military government gave up power to an elected government.

BIOGRAPHY

Eva Perón
(1919–1952)

Known affectionately as Evita, Eva Perón helped improve the living conditions of people in Argentina, particularly the poor. As the wife of Argentina's president, Juan Perón, Evita established thousands of hospitals and schools throughout Argentina. She also helped women gain the right to vote. After years of battling cancer, Evita died at age 33. All of Argentina mourned her death for weeks.

Analyzing Why was Eva Perón able to help many people?

Critical Thinking: Summarizing

At Level

Effective Leaders

Research Required

1. Lead a class discussion about Eva Perón. Ask students to name characteristics that describe her. Record the characteristics on the board.

2. Ask students which characteristics helped make Eva Perón a great leader. Why?

3. Have each student conduct research and then write an obituary that discusses Perón's leadership abilities and other characteristics.

4. Ask students whether the characteristics that made great leaders in the past are the same as those that make today's leaders and heroes. Have students write a paragraph explaining their answer.

5. Ask volunteers to read their obituaries and paragraphs to the class. **LS** **Verbal/Linguistic**

    Alternative Assessment Handbook, Rubric 37: Writing Assignments

---

❷ Argentina Today

Argentina's capital, Buenos Aires, plays a large role in the country's government and economy today.

Recall What is the capital of Argentina? *Buenos Aires*

Describe What factors have contributed to the economy of Buenos Aires? *its well-educated population and its location on the coast and near the Pampas*

Explain What caused an economic crisis in Argentina in the late 1900s and early 2000s? *heavy debt and government spending*

Define What is the informal economy? *a part of the economy based on odd jobs that people perform without government regulation through taxes*

Interpreting Maps

Argentina: Population

Have students study the map and chart. Then ask the following questions:

What are Argentina's five largest cities, in order of size? *Buenos Aires, Córdoba, Rosario, Mendoza, San Miguel de Tucumán*

Which country shown is located farthest south? *Argentina*

▶ Map Zone Transparency: Argentina: Population

People and Culture

Argentina's historical ties to Europe still affect its culture. Most of Argentina's roughly 40 million people are descended from Spanish, Italian, or other European settlers. Argentine Indians and mestizos make up only about 3 percent of the population. Most Argentines are Roman Catholic.

Beef is still a part of Argentina's culture. A popular dish is parrilla (pah-REE-yah), which includes grilled sausage and steak. Supper is generally eaten late.

READING CHECK **Generalizing** What kind of governments did Argentina have in the 1900s?

Argentina Today

Today many more of Argentina's people live in **Buenos Aires** (BWAY-nohs EYE-rayz) than in any other city. Buenos Aires is the country's capital. It is also the second-largest urban area in South America. Much of Argentina's industry is located in and around Buenos Aires. Its location on the coast and near the Pampas has contributed to its economic development.

The Pampas are the country's most developed agricultural region. About 11 percent of Argentina's labor force works in agriculture. Large ranches and farms there produce beef, wheat, and corn for export to other countries.

Argentina's economy has always been affected by government policies. In the 1990s government leaders made economic reforms to help businesses grow. Argentina joined **Mercosur**—an organization that promotes trade and economic cooperation among the southern and eastern countries of South America. By the late 1900s and early 2000s, however, heavy debt and government spending brought Argentina into an economic crisis.

Argentina: Population

map zone

Geography Skills

Place Buenos Aires is home to nearly a third of all Argentines.

1. **Interpreting Graphs** How many times bigger is Buenos Aires than Argentina's second-largest city?
2. **Analyze** What might be a benefit and a drawback of having most of the country's population in one area?

THE WORLD ALMANAC
Facts about Countries

Argentina's Largest Cities

Population (in millions) — Cities: Buenos Aires, Córdoba, Rosario, Mendoza, San Miguel de Tucumán

hmhsocialstudies.com

Differentiating Instruction

Struggling Readers   **Below Level**

To help struggling readers, read aloud the name for each city in the chart. As you do, have students locate the city on the map. Remind students that this book has many illustrations that can help them learn. **LS** **Visual/Spatial**

📝 Alternative Assessment Handbook, Rubric 21: Map Reading

Advanced/Gifted and Talented Learners   **Above Level**

Have students discuss why the most populated areas also have the strongest economies. Ask students if they think this is the same for heavily populated cities in the United States. Have students explain why.

LS **Verbal/Linguistic, Visual/Spatial**

📝 Alternative Assessment Handbook, Rubric 11: Discussions

Answers

Reading Check *dictatorships and military governments*

Map Zone 1. *about 6;* 2. *possible answers—benefit: large work force; drawback: crowding*

218

Buenos Aires

Buenos Aires is a huge, modern city. Its main street is said to be the widest avenue in the world.

ANALYZING VISUALS What do the wide street and trees suggest about the people who built this city?

The economic crisis caused a political crisis. As a result, during 2001, Argentina's government changed hands four times as its leaders tried to solve the problems. By 2003 the economy had stabilized somewhat, but thousands of people's lives had changed forever. The crisis caused many people who once had professional careers to lose their jobs and join the informal economy. The **informal economy** is a part of the economy based on odd jobs that people perform without government regulation through taxes. Today many Argentines are still searching for ways to improve their economy.

READING CHECK Comparing and Contrasting What are some similarities and differences between Buenos Aires and the Pampas?

Uruguay

Tucked between Argentina and Brazil lies Uruguay. Its capital, Montevideo (mawn-tay-vee-DAY-oh), is located on the north shore of the Río de la Plata, not far from Buenos Aires. Uruguay has always been influenced by its larger neighbors.

Portugal claimed Uruguay during the colonial era, but the Spanish took over in the 1770s. By that time, few Uruguayan Indians remained. A few years later, in 1825, Uruguay declared independence from Spain. Since then, military governments have ruled Uruguay off and on. In general, however, the country has a strong tradition of respect for political freedom. Today Uruguay is a democracy.

People

As in Argentina, people of European descent make up the majority of Uruguay's population. Only about 12 percent of the population is mestizo, Indian, or of African descent. Roman Catholicism is the main religion in the country. Spanish is the official language, but many people also speak Portuguese because of Uruguay's location near Brazil.

More than 90 percent of Uruguay's people live in urban areas. More than a third of Uruguayans live in and near Montevideo. The country has a high literacy rate. In addition, many people there have good jobs and can afford a wide range of consumer goods and travel to Europe. However, many young people leave Uruguay to explore better economic opportunities elsewhere.

ATLANTIC SOUTH AMERICA **219**

Direct Teach

Main Idea

3 Uruguay

Uruguay has been influenced by its neighbors.

Identify What is the capital of Uruguay and where is it located? *Montevideo is located on the north shore of Río de la Plata, not far from Buenos Aires.*

Recall When did Uruguay claim its independence from Spain? *1825*

Describe Where does most of the population of Uruguay live? *More than 90 percent of Uruguay's people live in urban areas, with more than a third of those living in Montevideo.*

Activity Name Origins The name "Uruguay" means "river of the painted birds" in Guaraní, an Indian language. Why do you think it was given this name? Have students work in groups to learn how your city or town got its name. **LS** Verbal/Linguistic

Alternative Assessment Handbook, Rubric 30: Research

Critical Thinking: Analyzing   At Level

The People of Uruguay

1. Tell students that while some nations have very diverse populations, others do not.

2. To help students organize information about the population of Uruguay, copy the graphic organizer for students to see. Omit the blue, italicized answers. Have students copy and complete the graphic organizer on their own paper. **LS** Visual/Spatial, Verbal/Linguistic

Alternative Assessment Handbook, Rubric 13: Graphic Organizers

People of Uruguay

majority of population=European descent   *12%=mestizo, African, or Indian*

90%=live in urban areas

1/3=live in and near Montevideo

main religion=Roman Catholicism

Answers

Analyzing Visuals *possible answers—The people who built the highways planned for a future where many cars would be on the roads. They planted trees to make the area beautiful and pleasant for the citizens.*

Reading Check *Buenos Aires and the Pampas are both in Argentina. Buenos Aires is a large, urban area, while the Pampas is an agricultural region.*

④ Paraguay

Paraguay is the most rural country in the region.

Recall With which countries does Paraguay share a border? *Bolivia, Brazil, and Argentina*

Define What does landlocked mean? *completely surrounded by land*

Identify What is the capital of Paraguay, and where is it located? *Asunción is located along the Paraguay River near the border of Argentina.*

📄 **RF:** Biography, Agustín Barrios Mangoré

Interpreting Maps

Paraguay and Uruguay

Have students study the map and photographs. Then ask the following questions:

Why do many people in Paraguay live in rural areas? *Because the main economic activity is farming, there are few large cities in Paraguay.*

How does Uruguay benefit by sharing a border with Brazil and Argentina? *because its economy is tied to the economies of Brazil and Argentina*

▶ Map Zone Transparency: Paraguay and Uruguay

Answers

Focus on Reading *under Paraguay, highlighted*

Reading Check *The majority of people living in both countries are of European descent; the main religion in both countries is Roman Catholicism; people in both countries are generally well educated; both countries have large farming economies.*

Map Zone 1. *the Uruguay River;* **2.** *because Paraguay is landlocked and because Paraguay's main industry is farming*

Economy

FOCUS ON READING
Where can you find the definition of *landlocked*?

Just as Uruguay's culture is tied to its neighbors, its economy is tied to the economies of Brazil and Argentina. In fact, more than half of Uruguay's foreign trade is with these two Mercosur partners. Beef is an important export. As in Argentina, ranchers graze livestock on inland plains.

Agriculture, along with some limited manufacturing, is the basis of Uruguay's economy. Uruguay has few mineral resources. One important source of energy is hydroelectric power. Developing poor rural areas in the interior, where resources are in short supply, is a big challenge.

READING CHECK **Compare** In what ways is Uruguay similar to Argentina?

Paraguay

Paraguay shares borders with Bolivia, Brazil, and Argentina. It is a landlocked country. **Landlocked** means completely surrounded by land with no direct access to the ocean. The Paraguay River divides the country into two regions. East of the river is the country's most productive farmland. Ranchers also graze livestock in some parts of western Paraguay.

Paraguay was claimed by Spanish settlers in the mid-1530s. It remained a Spanish colony until 1811, when it won independence. From independence until 1989, Paraguay was ruled off and on by dictators. Today the country has elected leaders and a democratic government.

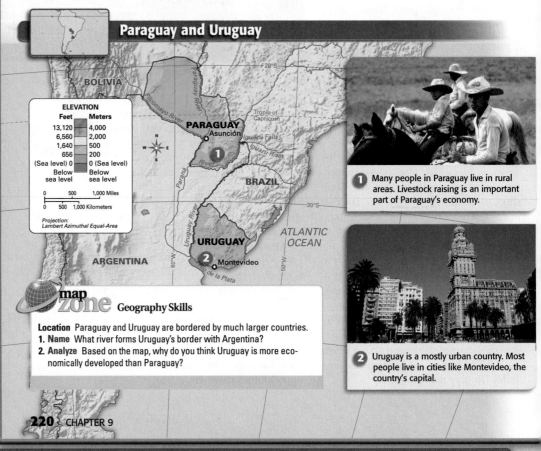

Paraguay and Uruguay

ELEVATION

Feet	Meters
13,120	4,000
6,560	2,000
1,640	500
656	200
(Sea level) 0	0 (Sea level)
Below sea level	Below sea level

0   500   1,000 Miles
0   500   1,000 Kilometers

Projection: Lambert Azimuthal Equal-Area

1 Many people in Paraguay live in rural areas. Livestock raising is an important part of Paraguay's economy.

2 Uruguay is a mostly urban country. Most people live in cities like Montevideo, the country's capital.

🌎 **map zone** **Geography Skills**

Location Paraguay and Uruguay are bordered by much larger countries.
1. Name What river forms Uruguay's border with Argentina?
2. Analyze Based on the map, why do you think Uruguay is more economically developed than Paraguay?

220 CHAPTER 9

Differentiating Instruction

At Level

English-Language Learners

1. Review with students the names of the three countries discussed in this section: Argentina, Uruguay, and Paraguay.

2. Hand out a sheet of paper to each student. Have students fold the paper equally in thirds, lengthwise so the paper has three columns. Have students write the name of each country at the top of each column. Have students write five facts about each country under the correct heading.

3. Organize the class into pairs. Have students read each other one fact at a time while their partners guess which country the fact is describing. Some facts may describe more than one country. **LS Verbal/Linguistic**

📄 Alternative Assessment Handbook, Rubric 14: Group Activity

People

A great majority—about 95 percent—of Paraguayans are mestizos. Indians and people of mostly European descent make up the rest of the population. Paraguay has two official languages. Almost all people in Paraguay speak both Spanish and Guarani (gwah-ruh-NEE), an Indian language. As in Uruguay, most people are Roman Catholic.

Paraguay's capital and largest city is Asunción (ah-soon-SYOHN). The city is located along the Paraguay River near the border with Argentina.

Economy

Much of Paraguay's wealth is controlled by a few rich families and companies. These families and companies have tremendous influence over the country's government.

Agriculture is an important part of the economy. In fact, nearly half of the country's workers are farmers. Many of these farmers grow just enough food to feed themselves and their families. They grow crops such as corn, cotton, soybeans, and sugarcane. Paraguay also has many small businesses but not much industry.

Paraguay's future may be promising as the country learns how to use its resources more effectively. For example, the country has built large hydroelectric dams on the Paraná River. These dams provide more power than Paraguay needs, so Paraguay is able to sell the surplus electricity to Brazil and Argentina.

READING CHECK **Contrast** How are the people of Paraguay different from the people of Argentina and Uruguay?

SUMMARY AND PREVIEW The people of Paraguay, Argentina, and Uruguay share some aspects of their European heritage. Their economies are also closely tied. In the next chapter you will learn about these countries' neighbors to the west.

Section 3 Assessment

hmhsocialstudies.com
ONLINE QUIZ

Reviewing Ideas, Terms, and Places

1. **a. Define** What is a **gaucho**?
   b. Explain Why is Argentina's population mostly of European descent?
2. **a. Identify** What is Argentina's biggest city?
   b. Make Inferences What benefits do you think being part of **Mercosur** brings to Argentina?
   c. Elaborate What are some benefits the **informal economy** provides, and what are some of its drawbacks?
3. **a. Recall** Where is Uruguay's capital located?
   b. Summarize How has Uruguay's location influenced its culture?
4. **a. Define** What does it mean to say a country is **landlocked**?
   b. Explain What is Paraguay's economy like?
   c. Predict What are some possible ways Paraguay may be able to improve its economy in the future?

Critical Thinking

5. **Comparing and Contrasting** Look over your notes on Uruguay and Paraguay. Then draw a diagram like the one here and use it to show similarities and differences between the two countries.

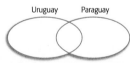

Uruguay   Paraguay

FOCUS ON WRITING

6. **Thinking about Argentina, Uruguay, and Paraguay** Add details about these countries to your notes for your Web site. What information on history, culture, and specific locations will you include? For each country, think of one image that would best illustrate it.

Teaching Tip

If students have difficulty remembering the capitals of each country, have them write sentences. Begin each word in the sentence with the first letters of each country and its capital. Sentences may be nonsensical. Here is an example:

Aunt (Argentina) Betty Ann (Buenos Aires) usually (Uruguay) makes (Montevideo) pickled (Paraguay) apples (Asunción).

• Review & Assess •

Close

Briefly review the similarities and differences among Argentina, Uruguay, and Paraguay.

Review

Online Quiz, Section 3

Assess

SE Section 3 Assessment
PASS: Section 3 Quiz
Alternative Assessment Handbook

Reteach/Classroom Intervention

Guided Reading Workbook, Section 3
Interactive Skills Tutor CD-ROM

Section 3 Assessment Answers

1. **a.** an Argentine cowboy
   b. because the country was colonized and settled by people from Europe
2. **a.** Buenos Aires
   b. It promotes trade and economic cooperation among the southern and eastern countries, which is good for the economy.
   c. It helps people who lost their jobs during the economic crisis find work, but they do not pay taxes to help support the government.
3. **a.** on the north shore of the Río de la Plata, not far from Buenos Aires

   b. Because Uruguay is located between Brazil and Argentina, its culture has been influenced by these larger countries.
4. **a.** It is completely surrounded by land.
   b. Agriculture is an important part of the economy, but much of Paraguay's wealth is controlled by rich families and companies.
   c. use its resources more effectively; sell surplus electricity to Brazil and Argentina
5. Students' Venn diagrams should include accurate details about the location, history, people, and economies of Uruguay and Paraguay.
6. Look over students' individual notes.

Answers

Reading Check *About 95 percent of Paraguayans are mestizos. Most people in Paraguay speak both Spanish and Guarani. Most people in Argentina and Uruguay are of European descent.*

Literature

The Gaucho Martín Fierro

As You Read Ask students what traits or character traits would help make a good gaucho. As they read, students should make a list of the traits revealed through Hernández's poem. *independence, physical strength, love of outdoors, good with horses, able to ride horses and use a lasso, able to live alone, able to work with others*

Info to Know

Influential People Gauchos were famous for being daring and skillful horsemen. Many also played an important role as revolutionary soldiers. They were a strong influence in the early years of the Argentine republic.

Meet the Writer

Protecting a Lifestyle José Hernández was born in 1834 in Buenos Aires, Argentina. He started the newspaper *El Río de la Plata*. He was against immigration because he thought it would harm pastoralism, which is a social organization based on raising livestock.

Gauchos spent a lot of time alone on the plains, but sometimes they got together for games and amusement.

GUIDED READING

WORD HELP

lassoing catching with a rope
steers cattle
keen happy, eager

❶ Notice Hernández's description of the Pampas.

❷ Hernández describes the work of gauchos.

What were some activities of gauchos?

Literature

from
The Gaucho Martín Fierro

by José Hernández

About the Reading *José Hernández spent part of his childhood on Argentina's Pampas. The gauchos lived freely on the plains there, herding cattle. In 1872 he published an epic poem about his days as an Argentine cowboy. The passage below is an excerpt.*

AS YOU READ Notice the emotion with which Hernández writes.

Even the poorest gaucho
had a string of matching horses;
he could always afford some amusement,
and people were ready for anything . . .
Looking out across the land
you'd see nothing but cattle and sky. ❶

When the branding-time came round
that was work to warm you up!
What a crowd! lassoing the running steers
and keen to hold and throw them . . . ❷
What a time that was! in those days surely
there were champions to be seen . . .

And the games that would get going
when we were all of us together!
We were always ready for them,
as at times like those
a lot of neighbors would turn up
to help out the regular hands.

Connecting Literature to Geography

1. **Identifying Points of View** Hernández had happy memories of his days as a gaucho. What words and phrases demonstrate how Hernández felt?

2. **Analyzing** Although few people still work as gauchos, they are popular subjects in Argentine literature. What aspects of gaucho life do you think modern readers find appealing?

222

Differentiating Instruction

English-Language Learners   Below Level

Have students illustrate the scene described in this excerpt. The drawing should convey the emotion of the poem. Have students reread the excerpt, noting the key words, phrases, and punctuation that help set the scene.
LS Visual/Spatial, Verbal/Linguistic
Alternative Assessment Handbook, Rubric 3: Artwork

Advanced/Gifted and Talented   Above Level

Have students study the line breaks and punctuation in the poem. Ask students why they think the author chose to start a new line or use ellipses. Have students write their own poems describing a scene they imagine in the life of a gaucho. **LS Visual/Spatial, Verbal/Linguistic**
Alternative Assessment Handbook, Rubric 26: Poems and Songs

Answers

Guided Reading *herding cattle, branding, games*

Connecting Literature to Geography 1. *"amusement" and "What a time that was!"* **2.** *living on the open plains, excitement of branding time, sense of community*

Chapter Review

Geography's Impact
video series
Review the video to answer the closing question:
What are some arguments for and against deforestation?

Visual Summary

Use the visual summary below to help you review the main ideas of the chapter.

QUICK FACTS

The lush Amazon rain forest covers a huge part of the region.

Brazil has many large cities as well as large rural areas.

Argentina, Uruguay, and Paraguay have large plains that are good for ranching.

Reviewing Vocabulary, Terms, and Places

For each group of terms below, write a sentence that shows how all the terms in the group are related.

1. estuary
   Río de la Plata
   Buenos Aires
2. megacity
   favelas
   aspects
3. gauchos
   Pampas
4. soil exhaustion
   deforestation
   Amazon River
5. Rio de Janeiro
   São Paulo
   Manaus

Comprehension and Critical Thinking

SECTION 1 *(Pages 206–209)*

6. **a. Recall** What kind of climate does the Amazon Basin have?

   b. Contrast How are northern Brazil and southern Argentina different?

   c. Elaborate How might the region's major physical features have influenced development and daily life in Atlantic South America?

SECTION 2 *(Pages 210–215)*

7. **a. Describe** What parts of Brazilian culture reflect African influences?

   b. Analyze What factors lead people from the northeast of Brazil to move to the southeast?

   c. Evaluate Is deforestation of the Amazon rain forest necessary? Explain your answer. What arguments might someone with a different opinion use?

ATLANTIC SOUTH AMERICA 223

Answers

Visual Summary

Review and Inquiry Have students use the visual summary to write a brief paragraph describing Atlantic South America as depicted in the illustrations.

▶ Quick Facts Transparency: Atlantic South America Visual Summary

Reviewing Vocabulary, Terms, and Places

1. <u>Buenos Aires</u> is a port city located on the <u>Río de la Plata</u>, an <u>estuary</u>.
2. One <u>aspect</u> of the <u>megacity</u>, São Paulo, is its <u>favelas</u> where many people live in poverty.
3. <u>Gauchos</u> herd cattle on the grassy plains of the <u>Pampas</u>.
4. <u>Soil exhaustion</u> and <u>deforestation</u> threaten the <u>Amazon River</u> Basin rain forest.
5. <u>Rio de Janeiro</u> is Brazil's second largest city and lies northeast of <u>São Paulo</u>, Brazil's largest city, while <u>Manaus</u> is a major city in the Amazon region.

Comprehension and Critical Thinking

6. **a.** humid tropical
   b. Northern Brazil has a humid tropical climate while Southern Argentina has a cool, desert climate.
   c. The region's river systems, plains, and plateaus made it a good place for farming and raising cattle.
7. **a.** religion, festivals, and food
   b. The northeast is Brazil's poorest region, and many people move to the southeast to find jobs.

Review and Assessment Resources

Review and Reinforce

SE Chapter Review

RF: Chapter Review

▶ Quick Facts Transparency: Atlantic South America Visual Summary

Spanish Chapter Summaries Audio CD Program

TOS Holt McDougal Puzzle View, Quiz Show for ExamView

Quiz Game CD-ROM

Assess

SE Standardized Test Practice

PASS: Chapter Test, Forms A and B

Alternative Assessment Handbook

TOS ExamView Test Generator, Chapter Test

Differentiated Instruction Modified Worksheets and Tests CD-ROM: Chapter Test

Online Assessment Program, in the Interactive Student Edition

Reteach/Intervene

Guided Reading Workbook

Differentiated Instruction Teacher Management System: Lesson Plans

Differentiated Instruction Modified Worksheets and Tests CD-ROM

Interactive Skills Tutor CD-ROM

↗ hmhsocialstudies.com
Chapter Resources

7. c. possible answer—Deforestation is necessary for the farmers and businesses who depend on it for their income. But people and animals living in the rain forest also need it to be protected.

8. a. Unlike most of South America, Argentina has few native peoples and its culture has been highly influenced by Europeans.
b. possible answer—Both were Spanish colonies; Paraguay is landlocked, and Uruguay is not.
c. possible answer—It will decline as people are able to find work.

Using the Internet

9. Go to hmhsocialstudies.com to access a rubric for this activity.

Social Studies Skills

10. Review students' graphic organizers to ensure that students include the main points about Atlantic South America's economies.

Map Activity

11. A. São Paulo
B. Paraná River
C. Amazon River
D. Patagonia
E. Río de la Plata
F. Pampas

Focus on Reading and Writing

12. Review students' work to ensure that they understand how to use context clues when reading.

📖 **RF:** Focus on Reading, Using Context Clues

13. Rubric Students' Web sites should
- include a home page that briefly describes the region
- include a page for each country discussed in the chapter
- have one well-written paragraph and one image for each country
- not overwhelm readers with too much text

📖 **RF:** Focus on Writing, Creating a Web site.

SECTION 3 *(Pages 216–221)*

8. a. Describe How is Argentina's culture different from other South American countries?

b. Contrast What is one difference between Uruguay and Paraguay?

c. Predict As Argentina's economy improves, what might happen to its informal economy?

Social Studies Skills

9. Connecting Ideas Draw a graphic organizer to help you organize information about the economy in Atlantic South America. One has been started for you below. You will need to add more ovals to contain the information.

Using the Internet 🌐21st CENTURY

10. Activity: Creating a Poster The Amazon River is the world's second-longest river. Through your online textbook, explore the many aspects of the river, including its wildlife, the rain forest it cuts through, the people who live alongside it, and the environmental issues surrounding it. Use the information you find and the interactive template provided to create a poster about the amazing Amazon River.

↗ hmhsocialstudies.com

Map Activity 🌐21st CENTURY

11. Atlantic South America On a separate sheet of paper, match the letters on the map with their correct labels.

São Paulo	Pampas	Patagonia
Paraná River	Río de la Plata	Amazon River

↗ hmhsocialstudies.com **INTERACTIVE MAP**

map zone

FOCUS ON READING AND WRITING

12. Using Context Clues Look through the chapter and pick out two difficult words that you had to figure out by using context clues. Then, note the context clues you used to help you figure out the definitions of the difficult words.

13. Creating a Web Site You can create a real Web site or a paper version of a Web site. First, look back through your notes and choose key ideas about each country to include. In designing your site, first include a home page that briefly describes the region. Indicate links for pages about each of the countries in the region. Each of your country pages should include one short paragraph and one image. Remember to keep the pages simple—too much text might overwhelm your readers and send them off to another site!

Standardized Test Prep

DIRECTIONS: Read questions 1 through 7 and write the letter of the best response. Then read question 8 and write your own well-constructed response.

1 In which country do most people speak Portuguese?

A Brazil

B Argentina

C Uruguay

D Paraguay

2 What major river flows through northwestern Brazil?

A Río de la Plata

B Uruguay River

C Paraná River

D Amazon River

3 Which of the following statements about Argentina is true?

A Most people are mestizos.

B Most people in Argentina live on the Pampas.

C Argentina is a member of Mercosur.

D Argentina has had a stable government and economy since 2000.

4 Which of the following was an effect of the "Dirty War" in Argentina?

A The country's economy suffered.

B Eva Perón became a popular political leader.

C Many Indians were killed on the Pampas.

D People elected military leaders to rule their country.

5 What is the most important part of the economy of Paraguay?

A mining

B agriculture

C manufacturing

D logging

Brazil's Urban and Rural Population (Estimates 1950–2000)

Source: Instituto Brasileiro de Geografia e Estatística

6 Based on the graph above, which of the following statements is false?

A Brazil's urban population is increasing while the rural population is decreasing.

B By 1960 more people in Brazil lived in urban areas than in rural areas.

C In 1950 more people in Brazil lived in rural areas than in urban areas.

D Brazil's total population is growing.

7 Based on the graph above, about how many people lived in urban areas of Brazil in 1990?

A 20 million

B 135 million

C 110 million

D 40 million

8 Extended Response Study the graph above and the information in your book about Brazil today. Then write a brief essay explaining how urban and rural landscapes in Brazil are changing. You will also want to discuss the causes and effects of this change.

ATLANTIC SOUTH AMERICA **225**

Answers

Standardized Test Prep

1. A

Break Down the Question This question requires students to recall factual information from Section 2.

2. D

Break Down the Question Refer students who missed the question to the physical map in Section 1.

3. C

Break Down the Question This question requires students to recall factual information from Section 3.

4. A

Break Down the Question Point out to students that an economic crisis resulted from the "Dirty War."

5. B

Break Down the Question This question requires students to recall factual information from Section 3.

6. B

Break Down the Question Remind students that the word *false* in this question signals that they should identify the choice that is incorrect.

7. C

Break Down the Question Point out that the line on the graph is between 100 and 125, which makes 110 the best choice.

8. Extended Response possible answer —Brazil's urban and rural landscapes are changing today because of population growth in its cities and new development in rainforest areas. Brazil's urban areas are sources of population growth and economic growth. However, urban areas have a lot of poverty. Many people are moving to the Amazon region for logging and mining opportunities. Both Brazil's urban and rural areas are thus under stress from population growth.

Reteach/Intervention Resources

Reproducible

- Guided Reading Workbook
- Differentiated Instruction Teacher Management System: Lesson Plans

Technology

- Quick Facts Transparency: Atlantic South America Visual Summary
- Differentiated Instruction Modified Worksheets and Tests CD-ROM
- Interactive Skills Tutor CD-ROM

Tips for Test Taking

Getting the Full Picture When a question refers to a graph, such as in questions 6–7 above, students should carefully study all the information in the graph, including headings, labels, and data plotted on the graph to determine any trends or oddities before they attempt to answer the questions.

Chapter 10 Planning Guide

Pacific South America

Overview	Instructional Resources	
CHAPTER 10 **Essential Question:** How has political unrest shaped the nations of Pacific South America? 🔊 **Focus on the Essential Question Podcast**	**TOS Differentiated Instruction Teacher Management System:** • Instructional Pacing Guides • Lesson Plans for Differentiated Instruction 📄 **Guided Reading Workbook** 📄 **Resource File:** • Chapter Review • Focus on Reading: Making Inferences • Focus on Speaking: Presenting an Interview • Social Studies Skills: Interpreting an Elevation Profile 📄 **Experiencing World History and Geography**	**TOS Calendar Planner** 💿 **Power Presentations with Media Gallery** 💿 **Differentiated Instruction Modified Worksheets and Tests CD-ROM** 💿 **Interactive Skills Tutor CD-ROM** 🔊 **Student Edition on Audio CD-ROM** 🔊 **The World's Music Audio Program** ▶️ **Map Zone Transparency:** Pacific South America: Political ▶️ **World Outline Maps: Transparencies and Activities** 📺 **Video:** Cliff Mummies of the Andes: Unwrapped
Section 1: **Physical Geography** **The Big Idea:** The Andes dominate Pacific South America's physical geography and influence the region's climate and resources.	**TOS Differentiated Instruction Teacher Management System:** Section 1 Lesson Plan 📄 **Guided Reading Workbook:** Section 1 📄 **Resource File:** • Vocabulary Builder: Section 1 • Geography for Life: Agricultural Patterns of Pacific South America	▶️ **Daily Bellringer Transparency:** Section 1 ▶️ **Map Zone Transparency:** Pacific South America: Physical ▶️ **Map Zone Transparency:** Bolivia: Resources 🔲 **Internet Activity:** Causes and Effects of El Niño
Section 2: **History and Culture** **The Big Idea:** Native cultures and Spanish colonization have shaped the history and culture of Pacific South America.	**TOS Differentiated Instruction Teacher Management System:** Section 2 Lesson Plan 📄 **Guided Reading Workbook:** Section 2 📄 **Resource File:** • Vocabulary Builder: Section 2 • Biography: Pachacuti • Primary Source: *Lost City of the Incas* by Hiram Bingham	▶️ **Daily Bellringer Transparency:** Section 2 ▶️ **Map Zone Transparency:** Languages in Pacific South America 📺 **Video:** Machu Picchu
Section 3: **Pacific South America Today** **The Big Idea:** The countries of Pacific South America are working to overcome challenges of poverty and political instability.	**TOS Differentiated Instruction Teacher Management System:** Section 3 Lesson Plan 📄 **Guided Reading Workbook:** Section 3 📄 **Resource File:** • Vocabulary Builder: Section 3 • Biography: Cecilia Muñoz • Literature: *My Invented Country* by Isabel Allende • Critical Thinking: The Demography of Pacific South America • Geography and History: Democratic Differences	▶️ **Daily Bellringer Transparency:** Section 3 ▶️ **Map Zone Transparency:** Settlements around Lima 🔲 **Internet Activity:** Cultures of the Andes

Chart Key:

Review, Assessment, Intervention

 The Americas Transparencies: Pacific South America Visual Summary

 Spanish Chapter Summaries Audio CD

 Progress Assessment Support System (PASS): Chapter Test

 Differentiated Instruction Modified Worksheets and Tests CD-ROM: Modified Chapter Test

TOS **ExamView® Assessment Suite (English/Spanish)**

 Alternative Assessment Handbook

Online Assessment Program, in the Interactive Student Edition

---

 PASS: Section 1 Quiz

 Online Quiz: Section 1

 Alternative Assessment Handbook

 PASS: Section 2 Quiz

 Online Quiz: Section 2

 Alternative Assessment Handbook

 PASS: Section 3 Quiz

 Online Quiz: Section 3

Alternative Assessment Handbook

Supporting Resources

- Multimedia Classroom Global History Series
- Global History Series Teacher's Guide

Maps Globes Graphs Level F

- Student Workbook
- Teacher's Guide

Social Studies Trade Library Collections

- NCSS Middle School Collection
- World Regions Trade Collection

Geography's Impact

Geography's Impact Video Program

- **Impact of the Andes Mountains**

For more information or to purchase go to hmhsocialstudies.com

---

Power Presentations with Media Gallery

Power Presentations with Media Gallery are visual presentations of each chapter's main ideas. Presentations can be customized by including Quick Facts charts, images from the text, and video clips.

CHAPTER 10 PLANNING GUIDE

Differentiating Instruction

How do I address the needs of varied learners?

The Target Resource acts as your primary strategy for differentiated instruction.

ENGLISH-LANGUAGE LEARNERS & STRUGGLING READERS

TARGET RESOURCE

The Americas Transparencies

- Pacific South America Visual Summary

Additional Resources

Differentiated Instruction Teacher Management System: Lesson Plans for Differentiated Instruction

Resource File:
- Vocabulary Builder Activities
- Social Studies Skills: Reading an Elevation Profile

Student Edition on Audio CD Program

Interactive Skills Tutor CD-ROM

Spanish Chapter Summaries Audio CD

Teacher One Stop:
- ExamView Assessment Suite, Spanish
- PuzzleView, Spanish

English-Language Learner Strategies and Activities

Spanish/English Guided Reading Workbook

SPECIAL NEEDS LEARNERS

TARGET RESOURCE

Differentiated Instruction Teacher Management System

Lesson Plans for Differentiated Instruction provide teachers with strategies to help plan instruction for all learners.

Additional Resources

Guided Reading Workbook

Resource File: Social Studies Skills: Reading an Elevation Profile

Student Edition on Audio CD Program

Interactive Skills Tutor CD-ROM

Graphic Organizer Transparencies with Support for Reading and Writing

ADVANCED/GIFTED AND TALENTED STUDENTS

TARGET RESOURCE

Resource File

The Resource File activities allow students to extend their knowledge of chapter-related places and people and to practice geography skills.

- Focus on Reading: Making Inferences
- Focus on Speaking: Presenting an Interview
- Literature: from *My Invented Country* by Isabel Allende

Additional Resources

Differentiated Instruction Teacher Management System: Lesson Plans for Differentiated Instruction

World History and Geography Document-Based Questions Activities

Geography, Science, and Cultures Activities

Experiencing World History and Geography

Differentiated Activities in the Teacher's Edition
- Using Map Terms, p. 229
- Creating a Sequence Diagram, p. 231

Teacher One Stop™

How can I manage the lesson plans and support materials for differentiated instruction?

With the Teacher One Stop, you can easily organize and print lesson plans, planning guides, and instructional materials for all learners. The Teacher One Stop includes the following materials to help you differentiate instruction:

- **Interactive Teacher's Edition**
- **Calendar Planner and pacing guides**
- **Editable lesson plans**
- **All reproducible ancillaries in Adobe Acrobat (PDF) format**
- **ExamView Assessment Suite (English & Spanish)**
- **Transparency and video previews**

Differentiated Activities in the Teacher's Edition
- Using Data from a Graph, p. 236

Interactive Student Edition

Complete online student edition with interactive multimedia support for chapter content assessment and reporting

- Interactive Maps and Notebook
- Standardized Test Prep
- Online Homework Practice and Research Activities
- Current Events
- Chapter-based Internet Activities
- Animated Geography Activities

Differentiated Activities in the Teacher's Edition
- Researching the Indigenous Languages of Pacific South America, p. 236

• Chapter Preview •

Essential Question

Introduce the Essential Question

- Have students locate the countries of Pacific South America on the map on pages 226–227. Challenge students to identify the physical feature that dominates the this region. Discuss how the Andes might impact people's lives.

- Explain that in the early 1800s, political unrest and the revolts that followed led to independence for Chile, Ecuador, Peru, and Bolivia.

- Invite students to suggest conditions that might lead to political unrest in a nation. Point out that all of the nations of Pacific South America have experienced poverty, unstable governments, and economic challenges in recent years and that people have different ideas about how best to combat these conditions.

Focus on Reading and Speaking

Reading The Resource File provides a worksheet to help students practice making inferences.

📖 **RF:** Focus on Reading, Making Inferences

Speaking The Resource File provides a worksheet to help students plan and present their interviews.

📖 **RF:** Focus on Speaking, Presenting an Interview

Key to Differentiating Instruction

Below Level

Basic-level activities designed for all students encountering new material

At Level

Intermediate-level activities designed for average students

Above Level

Challenging activities designed for honors and gifted and talented students

Standard English Mastery

Activities designed to improve standard English usage

LS Learning Styles

CHAPTER 10

Pacific South America

Essential Question How has political unrest shaped the nations of Pacific South America?

❓ What You Will Learn...

In this chapter you will learn about the Andes mountains that dominate the physical geography of Pacific South America. You will also study the history and culture of the region. In addition, you will learn about some of the struggles and progress happening today in Ecuador, Peru, Bolivia, and Chile.

FOCUS ON READING AND SPEAKING

Making Inferences An inference is a kind of guess. Sometimes an author does not give you complete information, and you have to make an inference. As you read, try to fill in gaps in information. Make guesses about things the writer does not tell you directly. **See the lesson, Making Inferences, on page 525.**

Interviewing Interviews with experts are a great way to learn new information. As you read about Pacific South America, you will identify questions for an interview. Then, with a partner, you will create a script for an interview about the region. One of you will play the role of the interviewer, and one will play the regional expert.

0° Equator
Galápagos Islands (ECUADOR)

PACIFIC OCEAN

Tropic of Capricorn

🌐 **map zone**

Geography Skills

Location The countries of Pacific South America lie on the western side of South America.
1. **Identify** Which country is landlocked?
2. **Analyze** How do you think Chile's shape affects life in that country?

Physical Geography The Andes are the second-highest mountain range in the world. These peaks are in a national park in Chile.

Introduce the Chapter

At Level

Getting to Know the Region

1. Name the countries of Pacific South America (Ecuador, Peru, Bolivia, and Chile) and ask students to share what they already know about them. Tell them that this chapter will help them learn more.

2. Ask students to find topics that they find especially interesting in the chapter by looking at the maps, illustrations, and photos and by reading the captions. Ask them to call out their topics and write them on the board.

3. Discuss why students find the topics interesting. Point out that people often want to learn about different topics and that it can be interesting to learn about a topic from someone else's point of view.

4. Encourage students to read other material ahead of time on the topics so that they can add to the class discussion when the topics are covered. **LS Verbal/Linguistic**

📖 Alternative Assessment Handbook, Rubric 14: Group Activity

COLOMBIA
Quito ⊛
ECUADOR
Guayaquil •

B R A Z I L

Amazon River

Equator — 0°

PERU

Lima • • Cuzco

BOLIVIA
⊛ La Paz
• Santa Cruz
⊛ Sucre

CHILE PARAGUAY

10°S

URUGUAY

20°S

— Tropic of Capricorn —

Valparaíso •
Santiago ⊛

ARGENTINA

ATLANTIC
OCEAN

30°S

40°S

⊛ National capital
• Other cities

0   300   600 Miles

0   300   600 Kilometers

Projection:
Lambert Azimuthal Equal-Area

Cliff Mummies of the
Andes: Unwrapped

hmhsocialstudies.com **VIDEO**

History Early
cultures made
beautiful gold
and silver art.

Culture Many people who live in the Andes
still wear traditional dress and speak native
languages. These women are from Peru.

227

227

• Chapter Preview •

Explore the Map and Pictures

Pacific South America: Political Draw students' attention to the islands on the map and the countries to which they belong. Have students note the Galápagos Islands off Ecuador's coast. Ask students what a group of islands like this is called. *(archipelago)* Have students find another archipelago on the map *(the islands at the tip of South America—called Tierra del Fuego).* Point out that the islands in this archipelago are divided between Chile and Argentina.

Analyzing Visuals What questions might you ask the Peruvian women pictured below? *possible answers—Is there a meaning to the colors and designs in your traditional dress? What language do you speak?*

▶ Map Zone Transparency: Pacific South America: Political

hmhsocialstudies.com
Teacher Resources

Critical Thinking: Analyzing Visuals

At Level

Beneath the Mask

1. Have students look at the gold mask shown here and ask them to write down the meaning it might have had for the person who created it. To guide students, ask them if they think the mask was an ornament, a religious object, or both.

2. Call on students to share their answers. Ask them to think about the qualities that gold has that make it a good material for such objects. Point out that the Inca worshipped the Sun God, Inti.

3. Ask students to look at the mask from the point of view of a Spanish conquistador. Explain that the conquistadors melted down massive amounts of similar objects after they conquered the Incas in 1532. Guide a class discussion exploring reasons for this.

LS Visual/Spatial, Verbal/Linguistic

Answers

Map Zone 1. *Bolivia;* **2.** *possible answers—The country is so long and narrow that people living in different parts of the country probably have little contact with one another. All parts of the country are affected by the mountains and coast.*

228 CHAPTER 10

Preteach

Bellringer

If YOU lived there. . . Use the **Daily Bellringer Transparency** to help students answer the question.

▶ Daily Bellringer Transparency, Section 1

Pacific South America — Daily Bellringer, Section 1

Preview Section 1

If YOU lived there ...
You and your family fish for herring in the cold waters off the coasts of Peru. Last year, however, an event called El Niño changed both the weather and the water. El Niño made the nearby ocean warmer. Without cold water, all the herring disappeared. You caught almost no fish at all. El Niño also caused terrible weather on the mainland.

Consider the effects on the OCEAN:
- ocean becomes warmer
- some fish leave; others appear
- ocean more pleasant for swimming

Consider the effects on the LAND:
- heavy rains in coastal areas
- flooding
- damage to property

How might another El Niño affect you?

Academic Vocabulary

Review with students the high-use academic term in this section.

cause to make something happen (p. 231)

✎ **RF:** Vocabulary Builder, Section 1

Taking Notes

Have students use the graphic organizer online to take notes on the section. This activity will prepare students for the Section Assessment, in which they will complete a graphic organizer that builds on the information using the Critical Thinking Skill: Categorizing.

Physical Geography

What You Will Learn...

Main Ideas

1. The Andes are the main physical feature of Pacific South America.
2. The region's climate and vegetation change with elevation.
3. Key natural resources in the region include lumber, oil, and minerals.

The Big Idea

The Andes dominate Pacific South America's physical geography and influence the region's climate and resources.

Key Terms and Places

altiplano, *p. 229*
strait, *p. 229*
Atacama Desert, *p. 231*
El Niño, *p. 231*

hmhsocialstudies.com
TAKING NOTES

Use the graphic organizer online to take notes on the physical geography of Pacific South America.

If YOU lived there...

You and your family fish for herring in the cold waters off the coast of Peru. Last year, however, an event called El Niño changed both the weather and the water. El Niño made the nearby ocean warmer. Without cold water, all the herring disappeared. You caught almost no fish at all. El Niño also caused terrible weather on the mainland.

How might another El Niño affect you?

BUILDING BACKGROUND Although most of the countries of Pacific South America lie along the coast, their landscapes are dominated by the rugged mountain range called the Andes. These mountains influence climates in the region. Ocean winds and currents also affect coastal areas here.

Physical Features

The countries of Pacific South America stretch along the Pacific coast from the equator, for which the country of Ecuador is named, south almost to the Arctic Circle. One narrow country, Chile (CHEE-lay), is so long that it covers about half the Pacific coast by itself. Not all of the countries in Pacific South America have coastlines, however. Bolivia is landlocked. But all of the countries in this region do share one major physical feature—the high Andes mountains.

Mountains

The Andes run through Ecuador, Peru, Bolivia, and Chile. Some ridges and volcanic peaks in the Andes rise more than 20,000 feet (6,800 m) above sea level. Because two tectonic plates meet at the region's edge, earthquakes and volcanoes are a constant threat. Sometimes these earthquakes disturb Andean glaciers, sending ice and mud rushing down mountain slopes.

Teach the Big Idea

At Level

Physical Geography

1. **Teach** Ask students the questions in the Main Idea boxes under Direct Teach.
2. **Apply** Create a chart on the board with four columns labeled "Ecuador," "Peru," "Bolivia," and "Chile." Have students copy the chart and fill in information on the countries. **LS Verbal/Linguistic, Visual/Spatial**
3. **Review** Fill in the chart on the board by calling on students to review their charts and contribute information from them.

4. **Practice/Homework** Ask students to write a brief essay about the country whose geography interests them most. Tell them to describe the country's geography and to explain why they find it so interesting.
   LS Verbal/Linguistic
   ✎ Alternative Assessment Handbook, Rubric 37: Writing Assignments

Landscapes in the Andes differ from south to north. In southern Chile, rugged mountain peaks are covered by ice caps. In the north, the Andes are more rounded than rugged, and there the range splits into two ridges. In southern Peru and Bolivia these ridges are quite far apart. A broad, high plateau called the **altiplano** lies between the ridges of the Andes.

Water and Islands

Andean glaciers are the source for many tributaries of the Amazon River. Other than the Amazon tributaries, the region has few major rivers. Rivers on the altiplano have no outlet to the sea. Water collects in two large lakes. One of these, Lake Titicaca, is the highest lake in the world that large ships can cross.

At the southern tip of the continent, the Strait of Magellan links the Atlantic and Pacific oceans. A **strait** is a narrow body of water connecting two larger bodies of water. The large island south of the strait is Tierra del Fuego, or "land of fire."

Chile and Ecuador both control large islands in the Pacific Ocean. Ecuador's volcanic Galápagos Islands have wildlife not found anywhere else in the world.

READING CHECK **Contrasting** How do the Andes differ from north to south?

COLOMBIA
ECUADOR
Galápagos Islands (ECUADOR)
0° Equator
Amazon River
PERU
BRAZIL
A N D E S
BOLIVIA
PACIFIC OCEAN
10°S
Lake Titicaca
Altiplano
Lake Poopó
Atacama Desert
PARAGUAY
20°S
Tropic of Capricorn
CHILE
30°S
URUGUAY
ARGENTINA
ATLANTIC OCEAN
40°S
Strait of Magellan
50°S
Tierra del Fuego
Cape Horn

ELEVATION

Feet	Meters
13,120	4,000
6,560	2,000
1,640	500
656	200
(Sea level) 0	0 (Sea level)
Below sea level	Below sea level

0   400   800 Miles
0   400   800 Kilometers

Projection: Lambert Azimuthal Equal-Area

map Zone **Geography Skills**

Regions The Andes stretch all through the countries of Pacific South America.
1. **Identify** To what country do the Galápagos Islands belong?
2. **Interpret** How do you think the Andes affect life in the region?

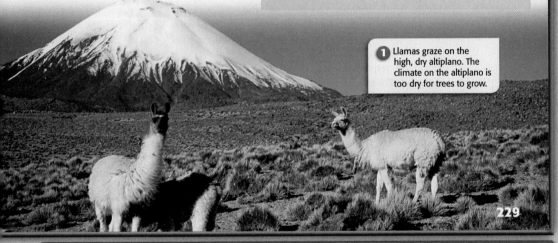

1 Llamas graze on the high, dry altiplano. The climate on the altiplano is too dry for trees to grow.

229

Differentiating Instruction

Above Level   Standard English Mastery

English-Language Learners

Prep Required

1. Create and distribute a map of Pacific South America for students to label with descriptive words from the text.

2. Read aloud the description of the Andes. Help students see that many of the words used to describe the Andes are opposites, such as *south/north*, *rounded/rugged*, and *ridge/plateau*. Guide students in a discussion about the meaning and usage of these words.

Have students write the words in the appropriate places on their maps.
🄻 **Visual/Spatial, Verbal/Linguistic**
📖 Alternative Assessment Handbook, Rubrics 11: Discussions; and 20: Map Creation

• ● **Direct Teach** ● •

Main Idea

❶ **Physical Features**

The Andes are the main physical feature of Pacific South America.

Explain What is the altiplano? *a broad high plateau that lies between the ridges of the Andes in southern Peru and Bolivia*

Identify Cause and Effect Why are earthquakes and volcanoes threats in the Andes? *because two tectonic plates meet at the region's edge*

Identify Where is the Strait of Magellan and what does it link? *at the southern tip of South America; the Atlantic and Pacific oceans*

▶ Map Zone Transparency: Pacific South America: Physical

Connect to Literature

The Lama Before reading this poem by American poet and humorist Ogden Nash (1902–1971), tell students that a lama is a Tibetan Buddhist priest. (The footnote is part of the original poem.)

The Lama

The one-l lama,
He's a priest.
The two-l llama,
He's a beast.
And I will bet
A silk pajama
There isn't any
*Three-l lllama.**

*The author's attention has been called to a type of conflagration known as a three-alarmer. Pooh.

Answers

Map Zone 1. *Ecuador;* **2.** *possible answers—limit transportation; make people dress warmly; cause danger because of volcanoes and earthquakes; cause mudslides; isolate people*

Reading Check *In the south the mountains are rugged and covered by ice; in the north, they are rounded and split into two ranges.*

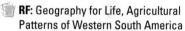

Main Idea

❷ Climate and Vegetation

The region's climate and vegetation change with elevation.

Recall What happens to air temperature as elevation increases? *It becomes cooler.*

Identify Where is the Atacama Desert? *in northern Chile*

Elaborate How does El Niño affect fishing in the waters off the Pacific coast? *It makes the waters too warm for the fish so they leave the area, leaving less for fishers to catch.*

📖 **RF:** Geography for Life, Agricultural Patterns of Western South America

Did you know. . .

Potatoes were first cultivated as early as 1,800 years ago in the Andes. A tough and durable crop, the potato grew well in the high elevations and poor soil of the region. Archaeologists working in the ancient ruins of Peru and Chile have found the remains of potatoes dating back to 500 BC. Evidence suggests that the potato was even worshipped by the ancient Incas, who buried potatoes with their dead. The first Europeans to see potatoes were the Spanish conquistadors. The potato was introduced to Europe in the second half of the 16ᵗʰ century, when Spanish explorers took it to Spain.

Answers

Analyzing Visuals *between 6,000 and 12,000 ft.*

Focus on Reading *possible answer— The location of mountains in Ecuador has a significant effect on the climate.*

230

Close-up

Climate Zones in the Andes

Five climate zones exist in the Andes. The different elevations support different types of plant and animal life.

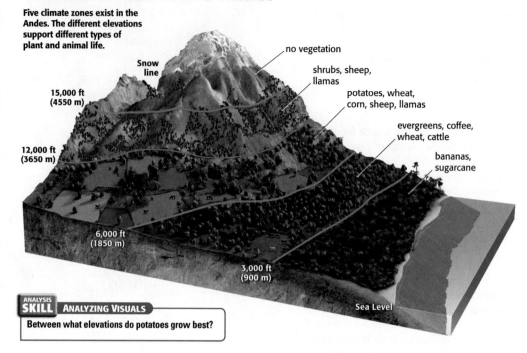

- no vegetation
- shrubs, sheep, llamas
- potatoes, wheat, corn, sheep, llamas
- evergreens, coffee, wheat, cattle
- bananas, sugarcane

Snow line

15,000 ft (4550 m)

12,000 ft (3650 m)

6,000 ft (1850 m)

3,000 ft (900 m)

Sea Level

ANALYSIS SKILL **ANALYZING VISUALS**

Between what elevations do potatoes grow best?

Climate and Vegetation

FOCUS ON READING

What can you infer about the location of mountains in Ecuador?

Climate, vegetation, and landscapes all vary widely in Pacific South America. We usually think of latitude as the major factor that affects climate. However, in Pacific South America, elevation has the biggest effect on climate and vegetation.

Elevation

Mountain environments change with elevation. For this reason, we can identify five different climate zones in the Andes. You can see these different climate zones on the diagram above.

The lowest zone includes the hot and humid lower elevations near sea level. Crops such as sugarcane and bananas grow

well there. This first zone is often found along the coast, but it is also found inland in eastern Ecuador and Peru and northern Bolivia. These regions are part of the Amazon basin. They have a humid tropical climate with thick, tropical rain forests.

As elevation increases, the air becomes cooler. The second elevation zone has moist climates with mountain forests. This zone is good for growing coffee. In addition, many of Pacific South America's large cities are located in this zone.

Higher up the mountains is a third, cooler zone of forests and grasslands. Farmers grow potatoes and wheat there. Many people in Pacific South America live and farm in this climate zone.

230 CHAPTER 10

Collaborative Learning

At Level

In the Zone

Research Required

1. Organize the class into five groups. Assign one of the zones in the Andes to each group. Tell the groups that they are to prepare an oral presentation on their climate zone.

2. Have students use the library, the Internet, or other resources to research their climate zone. Students in each group should divide the following topics among themselves: vegetation, climate, animals, people.

3. Ask each group to present its findings to the class, beginning with the lowest zone and proceeding up the zones in order. This will reinforce students' understanding of the gradual changes from zone to zone.

LS **Verbal/Linguistic, Interpersonal**

📖 Alternative Assessment Handbook, Rubrics 30: Research; and 24: Oral Presentations

At a certain elevation, the climate becomes too cool for trees to grow. This fourth climate zone above the tree line contains alpine meadows with grasslands and hardy shrubs. The altiplano region between the two ridges of the Andes lies mostly in this climate zone.

The fifth climate zone, in the highest elevations, is very cold. No vegetation grows in this zone because the ground is almost always covered with snow and ice.

Deserts

Pacific South America also has some climates that are not typical of any of the five climate zones. Instead of hot and humid climates, some coastal regions have desert climates.

Northern Chile contains the **Atacama Desert**. This desert is about 600 miles (965 km) long. Rain falls there less than five times a century, but fog and low clouds are common. They form when a cold current in the Pacific Ocean chills the warmer air above the ocean's surface. Cloud cover keeps the air near the ground from being warmed by the sun. As a result, coastal Chile is one of the cloudiest—and driest—places on Earth.

In Peru, some rivers cut through the dry coastal region. They bring snowmelt down from the Andes. Because they rely on melting snow, some of these rivers only appear at certain times of the year. The rivers have made some small settlements possible in these dry areas.

El Niño

About every two to seven years, this dry region experiences **El Niño**, an ocean and weather pattern that affects the Pacific coast. During an El Niño year, cool Pacific water near the coast warms. This change may cause extreme ocean and weather events that can have global effects.

As El Niño warms ocean waters, fish leave what is usually a rich fishing area. This change affects fishers. Also, El Niño **causes** heavy rains, and areas along the coast sometimes experience flooding. Some scientists think that air pollutants have made El Niño last longer and have more damaging effects.

ACADEMIC VOCABULARY
cause to make something happen

READING CHECK Finding Main Ideas How does elevation affect climate and vegetation?

Natural Resources

The landscapes of Pacific South America provide many valuable natural resources. For example, forests in southern Chile and in eastern Peru and Ecuador provide lumber. Also, as you have read, the coastal waters of the Pacific Ocean are rich in fish.

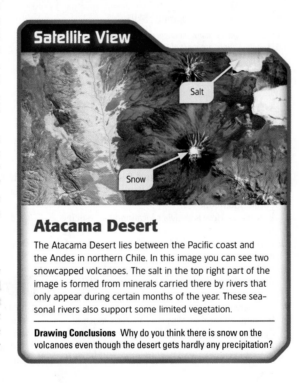

Satellite View

Atacama Desert

The Atacama Desert lies between the Pacific coast and the Andes in northern Chile. In this image you can see two snowcapped volcanoes. The salt in the top right part of the image is formed from minerals carried there by rivers that only appear during certain months of the year. These seasonal rivers also support some limited vegetation.

Drawing Conclusions Why do you think there is snow on the volcanoes even though the desert gets hardly any precipitation?

Bolivia: Resources

Gold	Tin
Lead	Zinc
Silver	

0   100   200 Miles
0   100   200 Kilometers
Projection: Lambert Azimuthal Equal-Area

BRAZIL

Madre de Dios

Beni River

Madeira R.

Guaporé River

BOLIVIA

Lake Titicaca

Mamoré River

Lake Poopó

−20°S

Pilcomayo River

CHILE   ARGENTINA   PARAGUAY

map Zone **Geography Skills**

Place Bolivia has many valuable mineral resources.
1. **Locate** Where are most of Bolivia's gold resources found?
2. **Interpret** What do you notice about the location of the mineral resources and the rivers?

In addition, the region has valuable oil and minerals. Ecuador in particular has large oil and gas reserves, and oil is the country's main export. Bolivia has some deposits of tin, gold, silver, lead, and zinc. Chile has copper deposits. In fact, Chile exports more copper than any other country in the world. Chile is also the site of the world's largest open pit mine.

Although the countries of Pacific South America have many valuable resources, one resource they do not have much of is good farmland. Many people farm, but the region's mostly cool, arid lands make it difficult to produce large crops for export.

READING CHECK **Categorizing** What types of resources do the countries of Pacific South America have?

SUMMARY AND PREVIEW The Andes are the main physical feature of Pacific South America. Next, you will learn how the Andes have affected the region's history and how they continue to affect life there today.

Section 1 Assessment

hmhsocialstudies.com
ONLINE QUIZ

Reviewing Ideas, Terms, and Places

1. **a. Identify** What is the main physical feature of Pacific South America?
   b. Analyze How is Bolivia's location unique in the region?
2. **a. Define** What is **El Niño**, and what are some of its effects?
   b. Draw Conclusions Why are parts of Ecuador, in the tropics, cooler than parts of southern Chile?
3. **a. Identify** What country in this region has large oil reserves?
   b. Make Inferences Why do you think much of the region is not good for farming?
   c. Elaborate What effects do you think copper mining in Chile might have on the environment?

Critical Thinking

4. **Categorizing** Review your notes on climate. Then use a diagram like this one to describe the climate and vegetation in each of the five climate zones.

FOCUS ON SPEAKING

5. **Describing Physical Geography** Note information about the physical features, climate and vegetation, and resources of Pacific South America. Write two questions and answers you can use in your interview.

232 CHAPTER 10

Section 1 Assessment Answers

1. **a.** the Andes
   b. It is landlocked.

2. **a.** an ocean weather pattern that causes heavy rains; flooding and disruption of ocean fishing
   b. They are at a higher elevation.

3. **a.** Ecuador
   b. possible answers—There is not much flat land; some areas are very dry.
   c. possible answers—Mining can pollute water; open pit mining may harm the land.

4. possible answers—characteristics of zones, from lowest to highest: hot, humid with tropical rain forests; comfortable, temperate, good coffee growing; cold, but potatoes and wheat grow; cool with no trees; cold with no vegetation

5. Students' notes and questions will vary but should reflect section content.

Interpreting an Elevation Profile

Learn

An elevation profile is a diagram that shows a side view of an area. This kind of diagram shows the physical features that lie along a line from point A to point B. Keep in mind that an elevation profile typically exaggerates vertical distances because vertical and horizontal distances are measured differently on elevation profiles. If they were not, even tall mountains would appear as tiny bumps.

> Vertical measurements are given on the sides of the diagram.

> The horizontal measurement is given along the bottom of the diagram.

Practice

Use the elevation profile above to answer the following questions.

1 What place does this elevation profile measure?

2 What is the highest point, and what is its elevation?

3 How can you tell that the vertical distance is exaggerated?

Apply

Look at the physical map of Pacific South America in Section 1 of this chapter. Choose a latitude line and create your own elevation profile for the land at that latitude. Be sure to pay attention to the scale and the legend so that you use correct measurements.

PACIFIC SOUTH AMERICA **233**

Social Studies Skills

Interpreting an Elevation Profile

Activity An Elevation Profile

Materials: building blocks (optional), yard sticks or rulers, graph paper, pencils

1. Have students create an elevation profile of part of the classroom, such as the furniture along a wall or a structure they build themselves out of building blocks.

2. Instruct students to measure and mark regular intervals horizontally along the structure. Then have them measure the height of the structure at each of these intervals. Have them decide on a vertical and a horizontal scale for their profile and label the lines on the graph paper accordingly. They should then plot each point on the graph paper and connect the points, as well as points for the ground or floor as a beginning and ending of zero.

3. Guide students in interpreting their elevation profiles. Discuss the amount of exaggeration in them.

4. Have students create questions about their profiles and then work in pairs to answer each other's questions.
   LS Visual/Spatial, Verbal/Linguistic

   Interactive Skills Tutor CD-ROM, Lesson 6: Interpret Maps, Graphs, Charts, Visuals, and Political Cartoons

   RF: Social Studies Skills, Interpreting an Elevation Profile

---

Social Studies Skills Activity: Interpreting an Elevation Profile

Everything in Proportion

At Level

1. Guide students in a discussion of how vertical distance is exaggerated on the elevation profile above. Tell them that they are going to find out how wide the horizontal distance would be if it used the same scale as the vertical distance.

2. Have students measure and compute how much distance an inch represents on the vertical scale. Remind them that a mile equals 5,280 feet.

3. Have students measure and compute how much distance an inch covers on the horizontal scale.

4. Students should find that an inch on the vertical distance represents about 3 miles, while on the horizontal distance it represents about 60 miles.

5. Help students as necessary to reach the final calculation: if the horizontal distance is measured in the same proportion as the vertical distance, it would have to be about 120 inches, or 10 feet wide.
   LS Visual/Spatial, Logical/Mathematical

   Alternative Assessment Handbook, Rubrics 11: Discussions; and 35: Solving Problems

Answers

Practice 1. *the northern part of Ecuador;* **2.** *Mt. Cayambe; about 20,000 feet;* **3.** *because 3 miles on the vertical scale takes up the same space (1 inch) as 60 miles on the horizontal scale*

Apply *Answers will vary depending on the latitude line chosen. Students should use the scale and the legend correctly to arrive at their measurements.*

Bellringer

If YOU lived there. . . Use the **Daily Bellringer Transparency** to help students answer the question.

▶ Daily Bellringer Transparency, Section 2

Key Terms

 RF: Vocabulary Builder, Section 2

Taking Notes

Have students use the graphic organizer online to take notes on the section. This activity will prepare students for the Section Assessment, in which they will complete a graphic organizer that builds on the information using the Critical Thinking Skill: Sequencing.

History and Culture

What You Will Learn...

Main Ideas

1. The countries of Pacific South America share a history influenced by the Inca civilization and Spanish colonization.
2. The culture of Pacific South America includes American Indian and Spanish influences.

The Big Idea

Native cultures and Spanish colonization have shaped the history and culture of Pacific South America.

Key Terms

viceroy, *p. 235*
Creoles, *p. 236*

hmhsocialstudies.com
TAKING NOTES

Use the graphic organizer online to take notes on the history and culture of Pacific South America.

If YOU lived there...

You live in Cuzco, the capital of the Inca Empire. You are required to contribute labor to the empire, and you have been chosen to work on a construction project. Hauling the huge stones will be difficult, but the work will be rewarding. You can either choose to help build a magnificent temple to the sun god or you can help build a road from Cuzco to the far end of the empire.

Which project will you choose? Why?

BUILDING BACKGROUND Before Spanish conquerors arrived in the early 1500s, a great American Indian empire ruled this region. Cuzco was the Inca capital. The Incas were such skilled engineers and builders that many of their forts and temples still stand today.

History

Thousands of years ago, people in Pacific South America tried to farm on mountainsides as steep as bleachers. Other people tried to farm where there was almost no rain. These early cultures learned how to adapt to and modify their environments.

Early Cultures

Peru's first advanced civilization reached its height in about 900 BC in the Andes. These people built stone terraces into the steep mountainside so they could raise crops. In coastal areas, people created irrigation systems to store water and control flooding.

Agriculture supported large populations, towns, and culture. In the Bolivian highlands one early culture, the Tiahuanaco (tee-uh-wuh-NAH-koh), made huge stone carvings near a lakeshore. In another civilization on the coast, people scratched outlines of animals and other shapes into the surface of the Peruvian desert. These designs, known as the Nazca lines, are so large they can only be recognized from the sky.

Teach the Big Idea

At Level

History and Culture

1. **Teach** Ask students the questions in the Main Idea boxes under Direct Teach.

2. **Apply** Divide the class into two groups. Have one group write notes about the influence of native cultures in the past and present on Pacific South America. Have the other group write notes about the influence of Spanish culture. **LS Interpersonal, Verbal/Linguistic**

3. **Review** Have the groups take turns reading their notes. Ask students to elaborate or give examples as needed.

4. **Practice/Homework** Ask students to draw a picture of a place of historical or cultural importance that they would like to visit in Pacific South America. Have students draw the place they would like to visit based on what they read or saw about it in the section. **LS Verbal/Linguistic, Visual/Spatial**

   Alternative Assessment Handbook, Rubrics 3: Artwork; and 14: Group Activity

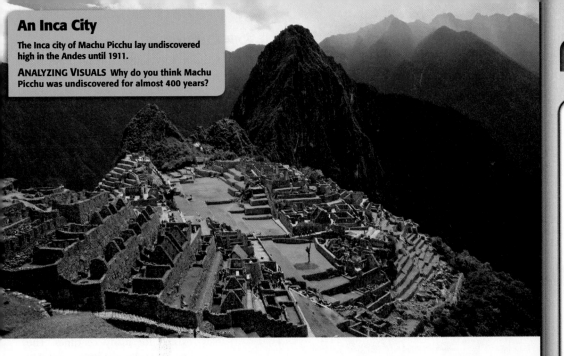

An Inca City

The Inca city of Machu Picchu lay undiscovered high in the Andes until 1911.

ANALYZING VISUALS Why do you think Machu Picchu was undiscovered for almost 400 years?

The Inca Empire

Eventually, one group of people came to rule most of the region. By the early 1500s, these people, the Incas, controlled an area that stretched from northern Ecuador to central Chile. The Inca Empire was home to as many as 12 million people.

The huge Inca Empire was highly organized. Irrigation projects turned deserts into rich farmland. Thousands of miles of stone-paved roads connected the empire. Rope suspension bridges helped the Incas cross the steep Andean valleys.

As advanced as their civilization was, the Incas had no wheeled vehicles or horses. Instead, relay teams of runners carried messages from one end of the empire to the other. Working together, a team of runners could carry a message up to 150 miles (240 km) in one day. The runners did not carry any letters, however, because the Incas did not have a written language.

Spanish Rule

In spite of its great organization, however, the Inca Empire did not last long. A new Inca ruler, on his way to be crowned king, met the Spanish explorer Francisco Pizarro. Pizarro captured the Inca king, who ordered his people to bring enough gold and silver to fill a whole room. These riches were supposed to be a ransom for the king's freedom. Instead, Pizarro ordered the Inca king killed. Fighting broke out, and by 1535 the Spaniards had conquered the Inca Empire.

The new Spanish rulers often dealt harshly with the South American Indians of the fallen Inca Empire. Many Indians had to work in gold or silver mines or on the Spaniards' plantations. A Spanish **viceroy**, or governor, was appointed by the king of Spain to make sure the Indians followed the Spanish laws and customs that had replaced native traditions.

HISTORY

VIDEO
Machu Picchu

hmhsocialstudies.com

FOCUS ON READING
How do you think the South American Indians felt about the viceroy?

Main Idea

❶ History

The countries of Pacific South America share a history influenced by the Inca civilization and Spanish colonization.

Describe How did Peru's first advanced civilization modify its environment to raise crops in the Andes? *They built stone terraces into steep mountainsides.*

Identify Who led the revolt against Spanish rule in Pacific South America? *Creoles, American-born descendants of Europeans*

Elaborate How did the Incas send messages across their empire? *They used relay teams of runners to carry messages over long distances.* Why did they rely on this method? *They had no wheeled vehicles or horses.*

🗎 **RF:** Biography, Pachacuti

🗎 **RF:** Primary Source, *Lost City of the Incas* by Hiram Bingham

---

MISCONCEPTION
ALERT

Chile's Mummies The mummies of ancient Egypt may be the most famous, but the oldest mummies in the world have been found in Chile. On the north coast of what is now Chile, a people known as the Chinchoros were mummifying their dead as early as 5,000 BC. That is approximately 2,000 years before the ancient Egyptians started making mummies.

Collaborative Learning

At Level

The Inca Empire

Research Required

1. Have students select one of the following research topics related to the Inca Empire and its culture:

   • the ruins of Machu Picchu

   • *quipu* (system of knots used to keep records and send messages)

   • Inca feats of engineering, especially stone masonry

   • the city of Cuzco in Inca times and today

   • Atahualpa (the last Inca ruler)

   • Inca religious beliefs and festivals

2. Have students work in groups with other students who chose the same topic (drop topics and reassign students, as necessary).

3. Have each member of the group work individually to write a short report on the overall topic. As a group, have students create a poster, model, or other multimedia project to support their reports.
   LS Visual/Spatial, Verbal/Linguistic

   🗎 Alternative Assessment Handbook, Rubrics 30: Research; and 42: Writing to Inform

---

Answers

Analyzing Visuals *possible answers—It was in a very remote area; it was covered with debris and vegetation.*

Focus on Reading *possible answer— They resented an outsider telling them how to live.*

Main Idea

❷ Culture

The culture of Pacific South America includes American Indian and Spanish influences.

Recall In which countries are two native languages official languages in addition to Spanish? *Bolivia and Peru*

Identify What is the religion of the majority of the people in Pacific South America? *Roman Catholicism* Where are ancient religious customs practiced? *in the Andes*

Summarize In what ways is culture in Pacific South America a blend of Spanish and Indian cultures? *possible answers—Most of the people are Roman Catholic, yet some still follow ancient religious customs; Spanish is the official language everywhere, but millions of Indians still speak their native languages.*

▶ Map Zone Transparency: Languages in Pacific South America

Did you know...

One piece in the traditional dress of Bolivian Indian women is the derby, a narrow-brimmed, dome-shaped hat first made in 1850 by William Bowler, a London hatter. The derby became popular with indigenous Bolivian women in the 1920s. A Bolivian merchant who had imported too many derbies decided to sell them as women's hats. The idea worked, and by the 1930s the Italian company Borsalino was mass-producing derbies specifically for exportation to the Andes. Today, many indigenous women have two derbies, one for everyday use and another one for special occasions.

Answers

Reading Check *The Incas built a strong civilization and an empire that was defeated by the Spanish.*

Map Zone 1. *Bolivia;* **2.** *possible answers—They live in remote areas; they prefer the ways of their ancestors.*

236

Independence

By the early 1800s, people in Pacific South America began to want independence. They began to revolt against Spanish rule. **Creoles**, American-born descendants of Europeans, were the main leaders of the revolts. The success of the revolts led to independence for Chile, Ecuador, Peru, and Bolivia by 1825.

READING CHECK **Evaluating** How did Inca civilization influence the history of the region?

hmhsocialstudies.com **INTERACTIVE MAP**

Languages in Pacific South America

- Spanish
- Aymara
- Guarani
- Quechua
- Mapuche

0 300 600 Miles
0 300 600 Kilometers
Projection: Lambert Azimuthal Equal-Area

map zone **Geography Skills**

Regions Spanish is an official language throughout the region, but many people speak native languages instead.

1. Interpreting Graphs Where do more people speak native languages than Spanish?

2. Analyze Why do you think many people do not speak Spanish?

THE **WORLD ALMANAC**
Facts about Countries

Languages in Pacific South America

- Speak mostly Spanish
- Speak mostly a native language

Population (in millions)

Ecuador Peru Bolivia Chile
Country

▶ hmhsocialstudies.com

Culture

Spanish and native cultures have both left their marks on Pacific South America. Most people in the region speak Spanish, and Spanish is the official language in all of the countries of the region.

However, people in many parts of the region also maintain much of their native culture. Millions of South American Indians speak native languages in addition to or instead of Spanish. In Bolivia, two native languages are official languages in addition to Spanish.

The people and customs of Pacific South America also reflect the region's Spanish and Indian heritage. For example, Bolivia's population has the highest percentage of South American Indians of any country on the continent. Many Bolivian Indians follow customs and lifestyles that have existed for many centuries. They often dress in traditional styles—full skirts and derby hats for the women and colorful, striped ponchos for the men.

Another part of the region's culture that reflects Spanish and Indian influences is religion. Most people in Pacific

236 CHAPTER 10

Differentiating Instruction

Special Needs Learners   **Below Level**

Have students look at the World Almanac graph, Languages in Pacific South America. Model how students can convert the data shown for each country into sentences. For example: *In Ecuador, nearly 10 million people speak mostly Spanish. About two and a half million speak mostly a native language.* Ask students to write similar sentences for the other countries.

LS **Logical/Mathematical, Verbal/Linguistic**

Alternative Assessment Handbook, Rubric 37: Writing Assignments

Advanced/Gifted and Talented   **Above Level**

Have students use the Internet or other resources to research the indigenous languages of Pacific South America: Aymara, Guaraní, Quechua, and Mapuche. Ask them to give a presentation covering topics such as origin of the language, related languages, number of speakers, countries where it is spoken, and whether it has a written form. Have students present their research to the class. **LS** **Verbal/Linguistic**

Alternative Assessment Handbook, Rubrics 24: Oral Presentations; and 30: Research

Andean Culture

Every May, high in the Andes, Bolivians gather in Macha, Bolivia for Tinku, a festival honoring *Pachamama*, or mother earth.

ANALYZING VISUALS What do you think the climate is like in Macha?

Music played on wooden flutes like these is popular in the Andes.

South America practice the religion of the Spanish—Roman Catholicism. Some people in the Andes, however, also still practice ancient religious customs. Every June, for example, people participate in a festival that was celebrated by the Incas to worship the sun. During festivals people wear traditional costumes, sometimes with wooden masks. They also play traditional instruments, such as wooden flutes.

READING CHECK **Generalizing** What traditional customs do people in the region still practice today?

SUMMARY AND PREVIEW Pacific South America was home to one of the greatest ancient civilizations in the Americas— the Inca. The Spanish conquered the Incas. Today the region's culture still reflects Inca and Spanish influences. Next, you will learn more about the governments and economies of Ecuador, Bolivia, Peru, and Chile today.

Section 2 Assessment

hmhsocialstudies.com
ONLINE QUIZ

Reviewing Ideas, Terms, and Places

1. **a. Recall** What ancient empire built paved roads through the Andes?
   b. Explain What role did **Creoles** play in the history of Pacific South America?
   c. Predict How might the Inca Empire have been different if the Incas had had wheels and horses?
2. **a. Recall** What country has the highest percentage of South American Indians in its population? *Bolivia*
   b. Make Generalizations What aspects of culture in Pacific South America reflect Spanish influence, and what aspects reflect Indian heritage?

Critical Thinking

3. **Sequencing** Look over your notes on the region's history. Then draw a graphic organizer like the one here and use it to put major historical events in chronological order.

Nazca lines drawn → □ → □ → □ → □

FOCUS ON SPEAKING

4. **Taking Notes on History and Culture** What information about the history and culture is important? Add two more questions, plus answers, to your notes.

PACIFIC SOUTH AMERICA **237**

Section 2 Assessment Answers

1. **a.** the Inca Empire
   b. They were the main leaders of independence movements.
   c. possible answer—They may have been better able to defend themselves against the Spanish.

2. **a.** Bolivia
   b. Spanish influence—language, architecture, Roman Catholicism; Indian heritage—language, music, clothing, religious festivals

3. possible answers—Incas control an area from northern Ecuador to central Chile; Spanish explorer Francisco Pizarro meets Inca king, 1535; Spaniards have conquered Inca Empire, 1800s; people in Pacific South America fight for independence.

4. Students' questions and answers will vary but should reflect section content.

Pacific South America Today

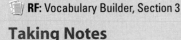
What You Will Learn...

Main Ideas

1. Ecuador struggles with poverty and political instability.
2. Bolivia's government is trying to gain stability and improve the economy.
3. Peru has made progress against poverty and violence.
4. Chile has a stable government and a strong economy.

The Big Idea

The countries of Pacific South America are working to overcome challenges of poverty and political instability.

Key Terms and Places

Quito, *p. 239*
La Paz, *p. 239*
Lima, *p. 240*
coup, *p. 241*
Santiago, *p. 242*

hmhsocialstudies.com
TAKING NOTES

Use the graphic organizer online to take notes on Pacific South America today.

If **YOU** lived there...

You are at a political rally in Valparaíso, Chile. Your family owns a vineyard nearby, so government policies about the economy affect you personally. You listen carefully to the speakers at the rally. Some politicians are in favor of more free trade with countries in North America. Others speak about different issues, such as housing and education.

What would you like to ask the politicians?

> **BUILDING BACKGROUND** All the countries of Pacific South America have faced similar issues in recent years. These include poverty, unstable governments, economic development, and how to encourage development and still protect the environment. Several of these countries are making progress, while others still have problems.

Ecuador Today

In recent decades, the countries of Pacific South America have all experienced periods of political instability. Ecuador, in particular, has faced recent instability. Widespread poverty is a constant threat to a stable government in this country.

Government

Ecuador has been a democracy since 1979. Still, the country has experienced great political instability and corruption. From 1996–2007, the country had nine different presidents. In 2004, Ecuadorian president Lucio Gutiérrez fired the majority of the nation's supreme court judges because they did not support him. Soon after, to quiet his political opponents, Gutiérrez declared a state of emergency. In response, the Ecuadorian Congress forced Gutiérrez from power in 2005. In 2006, Ecuadorians elected Rafael Correa president. In 2009, Correa was the first Ecuadorian president to be re-elected in more than 30 years.

238 CHAPTER 10

Economic Regions

Ecuador has three different economic regions. One region, the coastal lowlands, has agriculture and industry. The country's largest city, Guayaquil (gwy-ah-KEEL), is located there. It is Ecuador's major port and commercial center.

The Andean region of Ecuador is poorer. **Quito**, the national capital, is located there. Open-air markets and Spanish colonial buildings attract many tourists to Quito and other towns in the region.

A third region, the Amazon basin, has valuable oil deposits. The oil industry provides jobs that draw people to the region. Oil is also Ecuador's main export. But the oil industry has brought problems as well as benefits. The country's economy suffers if the world oil price drops. In addition, some citizens worry that drilling for oil could harm the rain forest.

READING CHECK **Generalizing** Why has Ecuador's government been unstable?

Bolivia Today

Like Ecuador, Bolivia is a poor country. Poverty has been a cause of political unrest in recent years.

Government

After years of military rule, Bolivia is a democracy. Bolivia's government is divided between two capital cities. The supreme court meets in Sucre (SOO-kray), but the congress meets in **La Paz**. Located at about 12,000 feet (3,660 m), La Paz is the highest capital city in the world. It is also Bolivia's main industrial center.

In the early 2000s, many Bolivians disagreed with their government's plans for fighting poverty. National protests forced several presidents to resign. Then in 2005, Bolivians elected an indigenous leader, Evo

Morales, as president. Re-elected president in 2009, Morales continues to work to improve the lives of Bolivia's poor.

Economy

Bolivia is the poorest country in South America. In the plains of eastern Bolivia there are few roads and little money for investment. However, foreign aid has provided funds for some development. In addition, the country has valuable resources, including metals and natural gas.

READING CHECK **Analyzing** Why might political revolts slow development?

CONNECTING TO Economics

The Informal Economy

Many people in the countries of Pacific South America are part of the informal economy. Street vendors, like the ones shown here in Quito, are common sights in the region's cities. People visit street vendors to buy items like snacks, small electronics, or clothing. The informal economy provides jobs for many people. However, it does not help the national economy because the participants do not pay taxes. Without income from taxes, the government cannot pay for services.

Analyzing How does the informal economy affect taxes?

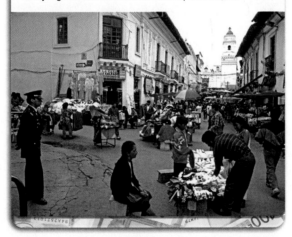

PACIFIC SOUTH AMERICA **239**

❸ Peru Today

Peru has made progress against poverty and violence.

Describe What is housing like in central Lima? *high-rise apartments and private houses, some from the colonial era*

Identify What was the Shining Path? *an anti-government terrorist group active during the 1980s and 1990s*

Evaluate What challenges do people who settle in "young towns" face? *poverty, building homes with poor materials, lack of services such as water and electricity*

▶ Map Zone Transparency: Settlements around Lima

📄 **RF: Critical Thinking,** The Demography of Pacific South America

📄 **RF: Literature,** *My Invented Country* by Isabel Allende

Activity Comparing

Governments Have students set up a chart or other graphic organizer to compare the different forms of government in the Pacific South American countries. Ask students to choose another country, either in Europe or in the Americas, to add to their charts. Then have students use a variety of resources to learn about that country's government and compare it with those in Pacific South America. Encourage students to use newspapers, television news reports, and interviews with community members in addition to books and the Internet when conducting their research.

Answers

Map Zone 1. *houses and apartments;* **2.** *because poor people can claim land on the outskirts and build their houses there*

240

Settlements around Lima

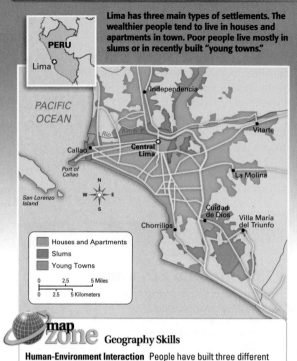

Lima has three main types of settlements. The wealthier people tend to live in houses and apartments in town. Poor people live mostly in slums or in recently built "young towns."

Houses and Apartments
Slums
Young Towns

0   2.5   5 Miles
0   2.5   5 Kilometers

map zone Geography Skills

Human-Environment Interaction People have built three different basic types of housing in and around Lima.
1. **Use the Map** What is the most common type of housing?
2. **Draw Conclusions** Why are most young towns built far from central Lima?

Houses and Apartments Most housing in Lima is made up of high-rise apartments and private houses, some of which are from the colonial era.

Peru Today

Peru is the largest and most populous country in Pacific South America. Today it is making some progress against political violence and poverty.

Lima

Peru's capital, **Lima** (LEE-muh), is the largest city in the region. Nearly one-third of all Peruvians live in Lima or the nearby port city of Callao (kah-YAH-oh). Lima has industry, universities, and government jobs, which attract many people from the countryside to Lima.

Lima was the colonial capital of Peru, and the city still contains many beautiful old buildings from the colonial era. It has high-rise apartments and wide, tree-lined boulevards. However, as in many big urban areas, a lot of people there live in poverty.

In spite of the poverty, central Lima has few slum areas. This is because most poor people prefer to claim land on the outskirts of the city and build their own houses. Often they can get only poor building materials. They also have a hard time getting water and electricity from the city.

Settlements of new self-built houses are called "young towns" in Lima. Over time, as people improve and add to their houses, the new settlements develop into large, permanent suburbs. Many of the people in Lima's young towns are migrants from the highlands. Some came to Lima to escape violence in their home villages.

240 CHAPTER 10

Cross-Discipline Activity: Music

At Level

Victor Jara, Chilean Folk Singer

Research Required   **Prep Required**

1. Explain to students that Victor Jara was a popular Chilean folk singer who was a victim of the 1973 coup in Chile. Tell them that he supported Chile's overthrown president, Salvador Allende, and had written songs against injustice.

2. Have students research the life and death of Victor Jara. Ask students to prepare a brief biographical fact sheet and to include information about how he is remembered today.

3. In advance, find a CD at the library with one of Victor Jara's most popular songs, *Te Recuerdo*

Amanda ("I Remember You, Amanda") and play it for the class. If possible, give students a printed translation of the song. Tell students that Jara's songs celebrated the simple people of Chile and denounced the poverty and injustice in their lives.

4. Have students share information from their biographical fact sheets. Discuss Victor Jara and how he is remembered today.
LS **Verbal/Linguistic, Auditory/Musical**

📄 Alternative Assessment Handbook, Rubrics 26: Poems and Songs; and 30: Research

Slums Just outside downtown and near the port area, many people live in slum housing. These buildings are permanent, but run-down.

Young Towns Many poor people in recent years have taken over land on the outskirts of Lima and have built their own shelters.

Government

In the 1980s and 1990s, a terrorist group called the Shining Path was active. This group carried out deadly attacks because it opposed government policies. Some 70,000 people died in violence between the Shining Path and government forces, and Peru's economy suffered. However, after the arrest of the group's leaders, Peru's government began making progress against political violence and poverty. The country has an elected president and congress.

Resources

Peru's resources are key factors in its economic progress. Some mineral deposits are located near the coast, and hydroelectric projects on rivers provide energy. Peru's highlands are less developed than the coastal areas. However, many Peruvian Indians grow potatoes and corn there.

READING CHECK Identifying Cause and Effect How did the Shining Path affect Peru?

Chile Today

Like Peru, Chile has ended a long violent period. Chile now has a stable government and a growing economy.

Government

In 1970 Chileans elected a president who had some ideas influenced by communism. A few years later he was overthrown and died in a U.S.-backed military coup (KOO). A **coup** is a sudden overthrow of a government by a small group of people.

In the years after the coup, military rulers tried to crush their political enemies. Chile's military government was harsh and often violent. It imprisoned or killed thousands of people.

In the late 1980s Chile's military dictatorship weakened and Chileans created a new, democratic government. In 2006 Chileans elected their first female president, Michelle Bachelet, and in 2010 they elected business leader Sebastián Piñera president.

FOCUS ON READING

What can you infer about the reason for the end of the military government?

Info to Know

Chile's Copper Since the beginning of the 1800s, copper has been crucial to the Chilean economy and has helped Chile industrialize and develop much faster than other South American countries. By 1825 foreign investors were competing fiercely to control Chile's copper market. By 1860 copper accounted for more than half of the country's revenue. Today Chile is the world leader in copper production. Yet this productivity has come at a cost to the environment around the mines, which has been heavily polluted with arsenic and carbon-monoxide from the factories where copper ore is refined.

Review & Assess

Close

Briefly review how each country has been affected by poverty and political instability.

Review

 Online Quiz, Section 3

Assess

SE Section 3 Assessment

PASS: Section 3 Quiz

Alternative Assessment Handbook

Reteach/Classroom Intervention

Guided Reading Workbook, Section 3

Interactive Skills Tutor CD-ROM

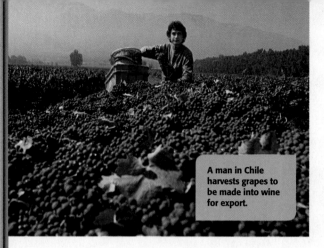

A man in Chile harvests grapes to be made into wine for export.

Mediterranean climate allows farmers to grow many crops. For example, grapes grow well there, and Chilean fruit and wine are exported around the world.

Farming, fishing, forestry, and mining form the basis of Chile's economy. Copper mining is especially important. It accounts for more than one-third of Chile's exports.

Chile's economic stability was rocked by a massive earthquake that struck on February 27, 2010. The quake killed about 500 Chileans and caused about $30 billion of damage to buildings, homes, and streets. Today, Chile's people and government continue to rebuild their nation.

Resources and Economy

Chile's economy is the strongest in the region. Poverty rates have decreased, and Chile's prospects for the future seem bright. Small businesses and factories are growing quickly. More Chileans are finding work, and wages are rising.

About one-third of all Chileans live in central Chile. This region includes the capital, **Santiago**, and a nearby seaport, Valparaíso (bahl-pah-rah-EE-soh). Its mild

READING CHECK **Identifying Points of View** Why might Chile want to join a free trade group?

SUMMARY AND PREVIEW In recent years Ecuador, Peru, Bolivia, and Chile have struggled with political violence and poverty. However, Peru and Chile are recovering. Next, you will study the culture and economy of the United States.

Section 3 Assessment

hmhsocialstudies.com
ONLINE QUIZ

Reviewing Ideas, Terms, and Places

1. **a. Identify** What is Ecuador's largest city?
   b. Make Generalizations Why have Ecuadorians been unhappy with their government in recent years?
2. **a. Identify** What are Bolivia's two capital cities?
   b. Analyze Why might Bolivia's economy improve in the future?
3. **a. Recall** Why did many Peruvians move to Lima from the highlands in the 1980s?
   b. Elaborate What challenges do you think people who move to **Lima** from the highlands face?
4. **a. Define** What is a **coup**?
   b. Make Inferences What might happen to Chile's economy if the world price of copper drops?

Critical Thinking

5. **Solving Problems** Review your notes. Then, in a diagram like the one here, write one sentence about each country, explaining how that country is dealing with poverty or government instability.

Ecuador	
Bolivia	
Peru	
Chile	

FOCUS ON SPEAKING

6. **Thinking about Pacific South America Today** Add questions about each country in Pacific South America to your notes. How might you answer these questions in your interview? Write down the answer to each question.

Section 3 Assessment Answers

1. **a.** Guayaquil
   b. Reforms have not come quickly enough.
2. **a.** La Paz and Sucre
   b. Bolivia may begin to export more natural gas and metals.
3. **a.** to escape violence and look for work
   b. poor services, such as water and electricity; overcrowding; poor-quality housing
4. **a.** a sudden overthrow of a government by a small group of people
   b. It might grow weaker because of the jobs and profits lost.

5. possible answers—The economic regions of Ecuador are helping to overcome poverty. Poverty and political instability in Bolivia may change with the export of natural gas and metals. Peru has an elected president and congress and many resources to help the economy. Chile has a stable government and growing economy.

6. Students questions and answers will vary but should reflect section content.

Answers

Reading Check *to increase their trade in the western hemisphere*

Geography's Impact
video series
Review the video to answer the closing question:
Why do descendants of the Incas still live in the difficult high altitudes of the Andes?

Visual Summary

Use the visual summary below to help you review the main ideas of the chapter.

QUICK FACTS

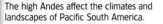

The high Andes affect the climates and landscapes of Pacific South America.

Many South American Indians maintain traditional customs and ways of life in the Andes.

Today the countries of Pacific South America are working toward development and improved economies.

Reviewing Vocabulary, Terms, and Places

Write each word defined below, circling each letter that is marked by a star. Then write the word these letters spell.

1. _ _ * _ _ _ _ _ _ _ _ _ _ _ _—a desert in northern Chile that is one of the cloudiest and driest places on Earth

2. * _ _ _ _—the capital of Peru

3. _ _ _ _ * _—the capital of Ecuador

4. _ * _ _ _ _ _ _ _—a governor appointed by the king of Spain

5. _ _ _ * _ _ _—one of the capitals of Bolivia

6. _ _ _ _ _ * _ _—an American-born descendant of Europeans

7. _ _ _ _ * _ _ _—a narrow passageway that connects two large bodies of water

8. _ _ _ * _ _ _ _—an ocean and weather pattern that affects the Pacific coast

9. _ * _ _ _—a sudden overthrow of a government by a small group of people

Comprehension and Critical Thinking

SECTION 1 *(Pages 228–232)*

10. **a. Describe** What are climate and vegetation like on the altiplano?

b. Compare and Contrast What are two differences and one similarity between the Atacama Desert and the altiplano?

c. Evaluate What elevation zone would you choose to live in if you lived in Pacific South America? Why would you choose to live there?

SECTION 2 *(Pages 234–237)*

11. **a. Describe** How did the Incas organize their huge empire?

b. Analyze How have Spanish and native cultures left their marks on culture in Pacific South America?

c. Elaborate Why do you think Pizarro killed the Inca king even though he had received riches as ransom?

PACIFIC SOUTH AMERICA **243**

Answers

Visual Summary

Review and Inquiry Have students use the visual summary to help them review the physical geography, culture, and current conditions in Pacific South America.

Quick Facts Transparency: Pacific South America Visual Summary

Reviewing Vocabulary, Terms, and Places

1. Atacama Desert
2. Lima
3. Quito
4. viceroy
5. La Paz

6. Creole
7. strait
8. El Niño
9. coup

mystery word—**altiplano**

Comprehension and Critical Thinking

10. **a.** The climate is cool; the vegetation is grasslands and hearty shrubs.

b. differences—The Atacama Desert is cloudier and drier; similarity—Trees do not grow in either place.

c. Answers will vary but should reflect an understanding of section content.

11. **a.** Irrigation turned deserts into farmland; stone-paved roads and suspension bridges connected the empire; relay runners carried messages.

b. Spanish—Roman Catholicism, Spanish language; native cultures—religious festivals, languages, music and instruments, clothing

c. possible answers—Pizarro wanted all of the riches, not just some of them.

Review and Assessment Resources

Review and Reinforce

SE Chapter Review

RF: Chapter Review

Quick Facts Transparency: Pacific South America Visual Summary

Spanish Chapter Summaries Audio CD Program

TOS Holt McDougal Puzzle View, Quiz Show for ExamView

Quiz Game CD-ROM

Assess

SE Standardized Test Practice

PASS: Chapter Test, Forms A and B

Alternative Assessment Handbook

TOS ExamView Test Generator, Chapter Test

Differentiated Instruction Modified Worksheets and Tests CD-ROM; Chapter Test

Online Assessment Program, in the Interactive Student Edition

Reteach/Intervene

Guided Reading Workbook

Differentiated Instruction Teacher Management System: Lesson Plans

Differentiated Instructions Modified Worksheets and Tests CD-ROM

Interactive Skills Tutor CD-ROM

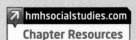

hmhsocialstudies.com

Chapter Resources

12 a. Chile

b. poverty; dissatisfaction with government policies

c. benefits—jobs, escaping violence; drawbacks—overcrowded conditions, lack of services, having to leave family and home

Using the Internet

13. Go to ⟋ hmhsocialstudies.com to access a rubric for this activity.

Social Studies Skills

14. to show the physical features that lie along a line between two points

15. on the sides of the diagram

16. 360 miles

17. sea level

Map Activity

18. A. Strait of Magellan
B. Andes
C. Atacama Desert
D. La Paz, Bolivia
E. Quito, Ecuador
F. Santiago, Chile

Focus on Reading and Speaking

19. a guess to decide what pieces of information were not given by an author

20. few people live there; little rain falls, and people and crops need water

📋 **RF:** Focus on Reading, Making Inferences

21. Rubric Students' interviews should

• sound natural

• cover important, interesting details

• show smooth communication between partners

• use an enthusiastic, lively tone

📋 **RF:** Focus on Speaking, Presenting an Interview

SECTION 3 *(Pages 238–242)*

12. a. Identify What country in Pacific South America has the healthiest economy?

b. Analyze What problems in Ecuador and Bolivia cause political unrest?

c. Evaluate What would be some benefits and drawbacks of moving from the highlands to one of Lima's "young towns"?

Using the Internet

13. Activity: Analyzing Climate Chile has steep mountains, volcanoes, a desert, a rich river valley, and thick forests. These diverse areas contain many different climates. Click on the links given in your online textbook to explore the many climates of Chile. Then test your knowledge by taking an online quiz.

⟋ hmhsocialstudies.com

Social Studies Skills

Interpreting an Elevation Profile *Use the elevation profile on the Social Studies Skills page to answer the following questions.*

14. What is the purpose of an elevation profile?

15. Where can you find the vertical measurements on an elevation profile?

16. What horizontal distance does the elevation profile measure?

17. What is the elevation of the Amazon basin?

Map Activity

18. Pacific South America On a separate sheet of paper, match the letters on the map with their correct labels.

Strait of Magellan	Santiago, Chile
Quito, Ecuador	Atacama Desert
Andes	La Paz, Bolivia

FOCUS ON READING AND SPEAKING

Making Inferences *Use the information in this chapter to answer the following questions.*

19. What is an inference?

20. What can you infer about the size of the population in the Atacama Desert? What clues led you to make this inference?

21. Presenting an Interview Now that you have questions and answers, work with a partner to write an interview script. Read through your script several times so that you know it well enough to sound natural during the interview. Remember to use a lively tone as you speak so that your audience will pay attention.

DIRECTIONS: *Read questions 1 through 7 and write the letter of the best response. Then read question 8 and write your own well-constructed response.*

1 The main mountain range located in Pacific South America is called the

A altiplano.

B Andes.

C Strait of Magellan.

D Pampas.

2 Which of the following conditions is a result of El Niño?

A increased greenhouse gases

B more fish in a usually poor fishing area

C drought on the Pacific coast

D warmer waters near the Pacific coast

3 What early culture had a huge empire in Pacific South America in the early 1500s?

A Inca

B Aztec

C Tiahuanaco

D Nazca

4 Which of the following statements about culture in Pacific South America is false?

A Most people speak Spanish.

B Chile has a higher percentage of Indians than any other country in South America.

C Religion in the region often combines Catholic and ancient native customs.

D Wooden flutes and drums are traditional instruments.

5 Which country's main export is oil?

A Bolivia

B Chile

C Ecuador

D Peru

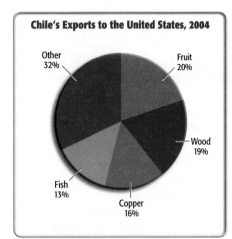

Chile's Exports to the United States, 2004

Other 32%
Fruit 20%
Wood 19%
Copper 16%
Fish 13%

Source: International Trade Administration, TradeStats Express

6 Based on the graph above, what one product is Chile's main export to the United States?

A fish

B wood

C fruit

D copper

7 What has been a major cause of political unrest in the region?

A dissatisfaction with economic policies

B arrest of the leaders of the Shining Path

C development of "young towns" in Peru

D high unemployment in Chile

8 **Extended Response** Using the graph above and your knowledge of Pacific South America today, compare and contrast the economic situations in each of the four countries.

PACIFIC SOUTH AMERICA **245**

Answers

Standardized Test Prep

1. B
Break Down the Question This question requires students to recall factual information from Section 1.

2. D
Break Down the Question This question requires students to recall factual information from Section 1.

3. A
Break Down the Question This question requires students to recall factual information from Section 2.

4. B
Break Down the Question This question requires students to recall factual information from Section 2.

5. C
Break Down the Question This question requires students to recall factual information from Section 3.

6. C
Break Down the Question This question requires students to accurately read the chart.

7. A
Break Down the Question This question requires students to recall factual information from Section 3.

8. Extended Response Answers will vary but should reflect an understanding that Ecuador, Bolivia, Peru, and Chile each have valuable resources that they can use and export to help economic progress. The political situation in each country affects their economies. All four countries have been affected negatively by political instability. However, Chile is now stable and is making significant progress economically.

Reteach/Intervention Resources

Reproducible

- Guided Reading Workbook
- Differentiated Instruction Teacher Management System: Lesson Plans

Technology

- Quick Facts Transparency: Pacific South America Visual Summary
- Differentiated Instruction Modified Worksheets and Tests CD-ROM
- Interactive Skills Tutor CD-ROM

Tips for Test Taking

Anticipate the Answers Provide this tip to students: Before you read the answer choices, answer the question yourself. Then, read the choices. If the answer you gave is among the choices listed, it is probably correct!

Chapter 11 Planning Guide

The United States

Overview	Instructional Resources	
CHAPTER 11 **Essential Question:** What are the unique characteristics of the different regions of the United States? 🔊 **Focus on the Essential Question Podcast**	**TOS** **Differentiated Instruction Teacher Management System:** • Instructional Pacing Guides • Lesson Plans for Differentiated Instruction **Guided Reading Workbook** **Resource File:** • Chapter Review • Focus on Reading: Categorizing • Focus on Viewing : Creating a Collage • Social Studies Skills: Using a Political Map **Experiencing World History and Geography**	**TOS** **Calendar Planner** **Power Presentations with Media Gallery** **Differentiated Instruction Modified Worksheets and Tests CD-ROM** **Interactive Skills Tutor CD-ROM** **Student Edition on Audio CD-ROM** **The World's Music Audio Program** **Map Zone Transparency:** The United States: Political **World Outline Maps: Transparencies and Activities** **Video:** Paving America
Section 1: **Physical Geography** **The Big Idea:** The United States is a large country with diverse physical features, climates, and resources.	**TOS** **Differentiated Instruction Teacher Management System:** Section 1 Lesson Plan **Guided Reading Workbook:** Section 1 **Resource File:** • Vocabulary Builder: Section 1	**Daily Bellringer Transparency:** Section 1 **Map Zone Transparency:** United States: Physical **Map Zone Transparency:** United States: Climate **Map Zone Transparency:** United States, Canada, and Mexico: Political **Internet Activity:** Climates of the U.S.
Section 2: **History and Culture** **The Big Idea:** Democratic ideas and immigration have shaped the history and culture of the United States.	**TOS** **Differentiated Instruction Teacher Management System:** Section 2 Lesson Plan **Guided Reading Workbook:** Section 2 **Resource File:** • Vocabulary Builder: Section 2 • Biography: Sacagawea • Geography and History: The Transcontinental Railroad • Literature: *The Adventures of Tom Sawyer* by Mark Twain • Primary Source: *Up from Slavery* by Booker T. Washington	**Daily Bellringer Transparency:** Section 2 **Map Zone Transparency:** Western Expansion of the United States **Map Zone Transparency:** Distribution of Selected Ethnic Groups **Internet Activity:** The Civil War **Animated Geography:** Growth of the United States
Section 3: **The United States** **The Big Idea:** The United States has four main regions and faces opportunities and challenges.	**TOS** **Differentiated Instruction Teacher Management System:** Section 3 Lesson Plan **Guided Reading Workbook:** Section 3 **Resource File:** • Vocabulary Builder: Section 3 • Biography: *Apollo 11* Mission Crew • Critical Thinking: Why Cities Are Where They Are • Geography for Life: What Region Do You Live In?	**Daily Bellringer Transparency:** Section 3 **Map Zone Transparency:** Regions of the United States **Map Zone Transparency:** United States: Land Use and Resources

Review, Assessment, Intervention

 The Americas Transparencies: The United States Visual Summary

 Spanish Chapter Summaries Audio CD

Progress Assessment Support System (PASS): Chapter Test

 Differentiated Instruction Modified Worksheets CD-ROM: Modified Chapter Test

TOS **ExamView® Assessment Suite (English/Spanish)**

Alternative Assessment Handbook

 Online Assessment Program, in the Interactive Student Edition

---

PASS: Section 1 Quiz

Online Quiz: Section 1

Alternative Assessment Handbook

PASS: Section 2 Quiz

Online Quiz: Section 2

Alternative Assessment Handbook

PASS: Section 3 Quiz

Online Quiz: Section 3

Alternative Assessment Handbook

Supporting Resources

HISTORY.

• Multimedia Classroom Global History Series
• Global History Teacher's Guide

Maps Globes Graphs Level F

• Student Workbook
• Teacher's Guide

Social Studies Trade Library Collections

• NCSS Middle School Trade Collection
• World Regions Trade Collection

Geography's Impact

Geography's Impact Video Program

• **Impact of Immigration**

For more information or to purchase go to hmhsocialstudies.com

Power Presentations with Media Gallery

Power Presentations with Media Gallery are visual presentations of each chapter's main ideas. Presentations can be customized by including Quick Facts charts, images from the text, and video clips.

CHAPTER 11 PLANNING GUIDE

Differentiating Instruction

How do I address the needs of varied learners?

The Target Resource acts as your primary strategy for differentiated instruction.

ENGLISH-LANGUAGE LEARNERS & STRUGGLING READERS

TARGET RESOURCE
Interactive Reader and Study Guide

The activities in the Interactive Reader and Study Guide engage students with questions while presenting summaries of chapter content and provide opportunities for students to practice critical thinking skills.

Additional Resources

Differentiated Instruction Teacher Management System: Lesson Plans for Differentiated Instruction

Resource File:
- Vocabulary Builder Activities
- Social Studies Skills: Using a Political Map

Spanish/English Guided Reading Workbook

Student Edition on Audio CD Program

Interactive Skills Tutor CD-ROM

Spanish Chapter Summaries Audio CD

Teacher One Stop:
- ExamView Assessment Suite, Spanish
- PuzzleView, Spanish

English-Language Learner Strategies and Activities

SPECIAL NEEDS LEARNERS

TARGET RESOURCE
Differentiated Instruction Modified Worksheets and Tests CD-ROM

- Vocabulary Flash Cards
- Modified Vocabulary Builder Activities
- Modified Chapter Review Activity
- Modified Chapter Test

Additional Resources

Differentiated Instruction Teacher Management System: Lesson Plans for Differentiated Instruction

Guided Reading Workbook

Resource File: Social Studies Skills: Using a Political Map

Student Edition on Audio CD Program

Interactive Skills Tutor CD-ROM

Graphic Organizer Transparencies with Support for Reading and Writing

ADVANCED/GIFTED AND TALENTED STUDENTS

TARGET RESOURCE
Resource File

The Resource File activities allow students to extend their knowledge of chapter-related places and people and to practice geography skills.

- Focus on Reading: Categorizing
- Focus on Viewing: Creating a Collage
- Literature: from *The Adventures of Tom Sawyer* by Mark Twain

Additional Resources

Differentiated Instruction Teacher Management System: Lesson Plans for Differentiated Instruction

World History and Geography Document-Based Questions Activities

Geography, Science, and Cultures Activities

Experiencing World History and Geography

Differentiated Activities in the Teacher's Edition

- Reading a Map, p. 247
- Listing Events in Chronological Order, p. 247
- Using Maps, p. 263
- Using a Map Key, p. 266
- Writing a Travel Brochure about the West, p. 268
- Using a Graphic Organizer, p. 269

Differentiated Activities in the Teacher's Edition

- Discussing the Effects of Natural Disasters, p. 255

Differentiated Activities in the Teacher's Edition

- Understanding How Climates Affect Food Crops, p. 251
- Creating a Report on Natural Disasters, p. 255
- Understanding the Use of Natural Resources, p. 266

Teacher One Stop™

How can I manage the lesson plans and support materials for differentiated instruction?

With the Teacher One Stop, you can easily organize and print lesson plans, planning guides, and instructional materials for all learners. The Teacher One Stop includes the following materials to help you differentiate instruction:

- **· Interactive Teacher's Edition**
- **· Calendar Planner and pacing guides**
- **· Editable lesson plans**
- **· All reproducible ancillaries in Adobe Acrobat (PDF) format**
- **· ExamView Assessment Suite (English & Spanish)**
- **· Transparency and video previews**

Interactive Student Edition

Complete online student edition with interactive multimedia support for chapter content assessment and reporting

- Interactive Maps and Notebook
- Standardized Test Prep
- Online Homework Practice and Research Activities
- Current Events
- Chapter-based Internet Activities
- Animated Geography Activities

DIFFERENTIATED INSTRUCTION PLANNING GUIDE

Essential Question

Introduce the Essential Question

- Discuss how physical features can distinguish regions. Compare ways in which the eastern United States is different from the western part of the country. Have students predict how those differences might affect people and their ways of life.

- Tell students that as the United States expanded west after gaining its independence, the search for land and other resources, the development of new industries, and the influx of immigrants affected different regions of the United States in different ways.

- Explain that geographers often divided the United States into four large regions—the Northeast, South, Midwest, and the West. Challenge students to speculate ways in which those regions are similar and different.

Focus on Reading and Viewing

Reading The Resource File provides a worksheet to help students practice categorizing.

📃 **RF:** Focus on Reading, Categorizing

Viewing The Resource File provides a worksheet to help students create a collage.

📃 **RF:** Focus on Viewing, Creating a Collage

Key to Differentiating Instruction

Below Level

Basic-level activities designed for all students encountering new material

At Level

Intermediate-level activities designed for average students

Above Level

Challenging activities designed for honors and gifted and talented students

Standard English Mastery

Activities designed to improve standard English usage

LS Learning Styles

246 CHAPTER 11

CHAPTER **11**

The United States

Essential Question What are the unique characteristics of the different regions of the United States?

❓ What You Will Learn...

In this chapter you will learn about the physical features, climates, and resources of the United States. You will also discover how democratic ideas and immigration have shaped the United States. Finally, you will learn about our country's different regions, diverse population, and the challenges we face as a nation.

FOCUS ON READING AND VIEWING

Categorizing A good way to make sense of what you read is to separate facts and details into groups, called categories. For example, you could sort facts about the United States into categories like natural resources, major cities, or rivers. As you read this chapter, look for ways to categorize details under each topic. **See the lesson, Categorizing, on page 526.**

Creating a Collage Artists create collages by gluing art and photographs onto a flat surface, such as a poster board. As you read this chapter, you will collect ideas for a collage about the United States. After you create your own collage, you will view and evaluate the collages of other students in your class.

Culture People of many different ethnic groups and cultures make up the population of the United States.

Introduce the Chapter

At Level

Exploring the United States

1. Ask students to imagine that they have a friend living in another country who wants to learn about the United States. Ask students to think about what makes the United States interesting or special. Remind students that the United States is a large country with many different climates, landscapes, and people.

2. Explain to students that they are going to learn about how the size and diverse climate and population of the United States contributes to its strength as a nation.

3. Ask students to keep track of the different physical features, climates, and cultures they learn about and how these characteristics make the United States unique.

LS Verbal/Linguistic, Interpersonal

📃 Alternative Assessment Handbook, Rubric 11: Discussions

The United States: Political

CANADA

ND
Fargo
MN
SD Minneapolis WI
WY
Cheyenne
NE
Milwaukee
IA Chicago
Lincoln
Des Moines
Denver
CO
KS Kansas City
MO St. Louis
Santa Fe
OK Oklahoma City
AR Little Rock
NM
TX Dallas
Houston
New Orleans
LA
MS Montgomery
AL
MI Detroit
IL Indianapolis
IN OH Cleveland
Lexington
KY
Nashville
TN
Memphis
GA Atlanta
L. Superior
L. Michigan
L. Huron
L. Erie
L. Ontario
St. Lawrence R.
ME
VT NH Boston
NY MA CT RI
PA Philadelphia New York
Baltimore NJ
Washington, D.C. DE
WV VA MD
NC Charlotte
SC Charleston
FL
Jacksonville
Miami
Lake Okeechobee
Gulf of Mexico
MEXICO
Rio Grande
Red R.
Mississippi R.
Missouri R.
Ohio R.
River

ATLANTIC OCEAN

40°N
30°N
80°W
90°W

⊕ National capital
● Other cities

0   200   400 Miles
0   200   400 Kilometers
Projection: Albers Equal Area

N
W E
S

HISTORY Paving America
↗ hmhsocialstudies.com **VIDEO**

map zone

Geography Skills

Place The United States is made up of 50 states.

1. **Locate** What two countries border the United States?
2. **Contrast** How is Maryland's size and location different from California's size and location?

Geography The Grand Canyon in Arizona is one example of the many spectacular landscapes in the United States.

History The Statue of Liberty in New York Harbor symbolizes our freedom and our history as a democratic nation.

247

Explore the Map and Pictures

The United States: Political The United States is one of the largest countries in the world. This map shows the geography of our country, including national and state boundaries and the bodies of water that border the United States.

Analyzing Visuals What four states border Mexico? *California, Arizona, New Mexico, and Texas* Which ocean borders the east coast? *Atlantic Ocean* Which state is larger: Ohio or Idaho? *Idaho* Why do you think the Grand Canyon attracts visitors from around the world? *It is an unusual and beautiful area.*

Info to Know

Age of the U.S. The United States is actually a young country compared to other nations of the world. The United States Constitution was written in 1787, only a little more than 200 years ago.

↗ hmhsocialstudies.com
Teacher Resources

Differentiating Instruction

Below Level

Struggling Readers

1. United States maps may overwhelm some students because of the amount of information they show. For example, the locations of Alaska and Hawaii may be confusing.

2. Read the map with students to help them better understand the information it shows about the United States.

3. Ask them to locate and name some of the major bodies of water, both in and bordering the United States. *possible responses—in the U.S.: Mississippi River, Colorado River,*

Lake Michigan; bordering the U.S.: Atlantic Ocean, Pacific Ocean, Gulf of Mexico

4. Ask which state is farthest west. East? North? South? *Hawaii; Maine; Alaska; Hawaii*

5. To help them better understand the location of your home state, ask which state(s) are north of your home state. South? East? West? *Answers will vary.*

LS Visual/Spatial, Verbal/Linguistic

Alternative Assessment Handbook, Rubric 21: Map Reading

Answers

Map Zone 1. *Mexico and Canada;* **2.** *Maryland is small in size and is located on the East coast. California is large in size and is located on the West coast.*

Preteach

Bellringer

If YOU lived there. . . Use the **Daily Bellringer Transparency** to help students answer the question.

▶ Daily Bellringer Transparency, Section 1

Key Terms and Places

📖 **RF:** Vocabulary Builder, Section 1

Taking Notes

Have students use the graphic organizer online to take notes on the section. This activity will prepare students for the Section Assessment, in which they will complete a graphic organizer that builds on the information using the Critical Thinking Skill: Categorizing.

Physical Geography

What You Will Learn...

Main Ideas

1. Major physical features of the United States include mountains, rivers, and plains.
2. The climate of the United States is wetter in the East and South and drier in the West.
3. The United States is rich in natural resources such as farmland, oil, forests, and minerals.

The Big Idea

The United States is a large country with diverse physical features, climates, and re-sources.

Key Terms and Places

Appalachian Mountains, *p. 248*
Great Lakes, *p. 249*
Mississippi River, *p. 249*
tributary, *p. 249*
Rocky Mountains, *p. 250*
continental divide, *p. 250*

📱 **hmhsocialstudies.com**
TAKING NOTES

Use the graphic organizer online to take notes on the physical geography of the United States.

If YOU lived there...

You live in St. Louis, Missouri, which is located on the Mississippi River. For the next few days, you will travel down the river on an old-fashioned steamboat. The Mississippi begins in Minnesota and flows south through 10 states in the heart of the United States. On your trip, you bring a video camera to film life along this great river.

What will you show in your video about the Mississippi?

BUILDING BACKGROUND The United States stretches from sea to sea across North America. To the north is Canada and to the south lies Mexico. Because it is so large, the United States has a great variety of landscapes and climates.

Physical Features

The United States is the third largest country in the world behind Russia and Canada. Our country is home to an incredible variety of physical features. All but two of the 50 states—Alaska and Hawaii—make up the main part of the country. Look at the physical map of the United States on the next page. It shows the main physical features of our country. Use the map as you read about America's physical geography in the East and South, the Interior Plains, and the West.

The East and South

If you were traveling across the United States, you might start on the country's eastern coast. This low area, which is flat and close to sea level, is called the Atlantic Coastal Plain. As you go west, the land gradually rises higher to a region called the Piedmont. The **Appalachian Mountains**, which are the main mountain range in the East, rise above the Piedmont. These mountains are very old. For many millions of years, rain, snow, and wind

---

Teach the Big Idea

Physical Geography

1. **Teach** Ask students the questions in the Main Idea boxes under Direct Teach.

2. **Apply** Have each student choose a word from the "Key Terms and Places" list to learn more about physical features or areas of the United States, such as the Rocky Mountains. Have students find photographs on the Internet or in magazines of the area or physical feature they choose.

3. **Review** Ask students to share and describe their photograph with the class.

4. **Practice/Homework** Have students research the exact location of the feature or area in their photograph and write one or two paragraphs describing its location and surrounding physical features.
   📊 **Visual/Spatial, Verbal/Linguistic**
   📖 Alternative Assessment Handbook, Rubric 30: Research

United States: Physical

ELEVATION

Feet	Meters
13,120	4,000
6,560	2,000
1,640	500
656	200
(Sea level) 0	0 (Sea level)
Below sea level	Below sea level

0   200   400 Miles
0   200   400 Kilometers

Projection: Albers Equal Area

map zone Geography Skills

Place The western United States is higher in elevation than the east.
1. **Locate** Where is the highest elevation in the United States located?
2. **Analyze** How do you think the Appalachians have influenced settlement in the United States?

have eroded and smoothed their peaks. As a result, the highest mountain in the Appalachians is about 6,700 feet (2,040 m).

The Interior Plains

As you travel west from the Appalachians, you come across the vast Interior Plains that stretch to the Great Plains just east of the Rocky Mountains. The Interior Plains are filled with hills, lakes, and rivers. The first major water feature that you see here

is called the **Great Lakes**. These lakes make up the largest group of freshwater lakes in the world. The Great Lakes are also an important waterway for trade between the United States and Canada.

West of the Great Lakes lies North America's largest and most important river, the **Mississippi River**. Tributaries in the interior plains flow to the Mississippi. A **tributary** is a smaller stream or river that flows into a larger stream or river.

Appalachians The smooth peaks of the Appalachian Mountains dominate the landscape of western North Carolina.

THE UNITED STATES   **249**

Cause-and-Effect Posters

1. Discuss with students why the physical features of the United States made it so attractive to early settlers. Ask students to imagine how different the country would be if one of these physical features were to change dramatically. For example, what if the Mississippi River dried up? Encourage students to take notes about the discussion.

2. Have each student make a map of the United States on poster board, showing its major physical features. Next to each feature, have

students write a sentence explaining why it is important, and what might happen without it.

3. Ask volunteers to share their cause-and-effect posters with the class.
LS Visual/Spatial, Verbal/Linguistic

Alternative Assessment Handbook, Rubrics 6: Cause and Effect; and 28: Posters

---

Direct Teach

Main Idea

❶ Physical Features

Major physical features of the United States include mountains, rivers, and plains.

Identify What is a *tributary*? Name two rivers that are large tributaries of the Mississippi River. *a stream or river that flows into a larger stream or river; Missouri and Ohio Rivers*

Explain What are the *Interior Plains? a series of rolling hills, lakes, and large rivers stretching from the Appalachian Mountains westward to the Rocky Mountains*

Summarize Describe how the physical landscape changes from east to west. *In the east, the Atlantic Coastal Plain is flat and close to sea level. The land rises to the west in the Piedmont region then rises again at the Appalachian Mountains. West of the Appalachians are the Interior Plains. Farther west are the Great Plains, which are vast areas of grasslands. The elevation climbs again at the Rocky Mountains. Finally, you reach the Sierra Nevada and Cascade Range and the Pacific Coast on the far west.*

▶ Map Zone Transparency: United States: Physical

Info to Know

A Very Long River The Mississippi River is the world's fourth longest river. It stretches approximately 2,348 miles. Long before Europeans arrived in North America, Native Americans used the Mississippi River and its watershed for trading, food, and water. Today, the river continues to be a valuable resource.

Answers

Map Zone 1. *Alaska;* **2.** *They were probably difficult for people to cross, so more people settled east of the Appalachians.*

249

Info to Know

The Continental Divide All continents have a continental divide except Antarctica. Continental divides are a section of elevated terrain forming a border between two watersheds. This means that along the border, water flows on both sides of the line and travels in opposite directions. The Continental Divide in North America is sometimes called the Great Divide.

Mississippi River Delta Look closely at the Satellite View of the Mississippi River Delta. How does sediment from the Mississippi change the area where the land meets the Gulf of Mexico? *Deposits of sediment from the river make gulf waters shallower.*

Did you know. . .

One of the biggest threats to America's rivers is urban sprawl. As cities and suburban areas expand outward, it can significantly drain rivers and pollute them. Urban sprawl can also damage ecosystems, affecting fish and other wildlife. One river at risk is the Missouri River, especially along Iowa's western border.

Answers

Focus on Reading *rivers that flow eastward and rivers that flow westward*

Reading Check *Atlantic Coastal Plain, Appalachian Mountains, Great Lakes, Mississippi River, Rocky Mountains*

Satellite View *flooding, poor water quality*

250

Along the way, these rivers deposit rich silt. The silt creates fertile farmlands that cover most of the Interior Plains. The Missouri and Ohio rivers are huge tributaries of the Mississippi. They help drain the entire Interior Plains.

Look at the map on the previous page. Notice the land begins to increase in elevation west of the Interior Plains. This higher region is called the Great Plains. Vast areas of grasslands cover these plains.

The West

In the region called the West, several of the country's most rugged mountain ranges make up the **Rocky Mountains**. These enormous mountains, also called the Rockies, stretch as far as you can see. Many of the mountains' jagged peaks rise above 14,000 feet (4,270 m).

FOCUS ON READING
Into what two categories might you group the details on rivers?

In the Rocky Mountains is a line of high peaks called the Continental Divide. A **continental divide** is an area of high ground that divides the flow of rivers towards opposite ends of a continent.

Rivers east of the divide in the Rockies mostly flow eastward and empty into the Mississippi River. Most of the rivers west of the divide flow westward and empty into the Pacific Ocean.

Farther west, mountain ranges include the Cascade Range and the Sierra Nevada. Most of the mountains in the Cascades are dormant volcanoes. One mountain, Mount Saint Helens, is an active volcano. A tremendous eruption in 1980 blew off the mountain's peak and destroyed 150 square miles (390 sq km) of forest.

Mountains also stretch north along the Pacific coast. At 20,320 feet (6,194 m), Alaska's Mount McKinley is the highest mountain in North America.

Far out in the Pacific Ocean are the islands that make up the state of Hawaii. Volcanoes formed these islands millions of years ago. Today, hot lava and ash continue to erupt from the islands' volcanoes.

READING CHECK **Summarizing** What are the major physical features of the United States?

Satellite View

The river branches out in several places here as it tries to find the shortest way to the ocean.

The Mississippi River Delta

From its source in Minnesota, the Mississippi River flows south across the central United States. It ends at the tip of Louisiana, which is shown here. This satellite image shows the area where the Mississippi River meets the Gulf of Mexico. This area is called a delta. A river's delta is formed from sediment that a river carries downstream to the ocean. Sediment is usually made up of rocks, soil, sand, and dead plants. Each year, the Mississippi dumps more than 400 million tons of sediment into the Gulf of Mexico.

The light blue and green areas in this image are shallow areas of sediment. The deeper water of the Gulf of Mexico is dark blue. Also, notice that much of the delta land looks fragile. This is new land that the river has built up by depositing sediment.

Making Inferences What natural hazards might people living in the Mississippi Delta experience?

Collaborative Learning

At Level | Standard English Mastery

Follow the River

1. Organize the class into small groups. Have each group choose a river that flows from the Continental Divide. Have students trace the river's journey to its outlet into an ocean or sea. Have students research their river's length, the number of states and major cities it passes, and ways that their river is unique.

2. Have each group describe its river to the rest of the class.

3. As a class, discuss the value of our nation's rivers and in what ways we depend on them.

You might want to ask the following questions: What might happen if this river becomes overly polluted? What might happen if this river dried up? Who would be affected?

4. Have students write letters or emails to U.S. government officials, summarizing their findings and asking that steps be taken to protect the nation's rivers. For addresses, visit www.firstgov.gov. **LS** **Verbal/Linguistic**

Alternative Assessment Handbook, Rubrics 14: Group Activity; and 29: Presentations

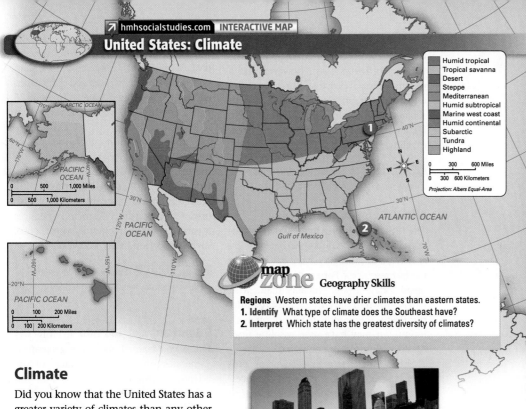

United States: Climate

hmhsocialstudies.com INTERACTIVE MAP

Legend:
- Humid tropical
- Tropical savanna
- Desert
- Steppe
- Mediterranean
- Humid subtropical
- Marine west coast
- Humid continental
- Subarctic
- Tundra
- Highland

Projection: Albers Equal-Area

map zone — Geography Skills

Regions Western states have drier climates than eastern states.
1. **Identify** What type of climate does the Southeast have?
2. **Interpret** Which state has the greatest diversity of climates?

Climate

Did you know that the United States has a greater variety of climates than any other country? Look at the map above to see the different climates of the United States.

The East and South

The eastern United States has three climate regions. In the Northeast, people live in a humid continental climate with snowy winters and warm, humid summers. Southerners, on the other hand, experience milder winters and the warm, humid summers of a humid subtropical climate. Most of Florida is warm all year.

The Interior Plains

Temperatures throughout the year can vary greatly in the Interior Plains. Summers are hot and dry in the Great Plains. However, most of the region has a humid continental climate with long, cold winters.

1 With a humid continental climate, New York City experiences cold winters with snowfall. In this climate people can ice skate during the winter.

2 With a humid subtropical climate, most of Florida has warm sunny days during most of the year. In this climate people can enjoy the region's beaches.

THE UNITED STATES **251**

Direct Teach

Main Idea

② Climate

The climate of the United States is wetter in the East and South and drier in the West.

Explain What types of climates can be found in the eastern part of the United States? *The Northeast is humid continental, with snowy winters and warm, humid summers. Farther south it is humid subtropical. Winters are milder, and summers are more humid. Farthest south in the tropical savanna, it is warm year-round.*

Identify Look at the map. Which state has a "humid tropical" climate? *Hawaii* What types of climate does Alaska have? *tundra and subarctic*

▶ Map Zone Transparency: United States: Climate

MISCONCEPTION ALERT

The Weather or Climate of the U.S.? Some students may think that a certain region of the United States is always "cold" or "hot," for example. Encourage students to review descriptions of the various climates the United States experiences. You may want to also remind them of the difference between *weather* (short-term changes in the air) and *climate* (a region's average weather conditions over a long period).

hmhsocialstudies.com

Online Resources
Activity: Climates of the U.S.

Differentiating Instruction

Struggling Readers
Below Level

To help struggling readers, have them match the color in the legend to the color shown on the map. Read aloud the climate description. As you do, have students trace the region with that climate with their finger. Remind students that this book has many illustrations that can help them learn. **LS** Visual/Spatial, Verbal/Linguistic

Alternative Assessment Handbook, Rubric 21: Map Reading

Advanced/Gifted and Talented
Above Level

Have students discuss how different climates affect what types of foods can be grown in certain regions of the country and for how long. Ask students how a change in these climates might affect farming in our country. **LS** Verbal/Linguistic

Alternative Assessment Handbook, Rubric 6: Cause and Effect

Answers

Map Zone 1. *humid subtropical;*
2. *California*

251

252

Direct Teach

Main Idea

③ Natural Resources

The United States is rich in natural resources such as farmland, oil, forests, and minerals.

Explain How are our lives affected by natural resources? *We depend on natural resources from all over the country for food, fuel, electricity, and many other daily needs.*

Make Inferences Why does the United States have such productive farmland? *because of the climate, fertile soils in the Interior Plains, and its many rivers*

Review & Assess

Close

Discuss with students the importance of physical features, climate, and natural resources in the United States.

Review

↗ Online Quiz, Section 1

Assess

SE Section 1 Assessment

PASS: Section 1 Quiz

Alternative Assessment Handbook

Reteach/Classroom Intervention

Guided Reading Workbook, Section 1

Interactive Skills Tutor CD-ROM

Answers

Reading Check (left) *humid tropical, tropical savanna, desert, steppe, Mediterranean, humid subtropical, marine west coast, humid continental, subarctic, tundra, and highland*

Reading Check *soil, oil, minerals, forests*

252

The West

Climates in the West are mostly dry. The Pacific Northwest coast, however, has a wet, mild coastal climate. The region's coldest climates are in Alaska, which has both subarctic and tundra climates. In contrast, Hawaii is the only state with a warm, tropical climate.

READING CHECK **Identifying** What types of climates are found in the United States?

Natural Resources

The United States is extremely rich in natural resources. Do you know that your life is affected in some way every day by these natural resources? For example, if you ate bread today, it was probably made with wheat grown in the fertile soils of the Interior Plains. If you rode in a car or on a bus recently, it may have used gasoline from Alaska, California, or Louisiana.

The United States is a major oil producer but uses more oil than it produces. In fact, we import more than one half of the oil we need.

Valuable minerals are mined in the Appalachians and Rockies. One mineral, coal, supplies the energy for more than half of the electricity produced in the United States. The United States has about 25 percent of the world's coal reserves and is a major coal exporter.

Other important resources include forests and farmland, which cover much of the country. The trees in our forests provide lumber that is used in constructing buildings. Wood from these trees is also used to make paper. Farmland produces a variety of crops including wheat, corn, soybeans, cotton, fruits, and vegetables.

READING CHECK **Summarizing** What are important natural resources in the U.S.?

SUMMARY AND PREVIEW In this section you learned about the geography, climates, and natural resources of the United States. In the next section, you will learn about the history and culture of the United States.

Section 1 Assessment

↗ hmhsocialstudies.com
ONLINE QUIZ

Reviewing Ideas, Terms, and Places

1. **a. Define** What is a **tributary**?
   b. Contrast How are the **Appalachian Mountains** different from the **Rocky Mountains**?
   c. Elaborate Why are the **Great Lakes** an important waterway?
2. **a. Describe** What is the climate like in the Northeast?
   b. Draw Conclusions What would winter be like in Alaska?
3. **a. Recall** What kinds of crops are grown in the United States?
   b. Explain Why is coal an important resource?
   c. Predict What natural resources might not be as important to your daily life in the future?

Critical Thinking

4. **Categorizing** Copy the graphic organizer below. Use it to organize your notes on physical features, climate, and resources by region of the country.

East and South	Interior Plains	West

FOCUS ON VIEWING

5. **Thinking about Physical Geography** Jot down key words that describe the physical features and climate of the United States. Think of at least three objects or images you might use to illustrate physical features and climate.

252 CHAPTER 11

Section 1 Assessment Answers

1. **a.** A tributary is a stream or river that flows into a larger stream or river.
   b. The Appalachians have lower, smoother peaks than the Rockies because of erosion. The Rockies have tall, jagged peaks.
   c. The Great Lakes, the world's largest freshwater lake system, are an important waterway for U.S.–Canada trade.
2. **a.** The Northeast climate is cold and snowy in the winter and warm and humid in the summer.
   b. Winter in Alaska would be extremely cold.
3. **a.** wheat, corn, soybeans, cotton, fruits, and vegetables

b. Coal is used to make electricity. The U.S. also exports coal to other countries.
c. Oil and coal may become less important as scarcity and environmental concerns limit their use.

4. Answers will vary, but students' notes should be categorized by region.

5. Descriptions might include rivers, mountains, plains, and climate types found in the United States.

Social Studies Skills

Using a Political Map

Learn

Many types of maps are useful in studying geography. Political maps are one of the most frequently used types of maps. These maps show human cultural features such as cities, states, and countries. Look at the map's legend to figure out how these features are represented on the map.

Most political maps show national boundaries and state boundaries. The countries on political maps are sometimes shaded different colors to help you tell where the borders of each country are located.

Practice

Use the political map here to answer the following questions.

- What countries does this map show?
- How does the map show the difference between state boundaries and national boundaries?
- What is the capital of Canada?

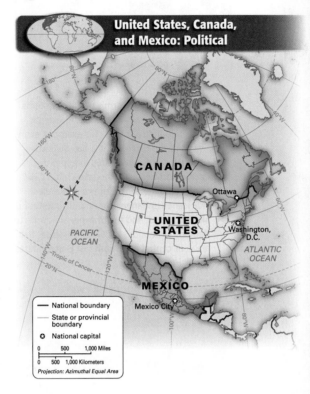

United States, Canada, and Mexico: Political

CANADA
Ottawa

UNITED STATES
Washington, D.C.

PACIFIC OCEAN

ATLANTIC OCEAN

MEXICO
Mexico City

— National boundary
‑‑‑ State or provincial boundary
✪ National capital

0   500   1,000 Miles
0   500 1,000 Kilometers
Projection: Azimuthal Equal Area

Apply

Using an atlas or the Internet, find a political map of your state. Use that map to answer the following questions.

1. What is the state capital and where is it located?
2. What other states or countries border your state?
3. What are two other cities in your state besides the capital and the city you live in?

Social Studies Skills Activity: Using a Political Map [At Level]

Identifying a Political Map

1. Review with students what features are found on a political map. *national and state borders, cities, and other human features*

2. Working with a partner, have each student find any map in their textbook and cover the title and legend with a sticky note.

3. Each student should show the map to his or her partner and have them say if it is a political map or not. Students should give reasons why or why not.

4. Students should then remove the sticky notes to see if their partner was correct.
   LS Visual/Spatial, Interpersonal

   Alternative Assessment Handbook, Rubric 21: Map Reading

Social Studies Skills

Using a Political Map

Activity Make a Map

Materials: research materials, such as an atlas or the Internet; art paper, colored pencils, rulers

1. Ask students to choose any country that they would like to learn more about.

2. Have students use research materials to locate a political map of the country they chose.

3. Students should use art supplies and a ruler to create a political map of their country.

4. Encourage students to use colored pencils to shade different states or provinces within their country. Students should mark at least three cities on their maps, including the country's capital. Remind students to include a legend, scale, compass, and map title. **LS Verbal/Linguistic**

   Alternative Assessment Handbook, Rubric 20: Map Creation

   Interactive Skills Tutor CD-ROM, Lesson 6: Interpret Maps, Graphs, Charts, Visuals, and Political Cartoons

Answers

Practice 1. *Canada, United States, Mexico;* **2.** *National boundaries are slightly heavier than state boundaries and have a darker shade of the color used to differentiate each country.* **3.** *Ottawa*

Apply *Students' answers will vary based on the location of your home state.*

Case Study

Info to Know

Earthquakes Southern California has about 10,000 earthquakes a year. Most of them are so small you can't feel them. The first earthquake was reported in California in 1769. The explorer Gaspar de Portola's expedition was camping about 30 miles (48 km) southeast of what is now Los Angeles when the group felt the earthquake.

Activity **Journal Entry** Ask students to imagine they are on Gaspar de Portola's expedition during the earthquake. Have students write a journal entry describing what they felt and what they thought might be the cause of the movement. Ask volunteers to share their journal entries with the class.

LS Verbal/Linguistic

Alternative Assessment Handbook, Rubric 40: Writing to Describe

Case Study

Natural Hazards
in the United States

Background Earth's physical systems create patterns around us, and these patterns influence our lives. For example, every region of the United States has distinctive natural hazards. Volcanoes threaten the Pacific Northwest. Earthquakes rattle California. Wildfires strike forests in the West. Hurricanes endanger the Atlantic and Gulf of Mexico coasts, and major rivers are prone to flooding. Tornadoes regularly rip across flat areas of central and southeast United States.

In fact, the United States lies in danger of getting hit by an average of six hurricanes a year. Formed by the warm waters of the Atlantic Ocean and Caribbean Sea and the collision of strong winds, hurricanes are the most powerful storms on Earth. Most hurricanes look like large doughnuts with a hole, or eye, in the middle of the storm. Around the eye, high winds and rain bands rotate counterclockwise. Once the hurricane moves over land or cold water it weakens.

Natural Hazards in the United States

Tornado Alley

Earthquakes — Volcanoes
Wildfires — Tornadoes
Hurricanes — Tornado Risk
Flood areas — Moderate / High

map zone

Collaborative Learning

At Level

Natural Hazards Facts

Research Required

1. Organize the class into three groups. Assign one group tornadoes, one group earthquakes, and one group hurricanes.

2. Ask each group to research their assigned topic, looking for ten interesting facts.

3. Have each group write their facts on poster board or a large piece of paper.

4. Students should decorate their posters with drawings and/or magazine and newspaper cutouts.

5. Ask each group to choose a member to present their poster to the rest of the class.

LS Verbal/Linguistic, Visual/Spatial

Alternative Assessment Handbook, Rubrics 14: Group Activity; and 24: Oral Presentations

After Hurricane Katrina hit New Orleans, people escaped the floodwaters by fleeing to rooftops and high-rise apartment buildings like this one.

Using satellite images like this one of Hurricane Katrina, scientists saw how large the storm was and warned people along the Gulf coast to evacuate.

Checking for Understanding

True or False Answer each statement T if it is true or F if it is false. If false, explain why.

1. Volcanoes threaten Maine, Ohio, and the South. *F: Volcanoes threaten the Pacific Northwest.*
2. The area where tornadoes hit the hardest is called "Tornado Town." *F: The area is called "Tornado Alley."*
3. Hurricanes are the most powerful storms on Earth. *T*

Hurricane Katrina On August 29, 2005, one of the most destructive hurricanes ever hit the United States. Hurricane Katrina devastated coastal regions of Louisiana, the city of New Orleans, and the entire coast of Mississippi.

With winds as high as 145 mph (235 km), Katrina destroyed hundreds of thousands of homes and businesses. In addition, the force of Katrina's storm surge pushed water from the Gulf of Mexico onto land to a height of about two stories tall. As a result, low-lying areas along the Gulf coast experienced massive flooding.

The storm surge also caused several levees that protected New Orleans from the waters of Lake Pontchartrain to break. The loss of these levees caused the lake's waters to flood most of the city. About 150,000 people who did not evacuate before the storm were left stranded in shelters, high-rise buildings, and on rooftops. Using boats and helicopters, emergency workers rescued thousands of the city's people. Total damages from the storm along the Gulf coast was estimated to be nearly $130 billion. More than 1,300 people died and over a million were displaced.

What It Means Natural hazards can influence where we live, how we build our homes, and how we prepare for storms. In addition to hurricanes, other hazards affect the United States. For example, Tornado Alley is a region of the Great Plains that experiences a high number of tornadoes, or "twisters"—rapidly spinning columns of air that stay in contact with the ground. In Tornado Alley, special warning sirens go off when storms develop that might form a dangerous tornado.

Geography for Life Activity

1. How are hurricanes formed?

2. Many people train and volunteer as storm chasers. They may follow storms for hundreds of miles to gather scientific data, take photographs, or file news reports. What might be the risks and rewards of such activity? Would it interest you?

3. **Comparing Windstorms** Do some research to find out how tornadoes and hurricanes differ. Summarize the differences in a chart that includes information about how these storms start, where and when they tend to occur in the United States, and their wind strength.

THE UNITED STATES **255**

Preparing for Natural Hazards

Activity Talk with students about the type of damage natural hazards can cause. For example, homes and businesses can be destroyed and floods may occur. Have students think of ways they could help a community prepare for a hurricane, tornado, earthquake, or other disaster. **LS Verbal/Linguistic**

📖 Alternative Assessment Handbook, Rubrics 6: Cause and Effect; and 35: Solving Problems

Differentiating Instruction

Special Needs Learners
Below Level

1. Lead the class in a discussion about the effects of natural hazards in the United States.

2. Ask students how landslides and floods might affect people and animals living in the area.

3. Have students think of ways they could help people recover from a natural disaster. **LS Visual/Spatial**

📖 Alternative Assessment Handbook, Rubrics 6: Cause and Effects; and 11: Discussions

Advanced/Gifted and Talented
Above Level

1. Have students use the library, Internet, or other resources to learn about a natural disaster that has occurred in the region in which you live.

2. Have students prepare a one-page report describing the event.

3. Ask volunteers to share their reports with the class. **LS Verbal/Linguistic**

📖 Alternative Assessment Handbook, Rubrics 1: Acquiring Information; and 42: Writing to Inform

Answers
Geography for Life Activity
1. *by the warm waters of the Atlantic Ocean and Caribbean Sea and the collision of strong winds*
2. *risks—dangerous, unpredictable; rewards—thrilling experience, good photographs; Answers will vary, but students should provide reasons to support their answer.* 3. *Students' charts will vary, but should include the required information.*

255

256 CHAPTER 11

Bellringer

If YOU lived there. . . Use the **Daily Bellringer Transparency** to help students answer the question.

▶ Daily Bellringer Transparency, Section 2

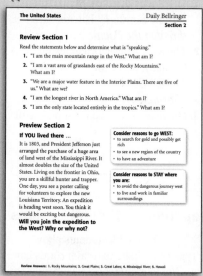

Academic Vocabulary

Review with students the high-use academic term in this section.

development the process of growing or improving (p. 258)

RF: Vocabulary Builder, Section 2

Taking Notes

Have students use the graphic organizer online to take notes on the section. This activity will prepare students for the Section Assessment, in which they will complete a graphic organizer that builds on the information using the Critical Thinking Skill: Summarizing.

History and Culture

What You Will Learn...

Main Ideas

1. The United States is the world's first modern democracy.
2. The people and culture of the United States are very diverse.

The Big Idea

Democratic ideas and immigration have shaped the history and culture of the United States.

Key Terms and Places

colony, *p. 256*
Boston, *p. 256*
New York, *p. 256*
plantation, *p. 257*
pioneers, *p. 258*
bilingual, *p. 260*

hmhsocialstudies.com
TAKING NOTES

Use the graphic organizer online to take notes on the history and culture of the United States.

If YOU lived there...

It is 1803, and President Jefferson just arranged the purchase of a huge area of land west of the Mississippi River. It almost doubles the size of the United States. Living on the frontier in Ohio, you are a skillful hunter and trapper. One day, you see a poster calling for volunteers to explore the new Louisiana Territory. An expedition is heading west soon. You think it would be exciting but dangerous.

Will you join the expedition to the West? Why or why not?

BUILDING BACKGROUND From 13 colonies on the Atlantic coast, the territory of the United States expanded all the way to the Pacific Ocean in about 75 years. Since then, America's democracy has attracted immigrants from almost every country in the world. Looking for new opportunities, these immigrants have made the country very diverse.

First Modern Democracy

Long before Italian explorer Christopher Columbus sailed to the Americas in 1492, native people lived on the land that is now the United States. These Native Americans developed many distinct cultures. Soon after Columbus and his crew explored the Americas, other Europeans began to set up colonies there.

The American Colonies

Europeans began settling in North America and setting up colonies in the 1500s. A **colony** is a territory inhabited and controlled by people from a foreign land. By the mid-1700s the British Empire included more than a dozen colonies along the Atlantic coast. New cities in the colonies such as **Boston** and **New York** became major seaports.

Teach the Big Idea

At Level

History and Culture

1. **Teach** Ask students the questions in the Main Idea boxes under Direct Teach.

2. **Apply** Have students create a three-column chart on their own paper. In the first column, ask students to write down any headings, subheadings, or important terms from the section. In the second column, have students create one or two questions for each term or heading in the first column. In the third column, have students write the answers to their questions.

3. **Review** Pair students and have them ask each other the questions they wrote.

4. **Practice/Homework** Have students use their charts to create five multiple-choice questions about the section. Remind students to provide an answer key and an explanation of why each answer is correct.
   LS Verbal/Linguistic

   Alternative Assessment Handbook, Rubrics 1: Acquiring Information; and 7: Charts

Some people living in the British colonies lived on plantations. A **plantation** is a large farm that grows mainly one crop. Many of the colonial plantations produced tobacco, rice, or cotton. Thousands of enslaved Africans were brought to the colonies and forced to work on plantations.

By the 1770s many colonists in America were unhappy with British rule. They wanted independence from Britain. In July 1776, the colonial representatives adopted the Declaration of Independence. The document stated that "all men are created equal" and have the right to "life, liberty, and the pursuit of happiness." Although not everyone in the colonies was considered equal, the Declaration was a great step toward equality and justice.

To win their independence, the American colonists fought the British in the Revolutionary War. First, colonists from Massachusetts fought in the early battles of the war in and around Boston. As the war spread west and south, soldiers from all the American colonies joined the fight against Britain.

In 1781 the American forces under General George Washington defeated the British army at the Battle of Yorktown in Virginia. With this defeat, Britain recognized the independence of the United States. As a consequence, Britain granted all its land east of the Mississippi River to the new nation.

Expansion and Industrial Growth

After independence, the United States gradually expanded west. Despite the challenges of crossing swift-moving rivers and traveling across rugged terrain and huge mountains, people moved west for land and plentiful resources.

BIOGRAPHY

George Washington
(1732–1799)

As the first president of the United States, George Washington is known as the Father of His Country. Washington was admired for his heroism and leadership as the commanding general during the Revolutionary War. Delegates to the Constitutional Convention chose him to preside over their meetings. Washington was then elected president in 1789 and served two terms.

Drawing Inferences Why do you think Washington was elected president?

Fight for Independence

This painting shows General George Washington leading American troops across the Delaware River to attack British forces.

THE UNITED STATES **257**

Cross-Discipline Activity: Language Arts

Writing a Biography

1. Review the information about George Washington with students, including the biography feature above. Explain that one way historians record information is through biographies.

2. Ask each student to imagine that he or she has been asked to write a biography about George Washington. Have students choose one event or accomplishment from Washington's life.

3. Have each student write about the event or accomplishment. Students should include

why they think this event was important in American history. Ask students to consider how things might be different today if that event had not happened.

4. Have volunteers share their biographies with the class. **LS Verbal/Linguistic**

   Alternative Assessment Handbook, Rubrics 4: Biographies; and 37: Writing Assignments

257

Map Zone: Western Expansion of the United States Review the map with students. Ask the following questions:

Recall The discovery of what natural resource brought nearly 80,000 people to California in the late 1840s? *gold*

Analyze What was the first territory gained after 1783? *Louisiana*

▶ Map Zone Transparency: Western Expansion of the United States

Activity **Imagining Life on the Oregon Trail** Have students imagine they are among the first pioneers to travel the Oregon Trail. Have them write five diary entries describing the landscape, what they ate, how they traveled, and who traveled with them. Finally, have students describe the place where they chose to settle. Ask volunteers to share their diaries with the rest of the class. **LS Verbal/Linguistic**

📝 Alternative Assessment Handbook, Rubric 40: Writing to Describe

📖 RF: Literature, *The Adventures of Tom Sawyer* by Mark Twain

📖 RF: Geography and History, *The Transcontinental Railroad*

↗ **hmhsocialstudies.com**

Online Resources
Activity: The Civil War

These first settlers that traveled west were called **pioneers**. Many followed the 2,000-mile Oregon Trail west from Missouri to the Oregon Territory. Groups of families traveled together in wagons pulled by oxen or mules. The trip was harsh. Food, supplies, and water were scarce.

ACADEMIC VOCABULARY
development the process of growing or improving

While many pioneers headed west seeking land, others went in search of gold. The discovery of gold in California in the late 1840s had a major impact on the country. Tens of thousands of people moved to California.

By 1850 the population of the United States exceeded 23 million and the country stretched all the way to the Pacific Ocean. As the United States expanded, the nation's economy also grew. By the late 1800s, the country was a major producer of goods like steel, oil, and textiles, or cloth products. The steel industry grew around cities that were located near coal and iron ore deposits. Most of those new industrial cities were in the Northeast and Midwest. The country's economy also benefited from the **development** of waterways and railroads. This development helped industry and people move farther into the interior.

Attracted by a strong economy, millions of people immigrated, or came to, the United States for better jobs and land. Immigration from European countries was especially heavy in the late 1800s and early 1900s. As a result of this historical pattern of immigration, the United States is a culturally diverse nation today.

Western Expansion of the United States

↗ hmhsocialstudies.com
ANIMATED GEOGRAPHY

map zone Geography Skills

Movement The United States expanded in about 100 years as the government gained territory and people moved west.
1. **Identify** What territory did the United States acquire in 1846?
2. **Analyzing** How were Louisiana and Alaska acquired?

258 CHAPTER 11

Differentiating Instruction

Below Level

English-Language Learners

1. Review the Western Expansion map with students. Point to and read aloud the date for each territory.

2. Have students fold a clean sheet of paper in half to create a crease down the center of the paper. Ask students to list each territory from east to west on the left half of the paper. On the right half of the paper, have students arrange the list in chronological order, from earliest to latest.

3. Point out that the land within the borders of the United States today was acquired in just over 100 years. **LS Visual/Spatial**

📝 Alternative Assessment Handbook, Rubric 7: Charts

Wars and Peace

The United States fought in several wars during the 1900s. Many Americans died in two major wars, World Wars I and II. After World War II, the United States and the Soviet Union became rivals in what was known as the Cold War. The Cold War lasted until the early 1990s, when the Soviet Union collapsed. U.S. troops also served in long wars in Korea in the 1950s and in Vietnam in the 1960s and 1970s. In 1991, the U.S. fought Iraq in the Persian Gulf War. More recently, the U.S. invaded Iraq in 2003 and is helping Iraqis rebuild their country today.

Today the United States is a member of many international organizations. The headquarters of one such organization, the United Nations (UN), is located in New York City. About 190 countries are UN members. The United States is one of the most powerful members.

Government and Citizenship

The United States has a limited, democratic government based on the U.S. Constitution. This document spells out the powers and functions of the branches of the federal government. The federal government includes an elected president and Congress. In general, the federal government handles issues affecting the whole country, but many powers are left to the 50 state governments. Counties and cities also have their own local governments. Many of these local governments provide services to the community such as trash collection, road building, electricity, and public transportation.

Rights and Responsibilities

American citizens have many rights and responsibilities, including the right to vote. Starting at age 18, U.S. citizens are allowed to vote. They are also encouraged

to play an active role in government. For example, Americans can call or write their public officials to ask them to help solve problems in their communities. Without people participating in their government, the democratic process suffers.

READING CHECK Sequencing What were some major events in the history of the United States?

Primary Source

HISTORIC DOCUMENT
The Constitution

On September 17, 1787, state delegates gathered in Philadelphia to create a constitution, a written statement of the powers and functions of the new government of the United States. The Preamble, or introduction, to the U.S. Constitution is shown below. It states the document's general purpose.

"*We the People* of the United States, in order to form a more perfect Union, establish justice, insure domestic tranquillity, provide for the common defense, promote the general welfare, and secure the blessings of liberty to ourselves and our posterity, do ordain and establish this Constitution for the United States of America."

Americans wanted peace within the United States and a national military force.

preamble

They wanted to ensure freedoms for themselves and for future generations.

ANALYSIS SKILL ANALYZING PRIMARY SOURCES

How do you think the ideas that appear in the Preamble affect your daily life?

THE UNITED STATES **259**

259

❷ People and Culture

The people and culture of the United States are very diverse.

Recall Why are so many religious holidays celebrated in the United States? *because different cultures practice different religions*

Identify What does it mean to be bilingual? *to speak two different languages*

Recall From which continent did the ancestors of most Americans come? *Europe*

Explain What is one reason that the United States population is so diverse? *Immigrants came and still come to the United States from around the world. They brought different languages, religions, and cultural practices.*

Activity **Immigration Pros and Cons** Organize students into two groups. Direct students to research the possible advantages and disadvantages of immigration to the United States. Then hold a debate on the issue. To extend this activity, have students research immigration policies of other countries, such as Canada, Costa Rica, and Brazil, and compare their policies to those of the United States.

LS Verbal/Linguistic

📄 Alternative Assessment Handbook, Rubric 10: Debates

📄 **RF:** Primary Source: *Up from Slavery*

People and Culture

About 7 out of 10 Americans are descended from European immigrants. However, the United States is also home to people of many other cultures and ethnic groups. As a result, the United States is a diverse nation where many languages are spoken and different religions and customs are practiced. The blending of these different cultures has helped produce a unique American culture.

Ethnic Groups in the United States

FOCUS ON READING
What details would be included under a category called *ethnic groups*?

Some ethnic groups in the United States include Native Americans, African Americans, Hispanic Americans, and Asian Americans. As you can see on the maps on the next page, higher percentages of these ethnic groups are concentrated in different areas of the United States.

For thousands of years, Native Americans were the only people living in the Americas. Today, most Native Americans live in the western United States. Many Native Americans are concentrated in Arizona and New Mexico.

Even though African Americans live in every region of the country, some areas of the United States have a higher percentage of African Americans. For example, a higher percentage of African Americans live in southern states. Many large cities also have a high percentage of African Americans. On the other hand, descendants of people who came from Asian countries, or Asian Americans, are mostly concentrated in California.

Many Hispanic Americans originally migrated to the United States from Mexico, Cuba, and other Latin American countries. As you can see on the map of Hispanic Americans, a higher percentage of Hispanic Americans live in the southwestern states. These states border Mexico.

Language

What language or languages do you hear as you walk through the hall of your school? Since most people in the United States speak English, you probably hear English spoken every day. However, in many parts of the country, English is just one of many languages you might hear. Are you or is someone you know bilingual? People who speak two languages are **bilingual**.

Today more than 55 million U.S. residents speak a language in addition to English. These languages include Spanish, French, Chinese, Russian, Arabic, Navajo, and many others.

After English, Spanish is the most widely spoken language in the United States. About 34 million Americans speak Spanish at home. Many of these people live near the border between the United States and Mexico and in Florida.

Religion

Americans also practice many religious faiths. Most people are Christians. However, some are Jewish or Muslim. A small percentage of Americans are Hindu or Buddhist. What religions are practiced in your community? Your community might have Christian churches, Jewish synagogues, and Islamic mosques, as well as other places of worship. Religious variety adds to our country's cultural diversity.

With so many different religions, many religious holidays are celebrated in the United States. These holidays include the Christian celebrations of Christmas and Easter and the Jewish holidays of Hanukkah, Yom Kippur, and Rosh Hashanah. Some African Americans also celebrate Kwanzaa, a holiday that is based on a traditional African festival. Muslims celebrate the end of the month of Ramadan with a large feast called 'Id al-Fitr.

260 CHAPTER 11

Collaborative Learning

At Level

Diversity in the Community

Prep Required

Materials: information about immigrants to your community

1. Obtain information about your community's history. Ask students in what countries community members lived before coming to America. Write the countries on the board.

2. Have students interpret the results. How many countries were listed? From which continent did most community members come? Using a globe or world map, have each student locate the countries.

3. Find out how much students know about the cultures of their community. What language(s) were originally spoken? Do people celebrate special holidays or traditions?

4. Have students write about a community tradition they enjoy. Ask volunteers to share their stories with the class.

LS Visual/Spatial, Verbal/Linguistic

📄 Alternative Assessment Handbook, Rubrics 11: Discussions; 14: Group Activity; and 37: Writing Assignments

Answers

Focus on Reading *possible answers—Native Americans are concentrated in the Southwest; many African Americans live in southern states; many Asian Americans live in or near New York and California; many Hispanic Americans live in states bordering Mexico.*

Distribution of Selected Ethnic Groups, 2000

Legend (Hispanic Americans):
- 0%–5%
- 6%–10%
- 11%–25%
- 26%–98%

Hispanic Americans

Legend (Native Americans):
- 0%–2%
- 3%–10%
- 11%–25%
- 26%–95%

Native Americans

Diverse America
People of different ethnic groups enjoy a concert in Miami, Florida. Like most large American cities, Miami has a very diverse population. More than half of all Hispanic Americans of Cuban descent live in Miami.

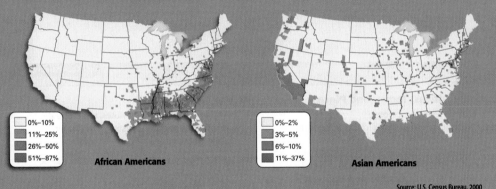

Legend (African Americans):
- 0%–10%
- 11%–25%
- 26%–50%
- 51%–87%

African Americans

Legend (Asian Americans):
- 0%–2%
- 3%–5%
- 6%–10%
- 11%–37%

Asian Americans

Source: U.S. Census Bureau, 2000

map zone
Geography Skills

Regions These maps show population information from the U.S. Census. Every 10 years, Americans answer census questions about their race or ethnic group.

1. **Locate** In what region of the United States does the highest percentage of African Americans live?
2. **Analyze** Why do you think many Hispanic Americans live in the southwestern United States?

THE UNITED STATES **261**

Linking to Today

Diversity America's history is directly linked to today's diverse population and culture. Lawmakers still look to the U.S. Constitution to run our government and to ensure the safety of and equal rights for all U.S. citizens, regardless of race or ethnicity.

• Review & Assess •

Close

Discuss with students how the United States became a nation and how its history influenced America's diverse culture.

Review

📝 Online Quiz, Section 2

Assess

SE Section 2 Assessment
📄 PASS: Section 2 Quiz
📄 Alternative Assessment Handbook

Reteach/Classroom Intervention

📄 Guided Reading Workbook, Section 2
💿 Interactive Skills Tutor CD-ROM

Answers

Reading Check *It has led to the introduction of many types of traditions, religions, foods, music, and other cultural practices.*

262

Foods and Music

Diversity shows itself through cultural practices. In addition to language and religion, cultural practices include the food we eat and the music we listen to.

America's food is as diverse as the American people. Think about some of the foods you have eaten this week. You may have eaten Mexican tacos, Italian pasta, or Japanese sushi. These dishes are now part of the American diet.

Different types of music from around the world have also influenced American culture. For example, salsa music from Latin America is popular in the United States today. Many American musicians now combine elements of salsa into their pop songs. However, music that originated in the United States is also popular in other countries. American musical styles include blues, jazz, rock, and hip hop.

American Popular Culture

As the most powerful country in the world, the United States has tremendous influence around the world. American popular culture, such as movies, television programs, and sports, is popular elsewhere. For example, the *Star Wars* movies are seen by millions of people around the world. Other examples of American culture in other places include the popularity of baseball in Japan, Starbucks coffee shops in almost every major city in the world, and an MTV channel available throughout Asia. As you can see, Americans influence the rest of the world in many ways through their culture.

READING CHECK **Generalizing** How has cultural diversity enriched life in the United States?

SUMMARY AND PREVIEW The history of the United States has helped shape the democratic nation it is today. Drawn to the United States because of its democracy, immigrants from around the world have shaped American culture. In the next section, you will learn about the different regions of the United States and the issues the country is facing today.

Section 2 Assessment

hmhsocialstudies.com
ONLINE QUIZ

Reviewing Ideas, Terms, and Places

1. **a. Define** What is a **colony**?
   b. Make Inferences Why did the pioneers move west?
   c. Elaborate What is an example of the rights and responsibilities that American citizens have?
2. **a. Recall** What language other than English is widely spoken in the United States?
   b. Summarize What are some religions practiced in the United States?
   c. Predict How do you think American culture will be different in the future, and what influences do you think will bring about the changes?

Critical Thinking

3. **Summarizing** Using your notes, write one descriptive sentence about the history, government, people, and culture of the United States.

People — History

Government — Culture

FOCUS ON VIEWING

4. **Thinking about History and Culture** How would you describe the history and culture of the United States? Identify two images for your collage.

262 CHAPTER 11

Section 2 Assessment Answers

1. **a.** A colony is a territory controlled by people from a foreign land.
   b. for land and resources
   c. possible answer—Citizens have the right to vote, and they have the responsibility to participate in government.
2. **a.** Spanish
   b. Americans practice Buddhism, Christianity, Hinduism, Islam, and Judaism.
   c. American culture may become more diverse if immigration continues.

3. Answers will vary, but students' sentences should use descriptive language based on information in this section.

4. possible answer—U.S. history includes several wars and changes to its boundaries. The culture of the United States is very diverse because of immigration. Students' descriptions of images for their collages will vary.

from
Bearstone

by Will Hobbs

About the Reading *In* Bearstone, *writer Will Hobbs tells about an orphaned Native American boy named Cloyd who lives on a Colorado farm. While roaming the nearby canyons, Cloyd finds a relic from his ancestors. The relic is a stone in the shape of a turquoise bear, which becomes his Bearstone, the title of this story.*

AS YOU READ Identify what the mountains mean to Cloyd.

. . . This was a shining new world. To the north and east, peaks still covered with snow shone in the cloudless blue sky. He'd never seen mountains so sharp and rugged, so fierce and splendid. Below him, an eagle soared high above the old man's field. It was a good sign.

Then he remembered his grandmother's parting words as he left for Colorado. She told him something he'd never heard before: their band of Weminuche Utes ❶ hadn't always lived at White Mesa. ❷ Colorado, especially the mountains above Durango, had been their home until gold was discovered there and the white men wanted them out of the way. Summers the people used to hunt and fish in the high mountains, she'd said; they knew every stream, places so out of the way that white men still hadn't seen them. 'So don't feel bad about going to Durango,' she told him.

Cloyd regarded the distant peaks with new strength, a fierce kind of pride he'd never felt before. These were the mountains where his people used to live.

Connecting Literature to Geography

1. **Describing** What details in the first paragraph show us that Cloyd feels happy and at home in these mountains? Which details describe the physical features of these mountains?

2. **Making Inferences** Why did Cloyd's grandmother think he shouldn't feel bad about going to Durango? How does this fact affect his feelings about the mountains of Colorado?

In this book, a Native American boy named Cloyd learns more about his ancestors.

GUIDED READING

WORD HELP

band a group of Native American families

❶ Weminuche Utes are a band of Utes, a Native American cultural group.

❷ White Mesa is a Ute community in Utah where Cloyd lived before he moved to Colorado.

263

Literature

Bearstone

Bearstone

As You Read Ask students how mountains could seem both fierce and splendid. As they read, students should make a list of the things Cloyd's grandmother told him about the mountains. The Weminuche Utes were forced from the mountains by white men who discovered gold there. Until then, the Weminuche Utes had hunted and fished in the high mountains during the summer.

Info to Know

Cloyd's Character Will Hobbs, the author of *Bearstone*, based the character of Cloyd on a Ute boy whom his wife, a teacher, taught to read. The 13-year-old boy was originally from Utah. He had been sent to a Native American group home in Durango, and he was very homesick.

Did you know. . .

Each year a dance is held to honor the grizzly bear. The grizzly bear is thought to teach the Ute people strength, wisdom, and survival.

Cross-Discipline Activity: Literature

At Level | **Standard English Mastery**

Writing What Happens Next

1. Talk with students about what they know of Cloyd's story. Write notes on the board as students list points in the story that reveal something about Cloyd's past, present, and future.

2. Find out what students know of Cloyd's character. Reread the introduction and ask students to think about why Cloyd might secretly name himself "Lone Bear."

3. Have students look up five unfamiliar words from the reading in a dictionary. Have them write the definitions in their own words.

4. Have students write an extension of Cloyd's story, describing what they think happens after Cloyd remembers his grandmother's words. Students should include the words they looked up in Step 3.

5. Ask volunteers to share their story extensions with the class. **LS Verbal/Linguistic**

   Alternative Assessment Handbook, Rubrics 1: Acquiring Information; 11: Discussions; and 39: Writing to Create

Answers

Connecting Literature to Geography 1. *Cloyd describes the world before him as shining and new and mentioned the eagle as a good sign; sharp, rugged, fierce, splendid;* **2.** *Cloyd's grandmother probably told Cloyd not to feel bad about going to Durango because that was where his family originally came from. Cloyd seemed to feel hopeful about going to the mountains.*

264 CHAPTER 11

Bellringer

If YOU lived there. . . Use the **Daily Bellringer Transparency** to help students answer the question.

 Daily Bellringer Transparency, Section 3

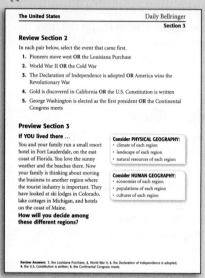

The United States   Daily Bellringer
Section 3

Review Section 2
In each pair below, select the event that came first.

1. Pioneers move west **OR** the Louisiana Purchase
2. World War II **OR** the Cold War
3. The Declaration of Independence is adopted **OR** America wins the Revolutionary War
4. Gold is discovered in California **OR** the U.S. Constitution is written
5. George Washington is elected as the first president **OR** the Continental Congress meets

Preview Section 3

If YOU lived there ...
You and your family run a small resort hotel in Fort Lauderdale, on the east coast of Florida. You love the sunny weather and the beaches there. Now your family is thinking about moving the business to another region where the tourist industry is important. They have looked at ski lodges in Colorado, lake cottages in Michigan, and hotels on the coast of Maine.
How will you decide among these different regions?

Consider PHYSICAL GEOGRAPHY:
· climate of each region
· landscape of each region
· natural resources of each region

Consider HUMAN GEOGRAPHY:
· economies of each region
· populations of each region
· cultures of each region

Review Answers: 1. the Louisiana Purchase; 2. World War II; 3. the Declaration of Independence is adopted; 4. the U.S. Constitution is written; 5. the Continental Congress meets

Academic Vocabulary

Review with students the high-use academic term in this section.

process a series of steps by which a task is accomplished (p. 268)

📝 **RF:** Vocabulary Builder, Section 3

Taking Notes

Have students use the graphic organizer online to take notes on the section. This activity will prepare students for the Section Assessment, in which they will complete a graphic organizer that builds on the information using the Critical Thinking Skill: Finding Main Ideas.

What You Will Learn...

Main Ideas

1. The United States has four regions—the Northeast, South, Midwest, and West.
2. The United States has a strong economy and a powerful military but is facing the challenge of world terrorism.

The Big Idea

The United States has four main regions and faces opportunities and challenges.

Key Terms and Places

megalopolis, *p. 265*
Washington, D.C., *p. 265*
Detroit, *p. 267*
Chicago, *p. 267*
Seattle, *p. 268*
terrorism, *p. 270*

⬇️ **hmhsocialstudies.com**
    TAKING NOTES

Use the graphic organizer online to take notes on the United States today.

The United States Today

If YOU lived there...

You and your family run a small resort hotel in Fort Lauderdale, on the east coast of Florida. You love the sunny weather and the beaches there. Now your family is thinking about moving the business to another region where the tourist industry is important. They have looked at ski lodges in Colorado, lake cottages in Michigan, and hotels on the coast of Maine.

How will you decide among these different regions?

BUILDING BACKGROUND Geography, history, climate, and population give each region of the United States its own style. Some differences between the regions are more visible than others. For example, people in each region speak with different accents and have their favorite foods. Even with some differences, however, Americans are linked by a sense of unity in confronting important issues.

Regions of the United States

Because the United States is such a large country, geographers often divide it into four main regions. These are the Northeast, South, Midwest, and the West. You can see the four regions on the map on the next page. Find the region where you live. You probably know more about your own region than you do the three others. The population, resources, and economies of the four regions are similar in some ways and unique in others.

The Northeast

The Northeast shares a border with Canada. The economy in this region is heavily dependent on banks, investment firms, and insurance companies. Education also contributes to the economy. The area's respected universities include Harvard and Yale.

Teach the Big Idea   At Level

The United States Today

1. **Teach** Ask students the questions in the Main Idea boxes under Direct Teach.
2. **Apply** Have students create their own regional maps of the United States. Ask students to jot down facts they learn about each region.
3. **Review** Have students form groups of three or four to share and compare their completed maps. Have students add any facts they might have missed.

4. **Practice/Homework** Have students add details to their maps using colored pencils. For example, they can create symbols to represent natural resources most valuable to each region. Have students share their finished maps with the class.
   🔲 **Visual/Spatial**
   📄 Alternative Assessment Handbook, Rubrics 3: Artwork; and 20: Map Creation

map zone

Geography Skills

Regions The United States has four geographic and economic regions.

1. **Locate** What region is located on the Pacific Ocean?
2. **Analyze** What region does not border Canada?

THE WORLD ALMANAC
Facts about Countries

Population of Major U.S. Cities

	City	Population
1	New York	8,363,710
2	Los Angeles	3,833,995
3	Chicago	2,853,114
4	Houston	2,242,193
5	Phoenix	1,567,924

New York, New York

hmhsocialstudies.com

Some natural resources of the Northeast states include rich farmland and huge pockets of coal. Used in the steelmaking process, coal remains very important to the region's economy. The steel industry helped make Pittsburgh, in western Pennsylvania, the largest industrial city in the Appalachians.

Today fishing remains an important industry in the Northeast. Major seaports allow companies to ship their products to markets around the world. Cool, shallow waters off the Atlantic coast are good fishing areas. Cod and shellfish such as lobster are the most valuable seafood.

The Northeast is the most densely populated region of the United States. Much of the Northeast is a **megalopolis**, a string of large cities that have grown together. This area stretches along the Atlantic coast from Boston to **Washington, D.C.** The three other major cities in the megalopolis are New York, Philadelphia, and Baltimore.

THE UNITED STATES **265**

265

Direct Teach

Interpreting Maps

United States: Land Use and Resources Review the map and map keys with the students. Ask the following questions:

1. In which state are gold and silver major resources? *Nevada*

2. What is a major resource along the Atlantic coast? *fish*

3. Which region is a major source of coal? *the Northeast*

▶ Map Zone Transparency: United States: Land Use and Resources

Activity **Imports and Exports**
Have groups of students use the Internet or library sources to research major imports and exports of your home state. Have them also research major national imports and exports. Ask students to create a graph or a chart in order to compare and contrast the major national imports and exports with those of your home state.

LS Logical/Mathematical

Alternative Assessment Handbook, Rubric 7: Charts

Linking to Today

Megalopolis and Urban Sprawl Some researchers think that the Northeast megalopolis was at first largely a result of geography. For example, they cite the region's access to the coastline and its quality harbors as key factors in its early development. However, with the growing popularity of the automobile, suburbs—smaller, mainly residential communities near large cities—grew. The result has been an expanded urban landscape, or urban sprawl. Today, other urban areas across the U.S. are expanding, or sprawling, as well. A future map of the U.S. may include another megalopolis—or two!

Answers

Map Zone 1. *coal;* 2. *Commercial farming is done in the Northeast while livestock raising is a major land use in the West.*

266

United States: Land Use and Resources

Major Resources
- 🪨 Coal
- Copper
- Fish
- Gold
- Natural gas
- Oil
- Silver

Land Use
Cotton Major products
- Commercial farming
- Livestock raising
- Forests
- Limited economic activity

0   250   500 Miles
0   250   500 Kilometers
Projection: Albers Equal Area

map zone
Geography Skills

Human-Environment Interaction This map shows the major land uses and resources of the United States that affect the daily lives of Americans.

1. **Identify** What major natural resource is found in Pennsylvania?
2. **Contrast** How is land use in the Northeast different from land use in the West?

At least 40 million people live in this urban area. All of these cities were founded during the colonial era. They grew because they were important seaports. Today these cities are industrial and financial centers.

The South

The South is a region that includes long coastlines along the Atlantic Ocean and the Gulf of Mexico. Along the coastal plains rich soils provide farmers with abundant crops of cotton, tobacco, and citrus fruit.

In recent years, the South has become more urban and industrial and is one of the country's fastest-growing regions. The

South's cities, such as Atlanta, have grown along with the economy. The Atlanta metropolitan area has grown from a population of only about 1 million in 1960 to more than 5 million today.

Other places in the South have also experienced growth in population and industry. The Research Triangle in North Carolina is an area of high-tech companies and several large universities. The Texas Gulf Coast and the lower Mississippi River area have huge oil refineries and petrochemical plants. Their products, which include gasoline, are mostly shipped from the ports of Houston and New Orleans.

266 CHAPTER 11

Differentiating Instruction

Struggling Readers   Below Level

To help struggling readers, have them match the symbols in the key to the symbols on the map. Read aloud the name for each symbol and have students find the symbols on the map.

LS Visual/Spatial

Alternative Assessment Handbook, Rubric 21: Map Reading

Advanced/Gifted and Talented   Above Level

Discuss how today's economy supports the resources shown on the map above. Ask students how resources in your region are used. Remind students that people all over the country depend on its resources.

LS Verbal/Linguistic, Visual/Spatial

Alternative Assessment Handbook, Rubric 11: Discussions

1 Farms with fertile soils like this one in Wisconsin cover much of the rural Midwest.

2 Large white containers, shown here at the Port of Houston, store oil from the Gulf Coast.

Millions of Americans vacation in the South, which makes the travel industry profitable in the region. Warm weather and beautiful beaches draw many vacationers to resorts in the South. You may not think of weather and beaches when you think about industry, but you should. Resort areas are an industry because they provide jobs and help local economies grow.

Many cities in the South trade goods and services with Mexico and countries in Central and South America. This trade is possible because several of the southern states are located near these countries. For example, Miami is an important trading port and travel connection with Caribbean countries, Mexico, and South America. Atlanta, Houston, and Dallas are also major transportation centers.

The Midwest

The Midwest is one of the most productive farming regions in the world. The Mississippi River and many of its tributaries carry materials that help create the region's rich soils, which are good for farming. Midwestern farmers grow mostly corn, wheat, and soybeans. Farmers in the region also raise livestock such as dairy cows.

The core of the Midwest's corn-growing region stretches from Ohio to Nebraska. Much of the corn is used to feed livestock, such as beef cattle and hogs.

To the north of the corn-growing region is an area of dairy farms. States with dairy farms are major producers of milk, cheese, and other dairy products. This area includes Wisconsin and most of Michigan and Minnesota. Much of the dairy farm region is pasture, but farmers also grow crops to feed dairy cows.

Many of the Midwest's farm and factory products are shipped to markets by water routes, such as those along the Ohio and Mississippi rivers. The other is through the Great Lakes and the Saint Lawrence Seaway to the Atlantic Ocean.

Most major cities in the Midwest are located on rivers or the Great Lakes. As a result, they are important transportation centers. Farm products, coal, and iron ore are easily shipped to these cities from nearby farms and mines. These natural resources support industries such as automobile manufacturing. For example, **Detroit**, Michigan, is the country's leading automobile producer.

One of the busiest shipping ports on the Great Lakes is **Chicago**, Illinois. The city also has one of the world's busiest airports. Chicago's industries attracted many immigrants in the late 1800s. People moved here to work in the city's steel mills. Today Chicago is the nation's third-largest city.

FOCUS ON READING
As you read about the Midwest, sort the details into three categories.

THE UNITED STATES **267**

Linking to Today

Sustainable Farming Limited water resources, increasing fuel costs, and soil depletion are just some of the key issues facing American farmers today. A possible solution is sustainable farming—farming systems that are self-sustaining and do not deplete natural resources or pollute the environment. For example, some farmers use soil-conservation techniques that limit erosion and protect water resources. To learn more about sustainable farming, contact the National Sustainable Agriculture Information Service at www.attra.org.

Activity Irrigation Diagram Have students draw diagrams of the irrigation system described on this page. Have students number the diagram and write a short description of how each major part works. Talk with students about how irrigation systems have helped improve the farming industry in the United States and around the world.

LS Visual/Spatial, Verbal/Linguistic

Alternative Assessment Handbook, Rubric 3: Artwork

Info to Know

Strip Mining Strip mining is considered the least expensive type of mining in the United States. Strip mining involves removing a layer of earth above a coal deposit. Large machines remove the earth and rocks above the coal supply, or seam. Then the machines lift the uncovered coal from the earth. Removing coal from several seams along a slope of land creates a strange-looking landscape. From a distance, it looks almost like a pyramid or like several boxes stacked on top of each other. Because this type of mining has a large impact on the environment, laws require miners to restore mined areas.

The West

The West is the largest region in the United States. Many western states have large open spaces with few people. The West is not all open spaces, however. Many large cities are on the Pacific coast.

One state on the coast, California, is home to more than 10 percent of the U.S. population. California's mild climate and wealth of resources attract people to the state. Most Californians live in Los Angeles, San Diego, and the San Francisco Bay area. The center of the country's entertainment industry, Hollywood, is in Los Angeles. Farming and the technology industry are also important to California's economy.

The economy of other states in the West is dependent on ranching and growing wheat. Wheat is grown mostly in Montana, Idaho, and Washington.

Much of the farmland in the West must be irrigated, or watered. One method of irrigation uses long sprinkler systems mounted on huge wheels. The wheels

ACADEMIC VOCABULARY
process a series of steps by which a task is accomplished

rotate slowly. This sprinkler system waters the area within a circle. From the air, parts of the irrigated Great Plains resemble a series of green circles.

The West also has rich deposits of coal, oil, gold, silver, copper, and other minerals. However, mining these minerals can cause problems. For example, coal miners in parts of the Great Plains use a **process** called strip mining, which strips away soil and rock. This kind of mining leads to soil erosion and other problems. Today laws require miners to restore mined areas.

In Oregon and Washington, forestry and fishing are two of the most important economic activities. **Seattle** is Washington's largest city. The Seattle area is home to many important industries, including a major computer software company. More than half of the people in Oregon live in and around Portland.

Alaska's economy is largely based on oil, forests, and fish. As in Washington and Oregon, people debate over developing

Olympic National Park

One of the largest sections of coastal wilderness in the United States, shown here, stretches along the Pacific coast in Washington's Olympic National Park.

Differentiating Instruction

Below Level

Struggling Readers

1. Have students work in pairs to write a travel brochure that promotes the West. In the brochure, have students describe the climate, economy, and three major industries (such as farming, mining, forestry, and fishing). You may wish to pair students with good writing skills with struggling readers to complete this activity.

2. Have students include two major cities in the West and explain why they are important to the West's economy.

3. Allow students to decorate their brochures with drawings, clip art, and/or magazine cutouts.

4. Ask volunteers to present their brochures to the class. **LS** Visual/Spatial, Verbal/Linguistic

Alternative Assessment Handbook, Rubrics 3: Artwork; and 14: Group Activity these resources. For example, some people want to limit oil drilling in wild areas of Alaska. Others want to expand drilling to produce more oil.

Hawaii's natural beauty, mild climate, and fertile soils are its most important resources. The islands' major crops are sugarcane and pineapples. Millions of tourists visit the islands each year.

READING CHECK **Comparing** How is the economy of the West different from the economy of the South?

Changes in the Nation

Because of its economic and military strength, the United States is often called the world's only superpower. In recent years, however, the United States has faced many challenges and changes.

Economy

An abundance of natural resources, technology, and plentiful jobs have helped make the U.S. economy strong. The United States also benefits by trading with other countries. The three largest trading partners of the United States are Canada, China, and Mexico. In 1992 the United States, Mexico, and Canada signed the North American Free Trade Agreement, or NAFTA. This agreement made trade easier and cheaper between the three neighboring nations.

Still, the U.S. economy has experienced significant ups and downs since the 1990s. In the 1990s the nation experienced the longest period of economic growth in its history. By the end of 2007, the United States faced a recession, or a sharp decrease in economic activity. In this recession, the housing market collapsed, major banks and businesses failed, and an estimated 8.4 million jobs were lost in the United States.

The War on Terror

In the 1990s the United States began to experience acts of terrorism against its people. Terrorism is the threat or use of violence to intimidate or cause fear for political or social reasons. Some terrorists have been from foreign countries, whereas others have been U.S. citizens.

On September 11, 2001, the United States suffered the deadliest terrorist attack in the country's history. Wanting to disrupt the U.S. economy, 19 Islamic extremist terrorists hijacked four American jets. They crashed two into the World Trade Center and one into the Pentagon.

In response, U.S. President George W. Bush declared a "war on terrorism." He sent military forces to Afghanistan, to kill or capture members of a terrorist group called al-Qaeda, which had planned the September 11 attacks. The United States then turned its attention to Iraq. President Bush believed that Iraqi leader Saddam Hussein was another threat to Americans. In March 2003 Bush sent U.S. troops into Iraq to remove Hussein from power.

Today world leaders are working with the United States to combat terrorism. In the United States, the Department of Homeland Security was established to prevent terrorist attacks on American soil. Many other countries have also increased security within their borders, especially at international airports.

Government

The 2008 presidential election pitted Republican senator John McCain and his running mate Governor Sarah Palin against Democratic senator Barack Obama and his running mate Joe Biden, a fellow senator. The two presidential candidates differed in many ways. For example, McCain was 25 years older than Obama and he held opposing views on the war in Iraq.

THE UNITED STATES **269**

270

Direct Teach

Checking for Understanding

True for False Answer each statement T if it is true or F if it is false. If false, explain why.

1. The deadliest terrorist attack in U.S. history occurred on September 11, 2001. *T*
2. George W. Bush declared the defeat of terrorism. *F: George W. Bush declared war on terrorism.*
3. The Department of Homeland Security helps protect our country. *T*

Review & Assess

Close

Ask students to write a short paragraph summarizing how the economies of different regions in the U.S. are alike and different.

Review

🔲 Online Quiz, Section 3

Assess

SE Section 3 Assessment
📋 PASS: Section 3 Quiz
📋 Alternative Assessment Handbook

Reteach/Classroom Intervention

📋 Guided Reading Workbook, Section 3
💿 Interactive Skills Tutor CD-ROM

Answers

Reading Check *the economy, the war in Iraq, healthcare, and terrorism.*

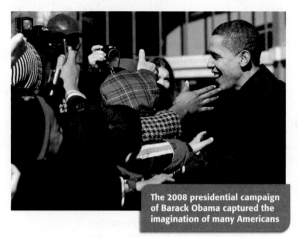

The 2008 presidential campaign of Barack Obama captured the imagination of many Americans

On election day, about 128 million people voted, the highest voter turnout for any election in U.S. history. Barack Obama won the election, winning 365 electoral votes to McCain's 173. Obama became the nation's first African American president.

READING CHECK **Summarizing** What issues shaped the 2008 presidential election?

McCain, a distinguished military veteran, thought that U.S. forces should stay in Iraq indefinitely. Obama supported plans to withdraw U.S. troops as soon as possible. The two also differed over how best to address the economy, taxes, and health care.

SUMMARY AND PREVIEW In this section, you learned about the geographic features, resources, and economic activities found in different regions of the United States. You also learned that the economy and terrorism are two important issues facing the country today. In the next chapter, you will learn about Canada, our neighbor to the north of the United States.

Section 3 Assessment

hmhsocialstudies.com
ONLINE QUIZ

Reviewing Ideas, Terms, and Places

1. **a. Define** What is a **megalopolis**? What major cities are part of the largest megalopolis in the United States?
   b. Compare and Contrast How is land use in the Midwest similar to and different from land use in the South?
   c. Elaborate How are the regions of the United States different from one another?
2. **a. Define** What is **terrorism**? What terrorist attack occurred in September 2001?
   b. Explain How did a recession affect the U.S. economy in 2007?
   c. Elaborate What steps are the United States and other countries taking in an attempt to combat world terrorism?

Critical Thinking

3. **Finding Main Ideas** Use your notes to help you list at least one main idea about the population, resources, and economy of each region.

	Northeast	South	Midwest	West
Population				
Resources				
Economy				

FOCUS ON VIEWING

4. **Thinking about the United States Today** You have read about the regions of the United States, as well as issues facing the country today. What key words, images, and objects might represent what you have learned?

Section 3 Assessment Answers

1. **a.** A megalopolis is a string of large cities that have grown together; Boston, Washington, D.C., New York, Philadelphia, Baltimore
   b. Land is used for farming in the Midwest and in the South. Southern farms produce cotton and citrus fruit; the Midwest produces corn, wheat, and soy.
   c. Each region has its own natural resources and methods of land use.
2. **a.** Terrorism is a violent attack that causes fear. Terrorists attacked the World Trade Center and the Pentagon on September 11, 2001.

   b. The United States is wealthy and has a powerful military.
   c. The United States and other countries are increasing their national security.
3. Answers will vary, but main ideas should fit the appropriate category on the chart.
4. Answers will vary, but students' descriptions, images, and objects should summarize information from Section 3.

Geography's Impact
video series
Review the video to answer the closing question:
What do you think it would be like to live in a country that had no cultural diversity?

Visual Summary

Use the visual summary below to help you review the main ideas of the chapter.

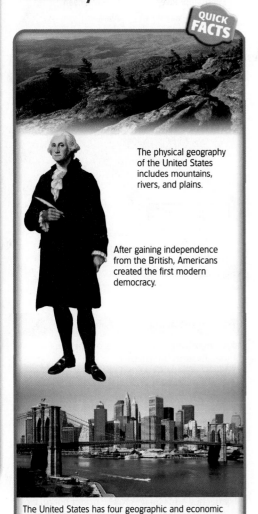

QUICK FACTS

The physical geography of the United States includes mountains, rivers, and plains.

After gaining independence from the British, Americans created the first modern democracy.

The United States has four geographic and economic regions—the Northeast, South, Midwest, and the West.

Reviewing Vocabulary, Terms, and Places

Match the terms or places with their definitions or descriptions.

a. Boston
b. Great Lakes
c. tributary
d. Rocky Mountains
e. colony
f. Appalachian Mountains
g. pioneers
h. bilingual
i. megalopolis
j. Washington, D.C.
k. Chicago
l. terrorism

1. a string of cities that have grown together
2. major seaport in the British colonies
3. stream or river that flows into a larger stream or river
4. violent attacks that cause fear
5. first settlers
6. largest freshwater lake system in the world
7. major mountain range in the West
8. capital of the United States
9. third-largest city in the United States
10. major mountain range in the East
11. having the ability to speak two languages
12. territory controlled by people from a foreign land

Comprehension and Critical Thinking

SECTION 1 *(Pages 248–252)*

13. a. **Identify** What river drains the entire Interior Plains and is the longest river in North America?

Answers

13. c. possible answers—Coal makes electricity. Oil makes gas that fuels your car. Foods grown around the country make up your meals.

14. a. the first settlers to move West
b. possible answer—They come for greater economic opportunities.
c. possible answer—Large entertainment and food companies market their products in other countries.

15. a. the Northeast, the South, the Midwest, the West
b. the Midwest
c. possible answers—increase security at airports, use the Department of Homeland Security

Using the Internet

16. Go to [hmhsocialstudies.com] to access a rubric for this activity.

Social Studies Skills

17. California, Arizona, New Mexico, Texas

18. the Mississippi River

Map Activity

19. A. Pacific Ocean
B. Great Lakes
C. Alaska
D. Atlantic Ocean
E. Mississippi River
F. Rocky Mountains

Focus on Reading and Viewing

20. Students will categorize information from the chapter in a graphic format.

RF: Focus on Reading, Categorizing

21. Rubric Students' collages should include
- at least six descriptions of the United States based on information from all three sections of the chapter
- pictures and objects organized by region
- labels to identify each grouping
- a title for the entire collage

RF: Focus on Viewing, Creating a Collage

SECTION 1 *(continued)*
b. Contrast How are the Appalachians different from the Rocky Mountains?
c. Elaborate What natural resources affect your daily life?

SECTION 2 *(Pages 256–262)*
14. a. Define Who were the pioneers?
b. Draw Conclusions Why do you think people immigrate to the United States?
c. Elaborate How has American culture influenced cultures around the world?

SECTION 3 *(Pages 264–270)*
15. a. Recall What are the four regions of the United States?
b. Compare Is corn grown mostly in the Midwest or the South?
c. Elaborate How should the United States protect itself from terrorism?

Using the Internet

16. Activity: Making a Brochure The United States is a country with a diverse population. This diversity is seen in many of the holidays Americans celebrate. Through your online textbook, research holidays celebrated in the United States. Take notes on what you find. Then use your notes to create an illustrated brochure about three holidays. Be sure to tell about the history, background, and traditions of each holiday.

[hmhsocialstudies.com]

Social Studies Skills

Reading a Political Map Look at the political map of the United States at the beginning of this chapter. Then answer the following questions.
17. What four states border Mexico?
18. What river forms the boundary between Illinois and Missouri?

Map Activity

19. The United States On a sheet of paper, match the letters on the map with their correct labels.

Great Lakes	Rocky Mountains
Mississippi River	Pacific Ocean
Atlantic Ocean	Alaska

[hmhsocialstudies.com] **INTERACTIVE MAP**

FOCUS ON READING AND VIEWING

20. Categorizing For each category below, list details from the chapter.

Geography	People	Regions

21. Creating a Collage Gather the information and images you need to create a collage about the United States. Next, decide how to organize your collage. You might, for example, organize it by region or by time period. After you have attached your images to the poster board, create a label for each grouping. Finally, write a title for the entire collage. Be prepared to display your work and evaluate your classmates' collages for organization and clarity.

Standardized Test Prep

DIRECTIONS: Read questions 1 through 7 and write the letter of the best response. Question 8 will require a brief essay.

1 What physical feature does the Mississippi River and its tributaries drain?

A Piedmont

B Rocky Mountains

C Interior Plains

D Great Lakes

2 What country did the United States gain independence from?

A Britain

B France

C Canada

D Mexico

3 Many pioneers moved west hoping to find

A silver.

B diamonds.

C coal.

D gold.

4 People who are bilingual speak how many languages?

A one

B five

C two

D three

5 NAFTA is a trade agreement among the United States, Mexico, and

A Brazil.

B Canada.

C Britain.

D Australia.

Regions of the United States

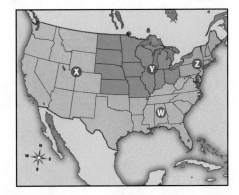

6 Based on the map above, which region is the Midwest?

A X

B W

C Z

D Y

7 Which region is known for its dense population?

A Z

B W

C Y

D X

8 **Extended Response** Look at the map of U.S. regions and the chart of major U.S. cities in Section 3. Write a short essay describing the population, resources, and economies of each region of the United States.

Answers

Standardized Test Prep

1. C

Break Down the Question This question requires students to recall factual information. Refer students who miss it to Section 1.

2. A

Break Down the Question This question requires students to recall factual information. Refer students who miss it to Section 2.

3. D

Break Down the Question While the other three choices list natural resources found in the West, the discovery of gold drove many pioneers westward.

4. C

Break Down the Question This question requires students to recall the definition of a key term in Section 2.

5. B

Break Down the Question NAFTA is a free trade agreement among nations in North America. Canada is the only choice that is located in North America.

6. D

Break Down the Question The Midwest is the green section on the map. Refer students who missed this question to the regional map in Section 3.

7. A

Break Down the Question The Northeast contains a megalopolis, which is a string of large cities close together. Refer students who missed this question to Section 3.

8. Extended Response Students' essays should reflect concepts learned in the chapter and information from the map and chart in Section 1 about the population, resources, and economies of each of the four regions in the United States.

Intervention Resources

Reproducible

- Guided Reading Workbook
- Differentiated Instruction Teacher Management System: Lesson Plans

Technology

- Quick Facts Transparency: The United States Visual Summary
- Differentiated Instruction Modified Worksheets and Tests CD-ROM
- Interactive Skills Tutor CD-ROM

Tips for Test Taking

Read It Again Encourage students to read each item carefully when taking a multiple-choice test. Sometimes, more than one of the answer choices may be correct.

- The correct answer may be "all of the above" or "none of the above."
- The question may be asking for the *best* answer.

Multimedia Classroom

The **HISTORY™ Multimedia Classroom** is a set of exciting new social studies teaching tools featuring award-winning program content. These comprehensive lesson plans, correlated to individual state and national curriculum standards, are easy to use for both teachers and students.

Each lesson contains the following:
- Short video segments that bring history topics to life
- Maps and visual materials
- Discussion and review questions
- Easily printable primary source documents
- Classroom activities and Internet-based activity links

The Multimedia Classroom has been specially designed to be versatile and easily adaptable to existing courses, lesson plans, and syllabi. Every lesson is designed to offer maximum flexibility. Teachers can select entire plans or only the elements they need, allowing them to individually tailor each lesson. Each multimedia lesson is available in CD-ROM format and is accompanied by full-length award-winning programs on DVD from HISTORY™.

For more information or to purchase go to ⬈ hmhsocialstudies.com

Because some of these lessons may contain video material of a sensitive nature, we recommend that teachers and parents review these materials in their entirety before screening them to students.

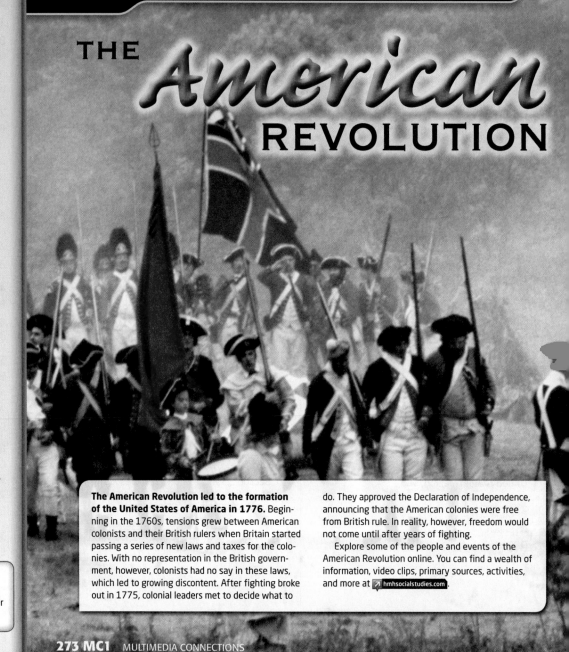

THE *American* REVOLUTION

The American Revolution led to the formation of the United States of America in 1776. Beginning in the 1760s, tensions grew between American colonists and their British rulers when Britain started passing a series of new laws and taxes for the colonies. With no representation in the British government, however, colonists had no say in these laws, which led to growing discontent. After fighting broke out in 1775, colonial leaders met to decide what to do. They approved the Declaration of Independence, announcing that the American colonies were free from British rule. In reality, however, freedom would not come until after years of fighting.

Explore some of the people and events of the American Revolution online. You can find a wealth of information, video clips, primary sources, activities, and more at ⬈ hmhsocialstudies.com .

273 MC1 MULTIMEDIA CONNECTIONS

The American Revolution

Resources ⬈ hmhsocialstudies.com

The following resources come with printable introductions, comprehension and critical thinking questions, transcripts, and vocabulary support.

Full Length DVD

The American Revolution (30 mins)

Video Clips

- Seeds of Revolution (3:02)
- Bloodshed in Boston (2:36)
- Rebellion Arises (1:48)
- Independence! (2:36)
- A Moment of Retreat (1:28)
- The Times That Try Men's Souls (3:31)
- Victory at Saratoga (2:29)
- Final Battle (2:02)
- Victory! (1:42)

Primary Sources

- "Give Me Liberty or Give Me Death"
- The Declaration of Independence
- A Quote from *The Crisis*
- *Crossing the Delaware*
- An Account from Saratoga

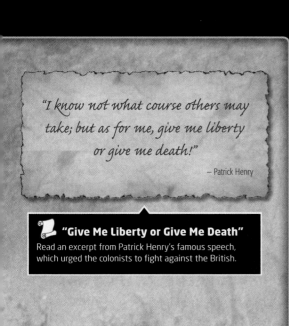

"I know not what course others may take; but as for me, give me liberty or give me death!"

— Patrick Henry

"Give Me Liberty or Give Me Death"
Read an excerpt from Patrick Henry's famous speech, which urged the colonists to fight against the British.

Seeds of Revolution
Watch the video to learn about colonial discontent in the years before the Revolutionary War.

Independence!
Watch the video to learn about the origins of the Declaration of Independence.

Victory!
Watch the video to learn how the American colonists won the Revolutionary War.

THE AMERICAN REVOLUTION **273 MC2**

Lesson Preview

"Give Me Liberty or Give Me Death"

Patrick Henry was a colonial leader of Virginia and a well-known orator during the Revolutionary War. On March 23, 1775, he gave his most famous speech, titled "Give Me Liberty or Give Me Death," to the Virginia Convention at St. John's Church in Richmond, Virginia. In his speech, Henry urged Virginians to organize and prepare for war against the British. His words helped unite many American colonists.

Seeds of Revolution

In the early 1760s, most American colonists felt loyalty toward Britain's King George III and were satisfied living under British rule. But that began to change. Over the next 10 years, the colonists grew frustrated by new laws and taxes the British enacted for the colonies and by their lack of political representation in the British Parliament. The colonists' frustration turned to anger and led many to question their loyalty to a distant ruler and to think about their freedom.

Independence!

When the first battles of the Revolutionary War broke out between American colonists and British soldiers, the colonists lacked organization. But soon the colonists developed better military and political structures. In June of 1775, the Continental Congress appointed Virginian George Washington to head the army. The next year the Continental Congress approved a Declaration of Independence from Britain.

Victory!

After several years of fighting the American colonists, the British began to lack the will and resources to continue the war. In 1782, the British initiated peace talks and the next year signed the Treaty of Paris, officially ending the war. The Americans had won their independence from British rule. With this victory, Americans had much work ahead in their new nation.

Activities
- Blueprint for a Boycott
- History as It Happens
- The Midnight Ride: Fact and Fiction
- What would you Declare?
- The Landscape of War
- Proclaiming Freedom
- "Turning Points"
- Giving Up the Fight
- Moving on: The Treaty of Paris
- Extended Activities

Extended Activities

? **General Review Questions**

? **General Discussion Questions**

📖 **Web Links**

📖 **Bibliography**

Chapter 12 Planning Guide

Canada

Overview	Instructional Resources	
CHAPTER 12 **Essential Question:** How has geography and climate shaped the development of Canada's provinces? 🔊 **Focus on the Essential Question Podcast**	**TOS Differentiated Instruction Teacher Management System:** • Instructional Pacing Guides • Lesson Plans for Differentiated Instruction 📄 **Guided Reading Workbook** 📄 **Resource File:** • Chapter Review • Focus on Reading: Understanding Lists • Focus on Speaking: Creating a Radio Ad • Social Studies Skills: Using Mental Maps and Sketch Maps Experiencing World History and Geography 📄 **Experiencing World History and Geography**	**TOS Calendar Planner** 💿 **Power Presentations with Media Gallery** 💿 **Differentiated Instruction Modified Worksheets and Tests CD-ROM** 💿 **Interactive Skills Tutor CD-ROM** 🔊 **Student Edition on Audio CD-ROM** 🔊 **The World's Music Audio Program** 📺 **Map Zone Transparency:** Canada: Political 📺 **World Outline Maps: Transparencies and Activities** 📹 **Video:** Tech of the Ice Road 📹 **Multimedia Connections** Mexico: Conquest and Courage
Section 1: **Physical Geography** **The Big Idea:** Canada is a huge country with a northerly location, cold climates, and rich resources.	**TOS Differentiated Instruction Teacher Management System:** Section 1 Lesson Plan 📄 **Guided Reading Workbook:** Section 1 📄 **Resource File:** • Vocabulary Builder: Section 1 • Geography for Life: The Changing Geography of Ice Hockey • Primary Source: "O Canada"	📺 **Daily Bellringer Transparency:** Section 1 📺 **Map Zone Transparency:** Canada: Physical
Section 2: **History and Culture** **The Big Idea:** Canada's history and culture reflect Native Canadian and European settlement, immigration, and migration to cities.	**TOS Differentiated Instruction Teacher Management System:** Section 2 Lesson Plan 📄 **Guided Reading Workbook:** Section 2 📄 **Resource File:** • Vocabulary Builder: Section 2 • Geography and History: One Country, Many Cultures • Critical Thinking: Can Canada Survive? • Biography: Mary Pickford • Literature: *Anne of Green Gables* by Lucy Maud Montgomery	📺 **Daily Bellringer Transparency:** Section 2 📺 **Map Zone Transparency:** Canada's Major Languages ↗️ **Internet Activity:** Canada's First Nations
Section 3: **Canada Today** **The Big Idea:** Canada's democratic government oversees the country's regions and economy.	**TOS Differentiated Instruction Teacher Management System:** Section 3 Lesson Plan 📄 **Guided Reading Workbook:** Section 3 📄 **Resource File:** • Vocabulary Builder: Section 3 • Biography: Douglas Jung	📺 **Daily Bellringer Transparency:** Section 3 📺 **Map Zone Transparency:** Regions of Canada ↗️ **Internet Activity:** States vs. Provinces

Review, Assessment, Intervention

 The Americas Transparencies: Canada Visual Summary

 Spanish Chapter Summaries Audio CD

 Progress Assessment Support System (PASS): Chapter Test

 Differentiated Instruction Modified Worksheets CD-ROM: Modified Chapter Test

TOS   ExamView® Assessment Suite (English/Spanish)

 Alternative Assessment Handbook

 Online Assessment Program, in the Interactive Student Edition

---

 PASS: Section 1 Quiz

 Online Quiz: Section 1

 Alternative Assessment Handbook

 PASS: Section 2 Quiz

 Online Quiz: Section 2

 Alternative Assessment Handbook

 PASS: Section 3 Quiz

 Online Quiz: Section 3

 Alternative Assessment Handbook

Supporting Resources

HISTORY

- Multimedia Classroom Global History Series
- Global History Teacher's Guide

Maps Globes Graphs Level F

- Student Workbook
- Teacher's Guide

Social Studies Trade Library Collections

- NCSS Middle School Trade Collection
- Native American Trade Collection

Geography's Impact

Geography's Impact Video Program

- Impact of Immigration

For more information or to purchase go to hmhsocialstudies.com

Power Presentations with Media Gallery

Power Presentations with Media Gallery are visual presentations of each chapter's main ideas. Presentations can be customized by including Quick Facts charts, images from the text, and video clips.

Differentiating Instruction

How do I address the needs of varied learners?
The Target Resource acts as your primary strategy for differentiated instruction.

ENGLISH-LANGUAGE LEARNERS & STRUGGLING READERS

Student Edition on Audio CD Program

Spanish Resources

Spanish Chapter Summaries Audio CD

Teacher One Stop:
- ExamView Assessment Suite, Spanish
- PuzzleView, Spanish

English-Language Learner Strategies and Activities

Additional Resources

Differentiated Instruction Teacher Management System: Lesson Plans for Differentiated Instruction

Resource File:
- Vocabulary Builder Activities
- Social Studies Skills: Using Mental Maps and Sketch Maps

Quick Facts Transparencies:
- Canada Visual Summary

Interactive Skills Tutor CD-ROM

Spanish/English Guided Reading Workbook

SPECIAL NEEDS LEARNERS

The Americas Transparencies
- Canada Visual Summary

Additional Resources

Differentiated Instruction Teacher Management System: Lesson Plans for Differentiated Instruction

Guided Reading Workbook

Resource File: Social Studies Skills: Using Mental Maps and Sketch Maps

Student Edition on Audio CD Program

Interactive Skills Tutor CD-ROM

Graphic Organizer Transparencies with Support for Reading and Writing

ADVANCED/GIFTED AND TALENTED STUDENTS

Differentiated Instruction Teacher Management System

Lesson Plans for Differentiated Instruction provide teachers with strategies to help plan instruction for all learners.

Additional Resources

Resource File:
- Focus on Reading: Understanding Lists
- Focus on Speaking: Creating a Radio Ad
- Literature: *Anne of Green Gables* by Lucy Maud Montgomery

World History and Geography Document-Based Questions Activities

Geography, Science, and Cultures Activities

Experiencing World History and Geography

Differentiated Activities in the Teacher's Edition

- Working with a Globe, p. 277
- Creating a Postcard from Canada, p. 277
- Discussing Cultural Celebrations, Holidays, and Festivals, p. 282

Differentiated Activities in the Teacher's Edition

- Creating a Sequence Chart, p. 283

Differentiated Activities in the Teacher's Edition

- Exploring the St. Lawrence Seaway, p. 277
- Researching Canada's Transcontinental Railroad, p. 282

Teacher One Stop™

How can I manage the lesson plans and support materials for differentiated instruction?

With the Teacher One Stop, you can easily organize and print lesson plans, planning guides, and instructional materials for all learners. The Teacher One Stop includes the following materials to help you differentiate instruction:

- **· Interactive Teacher's Edition**
- **· Calendar Planner and pacing guides**
- **· Editable lesson plans**
- **· All reproducible ancillaries in Adobe Acrobat (PDF) format**
- **· ExamView Assessment Suite (English & Spanish)**
- **· Transparency and video previews**

Interactive Student Edition

Complete online student edition with interactive multimedia support for chapter content assessment and reporting

- Interactive Maps and Notebook
- Standardized Test Prep
- Online Homework Practice and Research Activities
- Current Events
- Chapter-based Internet Activities
- Animated Geography Activities

Essential Question

Introduce the Essential Question

- Point out that because the United States and Canada share such a long border, the two countries have some of the same physical environments. However, Canada is farther north and has a colder climate. Ask students to analyze how this might impact population distribution in Canada.

- Explain that immigrants came to Canada to work on railroads and farms and in mines, forests, and factories. Others were lured by the discovery of gold. Tell students that immigrants contributed to an economic boom in the early 1900s.

- Tell students that the four regions of Canada are separated by vast distances, economic activities, and culture. Discuss how this has impacted Canada's development.

Focus on Reading and Speaking

Reading The Resource File provides a worksheet to help students practice understanding lists.

📑 **RF:** Focus on Reading, Understanding Lists

Speaking The Chapter Resource File provides a worksheet to help students create a radio ad.

📑 **RF:** Focus on Speaking, Creating a Radio Ad

Key to Differentiating Instruction

Below Level

Basic-level activities designed for all students encountering new material

At Level

Intermediate-level activities designed for average students

Above Level

Challenging activities designed for honors and gifted and talented students

Standard English Mastery

Activities designed to improve standard English usage

LS Learning Styles

CHAPTER 12

Canada

Essential Question How has geography and climate shaped the development of Canada's provinces?

❓ What You Will Learn...

In this chapter you will learn about the physical features, climates, and resources of Canada. You will study the history of Canada and the country's different cultures. Finally, you will learn about Canada's government, regions, and economy.

SECTION 1: Physical Geography 276

The Big Idea Canada is a huge country with a northerly location, cold climates, and rich resources.

SECTION 2: History and Culture 280

The Big Idea Canada's history and culture reflect Native Canadian and European settlement, immigration, and migration to cities.

SECTION 3: Canada Today 286

The Big Idea Canada's democratic government oversees the country's regions and economy.

FOCUS ON READING AND SPEAKING

Understanding Lists Identifying a list of the interesting facts that you read about may help you understand the topic you are studying. For example, you could identify facts about Canada's physical features, regions, government, or economy. As you read this chapter, look for lists of facts. **See the lesson, Understanding Lists, on page 527.**

Creating a Radio Ad You are a member of the Canadian tourism board and your job is to develop a radio ad to attract visitors to Canada. Read about Canada in this chapter. Then, write a script for a one-minute radio ad. Be ready to present your ad to the class.

274 CHAPTER 12

Culture Ice hockey is Canada's national sport. Many Canadians grow up playing on frozen lakes.

Map legend:
- ✪ National capital
- ★ Provincial capitals
- ● Other cities

0   250   500 Miles
0   250   500 Kilometers
Projection: Lambert Azimuthal Equal-Area

ARCTIC OCEAN
Alaska (UNITED STATES)
YUKON TERRITORY — ★Whitehorse
NORTHWEST TERRITORIES — Yellowknife
BRITISH COLUMBIA
ALBERTA — ★Edmonton
Vancouver Island — Vancouver — Calgary
Victoria★
PACIFIC OCEAN

Introduce the Chapter

At Level

Good Neighbor Canada

1. Tell students that Canada and the United States have the longest undefended border in the world. Although security has tightened since the 2001 terrorist attacks, citizens of both countries, as well as trade goods, move relatively freely across this border.

2. Focus discussion on reasons why U.S.-Canada relations have remained peaceful. Possible response: *shared history, trade ties, language, democratic values*

3. As a class make a graphic organizer (Venn diagram) of ways the two countries might be alike and different. Areas for consideration can include landforms, natural resources, climate, language, customs, religions, government, population, trade ties, economy, and foreign policy.

4. Ask students to create a list of questions about Canada and look for answers in the chapter. **LS** Verbal/Linguistic, Visual/Spatial

📑 Alternative Assessment Handbook, Rubric 1: Acquiring Information

GREENLAND
(DENMARK)

Baffin
Bay

Arctic
Circle

Iqaluit

NUNAVUT

Labrador
Sea

Hudson
Bay

NEWFOUNDLAND
AND LABRADOR

SASKATCHEWAN

Saskatchewan
R.

MANITOBA

QUEBEC

ATLANTIC
OCEAN

★ St. John's

Regina

Lake
Winnipeg

Winnipeg

ONTARIO

PRINCE EDWARD ISLAND

Charlottetown ★

Fredericton ★

NOVA SCOTIA
★ Halifax

Quebec ★

Montreal ★

St. Lawrence R.

NEW BRUNSWICK

Lake
Huron

Ottawa ⊛

Lake
Superior

Toronto ★

UNITED STATES

Lake
Michigan

Windsor ★

Lake
Ontario

Lake
Erie

HISTORY

Technology of the
Ice Road

hmhsocialstudies.com VIDEO

map zone

Geography Skills

Place Ten provinces and three
territories make up Canada.

1. **Locate** What is the provincial capital of Manitoba?
2. **Make Inferences** What do
you think the climate is like in
the Yukon Territory? Why?

History Since 1867,
leaders of Canada's
democratic government
have met in the nation's
parliament building in
Ottawa.

Geography Canada's physical geography ranges
from the rocky Atlantic coast shown here to vast
interior plains and mountains in the west.

275

Explore the Map and Pictures

Canada: Political Tell students that
Canada has the longest coastline in
the world. Have them study the map
to explain what makes its coastline so
long. Emphasize the many peninsulas,
islands, and inlets as well as Canada's
size. Ask: On which coast might ports
be closed part of the year? Why? *Arctic
coast, icebound* Have students name
three bodies of water that Canada and
the United States share. *Atlantic Ocean,
Pacific Ocean, Great Lakes*

Analyzing Visuals Why is ice hockey
a popular sport in Canada? *long cold
winters with many frozen lakes for
hockey games* Why might the nation's
capital be located in southern Canada?
warmer climate, better transportation
What economic activity might be important on the Atlantic coast? *fishing*

▶ Map Zone Transparency: Canada:
Political

↗ hmhsocialstudies.com
Teacher Resources

Differentiating Instruction

At Level

Struggling Readers

Materials: globe

1. On a globe, have students find the area shown
on the map. Note Canada's location relative
to the North Pole. Have students name other
countries that surround the North Pole. Have
students describe what they know about the
climates of these countries and then make
predictions about Canada's climate.

2. Define the term *Arctic Circle* and note its
location at approximately 66°30 N. Explain
that within the area from the Arctic Circle to the

North Pole, the sun does not rise at all for one
or more days each year. Usually this period of
darkness begins around December 21. In the
summer, the reverse is true with nearly 24 hours
of daylight beginning around June 21. It remains
dark at the North Pole for 6 months of the year.

3. Have students write paragraphs explaining
how they would like living within the Arctic
Circle on the shortest and longest days of the
year. LS **Visual/Spatial, Verbal/Linguistic**

📝 Alternative Assessment Handbook, Rubric 41:
Writing to Express

Answers

Map Zone 1. *Winnipeg;* **2.** *cold,
because it is close to the Arctic Ocean*

Preteach

Bellringer

If YOU lived there. . . Use the **Daily Bellringer Transparency** to help students answer the question.

▶️ Daily Bellringer Transparency, Section 1

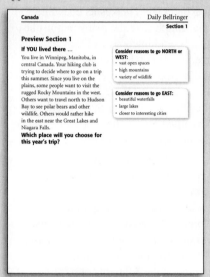

Key Terms and Places

📝 **RF:** Vocabulary Builder, Section 1

Taking Notes

Have students use the graphic organizer online to take notes on the section. This activity will prepare students for the Section Assessment, in which they will complete a graphic organizer that builds on the information using the Critical Thinking Skill: Generalizing.

SECTION 1

Physical Geography

What You Will Learn...

Main Ideas

1. A huge country, Canada has a wide variety of physical features, including rugged mountains, plains, and swamps.
2. Because of its northerly location, Canada is dominated by cold climates.
3. Canada is rich in natural resources like fish, minerals, fertile soil, and forests.

The Big Idea

Canada is a huge country with a northerly location, cold climates, and rich resources.

Key Terms and Places

Rocky Mountains, *p. 276*
St. Lawrence River, *p. 276*
Niagara Falls, *p. 276*
Canadian Shield, *p. 277*
Grand Banks, *p. 278*
pulp, *p. 279*
newsprint, *p. 279*

hmhsocialstudies.com
TAKING NOTES

Use the graphic organizer online to take notes on the physical geography of Canada.

If **YOU** lived there...

You live in Winnipeg, Manitoba, in central Canada. Your hiking club is trying to decide where to go on a trip this summer. Since you live on the plains, some people want to visit the rugged Rocky Mountains in the west. Others want to travel north to Hudson Bay to see polar bears and other wildlife. Others would rather hike in the east near the Great Lakes and Niagara Falls.

Which place will you choose for this year's trip?

> **BUILDING BACKGROUND** A long international boundary separates Canada and the United States. With the exception of the St. Lawrence River and the Great Lakes, there is no actual physical boundary between the two countries. Rivers, lakes, prairies, and mountain ranges cross the border.

Physical Features

Did you know that Canada is the second-largest country in the world? Russia is the only country in the world that is larger than Canada. The United States is the third-largest country in the world and shares many physical features with Canada.

As you look at the map on the following page, see if you can find the physical features that the United States and Canada share. You may notice that mountains along the Pacific coast and the **Rocky Mountains** extend north into western Canada from the western United States. Broad plains stretch across the interiors of both countries. In the east, the two countries share a natural border formed by the **St. Lawrence River**. An important international waterway, the St. Lawrence links the Great Lakes to the Atlantic Ocean.

The United States and Canada also share a spectacular physical feature called **Niagara Falls**. The falls are located on the Niagara River between the province of Ontario and New York State.

Teach the Big Idea

At Level

Physical Geography

1. **Teach** Ask students the questions in the Main Idea boxes under Direct Teach.

2. **Apply** Have students make a three-columned chart, labeling the columns: *physical features, climate,* and *resources.* As they read the section, have them list words or phrases that describe each aspect of Canada's geography. After completing the chart, have students circle the items that are assets or advantages for Canada and underline any geographic features that have

disadvantages. Some, such as the Canadian Shield and Rocky Mountains, will have both.

3. **Review** Have students discuss both advantages and disadvantages of Canada's size, location, climate, and landforms.

4. **Practice/Homework** Have students pick one geographic feature they would change and write a paragraph telling why.

📘 **Verbal/Linguistic, Interpersonal, Intrapersonal**

Alternative Assessment Handbook, Rubric 7: Charts

Created by the waters of the Niagara River, the falls flow between two of the Great Lakes—Lake Erie and Lake Ontario. The falls here plunge an average of 162 feet (50 m) down a huge ledge. That is higher than many 15-story buildings!

Canada has a region of rocky uplands, lakes, and swamps called the **Canadian Shield**. See on the map how this feature curves around Hudson Bay. The Shield covers about half the country.

Farther north, Canada stretches all the way up to the Arctic Ocean. The land here is covered with ice year-round. Ellesmere Island is very rugged with snow-covered mountains and jagged coastlines. Very few people live this far north, but wildlife such as the polar bear and the Arctic wolf have adapted to the harsh environment.

READING CHECK **Summarizing** What are the major physical features of Canada?

hmhsocialstudies.com INTERACTIVE MAP
Canada: Physical

Geography Skills

Place Canada is located between the United States and the Arctic Ocean.
1. **Locate** What mountain range has the highest elevation?
2. **Draw Conclusions** How does Canada's northerly location affect its climate?

ELEVATION

Feet	Meters
13,120	4,000
6,560	2,000
1,640	500
656	200
(Sea level) 0	0 (Sea level)
Below sea level	Below sea level

Projection: Lambert Azimuthal Equal-Area

Mist rises over Niagara Falls where the Niagara River forms a natural boundary between the United States and Canada.

CANADA **277**

• **Direct Teach** •

Main Idea

❶ **Physical Features**

A huge country, Canada has a wide variety of physical features, including rugged mountains, plains, and swamps.

Recall What are three physical features shared by Canada and the United States? What bodies of water form part of Canada's southern border? *Coast Mountains, Rocky Mountains, St. Lawrence River, Niagara Falls; St. Lawrence River, Great Lakes*

Evaluate Would the Canadian Shield be a good region for farming? Why or why not? *no, land is rocky not flat, hard to plow, filled with lakes and swamps*

RF: Geography for Life, The Changing Geography of Ice Hockey

Map Zone Transparency: Canada: Physical

Did you know. . .

Niagara Falls is still a popular spot for honeymooners and tourists, but in the late 1800s and early 1900s it also attracted many thrill seekers. They took their chances going over the falls in barrels, boats, and rubber balls. The most celebrated was the French acrobat Blondin. He walked across a tightrope 1,100 feet long strung 160 feet above the falls for the first time in 1859. Stunting was outlawed in 1912.

Differentiating Instruction

Struggling Readers
Below Level

Have students take turns locating Canada's physical features, including those shared with the United States, on a wall map of North America. Have students work in pairs to create a postcard from Canada. Ask them to draw a physical feature on one side and a note to a friend describing where the feature is located and what it looks like on the other side.

Verbal/Linguistic

Alternative Assessment Handbook Rubric 40: Writing to Describe

Advanced/Gifted and Talented
At Level
Research Required

Have students use the library, Internet, or other resources to find out how locks and canals are used on the St. Lawrence Seaway. Have students give a short talk on how the system of canals and locks works using an illustration or diagram to explain the process of raising or lowering ships.

Verbal/Linguistic

Alternative Assessment Handbook Rubric 29: Presentations

Answers

Reading Check *rugged mountains, broad plains, Canadian Shield, Niagara Falls*

Map Zone 1. *Coast Mountains;* **2.** *It provides Canada with cool to freezing temperatures year-round.*

Main Idea

❷ Climate

Because of its northerly location, Canada is dominated by cold climates.

Explain Why does Canada have a colder climate than the United States? *farther from equator, at much higher latitudes*

Analyze Why does southern Canada have a warmer climate than northern Canada? *closer to equator and at lower latitudes*

Make Inferences What is one factor that contributes to the mild climate along the coast of British Columbia? *location on Pacific Ocean*

Connect to Science

Equator to Poles The sun's rays fall most directly at the equator and less directly closer to the poles. The farther away from the equator the sun shines, the more indirect, slanted, and diffuse its rays are. Less intense rays produce lower temperatures, resulting in colder climates.

Linking to Today

All Fished Out For centuries fishing boats traveled from Japan, Russia, Europe, and elsewhere to fish for cod and other fish in the Grand Banks. In the 1970s declining fish catches led Canada to ban foreign fishing in its waters. Some foreign ships ignored the ban and some Canadian fishermen continued to overfish. By the 1990s cod had all but disappeared. From 1992 to 1998 Canada closed the Grand Banks to cod fishing. Some fishing is now allowed, but fish stocks are not yet back to normal.

Answers

Focus on Reading *subarctic, tundra, ice cap, humid and relatively mild*

Reading Check *far north has tundra and ice cap climates, central and northern Canada subarctic climate, central and eastern humid and relatively mild, British Columbia coast mild, inland southern Canada colder and drier*

278

Climate

FOCUS ON READING
What climates would you include in a list of the climates of Canada?

Canada's location greatly influences the country's climate. Canada is located far from the equator at much higher latitudes than the United States. This more northerly location gives Canada cool to freezing temperatures year-round.

The farther north you go in Canada, the colder it gets. The coldest areas of Canada are located close to the Arctic Circle. Much of central and northern Canada has a subarctic climate. The far north has tundra and ice cap climates. About half of Canada lies in these extremely cold climates.

The central and eastern parts of southern Canada have a much different climate. It is humid and relatively mild. However, the mildest area of Canada is along the coast of British Columbia. This location on the Pacific coast brings rainy winters and mild temperatures. Inland areas of southern Canada are colder and drier.

READING CHECK **Categorizing** What are Canada's climates?

Resources

Canada is incredibly rich in natural resources such as fish, minerals, and forests. Canada's Atlantic and Pacific coastal waters are among the world's richest fishing areas. Off the Atlantic coast lies a large fishing ground near Newfoundland and Labrador called the **Grand Banks**. Here, cold waters from the Labrador Sea meet the warm waters of the Gulf Stream. These conditions are ideal for the growth of tiny organisms, or plankton, that fish like to eat. As a result, large schools of fish gather at the Grand Banks. However, recent overfishing of this region has left many fishers in Canada unemployed.

Minerals are also valuable resources in Canada. The Canadian Shield contains many mineral deposits. Canada is a main source of the world's nickel, zinc, and uranium. Lead, copper, gold, and silver are also important resources. Saskatchewan has large deposits of potash, a mineral used to make fertilizer. Alberta produces most of Canada's oil and natural gas.

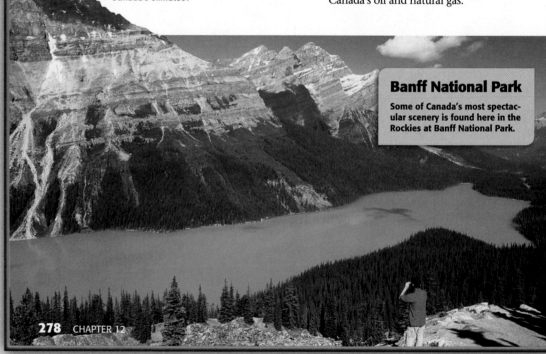

Banff National Park
Some of Canada's most spectacular scenery is found here in the Rockies at Banff National Park.

278 CHAPTER 12

Collaborative Learning

Predicting Effects

1. Divide students into three groups called *Physical Features, Climate,* and *Natural Resources.* Have each group make predictions that answer these questions: What effect might Canada's physical features/climate/natural resources have on where people live, how they earn a living, and the kinds of sports and recreation they enjoy?

2. Have each group create a cause-and-effect chart showing its predictions. Have the groups share their charts with the class, giving reasons for choices.

Causes → Effects

3. Conclude by asking students which geographic factor they think most heavily influences how people in their community live today. **LS Interpersonal, Verbal/Linguistic**

Alternative Assessment Handbook, Rubrics 6: Cause and Effect; and 13: Graphic Organizers

Satellite View

The city of Windsor, Ontario, lies across the Detroit River from Detroit, Michigan.

Agriculture in Ontario

In this satellite image, crop fields in different stages of growth appear scattered throughout the province of Ontario. These rectangular fields of vegetation appear red at their height of growth and white after the crops are harvested. Rich soils and a mild climate in this region, which lies north of Lake Erie, make it one of Canada's most fertile regions. Crops grown here include wheat, soybeans, corn, and a variety of vegetables. Some of these crops are exported to the United States through the Canadian port of Windsor to Detroit, Michigan, just across the Detroit River. Both cities appear in this image as shades of blue and brown.

Drawing Conclusions What is the economy of southern Ontario based on?

Vast areas of forests stretch across most of Canada from Labrador to the Pacific coast. These trees provide lumber and pulp. **Pulp**—softened wood fibers—is used to make paper. The United States, the United Kingdom, and Japan get much of their newsprint from Canada. **Newsprint** is cheap paper used mainly for newspapers.

READING CHECK **Drawing Conclusions** How do Canada's major resources affect its economy?

SUMMARY AND PREVIEW In this section, you learned that Canada shares many physical features with the United States. However, Canada's geography is also different. Due to its northerly location, Canada has a cold climate. Fish, minerals, fertile soil, and forests are all important natural resources. In the next section, you will learn about the history and culture of Canada.

Section 1 Assessment

hmhsocialstudies.com
ONLINE QUIZ

Reviewing Ideas, Terms, and Places

1. **a. Recall** What river links the Great Lakes to the Atlantic Ocean?
   b. Explain What physical features does **Niagara Falls** flow between?
   c. Develop If you were to live in Canada, where would you not want to live?
2. **a. Describe** How is Canada's climate related to its northerly location?
   b. Draw Conclusions Where would you expect to find Canada's coldest climate? Why?
3. **a. Define** What is the **Grand Banks**?
   b. Interpret How are Canada's forests a valuable resource?

Critical Thinking

4. **Generalizing** Using your notes on Canada's resources, identify the location of each type of resource.

Resources → Location

FOCUS ON SPEAKING

5. **Writing about Physical Geography** What information about Canada's physical features, climate, and resources might visitors find appealing? Jot down what descriptions you want to include in your radio ad.

CANADA **279**

279

Bellringer

If YOU lived there. . . Use the **Daily Bellringer Transparency** to help students answer the question.

Daily Bellringer Transparency, Section 2

Canada   Daily Bellringer
                                                Section 2

Review Section 1

Indicate whether each sentence below is **TRUE** or **FALSE**. If the sentence is false, change the underlined word to make the sentence true.

1. The Canadian Shield is an important seaway that links the Great Lakes to the Atlantic Ocean.
2. The Grand Banks stretch into western Canada from the western United States.
3. Newsprint is thin paper that is made from pulp.

Preview Section 2

If YOU lived there …

You own a general store in Calgary, Alberta, in the early 1880s. Your town is a center for agriculture and ranching on the prairies around you. Still, it sometimes feels very isolated. You miss your family in Ontario. Now the news comes that the Canadian Pacific Railway will soon reach Calgary. It will connect the town with all of central and eastern Canada. **How will the railroad change your life?**

Consider how the railroad will affect your FAMILY:
• easier to visit family in Ontario
• easier for family to come to Calgary
• some family members might want to move to Calgary

Consider how the railroad will affect your BUSINESS:
• more people will come to Calgary
• the store should get more business
• you may be able to expand store

Review Answers: 1. F, St. Lawrence River; 2. F, Rocky Mountains; 3. T

Academic Vocabulary

Review with students the high-use academic term in this section.

establish to set up or create (p. 281)

RF: Vocabulary Builder, Section 2

Taking Notes

Have students use the graphic organizer online to take notes on the section. This activity will prepare students for the Section Assessment, in which they will complete a graphic organizer that builds on the information using the Critical Thinking Skill: Analyzing.

SECTION 2

History and Culture

Main Ideas

1. Beginning in the 1600s, Europeans settled the region that would later become Canada.
2. Immigration and migration to cities have shaped Canadian culture.

The Big Idea

Canada's history and culture reflect Native Canadian and European settlement, immigration, and migration to cities.

Key Terms and Places

provinces, *p. 282*
Quebec, *p. 282*
British Columbia, *p. 282*
Toronto, *p. 284*

hmhsocialstudies.com
TAKING NOTES

Use the graphic organizer online to take notes on the history and culture of Canada.

If **YOU** lived there...

You own a general store in Calgary, Alberta, in the early 1880s. Your town is a center for agriculture and ranching on the prairies around you. Still, it sometimes feels very isolated. You miss your family in Ontario. Now the news comes that the Canadian Pacific Railway will soon reach Calgary. It will connect the town with all of central and eastern Canada.

How will the railroad change your life?

BUILDING BACKGROUND Canada is a close neighbor with the United States. The two countries are linked by a common language and a history of British colonial rule. But the two countries developed in different ways. Canada's diverse population developed its own culture and way of life.

History

As the ice sheets of the ice ages melted, people moved into all areas of what is now Canada. As they did elsewhere in the Americas, these ancient settlers adapted to the physical environment.

Canada's History

Native Canadians
Thousands of years ago, Indians and Inuit settled Canada.

New France
Known as the Father of New France, explorer Samuel de Champlain established Quebec in 1608.

Teach the Big Idea

At Level

History and Culture

1. **Teach** Ask students the questions in the Main Idea boxes under Direct Teach.

2. **Apply** Point out that just as wind, rain, and other physical forces shape landforms, historical events shape culture. As students read, have them list one way each of these events helped to shape Canadian culture: French settlement, British settlement, creation of the Dominion of Canada, construction of the transcontinental railroad, immigration from Europe and Asia, and movement from farms to cities.

3. **Review** Have students write a short paragraph explaining the causes and effects of one of the events chosen.

4. **Practice/Homework** Have students write newspaper headlines for three historical events. Have students exchange headlines with each other and write short articles on headline topic. **LS Verbal/Linguistic**

Alternative Assessment Handbook, Rubric 37: Writing Assignment

Native Canadians

Indians and the Inuit (IH-nu-wuht) people were the first Canadians. Over the years, some of these native peoples divided into groups that became known as the First Nations. One group living on Canada's vast interior plains, the Cree, were skilled bison hunters. In the far north the Inuit adapted to the region's extreme cold, where farming was impossible. By hunting seals, whales, walruses, and other animals, the Inuit could feed, clothe, and house themselves. Today about 400,000 Indians and Inuit live in Canada.

European Settlement

Other people migrated to Canada from Europe. The first Europeans in Canada were the Vikings, or Norse. They settled on Newfoundland Island in about AD 1000, but later abandoned their settlements. In the late 1400s other Europeans arrived and explored Canada. Soon more explorers and fishermen from western Europe began crossing the Atlantic.

Trade quickly developed between the Europeans and Native Canadians. Europeans valued the furs that Native Canadians supplied. The Canadians wanted European metal goods like axes and guns. Through trading, they began to also exchange foods, clothing, and methods of travel.

New France

France was the first European country to successfully settle parts of what would become Canada. The French **established** Quebec City in 1608. They called their new territories New France. At its height, New France included much of eastern Canada and the central United States.

New France was important for several reasons. It was part of the French Empire, which provided money and goods to French settlers. It also served as a base to spread French culture.

France had to compete with Britain, another European colonial power, for control of Canada. To defend their interests against the British, the French built trade and diplomatic relationships with Native Canadians. They exported furs, fish, and other products from New France to other parts of their empire. In addition, the French sent manufactured goods from France to New France. French missionaries also went to New France to convert people to Christianity.

All of these efforts protected French interests in New France for 150 years, until the British finally defeated the French. Although it did not last, New France shaped Canada's cultural makeup. The descendants of French settlers form one of Canada's major ethnic groups today.

Monty

British Settlement
The British built forts throughout Canada like this one in Halifax, Nova Scotia.

Dominion of Canada
After 1867, Canadians created their own government and a mounted police force patrolled the border with the United States.

CANADA **281**

Main Idea

History, *continued*

Explain How did the French and Indian War affect New France? *After the French defeat, Britain took control of New France and divided Quebec into two colonies.*

Draw Conclusions What did Canada's leaders hope to achieve by building a railroad across the country? *increase trade, open up new areas for settlement, and, most importantly, build a national identity*

Did you know. . .

Chinese, Italians, and workers of other nationalities helped build the Canadian Pacific Railway. It was hard and dangerous work. Risks included rockslides, disease, dynamite explosions, searing heat, and bitter cold. Chinese workers laid tracks east through the canyons and passes of British Columbia, fulfilling a pledge by the central government to complete a railroad to the Pacific coast. In return British Columbia agreed to join the Canada Confederation.

British Conquest

In the mid-1700s, the rivalry between France and England turned to war. The conflict was called the French and Indian War. This was the war that resulted in the British taking control of New France away from the French. A small number of French went back to France. However, the great majority stayed. For most of them, few changes occurred in their daily activities. They farmed the same land, prayed in the same churches, and continued to speak French. Few English-speaking settlers came to what is now called **Quebec**.

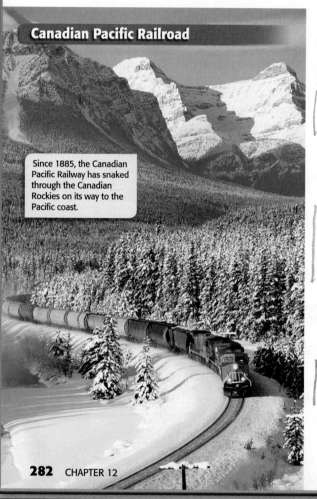

Canadian Pacific Railroad

Since 1885, the Canadian Pacific Railway has snaked through the Canadian Rockies on its way to the Pacific coast.

The British divided Quebec into two colonies. Lower Canada was mostly French-speaking, and Upper Canada was mostly English-speaking. The boundary between Upper and Lower Canada forms part of the border between the provinces of Quebec and Ontario today. **Provinces** are administrative divisions of a country. To the east, the colony of Nova Scotia (noh-vuh SKOH-shuh) was also divided. A new colony called New Brunswick was created where many of the British settlers lived.

Creation of Canada

For several decades these new colonies developed separately from each other. The colonists viewed themselves as different from other parts of the British Empire. Therefore, the British Parliament created the Dominion of Canada in 1867. A dominion is a territory or area of influence. For Canadians, the creation of the Dominion was a step toward independence from Britain. The motto of the new Dominion was "from sea to sea."

How would Canadians create a nation from sea to sea? With railroads. When the Dominion was established, Ontario and Quebec were already well served by railroads. **British Columbia**, on the Pacific coast, was not. To connect British Columbia with the provinces in the east, the Canadians built a transcontinental railroad. Completed in 1885, the Canadian Pacific Railway was Canada's first transcontinental railroad.

After the Canadian Pacific Railway linked the original Canadian provinces to British Columbia, Canada acquired vast lands in the north. Much of this land was bought from the Hudson's Bay Company, a large British fur-trading business. Most of the people living in the north were Native Canadians and people of mixed European and native ancestry. With the building

Differentiating Instruction

Advanced/Gifted and Talented

1. Have students research the route of Canada's transcontinental railroad. Ask them to compare this route with a physical map of Canada and identify the obstacles that railroad builders encountered as they moved west. Engineers had to solve problems of laying tracks through swamps and muskeg, finding passes through high mountains, and building bridges over deep, icy rivers.

At Level

2. Have students work in pairs to research the problems the builders of the railroad faced from the physical environment and how they solved these problems. Have each group pick a location on the Canadian Pacific Railway and create an historical marker honoring a person or group that took part in building the railroad.
LS Verbal/Linguistic, Visual/Spatial
📝 Alternative Assessment Handbook, Rubric 37: Writing Assignments

English-Language Learners

At Level

1. Ask students to describe the ways families mark events in their personal history through birthday parties and other celebrations.

2. Discuss the term *culture*. Have students describe holidays or festivals in their country of origin or local community. Pick a Canadian holiday like Dominion Day and talk about how it is celebrated.
LS Verbal/Linguistic
📝 Alternative Assessment Handbook, Rubric 11: Discussions

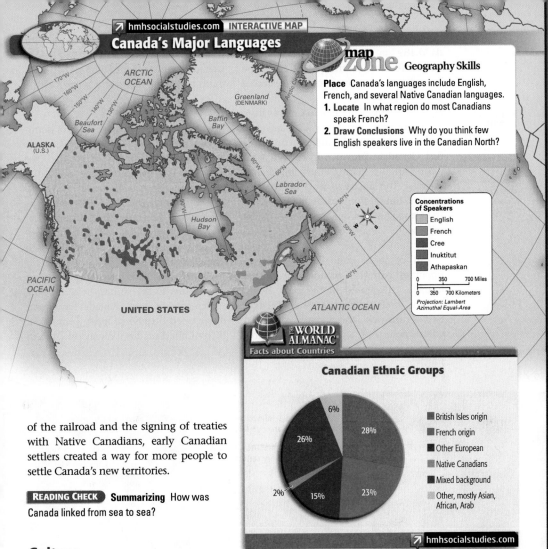

Place Canada's languages include English, French, and several Native Canadian languages.
1. **Locate** In what region do most Canadians speak French?
2. **Draw Conclusions** Why do you think few English speakers live in the Canadian North?

Concentrations of Speakers
- English
- French
- Cree
- Inuktitut
- Athapaskan

0   350   700 Miles
0   350   700 Kilometers
Projection: Lambert Azimuthal Equal-Area

THE WORLD ALMANAC
Facts about Countries

Canadian Ethnic Groups

- British Isles origin — 28%
- French origin — 23%
- Other European — 15%
- Native Canadians — 2%
- Mixed background — 26%
- Other, mostly Asian, African, Arab — 6%

↗ hmhsocialstudies.com

of the railroad and the signing of treaties with Native Canadians, early Canadian settlers created a way for more people to settle Canada's new territories.

READING CHECK **Summarizing** How was Canada linked from sea to sea?

Culture

Canada's people reflect a history of British and French colonial rule. In addition, the country has experienced waves of immigration. The country is home to a great variety of people who belong to different ethnic groups and cultures. Although individual groups still keep their own cultural ways, many Canadians have tried to create a single national identity.

Immigration

During the late 1800s and early 1900s, many immigrants came to Canada from Europe. Most were from Britain, Russia, and Germany. Some people also came from the United States. While most of these immigrants farmed, others worked in mines, forests, and factories.

CANADA **283**

Direct Teach

Linking to Today

Language of the Law In the 2001 Census almost 60 percent of Canadians reported English as their first language. About one-fourth of the population listed French as their first language. The Canadian government implements its bilingual policy through many different laws. Some give all Canadians the right to appear before the federal courts speaking either English or French. All federal laws, statutes, and official documents must be printed in both languages. Lawmakers can use English or French in Parliament. The French language is spoken throughout Quebec province, but many French speakers also speak English. Only a small percentage of English speakers outside of Quebec can speak French. Chinese is Canada's third most commonly spoken language. In the 2001 Census about 3 percent of Canadians reported that one of the Chinese languages was their first language.

- **RF:** Critical Thinking, Can Canada Survive?
- **Map Transparency:** Canada's Major Languages

↗ **hmhsocialstudies.com**

Online Resources
Activity: Canada's First Nations

Differentiating Instruction

Below Level

Special Needs Learners

1. Make a large drawing of the graphic organizer sequence chart on the board. List six events from Canadian history on the board in random order. Have students take turns picking the event that occurred next and entering this information on the graphic organizer.

2. Ask each student to pick one more event to add to the chart and place it chronologically.
LS Visual/Spatial, Verbal/Linguistic

Alternative Assessment Handbook, Rubric 13: Graphic Organizers

First Nations Arrive → New France Settled → Britain Wins French and Indian War ↓ Upper and Lower Canada Created ← Dominion Status for Canada

Answers

Map Zone 1. *in the east, Quebec;* **2.** *possible answer—Because of the harsh climate, few English immigrants likely settled there.*

Reading Check *by railroads*

283

Main Idea

❷ Culture

Immigration and migration to cities have shaped Canadian culture.

Recall In the late 1800s where did the first wave of immigrants to Canada come from? *Britain, Russia, Germany, and the United States as well as China, Japan, and India*

Analyze How did immigrants contribute to the economic boom of the early 1900s? *worked on farms and railroads and in factories, mines, and forests*

Explain How has the movement to cities affected rural Canada? *Many smaller settlements disappeared because so many people left.*

📖 **RF:** Biography, *Mary Pickford*

📖 **RF:** Literature, *Anne of Green Gables* by Lucy Maud Montgomery

Info to Know

A Changing Population Canada is the world's second-largest country in area, but it has slightly fewer citizens than the state of California. Increasingly, immigration is the key factor in Canada's population growth. Today close to three-fourths of Canada's population growth comes from immigration. In the 1950s, about 9 out of every 10 immigrants came from the United Kingdom or other European countries. In the 1990s, only 2 in 10 did. More than half of newer immigrants came from Asia and the Middle East.

Answers

Focus on Reading *Asian immigrants to Canada came mainly from China, Japan, and India.*

Analyzing Visuals *Many modern glass and steel buildings and one older brick building reflect how Toronto has changed over time.*

Other immigrants were lured to Canada in 1897 by the discovery of gold in the Yukon Territory. Many people from the United States migrated north in search of Canada's gold.

FOCUS ON READING
What details of this paragraph could you add to a list of countries from which immigrants came?

Immigrants also came to Canada from Asian countries, especially China, Japan, and India. British Columbia became the first Canadian province to have a large Asian minority. Many Chinese immigrants migrated to Canada to work on the railroads. Chinese immigrants built most of the Canadian Pacific Railway, one of the railroad lines linking eastern Canada to the Pacific coast.

All of these immigrants played an important part in an economic boom that Canada experienced in the early 1900s. During these prosperous times, Quebec, New Brunswick, and Ontario produced wheat, pulp, and paper. British Columbia and Ontario supplied the country with minerals and hydroelectricity. As a result, Canadians enjoyed one of the highest standards of living in the world by the 1940s.

Movement to Cities

After World War II, another wave of immigrants from Europe arrived in Canada. Many settled in Canada's large cities. For example, **Toronto** has become one of the most culturally diverse cities in the world. The Europeans were joined by other people from Africa, the Caribbean, Latin America, and particularly Asia. Asian businesspeople have brought a great deal of wealth to Canada's economy. *India*

Many Canadians have recently moved from farms to the country's cities. Some settlements in rural Canada have even disappeared because so many people left. Many Canadians have moved to cities in

Toronto

With about 5 million people, Toronto is Canada's largest city.

ANALYZING VISUALS How is Toronto's history reflected in this city square?

284 CHAPTER 12

Critical Thinking: Understanding Cause and Effect
Above Level

Writing an Editorial

1. Explore with students the effects of immigration and urbanization on Canadian life. Begin by discussing how these trends are changing the United States. Then have students describe reasons why immigrants come and suggest ways cultural diversity and the growth of cities has changed Canada. Consider both positive and negative aspects of these changes.

2. Have students describe how they think life in Canada would be different if immigration and urbanization had not occurred.

3. Ask students whether they think these trends will continue in this century and, if so, how Canada might change in the future as a result. Have students write a short editorial expressing an opinion on this question and giving reasons for their opinion.
LS **Verbal/Linguistic**

📖 Alternative Assessment Handbook, Rubric 41: Writing to Express

Vancouver's Chinatown

If you walked around Vancouver, British Columbia, you would quickly realize when you entered the neighborhood of Chinatown. First you would notice that most signs are in Chinese and you would hear some people speaking Chinese. Then you would realize most restaurants serve Chinese food, and shops sell colorful silk clothing, herbs, and art imported from China. If you were in the city for the Chinese New Year, you would probably see a parade of people in traditional Chinese dress. Vancouver's Chinatown is a unique place where Chinese culture is kept alive in Canada today.

Drawing Conclusions How is Vancouver's Chinatown a unique neighborhood?

Ontario to find jobs. Others moved to Vancouver, British Columbia, for its good job opportunities, mild climate, and location near plentiful resources. Resources such as oil, gas, potash, and uranium have provided wealth to many cities in the Western Provinces. However, the political and economic center of power remains in the cities of Ottawa, Toronto, and Montreal.

READING CHECK **Analyzing** How has immigration changed Canada?

SUMMARY AND PREVIEW In this section, you learned that Canada was greatly influenced by British and French settlement, the building of the railroad to the Pacific coast, immigration, and movement to cities. In the next section you will learn about Canada's regions and economy today.

Section 2 Assessment

hmhsocialstudies.com
ONLINE QUIZ

Reviewing Ideas, Terms, and Places

1. **a. Recall** What is a **province**?
   b. Summarize How did Britain gain control of New France from the French?
   c. Elaborate How do you think the Canadian Pacific Railway changed Canada?
2. **a. Identify** What immigrant group helped build the railroads?
   b. Draw Conclusions Why did people migrate to Canada?
   c. Elaborate Why do you think many Canadians moved from farms to the cities?

Critical Thinking

3. **Analyzing** Draw a diagram like the one below. Using your notes, write a sentence in each box about how each topic influenced the next topic.

Railroad → Immigration → Cities

FOCUS ON SPEAKING

4. **Adding Details** Add information about the history and culture of Canada to your notes. Which details would most interest potential visitors?

CANADA **285**

Did you know. . .

Today more than half of all Canadian immigrants live in Toronto, Vancouver, or Montreal. Immigrants cite diverse reasons for choosing each city. Many say their main reason for choosing Toronto is job opportunities. Immigrants choose Montreal for its French language and culture and Vancouver for its mild climate. Ask students why they think many immigrants choose to live in big cities rather than small towns.

• Review & Assess •

Close

Have students pick three events from the Summary and Preview and write a sentence telling how each changed Canada.

Review

⬀ Online Quiz, Section 2

Assess

SE   Section 2 Assessment
PASS: Section 2 Quiz
Alternative Assessment Handbook

Reteach/Classroom Intervention

Guided Reading Workbook, Section 2
Interactive Skills Tutor CD-ROM

Section 2 Assessment Answers

1. **a.** administrative division of a country
   b. defeated France in the French and Indian War
   c. united the country by linking the original provinces to British Columbia, provided an easier way for people and goods to get across rugged terrain and through harsh weather more safely and quickly

2. **a.** Chinese
   b. greater economic opportunity especially for farmers, but also to find jobs in mines, forests, and factories; to prospect for gold in the Yukon
   c. to find jobs

3. possible answer—The railroad made immigration across Canada easier; immigration added to the population and cultural diversity of cities; the cities of Ottawa, Toronto, and Montreal are economic centers of power.

4. possible answers—great variety of ethnic groups and cultures, large cities with interesting stores and cultural events, high standard of living; students will choose different details of interest to visitors.

Answers

Drawing Conclusions *many signs in Chinese, people speaking Chinese, restaurants serving Chinese foods, shops selling Chinese imports, people wearing traditional Chinese dress for Chinese New Year*

Reading Check *Immigrants played a key role in the economic boom that began in the early 1900s and have helped large cities like Toronto become more culturally diverse.*

Bellringer

If YOU lived there. . . Use the **Daily Bellringer Transparency** to help students answer the question.

▶ Daily Bellringer Transparency, Section 3

Canada   Daily Bellringer
                                    Section 3

Review Section 2

Read the lists of events below and put them in the correct order.

a. The French found Quebec City and establish New France.

b. The Canadian Pacific railroad is built, linking eastern Canada to the Pacific Coast.

c. England wins the French and Indian War.

d. The Vikings settle on Newfoundland Island.

Preview Section 3

If YOU lived there ...

You and your family live in Toronto, Ontario. Your parents, who are architects, have been offered an important project in Montreal. If they accept it, you would live there for two years. Montreal is a major city in French-speaking Quebec. You would have to learn a new language. In Montreal, most street signs and advertisements are written in French. **How do you feel about moving to a city with a different language and culture?**

Consider reasons to MOVE:
• good opportunity for parents
• chance to learn a new language
• exposure to a new culture

Consider reasons to STAY:
• no language barrier
• won't have to leave friends and neighbors
• familiar with culture

Review Answers: d, a, c, b

Academic Vocabulary

Review with students the high-use academic term in this section.

distinct separate (p. 290)

📝 RF: Vocabulary Builder, Section 3

Taking Notes

Have students use the graphic organizer online to take notes on the section. This activity will prepare students for the Section Assessment, in which they will complete a graphic organizer that builds on the information using the Critical Thinking Skill: Comparing and Contrasting.

Answers

Reading Check *Both have a democratic government, federal system, strong central government, two-house legislature, and strong head of state.*

Canada Today

What You Will Learn...

Main Ideas

1. Canada has a democratic government with a prime minister and a parliament.
2. Canada has four distinct geographic and cultural regions.
3. Canada's economy is largely based on trade with the United States.

The Big Idea

Canada's democratic government oversees the country's regions and economy.

Key Terms and Places

regionalism, *p. 287*
maritime, *p. 287*
Montreal, *p. 288*
Ottawa, *p. 289*
Vancouver, *p. 290*

hmhsocialstudies.com
TAKING NOTES

Use the graphic organizer online to take notes on present-day Canada.

If **YOU** lived there...

You and your family live in Toronto, Ontario. Your parents, who are architects, have been offered an important project in Montreal. If they accept it, you would live there for two years. Montreal is a major city in French-speaking Quebec. You would have to learn a new language. In Montreal, most street signs and advertisements are written in French.

How do you feel about moving to a city with a different language and culture?

BUILDING BACKGROUND Canada today has been shaped by both history and geography. Canada's first European settlers were French, but the British eventually controlled the territory. Differences in culture still remain, however. In addition, the four regions of Canada are separated by vast distances, economic activities, and culture.

Canada's Government

"Peace, order, and good government" is a statement from Canada's constitution that Canadians greatly value. Canadians are proud of their democratic government, which is led by a prime minister. Similar to a president, a prime minister is the head of a country's government.

Canada's prime minister oversees the country's parliament, Canada's governing body. Parliament consists of the House of Commons and the Senate. Canadians elect members of the House of Commons. However, senators are appointed by the prime minister.

Canada's 10 provincial governments are each led by a premier. These provincial governments are much like our state governments. Canada's central government is similar to our federal government. The Canadian federal system lets people keep their feelings of loyalty to their own province.

READING CHECK **Comparing** How is Canada's government similar to that of the United States?

Teach the Big Idea

At Level

Canada Today

1. **Teach** Ask students the questions in the Main Idea boxes under Direct Teach.

2. **Apply** Have students make a three-column chart labeled *Government, Regions,* and *Economy*. Before teaching the section, have them describe what they already know about each of these topics. Then have them list three questions about each topic. As they read, have them write down what they learned about each from reading the section.

3. **Review** As a review of the section, have students create five completion questions. Then have students quiz each other with the questions they have created.

4. **Practice/Homework** Have students write down one big idea sentence for each section heading. 🔲 **Verbal/Linguistic**

📝 Alternative Assessment Handbook, Rubric 1: Acquiring Information

Canada's Regions

Canada's physical geography separates the country into different regions. For example, people living on the Pacific coast in British Columbia are isolated from Canadians living in the eastern provinces on the Atlantic coast. Just as geographic distance separates much of Canada, differences in culture also define regions.

Regionalism

The cultural differences between English-speaking and French-speaking Canadians have led to problems. English is the main language in most of Canada. In Quebec, however, French is the main language. When Canadians from different regions discuss important issues, they are often influenced by regionalism. **Regionalism** refers to the strong connection that people feel toward the region in which they live.

In some places, this connection is stronger than people's connection to their country as a whole. To better understand regionalism in Canada, we will now explore each region of the country. As you read, refer to the map below to locate each region.

The Eastern Provinces

The region called the Eastern Provinces is a region that lies on the Atlantic coast of Canada. The provinces of New Brunswick, Nova Scotia, and Prince Edward Island are often called the Maritime Provinces. **Maritime** means on or near the sea. The province of Newfoundland and Labrador is usually not considered one of the Maritime Provinces. It includes the island of Newfoundland and a large region of the mainland called Labrador.

A short growing season limits farming in the Eastern Provinces. However, farmers in Prince Edward Island grow potatoes.

⬈ hmhsocialstudies.com INTERACTIVE MAP

Regions of Canada

Legend:
- The Eastern Provinces
- The Heartland
- The Western Provinces
- The Canadian North

0 — 500 — 1,000 Miles
0 — 500 — 1,000 Kilometers
Projection: Lambert Azimuthal Equal-Area

map zone

Geography Skills

Regions Canada has four distinct regions.

1. **Locate** What region is located on the Atlantic coast?
2. **Draw Conclusions** Why do you think few people live in the Canadian North?

CANADA **287**

Direct Teach

Main Idea

❶ Canada's Government

Canada has a democratic government with a prime minister and a parliament.

Identify What is the role of the prime minister? *head of government*

Contrast How is the Canadian Parliament different from the U.S. Congress? *Canadian senators are appointed by the prime minister.*

Infer What common roots do the Canadian and U.S. political systems have? *Both countries had ties to Britain and British settlers, who brought British political traditions to North America.*

📄 **RF:** Biography, Douglas Jung

▶ Map Zone Transparency: Regions of Canada

Info to Know

Canada and Britain In many ways Canada's government resembles the British system. Like Britain, the executive legislative functions are combined in the Parliament and Cabinet ministries. Canada's ceremonial head of state is Britain's monarch. The monarch chooses a Canadian governor general to represent the Crown in Canada.

⬈ **hmhsocialstudies.com**

Online Resources
Activity: States vs. Provinces

Differentiating Instruction

At Level

Struggling Readers

1. Divide students into three groups. Have each group create a page for a Citizen's Handbook for new immigrants.

2. One group can write the introduction explaining why it is important for immigrants to understand how Canada's government works if they want to become citizens. A second group can make drawings or a chart showing how the government is organized.

The third group can create a cover for the book and a glossary explaining these terms: *prime minister, Parliament, Senators,* and *House of Commons.*

LS Verbal/Linguistic, Visual/Spatial

📄 Alternative Assessment Handbook, Rubric 42: Writing to Inform

Answers

Map Zone: 1. *Eastern Provinces;*
2. *harsh climate, fewer job opportunities*

287

Main Idea

2 Canada's Regions

Canada has four distinct geographic and cultural regions.

Recall Why are three of the eastern provinces called the Maritime Provinces? Why do many people in the eastern provinces live near the coast? *They are "on or near the sea"; They can find jobs in coastal cities that serve as fishing and shipping ports and have industrial plants.*

Describe What makes the Heartland unique? *more than half of all Canadians live there; country's most urbanized area*

Analyze Why might so many Canadians live in the Heartland? *milder climate and more job opportunities in Canada's major cities*

Connect to Today

Separatists For over 40 years Quebec has had a separatist movement that favors independence for Quebec. Its political party, the Parti Quebecois, once had strong support throughout Quebec. In the 1970s and 1980s, many English speakers left Quebec. In 1995 voters narrowly defeated a referendum on separation. Since then support for the movement has declined. Quebec now has many immigrants from Eastern Europe, Africa, the Caribbean, and Asia who do not support this cause.

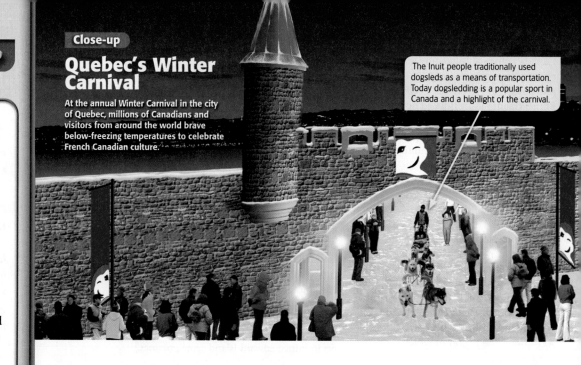

Close-up

Quebec's Winter Carnival

At the annual Winter Carnival in the city of Quebec, millions of Canadians and visitors from around the world brave below-freezing temperatures to celebrate French Canadian culture.

The Inuit people traditionally used dogsleds as a means of transportation. Today dogsledding is a popular sport in Canada and a highlight of the carnival.

Most of the economy in Canada's Eastern Provinces is related to the forestry and fishing industries.

Many people in the Eastern Provinces are descendants of immigrants from the British Isles. In addition, French-speaking families have moved from Quebec to New Brunswick. Most of the region's people live in coastal cities. Many cities have industrial plants and serve as fishing and shipping ports. Along the Atlantic coast lies Halifax, Nova Scotia, the region's largest city.

The Heartland

FOCUS ON READING

In the paragraphs under The Heartland sort the facts into different lists.

Inland from the Eastern Provinces are Quebec and Ontario, which together are sometimes referred to as the Heartland. More than half of all Canadians live in these two provinces. In fact, the chain of cities that extends from Windsor, Ontario, to the city of Quebec is the country's most urbanized region.

The provincial capital of Quebec is also called Quebec. The city's older section has narrow streets, stone walls, and French-style architecture. **Montreal** is Canada's second-largest city and one of the largest French-speaking cities in the world. About 3.5 million people live in the Montreal metropolitan area. It is the financial and industrial center of the province. Winters in Montreal are very cold. To deal with this harsh environment, Montreal's people use underground passages and overhead tunnels to move between buildings in the city's downtown.

In Canada many residents of Quebec, called Quebecois (kay-buh-KWAH), believe their province should be given a special status. Quebecois argue that this status would recognize the cultural differences between their province and the rest of Canada. Some even want Quebec to become an independent country.

Critical Thinking: Analyzing

At Level

Holding a Debate

1. Discuss the term *regionalism* with students. Ask them to describe the ways the Quebecois have expressed their regionalism. Explain that Quebec has a political party that wants Quebec to separate from Canada.

2. Divide students into groups. Have each group create a list of advantages and disadvantages of regionalism for Quebec and for Canada. Discuss why it is important to recognize and appreciate cultural differences and identify ways regionalism can sometimes cause problems for the nation.

3. Ask each group to prepare arguments supporting and opposing the following statement: *Because of its special heritage, Quebec should be allowed to separate from Canada.* Pick two (or more) students to debate this question. **LS Verbal/Linguistic**

   Alternative Assessment Handbook, Rubric 10: Debates

Answers

Focus on Reading *Answers will vary. Students should organize facts into lists such as for Quebec, Montreal, Ottawa.*

Many of the city's buildings reflect French architecture.

ANALYSIS SKILL **ANALYZING VISUALS**

From the clues you see in this scene, what do you think is unique about French Canadian culture?

Ice sculptures created by Canadian and international artists line the carnival's grounds.

The carnival's mascot is a snowman who wears a traditional Canadian sash and hat.

On the other hand, many English-speaking Canadians think Quebec already has too many privileges. Most Canadians, however, still support a united Canada. Strong feelings of regionalism will continue to be an important issue.

With an even larger population than Quebec, the province of Ontario is Canada's leading manufacturing province. Hamilton, Ontario, is the center of Canada's steel industry. Canada exports much of its steel to the United States.

Ontario's capital, Toronto, is a major center for industry, finance, education, and culture. Toronto's residents come from many different parts of the world, including China, Europe, and India.

Canada's national capital, **Ottawa**, is also in Ontario. In Ottawa many people speak both English and French. The city is known for its grand government buildings, parks, and several universities.

The Western Provinces

West of Ontario are the prairie provinces of Manitoba, Saskatchewan, and Alberta. On the Pacific coast is the province of British Columbia. Together, these four provinces make up Canada's Western Provinces.

More people live in Quebec than in all of the prairie provinces combined. The southern grasslands of these provinces are part of a rich wheat belt. Farms here produce far more wheat than Canadians need. The extra wheat is exported. Oil and natural gas production is a very important economic activity in Alberta. The beauty of the Canadian Rockies attracts many visitors to national parks in western Alberta and eastern British Columbia.

British Columbia is Canada's westernmost province and home to almost 4 million people. This mountainous province has rich natural resources, including forests, salmon, and valuable minerals.

CANADA **289**

Direct Teach

Main Idea

Canada's Regions, *continued*

Recall What are the most important resources of the Western Provinces? *prairie provinces—fertile soil, oil and natural gas; British Columbia—forests, salmon, minerals*

Analyze How has Vancouver's location helped its economy? *Pacific coast location has enabled it to trade more easily with Asia*

Drawing Conclusions What evidence can you find that Canada's population is not equally distributed? *Northern Canada makes up more than one-third of the land area, but has only about 100,000 people, while more than half of all Canadians live within the Heartland.*

Collaborative Learning

Above Level

Creating a Television Commercial

1. Organize students into small groups. Ask students to imagine that they are public affairs directors for their province. Their job is to promote economic development and tourism for their region.

2. Assign each group a region. Have groups create a television commercial that highlights their region. Encourage groups to come up with a creative and catchy slogan for their ad. The commercial should tell viewers where the region is located and why it is a good place to live and work.

3. Have each group record its commercial or perform it live for the class.
   LS **Interpersonal, Visual/Spatial**
   Alternative Assessment Handbook, Rubrics 2: Advertisements; and 29: Presentations

Answers

Analyzing Visuals *possible answer—The old coexists with the new.*

289

❸ Canada's Economy

Canada's economy is largely based on trade with the United States.

Recall What is Canada's major type of export to other countries? What is Canada's fastest-growing service industry? *natural resources; tourism*

Analyze What country is Canada's top trading partner? Why do you think it's Canada's top trading partner? *United States; share similar culture and a relatively open border*

Analyze How have the Heartland's many large cities affected the region's growth? *helped it grow by attracting people to jobs in manufacturing, industry, finance, education, and government*

Did you know. . .

Canada's newest territory was created in 1999 as the result of a land claims settlement with the Inuit people. Nunavut is a vast territory. It is one-fifth the size of Canada, but it is sparsely populated. Its population density is only one person for every 70 square kilometers. Nunavut consists of 26 communities that range in size from 25 people in Bathurst Inlet to almost 6,000 in the capital Iqaluit. Many communities cannot be reached by road or rail, so everything that residents need from fuel to food must be brought in by plane. The government is the largest employer in the territory.

Answers

Reading Check *Prairies are good for growing wheat, a key export; British Columbia's coastal location has helped it build strong trade ties with Asia.*

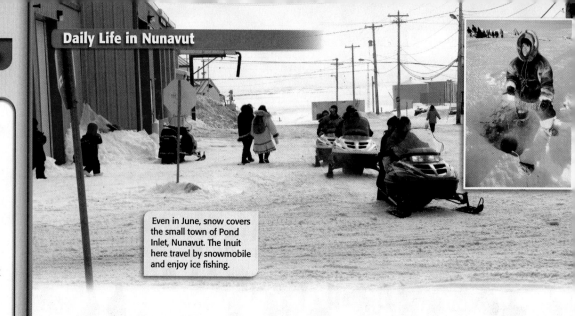

Daily Life in Nunavut

Even in June, snow covers the small town of Pond Inlet, Nunavut. The Inuit here travel by snowmobile and enjoy ice fishing.

Nearly half of British Columbia's population lives in and around the coastal city of **Vancouver**. The city's location on the Pacific coast helps it to trade with countries in Asia.

The Canadian North

Northern Canada is extremely cold due to its location close to the Arctic Circle. The region called the Canadian North includes the Yukon Territory, the Northwest Territories, and Nunavut (NOO-nuh-voot). These three territories cover more than a third of Canada but are home to only about 100,000 people.

Nunavut is a new territory created for the native Inuit people who live there. Nunavut means "Our Land" in the Inuit language. Even though Nunavut is part of Canada, the people there have their own **distinct** culture and government. About 30,000 people live in Nunavut.

The physical geography of the Canadian North includes forests and tundra. The frozen waters of the Arctic Ocean separate

ACADEMIC VOCABULARY
distinct separate

isolated towns and villages. During some parts of the winter, sunlight is limited to only a few hours.

READING CHECK **Drawing Conclusions** How does geography affect the location of economic activities in the Western Provinces?

Canada's Economy

As you learned in Section 1, Canada has many valuable natural resources. Canada's economy is based on the industries associated with these resources. In addition, Canada's economy also benefits from trade.

Industries

Canada is one of the world's leading mineral producers. Canadians mine valuable titanium, zinc, iron ore, gold, and coal. Canada's iron and steel industry uses iron ore to manufacture products like planes, automobiles and household appliances. However, most Canadians work in the services industry. For example, tourism is

---

Critical Thinking: Analyzing Information   At Level

Make a Chart and Map

1. Organize students into four groups. Have each group create a chart with four columns and four rows. Have students label the columns *Eastern Provinces*, *Heartland*, *Western Provinces*, and *Far North*. Label the rows *location*, *climate*, *natural resources*, and *economic activities*.

2. After groups have completed their charts, ask: How are the economic activities of each region linked to its natural resources and location? Have each group make a map of one

of Canada's regions, showing the provincial capital and a symbol for each region that reflects its economy, resources, or other unique feature. Maps should include a title, a compass rose, and a scale.

3. Conclude by having each student pick the region they would like to live in and explain why. **LS Verbal/ Linguistic, Visual/Spatial**

Alternative Assessment Handbook, Rubrics 7: Charts; and Rubric 20: Map Creation

Canada's fastest-growing services industry. Canada's economy also benefits from the millions of dollars visitors spend in the country each year.

Trade

Canada's economy depends on trade. Many of Canada's natural resources that you have learned about are exported to countries around the world. Canada's leading trading partner is the United States.

As the world's largest trading relationship, Canada and the United States rely heavily on each other. About 60 percent of Canada's imported goods are from the United States. About 85 percent of Canada's exports, such as lumber, goes to the United States.

However, the United States placed tariffs, or added fees, on Canadian timber. American lumber companies accused Canada of selling their lumber at unfairly low prices. Canada argued that the tariffs were unfair according to the North American Free Trade Agreement (NAFTA).

The export of cattle to the United States is another area of dispute between the two countries. When a Canadian cow was discovered with mad cow disease in 2003, the United States banned the import of all cattle from Canada. Canadian ranchers now claim that all their cows are free of the disease. After a two-year ban, the United States imports Canadian cattle and beef again.

READING CHECK Summarizing What goods does Canada export?

SUMMARY In this section you learned that Canada has distinct regions that are separated by both geography and culture. The U.S. and Canada are trading partners that share a common colonial history, a border, and the English language.

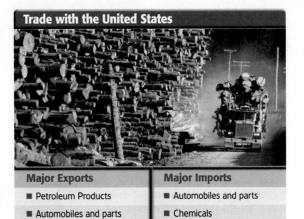

Trade with the United States

Major Exports	Major Imports
■ Petroleum Products	■ Automobiles and parts
■ Automobiles and parts	■ Chemicals
■ Lumber	■ Plastics

Section 3 Assessment hmhsocialstudies.com ONLINE QUIZ

Reviewing Ideas, Terms, and Places

1. **a.** Recall What office heads Canada's government?
   b. Summarize How is Canada's parliament structured?
2. **a.** Define What is **regionalism**?
   b. Contrast How are Canada's Western Provinces different from the Canadian North?
   c. Evaluate Why do you think the Quebecois want to break away from Canada?
3. **a.** Describe How are Canada's natural resources important to the country's economy?
   b. Draw Conclusions Why do Canada and the United States rely on each other as trading partners?

Critical Thinking

4. **Comparing and Contrasting** Use your notes to complete this chart. List the similarities and differences between the Eastern Provinces and Western Provinces.

Similarities	Differences
1.	1.
2.	

FOCUS ON SPEAKING

5. **Presenting Canada Today** Add details about present-day Canada to your notes. Consider which images you will use to persuade your audience to visit Canada after they listen to your ad.

CANADA **291**

Section 3 Assessment Answers

1. **a.** a prime minister
   b. It's made up of a House of Commons and the Senate.
2. **a.** strong connection that people feel toward their region
   b. Western Provinces—farming areas in prairies, British Columbia has many resources, milder climate, and large city, Vancouver. Canadian North—much colder, harsher climate, fewer resources, and no large cities, large Inuit population
   c. Students might suggest that they want to maintain their French identity and culture.

3. **a.** key exports for trade
   b. Canada has many natural resources that the U.S. needs for manufacturing. Canada and the U.S. are neighbors, so transportation costs may be less.

4. possible answers: similarities—north of the equator, English main language, influenced by regionalism; differences—levels of population, climate, economy, physical geography

5. Answers will vary, but should reflect information from the text.

Answers

Reading Check *minerals such as titanium, zinc, iron ore, gold, and coal; timber and wood pulp, automobiles and parts, aircraft, beef*

291

Social Studies Skills

Using Mental Maps and Sketch Maps

Activity Make a Sketch Map

Materials: paper, colored pencils

1. Ask students to think about a place that they could draw a sketch map of, such as their school, country, or community.

2. Once students decide what their maps will show, have them determine how much space it needs to cover.

3. Students should use art supplies to create their sketch maps. Remind them that sketch maps show the relative size and shape of places.

4. Encourage students to use colored pencils to shade different parts of their maps. Students should include at least five shapes on their maps. Remind them to include a compass rose.

LS Visual/Spatial

RF: Social Studies Skills, Using Mental Maps and Sketch Maps

Alternative Assessment Handbook, Rubric 20: Map Creation

Interactive Skills Tutor CD-ROM, Lesson 6: Interpret Maps, Graphs, Charts, Visuals, and Political Cartoons

Using Mental Maps and Sketch Maps

Learn

We create maps in our heads of all kinds of places—our schools, communities, country, and the world. These images, or mental maps, are shaped by what we see and experience.

We use mental maps of places when we draw sketch maps. A sketch map uses very simple shapes to show the relationship between places and the relative size of places. Notice the sketch map of the world shown here. It may not look like any other map in your book, but it does give you an idea of what the world looks like.

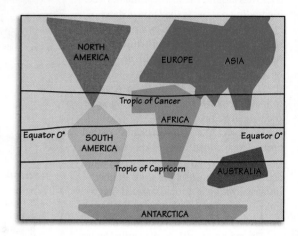

Practice

Does your mental map of the world look like the sketch map here? It is alright if they do not look exactly alike. Now think about the places in your own neighborhood. Use your mental map to draw a sketch map of your neighborhood. Then use your sketch map to answer the following questions.

- What are the most important features of your map?
- What is the largest building in your neighborhood?
- What labels did you use on your map?

Apply

Draw a sketch map of Canada. Make sure to include the cities and physical features you learned about in this chapter. Then exchange your map with another student. Ask your partner to make corrections to your map if he or she does not understand it.

292 CHAPTER 12

Social Studies Skills Activity: Using Mental Maps and Sketch Map

Creating Sketch Maps

At Level

Materials: paper, colored pencils

1. Review with students what they have learned about using mental and sketch maps.

2. Working with a partner, have students think of the events of a familiar poem or story that they could use to create a sketch map.

3. Students should then work together to draw the map. Have them discuss what elements to include and why it is important to include them.

4. Ask for volunteers to share their maps with the class. Give other students a chance to interpret the maps and to ask questions.

5. Display students' sketch maps around the classroom. **LS Visual/Spatial, Verbal/Linguistic**

Alternative Assessment Handbook, Rubrics 14: Group Activity; and 20: Map Creation

Answers

Practice *Answers will vary, but students should note the most important features on their map and be able to explain why they included them.*

Apply *Students' sketch maps of Canada will vary, but should include cities such as Montreal, Ottawa, and Vancouver and physical features such as the Rocky Mountains, St. Lawrence River, and Niagara Falls.*

292

Geography's Impact
video series
Review the video to answer the closing question:
Why did the people of Nunavut want their own territory?

Visual Summary

Use the visual summary below to help you review the main ideas of the chapter.

QUICK FACTS

Native Canadian and European settlement has influenced Canadian culture.

Canada has cold climates and its physical features include rugged mountains.

Canada has distinctive cultural regions today.

Reviewing Vocabulary, Terms, and Places

Choose the letter of the answer that best completes each statement below.

1. A physical feature of rocky uplands, lakes, and swamps in Canada is called the
   a. Niagara Falls.
   b. Great Lakes.
   c. Grand Banks.
   d. Canadian Shield.

2. Which part of Canada did the French settle?
   a. Ontario
   b. New Brunswick
   c. Quebec
   d. British Colombia

3. What province was the first to have a large Asian population?
   a. Manitoba
   b. British Columbia
   c. Quebec
   d. Saskatchewan

4. A strong connection that people feel toward their region is called
   a. maritime.
   b. province.
   c. heartland.
   d. regionalism.

Comprehension and Critical Thinking

SECTION 1 *(Pages 276–279)*

5. a. **Define** What is pulp?
   b. **Make Inferences** What is the coldest area in Canada?
   c. **Evaluate** What makes the Grand Banks an ideal fishing ground?

SECTION 2 *(Pages 280–285)*

6. a. **Identify** Who were the first Canadians?
   b. **Draw Conclusions** Why did Canadians build a rail line across Canada?
   c. **Predict** Do you think Canada's cities will increase or decrease in population in the future? Explain your answers.

SECTION 3 *(Pages 286–291)*

7. a. **Recall** What kind of government does Canada have?

CANADA **293**

Answers

Visual Summary

Review and Inquiry Have students use the visual summary to write a brief paragraph summarizing the important themes depicted in the illustrations.

▶ Quick Facts Transparency: Canada Visual Summary

Reviewing Vocabulary, Terms, and Places

1. d
2. c
3. b
4. d

Comprehension and Critical Thinking

5. a. softened wood fibers used to make paper
   b. areas close to the Arctic Circle
   c. The cold water from the Labrador Sea meets with the warm water of the Gulf Stream, creating ideal conditions for growing organisms that fish like to eat. Large schools of fish gather to eat there.

6. a. Indians and Inuit people
   b. to link British Columbia with the provinces in the east
   c. Answers will vary, but students may answer that Canada's cities will probably grow in the future due to continuing immigration and more job opportunities.

7. a. a democratic government led by a prime minister

Review and Assessment Resources

Review and Reinforce

SE Chapter Review

📖 **RF:** Chapter Review

▶ Quick Facts Transparency: Canada Visual Summary

🔊 Spanish Chapter Summaries Audio CD Program

TOS Holt McDougal PuzzleView, Quiz Show for ExamView

💿 Quiz Game CD-ROM

Assess

SE Standardized Test Practice

📖 PASS: Chapter Test, Forms A and B

📖 Alternative Assessment Handbook

TOS ExamView Test Generator, Chapter Test

💿 Differentiated Instruction Modified Worksheets and Tests CD-ROM: Chapter Test

↗ Online Assessment Program, in the Interactive Student Edition

Reteach/Intervene

📖 Guided Reading Workbook

📖 Differentiated Instruction Teacher Management System: Lesson Plans

💿 Differentiated Instruction Modified Worksheets and Tests CD-ROM

💿 Interactive Skills Tutor CD-ROM

↗ hmhsocialstudies.com
Chapter Resources

7. b. The Eastern Provinces are on or near the sea; farming is difficult due to a short growing season and poor soils, region's economy is related to farming and fishing. The Western Provinces are the prairie provinces and British Columbia; prairies are part of a rich wheat belt; British Columbia has rich resources, and trades with Asia.

c. They believe that their province should be given a special status that would recognize the cultural differences between Quebec and the rest of Canada.

Using the Internet

8. Go to hmhsocialstudies.com to access a rubric for this activity.

Social Studies Skills

9. Students' sketch maps will vary, but should resemble Canada and include important physical features and a compass rose.

Map Activity

10. A. St. Lawrence River
B. Manitoba
C. Vancouver
D. Rocky Mountains
E. Nunavut

Focus on Reading and Speaking

11. Students' lists should include important facts from the text about Canada's physical geography, history and culture, and life there today.

12. Rubric Students' radio ads should

- be one minute long
- have an introduction, body, and summary
- use persuasive and descriptive language
- include vivid details

RF: Focus on Speaking, Creating a Radio Ad

SECTION 3 *(continued)*

b. Compare and Contrast How are the Eastern Provinces different than the Western Provinces?

c. Evaluate Why do the Quebecois see themselves as different from other Canadians?

Using the Internet

8. Activity: Writing Newspaper Articles You are a reporter for The Quebec Chronicle assigned to write articles for the next issue of the newspaper. Through your online textbook, explore the people of Quebec and find background information for your articles covering Quebec. Use the links provided to conduct your research and then write three short articles. Go to press using the interactive template and publish your Canadian newspaper.

↗ hmhsocialstudies.com

Social Studies Skills

9. Using Mental Maps and Sketch Maps Without looking at a map of Canada think about what the Eastern Provinces look like. Then create a sketch map of the Eastern Provinces. Make sure to include a compass rose and important physical features.

Map Activity

10. Canada On a separate sheet of paper, match the letters on the map with their correct labels.

Rocky Mountains   Manitoba
Nunavut   St. Lawrence River
Vancouver

↗ hmhsocialstudies.com **INTERACTIVE MAP**

FOCUS ON READING AND SPEAKING

11. Understanding Lists Use your notes about Canada to create a list of important facts for each section. Organize your lists using this chart.

Physical Geography	History and Culture	Canada Today

12. Creating a Tourism Ad Now that you have collected notes on Canada's geography, history, and culture, choose the information you think will most appeal to visitors. Write a one-minute radio script, using descriptive and persuasive language to convince your audience to visit Canada. Describe Canada in a way that will capture your audience's imagination. Ask the class to listen carefully as you read your radio ad to them. Then ask the class to evaluate your ad on how persuasive it was or was not.

Standardized Test Prep

DIRECTIONS: Read questions 1 through 7 and write the letter of the best response. Then read question 8 and write your own well-constructed response.

1 The United States and Canada share which physical feature?
- A Canadian Shield
- B Rocky Mountains
- C Hudson Bay
- D Saskatchewan River

2 What resource in Canada provides pulp and newsprint?
- A forests
- B nickel
- C potash
- D fish

3 Many Canadians moved from farms to cities to find
- A gold.
- B good schools.
- C jobs.
- D better weather.

4 Canada's prime minister oversees the country's
- A railroads.
- B parliament.
- C provincial governments.
- D city governments.

5 Canada's capital, Ottawa, is located in
- A Northwest Territories.
- B Nova Scotia.
- C Ontario.
- D British Columbia.

Climate of British Columbia

6 Based on the map above, which climate type does the Pacific coast of British Columbia experience?
- A subarctic
- B marine west coast
- C highland
- D steppe

7 About 60 percent of Canada's imported goods come from which country?
- A Mexico
- B Greenland
- C Russia
- D United States

8 **Extended Response** Look at the political map of Canada at the beginning of this chapter. Using information from the map, explain why the United States and Canada are major trading partners.

CANADA **295**

Answers

Standardized Test Prep

1. B
Break Down the Question This question requires students to recall factual information. Refer students who miss it to Section 1.

2. A
Break Down the Question This question requires students to recall the definition of a key term in Section 1.

3. C
Break Down the Question This question requires students to recall factual information. Refer students who miss it to Section 2.

4. B
Break Down the Question Students should remember that a prime minister's position is similar to that of a president.

5. C
Break Down the Question Refer students who missed the question to the map in the Chapter Preview.

6. B
Break Down the Question Remind students to study the map closely, to avoid mistaking the part of Alaska that lies between the Pacific Ocean and the northern part of British Columbia.

7. D
Break Down the Question This question requires students to recall that the United States and Canada are major trading partners. Refer students who miss it to Section 3.

8. Extended Response Students' explanations should reflect concepts learned in the chapter and information from the chapter opener map. Possible reasons students may note are the cultural ties and relatively open border they share.

Intervention Resources

Reproducible
- Guided Reading Workbook
- Differentiated Instruction Teacher Management System: Lesson Plans

Technology
- Quick Facts Transparency: Canada Visual Summary
- Differentiated Instruction Modified Worksheets and Tests CD-ROM
- Interactive Skills Tutor CD-ROM

Tips for Test Taking

Take It All In Encourage students to preview the test to get a mental map of their tasks.
- Know how many questions there are.
- Know where to stop.
- Set time checkpoints.
- Do the easy sections first. Easy questions can be worth just as many points as hard ones.

Describing a Place

What are the physical features of a country? What is the weather like? What drives the economy? The answers to questions like these are often cold, hard facts and statistics. But they can bring life to a description of a place.

Assignment
Write a paper describing one of these places in the Americas:
- a city
- a country

1. Prewrite

Identify a Topic and Big Idea
- Choose one of the topics above to write about.
- Turn your topic into a big idea, or thesis. For example, your big idea might be, "Cuba's government greatly influences life in the country."

> **TIP** **Precise Language** Describe your place with specific nouns, verbs, adjectives, and adverbs. For example, rather than writing "Buenos Aires is big," write "Buenos Aires is the largest city in Argentina."

Gather and Organize Information
- Look for information about your place in the library or on the Internet. Organize your notes in groupings such as physical features, economy, or culture. Decide which facts about the place you are describing are most important or unique.

2. Write

Use a Writer's Framework

> **A Writer's Framework**
>
> **Introduction**
> - Start with an interesting fact or question.
> - Identify your big idea and provide any necessary background information.
>
> **Body**
> - Write at least one paragraph for each category. Include facts that help explain each detail.
> - Write about each detail in order of importance.
>
> **Conclusion**
> - Summarize your description in your final paragraph.

3. Evaluate and Revise

Review and Improve Your Paper
- Re-read your paper and use the questions below to identify ways to revise your paper.
- Make the changes needed to improve your paper.

Evaluation Questions for a Description of a Place
1. Do you begin with an interesting fact or question?
2. Does your introduction identify your big idea? Do you provide background information to help your readers better understand your idea?
3. Do you have at least one paragraph for each category?
4. Do you use order of importance to organize the details of your description?
5. Are there more details you would like to know about your place? If so, what are they?

4. Proofread and Publish

Give Your Description the Finishing Touch
- Make sure you used commas correctly when listing more than two details in a sentence.
- Check your spelling of the names of places.
- Share your description with classmates or with students in another social studies class.

5. Practice and Apply

Use the steps and strategies outlined in this workshop to write your description of a place. Share your description with classmates. With your classmates, group the descriptions by country and then identify the places you would like to visit.

296

Europe and Russia

Direct Teach

Introduce the Unit

Share the information in the chapter overviews with students.

Chapter 13 Ancient Greek culture, the civilization of the Roman Empire, and the spread of Christianity shaped Europe's early history.

Chapter 14 Developments such as the Renaissance, the Reformation, the rise of science, and global exploration and expansion created early modern Europe.

Chapter 15 Modern Europe has witnessed devastating world wars and a divisive Cold War but is now working toward unity.

Chapter 16 Climate affects life in the Mediterranean region, as do its countries' long histories.

Chapter 17 A variety of landscapes and cultures have shaped life in West-Central Europe. The region is prosperous.

Chapter 18 The British Isles have a rich history and culture. Scandinavia has become one of Europe's most stable and prosperous regions.

Chapter 19 The landforms and cultures of Eastern Europe are diverse. Since the 1990s Eastern Europe has experienced major changes.

Chapter 20 Russia is the world's largest country. The Caucasus countries are southwest of Russia. The region is marked by a history of strict rule and ethnic diversity.

The Alps

The Alps, one of Europe's major mountain ranges, stretch across the heart of central Europe.

Islands and Peninsulas

Islands and peninsulas surround the edges of Europe, drawing people to the sea to work, travel, and trade.

B EUROPE AND RUSSIA

Unit Resources

Planning

- Differentiated Instruction Teacher Management System: Pacing Guide
- **TOS** Calendar Planner
- Power Presentations with Video CD-ROM

Differentiating Instruction

- Differentiated Instruction Teacher Management System: Lesson Plans for Differentiated Instruction
- Differentiated Instruction Modified Worksheets and Tests CD-ROM

Enrichment

- **RF:** Interdisciplinary Projects
  - Early History of Europe: The Black Death

- Modern European History: Reading and Writing Allegories; Current Events: Letting Historical Figures Solve Today's Problems
- Eastern Europe: Eastern Europe's Economy
- Russia and the Caucasus: The Russian Space Program

- Geography, Science, and Culture Activities with Answer Key

Assessment

- PASS: Benchmark Test
- **TOS** ExamView Test Generator: Benchmark Test
- Online Assessment Program, in the Interactive Student Edition
- Alternative Assessment Handbook

B

Northern European Plain

Rolling across northern Europe is a vast lowland called the Northern European Plain.

Europe and Russia

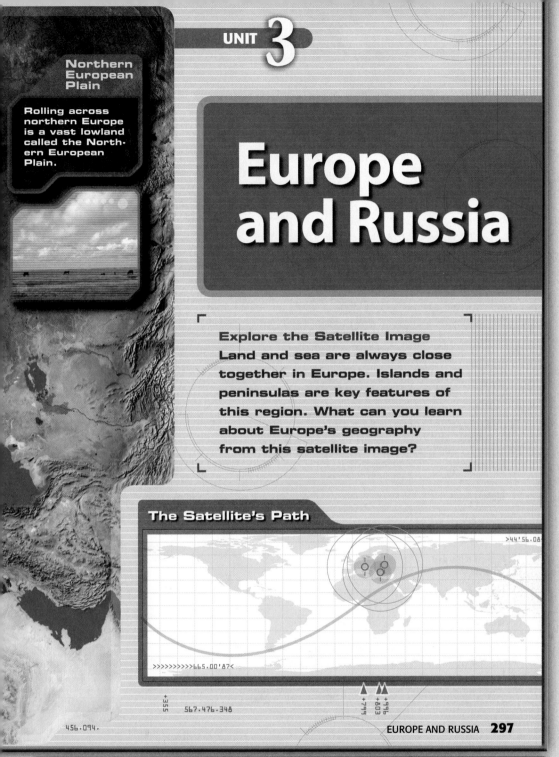

Explore the Satellite Image
Land and sea are always close together in Europe. Islands and peninsulas are key features of this region. What can you learn about Europe's geography from this satellite image?

The Satellite's Path

>44'56.08

>>>>>>>>>665.00'87<

+355   567.476.348   +799   +603
                     +99%
456.094.

EUROPE AND RUSSIA **297**

1. Divide students into three groups. Have each group brainstorm solutions to the following problem: What can be done to promote the distribution of wealth in Europe and Russia?

2. Students should use the maps in the atlas section to acquire information about Europe and Russia and to help them come up with creative solutions.

3. After brainstorming, each group should select one solution to elaborate on and share with the rest of the class. Emphasize that creativity is an important factor in choosing a solution.

4. Have groups take turns sharing their solutions. Then have an anonymous class vote for the most creative solution to the problem of wealth distribution in Europe and Russia.

LS Interpersonal, Verbal/Linguistic

Alternative Assessment Handbook, Rubrics 14: Group Activity; and 35: Solving Problems

Direct Teach

Connect to the Unit

Activity **Plan a Defense Strategy** Divide students into three groups. Assign each group one of these regions: Western Europe, Eastern Europe, and Russia. Have the groups study the maps in the atlas section and make generalizations about climate, landforms, population, and transportation. Then have each group plan a defense strategy that will protect its region from invasion. Where are the borders vulnerable? Where are they strong? Are some countries within a region stronger than others?

During the study of Europe and Russia, have students think about how geography has affected politics and economics in the region.

LS Interpersonal, Visual/Spatial

Alternative Assessment Handbook, Rubric 21: Map Reading

Explore the Photographs

Point out the Alps and the Northern European Plain in the satellite image and photographs. Ask: Where do you think more Europeans live: in or near the Alps or on the Northern European Plain? Why? *possible answer—Most people probably live on the Northern European Plain; the climate is mild, and there is good land for farming and rivers for irrigation and trade.* Based on the photograph of the seaside town, what can students learn about climate and work of the region? *possible answer—The climate is probably warm. Some people may fish or trade for a living.*

Map Zone Transparency: Europe and Russia Satellite Image

Answers

Explore the Satellite Image *possible answer—The geography of Europe is diverse, with mountains, plains, lakes, rivers, and access to oceans. Most of Europe is covered in lush vegetation; Spain and Portugal are drier than the rest of Europe; Iceland and parts of Scandinavia are covered in ice.*

297

Explore the Map

Europe and Russia: Physical As students examine the map on these pages, ask the following questions:

Location What are six mountain ranges located in Russia? *Ural, Caucasus, Sayan, Yablonovy, Stanovoy, Kolyma*

Region What are the countries in the Caucasus region? *Georgia, Armenia, Azerbaijan*

Human/Environment Interaction In which European country would you prefer to live if you enjoyed mountain climbing? Why? *Answers will vary, but students should choose a country near one or more mountain ranges.*

▶ Map Zone Transparency: Europe and Russia: Physical

UNIT 3 REGIONAL ATLAS

Europe and Russia: Physical

THE WORLD ALMANAC Facts about the World
Geographical Extremes: Europe and Russia

Longest River	Volga River, Russia: 2,290 miles (3,685 km)
Highest Point	Mount Elbrus, Russia: 18,510 feet (5,642 m)
Lowest Point	Caspian Sea, Russia/Azerbaijan: 92 feet (28 m) below sea level
Highest Recorded Temperature	Seville, Spain: 122°F (50°C)
Lowest Recorded Temperature	Ust'Shchugor, Russia: –67°F (–55°C)
Wettest Place	Crkvica, Bosnia and Herzegovina: 183 inches (464.8 cm) average precipitation per year
Driest Place	Astrakhan, Russia: 6.4 inches (16.3 cm) average precipitation per year

↗ hmhsocialstudies.com

ELEVATION

Feet		Meters
13,120		4,000
6,560		2,000
1,640		500
656		200
(Sea level) 0		0 (Sea level)
Below sea level		Below sea level

0   400   800 Miles
0   400   800 Kilometers
Projection: Robinson

298 REGIONAL ATLAS

Differentiating Instruction

Struggling Readers   `Below Level`

1. Focus students' attention on the physical map and World Almanac chart on this page. Read the facts in the chart out loud one by one.

2. As you read each fact, ask a volunteer to locate that place on a large classroom map of the region. The other students should locate the place on the map in their textbooks.
LS Visual/Spatial

📖 Alternative Assessment Handbook, Rubric 21: Map Reading

Advanced/Gifted and Talented Students   `Above Level`

1. Have students select one fact from the World Almanac chart to research in-depth.

2. Students should then prepare and deliver a persuasive speech, trying to convince tourists to visit that place. **LS Verbal/Linguistic**

📖 Alternative Assessment Handbook, Rubrics 24: Oral Presentations; and 43: Writing to Persuade

Europe and Russia

Size Comparison: The United States and Europe and Russia

map Zone
Geography Skills

Place Europe is a small continent. Russia stretches from Eastern Europe across northern Asia.

1. **Name** What is the large region located in eastern Russia called?
2. **Make Inferences** Based on its latitude, what do you think the environment of Siberia is like?

Europe and Russia

Activity **Compare Size** Give each student a blank transparency. Have students locate a map of the United States in the atlas section in their textbook. Students should lay the transparency over the U.S. map and trace its outside boundary, or perimeter (not including Hawaii and Alaska). Students should also outline the boundaries for the state in which they live. Have students write the scale of the map somewhere on their transparency.

Next have students lay their transparencies over other maps and regions around the world. (These maps can also be found in the atlas section of their textbooks.) Have students look for countries that have about the same area as the state in which they live. Challenge students to find a country that covers roughly the same area as the continental United States.

Have students come together as a class and share their findings. Did students find the same countries? Verify each other's findings and evaluate whether or not the areas are similar. Emphasize that when comparing maps, the two maps should have the same scale. Discuss reasons why the map scales must be the same. Ask students how this activity helped them better understand the approximate sizes of countries in other world regions. **LS** **Visual/Spatial**

📒 Alternative Assessment Handbook, Rubrics 9: Comparing and Contrasting; and 20: Map Creation

💿 Interactive Skills Tutor CD-ROM, Lesson 1: Compare and Contrast

Differentiating Instruction

Struggling Readers
Below Level

1. Pair struggling readers with two other students. Have one partner dictate a question about the physical map while another student writes or types it. The third partner should answer the question.

2. Switch roles and repeat the activity until everyone has asked, written, and answered three questions. **LS** **Visual/Spatial, Verbal/Linguistic**

📒 Alternative Assessment Handbook, Rubric 21: Map Reading

English-Language Learners
Below Level

1. Have students draw a two-columned chart on notebook paper with the headings *nouns* and *adjectives*. As students examine the physical map on this page, have them list words in the appropriate column that describe what they see.

2. Have students compare lists with one another when they are finished. **LS** **Visual/Spatial, Verbal/Linguistic**

📒 Alternative Assessment Handbook, Rubrics 21: Map Reading; and 40: Writing to Describe

Answers

Map Zone 1. *Siberia;* 2. *possible answer—cold and harsh with sparse vegetation*

299

Explore the Map

Europe: Political Explain that Europe is often referred to as a peninsula of peninsulas. Trace the outline of Europe on a large wall map so that students can see how the entire continent of Europe is a peninsula. Ask students to examine the political map on this page and identify countries or pairs of countries that are peninsulas. *Spain and Portugal, Italy, Denmark, Norway and Sweden, Greece*

Ask volunteers to name the country to which each of the following islands belong: Sardinia *Italy*; Shetland Islands *U.K.*; Crete *Greece*; Balearic Islands *Spain*; Faeroe Islands *Denmark*; Corsica *France*

▶ Map Zone Transparency: Europe: Political

○ National capital
• Other city

0   200   400 Miles
0 200 400 Kilometers

Projection: Azimuthal Equal-Area

map zone
Geography Skills

Place Europe includes many small countries.
1. Name Which European countries are island countries?

2. Make Generalizations Based on this map, which countries do you think might have the largest populations? Why?

Collaborative Learning

At Level

Play a Quiz Game

1. Divide students into six groups and assign each group one color represented on the political map on this page. (Remind students that the colors on political maps have no particular meaning; they are shaded only to better emphasize the boundaries and shapes of the countries.)

2. Each group should begin by making a list of countries shaded their assigned color on the map. Then have students use an encyclopedia or almanac to write five Frequently Asked Questions (FAQs) about each country. The

questions should be written on index cards, and the answers should be written on the backs of the cards.

3. Have groups trade sets of cards and read the questions and answers out loud to one another.

4. Combine all the cards together and host a class Quiz Show, where teams compete to answer the questions correctly. **LS Verbal/Linguistic**

📝 Alternative Assessment Handbook, Rubrics 1: Acquiring Information; and 14: Group Activity

Answers

Map Zone 1. *Ireland, United Kingdom, Iceland;* **2.** *possible answers—probably countries in the mid-latitudes, which have mild climates; access to the Mediterranean Sea, the Atlantic Ocean, and the North Sea facilitates trade opportunities and the ability to support large populations.*

Europe and Russia

Russia and the Caucasus: Political

ATLANTIC OCEAN

ARCTIC OCEAN

North Sea

Barents Sea

Baltic Sea

Kaliningrad

EUROPE

St. Petersburg

Moscow

Nizhniy Novgorod

Volga River

Yekaterinburg

Samara

Black Sea

GEORGIA

Tbilisi

ARMENIA

Yerevan

Baku

AZERBAIJAN

Caspian Sea

KAZAKHSTAN

Ob River

Yenisey River

R U S S I A

Novosibirsk

Lena River

Sea of Okhotsk

Vladivostok

JAPAN

MONGOLIA

Bering Strait

Bering Sea

PACIFIC OCEAN

CHINA

Tropic of Cancer

- ⊙ National capital
- • Other city

0   300   600 Miles

0   300   600 Kilometers

Projection: Two-Point Equidistant

map Zone Geography Skills

Place Russia is the largest country in the world.

1. Use the Map About how many miles is Russia from west to east?

2. Analyze Where does Russia have access to the ocean? How do you think that affects trade?

EUROPE AND RUSSIA **301**

Explore the Map

Russia and the Caucasus: Political
As students look at the political map on this page, ask: What is the first thing you notice about Russia? *Many students will probably note its size.* What country in the Caucasus region consists of two separate areas? *Azerbaijan* Why do you think this is? *possible answers—as a result of war; because of the break-up of the Soviet Union; Armenia may have once been under Azerbaijan's control.*

▶ Map Zone Transparency: Russia and the Caucasus: Political

Cross-Discipline Activity: Mathematics

At Level

Measure Perimeter and Distance

1. Make enlarged copies of the political map on this page. Using the map scale, have students estimate the distance (in miles) of Russia's perimeter. Record students' estimates on the board.

2. Give each student a piece of string about 20 inches long. Have students lay the string around Russia's outside border. Students may use tape to hold the string in place. Have students cut the string where the two ends meet then pull the string off the map.

3. Using the map scale and string, ask students to calculate the distance of Russia's border. Have students compare string lengths and calculations.

4. When the entire class has agreed on one solution, compare the answer with the estimates students gave at the beginning of the activity. **LS Logical/Mathematical, Kinesthetic**

   Alternative Assessment Handbook, Rubrics 14: Group Activity; and 35: Solving Problems

Answers

Map Zone 1. *about 3,900 miles;*
2. *in the west, access to the Atlantic Ocean by way of the Baltic Sea; in the east, access to the Pacific Ocean by way of the Sea of Okhotsk and the Bering Sea; possible answer—With access to both the Atlantic and Pacific, Russia is able to trade with many countries around the world.*

301

Direct Teach

Explore the Map

Europe: Population Have students compare the population map on this page with the political map of the same region. Then have students answer the following questions: What two countries have between 25 and 130 people per square mile in all areas? *Latvia and Lithuania* Which island has the highest population density? *United Kingdom*

▶ Map Zone Transparency: Europe: Population

Answers

Map Zone 1. *Northern Europe is more heavily populated than the rest of Europe.*
2. *Northern European Plain*

302

Europe: Population

ARCTIC OCEAN

Denmark Strait

Norwegian Sea

Arctic Circle

70°N

60°N

50°N

40°N

30°W

20°W

10°W

ATLANTIC OCEAN

North Sea

Baltic Sea

RUSSIA

Kaliningrad (RUSSIA)

London

Berlin

Warsaw

Kiev

Paris

Vienna

Bucharest

Black Sea

Madrid

Barcelona

Rome

Adriatic Sea

ASIA

Aegean Sea

Strait of Gilbraltar

AFRICA

Mediterranean Sea

Persons per square mile	Persons per square km
520	200
260	100
130	50
25	10
3	1
0	0

● Major cities over 2 million

0   150   300 Miles
0   150   300 Kilometers

Projection: Azimuthal Equal-Area

map Zone
Geography Skills

Place Although Europe is small, it is densely populated.
1. Use the Map How does the population density of Northern Europe compare to the rest of Europe?
2. Compare Compare this map to the physical map. What large plain in Europe has a high population density?

302 REGIONAL ATLAS

Critical Thinking: Interpreting Maps

At Level

Analyze Population Near Rivers

1. As students examine the population map on this page, have them look for areas that are most and least populated.

2. Point out that many European cities are located on or near rivers. Have students compare this map to the physical map of Europe in the Atlas. Have students identify cities with large populations and determine what river or rivers those cities are near.

3. Students should draw a chart on a separate sheet of paper and record their findings in the chart.

Encourage them to use the population map to identify the metropolitan areas with more than two million residents. These cities should be included on their charts.

4. As a class, discuss reasons why these densely populated areas are usually located on or near major rivers. **LS Visual/Spatial, Verbal/Linguistic**

Alternative Assessment Handbook, Rubrics 12: Drawing Conclusions; and 21: Map Reading

Europe and Russia

Russia and the Caucasus: Climate

Climate Types
- Steppe
- Mediterranean
- Humid subtropical
- Humid continental
- Subarctic
- Tundra
- Highland

0   300   600 Miles
0   300   600 Kilometers

Projection: Two-Point Equidistant

map zone
Geography Skills

Regions Russia is dominated by cold climates.

1. Name Which climates cover large parts of Russia?

2. Analyze Based on this map, where do you think Russia's population is concentrated? Why? Which areas would you expect to have a low population density?

Explore the Map

Russia and the Caucasus: Climate Have students use the climate map on this page to answer the questions below:

Place What climate type dominates most of Russia? *subarctic*

Location What are some factors that may affect the climate in central and eastern Russia? *possible answers—northern latitude, large land mass, distance from the ocean*

▶ Map Zone Transparency: Russia and the Caucasus: Climate

Differentiating Instruction

Below Level   Standard English Mastery

English-Language Learners

1. Draw a graphic organizer on the board with "Siberia's climate" in the center with several smaller circles around it. Ask students to identify the climate type in Siberia. Ask for words that might describe the weather there and write the words in the smaller circles of the graphic organizer.

2. Tell students that because of Siberia's harsh climate, few people live there, and the area is very isolated compared to the rest of Russia. Discuss the meanings of the words *isolated* and *isolation*.

3. Then have students use standard English to write a letter from the perspective of someone who lives in Siberia to a friend who lives in Moscow. Have them imagine how that person might feel—based on the climate, weather, and effects of isolation—and express these feelings in their personal letters.

LS Verbal/Linguistic, Intrapersonal

Alternative Assessment Handbook, Rubrics 25: Personal Letters; and 41: Writing to Express

Answers

Map Zone 1. *humid continental, subarctic, tundra, steppe;* **2.** *possible answer—probably in the western part of the country, where the climate is milder. The eastern and far northern parts of the country have more severe climates and probably have a low population density.*

303

The World Almanac: Facts about Countries

Activity **Top Ten List** Have students use the data in the World Almanac chart on these pages to create a "Top Ten" list. Students may work individually or with a partner to create a multimedia presentation, in which they will present their list. Students can choose what their category will be. (i.e., countries with fewest number of TVs; highest population, highest per capita GDP, easternmost countries, highest life expectancy at birth, etc.)

Presentations should include images, music, sound effects, moving text, etc. If available, students should use multimedia software to create the presentation.

Have students take turns presenting to the rest of the class. **LS Visual/Spatial, Auditory/Musical, Verbal/Linguistic**

- Alternative Assessment Handbook, Rubric 22: Multimedia Presentations
- Interactive Skills Tutor CD-ROM, Lesson 8: Create Written, Visual, Oral Presentations

THE WORLD ALMANAC® Facts about Countries

Europe and Russia

COUNTRY Capital	FLAG	POPULATION	AREA (sq mi)	PER CAPITA GDP (U.S. $)	LIFE EXPECTANCY AT BIRTH	TVS PER 1,000 PEOPLE
Albania Tirana		3.6 million	11,100	$6,000	77.9	146
Andorra Andorra la Vella		83,888	181	$42,500	82.7	440
Armenia Yerevan		3 million	11,506	$6,300	72.7	241
Austria Vienna		8.2 million	32,382	$40,200	79.5	526
Azerbaijan Baku		8.2 million	33,436	$9,500	66.6	257
Belarus Minsk		9.6 million	80,155	$11,800	70.5	331
Belgium Brussels		10.4 million	11,787	$37,400	79.2	532
Bosnia and Herzegovina: Sarajevo		4.6 million	19,741	$6,500	78.5	112
Bulgaria Sofia		7.2 million	42,823	$12,900	73	429
Croatia Zagreb		4.5 million	21,831	$18,300	75.3	286
Czech Republic Prague		10.2 million	30,450	$25,900	76.7	487
Denmark Copenhagen		5.5 million	16,639	$37,100	78.2	776
Estonia Tallinn		1.3 million	17,462	$21,000	72.8	567
Finland Helsinki		5.3 million	130,559	$36,900	78.9	643
France Paris		64 million	211,209	$33,200	81	620
United States Washington, D.C.		307.2 million	3,718,711	$46,900	78.2	844

304 FACTS ABOUT COUNTRIES

Differentiating Instruction

Below Level

Special Needs Learners

Prep Required

Materials: scraps of cloth in a variety of colors

1. Pair special needs learners with other students. Pairs should choose a European country from the World Almanac chart. They will work together to research the meaning of the symbols on their selected country's flag.

2. Have either student use the scraps of cloth to create a reproduction of the country's flag. Students should cut the pieces of cloth into the correct shapes and sizes, then glue them onto a piece of cardstock or cardboard.

Meanwhile, their partners should write a paragraph explaining the meaning of the symbols on their flag based on their research.

3. When both tasks are complete, have each pair present their flag and paragraph to the rest of the class. Display the paragraphs and flags on a bulletin board. **LS Verbal/Linguistic, Kinesthetic, Interpersonal**

- Alternative Assessment Handbook, Rubric 30: Research

COUNTRY Capital	FLAG	POPULATION	AREA (sq mi)	PER CAPITA GDP (U.S. $)	LIFE EXPECTANCY AT BIRTH	TVS PER 1,000 PEOPLE
Georgia T'bilisi		4.6 million	26,911	$4,600	76.8	516
Germany Berlin		82.3 million	137,847	$35,400	79.2	581
Greece Athens		10.7 million	50,942	$32,000	79.6	480
Hungary Budapest		9.9 million	35,919	$19,800	73.3	447
Iceland Reykjavik		306,694	39,769	$41,800	80.6	505
Ireland Dublin		4.2 million	27,135	$45,300	78.2	406
Italy Rome		58.1 million	116,306	$31,300	80.2	492
Kosovo Pristina		1.8 million	4,203	$2,300	69.5	Not available
Latvia Riga		2.2 million	24,938	$17,300	72	757
Liechtenstein Vaduz		34,761	62	$118,000	80	469
Lithuania Vilnius		3.6 million	25,174	$17,800	74.8	422
Luxembourg Luxembourg		491,775	998	$81,000	79.3	599
Macedonia Skopje		2 million	9,781	$9,100	74.6	273
Malta Valletta		405,165	122	$24,700	79.4	549
Moldova Chişinau		4.3 million	13,067	$2,500	70.6	297
United States Washington, D.C.		307.2 million	3,718,711	$46,900	78.2	844

Direct Teach

The World Almanac: Facts about Countries

Interpret According to the chart, which country has the longest life expectancy? *Andorra has a life expectancy of 82.7*

Analyze Lead a class discussion about the countries with the lowest life expectancies. Have students find the five lowest life expectancies. *Azerbaijan, 66.6; Russia, 66.2; Ukraine, 68.2; Belarus, 70.5; Kosovo, 69.5.* Ask students to locate these countries on the political map and discuss why the region may have lower life expectancies. *possible answers—political unrest, diet and lifestyle, poverty*

Cross Discipline Activity: Music

At Level

Research National Anthems

1. Have individual students or small groups choose a European country to explore the history behind and lyrics of its national anthem.

2. Students can conduct research using the Internet or local library resources. Students should also find a recording of their country's national anthem.

3. Ask students to write a brief summary relating the history behind their country's national anthem. Students should type or print the lyrics of the song to be compiled in a class song book. Make copies of the song book for each student.

4. Have students take turns reading their summaries and playing their country's national anthem for the rest of the class. As students listen, they can follow the lyrics and sing along if they wish. **LS Auditory/Musical, Verbal/Linguistic**

🗒 Alternative Assessment Handbook, Rubrics 18: Listening; 26: Poems and Songs; and 30: Research

THE WORLD ALMANAC® Facts about Countries

COUNTRY / Capital	FLAG	POPULATION	AREA (sq mi)	PER CAPITA GDP (U.S. $)	LIFE EXPECTANCY AT BIRTH	TVS PER 1,000 PEOPLE
Monaco Monaco		32,965	1	$30,000	80.1	758
Montenegro Cetinje, Podgorica		672,180	5,415	$10,100	77.3	Not available
Netherlands Amsterdam		16.7 million	16,033	$40,400	79.4	540
Norway Oslo		4.7 million	125,182	$59,300	79.9	653
Poland Warsaw		38.5 million	120,728	$17,300	75.6	387
Portugal Lisbon		10.7 million	35,672	$22,200	78.2	567
Romania Bucharest		22.2 million	91,699	$12,200	72.3	312
Russia Moscow		140 million	6,592,772	$16,100	66.2	421
San Marino San Marino		30,324	24	$41,900	82	875
Serbia Belgrade		7.4 million	39,518	$10,800	75.4	277
Slovakia Bratislava		5.5 million	18,859	$21,900	75.3	418
Slovenia Ljubljana		2 million	7,827	$29,600	76.9	362
Spain Madrid		40.5 million	194,897	$34,700	80.1	555
Sweden Stockholm		9 million	173,732	$38,100	80.8	551
Switzerland Bern		7.6 million	15,942	$41,800	80.8	457
United States Washington, D.C.		307.2 million	3,718,711	$46,900	78.2	844

306 FACTS ABOUT COUNTRIES

Collaborative Activity

At Level

Research Required

Create an Awareness Campaign

1. Divide students into small groups to create awareness campaigns about the countries of the Caucasus.

2. Have groups use the information in the World Almanac chart about the Caucasus countries to come up with a slogan. Students should also do outside research to learn more quick facts about these.

3. Have each group create a banner displaying their slogan. Students should also create pamphlets, brochures, posters, maps, or other materials providing information about the Caucasus region.

4. Lead a class discussion about the Caucasus. Find out how many students were unfamiliar with the Caucasus region until now. Ask students how creating a campaign increased their own awareness about the Caucasus countries. **LS Verbal/Linguistic, Visual/Spatial, Interpersonal**

📓 Alternative Assessment Handbook, Rubrics 1: Acquiring Information; and 34: Slogans and Banners

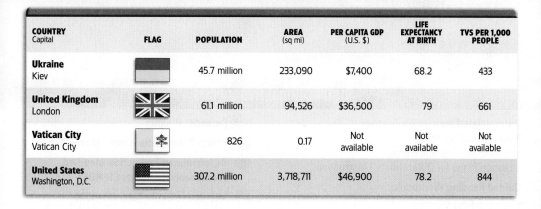

COUNTRY Capital	FLAG	POPULATION	AREA (sq mi)	PER CAPITA GDP (U.S. $)	LIFE EXPECTANCY AT BIRTH	TVS PER 1,000 PEOPLE
Ukraine Kiev		45.7 million	233,090	$7,400	68.2	433
United Kingdom London		61.1 million	94,526	$36,500	79	661
Vatican City Vatican City		826	0.17	Not available	Not available	Not available
United States Washington, D.C.		307.2 million	3,718,711	$46,900	78.2	844

World's Highest Per Capita GDPs

Liechtenstein
Qatar
Luxembourg
Norway
Kuwait
Brunei
Singapore
United States
Ireland
Andorra

■ European Countries
■ Other Countries

0 20 40 60 80 100 120
Per capita GDP
(in thousands of U.S. dollars)

Europe includes some of the wealthiest countries in the world. In fact, five of the ten countries with the highest per capita GDPs are in Europe.

Densely Populated Countries: Europe

Country	Population Density (per square mile)
Netherlands	1,278
Belgium	891
United Kingdom	655
Germany	611
Italy	512
Switzerland	495
Denmark	336
Poland	327
United States	87

Many European countries are densely populated, especially when compared to the United States.

ANALYSIS SKILL **ANALYZING INFORMATION**

1. What are the three most densely populated countries in Europe? How do their densities compare to that of the United States?
2. Which countries in Europe seem to have the lowest per capita GDPs? Look at the atlas political map. Where are these countries located in Europe?

EUROPE AND RUSSIA **307**

CHAPTER 13 PLANNING GUIDE

Overview	Instructional Resources

CHAPTER 13

Essential Question: What are the major political and cultural legacies from Europe's early history?

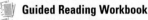 **Focus on the Essential Question Podcast**

TOS **Differentiated Instruction Teacher Management System:**
- Instructional Pacing Guides
- Lesson Plans for Differentiated Instruction

Guided Reading Workbook

Resource File:
- Chapter Review
- Focus on Reading: Re-reading
- Focus on Writing: Writing a Myth
- Social Studies Skills: Interpreting a Historical Map

Experiencing World History and Geography

TOS **Calendar Planner**

Power Presentations with Media Gallery

Differentiated Instruction Modified Worksheets and Tests CD-ROM

Interactive Skills Tutor CD-ROM

Student Edition on Audio CD-ROM

The World's Music Audio Program

World Outline Maps: Transparencies and Activities

Video: Origins of Western Culture

Section 1:

Ancient Greece

The Big Idea: Through colonization, trade, and conquest, the Greeks spread their culture in Europe and Asia.

TOS **Differentiated Instruction Teacher Management System:** Section 1 Lesson Plan

Guided Reading Workbook: Section 1

Resource File:
- Vocabulary Builder: Section 1
- Biography: Alexander the Great

Daily Bellringer Transparency: Section 1

Map Zone Transparency: Greek City-States and Colonies, c. 600 BC

Map Zone Transparency: Alexander the Great's Empire, c. 323 BC

Internet Activity: Alexander the Great

Animated Geography: The Empire of Alexander the Great

Video: Mysteries and Discoveries

Section 2:

The Roman World

The Big Idea: The Romans unified parts of Europe, Africa, and Asia in one of the ancient world's greatest civilizations.

TOS **Differentiated Instruction Teacher Management System:** Section 2 Lesson Plan

Guided Reading Workbook: Section 2

Resource File:
- Vocabulary Builder: Section 2
- Biography: Octavia Thurina Minor
- Primary Source: The Deeds of the Divine Augustus
- Geography and History: Rome's Trade Routes, First Century AD
- Critical Thinking: The Roads of Ancient Rome

Daily Bellringer Transparency: Section 2

Map Zone Transparency: Expansion of Rome, 100 BC–AD 117

Map Zone Transparency: Early Christianity in the Roman Empire

Internet Activity: Stadiums—Ancient and Modern

Animated Geography: Roman Aqueduct

Video: The Glory of Rome's Forum

Video: Ancient Rome: The Mobile Security

Section 3:

The Middle Ages

The Big Idea: Christianity and social systems influenced life in Europe in the Middle Ages.

TOS **Differentiated Instruction Teacher Management System:** Section 3 Lesson Plan

Guided Reading Workbook: Section 3

Resource File:
- Vocabulary Builder: Section 3
- Literature: "The Knight's Tale" from *The Canterbury Tales* by Geoffrey Chaucer
- Geography for Life: Transportation in Europe: Then and Now
- Interdisciplinary Project: Research Project: The Black Death

Daily Bellringer Transparency: Section 3

Map Zone Transparency: The First Crusade, 1096

Map Zone Transparency: The Black Death

Map Zone Transparency: Western Europe, 1000

Animated Geography: European Feudalism

Video: The Black Death

Chart Key:

 SE Student Edition   Presentation Resource 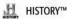 MP3 Audio

TOS Teacher One Stop   DVD/CD-ROM HISTORY™

 Printable Resource

Program Resources available on **TOS** and @ **hmhsocialstudies.com**

Review, Assessment, Intervention

 Europe and Russia Transparencies: Early History of Europe Visual Summary

 Spanish Chapter Summaries Audio CD

 Progress Assessment Support System (PASS): Chapter Test

 Differentiated Instruction Modified Worksheets CD-ROM: Modified Chapter Test

TOS **ExamView® Assessment Suite (English/Spanish)**

 Alternative Assessment Handbook

 Online Assessment Program, in the Interactive Student Edition

---

 PASS: Section 1 Quiz

 Online Quiz: Section 1

Alternative Assessment Handbook

 PASS: Section 2 Quiz

 Online Quiz: Section 2

 Alternative Assessment Handbook

PASS: Section 3 Quiz

Online Quiz: Section 3

Alternative Assessment Handbook

Supporting Resources

 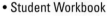

• Multimedia Classroom Global History Series
• Global History Teacher's Guide

Maps Globes Graphs Level F

• Student Workbook
• Teacher's Guide

Social Studies Trade Library Collections

• NCSS Middle School Trade Collection
• World Regions Trade Collection

Geography's Impact

Geography's Impact Video Program

• **Impact of Greek Scholars**

For more information or to purchase go to **hmhsocialstudies.com**

Power Presentations with Media Gallery

Power Presentations with Media Gallery are visual presentations of each chapter's main ideas. Presentations can be customized by including Quick Facts charts, images from the text, and video clips.

CHAPTER 13 PLANNING GUIDE

Differentiating Instruction

How do I address the needs of varied learners?

The Target Resource acts as your primary strategy for differentiated instruction.

ENGLISH-LANGUAGE LEARNERS & STRUGGLING READERS

TARGET RESOURCE

Resource File

The Resource File activities allow students to extend their knowledge of chapter-related places and people and to practice geography skills.

- Vocabulary Builder Activities
- Social Studies Skills: Interpreting a Historical Map

Additional Resources

Differentiated Instruction Teacher Management System: Lesson Plans for Differentiated Instruction

Europe and Russia Transparencies:
- Early History of Europe Visual Summary

Student Edition on Audio CD Program

Interactive Skills Tutor CD-ROM

Spanish Chapter Summaries Audio CD Program

Teacher One Stop:
- ExamView Assessment Suite, Spanish
- PuzzleView, Spanish

English-Language Learner Strategies and Activities

Spanish/English Guided Reading Workbook

SPECIAL NEEDS LEARNERS

TARGET RESOURCE

Guided Reading Workbook

The activities in the Guided Reading Workbook engage students with questions while presenting summaries of chapter content and provide opportunities for students to practice critical thinking skills.

Additional Resources

Differentiated Instruction Teacher Management System: Lesson Plans for Differentiated Instruction

Resource File: Social Studies Skills: Interpreting a Historical Map

Student Edition on Audio CD Program

Interactive Skills Tutor CD-ROM

Graphic Organizer Transparencies with Support for Reading and Writing

ADVANCED/GIFTED AND TALENTED STUDENTS

TARGET RESOURCE

Differentiated Instruction Teacher Management System

Lesson Plans for Differentiated Instruction provide teachers with strategies to help plan instruction for all learners.

Additional Resources

Resource File:
- Focus on Reading: Re-reading
- Focus on Writing: Writing a Myth
- Literature: "The Knight's Tale" from *The Canterbury Tales* by Geoffrey Chaucer

World History and Geography Document-Based Questions Activities

Geography, Science, and Cultures Activities

Experiencing World History and Geography

Differentiated Activities in the Teacher's Edition

- Identifying Rights of Roman Citizens, p. 319
- Understanding Cause and Effect, p. 324
- Matching Text and Images, p. 326
- Understanding Feudalism, p. 332
- Analyzing Homonyms, p. 333

Teacher One Stop™

How can I manage the lesson plans and support materials for differentiated instruction?

With the Teacher One Stop, you can easily organize and print lesson plans, planning guides, and instructional materials for all learners. The Teacher One Stop includes the following materials to help you differentiate instruction:

- **Interactive Teacher's Edition**
- **Calendar Planner and pacing guides**
- **Editable lesson plans**
- **All reproducible ancillaries in Adobe Acrobat (PDF) format**
- **ExamView Assessment Suite (English & Spanish)**
- **Transparency and video previews**

Differentiated Activities in the Teacher's Edition

- Understanding City Planning, p. 311
- Discussing Importance of Roads, p. 326
- Making a Travel Collage, p. 329

Interactive Student Edition

Complete online student edition with interactive multimedia support for chapter content assessment and reporting

- Interactive Maps and Notebook
- Standardized Test Prep
- Online Homework Practice and Research Activities
- Current Events
- Chapter-based Internet Activities
- Animated Geography Activities

Differentiated Activities in the Teacher's Edition

- Choosing Between Alternatives, p. 311
- Developing Maps, p. 329
- Creating Annotated Time Lines, p. 337

DIFFERENTIATED INSTRUCTION PLANNING GUIDE

308 CHAPTER 13

Chapter Preview

Essential Question

Introduce the Essential Question

• Lead students to understand that people in the United States help make decisions about their community, state, and nation by voting. Tell students that one of the earliest peoples to use voting to make major decisions was the ancient Greeks. In fact, Athens was the world's first democracy.

• Describe how the culture of Rome continues to influence government, architecture, languages, and legal systems in the world today.

• Explain that the Magna Carta, signed by King John of England in 1215, is considered to be one of the first steps toward democracy in modern Europe. It limited the king's power and established the law—not the king—as the supreme power in England.

Focus on Reading and Writing

Reading The Resource File provides a worksheet to help students practice re-reading.

📋 **RF:** Focus on Reading, Re-reading

Writing The Resource File provides a worksheet to help students organize and write their myths.

📋 **RF:** Focus on Writing, Writing a Myth

Key to Differentiating Instruction

Below Level

Basic-level activities designed for all students encountering new material

At Level

Intermediate-level activities designed for average students

Above Level

Challenging activities designed for honors and gifted and talented students

Standard English Mastery

Activities designed to improve standard English usage

LS Learning Styles

CHAPTER **13**

Early History of Europe

2000 BC–AD 1500

Essential Question What are the major political and cultural legacies from Europe's early history?

❓ What You Will Learn...

In this chapter you will learn about three major periods in the early history of Europe. First you will learn about ancient Greece, a culture whose ideas still shape the world. Then you will learn about Rome, one of the most powerful civilizations in all of world history. Finally, you will read about the Middle Ages, a time of great changes in Europe.

FOCUS ON READING AND WRITING

Re-reading Sometimes a single reading is not enough to fully understand a passage of text. If you feel like you do not fully understand a passage after you read it, it may help to re-read the passage more slowly. **See the lesson, Re-reading, on page 528.**

Writing a Myth A myth is a story that tries to explain why something happened. Throughout history, people have used myths to explain natural and historical events. After you read this chapter, you will write a myth that people might have used to explain a major event in European history.

308 CHAPTER 13

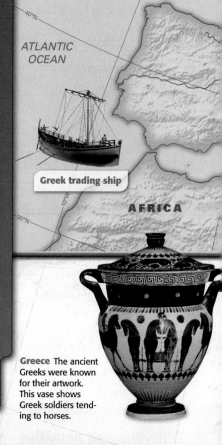

map zone

Geography Skills

Place Europe was home to some of the world's great civilizations.

1. **Locate** In what city was the Colosseum built?

2. **Analyze** Which of the buildings pictured on this map do you think is most impressive? Why?

ATLANTIC OCEAN

Greek trading ship

AFRICA

Greece The ancient Greeks were known for their artwork. This vase shows Greek soldiers tending to horses.

Introduce the Chapter

At Level

Building on the Past

1. Tell students that an ancient civilization flourished in Greece more than 2,000 years ago. Ask them to imagine that they are living there. Ask them what they think their lives would be like?

2. Explain that the people of the Roman Empire were inspired by Greek culture, and the people of the Middle Ages built on the achievements of both the Greeks and the Romans. Discuss how one period in history can influence another. Tell students that

in this chapter they will learn how ancient Greece and Rome and the world of the Middle Ages continue to affect their lives today.

3. Have students work in pairs to examine the chapter's visuals. Encourage them to look for connections between these images and the world as they know it today. **LS** Visual/Spatial

📋 Alternative Assessment Handbook, Rubrics 1: Acquiring Information; and 6: Cause and Effect

Europe, 2000 BC–AD 1500

North
Sea

Baltic Sea

Westminster Abbey in London

London

Paris

EUROPE

The Colosseum in Rome

Rome

Crusaders

ASIA

The Parthenon in Athens

Athens

Mediterranean Sea

0   100   300 Miles
0   100   200 Kilometers
Projection: Azimuthal Equal Area

HISTORY
Origins of Western Culture
hmhsocialstudies.com   VIDEO

Rome The forum, or town square, was central to life in ancient Rome. The ruins of the forum can still be seen in Rome.

Middle Ages
Warriors called knights were key to the political system of Europe in the Middle Ages. Knights wore suits of armor like this one into battle.

309

Chapter Preview

Explore the Map and Pictures

Europe, 2000 BC–AD 1500 Point out how relatively small (in land area) Greece and Italy are compared to the rest of Europe. Explain that much of the culture of ancient Greece and Rome was confined to the Mediterranean, while the culture of the Middle Ages spread across the entire continent.

Analyzing Visuals Have students study the images of the Colosseum and the Parthenon. Ask them if they have seen similar types of buildings today, and, if so, what this tells them about the influence of ancient Greece and Rome. Explain that many of the structures that the Greeks and Romans built centuries ago are still standing.

Tell students that Greeks often used vases such as the one shown here to store and carry wine and water.

▶ Map Zone Transparency: Europe, 2000 BC–AD 1500

hmhsocialstudies.com
Teacher Resources

Critical Thinking: Comparing

Comparing Maps

1. Have students compare physical, political, and historical maps of the region.

2. Begin by having students examine the map above and the other maps in this chapter, paying attention to the location of cities, colonies, and regions, such as the empires of Rome and Alexander the Great. Then have them study a physical map of the continent and make a list of general statements comparing the maps. For example, the Mediterranean world was densely settled by

the Greeks and Romans at different times. What is the climate of the region? What are its landforms? How might people make a living there?

3. Remind students that comparing physical and political maps can help them as they study a region or a historical period. **LS Visual/Spatial**

📝 Alternative Assessment Handbook, Rubrics 9: Comparing and Contrasting; and 21: Map Reading

Answers

Map Zone 1. *Rome;* **2.** *Responses will vary but should refer to Westminster Abbey, the Colosseum, or the Parthenon.*

Bellringer

If YOU lived there. . . Use the **Daily Bellringer Transparency** to help students answer the question.

▶ Daily Bellringer Transparency, Section 1

Early History of Europe   Daily Bellringer
                                                    Section 1

Preview Section 1

If YOU lived there ...
You live in the ancient city of Athens, one of the largest cities in Greece. Your brother, just two years older than you, is excited. He is finally old enough to take part in the city's government. He and your father, along with the other free men in the city, will meet to vote on the city's laws and leaders. Your mother and your sisters, however, cannot take part in the process.

Why is your brother excited about voting?

Consider being ABLE to vote:
• Your views are represented.
• You can help make new laws or improve old ones.
• You can feel proud about helping to rule Athens.

Consider NOT BEING ABLE to vote:
• Your views are not considered.
• You have no power to change things.
• You feel left out.

Key Terms and Places

📖 **RF:** Vocabulary Builder, Section 1

Taking Notes

Have students use the graphic organizer online to take notes on the section. This activity will prepare students for the Section Assessment, in which they will complete a graphic organizer that builds on the information using the Critical Thinking Skill: Analyzing.

SECTION 1

Ancient Greece

If YOU lived there...

You live in the ancient city of Athens, one of the largest cities in Greece. Your brother, just two years older than you, is excited. He is finally old enough to take part in the city's government. He and your father, along with the other free men in the city, will meet to vote on the city's laws and leaders. Your mother and your sisters, however, cannot take part in the process.

Why is your brother excited about voting?

What You Will Learn...

Main Ideas

1. Early Greek culture saw the rise of the city-state and the creation of colonies.
2. The golden age of Greece saw advances in government, art, and philosophy.
3. Alexander the Great formed a huge empire and spread Greek culture into new areas.

The Big Idea

Through colonization, trade, and conquest, the Greeks spread their culture in Europe and Asia.

Key Terms and Places

city-states, *p. 310*
golden age, *p. 312*
Athens, *p. 313*
Sparta, *p. 315*
Hellenistic, *p. 316*

hmhsocialstudies.com
TAKING NOTES

Use the graphic organizer online to take notes on key events in Greek history.

BUILDING BACKGROUND In ancient times, people in most cultures lived under the rule of a king. In Greece, however, life was different. There was no ruler who held power over all of Greece. Instead, people lived in independent cities. Each of these cities had its own government, culture, and way of life.

Early Greek Culture

Suppose you and some friends wanted to go to the movies, but you could not decide which movie to see. Some of you might want to see the latest action thriller, while others are more in the mood for a comedy. How could you decide which movie you would go to see? One way to decide would be to take a vote. Whichever movie got more votes would be the one you saw.

Did you know that by voting you would be taking part in a process invented some 2,500 years ago? It is true. One of the earliest peoples to use voting to make major decisions was the ancient Greeks. Voting was only one of the many contributions the Greeks made to our culture, though. In fact, many people call ancient Greece the birthplace of modern civilization.

City-States

Early Greece could be a dangerous place. Waves of invaders swept through the land, and violence was common. Eventually, people began to band together in groups for protection. Over time, these groups developed into **city-states**, or political units made up of a city and all the surrounding lands.

Teach the Big Idea   At Level

Ancient Greece

1. **Teach** Ask students the questions in the Main Idea boxes under Direct Teach.

2. **Apply** Have students draw a time line that includes the key events in the section, including information presented in the section's maps, visuals, and captions. Encourage students to share their time lines with the class. 🔲 **Visual/Spatial**

3. **Review** As a review of the section, have students create five multiple-choice

questions. Then have students quiz each other with the questions they have created.

4. **Practice/Homework** Have students illustrate their time lines with at least three events, people, or places mentioned in the section. 🔲 **Visual/Spatial**

📖 Alternative Assessment Handbook, Rubrics 3: Artwork; and 36: Time Lines

Greek City-States and Colonies, c. 600 BC

ATLANTIC OCEAN

EUROPE

Massilia
(Marseille)

ITALY

Adriatic Sea

Neapolis
(Naples)

Byzantium
(Istanbul)

Black
Sea

Corinth

ASIA
MINOR

GREECE

Athens

Mediterranean Sea

AFRICA

Cyrene

EGYPT

Area of Greek
influence

● Greek city-state
or colony

— Trade route

0   150   300 Miles
0 150 300 Kilometers

Projection: Azimuthal Equal Area

map zone
Geography Skills

Place The ancient Greeks set up colonies and traded goods and ideas with them.

1. **Locate** Around which bodies of water were Greek colonies established?
2. **Interpret** Why do you think Greek trade routes usually followed coastlines?

In the center of most city-states was a fortress on a hill. This hill was called the acropolis (uh-KRAH-puh-luhs), which is Greek for "top city." In addition to the fortress, many city-states built temples and other public buildings on the acropolis.

Around the acropolis was the rest of the city, including houses and markets. High walls usually surrounded the city for protection. In wartime, farmers who lived outside the walls could seek safety inside.

Living in city-states provided many advantages for the Greeks. The city was a place where people could meet and trade. In addition, the city-state gave people a new sense of identity. People thought of themselves as residents of a particular city-state, not as Greeks.

Colonies

In time, some city-states established new outposts, or colonies, around the Black and Mediterranean seas. You can see these colonies on the map above. Some of them still exist today as modern cities, such as Naples, Italy, and Marseille, France.

Although they were independent, most colonies kept ties with the older cities of Greece. They traded goods and shared ideas. These ties helped strengthen the economies of both cities and colonies, and they kept Greek culture strong. Because they stayed in contact, Greek cities all over Europe shared a common culture.

READING CHECK **Summarizing** Where did the ancient Greeks establish colonies?

EARLY HISTORY OF EUROPE **311**

Direct Teach

Main Idea

❶ **Early Greek Culture**

Early Greek culture saw the rise of the city-state and the creation of colonies.

Define What is a city-state? *a political unit made up of a city and the land surrounding it*

Describe In what ways was the acropolis the center of the city-state? *Not just a fortress, the acropolis was also where temples and public structures were built. Houses and markets were located around the acropolis.*

Make Inferences How did colonies help keep Greek culture strong? *by trading goods and sharing ideas with Greece*

▶ Map Zone Transparency: Greek City-States and Colonies, c. 600 BC

Info to Know

Cultural Origins The origins of Greek culture can be found in the Mycenaean age, which lasted from about 1600 BC to 1100 BC. People of this time were the first to worship many of the gods later worshipped by the Greeks. Other aspects of culture during this period, including architecture, inspired the Greeks. The stories of the heroes of this time, such as Achilles and Odysseus, were later related by the Greek poet Homer in his epic poems the *Iliad* and the *Odyssey* (8th century BC).

Differentiating Instruction

Special Needs Learners
Below Level

Have students discuss why the Greeks built their most prominent buildings on a hill, or acropolis. Then have them draw a picture of what a city-state might look like, including the acropolis, the houses, the markets, and the wall around the city.

LS **Visual/Spatial**

📖 Alternative Assessment Handbook, Rubric 3: Artwork

Advanced/Gifted and Talented
Above Level

Research Required

Ask students to imagine that they live in a Greek city-state, but have to move to a new colony in Spain or Italy. Suggest they do research to help them make their decision. With a partner, have them write a list of pros and cons. Then have them evaluate the list and make a decision.

LS **Verbal/Linguistic**

📖 Alternative Assessment Handbook, Rubric 16: Judging Information

Answers

Map Zone 1. *Mediterranean Sea, Black Sea;* **2.** *Most city-states and colonies were located on the coast.*

Reading Check *around the Black and Mediterranean seas*

Direct Teach

Main Idea

❷ The Golden Age of Greece

The golden age of Greece saw advances in government, art, and philosophy.

Recall Why did the Greek city-states band together around 500 BC? *to defend themselves against the invading Persians*

Identify Cause and Effect In what way did the armed struggle between the Greeks and the Persians make the golden age possible? *The Greeks were able to defeat the Persians, thus gaining confidence and the realization that they were capable of great achievements.*

Predict What might have happened if the city-states had not banded together? *They might all have been conquered.*

Close-up
The Parthenon

Athena Tell students that Athena, after whom Athens was named, was the goddess of war and handicrafts. She was also the goddess of wisdom, or reason, and was associated with owls. The owl became the symbol of Athens as well. Point out the owl on Athena's staff as well as on her spear and military dress.

Linking to Today

Return of the Stones? In the early 1800s, many parts of the Parthenon—columns and sculptures—were moved to London. Today, they still reside there, at the British Museum. Many people around the world believe they should be returned to Greece, to restore the cultural integrity of the Parthenon. To learn more, visit www.parthenonuk.com.

About the Illustration
This illustration is an artist's conception based on available sources. However, historians are uncertain exactly what this scene looked like.

The Golden Age of Greece

When most people think of ancient Greek culture today, certain images come to mind. They think of the ruins of stately temples and of realistic statues. They also think of great writers, philosophers, and scientists whose ideas changed the world.

These images represent some of the many contributions the Greeks made to world history. Remarkably, most of these contributions were developed during a relatively short time, between 500 and 300 BC. For that reason, this period is often called a **golden age**, a period in a society's history marked by great achievements.

The Growth of Greek Power

Early in Greece's history, city-states remained fiercely independent. Each city-state focused on its own concerns and did not interfere in the others' affairs.

Around 500 BC, however, an invading army caused the Greeks to band together against a common enemy. That invasion came from Persia, a powerful empire in central Asia. The Persian army was huge, well-trained, and experienced. Greece, on the other hand, had no single army. Each city-state had an army, but none was as large as Persia's. As a result, the Persians expected a quick victory.

HISTORY
VIDEO
Mysteries and Discoveries
hmhsocialstudies.com

Close-up

The Parthenon

The Parthenon is often seen as a symbol of ancient Athens. It was a beautiful temple to the goddess Athena, whom the people of Athens considered their protector. The temple is now in ruins, but this illustration shows how it may have looked when it was built around 440 BC.

The Parthenon was decorated with carvings of events from Greek history and mythology.

Once a year, the people of Athens held a great festival in honor of Athena. Part of the festival included a great procession that wound through the city.

312 CHAPTER 13

Critical Thinking: Drawing Conclusions

Above Level

Debating Progress vs. Preservation

Research Required

1. Tell students that air pollution is a serious problem in Athens today, damaging the marble of the Parthenon and other monuments.

2. Have students search the Internet or library to learn more about the sources and effects of the pollution. Ask them to also research what is being done to prevent the damage.

3. Assign groups different sides in a debate. Tell them that there is only enough money to either repair the monuments (preservation)

or finish new projects in Athens (progress). Have each group gather reasons to support its position.

4. Have students debate the issue. Afterward, have them explain whether or not they were persuaded by the other side's arguments, and why. **Verbal/Linguistic, Interpersonal**

Alternative Assessment Handbook, Rubrics 10: Debates; and 30: Research

Nevertheless, the Greeks took up arms against the Persians. Led by **Athens**, a city-state in eastern Greece, the Greeks were able to defeat the Persians and keep Greece from being conquered. When the Persians invaded again 10 years later, the Athenians once again helped defeat them.

The victory over the Persians increased the confidence of people all over Greece. They realized that they were capable of great achievements. In the period after the Persian invasion, the people of Greece made amazing advances in art, writing, and thinking. Many of these advances were made by the people of Athens.

Athenian Culture

In the century after the defeat of Persia, Athens was the cultural center of Greece. Some of history's most famous politicians, artists, and thinkers lived in Athens during this time.

One reason for the great advances the Athenians made during this time was their city's leadership. Leaders such as Pericles (PER-uh-kleez), who ruled Athens in the 400s BC, supported the arts and encouraged the creation of great works. For example, Pericles hired great architects and artists to construct and decorate the Parthenon, the temple shown below.

marathon

Inside the Parthenon was a magnificent statue of Athena by the sculptor Phidias. Many people consider him the greatest sculptor in all of Greece.

Like most Greek temples, the Parthenon had huge marble columns to support its roof.

ANALYSIS SKILL   ANALYZING VISUALS
Why do you think people consider the Parthenon to be a symbol of ancient Athens?

313

313

Main Idea

❷ The Golden Age of Greece, *continued*

The golden age of Greece saw advances in government, art, and philosophy.

Recall Which war led to the end of the golden age in Greece? *the war between Sparta and Athens*

Make Generalizations What did Greek artists, scientists, and philosophers have in common? *They all closely studied human beings.*

Connect to Civics

Pericles The following text is from a famous funeral oration given by Pericles after the first battles between Athens and Sparta.

"Our constitution does not copy the laws of neighboring states; we are rather a pattern to others than imitators ourselves. Its administration favors the many instead of the few; this is why it is called a democracy. If we look to the laws, they afford equal justice to all in their private differences; if no social standing, advancement in public life falls to reputation for capacity . . . ; nor again does poverty bar the way, if a man is able to serve the state, he is not hindered by the obscurity of his condition."

Teaching Tip

Read the excerpt aloud, pausing after each clause or sentence to clarify difficult vocabulary or concepts.

About the Illustration

This illustration is an artist's conception based on available sources. However, historians are uncertain exactly what this scene looked like.

Athenian Democracy

Athens was governed as a democracy. Once a month, all adult men in the city gathered together in an assembly to make the city's laws.

Men spoke in the assembly to support or argue against ideas. Sometimes, people in the crowd argued with them.

Voting was done either by show of hands or by secret ballot. The ballots used were broken pieces of pottery.

BIOGRAPHY

Pericles
(c. 495–429 BC)

Pericles, the most famous leader in all of Athenian history, wanted the city's people to be proud of their city. In his speeches, he emphasized the greatness of Athenian democracy and encouraged everyone to take part. He also worked to make the city beautiful. He hired the city's best architects to build monuments, such as the Parthenon, and hired great artists to decorate them. He also supported the work of writers and poets in order to make Athens the cultural center of all Greece.

Athenian Democracy

Leaders like Pericles had great power in Athens, but they did not rule alone. The city of Athens was a democracy, and its leaders were elected. In fact, Athens was the world's first democracy. No one else in history had created a government in which people ruled themselves.

In Athens most power was in the hands of the people. All the city's leaders could do was suggest ideas. Those ideas had to be approved by an assembly made up of the city's free men before they were enacted. As a result, it was vital that all the men of Athens took part in making government decisions.

The people of Athens were very proud of their democracy, and also of their city in general. This pride was reflected in their city's buildings and art.

Turn back to the previous page and look at the picture of the Parthenon again. Why do you think the temple was so large and so elaborately decorated? Like many Greek buildings, it was designed to be a symbol of the city. It was supposed to make people see Athens as a great and glorious city.

Architecture and Art

The Parthenon may be the most famous building from ancient Greece, but it is only one of many magnificent structures built by the Greeks. All over Greece, builders created beautiful marble temples. These temples were symbols of the glory of the cities in which they were built.

Greek temples and other buildings were often decorated with statues and carvings. These works by Greek artists are still admired by people today.

314 CHAPTER 13

Critical Thinking: Comparing and Contrasting   **At Level**

Writing a Comparison-Contrast Essay   **Research Required**

1. Have students research the similarities and differences between U.S. and Athenian democracy. Ask them to focus on institutions, citizens' rights/responsibilities, and lawmaking.

2. Have students write a comparison-contrast essay. Have them use a graphic organizer such as the one shown to organize their information.

	U.S.	Athenian
Institutions		
Citizens' rights/responsibilities		
Lawmaking		

LS Verbal/Linguistic, Visual/Spatial

Alternative Assessment Handbook, Rubrics 9: Comparing and Contrasting; 13: Graphic Organizers; and 42: Writing to Inform

Greek art is so admired because of the skill and careful preparation of ancient Greek artists. These artists wanted their works to look realistic. To achieve their goals, they watched people as they stood and moved. They wanted to learn exactly what the human body looked like while it was in motion. The artists then used what they learned from their observations to make their statues as lifelike as possible.

Science, Philosophy, and Literature

Artists were not the only people in ancient Greece to study other people. Scientists, for example, studied people to learn how the body worked. Through these studies, the Greeks learned a great deal about medicine and biology. Other Greek scholars made great advances in math, astronomy, and other areas of science.

Greek philosophers, or thinkers, also studied people. They wanted to figure out how people could be happy. Three of the world's most influential philosophers—Socrates, Plato, and Aristotle—lived and taught in Athens during this time. Their ideas continue to shape how we live and think even today.

The ancient Greeks also made huge contributions to world literature. Some of the world's timeless classics were written in ancient Greece. They include stories of Greek heroes and their daring adventures, poems about love and friendship, and myths meant to teach lessons about life. Chances are that you have read a book, seen a film, or watched a play inspired by— or even written by—the ancient Greeks.

Actually, if you have ever seen a play at all then you have the Greeks to thank. The ancient Greeks were the first people to write and perform drama, or plays. Once a part of certain religious ceremonies, plays became one of the most popular forms of entertainment in Greece.

The Decline of the City-States

As great as it was, the Greek golden age could not last forever. In the end, Greece was torn apart by a war between Athens and its rival city-state, **Sparta**.

Sparta was a military city with one of the strongest armies in Greece. Jealous of the influence Athens had over other city-states, the Spartans attacked Athens.

The war between these two powerful city-states devastated Greece. Other city-states joined the war, supporting one side or the other. For years the war went on. In the end, Sparta won, but Greece was in shambles. Thousands of people had been killed and whole cities had been destroyed. Weakened, Greece lay open for a foreign conqueror to swoop in and take over.

READING CHECK Analyzing Why is the period between 500 and 300 BC called a golden age in Greece?

Greek Art

The ancient Greeks took great care to make their art lifelike. This statue shows Athena, a goddess from Greek mythology.

ANALYZING VISUALS What details make this statue lifelike?

EARLY HISTORY OF EUROPE **315**

Connect to Math and Science

More than Pi Greek scientists and mathematicians made many advances during and after the golden age. Euclid published theories that became the foundation of modern geometry, and Archimedes calculated the value of pi. Greek geographers correctly calculated the circumference of the earth. They also knew that the earth rotated on its axis and revolved around the sun. (This knowledge would not be widely accepted for nearly 2,000 years.) Other scientists invented machines operated by air, water pressure, and steam. However, the technology did not yet exist to build many of them. Medical scientists also made many discoveries based on their studies of the human body. The Hippocratic oath, describing the Greeks' notion of ethical medical behavior, is still sworn by doctors today.

History Humor

Why is a museum like an old frying pan? *because it's full of ancient Greece*

Connect to English/ Language Arts

Greek Roots The word for city-state in Greek is *polis*. This word is the root of several English words having to do with cities and government, including *politics, policy, politician, cosmopolitan, and metropolis.*

Reading Poetry Aloud

Materials: samples of Greek poetry

1. Provide students with samples of Greek lyric and epic poetry. Read one or two of the poems aloud.

2. Have students prepare to read the poems aloud by reading them several times—first silently to themselves and then aloud to a partner. Encourage them to pay attention to mood, subject matter, rhyme patterns, and rhythm.

3. Have students read their poems to the class. Ask listeners to give feedback, both about the content of the poems and the style in which they were read.

4. Tell students that the Greeks have inspired many modern writers, including the American poet H.D. (Hilda Doolittle). Have them find some of H.D.'s poems and read them aloud to the class. **LS Verbal/Linguistic**

   Alternative Assessment Handbook, Rubrics 18: Listening; and 26: Poems and Songs

Answers

Reading Check *because the Greeks made many contributions to culture— art, architecture, literature, philosophy, science, drama, and democracy—during this period*

Greek Art *the facial features, the arm and hand, the folds in the clothing*

❸ **The Empire of Alexander**

Alexander the Great formed a huge empire and spread Greek culture into new areas.

Recall How many years did it take Alexander to establish his empire? *about 11 years*

Explain Why did Alexander turn back toward home in 325 BC? *His troops were tired and far from home, and they demanded that Alexander turn back.*

Sequence Which was the first place that Alexander conquered? *Greece* Which was the last? *western India*

Elaborate Imagine that you are a Greek arriving in a new land that is part of Alexander the Great's empire. What part of your culture would you most want to share with your new neighbors? Why? *Students' responses will vary, but should reflect section content.*

📖 **RF:** Biography, Alexander the Great

▶️ Map Zone Transparency: Alexander the Great's Empire, c. 323 BC

The Empire of Alexander

In fact, a conqueror did take over all of Greece in the 330s BC. For the first time in its history, all of Greece was unified under a single ruler. He was from an area called Macedonia just north of Greece, an area that many Greeks considered uncivilized. He was known as Alexander the Great.

Alexander's Conquests

Alexander swept into Greece with a strong, well-trained army in 336 BC. In just a few years, he had conquered all of Greece.

Alexander, however, was not satisfied to rule only Greece. He wanted to create a huge empire. In 334 BC he set out to do just that. As you can see on the map, he was quite successful.

At its greatest extent, Alexander's empire stretched from Greece in the west all the way to India in the east. It included nearly all of central Asia—including what had been the Persian Empire—and Egypt. Alexander had dreams of extending his empire even farther east, but his troops refused to keep fighting. Tired and far from home, they demanded that Alexander turn back. He did, turning back toward home in 325 BC. On his way back home, however, Alexander became ill and died. He was 33.

The Spread of Greek Culture

FOCUS ON READING

After you read this passage, reread it to make sure you understand all the details.

During his life, Alexander wanted Greek culture to spread throughout his empire. To help the culture spread, he built cities in the lands he conquered and urged Greek people to move there. He named many of the cities Alexandria after himself.

As Greek people moved to these cities, however, they mingled with the people and cultures in the area. As a result, Greek culture blended with other cultures. The result was a new type of culture that mixed elements from many people and places.

Because the Greek word for Greek is Hellenic, historians often refer to these blended cultures as **Hellenistic**, or Greek-like. Hellenistic culture helped shape life in Egypt, central Asia, and other parts of the world for many years.

READING CHECK Finding Main Ideas What lands were included in Alexander's empire?

SUMMARY AND PREVIEW Greece was the location of the first great civilization in Europe. In time, though, it was defeated by a new power, the Roman Empire.

Map legend:
- Empire c. 323 BC
- ✶ Major battle site
- → Route of Alexander and his armies

0   150   300 Miles
0   150   300 Kilometers

Projection: Two-Point Equidistant

Cross-Discipline Activity: Art

At Level

Creating a Political Cartoon

Materials: copies of political cartoons

1. Have students work individually or in pairs to create a political cartoon based on one or more details from the section. Before they begin, distribute copies of current political cartoons. Then lead a discussion about what makes the cartoons "work."

2. Students should first review the section, looking for events, places, or people that could be satirized in a cartoon. Once they

have chosen their subject, they may begin with the illustration or the caption. Encourage them to experiment with different styles.

3. Have students display their cartoons. Discuss how political cartoons can help us view historical and current events in new ways.

   LS Visual/Spatial

📖 Alternative Assessment Handbook, Rubric 27: Political Cartoons

---

Answers

Reading Check *lands from Greece and Egypt in the west across southern Asia to India in the east*

Alexander the Great's Empire, c. 323 BC

CAUCASUS MOUNTAINS

Caspian Sea

Jaxartes River (Syr Darya)

Alexandria Eskhata

Oxus River (Amu Darya)

BACTRIA

HINDU KUSH

Alexandria on the Caucasus

Alexandropolis

Kabul

Alexandria Nicaea

Alexandria Bucephala

Gaugamela 331 BC

PARTHIA

Ecbatana

Alexandria Areia

PERSIAN EMPIRE

Alexandria Arachoton (Kandahar)

Indus River

Alexandria Opiana

Susa

Babylon

Euphrates River

Pasargadae

INDIA

Alexandria

Persepolis

Alexandria Carmana

Arabian Peninsula

Persian Gulf

Alexandria

Pattala

Arabian Sea

map zone
Geography Skills

Regions Alexander the Great's empire included much of central Asia, Europe, and Egypt.

1. **Identify** What rivers did Alexander cross?
2. **Analyze** About how long was the route of Alexander from Pella to Babylon?

Section 1 Assessment

Reviewing Ideas, Terms, and Places

1. **a. Describe** What did an ancient Greek **city-state** include?
   b. Explain Why did the Greeks form city-states?
2. **a. Identify** What were some major achievements in Greece between 500 and 300 BC?
   b. Summarize What was the government of ancient Athens like?
   c. Evaluate Would you have liked living in ancient Greece? Why or why not?
3. **a. Describe** How did Alexander the Great try to spread Greek culture in his empire?
   b. Drawing Conclusions How might Greek history have been different if Alexander had not existed?

Critical Thinking

4. **Analyzing** Using your notes, draw a time line of major events in Greek history. For each event you list on your time line, write a sentence explaining why it was important.

FOCUS ON WRITING

5. **Choosing Characters** Many ancient myths focused on the deeds of heroes or other great figures. What people from ancient Greece might feature in such a myth? Write some ideas in your notebook.

EARLY HISTORY OF EUROPE **317**

Did you know...

According to the Greek historian Plutarch, Alexander the Great founded over 70 new cities in his effort to spread Greek culture.

Review & Assess

Close

Briefly review the sequence of events in the chapter, from the early days of Greece through the death of Alexander the Great.

Review

Online Quiz, Section 1

Assess

SE Section 1 Assessment
PASS: Section 1 Quiz
Alternative Assessment Handbook

Reteach/Classroom Intervention

Guided Reading Workbook, Section 1
Interactive Skills Tutor CD-ROM

Section 1 Assessment Answers

1. **a.** a city and all the surrounding lands
   b. for protection against invaders

2. **a.** government (democracy), architecture and art (Parthenon), science, philosophy, and literature (drama)
   b. a democracy, with most power in the hands of the people. Leaders' ideas had to be approved by an assembly of free men.
   c. Students' answers will vary, but should reflect section content.

3. **a.** by building cities in the conquered lands and urging Greeks to move there

   b. Greece may not have become unified; Greek culture may not have spread.

4. Students should list the major events on the time line, such as the establishment of city-states and colonies, Athens's defeat of the Persians, the golden age, war with Sparta, and Alexander's conquest of Greece.

5. Students' ideas about characters will vary. They should record their ideas in their notebooks.

Answers
Map Zone 1. *the Nile, Tigris, Indus, and Oxus rivers;* **2.** *about 3,000 miles*

Bellringer

If YOU lived there. . . Use the **Daily Bellringer Transparency** to help students answer the question.

▶️ Daily Bellringer Transparency, Section 2

Academic Vocabulary

Review with students the high-use academic term in this section.

facilitate to make easier (p. 321)

📄 RF: Vocabulary Builder Activity, Section 2

Taking Notes

Have students use the graphic organizer online to take notes on the section. This activity will prepare students for the Section Assessment, in which they will complete a graphic organizer that builds on the information using the Critical Thinking skill: Identifying Cause and Effect.

The Roman World

What You Will Learn...

Main Ideas

1. The Roman Republic was governed by elected leaders.
2. The Roman Empire was a time of great achievements.
3. The spread of Christianity began during the empire.
4. Various factors helped bring about the decline of Rome.

The Big Idea

The Romans unified parts of Europe, Africa, and Asia in one of the ancient world's greatest civilizations.

Key Terms and Places

Rome, *p. 318*
republic, *p. 319*
Senate, *p. 319*
citizens, *p. 319*
Carthage, *p. 320*
empire, *p. 320*
aqueducts, *p. 322*

hmhsocialstudies.com
TAKING NOTES

Use the graphic organizer online to take notes on Roman history and culture.

If YOU lived there...

You live in Rome in about 50 BC. Times are difficult for ordinary Romans. Bread is scarce in the city, and you are finding it hard to find work. Now a popular general is mounting a campaign to cross the mountains into a territory called Gaul. He wants to try to conquer the barbarians who live there. It might be dangerous, but being a soldier guarantees work and a chance to make money.

Will you join the army? Why or why not?

BUILDING BACKGROUND Rome's well-trained army helped it conquer large parts of Europe, Africa, and Asia. Through these conquests, Rome built a long-lasting empire that left its mark on the languages, cultures, and government of Europe.

The Roman Republic

"All roads lead to Rome." "Rome was not built in a day." "When in Rome, do as the Romans do." Have you heard these sayings before? All of them were inspired by the civilization of ancient Rome, a civilization that collapsed more than 1,500 years ago.

Why would people today use sayings that relate to so old a culture? They refer to Rome because it was one of the greatest and most influential civilizations in history. In fact, we can still see the influence of ancient Rome in our lives.

Rome's Early History

Rome was not always so influential, however. At first it was just a small city in Italy. According to legend, the city of **Rome** was established in the year 753 BC by a group called the Latins.

For many years, the Romans were ruled by kings. Not all of these kings were Latin, though. For many years the Romans were ruled by a group called the Etruscans. The Romans learned a great deal from the Etruscans. For example, they learned about written language and how to build paved roads and sewers. Building on what they learned from the Etruscans, the Romans made Rome into a large and successful city.

Teach the Big Idea

At Level

The Roman World

1. **Teach** Ask students the questions in the Main Idea boxes under Direct Teach.

2. **Apply** Have students create a chart with four columns labeled *People, Places, Events,* and *Ideas.* As they read, have them fill in the columns with details from the section. **LS Visual/Spatial**

3. **Review** Have students compare the entries on their charts. Then have them quiz each other about their entries.

4. **Practice/Homework** Have students choose one detail from each column and write one paragraph on each, describing the importance of that person, place, event, or idea. **LS Verbal/Linguistic**

📄 Alternative Assessment Handbook, Rubric 7: Charts /p

The Beginning of the Republic

Not all of Rome's kings were good leaders, or good people. Some were cruel, harsh, and unfair. The last king of Rome was so unpopular that he was overthrown. In 509 BC a group of Roman nobles forced the king to flee the city.

In place of the king the people of Rome created a new type of government. They formed a **republic**, a type of government in which people elect leaders to make laws for them. Once elected, these leaders made all government decisions.

To help make some decisions, Rome's leaders looked to the **Senate**, a council of rich and powerful Romans who helped run the city. By advising the city's leaders, the Senate gained much influence in Rome.

For Rome's republican government to succeed, **citizens**, or people who could take part in the government, needed to be active. Rome's leaders encouraged citizens to vote and to run for office. As a result, speeches and debates were common in the city. One popular place for these activities was in the forum, the city's public square.

HISTORY

VIDEO
The Glory of Rome's Forum

hmhsocialstudies.com

Close-up

The Roman Forum

The forum was a large public square that stood in the center of the city. Roman citizens often met in the forum to discuss city affairs and politics.

Government buildings and temples stood on the hills around the forum.

Only citizens, or people who could vote, were allowed to wear this article of clothing, called a toga.

Many people met in the forum to discuss politics, current affairs, and other issues.

ANALYSIS SKILL **ANALYZING VISUALS**
What are some places in your local community that serve the same function as the forum did?

319

319

Did you know. . .

Upon becoming emperor, Augustus was referred to as the *princeps*, or "first citizen." He led a relatively simple life, with little interest in personal luxury.

📄 **RF:** Biography, Octavia Thurina Minor

📄 **RF:** Primary Source, *The Deeds of the Divine Augustus*

Did you know. . .

Most men of the ancient world did not shave, although Rome encouraged its soldiers to shave (supposedly to look "manly" and for hygiene). The first Roman to shave every day was thought to be the Roman general Scipio Africanus (256–184 BC).

About the Illustration

This illustration is an artist's conception based on available sources. However, historians are uncertain exactly what this scene looked like.

FOCUS ON READING
After you read this passage, re-read it. Make a list of details you did not notice in your first reading.

Growth and Conquest

After the creation of the republic, the Romans began to expand their territory. They started this expansion in Italy. As the map at right shows, however, the republic kept growing. By 100 BC the Romans ruled much of the Mediterranean world.

The Romans were able to take so much land because of their strong, organized army. They used this army to conquer their rivals. For example, the Romans fought the people of **Carthage**, a city in North Africa, and took over their lands.

Rome's expansion did not stop in 100 BC. In the 40s BC a general named Julius Caesar conquered many new lands for Rome. Caesar's conquests made him very powerful and very popular in Rome. Afraid of Caesar's power, a group of Senators decided to put an end to it. They banded together and killed Caesar in 44 BC.

READING CHECK Summarizing How did the Romans expand their territory?

The Roman Empire

The murder of Julius Caesar changed Roman society completely. The Romans were shocked and horrified by his death, and they wanted Caesar's murderers to be punished. One of the people they called on to punish the murderers was Caesar's adopted son, Octavian. Octavian's actions would reshape the Roman world. Under his leadership, Rome changed from a republic to an **empire**, a government that includes many different peoples and lands under a single rule.

The First Emperor

Octavian moved quickly to punish his uncle's murderers. He led an army against them and, before long, defeated them all.

After defeating his enemies, Octavian became more powerful. One by one, he eliminated his rivals for power. Eventually, Octavian alone ruled the entire Roman world as Rome's first emperor.

Roman Conquests

The Roman army was both powerful and flexible, which allowed it to take on and defeat many foes. Even the huge elephants ridden by the soldiers of Carthage were no match for the Romans' bravery and cleverness.

ANALYZING VISUALS What kind of equipment did the Roman army use?

320 CHAPTER 13

Critical Thinking: Making Generalizations   [At Level]

Analyzing the Qualities of a Good Leader

1. In small groups, have students discuss what qualities they think a good leader should have. Encourage them to reread the material about Caesar, Augustus, and Pericles in the previous section. Have them discuss other leaders, either contemporary or historical. Then have them make a list of the qualities that a good leader should possess.

2. Have students write an instruction manual for a good leader to follow. In the manual, have them explain to the leader why he or she needs to take certain actions or have certain policies. Have them support their argument with details about a contemporary or historical leader.

3. Have groups share their instruction manuals and discuss their conclusions.
   LS Interpersonal, Verbal/Linguistic

   📄 Alternative Assessment Handbook, Rubrics 14: Group Activity; and 43: Writing to Persuade

---

Answers

Reading Check *by using their strong, flexible, and well-organized army to conquer their rivals*

Analyzing Visuals *shields, spears, helmets, armor*

Expansion of Rome, 100 BC–AD 117

North
Sea

ATLANTIC
OCEAN

BRITAIN

EUROPE

GAUL

ALPS

Rhine River

Danube River

SPAIN

Rome

Carthage

Mediterranean Sea

AFRICA

Black Sea

Byzantium

GREECE

ASIA MINOR

Athens

Caspian Sea

Tigris River

Euphrates River

Jerusalem

Alexandria

ASIA

EGYPT

Nile River

Red Sea

Roman Republic, 100 BC
Republic at Caesar's death, 44 BC
Empire at Augustus's death, AD 14
Greatest extent of empire, AD 117

0   200   400 Miles
0   200   400 Kilometers

Projection: Azimuthal Equal Area

map zone **Geography Skills**

Place The Roman Empire grew greatly by AD 117.
1. **Locate** Where were the borders of the Roman Empire in 117?
2. **Draw Conclusions** The Romans called the Mediterranean "Our Sea." Why do you think this is so?

As emperor, Octavian was given a new name, Augustus, which means "honored one." The people of Rome respected and admired Augustus. This respect was mainly the result of his many accomplishments. As the map above shows, Augustus added a great deal of territory to the empire. He also made many improvements to lands already in the empire. For example, he built monuments and public buildings in the city of Rome. He also improved and expanded Rome's network of roads, which **facilitated** both travel and trade.

The Pax Romana

The emperors who ruled after Augustus tried to follow his example. Some of them worked to add even more land to the empire. Others focused their attentions on improving Roman society.

Because of these emperors' efforts, Rome experienced a long period of peace and achievement. There were no major wars or rebellions within the empire, and trade increased. This period, which lasted for about 200 years, was called the Pax Romana, or the Roman Peace.

ACADEMIC VOCABULARY

facilitate
(fuh-SI-luh-tayt)
to make easier

EARLY HISTORY OF EUROPE **321**

Direct Teach

History Humor

A teacher quizzed the class, "When was Rome built?"

One student replied, "At night."

"Why do you think at night?" asked the teacher.

"Because we all know that Rome wasn't built in a day!" answered the student.

Connect to Technology

Roman Aqueducts To bring water to its huge population, the Romans built 11 major aqueducts. The longest was nearly 60 miles long. Many were built above ground and supported by arches. Others were built underground. Some of the water went directly to the emperor and to the homes of the wealthy. The rest went to public fountains and bath complexes. Today the ruins of aqueducts can be seen throughout the former Roman Empire, from southern Europe to northern Africa and Asia Minor.

Linking to Today

Welcome to the Colosseum Over two million people visit this ancient wonder each year. Ongoing restoration projects allow visitors greater access to it and, perhaps more importantly, provide researchers with important new information about the site.

hmhsocialstudies.com

Online Resources
Activity: Stadiums—
Ancient and Modern

CONNECTING TO Technology

Built to Last

Think about the buildings in your neighborhood. Can you imagine any of them still standing 1,000 years from now? The ancient Romans could. Many structures that they built nearly 2,000 years ago are still standing today. How is that possible?

The Romans knew many techniques for building strong, long-lasting structures. Look at the Colosseum, pictured here. Notice how many arches were used in its design. Arches are one of the strongest shapes you can use in construction, a fact the Romans knew well. They also invented materials like cement to make their buildings stronger.

Making Generalizations How did technology help the Romans build strong and lasting structures?

hmhsocialstudies.com

ANIMATED GEOGRAPHY
Roman Aqueduct

Roman Building and Engineering

Because the Pax Romana was a time of stability, the Romans were able to make great cultural achievements. Some of the advances made during this time continue to affect our lives even today.

One of the areas in which the Romans made visible advances was architecture. The Romans were great builders, and many of their structures have stood for centuries. In fact, you can still see Roman buildings in Europe today, almost 2,000 years after they were built. This is because the Romans were skilled engineers who knew how to make their buildings strong.

Buildings are not the only structures that the Romans built to last. Ancient roads, bridges, and **aqueducts**—channels used to carry water over long distances—are still seen all over Europe. Planned by skilled Roman engineers, many of these structures are still in use.

Roman Language and Law

Not all Roman achievements are as easy to see as buildings, however. For example, the Romans greatly influenced how we speak, write, and think even today. Many of the languages spoken in Europe today, such as Spanish, French, and Italian, are based on Latin, the Romans' language. English, too, has adopted many words from Latin.

The Romans used the Latin language to create great works of literature. Among these works were some of the world's most famous plays, poems, and stories. Many of them are read and enjoyed by millions of people around the world today.

Even more important to the world than their literary achievements, however, were the Romans' political contributions. All around the world, people use legal systems based on ancient Roman law. In some countries, the entire government is based largely on the ancient Roman system.

One such country is the United States. The founders of our country admired the Roman government and used it as a model for our government. Like ancient Rome, the United States is a republic. We elect our leaders and trust them to make our laws. Also like the Romans, we require all people to obey a set of basic written laws. In ancient Rome, these laws were carved on stone tablets and kept on display. In the United States, they are written down in a document, the Constitution.

READING CHECK **Finding Main Ideas** What were some of the Romans' main achievements?

Collaborative Learning

At Level

Analyzing Cultural Influence

1. Remind students about the spread of Hellenistic culture under Alexander the Great. Explain that the Romans admired Greek culture, which greatly influenced their own.

2. Create small groups, and have each research a topic on Roman culture—art, architecture, philosophy, literature, and so on. Ask the group to determine how much influence Greek culture had on this aspect of Roman culture.

3. Have the groups compile their findings and create a poster for their topic. Remind them to make clear how Greek culture influenced the Romans.

4. Have groups display and discuss their posters.
LS **Interpersonal, Verbal/Linguistic, Visual/Spatial**

Alternative Assessment Handbook, Rubrics 16: Judging Information; and 28: Posters

---

Answers

Connecting to Technology *They used arches to help build strong structures; they invented cement and other materials to make their buildings stronger.*

Reading Check *building and engineering; influence on language and legal systems; contributions of literature; ideas about government*

The Spread of Christianity

In addition to art and law, the ancient Romans also had a tremendous influence on religion. One of the world's major religions, Christianity, first appeared and spread in the Roman world.

The Beginnings of Christianity

Christianity is based on the life, actions, and teachings of Jesus of Nazareth. He and his early followers lived in the Roman territory of Judea in southwest Asia. They converted many people in Jerusalem and other cities in Judea to Christianity.

However, Christianity quickly spread far beyond the borders of Judea. Jesus's followers traveled widely, preaching and spreading his teachings. Through their efforts, communities of Christians began to appear in cities throughout the Roman world. Christian ideas spread quickly through these cities, as more and more people converted to Christianity.

Persecution and Acceptance

The rapid spread of Christianity worried some Roman leaders. They feared that Christianity would soon grow larger than all other religions in the empire. If that ever happened, they feared, the Christians might rebel and take over Rome.

To prevent a rebellion, some emperors began to persecute, or punish, Christians. They arrested, fined, or even killed any Christians they found.

The persecution did not cause people to abandon Christianity, however. Instead, Christians began to meet in secret, hiding their religion from the government.

Eventually, the persecution was ended. In the 300s a powerful emperor named Constantine became a Christian himself. Once the emperor had converted, the Christian faith was openly accepted even more widely in the empire. Look at the map below to see how Christianity spread between 300 and 400.

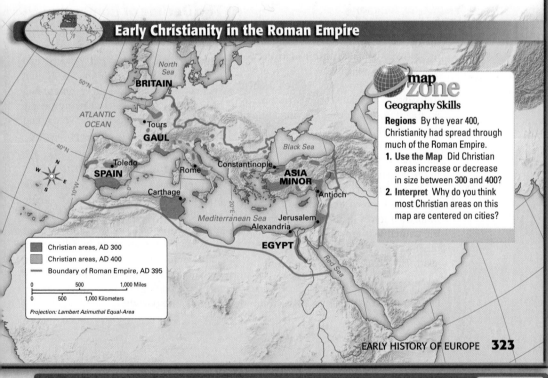

Early Christianity in the Roman Empire

map zone

Geography Skills

Regions By the year 400, Christianity had spread through much of the Roman Empire.

1. **Use the Map** Did Christian areas increase or decrease in size between 300 and 400?
2. **Interpret** Why do you think most Christian areas on this map are centered on cities?

Christian areas, AD 300
Christian areas, AD 400
Boundary of Roman Empire, AD 395

0   500   1,000 Miles
0   500   1,000 Kilometers
Projection: Lambert Azimuthal Equal-Area

EARLY HISTORY OF EUROPE **323**

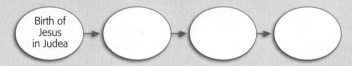

❹ The Decline of Rome

Various factors helped bring about the decline of Rome.

Describe Where did Constantine establish a new Roman capital, Constantinople? *in present-day Turkey* Why? *to move Rome's capital to a more central location in the empire*

Analyze Why did the barbarian invasions of Rome succeed? *the barbarians had strong leaders; the Romans were weak from internal problems and could not fend off the attacks*

Activity **Making a Time Line**
Have students create a time line showing the series of events that led to the downfall of Rome. **LS** Visual/Spatial

📖 Alternative Assessment Handbook, Rubric 36: Time Lines

Info to Know

Istanbul or Constantinople? Constantinople remained a Christian city for about a thousand years, until falling to the Turks in 1453. Now called Istanbul, it is the capital city of Turkey.

About the Illustration

This illustration is an artist's conception based on available sources. However, historians are uncertain exactly what this scene looked like.

Answers

Analyzing Visuals *internal—bad emperors, high taxes, poverty, fighting between rival military leaders; external—invasions, the overthrow of the Roman emperor in 476*

Reading Check *After Constantine converted in the 300s, Christianity spread widely throughout the empire. Support for Christianity grew, and soon all other religions were banned.*

324

The Decline of Rome

Beginning around 200, the once-mighty Roman Empire began to weaken. Factors from inside and outside the empire caused many problems for Rome's leaders and led to the empire's collapse in the late 400s.

Barbarian invaders

ANALYSIS SKILL **ANALYZING VISUALS**
Which factors in Rome's decline were internal? Which came from outside the empire?

Reasons for the Decline of Rome

- Poor leaders cared less for the people of Rome than they did for their own happiness.
- Taxes and prices rose, increasing poverty.
- People became less loyal to Rome.
- Military leaders fought each other for power.
- The empire was too large for a single person to govern well.
- Barbarians invaded the empire from outside.

Official Religion

Even after Constantine became Christian, many people in the Roman Empire did not convert. Romans continued to practice many different religions.

Over time, however, Rome's leaders supported Christianity more and more. By the 380s, support for Christianity had grown so much that an emperor chose to ban all other religions. With that ban, Christianity was the only religion allowed in the Roman Empire.

By the end of the 300s, the Christian church had grown into one of the most influential forces in the Roman world. As the church was growing, however, many other parts of Roman society were falling apart. The Roman Empire was ending.

READING CHECK **Sequencing** How did the Christian church gain influence in Rome?

The Decline of Rome

Rome's problems had actually started long before 300. For about a century, crime rates had been rising and poverty had been increasing. In addition, the Roman systems of education and government had begun breaking down, and many people no longer felt loyal to Rome. What could have happened to cause these problems?

Problems in the Government

Many of Rome's problems were the result of poor government. After about 200, Rome was ruled by a series of bad emperors. Most of these emperors were more interested in their own happiness than in ruling well. Some simply ignored the needs of the Roman people. Others raised taxes to pay for new buildings or wars, driving many Romans into poverty.

324 CHAPTER 13

Differentiating Instruction

Below Level

Struggling Readers

1. Pair struggling readers with more proficient readers. Have them create a cause-and-effect chart like the following example, labeling the boxes on the left *Internal* and *External* and the box on the right *Decline of Rome*.

2. As they review the information about the causes for the decline of Rome, have them complete the chart. **LS** Verbal/Linguistic, Visual/Spatial

📖 Alternative Assessment Handbook, Rubrics 6: Cause and Effect; and 13: Graphic Organizers

| Internal | → | Decline of Rome |
| External | → | |

Frustrated by these bad emperors, some military leaders tried to take over and rule Rome in their place. In most cases, though, these military leaders were no better than the emperors they replaced. Most of them were poor leaders. In addition, fighting between rival military leaders almost led to civil war on many occasions.

Rome did have a few good emperors who worked furiously to save the empire. One emperor feared that the empire had grown too large for one person to rule. To correct this problem, he divided the empire in half and named a co-ruler to help govern. Later, the emperor Constantine built a new capital, Constantinople, in what is now Turkey, nearer to the center of the Roman Empire. He thought that ruling from a central location would help keep the empire together. These measures helped restore order for a time, but they were not enough to save the Roman Empire.

Invasions

Although internal problems weakened the empire, they alone probably would not have destroyed it. However, as the empire was getting weaker from within, invaders from outside also began to attack in the late 300s and 400s. Already suffering from their own problems, the Romans could not fight off these invasions.

Most Roman people considered the various groups who invaded their empire barbarians, uncivilized and backward. In truth, however, some of these so-called barbarian groups had their own complex societies and strong, capable leaders. As a result, they were able to defeat Roman armies and take lands away from the empire. In the end, the barbarians were even able to attack and destroy the city of Rome itself. In 476 the last emperor of Rome was overthrown and replaced by the leader of an invading group.

Most historians consider the capture of the Roman emperor in 476 the end of the Roman Empire in western Europe. Although people continued to think of themselves as Romans, there was no empire to tie them together. As a result, European society slowly broke apart.

READING CHECK **Generalizing** Why did the Roman Empire decline?

SUMMARY AND PREVIEW In this section you learned that the Romans brought a vast territory under one government. Next, you will learn what happened after that government collapsed, in a period called the Middle Ages.

Section 2 Assessment

hmhsocialstudies.com
ONLINE QUIZ

Reviewing Ideas, Terms, and Places

1. **a. Describe** What was the government of the Roman **Republic** like?
   b. Contrast How was **Rome**'s government in the republic unlike the government under kings?
2. **a. Identify** Who was Augustus?
   b. Explain How did the Pax Romana help the Romans make great achievements?
3. **Generalize** How did Rome's emperors affect the spread of Christianity?
4. **a. Identify** What threats to the Roman Empire appeared in the 200s, 300s, and 400s?
   b. Evaluate Do you think internal problems or invasions were more responsible for Rome's fall? Why?

Critical Thinking

5. **Identifying Causes** Draw a graph like the one at right. On the left side, list the main causes of Rome's growth. On the right, list the main causes of its decline.

Growth	Decline

FOCUS ON WRITING

6. **Finding a Setting** Where will your myth be set? Think back over this section and the previous one to find an appropriate location for your myth.

EARLY HISTORY OF EUROPE **325**

Section 2 Assessment Answers

1. **a.** citizens elected leaders to make laws and all government decisions
   b. Kings were often cruel, harsh, and unfair. They could not be voted out. Under the republican system, citizens could elect leaders.
2. **a.** Rome's first emperor, he expanded the empire, built monuments and public buildings, and improved roads.
   b. Lack of warfare and rebellion made it possible for trade and culture to expand.
3. Constantine's conversion helped Christianity spread. Another emperor banned all other religions.

4. **a.** 200s—bad emperors, breakdowns in education and government, poverty, crime, high taxes, rebellion by military leaders; 300s and 400s—invasions, overthrow of the emperor
   b. Responses will vary, but students should use text examples to support their answers.
5. Responses will vary. Students should list factors that explain Rome's growth and decline.
6. Locations will vary.

Answers

Reading Check *Internal and external forces brought about the empire's decline. Internal forces included crime, poverty, high taxes, the break-down of educational and governmental systems, and struggles for power by rival military leaders. External forces included invasions in the late 300s and 400s and the overthrow of the last Roman emperor in 476.*

325

Info to Know

The Postal Service One of the most important uses of the Roman road system was the *cursus publicus,* or postal service. Although average citizens were not allowed to use the postal service, it provided the Roman government with an important means of sending information and instructions across the empire.

Teaching Tip

Map Distortion Explain to students that the drawing of the map of Europe in this feature is distorted. Have them compare this map with the map in the Atlas or other maps in this chapter to get another view of the extent of the Roman roads.

RF: Critical Thinking, The Roads of Ancient Rome

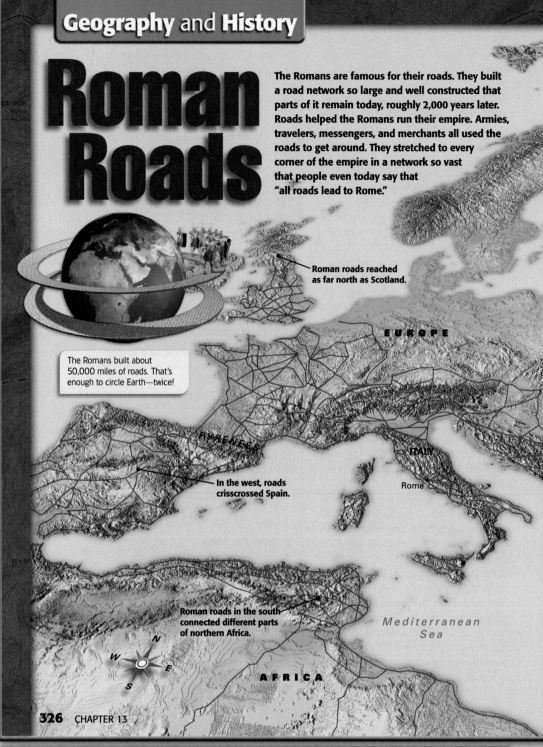

Geography and History

Roman Roads

The Romans are famous for their roads. They built a road network so large and well constructed that parts of it remain today, roughly 2,000 years later. Roads helped the Romans run their empire. Armies, travelers, messengers, and merchants all used the roads to get around. They stretched to every corner of the empire in a network so vast that people even today say that "all roads lead to Rome."

Roman roads reached as far north as Scotland.

The Romans built about 50,000 miles of roads. That's enough to circle Earth—twice!

EUROPE

PYRENEES

ITALY

Rome

In the west, roads crisscrossed Spain.

Roman roads in the south connected different parts of northern Africa.

Mediterranean Sea

AFRICA

326 CHAPTER 13

Differentiating Instruction

Struggling Readers   Below Level

To help struggling readers, have them match the text to the images in the feature. Read aloud the introduction and each caption. As you do, have students identify images and map elements that correspond to the text. **LS** Visual/Spatial, Verbal/Linguistic

Alternative Assessment Handbook, Rubric 1: Acquiring Information

Special Needs Learners   At Level

Have students discuss how people rely on roads today. Have them talk about the roads they travel every day and speculate about how difficult it would be to get around if there were no roads. Suggest that they give several examples. **LS** Verbal/Linguistic

Alternative Assessment Handbook, Rubric 11: Discussions

Paving stones

Drainage ditch

Curbstones

Sand, clay,
and gravel

Stone chips
Gravel concrete

Roman roads were built to last. They were
constructed of layers of sand, concrete, rock,
and stone. Drainage ditches let water drain
off, preventing water damage.

The roads were built by and for
the military. The main purpose of the
roads was to allow Rome's armies to
travel quickly throughout the empire.

In the east, Roman roads
stretched into Southwest Asia.

The Romans built tall
"milestones" along their roads
to mark distances. Just like
modern highway signs, the
markers told travelers how far
it was to the next town.

ANALYSIS SKILL ANALYZING VISUALS

1. **Movement** Why did the Romans build their roads?
2. **Location** How does the map show that "all roads lead to Rome"?

327

Geography and History

Info to Know

Not a One-Way Street Rome's vast network of roads helped the empire expand and also contributed to its prosperity. But when Rome began to weaken, the roads also made it easier for invaders.

MISCONCEPTION /// ALERT \\\

Who Were Rome's Road Builders?
Much of Rome's vast network of roads was built by its own soldiers. Planning and prep work was done by surveyors and engineers.

About the Illustration
This illustration is an artist's conception based on available sources. However, historians are uncertain exactly what this scene looked like.

Cross-Discipline Activity: Literature

At Level

Writing a Dialogue

1. Have students work in pairs to write a dialogue that could be the first scene of a play about traveling through the Roman Empire.

2. Have students begin by identifying the characters in the play. These might include poor or wealthy travelers, soldiers, peasants, innkeepers, thieves, or traders. Then have them write a dialogue based on a conflict between two characters or a problem that affects two characters.

3. Remind students what they've learned about the Roman world, including the system of roads. Encourage them to include some of these details in their dialogues.

4. Have students perform their dialogues before the class. **LS Interpersonal, Verbal/Linguistic**

Alternative Assessment Handbook, Rubric 33: Skits and Reader's Theater

Answers

Analyzing Visuals 1. *mainly to allow their armies to travel quickly throughout the empire;* **2.** *Rome is at the center of the map; any road on the map will link to another road and eventually lead to Rome.*

Bellringer

If YOU lived there. . . Use the **Daily Bellringer Transparency** to help students answer the question.

 Daily Bellringer Transparency, Section 3

Key Terms and Places

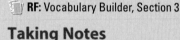 **RF:** Vocabulary Builder, Section 3

Taking Notes

Have students use the graphic organizer online to take notes on the section. This activity will prepare students for the Section Assessment, in which they will complete a graphic organizer that builds on the information using the Critical Thinking Skill: Analyzing.

SECTION 3

The Middle Ages

If YOU lived there...

You are the youngest child of a noble family in medieval France. One day your father tells you that you are being sent to the court of another noble family. There you will learn fine manners and proper behavior. You will also learn music and drawing. You know it is a great honor, but you will miss your own home.

How do you feel about this change in your life?

What You Will Learn...

Main Ideas

1. The Christian church influenced nearly every aspect of society in the Middle Ages.
2. Complicated political and economic systems governed life in the Middle Ages.
3. The period after 1000 was a time of great changes in medieval society.

The Big Idea

Christianity and social systems influenced life in Europe in the Middle Ages.

Key Terms and Places

Middle Ages, *p. 328*
pope, *p. 329*
Crusade, *p. 329*
Holy Land, *p. 329*
Gothic architecture, *p. 330*
feudal system, *p. 331*
manor, *p. 332*
nation-state, *p. 335*

hmhsocialstudies.com
TAKING NOTES

Use the graphic organizer online to take notes on medieval society.

BUILDING BACKGROUND When people think of the Middle Ages today, they usually think of castles, princesses, and knights in shining armor. Although these were all part of the Middle Ages, they do not tell the whole story. The Middle Ages was a time of great change in Europe, as the influence of the ancient world faded away.

The Christian Church and Society

When historians talk about the past, they often divide it into three long periods. The first period is the ancient world, the time of the world's earliest civilizations, such as Egypt, China, Greece, and Rome. The last period historians call the modern world, the world since about 1500. Since that time, new ideas and contacts between civilizations changed the world completely.

What happened between ancient and modern times? We call this period, which lasted from about 500 until about 1500, the **Middle Ages**. We also call it the medieval (mee-DEE-vuhl) period. The word *medieval* comes from two Latin words that mean "middle age." It was a time of great changes in Europe, many of them inspired by the Christian church.

The Importance of the Church

When the Roman Empire fell apart in the late 400s, the people of Europe were left without a single dominant government to unite them. In the absence of strong leaders, Europe broke into many small kingdoms. Each of these kingdoms had its own laws, customs, and language. Europe was no longer the same place it had been under the Romans.

328 CHAPTER 13

Teach the Big Idea
At Level

The Middle Ages

1. **Teach** Ask students the questions in the Main Idea boxes under Direct Teach.

2. **Apply** Ask students to imagine that they will interview three people from the Middle Ages. These might include a woman, a Crusader, a noble, a peasant, a king, or others. Have them write at least three interview questions (based on material in the chapter) to ask each person.

3. **Review** Have students take turns interviewing each other and answering the questions.

4. **Practice/Homework** Have students write the responses next to their interview questions. Then have them work to come up with more questions. **LS Verbal/Linguistic**

   Alternative Assessment Handbook, Rubrics 1: Acquiring Information; and 37: Writing Assignments

North Sea

ENGLAND

HOLY
ROMAN
EMPIRE

FRANCE

Regensburg • Vienna
Lyon •
• Trieste
• Genoa • Zadar
Corsica
• Rome
Sardinia
Mediterranean Sea
Sicily
Crete

Black Sea

Constantinople
SELJUK
TURKS

BYZANTINE
EMPIRE

• Edessa
• Antioch
• Tripoli
• Acre   HOLY
LAND
Jerusalem

ATLANTIC
OCEAN

	Christian lands, 1095
	Muslim lands, 1095
—	First Crusade, 1096–1099

0   100   200 Miles
0   100   200 Kilometers
Projection: Azimuthal Equal Area

map Zone Geography Skills

Movement In 1096, the pope called on Christian Crusaders to take the Holy Land away from the Muslims who controlled it.
1. **Use the Map** Which direction did the Crusaders travel?
2. **Analyze** Which do you think was more difficult, the trip from Vienna to Constantinople or from Constantinople to Antioch? Why?

One factor, however, continued to tie the people of Europe together—religion. Nearly everyone in Europe was Christian, and so most Europeans felt tied together by their beliefs. Over time, the number of Christians in Europe increased. People came to feel more and more like part of a single religious community.

Because Christianity was so important in Europe, the Christian church gained a great deal of influence. In time, the church began to influence the politics, art, and daily lives of people all over the continent. In fact, almost no part of life in Europe in the Middle Ages was unaffected by the church and its teachings.

The Christian Church and Politics

As the Christian church gained influence in Europe, some church leaders became powerful. They gained political power in addition to their religious authority.

The most powerful religious leader was the **pope**, the head of the Christian church. The pope's decisions could have huge effects on people's lives. For example, one pope decided to start a religious war, or **Crusade**, against the church's enemies in Southwest Asia. He wanted Europeans to take over the **Holy Land**, the region in which Jesus had lived. For many years, the region had been in the hands of another religious group, the Muslims.

EARLY HISTORY OF EUROPE **329**

Main Idea

❶ The Christian Church and Society, *continued*

The Christian church influenced nearly every aspect of society in the Middle Ages.

Recall What events did people attend at their churches? *markets, festivals, religious ceremonies*

Cause and Effect What long-term effects did the Crusades have on Europe? *trade increased along with a demand for goods from Southwest Asia; relations between Christians and Muslims became worse*

Analyze Why was most art during the Middle Ages concerned with religious themes? *because it was influenced by the church*

Activity **The Children's Crusade** Tell students that not all of the Crusades were launched by religious leaders. The Children's Crusade was a popular movement begun by a young boy. Have them research and write a report about the Children's Crusade. 🅛🅢 **Verbal/Linguistic**

📝 Alternative Assessment Handbook, Rubrics 30: Research; and 40: Writing to Describe

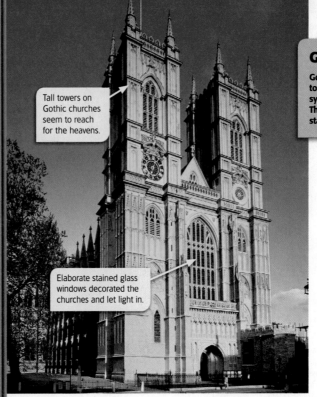

Tall towers on Gothic churches seem to reach for the heavens.

Elaborate stained glass windows decorated the churches and let light in.

Gothic Architecture

Gothic churches were designed to tower over medieval cities as symbols of the church's greatness. This cathedral, Westminster Abbey, stands in London, England.

VIDEO
The Crusades' Aftermath
🔗 hmhsocialstudies.com

Thousands of people answered the pope's call for a Crusade. As the map on the previous page shows, they traveled thousands of miles to fight the church's enemies. This Crusade was the first of eight attempts by Christians over two centuries to win back the Holy Land.

In the end, the Crusades did not drive the Muslims from the Holy Land. They did, however, lead to sweeping changes in Europe. Crusaders brought new goods and ideas back to Europe with them. Europeans began to want more of these goods, so trade between Europe and Asia increased. At the same time, though, relations between Christians and Muslims grew worse. For years to come, followers of the religions distrusted and resented each other.

The Church and Art

Politics was not the only area in which the church had great influence. Most art of the Middle Ages was also influenced by the church. Medieval painters and sculptors, for example, used religious subjects in their works. Most music and literature from the period is centered on religious themes.

The greatest examples of religious art from the Middle Ages are church buildings. Huge churches like the one shown on this page were built all over Europe. Many of them are examples of **Gothic architecture**, a style known for its high pointed ceilings, tall towers, and stained glass windows. People built Gothic churches as symbols of their faith. They believed that building these amazing structures would show their love for God. The insides of such churches are as elaborate and ornate as the outsides.

The Church and Daily Life

Most people in Europe never saw a Gothic church, especially not the inside. Instead they worshipped at small local churches. In fact, people's lives often centered around their local church. Markets, festivals, and religious ceremonies all took place there. Local priests advised people on how to live and act. In addition, because most people could not read or write, they depended on the church to keep records for them.

READING CHECK **Summarizing** How did the Christian church shape life in the Middle Ages?

Critical Thinking: Analyzing Information
At Level

Writing a Letter

1. Have students explore images of artifacts, women, religious figures, knights, and Crusaders. A good source for images is the Web site: www.newyorkcarver.com/museum.htm, which has links to nearly 30 medieval art collections.

2. Ask students to imagine that they are traveling with the Crusaders. Have them write letters to their families. Suggest that they use the images they find as a starting point for details they can include in their letters. The letters might describe what they have seen on the journey or what they miss from home. Some students may wish to write an exchange of letters (from those on the road and from those left behind).

3. Have volunteers read their letters aloud and display the images they have found. 🅛🅢 **Verbal/Linguistic**

📝 Alternative Assessment Handbook, Rubrics 1: Acquiring Information; and 25: Personal Letters

Answers

Reading Check *The church was a place to worship, but also the center of people's lives. The church influenced politics, the economy, and the culture.*

Life in the Middle Ages

Christianity was a major influence on people's lives in the Middle Ages, but it was not the only one. Much of European society was controlled by two systems of relationships. They were the feudal (FYOO-duhl) system and the manor system.

The Feudal System

Medieval Europe was divided into many small kingdoms. In most kingdoms, the king owned all the land. Sometimes, kings gave parts of their land to nobles—people born into wealthy, powerful families. In turn, these nobles gave land to knights, or trained warriors, who promised to help them defend both their lands and the king. This system of exchanging land for military service is called the **feudal system**, or feudalism (FYOO-duh-li-zuhm).

Everyone involved in the feudal system had certain duties to perform. The kings and nobles provided land and promised to protect the people who served them and to treat everyone fairly. In return, the knights who received land promised to serve the nobles dutifully, especially in times of war. The set of relationships between knights and nobles was the heart of Europe's feudal system.

The feudal system was very complex. Its rules varied from kingdom to kingdom and changed constantly. Feudal duties in France, for example, were not the same as those in Germany or England. Also, it was possible for one knight to owe service to more than one noble. If the two nobles he served went to war, the poor knight would be torn between them. In such situations, feudal relationships could be confusing or even dangerous.

FOCUS ON READING
After you read this passage, reread it. Make a list of details you did not notice in your first reading.

Feudal Relationships

Europe's feudal system was based on relationships between knights and nobles. Each had certain duties that he or she had to perform.

ANALYZING VISUALS Who had to provide military service as one of his duties?

hmhsocialstudies.com
ANIMATED GEOGRAPHY

Noble's duties
- Provide knight with land
- Treat knights fairly and honestly

Knight's duties
- Provide military service
- Supply food and shelter for noble during visits

EARLY HISTORY OF EUROPE **331**

Info to Know

Role of Women For the most part, women on manors stayed in the home sewing, baking, weaving, and spinning. However, women also hunted and learned how to use weapons to fight in battles and defend their homes. Some women specialized in occupations such as painting, writing and blacksmithing.

Checking for Understanding

Are the following statements true or false?

1. Estate owners and peasants exchanged land for military service. *false*
2. The relationships between knights and nobles were central to the feudal system. *true*
3. The workers on a manor often lived in villages. *true*
4. The population of cities declined after 1000. *false*

The Manor System

The feudal system was only one set of guidelines that governed life in the Middle Ages. Another system, the manor system, controlled most economic activities in Europe during this period.

At the center of the manor system was the **manor**, a large estate owned by a noble or knight. Every manor was different, but most included a large house or castle, fields, pastures, and forests. A manor also had a village where workers lived. They traveled back and forth to the fields each day.

The owner of a manor did not farm his own land. Instead, he had workers to farm it for him. Most of the crops grown on the manor went to the owner. In exchange for their work, the workers got a place to live and a small piece of land on which they could grow their own food.

The workers on most manors included either free peasants or serfs. Peasants were free farmers. Serfs, on the other hand, were not free. Although they were not slaves, they were not allowed to leave the land on which they worked.

Close-up

Life on a Manor

Manors were large estates that developed during the Middle Ages. Many manors were largely self-sufficient, producing most of the food and goods they needed. This picture shows what a manor in England might have looked like.

The owner of the manor lived in a large stone house called the manor house.

Peasants grew vegetables in small gardens located near their houses.

In late spring, peasants harvested crops like wheat.

332 CHAPTER 13

Differentiating Instruction

Struggling Readers

1. To help students understand feudalism, the manor system, and urban life in the Middle Ages, draw the following chart for students to see. Complete the chart with details from the section, or ask volunteers to do so.

2. Encourage students to explain which way of life they would have prefered and why.
   LS Verbal/Linguistic, Visual/Spatial

   Alternative Assessment Handbook, Rubrics 7: Charts; and 13: Graphic Organizers

Feudal	Manor	Urban

Towns and Trade

Not everyone in the Middle Ages lived on manors. Some people chose to live in towns and cities like Paris or London. Compared to our cities today, most of these medieval cities were small, dirty, and dark.

Many of the people who lived in cities were traders. They bought and sold goods from all over Europe and other parts of the world. Most of their goods were sold at trade fairs. Every year, merchants from many places in Europe would meet at these large fairs to sell their wares.

Before the year 1000, trade was not very common in Europe. After that year, however, trade increased. As it did, more people began to move to cities. Once small, these cities began to grow. As cities grew, trade increased even more, and the people who lived in them became wealthier. By the end of the Middle Ages, cities had become the centers of European culture and wealth.

READING CHECK **Finding Main Ideas** What were two systems that governed life in Europe during the Middle Ages? How did they differ?

The village church was built on a small piece of land that belonged to the lord.

Sheep grazed on grassy fields, and villagers used sheep's wool to make clothes.

The village blacksmith made iron tools for farming.

ANALYSIS SKILL ANALYZING VISUALS
What goods can you see being produced on this manor? How do you think the lives of peasants on this manor differed from the life of the owner?

Peasants took wheat to the mill to be ground into flour, which they used to make bread.

333

Direct Teach

Did you know. . .

One factor in the growth of cities was that agriculture become more productive, or efficient. Use of a heavy plow pulled by horses and increased cultivation of peas and beans improved soil fertility and people's nutrition. As a result, the peasant population grew, while at the same time fewer people were needed to work in agriculture. Some of these "surplus" workers learned trades and began providing goods and services to city dwellers, and many moved into the cities. As cities grew, many more traders and artisans were needed. Also needed were cobblers, bakers, lawyers, barbers, butchers, cooks, tailors, scribes, teachers, and physicians, just to name a few.

About the Illustration

This illustration is an artist's conception based on available sources. However, historians are uncertain exactly what this scene looked like.

Differentiating Instruction

| At Level | Standard English Mastery |

English-Language Learners

1. Explain that homonyms are words that sound the same, but are spelled differently and have different meanings.

2. Point out these homonyms in the "Life in the Middle Ages" section: *knight (night), manor (manner),* and *serf (surf)*

3. Pair English learners with more proficient readers and have them work together to create a chart defining these words. Encourage them to find other homonyms from the section, and add these to their charts. Have students use standard English to write sentences using each term and its homonym.

Term	Definition	Homonym	Definition
knight		night	
manor		manner	
serf		surf	

LS **Verbal/Linguistic**
Alternative Assessment Handbook, Rubric 7: Charts

Answers

Reading Check *feudal system and manor system—different in these ways: the feudal system determined relations between knights and nobles; the manor system determined relations between the rich (owners) and poor (workers)*

Analyzing Visuals *flour, iron tools, wool, vegetables, wheat; possible response—The peasants had a difficult life with much physical labor. They lived in smaller homes and had fewer possessions.*

333

Main Idea

❸ Changes in Medieval Society

The period after 1000 was a time of great changes in medieval society.

Identify Who was William the Conqueror? *a noble from France who in 1066 overthrew the English king and became king of England*

Recall How did the Black Death affect Europe's population? *up to a third of the population died; a labor shortage resulted*

Analyze Why did England's nobles force King John to sign Magna Carta? *The king had raised taxes, indicating that he believed he was the supreme ruler, while the nobles believed in the power of law.*

Make Inferences How would eliminating feudalism increase the power of kings? *possible answer—Nobles would have less power and influence if feudalism were eliminated.*

Primary Source

To help students understand the provisions of Magna Carta, create a web diagram such as the one below and work with students to fill in details about its provisions.

Magna Carta

Answers

Primary Source *They state the rights of ordinary people to be free, to own property, and to receive a fair trial. These are basic rights in a democracy.*

Changes in Medieval Society

Life in the Middle Ages changed greatly after the year 1000. You have already seen how cities grew and trade increased. Even as these changes were taking place, bigger changes were sweeping through Europe.

THE IMPACT TODAY

The ideas of Magna Carta influenced later documents, including our Constitution.

Political Changes in England

One of the countries most affected by change in the Middle Ages was England. In the year 1066 a noble from northern France, William the Conqueror, sailed to England and overthrew the old king. He declared himself the new king of England.

William built a strong government in England, something the English had not had before. Later kings of England built on William's example. For more than a century, these kings increased their power. By the late 1100s England's king was one of the most powerful men in Europe.

When William's descendant John took the throne, however, he angered many nobles by raising taxes. John believed that the king had the right to do whatever he wanted. England's nobles disagreed.

In 1215 a group of nobles forced King John to sign Magna Carta, one of the most important documents in English history. Magna Carta stated that the law, not the king, was the supreme power in England. The king had to obey the law. He could not raise taxes without the nobles' permission.

Many people consider Magna Carta to be one of the first steps toward democracy in modern Europe and one of history's most important documents. By stating that the king was not above the law, Magna Carta set limits on his power. In addition, it gave a council of nobles the power to advise the king. In time, that council developed into Parliament (PAHR-luh-muhnt), the elected body that governs England today.

Primary Source

HISTORIC DOCUMENT

Magna Carta

Magna Carta was one of the first documents to protect the rights of the people. Magna Carta was so influential that the British still consider it part of their constitution. Some of its ideas are also in the U.S. Constitution. Included in Magna Carta were 63 demands that English nobles made King John agree to follow. A few of these demands are listed here.

Demand number 31 defended people's right to property, not just wood.

Magna Carta guaranteed that free men had the right to a fair trial.

To all free men of our kingdom we have also granted, for us and our heirs for ever, all the liberties written out below, to have and to keep for them and their heirs, of us and our heirs.

(16) No man shall be forced to perform more service for a knight's 'fee,' or other free holding of land, than is due from it.

(31) Neither we nor any royal official will take wood for our castle, or for any other purpose, without the consent [permission] of the owner.

(38) In future no official shall place a man on trial upon his own unsupported statement, without producing credible [believable] witnesses to the truth of it.

—Magna Carta, from a translation by the British Library

ANALYSIS SKILL **ANALYZING PRIMARY SOURCES**

In what ways do you think the ideas listed above influenced modern democracy?

334 CHAPTER 13

Collaborative Learning

At Level

Role-Playing the Creation of Magna Carta

1. Organize students into small groups. Tell students they are going to role-play the creation of Magna Carta.

2. Have students begin by reviewing the information in the section about Magna Carta. (You may also have them research information from outside sources.) To make sure they cover all the important points, have each group create an outline before they begin.

3. Assign roles or have students select them. Have groups perform their plays before the

class. Remind them that the nobles should describe the provisions of Magna Carta and try to win over the king to their position. Likewise, the king should try to win over the nobles to his position.

4. Discuss with students insights they have obtained about how Magna Carta affects their lives today. **LS Interpersonal, Verbal/Linguistic**

📝 Alternative Assessment Handbook, Rubrics 14: Group Activity; and 33: Skits and Reader's Theater

The Black Death

Not all of the changes that struck medieval Europe had such positive results. In 1347 a disease called the Black Death swept through Europe. Up to a third of Europe's people died from the disease. Even such a disaster, however, had some positive effects. With the decrease in population came a labor shortage. As a result, people could demand higher wages for their work.

The Fight for Power

Even as the Black Death was sweeping across Europe, kings fought for power. In 1337 the Hundred Years' War broke out between England and France. As its name suggests, the war lasted more than 100 years. In the end, the French won.

Inspired by the victory, France's kings worked to increase their power. They took land away from nobles to rule themselves. France became a **nation-state**, a country united under a single strong government.

Around Europe, other rulers followed the French example. As nation-states arose around Europe, feudalism disappeared, and the Middle Ages came to an end.

READING CHECK Finding Main Ideas What changes occurred in Europe after 1000?

BIOGRAPHY

Joan of Arc
(c. 1412–1431)

One of the most famous war leaders in all of European history was a teenage girl. Joan of Arc, a leader of French troops during the Hundred Years' War, was only 16 when she first led troops into battle. She won many battles against the English but was captured in battle in 1430, tried, and executed. Nevertheless, her courage inspired the French, who went on to win the war. Today Joan is considered a national hero in France.

Make Inferences Why do you think Joan is considered a hero in France?

SUMMARY AND PREVIEW In this chapter you read about early Europe, a time that still influences how we live today. From the earliest civilizations of Greece and Rome to the Middle Ages, the people of Europe helped shape Western society. Next, you will learn about later periods that also affect our lives.

Section 3 Assessment

Reviewing Ideas, Terms, and Places
1. **a. Recall** Why did the **pope** call for a **Crusade**?
   b. Generalize How did the Christian church affect art in the Middle Ages?
2. **a. Define** What was the **feudal system**?
   b. Explain How did the **manor** system work?
   c. Elaborate What made the feudal system so complex?
3. **a. Describe** How did the Black Death affect Europe?
   b. Explain How did England's government change after 1000?

Critical Thinking
4. **Analyzing** Use your notes to complete a table like the one on the right. List ways the Church shaped medieval politics, life, and art.

```
        The Christian
           Church
      ┌──────┴──────┐
   Politics        Art
      └──────┬──────┘
          Daily
           Life
```

FOCUS ON WRITING
5. **Selecting a Topic** Now you have read about events and people in the Middle Ages. Choose one that could be the subject of your myth.

EARLY HISTORY OF EUROPE **335**

Section 3 Assessment Answers

1. **a.** to take over the Holy Land from the Muslims
   b. Painting, sculpture, music, and literature all centered on religious themes.
2. **a.** a system of exchanging land for military service, between nobles and knights
   b. Owners of manors provided workers with a place to live and some land to farm in exchange for most of the crops they produced.
   c. Its rules varied from place to place and changed constantly. A knight's loyalty could be torn if he owed service to more than one noble.
3. **a.** It killed up to one third of Europe's population. It also created a labor shortage.

   b. First, William the Conqueror built a strong government. Then Magna Carta reduced the power of England's kings.
4. possible answers—politics: Crusades, government; art: Gothic architecture, religious themes; daily life: markets and festivals at local church, advice from priests
5. Responses will vary but should relate to chapter content.

Direct Teach

MISCONCEPTION ALERT

Tiny, but Deadly, Bites Many people think that the Black Death was spread by rats. That's only partly true. It was actually the fleas on the rats whose bites infected people with the disease—not rat bites.

About the Illustration
This illustration is an artist's conception based on available sources. However, historians are uncertain exactly what Joan of Arc looked like.

Review & Assess

Close
Review with students how medieval society was affected by the feudal system, the manor system, and Christianity.

Review
↗ Online Quiz, Section 3

Assess
SE Section 3 Assessment
PASS: Section 3 Quiz
Alternative Assessment Handbook

Reteach/Classroom Intervention
Guided Reading Workbook, Section 3
Interactive Skills Tutor CD-ROM

Answers

Biography *She was a brave leader who inspired the French to win the war, even after her death.*

Reading Check *political changes, including a new, strong government in England and the signing of Magna Carta; the Black Death; the Hundred Years' War, which led to the elimination of the feudal system and increased the power of kings*

335

Info to Know

Death Statistics Approximately 25 million people in Europe died during the Black Death. Several million are also estimated to have died in the Middle East and Asia, which is considered the most probable source of the plague. In Europe, about one-third to one-half of Europe's population died in just a two-year period, between 1347 and 1351.

Linking to Today

Plague Is Still Here Outbreaks of plague still occur today, mostly in rural communities or in urban areas with infected rats and rat fleas. In the United States about 10 to 15 cases of plague appear every year, mostly in the southwestern states. Worldwide, about 1,000 to 3,000 cases are reported. Today antibiotics, which did not exist in the Middle Ages, can cure plague if the patient is treated in time.

Connect to Science

Low Immunity When the Black Death hit Europe, the population was especially vulnerable to disease. Many people had a low level of immunity resulting from a famine between 1315 and 1322. A typhoid epidemic and an occurrence of anthrax in animals also led to economic hardship throughout Europe.

📑 **RF:** Interdisciplinary Project: The Black Death

About the Illustration

This illustration is an artist's conception based on available sources. However, historians are uncertain exactly what this scene looked like.

Geography and History

The Black Death

"And they died by the hundreds," wrote one man who saw the horror, "both day and night." The Black Death had arrived. The Black Death was a series of deadly plagues that hit Europe between 1347 and 1351, killing millions. People didn't know what caused the plague. They also didn't know that geography played a key role in its spread—as people traveled to trade, they unwittingly carried the disease with them to new places.

EUROPE

CENTRAL ASIA

Kaffa

CHINA

AFRICA

The plague probably began in central and eastern Asia. These arrows show how it spread into and through Europe.

This ship has just arrived in Europe from the east with trade goods—and rats with fleas.

The fleas carry the plague and jump onto a man unloading the ship. Soon, he will get sick and die.

336 CHAPTER 13

Critical Thinking: Understanding Cause and Effect
At Level

Charting the Black Death's Effects

1. Have students clarify the effects of the Black Death by creating a cause-and-effect diagram.

2. Ask students to review the information about the Black Death in their textbooks. Then have them record its effects in a cause-and-effect flow chart. **LS** **Visual/Spatial, Verbal/Linguistic**

📑 Alternative Assessment Handbook, Rubrics 6: Cause and Effect; and 13: Graphic Organizers

Causes   Effects

Black Death

The plague is so terrifying that many people think it's the end of the world. They leave town for the country, spreading the Black Death even further.

People dig mass graves to bury the dead. But often, so many victims are infected that there is no one left to bury them.

The garbage and dirty conditions in the town provide food and a home for the rats, allowing the disease to spread even more.

So many people die so quickly that special carts are sent through the streets to gather the bodies.

HISTORY

VIDEO
The Black Death

hmhsocialstudies.com

ANALYSIS SKILL   ANALYZING VISUALS

1. **Movement** How did the Black Death reach Europe from Asia?
2. **Place** What helped spread the plague within Europe?

EARLY HISTORY OF EUROPE **337**

Geography and History

Info to Know

Three Types of Plague There are three types of plague. The first, bubonic plague, is the most common. Symptoms include swellings (buboes) on the neck and in the armpit and groin areas, as well as high fever. Bubonic plague is generally spread by fleas, which carry the bacteria from person to person. The second is a more deadly type of the disease, pneumonic plague, which attacks the lungs. It is highly contagious—the exhaled breath of infected persons spreads it. The third type is septicemic plague, which attacks the blood system and leads to brain damage.

Did you know. . .

The familiar nursery rhyme "Ring Around the Rosie" might have had its origins in the Black Death. The rhyme's lyrics are "Ring around the rosie/ a pocket full of posies/ Ashes, ashes, we all fall down."

Connect to Literature

Read All About It Many works of great literature from the Middle Ages mention the Black Death. Some of these works include *The Decameron* (Boccaccio), *The Canterbury Tales* (Chaucer), and *Piers Plowman* (Langland).

Social Studies Skills

Interpreting a Historical Map

Activity Comparing Historical Maps

Materials: two historical maps of the same region (ideally of Greece, Rome, or Western Europe) at different points in time

1. Distribute copies of the maps. Have students examine the maps' features, especially titles, labels, and keys. If both maps shows political boundaries, have students compare them. Some maps may illustrate events, such as battles and movements of people. Have students work individually or in pairs to analyze these elements.

2. Have students point out at least two changes that occurred between the time periods covered by the maps. Then have them point out at least two features on the maps that remained the same. Have them write this information at the bottom of the second map.

3. Have students write one or two paragraphs about the maps, briefly describing the changes they illustrate and the features that have remained the same. **LS** Visual/Spatial

- Alternative Assessment Handbook, Rubrics 9: Comparing and Contrasting; and 21: Map Reading
- Interactive Skills Tutor CD-ROM, Lesson 6: Interpret Maps
- **RF:** Social Studies Skills, Interpreting a Historical Map
- Map Zone Transparency: Western Europe, 1000

Answers

Practice 1. *Western Europe, Middle Ages;* **2.** *Christian lands;* **3.** *Burgundy;* **4.** *Caliphate of Córdoba (southern part of present-day Spain) and Sicily*

Apply *Students' questions will vary, but should be based only on the map.*

338

Interpreting a Historical Map

Learn

History and geography are closely related. You cannot truly understand the history of a place without knowing where it is and what it is like. For that reason, historical maps are important in the study of history. A historical map is a map that shows what a place was like at a particular time in the past.

Like other maps, historical maps use colors and symbols to represent information. One color, for example, might represent the lands controlled by a certain kingdom or the areas in which a particular religion or type of government was common. Symbols might identify key cities, battle sites, or other major locations.

Practice

Use the map on this page to answer the following questions.

1 Read the map's title. What area does this map show? What time period?

2 Check the map's legend. What does the color purple represent on this map?

3 According to the map, what territory lay between France and the Holy Roman Empire at this time?

4 What parts of Europe were Muslim in the year 1000?

Western Europe, 1000

Christian lands
Muslim lands

0   250   500 Miles
0   250   500 Kilometers
Projection: Azimuthal Equal Area

NORWAY
SCOTLAND
SWEDEN
IRELAND   ENGLAND   North Sea   DENMARK
WALES
NAVARRE   FRANCE   HOLY ROMAN EMPIRE
LEÓN   BURGUNDY
ATLANTIC OCEAN   CALIPHATE OF CÓRDOBA   BARCELONA   Rome
SICILY

map Zone

Apply

Look back at the map called Early Christianity in the Roman Empire in Section 2 of this chapter. Study the map, and then write five questions that you might see about such a map on a test. Make sure that the questions you ask can be answered with just the information on the map.

338 CHAPTER 13

Social Studies Skills Activity: Interpreting a Historical Map

Comparing Maps

At Level

Materials copies of city or state maps from different periods

Distribute copies of two maps of your state or city from time periods at least 50 years apart. Discuss differences between the two maps, such as city size and landmarks. Show students how the maps' titles, labels, and keys can give them clues about these differences. Have students write four sentences—two describing major changes and two describing features in the state or city that have not changed. **LS** Visual/Spatial, Verbal/Linguistic

- Alternative Assessment Handbook, Rubrics 21: Map Reading; and 40: Writing to Describe

Chapter Review

Geography's Impact
video series
Review the video to answer the closing question:
What are three ways in which Greek scholars have influenced education in America?

Visual Summary

Use the visual summary below to help you review the main ideas of the chapter.

QUICK FACTS

Ancient Greece was the birthplace of democracy, theater, and many other advances of Western society.

The Romans were master builders who created one of the largest empires in world history.

During the Middle Ages, new political and economic systems took hold in Europe, and religion dominated society.

Reviewing Vocabulary, Terms, and Places

For each group of terms below, write the letter of the term that does not relate to the others. Then write a sentence that explains how the other two terms are related.

1. **a.** Athens
   b. Sparta
   c. Rome
2. **a.** feudal system
   b. aqueduct
   c. manor
3. **a.** Crusade
   b. republic
   c. empire
4. **a.** Senate
   b. citizen
   c. colony

Comprehension and Critical Thinking

SECTION 1 *(Pages 310–317)*

5. **a. Identify** What was the basic political unit in ancient Greece? What is one example?
   b. Contrast How was life in Greece different under Alexander than it had been during the golden age?
   c. Evaluate What do you think was the greatest achievement of the ancient Greeks? Why?

SECTION 2 *(Pages 318–325)*

6. **a. Define** What was the Pax Romana? What happened during that time?
   b. Summarize How did Rome's government change after the republic fell apart?
   c. Elaborate What role did Rome's leaders play in the spread of Christianity?

EARLY HISTORY OF EUROPE **339**

Answers

Visual Summary

Review and Inquiry Have students use the visual summary to review main ideas related to ancient Greece, ancient Rome, and the Middle Ages.

Reviewing Vocabulary, Terms and Places

1. c; Athens and Sparta were Greek city-states.
2. b; The feudal system and manor system were relationship systems during the Middle Ages.
3. a; A republic, like an empire, is a political entity.
4. c; In Rome, citizens and members of the Senate worked together to create laws.

Comprehension and Critical Thinking

5. **a.** city-state: possible answers—Sparta, Athens
   b. All of Greece was now unified.
   c. possible answers—democracy, architecture, art, science, philosophy; reasons will vary
6. **a.** A long period of peace and achievement in the Roman Empire during which there were no major wars or rebellions and there were advances in building, engineering, and law.
   b. The Roman Empire was destroyed and Rome was ruled by invaders.
   c. Constantine converted to Christianity, which then spread quickly. Another emperor later banned all other religions in the empire.

Review and Assessment Resources

Review and Reinforce

SE Chapter Review

CRF: Chapter Review

Quick Facts Transparency: Early History of Europe Visual Summary

Spanish Chapter Summaries Audio CD Program

TOS Holt McDougal PuzzleView®; Quiz Show for ExamView

Quiz Game CD-ROM

Assess

SE Standardized Test Practice

PASS: Chapter Test Forms A and B

Alternative Assessment Handbook

TOS ExamView Test Generator, Chapter Test

Differentiated Instruction Modified Worksheets and Tests CD-ROM: Chapter Test

Online Assessment Program, in the Interactive Student Edition

Reteach/Intervene

Guided Reading Workbook

Differentiated Instruction Teacher Management System: Lesson Plans

Differentiated Instruction Modified Worksheets and Tests CD-ROM

Interactive Skills Tutor CD-ROM

hmhsocialstudies.com
Chapter Resources

7. a. possible responses—the first step toward democracy with Magna Carta; the Black Death, which reduced the population and led to a labor shortage; the Hundred Years' War, which led to the elimination of the feudal system and increased power for kings

b. to provide military service to the nobles

c. The Christian church was largely the center of life during the Middle Ages.

Using the Internet

8. Go to hmhsocialstudies.com to access a rubric for this activity.

Social Studies Skills

9. 100 BC–AD 117

10. the Roman Empire's borders around 100 BC

11. before

12. Spain

13. 44 BC–AD 14

Map Activity

14. A. Rome
B. Athens
C. Holy Land
D. Alexandria
E. Carthage
F. Gaul

Focus on Writing

15. Main ideas: The manor system controlled most economic activities; the manor was the center of the system; the manor's owner did not farm his own land, but had workers farm it for him; the workers were peasants or serfs.

RF: Focus on Reading, Re-reading

16. Rubric Students' myths should

• focus on one event

• explain the event as someone in the past might have

• have a beginning, middle, and end

• use descriptive details

RF: Focus on Writing, Writing a Myth

SECTION 3 (Pages 328–335)

7. a. Describe What were two changes that affected Europe in the late Middle Ages?

b. Explain What duties did knights have under the feudal system?

c. Develop Why do you think so much of the art created in the Middle Ages was religious?

Using the Internet

8. Activity: Exploring Ancient Greece The golden age of Greece was an amazing time—the Greeks helped shape our government, art, philosophy, writing, and more! Through your online textbook, learn more about the ancient Greek world. Imagine you have traveled through time, back to ancient Greece. What are the people doing? What kinds of buildings do you see? What is the area like? Draw a picture or make a collage to record your observations.

 hmhsocialstudies.com

Social Studies Skills

Interpreting a Historical Map *Use the map on the Expansion of Rome in Section 2 of this chapter to answer the following questions.*

9. What time period is shown on this map?

10. What does the orange color on this map represent?

11. Did the areas shown on the map in gold become part of Rome before or after the areas shown in light green?

12. Which was conquered by the Romans first—Spain or Gaul?

13. Between which two years did Egypt become a Roman territory?

Map Activity

14. Europe, 2000 BC–AD 1500 On a separate sheet of paper, match the letters on the map with their correct labels.

Athens	Carthage	Rome
Gaul	Holy Land	Alexandria

---

hmhsocialstudies.com **INTERACTIVE MAP**

map zone

FOCUS ON READING AND WRITING

15. Re-Reading Read the passage titled The Manor System in Section 3. After you read, write down the main ideas of the passage. Then go back and re-read the passage carefully. Add to your list of main ideas anything more that you noticed in your second reading. How much more did you learn from the passage when you re-read it?

16. Writing Your Myth Now that you have learned about the events and people of ancient and medieval Europe, you can write a myth about one of them. Remember that your myth should try to explain the person or the event in a way that people of the time might have. For example, they might have thought that Caesar was the son of a goddess or that the Black Death was caused by a terrible unknown monster. Try to include descriptive details that will help bring your myth to life for the people who read it.

DIRECTIONS: Read questions 1 through 7 and write the letter of the best response. Then read question 8 and write your own well-constructed response.

1 Democracy was first practiced in which city-state of ancient Greece?

A Athens
B Carthage
C Rome
D Sparta

2 A large estate owned by a noble or knight in the Middle Ages was called a

A city-state.
B republic.
C empire.
D manor.

3 The first Roman emperor to become a Christian was named

A Julius Caesar.
B Augustus.
C Constantine.
D Jesus of Nazareth.

4 Which of the following was first created in the Middle Ages?

A aqueducts
B Gothic architecture
C drama
D democracy

5 The blended culture that was created in Alexander the Great's empire is called

A Greek
B Hellenistic ✓
C Roman
D Medieval

Europe, AD 117

6 Study the map above. The area shown in orange on this map was ruled by the

A Greeks
B Etruscans
C Romans
D French

7 Which document limited the powers of the king of England?

A Black Death
B Crusade
C Feudal system
D Magna Carta

8 **Extended Response** As the map above shows, much of Europe was unified under a single government in 117. By the Middle Ages, though, that government had fallen apart. Write a brief paragraph in which you explain two ways in which European society was different in the Middle Ages than it had been in earlier times.

EARLY HISTORY OF EUROPE **341**

Answers

Standardized Test Prep

1. A
Break Down the Question Neither B nor C is correct, because neither Carthage nor Rome are in Greece. Sparta was a city-state, but democracy began in Athens.

2 D
Break Down the Question A refers to Greece; B and C refer to Rome. D is the only correct answer.

3. C
Break Down the Question Julius Caesar and Augustus ruled before Christianity. Jesus was not a Roman emperor. The correct answer is C; Constantine converted in the 330s.

4. B
Break Down the Question Drama, democracy, and aqueducts existed during the Middle Ages, but they were created earlier in ancient Greece and Rome. So A, C, and D are incorrect. Gothic architecture was first created in the Middle Ages.

5. B
Break Down the Question Greek and Roman cultures weren't truly blended cultures, so A and C are incorrect. Alexander the Great lived long before the Middle Ages. Hellenistic means "Greeklike." B is the correct answer.

6. C
Break Down the Question The Romans were the only people to rule this area so C is the correct answer.

7. D
Break Down the Question A, B, and C are not documents. D is the correct answer.

8. Extended Response Answers will vary but students may mention that Christianity was the major influence on society and that small kingdoms had their own customs, laws, and language.

Reteach/Intervention Resources

Reproducible
- Guided Reading Workbook
- Differentiated Instruction Teacher Management System: Lesson Plans

Technology
- Quick Facts Transparency: Early History of Europe Visual Summary
- Differentiated Instruction Modified Worksheets and Tests CD-ROM
- Interactive Skills Tutor CD-ROM

Tips for Test Taking

Master the Question Have you ever said, "I knew the answer, but I thought the question asked something else?" Be very sure that you know what a question is asking. Read the question at least twice before reading the answer choices. Approach it as you would a mystery story or a riddle. Look for clues. Watch especially for words like not and except—they tell you to look for the choice that is false or different from the other choices or opposite in some way.

Multimedia Classroom

The **HISTORY™ Multimedia Classroom** is a set of exciting new social studies teaching tools featuring award-winning program content. These comprehensive lesson plans, correlated to individual state and national curriculum standards, are easy to use for both teachers and students.

Each lesson contains the following:
- Short video segments that bring history topics to life
- Maps and visual materials
- Discussion and review questions
- Easily printable primary source documents
- Classroom activities and Internet-based activity links

The Multimedia Classroom has been specially designed to be versatile and easily adaptable to existing courses, lesson plans, and syllabi. Every lesson is designed to offer maximum flexibility. Teachers can select entire plans or only the elements they need, allowing them to individually tailor each lesson. Each multimedia lesson is available in CD-ROM format and is accompanied by full-length award-winning programs on DVD from HISTORY™.

For more information or to purchase go to ⊐ hmhsocialstudies.com

Because some of these lessons may contain video material of a sensitive nature, we recommend that teachers and parents review these materials in their entirety before screening them to students.

ANCIENT GREECE

The Acropolis of Athens symbolizes the city and represents the architectural and artistic legacy of ancient Greece. *Acropolis* means "highest city" in Greek, and there are many such sites in Greece. Historically, an acropolis provided shelter and defense against a city's enemies. The Acropolis of Athens—the best known of them all—contained temples, monuments, and artwork dedicated to the Greek gods. Archaeological evidence indicates that the Acropolis was an important place to inhabitants from much earlier eras. However, the structures that we see today on the site were largely conceived by the statesman Pericles during the Golden Age of Athens in the 5th century B.C.

Explore the Acropolis of ancient Greece and learn about the legacy of Greek civilization. You can find a wealth of information, video clips, primary sources, activities, and more at ⊐ hmhsocialstudies.com.

341 MC1 MULTIMEDIA CONNECTIONS

Ancient Greece

Resources ⊐ hmhsocialstudies.com

The following resources come with printable introductions, comprehension and critical thinking questions, transcripts, and vocabulary support.

Full Length DVD

Ancient Greece (45 minutes)

Video Clips
- Athens' Spiritual Citadel (1:43)
- Athena as Divine Guardian (1:47)
- At War with the Persians (1:56)
- Pericles and the Golden Age (3:37)
- The Panathenaia Festival (3:52)
- Origins of Western Culture (4:29)
- Dionysus and Greek Theater (1:57)
- The Death of a Philosopher (1:13)
- Bringing Down the Parthenon (4:10)
- Elgin's Contested Collection (1:43)
- Mysteries and Discoveries (5:11)

Primary Sources
- *Oedipus Rex*
- *The Republic*
- *The Histories*
- The Porch of the Caryatids
- A Panathenaic Amphora
- Greek Fables
- A Greek Funeral Stele

The Parthenon

Watch the video to see what the Parthenon, one of the most important temples on the Acropolis, might have looked like after it was completed.

The Persian Wars

Watch the video to find out how Athens emerged as the principal Greek city-state at the conclusion of the Persian Wars.

The Goddess Athena

Watch the video to learn how, according to Greek mythology, Athena became the protector of Athens.

Legacy of Greece

Watch the video to analyze *The School of Athens*, a painting by the Italian Renaissance artist Raphael, which pays tribute to the legacy of ancient Greece in philosophy and science.

ANCIENT GREECE **341 MC2**

Lesson Preview

The Parthenon

No other building on the Acropolis was as magnificent as the Parthenon. Begun by Pericles in 447 B.C., the Parthenon took about 15 years to build. When finished, the marble temple was more than 225 feet long and 100 feet wide. However, the Parthenon was impressive for the elegant proportion of its columns, not for its size. Visitors did not enter the temple; they could only view it from outside. As they walked around the Parthenon, visitors admired the colorful sculptures that rose in the frieze above its columns until they finally glimpsed the huge gold and ivory statue of Athena standing within.

The Persian Wars

From about 490 to 479 B.C., the Greek city-states fought the vast and powerful Persian Empire. Surprisingly, Greece defeated the Persians at their first major battle at Marathon, a town that lay not far from Athens. According to legend, an Athenian messenger ran from Marathon to Athens after the battle to announce the Greeks' victory. He completed the 26-mile run but died from exhaustion after he delivered the message. This legend inspired the modern marathon race.

The Goddess Athena

According to Greek mythology, Athena, the goddess of wisdom, and Poseidon, the god of the sea, competed for a city in Greece by presenting it with valuable gifts. Poseidon gave the city a spring, but the people had little use for its salty water. Athena planted an olive tree, which would provide the city with food, oil, and wood. The goddess won and named her city Athens.

Legacy of Greece

Raphael's *The School of Athens* depicts the great philosophers of ancient Greece. Its central figures are Plato on the left—portrayed as Leonardo da Vinci—and his student, Aristotle, on the right. Raphael portrayed himself in a less significant area of the painting, peering out from among a group of scholars.

Chapter 14 Planning Guide

History of Early Modern Europe

Overview	Instructional Resources	
CHAPTER 14 **Essential Question:** What important events shaped Europe from the Middle Ages to modern times? 🔊 **Focus on the Essential Question Podcast**	**TOS Differentiated Instruction Teacher Management System:** • Instructional Pacing Guides • Lesson Plans for Differentiated Instruction **Guided Reading Workbook** **Resource File:** • Chapter Review • Focus on Reading: Understanding Chronological Order • Focus on Writing: Creating a Travel Brochure • Social Studies Skills: Making Economic Choices **Experiencing World History and Geography**	**TOS Calendar Planner** 🔘 **Power Presentations with Media Gallery** 🔘 **Differentiated Instruction Modified Worksheets and Tests CD-ROM** 🔘 **Interactive Skills Tutor CD-ROM** 🔊 **Student Edition on Audio CD-ROM** 🔊 **The World's Music Audio Program** ▶️ **Map Zone Transparency:** Europe, 1500–1900 ▶️ **World Outline Maps: Transparencies and Activities** Ⓗ **Video:** Da Vinci Tech
Section 1: **The Renaissance and Reformation** **The Big Idea:** The periods of the Renaissance and the Reformation introduced new ideas and new ways of thinking into Europe.	**TOS Differentiated Instruction Teacher Management System:** Section 1 Lesson Plan **Guided Reading Workbook:** Section 1 **Resource File:** • Vocabulary Builder: Section 1 • Primary Source: The Notebooks of Leonardo da Vinci • Geography for Life: Italian Renaissance Cities: A Modern Way of Life?	▶️ **Daily Bellringer Transparency:** Section 1 ▶️ **Map Zone Transparency:** Major Trade Routes, 1350–1500 ▶️ **Map Zone Transparency:** Religion in Europe, 1600 ↗️ **Internet Activity:** Technology and Exploration ↗️ **Animated Geography:** The Renaissance Ⓗ **Video:** Humanism Triggers the Renaissance
Section 2: **Science and Exploration** **The Big Idea:** New inventions and knowledge led to European exploration and empires around the world.	**TOS Differentiated Instruction Teacher Management System:** Section 2 Lesson Plan **Guided Reading Workbook:** Section 2 **Resource File:** • Vocabulary Builder: Section 2 • Biography: Galileo • Geography and History: Magellan's Voyage around the World	▶️ **Daily Bellringer Transparency:** Section 2 ▶️ **Map Zone Transparency:** European Exploration, 1487–1580 ▶️ **Map Zone Transparency:** European Empires in the Americas, 1700 Ⓗ **Video:** Sir Isaac Newton: The Gravity of Genius
Section 3: **Political Change in Europe** **The Big Idea:** Ideas of the Enlightenment inspired revolutions and new governments in Europe.	**TOS Differentiated Instruction Teacher Management System:** Section 3 Lesson Plan **Guided Reading Workbook:** Section 3 **Resource File:** • Vocabulary Builder: Section 3 • Biography: Napoleon Bonaparte	▶️ **Daily Bellringer Transparency:** Section 3 ▶️ **Map Zone Transparency:** Europe after the Congress of Vienna, 1815
Section 4: **The Industrial Revolution** **The Big Idea:** Driven by new ideas and technologies, much of Europe developed industrial societies in the 1700s and 1800s.	**TOS Differentiated Instruction Teacher Management System:** Section 4 Lesson Plan **Guided Reading Workbook:** Section 4 **Resource File:** • Vocabulary Builder: Section 4 • Literature: *Frankenstein* by Mary Wollstonecraft Shelley	▶️ **Daily Bellringer Transparency:** Section 4 ↗️ **Internet Activity:** Life of a British Textile Factory Worker

Review, Assessment, Intervention

 Europe and Russia Transparencies: History of Early Modern Europe Visual Summary

 Spanish Chapter Summaries Audio CD

 Progress Assessment Support System (PASS): Chapter Test

 Differentiated Instruction Modified Worksheets and Tests CD-ROM: Modified Chapter Test

TOS **ExamView® Assessment Suite (English/Spanish)**

 Alternative Assessment Handbook

 Online Assessment Program, in the Interactive Student Edition

---

 PASS: Section 1 Quiz

 Online Quiz: Section 1

 Alternative Assessment Handbook

 PASS: Section 2 Quiz

 Online Quiz: Section 2

 Alternative Assessment Handbook

 PASS: Section 3 Quiz

 Online Quiz: Section 3

 Alternative Assessment Handbook

 PASS: Section 4 Quiz

 Online Quiz: Section 4

 Alternative Assessment Handbook

Supporting Resources

- Multimedia Classroom Global History Series
- Global History Series Teacher's Guide

Maps Globes Graphs Level F

- Student Workbook
- Teacher's Guide

Social Studies Trade Library Collections

- NCSS Middle School Trade Collection
- Women in History Trade Collection

Geography's Impact

Geography's Impact Video Program

- **Impact of the Renaissance and Reformation**

For more information or to purchase go to   hmhsocialstudies.com

Power Presentations with Media Gallery

Power Presentations with Media Gallery are visual presentations of each chapter's main ideas. Presentations can be customized by including Quick Facts charts, images from the text, and video clips.

CHAPTER 14 PLANNING GUIDE

Differentiating Instruction

How do I address the needs of varied learners?
The Target Resource acts as your primary strategy for differentiated instruction.

ENGLISH-LANGUAGE LEARNERS & STRUGGLING READERS

Interactive Skills Tutor CD-ROM

The Interactive Skills Tutor CD-ROM contains lessons that provide additional practice for 20 different critical thinking skills.

Additional Resources

Differentiated Instruction Teacher Management System: Lesson Plans for Differentiated Instruction

Resource File:
- Vocabulary Builder Activities
- Social Studies Skills: Making Economic Choices

Europe and Russia Transparencies:
- History of Early Modern Europe Visual Summary

Spanish/English Guided Reading Workbook

Spanish Chapter Summaries Audio CD

Teacher One Stop:
- ExamView Assessment Suite, Spanish
- PuzzleView, Spanish

English-Language Learner Strategies and Activities

SPECIAL NEEDS LEARNERS

Differentiated Instruction Modified Worksheets and Tests CD-ROM

- Vocabulary Flash Cards
- Modified Vocabulary Builder Activities
- Modified Chapter Review
- Modified Chapter Test

Additional Resources

Differentiated Instruction Teacher Management System: Lesson Plans for Differentiated Instruction

Guided Reading Workbook

Resource File: Social Studies Skills: Making Economic Choices

Student Edition on Audio CD Program

Interactive Skills Tutor CD-ROM

Graphic Organizer Transparencies with Support for Reading and Writing

ADVANCED/GIFTED AND TALENTED STUDENTS

Resource File

The Resource File activities allow students to extend their knowledge of chapter-related places and people and to practice geography skills.
- Focus on Reading: Understanding Chronological Order
- Focus on Writing: Creating a Travel Brochure
- Literature: *Frankenstein* by Mary Wollstonecraft Shelley

Additional Resources

Differentiated Instruction Teacher Management System: Lesson Plans for Differentiated Instruction

World History and Geography Document-Based Questions Activities

Geography, Science, and Cultures Activities

Experiencing World History and Geography

Differentiated Activities in the Teacher's Edition

- Identifying European Colonies in the Americas, p. 356
- Decoding *Enlightenment*, p. 350
- Analyzing Social Classes in France, p. 362
- Identifying Great Britain's Resources, p. 367

Differentiated Activities in the Teacher's Edition

- Creating a Commemorative Stamp, p. 352

Differentiated Activities in the Teacher's Edition

- Analyzing a Quotation, p. 362

Teacher One Stop™

How can I manage the lesson plans and support materials for differentiated instruction?

With the Teacher One Stop, you can easily organize and print lesson plans, planning guides, and instructional materials for all learners. The Teacher One Stop includes the following materials to help you differentiate instruction:

· **Interactive Teacher's Edition**
· **Calendar Planner and pacing guides**
· **Editable lesson plans**
· **All reproducible ancillaries in Adobe Acrobat (PDF) format**
· **ExamView Assessment Suite (English & Spanish)**
· **Transparency and video previews**

Interactive Student Edition

Complete online student edition with interactive multimedia support for chapter content assessment and reporting

- Interactive Maps and Notebook
- Standardized Test Prep
- Online Homework Practice and Research Activities
- Current Events
- Chapter-based Internet Activities
- Animated Geography Activities

DIFFERENTIATED INSTRUCTION PLANNING GUIDE

Essential Question

Introduce the Essential Question

- Explain that at the end of the Middle Ages, new ideas and discoveries ushered in the Renaissance, a period of artistic achievements, scientific knowledge, and inventions.

- Explain that modern science, which had its birth between about 1540 and 1700, led to European exploration and empires around the world.

- Point out that in the 1600s and 1700s, Europe experienced a period called the Enlightenment, during which people used reason to develop new ideas about government and people's rights.

- Discuss how new technologies led to industrial societies in Europe and how machines changed how people lived and worked.

Focus on Reading and Writing

Reading The Resource File provides a worksheet to help students practice understanding chronological order.

📝 **RF:** Focus on Reading, Understanding Chronological Order

Writing The Resource File provides a worksheet to help students organize and write their travel brochures.

📝 **RF:** Focus on Writing, Creating a Travel Brochure

Key to Differentiating Instruction

Below Level

Basic-level activities designed for all students encountering new material

At Level

Intermediate-level activities designed for average students

Above Level

Challenging activities designed for honors and gifted and talented students

Standard English Mastery

Activities designed to improve standard English usage

LS Learning Styles

History of Early Modern Europe

Essential Question What important events shaped Europe from the Middle Ages to modern times?

❓ What You Will Learn...

In this chapter you will learn about European history from the end of the Middle Ages to 1900. During this period new ideas and innovations changed life and expanded knowledge across Europe.

FOCUS ON READING AND WRITING

Understanding Chronological Order Chronological means "related to time." Many of the events in this chapter are described in sequence, or in the order in which they occurred. Words such as first, before, next, and later can signal chronological order. **See the lesson, Understanding Chronological Order, on page 529.**

Creating a Travel Brochure Your job is to encourage people to visit a time from Europe's exciting past. Read about Europe's history from the Renaissance through the Industrial Revolution. Then choose one time period and create a travel brochure to convince others to visit Europe during that period. What exciting changes might visitors see? What experiences might they have? Describe it all in your brochure.

ATLANTIC OCEAN

Explorer's ship

Madrid

AFRICA

The Reformation In 1517 Martin Luther, a German monk, posted problems he saw in the Catholic Church.

Introduce the Chapter

At Level

What Is Modern?

1. Direct students' attention to the chapter title. Ask several students what *modern* means.

2. Ask students if the images on the map seem modern to them. From what perspective would the printing press, steam train, and ship be seen as new and innovative?

3. Have students identify the functions of the printing press, steam train, and ship and describe reasons why these inventions might represent significant advances that set this

period apart from earlier periods in European history.

4. As a class, have students suggest images they would choose for a map today. What inventions would they pick? What historical events? Would students put any people or buildings on their lists? Make a list of these images. As students make suggestions, have them give reasons for their choices that show how these inventions or events have changed how people live today. **LS Verbal/Linguistic**

Steam train

North Sea

Baltic Sea

Printing press

Wittenberg

Paris

French Revolution

EUROPE

Milan

Venice

Florence

Rome

Duomo, a cathedral in Florence

Mediterranean Sea

HISTORY Da Vinci Tech

↗ hmhsocialstudies.com VIDEO

| 0 | 100 | 300 Miles |
| 0 | 100 | 200 Kilometers |

Projection: Azimuthal Equal Area

map zone Geography Skills

Place The nations and kingdoms of Europe underwent many changes during this period.

1. Identify What city is connected with the French Revolution?

2. Analyze Based on the images on the map, what types of changes do you think occurred during this period of Europe's history?

The Age of Exploration Italian sailor Christopher Columbus led a voyage that reached the Americas in 1492.

The Industrial Revolution First used in factories, the steam engine later powered trains and ships. Inventions such as the steam engine changed life in Europe during the 1700s and 1800s.

343

Chapter Preview

Explore the Map and Pictures

Europe, 1500–1900 Tell students that during this 400-year period, Europe experienced enormous changes due to war, conflict within the church, the exploration of new lands, and scientific, industrial, and political revolutions. These revolutions sparked new inventions and new ways of thinking about the world.

Analyzing Visuals What sources of energy do you see here? *wind, steam* What were main sources of energy before steam engine was invented? *wind, water, horse, foot power* How might the invention of the steam engine have changed how Europeans lived? *possible answers—could go farther faster, carry heavier loads, live farther from water*

▶ Map Zone Transparency: Europe, 1500–1900

Info to Know

Duomo in Florence *Duomo* is an Italian word that means *cathedral*. The cathedral on the map is famous throughout the world as a symbol of the city of Florence. The architect Filippo Brunelleschi started work on the octagonal dome in 1420 and finished it 16 years later.

↗ hmhsocialstudies.com **Teacher Resources**

Critical Thinking: Analyzing Visuals [At Level]

Asking Historical Questions

1. Have students examine the pictures at the bottom of the page and write down three predictions about how the actions of Martin Luther and Christopher Columbus might have affected events in the historical period students are about to study.

2. Ask students to think about the following questions. What risks might be associated with the actions of each? What might each hope to gain?

3. Then ask students what they can learn from examining the images on the map about how this period might be different from earlier

periods in European history. Is it similar in any ways?

4. Have students describe what other information they can learn from the map and pictures. Ask them to consider how their lives might be different today if certain events or inventions did not take place. **LS Verbal/Linguistic**

📖 Alternative Assessment Handbook, Rubric 11: Discussions

Answers

Map Zone 1. *Paris;* **2.** *possible answer—changes in transportation, communications, knowledge of world, architecture, religion, politics*

Bellringer

If YOU lived there. . . Use the **Daily Bellringer Transparency** to help students answer the question.

▶ Daily Bellringer Transparency, Section 1

History of Early Modern Europe | Daily Bellringer
Section 1

Preview Section 1

If YOU lived there ...
You live in Florence, Italy, in the 1400s. Your father, a merchant, has just hired a tutor from Asia Minor to teach you and your sisters and brothers. Your new teacher starts by stating, "Nothing good has been written in a thousand years." He insists that you learn to read Latin and Greek so that you can study Roman and Greek books that were written long ago.
What can you learn from these ancient books?

Consider what you can learn from ANCIENT ROMAN books:
• a knowledge of architecture, such as for building roads and bridges
• a model for government and written laws
• a better understanding of languages, since many are based on Latin

Consider what you can learn from ANCIENT GREEK books:
• how democracy works
• a knowledge of science and math
• reading classic literature that can teach lessons about life

Key Terms and Places

📖 **RF:** Vocabulary Builder, Section 1

Taking Notes

Have students use the graphic organizer online to take notes on the section. This activity will prepare students for the Section Assessment, in which they will complete a graphic organizer that builds on the information using the Critical Thinking Skill: Finding Main Ideas.

The Renaissance and Reformation

What You Will Learn...

Main Ideas

1. The Renaissance was a period of new learning, new ideas, and new advances in art, literature, and science.
2. The Reformation changed the religious map of Europe.

The Big Idea

The periods of the Renaissance and the Reformation introduced new ideas and new ways of thinking into Europe.

Key Terms and Places

Renaissance, *p. 344*
Florence, *p. 344*
Venice, *p. 344*
humanism, *p. 345*
Reformation, *p. 348*
Protestants, *p. 349*
Catholic Reformation, *p. 349*

hmhsocialstudies.com
TAKING NOTES

Use the graphic organizer online to take notes on the Renaissance and the Reformation.

If YOU lived there...

You live in Florence, Italy, in the 1400s. Your father, a merchant, has just hired a tutor from Asia Minor to teach you and your sisters and brothers. Your new teacher starts by stating, "Nothing good has been written in a thousand years." He insists that you learn to read Latin and Greek so that you can study Roman and Greek books that were written long ago.

What can you learn from these ancient books?

BUILDING BACKGROUND The end of the Middle Ages brought important changes to European politics and society. These changes set the stage for an exciting new period of learning and creativity. During this period, new ideas influenced the arts, science, and attitudes toward religion.

The Renaissance

Do you ever get the urge to do something creative? If so, how do you express your creativity? Do you like to draw or paint? Maybe you prefer to write stories or poems or create music.

At the end of the Middle Ages, people across Europe found the urge to be creative. Their creativity was sparked by new ideas and discoveries that were sweeping through Europe at the time. This period of creativity, of new ideas and inspirations, is called the **Renaissance** (REN-uh-sahns). It lasted from about 1350 through the 1500s. *Renaissance* is French for "rebirth." The people who named this period believed it represented a new beginning, or rebirth, in Europe's history and culture.

New Ideas

The Renaissance started in Italy. During and after the Crusades, Italian cities such as **Florence** and **Venice** became rich through trade. Goods from faraway Asia moved through these cities.

Teach the Big Idea
At Level

The Renaissance and Reformation

1. **Teach** Ask students the questions in the Main Idea boxes under Direct Teach.

2. **Apply** Have students make a three-column chart, labeled Causes, Event, and Effects. In the Event column, have them list *Renaissance* and *Reformation,* leaving at least ten lines of space between the two terms. As they read the lesson, have students list causes of these two events in column one and the effects on European culture in column three. 📖 **Verbal/Linguistic**

3. **Review** As you review the section's main ideas, discuss how advances in art, literature, and science were influenced by humanism.

4. **Practice/Homework** Have students pick one change that occurred during the Renaissance or Reformation and describe how it has affected art, literature, belief systems, or another aspect of culture. 📖 **Verbal/Linguistic**

📝 Alternative Assessment Handbook, Rubrics 6: Cause and Effect; and 7: Charts

These goods made the people who lived there curious about the larger world. At the same time, scholars from other parts of the world came to Italy. They brought books written by ancient Greeks and Romans.

Inspired by these books and by the ancient ruins around them, some people in Italy became interested in ancient cultures. These people began reading works in Greek and Latin and studying subjects that had been taught in Greek and Roman schools.

These subjects, known as the humanities, included history, poetry, and grammar. Increased study of the humanities led to a new way of thinking and learning known as humanism.

Humanism emphasized the abilities and accomplishments of human beings. The humanists believed that people were capable of great things. As a result, they admired artists, architects, leaders, writers, scientists, and other talented individuals.

Major Trade Routes, 1350–1500

ENGLAND
EUROPE
FRANCE
Paris
Augsburg
Lyon
Genoa
Milan
Venice
Marseille
Pisa
Florence
SPAIN
Rome
Valencia
Naples
Granada
Tunis
Sicily (SPAIN)
AFRICA
Mediterranean Sea
RUSSIA
Kaffa
Black Sea
Constantinople
BYZANTINE EMPIRE
Antioch
SYRIA
Damascus
Cairo
EGYPT
To China
To India
To India
ATLANTIC OCEAN
50°N
40°N
20°E
30°E

Trade routes controlled by Italian city-states
0   200   400 Miles
0   200   400 Kilometers
Projection: Azimuthal Equal Area

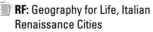

Geography Skills

Movement Traders brought goods to Europe from distant lands, including Africa and Asia.
1. **Identify** Which seas served as routes for trade?
2. **Analyze** How do you think the geographic location of the Italian trading cities helped them control trade in the Mediterranean region?

Florence Florence was a banking and trade center. The city's wealthy leaders used their money to beautify Florence.

Venice Venice was the most successful of the Italian trading cities. Traders brought goods to Venice from as far away as China and India.

HISTORY OF EARLY MODERN EUROPE **345**

The Renaissance

The Renaissance was a period of great creativity and advances in art, literature, and science.

Renaissance sculptors were careful to show the tiniest details in their works. This statue by Michelangelo is of David, a king of ancient Israel.

Painters like Hans Holbein the Younger wanted to show what real life was like for people in Europe.

Direct Teach

Main Idea

The Renaissance, *continued*

Identify How was Leonardo da Vinci an example of the Renaissance ideal? *He was not just a painter, but also sculptor, architect, engineer, and scientist.*

Describe How did the writings of the Greeks and Romans lead to new inventions? *Inspired by Greek and Roman knowledge, people began to study math, astronomy, and other sciences. They used this new knowledge to create new techniques and inventions.*

Make Inferences What effect did the printing press have on the Renaissance? *It helped spread knowledge of new ideas in art, literature, and science, which resulted in new inventions and other changes.*

📝 **RF:** Primary Source, The Notebooks of Leonardo da Vinci

Did you know. . .

In the 1490s, Leonardo da Vinci began to fill notebooks with quick sketches of what he saw around him. He first made drawings on tiny paper pads and then copied them into his notebooks. Some drawings reflect his interest in human anatomy, painting, or architecture. Others show his interest in mechanics. One intriguing feature of the notebooks is his use of mirror writing. He wrote his notes in reverse from right to left. To read a page, it had to be held up to a mirror. Scholars are unsure why he wrote this way.

HISTORY

VIDEO
Humanism Triggers the Renaissance

hmhsocialstudies.com

Renaissance Art

The Renaissance was a period of talented artistic achievements. Artists of the period created new techniques to improve their work. For example, they developed the technique of perspective, a method of showing a three-dimensional scene on a flat surface so that it looks real.

Many Renaissance artists were also humanists. Humanist artists valued the achievements of individuals. These artists wanted their paintings and sculptures to show people's unique personalities. One of the artists best able to show this sense of personality in his works was the Italian Michelangelo (mee-kay-LAHN-jay-loh). He was both a great painter and sculptor. His statues, like the one of King David above, seem almost to be alive.

Another famous Renaissance artist was Leonardo da Vinci. Leonardo achieved the Renaissance goal of excelling in many areas. He was not only a great painter and sculptor but also an architect, scientist, and engineer. He sketched plants and animals as well as inventions such as a submarine.

He collected knowledge about the human body. Both Leonardo and Michelangelo are examples of what we call Renaissance people—people who can do practically anything well.

Renaissance Literature

Like artists, Renaissance writers expressed the attitudes of the time. The most famous Renaissance writer is probably the English dramatist William Shakespeare. He wrote excellent poetry, but Shakespeare is best known for his plays. They include more than 30 comedies, histories, and tragedies. In his plays, Shakespeare turned popular stories into great drama. His writing shows a deep understanding of human nature and skillfully expresses the thoughts and feelings of his characters. For these reasons, Shakespeare's plays are still highly popular in many parts of the world.

Renaissance writings were read and enjoyed by a larger audience than earlier writings had been. This change was largely due to advances in science and technology, such as the printing press.

346 CHAPTER 14

Collaborative Learning
At Level

Creating an Invitation

1. Organize the class into small groups. Ask students to imagine that they work in the publicity department at a local museum. Their job is to let people in their community know about the opening of a new exhibit on the Renaissance.

2. Assign each group one of these topics: Renaissance Art, Renaissance Drama and Literature, or Renaissance Science and Inventions.

3. As a class, decide when, where, and at what time the exhibit will open. Then have each group prepare an invitation to be sent to community members. The invitation should tell what the exhibit will contain, why people will enjoy it, and what they will learn. It should also give basic information such as time, date, place, and cost.

LS **Interpersonal, Verbal/Linguistic**

📄 Alternative Assessment Handbook, Rubrics 2: Advertisements; and 14: Group Activity

Leonardo da Vinci drew sketches of many devices that were not invented until centuries after his death. This model of a type of helicopter was based on the sketch by Leonardo shown below.

William Shakespeare is considered the greatest of all Renaissance writers. His plays are still read and performed today.

ANALYSIS SKILL **ANALYZING VISUALS**

Based on the sculpture of David and on the Holbein painting, how would you describe Renaissance art?

Renaissance Science

Some of the ancient works rediscovered during the Renaissance dealt with science. For the first time in centuries, Europeans could read about early Greek and Roman scientific advances. Inspired by what they read, some people began to study math, astronomy, and other fields of science.

Using this new scientific knowledge, Europeans developed new inventions and techniques. For example, they learned how to build enormous domes that could rise higher than earlier buildings.

Another invention of the Renaissance was the movable type printing press. A German named Johann Gutenberg built the first movable type printing press in the mid-1400s. This type of printing press could print books quickly and cheaply. For the first time, people could easily share ideas with others in distant areas. The printing press helped the ideas of the Renaissance spread beyond Italy.

READING CHECK Summarizing How did life in Europe change during the Renaissance?

CONNECTING TO Technology

The Printing Press

Printing was not a new idea in Renaissance Europe. What was new was the method of printing. Johann Gutenberg designed a printing system called movable type. It used a set of tiny lead blocks, each carved with a letter of the alphabet. These blocks could then be used to spell out an entire page of text for printing. Once copies of the page were made, the printer could reuse the blocks to spell out another page. This was much faster and easier than earlier systems had been.

Generalizing How did movable type improve printing?

Direct Teach

Info to Know

Gutenberg Bible With his movable type, Gutenberg could make 16 copies of a page in an hour. His first book, known today as the Gutenberg Bible, was a Latin Bible. It took him about 15 years to raise the money for the project. During that time, he kept his invention secret. When the printing began, Gutenberg and six printers worked full time for more than a year to produce it. Scholars do not know how many copies Gutenberg made originally, but 40 copies of this famous Bible still exist. Some are in the United States. Visitors can see them at the U.S. Library of Congress, the New York Public Library, and at the Harvard University and Yale University libraries.

Activity Cooperation or Conflict? Have students create a three-column chart with the headings: Contribution, Cooperation, and Conflict. Explain that developments in the arts, literature, media, technology, and languages often foster cooperation among people or perpetuate conflict. As students read the chapter, have them record contributions brought on during the Renaissance in the first column of their charts. Then have students write a sentence explaining how each contribution led to cooperation or conflict in Europe in the corresponding column of their charts.

Cross-Discipline Activity: Language Arts   At Level

Writing a Descriptive Essay

1. Have students discuss the ways Gutenberg's invention of movable type changed life in Europe, such as the spreading of new ideas.

2. As a prewriting activity, list on the board students' ideas of the ways people today rely on printed information, such as newspapers, books, magazines, recipes, and instructions for assembling products.

3. Then have each student write a descriptive essay showing what life in school today

might be like if Gutenberg had not invented the printing press.

4. Ask for volunteers to read their essays to the class or print the essays in a class newspaper.

LS Verbal/Linguistic, Intrapersonal

Alternative Assessment Handbook, Rubrics 11: Discussions; and 40: Writing to Describe

Answers

Reading Check *possible answer— People spent their free time doing creative hobbies, such as painting or writing; people started reading books; schools were filled with people wanting to learn.*

Analyzing Visuals *realistic, because of the attention to detail (David) and emphasis on the lives of ordinary people (Holbein)*

Connecting to Technology *It was faster, easier, and cheaper than earlier printing because type was reusable.*

Main Idea

2 The Reformation

The Reformation changed the religious map of Europe.

Describe Why did Europeans want reform? *Church officials had become too focused on their own power instead of their religious duties.*

Explain What part did Martin Luther play in the Protestant Reformation? *He started the Reformation by posting complaints on a church door in Wittenberg in 1517. Luther's followers then formed their own religion, becoming the first Protestants.*

Draw Conclusions Why did Catholic officials decide to make the reforms known as the Catholic Reformation? *because the Catholic Church wanted to focus more on spiritual matters and help make church teachings easier to understand*

▶ Map Zone Transparency: Religion in Europe, 1600

The Reformation

By the early 1500s some Europeans had begun to complain about problems they saw in the Roman Catholic Church. For example, they thought the church had become corrupt. In time, their complaints led to a religious reform movement called the **Reformation** (re-fuhr-MAY-shuhn).

The Protestant Reformation

Although people called for church reform in other places, the Reformation began in what is now Germany. This area was part of the Holy Roman Empire. Some people there thought church officials were too focused on their own power and had lost sight of their religious duties.

↗ hmhsocialstudies.com **INTERACTIVE MAP**
Religion in Europe, 1600

Legend:
- Protestant
- Roman Catholic
- Roman Catholic with Protestant minorities
- Eastern Orthodox
- Muslim
- Boundary of the Holy Roman Empire

0 — 250 — 500 Miles
0 — 250 — 500 Kilometers

Projection: Lambert Azimuthal Equal-Area

map zone Geography Skills

Regions By the Reformation's end, parts of Europe were still Catholic, while others had become mostly Protestant.

1. **Locate** In which part of Europe were most people Protestant?
2. **Analyze** How were religious areas spread across the Holy Roman Empire?

Differentiating Instruction

Below Level | Standard English Mastery

English-Language Learners

1. Give students practice in decoding new words by looking at the words *reform* and *reformation*.

2. Begin by noting that the prefix *re-* means to do something again as in *retell* or to go back and do over as in *return* and *reapply*.

3. Have students take turns suggesting more words that begin with this prefix while other students suggest definitions.

4. Then focus on the word *reformation*. Tell students that the suffix *–ation* means "the act of doing something." Have students use a dictionary to find and define the root word *reform* and then the word *reformation*.

5. Ask students to use standard English to explain why these Protestant and Catholic movements are called *reformations*.

LS Verbal/Linguistic

Alternative Assessment Handbook, Rubric 1: Acquiring Information

Answers

Map Zone 1. *northern Europe;*
2. *The northern part of the empire and Geneva were mainly Protestant; the western and southern parts were mainly Roman Catholic; the eastern part was mainly Roman Catholic with Protestant minorities.*

One of the first people to express protests against the Catholic Church was a German monk named Martin Luther. In 1517 Luther nailed a list of complaints to a church door in the town of Wittenberg. Luther's protests angered church officials, who soon expelled him from the church. In response, Luther's followers formed a separate church. They became the first **Protestants**, Christians who broke from the Catholic Church over religious issues.

Other reformers who followed Luther began creating churches of their own as well. The Roman Catholic Church was no longer the only church in Western Europe. As you can see on the map, many areas of Europe had become Protestant by 1600.

The Catholic Reformation

Protestants were not the only ones who called for reform in the Roman Catholic Church. Many Catholic officials wanted to reform the church as well. Even as the first Protestants were breaking away from the church, Catholic officials were launching a series of reforms that became known as the **Catholic Reformation**.

As part of the Catholic Reformation, church leaders began focusing more on spiritual concerns and less on political power. They also worked to make church teachings easier for people to understand. To tell people about the changes, church leaders sent priests and teachers all over Europe. Church leaders also worked to spread Catholic teachings into Asia, Africa, and other parts of the world.

Religious Wars

The Reformation caused major changes to the religious map of Europe. Catholicism, once the main religion in most of Europe, was no longer so dominant. In many areas, especially in the north, Protestants now outnumbered Catholics.

In some parts of Europe, Catholics and Protestants lived together in peace. In some other places, however, this was not the case. Bloody religious wars broke out in France, Germany, the Netherlands, and Switzerland. Wars between religious groups left parts of Europe in ruins.

These religious wars led to political and social changes in Europe. For example, many people began relying less on what church leaders and other authority figures told them. Instead, people raised questions and began looking to science for answers.

FOCUS ON READING

Dates in a text, such as the dates 1517 and 1600 in the text at left, help you keep events in order in your mind.

READING CHECK **Finding Main Ideas** How did Europe change after the Reformation?

SUMMARY AND PREVIEW In the 1300s through the 1500s, new ideas changed Europe. Next, you will learn about other ideas and events that brought changes.

Section 1 Assessment

hmhsocialstudies.com
ONLINE QUIZ

Reviewing Ideas, Terms, and Places

1. **a. Define** What was the **Renaissance**?
   b. Summarize What were some changes made in art during the Renaissance?
   c. Elaborate How did the printing press help spread Renaissance ideas?
2. **a. Describe** What led to the **Reformation**?
   b. Explain Why did church leaders launch the series of reforms known as the **Catholic Reformation**?

Critical Thinking

3. **Finding Main Ideas** Draw a chart like the one shown. Use your notes to describe new ideas of the Renaissance and the Reformation. Add rows as needed.

Idea	Description

FOCUS ON WRITING

4. **Describing the Renaissance and the Reformation** Note things about these two periods that might interest visitors. For example, visitors might want to see Renaissance art.

HISTORY OF EARLY MODERN EUROPE **349**

Section 1 Assessment Answers

1. **a.** period from about 1350 to 1500 that focused on creativity, new ideas, and inventions
   b. perspective, greater attention to detail, people in artworks became individuals, focus on life of ordinary Europeans
   c. Books became faster, easier, and less costly to create.
2. **a.** Church officials focused more on power than on religious duties.
   b. to focus more on spiritual matters and spread Catholic teachings

3. possible responses—perspective: shows three dimensions; movable type: made books more available; Protestantism: called for church reform
4. Students might mention painters, sculptures, Shakespeare, printing press, and Wittenberg.

Bellringer

If YOU lived there... Use the **Daily Bellringer Transparency** to help students answer the question.

▶ Daily Bellringer Transparency, Section 2

Academic Vocabulary

Review with students the high-use academic term in this section.

logical reasoned, well thought out (p. 351)

📝 **RF:** Vocabulary Builder, Section 2

Taking Notes

Have students use the graphic organizer online to take notes on the section. This activity will prepare students for the Section Assessment, in which they will complete a graphic organizer that builds on the information using the Critical Thinking Skill: Identifying Cause and Effect.

Answers

Analyzing Visuals *The compass and astrolabe became essential tools for navigation; the telescope led to new ways of looking at Earth and the universe.*

350

SECTION 2

Science and Exploration

Main Ideas

1. During the Scientific Revolution, discoveries and inventions expanded knowledge and changed life in Europe.
2. In the 1400s and 1500s, Europeans led voyages of discovery and exploration.
3. As Europeans discovered new lands, they created colonies and new empires all over the world.

The Big Idea

New inventions and knowledge led to European exploration and empires around the world.

Key Terms

Scientific Revolution, *p. 351*
New World, *p. 355*
circumnavigate, *p. 355*

hmhsocialstudies.com
TAKING NOTES

Use the graphic organizer online to take notes on science and exploration.

If YOU lived there...

You are an adviser to a European king in the 1500s. The rulers of several other countries have sent explorers to search for new trade routes. Your king does not want to fall behind. Now a young sea captain has come to the royal court with a daring plan. The king is interested, but funding such a voyage could be costly.

What will you advise the king to do?

BUILDING BACKGROUND The Renaissance made Europeans more curious about science and the world. This curiosity led to new inventions and technologies that helped people explore the world. As a result, a spirit of adventure swept across Europe.

The Scientific Revolution

Can you imagine what your life would be like without science? Think of all the things that science has provided in our daily lives. Without it, we would have no electricity, no automobiles, no plastic. Our lives would be totally different.

Scientific Advances and Exploration

Several inventions and technical advances enabled people to explore the world and to study the heavens.

ANALYZING VISUALS Why do you think these inventions and advances contributed to increased exploration of the world?

Astrolabe With an astrolabe, sailors could use the stars to calculate a ship's exact location.

Teach the Big Idea

At Level

Science and Exploration

1. **Teach** Ask students the questions in the Main Idea boxes under Direct Teach.

2. **Apply** Have each student create a two-column chart. Label the first column *Belief/ Invention/Discovery* and the second column, *Importance*. As students read the lesson, have them fill in the chart with the names of specific ideas, inventions or discoveries and explain why this belief, invention, or discovery was important. **LS** Verbal/Linguistic

3. **Review** Have pairs of students compare charts and add information.

4. **Practice/Homework** Have students use their charts to create five true/false or fill-in-the blank questions about the section. Remind students to provide an answer key and an explanation of why each answer is correct. **LS** Verbal/Linguistic, Interpersonal

   📝 Alternative Assessment Handbook, Rubrics 1: Acquiring Information; and 7: Charts

Did you know that there was a time when people lived without the benefits of modern science? In fact, it was not until the 1500s and 1600s that most people in Europe began to appreciate what science and technology could do to improve life.

A New View of Science

Before the 1500s, most educated people who studied the world relied on authorities such as ancient Greek writers and church officials. People thought these authorities could tell them all they needed to know. Europeans had little need for science.

Between about 1540 and 1700, though, European views about how to study the world changed. This widespread change in views was part of the **Scientific Revolution**, the series of events that led to the birth of modern science. People began placing more importance on what they observed and less on what they were told. They used their observations to come up with **logical** explanations for how the world worked. This new focus on observation marked the start of modern science.

Why is the birth of modern science called a revolution? The new approach to science was a radical idea. In the same way a political revolution changes a country, this new view of science changed society.

Science and Religion

Not everyone was happy with the new role of science in society. Some people feared that scientific ideas would eventually lead to the breakdown of European society.

Many of the people who most feared the increasing influence of science were church officials. They tended to oppose science when it went against the teachings of the church. For example, the church taught that Earth was at the center of the universe. Some scientists, though, had observed through telescopes that Earth orbited the sun. This observation went against the church's teaching.

This growing tension between religion and science came to a head in 1632. That year, an Italian scientist named Galileo (gal-uh-LEE-oh) published a book in which he stated that Earth orbited the sun. He was arrested and put on trial. Afraid that the church would expel him, Galileo publicly stated that his writings were wrong. Privately, though, he held to his beliefs.

Despite conflicts such as these, science and religion were able to exist together in Europe. In fact, many scientists saw a connection between science and religion. These scientists believed that science could better explain church teachings. Science continued developing rapidly as a result.

ACADEMIC VOCABULARY
logical
reasoned, well thought out

Compass The compass, which always points north, helped sailors find their way at sea.

Telescope With the telescope, scientists could study the heavens like never before.

HISTORY OF EARLY MODERN EUROPE **351**

Did you know...

Isaac Newton gained his first understanding of gravity while sitting under an apple tree. According to a popular legend, Newton's insight came when an apple fell on his head. For many years, scholars distrusted this story, but in 1936, the memoir of one of Newton's close friends was found. It repeated the apple story. Some scholars still think it more likely that Newton watched, rather than felt, the apple fall.

Connect to Science

Innovations in Sailing Until the invention of the caravel, most ships had square sails rather than lateen, or triangular, ones. Square sails work well when going with the wind. They fill up with air like a parachute and push the ship along. However, when sailing against the wind, triangular sails work better. They also work well when wind patterns are unpredictable or shifting— as they often were when Portuguese ships sailed close to the coast of Africa rather than on the open sea.

↗ **hmhsocialstudies.com**

Online Resources
Activity: Technology and Exploration

Close-up
A Caravel

Many of the explorers who set out from Europe in the 1400s and 1500s did so in a new type of ship, the caravel. These ships could sail across huge distances because of some important advances in shipbuilding technology.

Triangular sails enabled the caravel to sail into the wind.

The caravel's smooth, rounded hull, or frame, could stand up to even rough seas.

A large center rudder made the ship easier to move and enabled quick turns.

ANALYSIS SKILL **ANALYZING VISUALS**
What features made the caravel an excellent ship for sailing across long distances?

Discoveries and Inventions

HISTORY
VIDEO
Sir Isaac Newton: The Gravity of Genius
↗ hmhsocialstudies.com

The Scientific Revolution was a period of great advances in many fields of science. With increased interest in science came discoveries in astronomy, biology, physics, and other fields. For example, astronomers discovered how the stars and the planets move in the sky. Biologists learned how blood circulates throughout the human body. Physicists figured out how mirrors and pendulums worked.

Some of the greatest advances of the Scientific Revolution were made by one man, Sir Isaac Newton. He made exciting contributions to both math and physics.

Newton is probably best known today for his observations about gravity, the force that attracts objects to each other. Before his observations, scientists knew very little about how gravity works.

Many of the discoveries of the Scientific Revolution were possible because of new inventions. Devices such as the telescope, the microscope, and the thermometer were invented at this time. Some of these new inventions helped contribute to another exciting time—the Age of Exploration.

READING CHECK **Summarizing** What happened during the Scientific Revolution?

352 CHAPTER 14

Differentiating Instruction

Below Level

Special Needs Learners

Prep Required **Research Required**

1. Show students examples of commemorative postage stamps. Have them suggest reasons why each of the images on these stamps was selected.

2. Then have students pick an invention, such as the caravel, telescope, microscope, thermometer, astrolabe, or compass. Have students use a reference book, encyclopedia, or the Internet to learn more about this invention.

3. Have students use the examples of the commemorative stamps as a model to create

a postage stamp of the invention they chose. They could do this on paper or on a computer with a graphics program.

4. Below their picture of the stamp or on a separate sheet of paper, have students write a paragraph explaining the importance of the invention. Ask students to display their stamps and paragraph.

LS **Visual/Spatial, Verbal/Linguistic**

📄 Alternative Assessment Handbook, Rubrics 22: Multimedia Presentations; and 30: Research

Answers

Analyzing Visuals *triangular sails, rounded hull, center rudder*

Reading Check *Science assumed a more central role in European society, great advances took place in many scientific fields, and new inventions made many scientific discoveries possible.*

The Voyages of Discovery

Some advances in science and technology enabled people to make longer, safer sea voyages. New compasses and astrolabes helped sailors figure out where they were even when far from land. Improvements in mapmaking helped people plan safer routes for their journeys. In addition, new ships, such as the caravel, made sea travel safer. The caravel could sail farther than earlier ships could.

Equipped with these new advances, many Europeans set out on great voyages of discovery. They sailed into unknown waters hoping to find new trade routes to faraway places. They would succeed in their quest, and their discoveries would change the world.

The Drive to Discover

Why were Europeans so eager to explore? They had many reasons. Some explorers were curious about the unknown. They hoped to find out what lay beyond the horizon. Others sought adventure and the excitement of life at sea. Still others had religious reasons. These explorers wanted to spread the Christian faith.

Another reason to explore was the desire to get rich. Some explorers wanted to find new lands that had products they could sell in Europe. The explorers hoped to sell these goods for lots of money and to become rich.

In addition, some European leaders promoted exploration in hope it would benefit their countries. Prince Henry, a member of the Portuguese royal family, encouraged explorers to find a route to India's rich spice trade. Queen Isabella of Spain also promoted exploration. She paid for explorers to seek out new lands and claim them for Spain. She hoped these lands would bring Spain wealth.

Voyages to the East

In the mid-1400s, explorers from Europe began searching for an all-water route to Asia. They wanted to reach Asia to get goods from China and India. During the Middle Ages, Europeans had discovered the exotic goods available in Asia. Many of them, such as silk and spices, were not found in Europe. These Asian goods were costly, because traders had to bring them long distances over land. Further, Italian traders controlled the sale of such goods in Europe—and these Italian traders had become very rich.

Other European countries wanted to break the hold the Italians had on trade with Asia. The Italians controlled all the trade routes in the eastern Mediterranean. If other countries could find an all-water route to Asia, they would not have to pay Italian traders to get exotic Asian goods.

BIOGRAPHY

Queen Isabella
(1451–1504)

Christopher Columbus's voyage to the Americas would not have been possible without the support of Queen Isabella of Spain. In 1492 Columbus approached the queen in search of money to pay for his voyage. He had already been turned down by the king of Portugal, who thought Columbus's plan was foolhardy. Isabella liked his plan, however. She gave Columbus money and ships to help make his voyage. With the support of the queen and others, he was able to complete his journey. It would change the history of Europe, the Americas, and the world forever.

Analyzing How did Isabella make Columbus's voyage possible?

353

353

The Voyages of Discovery, continued

Describe What was the goal of the voyages of Vasco da Gama and the other early Portuguese explorers? *to find a water route to Asia*

Explain Why was Columbus's discovery of America an accident? *He was searching for an all-water route to Asia so he sailed west across the Atlantic and landed off the coast of North America believing he was in Asia.*

Make Inferences What sparked European interest in exploring the Americas? *the continued search for an all-water route to China and India; belief that native peoples had gold and other precious metals; seeking glory*

▶ Map Zone Transparency: European Exploration, 1487–1580

hmhsocialstudies.com **INTERACTIVE MAP**

European Exploration, 1487–1580

map zone
Geography Skills

Movement During the 1400s and 1500s, explorers set out from many countries in Europe. Their voyages carried them to places all around the world.

1. **Identify** Which explorers' expeditions went around the world?
2. **Contrast** How did later explorers' destinations differ from those of earlier explorers?

FOCUS ON READING
What signal words on this page give you clues about the chronological order of events?

The first explorers to search for a sea route to Asia were from Portugal. Under the direction of Prince Henry, they sailed south along Africa's west coast. As they went, they set up trading posts along the Atlantic coast of Africa. In time, explorers sailed farther south.

In 1497–1498 a Portuguese explorer named Vasco da Gama sailed around the southern tip of Africa and on to the west coast of India. You can see his route on the map above. Portugal had found a new sea route to Asia.

Voyages to America

Meanwhile, other countries had also been sending explorers out to find new routes to Asia. The most important expedition came from Spain. In 1492 Queen Isabella of Spain helped pay for a voyage led by Christopher Columbus, an Italian sailor. Columbus hoped to reach Asia by sailing west across the Atlantic. The voyage was long and difficult, but he finally reached land after several months at sea. He landed on an island in what is now the Bahamas. Columbus had reached a new land.

354 CHAPTER 14

Cross-Discipline Activity: English/Language Arts

Making the Case for Exploration

1. Divide the class into two groups. One will act as explorers writing pleas to a monarch for money and supplies for a voyage of exploration. The second group will act as monarchs, reading the pleas and writing decisions explaining who will or will not get the support and why.

2. The explorers must persuade the monarch of their qualifications as sailors and explorers, their need for specific supplies, and the glory or profits they will bring the country.

3. Distribute the petitions among the group of monarchs. Assign each monarch to read a plea and write a response explaining why the plea is accepted or rejected. Have volunteers read the pleas and responses to the class.

LS Verbal/Linguistic

📄 Alternative Assessment Handbook, Rubric 43, Writing to Persuade

Answers

Map Zone 1. *Magellan, Drake;* **2.** *possible answer—Later explorers sailed longer distances.*

Focus on Reading *first, in time, meanwhile, finally*

PORTUGAL
→ Dias 1487–1488
⇢ Da Gama 1497–1498

SPAIN
→ Columbus 1492–1493
⇢ Magellan 1519–1522

FRANCE
→ Cartier 1534–1535

ENGLAND
→ Drake 1577–1580
⇢ Cabot 1497–1498

0   1,000   2,000 Miles
0   1,000   2,000 Kilometers
Projection: Miller Cylindrical

ASIA

30°N

PACIFIC OCEAN

MAGELLAN

DRAKE

0° Equator

East Indies

AUSTRALIA

30°S

120°E   150°E   180°

Columbus thought he had found a route to Asia, which Europeans called the Indies. Europeans came to realize that he had reached a land unknown to them. They called this land, which in time came to be known as **America, the New World**.

Excited by the new discovery, explorers set out from Europe to learn more about the new land. Led by Spain, explorers from Portugal, France, England, and the Netherlands set sail for North and South America. Before long, little of the Americas would remain unexplored.

This wave of European exploration of the Americas had many different causes. Some explorers were still looking for the best water route to Asia. They hoped to find a passage through the Americas by which ships could sail to India or China.

Other explorers led voyages in search of riches. These explorers had heard that the native people of the Americas had lots of gold—more gold than most Europeans had ever seen. These explorers dreamed of the glory and riches they hoped to gain from conquering the lands and people of the Americas.

Voyages around the World

For some Europeans, their new knowledge of the Americas made them more curious about the world. Since they had not known about the Americas, they wondered what else about the world they did not know. One way to learn more about the world, they decided, would be to **circumnavigate**, or travel all the way around, Earth.

The first person to try such a journey was Ferdinand Magellan (muh-JEHL-uhn), a Portuguese sailor. Magellan sailed west from Spain around the southern tip of South America. From there he continued into the Pacific Ocean, where no European had sailed before. Magellan made it as far as the Philippines, where he was killed in a conflict with natives. His crew pushed on, however, and finally reached Spain to complete their trip around the world.

The voyages of explorers like Magellan taught Europeans much about the world. In time, they even achieved the goal of Christopher Columbus—to reach Asia by sailing west from Europe. In addition, they paved the way for European settlement and colonization of the Americas.

READING CHECK **Identifying Cause and Effect** What were two causes of exploration?

Direct Teach

Info to Know

The Diet of Magellan's Crew By the time Magellan's Pacific crossing began, Magellan and his crew had almost no food left. They survived on worm-eaten biscuits. When they could, the crew caught flying fish and tuna, but most of the time they ate rats and boiled leather. Scurvy killed many crew members. There would have been no survivors—and no completed voyage—if the ships had not reached Guam, where the desperate sailors found fruit and fresh water.

RF: Geography and History, Magellan's Voyage around the World

Collaborative Learning

At Level

Fill in the Headlines

1. Organize the class into small groups.

2. Have each group study the map on these pages and write a headline on a notecard for an article about one explorer's expedition. For example, a headline might read: "Magellan's Crew Completes Voyage around World without Captain" or "Columbus Sets Sail on Voyage to India."

3. Have groups exchange headlines and write a one-paragraph article about the headline they have been given.

4. Remind students to include answers to these five questions: Who? What? Where? When? Why? **LS** **Interpersonal, Verbal/Linguistic**

Alternative Assessment Handbook, Rubric 42: Writing to Inform

Answers

Reading Check *Causes for exploration included the search for the best water route to Asia and the search for glory and riches.*

Main Idea

❸ New Empires

As Europeans discovered new lands, they created colonies and new empires all over the world.

Recall What factors contributed to Spain's defeat of the Aztec and Inca armies? *steel swords, firearms, horses, exposure to diseases brought by the Spanish*

Evaluate How did conquests in the Americas change Spain? *It made Spain the wealthiest country in Europe and enabled it to build and equip a large, powerful military force—becoming head of a huge empire.*

Contrast Why did Spain become rich from its empire in the Americas more quickly than the other European countries that established colonies there? *Spain found gold, which gave it great wealth and power; other nations grew rich more slowly through natural resources, such as wood and fur.*

▶ Map Zone Transparency: European Empires in the Americas, 1700

Info to Know

The Columbian Exchange The exchange of plants, animals, and diseases between Europe and the Americas began with Columbus's first voyage of discovery. For this reason, this exchange is known as the Columbian Exchange. For native peoples, this exchange was largely disastrous. Europeans unknowingly introduced smallpox, measles, chicken pox, and other diseases. Native peoples had no immunities to these diseases. As a result, entire tribes and villages were wiped out.

Answers

Map Zone 1. *Spain;* **2.** *England—eastern seaboard of North America and parts of what is now Canada; France—eastern Canada and a central area of North America; possible answer—Conflict could arise because of their close location to each other and competition for more or better-located land and resources.*

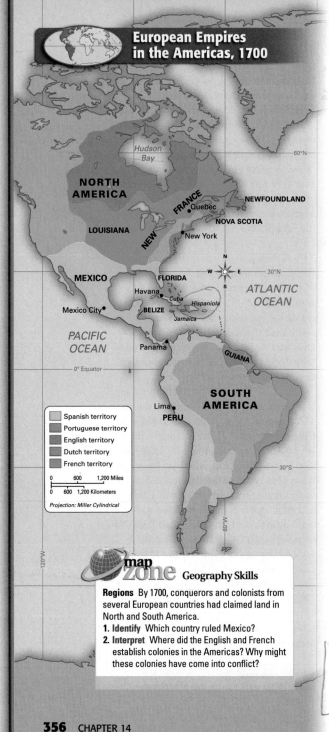

European Empires in the Americas, 1700

Hudson Bay

NORTH AMERICA

NEW FRANCE

• Quebec

NEWFOUNDLAND

NOVA SCOTIA

LOUISIANA

• New York

MEXICO

FLORIDA

Havana

Cuba

Hispaniola

ATLANTIC OCEAN

Mexico City •

BELIZE

Jamaica

PACIFIC OCEAN

0° Equator

Panama •

GUIANA

SOUTH AMERICA

Lima •

PERU

30°S

Spanish territory
Portuguese territory
English territory
Dutch territory
French territory

0   600   1,200 Miles
0 600 1,200 Kilometers

Projection: Miller Cylindrical

map zone **Geography Skills**

Regions By 1700, conquerors and colonists from several European countries had claimed land in North and South America.
1. **Identify** Which country ruled Mexico?
2. **Interpret** Where did the English and French establish colonies in the Americas? Why might these colonies have come into conflict?

356 CHAPTER 14

New Empires

As European explorers discovered new lands in the Americas and elsewhere, they claimed these lands for their countries. These land claims formed the basis for new European empires that stretched across the sea into lands far from Europe.

Conquests and Empires

The Spanish, who were the first Europeans to reach the Americas, claimed large areas of land there. In some places, the Spanish met powerful native empires. These native people fought to defend their lands.

Before long, though, the Spanish had defeated the two most powerful empires in the Americas. These empires were the Aztecs in what is now Mexico and the Incas in what is now Peru. The Spanish had steel swords, firearms, and horses—all unknown in the Americas. This advantage helped the Spanish defeat the Aztec and Inca armies. In addition, diseases that the Spanish carried killed many thousands of Native Americans. By the mid-1500s, Spain ruled a huge area in the Americas.

One of Spain's central goals in the Americas was to gain wealth. The Spanish wanted the gold and silver that could be found in Mexico and some other places. To get these riches, the Spanish enslaved Native Americans and forced them to work in mines. In addition, the Spanish brought African slaves to the Americas to work in the mines. Soon, ships full of gold and silver from these mines were crossing the Atlantic Ocean back to Spain.

Riches from the Americas made Spain the wealthiest country in Europe. Spain's rulers used this money to buy equipment for its armies and to produce ships for its navy. With this powerful military, Spain became Europe's mightiest country, the center of a huge empire.

Differentiating Instruction

Below Level

Struggling Readers

1. To help students learn what regions of North and South America the five European countries claimed, copy the graphic organizer to the right on the board.

2. Have each student copy and complete the graphic organizer for each of the five European countries. When students are finished, review the answers with the class.

LS **Verbal/Linguistic, Visual/Spatial**

✎ Alternative Assessment Handbook, Rubric 13: Graphic Organizers

Spain

Other Colonies

Other European countries envied Spain's wealth and power. They wanted a share of the wealth that Spain was finding in the Americas. In hope of finding similar wealth, these countries began to establish colonies in the lands they explored. As the map shows, colonists from England, France, the Netherlands, and Portugal had settled in the Americas by 1700.

Like the Spanish, these colonists found Native Americans living in the places they settled. In some cases, new colonists lived peacefully with Native Americans. In other cases, conflict occurred, and colonists and Native Americans fought bloody wars.

Unlike the Spanish, other European colonists in the Americas did not find huge deposits of gold or silver. They did find other valuable resources, though. Among these resources were wood, furs, rich soil, and different foods. These resources helped the countries of England, France, Portugal, and the Netherlands grow wealthy.

READING CHECK **Analyzing** How did the Spanish create an empire in the Americas?

Conquest of Mexico
The Spanish soldiers who conquered Mexico had better armor and more advanced weapons than the Aztecs.

SUMMARY AND PREVIEW The Scientific Revolution and the Age of Exploration expanded knowledge and led to changes around the world. Next, you will read about another time of great change. Called the Enlightenment, this period led to major political changes in Europe.

Section 2 Assessment

hmhsocialstudies.com
ONLINE QUIZ

Reviewing Ideas, Terms, and Places

1. **a. Describe** How did European attitudes toward science change in the 1500s and 1600s?
   b. Evaluate What do you think is the greatest advance of the **Scientific Revolution**? Why?
2. **a. Identify** Who was Christopher Columbus?
   b. Explain What drove Europeans to launch the voyages of discovery?
   c. Elaborate What challenges do you think made it difficult for explorers to **circumnavigate** the world for the first time?
3. **a. Describe** What enabled Spain to create a huge, powerful empire in the Americas?
   b. Contrast How did other countries' American colonies differ from Spain's?

Critical Thinking

4. **Identifying Cause and Effect** Draw a diagram like the one shown. Using your notes for information, on the left list the causes of European exploration. On the right, list the effects of that exploration.

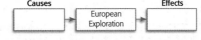

Causes → European Exploration → Effects

FOCUS ON WRITING

5. **Describing the Scientific Revolution and the Age of Exploration** What were Europeans discovering and inventing? Where were Europeans traveling? How did these events change Europe? Take notes on events and changes that might interest visitors.

HISTORY OF EARLY MODERN EUROPE **357**

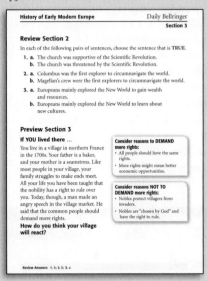
Political Change in Europe

What You Will Learn...

Main Ideas

1. During the Enlightenment, new ideas about government took hold in Europe.
2. The 1600s and 1700s were an Age of Revolution in Europe.
3. Napoleon Bonaparte conquered much of Europe after the French Revolution.

The Big Idea

Ideas of the Enlightenment inspired revolutions and new governments in Europe.

Key Terms

Enlightenment, *p. 358*
English Bill of Rights, *p. 360*
Declaration of Independence, *p. 361*
Declaration of the Rights of Man and of the Citizen, *p. 362*
Reign of Terror, *p. 362*

hmhsocialstudies.com
TAKING NOTES

Use the graphic organizer online to take notes on Enlightenment ideas and the events they inspired.

If YOU lived there...

You live in a village in northern France in the 1700s. Your father is a baker, and your mother is a seamstress. Like most people in your village, your family struggles to make ends meet. All your life you have been taught that the nobility has a right to rule over you. Today, though, a man made an angry speech in the village market. He said that the common people should demand more rights.

How do you think your village will react?

BUILDING BACKGROUND The Scientific Revolution and the Age of Exploration expanded Europeans' knowledge and changed life in many ways. The 1600s and 1700s brought still more changes. Some people began to use reason to improve government and society.

The Enlightenment

Think about the last time you faced a problem that required careful thought. Perhaps you were working a complex math problem or trying to figure out how to win a game. Whatever the problem, when you thought carefully about how to solve it, you were using your power to reason, or to think logically.

The Age of Reason

During the 1600s and 1700s a number of people began to put great importance on reason, or logical thought. They started using reason to challenge long-held beliefs about education, government, law, and religion. By using reason, these people hoped to solve problems such as poverty and war. They believed the use of reason could achieve three great goals—knowledge, freedom, and happiness—and thereby improve society. The use of reason in shaping people's ideas about society and politics defined a period called the **Enlightenment**. Because of its focus on reason, this period is also known as the Age of Reason.

358 CHAPTER 14

The Enlightenment

This 1764 painting shows a salon, a social gathering where people met to discuss Enlightenment ideas. The artist is Michel-Barthelemy Ollivier.

INTERPRETING CHARTS What were the key Enlightenment ideas about natural laws?

Key Enlightenment Ideas

- The ability to reason is unique to humans.
- Reason can be used to solve problems and to improve people's lives.
- Reason can free people from ignorance.
- The natural world is governed by laws that can be discovered through reason.
- Natural laws also govern human behavior.
- Governments should reflect natural laws and encourage education and debate.

New Ideas about Government

During the Enlightenment, some people used reason to examine government. They questioned how governments worked and what the purpose of government should be. In doing so, these people developed completely new ideas about government. These ideas would help lead to the creation of modern democracy.

At the time of the Enlightenment, monarchs, or kings and queens, ruled in most of Europe. Many of these monarchs believed they ruled through divine right. That is, they thought God gave them the right to rule however they chose.

Some people challenged rule by divine right. They thought rulers' powers should be limited to protect people's freedoms. These people said government's purpose was to protect and to serve the people.

John Locke, an English philosopher, had a major influence on Enlightenment thinking about the role of government.

Locke thought government should be a **contract** between a ruler and the people. A contract binds both sides, so it would limit the ruler's power. Locke also believed that all people had certain natural rights, such as life, liberty, and property. If a ruler did not protect these natural rights, people had the right to change rulers.

Other scholars built on Locke's ideas. One was Jean-Jacques Rousseau (roo-SOH). He said government should express the will, or desire, of the people. According to Rousseau, citizens give the government the power to make and enforce laws. But if these laws do not serve the people, the government should give up its power.

These Enlightenment ideas spread far and wide. In time, they would inspire some Europeans to rise up against their rulers.

READING CHECK **Contrasting** How did Enlightenment ideas about government differ from the views of most monarchs?

ACADEMIC VOCABULARY

contract
a binding legal agreement

Direct Teach

Main Idea

❶ The Enlightenment

During the Enlightenment, new ideas about government took hold in Europe.

Identify What was the Enlightenment? *a period in European history when people began to use reason to shape their ideas about society and politics*

Explain How did ideas about monarchies change? *Thinkers challenged the idea of divine right, believing that rulers' powers should be limited and that one role of government should be to protect people's freedoms.*

Evaluate In what ways did Rousseau's ideas build on Locke's ideas? *Locke believed all people had certain natural rights. If a ruler did not protect these rights, people had the right to change rulers. Rousseau went a step further, believing government's role was to express the will of the people and when the laws it made did not serve the people, the government should give up power.*

Activity **Thinking About How Ideas Spread** Although most leaders of the Enlightenment were men, a few women—such as Madame Marie Therese Rodet Geoffrin in Paris—played key roles in the spread of ideas. They used their homes for salons, or weekly gatherings to talk and share ideas. Ask students how people share ideas today. Examples include the Internet, email, telephones, TV, radio, and newspapers. Have them discuss which method they consider most effective and explain why.

Differentiating Instruction

At Level

English-Language Learners

Standard English Mastery

1. Write the term *Enlightenment* on the board. Have a student come to the board and find the root word *light*. Have students suggest any connections the word *light* might have to the period students are learning about.

2. Using a different color, circle *Enlighten*. Have students suggest possible meanings for this word. (*to shed light on, instruct or teach, furnish knowledge of, or free from superstition or misinformation*)

3. Have students review the Enlightenment chart on this page. Ask them to explain why the main ideas outlined in this chart were described as *enlightened*.

4. For additional practice, students might decode the words *enlarge, enlargement, enslave,* and *enslavement*, looking at prefixes and suffixes as well as root words, and use them in complete sentences.
   LS **Verbal/Linguistic**
   Alternative Assessment Handbook, Rubric 1: Acquiring Information

Answers

Interpreting Charts *Natural laws govern human behavior; government should reflect natural laws.*

Reading Check *Most monarchs believed they ruled through divine right and had the power to rule however they chose. Enlightenment thinkers wanted to limit the powers of monarchs and challenged the idea of divine right.*

❷ The Age of Revolution

The 1600s and 1700s were an Age of Revolution in Europe.

Recall What did the English Bill of Rights do? *listed the rights of the Parliament and the English people; gave Parliament the power to pass laws and raise taxes*

Explain How did the English Bill of Rights and the Magna Carta change the relationship between the monarchy and the Parliament in England? *ended monarch's divine right to rule and gave most political power to Parliament*

Analyze How did the Declaration of the Rights of Man and of the Citizen respond to the problems that led to the French Revolution? *gave more rights and freedoms to Third Estate; greater voice in government through National Assembly; made taxation fairer*

Connect to Government

Bill of Rights Many of the rights guaranteed to American citizens by the Bill of Rights in the U.S. Constitution, came from the English Bill of Rights and Magna Carta. These documents greatly influenced the framers of the U.S. Constitution. The English Bill of Rights gave no new rights to Englishmen, but restated their existing rights, such as trial by jury and denial of cruel and unusual punishment.

Answers

Focus on Reading *1215; previous 400 years and future rulers*

Analyzing Visuals *U.S. Declaration of Independence, French Declaration of the Rights of Man and of the Citizen*

360

The Age of Revolution

The 1600s and 1700s were a time of great change in Europe. Some changes were peaceful, such as those in science. Other changes were more violent. In England, North America, and France, new ideas about government led to war and the Age of Revolution.

Civil War and Reform in England

FOCUS ON READING
Read the paragraph about Magna Carta. What date and signal words help you tell that this document was written long before the English Bill of Rights?

In England, Enlightenment ideas led to conflict between the monarchs, or rulers, and Parliament, the lawmaking body. For many years England's rulers had shared power with Parliament. The relationship was an uneasy one, however. As rulers and Parliament fought for power, the situation grew worse.

In 1642 the power struggle erupted in civil war. Supporters of Parliament forced King Charles I from power. He was later tried and beheaded. A new government then formed, but it was unstable.

By 1660 many of the English were tired of instability. They wanted to restore the monarchy. They asked the former king's son to rule England as Charles II. However, Charles had to agree to let Parliament keep powers it had gained during the civil war.

In 1689 Parliament further limited the monarch's power. That year, it approved the **English Bill of Rights**. This document listed rights for Parliament and the English people. For example, it gave Parliament the power to pass laws and to raise taxes.

In addition, Parliament made the king promise to honor Magna Carta. Signed in 1215, this document limited the English ruler's power and protected some rights of the people. However, few monarchs had honored it during the previous 400 years. Parliament wanted to be sure future rulers honored Magna Carta.

By 1700 Parliament held most of the political power in England. Divine right to rule had ended for England's monarchy.

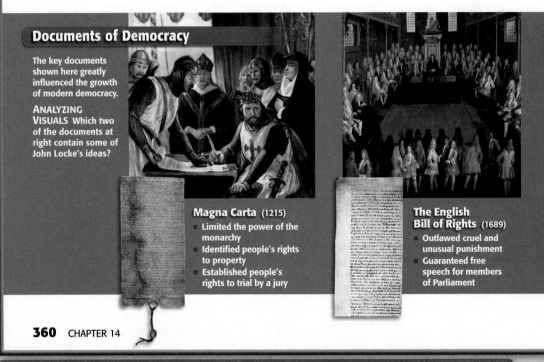

Documents of Democracy

The key documents shown here greatly influenced the growth of modern democracy.

ANALYZING VISUALS Which two of the documents at right contain some of John Locke's ideas?

Magna Carta (1215)
- Limited the power of the monarchy
- Identified people's rights to property
- Established people's rights to trial by a jury

The English Bill of Rights (1689)
- Outlawed cruel and unusual punishment
- Guaranteed free speech for members of Parliament

360 CHAPTER 14

Critical Thinking: Comparing

Writing an Opinion Piece

1. Have students make a three-columned chart comparing the power struggles or revolutions that occurred during the Age of Revolution. Have students label the columns: *England*, *United States*, *France*.

2. Then have students compare, one at a time, the English civil war and reforms, the American Revolution, and the French Revolution in terms of their causes, goals, methods, achievements, and long-term consequences.

3. When students have completed their comparisons, have them pick the conflict they consider most successful. Students should then write a short opinion piece explaining their choice. **LS Verbal/Linguistic**

   📄 Alternative Assessment Handbook, Rubric 43, Writing to Persuade

The American Revolution

In time, Enlightenment ideas spread to the British colonies in North America. There, the British ruler's power was not limited as it was in England. For this reason, many colonists had grown unhappy with British rule. These colonists began to protest the British laws that they thought were unfair.

In 1775 the protests turned to violence, starting the Revolutionary War. Colonial leaders, influenced by the ideas of Locke and Rousseau, claimed Great Britain had denied their rights. In July 1776 they signed the **Declaration of Independence**. Largely written by Thomas Jefferson, this document declared the American colonies' independence from Britain. A new nation, the United States of America, was born.

In 1783 the United States officially won its independence. The colonists had successfully put Enlightenment ideas into practice. Their success would inspire many other people, particularly in France.

The French Revolution

The people of France closely watched the events of the American Revolution. Soon, they grew inspired to fight for their own rights in the French Revolution.

A major cause of the French Revolution was anger over the differences between social classes. In France, the king ruled over a society split into three classes called estates. The Catholic clergy made up the First Estate. They enjoyed many benefits. Nobles belonged to the Second Estate. These people held important positions in military, government, and the courts. The majority of the French people were members of the Third Estate. This group included peasants, craftworkers, and shopkeepers.

Many Third Estate members thought France's classes were unfair. These people were poor and often hungry. Yet, they paid the highest taxes. While they suffered, King Louis XVI held fancy parties, and Queen Marie-Antoinette wore costly clothes.

MISCONCEPTION
ALERT

Queen Marie-Antoinette Marie-Antoinette of France is often noted for saying, "Let them eat cake." She is thought to have said this to answer complaints that the poor people had no bread and that the privileged classes were letting them starve. However, there is no firm proof that she ever said this. The quote comes from Rousseau's book *Confessions*. He attributed the callous remark to an unnamed "young princess." Like her husband, King Louis XVI, Marie-Antoinette was also guillotined.

The U.S. Declaration of Independence (1776)
- Declared that people have natural rights that governments must protect
- Argued that people have the right to replace their governments

The French Declaration of the Rights of Man and of the Citizen (1789)
- Stated that the French government received its power from the people
- Strengthened individual rights and equality among citizens

HISTORY OF EARLY MODERN EUROPE **361**

Collaborative Learning

At Level | Research Required

Documents of Democracy Hall of Fame

1. Organize the class into four groups. Assign each group one these documents: English Bill of Rights, Magna Carta, Declaration of Independence, and Declaration of the Rights of Man and of the Citizen.

2. Have each group prepare a large poster that includes the date of the document, key ideas, and an illustration showing at least one of its key ideas.

3. Using books, encyclopedias, or the Internet, have each group choose one quote from or about this document to include on the poster. Each group should also choose a spokesperson. Have each group prepare a short speech for their spokesperson, explaining their poster and why their document should be in the Documents of Democracy Hall of Fame.

4. When all groups have completed their posters and speech, ask the spokespersons to stand in different parts of the room with their posters. These areas will be listening stations. Have the rest of the groups circulate around the room, viewing the other posters and listening to each speech in turn.

5. When groups have visited the other stations, ask them to explain why each document should—or should not—be included in the Documents of Democracy Hall of Fame. **LS Visual/Spatial, Kinesthetic**

Alternative Assessment Handbook, Rubrics 28: Posters; and 29: Presentations

Info to Know

Info to Know

Bastille Day In France, July 14 is an official holiday known as Bastille Day. For the more than 125 years since it was first declared an official holiday, French people throughout the world have celebrated it with music, fireworks, and parades. This holiday commemorates the day in 1789 when revolutionaries captured the Bastille and released the seven prisoners there. The prison had long been a symbol for the harsh rule of France's kings. However, by the late 1700s, the prison was rarely used. Nonetheless, it became a focal point for the anger of the mob.

Did you know. . .

The French national anthem, *La Marseillaise*, was written during the French Revolution by an army captain, Rouget de Lisle, at the request of the army's general who wanted a battle march for his troops. Revolutionaries gave copies of the song to troops marching from the port city of Marseilles to Paris. They came into Paris singing it and thus it became known as *La Marseillaise*. During the French Empire, Napoleon banned the song—as did a later French king and Napoleon III.

Meanwhile, France's government was deeply in debt. To raise money, Louis XVI wanted to tax the wealthy. He called a meeting of the representatives of the three estates to discuss a tax increase.

The meeting did not go smoothly. Some members of the Third Estate were familiar with Enlightenment ideas. These members demanded a greater voice in the meeting's decisions. Eventually, the Third Estate members formed a separate group called the National Assembly. This group demanded that the French king accept a constitution limiting his powers.

Louis XVI refused, which angered the common people of Paris. On July 14, 1789, this anger led a mob to storm the Bastille, a prison in Paris. The mob released the prisoners and destroyed the building. The French Revolution had begun.

The Storming of the Bastille

On July 14, 1789, a mob stormed and destroyed the Bastille, a prison in Paris. To many French people, this prison symbolized the king's harsh rule.

ANALYZING VISUALS What were some weapons used in the French Revolution?

The French Revolution quickly spread to the countryside. In events called the Great Fear, peasants took revenge on landlords and other nobles for long years of poor treatment. In their rage, the peasants burned down houses and monasteries.

At the same time, other leaders of the revolution were taking peaceful steps. The National Assembly wrote and approved the **Declaration of the Rights of Man and of the Citizen**. This 1789 French constitution guaranteed French citizens some rights and made taxes fairer. Among the freedoms the constitution supported were the freedoms of speech, of the press, and of religion.

The French Republic

In time, revolutionary leaders created a French republic. The new republic did not end France's many growing problems, however. Unrest soon returned.

In 1793 the revolutionaries executed Louis XVI. His execution was the first of many as the government began arresting anyone who questioned its rule. The result was the **Reign of Terror**, a bloody period of the French Revolution during which the government executed thousands of its opponents and others at the guillotine (GEE-uh-teen). This device beheaded victims with a large, heavy blade. The Reign of Terror finally ended when one of its own leaders was executed in 1794.

Although a violent period, the French Revolution did achieve some of its goals. French peasants and workers gained new political rights. The government opened new schools and improved wages. In addition, it ended slavery in France's colonies.

The French republic's leaders struggled, though. As problems grew worse, a strong leader rose up to take control.

READING CHECK Analyzing Why did many members of the Third Estate support revolution?

Differentiating Instruction

Struggling Readers   `Below Level`

1. Have students review the information on the French Revolution. Then ask them to make a graphic organizer, showing the three social classes, or estates, that made up French society at the time of the French Revolution (*for example, a pyramid with three levels*).

2. Have students write labels for each class and add two or three symbols to represent the people of each class. **LS Visual/Spatial**

📖 Alternative Assessment handbook, Rubric 13: Graphic Organizers

Advanced/Gifted and Talented   `Above Level`

1. Read aloud the following quote from John Locke: "The end [purpose] of law is not to abolish or restrain, but to preserve and enlarge freedom . . . where there is no law there is no freedom." Have students discuss what they think Locke meant by this quote.

2. Then ask each student to write a paragraph explaining how the quote applies to the Reign of Terror. **LS Verbal/Linguistic**

📖 Alternative Assessment Handbook, Rubric 42: Writing to Inform

Answers

Analyzing Visuals *cannons, guns, spears, clubs*

Reading Check *They were familiar with Enlightenment ideas and opposed to the unfair class system, unfair taxes, and the failure of Louis XVI to accept constitutional limits on his powers.*

Napoleon Bonaparte

Jacques-Louis David painted this scene of Napoleon crowning his wife, Josephine, empress after crowning himself emperor. The coronation took place in 1804 in Notre Dame Cathedral in Paris, France.

ANALYZING VISUALS How does the event show Napoleon's power?

Napoleonic Empire, 1812

Napoleon Bonaparte

In 1799 France was ripe for a change in leadership. That year, Napoleon Bonaparte, a 30-year-old general, took control. Many French people welcomed him because he seemed to support the Revolution's goals. His popularity grew quickly, and in 1804 Napoleon crowned himself emperor.

Military Conquests and Rule

Napoleon was a brilliant military leader. Under his command, the French army won a series of dazzling victories. By 1810 France's empire stretched across Europe.

In France, Napoleon restored order. He created an efficient government, made taxes fairer, and formed a system of public education. Perhaps his most important accomplishment was the creation of a new French legal system, the Napoleonic Code.

This legal code reflected the ideals of the French Revolution, such as equality before the law and equal civil rights.

With these many accomplishments, Napoleon sounds like a perfect leader. But he was not. He harshly punished anyone who opposed or questioned his rule.

Napoleon's Defeat

In the end, bad weather contributed to Napoleon's downfall. In 1812 he led an invasion of Russia. The invasion was a disaster. Bitterly cold weather and smart Russian tactics forced Napoleon's army to retreat. Many French soldiers died.

Great Britain, Prussia, and Russia then joined forces and in 1814 defeated Napoleon's weakened army. He returned a year later with a new army, but was again defeated. The British then exiled him to an island, where he died in 1821.

Elba

HISTORY OF EARLY MODERN EUROPE **363**

Info to Know

Congress of Vienna Most European nations attended the conference that redrew the map of Europe. However, just four nations—Austria, Prussia, Russia, and Great Britain—made the real decisions. These four nations had been most responsible for Napoleon's defeat. Despite France's defeat, the negotiating skills of the French diplomat Talleyrand enabled France to be admitted to the bargaining table. The resulting settlement lasted almost half a century.

▶ Map Zone Transparency: Europe after the Congress of Vienna, 1815

Review & Assess

Close

Have students explain how ideas of the Enlightenment influenced the revolutions and reforms of the 1600s and 1700s in Europe.

Review

↗ Online Quiz, Section 3

Assess

SE Section 3 Assessment
PASS: Section 3 Quiz
Alternative Assessment Handbook

Reteach/Classroom Intervention

Guided Reading Workbook, Section 3
Interactive Skills Tutor CD-ROM

Answers

Map Zone 1. *Corsica;* 2. *rise—bordered by many of the states it conquered, shorter supply lines; fall—far from Russia, long supply lines*

Reading Check *possible answer—His armies had conquered them and made them subjects of the French Empire.*

364

Europe after the Congress of Vienna, 1815

map zone

Geography Skills

Regions After the defeat of Napoleon in 1814, the Congress of Vienna reorganized Europe.
1. **Name** What were Europe's largest empires in 1815?
2. **Analyze** How might France's location have contributed to Napoleon's rise and fall?

In 1814 European leaders met at the Congress of Vienna. There, they redrew the map of Europe. Their goal was to keep any country from ever becoming powerful enough to threaten Europe again.

READING CHECK **Drawing Inferences** Why did other countries want to defeat Napoleon?

SUMMARY AND PREVIEW You have read how new ideas about government arose out of the Enlightenment. These ideas led to revolutions and political change in Europe and elsewhere. Next, you will read about the growth of industry and how it changed European society.

Section 3 Assessment

hmhsocialstudies.com
ONLINE QUIZ

Reviewing Ideas, Terms, and Places

1. **a. Define** What does divine right mean?
   b. Explain What did **Enlightenment** thinkers believe the purpose of government should be?
2. **a. Describe** What was the significance of the **English Bill of Rights**?
   b. Make Inferences Why do you think many Americans consider Thomas Jefferson a hero?
   c. Evaluate How successful do you think the French Revolution was? Explain your answer.
3. **a. Identify** Who was Napoleon Bonaparte, and what were his main accomplishments?
   b. Analyze How were Napoleon's forces weakened and then defeated?

Critical Thinking

4. **Sequencing** Review your notes. Then use a time line like the one here to list the main events of the Age of Revolution. List the events in the order in which they occurred.

FOCUS ON WRITING

5. **Describing Political Change in Europe** Take notes on the political changes that occurred during this period. What exciting and dramatic events might interest visitors? For example, visitors might want to see the American Revolution firsthand.

364 CHAPTER 14

Section 3 Assessment Answers

1. **a.** Monarchs thought God gave them the right to rule however they chose.
   b. protect people's freedom and serve the people

2. **a.** limited the monarch's power by listing rights of Parliament and the English people
   b. He wrote the Declaration of Independence.
   c. It was a mixed success. Peasants and workers gained new rights, and slavery ended in French colonies. However, the Reign of Terror killed thousands and was followed by Napoleon's dictatorship.

3. **a.** ruler of France; created a French empire, efficient government, and new legal system
   b. weakened in Russia and defeated in 1814 and 1815 by combined European forces

4. Students' time lines will vary but might include: civil war in England (1642) and its approval of the Bill of Rights (1689), the Declaration of Independence (1776), and the storming of the Bastille (1789).

5. Students' notes will vary but should include events from this section that students think would interest visitors.

Social Studies Skills

Making Economic Choices

Learn

The economic choices that people make are a part of geography. For example, consider an economic choice you might make. You have a certain amount of spending money. You can either go to a movie with a friend or buy a CD. You cannot afford to do both, so you must make a choice.

Countries also must make economic choices. For example, a country might face a choice about whether to spend government money on improving defense, education, or health care.

Making economic choices involves sacrifices, or trade-offs. If you choose to spend your money on a movie, the trade-offs are the other things you want but cannot buy. By considering trade-offs, you can make better economic choices.

Practice

You are on the school dance committee. The committee has enough money to upgrade one item for the dance. As the diagram below shows, the committee can spend the money on fancy decorations, a live band, or a ballroom. The committee votes and chooses the fancy decorations.

1. Based on the diagram below, what are the trade-offs of the committee's choice?

2. What would have been the trade-offs if the committee had voted to spend the money on a ballroom instead?

3. How do you think creating a diagram like the one below might have helped the committee make its economic choice?

Fancy Decorations (instead of hand-made decorations) — Live Band (instead of playing CDs) — Ballroom (instead of the school gym)

Choice: Fancy Decorations

Apply

1. Describe an example of an economic choice you might face that has three possible trade-offs.

2. For each possible economic choice, identify what the trade-offs are if you make that choice.

3. What final choice will you make? Why?

4. How did considering trade-offs help you make your choice?

365

Social Studies Skills Activity: Making Economic Choices [At Level]

Taxes as Economic Choices

1. Remind students that protests over unfair taxes played a role in the reforms in England, the Revolutionary War, and the French Revolution. Brainstorm with students what they think makes a tax fair or unfair.

2. Divide the class into two groups. Tell students that your city or town wants to raise taxes, either to improve its schools or to fix its roads. Have students in one group create a chart of the trade-offs of raising taxes to improve schools. Have the other group create a chart of the trade-offs of fixing its roads.

3. Have volunteers share their answers, as you create master charts for the class to see. Then have students compare the two charts to evaluate how the taxes would best be used.

LS Logical/Mathematical, Visual/Spatial

Alternative Assessment Handbook, Rubric 35: Solving Problems

Social Studies Skills

Making Economic Choices

Activity **Evaluating Trade-Offs for a Field Trip** Ask students to brainstorm ideas for a class field trip, such as visiting a local museum or historic site. Write their ideas on a board or chart. Then have students vote for their top three choices. Divide the class into groups of three to five students. Have each group create a chart similar to the one in their textbook, with the goal being to recommend one final choice for a field trip. Have each group list the trade-offs of their final choice. To extend the activity, have each group list the pros and cons, or advantages and disadvantages, for each of the three choices.

LS Logical/Mathematical, Interpersonal

Alternative Assessment Handbook, Rubric 35: Solving Problems

RF: Social Studies Skills, Making Economic Choices

Answers

Practice 1. *live band, ballroom;*
2. *live band, fancy decorations;*
3. *The committee would have understood all of their options and made the best economic choice for their budget.*

Apply 1. *Students' answers will vary but should include three trade-offs.*
2. *Students may choose to draw a chart to illustrate and organize their choices and the trade-offs for each choice.*
3. *Students' answers will vary but should include logical reasons for their final choice.* **4.** *Students should mention that seeing the consequences of their choices ahead of time helped them make better economic decisions.*

Bellringer

If YOU lived there. . . Use the **Daily Bellringer Transparency** to help students answer the question.

▶ Daily Bellringer Transparency, Section 4

Key Terms

📖 **RF:** Vocabulary Builder, Section 4

Taking Notes

Have students use the graphic organizer online to take notes on the section. This activity will prepare students for the Section Assessment, in which they will complete a graphic organizer that builds on the information using the Critical Thinking Skill: Identifying Cause and Effect.

The Industrial Revolution

What You Will Learn...

Main Ideas

1. Britain's large labor force, raw materials, and money to invest led to the start of the Industrial Revolution.
2. Industrial growth began in Great Britain and then spread to other parts of Europe.
3. The Industrial Revolution led to both positive and negative changes in society.

The Big Idea

Driven by new ideas and technologies, much of Europe developed industrial societies in the 1700s and 1800s.

Key Terms

Industrial Revolution, *p. 366*
textiles, *p. 368*
capitalism, *p. 368*
suffragettes, *p. 370*

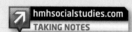
hmhsocialstudies.com
TAKING NOTES

Use the graphic organizer online to take notes on the Industrial Revolution.

If YOU lived there...

You live in Lancashire, England, in 1815. You and your family are weavers. You spin sheep's wool into thread. Then you weave the thread into fine woolen cloth to sell to local merchants. Now a mill is being built nearby. It will have large machines that weave cloth. The mill owner is looking for workers to run the machines. Some of your friends are going to work in the mill to earn more money.

What do you think about working in the mill?

BUILDING BACKGROUND In the mid-1700s great changes in industry revolutionized life in Europe. Like some earlier revolutions, the growth of industry was driven by new inventions and technology. This industrial growth would have far-reaching effects on society.

Start of the Industrial Revolution

Each day, machines from alarm clocks to dishwashers perform many jobs for us. In the early 1700s, however, people had to do most work themselves. They made most of the items they needed by hand. For power, they used animals or water or their own muscles. Then around the mid-1700s, everything changed. People began inventing machines to make goods and supply power. These machines completely changed the way people across Europe worked and lived. We call this period of rapid growth in machine-made goods the **Industrial Revolution**.

From Farmworker to Industrial Laborer

Changes in farming helped pave the way for industrial growth. Since the Middle Ages, farming in Europe had been changing. Wealthy farmers had started buying up land and creating larger farms. These large farms were more efficient. For this reason, many people who owned small farms lost their land. They then had to work for other farmers or move to cities.

366 CHAPTER 14

Teach the Big Idea

At Level

The Industrial Revolution

1. **Teach** Ask students the questions in the Main Idea boxes under Direct Teach.

2. **Apply** Have each student create an illustrated time line of the Industrial Revolution. The time line should include dates of inventions and drawings related to farming or industry, along with short captions that explain why each invention was important. Have students display their time lines. **LS Visual/Spatial**

3. **Review** Remind students of the military revolutions they have read about in previous

sections of the chapter. Then ask them why the Industrial Revolution is so named when there was no military war. Ask how the two types of events are similar and how they differ.

4. **Practice/Homework** Have students make a list of inventions that are changing the way people live, work, and have fun in the early 2000s. **LS Verbal/Linguistic**

📝 Alternative Assessment Handbook, Rubric 36: Time Lines

At the same time, Europe's growing population was creating a need for more food. To meet this need, farmers began looking for ways to grow more and better crops. Farmers began to experiment with new methods. They also began improving farm technology. Englishman Jethro Tull, for example, invented a seed drill. This device made it possible to plant seeds in straight rows and at certain depths. As a result, more seeds grew into plants.

Better farming methods and technology had several effects. For one, farmers could grow more crops with less labor. With more crops available for food, the population grew even more. With less need for labor, however, many farmworkers lost their jobs. These workers then moved to cities. There, they created a large labor force for the coming industrial growth.

Great Britain's Resources

Great Britain provided the setting for the Industrial Revolution's start. Britain and its colonies had the resources needed for industrial growth. These resources included labor, raw materials, and money to invest. For example, Britain had a large workforce, rich supplies of coal, and many rivers for waterpower.

In addition, Great Britain's colonial markets and its growing population were increasing the demand for manufactured goods. Increased demand led people to look for ways to make goods faster or more easily. In Britain all these things came together to start the Industrial Revolution.

READING CHECK Identifying Cause and Effect How did new technology and better farming methods affect agriculture in Europe?

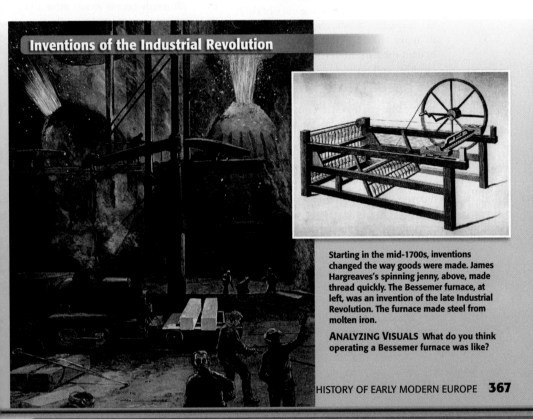

Inventions of the Industrial Revolution

Starting in the mid-1700s, inventions changed the way goods were made. James Hargreaves's spinning jenny, above, made thread quickly. The Bessemer furnace, at left, was an invention of the late Industrial Revolution. The furnace made steel from molten iron.

ANALYZING VISUALS What do you think operating a Bessemer furnace was like?

HISTORY OF EARLY MODERN EUROPE **367**

367

Main Idea

❷ Industrial Growth

Industrial growth began in Great Britain and then spread to other parts of Europe.

Recall How did the Industrial Revolution change how cloth was made? *went from threads for cloth made one at a time on spinning wheels to machines that quickly produced large amounts of cloth*

Evaluate Why did the invention of the steam engine have such a powerful effect on industrial growth? *provided a new energy source that allowed factories to move from nearby rivers to cities; increased demand for coal and iron; led Bessemer to develop a cheap way to convert iron into steel in 1856; led to improved transportation by boat and train*

Compare In what ways was capitalism a new economic system? *Individuals, rather than monarchs or feudal landowners, now owned most businesses and resources; people could invest in businesses, not just land, to make a profit.*

Did you know...

Many English workers were upset at the Industrial Revolution's changes. They were afraid of losing their livelihoods to machines. In 1811, for example, bands of workers began breaking into factories at night, destroying textile machines. They called themselves Luddites—and sometimes clashed violently with law enforcement officials. Today a person who is against technological change may be called a Luddite.

Answers

Focus on Reading *Arkwright's; his invention was in 1769 while Bessemer's was in 1855.*

Reading Check *possible answers—leave farm for job opportunities, more money to live on; stay on farm to be close to family and friends, to avoid working conditions in a factory, to have a slower pace of life*

Industrial Growth

Industrial growth began with **textiles**, or cloth products. In the early 1700s people made cloth by hand. They used spinning wheels to make thread and looms to weave it into cloth. Given the time and effort this took, it is not surprising that people would want a way to make cloth quickly.

THE IMPACT TODAY

New inventions continue to make communication faster and easier. Cell phones and e-mail are just two examples.

FOCUS ON READING
Which came first, Arkwright's invention or Bessemer's? How can you tell?

The Textile Industry

A big step toward manufactured clothing came in 1769. That year, an Englishman named Richard Arkwright invented a waterpowered spinning machine. Called a water frame, this machine could produce dozens of threads at one time. In contrast, a person using a traditional spinning wheel could produce only one thread at a time.

Other machines sped up production even more. With these new machines, workers could produce large amounts of cloth quickly. As a result, the price of cloth fell. Soon, the British were using machines to make many types of goods. People housed these machines in buildings called factories, and the factories needed power.

Other Inventions

Most early machines ran on waterpower. Thus, factories had to be located by rivers. Although Britain had many rivers, they were not always in desirable locations.

Steam power provided a solution. In the 1760s James Watt, a Scot, built the first modern steam engine. Soon, steam powered most machines. Factories could now be built in better places, such as in cities.

Steam power increased the demand for coal and iron, which were needed to make machinery. Iron can be a brittle metal, though, and iron parts often broke. Then in 1855 Englishman Henry Bessemer developed a cheap way to convert iron into steel, which is stronger. This invention led to the growth of the steel industry.

In addition, new inventions improved transportation and communication. Steam engines powered riverboats and trains, speeding up transportation. The telegraph made communication faster. Instead of sending a note by boat or train, people could go to a telegraph office and instantly send a message over a long distance.

The Factory System

Industrial growth led to major changes in the way people worked and lived. Before, most people had worked on farms or in their homes. Now, more people were going to work in factories. Many of these workers were young women and children, whom owners paid lower wages.

Factory work was long, tiring, and dangerous. Factory workers did the same tasks for 12 hours or more a day, six days a week. Breaks were few, and rules were strict. Although people made more than on farms, wages were still low.

To add to the toil, factory conditions were miserable and unsafe. Year-round, the air was thick with dust, which could harm workers' lungs. In addition, the large machines were dangerous and caused many injuries. Even so, factory jobs were desirable to people with few alternatives.

Spread of Industry

In time, the Industrial Revolution spread from Great Britain to other parts of Europe. By the late 1800s, factories were making goods across much of Western Europe.

The growth of industry helped lead to a new economic system, **capitalism**. In this system, individuals own most businesses and resources. People invest money in businesses in the hope of making a profit.

READING CHECK **Evaluating** If you had lived at this time, would you have left a farm to work in a factory for more money? Why, or why not?

Collaborative Learning

At Level

Creating a Political Cartoon

1. Show students examples of political cartoons. Explain that these cartoons differ from comic books because, like letters to the editor, political cartoons try to persuade the audience of a particular point of view or opinion on a topic.

2. Divide students into small groups. Ask them to imagine that they are political cartoonists living in Britain during the Industrial Revolution. Have them brainstorm ideas about factory conditions. Have students each sketch a rough political cartoon. Then have the group select one draft or parts of several for a chosen artist to draw.

3. Have groups create a caption for their cartoon. Display all cartoons. Have students identify each cartoon's point of view.

LS Interpersonal, Visual/Spatial

Alternative Assessment Handbook, Rubrics 27: Political Cartoons; and 14: Group Activity

Close-up

A British Textile Factory

In early textile factories, workers ran machines in a large room. A supervisor kept a watchful eye. Conditions in factories were poor, and the work was long, tiring, and dangerous. Even so, young women and children as young as six worked in many early factories.

Dust and cotton fibers fill the air, causing breathing problems.

Factory owners keep windows shut to prevent air from blowing the threads. This creates a hot, stuffy room.

One task is to straighten threads as they come out of the machines. This task can cut workers' hands.

Machines are loud. Workers must shout to be heard over the deafening roar.

To avoid being injured or killed, girls must tie back their hair to keep it from getting caught in the machines.

ANALYSIS SKILL | **ANALYZING VISUALS**

Why do you think the machines in early textile factories caused so many injuries?

Critical Thinking: Solving Problems

At Level

Inside the Factory

1. Divide students into small groups. Have each group study the picture of the textile factory and list the dangers and other safety problems they see.

2. Have each group brainstorm ways to modernize the factory by improving working conditions and safety. Ideas might include safety devices such as air-filtering masks and changes in room design or machinery. Ask each group to list the improvements they would make.

3. Have each group draw a picture of the same textile factory, showing the changes they would make to improve working conditions and safety.

4. As a large group, discuss what changes were possible in the 1800s. Ask students to brainstorm how factory conditions could realistically have been improved back then.
   LS Visual/Spatial, Verbal/Linguistic

   Alternative Assessment Handbook, Rubric 35: Solving Problems

---

Direct Teach

Close-up

A British Textile Factory

Factory Conditions Review the illustration of an early textile factory with students. Ask the following questions:

Identify What might cause hearing damage? *roar of machines*

Explain What made the air hazardous to health? *dust and cotton fibers caused breathing problems and damaged lungs*

Draw Conclusions Why were people willing to work in such dangerous conditions? *few other options for poor, jobless farmworkers; possibly an improvement over drudgery of farm work*

Connect to Civics

Property Rights of British Women In the late 1800s and early 1900s, British women fought for property rights. Until 1870, when a woman married, all her property was legally given to her husband. If she divorced, she lost any property she brought into the marriage. In 1870, Parliament passed the Married Women's Property Act, giving married women the right to keep their earnings and inherit personal property. In 1882, new laws gave married women the right to all property—whether owned before or after marriage.

↗ hmhsocialstudies.com

Online Resources
Activity: Life of a British Textile Factory Worker

Answers

Analyzing Visuals *possible answers—workers not protected from contact with dangerous machine parts that could kill or hurt them; dust made it hard to see and breathe; loud noises may have been distracting.*

369

❸ Changes in Society

The Industrial Revolution led to both positive and negative changes in society.

Recall How did the Industrial Revolution make life in Europe better? Worse? *better—manufactured goods cheaper and more available, new inventions made some tasks easier, more people joined middle class; worse—cities became dirty, noisy, and crowded while workers remained poor with dangerous and unhealthy living conditions*

Evaluate Why was gaining political power important to workers? *possible answer—with political power, voters could pressure lawmakers to pass laws requiring better working conditions.*

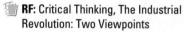 **RF:** Critical Thinking, The Industrial Revolution: Two Viewpoints

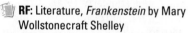 **RF:** Literature, *Frankenstein* by Mary Wollstonecraft Shelley

Close

Have students describe how new inventions and technologies changed life in Europe.

Review

 Online Quiz, Section 4

Assess

SE Section 4 Assessment

 PASS: Section 4 Quiz

Alternative Assessment Handbook

Reteach/Classroom Intervention

Guided Reading Workbook, Section 4

● Interactive Skills Tutor CD-ROM

Answers

Reading Check *Cities grew rapidly, becoming dirty, noisy, and crowded.*

370

Reform efforts addressed the workplace, society, and government. Here, British suffragettes campaign for the right to vote.

Changes in Society

The Industrial Revolution improved life in Europe in many ways. Manufactured goods became cheaper and more available. Inventions made life easier. More people grew wealthier and joined the middle class. These people could afford to live well.

At the same time, industrial growth made life worse in other ways. Cities grew rapidly. They became dirty, noisy, and crowded. Many workers remained poor. They often had to live crammed together in shabby, unsafe apartments. In these conditions, diseases spread rapidly as well.

Such problems led to efforts to reform society and politics. People worked to have laws passed improving wages and factory conditions. Others worked to make cities cleaner and safer. Efforts to gain political power were led by **suffragettes**, women who campaigned to gain the right to vote. In 1928 British suffragettes won the right to vote for women in Great Britain. Changes like these helped usher in the modern age.

READING CHECK **Summarizing** How did the Industrial Revolution affect cities in Europe?

SUMMARY AND PREVIEW As you have read, industrial growth greatly changed how many Europeans lived and worked. In the next chapter you will learn about Europe's modern history.

Section 4 Assessment

hmhsocialstudies.com
ONLINE QUIZ

Reviewing Ideas, Terms, and Places

1. a. Recall In which country did the start of the **Industrial Revolution** take place?
b. Draw Conclusions How did changes in farming help pave the way for industrial growth?
c. Develop Write a few sentences defending the idea that Great Britain was ready for industrial growth in the early 1700s.

2. a. Identify What were two inventions that contributed to industrial growth during this period?
b. Make Inferences How do you think work in a factory differed from that on a farm?

3. a. Recall What did the **suffragettes** achieve?
b. Summarize What problems did industry create? How did people work to solve these problems?

Critical Thinking

4. Identifying Cause and Effect Review your notes. Then use a diagram like the one shown to explain how each change in society led to the next.

| Changes in Farming | → | New Inventions | → | Factory System | → | New Ways of Life |

FOCUS ON WRITING

5. Describing the Industrial Revolution What might encourage people to visit Europe during the Industrial Revolution? Jot down some ideas in your notes. For example, people might want to see what it was like to work in an early factory.

370 CHAPTER 14

Section 4 Assessment Answers

1. a. Great Britain
b. Increased farm productivity forced workers to move to cities, creating a needed labor force.
c. possible answer—Britain had a large labor force, ample coal, and many rivers for waterpower. Its growing population increased demand for more and better manufactured goods.

2. a. water-powered spinning machine, steam engine, Bessemer steel
b. factory work—plentiful, repetitive, dangerous, unhealthy; farm work—scarce, safer, healthier, weather dependent

3. a. the right for women to vote
b. problems—Cities became dirty, noisy, crowded, disease-ridden; solutions—Reformers worked for laws to raise wages and improve factory conditions.

4. Students' answers will vary but should include information from the section to support their explanations.

5. Answers will vary but might include examples such as seeing new inventions, new ways of producing goods, new farming techniques, and what factories were really like.

Geography's Impact
video series
Review the video to answer the closing question:
How did the Renaissance and Reformation change Europe?

Visual Summary

Use the visual summary below to help you review the main ideas of the chapter.

QUICK FACTS

The Renaissance and the Reformation introduced new ideas, art, and ways of thinking into Europe.

Advances of the Scientific Revolution, such as the astrolabe, led to European exploration and empires.

The new ideas of the Enlightenment led to European revolutions, such as the French Revolution.

Driven by new technologies, much of Europe developed industrial societies in the 1700s and 1800s.

Reviewing Vocabulary, Terms, and Places

Copy each sentence onto your own paper and fill in the blank with the word or place in the pair that best completes each sentence.

1. Two important Italian trading cities were Venice and _____ (Florence/Wittenberg).

2. A way of thinking and learning that stresses the importance of human abilities is called _____ (humanism/perspective).

3. The _____ (Renaissance/Reformation) was a movement to reform the Catholic Church.

4. Magellan led a voyage that became the first to _____ (circumnavigate/navigate) Earth.

5. The first European country to build an American empire was _____ (Spain/Portugal).

6. The _____ (Renaissance/Enlightenment) is the period during which people used reason to examine society and politics.

7. John Locke thought government should be a _____ (contract/divine right) between the ruler and the people.

8. The Industrial Revolution began in _____ (steel/textiles).

9. Industrial growth led to a new economic system called _____ (capitalism/communism).

10. British women called _____ (suffragettes/reformers) campaigned for the right to vote.

Comprehension and Critical Thinking

SECTION 1 *(Pages 344–349)*

11. **a. Describe** What was the Reformation?

    b. Summarize How did the Renaissance affect art, literature, and science?

    c. Evaluate Do you think the Renaissance was truly a rebirth of Europe? Why, or why not?

Answers

Visual Summary

Review and Inquiry Have students use the visual summary to discuss details related to the effects of the Renaissance and Reformation, Scientific Revolution, Enlightenment and European revolutions, and Industrial Revolution on life in Europe.

Quick Facts Transparency: History of Early Modern Europe Visual Summary

Reviewing Vocabulary, Terms, and Places

1. Florence
2. humanism
3. Reformation
4. circumnavigate
5. Spain
6. Enlightenment
7. contract
8. textiles
9. capitalism
10. suffragettes

Comprehension and Critical Thinking

11. **a.** religious reform movement begun by Martin Luther in the 1500s

    b. Artists used new techniques, such as perspective; artists and writers reflected humanism in subjects and themes; scientists were inspired by the ancient Greeks and Romans to learn and create new techniques and inventions.

    c. possible responses—Yes, it was a rebirth because new ideas and inventions changed Europe. No, because the Catholic Church was still a dominant force in society and did not reform until later.

Review and Assessment Resources

Review and Reinforce

SE Chapter Review

RF: Chapter Review

Quick Facts Transparency: History of Early Modern Europe Visual Summary

Spanish Chapter Summaries Audio CD Program

TOS Holt McDougal Puzzle View, Quiz Show for ExamView

Quiz Game CD-ROM

Assess

SE Standardized Test Practice

PASS: Chapter Test, Forms A and B

Alternative Assessment Handbook

TOS ExamView Test Generator, Chapter Test

Differentiated Instruction Modified Worksheets and Tests CD-ROM: Chapter Test

Online Assessment Program, in the Interactive Student Edition

Reteach/Intervene

Guided Reading Workbook

Differentiated Instruction Teacher Management System: Lesson Plans

Differentiated Instruction Modified Worksheets and Tests CD-ROM

Interactive Skills Tutor CD-ROM

hmhsocialstudies.com
Chapter Resources

12. a. Columbus was the first European to discover the Americas; Magellan's crew circumnavigated the world.
b. provided navigation tools and better ships, enabling European explorers to make longer, safer voyages
c. began European rivalry for colonies, made many nations rich

13. a. knowledge, freedom, happiness
b. People can change rulers if laws do not protect rights.
c. weakened the power of monarchs by giving more power to Parliament and protecting the rights of citizens

14. a. Great Britain
b. goods cheaper; inventions made life easier; more people joined middle class; development of capitalism
c. Answers will vary, but should use information from the chapter.

Using the Internet

15. Go to ⏎ hmhsocialstudies.com to access a rubric for this activity.

Social Studies Skills

16. You can't buy shoes or a book.
17. You can't buy shoes or a DVD.

Map Activity

18. A. Florence
B. Paris
C. Wittenberg
D. London
E. Madrid
G. Venice

Focus on Reading and Writing

19. Answers will vary. Some possible choices include: Queen Isabella backs Columbus's voyage (1492); Reformation begins (1517); English Bill of Rights passes (1689); storming of the Bastille (1789); Reign of Terror ends (1794); Napoleon Bonaparte takes control (1799); Russians defeat Napoleon (1812); Bessemer converts iron to steel (1855); women in Britain win right to vote (1928)

RF: Focus on Reading, Understanding Chronological Order

SECTION 2 (Pages 350–357)

12. a. Identify What did Christopher Columbus and Ferdinand Magellan achieve?
b. Identify Cause and Effect How did the Scientific Revolution help contribute to the Age of Exploration?
c. Elaborate How did European colonization of the Americas affect European society?

SECTION 3 (Pages 358–364)

13. a. Recall What three goals did Enlightenment thinkers believe the use of reason could achieve?
b. Compare What ideas did John Locke and Jean-Jacques Rousseau share?
c. Elaborate How did the English Bill of Rights and the Declaration of the Rights of Man and of the Citizen change the power of monarchs?

SECTION 4 (Pages 366–370)

14. a. Recall In which country did the Industrial Revolution start?
b. Identify Cause and Effect How did industrial growth lead to improvements in society?
c. Evaluate Which Industrial Revolution invention do you think was most significant? Why?

Using the Internet

15. Activity: Creating a Biography The period of the Renaissance saw many advances in art and literature. Through your online textbook, learn about some of the artists and writers of the Renaissance. Then choose one artist or writer to learn more about and write a brief biography of his or her life. Be sure to include information on the person's accomplishments and significance.

⏎ hmhsocialstudies.com

Social Studies Skills

Making Economic Choices *You have enough money to buy one of the following items: shoes, a DVD, or a book.*

16. What are the trade-offs if you buy the DVD?
17. What are the trade-offs if you buy the book?

Map Activity

18. Europe, 1500–1900 On a separate sheet of paper, match the letters on the map with their correct labels.

Florence   Madrid   Venice
London   Paris   Wittenberg

↗ hmhsocialstudies.com **INTERACTIVE MAP**

FOCUS ON READING AND WRITING

19. Understanding Chronological Order Create a time line that lists 10 significant events covered in this chapter. List the events in the order in which they occurred and provide a date and label for each event.

20. Creating a Travel Brochure By now you should know which time period you want to cover. Create a travel brochure to encourage people to visit Europe during that time period. Use images and descriptive language to convince your readers to travel to the period. In your brochure, highlight interesting historical events that visitors might witness, interesting people they might meet, or new ideas they might learn.

---

20. Rubric Students' travel brochures should

- encourage people to visit the selected time period
- include interesting information about key people and events from the selected time period
- describe the selected time period accurately

RF: Focus on Writing, Creating a Travel Brochure

DIRECTIONS: *Read questions 1 through 7 and write the letter of the best response. Then read question 8 and write your own well-constructed response.*

1 Which person played an important role in spreading the ideas of the Renaissance beyond Italy?

A Johann Gutenberg

B Leonardo da Vinci

C Martin Luther

D William Shakespeare

2 What land did Christopher Columbus reach on his voyage in 1492?

A America

B China

C India

D Spain

3 Which event marked the beginning of the French Revolution?

A Congress of Vienna

B Great Fear

C Reign of Terror

D Storming of the Bastille

4 The Industrial Revolution began in which of the following countries?

A France

B Germany

C Great Britain

D Spain

5 A period of rapid growth in machine-made goods during the 1700s and 1800s is the

A American Revolution.

B French Revolution.

C Industrial Revolution.

D Scientific Revolution.

Religions in Europe, 1600

6 On the map above, which letter marks a Protestant area?

A V

B W

C Y

D Z

7 On the map, which letter indicates Rome?

A V

B W

C X

D Y

8 **Extended Response** Examine the Section 2 map European Exploration, 1487–1580. Select the two voyages that you think are most significant in European history. Describe each voyage, identify who led it, and explain its significance.

Answers

Standardized Test Prep

1. A
Break Down the Question Although the other choices were people whose ideas did spread, the one who was most important was Gutenberg, or choice A. Refer students who miss it to Section 1.

2. A
Break Down the Question This question requires students to recall factual information from Section 2.

3. D
Break Down the Question Choices A, B, and C can be eliminated, as each took place after the storming of the Bastille. Refer students who miss it to Section 3.

4. C
Break Down the Question This question requires students to recall factual information from Section 4.

5. C
Break Down the Question This question requires students to recall factual information from Section 4.

6. C
Break Down the Question Although letter X on the map is a Protestant area, it is not an answer choice. This question requires students to accurately read the map and answer choices and to recall information from Section 1.

7. A
Break Down the Question This question requires students to accurately read the map and recall factual information from Section 1.

8. Extended Response possible answer—Da Gama's voyage from Portugal, around Africa, to Asia established a long-sought water route from Europe to Asia. Columbus's voyage from Spain to the Americas led to the colonization of the Americas and European empire building.

Reteach/Intervention Resources

Reproducible

- Guided Reading Workbook
- Differentiated Instruction Teacher Management System: Lesson Plans

Technology

- Quick Facts Transparency: History of Early Modern Europe Visual Summary
- Differentiated Instruction Modified Worksheets and Tests CD-ROM
- Interactive Skills Tutor CD-ROM

Tips for Test Taking

Take It All In Encourage students to preview the test to get a mental map of their tasks:

- Know how many questions there are.
- Know where to stop.
- Set time checkpoints.
- Do the easy sections first; easy questions can be worth just as many points as hard ones.

Modern European History

Overview	Instructional Resources	

CHAPTER 15

Essential Question: How have major conflicts shaped the history of modern Europe?

🔊 **Focus on the Essential Question Podcast**

TOS Differentiated Instruction Teacher Management System:
- Instructional Pacing Guides
- Lesson plans for Differentiated Instruction

Guided Reading Workbook

Resource File:
- Chapter Review
- Focus on Reading: Using Context Clues–Contrast
- Focus on Writing: Writing a Diary Entry
- Social Studies Skills: Interpreting Political Cartoons

Experiencing World History and Geography

TOS Calendar Planner
- 💿 **Power Presentations with Media Gallery**
- 💿 **Differentiated Instruction Modified Worksheets and Tests CD-ROM**
- 💿 **Interactive Skills Tutor CD-ROM**
- 🔊 **Student Edition on Audio CD-ROM**
- 🔊 **The World's Music Audio Program**
- 🗺 **Map Zone Transparency:** Europe: 1900–Today
- 🗺 **World Outline Maps: Transparencies and Activities**
- 📺 **Video:** Battle of Britain

Section 1:

World War I

The Big Idea: World War I and the peace treaty that followed brought tremendous change to Europe.

TOS Differentiated Instruction Teacher Management System: Section 1 Lesson Plan

Guided Reading Workbook: Section 1

Resource File:
- Vocabulary Builder: Section 1
- Biography: Vladimir Lenin
- Geography and History: Europe and World War I

- 🗺 **Daily Bellringer Transparency:** Section 1
- 🗺 **Map Zone Transparency:** European Alliances, 1914
- 💬 **Internet Activity:** Trench Warfare

Section 2:

World War II

The Big Idea: Problems in Europe led to World War II, the deadliest war in history.

TOS Differentiated Instruction Teacher Management System: Section 2 Lesson Plan

Guided Reading Workbook: Section 2

Resource File:
- Vocabulary Builder: Section 2
- Biography: Anne Frank
- Primary Source: Charter of the United Nations
- Interdisciplinary Project: Reading and Writing Allegories

- 🗺 **Daily Bellringer Transparency:** Section 2
- 🗺 **Map Zone Transparency:** World War II in Europe, 1941
- 🔗 **Internet Activity:** D-Day Invasion
- 📺 **Video:** BBC Report on D-Day

Section 3:

Europe since 1945

The Big Idea: After years of division during the Cold War, today Europe is working toward unity.

TOS Differentiated Instruction Teacher Management System: Section 3 Lesson Plan

Guided Reading Workbook: Section 3

Resource File:
- Vocabulary Builder: Section 3
- Literature: *Animal Farm* by George Orwell
- Geography for Life: The Soviet "Game of the Name"
- Critical Thinking: Disaster at Chernobyl
- Interdisciplinary Project: Current Events: Letting Historical Figures Solve Today's Problems

- 🗺 **Daily Bellringer Transparency:** Section 3
- 🗺 **Map Zone Transparency:** A Divided Europe, 1955

Chart Key:

 SE Student Edition   Presentation Resource   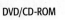 MP3 Audio

TOS Teacher One Stop   DVD/CD-ROM   HISTORY™

 Printable Resource

Program Resources available on **TOS** and @ **hmhsocialstudies.com**

Review, Assessment, Intervention

 Europe and Russia Transparencies: Modern European History Visual Summary

 Spanish Chapter Summaries Audio CD

 Progress Assessment Support System (PASS): Chapter Test

 Differentiated Instruction Modified Worksheets and Tests CD-ROM: Modified Chapter Test

TOS **ExamView® Assessment Suite (English/Spanish)**

 Alternative Assessment Handbook

 Online Assessment Program, in the Interactive Student Edition

 PASS: Section 1 Quiz

 Online Quiz: Section 1

 Alternative Assessment Handbook

 PASS: Section 2 Quiz

 Online Quiz: Section 2

Alternative Assessment Handbook

 PASS: Section 3 Quiz

 Online Quiz: Section 3

 Alternative Assessment Handbook

Supporting Resources

HISTORY®

• Multimedia Classroom Global History Series
• Global History Teacher's Guide

Maps Globes Graphs Level F

• Student Workbook
• Teacher's Guide

Social Studies Trade Library Collections

• Premier Primary Trade Collection
• World Regions Trade Collection
• NCSS Middle School Trade Collection

Geography's Impact

Geography's Impact Video Program

• **Impact of the European Union**

For more information or to purchase go to **hmhsocialstudies.com**

Power Presentations with Media Gallery

Power Presentations with Media Gallery are visual presentations of each chapter's main ideas. Presentations can be customized by including Quick Facts charts, images from the text, and video clips.

CHAPTER 15 PLANNING GUIDE

Differentiating Instruction

How do I address the needs of varied learners?
The Target Resource acts as your primary strategy for differentiated instruction.

ENGLISH-LANGUAGE LEARNERS & STRUGGLING READERS

TARGET RESOURCE

Graphic Organizer Transparencies with Support for Reading and Writing

Spanish Resources

Spanish Chapter Summaries Audio CD
Teacher One Stop:
- ExamView Assessment Suite, Spanish
- PuzzleView, Spanish

English-Language Learner Strategies and Activities

Additional Resources

Differentiated Instruction Teacher Management System: Lesson Plans for Differentiated Instruction
Resource File:
- Vocabulary Builder Activities
- Social Studies Skills: Interpreting Political Cartoons

Europe and Russia Transparencies:
- Modern European History Visual Summary

Student Edition on Audio CD Program
Interactive Skills Tutor CD-ROM
Spanish/English Guided Reading Workbook

SPECIAL NEEDS LEARNERS

TARGET RESOURCE

Resource File

The Resource File activities allow students to extend their knowledge of chapter-related places and people and to practice geography skills.
- Vocabulary Builder Activities
- Social Studies Skills: Interpreting Political Cartoons

Additional Resources

Differentiated Instruction Teacher Management System: Lesson Plans for Differentiated Instruction
Guided Reading Workbook
Student Edition on Audio CD Program
Interactive Skills Tutor CD-ROM
Graphic Organizer Transparencies with Support for Reading and Writing

ADVANCED/GIFTED AND TALENTED STUDENTS

TARGET RESOURCE

Differentiated Instruction Teacher Management System

Lesson Plans for Differentiated Instruction provide teachers with strategies to help plan instruction for all learners.

Additional Resources

Differentiated Instruction Teacher Management System: Lesson Plans for Differentiated Instruction
Resource File
- Focus on Reading: Using Context Clues–Contrast
- Focus on Writing: Writing a Diary Entry
- Literature: *Animal Farm* by George Orwell

World History and Geography Document-Based Questions Activities
Geography, Science, and Cultures Activities
Experiencing World History and Geography

Differentiated Activities in the Teacher's Edition

- Creating a Booklet on WWI Technology, p. 377
- Analyzing Characteristics of Dictators, p. 383
- Writing Letters from East and West Berlin, p. 391

Teacher One Stop™

How can I manage the lesson plans and support materials for differentiated instruction?

With the Teacher One Stop, you can easily organize and print lesson plans, planning guides, and instructional materials for all learners. The Teacher One Stop includes the following materials to help you differentiate instruction:

- **Interactive Teacher's Edition**
- **Calendar Planner and pacing guides**
- **Editable lesson plans**
- **All reproducible ancillaries in Adobe Acrobat (PDF) format**
- **ExamView Assessment Suite (English & Spanish)**
- **Transparency and video previews**

Differentiated Activities in the Teacher's Edition

- Writing about Trench Warfare, p. 381

Interactive Student Edition

Complete online student edition with interactive multimedia support for chapter content assessment and reporting

- Interactive Maps and Notebook
- Standardized Test Prep
- Online Homework Practice and Research Activities
- Current Events
- Chapter-based Internet Activities
- Animated Geography Activities

Differentiated Activities in the Teacher's Edition

- Researching the Geneva Convention, p. 378

• Chapter Preview •

Essential Question

Introduce the Essential Question

- Explain that intense rivalry among the countries of Europe led to World War I, which changed the government of some European countries and altered many of their borders.

- Tell students that economic and political problems after World War I led to the rise of dictatorships in Russia, Italy, and Germany. These dictators' actions caused World War II, which impacted the whole world and resulted in the creation of the United Nations.

- Summarize how tensions between the Western Allies and the Soviet Union divided Europe and led to the Cold War, a period of intense rivalry between Communist and non-Communist nations. Discuss how the European Union helped unify much of Europe after the Cold War ended.

Focus on Reading and Writing

Reading The Resource File provides a worksheet to help students practice Using Context Clues–Contrast.

📝 **RF:** Focus on Reading, Using Context Clues -Contrast.

Writing The Resource File provides a worksheet to help students organize and write their diary entries.

📝 **RF:** Focus on Writing, Writing a Diary Entry

Key to Differentiating Instruction

Below Level

Basic-level activities designed for all students encountering new material

At Level

Intermediate-level activities designed for average students

Above Level

Challenging activities designed for honors and gifted and talented students

Standard English Mastery

Activities designed to improve standard English usage

LS Learning Styles

374 CHAPTER 15

Modern European History

1900–Today

Essential Question How have major conflicts shaped the history of modern Europe?

What You Will Learn...

In this chapter you will learn about Europe since 1900. You will study the causes and effects of World Wars I and II. You will also learn about the Cold War and how it divided Europe. Finally, you will discover how Europe was reunited at the end of the Cold War.

SECTION 1: World War I 376
The Big Idea World War I and the peace treaty that followed brought tremendous change to Europe.

SECTION 2: World War II 382
The Big Idea Problems in Europe led to World War II, the deadliest war in history.

SECTION 3: Europe since 1945 388
The Big Idea After years of division during the Cold War, today Europe is working toward unity.

FOCUS ON READING AND WRITING

Using Context Clues—Contrast As you read, you may come across words you do not understand. When that happens, use context clues— words and sentences around the word—to guess at its meaning. Sometimes the clue to a word's meaning is a contrast clue. It tells you how the unknown word is different from a word you already know. **See the lesson, Using Context Clues—Contrast, on page 530.**

Writing a Diary Entry In this chapter you will read about European history since 1900. As you read, think about what it would have been like to live during this period. Later you will write a diary entry from the point of view of someone who lived during these times.

German U-boats

ATLANTIC OCEAN

🌐 map zone

Geography Skills

Place Modern European history was marked by huge conflicts and later reunification.
1. **Identify** Into what country are the German soldiers marching?
2. **Make Inferences** What do the icons on the map indicate to you about modern European history?

Madrid

AFRICA

World War I Soldiers from Europe's most powerful countries engaged in trench warfare during World War I.

Introduce the Chapter

At Level

Building Background

1. Ask students what they already know about Europe. Have them think about recent events in the news, foods that come from particular countries, relatives or ancestors they may have in Europe, languages they may know, and so on.

2. Have students look at the map to see if they can identify where countries are located. Ask them to interpret the drawings that are superimposed on the map. Tell students that many countries have changed their borders and governments in recent history.

3. Ask students if they can provide approximate dates for the images of World War I and World War II at the bottom of the page. Have students share their opinions about where the events depicted might be taking place.

4. Based on what they already know, challenge students to describe Europe in the 1900s using a single word. *(war, division)*
   LS Verbal/Linguistic, Visual/Spatial
   📝 Alternative Assessment Handbook, Rubric 14: Group Activity

North Sea

European Union

Baltic Sea

London

Berlin

Bombing damage in Warsaw

Paris

EUROPE

German troops invade France

Rome

Black Sea

ASIA

Mediterranean Sea

| 0 | 100 | 300 Miles |
| 0 | 100 | 200 Kilometers |

Projection: Azimuthal Equal Area

HISTORY **Battle of Britain**

⬀ hmhsocialstudies.com VIDEO

Vladimir Lenin

World War II The rise of strong dictators, like Germany's Adolf Hitler, led to the outbreak of the Second World War.

Europe since 1945 The end of the Cold War and the fall of the Berlin Wall helped to reunite Europe by the end of the 1900s.

375

Analyzing Visuals

Appealing to Emotions Explain to students that long before Hitler came to power, politicians used dramatic backdrops, stirring military music, colorful uniforms, and large crowds to present an image of strength and to stir feelings of national pride. Ask students to identify the elements that affect emotions in the picture of Adolf Hitler. Then ask them to look at the photo of Germans celebrating the fall of the Berlin Wall. What emotions does it produce?

Info to Know

1936 Olympics Adolf Hitler used huge demonstrations and military parades to instill national pride and consolidate his power. He also hoped to use the 1936 Olympic Games in Berlin to showcase the so-called superiority of the German race. His plan backfired when African American Jesse Owens dominated men's track and field, setting two new world records and tying another.

● **Chapter Preview** ●

Explore the Map and Pictures

Europe: 1900–Today Begin by having students look at Europe on a globe. Point out that Europe is much smaller than its neighboring continents, Africa and Asia. Yet Europe has had a huge impact on the world. Unfortunately, during the 1900s, much of that impact resulted in great suffering. Ask students to explain the pictures on the map that represent the warfare and destruction of the 1900s. Then draw students' attention to the Euro coins, and tell them that a new era of cooperation is dawning in Europe, making future conflicts less likely.

Analyzing Visuals What details in the picture show that Germany was unified after the fall of the Berlin Wall? *People are holding hands; people in the crowd are showing support just by being present.* How can you tell that Hitler was a strong dictator? *There are many people in the crowd; the signs in the background are very large.*

▶ Map Zone Transparency: Europe, 1900–Today

⬀ hmhsocialstudies.com
Teacher Resources

Answers

Map Zone 1. *France;* **2.** *There were military conflicts, strong leaders, and a desire for unity.*

Bellringer

If YOU lived there. . . Use the **Daily Bellringer Transparency** to help students answer the question.

▶ Daily Bellringer Transparency, Section 1

Modern European History   Daily Bellringer
           Section 1

Preview Section 1

If YOU lived there ...

It is 1914, and you live in London. For years you have heard about an important alliance between Great Britain, France, and Russia. Each country has promised to protect the others. Just days ago, you learned that war has broken out in Eastern Europe. Russia and France are preparing for war. People are saying that Britain will fight to protect its allies. If that happens, Europe's most powerful countries will be at war.

How do you feel about the possibility of war?

Consider your feelings AGAINST the war:
• feel country's allies are being reckless
• feel country would be safer avoiding war
• don't want to fight for a cause you disagree with

Consider your feelings FOR the war:
• feel it's important to keep promises made to allies
• want to support allies
• feel this war is honorable

Academic Vocabulary

Review with students the high-use academic term in this section.

strategy a plan for fighting a battle or war (p. 378)

📑 **RF:** Vocabulary Builder, Section 1

Taking Notes

Have students use the graphic organizer online to take notes on the section. This activity will prepare students for the Section Assessment, in which they will complete a graphic organizer that builds on the information using the Critical Thinking Skill: Categorizing.

World War I

If YOU lived there...

It is 1914, and you live in London. For years you have heard about an important alliance between Great Britain, France, and Russia. Each country has promised to protect the others. Just days ago, you learned that war has broken out in Eastern Europe. Russia and France are preparing for war. People are saying that Britain will fight to protect its allies. If that happens, Europe's most powerful countries will be at war.

How do you feel about the possibility of war?

What You Will Learn...

Main Ideas

1. Rivalries in Europe led to the outbreak of World War I.
2. After a long, devastating war, the Allies claimed victory.
3. The war's end brought great political and territorial changes to Europe.

The Big Idea

World War I and the peace treaty that followed brought tremendous change to Europe.

Key Terms

nationalism, *p. 376*
alliance, *p. 377*
trench warfare, *p. 378*
Treaty of Versailles, *p. 379*
communism, *p. 380*

hmhsocialstudies.com
TAKING NOTES

Use the graphic organizer online to take notes on the causes and effects of World War I.

> **BUILDING BACKGROUND** The 1800s were a time of rapid change in Europe. Industries grew quickly. Cities expanded. The countries of Europe raced to build empires and gain power. As each country tried to outdo the others, conflicts emerged. Europe was poised for war.

The Outbreak of War

In the early 1900s Europe was on the brink of war. Rivalries were building among Europe's strongest nations. One small spark would be enough to start World War I.

Causes of the War

During the 1800s nationalism changed Europe. **Nationalism** is devotion and loyalty to one's country. Some groups that were ruled by powerful empires wanted to build their own nation-states. For example, nationalism led some people in Bosnia and Herzegovina, a region in southeastern Europe, to demand their independence from the Austro-Hungarian Empire. Nationalism also created rivalries among many nations. By the early 1900s nationalism had grown so strong that countries were willing to go to war to prove their superiority over their rivals. A fierce competition emerged among the countries of Europe.

This competition for land, resources, and power drove many European countries to strengthen their armed forces. They built powerful armies and created stockpiles of new weapons. Each country wanted to show its strength and intimidate its rivals.

Teach the Big Idea
                                          At Level

World War I

1. **Teach** Ask students the questions in the Main Idea boxes under Direct Teach.

2. **Apply** Have students discuss reasons nations go to war. Tell them they can use examples from past or present wars. Remind students to think about the points of view from both sides of the conflict when they answer. List their reasons on the board.

3. **Review** When the list is finished, have students discuss what they think are the best,

the worst, and the most common reasons for going to war. 📢 **Verbal/Linguistic**

4. **Practice/Homework** Have students write a short persuasive essay explaining whether war should only be used as a last resort. Students should provide reasons to support their point of view.

📢 **Verbal/Linguistic, Interpersonal**

📑 Alternative Assessment Handbook, Rubrics 11: Discussions; and 43: Writing to Persuade

European Alliances, 1914

Triple Alliance
Triple Entente

0   200   400 Miles
0   200   400 Kilometers
Projection: Azimuthal Equal-Area

map Zone **Geography Skills**

Regions Rivalries split Europe into two opposing alliances—the Triple Alliance and the Triple Entente.
1. **Locate** Which alliance controlled central Europe?
2. **Draw Conclusions** Why do you think the location of the Triple Entente might have threatened the Triple Alliance?

Both Great Britain and Germany, for example, competed to build strong navies and powerful new battleships.

As tensions and suspicions grew, some European leaders hoped to protect their countries by creating alliances. An **alliance** is an agreement between countries. If one country is attacked, its allies—members of the alliance—help defend it. In 1882 Italy, Germany, and Austria-Hungary formed the Triple Alliance. In response, France, Great Britain, and Russia created their own alliance, the Triple Entente (ahn-TAHNT). As you can see in the map, these alliances divided Europe.

The Spark for War

By the summer of 1914, war in Europe seemed certain. Tensions between Austria-Hungary and Serbia arose over the control of Bosnia and Herzegovina, a province of Austria-Hungary and Serbia's neighbor. On June 28, 1914, a Serbian assassin shot and killed Archduke Francis Ferdinand, the heir to the throne of Austria-Hungary. Seeking revenge, Austria-Hungary declared war on Serbia. After Serbia turned to Russia for help, the alliance system quickly split Europe into two warring sides. On one side was Austria-Hungary and Germany, known as the Central Powers. The Allied Powers—Serbia, Russia, Great Britain, and France—were on the other side.

READING CHECK **Finding Main Ideas** What were the causes of World War I?

MODERN EUROPEAN HISTORY **377**

Main Idea

❷ War and Victory

After a long, devastating war, the Allies claimed victory.

Recall When did the Central Powers surrender? *in the fall of 1918*

Identify What new weapons were used in World War I? *machine guns, poison gas, tanks*

Make Inferences What did "going over the top" mean? *climbing out of the trench and attacking by running toward enemy positions*

Did you know. . .

Switzerland, a mountainous country in the center of Europe, has a well-deserved reputation for peace and neutrality. Most of Europe has recognized Switzerland's neutrality since 1815. Switzerland stayed out of both world wars, although fighting raged in neighboring countries. Though peaceful, Switzerland does have an army that it maintains for defensive purposes only. So devoted are the Swiss to avoiding international conflict that they did not join the United Nations until 2002.

↗ hmhsocialstudies.com

Online Resources
Activity: Trench Warfare

War and Victory

Germany struck the first blow in the war, sending a large army into Belgium and France. Allied troops, however, managed to stop the Germans just outside Paris. In the east, Russia attacked Germany and Austria-Hungary, forcing Germany to fight on two fronts. Hopes on both sides for a quick victory soon disappeared.

A New Kind of War

ACADEMIC VOCABULARY
strategy a plan for fighting a battle or war

A new military **strategy**, trench warfare, was largely responsible for preventing a quick victory. Early in the war both sides turned to trench warfare. **Trench warfare** is a style of fighting in which each side fights from deep ditches, or trenches, dug into the ground.

Both the Allies and the Central Powers dug hundreds of miles of trenches along the front lines. Soldiers in the trenches faced great suffering. Not only did they live in constant danger of attack, but cold, hunger, and disease also plagued them. Sometimes soldiers would "go over the top" of their trenches and fight for a few hours, only to retreat to the same position. Trench warfare cost millions of lives, but neither side could win the war.

To gain an advantage in the trenches, each side developed deadly new weapons. Machine guns cut down soldiers as they tried to move forward. Poison gas, first used by the Germans, blinded soldiers in the trenches. It was later used by both sides. The British introduced another weapon, the tank, to break through enemy lines.

Close-up

Trench Warfare

Both the Allied Powers and the Central Powers relied on trenches for defense during World War I. As a result, the war dragged on for years with no clear victor. Each side developed new weapons and technology to try to gain an advantage in the trenches.

Soldiers often threw or fired small bombs known as grenades.

Soldiers used gas masks to survive attacks of poison gas.

Trenches dug in zigzag patterns prevented the enemy from firing down the length of a trench.

378 CHAPTER 15

Differentiating Instruction

Above Level

Advanced/Gifted and Talented

Research Required

1. Review information about trench warfare with students. Ask them if they think there should be rules in warfare. For example, should soldiers be allowed to harm civilians? Record students' thoughts about rules of war on the board.

2. Assign students to groups to research a stage in the evolution of the Geneva Convention rules. (Meetings to decide on the rules of warfare were held in 1929 and 1949, among other years.) Have students report their findings to the class.

3. Have the class compare opinions about warfare with the rules of the Geneva Convention. Have students provide evidence of whether the rules of the Geneva Convention are being observed in current wars. **LS Verbal/Linguistic**

📝 Alternative Assessment Handbook, Rubrics 11: Discussions; and 29: Presentations

At sea, Britain used its powerful navy to block supplies from reaching Germany. Germany responded by using submarines, called U-boats. German U-boats tried to break the British blockade and sink ships carrying supplies to Great Britain.

The Allies Win

For three years the war was a stalemate—neither side could defeat the other. Slowly, however, the war turned in favor of the Allies. In early 1917 German U-boats began attacking American ships carrying supplies to Britain. When Germany ignored U.S. warnings to stop, the United States entered the war on the side of the Allies.

Help from American forces gave the Allies a fresh advantage. Soon afterward, however, the exhausted Russians pulled

out of the war. Germany quickly attacked the Allies, hoping to put an end to the war. Allied troops, however, stopped Germany's attack. The Central Powers had suffered a great blow. In the fall of 1918 the Central Powers surrendered. The Allied Powers were victorious.

READING CHECK Sequencing What events led to the end of World War I?

The War's End

After more than four years of fighting, the war came to an end on November 11, 1918. More than 8.5 million soldiers had been killed, and at least 20 million more were wounded. Millions of civilians had lost their lives as well. The war brought tremendous change to Europe.

Making Peace

Shortly after the end of the war, leaders from the Allied nations met at Versailles (ver-SY), near Paris. There, they debated the terms of peace for the Central Powers.

The United States, led by President Woodrow Wilson, wanted a just peace after the war. He did not want harsh peace terms that might anger the losing countries and lead to future conflict.

Other Allied leaders, however, wanted to punish Germany. They believed that Germany had started the war and should pay for it. They believed that weakening Germany would prevent future wars.

In the end, the Allies forced Germany to sign a treaty. The **Treaty of Versailles** was the final peace settlement of World War I. It forced Germany to accept the blame for starting the war. Germany also had to slash the size of its army and give up its overseas colonies. Additionally, Germany had to pay billions of dollars for damages caused during the war.

FOCUS ON READING
What does the term *just peace* mean? How can you tell?

Handwritten: Revolution 1917

Handwritten: 14 miles outside Paris Home to King/Queen

Each side used airplanes to observe troop movements and other actions behind enemy lines.

Armored vehicles, or tanks, were used to launch attacks across rough terrain.

ANALYSIS SKILL ANALYZING VISUALS
What advantages and disadvantages did trench warfare pose for soldiers?

MODERN EUROPEAN HISTORY **379**

Cross-Discipline Activity: Mathematics

Above Level

Calculating the Human Cost of War

Research Required

1. Using encyclopedias, almanacs, or the Internet, have students find data on the human cost of World War I. Have them find as many of the following data points as they can for each country involved:

   • number of soldiers wounded

   • number of soldiers killed

   • number of civilians killed

   • population of each country at the time

2. Have students create a chart or graph to present the data. For example, they might use two pie charts comparing a country's total population to its number of casualties. Allow students to work individually or in small groups.

3. Discuss with students what impact these casualties might have had on each country after the war. **LS Logical/Mathematical**

   Alternative Assessment Handbook, Rubric 7: Charts

Connect to Economics

Germany's Post-War Woes After the war, Germany adopted its first democratic constitution in the city of Weimar in 1919. However, the new government faced serious problems—unemployment and runaway inflation. For example, in 1923 the German mark lost its value at a rapid rate—late in the year, it took 4.2 trillion marks to buy one U.S. dollar. By 1928 both problems were under control, and the German people were gaining faith in democracy. Unfortunately, the Great Depression brought back economic woes, paving the way for Adolf Hitler, who convinced many people that he could solve Germany's economic problems.

Review & Assess

Close

Ask students what major mistakes European leaders made before and after World War I.

Review

 Online Quiz, Section 1

Assess

SE Section 1 Assessment

 PASS: Section 1 Quiz

Alternative Assessment Handbook

Reteach/Classroom Intervention

Guided Reading Workbook, Section 1

Interactive Skills Tutor CD-ROM

Answers

Reading Check *Communists took control of Russia; Germany became a democracy; Austria-Hungary was split in two; Finland, Estonia, Latvia, Lithuania, Poland, and Czechoslovakia gained independence; Yugoslavia was formed.*

380

Vladimir Lenin encouraged Russian workers to support his new Communist government.

A New Europe

World War I had a tremendous effect on the countries of Europe. It changed the governments of some European countries and the borders of others. For example, in Russia the war had caused great hardship for the people. A revolution then forced the Russian czar, or emperor, to give up power. Shortly after, Vladimir Lenin took over Russia's government and established a Communist government. **Communism** is a political system in which the government owns all property and controls all aspects of life in a country. An uprising toward the end of the war also forced the German emperor from power. A fragile republic replaced the German Empire.

World War I also altered the borders of many European countries. Austria and Hungary became separate countries. Poland and Czechoslovakia each gained their independence. Serbia, Bosnia and Herzegovina, and other Balkan states were combined to create Yugoslavia. Finland, Estonia, Latvia, and Lithuania, which had been part of Russia, became independent.

READING CHECK **Summarizing** How did World War I change Europe?

SUMMARY AND PREVIEW Intense rivalries among the countries of Europe led to World War I, one of the most devastating wars in history. In the next section you will learn about problems that plagued Europe and led to World War II.

Section 1 Assessment

hmhsocialstudies.com
ONLINE QUIZ

Reviewing Ideas, Terms, and Places

1. **a. Identify** What event triggered World War I?
   b. Analyze How did **nationalism** cause rivalries between some European countries?
   c. Evaluate Do you think **alliances** helped or hurt most countries? Explain your answer.
2. **a. Describe** What was **trench warfare** like?
   b. Draw Conclusions What difficulties did soldiers face as a result of trench warfare?
   c. Predict How might the war have been different if the United States had not entered it?
3. **a. Recall** How did the **Treaty of Versailles** punish Germany for its role in the war?
   b. Contrast How did the Allied leaders' ideas for peace with Germany differ?
   c. Elaborate Why do you think the war caused changes in government in Russia and Germany?

Critical Thinking

4. **Categorizing** Draw a chart like the one here. Use your notes to list the results of World War I in the appropriate category.

Political	Economic

FOCUS ON WRITING

5. **Writing about World War I** Think about the events of World War I. Imagine that you were present at one or more events during or after the war. What might you write about in your diary?

Section 1 Assessment Answers

1. **a.** Archduke Ferdinand was assassinated.
   b. Countries wanted to prove their superiority and competed for resources and power.
   c. helped by providing countries protection; hurt by dragging countries into war
2. **a.** Armies faced each other from parallel trenches that were easier to defend than attack. Soldiers suffered greatly.
   b. hunger, cold, disease, poison gas
   c. The war may have lasted even longer; the Central Powers may have won.
3. **a.** Germany was forced to reduce its army and pay war costs.

   b. America wanted a just peace, but others wanted to punish Germany.
   c. People were unhappy with the disastrous effects of the war.

4. possible answers: political—Lenin took power in Russia, Yugoslavia formed, Austria-Hungary broke up; economic—Germany made to pay billions of dollars for damages caused during the war

5. Events might include the assassination of Archduke Ferdinand or trench warfare.

from
All Quiet on the Western Front

by Erich Maria Remarque

About the Reading *In* All Quiet on the Western Front, *author Erich Maria Remarque provides a fictional account of the lives of soldiers during World War I. The book is considered one of the most realistic accounts of the war. In this selection, the book's narrator, twenty-year-old German soldier Paul Bäumer, describes a battle between German and British forces.*

AS YOU READ Note the words the speaker uses to describe the battle.

Our trenches have now for some time been shot to pieces, and we have an elastic line, so that there is practically no longer any proper trench warfare. ❶ When attack and counter-attack have waged backwards and forwards there remains a broken line and a bitter struggle from crater to crater. The front-line has been penetrated, and everywhere small groups have established themselves, the fight is carried on from clusters of shell-holes.

We are buried in a crater, the English are coming down obliquely, they are turning our flank and working in behind us. ❷ We are surrounded. It is not easy to surrender, fog and smoke hang over us, no one would recognize that we wanted to give ourselves up, and perhaps we don't want to, a man doesn't even know himself at such moments. We hear the explosions of the hand-grenades coming towards us. Our machine-gun sweeps over the semicircle in front of us . . . Behind us the attack crashes ever nearer.

Soldiers prepare to rush over the top of a trench during a battle in World War I.

GUIDED READING

WORD HELP

crater a hole in the ground made by the explosion of a bomb or shell

penetrated passed into or through

obliquely indirectly or underhandedly

❶ An elastic line describes a battle line that is pushed back and forth by enemy forces.

❷ "Turning our flank" refers to a tactic in which one military force moves around the side of the opposing force in order to surround them.

Connecting Literature to Geography

1. **Describing** What details in the first paragraph show that the technique of trench warfare is no longer working?

2. **Making Inferences** Why do you think the location of this trench is so important to the war and the people fighting in it?

381

Literature

from *All Quiet on the Western Front*

As You Read Ask students to imagine what Paul Bäumer is experiencing. Have them make a five-columned chart using the five senses as headings. Entries in the chart should include descriptive words that help portray Bäumer's experience in the trenches.

Meet the Writer

Erich Maria Remarque (1898–1970) Born in Osnabrück, Germany, Erich Maria Remarque wrote *All Quiet on the Western Front* in 1929. He based it on his personal war experiences. It was a huge bestseller, and he followed up with other popular novels that told of life in Germany during the Weimar Republic and the early Nazi era. *All Quiet on the Western Front* was banned in Germany in the 1930s. Remarque fled to Switzerland, then moved to the U.S., where he became a citizen. He returned to Switzerland and lived there until his death in 1970.

Info to Know

Post-war Literature Many young men were horrified by what they saw in World War I and wrote eloquent anti-war plays, poems, and novels. Their writing portrayed a realistic view of war, not a romanticized one.

Differentiating Instruction

At Level

Special Needs Learners

Materials: Student Edition on Audio CD Program

1. Play the literature selection on audio CD or read the excerpt aloud for students with visual impairments.

2. Review with students what they have learned about what fighting in World War I was like. Include the information students read in the chapter as well as the excerpt from *All Quiet on the Western Front.*

3. Using the list of words students compiled in the *As You Read* activity above, have students

write a short fictional passage. Remind them to write vivid descriptions of trench warfare, using as many of the words from their lists as possible. Students may wish to record their short stories on audio cassette instead of writing or typing them.

4. Ask volunteers to share their passages with the class. **LS Verbal/Linguistic, Auditory/Musical**

Alternative Assessment Handbook, Rubrics 18: Listening; and 40: Writing to Describe

Answers

Connecting Literature to Geography 1. *Trenches have been shot to pieces; we have an elastic line; the front-line has been penetrated; the fight is carried on from clusters;* **2.** *The front line is supposed to be the strongest line; if it is penetrated, the battle or war may be lost.*

Bellringer

If YOU lived there. . . Use the **Daily Bellringer Transparency** to help students answer the question.

▶️ Daily Bellringer Transparency, Section 2

Key Terms

 RF: Vocabulary Builder, Section 2

Taking Notes

Have students use the graphic organizer online to take notes on the section. This activity will prepare students for the Section Assessment, in which they will complete a time line that builds on the information using the Critical Thinking Skill: Sequencing.

World War II

If YOU lived there...

It is 1922, and you are part of a huge crowd in one of Rome's public squares. Everyone is listening to the fiery speech of a dynamic new leader. He promises to make Italy great again, as it was in the days of ancient Rome. You know that your parents and some of your teachers are excited about his ideas. Others are concerned that he may be too forceful.

What do you think of this new leader's message?

What You Will Learn...

Main Ideas

1. Economic and political problems troubled Europe in the years after World War I.
2. World War II broke out when Germany invaded Poland.
3. Nazi Germany targeted the Jews during the Holocaust.
4. Allied victories in Europe and Japan brought the end of World War II.

The Big Idea

Problems in Europe led to World War II, the deadliest war in history.

Key Terms

Great Depression, *p. 382*
dictator, *p. 383*
Axis Powers, *p. 385*
Allies, *p. 385*
Holocaust, *p. 385*

hmhsocialstudies.com
TAKING NOTES

Use the graphic organizer online to take notes on the important dates and events of World War II.

BUILDING BACKGROUND Many countries faced deep economic and political problems as a result of World War I. Dictators rose to power in a number of countries, but did not bring solutions. Instead, they attacked their neighbors and plunged the world back into war.

Problems Trouble Europe

After World War I, Europeans began rebuilding their countries. Just as they had started to recover, however, many economic and political problems emerged. These problems threatened the peace and security of Europe.

The Great Depression

World War I left much of Europe in shambles. Factories and farmland had been destroyed, and economies were in ruins. Countries that had lost the war, like Germany and Austria, owed billions in war damages. Many countries turned to the United States for help. During the 1920s the U.S. economy was booming. Loans from American banks and businesses helped many European nations recover and rebuild after World War I.

In 1929, however, the recovery fell apart. A stock market crash in the United States triggered a global economic crisis in the 1930s known as the **Great Depression**. As the U.S. economy faltered, American banks stopped lending to Europe. Without U.S. loans and investments, European economies declined. Unemployment skyrocketed as businesses and farms, as well as banks, went bankrupt.

Teach the Big Idea

World War II

1. **Teach** Ask students the questions in the Main Idea boxes under Direct Teach.

2. **Apply** Ask students the following question: *Could World War II have been prevented?* Invite students to list causes that contributed to the war. Record causes on the board. Then ask students to suggest ways that those causes could have been dealt with more effectively. Write students' ideas next to each cause.
LS Interpersonal

3. **Review** Review the list and have the class evaluate each item. Have students choose the idea they think would have been the most likely to prevent war.

4. **Practice/Homework** Based on their decisions in Step 3, have students write a short persuasive essay on how WW II could have been prevented. **LS Verbal/Linguistic**

📋 Alternative Assessment Handbook, Rubrics 11: Discussions; and 43: Writing to Persuade

The Rise of Dictators

The Great Depression added to Europe's problems. Blaming weak governments for the hard times, some Europeans turned to dictators to strengthen their countries and improve their lives. A **dictator** is a ruler who has total control. Dictators rose to power in Russia, Italy, and Germany.

One of the first dictators in Europe was Russia's Vladimir Lenin. Lenin gained power as a result of a 1917 revolution. He formed the first Communist government and took control of businesses and private property. He also united Russia and other republics to create the Soviet Union. After Lenin's death in 1924, Joseph Stalin took power. As dictator, he made all economic decisions, restricted religious worship, and used secret police to spy on citizens.

Benito Mussolini of Italy was another powerful dictator during this period. In the 1920s Mussolini won control of the Italian government and made himself dictator. He promised to make Italy stronger and to revive the economy. He even spoke of restoring the glory of the former Roman Empire. As dictator, however, Mussolini suspended basic rights like freedom of speech and trial by jury.

By the 1930s many Germans had lost faith in their government. They turned to a new political party, the Nazi Party. The party's leader, Adolf Hitler, promised to strengthen Germany. He vowed to rebuild Germany's military and economy. After years of struggle, many Germans listened eagerly to his message. In 1933 Hitler rose to power and soon became dictator. He banned all parties except the Nazi Party. He also began discriminating against so-called inferior races, particularly Germany's Jews.

READING CHECK **Generalizing** Why did some people support the rise of dictators?

European Dictators

Popular dictators rose to power in Europe in the 1920s and 1930s. Adolf Hitler in Germany and Benito Mussolini in Italy gained public support with promises to make life better and to strengthen their countries.

383

Direct Teach

Main Idea

1 Problems Trouble Europe

Economic and political problems troubled Europe in the years after World War I.

Recall What dictator rose to power in Italy in the 1920s? *Benito Mussolini*

Identify What did Mussolini promise the people of Italy? *to make Italy stronger and to revive its economy*

Identify Cause and Effect How did the American economy help Europe in the 1920s? *The booming American economy made loan money available to help rebuild Europe.*

MISCONCEPTION ALERT

Seizing Power? Adolf Hitler did not seize power in Germany, but gained it through legal means. In the late 1920s, Germany was a democracy, and Hitler's Nazi party was one of several political parties. In 1932, Hitler ran for president, and was soundly defeated. But the Nazis had won the largest number of seats in the Reichstag, or parliament. After some maneuvering, Hitler became Chancellor. In the next election, during a period of violence, the Nazis won a true majority in the Reichstag, which then legally voted to give Hitler the powers of a dictator.

Differentiating Instruction

Below Level

Struggling Readers

Have students read the section and write, in the left column of a graphic organizer like the one shown here, words and phrases that describe what people want from dictators. For example "to be strong" or "to share wealth." Then have students complete the sentence by writing a reason in the second column. **LS Verbal/Linguistic, Visual/Spatial**

Alternative Assessment Handbook, Rubrics 12: Drawing Conclusions; and 13: Graphic Organizers

People like dictators. . .	because. . .
to be strong	they want to be protected from foreign armies

Answers

Reading Check *possible answers— People wanted strong rulers who could improve their lives. Dictators made people feel proud and promised an ideal society in which people would share wealth.*

❷ War Breaks Out

World War II broke out when Germany invaded Poland.

Recall What African country did Italy invade in 1935? *Ethiopia*

Identify Cause and Effect Why did France and England declare war on Germany in 1939? *Germany invaded Poland.*

Contrast Why did the Allies react differently when Germany attacked Poland in 1939 than when Germany occupied Czechoslovakia in 1938? *In 1938 they still believed Germany would keep its word and that war could be avoided.*

▶ Map Zone Transparency: World War II in Europe, 1941

Connect to Art

Pablo Picasso's *Guernica* In the 1930s another European dictator seized power—General Francisco Franco of Spain. Franco, with the support of Hitler and Mussolini, led a revolt called the Spanish Civil War against the elected government. To help Franco succeed in 1937, the German air force bombed a government stronghold, the Spanish town of Guernica, deliberately killing more than a third of its people. The Spanish artist Pablo Picasso, outraged at the cruelty of this brutal war crime, painted the famous mural *Guernica* to tell the world what was happening to his people.

Answers

Map Zone 1. *Great Britain and the Soviet Union;* **2.** *An army and all its equipment could not easily cross water.*

Focus on Reading *The contrast clues "attempts at peace" and "instead of peace" can help students understand that aggression means "attack" or "use of force."*

↗ hmhsocialstudies.com **INTERACTIVE MAP**
World War II in Europe, 1941

- Axis powers
- Axis controlled
- Allied powers
- Allied controlled
- Neutral countries

0   150   300 Miles
0   150   300 Kilometers
Projection: Azimuthal Equal-Area

mapzone Geography Skills

Regions By 1941 the Axis Powers controlled much of Europe.
1. **Locate** What two Allied Powers remained standing by 1941?
2. **Analyzing** Why do you think the Axis was unable to conquer Great Britain?

War Breaks Out

As dictators, Hitler and Mussolini were determined to strengthen their countries at any cost. Their actions led to history's deadliest war—World War II.

Threats to Peace

After World War I, European countries wanted peace. Many countries hoped to prevent another deadly war. By the late 1930s, however, attempts at peace had failed. Instead of peace, Italian and German aggression forced Europe into a second world war.

In 1935 Benito Mussolini ordered his Italian troops to invade Ethiopia, a country in East Africa. Other nations were shocked by his actions, but none tried to turn back the invasion. Meanwhile, the Italian leader and Germany's Adolf Hitler joined together to form an alliance known as the Rome-Berlin Axis.

Hitler was next to act. In 1938 he broke the Treaty of Versailles when he annexed, or added, Austria to Germany's territory. Although Britain and France protested, they did not attempt to stop Germany.

Later that year, Hitler announced his plan to take Czechoslovakia as well. Many European leaders were worried, but they still hoped to avoid a war. They allowed Hitler to annex part of Czechoslovakia in return for his promise of peace. By the spring of 1939, however, Germany had conquered the rest of Czechoslovakia.

FOCUS ON READING
How do contrast clues help you understand the meaning of the word *aggression*?

Cross-Discipline Activity: Art

At Level

Relating to Picasso's *Guernica*

Prep Required

1. Bring a reproduction of Pablo Picasso's *Guernica* to class. Lead a discussion of what the images in the picture symbolize. Tell students that Picasso said, "It isn't up to the painter to define the symbols. Otherwise it would be better if he wrote them out in so many words."

2. Point out to students that even though the painting is about an attack by bombers, no images of airplanes appear. Solicit and record students' observations about possible meanings of symbols in the painting.

3. Have students either draw a picture in reaction to the bombing of Guernica or write a paragraph describing the symbolism of *Guernica*. **LS Visual/Spatial, Verbal/Linguistic**

📖 Alternative Assessment Handbook, Rubrics 3: Artwork; and 11: Discussions

Italy quickly moved to occupy Albania in the Balkans. Attempts to keep the peace had failed.

Eventually, Great Britain and France realized they could not ignore Hitler's actions. When Germany threatened to take Polish territory, the Allies vowed to protect Poland at all costs. On September 1, 1939, German forces launched an all-out attack on Poland. Two days later, Great Britain and France responded by declaring war on Germany. World War II had begun.

Allies Lose Ground

Germany's invasion of Poland triggered the Second World War. Germany, Italy, and Japan formed an alliance called the **Axis Powers**. Against them stood the **Allies**—France, Great Britain, and other countries that opposed the Axis.

Germany struck first. After defeating Poland, Germany moved on to a series of quick victories in Western Europe. One by one, countries fell to German forces. In June 1940 Germany invaded and quickly defeated one of Europe's greatest powers, France. In less than a year, Hitler had gained control of almost all of Western Europe.

Next, Germany set its sights on Britain. The German air force repeatedly attacked British cities and military targets. Hitler hoped the British would surrender. Rather than give in, however, the British persevered.

Unable to defeat Great Britain, the Axis Powers turned their attention elsewhere. As German troops marched into Eastern Europe, Italian forces invaded North Africa. By the end of 1941 Germany had invaded the Soviet Union, and Japan had attacked the United States at Pearl Harbor, Hawaii. The Allies were losing ground in the war.

READING CHECK Drawing Inferences Why do you think the Axis Powers easily gained the advantage in the early years of the war?

The Holocaust

One of the most horrifying aspects of the war was the Holocaust (HOH-luh-kawst). The **Holocaust** was the attempt by the Nazi government during World War II to eliminate Europe's Jews. Believing that the Germans were a superior race, the Nazis tried to destroy people who they believed were inferior, especially the Jews.

Even before the war began, the Nazi government began restricting the rights of Jews and others in Germany. For example, laws restricted Jews from holding government jobs or attending German schools. Nazis imprisoned countless Jews in camps.

Primary Source

JOURNAL ENTRY
The Diary of Anne Frank

Anne Frank and her family fled to Amsterdam to escape Nazi persecution of Jews in Germany. In 1942, when Nazis began rounding up Jews in the Netherlands, the Franks were forced to hide. Anne kept a diary of her time in hiding.

" *Countless friends and acquaintances have gone to a terrible fate. Evening after evening the green and gray army lorries [trucks] trundle past. The Germans ring at every front door to inquire if there are any Jews living in the house. If there are, then the whole family has to go at once. If they don't find any, they go on to the next house. No one has a chance of evading them unless one goes into hiding.* "

—from *The Diary of a Young Girl*

ANALYSIS SKILL **ANALYZING PRIMARY SOURCES**

What likely happened to the Jews that were rounded up by German officials?

MODERN EUROPEAN HISTORY **385**

385

Direct Teach

Main Idea

❸ **The Holocaust**

Nazi Germany targeted the Jews during the Holocaust.

Recall Where did Jews stage an uprising against the Nazis? *Warsaw, Poland*

Explain How did Oskar Schindler save some Jews during the Holocaust? *He gave them jobs in his factory.*

Draw a Conclusion: Why didn't more Jews fight back? *possible answer—They didn't believe Hitler would actually try to wipe out all the Jews in Eastern Europe.*

📰 RF: Biography, Anne Frank

Info to Know

Stalin-Hitler Pact of 1939 In the summer of 1939 many Europeans feared that war was coming. Since the Communists and the Nazis were the bitterest of political enemies, most people assumed the Soviet Union would fight with the Allies. But the world was shocked on August 23, 1939, when Germany and the Soviet Union signed a non-aggression pact. People in western Europe realized they would have to fight the powerful Axis war machine alone. What they did not know was even more shocking: Hitler and Stalin had made a secret agreement to divide Poland between them. On September 1, Germany attacked Poland. The non-aggression pact ended in 1941, when Germany reneged on the agreement and invaded the Soviet Union.

Collaborative Learning

Responding to the Holocaust

At Level

Research Required

1. Point out to students that the Nazis also sought to eliminate groups other than Jews. Tell students they will be researching an aspect of the Holocaust. (For sources, students may start with the Holocaust Encyclopedia on the Web site for the U.S. Holocaust Museum.) Have groups preview material on various topics before choosing one.

   • the Roma
   • the 1935 Nuremberg Laws
   • Jehovah's Witnesses

   • "Degenerate" art (Hitler's label for abstract art)
   • the system of badges that victims were required to wear

2. After groups have chosen and researched a topic, have each group design, create, and present a poster to the class of what they learned. Each group member should have a specific role in the poster project and presentation. **LS Visual/Spatial, Verbal/Linguistic**

   📰 Alternative Assessment Handbook, Rubrics 28: Posters; and 30: Research

Answers

Reading Check *Students may say that the Allies hoped to avoid war and gave up some territory without a fight; the Axis attacked some weak nations first; Britain could not transport its land army to the continent; the U.S. and the Soviet Union were not yet in the war; the Axis had superior weapons and tactics.*

Analyzing Primary Sources *They were likely killed.*

Direct Teach

Main Idea

❹ End of the War

Allied victories in Europe and Japan brought the end of World War II.

Define What is the United Nations? *an international peace-keeping organization*

Identify What happened on D-Day, and when did it occur? *The Allies landed on the beaches of Normandy, France; June 6, 1944*

Sequence What events led to the defeat of the Axis Powers in 1945? *British forces gained control of North Africa; Mussolini surrendered; Soviet troops forced Germany to retreat; the Allies landed at Normandy; the Allies entered German territory; Germany surrendered in May 1945; the U.S. used the atomic bomb; Japan surrendered in August 1945*

📖 **RF:** Primary Source, Charter of the United Nations

Biography

Wernher von Braun (1912–1977) If ever there was a "rocket scientist," it was Germany's Wernher von Braun. Inspired by the novels of Jules Verne, von Braun began studying rockets in his teens. During World War II, he headed the team that designed the V-2 rocket, which rained huge bombs on terrorized Londoners from 500 miles away. As the war ended, von Braun arranged for 500 of his fellow rocket scientists to surrender to the American army, rather than to the Soviets. The scientists were taken to the U.S. where they helped design and build the rockets for the American space program of the 1960s.

↗ **hmhsocialstudies.com**

Online Resources
Activity: D-Day Invasion

Answers

Reading Check *The Nazis considered the Jews an inferior race.*

386

Time Line

World War II

September 1–3, 1939
German forces invade Poland; Britain and France declare war.

June 22, 1941
Germany launches invasion of the Soviet Union.

| 1940 | 1941 | 1942 | 1943 |

June 22, 1940
France falls to German forces.

July–September 1940
Germany bombs London during the Battle of Britain.

Thousands of Jews fled Germany to escape persecution, but many had to remain behind because they were not allowed into other countries.

Germany's expansion into Eastern Europe brought millions more Jews under Hitler's control. In 1942 the Nazi government ordered the destruction of Europe's entire Jewish population. The Nazis used mass executions and concentration camps, like Auschwitz in Poland, to murder 6 million Jews.

The Nazis did face resistance. Some Jews fought back. For example, Jews in Warsaw, Poland, staged an uprising. Some non-Jewish Europeans tried to save Jews from the Nazis. German businessman Oskar Schindler, for example, saved Jews by employing them in his factories. By the time the Nazis were defeated, they had killed about two-thirds of Europe's Jews and several million non-Jews.

READING CHECK **Analyzing** Why did Hitler's Nazi government attempt to destroy the Jews?

386 CHAPTER 15

End of the War

The Allies did not fare well in the early years of the war. Victories in 1943 and 1944, though, helped them end World War II.

Allies Are Victorious

In early 1943 U.S. and British forces gained control of North Africa and Italy, forcing Mussolini to surrender. That same year, the Allies defeated the Japanese in several key battles. In the east, Soviet troops forced Germany to retreat.

In June 1944 Allied forces landed on the beaches of Normandy, France. The invasion, or D-Day as it was called, dealt a serious blow to the Axis. It paved the way for Allied forces to advance on Germany.

By the spring of 1945 Allied troops had crossed into German territory. In May 1945 Germany surrendered. In August 1945 the United States used a powerful new weapon, the atomic bomb, to bring the war with Japan to an end. After almost six years of fighting, World War II was over.

Hiroshima

Critical Thinking: Analyzing Information

Above Level

Exploring the UN Charter

1. Obtain copies of the Preamble of the United Nations Charter or go to the United Nations Web site. Have students make a two-columned table. In the first column, have them write each bullet point of the Preamble.

2. In the second column, have students cite a supporting source from their text by placing the heading title and page number in parentheses in an appropriate slot. Each entry should explain or support a point of the Preamble.

3. For any item lacking support, students should supply their own explanation, labeled "Personal Opinion."

4. Using the information in their tables, have students write a short paper explaining why the members of the United Nations agreed to the wording of the Charter's Preamble.

LS Verbal/Linguistic

📖 Alternative Assessment Handbook, Rubrics 30: Research; and 42: Writing to Inform.

February 1945
Allied leaders plan the final defeat of the Axis Powers.

April 1945
Allied troops begin liberation of Nazi concentration camps.

1944

1945

1946

June 6, 1944
Allied forces launch D-Day invasion in Normandy, France.

May 7, 1945
Germany surrenders to Allied Powers.

PA 1-27

HISTORY

VIDEO
BBC Report on D-Day
hmhsocialstudies.com

ANALYSIS SKILL **READING TIME LINES**

About how long after the beginning of the war did Germany invade the Soviet Union?

Results of the War

The war had a huge impact on the world. It resulted in millions of deaths, tensions between the Allies, and the creation of the United Nations.

World War II was the deadliest conflict in history. More than 50 million people lost their lives. Millions more were wounded.

The United States and the Soviet Union emerged from the war as the most powerful countries in the world. An intense rivalry developed between the two countries.

After the war, people hoped to prevent another deadly conflict. In 1945 some 50 nations formed the United Nations, an international peacekeeping organization.

NYC

READING CHECK **Summarizing** What were the main results of World War II?

SUMMARY AND PREVIEW World War II was the deadliest war in history. Next, you will learn about developments in Europe during the postwar period.

Section 2 Assessment
hmhsocialstudies.com
ONLINE QUIZ

Reviewing Ideas, Terms, and Places

1. **a. Define** What was the **Great Depression**?
   b. Explain How did economic problems in the United States lead to the Great Depression?
2. **a. Describe** What led to the outbreak of World War II?
   b. Predict What might have happened if Great Britain had fallen to Germany?
3. **a. Identify** What was the **Holocaust**?
   b. Draw Inferences Why did the Nazis target certain groups for elimination?
4. **a. Recall** What events led to Germany's surrender?
   b. Analyze How did World War II change Europe?

Critical Thinking

5. **Sequencing** Draw a time line like this one. Using your notes on important events, place the main events and their dates on the time line.

1917   1945

FOCUS ON WRITING

6. **Telling about World War II** Imagine that you are an adult during the Second World War. Where might you have lived? What might you have seen and done there? Write down some ideas in your notebook.

MODERN EUROPEAN HISTORY **387**

Bellringer

If YOU lived there. . . Use the **Daily Bellringer Transparency** to help students answer the question.

▶ Daily Bellringer Transparency, Section 3

Modern European History | Daily Bellringer
Section 3

Review Section 2
In each pair below, select the event that came first.
1. Dictators rise to power in Europe **OR** World War II begins
2. The United Nations is set up **OR** World War II ends
3. Germany invades Poland **OR** France falls to Germany

Preview Section 3
If YOU lived there ...
It is November 1989, and you live on the East German side of Berlin. For years the Berlin Wall has divided your city in two. The government has carefully controlled who could cross the border. One night, you hear an exciting rumor—the gate through the Wall is open. People in East and West Berlin can now travel back and forth freely. Young Berliners are celebrating in the streets.
What will this change mean for your country?

Consider the CHALLENGES:
- adapting to change
- creating new economic and political systems
- having many more choices and responsibilities

Consider the OPPORTUNITIES:
- freedom to live and travel wherever you choose
- access to new ideas and economic opportunities
- new rights, such as freedom of speech

Review Answers: 1. Dictators rise to power in Europe; 2. World War II ends; 3. Germany invades Poland

Academic Vocabulary

Review with students the high-use academic term in this section.

advocate to plead in favor of (p. 391)

▶ RF: Vocabulary Builder, Section 3

Taking Notes

Have students use the graphic organizer online to take notes on the section. This activity will prepare students for the Section Assessment, in which they will complete a chart that builds on the information using the Critical Thinking Skill: Summarizing.

Europe since 1945

If YOU lived there...

It is November 1989, and you live on the East German side of Berlin. For years the Berlin Wall has divided your city in two. The government has carefully controlled who could cross the border. One night, you hear an exciting rumor—the gate through the Wall is open. People in East and West Berlin can now travel back and forth freely. Young Berliners are celebrating in the streets.

What will this change mean for your country?

BUILDING BACKGROUND In the years after World War II, tensions between the Western Allies and the Soviet Union divided Europe into East and West. By the late 1980s, those tensions were at last coming to an end. Europe could finally work toward unity.

The Cold War

Although Europeans were relieved when World War II ended, new problems soon arose. Countries whose governments and economies had been weakened during the war had to work to strengthen them. Entire cities had to be rebuilt. Most importantly, postwar tensions between the Allies divided Europe.

Superpowers Face Off

The United States and the Soviet Union emerged from World War II as the world's most powerful nations. Allies during the war, the two **superpowers**, or strong and influential countries, now distrusted each other. Growing hostility between the superpowers led to the **Cold War**, a period of tense rivalry between the United States and the Soviet Union.

Much of the hostility between the Soviet Union and the United States focused on political and economic differences. The United States is a democracy with an economy based on free enterprise. The Soviet Union was a Communist country, in which individual freedoms were limited. Its leaders exerted strict control over the political system and the economy. These basic differences separated the two countries.

What You Will Learn...

Main Ideas
1. The Cold War divided Europe between democratic and Communist nations.
2. Many Eastern European countries changed boundaries and forms of government at the end of the Cold War.
3. European cooperation has brought economic and political change to Europe.

The Big Idea
After years of division during the Cold War, today Europe is working toward unity.

Key Terms
superpowers, *p. 388*
Cold War, *p. 388*
arms race, *p. 390*
common market, *p. 392*
European Union (EU), *p. 392*

hmhsocialstudies.com
TAKING NOTES

Use the graphic organizer online to take notes on events in Europe since 1945.

Teach the Big Idea

At Level

Europe since 1945

1. **Teach** Ask students the questions in the Main Idea boxes under Direct Teach.

2. **Apply** Draw a line on the board and tell students that you will be creating a time line together. Tell them, however, that you will be working backwards, beginning on the right side with the fall of the Berlin Wall. As you work backward in time, encourage students to identify significant events as well as their causes. **LS Visual/Spatial**

3. **Review** Have students copy the time line on a piece of paper and add other notable events.

4. **Practice/Homework** Have students write a narrative emphasizing the causes and effects of Cold War events listed on the time line. **LS Verbal/Linguistic**

📓 Alternative Assessment Handbook, Rubrics 36: Time Lines; and 37: Writing Assignments

A Divided Europe, 1955

NATO countries
Warsaw Pact countries
Other Communist countries
Neutral countries

0   200   400 Miles
0   200   400 Kilometers
Projection: Azimuthal Equal Area

Geography Skills

Regions The Cold War divided Europe into two distinct alliances—NATO and the Warsaw Pact.
1. **Identify** Which Communist country was not a member of the Warsaw Pact?
2. **Analyze** How was Germany affected by the alliances?

Causes and Effects of the Cold War

Causes	Effects
■ Rivalry develops between the United States and the Soviet Union after World War II.	■ Alliances divide Europe between Communist and non-Communist countries.
■ Hostilities between democratic and Communist governments increase.	■ Germany is divided into two separate countries.
■ The superpowers dispute the division of Germany after World War II.	■ The United States and the Soviet Union engage in a nuclear arms race.

A Divided Europe

The Cold War divided Europe into non-Communist and Communist countries. Most of Western Europe supported democracy and the United States. Much of Eastern Europe practiced Soviet-style communism. British prime minister Winston Churchill described the split that existed in Europe:

❝ …an iron curtain has descended across the Continent. Behind that line lie all the capitals of the ancient states of Central and Eastern Europe. …all are subject…not only to Soviet influence but to…control from Moscow. ❞

—from Winston Churchill's 1946 speech at Westminster College in Fulton, Missouri

Within this divided Europe was a divided Germany. After World War II, the Allies had separated Germany into four zones. By 1948 the Western Allies were ready to reunite their zones. However, the Soviet government feared the threat that a united Germany might pose. The next year, the Western zones were joined to form the Federal Republic of Germany, or West Germany. The Soviets helped to establish the German Democratic Republic, or East Germany. The city of Berlin, located within East Germany, was itself divided into East and West. In 1961 Communist leaders built the Berlin Wall to prevent any East Germans from fleeing to the West.

New alliances divided Europe even further. In 1949 the United States joined with several Western nations to create a powerful new alliance known as NATO, or the North Atlantic Treaty Organization.

MODERN EUROPEAN HISTORY **389**

Main Idea

❶ The Cold War

The Cold War divided Europe between democratic and Communist nations.

Define What is a superpower? *a strong and influential country*

Identify Who was Winston Churchill? *Prime Minister of Britain*

Elaborate What was life like in Eastern Europe during the Cold War? *Many aspects of life were strictly controlled by the government; people suffered from many shortages; they often lacked food and goods such as clothing and automobiles.*

▶ Map Zone Transparency: A Divided Europe, 1955

📄 **RF:** Literature, *Animal Farm* by George Orwell

Info to Know

Berlin Airlift After World War II both Germany and the city of Berlin were split into eastern and western parts. West Berlin was surrounded entirely by Communist East Germany, and the Soviet Union tried to take advantage of that fact in 1948. They blockaded the city, hoping the West would abandon it. Instead, Western democracies began supplying the city by air. At one point 8,000 tons of supplies a day were airlifted into West Berlin. The Soviet Union dropped the blockade about a year after it had started, and West Berlin survived.

Collaborative Learning

At Level

Presenting the Space Race

Research Required

1. Tell students that one area of competition between the East and the West during the Cold War was the space race. Divide students into groups to research one of the following topics:

   • Sputnik
   • animals in space
   • Telstar
   • first view of the far side of the moon
   • Project Mercury
   • first man, first woman in space
   • Ranger 9 crash on the moon

   • Apollo 11 mission
   • Saturn V rocket
   • Apollo 13 mission

2. Have students choose a medium to present the results of their research. Some ideas include reports, posters, models, or dioramas. Each group member must have a specific role in the project and presentation. 🆂 **Verbal/Linguistic, Visual/Spatial**

   📄 Alternative Assessment Handbook, Rubrics 29: Presentations; and 30: Research

Answers

Map Zone 1. *Yugoslavia;* **2.** *Germany was divided into two separate countries, and Berlin was also divided in two.*

389

❷ The End of the Cold War

Many Eastern European countries changed boundaries and forms of government at the end of the Cold War.

Define What is an arms race? *a competition between countries to build superior weapons*

Explain What caused violence after the break-up of Yugoslavia? *ethnic tensions*

Summarize Who was Mikhail Gorbachev, and what did he do? *the leader of the Soviet Union in the 1980s; introduced reforms that led to the breakup of the Soviet Union and its empire*

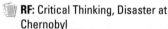 **RF:** Critical Thinking, Disaster at Chernobyl

Info to Know

MAD Strategy During the Cold War, both the United States and the Soviet Union built huge stockpiles of nuclear weapons. America's nuclear strategy was based on the idea of *mutual assured destruction*, or MAD. The idea of MAD was this: as long as both sides could survive a surprise nuclear attack and return a devastating counter-attack, neither side would dare strike first. All nuclear treaties negotiated during those times relied on the idea of mutual assured destruction. That is, the treaties prevented either side from building an effective missile defense system. The theory was very controversial, but it worked.

Answers

Reading Check *It divided Europe into Western Europe, which was democratic, and Eastern Europe, which was Communist. Western Europe's economy grew while Eastern Europe's did not.*

Biography *possible answers: yes—Some were in favor of the reforms, expanded freedoms, and modernization; no—Some people don't like change; communists lost power and influence.*

390

THE IMPACT TODAY NATO is still a powerful alliance today with 26 member nations in Europe and North America.

The members of NATO agreed to protect each other if attacked. In response, the Soviet Union formed its own alliance, the Warsaw Pact. Most Eastern European countries joined the Warsaw Pact. The two alliances used the threat of nuclear war to defend themselves. By the 1960s the United States, the Soviet Union, Britain, and France all had nuclear weapons.

The postwar division of Europe into East and West had a lasting effect on both sides. With U.S. assistance, many Western countries experienced economic growth. The economies of Communist Eastern Europe, however, failed to develop. Due to their lack of a market economy and strong industries, they suffered many shortages. They often lacked enough food, clothing, and automobiles to meet demand.

READING CHECK **Summarizing** How did the Cold War affect Europe?

BIOGRAPHY

Mikhail Gorbachev
(1931–)

Mikhail Gorbachev was a key figure in bringing the Cold War to an end. In 1985 Communist officials appointed Gorbachev the leader of the Soviet Union. He quickly enacted reforms to modernize his country. He expanded basic freedoms, such as freedom of speech and freedom of the press. His democratic reforms helped bring an end to communism in the Soviet Union. In 1990 Mikhail Gorbachev won the Nobel Peace Prize for his efforts to end the Cold War and promote peace.

Evaluating Do you think Gorbachev was a popular ruler? Why or why not?

The End of the Cold War

In the late 1980s tensions between East and West finally came to an end. The collapse of communism and the end of the Cold War brought great changes to Europe.

Triumph of Democracy

During the Cold War the United States and the Soviet Union competed against each other in an arms race. An **arms race** is a competition between countries to build superior weapons. Each country tried to create more-advanced weapons and to have more nuclear missiles than the other. This arms race was incredibly expensive. The high cost of the arms race eventually damaged the Soviet economy.

By the 1980s the Soviet economy was in serious trouble. Soviet leader Mikhail Gorbachev (GAWR-buh-chawf) hoped to solve the many problems his country faced. He reduced government control of the economy and introduced democratic elections. He improved relations with the United States. Along with U.S. president Ronald Reagan, Gorbachev took steps to slow the arms race.

In part because of these new policies, reform movements soon spread. Beginning in 1989, democratic movements swept through the East. For example, Poland and Czechoslovakia threw off Communist rule. Joyful Germans tore down the Berlin Wall that separated East and West. Several Soviet republics began to demand their independence. Finally, in December 1991 the Soviet Union broke apart.

Changes in Eastern Europe

The end of the Cold War brought many changes to Eastern Europe. These changes resulted from Germany's reunification, the creation of new countries, and rising ethnic tensions in southeastern Europe.

Critical Thinking: Comparing and Contrasting [At Level]

Using a Venn Diagram

Review with students the information in this section describing the confrontation between the East and West during the Cold War. Point out that although the two sides had very different political and economic approaches, they also had much in common. Draw the graphic organizer on the board and have students compare and contrast the Cold War rivals.

LS **Verbal/Linguistic, Visual/Spatial**

Alternative Assessment Handbook, Rubrics 9: Comparing and Contrasting; and 11: Discussions

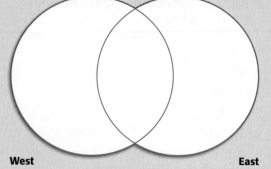

West   East

Reforms in the Soviet Union in the 1980s encouraged support for democracy throughout Eastern Europe.

ANALYZING VISUALS What role did the people play in communism's collapse?

Fall of the Berlin Wall East and West Germans celebrate the fall of the Berlin Wall.

Democracy in Czechoslovakia
In 1989 pro-democracy demonstrations swept Czechoslovakia. Rallies like this one led to the collapse of Czechoslovakia's Communist government.

The reunification of East and West Germany was one of many changes in Eastern Europe that marked the end of the Cold War. After the fall of the Berlin Wall in 1989, thousands of East Germans began demanding change. In early 1990 the Communist government crumbled. A few months later, the governments of East and West Germany agreed to reunite. After 45 years of division, Germany was reunited.

Other important changes occurred in Eastern Europe after the Cold War. The breakup of the Soviet Union created more than a dozen independent nations. The Russian Federation is the largest and most powerful of these new countries. Ukraine, Lithuania, Belarus, and others also emerged from the former Soviet Union.

Ethnic conflicts have also transformed Eastern Europe since the end of the Cold War. For example, tensions between ethnic groups in Czechoslovakia and Yugoslavia led to the breakup of both countries.

In Czechoslovakia, ethnic tensions divided the country. Disputes between the country's two main ethnic groups emerged in the early 1990s. Both the Czechs and the Slovaks **advocated** separate governments. In January 1993 Czechoslovakia peacefully divided into two countries—the Czech Republic and Slovakia.

While ethnic problems in the former Czechoslovakia were peaceful, ethnic tension in Yugoslavia triggered violence. After the collapse of communism, several Yugoslav republics declared their independence. Different ethnic groups fought each other for control of territory. Yugoslavia's civil wars resulted in years of fighting and thousands of deaths. By 1994 Yugoslavia had split into five countries—Bosnia and Herzegovina, Croatia, Macedonia, Serbia and Montenegro, and Slovenia.

ACADEMIC VOCABULARY

advocate
to plead in favor of

READING CHECK Drawing Conclusions How did the end of the Cold War affect Europe?

Biography

Lech Walesa (1943–) Lech Walesa was one of many people who struggled against Soviet-style communism in Eastern Europe. In 1976 Walesa, an electrician in a Polish shipyard, took an active role in an anti-government labor union—and was removed from his job. He was jailed several times over the next decade until 1980, when some workers' rights were granted. The next year, Walesa was elected chairman of Solidarity, a group that began as a labor union and evolved into a political party. Solidarity's struggle was not easy—the Soviet Union forced the Polish government to declare martial law and crack down on the unruly Polish people. Walesa was awarded the Nobel Peace Prize in 1983. This recognition gave hope to his embattled followers. In the late 1980s when Mikhail Gorbachev was reforming the Soviet Union, Poland was already moving toward democracy. In 1990 Poland elected Lech Walesa as the first President of the Republic of Poland.

Differentiating Instruction

Below Level | Standard English Mastery

English-Language Learners

1. Divide students into two groups—West Berlin and East Berlin. Have students imagine that they have a cousin living on the other side of the Berlin Wall in the early 1980s. Have them use standard English to write a letter describing what life is like on their side.

2. Ask volunteers to read the letters that they have received to the rest of the class. After each letter is read, lead a class discussion. Alternate choosing volunteers from West Berlin and East Berlin.

3. Have students imagine that it is 1989, shortly before the fall of the Berlin Wall. Have them use standard English to engage in a similar exchange of letters. **Verbal/Linguistic, Interpersonal**

   Alternative Assessment Handbook, Rubric 40: Writing to Describe

---

Answers

Analyzing Visuals *Large crowds demonstrated at rallies and demanded freedom.*

Reading Check *Germany was reunited; Czechoslovakia and Yugoslavia were split apart; new democracies were formed.*

Main Idea

❸ European Cooperation

European cooperation has brought economic and political change to Europe.

Recall What is the currency used by many countries in Europe today? *the euro*

Identify What is the European Union? *an organization that promotes political and economic cooperation in Europe*

Compare and Contrast How is the European Union like an alliance, and how is it different? *alike—It is an agreement between nations; different—It is concerned with economic and political cooperation, not conflict or warfare.*

📑 **RF:** Geography for Life, The Soviet "Game of the Name"

Info to Know

Airbus: European Cooperation in Action As part of their increasing cooperation, four European countries joined together to create the world's largest commercial aircraft manufacturer, Airbus. In 1970 France and Germany started the company; later Spain and the United Kingdom joined Airbus, which has overtaken its American rival, Boeing. In 2004, Airbus outperformed its major competitor by delivering more airplanes—and receiving more orders. Airbus has since received orders from airlines for the world's largest commercial plane, its 555-seat A380.

Answers

Drawing Conclusions *Germany, France, Italy, United Kingdom, Spain, and Poland because they have the most representatives*

392

THE WORLD ALMANAC
Facts about Countries — The European Union

Country	Year Admitted	Monetary Unit	Representatives in the European Parliament
Austria	1995	Euro	17
Belgium	1952	Euro	22
Bulgaria	2007	Lev	17
Cyprus	2004	Pound	6
Czech Republic	2004	Koruna	22
Denmark	1973	Krone	13
Estonia	2004	Kroon	6
Finland	1995	Euro	13
France	1952	Euro	72
Germany	1952	Euro	99
Greece	1979	Euro	22
Hungary	2004	Forint	22
Ireland	1973	Euro	12
Italy	1952	Euro	72
Latvia	2004	Lats	8
Lithuania	2004	Litas	12
Luxembourg	1952	Euro	6
Malta	2004	Lira	5
The Netherlands	1952	Euro	25
Poland	2004	Zloty	50
Portugal	1986	Euro	22
Romania	2007	Leu	33
Slovakia	2004	Koruna	13
Slovenia	2004	Euro	7
Spain	1986	Euro	50
Sweden	1995	Krona	18
United Kingdom	1973	Pound	72

Drawing Conclusions What are the most powerful countries in the European Parliament?

🔗 hmhsocialstudies.com

European Cooperation

Many changes shaped postwar Europe. One of the most important of those changes was the creation of an organization that now joins together most of the countries of Europe.

A European Community

Two world wars tore Europe apart in the 1900s. After World War II many of Europe's leaders began to look for ways to prevent another deadly war. Some people believed that creating a feeling of community in Europe would make countries less likely to go to war. Leaders like Great Britain's Winston Churchill believed the countries of Europe should cooperate rather than compete. They believed strong economic and political ties were the key.

Six countries—Belgium, France, Italy, Luxembourg, the Netherlands, and West Germany—took the first steps toward European unity. In the early 1950s these six countries joined to create a united economic community. The organization's goal was to form a **common market**, a group of nations that cooperates to make trade among members easier. This European common market, created in 1957, made trade easier among member countries. Over time, other nations joined. Europeans had begun to create a new sense of unity.

The European Union

Since its beginning in the 1950s, many new nations have become members of this European community, now known as the European Union. The **European Union (EU)** is an organization that promotes political and economic cooperation in Europe. Today the European Union has more than 25 members. Together, they deal with a wide range of issues, including trade, the environment, and migration.

Cross-Discipline Activity: Mathematics   **Above Level**

Interpreting EU Data
Research Required

Point out the data in the fourth column of the European Union table *Representatives in the EU Parliament*. Ask students to decide if countries are represented fairly in the EU. Allow students to use the table to aid their process.

1. Decide if students will research data for all countries or only a sample; then assign them to look up current populations of selected EU countries.

2. For each country, divide the number of people in the country by the number of EU representatives. This is the country's *representation quotient.*

3. Arrange the results in an ordered list, and then decide how best to display the results. (A bar graph is a likely choice.)

4. If students chose to exhaustively compile data for all EU countries, they may compute the average representation quotient and draw it as a reference line on their bar graph.

LS Logical/Mathematical, Visual/Spatial

📑 Alternative Assessment Handbook, Rubric 7: Charts

The European Union has executive, legislative, and judicial branches. The EU is run by a commission made up of one representative from each member nation. Two legislative groups, the Council of the European Union and the European Parliament, debate and make laws. Finally, the Court of Justice resolves disputes and enforces EU laws.

Through the European Union, the countries of Europe work together toward common economic goals. The EU helps its member nations compete with economic powers like the United States and Japan. In 1999 the EU introduced a common currency, the euro, which many member countries now use. The euro has made trade much easier.

The European Union has helped unify Europe. In recent years many countries from Eastern Europe have joined the EU. Other countries hope to join in the future. Despite difficulties, EU leaders hope to continue their goal to bring the nations of Europe closer together.

READING CHECK **Finding Main Ideas** How has cooperation in Europe affected the region?

In 2005 French and Dutch voters rejected a proposed constitution for the European Union. Here, voters in France demand that their vote be upheld.

SUMMARY AND PREVIEW In this section you learned how the European Union helped unify much of Europe after years of division during the Cold War. In the next chapter, you will learn about Southern Europe's physical geography and culture.

Section 3 Assessment

hmhsocialstudies.com
ONLINE QUIZ

Reviewing Ideas, Terms, and Places

1. **a. Recall** What was the **Cold War**?
   b. Analyze Why was Europe divided during the Cold War?
2. **a. Identify** What new countries were formed after the end of the Cold War?
   b. Compare and Contrast How were ethnic tensions in Czechoslovakia and Yugoslavia similar and different?
   c. Evaluate Do you think the end of the Cold War helped or hurt the nations of Eastern Europe?
3. **a. Define** What is a **common market**?
   b. Make Inferences Why did some Europeans believe stronger economic and political ties could prevent war in Europe?

Critical Thinking

4. **Summarizing** Use your notes and the chart below to summarize the effect that each event had on the different regions of Europe. Write a sentence that summarizes the effect of each event.

	Cold War	End of Cold War	European Union
Western Europe			
Eastern Europe			

FOCUS ON WRITING

5. **Thinking about Europe since 1945** You are now in your mid-80s. How might events during and after the Cold War have affected your life?

MODERN EUROPEAN HISTORY **393**

Direct Teach

Did you know. . .

Completed in 1994, the 31-mile long tunnel under the English Channel connects England with the European continent physically for the first time in history. On average, the Chunnel is 150 feet below the level of the seabed. A high-speed train, the Eurostar, takes passengers between London and Paris in about three hours. The Chunnel also accommodates motorized traffic. Many heavy goods that once had to cross the English Channel by sea are now driven across in trucks.

Review & Assess

Close

Discuss with students which European country they would most like to visit.

Review

↗ Online Quiz, Section 3

Assess

SE Section 3 Assessment
PASS: Section 3 Quiz
Alternative Assessment Handbook

Reteach/Classroom Intervention

Guided Reading Workbook, Section 3
Interactive Skills Tutor CD-ROM

Section 3 Assessment Answers

1. **a.** a period of tense rivalry between the United States and the Soviet Union
   b. Much of Eastern Europe was loyal to the Soviet Union; much of Western Europe was loyal to the U.S.
2. **a.** Russia, Belarus, Ukraine, Lithuania, the Czech Republic, Slovakia, Bosnia and Herzegovina, Croatia, Serbia and Montenegro, Macedonia, and Slovenia
   b. similar—Ethnic tensions resulted in the break-up of the two countries; different—Czechoslovakia split peacefully, while Yugoslavia broke up violently.

c. Answers will vary but students should support their response with information from the text.

3. **a.** a group of nations that cooperates to make trade easier among its members
   b. possible answer—Countries that cooperate are less likely to go to war.

4. Students' summaries will vary but should be based on section content.

5. possible answer: during—fears of nuclear war and of communism spreading; after—hopes for lasting peace and greater political freedoms and economic opportunities

Answers

Reading Check *It has helped to unify Europe through trade and politics.*

393

Social Studies Skills

Interpreting Political Cartoons

Activity Political Cartoons and Posters

Materials: copies of political cartoons and posters—especially of the World War I and World War II era—representing both sides of each conflict

1. Tell students that political cartoons and political posters use many of the same techniques.

2. Have students look at a variety of cartoons and posters and ask questions, such as the following:

   How are allies and enemies depicted in the drawings?

   What are some of the symbols used to identify which side countries, people, or armies belong to?

   Are events portrayed truthfully, dishonestly, or somewhere in between?

   LS Visual/Spatial

- Alternative Assessment Handbook, Rubrics 27: Political Cartoons
- Interactive Skills Tutor CD-ROM, Lesson 6: Interpret Maps, Graphs, Charts, Visuals, and Political Cartoons

Social Studies Skills

Chart and Graph | **Critical Thinking** | Geography | Study

Interpreting Political Cartoons

Learn

Political cartoons are drawings that express views on important political or social issues. The ability to interpret political cartoons will help you understand issues and people's attitudes about them.

Political cartoons use images and words to convey a message about a particular event, person, or issue in the news. Most political cartoons use symbols to represent those ideas. For example, political cartoonists often use Uncle Sam to represent the United States. They also use titles and captions to express their point of view.

Practice

Examine the cartoon on this page. Then, answer the following questions to interpret the message of the cartoon.

❶ Read any title, labels, or captions to identify the subject of the cartoon. What information does the caption for this cartoon give you? To what event does this cartoon refer?

❷ Identify the people and symbols in the cartoon. What person is pictured in this cartoon? What does the crushed hammer and sickle represent?

❸ What message is the cartoonist trying to convey?

Soviet leader Mikhail Gorbachev examines a broken hammer and sickle.

Apply

Use your new skills to interpret a recent political cartoon. Locate a political cartoon that deals with an issue or event that has been in the news recently. Then answer the questions below.

1. What issue or event does the cartoon address?

2. What people or symbols are represented in the cartoon?

3. What point is the cartoon attempting to make?

394 CHAPTER 15

Social Studies Skills Activity: Interpreting Political Cartoons

Symbols in Political Cartoons

Below Level

1. Have students brainstorm symbols that they use and see in daily life. Common symbols include the dollar sign, eagle, dove, fist, heart, flower, flag, skull and crossbones, lightning bolt, donkey, elephant, maple leaf, flame, rainbow, shamrock, lion, black cat, equal sign, question mark, stop sign, arrow, and musical notes.

2. Tell students to choose ten symbols and label them with a word or phrase explaining each symbol's meaning.

3. Have students draw their own political cartoon using at least one symbol to help illustrate their idea. (The cartoon may also use captions or names as political cartoons do.) **LS** Visual/Spatial

- Alternative Assessment Handbook, Rubric 27: Political Cartoons

Answers

Practice 1. *name of the person depicted; break-up of the Soviet Union;* 2. *Mikhail Gorbachev; the Soviet Union;* 3. *The Soviet Union broke up under the leadership of Mikhail Gorbachev.*

Apply *Answers will vary depending on the political cartoon selected.*

Geography's Impact
video series
Review the video to answer the closing question: *Why do you think the creation of the European Union was important to many Europeans?*

Visual Summary

Use the visual summary below to help you review the main ideas of the chapter.

QUICK FACTS

World War I introduced many changes to Europe, including a new type of fighting called trench warfare.

The Allied and Axis powers faced off in World War II, the deadliest war in the world's history.

After years of division, the end of the Cold War finally reunited the nations of Europe.

Reviewing Vocabulary, Terms, and Places

Match the words or names with their definitions or descriptions.

1. arms race   **4.** nationalism

2. Axis Powers   **5.** strategy

3. dictator   **6.** trench warfare

a. a powerful ruler that exerts complete control and often rules by force

b. a style of fighting in which each side fights from deep ditches dug into the ground

c. a plan for fighting a battle or war

d. the alliance of Germany, Italy, and Japan in World War II

e. devotion and loyalty to one's country

f. a competition between countries for superior weapons

Comprehension and Critical Thinking

SECTION 1 *(Pages 376–380)*

7. a. Recall What causes led to the outbreak of World War I?

    b. Draw Conclusions How did the U.S. entry into World War I affect the war's outcome?

    c. Elaborate Why do you think World War I led to revolutions in some countries?

SECTION 2 *(Pages 382–387)*

8. a. Identify What two alliances fought in World War II? What countries belonged to each?

    b. Compare In what ways were Joseph Stalin, Benito Mussolini, and Adolf Hitler similar?

    c. Elaborate In your opinion, how were the Allies able to win World War II?

SECTION 3 *(Pages 388–393)*

9. a. Identify Into what alliances was Europe divided during the Cold War?

MODERN EUROPEAN HISTORY **395**

Answers

Visual Summary

Review and Inquiry Have students use the visual summary to write a brief paragraph explaining why there was so much violence in Europe in the 1900s.

▶ Quick Facts Transparency: Modern European History, 1900–Today Visual Summary

Reviewing Vocabulary, Terms, and Places

1. f   **4.** e

2. d   **5.** c

3. a   **6.** b

Comprehension and Critical Thinking

7. a. nationalism; competition for land, power, and resources; alliances; assassination of Archduke Ferdinand
    b. Allied Powers had renewed energy.
    c. People were dissatisfied with their ruined countries and the many deaths and wanted new leadership.

8. a. Axis Powers—Germany, Italy, Japan, and other countries; Allies—Soviet Union, Great Britain, United States, France, and other countries
    b. They were all dictators.
    c. possible answers—U.S. and Britain forced Mussolini to surrender; Allies defeated Japan in key battles; Soviets forced Germany to retreat; Allies advanced on Germany with D-Day invasion.

9. a. western—non-Communist, loyal to U.S.; eastern—Communist, loyal to Soviet Union

---

Review and Assessment Resources

Review and Reinforce

SE Chapter Review

📖 RF: Chapter Review

▶ Quick Facts Transparency: Modern European History, 1900–Today Visual Summary

🔊 Spanish Chapter Summaries Audio CD

TOS Holt McDougal PuzzleView®; Quiz Show for ExamView

💿 Quiz Game CD-ROM

Assess

SE Standardized Test Practice

📖 PASS: Chapter Test, Forms A and B

📖 Alternative Assessment Handbook

TOS ExamView Test Generator, Chapter Test

💿 Differentiated Instruction Modified Worksheets and Tests CD-ROM: Chapter Test

↗ Online Assessment Program, in the Interactive Student Edition

Reteach/Intervene

📖 Guided Reading Workbook

SE Differentiated Instruction Teacher Management System: Lesson Plans

💿 Differentiated Instruction Modified Worksheets and Tests CD-ROM

💿 Interactive Skills Tutor CD-ROM

↗ hmhsocialstudies.com
Chapter Resources

9. b. possible answer—The U.S. helped Western Europe prosper while Eastern Europe struggled. Soviet leader Gorbachev worked with U.S. president Reagan to slow the arms race. Other reforms in the Soviet Union led to democratic movements, which resulted in new countries forming and the break-up of the Soviet Union.

c. possible answers: help—develop a good sense of community among nations, strengthen the economies of the member nations, bring cooperation and peace to Europe; hurt—nations may become too dependent on one another; EU limits government roles.

Using the Internet

10. Go to hmhsocialstudies.com to access a rubric for this activity.

Social Studies Skills

11. the D-Day invasion of Normandy, France

12. Adolf Hitler—Axis Powers; tanks, airplanes, and bombs—planned invasion; giant wave—overwhelming military siege by the Allies

13. possible answer—The Allies had more capacity to produce weapons than the Axis Powers, and that capacity proved decisive in the conflict.

Map Activity

14. A. London
B. Paris
C. West Germany
D. Berlin
E. Poland
F. Yugoslavia
G. Moscow

SECTION 3 *(continued)*

b. Analyze How did the Cold War come to an end?

c. Predict Do you think that the European Union will hurt or help Europe? Explain.

Using the Internet

10. Activity: Creating a Poster The D-Day invasion of Normandy was crucial to the Allies' victory in World War II. Through your online textbook, find out more about D-Day. Then create a poster that celebrates the anniversary of the D-Day invasion. Be sure to include a short statement explaining why the invasion was important and images that grab your audience's attention.

⤤ hmhsocialstudies.com

Social Studies Skills

Interpreting Political Cartoons *Examine the political cartoon below, then answer the questions that follow.*

11. What event does the cartoon depict?

12. What symbols does the cartoon use? To what do those symbols refer?

13. What point is the artist trying to make?

Map Activity

14. Europe, 1989 On a separate sheet of paper, match the letters on the map with their correct labels.

Berlin   Poland   West Germany
London   Moscow   Yugoslavia
Paris

⤤ hmhsocialstudies.com   **INTERACTIVE MAP**

FOCUS ON READING AND WRITING

Using Context Clues—Contrast *Use context clues to determine the meaning of the underlined words in the sentences below.*

15. During World War II, people who aided Jews were often underlined detained rather than set free.

16. Many celebrations at the end of the Cold War were frenzied, not calm and orderly.

17. European dictators who rose to power were ruthless as opposed to kind.

Writing a Diary Entry *Use your notes and the directions below to write a diary entry.*

18. Review your notes to organize the diary of your imaginary person. Divide your diary into three periods—World War I, World War II, and 1945–today. Describe the events your imaginary person experienced from his or her point of view. Remember to describe his or her thoughts and feelings about each event.

Focus on Reading and Writing

15. Detained means the opposite of set free.

16. Frenzied means the opposite of calm and orderly.

17. Ruthless means the opposite of kind.

📋 **RF:** Focus on Reading, Using Context Clues–Contrast

18. Rubric Students' diary entries should

• be written from the perspective of someone in history

• include a detailed description of the events surrounding the person from his or her point of view

• include thoughts or feelings about each event from the person's point of view

📋 **RF:** Focus on Writing, Writing a Diary Entry

Standardized Test Prep

DIRECTIONS: Read questions 1 through 7 and write the letter of the best response. Question 8 will require a brief essay.

1 **Which world leader was *most* involved in the end of the Cold War?**

A Francis Ferdinand

B Joseph Stalin

C Mikhail Gorbachev

D Winston Churchill

2 **The fall of the Berlin Wall is an important symbol of**

A the Communist revolution in Russia.

B the Allied victory in World War II.

C the collapse of communism in Europe.

D the formation of the European Union.

3 **Which of the following was a result of World War II?**

A The United Nations was formed.

B Adolf Hitler was charged with war crimes.

C A Communist revolution took place in Russia.

D The U.S. economy collapsed.

4 **Which of the following was a key cause of World War I?**

A The United Nations failed to negotiate a peaceful settlement between East and West.

B Germany and Italy launched invasions.

C Competition between the countries of Europe created fierce rivalries.

D Countries feared that communism would spread throughout Europe.

5 **Who was the first leader of Communist Russia?**

A Benito Mussolini

B Joseph Stalin

C Mikhail Gorbachev

D Vladimir Lenin

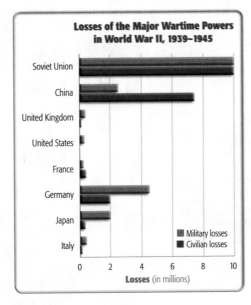

Losses of the Major Wartime Powers in World War II, 1939–1945

Military losses
Civilian losses

Losses (in millions)

6 **Based on the information in the chart above, which Allied power lost the *fewest* civilians in World War II?**

A France

B United Kingdom

C Italy

D United States

7 **Ethnic tensions at the end of the Cold War divided which of the following countries?**

A France

B Germany

C United States

D Yugoslavia

8 **Extended Response** Tensions after World War II led to the Cold War between the United States and the Soviet Union. Use the map in Section 3 to explain how the Cold War affected Europe.

MODERN EUROPEAN HISTORY **397**

Standardized Test Prep

1. C
Break Down the Question This question requires students to recall factual information from Section 3.

2. C
Break Down the Question This question requires students to recall factual information from Section 3.

3. A
Break Down the Question This question requires students to recall factual information from Section 2.

4. C
Break Down the Question This question requires students to recall factual information from Section 1.

5. D
Break Down the Question This question requires students to recall factual information from Section 1.

6. D
Break Down the Question This question requires students to accurately read the chart.

7. D
Break Down the Question This question requires students to recall factual information from Section 3.

8. Extended Response Students should say that most European countries were divided between two alliances—NATO and the Warsaw Pact. People in Western Europe lived in democracies, and their economies did well. People in Eastern Europe had very few rights and suffered economically.

Reteach/Intervention Resources

Reproducible

Guided Reading Workbook

Differentiated Instruction Teacher Management System: Lesson Plans

Technology

Quick Facts Transparency: Modern European History, 1900–Today Visual Summary

Differentiated Instruction Modified Worksheets and Tests CD-ROM

Interactive Skills Tutor CD-ROM

Tips for Test Taking

I'm Stuck! Suggest to students the following tips if they come across a test question that stumps them. Don't get frustrated. First master the question to make sure you understand what is being asked. Then work through the strategies you have already learned. If you are still stuck, circle the question and go on to others. Come back to it later. What if you still have no idea? Practice the 50/50 strategy and make an educated guess.

The **HISTORY™ Multimedia Classroom** is a set of exciting new social studies teaching tools featuring award-winning program content. These comprehensive lesson plans, correlated to individual state and national curriculum standards, are easy to use for both teachers and students.

Each lesson contains the following:

- Short video segments that bring history topics to life
- Maps and visual materials
- Discussion and review questions
- Easily printable primary source documents
- Classroom activities and Internet-based activity links

The Multimedia Classroom has been specially designed to be versatile and easily adaptable to existing courses, lesson plans, and syllabi. Every lesson is designed to offer maximum flexibility. Teachers can select entire plans or only the elements they need, allowing them to individually tailor each lesson. Each multimedia lesson is available in CD-ROM format and is accompanied by full-length award-winning programs on DVD from HISTORY™.

For more information or to purchase go to ⬈ hmhsocialstudies.com

Because some of these lessons may contain video material of a sensitive nature, we recommend that teachers and parents review these materials in their entirety before screening them to students.

MULTIMEDIA CONNECTIONS
HISTORY
Dear home: LETTERS FROM WWI

When U.S. troops arrived in Europe in 1917 to fight in World War I, the war had been dragging on for nearly three years. The American soldiers suddenly found themselves in the midst of chaos. Each day, they faced the threats of machine gun fire, poison gas, and aerial attacks. Still, the arrival of American reinforcements had sparked a new zeal among the Allies, who believed the new forces could finally turn the tide in their favor. The letters soldiers wrote to their families back home reveal the many emotions they felt on the battlefield: confusion about their surroundings, fear for their own safety, concern for friends and loved ones, and hope that the war would soon be over.

Explore World War I online through the eyes of the soldiers who fought in it. You can find a wealth of information, video clips, primary sources, activities, and more at ⬈ hmhsocialstudies.com.

397 MC1 MULTIMEDIA CONNECTIONS

Letters from World War I

Resources ⬈ hmhsocialstudies.com

The following resources come with printable introductions, comprehension and critical thinking questions, transcripts, and vocabulary support.

Full Length DVD

Dear Home: Letters from WWI (1 hr 40 mins)

Video Clips

- Europe at War (1:59)
- The End of Isolation (2:16)
- Signing Up (3:22)
- Over There (2:20)
- At Home and at War (3:57)
- Letters Home (2:07)
- War on the Western Front (2:58)
- Surrender (2:57)
- Building a League of Nations (3:08)

Primary Sources

- Wilson's Address to Congress
- Letter from France
- The Fourteen Points

"I have been on every front in France. You cant imagine how torn up this country really is. Every where there are wire entanglements and trenches and dugouts. Even out of the war zone there are entanglements and dugouts to protect the civilians from air raids."

-Corp. Albert Smith, U.S. soldier

Letter from France
Read the document to learn about one soldier's observations of wartime life.

Over There
Watch the video to learn about the experiences of American soldiers on the way to Europe and upon their arrival.

War on the Western Front
Watch the video to hear one soldier's vivid account of battle and its aftermath.

Surrender!
Watch the video to experience soldiers' reactions to the news that the war was finally over.

Lesson Preview

Letter from France
In his letter home of October, 1918, Corp. Albert Smith proudly told his brother that France would be "the most peaceable country in the world in about 60 days." He was correct in predicting that the war would end by that time. But one may wonder how much longer Smith had to go before enjoying a bath, or if he was able to shave often enough that his gas mask continued to fit properly. And did he ever make it back to his beloved Tennessee?

Over There
The Great War, as it was called at the time, had been dragging on in Europe for more than two years when the United States finally began sending soldiers to help the Allied cause. The troops came by ship across the Atlantic, where days of tedium were sometimes shattered by attacks from German U-boats hidden below the waves. The troops that made the voyage safely were welcomed by the English and the French. But would the Americans be able to turn the tide?

War on the Western Front
World War I was the first war for which there is a large archive of motion picture footage. Those images, along with the letters sent home from the front, provide vivid evidence of the war's horrors—the stinking trenches, constant noise, sudden attacks, terrible injuries, and the dead and wounded lying in heaps in no-man's-land.

Surrender!
By the autumn of 1918, both sides were exhausted. Yet when rumors of a compromise began to circulate, Allied soldiers were outraged. Only a complete and unconditional surrender would suffice. When an armistice was finally signed, it was clear that the enemy was just as anxious to stop the fighting as were the Allied troops. German and Allied soldiers celebrated together at the front.

Activities
- Breaking News: *The Lusitania Sinks*
- Time for War:
- To the Folks Back Home
- Friend or Foe:
- Reports from the Frontline
- Sense in Censorship?
- The Causes and Consequences of War
- From Armistice Day to Veterans Day
- Voting on the Treaty of Versailles
- Extended Activities

Extended Activities
? **General Review Questions**
? **General Discussion Questions**
📖 **Web Links**
📖 **Bibliography**

Chapter 16 Planning Guide

Southern Europe

Overview	Instructional Resources	

CHAPTER 16

Essential Question: How has climate influenced the land and people of Southern Europe?

🔊 **Focus on the Essential Question Podcast**

TOS Differentiated Instruction Teacher Management System:
- Instructional Pacing Guides
- Lesson Plans for Differentiated Instruction

Guided Reading Workbook

Resource File:
- Chapter Review
- Focus on Reading: Asking Questions
- Focus on Writing: Writing a News Report
- Social Studies Skills: Reading a Climate Map

Experiencing World History and Geography

TOS Calendar Planner

💿 **Power Presentations with Media Gallery**

💿 **Differentiated Instruction Modified Worksheets and Tests CD-ROM**

💿 **Interactive Skills Tutor CD-ROM**

🔊 **Student Edition on Audio CD-ROM**

🔊 **The World's Music Audio Program**

▶️ **Map Zone Transparency:** Southern Europe: Political

▶️ **World Outline Maps: Transparencies and Activities**

Video: Humanism Triggers the Renaissance

Section 1:

Physical Geography

The Big Idea: The peninsulas of Southern Europe have rocky terrains and sunny, mild climates.

TOS Differentiated Instruction Teacher Management System: Section 1 Lesson Plan

Guided Reading Workbook: Section 1

Resource File:
- Vocabulary Builder: Section 1
- Geography for Life: The Mediterranean Sea

▶️ **Daily Bellringer Transparency:** Section 1

▶️ **Map Zone Transparency:** Southern Europe: Physical

▶️ **Map Zone Transparency:** Europe: Climate

📄 **Internet Activity:** Islands of the Mediterranean

Section 2:

Greece

The Big Idea: The home of one of the Western world's oldest civilizations, Greece is trying to reclaim its place as a leading country in Europe.

TOS Differentiated Instruction Teacher Management System: Section 2 Lesson Plan

Guided Reading Workbook: Section 2

Resource File:
- Vocabulary Builder: Section 2
- Biography: Aristotle

▶️ **Daily Bellringer Transparency:** Section 2

▶️ **Map Zone Transparency:** Greece: Population

📄 **Internet Activity:** Greek Mythology

Section 3:

Italy

The Big Idea: Once the center of a huge empire, Italy is now one of the most prosperous countries in Europe.

TOS Differentiated Instruction Teacher Management System: Section 3 Lesson Plan

Guided Reading Workbook: Section 3

Resource File:
- Vocabulary Builder: Section 3
- Primary Source: "The Creation of Adam" by Michelangelo
- Geography and History: Northern and Southern Italy

▶️ **Daily Bellringer Transparency:** Section 3

▶️ **Map Zone Transparency:** Satellite View: Venice

Section 4:

Spain and Portugal

The Big Idea: Spain and Portugal have rich cultures, stable governments, and growing economies.

TOS Differentiated Instruction Teacher Management System: Section 4 Lesson Plan

Guided Reading Workbook: Section 4

Resource File:
- Vocabulary Builder: Section 4
- Biography: Amália Rodrigues
- Literature: *Don Quixote* by Miguel de Cervantes

▶️ **Daily Bellringer Transparency:** Section 4

Chart Key:

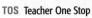

SE Student Edition

TOS Teacher One Stop

 Printable Resource

 Presentation Resource

 DVD/CD-ROM

MP3 Audio

HISTORY™

Program Resources available on **TOS** and @ hmhsocialstudies.com

---

Review, Assessment, Intervention

Europe and Russia Transparencies: Southern Europe Visual Summary

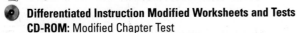 **Spanish Chapter Summaries Audio CD**

Progress Assessment Support System (PASS): Chapter Test

Differentiated Instruction Modified Worksheets and Tests CD-ROM: Modified Chapter Test

TOS ExamView® Assessment Suite (English/Spanish)

Alternative Assessment Handbook

Online Assessment Program, in the Interactive Student Edition

---

 PASS: Section 1 Quiz

Online Quiz: Section 1

Alternative Assessment Handbook

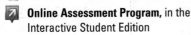 **PASS:** Section 2 Quiz

Online Quiz: Section 2

Alternative Assessment Handbook

PASS: Section 3 Quiz

Online Quiz: Section 3

Alternative Assessment Handbook

PASS: Section 4 Quiz

Online Quiz: Section 4

Alternative Assessment Handbook

Supporting Resources

- Multimedia Classroom Global History Series
- Global History Teacher's Guide

Maps Globes Graphs Level F

- Student Workbook
- Teacher's Guide

Social Studies Trade Library Collections

- World Regions Trade Collection
- NCSS Middle School Trade Collection

Geography's Impact

Geography's Impact Video Program

- **Impact of the Olympics on Athens**

For more information or to purchase go to hmhsocialstudies.com

---

Power Presentations with Media Gallery

Power Presentations with Media Gallery are visual presentations of each chapter's main ideas. Presentations can be customized by including Quick Facts charts, images from the text, and video clips.

Differentiating Instruction

How do I address the needs of varied learners?

The Target Resource acts as your primary strategy for differentiated instruction.

ENGLISH-LANGUAGE LEARNERS & STRUGGLING READERS

TARGET RESOURCE

Interactive Skills Tutor CD-ROM

The Interactive Skills Tutor CD-ROM contains lessons that provide additional practice for 20 different critical thinking skills.

Additional Resources

Differentiated Instruction Teacher Management System: Lesson Plans for Differentiated Instruction

Resource File:
- Vocabulary Builder Activities
- Social Studies Skills: Reading a Climate Map

Quick Facts Transparencies:
- Southern Europe Visual Summary

Spanish/English Guided Reading Workbook

Spanish Chapter Summaries Audio CD

Teacher One Stop:
- ExamView Assessment Suite, Spanish
- PuzzleView, Spanish

English-Language Learner Strategies and Activities

SPECIAL NEEDS LEARNERS

TARGET RESOURCE

Resource File

The Resource File activities allow students to extend their knowledge of chapter-related places and people and to practice geography skills.
- Vocabulary Builder Activities
- Social Studies Skills: Interpreting Political Cartoons

Additional Resources

Differentiated Instruction Teacher Management System: Lesson Plans for Differentiated Instruction

Resource File: Social Studies Skills: Reading a Climate Map

Student Edition on Audio CD Program

Interactive Skills Tutor CD-ROM

Graphic Organizer Transparencies with Support for Reading and Writing

ADVANCED/GIFTED AND TALENTED STUDENTS

TARGET RESOURCE

Differentiated Instruction Teacher Management System

Lesson Plans for Differentiated Instruction provide teachers with strategies to help plan instruction for all learners.

Additional Resources

Resource File:
- Focus on Reading: Asking Questions
- Focus on Writing: Writing a News Report
- Literature: *Don Quixote* by Miguel de Cervantes

World History and Geography Document-Based Questions Activities

Geography, Science, and Cultures Activities

Experiencing World History and Geography

Differentiated Activities in the Teacher's Edition

- Discussing Images, p. 399
- Analyzing Visuals, p. 402
- Discussing Languages in Spain and Portugal, p. 416

Teacher One Stop™

How can I manage the lesson plans and support materials for differentiated instruction?

With the Teacher One Stop, you can easily organize and print lesson plans, planning guides, and instructional materials for all learners. The Teacher One Stop includes the following materials to help you differentiate instruction:

- · **Interactive Teacher's Edition**
- · **Calendar Planner and pacing guides**
- · **Editable lesson plans**
- · **All reproducible ancillaries in Adobe Acrobat (PDF) format**
- · **ExamView Assessment Suite (English & Spanish)**
- · **Transparency and video previews**

Differentiated Activities in the Teacher's Edition

- Learning about Religious Festivals, p. 407

Interactive Student Edition

Complete online student edition with interactive multimedia support for chapter content assessment and reporting

- Interactive Maps and Notebook
- Standardized Test Prep
- Online Homework Practice and Research Activities
- Current Events
- Chapter-based Internet Activities
- Animated Geography Activities

Differentiated Activities in the Teacher's Edition

- Giving an Oral Report, p. 399

Introduce the Essential Question

- Have students locate Greece, Italy, Spain, and Portugal on the map on pages 398–399. Explain that all four countries enjoy a mild climate that attracts millions of tourists each year.
- Ask students to relate what they know about Greece. Point out that traditional Greek foods such as lamb and olives do well in Greece's mild climate and rugged landscape.
- Explain that the climate in Italy is favorable for agriculture and that the most productive farmland is in the Po Valley.
- Tell students that the climate of the Iberian Peninsula is conducive to agriculture. Portugal is also noted for grapes and cork.

Focus on Reading and Writing

Reading The Resource File provides a worksheet to help students practice asking questions.

RF: Focus on Reading, Asking Questions

Writing The Resource File provides a worksheet to help students write a news report.

RF: Focus on Writing, Writing a News Report

Key to Differentiating Instruction

Below Level

Basic-level activities designed for all students encountering new material

At Level

Intermediate-level activities designed for average students

Above Level

Challenging activities designed for honors and gifted and talented students

Standard English Mastery

Activities designed to improve standard English usage

LS **Learning Styles**

CHAPTER **16**

Southern Europe

Essential Question How has climate influenced the land and people of Southern Europe?

? What You Will Learn...

In this chapter you will learn about four large countries located in Southern Europe—Greece, Italy, Spain, and Portugal. You will learn about the countries' long histories and the many groups that have influenced their societies. Finally, you will see how the countries' histories still affect their cultures and governments.

FOCUS ON READING AND WRITING

Asking Questions As you read a text, it can be helpful to ask yourself questions about what you are reading to be sure you understand it. One set of questions that you can use to test your understanding of a passage is the five Ws—who, what, when, where, and why. **See the lesson, Asking Questions, on page 531.**

Writing a News Report You are a newspaper reporter on special assignment in Southern Europe. Your editor has told you that many readers know about Southern Europe's past but not about the region today. After you read this chapter, you will write a news report about an imaginary event in a Southern European country today.

398 CHAPTER 16

Map showing Southern Europe with legend:
⬦ National capital
• Other city
0 — 100 — 200 Miles
0 — 100 — 200 Kilometers
Projection: Azimuthal Equal Area

ATLANTIC OCEAN

PORTUGAL — Porto, Douro R., Tagus River, Lisbon

SPAIN — Bilbao, Madrid, Valencia, Seville, Guadalquivir River, Granada, Ebro River

Strait of Gibraltar, Gibraltar (U.K.)

MOROCCO

Geography Mountains cover large areas of Southern Europe. The Dolomites, shown here, are in northern Italy.

Introduce the Chapter

At Level

Southern Europe

1. Draw attention to the map of Southern Europe. Have students locate each of the four countries. Then have them study the pictures in Section 1. What physical features do they notice? *rock formations, water, farmland, beaches*

2. Ask volunteers to tell what they already know about any of these countries. List their suggestions under each country's name on the board. Students who have family backgrounds related to one of these countries might be especially helpful. Have students copy the completed list on a sheet of paper. Explain that students can compare these lists with what they have learned after studying the history, culture, and present-day life of people in Portugal, Spain, Italy, and Greece.

LS **Verbal/Linguistic, Visual/Spatial**

Alternative Assessment Handbook, Rubric 11: Discussions

GERMANY

FRANCE

SWITZERLAND

AUSTRIA

Milan

Venice

Po River

Genoa

ITALY

SAN MARINO

Florence

ANDORRA

Barcelona

VATICAN CITY ☩ Rome

Balearic Islands

Sardinia

Naples

Adriatic Sea

Tyrrhenian Sea

Palermo

Ionian Sea

Sicily

ALGERIA

MALTA

TUNISIA

Mediterranean Sea

Thessaloniki

GREECE

TURKEY

Athens ☩

Aegean Sea

Crete

20°E

HISTORY

Humanism Triggers the Renaissance

↗ hmhsocialstudies.com **VIDEO**

map zone Geography Skills

Place Southern Europe occupies three large peninsulas and thousands of small islands in the Mediterranean Sea.
1. Identify What is the capital of Greece?
2. Interpret Why is Southern Europe also called Mediterranean Europe?

History Greece was the home of Europe's first great civilization. The ruins in Delphi are more than 2,300 years old.

Culture Bullfights are popular events in parts of Spain. Bullfighters, called matadors, are honored members of society.

399

Chapter Preview

Explore the Map and Pictures

Southern Europe: Political This map highlights the three large peninsulas of southern Europe: the Iberian Peninsula (Spain and Portugal), the Italian Peninsula (Italy), and the Balkan Peninsula (Greece). Remind students that a peninsula is a piece of land almost surrounded by water. Students should note that water surrounds most of Spain, Italy, and Greece. About half of Portugal borders water.

Analyzing Visuals Direct students' attention to the three pictures on these pages. What do students think of when they look at the snow-capped mountains? Do they admire the matador? The ruins in Delphi mark a sacred place for the ancient Greeks. Tell students they will learn more about ancient Greece in Section 2 of this chapter.

▶ Map Zone Transparency: Southern Europe: Political

↗ **hmhsocialstudies.com**
Teacher Resources

Differentiating Instruction

Struggling Readers [Below Level]

Allow students time to study the pictures in this chapter. Have them choose one or two pictures that interest them the most. Ask volunteers to identify their favorites. What interests them about the subjects of the pictures? What more would they like to learn about the subjects? On the board, list the subjects that students have chosen. **LS Verbal/Linguistic, Visual/Spatial**

📝 Alternative Assessment Handbook, Rubric 11: Discussions

Advanced/Gifted and Talented [Above Level]

Ask volunteers to research a few important facts about one subject from the list created in the Introduce the Chapter activity and prepare a brief oral report for the class. As time permits, students can present their reports at appropriate times during the teaching of this chapter.
LS Verbal/Linguistic

📝 Alternative Assessment Handbook, Rubric 24: Oral Presentations

Answers

Map Zone 1. *Athens;* **2.** *Most of the coastline borders the Mediterranean Sea.*

400 CHAPTER 16

Preteach

Bellringer

If YOU lived there. . . Use the **Daily Bellringer Transparency** to help students answer the question.

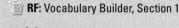 Daily Bellringer Transparency, Section 1

Southern Europe   Daily Bellringer
      Section 1

Preview Section 1

If YOU lived there . . .

You are in a busy fish market in a small town on the coast of Italy, near the Mediterranean Sea. It is early morning. Colorful fishing boats have just pulled into shore with their catch of fresh fish and seafood. They unload their nets of slippery octopus and wriggling shrimp. Others bring silvery sea bass. You are looking forward to lunch—perhaps a tasty fish soup or pasta dish.

How does the Mediterranean affect your life?

Consider how it affects what you EAT:
- variety of fresh fish and seafood
- fresh farm products, because of mild climate
- recipes reflect Mediterranean cuisine

Consider how it affects what you DO:
- good for swimming
- could go sailing or boating
- can fish year-round

Key Terms and Places

 RF: Vocabulary Builder, Section 1

Taking Notes

Have students use the graphic organizer online to take notes on the section. This activity will prepare students for the Section Assessment, in which they will complete a graphic organizer that builds on the information using the Critical Thinking Skill: Finding Main Ideas.

Physical Geography

What You Will Learn...

Main Ideas

1. Southern Europe's physical features include rugged mountains and narrow coastal plains.
2. The region's climate and resources support such industries as agriculture, fishing, and tourism.

The Big Idea

The peninsulas of Southern Europe have rocky terrains and sunny, mild climates.

Key Terms and Places

Mediterranean Sea, *p. 400*
Pyrenees, *p. 401*
Apennines, *p. 401*
Alps, *p. 401*
Mediterranean climate, *p. 402*

hmhsocialstudies.com
TAKING NOTES

Use the graphic organizer online to take notes on the physical geography of Southern Europe.

If YOU lived there...

You are in a busy fish market in a small town on the coast of Italy, near the Mediterranean Sea. It is early morning. Colorful fishing boats have just pulled into shore with their catch of fresh fish and seafood. They unload their nets of slippery octopus and wriggling shrimp. Others bring silvery sea bass. You are looking forward to lunch—perhaps a tasty fish soup or pasta dish.

How does the Mediterranean affect your life?

BUILDING BACKGROUND The Mediterranean Sea has shaped the geography, climate, and culture of Southern Europe. All of these countries have long coastlines, with good harbors and beautiful beaches. Because much of the interior is rugged and mountainous, the sea has also been a highway for trade and travel.

Physical Features

The continent of Europe has often been called a peninsula of peninsulas. Why do you think this is so? Look at the map of Europe in this book's Atlas to find out. Notice how Europe juts out from Asia like one big peninsula. Also, notice how smaller peninsulas extend into the many bodies of water that surround the continent.

Look at the map of Europe again. Do you see the three large peninsulas that extend south from Europe? From west to east, these are the Iberian Peninsula, the Italian Peninsula, and the Balkan Peninsula. Together with some large islands, they form the region of Southern Europe.

Southern Europe is also known as Mediterranean Europe. All of the countries of Southern Europe have long coastlines on the **Mediterranean Sea**. In addition to this common location on the Mediterranean, the countries of Southern Europe share many common physical features.

Teach the Big Idea
At Level

Physical Geography

1. **Teach** Ask students the questions in the Main Idea boxes under Direct Teach.

2. **Apply** Divide the class into three groups. Ask one group to name and describe the landforms of southern Europe, another group the bodies of water, and a third group the climate and resources. Allow the groups time to share opinions. **LS Verbal/Linguistic**

3. **Review** Have each group report to the class. After each group is finished, have the class add information if appropriate.

4. **Practice/Homework** Have students write one paragraph describing the landforms of southern Europe and another describing the climate and resources. **LS Verbal/Linguistic**

    Alternative Assessment Handbook, Rubric 40: Writing to Describe

Landforms

The three peninsulas of Southern Europe are largely covered with rugged mountains. In Greece, for example, about three-fourths of the land is mountainous. Because much of the land is so rugged, farming and travel in Southern Europe can be a challenge.

The mountains of Southern Europe form several large ranges. On the Iberian Peninsula, the **Pyrenees** (PIR-uh-neez) form a boundary between Spain and France to the north. Italy has two major ranges. The **Apennines** (A-puh-nynz) run along the whole peninsula, and the **Alps**—Europe's highest mountains—are in the north. The Pindus Mountains cover much of Greece.

Southern Europe's mountains extend into the sea as well, where they rise above the water to form islands. The Aegean Sea east of Greece is home to more than 2,000 such islands. Southern Europe also has many larger islands formed by undersea mountains. These include Crete, which is south of Greece; Sicily, at the southern tip of Italy; and many others.

Not all of Southern Europe is rocky and mountainous, though. Some flat plains lie in the region. Most of these plains are along the coast and in the valleys of major rivers. It is here that most farming in Southern Europe takes place. It is also here that most of the region's people live.

FOCUS ON READING

As you read, ask yourself this question: Where are the Pyrenees?

Southern Europe: Physical

ELEVATION

Feet		Meters
13,120		4,000
6,560		2,000
1,640		500
656		200
(Sea level) 0		0 (Sea level)
Below sea level		Below sea level

Projection: Azimuthal Equal-Area

Geography Skills

Region The countries of Southern Europe lie on three peninsulas that extend into the Mediterranean Sea.
1. **Name** What mountain range separates Spain from the rest of Europe?
2. **Interpret** In what ways might mountains affect life in this region?

Southern Europe is known for mountains and seas. On Greece's coast, these two features come together to create a dramatic landscape.

401

hmhsocialstudies.com INTERACTIVE MAP

Direct Teach

Main Idea

① Physical Features

Southern Europe's physical features include rugged mountains and narrow coastal plains.

Recall What type of landform covers much of southern Europe? *rugged mountains*

Identify What areas of southern Europe are ideal for farming? *coastal plains and river valleys*

Draw Conclusions Why do you think most people live in the coastal plains and river valleys? *There are more ways to earn a living.*

▶ Map Zone Transparency: Southern Europe: Physical

📑 RF: Geography for Life, The Mediterranean Sea

📑 RF: Critical Thinking, Is Venice Slipping Away?

Did you know...

The highest peak in the
- Alps is Mont Blanc on the French-Italian border—15,771 ft.
- Pyrenees is Aneto—11,168 ft.
- Apennines is the Great Rock of Italy—9,554 ft.
- Pindus is Mount Smolikos—8,652 ft.
- U.S. is Mount McKinley (Alaska)—20,320 ft.
- world is Mount Everest (Nepal/Tibet)—29,035 ft.

🔗 hmhsocialstudies.com
Online Resources
Activity: The Mediterranean

Critical Thinking: Analyzing Maps

At Level

Studying Southern Europe

1. Allow students time to study the physical map of southern Europe on this page.

2. Have students locate the three peninsulas, four mountain ranges, four seas, and two rivers mentioned in the text.

3. Draw attention to the Map Zone feature and ask volunteers to answer the questions. Follow up with these questions: What sea borders Greece on the west? *Ionian* What sea does the river Po empty into? *Adriatic* Where does the Po begin? *in the Alps* Through what two countries does the Tagus River flow? *Spain and Portugal* What areas of southern Europe have the lowest elevation? *coastal areas, particularly the west coast of Portugal and the northeast and east coast of Italy* Where is the highest elevation? *in the Alps* What separates Spain from northern Africa? *the Strait of Gibraltar*

🅛🅢 **Verbal/Linguistic, Visual/Spatial**

📖 Alternative Assessment Handbook, Rubric 21: Map Reading

Answers

Focus on Reading *in northern Spain*
Map Zone 1. *travel, transportation, industry;* **2.** *because it borders the Mediterranean Sea*

401

Main Idea

❷ Climate and Resources

The region's climate and resources support such industries as agriculture, fishing, and tourism.

Recall Name two important resources in southern Europe. *climate, the sea*

Analyze Why is the sea important to southern Europe's economy? *Port cities ship goods around the world, and fish and shellfish support the fishing industry.*

Draw Conclusions What kinds of things might this region export? *citrus fruits, grapes, olives, wheat, fish*

Info to Know

Two Important Rivers The Tagus River, which is 626 miles long, begins in central Spain and flows west through Portugal to the Atlantic Ocean. It empties at Lisbon, one of Europe's major port cities. The Po River, which is about 405 miles long, flows from the Alps to the Adriatic Sea. Ships from the Adriatic carry freight up the Po as far as Turin, which is an important industrial city in northern Italy.

Answers

Reading Check *rugged mountains, coastal plains, river valleys, islands, seas, and rivers*

402

Close-up

Mediterranean Climate

Southern Europe is known for its Mediterranean climate, which features warm, dry summers and mild, wet winters. This climate affects nearly every aspect of life in the region.

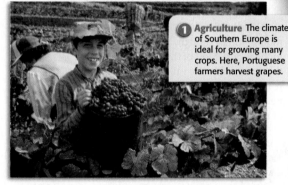

❶ **Agriculture** The climate of Southern Europe is ideal for growing many crops. Here, Portuguese farmers harvest grapes.

PORTUGAL
SPAIN
1
2

❷ **Tourism** The region's mild and sunny climate draws millions of tourists to places like this beach in Ibiza, Spain.

Water Features

Since Southern Europe is mostly peninsulas and islands, water is central to the region's geography. No place in Southern Europe is very far from a major body of water. The largest of these bodies of water is the Mediterranean, but the Adriatic, Aegean, and Ionian seas are also important to the region. For many centuries, these seas have given the people of Southern Europe food and a relatively easy way to travel around the region.

Only a few large rivers run through Southern Europe. The region's longest river is the Tagus (TAY-guhs), which flows across the Iberian Peninsula. In northern Italy, the Po runs through one of Southern Europe's most fertile and densely populated areas. Other rivers run out of the mountains and into the many surrounding seas.

READING CHECK **Finding Main Ideas** What are the region's major features?

Climate and Resources

Southern Europe is famous for its pleasant climate. Most of the region enjoys warm, sunny days and mild nights for most of the year. Little rain falls in the summer, falling instead during the mild winter. In fact, the type of climate found across Southern Europe is called a **Mediterranean climate** because it is common in this region.

The region's climate is also one of its most valuable resources. The mild climate is ideal for growing a variety of crops, from citrus fruits and grapes to olives and wheat. In addition, millions of tourists are drawn to the region each year by its climate, beaches, and breathtaking scenery.

402 CHAPTER 16

Differentiating Instruction

Below Level

Struggling Readers

1. Draw attention to the Close-up feature on Mediterranean climate. Point out the numbers on each picture and the numbered locations on the map. Explain to students that the pictures illustrate scenes from the numbered locations on the map.

2. Have students study the first picture and read its caption. Then ask: Where was this picture taken? *in wine-growing region of Portugal* What aspect of life is affected by the climate in this picture? *the growing of crops*

3. Repeat this procedure with the other three pictures. (For the second picture, point out that Ibiza is an island.) Use the Analyzing Visuals question to review the influence of climate on southern Europe.

LS **Verbal/Linguistic, Visual/Spatial**

📖 Alternative Assessment Handbook, Rubric 21: Map Reading

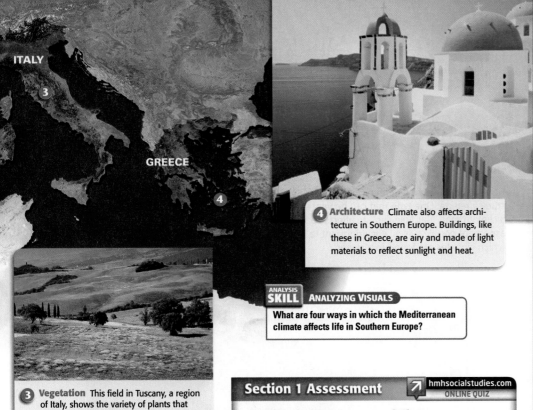

ITALY

GREECE

4 Architecture Climate also affects architecture in Southern Europe. Buildings, like these in Greece, are airy and made of light materials to reflect sunlight and heat.

ANALYSIS SKILL ANALYZING VISUALS

What are four ways in which the Mediterranean climate affects life in Southern Europe?

3 Vegetation This field in Tuscany, a region of Italy, shows the variety of plants that thrive in Southern Europe's climate.

The sea is also an important resource in Southern Europe. Many of the region's largest cities are ports, which ship goods all over the world. In addition, the nearby seas are full of fish and shellfish, which provide the basis for profitable fishing industries.

READING CHECK Generalizing How is a mild climate important to Southern Europe?

SUMMARY AND PREVIEW In this section you learned about the physical features of Southern Europe. In the next section you will learn how those features affect life in one country—Greece.

Section 1 Assessment

hmhsocialstudies.com
ONLINE QUIZ

Reviewing Ideas, Terms, and Places

1. **a. Recall** Which three peninsulas are in Southern Europe?
   b. Explain Why is the sea important to Southern Europe?
   c. Elaborate Why do you think most people in Southern Europe live on coastal plains or in river valleys?
2. **a. Describe** What is the **Mediterranean climate** like?
   b. Generalize How is climate an important resource for the region?

Critical Thinking

3. **Finding Main Ideas** Draw a diagram like the one shown here.

   Landforms   Climate

   In the left oval, use your notes to explain how landforms affect life in Southern Europe. In the right oval, explain how climate affects life in the region.

Focus on Writing

4. **Describing the Setting** Your news report will be about an imaginary event someplace in Southern Europe. That event might happen on a beach, in the mountains, or on a farm. Write some ideas in your notebook.

SOUTHERN EUROPE **403**

Direct Teach

Did you know. . .

The climate of a particular location depends on five factors: latitude, altitude, surface features, distance from large bodies of water, and circulation of the atmosphere. Southern Europe's Mediterranean climate is also considered a subtropical dry summer climate.

Info to Know

The Highland Climate A highland climate is common in mountainous regions. This climate varies with the altitude. A location in this climate might be mild in the foothills, much cooler further up, and very cold at the top.

Review & Assess

Close

Have students discuss the major physical features of southern Europe and the ways in which climate and resources affect life in the region.

Review

Online Quiz, Section 1

Assess

SE Section 1 Assessment
PASS: Section 1 Quiz
Alternative Assessment Handbook

Reteach/Classroom Intervention

Guided Reading Workbook, Section 1
Interactive Skills Tutor CD-ROM

Section 1 Assessment Answers

1. **a.** Iberian, Italian, and Baltic
   b. It provides food and a way to travel and transport goods through the region.
   c. more ways to earn a living
2. **a.** hot, dry summers and mild, wet winters
   b. It's ideal for growing crops and bringing tourists.
3. possible answers: Landforms—The rugged mountains are less populated; The coastal plains and river valleys are ideal for farming; Most of the people live there; Climate—It is good for agriculture, tourism, and has lush

vegetation; Because of the sunlight and heat, buildings are airy and made of light materials.

4. Students' notes will vary but should be based on details from this section.

Answers

Reading Check *It is ideal for growing crops, and it encourages tourism.*
Analyzing Visuals *agriculture, tourism, vegetation, and architecture*

Social Studies Skills

Reading a Climate Map

Activity Read a U.S. Climate Map

Materials: U.S. climate map, U.S. political map

1. Tell students they are going to use information from a climate map to describe the climates of various locations in the United States.

2. Distribute copies of a U. S. climate map. As a class, locate your local community (the general area) and have students identify its type of climate. Ask volunteers to offer examples of weather patterns that illustrate this type of climate.

3. Have students work in pairs. Choose four major cities and assign each pair one of these cities. (If major cities are not shown on the climate map, supply students with a political map as well.)

4. Ask each pair to brainstorm what they already know about the climate of the city they have been assigned. Then have them compare their ideas to the description in the map key.

5. As a class, review the climates of the four cities. Discuss how students' ideas compared to the descriptions in the map key. **LS** **Visual/Spatial**

- Alternative Assessment Handbook, Rubric 21: Map Reading
- Interactive Skills Tutor CD-ROM, Lesson 6: Interpret Maps, Graphs, Charts, Visuals, and Political Cartoons
- RF: Social Studies Skills, Reading a Climate Map

Answers

Practice 1. *steppe;* 2. *Bern;*
3. *Mediterranean*

Apply *Students should offer trip preparation details that are appropriate to the climate they have selected.*

404

Reading a Climate Map

Learn

Geographers use many different types of maps to study a region. One type that can be very useful is a climate map. Because climate affects so many aspects of people's lives, it is important to know which climates are found in a region.

Practice

Use the climate map of Europe below to answer the following questions.

1 What does orange mean on this map?

2 What city has a highland climate?

3 What is the dominant climate in the countries of Southern Europe?

Europe: Climate

Climate Types
- Steppe
- Mediterranean
- Humid subtropical
- Marine west coast
- Humid continental
- Subarctic
- Tundra
- Ice cap
- Highland

0   300   600 Miles
0   300   600 Kilometers

Projection: Azimuthal Equal-Area

ATLANTIC OCEAN

Stockholm
London
Paris
Bern
Lisbon   Madrid   Rome
Mediterranean Sea
Athens
Black Sea

Apply

Choose one of the cities shown on the map above. Imagine that you are planning a trip to that city and need to know what the climate is like so you can prepare. Use the map to identify the type of climate found in your chosen city. Then use the library or the Internet to find out more about that type of climate. Write a short description of the climate and how you could prepare for it.

404 CHAPTER 16

Social Studies Skills Activity

Below Level

Reading a Climate Map

1. For students having difficulty interpreting the map in the textbook or in the activity on this page, monitor students' progress in reading the map. Draw their attention to the key. Point out the colors (or background pattern if the map is black and white) assigned to each climate type and connect them to the colors on the map. Model the connection by pointing to a color on the map and having students find it in the key.

2. Discuss why climate maps are useful. Have students explain how they can use a climate map to help them make decisions about where they want to travel and how they need to prepare. Ask volunteers to explain their ideas. Can a climate map affect the time of year they travel, the activities they plan, or what they bring on a trip? How? **LS** **Verbal/Linguistic, Visual/Spatial**

- Alternative Assessment Handbook, Rubric 21: Map Reading

Greece

If **YOU** lived there...

You live in a small town on one of the many Greek islands. White houses perch on steep streets leading down to the sea. Many tourists come here by boat after visiting the busy capital city of Athens. They tell you about the beautiful ancient buildings they saw there. But your island has ancient statues and temple sites too. Still, some of your friends talk about moving to the city.

What might make people move to the city?

> **BUILDING BACKGROUND** In recent years, many people have moved out of Greece's small towns and villages into cities, especially Athens. Now the capital of Greece, Athens is an ancient city. It was home to one of Europe's greatest civilizations, one whose influence is still felt today all around the world.

History

Greece is a country steeped in history. Home to one of the world's oldest civilizations, it has been called the birthplace of Western culture. Even today, remnants of ancient Greece can be found all over the country, and ideas from ancient thinkers continue to affect people's lives today.

Ancient Greece

Theater. Philosophy. Democracy. These are just a few of the ideas that the modern world owes to ancient Greece. The Greeks were pioneers in many fields, and their contributions still affect how we live and think.

In art, the Greeks created lifelike paintings and statues that served as examples for later artists to imitate. In architecture, they built stately temples of marble that continue to inspire architects around the world.

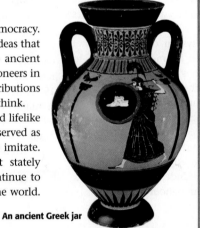
An ancient Greek jar

What You Will Learn...

Main Ideas

1. Early in its history, Greece was the home of a great civilization, but it was later ruled by foreign powers.
2. The Greek language, the Orthodox Church, and varied customs have helped shape Greece's culture.
3. In Greece today, many people are looking for new economic opportunities.

The Big Idea

The home of one of the Western world's oldest civilizations, Greece is trying to reclaim its place as a leading country in Europe.

Key Terms and Places

Orthodox Church, *p. 407*
Athens, *p. 408*

hmhsocialstudies.com
TAKING NOTES

Use the graphic organizer online to take notes on Greek history and culture.

Bellringer

If YOU lived there. . . Use the **Daily Bellringer Transparency** to help students answer the question.

Daily Bellringer Transparency, Section 2

Key Terms and Places

RF: Vocabulary Builder, Section 2

Taking Notes

Have students use the graphic organizer online to take notes on the section. This activity will prepare students for the Section Assessment, in which they will complete a graphic organizer that builds on the information using the Critical Thinking Skill: Categorizing.

Teach the Big Idea

At Level

Greece

1. **Teach** Ask students the questions in the Main Idea boxes under Direct Teach.

2. **Apply** Draw a three-column chart on the board and have students copy it and fill it in.

History	Culture	Greece Today

3. **Review** As a class, fill in the chart on the board. Have students volunteer facts from their own charts.

4. **Practice/Homework** Tell students to take their charts home and present the information to their families. Have them ask their families for questions about the information. Tell them to bring one question that their families asked to class. Discuss the answers for students to take home.

   LS Verbal/Linguistic, Interpersonal

   Alternative Assessment Handbook, Rubric 7: Charts

Main Idea

❶ History

Early in its history, Greece was the home of a great civilization, but it was later ruled by foreign powers.

Identify What did the ancient Greeks accomplish in art, literature, math, and government? *lifelike statues and paintings; new forms of literature, including history and drama; advances in geometry; creation of democracy*

Identify Who took over Greece during the 1300s and 1400s? *the Ottoman Turks*

Summarize How did Greece finally achieve a return to democracy? *They rebelled against the Turks and later got rid of a dictatorship.*

📖 **RF:** Biography, Aristotle

Biography

Alexander the Great As a young man, Alexander the Great was tutored by the Greek philosopher Aristotle. Aristotle believed that both the mind and the body should be trained. Alexander was taught literature, philosophy, and politics, as well as fitness and warfare. He conquered Greece at age eighteen. At age twenty, he became king. After his father died, he carried out his father's plan to conquer the Persian Empire. When he died, his empire stretched from Greece to India.

Answers

Connecting to Math *Architects used the Golden Mean, a mathematical formula for determining the height and width of a building.*

Focus on Reading *Alexander the Great*

Reading Check *the Romans, Byzantines, and Ottoman Turks*

CONNECTING TO Math

Proportion

The ancient Greeks were great admirers of mathematics. They thought math could be used in many areas of their lives. For example, they used it to design temples and other buildings.

Greek builders believed in a concept called the Golden Mean. This concept said that the height of a building should be a particular fraction of the building's width. If the building were too tall, they thought it would look flimsy. If it were too wide, it would look squat and ugly. As a result, these builders were very careful in planning their buildings. The Parthenon, the temple pictured below, was built using the Golden Mean. Many consider it to be the greatest of all Greek temples.

Generalizing How did mathematical ideas influence ancient Greek architecture?

FOCUS ON READING

As you read, ask yourself this question: Who conquered Greece in the 300s BC?

They invented new forms of literature, including history and drama, and made advances in geometry and other branches of math that we still study. In philosophy, they created a system of reasoning that is the foundation for modern science. In government, they created democracy, which inspired the government embraced by most people around the world today.

No ancient civilization lasted forever, though. In the 300s BC Greece became a part of Alexander the Great's empire, which also included Egypt and much of Southwest Asia. Under Alexander, Greek culture spread throughout his empire.

The Romans and the Turks

Alexander's empire did not last very long. When it broke up, Greece became part of another empire, the Roman Empire. For about 300 years, the Greeks lived under Roman rule.

After about AD 400 the Roman Empire was divided into two parts. Greece became part of the Eastern, or Byzantine, Empire. The rulers of the Byzantine Empire admired Greek culture and encouraged people to adopt the Greek language and customs. They also encouraged people to adopt their religion, Christianity.

Greece was part of the Byzantine Empire for about 1,000 years. In the 1300s and 1400s, however, Greece was taken over by the Ottoman Turks from central Asia. The Turks were Muslim, but they allowed the people of Greece to remain Christian. Some elements of Greek culture, though, began to fade. For example, many people began speaking Turkish instead of Greek.

Independent Greece

Many Greeks were not happy under Turkish rule. They wanted to be free of foreign influences. In the early 1800s, they rose up against the Turks. The rebellion seemed likely to fail, but the Greeks received help from other European countries and drove the Turks out. After the rebellion, Greece became a monarchy.

Greece's government has changed many times since independence. The country's first kings took steps toward restoring democracy, but for most of the 1900s the nation experienced instability. A military dictatorship ruled from 1967 to 1974. More recently, democracy has once again taken root in the country where it was born nearly 2,500 years ago.

READING CHECK **Sequencing** What groups have ruled Greece throughout history?

Collaborative Learning

Above Level

Using Graphic Organizers To Understand Concepts

Research Required

1. Create groups of four to five students. As a class, discuss the differences between a direct democracy and an indirect democracy. Point out that ancient Greece created a political form called direct democracy—all citizens voted on laws and for leaders.

2. Have each group do research to determine the positive and negative aspects of a direct democracy when compared to an indirect democracy. Encourage students to identify the characteristics and organization of indirect democracies and direct democracies.

3. Ask each group to create a compare and contrast chart of their research facts to use in a debate about whether direct or indirect democracy is more practical.

LS **Verbal/Linguistic, Visual/Spatial**

📖 Alternative Assessment Handbook, Rubrics 10: Debates; and 11: Discussions

Culture

Over the course of its history, many factors have combined to shape Greece's culture. These factors include the Greek language, Christianity, and customs adopted from the many groups who have ruled Greece.

Language and Religion

The people of Greece today speak a form of the same language their ancestors spoke long ago. In fact, Greek is one of the oldest languages still spoken in Europe today. The language has changed greatly over time, but it was never lost.

Although the Greeks maintained their language, their ancient religions have long since disappeared. Today nearly everyone in Greece belongs to the **Orthodox Church**, a branch of Christianity that dates to the Byzantine Empire. Religion is important to the Greeks, and holidays such as Easter are popular times for celebration.

Customs

Greek customs reflect the country's long history and its physical geography. Greek food, for example, is influenced both by products native to Greece and by groups who have ruled Greece over time.

Ingredients such as lamb, olives, and vegetables are easily available in Greece because they grow well there. As a result, the Greeks use lots of these ingredients in their cooking. Greek cuisine was later enhanced with ideas borrowed from other people. From the Turks, the Greeks learned to cook with yogurt and honey, and from the Italians they learned about pasta.

Greek meals are often eaten at family gatherings. For centuries, family has been central to Greek culture. Even as Greece is becoming more modernized, the family has remained the cornerstone of society.

READING CHECK **Summarizing** What are two dominant elements of Greek culture?

• **Direct Teach** •

Main Idea

❷ **Culture**

The Greek language, the Orthodox Church, and varied customs have helped shape Greece's culture.

Recall In what religion do most of the people in Greece believe? *the Orthodox Church*

Identify What is the cornerstone of Greek society? *the family*

Analyze How have Greece's history and its physical geography influenced its cuisine? *The Greeks rely on ingredients that grow well in their region, and they have borrowed recipe ideas from the Turks and the Italians.*

Connect to Literature

The Deities of Ancient Greece In ancient Greece, people believed in many gods and goddesses called *deities*. These deities had supernatural powers and the people believed the gods and goddesses controlled their lives. The most important deity was Zeus, ruler of Mount Olympus. Other major deities were Aphrodite, Apollo, and Athena. Myths about the adventures of these gods and goddesses have been handed down for centuries and are still read today. References to them pervade our popular culture—in literature, television, movies, and advertising.

↗ **hmhsocialstudies.com**

Online Resources
Activity: Greek Mythology

Easter in Greece

Easter is one of the most sacred days of the year for Orthodox Christians. All over Greece, people celebrate Easter with festivals, feasts, and special rituals.

ANALYZING VISUALS What evidence in this photo suggests that Easter is a major celebration?

The priests carry containers of holy water. Later, they will sprinkle this holy water on crowds as part of a blessing.

Priests wear richly decorated robes as part of their Easter celebration.

Many Easter ceremonies are led by an archbishop, a high-ranking official in the Orthodox Church.

SOUTHERN EUROPE **407**

Differentiating Instruction

At Level

Special Needs Learners

1. Draw attention to the photo on this page. Discuss the content, including the Analyzing Visuals question, after students have had time to read the introduction and the captions. Ask students familiar with the Orthodox religion to offer additional information.

2. Encourage students to share information about religious festivals and feasts they know about. If time permits, invite them to bring to class items related to such celebrations. Set aside 15 minutes for an informal show-and-tell.

3. Remind students that the family is the cornerstone of Greek society. Conclude by discussing how feasts help to bind families together. **LS** **Verbal/Linguistic, Visual/Spatial**

📃 Alternative Assessment Handbook, Rubric 29: Presentations

Answers

Reading Check *strong family ties, the Orthodox Church*

Analyzing Visuals *conducting a special Easter ritual, special robes*

❸ Greece Today

In Greece today, many people are looking for new economic opportunities.

Describe What is life like in Greece's rural mountain villages? *People are isolated. They grow crops and raise sheep and goats. They socialize in village squares.*

Cause and Effect What problem has resulted from the growth of industry in Athens? *air pollution, which damages the ancient ruins and people's health*

Summarize What is the state of Greece's economy? *It is not as strong as other European countries, but it is growing due to increased tourism.*

▶ Map Zone Transparency: Greece: Population

Info to Know

Rural Exodus In recent years more and more people have moved from the rural mountain regions of Greece to the cities, leaving small farms abandoned. The most successful farms today are located in the plains. Many Greeks who have moved to the cities maintain strong ties to the villages they came from, and some still own homes in those villages.

Answers

Map Zone 1. *Athens;* **2.** *Most people live on the plains or in cities where there are more job opportunities.*

408

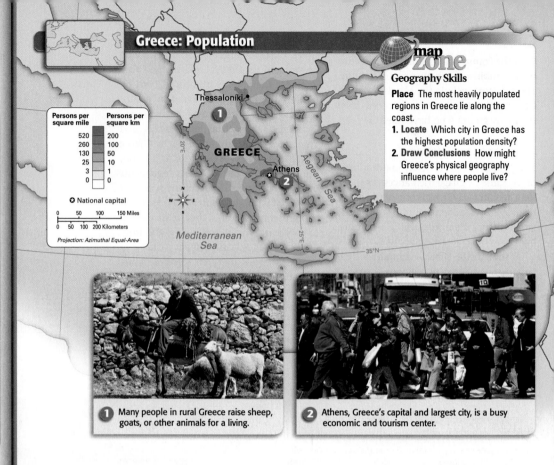

Greece: Population

Persons per square mile | Persons per square km
520 | 200
260 | 100
130 | 50
25 | 10
3 | 1
0 | 0

✪ National capital

0 50 100 150 Miles
0 50 100 200 Kilometers
Projection: Azimuthal Equal-Area

Thessaloníki ● ①
GREECE
Athens
②
Aegean Sea
Mediterranean Sea

map zone

Geography Skills

Place The most heavily populated regions in Greece lie along the coast.

1. Locate Which city in Greece has the highest population density?

2. Draw Conclusions How might Greece's physical geography influence where people live?

① Many people in rural Greece raise sheep, goats, or other animals for a living.

② Athens, Greece's capital and largest city, is a busy economic and tourism center.

Greece Today

When many people think of Greece now, they think about the country's history. In fact, Greece's past often overshadows its present. Today, though, Greece is a largely urbanized society with a rapidly growing and diverse economy.

Urban and Rural Greece

About three-fifths of all people in Greece today live in cities. Of these cities, **Athens**—the nation's capital—is by far the largest. In fact, almost one-third of the country's entire population lives in or around the city of Athens.

Athens is a huge city where old and new mix. Modern skyscrapers rise high above the ancient ruins of Greek temples. Most of the country's industry is centered there. However, this industry has resulted in air pollution, which damages the ancient ruins and causes health problems.

Outside of the city, Greek life is very different. People in rural areas still live largely as people have lived for centuries. Many live in isolated mountain villages, where they grow crops and raise sheep and goats. Village life often centers around the village square. People meet there to discuss local events and make decisions.

408 CHAPTER 16

Critical Thinking: Drawing Conclusions

At Level

Greece's Population and Economy

1. Have students study the population map on this page. Draw attention to the key and stress that the numbers in the key represent the average number of people who live within one square mile. Ask: What areas are the most populated? *areas near the coast* What areas are the least populated? *some of the small islands* What conclusion can you draw about some of the small islands? *They may not be very habitable.*

2. Have students study the economic chart on the next page. Solicit answers to the question at the bottom of the chart. Then ask: What conclusion can you draw from the information in the chart? *Greece's economy has shown steady growth in the last decade.*

3. Discuss why Greece's economy lags behind other European countries and outline Greece's plan for the future.

LS Verbal/Linguistic, Visual/Spatial

Alternative Assessment Handbook, Rubric 12: Drawing Conclusions

Greece's Economy

Although Greece is experiencing rapid economic growth, it still lags behind some other European nations. This lag is largely caused by a lack of resources. Greece has few mineral resources, and only about one-fifth of its land can be farmed. The rest of the land is too rugged.

One industry in which Greece excels is shipping. Greece has one of the largest shipping fleets in the world. Greek ships can be found in ports all around the world, loaded with cargo from countries in Europe and other parts of the world.

Another profitable industry in Greece is tourism. Millions of people from around the world visit every year. Some are drawn to ancient ruins in Athens and other parts of the country. Others prefer the sunny, sandy beaches of Greece's many islands. The Greek government actively promotes this tourism, and more people visit the country every year. Largely due to this tourism, Greece's GDP—the value of all its goods and services—has risen steadily in recent years.

READING CHECK Finding Main Ideas What are the most important industries in Greece?

THE WORLD ALMANAC
Facts about Countries

Per Capita GDP of Greece

Interpreting Graphs What was Greece's per capita GDP in 1994? What was it in 2004?

hmhsocialstudies.com

SUMMARY AND PREVIEW In this section you learned about Greece, a country with a long and varied history that still shapes its culture and economy today. In the next section you will learn about Italy, another country in the region that has been shaped by history.

Section 2 Assessment

hmhsocialstudies.com
ONLINE QUIZ

Reviewing Ideas, Terms, and Places

1. a. Identify What were two major achievements of the ancient Greeks?
b. Sequence What steps did the Greeks take to gain their independence?
2. a. Define What is the **Orthodox Church**?
b. Generalize What is one way in which Greece's history affects its culture today?
3. a. Describe What is life like in **Athens** today?
b. Explain Why is manufacturing not a major industry in Greece?
c. Evaluate Would you rather live in Athens or in rural Greece? Why?

Critical Thinking

4. Categorizing Draw a table like the one here. Use the table to organize your notes into columns about Greece's history, its culture, and Greece today.

Greece		
History	Culture	Today

FOCUS ON WRITING

5. Introducing Greece If you choose Greece for the site of your news report, what would be a good topic? The movement of people to the cities? An event at a historic site? Jot down your ideas.

SOUTHERN EUROPE **409**

Section 2 Assessment Answers

1. a. possible answers—created lifelike paintings and statues, invented new forms of writing, made advances in geometry
b. rebelled against Turks, overthrew dictatorship
2. a. branch of Christianity from Byzantine Empire
b. speak same language as ancestors, food influenced by groups who ruled them, have strong sense of family
3. a. crowded, filled with modern buildings and old ruins, heavily industrial, polluted

b. There are few natural resources.
c. Accept all reasonable responses.

4. possible answers: History—300s BC to early 1800s, ruled by Romans, Byzantines, and Turks; overthrew Turks and dictatorship to become independent; Culture—influenced by language, Eastern Orthodox church, history; Today—rural life isolated, most people in cities; economy lagging, but tourism helping it grow

5. Students' ideas will vary but could include information about Greece's population, industry, villages, and economy.

• **Direct Teach** •

Did you know. . .

The islands of Greece can be divided into three groups: the Aegean Islands, the Ionian Islands, and Crete.

The Aegean Islands are between Greece and Turkey. Within this group, many tourists are drawn to the island of Thira, which has been identified by some scholars as the site of the lost continent of Atlantis.

The Ionian Islands are west of Greece. A popular tourist attraction within this group is Ithaca, celebrated in Homer's *Odyssey* as the home of Ulysses.

Crete is south of Greece. Large numbers of tourists visit Crete annually to see the ancient Minoan ruins at Knossos.

• Review & Assess •

Close

Have students discuss the achievements of the ancient Greeks and how customs influence life in Greece today.

Review

Online Quiz, Section 2

Assess

SE Section 2 Assessment
PASS: Section 2 Quiz
Alternative Assessment Handbook

Reteach/Classroom Intervention

Guided Reading Workbook, Section 2
Interactive Skills Tutor CD-ROM

Answers

Interpreting Graphs *about $9,000; just over $20,000*
Reading Check *tourism and shipping*

409

Bellringer

If YOU lived there. . . Use the **Daily Bellringer Transparency** to help students answer the question.

▶ Daily Bellringer Transparency, Section 3

Southern Europe — Daily Bellringer
Section 3

Review Section 2

Indicate whether each sentence below is **TRUE** or **FALSE**. If the sentence is false, change the underlined word to make the sentence true.

1. Greece was once ruled by the Roman Empire, the Byzantine Empire, and the Ottoman Turks.
2. Greece's capital and largest city is Alexandria.
3. Although Greece lags behind some countries economically, it has one of the world's largest airplane fleets.
4. Nearly everyone in Greece belongs to the Protestant Church.

Preview Section 3

If YOU lived there ...

You live in Rome, the historic heart of Italy. Wherever you walk in Rome, you see reminders of the city's long and rich history. It may be a 600-year-old church or a 2,000-year-old market. One of your favorite spots to visit is the Colosseum. When you sit inside this ancient arena, you can imagine fierce gladiators and wild animals fighting there long ago. **How does history affect life in Italy?**

Consider effects on CULTURE:
• The history of its arts, architecture, cooking, and fashions are still part of daily life.
• Religion continues to be a major influence in many people's lives.
• Government and legal systems are based on ancient Rome's systems.

Consider effects on ECONOMY:
• Tourist visits are important to economy.
• Traditional arts provide jobs.
• Its history of trade keeps Italy an important world economic leader.

Review Answers: 1. T; 2. F, Athens; 3. F, shipping; 4. F, Orthodox

Academic Vocabulary

Review with students the high-use academic terms in this section.

contemporary modern (p. 412)

incentive something that leads people to follow a certain course of action (p. 413)

📖 **RF:** Vocabulary Builder, Section 3

Taking Notes

Have students use the graphic organizer online to take notes on the section. This activity will prepare students for the Section Assessment, in which they will complete a graphic organizer that builds on the information using the Critical Thinking Skill: Comparing and Contrasting.

What You Will Learn...

Main Ideas

1. Italian history can be divided into three periods: ancient Rome, the Renaissance, and unified Italy.
2. Religion and local traditions have helped shape Italy's culture.
3. Italy today has two distinct economic regions—northern Italy and southern Italy.

The Big Idea

Once the center of a huge empire, Italy is now one of the most prosperous countries in Europe.

Key Terms and Places

pope, *p. 412*
Vatican City, *p. 412*
Sicily, *p. 413*
Naples, *p. 413*
Milan, *p. 413*
Rome, *p. 414*

hmhsocialstudies.com
TAKING NOTES

Use the graphic organizer online to take notes on Italian history, life, and culture.

If YOU lived there...

You live in Rome, the historic heart of Italy. Wherever you walk in Rome, you see reminders of the city's long and rich history. It may be a 600-year-old church or a 2,000-year-old market. One of your favorite spots to visit is the Colosseum. When you sit inside this ancient arena, you can imagine fierce gladiators and wild animals fighting there long ago.

How does history affect life in Italy?

BUILDING BACKGROUND Italian history continues to affect life in Italy today, but its influence extends far beyond that one country. All around the world, people owe their ideas about art, government, law, and language to Italy and its people. Many of these ideas are ancient, but even today Italians help shape the world's culture.

History

Greece may have been the birthplace of the first civilization in Europe, but Italy was the home of the continent's greatest empire. For centuries, Italy was the heart of one of the largest and most powerful states the world has ever seen. Even after that state collapsed, Italy remained a major influence on Europe and other parts of the world.

Ancient Rome

The great civilization that developed in Italy was Rome. Built in the 700s BC as a tiny village, Rome grew to control nearly all the land around the Mediterranean Sea. At the height of the Roman Empire, the Romans controlled an empire that stretched from Britain in the northwest to the Persian Gulf. It included most of Europe as well as parts of southwest Asia and northern Africa.

Roman influences in the world can still be seen today. The Romans' art, architecture, and literature are still admired. Their laws and political ideas have influenced the governments and legal systems of many countries. In addition, the Romans helped spread Christianity, one of the world's major religions.

Teach the Big Idea

Italy

1. **Teach** Ask students questions in the Main Idea boxes under Direct Teach.

2. **Apply** Create questions on slips of paper, based on information in this section. Put them in an open container. Divide the class into two teams. Have one team draw a question from the container and answer it. Allow time for the team to share opinions before they answer. Repeat with the second team and continue until all questions have been answered. **LS Verbal/Linguistic**

3. **Review** Discuss answers as needed. Have students use their textbook to search for information and details to explain answers.

4. **Practice/Homework** Ask students to write down at least three questions that confused them or about which they would like to know more. **LS Verbal/Linguistic**

📖 Alternative Assessment Handbook, Rubric 11: Discussions

The Renaissance

The Roman Empire collapsed in the AD 400s, largely due to weak leadership and invasions from outside. With no central government to unite them, Italy's cities formed their own states. Each had its own laws, its own government, and its own army. Wars between them were common.

As time passed, the cities of Italy became major centers of trade. Merchants from these cities traveled to far-off places like China to bring goods back to Europe.

Many merchants became very rich from this trade. With the money they made, these merchants sponsored artists and architects. Their support of the arts helped lead to the Renaissance, a period of great creativity in Europe. It lasted from about 1350 through the 1500s. During the Renaissance artists and writers—many of them Italian—created some of the world's greatest works of art and literature.

Unified Italy

Italy remained divided into small states until the mid-1800s. At that time, a rise in nationalism, or strong patriotic feelings for a country, led people across Italy to fight for unification. As a result of their efforts, Italy became a unified kingdom in 1861.

In the 1920s a new government came to power. Under Benito Mussolini, Italy became a dictatorship. That dictatorship was short-lived, however. Mussolini joined Hitler to fight other countries of Europe in World War II. In 1945 Italy was defeated.

After World War II, Italy became a democracy. Since that time, power has rested in an elected Parliament and prime minister. Also since the end of the war, Italy has developed one of the strongest economies in Europe.

READING CHECK Summarizing What are some key periods in the history of Italy?

Italian History

The history of Italy stretches back nearly 3,000 years. This long span includes several key periods.

Ancient Rome

- According to legend, the city of Rome was built in the 700s BC.
- The Romans created a huge empire. At its height, the empire included parts of Europe, Southwest Asia, and northern Africa.
- Roman art, architecture, literature, and law still influence people today.
- Christianity arose and spread in the Roman Empire.

Roman statue

The Renaissance

- The Renaissance was a period of great advances in art, architecture, and literature.
- The Renaissance began in the 1300s in cities like Florence.
- From Italy, the Renaissance spread to other parts of Europe.
- Some of the world's greatest works of art were created at this time.

Leonardo da Vinci's *Mona Lisa*

Unified Italy

- Since the Middle Ages, Italy had been divided into small states.
- In the mid-1800s, increased feelings of nationalism led people across Italy to fight for unification.
- The fight for unification was led by Giuseppe Garibaldi.
- Italy was officially unified in 1861.

Giuseppe Garibaldi

SOUTHERN EUROPE **411**

Main Idea

❷ Culture

Religion and local traditions have helped shape Italy's culture.

Recall Give three reasons why religion is important in the lives of Italians. *Most Italians are Roman Catholic. The pope lives in the Italian Peninsula. Religious holidays and festivals are major events.*

Make Inferences How do local traditions affect Italy's cuisine? *Food preparation varies from region to region based on local preferences and products.*

Analyze Why has Italy always been known as a center of the arts? *It has a long history as an artistic trendsetter and has produced some of the world's great artists.*

📄 **RF:** Primary Source, "The Creation of Adam" by Michelangelo

Did you know. . .

Vatican City has
- 200 residents and another 800 who come in daily to work.
- a radio station, a daily newspaper, a bank, a post office, and some stores.
- many museums that are open to the public and contain some of the greatest art treasures in the world.
- an army of 90 men, called the Swiss Guard, who protect the pope.

Answers

Reading Check *possible answers—Roman Catholic Church, cuisine based on local preferences, history of artistic trendsetting*

Analyzing Visuals *Answers will vary but should be supported with details from the text.*

Culture

For centuries, people around the world have admired and borrowed from Italian culture. Italy's culture has been shaped by many factors. Among these factors are the Roman Catholic Church, local traditions, and regional geography.

Religion

Most people in Italy belong to the Roman Catholic Church. Historically, the church has been the single strongest influence on Italian culture. This influence is strong in part because the **pope**, the spiritual head of the Roman Catholic Church, lives on the Italian Peninsula. He resides in **Vatican City**, an independent state located within the city of Rome.

The lasting importance of the church can be seen in many ways in Italy. For example, the city of Rome alone is home to hundreds of Catholic churches from all periods of history. In addition, religious holidays and festivals are major events.

ACADEMIC VOCABULARY
contemporary
modern

Local Traditions

In addition to religion, local traditions have influenced Italian culture. Italian food, for example, varies widely from region to region. These variations are based on local preferences and products. All over Italy, people eat many of the same foods—olives, tomatoes, rice, pasta. However, the ways in which people prepare this food differ. In the south, for example, people often serve pasta with tomato sauces. In the north, creamy sauces are much more common.

Other traditions reflect Italy's past. For example, Italy has always been known as a center of the arts. The people of Italy have long been trendsetters, shaping styles that are later adopted by other people. As a result, the Italians are leaders in many **contemporary** art forms. For example, Italy has produced some of the world's greatest painters, sculptors, authors, composers, fashion designers, and filmmakers.

READING CHECK Finding Main Ideas What are two major influences on Italian culture?

Major Cities of Italy

Milan, Rome, and Naples are the three largest cities in Italy. Because of their varied histories and locations, each city has a distinct landscape and culture.

ANALYZING VISUALS Which city would you most like to visit?

Milan • Venice • Florence • **ITALY** • Rome • Naples

412 CHAPTER 16

Milan Milan, the largest city in Italy, is a global fashion capital. The clothes created there influence fashion designers around the world.

Collaborative Learning

At Level

Milan, Rome, and Naples

1. Have students work in pairs. If possible pair a struggling reader with a proficient one. Tell the pairs to identify the three cities pictured in the Major Cities of Italy feature and locate them on the map. Then have them read the information about these cities on the following pages.

2. Ask each pair to create a list of questions, using information they learned about each city. Have them exchange questions with another

pair and answer the questions they receive. Allow time for pairs to share opinions.

3. Ask volunteers from each pair to read and answer a question they received. Provide additional information as needed.

🔲 **Verbal/Linguistic**

📄 Alternative Assessment Handbook, Rubric 37: Writing Assignments

Italy Today

A shared language, the Roman Catholic Church, and strong family ties help bind Italians together. At the same time, though, major differences exist in the northern and southern parts of the country.

Southern Italy

Southern Italy is the country's poorer half. Its economy has less industry than the north and depends heavily on agriculture. Farming is especially important in **Sicily**, an island at the peninsula's tip. Tourism is also vital to the south's economy. Among the region's attractions are its dazzling beaches and ancient Roman ruins.

In recent decades, Italy's government has tried to promote industry in the south. It has offered <u>incentives</u>, such as lower taxes, to private companies that will build factories there. Many of these government efforts center on the city of **Naples**, a busy port and the largest city in southern Italy. Thanks to government programs, Naples is now also an industrial center.

Northern Italy

In contrast to southern Italy, the northern part of the country has a strong economy. Northern Italy includes the country's most fertile farmlands, its major trade centers, and its most popular tourist destinations.

The Po River valley in northern Italy has the country's most productive farmland. For decades, the Po valley has been called the breadbasket of Italy because most of the country's crops are grown there. Despite its fertile soils, farmers cannot grow enough to support Italy's population. Italy has to import much of its food.

The north is also home to Italy's major industrial centers. Busy factories in such cities as Turin and Genoa make appliances, automobiles, and other goods for export. **Milan** is also a major industrial center as well as a worldwide center for fashion design. The location of these cities near central Europe helps companies sell their goods to foreign customers. Railroads, highways, and tunnels make the shipment of goods through the Alps easy.

ACADEMIC VOCABULARY

incentive something that leads people to follow a certain course of action

Rome Rome, the capital of Italy, is in the central part of the country. A major center of banking and industry, Rome is also one of the world's most popular tourist sites.

Naples Naples is the most important city in southern Italy. Less glamorous than many northern cities, it is a port and manufacturing center.

SOUTHERN EUROPE **413**

Info to Know

Venice under Siege Twenty million tourists visit Venice every year. They represent just one of the reasons why Venice is in a constant battle to preserve itself. Other more important problems include a declining population, water pollution, air pollution, flooding, and sinking foundations. Many buildings are literally sinking in the water. Conservationists have been wrestling with these problems for years and are still searching for a permanent solution to Venice's predicament.

Review & Assess

Close

Have students discuss the three important periods in Italy's history and the differences between northern Italy and southern Italy today.

Review

⬀ Online Quiz, Section 3

Assess

SE   Section 3 Assessment

▤   PASS: Section 3 Quiz

▤   Alternative Assessment Handbook

Reteach/Classroom Intervention

▤   Guided Reading Workbook, Section 3

◉   Interactive Skills Tutor CD-ROM

Answers

Satellite View *Canals serve as roads through the city.*

Reading Check *Northern Italy has a stronger economy, more industry, better farmlands, and more popular tourist destinations than southern Italy.*

414

Satellite View

Venice

Venice, in northeastern Italy, is one of the country's most visited tourist attractions. Look at the image of Venice above, taken by an orbiting satellite. Does it look like other cities you have seen? What may not be obvious is that the paths that wind their way through the city are not roads, but canals. In fact, Venice has very few roads. This is because the city was built on islands—118 of them! People move about the city on boats that navigate along the canals. Every year, millions of tourists travel to Venice to see the sights as they are rowed along the scenic waterways.

Contrasting How is Venice unlike other cities you have studied?

Tens of millions of tourists visit the cities of northern Italy every year. They are drawn by the cities' rich histories and unique cultural features. Florence, for example, is a center of Italian art and culture. It was there that the Renaissance began in the 1300s. To the west of Florence is Pisa, famous for its Leaning Tower—the bell tower of the city's church. On the coast of the Adriatic Sea lies the city of Venice. Tourists are lured there by the romantic canals that serve as roads through the city.

Nestled in the center of the country is Italy's capital, **Rome**. With ties to both north and south, Rome does not fully belong to either region. From there, the country's leaders attempt to bring all the people of Italy together as one nation.

READING CHECK **Contrast** How are northern and southern Italy different?

SUMMARY AND PREVIEW In this section you read about Italy. The country's long history continues to affect life in Italy even today. Next, you will study two other countries whose pasts still affect life there—Spain and Portugal.

Section 3 Assessment

⬀ hmhsocialstudies.com
ONLINE QUIZ

Reviewing Ideas, Terms, and Places

1. **a. Describe** What was Renaissance Italy like?
   b. Interpret How did nationalism influence Italian history?
2. **a. Identify** What religion has had a major impact on Italian culture?
   b. Explain How have local traditions helped shape Italian culture?
3. **a. Recall** What is the main economic activity of southern Italy?
   b. Contrast How are the economies of **Milan**, **Rome**, and **Naples** different?
   c. Rate If you could visit any one city in Italy, which would it be? Why?

Critical Thinking

4. **Comparing and Contrasting** Draw two circles like the ones here. Using your notes, list details about southern Italy in the left circle and about northern Italy in the right circle. Where the circles overlap, list common features of the two.

   Southern Italy | Northern Italy

FOCUS ON WRITING

5. **Investigating Italy** What Italian event could you report on? Perhaps it could be a fashion show or a religious service at the Vatican. Make a list of events that could make an interesting report.

414 CHAPTER 16

Section 3 Assessment Answers

1. **a.** It was a period of great advances in art, architecture, and literature. Great works of art were created. This creativity spread to other parts of Europe.
   b. It inspired Italians to fight for unification.
2. **a.** the Roman Catholic Church
   b. Recipes vary from region to region, based on local preferences. Italy's reputation as a center for the arts makes it a worldwide trendsetter.
3. **a.** agriculture
   b. Milan—major industrial and fashion center; Rome—major center of banking, industry, and tourism; Naples—a busy port

c. Students should support their answers with details from the text.
4. possible answers: Northern Italy—fertile farmland, major industrial centers, center of fashion, most popular tourist destinations; Southern Italy—poorer than the north, relies on agriculture and tourism, receives incentives for building factories, has a busy port at Naples; Common features—same religion, same language, strong family ties, agriculture, tourism
5. Students' lists will vary but may include events such as a fashion show or a religious service.

Spain and Portugal

If YOU lived there...

You have just moved to southern Spain from a town in the far north. You cannot help noticing that many of the buildings here look different from those in your hometown. Many of the buildings here have rounded arches over the doorways and tall towers in front of them. In addition, some are decorated with ornate tiles.

Why do you think the buildings look different?

> **BUILDING BACKGROUND** Throughout history, many different groups have ruled parts of Spain and Portugal. Each group brought elements of its own culture to the region. As a result, parts of the two countries have cultures unlike those found anywhere else.

History

The countries of Spain and Portugal share the Iberian Peninsula, or **Iberia**, the westernmost peninsula in Europe. Although the two are different in many ways, they share a common history.

Across the centuries, several powerful empires controlled all or part of the Iberian Peninsula. By 700 BC, the Phoenicians, from the eastern Mediterranean, had colonized coastal areas of what is now Spain. After the Phoenicians came the Greeks. A few centuries later, all of Iberia became part of the Roman Empire.

After the Roman Empire fell apart, Iberia was invaded by the Moors, a group of Muslims from North Africa. For about 600 years, much of the Iberian Peninsula was under Muslim rule.

Moorish structures, such as this tower outside of Lisbon, Portugal, can still be seen all over Iberia.

What You Will Learn...

Main Ideas

1. Over the centuries, Spain and Portugal have been part of many large and powerful empires.
2. The cultures of Spain and Portugal reflect their long histories.
3. Having been both rich and poor in the past, Spain and Portugal today have growing economies.

The Big Idea

Spain and Portugal have rich cultures, stable governments, and growing economies.

Key Terms and Places

Iberia, *p. 415*
parliamentary monarchy, *p. 418*
Madrid, *p. 418*
Barcelona, *p. 418*
Lisbon, *p. 418*

hmhsocialstudies.com
TAKING NOTES

Use the graphic organizer online to take notes on Spain and Portugal.

SOUTHERN EUROPE **415**

Preteach

Bellringer

If YOU lived there. . . Use the **Daily Bellringer Transparency** to help students answer the question.

▶ Daily Bellringer Transparency, Section 4

Southern Europe	Daily Bellringer
	Section 4

Review Section 3

Read the list of events below and put them in the correct order.

a. Ancient Rome built a vast empire.
b. Italy became a unified country.
c. Italy was defeated in World War II.
d. The Renaissance began in cities such as Florence.

Preview Section 4

If YOU lived there ...
You have just moved to southern Spain from a town in the far north. You cannot help noticing that many of the buildings here look different from those in your hometown. Many of the buildings here have rounded arches over the doorways and tall towers in front of them. In addition, some are decorated with ornate tiles. **Why do you think the buildings look different?**

Consider influences on SOUTHERN Spain:
· Muslim influence was greater in southern Spain.
· Many buildings reflect traditional Muslim design elements.

Consider influences on NORTHERN Spain:
· Christian influence was greater in northern Spain.
· Many buildings reflect classical or Roman styles.

Key Terms and Places

▧ **RF:** Vocabulary Builder , Section 4

Taking Notes

Have students use the graphic organizer online to take notes on the section. This activity will prepare students for the Section Assessment, in which they will complete a graphic organizer that builds on the information using the Critical Thinking Skill: Categorizing.

Teach the Big Idea

At Level

Spain and Portugal

1. **Teach** Ask students the questions in the Main Idea boxes under Direct Teach.

2. **Apply** Allow time for students to take notes about Spain and Portugal, using the chart illustrated on this page. To help them find information, ask these questions: How are the two countries' histories similar? How are their cultures similar? How do they differ? In what ways are the two countries alike and different today? **LS Verbal/Linguistic**

3. **Review** As a class, discuss the notes that students have taken. Point out that although there are major differences between the two countries, they have many things in common.

4. **Practice/Homework** Ask students to review their notes to find one fact about either country, or both, that interests them. Have them write a short paragraph explaining why this fact interests them.
LS Verbal/Linguistic

▧ Alternative Assessment Handbook, Rubric 42: Writing to Inform

❶ History

Over the centuries, Spain and Portugal have been part of many large and powerful empires.

Identify What foreign powers have ruled all or part of Iberia? *Phoenicians, Greeks, Romans, and Moors*

Recall What empires did Spain and Portugal build? *They colonized territories in the Americas, Africa, and Asia.*

Cause and Effect What caused their empires to break up? *Most of their colonies rebelled and became independent.*

❷ Culture

The cultures of Spain and Portugal reflect their long histories.

Recall In what ways are the cultures of Spain and Portugal similar to those of other southern European countries? *They use the same ingredients in their cuisine. They share the same religion with Italy.*

Evaluate Why do you think the Basques want to break away from Spain? *because of their different language and customs*

▶ Map Zone Transparency: Spain and Portugal: Languages

📖 RF: Literature, Don Quixote by Miguel de Cervantes

Spain and Portugal: Languages

Bay of Biscay

ATLANTIC OCEAN

Bilbao

Barcelona

40°N

Madrid

PORTUGAL

SPAIN

Lisbon

Balearic Islands

Mediterranean Sea

Languages
- Spanish
- Portuguese
- Catalan
- Galician
- Basque

0   100   200 Miles
0   100   200 Kilometers
Projection: Azimuthal Equal-Area

Many Basque speakers take part in rallies like this one in support of independence. The banner in this photo reads "Basque Nation Arise" in the Basque language.

map zone — Geography Skills

Place Spanish and Portuguese are the most common languages of Spain and Portugal, but not the only ones.
1. **Identify** Which language is spoken in Barcelona?
2. **Draw Conclusions** Based on this map, which country do you think has a more unified culture? Why?

By the end of the 1400s, however, the Muslims were driven out of Iberia. The rulers of the Christian kingdoms of Spain and Portugal banded together to force non-Christians to leave Iberia. Those who refused to leave were made to convert or face severe punishments.

Spain and Portugal went on to build large empires that spanned the oceans. Both countries ruled huge territories in the Americas as well as smaller areas in Africa and Asia. These territories made the two kingdoms rich and powerful until most of their colonies broke away and became independent in the 1800s and 1900s.

READING CHECK **Summarizing** What empires have ruled Spain and Portugal?

Culture

In some ways, the cultures of Spain and Portugal are like those of other southern European countries. For example, the Spanish, Portuguese, Greeks, and Italians all cook with many of the same ingredients. The Catholic Church is very influential in Italy as well as Spain and Portugal. In other ways, Iberian cultures are unique.

Language

The most spoken languages in Iberia are, of course, Spanish and Portuguese. Various dialects of these languages are spoken in different parts of the peninsula. In addition, other languages are also spoken by many people in Iberia. The Catalan language of eastern Spain is similar to Spanish. Galician, which is spoken in northwest Spain, is more closely related to Portuguese.

In addition, the Basque (BASK) people of the Pyrenees have their own language, which is not related to either Spanish or Portuguese. The Basques also have their own customs and traditions, unlike those of the rest of Spain. As a result, many Basques have long wanted to form their own independent country.

Differentiating Instruction

Above Level

English-Language Learners

1. Draw attention to the language map of Spain and Portugal. Ask students to study the key and find the five language areas on the map.

2. Discuss where Galician is spoken. What language do the residents of Bilbao speak? Why might speaking a different language contribute to the Basques' desire to break away from Spain?

3. Have students answer the Map Zone two questions.

4. Discuss language differences. Ask students to comment on the disadvantages of speaking a language that is different from the one spoken by most of the population. How can these disadvantages be overcome?
   LS Verbal/Linguistic, Visual/Spatial

   Alternative Assessment Handbook, Rubric 21: Map Reading

Answers

Map Zone 1. *Catalan;* **2.** *Portugal; it has a single language.*

Reading Check *Phoenician, Greek, Roman, Moor*

Religion

Most people in both Spain and Portugal are Roman Catholic. People in both countries celebrate Christian holidays like Christmas and Easter. In addition, many towns hold fiestas, or festivals, in honor of their patron saints. At these festivals, people may gather to dance or to watch a bullfight.

Music and Art

Music and art have been central to Iberian culture for centuries. The Portuguese are famous for sad folk songs called fados. The Spanish are known for a style of song and dance called flamenco.

Many elements of Iberia's art and architecture reflect its Muslim past. Many buildings in the peninsula have elements of Muslim design, such as round arches and elaborate tilework.

READING CHECK **Comparing** What is one culture element that Spain and Portugal share?

Spain and Portugal Today

Like other countries in Western Europe, Spain and Portugal have rather strong economies. They do have some problems, however, problems that were largely brought on by past events.

Challenge of the Past

Spain and Portugal were once Europe's richest countries. Their wealth came from gold and silver found in their colonies.

When other countries in Europe began to build industrial economies, Spain and Portugal continued to rely on gold from their colonies. As those colonies became independent, that source of income was lost. As a result, Spain and Portugal were late in developing manufacturing.

Although Spain and Portugal are still poorer than other countries in Western Europe, they are growing rapidly. New industries such as tourism are making this new growth possible.

FOCUS ON READING

As you read, ask yourself this question: Why did Spain and Portugal fall behind other countries economically?

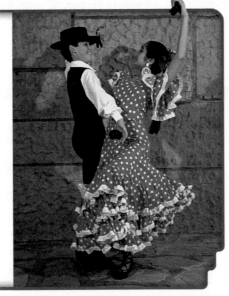

FOCUS ON CULTURE

Flamenco

Complex guitar rhythms, a heavy beat, and whirling dancers—these are all part of the traditional Spanish art form known as flamenco. The word *flamenco* refers both to a style of music and a style of dance. The most important instrument in the music is the guitar, which was itself a Spanish invention. Most of the time, the guitar is accompanied by other musical instruments and by singers.

When most people think of flamenco, however, they picture dancers. Flamenco dancers perform alone, in pairs, or in large groups. They wear brightly colored costumes as they perform complex steps. It is not unusual for dancers to clap their hands or snap their fingers to the beat or to play castanets as they dance. Castanets are small, hinged wooden instruments. The dancers clap the castanets together to make a clicking noise.

Finding Main Ideas What are the major elements of flamenco music and dancing?

SOUTHERN EUROPE **417**

Direct Teach

Main Idea

3 Spain and Portugal Today

Having been both rich and poor in the past, Spain and Portugal today have growing economies.

Explain What happened to the economies of Spain and Portugal when their colonies became independent? *They became poor because they had relied on gold from their colonies instead of developing industry.*

Analyze Which country's government is most similar to the one in the United States? *Portugal, because it is a republic where the leaders are elected by the people and there is no king*

RF: Biography, Amália Rodrigues

Focus on Culture

Flamenco Although people around the world enjoy flamenco, its traditional form originated in Andalusia, in southern Spain. The history of flamenco is not clear, but its present-day form began in the nineteenth century. Dancers who perform flamenco in the traditional way do not follow rigid patterns. They improvise steps, using some basic movements and the rhythm of the guitar to express their feelings.

Cross-Discipline Activity: Music

At Level

Analyzing Musical Art Forms

1. Find recordings of Portuguese fado songs and Spanish flamenco music.

2. Play the recordings for the class. As students listen to the music, ask them to think about the mood that is evoked in each and the feelings that are expressed.

3. Ask students to discuss their impressions of these two art forms. What does the music reveal about the people of Spain and Portugal?

4. If time permits, ask volunteers to do more research on one of these traditions and present what they learn to the class.

5. Expand the discussion by asking students to talk about musical traditions in the United States. What type of music best reflects our culture? Encourage a lively debate.

LS **Verbal/Linguistic, Auditory/Musical**

Alternative Assessment Handbook, Rubrics 11: Discussions; and 18: Listening

Answers

Reading Check *possible answers— Roman Catholic religion, festivals for patron saints, music influenced Muslim art and architecture*

Focus on Reading *They did not build an industrial economy.*

Focus on Culture *complex guitar rhythms, heavy beat, whirling dancers, singers, colorful costumes, clapping, snapping fingers, castanets*

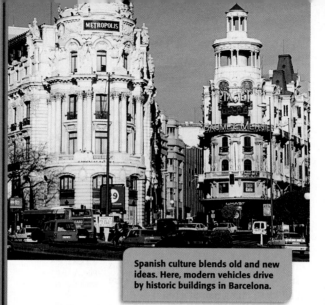

Spanish culture blends old and new ideas. Here, modern vehicles drive by historic buildings in Barcelona.

Spain Today

The people of Spain have kept many aspects of their history alive. For example, Spain is still governed by a king, a descendant of the kings who ruled the country long ago. Unlike in the past, however, Spain today is a **parliamentary monarchy**, which means that the king rules with the help of an elected parliament.

In other ways, Spain has become a more modern country. Agriculture was once the major economic activity, but factories now create automobiles and other high-tech products. Cities such as **Madrid**—the capital—and **Barcelona** are centers of industry, tourism, and culture.

Portugal Today

Unlike Spain, Portugal is not a monarchy. It is a republic with elected leaders. As in Spain, the economy is based largely on industries centered in large cities, especially **Lisbon**. In many rural areas, though, people depend on agriculture. Farmers there grow many crops but are most famous for grapes and cork. Farmers harvest cork from the bark of a particular type of oak tree. Once it is dried, the cork is used to make bottle stoppers and other products.

READING CHECK Contrasting How are Spain and Portugal's governments different?

SUMMARY AND PREVIEW You have just learned about the countries of Southern Europe. Next, you will move north to study West-Central Europe.

Section 4 Assessment

hmhsocialstudies.com
ONLINE QUIZ

Reviewing Ideas, Terms, and Places

1. **a. Recall** What is **Iberia**? What two countries are located there?
   b. Sequence What people have ruled Iberia, and in what order did they rule it?
2. **a. Identify** What is the most common religion in Spain and Portugal?
   b. Generalize How is Spain's history reflected in its architecture?
   c. Elaborate Why do you think many Basques want to become independent from Spain?
3. **a. Identify** What are two crops grown in Portugal?
   b. Analyze What is Spain's government like?

Critical Thinking

4. **Categorizing** Draw a diagram like the one here. Using your notes, record information about the cultures and economies of Spain and Portugal.

	Spain	Portugal
Culture		
Economy		

Focus on Writing

5. **Writing about Spain and Portugal** What details about Spain and Portugal will grab your readers' attention? Look back through your notes to choose the topic for your article.

418 CHAPTER 16

Section 4 Assessment Answers

418

Geography's Impact
video series
Review the video to answer the closing question:
Why did the 2004 Olympics have so great an impact on Athens?

Visual Summary

Use the visual summary below to help you review the main ideas of the chapter.

QUICK FACTS

Greece
The birthplace of democracy, Greece is working to improve its economy.

Italy
Italy is one of Europe's leading cultural and economic countries.

Spain and Portugal
The rich cultures of Spain and Portugal are shaped by their histories.

Reviewing Vocabulary, Terms, and Places

Fill in the blanks with the correct term or location from this chapter.

1. The climate found in most of Southern Europe is the _____.
2. The _____ is the head of the Roman Catholic Church.
3. The highest mountains in Europe are the _____.
4. _____ is the capital of Greece.
5. A _____ is a government in which a king rules with the help of an elected body.
6. Italy's capital, _____, was the birthplace of an ancient civilization.
7. _____ is an independent state located within the city of Rome.
8. Spain and Portugal are located on a peninsula known as _____.

Comprehension and Critical Thinking

SECTION 1 *(Pages 400–403)*

9. **a. Describe** What are two physical features that all the countries of Southern Europe have in common?
   b. Draw Conclusions Why has Southern Europe's climate been called its most valuable resource?
   c. Predict How would daily life in Southern Europe be different if it were not a coastal region?

SECTION 2 *(Pages 405–409)*

10. **a. Identify** What is the largest city in Greece? How would you describe the city?
    b. Generalize How has Greece's economy changed in the last decade? What is largely responsible for this change?
    c. Elaborate How does Greek history still affect the country today?

SOUTHERN EUROPE **419**

Answers

Visual Summary

Review and Inquiry Have students use the visual summary to provide details about the chapter's main ideas.

▶ Quick Facts Transparency: Southern Europe Visual Summary

Reviewing Vocabulary, Terms, and Places

1. Mediterranean climate
2. pope
3. Alps
4. Athens
5. parliamentary monarchy
6. Rome
7. Vatican City
8. Iberia

Comprehension and Critical Thinking

9. **a.** rugged mountains, coastal plains
   b. Its hot summers aid agriculture and attract tourists.
   c. would be no fishing industry, no ports, no sea transportation
10. **a.** Athens; modern skyscrapers, old ruins, heavily populated, industry, air pollution
    b. Greece's economy has steadily grown in the last decade; tourism
    c. People speak the same language and eat foods influenced by their past; religion and family remain important parts of life.

Review and Assessment Resources

Review and Reinforce

SE Chapter Review
RF: Chapter Review
▶ Quick Facts Transparency: Southern Europe Visual Summary
🔊 Spanish Chapter Summaries Audio CD Program
TOS Holt McDougal Puzzle View, Quiz Show for ExamView
● Quiz Game CD-ROM

Assess

SE Standardized Test Practice
PASS: Chapter Test, Forms A and B
Alternative Assessment Handbook
TOS ExamView Test Generator, Chapter Test
● Differentiated Instruction Modified Worksheets and Tests CD-ROM: Chapter Test
↗ Online Assessment Program, in the Interactive Student Edition

Reteach/Intervene

Guided Reading Workbook
Differentiated Instruction Teacher Management System: Lesson Plans
● Differentiated Instruction Modified Worksheets and Tests CD-ROM
● Interactive Skills Tutor CD-ROM

↗ hmhsocialstudies.com
Chapter Resources

Answers

11. a. northern Italy; because it has more industry, better farmland, and more tourists

b. the Renaissance period, a unified Italy; The country divided into city-states and fighting broke out among them; these cities became major centers of trade.

c. Italy produced great works of art that are still appreciated today. It was the birthplace of Christianity. It sets trends in art and fashion. Roman art, architecture, law, and philosophy still influence world culture.

12. a. a population in northern Spain with a separate language and unique customs

b. alike—common history, religion, rapidly growing economies; different—Spain has diverse languages, more dependence on industry, flamenco music, parliamentary monarchy; Portugal has unified language, less industry but more agriculture, fado songs, a republic.

c. possible answer—The Moors invaded from North Africa and brought Muslim influences with them.

Social Studies Skills

13. marine west coast

14. subarctic

15. northeastern Italy and above northeastern Greece

Using the Internet

16. Go to hmhsocialstudies.com to access a rubric for this activity.

Map Activity

17. A. Sicily
B. Mediterranean Sea
C. Spain
D. Rome, Italy
E. Po River
F. Lisbon, Portugal
G. Aegean Sea
H. Athens, Greece

SECTION 3 *(Pages 410–414)*

11. a. Recall Which region of Italy has the stronger economy? Why?

b. Sequence What periods followed the Roman Empire in Italy? What happened during those periods?

c. Elaborate What are some ways in which the Italians have influenced world culture?

SECTION 4 *(Pages 415–418)*

12. a. Identify Who are the Basques?

b. Compare and Contrast How are Spain and Portugal alike? How are they different?

c. Elaborate How do you think Iberia's history makes it different from other places in Europe?

Social Studies Skills

Reading a Climate Map *Use the climate map from the Social Studies Skills lesson of this chapter to answer the following questions.*

13. What type of climate does London have?

14. What climate is found only in the far north?

15. Where in Europe would you find a humid subtropical climate?

Using the Internet

16. Activity: Exploring Italian Cuisine Pizza. Pasta. Mozzarella. Olive oil. These are some of the most popular elements of Italian food, one of the world's favorites. Through your online textbook, learn more about the history and variety of Italian cooking. Then test your knowledge with the interactive activity.

 hmhsocialstudies.com

Map Activity

17. Southern Europe On a separate sheet of paper, match the letters on the map with their correct labels.

Mediterranean Sea	Lisbon, Portugal
Athens, Greece	Po River
Sicily	Rome, Italy
Spain	Aegean Sea

---

hmhsocialstudies.com **INTERACTIVE MAP**

map zone

FOCUS ON READING AND WRITING

Asking Questions *Read the passage below. After you read it, answer the questions below to be sure you have understood what you read.*

> Spain is a democracy, but it has not always been. From 1939 to 1975, a dictator named Francisco Franco ruled the country. He came to power as a result of a bloody civil war and was unpopular with the Spanish people.

18. Who is this paragraph about?
19. What did the people in this passage do?
20. When did the events described take place?
21. Where did the events described take place?
22. Why did the events happen?

Writing Your News Report *Use your notes and the instructions below to help you create your news report.*

23. Select a topic for your news report. Create a plan for your report by answering these questions: What is the scene or setting of the event? Who is there? Why is it important enough to include in the news? What happened? Start your news report with a dateline, for example: Rome, May 5, 2009. Begin your first paragraph with an interesting observation or detail. Explain the event in two or three short paragraphs. Close with an important piece of information or interesting detail.

Focus on Reading and Writing

18. Francisco Franco

19. fought a civil war

20. from 1939 to 1975

21. in Spain

22. due to a bloody civil war

📝 **RF:** Focus on Reading, Asking Questions

23. Rubric Students' news reports should

- write about an event
- describe the scene and setting
- explain who was there
- explain why the event is important and what happened
- include interesting details

📝 **RF:** Focus on Writing, Writing a News Report

DIRECTIONS: Read questions 1 through 7 and write the letter of the best response. Then read question 8 and write your own well-constructed response.

1 **In which country of Southern Europe is the Orthodox Church dominant?**

A Portugal

B Spain

C Italy

D Greece

2 **Two of the most common foods in Southern European cooking are**

A grapes and olives.

B corn and barley.

C beans and squash.

D beef and pork.

3 **The form of government for which ancient Greece is best known is**

A monarchy.

B dictatorship.

C democracy.

D parliamentary monarchy.

4 **The Moors were Muslims who conquered**

A Spain.

B Greece.

C Crete.

D Italy.

5 **Which of these cities is in Portugal?**

A Rome

B Athens

C Lisbon

D Madrid

Spain and Portugal: Climates

Climate Types

- Steppe
- Mediterranean
- Marine west coast

0   100   200 Miles
0   100   200 Kilometers

6 **Based on the map above, which city in Spain lies in an area with a steppe climate?**

A Bilbao

B Cartagena

C Lisbon

D Madrid

7 **Based on the map on this page, which is the most common climate in Spain?**

A Steppe

B Mediterranean

C Marine west coast

D Tropical

8 **Extended response** Climate influences many aspects of people's lives in Southern Europe. Write a short paragraph that describes the region's climate. At the end of the paragraph, list two ways in which climate affects how people live.

SOUTHERN EUROPE **421**

Reteach/Intervention Resources

Reproducible

- Guided Reading Workbook
- Differentiated Instruction Teacher Management System: Lesson Plans

Technology

- Quick Facts Transparency: Southern Europe Visual Summary
- Differentiated Instruction Modified Worksheets and Tests CD-ROM
- Interactive Skills Tutor CD-ROM

Tips for Test Taking

Answering Questions About Maps When a question refers to a map, such as questions 6 and 7 above, encourage students to first study the information given in the map's key and relate that information to the items shown on the map, before answering the question.

Chapter 17 Planning Guide

West-Central Europe

Overview	Instructional Resources	
CHAPTER 17 **Essential Question:** What geographic and cultural features characterize West-Central Europe? 🔊 **Focus on the Essential Question Podcast**	**TOS Differentiated Instruction Teacher Management System:** • Instructional Pacing Guides • Lesson Plans for Differentiated Instruction **Guided Reading Workbook** **Resource File:** • Chapter Review • Focus on Reading: Recognizing Word Origins • Focus on Speaking: Presenting a Persuasive Speech • Social Studies Skills: Analyzing a Circle Graph **Experiencing World History and Geography**	**TOS Calendar Planner** **Power Presentations with Media Gallery** **Differentiated Instruction Modified Worksheets and Tests CD-ROM** **Interactive Skills Tutor CD-ROM** **Student Edition on Audio CD-ROM** **The World's Music Audio Program** **Map Zone Transparency:** West-Central Europe: Political **World Outline Maps: Transparencies and Activities**
Section 1: **Physical Geography** **The Big Idea:** West-Central Europe has a range of landscapes, a mild climate, and rich farmland.	**TOS Differentiated Instruction Teacher Management System:** Section 1 Lesson Plan **Guided Reading Workbook:** Section 1 **Resource File:** • Vocabulary Builder: Section 1	**Daily Bellringer Transparency:** Section 1 **Map Zone Transparency:** West-Central Europe: Physical **Map Zone Transparency:** Satellite View: The Swiss Alps **Map Zone Transparency:** West-Central Europe: Land Use and Resources
Section 2: **France and the Benelux Countries** **The Big Idea:** France and the Benelux Countries have strong economies and rich cultural traditions.	**TOS Differentiated Instruction Teacher Management System:** Section 2 Lesson Plan **Guided Reading Workbook:** Section 2 **Resource File:** • Vocabulary Builder: Section 2 • Biography: Jacques-Yves Cousteau • Literature: *The Lily of the Valley* by Honoré de Balzac • Primary Source: "Above the Clouds, the French Glimpse the Old Grandeur" by Elaine Sciolino • Geography and History: Countries in the European Union • Critical Thinking: A Taste of France	**Daily Bellringer Transparency:** Section 2 **Map Zone Transparency:** The European Union **Internet Activity:** French Landmarks
Section 3: **Germany and the Alpine Countries** **The Big Idea:** Germany and the Alpine Countries are prosperous countries with similar cultures.	**TOS Differentiated Instruction Teacher Management System:** Section 3 Lesson Plan **Guided Reading Workbook:** Section 3 **Resource File:** • Vocabulary Builder: Section 3 • Biography: Emmy Noether • Geography for Life: The EU and NATO: Past, Present, and Future	**Daily Bellringer Transparency:** Section 3 **Map Zone Transparency:** Germany: Political **Map Zone Transparency:** Switzerland: Language Regions **Internet Activity:** German Customs

Review, Assessment, Intervention

- **Europe and Russia Transparencies:** West-Central Europe Visual Summary
- **Spanish Chapter Summaries Audio CD**
- **Progress Assessment Support System (PASS):** Chapter Test
- **Differentiated Instruction Modified Worksheets and Tests CD-ROM:** Modified Chapter Test
- **TOS** **ExamView® Assessment Suite (English/Spanish)**
- **Alternative Assessment Handbook**
- **Online Assessment Program,** in the Interactive Student Edition

---

- **PASS:** Section 1 Quiz
- **Online Quiz:** Section 1
- **Alternative Assessment Handbook**

- **PASS:** Section 2 Quiz
- **Online Quiz:** Section 2
- **Alternative Assessment Handbook**

- **PASS:** Section 3 Quiz
-   **Online Quiz:** Section 3
-   **Alternative Assessment Handbook**

Supporting Resources

- Multimedia Classroom Global History Series
- Global History Teacher's Guide

Maps Globes Graphs Level F

- Student Workbook
- Teacher's Guide

Social Studies Trade Library Collections

- World Regions Trade Collection
- NCSS Middle School Trade Collection

Geography's Impact

Geography's Impact Video Program
- **Impact of Living Below Sea Level**

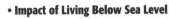

For more information or to purchase go to hmhsocialstudies.com

Power Presentations with Media Gallery

Power Presentations with Media Gallery are visual presentations of each chapter's main ideas. Presentations can be customized by including Quick Facts charts, images from the text, and video clips.

Differentiating Instruction

How do I address the needs of varied learners?

The Target Resource acts as your primary strategy for differentiated instruction.

ENGLISH-LANGUAGE LEARNERS & STRUGGLING READERS

Differentiated Instruction Teacher Management System

Lesson Plans for Differentiated Instruction provide teachers with strategies to help plan instruction for all learners.

Additional Resources

Resource File:
- Vocabulary Builder Activities
- Social Studies Skills: Analyzing a Circle Graph

Quick Facts Transparencies:
- West-Central Europe Visual Summary

Student Edition on Audio CD Program

Interactive Skills Tutor CD-ROM

Spanish Chapter Summaries Audio CD Program

Teacher One Stop:
- ExamView Assessment Suite, Spanish
- PuzzleView, Spanish

English-Language Learner Strategies and Activities

Spanish/English Guided Reading Workbook

SPECIAL NEEDS LEARNERS

Guided Reading Workbook

The activities in the Guided Reading Workbook engage students with questions while presenting summaries of chapter content and provide opportunities for students to practice critical thinking skills.

Additional Resources

Differentiated Instruction Teacher Management System: Lesson Plans for Differentiated Instruction

Resource File: Social Studies Skills: Analyzing a Circle Graph

Student Edition on Audio CD Program

Interactive Skills Tutor CD-ROM

Graphic Organizer Transparencies with Support for Reading and Writing

ADVANCED/GIFTED AND TALENTED STUDENTS

Resource File

The Resource File activities allow students to extend their knowledge of chapter-related places and people and to practice geography skills.

- Focus on Reading: Recognizing Word Origins
- Focus on Speaking: Presenting a Persuasive Speech
- Literature: *Lily of the Valley* by Honoré de Balzac

Additional Resources

Differentiated Instruction Teacher Management System: Lesson Plans for Differentiated Instruction

World History and Geography Document-Based Questions Activities

Geography, Science, and Cultures Activities

Experiencing World History and Geography

Differentiated Activities in the Teacher's Edition

- Understanding Geographic Terms, p. 425
- Analyzing the Euro, p. 434
- Creating a Time Line of German History, p. 437

Teacher One Stop™

How can I manage the lesson plans and support materials for differentiated instruction?

With the Teacher One Stop, you can easily organize and print lesson plans, planning guides, and instructional materials for all learners. The Teacher One Stop includes the following materials to help you differentiate instruction:

- **· Interactive Teacher's Edition**
- **· Calendar Planner and pacing guides**
- **· Editable lesson plans**
- **· All reproducible ancillaries in Adobe Acrobat (PDF) format**
- **· ExamView Assessment Suite (English & Spanish)**
- **· Transparency and video previews**

Differentiated Activities in the Teacher's Edition

- Understanding Cultural Identity, p. 430

Interactive Student Edition

Complete online student edition with interactive multimedia support for chapter content assessment and reporting

- Interactive Maps and Notebook
- Standardized Test Prep
- Online Homework Practice and Research Activities
- Current Events
- Chapter-based Internet Activities
- Animated Geography Activities

Differentiated Activities in the Teacher's Edition

- Researching Artists and their Works, p. 430
- Advertising EU Membership, p. 434

Essential Question

Introduce the Essential Question

- Point out that the countries of West-Central Europe are among the world's most prosperous countries. This is due to mild climates, good farmland, navigable rivers, market economies, and stable governments.

- Tell students that France is the largest country in the West-Central Europe region. France and the Benelux Countries have strong economies. Have students discuss how the economies of these countries are affected by their geography and culture.

- Point out that Germany and the Alpine Countries share some cultural traditions. Discuss which cultural traditions unite these countries.

Focus and Reading and Speaking

Reading The Resource File provides a worksheet to help students recognize word origins.

RF: Focus on Reading, Recognizing Word Origins

Speaking The Resource File provides a worksheet to help students present a persuasive speech.

RF: Focus on Speaking, Presenting a Persuasive Speech

Key to Differentiating Instruction

Below Level

Basic-level activities designed for all students encountering new material

At Level

Intermediate-level activities designed for average students

Above Level

Challenging activities designed for honors and gifted and talented students

Standard English Mastery

Activities designed to improve standard English usage

LS Learning Styles

CHAPTER 17
West-Central Europe

Essential Question What geographic and cultural features characterize West-Central Europe?

 What You Will Learn...

In this chapter you will learn about the physical features, climate, and natural resources of West-Central Europe. You will also study the histories and cultures of the countries in this region. Finally, you will learn about life in these countries today.

FOCUS ON READING AND SPEAKING

Recognizing Word Origins Many of the words we use today came into English from other languages, such as Latin, French, or German. As you read this chapter, think about the origin, or sources, of words. Knowing a word's origin can help you remember the word's meaning. **See the lesson, Recognizing Word Origins, on page 532.**

Writing a Persuasive Speech As you read about West-Central Europe, you will discover some issues. Issues are topics that people disagree about. Think about which of the issues seem important to you. Later, you will take a stand on one of these issues by writing and presenting a persuasive speech.

422 CHAPTER 17

History The Eiffel Tower in Paris, France, was completed in 1889. It was the world's tallest structure until 1930.

Map labels: National capital · Other city · 0 75 150 Miles · 0 75 150 Kilometers · Projection: Azimuthal Equal-Area · UNITED KINGDOM · 50°N · ATLANTIC OCEAN · English Channel · Bay of Biscay · Bordeaux · SPAIN

Introduce the Chapter

At Level

The Heart of Europe

1. Direct students' attention to the map. Note that this region has been called the Heart of Europe because of its prominent role in European history. It has some of the world's most famous cities such as Paris, Amsterdam, and Berlin. Ask students to describe what they already know about some of these cities.

2. Have students note how varied the countries of the region are in size. Discuss briefly the benefits and challenges of being a large or very small country. Then have students find the landlocked countries in the region. Discuss whether being a landlocked country was a serious disadvantage in the past and if it is still one today.

3. Point out the many rivers that run through the region. Have students speculate on what role these rivers play in the economy of the region today. **LS Verbal/Linguistic**

   Alternative Assessment Handbook, Rubric 11: Discussions

North Sea

Kiel Canal

Hamburg

NETHERLANDS

Amsterdam

Rotterdam

RUHR

Antwerp

Lille Brussels

BELGIUM

GERMANY

Berlin

Elbe River

Oder River

Weser River

Neisse River

Rhine River

LUXEMBOURG
Luxembourg

Frankfurt

Seine River

Paris

CZECH REPUBLIC

Loire River

Danube River

Munich

Vienna

FRANCE

LIECHTENSTEIN Salzburg

Zurich

Bern

SWITZERLAND

Lake Geneva

Geneva

Lyon

Innsbruck

AUSTRIA

HUNGARY

Adriatic Sea

Rhône River

ITALY

Marseille

MONACO

Corsica (FRANCE)

Mediterranean Sea

map zone Geography Skills

Regions The countries of West-Central Europe are some of the most industrialized and richest countries in the world.

1. **Identify** Which countries make up this region?
2. **Make Inferences** Why do you think some of the countries in this region might want to join together to promote economic growth?

Geography The Netherlands is famous for its fields of brightly colored tulips.

Culture A German teen participates in a Bavarian cow festival.

423

Connect to Economics

The Tulip Craze Tulips were brought to Holland, now the Netherlands, from Turkey in the mid-1500s. At first, people bought them for their beauty. Prices rose as people sought rare tulips. Hoping to become rich, many people took out loans so they could invest in tulips. They planned to sell tulips for even higher prices. Unfortunately, prices rose so high that no more buyers could be found. As a result, prices for tulips fell—and kept falling. By the 1630s, many people had lost everything they had invested in tulips, including their home and businesses. At one time during the craze, tulips sold for hundreds of dollars! Today you can buy one for less than a dollar.

Info to Know

The Eiffel Tower This most famous Parisian landmark was built for the International Exposition of 1889 celebrating the hundred-year anniversary of the French Revolution. A committee chose bridge engineer Gustave Eiffel's plan from among the 100 plans submitted to the design competition. When Eiffel created his tower, nothing like it had ever been built. It was twice as high as the dome of St. Peter's church in Rome or Egypt's tallest pyramid. It remained the tallest building in the world until 1930 when the Chrysler Building in New York City knocked it out of first place.

Chapter Preview

Explore the Map and Pictures

West-Central Europe: Political
Tell students that the countries of West-Central Europe have much in common. They are all thriving economically, have strong democratic governments and many vibrant cities, and have made remarkable recoveries from the devastation of two world wars. As the pictures suggest, they are also quite different from each other. Unlike the Scandinavian or Mediterranean countries, they do not have a shared religion or common customs and cultural traits.

Analyzing Visuals Ask students why they think the Eiffel Tower became a key landmark for Paris? *height, uniqueness, and technologically advanced at time it was built* Judging by this tulip field, what is the terrain and climate of the Netherlands? *flat; mild climate with enough rain, sun, and fertile soil to grow tulips commercially* What can geographers learn about a place by studying its festivals? *about cultural or religious values, beliefs, customs, and history of a place*

▶ Map Zone Transparency: West-Central Europe: Political

⌐ hmhsocialstudies.com
Teacher Resources

Answers

Map Zone 1. *France, Germany, Austria, Switzerland, Netherlands, Belgium, Luxembourg;* **2.** *possible answer—Many of the countries of the region such as the Netherlands, Belgium, Luxembourg, and Switzerland are small and could benefit from joining forces to create a larger market for their crops and manufactured goods.*

Bellringer

If YOU lived there. . . Use the **Daily Bellringer Transparency** to help students answer the question.

▶️ Daily Bellringer Transparency, Section 1

West-Central Europe   Daily Bellringer
                    Section 1

Preview Section 1

If YOU lived there . . .
You are a photographer planning a book about the landscapes of West-Central Europe. You are trying to decide where to find the best pictures of rich farmland, forested plateaus, and rugged mountains. So far, you are planning to show the colorful tulip fields of the Netherlands, the hilly Black Forest region of Germany, and the snow-covered Alps in Switzerland. **What other places might you want to show?**

Consider other UPLANDS AND MOUNTAINS:
• scene from the Massif Central in France
• view from the Alps in Austria
• walls to hold back the sea in the Netherlands

Consider other PLAINS:
• Lavender fields in Provence, a region in southern France
• livestock farms in Belgium
• farms along the Danube and Rhine rivers

Key Terms and Places

📖 **RF:** Vocabulary Builder, Section 1

Taking Notes

Have students use the graphic organizer online to take notes on the section. This activity will prepare students for the Section Assessment in which they will complete a graphic organizer that builds on the information using the Critical Thinking Skill: Categorizing.

Physical Geography

What You Will Learn...

Main Ideas

1. The physical features of West-Central Europe include plains, uplands, mountains, rivers, and seas.
2. West-Central Europe's mild climate and resources support agriculture, energy production, and tourism.

The Big Idea

West-Central Europe has a range of landscapes, a mild climate, and rich farmland.

Key Terms and Places

Northern European Plain, *p. 424*
North Sea, *p. 426*
English Channel, *p. 426*
Danube River, *p. 426*
Rhine River, *p. 426*
navigable river, *p. 426*

hmhsocialstudies.com
TAKING NOTES

Use the graphic organizer online to take notes on the physical geography of West-Central Europe.

If YOU lived there...

You are a photographer planning a book about the landscapes of West-Central Europe. You are trying to decide where to find the best pictures of rich farmland, forested plateaus, and rugged mountains. So far, you are planning to show the colorful tulip fields of the Netherlands, the hilly Black Forest region of Germany, and the snow-covered Alps in Switzerland.

What other places might you want to show?

BUILDING BACKGROUND The countries of West-Central Europe are among the most prosperous and powerful countries in the world. The reasons include their mild climates, good farmland, many rivers, market economies, and stable governments. In addition, most of these countries cooperate as members of the European Union.

Physical Features

From fields of tulips, to sunny beaches, to icy mountain peaks, West-Central Europe offers a wide range of landscapes. Even though the region is small, it includes three major types of landforms—plains, uplands, and mountains. These landforms extend in wide bands across the region.

Plains, Uplands, and Mountains

Look at the map at right. Picture West-Central Europe as an open fan with Italy as the handle. The outer edge of this imaginary fan is a broad coastal plain called the **Northern European Plain**. This plain stretches from the Atlantic coast into Eastern Europe.

Most of this plain is flat or rolling and lies less than 500 feet (150 m) above sea level. In the Netherlands, parts of the plain dip below sea level. There, people must build walls to hold back the sea. In Brittany in northwestern France, the land rises to form a plateau above the surrounding plain.

424 CHAPTER 17

Teach the Big Idea

Physical Geography

1. **Teach** Ask students the questions in the Main Idea boxes under Direct Teach.

2. **Apply** Have students make a four-columned chart and label the columns: *Landforms, Water Features, Climate,* and *Resources.* As they read the lesson, have them list words or phrases that describe each aspect of the geography of West-Central Europe. Then write the terms *agriculture, energy production,* and *tourism* on the board. Have students identify aspects of the region's physical geography that make these economic activities possible.
LS Verbal/Linguistic

3. **Review** Have students rank the region's geographic assets in order of importance and explain their choices.

4. **Practice/Homework** Have students pick an area they might enjoy living in and write a paragraph telling why. **LS Verbal/Linguistic, Interpersonal**

📋 Alternative Assessment Handbook, Rubrics 13: Graphic Organizers; and 37: Writing Assignments

The Northern European Plain provides the region's best farmland. Many people live on the plain, and the region's largest cities are located there.

The Central Uplands extend across the center of our imaginary fan. This area has many rounded hills, small plateaus, and valleys. In France, the uplands include the <u>Massif</u> Central (ma-SEEF sahn-TRAHL), a plateau region, and the Jura Mountains.

This range is on the French-Swiss border. In Germany, uplands cover much of the southern two-thirds of the country. Dense woodlands, such as the Black Forest, blanket many of the hills in this area.

The Central Uplands have many productive coalfields. As a result, the area is important for mining and industry. Some valleys provide fertile soil for farming, but most of the area is too rocky to farm.

FOCUS ON READING
Look up the origin of *massif* in a dictionary. How does its origin relate to the description of the Massif Central?

hmhsocialstudies.com **INTERACTIVE MAP**

West-Central Europe: Physical

DENMARK
Baltic Sea
IRELAND
North Sea
UNITED KINGDOM
NETHERLANDS
NORTHERN EUROPEAN PLAIN
BELGIUM
English Channel
Rhine River
GERMANY
LUXEMBOURG
CZECH REPUBLIC
Bohemian Forest
Seine River
CENTRAL UPLANDS
Black Forest
Danube River
ATLANTIC OCEAN
BRITTANY
LIECHTENSTEIN
JURA MTS.
FRANCE
ALPS
AUSTRIA
HUNGARY
Bay of Biscay
Mont Blanc 15,771 ft (4,807 m)
SWITZERLAND
MASSIF CENTRAL
Rhône River
Adriatic Sea
1
PYRENEES
FRENCH RIVIERA
MONACO
ITALY
SPAIN
Mediterranean Sea

ELEVATION

Feet	Meters
13,120	4,000
6,560	2,000
1,640	500
656	200
(Sea level) 0	0 (Sea level)
Below sea level	Below sea level

0   100   200 Miles
0   100   200 Kilometers
Projection: Azimuthal Equal Area

map zone Geography Skills

Place The land of West-Central Europe rises from the low Northern European Plain to the Central Uplands to the high Alps.
1. **Name** What bodies of water surround the countries of West-Central Europe?
2. **Draw Conclusions** How might the elevation of the Netherlands affect life there?

1 Each summer, lavender blooms across Provence, a region of southern France. Lavender is used in perfumes and soaps.

WEST-CENTRAL EUROPE **425**

Differentiating Instruction

Below Level

English-Language Learners

1. Review with students the definitions of the terms *plains*, *uplands*, and *mountains*. Have them identify the landform types most common in their area and describe those in other places they have lived or visited.

2. Review the terms *elevation* and *sea level*. Remind students that sea level is the level of the ocean's surface used as a reference point for measuring elevation, heights, and depths on Earth's surface, in feet or meters.

3. Check understanding by having students predict in what landform areas these elevations would be found:

   13,120 ft. (mountains, such as the Alps)

   500 ft. (plains, such as the Northern European Plain)

4. Working in pairs, have students make up a similar question and answer to share with the class.
   LS Verbal/Linguistic
   📖 Alternative Assessment Handbook, Rubric 1: Acquiring Information

Direct Teach

Main Idea

① **Physical Features**

The physical features of West-Central Europe include plains, uplands, mountains, rivers, and seas.

Recall Where is the best farmland in West-Central Europe found? *North European Plain*

Describe What are the natural resources or distinctive features of each of the landform regions? *plains—very good farmland; uplands—forests, coal, and some areas with fertile soil; mountains—scenic beauty*

Draw Conclusions How might the region's water features have affected its economic development? *Navigable rivers and nearness to seas and ocean encouraged the growth of trade.*

▶️ Map Zone Transparency: West-Central Europe: Physical

Info to Know

Disappearing Forests Much of Europe was once covered by forests, which have disappeared as a result of human activities, such as farming. Today, forests are impacted by air pollution, pest outbreaks, drought, and fires.

Connect to Science

Lavender French farmers in Provence grow lavender plants. Lavender's smell comes from oil glands found among the tiny hairs that cover its flowers, leaves, and stems. This oil is extracted from the flowers for use in perfumes, soaps, skin lotions, and other cosmetics.

Answers

Focus on Reading *It's a French term for a large mountain mass and the Massif Central is a mountainous region.*

Map Zone 1. *Baltic Sea, North Sea, English Channel, Atlantic Ocean, Bay of Biscay, Mediterranean Sea;* **2.** *possible answer—The low elevations would affect where buildings could be built and increase the danger of flooding.*

425

Main Idea

② Climate and Resources

West-Central Europe's mild climate and resources support agriculture, energy production, and tourism.

Describe How is the climate of the Alps different from the climate in most of West-Central Europe? Why? *wetter and colder than most of region which has marine west coast climate with cold winters and mild summers; at higher altitude*

Analyze Why is climate a natural resource for the region? *Mild climate combined with ample rainfall and rich soil make region's farmlands highly productive.*

Make Inferences How do the region's natural resources support industry? *coal, natural gas, hydro-electric power, uranium for nuclear power provide energy; iron ore used in manufacturing products*

▶ Map Zone Transparency: West-Central Europe: Land Use and Resources

Linking to Today

Avalanche Prevention The Swiss Federal Snow and Avalanche Research Institute in Davos, Switzerland, is a world leader in avalanche risk assessment and prevention. The Institute estimates that about 150 skiers, snowboarders, and mountaineers are killed by avalanches each year in Europe and North America. The center trains skiers and climbers, as well as rescue dogs, mostly collies and German shepherds. The dogs can cover terrain eight times faster than humans and work in colder and harsher conditions. These dogs are trained to pick up the scent of humans buried deep in the snow. After an avalanche, rescue dogs are brought to the scene by helicopter or by lift systems at ski resorts.

Answers

Satellite View *Snow does not melt, but instead builds up and turns to ice.*
Reading Check *plains, uplands, mountains*

426

Along the inner part of our imaginary fan, the land rises dramatically to form the alpine mountain system. This system includes the Alps and the Pyrenees, which you read about in the last chapter.

As you have read, the Alps are Europe's highest mountain range. They stretch from southern France to the Balkan Peninsula. Several of the jagged peaks in the Alps soar to more than 14,000 feet (4,270 m). The highest peak is Mont Blanc (mawn BLAHN), which rises to 15,771 feet (4,807 m) in France. Because of the height of the Alps, large snowfields coat some peaks.

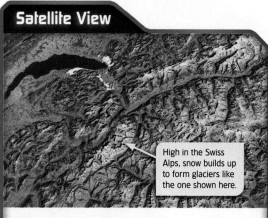

Satellite View

High in the Swiss Alps, snow builds up to form glaciers like the one shown here.

The Swiss Alps

At high elevations in the Alps, snow does not melt. For this reason, the snow builds up over time. As the snow builds up, it turns to ice and eventually forms glaciers. A glacier is a large, slow-moving sheet or river of ice. The satellite image above shows glaciers in the Swiss Alps. The white regions are the glaciers, and the blue areas are alpine lakes.

The buildup of snow and ice in the Alps can cause avalanches at lower elevations. An avalanche is a large mass of snow or other material that suddenly rushes down a mountainside. Avalanches pose a serious danger to people.

Analyzing Why do glaciers sometimes form at higher elevations in the Alps?

426 CHAPTER 17

Water Features

Several bodies of water are important to West-Central Europe's physical geography. The **North Sea** and **English Channel** lie to the north. The Bay of Biscay and Atlantic Ocean lie to the west. The Mediterranean Sea borders France to the south.

Several rivers cross the region as well. Look at the map on the previous page to identify them. Two important rivers are the **Danube** (DAN-yoob) and the **Rhine** (RYN). For centuries people and goods have traveled these rivers, and many cities, farms, and industrial areas line their banks.

Several of West-Central Europe's rivers are navigable. A **navigable river** is one that is deep and wide enough for ships to use. These rivers and a system of canals link the region's interior to the seas. These waterways are important for trade and travel.

READING CHECK **Finding Main Ideas** What are the region's three major landform areas?

Climate and Resources

A warm ocean current flows along Europe's northwestern coast. This current creates a marine west coast climate in most of West-Central Europe. This climate makes much of the area a pleasant place to live. Though winters can get cold, summers are mild. Rain and storms occur often, though.

At higher elevations, such as in the Alps, the climate is colder and wetter. In contrast, southern France has a warm Mediterranean climate. Summers are dry and hot, and winters are mild and wet.

West-Central Europe's mild climate is a valuable natural resource. Mild temperatures, plenty of rain, and rich soil have made the region's farmlands highly productive. Farm crops include grapes, grains, and vegetables. In the uplands and Alps, pastures and valleys support livestock.

Critical Thinking: Making Generalizations   [At Level]

Important Natural Resources

1. Point out that the countries of West-Central Europe are among Earth's most prosperous. Discuss the natural resources that have helped create a high standard of living and prosperity. Note differences between natural resources and human resources. Point out that tourism depends on human and natural resources.

2. Focus discussion on energy resources. Have students look at the map on the next page and identify places where oil and natural

gas are found. Have them write a statement describing the relationship between the two resources. Discuss why energy resources are important to economic growth.

3. Have students examine the map and write three sentences describing how land use and energy resources are related in West-Central Europe. **LS** **Verbal/Linguistic, Visual/Spatial**

📝 Alternative Assessment Handbook, Rubric 21: Map Reading

INTERACTIVE MAP

West-Central Europe: Land Use and Resources

map zone Geography Skills

Human-Environment Interaction The land and resources of West-Central Europe support farming, mining, and industry.

1. **Identify** What cities serve as major manufacturing centers?
2. **Draw Conclusions** Why is hydroelectric power found along alpine rivers?

Land Use
- Commercial farming
- Livestock raising
- Primarily forestland
- Manufacturing
- Limited economic activity

Major Resources
- Coal
- Natural gas
- Oil
- Uranium
- Other minerals
- Fishing
- Nuclear power
- Hydroelectric power
- Major manufacturing and trade centers

0   100   200   300 Miles
0   100   200   300 Kilometers
Projection: Azimuthal Equal-Area

Energy and mineral resources are not evenly distributed across the region, as the map shows. France has coal and iron ore, Germany also has coal, and the Netherlands has natural gas. Fast-flowing alpine rivers provide hydroelectric power. Even so, many countries must import fuels.

Another valuable natural resource is found in the breathtaking beauty of the Alps. Each year, tourists flock to the Alps to enjoy the scenery and to hike and ski.

READING CHECK **Summarizing** What natural resources contribute to the region's economy?

SUMMARY AND PREVIEW West-Central Europe includes low plains, uplands, and mountains. The climate is mild, and natural resources support farming, industry, and tourism. Next, you will read about France and the Benelux Countries.

Section 1 Assessment

hmhsocialstudies.com ONLINE QUIZ

Reviewing Ideas, Terms, and Places

1. **a. Describe** What are the main physical features of the **Northern European Plain**?
   b. Analyze How does having many **navigable** rivers benefit West-Central Europe?
2. **a. Recall** What is the region's main climate?
   b. Make Inferences How might an uneven distribution of mineral resources affect the region?

Critical Thinking

3. **Categorizing** Draw a fan like this one. Label each band with the landform area in West-Central Europe it represents. Using your notes, identify each area's physical features, climate, and resources.

FOCUS ON SPEAKING

4. **Noting the Physical Geography** What issues related to land use and resources can you think of? Could mining coal or importing fuel be an issue? Jot down ideas.

WEST-CENTRAL EUROPE **427**

Section 1 Assessment Answers

1. **a.** broad coastal plain, lies less than 500 feet above sea level, good farmland, large cities
   b. facilitate transportation, trade, travel, tourism
2. **a.** marine west coast with cold winters and mild summers
   b. Some countries have to import more energy or fuel than others.
3. European Plain (outer band)—flat or rolling with most of it lying less than 500 feet above sea level, good farmland, location of largest

cities; Central Uplands (middle band)—many rounded hills, small plateaus, valleys, dense forests on some hills, coal fields, most areas too rocky for farming; Alpine mountain system (inner band)—highest European mountain range, large snowfields, colder, wetter climate

4. Accept reasonable answers based on the text. Possible answers include mining coal, importing fuel, farming and the environment, tourism, and water usage.

Direct Teach

Info to Know

Uranium This ore is a key resource for production of nuclear power. Sources of this radioactive metal are found in France, especially on the Massif Central, a mountainous plateau in the center of the country. France gets three-fourths of its electricity from nuclear energy. It has dozens of nuclear reactors. The nation has become a leader in nuclear technology and reactor construction.

Review & Assess

Close

Ask students to describe West-Central Europe's physical features, climate, and natural resources.

Review

Online Quiz, Section 1

Assess

SE Section 1 Assessment
PASS: Section 1 Quiz
Alternative Assessment Handbook

Reteach/Classroom Intervention

Guided Reading Workbook, Section 1
Interactive Skills Tutor CD-ROM

Answers

Map Zone 1. *Marseille, Paris, Brussels, Rotterdam, Essen, Bremen, Hamburg, Rostock, Berlin, Frankfurt, Munich, Zurich, Lyon, Vienna;* **2.** *In the mountains the rivers flow rapidly downhill, providing power to create electricity.*

Reading Check *mild climate, ample rainfall, rich soil, iron ore, uranium, coal, natural gas, hydroelectric power from fast-flowing alpine rivers, scenic beauty of Alps*

Bellringer

If YOU lived there. . . Use the **Daily Bellringer Transparency** to help students answer the question.

▶ Daily Bellringer Transparency, Section 2

West-Central Europe   Daily Bellringer
Section 2

Review Section 1

Read the statements below and determine what is "speaking."

1. "I am the highest peak in the Alps." What am I?
2. "Along with the Danube River, I am an important river in Europe, and I flow through Germany." What am I?
3. "I am a kind of river that is deep and wide enough for ships to use." What am I?

Preview Section 2

If YOU lived there ...
You are strolling through one of the many open-air markets in a Paris neighborhood. You stop to buy some fruit, then go into a bakery to buy bread, cheese, and lemonade. You sit on a park bench to eat lunch. You end your day with a stroll along the banks of the Seine River, where you look at books and postcards.

Why do you think people enjoy living in Paris?

Consider CULTURAL reasons:
· good food
· beautiful parks and neighborhoods
· tradition of arts and culture

Consider GEOGRAPHIC reasons:
· the scenery of the Seine
· pleasant climate
· located near other beautiful landscapes

Review Answers: 1. Mont Blanc; 2. Rhine; 3. navigable river

Key Terms and Places

RF: Vocabulary Builder, Section 2

Taking Notes

Have students use the graphic organizer online to take notes on the section. This activity will prepare students for the Section Assessment in which they will complete a graphic organizer that builds on the information using the Critical Thinking Skill: Categorizing.

France and the Benelux Countries

What You Will Learn...

Main Ideas

1. During its history France has been a kingdom, empire, colonial power, and republic.
2. The culture of France has contributed to the world's arts and ideas.
3. France today is a farming and manufacturing center.
4. The Benelux Countries have strong economies and high standards of living.

The Big Idea

France and the Benelux Countries have strong economies and rich cultural traditions.

Key Terms and Places

Paris, *p. 431*
Amsterdam, *p. 433*
The Hague, *p. 433*
Brussels, *p. 433*
cosmopolitan, *p. 433*

hmhsocialstudies.com
TAKING NOTES

Use the graphic organizer online to take notes on the Benelux countries.

If YOU lived there...

You are strolling through one of the many open-air markets in a Paris neighborhood. You stop to buy some fruit, then go into a bakery to buy bread, cheese, and lemonade. You sit on a park bench to eat lunch. You end your day with a stroll along the banks of the Seine River, where you look at books and postcards.

Why do you think people enjoy living in Paris?

BUILDING BACKGROUND For centuries, France has played a major role not only in Europe but also in the histories of the United Kingdom and the United States. The Norman Conquest in 1066 brought French influences into English language, law, and culture. France later helped the American colonists win their independence.

History of France

In southwest France, Lascaux (lah-SKOH) Cave holds a treasure from the past. Inside, prehistoric paintings of bulls run and jump along the stone walls. More than 15,000 years old, these paintings show how long people have lived in what is now France.

Early History

In ancient times, France was part of a region called Gaul (GAWL). Centuries ago, Celtic peoples from eastern Europe settled in Gaul. In the 50s BC, the Romans conquered the region. They introduced Roman law. The Romans also established a Latin-based language that in time developed into French.

Roman rule in Gaul lasted until the AD 400s. The Franks, a Germanic people, then conquered much of Gaul. It is from the Franks that France gets its name. The Franks' greatest ruler was Charlemagne (SHAHR-luh-mayn), who built a powerful Christian empire. After he had conquered much of the old Roman Empire, the pope crowned him Emperor of the Romans in 800.

428 CHAPTER 17

Teach the Big Idea

France and the Benelux Countries

1. **Teach** Ask students the questions in the Main Idea boxes under Direct Teach.

2. **Apply** Locate France and the Benelux countries on a map of Europe. Have students read the section and record three ways France and the Benelux countries differ in size, population, and physical geography. Have them share responses and predict how the differences might affect economic development. **LS Visual/Spatial, Verbal/Linguistic**

3. **Review** After completing the section, have students note the ways France and the Benelux countries have built strong economies.

4. **Practice/Homework** Have students write a paragraph identifying the natural and human resources one country used to become a modern, industrialized nation. **LS Verbal/Linguistic**

   📄 Alternative Assessment Handbook, Rubrics 21: Map Reading; and 37: Writing Assignments

After Charlemagne's death, many invaders attacked the Franks. One such group, the Normans, settled in northwestern France. This area is called Normandy.

In 1066 the Normans conquered England. William the Conqueror, the duke of Normandy, became king of England. He now ruled England as well as part of France. In the 1300s England's king tried to claim the French throne to gain control of the rest of France. This event led to the Hundred Years' War (1337–1453). The French eventually drove out the English.

Revolution and Empire

From the 1500s to the 1700s, France built a colonial empire. The French established colonies in the Americas, Africa, and Asia. At this time, most French people lived in poverty and had few rights. For these reasons, in 1789 the French people overthrew their king in the French Revolution.

A few years later a brilliant general named Napoleon took power. In time, he conquered much of Europe. Then in 1815 several European powers joined forces and defeated Napoleon. They exiled him and chose a new king to rule France.

Modern History

During both World War I and World War II, German forces invaded France. After each war, France worked to rebuild its economy. In the 1950s it experienced rapid growth.

During the 1950s and 1960s, many of of the French colonies gained their independence. Some people from these former colonies then moved to France.

France is now a republic with a parliament and an elected president. France still controls several overseas territories, such as Martinique in the West Indies.

READING CHECK Summarizing Which foreign groups have affected France's history?

France's History

During its long history, France has gone from strong kingdom to great empire, to colonial world power, to modern republic.

Early History

- Early Celtic peoples settle in Gaul.
- The Romans conquer Gaul and rule the region for hundreds of years.
- The Franks conquer Gaul. The ruler Charlemagne builds a powerful empire.
- Normans settle in northwestern France. In 1066 they conquer England and take the throne.
- France and England fight the Hundred Years' War.

Charlemagne

Revolution and Empire

- In the 1500s France begins to build a colonial empire.
- In 1789 the people rise up in the French Revolution.
- In 1799 Napoleon takes control. He soon conquers much of Europe.
- European powers unite to defeat Napoleon in 1815.

Arc de Triomphe

Modern History

- German forces invade France during World War I and World War II.
- Many French colonies declare independence in the 1950s and 1960s.
- Today France is a republic with a president and a democratic government.

WWII German occupation

WEST-CENTRAL EUROPE **429**

Main Idea

2 The Culture of France

The culture of France has contributed to the world's arts and ideas.

Identify What are two major contributions the French have made to art and architecture? *possible answers— impressionism, Gothic cathedrals, ideas about democracy, classic literature, arts, fashion, and film*

Draw Conclusions What aspects of French culture have helped unite the French? *pride in their long history as a European leader, French language, Catholicism, shared attitudes such as* joie de vivre, *appreciation of French cooking, shared celebrations, appreciation of the arts and literature*

 RF: Biography, Jacques-Yves Cousteau

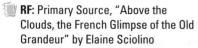 **RF:** Primary Source, "Above the Clouds, the French Glimpse of the Old Grandeur" by Elaine Sciolino

RF: Literature, *The Lily of the Valley* by Honoré de Balzac

Answers

Focus on Reading *It has Latin origins, from a word that meant kitchen—where chefs prepare fine cuisine, or food.*

430

FOCUS ON READING

Use a dictionary to find the origin of *cuisine*. How does the word's origin relate to the meaning of *cuisine* today?

The Culture of France

During their long history, the French have developed a strong cultural identity. Today French culture is admired worldwide.

Language and Religion

A common heritage unites the French. Most people speak French and are Catholic. At the same time, many immigrants have settled in France. These immigrants have their own languages, religions, and customs. For example, many Algerian Muslims have moved to France. This immigration is making France more culturally diverse.

Customs

The French have a phrase that describes their attitude toward life—*joie de vivre* (zhwah duh VEEV-ruh), meaning "enjoyment of life." The French enjoy good food, good company, and good conversation.

An enjoyment of food has helped make French cooking some of the best in the world. French chefs and cooking schools have worldwide reputations. The French have also contributed to the language of food. Terms such as *café,* *cuisine* (cooking), and *menu* all come from the French.

The French also enjoy their festivals. The major national festival is Bastille Day, held on July 14. On that date in 1789 a mob destroyed the Bastille, a Paris prison symbolizing the French king's harsh rule. The event began the French Revolution.

Ideas and the Arts

The French have made major contributions to the arts and ideas. In the Middle Ages, the French built majestic cathedrals in the Gothic style. This style has high pointed ceilings, stained-glass windows, and tall towers that reach heavenward. Notre Dame Cathedral in Paris is an example.

Close-up

Paris

Some 2,000 years old, Paris grew up along the banks of the Seine (SEN) River. Known as "the City of Light" for its gleaming beauty, Paris shines as one of Europe's most cultured cities. Wide tree-lined avenues, historic squares, and lovely gardens and parks grace the city center.

Notre Dame is France's most famous cathedral. It is a masterpiece of Gothic architecture.

The Seine River winds through the heart of Paris. Beautiful bridges cross the river, and in places booksellers line its banks.

430

Differentiating Instruction

Special Needs Learners

At Level

Prep Required

Review the term *cultural identity* with students. Show American identity cards such as a driver's license or school photo ID. Have students explain what purpose these cards serve. Discuss how a cultural identity is different from a legal or official identity. Have students give examples of beliefs, customs, or practices that are part of American cultural identity. **LS Verbal/Linguistic**

Alternative Assessment Handbook, Rubric 9: Comparing and Contrasting

Advanced/Gifted and Talented

Above Level

Research Required

Have students use art books and the Internet to learn about such painters as Degas, Monet, Manet, Renoir, and Mary Cassatt. Have each student pick one painter and give a short, illustrated talk about his or her life, style of painting, subjects for paintings, and most famous works. **LS Verbal/Linguistic, Visual/Spatial**

Alternative Assessment Handbook, Rubric 29: Presentations

In the 1700s France was a center of the Enlightenment, a period in which people used reason to improve society. French Enlightenment ideas about government inspired the American Revolution and the development of modern democracy.

In the 1800s France was the center of one of the most famous art movements of the modern age—impressionism. This style of painting uses rippling light to create an impression of a scene. During the same period, French authors wrote classics such as *The Three Musketeers* by Alexandre Dumas (doo-mah). Today France is known for art and its fashion and film industries.

READING CHECK Summarizing What are some main features of French culture?

France Today

France is now West-Central Europe's largest country. It plays a leading role in Europe and in the European Union (EU).

Today about 75 percent of the French live in cities. **Paris**, the capital, is by far the largest city, with about 10 million people.

Fashionable with a quick pace, Paris is a center of business, finance, learning, and culture. It boasts world-class museums, art galleries, and restaurants as well as famous landmarks such as the Eiffel Tower and Notre Dame Cathedral.

Other major cities include Marseille (mar-SAY), a Mediterranean seaport, and Lyon (LYAWN), located on the Rhone River. A modern system of highways, canals, and high-speed trains links France's cities.

France has a strong economy. It is the EU's top agricultural producer, and its major crops include wheat and grapes. French workers are also highly productive. Rich soil and efficient workers have made France a major exporter of goods, such as its famous perfumes and wines.

The Paris Métro, or subway, is known for its decorative wrought-iron entrances, built in the early 1900s.

Paris is known for its many sidewalk cafés, where people meet to eat, socialize, and relax.

ANALYSIS SKILL **ANALYZING VISUALS**
What examples do you see of the mixing of the new and the old in Paris?

431

4 The Benelux Countries

The Benelux Countries have strong economies and high standards of living.

Identify Why are the Benelux countries known as the Low Countries? *low elevation*

Summarize How has the location of the Benelux countries affected their history and economy? *led to frequent invasions, but also promoted trade and made cities there good places for international organizations, banking, and businesses*

Draw Conclusions What might be the advantages of living in a cosmopolitan city? *variety of arts, cuisine, and entertainment offered, possibly acceptance of diversity among residents, access to and knowledge of different cultures and new ideas*

RF: Geography and History, Countries in the European Union

Connect to Technology

Staying Dry In the Netherlands, scientists and government officials take global warming seriously. Some scientists predict a rise of 4 to 36 inches in sea levels in the next 100 years. Since much of the land is below sea level, such a rise could cause serious problems. A Dutch company hopes to create a floating housing development on the sea near Amsterdam. The houses are to be connected by walkways.

Answers

Connecting to Technology *by building dikes and then pumping out the water from behind dikes to create polders; by creating a national system of dikes, dams, and floodgates to hold back the sea*

Reading Check *It has outstanding museums and restaurants, famous landmarks such as the Eiffel Tower and Notre Dame Cathedral, and is a center of business, finance, learning, and culture.*

432

Dutch Polders

More than 25 percent of the Netherlands lies below sea level. For centuries, the Dutch have reclaimed land from the sea. These reclaimed lands are called polders.

To create polders, the Dutch build dikes near the shoreline. They then use pumps to remove the water behind the dikes. A national system of dikes, dams, floodgates, and storm barriers now holds back the sea.

Unfortunately, creating polders has caused sinking lowlands and other environmental damage. The Dutch are working to address these problems. For example, they are considering restoring some of the polders to wetlands, lakes, and the seas.

Finding Main Ideas How have the Dutch modified their environment to live in a region that lies below sea level?

Tourism is also vital to the economy. Each year, millions of people visit Paris, the French Alps, and the sunny French Riviera, a resort area on the Mediterranean coast.

READING CHECK **Drawing Conclusions** Why do you think tourists might want to visit Paris?

The Benelux Countries

Belgium, the Netherlands, and Luxembourg are called the Benelux Countries. *Benelux* combines the first letters of each country's name. They are also called the Low Countries because of their elevation.

History

Many nations and empires dominated the Benelux region. In 1648 the Netherlands gained its independence. It ruled Belgium until 1830, and Luxembourg until 1867, when they gained independence.

In World War II, Germany occupied the Benelux Countries. After the war, they joined the North Atlantic Treaty Organization (NATO) for protection. NATO is an alliance of nations. In the 1950s the Benelux Countries joined the group of nations now known as the EU.

Today the Benelux Countries each have a parliament and ceremonial monarch. The tiny, densely populated countries lie between larger, stronger countries. This location has led to invasions but has also promoted trade. The Benelux Countries now have wealthy economies.

The Netherlands

Bordering the North Sea, the Netherlands is low and flat. Some of the land lies below sea level. The Netherlands includes the historical region of Holland and is sometimes called Holland. The people here are the Dutch, and the language they speak is also called Dutch.

Critical Thinking: Solving Problems

At Level

Reclaiming Land from the Sea

1. Remind students that geographers study both how people adapt to their environments and how they use technology to change their environments. Have students describe ways humans have modified the environment (e.g., dams, flood control projects, irrigation, highways, artificial lakes for recreation).

2. With 991 people per square mile, the Netherlands is among the most densely populated countries in the world. Have students identify the problems that the Netherlands faced as a result of its location

and explain why the Dutch wanted more land. Have them identify various ways European countries have met the need for more land (*war, conquest, annexation*) and explain how the Dutch solved this problem.

3. Have students create a poster identifying this problem, and describing how it was solved and the positive and negative consequences of the solution. **LS Verbal/Linguistic, Visual/Spatial**

Alternative Assessment Handbook, Rubric 28: Posters

Excellent harbors on the North Sea have made the Netherlands a center of international trade. The city of Rotterdam is one of the world's busiest seaports. It is also part of a highly industrial and urban, or city-based, area. This area includes **Amsterdam**, the capital, and **The Hague** (HAYG), the seat of government. Agriculture is also important to the Dutch economy, and Dutch cheese and tulips are world famous.

Belgium

Belgium is a highly urban country. More than 95 percent of the people of Belgium live in cities. The capital city, **Brussels**, serves as the headquarters for many international organizations, including the EU and NATO. The city of Brussels is as a result highly **cosmopolitan**, or characterized by many foreign influences.

Language divides Belgium. The coast and north are called Flanders. The people there speak Flemish. The southern interior is called Wallonia. The people there speak French and are called Walloons. These cultural differences have caused tensions.

Belgium is known for its cheeses, chocolate, cocoa, and lace. The city of Antwerp is a key port and diamond-cutting center.

Luxembourg

Luxembourg is a forested, hilly country. Although smaller than Rhode Island, it has one of the world's highest standards of living. Most of the people in Luxembourg are Roman Catholic and speak either French or German.

Luxembourg earns much of its income from services such as banking. The region also produces steel and chemicals. Its small cities are cosmopolitan centers of international business and government.

READING CHECK **Comparing** What do the Benelux Countries have in common?

SUMMARY AND PREVIEW As you have learned, France and the Benelux Countries are modern and urban with strong economies. Next, you will read about Germany and the Alpine Countries.

Section 2 Assessment

hmhsocialstudies.com
ONLINE QUIZ

Reviewing Ideas, Terms, and Places

1. **a. Identify** Who was Charlemagne?
   b. Explain Why is Napoleon considered a significant figure in French history?
   c. Develop Why might the French be proud of their long history?
2. **a. Define** What is impressionism?
   b. Summarize What are some major contributions of French culture?
   c. Elaborate How has immigration influenced French culture?
3. **a. Describe** Why is **Paris** an important city?
   b. Summarize What is the French economy like?
4. **a. Describe** How does language divide Belgium?
   b. Draw Conclusions Why might **Brussels** be such a **cosmopolitan** city?

Critical Thinking

5. **Categorizing** Draw a chart like the one here. Use your notes and enter information into each category. Within each category, organize the information by country.

FOCUS ON SPEAKING

6. **Describing France and the Benelux Countries** For each country, note one possible issue for your persuasive speech. For example, one issue might be language in Belgium. Should all Belgians have to speak the same language?

WEST-CENTRAL EUROPE **433**

Section 2 Assessment Answers

1. **a.** ruler of Franks, built Christian empire
   b. conquered much of Europe
   c. strong kingdom, great empire, colonial power, leader of Europe

2. **a.** style of painting using rippling light to create an impression of a scene
   b. cuisine, impressionism, cathedrals, ideas about government, fashion and film
   c. brought other languages, religions, customs

3. **a.** France's capital and largest city
   b. diverse, based on agriculture, manufacturing, trade, tourism

4. **a.** Flanders in north and coast speak Flemish; Walloons in southern interior speak French; these cultural differences have caused tensions
   b. It has many foreign influences since it's home to many international organizations.

5. Students' charts will vary, but should include details about each country's history, culture, government, and economic systems based on information from the text.

6. Students' answers will vary, but should be based on information from the text.

Direct Teach

Info to Know

Belgium's Language Divide In an effort to reduce the conflict between Flemings and Walloons, Belgian officials drew a line on a map of Belgium just south of Brussels. North of this line all public signs and government documents must be printed in Flemish. South of it they must be written in French. Brussels is officially bilingual with signs and documents in both languages. Belgium's conflict is somewhat similar to Canada's language tensions. In the province of Quebec, the leaders of the provincial government also worked with national leaders to develop a two-language policy.

Review & Assess

Close

Have students pick one event from France's modern history and explain how it has affected the nation.

Review

Online Quiz, Section 2

Assess

SE Section 2 Assessment
PASS: Section 2 Quiz
Alternative Assessment Handbook

Reteach/Classroom Intervention

Guided Reading Workbook, Section 2
Interactive Skills Tutor CD-ROM

Answers

Reading Check *low elevations; densely populated; lie between larger and stronger countries; strong economies; high standards of living; centers of international trade, business, and banking*

433

Geography and History

Geography and History

Activity **Cost/Benefit Chart** Have students create a three-columned chart labeled "Benefits and Costs". Under Benefits list *trade, currency, work,* and *travel advantages.* Ask: How does a common market with free trade help the economy of member nations? How does a common currency help member nations? Point out that work and travel changes are controversial issues for western European EU members. Some fear that newly admitted workers from eastern European nations will immigrate to western Europe and agree to accept lower wages. What might be the impact of this for western European workers? Complete the chart by describing any drawbacks or costs to EU members.

LS Visual/Spatial, Verbal/Linguistic

Alternative Assessment Handbook, Rubric 7, Charts

Linking to Today

Rejected EU Proposal In a blow to hopes for European unification, voters in France and the Netherlands, both founding members of the EU, rejected a proposed EU constitution in 2005. The document would have simplified the EU's decision-making process. All EU member states had to ratify the Constitution for it to become law by 2006. A major factor in creating a successful EU is finding ways to reconcile the economic and political interests of the separate member states with the goals of a supranational entity like the EU. Voters in smaller countries such as the Netherlands have concerns about immigration, EU expansion, loss of national identity, and domination by larger nations such as Germany and France. In France workers are concerned that companies will move factories to EU member nations in eastern Europe where wages and taxes are lower.

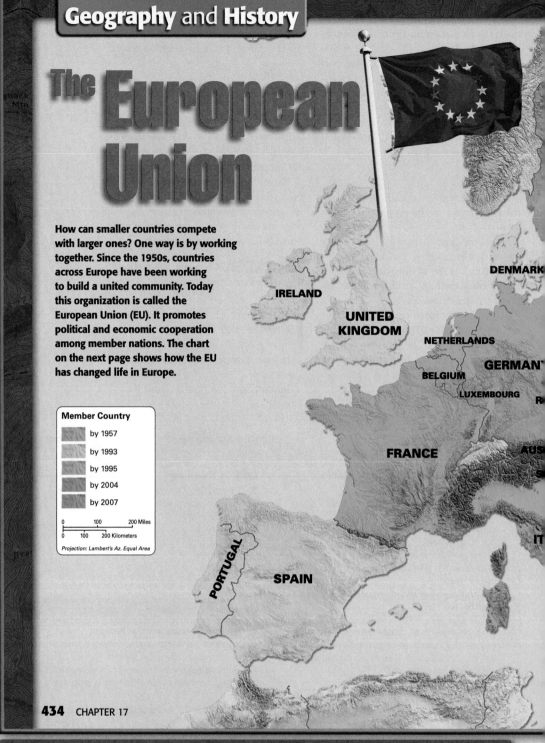

Geography and History

The European Union

How can smaller countries compete with larger ones? One way is by working together. Since the 1950s, countries across Europe have been working to build a united community. Today this organization is called the European Union (EU). It promotes political and economic cooperation among member nations. The chart on the next page shows how the EU has changed life in Europe.

Member Country

- by 1957
- by 1993
- by 1995
- by 2004
- by 2007

0   100   200 Miles
0 100   200 Kilometers
Projection: Lambert's Az. Equal Area

IRELAND
UNITED KINGDOM
DENMARK
NETHERLANDS
BELGIUM
GERMAN
LUXEMBOURG
FRANCE
AUS
PORTUGAL
SPAIN
IT

Differentiating Instruction

Struggling Readers
Below Level

Help students define the word *currency.* Have students describe the different types of images on these currencies. (*historical figures, national symbols*) Note that euro notes (that is, the paper currency) do not have such images. Euro notes feature maps of Europe, the EU flags, arches, bridges, and windows. Ask students why they think that is. Have them explain how the euro helps unite Europe. **LS** Visual/Spatial

Alternative Assessment Handbook, Rubric 16; Judging Information

Advanced/Gifted and Talented
Above Level

Have students imagine that they are EU officials in the public relations department. Their job is to create support among teenagers for participation in the EU. Have students create a jingle, poem, rap, slogan, banner, button, or bumper sticker that summarizes the benefits of EU membership and helps people remember their message. **LS** Visual/Spatial, Verbal/Linguistic

Alternative Assessment Handbook, Rubric 34; Slogans and Banners

FINLAND

ESTONIA

LATVIA

LITHUANIA

LAND

SLOVAKIA

UNGARY

ROMANIA

BULGARIA

TURKEY

GREECE

CYPRUS

Benefits of Membership in the European Union

Trade

Before	After
■ European countries had to pay customs duties, or taxes, on goods they traded with other European countries. ■ Many European countries' economies were small compared to those of larger nations such as the United States.	■ EU countries are part of a common market. They can trade freely with each other without paying duties. ■ EU countries create a combined economy that is one of the largest in the world.

Currency

Before	After
■ Each European country had its own separate currency, or form of money. ■ European countries and their citizens had to exchange currencies to buy goods from other European countries.	■ Most EU countries share one currency, the euro. ■ EU countries and their citizens can use the euro to buy goods and trade throughout the EU.

Work and Travel

Before	After
■ Europeans had to have passports or other special permits to travel from one European country to another. ■ Europeans had to obtain permission to live and work in other countries in Europe.	■ Citizens of EU countries do not need passports or special permits to travel throughout most of the EU. ■ Citizens of EU countries can live and work anywhere in the EU without having to obtain permission.

The Euro The front sides of euro coins all have the same image, but the backs feature a unique symbol for each country. Euro bills show symbols of unity.

ANALYSIS SKILL | ANALYZING VISUALS

1. **Name** Which six countries were the first to unite?
2. **Make Inferences** How do you think democracy's spread in Eastern Europe has affected the EU?
3. **Interpreting Charts** Based on the chart above, what are two benefits of EU membership?

WEST-CENTRAL EUROPE **435**

Connect to Geography

Movement One key goal of the formation of the European Union was to simplify and increase the movement of people and goods across borders. Removing taxes on products traded within the EU countries, sharing a single currency, eliminating passports and special permits for travel and work within the EU are three ways to further those goals.

Analyzing Visuals Have students examine the map. Which countries were founding members of the European Union? *France, Belgium, Germany, Luxembourg, Netherlands, Italy* In what year did many former communist Eastern European countries join? *2004* Which West-Central European country is not an EU member? *Switzerland*

Activity **Compare and Contrast** Tell students that many EU officials hope that Europe might one day become a "United States of Europe." Have students compare and contrast the challenges the United States faced in creating a union of states with the challenges faced by European nations today in forming such a union. How might cultural and historical differences make the task harder? Have students debate the following question: "Will the EU succeed in becoming a United States of Europe?" **LS Verbal/Linguistic**

Alternative Assessment Handbook, Rubric 10: Debates

Collaborative Learning

At Level

EU Decision Makers

1. Divide students into six groups. Assign each group one of the countries of West-Central Europe that is an EU member. Tell groups they are on a committee formed to create a new constitution for the EU. Explain that two questions facing the EU are how power should be shared among big and small member nations and what powers should be given to the EU government.

2. Review and discuss how power is shared in Congress among the states of the United States. Note that foreign policy and major tax decisions in the United States are made by the national government.

3. Have each group decide what kind of EU government would be best for their country given its size and economic interests. They must make a plan their citizens will accept.

4. Have each group write and present a proposal telling how the EU government should be organized. **LS Verbal/Linguistic**

Alternative Assessment Handbook, Rubric 24: Oral Presentations

Answers

Analyzing Visuals 1. *Belgium, France, Germany, Italy, Luxembourg, and the Netherlands;* **2.** *allowed more countries to join the European Union;* **3.** *possible answers—countries can trade freely without paying duties; most countries share one currency, the euro; citizens of the EU do not need passports to travel; citizens can live and work anywhere in the EU without obtaining permission.*

Bellringer

If YOU lived there. . . Use the **Daily Bellringer Transparency** to help students answer the question.

▶ Daily Bellringer Transparency, Section 3

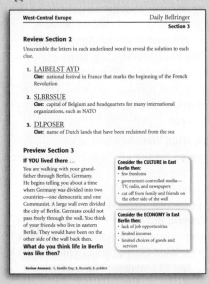

Academic Vocabulary

Review with students the high-use academic terms in this section.

purpose the reason something is done (p. 437)

neutral unbiased, not favoring either side in a conflict (p. 441)

 RF: Vocabulary Builder, Section 3

Taking Notes

Have students use the graphic organizer online to take notes on the section. This activity will prepare students for the Section Assessment in which they will complete a graphic organizer that builds on the information using the Critical Thinking Skill: Comparing and Contrasting.

Germany and the Alpine Countries

What You Will Learn…

Main Ideas

1. After a history of division and two world wars, Germany is now a unified country.
2. German culture, known for its contributions to music, literature, and science, is growing more diverse.
3. Germany today has Europe's largest economy, but eastern Germany faces challenges.
4. The Alpine Countries reflect German culture and have strong economies based on tourism and services.

The Big Idea

Germany and the Alpine Countries are prosperous countries with similar cultures.

Key Terms and Places

Berlin, *p. 437*
chancellor, *p. 439*
Vienna, *p. 441*
cantons, *p. 441*
Bern, *p. 441*

hmhsocialstudies.com
TAKING NOTES

Use the graphic organizer online to take notes on Germany and the Alpine countries.

If **YOU** lived there…

You are walking with your grandfather through Berlin, Germany. He begins telling you about a time when Germany was divided into two countries—one democratic and one Communist. A large wall even divided the city of Berlin. Germans could not pass freely through the wall. You think of your friends who live in eastern Berlin. They would have been on the other side of the wall back then.

What do you think life in Berlin was like then?

BUILDING BACKGROUND Since the Middle Ages, Germany and France have been the dominant countries in West-Central Europe. Both are large and prosperous with hardworking people and good farmland. The two countries have often been at war, but today they are partners in building a cooperative European Union.

History of Germany

Some countries have had a strong influence on world events. Germany is one of these countries. From its location in the heart of Europe, Germany has shaped events across Europe and the world—for both good and bad.

Growth of a Nation

In ancient times, tribes from northern Europe settled in the land that is now Germany. The Romans called this region Germania, after the name of one of the tribes. Over time, many small German states developed in the region. Princes ruled these states. With the support of the Roman Catholic Church, these states became part of the Holy Roman Empire.

For hundreds of years, Germany remained a loose association of small states. Then in 1871, Prussia, the strongest state, united Germany into one nation. As a unified nation, Germany developed into an industrial and military world power.

Teach the Big Idea
At Level

Germany and the Alpine Countries

1. **Teach** Ask students the questions in the Main Idea boxes under Direct Teach.

2. **Apply** Make a two-columned chart labeled *Strengths* and *Limitations*. Refer students to the map on land use and resources in Section 1. Have them identify natural resources of Germany and the Alpine countries. List their responses under *Strengths*. Note that Germany has more resources than the others, which are landlocked and mountainous. Have students describe the limitations of these features. Add these to the chart. **LS** **Visual/Spatial**

3. **Review** Note that despite these physical features, the Alpine nations have strong economies like Germany's.

4. **Practice/Homework** Ask students to write a paragraph describing how Austria or Switzerland have turned limitations into strengths to become prosperous nations. **LS** **Verbal/Linguistic**

   Alternative Assessment Handbook, Rubric 40: Writing to Describe

Germany: Political

The Brandenburg Gate, above, connects eastern and western Berlin. For 28 years, the Berlin Wall blocked the gate. It reopened in 1989.

Border of former East Germany
◎ National capital
● Other city

0   50   100 Miles
0   50   100 Kilometers
Projection: Azimuthal Equal-Area

map zone Geography Skills

Regions The former countries of East Germany and West Germany reunited in 1990 to form one country.
1. **Locate** Where is Germany's capital located?
2. **Contrast** How does river access to the sea differ between former East and West Germany?

War and Division

In 1914–1918, Germany fought and lost World War I. Payments for war damages and a major depression severely hurt the German economy. Looking for a strong leader, Germans found Adolf Hitler and his Nazi Party. Hitler promised the Germans to restore their country to its former glory.

In 1939 Germany attacked Poland, starting World War II. Soon, Germany had conquered much of Europe. The Nazis also sought to kill all European Jews in what is called the Holocaust. Germany lost the war, though. By 1945 it lay in ruins, defeated.

After the war, British, French, and U.S. troops occupied West Germany. The Soviet Union's troops occupied East Germany. Over time, two countries emerged.

The city of **Berlin** was in Communist East Germany. Even so, West Germany kept control of the western part of the city.

In 1961 Communist leaders built the Berlin Wall. The Wall's **purpose** was to prevent East Germans from fleeing to West Berlin.

A Reunited Germany

After World War II, U.S. aid helped West Germany rebuild rapidly. It soon became an economic power. East Germany rebuilt as well, but its economy lagged. In addition, its people had limited freedoms.

In 1989 movements for democracy swept through Eastern Europe. Communist governments began collapsing. Joyful East Germans tore down the Berlin Wall. In 1990 East and West Germany reunited.

ACADEMIC VOCABULARY
purpose the reason something is done

READING CHECK **Finding Main Ideas** What major challenges has Germany overcome?

WEST-CENTRAL EUROPE **437**

437

❷ Culture of Germany

German culture, known for its contributions to music, literature, and science, is growing more diverse.

Identify What famous classical composers have come from Germany? *Bach, Beethoven*

Describe What are some cultural differences among Germany's regions? *regional differences in religion, traditional crafts, dress, food, and celebrations*

Predict What challenges might Germany face as its population becomes more diverse? *integrating new languages, customs, and religions of immigrants such as the Turks, Italians, and refugees from Eastern Europe into German society*

Did you know. . .

The castle of Neuschwanstein in the Bavarian Alps was built by one of the members of Bavarian royalty. King Louis II was also known as "Mad Ludwig." He modeled his home on a medieval castle. It had an indoor garden, a two-story throne room, and an artificial cave. This castle was one of three the king built. The others were attempts to copy Versailles and other palaces of French King Louis XIV.

Answers

Reading Check *possible answers— classical music by composers Bach and Beethoven; literature through the works of Goethe; science*

German Culture

Germany's long history has enriched its culture. Historic castles dot the landscape, and long-held traditions continue. Blending with this history is a modern culture that includes a love of sports.

A Bavarian Castle King Ludwig II of Bavaria had the fairy-tale Neuschwanstein (noy-SHVAHN-shtyn) Castle built in the mid-1800s. The castle sits amid the Bavarian Alps in southern Germany.

Culture of Germany

Germans are known as hardworking and efficient people. At the same time, they enjoy their traditions and celebrating their cultural achievements.

People

Most Germans share a common heritage. About 90 percent are ethnic German, and most speak German. In recent years, significant numbers of immigrants have come to Germany to live and work as well. These immigrants include Turks, Italians, and refugees from Eastern Europe. Their influence is making German culture more diverse.

Religion

In 1517 Martin Luther, a German monk, helped start the Reformation. This religious reform movement led to the development of Protestant churches. Many Germanic states became Protestant; others remained Roman Catholic. Today in north and central Germany, most people are Protestant. In the south, most are Catholic. In eastern Germany, fewer Germans have religious ties, reflecting the area's Communist past.

Customs

Festivals and holidays tell us much about German culture. Religious festivals are very popular. For example, many areas hold festivals before the Christian season of Lent. In addition, Christmas is a major family event. The tradition of the Christmas tree even began in Germany.

Each region has local festivals as well. The best known is Oktoberfest in Bavaria, the region of southeast Germany. This festival is held each fall in Munich (MYOO-nik) to celebrate the region's food and drink.

The Arts and Sciences

Germany's contributions to the arts and sciences are widely admired. In music, Germany has produced famed classical composers, such as Johann Sebastian Bach and Ludwig van Beethoven. In literature, author Johann Wolfgang von Goethe (GOOH-tuh) ranks among Europe's most important writers. In science, Germans have made contributions in chemistry, engineering, medicine, and physics.

READING CHECK **Summarizing** What contributions have Germans made to world culture?

Cross-Discipline Activity: English/Language Arts — At Level

Writing a Letter — Standard English Mastery

1. Divide students into pairs. Have them imagine that they are on vacation together in Germany. Direct students' attention to the photographs in Section 3.

2. Tell them that the travelers have a free day when they can visit one of these places. Have students examine the photographs and decide which one to visit.

3. Have students use standard English to write a letter home telling a friend why they choose a particular place or event, what time of day

and season it was, how long they stayed, what the weather was like, and so on.

4. Then have students use the thesaurus or dictionary to add appropriate adjectives and descriptive phrases to their sentences.

Verbal/Linguistic

Alternative Assessment Handbook, Rubrics 40: Writing to Describe; and 25: Personal Letters

Soccer Fans German soccer fans celebrate a victory. Soccer is the most popular sport in Germany. The country hosted the soccer World Cup in 2006.

Christmas Markets German Christmas markets and fairs like this one have been popular for centuries. Booths sell trees, crafts, and food. Rides and music provide entertainment.

Germany Today

Despite a stormy history, Germany has endured. Today the country is a leading power in Europe and the world.

Government and Economy

Germany is a federal republic. A parliament chooses a **chancellor**, or prime minister, to run the government. The parliament also helps elect a president, whose duties are largely ceremonial. On the world stage, Germany belongs to the EU and NATO.

Germany's market economy has helped the country become an economic giant. It is Europe's largest economy, producing nearly one-fifth of all goods and services in the EU. The nation exports a wide range of products. You may be familiar with German cars, such as BMWs or Volkswagens.

The German economy is based on industry, such as chemicals, engineering, and steel. The main industrial district is the Ruhr, located in western Germany. Fewer Germans farm than in the past, but agriculture remains important. Major crops include grain, potatoes, and grapes. Timber is harvested in the south.

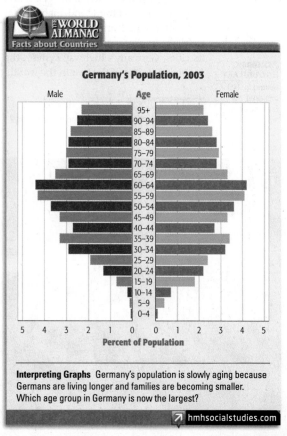

THE WORLD ALMANAC Facts about Countries

Germany's Population, 2003

Male — Age — Female

Percent of Population

Interpreting Graphs Germany's population is slowly aging because Germans are living longer and families are becoming smaller. Which age group in Germany is now the largest?

↗ hmhsocialstudies.com

WEST-CENTRAL EUROPE **439**

439

Main Idea

❹ The Alpine Countries

The Alpine Countries reflect German culture and have strong economies based on tourism and services.

Recall What are three ways Austria and Switzerland are alike? *landlocked, influenced by German culture, once part of the Holy Roman Empire*

Explain Why did the Habsburg Empire collapse and how did Austria change as a result? *on losing side in World War I; became a republic and grew into a modern industrialized nation*

Draw Conclusions Why might Switzerland's location help it remain neutral? *Because of the Alps, it is more isolated and less accessible than many European countries.*

▶ Map Zone Transparency: Switzerland: Language Regions

Linking to Today

Still Struggling The problems of reuniting Germany after 40 years have proven more difficult and costly than West German officials expected. Under its communist-controlled, command economy many factories in East Germany were inefficient and unproductive by West German standards. After East Germany's collapse, the government privatized or closed many of these state-run factories. Hundreds of thousands of East Germans lost their jobs and became dependent on government subsidies. At the same time, East Germany's roads, rail line, telephones and other infrastructure had deteriorated. Today the gap is closing, but unemployment remains higher in eastern Germany than in western Germany.

Answers

Focus on Reading *The word likely has Scandinavian roots, meaning* to go slowly, *which is similar to its current meaning.*

Reading Check *slowed economic growth*

Use a dictionary to find the origin of *lag*. How does the word's origin relate to its meaning here?

Economic growth has slowed since East and West Germany reunited, however. The economy of former East Germany continues to lag. The region also suffers high unemployment. Germany's government is working to solve these problems.

Cities

Most Germans live in cities. The largest city is Berlin, the capital. During World War II, Berlin suffered major destruction. Today Germans have restored their capital to its former splendor. A historic city, it has wide boulevards and many parks.

Other major German cities include Hamburg, a key port city on the North Sea, and Munich, a cultural and manufacturing center. Like France, Germany has an excellent transportation system that links its cities. Germany's highway system, the Autobahn, is one of the best in the world.

ACADEMIC VOCABULARY
neutral (p. 145) unbiased, not favoring either side in a conflict

READING CHECK **Analyzing** How has the reunification of Germany affected its economy?

The Alpine Countries

The beauty of the Alps draws many tourists to Austria and Switzerland. These countries are called the Alpine Countries after the Alps, which cover much of them.

Austria and Switzerland have many similarities. Both are landlocked. Both are heavily influenced by German culture and were once part of the Holy Roman Empire. Yet, the countries have their differences.

Austria

Austria was once the center of one of the most powerful empires in Europe. The royal Habsburg family came to control this empire. At its height, the Habsburg line ruled the Netherlands, Spain, and much of Germany, Italy, and Eastern Europe.

In 1918, however, the Habsburgs were on the losing side of World War I. After the war, Austria became a republic. Since then, Austria has grown into a modern, industrialized nation. Today it is a federal republic and EU member.

The Alpine Countries

440 CHAPTER 17

Austria and Switzerland draw millions of tourists each year. Above, tourists ride through Vienna, Austria, famous for its history and culture. At left, a mountain village shows the beauty of the Swiss Alps.

Collaborative Learning

At Level

Comparing and Contrasting

1. Divide students into four groups: Alpine Countries, Benelux Countries, France, and Germany. Have each group create a Fact File for their country or countries with information such as physical features, natural and human resources, economic activities, and cultural features and achievements.

2. After the Fact Files are completed, put the Benelux and Alpine groups together and France and Germany together. Have these larger groups share information and use it to compare and contrast their countries or subregions. Areas for comparison can also, include challenges each faced and how each met these challenges.

3. Encourage groups to present their findings in a variety of ways including computer presentations, panel discussions, skits, and posters. **LS Verbal/Linguistic, Interpersonal**

📄 Alternative Assessment Handbook, Rubrics 9: Comparing and Contrasting; and 29: Presentations

Most Austrians speak German and are Roman Catholic. The city of **Vienna** is Austria's capital and largest city. Located on the banks of the Danube, Vienna was once the center of Habsburg rule. Today historic palaces grace the city, which is a center of music and the fine arts.

Austria has a prosperous economy with little unemployment. Service industries, such as banking, are important and employ more than half of Austria's workforce. Tourism is important as well.

Switzerland

Since the 1600s Switzerland has been an independent country. Today it is a federal republic with 26 districts called **cantons**. Citizens are active in local government. In addition, all male citizens serve for a period in the militia, a citizen army.

Switzerland's location in the Alps has helped it remain <u>neutral</u> for centuries. To stay neutral, Switzerland has not joined the EU or NATO. The Swiss are active in international organizations, however.

As the map shows, the Swiss speak several languages. The main languages are German and French. Switzerland's capital, **Bern**, is centrally located to be near both German- and French-speaking regions.

Switzerland has one of the world's highest standards of living. It is famous for its banks, watches and other precision devices, and chocolate and cheese.

READING CHECK **Contrasting** How are the countries of Austria and Switzerland different?

SUMMARY AND PREVIEW You have read that Germany is an economic power with a rich culture, while the Alpine Countries are prosperous with beautiful mountain scenery. In the next chapter you will learn about Northern Europe.

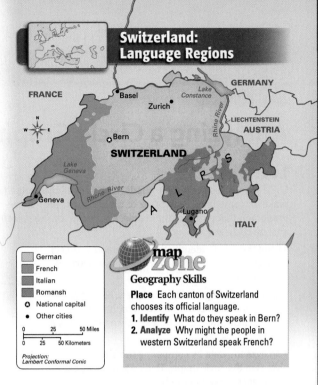

Switzerland: Language Regions

FRANCE · Basel · Zurich · GERMANY · Lake Constance · Rhine River · LIECHTENSTEIN · AUSTRITA · Bern · SWITZERLAND · Lake Geneva · Rhone River · A L P S · Geneva · Lugano · ITALY

- German
- French
- Italian
- Romansh
- ✪ National capital
- • Other cities

0   25   50 Miles
0   25   50 Kilometers

Projection:
Lambert Conformal Conic

map Zone

Geography Skills

Place Each canton of Switzerland chooses its official language.
1. **Identify** What do they speak in Bern?
2. **Analyze** Why might the people in western Switzerland speak French?

Section 3 Assessment
hmhsocialstudies.com
ONLINE QUIZ

Reviewing Ideas, Terms, and Places

1. **a. Identify** Why is Adolf Hitler significant in history?
   b. Sequence What events led to German reunification?
2. **a. Recall** What are some popular festivals in Germany?
   b. Contrast How does religion differ across Germany?
3. **a. Describe** What is the role of Germany's **chancellor**?
   b. Explain Why has Germany's economy slowed?
4. **a. Define** What are **cantons**, and where are they found?
   b. Analyze How are the Alps a valuable resource?

Critical Thinking

5. **Comparing and Contrasting** Draw a Venn diagram like this one. Use your notes to list the differences and similarities.

Germany   Alpine Countries

FOCUS ON SPEAKING

6. **Describing Germany and the Alpine Countries** For each country, note one issue for your speech. For example, you might argue that the Alps are the region's loveliest area.

WEST-CENTRAL EUROPE **441**

Section 3 Assessment Answers

1. **a.** led Germany into WW II, caused the Holocaust, left Germany divided and in ruins
   b. In 1989 democratic movements swept Eastern Europe, communism collapsed, and East Germans tore down Berlin Wall.

2. **a.** Oktoberfest, Christmas
   b. In north and central Germany, most people are Protestant; in south, most are Catholics; in east, many people have no religious ties.

3. **a.** runs the government, like a prime minister
   b. The economy of the former East Germany lags behind and has high unemployment.

4. **a.** districts within the Swiss republic; Switzerland
   b. The Alps are a major tourist attraction.

5. possible answer: alike—German culture, language, strong economies; different—Austria is mostly Catholic; French is also spoken in Switzerland.

6. Answers will vary, but should be based on information from the text.

Direct Teach

History Humor

Alpine Humor Yodeling is a unique form of Alpine singing. In this musical style higher and lower tones alternate. Yodeling has its origins in the calls of shepherds who took care of cows and goats grazing in Alpine meadows. Today yodeling is most often heard at Swiss and Austrian folk festivals. Here is a yodeling joke.

Knock, knock

Who's there?

Little old lady.

Little old lady who?

I didn't know you could yodel.

Review & Assess

Close

Have students write a paragraph comparing and contrasting Germany and the Alpine countries.

Review

↗ Online Quiz, Section 3

Assess

SE Section 3 Assessment
🗒 PASS: Section 3 Quiz
🗒 Alternative Assessment Handbook

Reteach/Classroom Intervention

🗒 Guided Reading Workbook, Section 3
💿 Interactive Skills Tutor CD-ROM

Answers

Map Zone 1. *German;* **2.** *They share a border with France.*

Reading Check *Austria—people speak German and are Roman Catholics, federal republic, EU member; Switzerland—people mainly speak German or French, not EU member, has neutral status, democratic confederation*

441

Analyzing a Circle Graph

Activity Reading a Circle Graph
Bring to class examples of circle graphs from local newspapers, magazines, or other sources. Many local government agencies send information to residents in the form of circle graphs. If unable to find one, have students create their own using a recent almanac or an Internet source such as the online CIA World Factbook to obtain data on such topics as major trading partners of specific West-Central European countries, major imports or exports to or from various countries, percentages of different religious or ethnic groups within a country, or other aspects of cultural geography. Have students describe the types of information that lend themselves to presentation as circle graphs and the types of information that are usually presented in line or bar graphs.

LS Logical/Mathematical, Visual/Spatial

- Alternative Assessment Handbook, Rubric 7: Charts
- Interactive Skills Tutor CD-ROM, Lesson 6: Interpret Maps, Graphs, Charts, Visuals, and Political Cartoons
- RF: Social Studies Skills, Analyzing a Circle Graph

Analyzing a Circle Graph

Learn

Circle graphs, also called pie charts, represent all the parts that make up something. Each piece of the circle, or "pie," shows what proportion that part is of the whole. Use the following guidelines to analyze circle graphs.

- Read the title to identify the circle graph's subject. The circle graph here shows the main languages spoken in Switzerland.
- Read the circle graph's other labels. Note what each part, or slice, of the circle graph represents. In the circle graph at right, each slice represents a different language.
- Analyze the data by comparing the size of the slices in the circle graph. Think about what the differences mean or imply.

Practice

1. Based on the circle graph at right, what are the three main languages spoken in Switzerland?

2. What language do less than 1 percent of the Swiss speak?

3. What percentage of the Swiss speak other languages not listed individually?

Languages in Switzerland

- Romansh 0.6%
- Other 8.9%
- Italian 7.6%
- French 19.2%
- German 63.7%

Source: Central Intelligence Agency, *The World Factbook 2002*

Apply

To answer the following questions, use the circle graph titled France's Current Export Partners in the Standardized Test Practice.

1. To which country does France send the highest percentage of its exports?

2. How many of France's main export partners belong to the European Union?

3. What percentage of French exports go to the United States?

Social Studies Skills Activity: Analyzing a Circle Graph **Below Level**

Special Needs Learners/ELL

Materials: protractor or circle template, markers, paper

1. Have students create their own data for a circle graph. Students can begin by making a list of up to five favorite places to visit in their community, favorite sports teams or leisure-time activities, most important community issues, or another topic of interest.

2. To collect data, have students either survey the class or poll friends and family on their preferences from among the five choices.

Have students write down and report responses. Tally responses and make a chart on the board showing totals. Then work with students to convert numbers to fractions or percentages for a circle graph. Then create a graph based on the data.

3. Have students discuss how viewing the data in chart and circle graph form is different. Then have each student make up three questions about the information on the circle graph.

LS Logical/Mathematical, Visual/Spatial

Alternative Assessment Handbook, Rubric 7: Charts

Answers

Practice 1. *German, French, Italian;*
2. *Romansh;* **3.** *8.9 percent*
Apply 1. *Germany;* **2.** *five;*
3. *7 percent*

Chapter Review

Geography's Impact
video series
Review the video to answer the closing question:
Do you think proximity to the sea has been more beneficial or harmful to the Netherlands?

Visual Summary

Use the visual summary below to help you review the main ideas of the chapter.

QUICK FACTS

France is a leading European nation and cultural center. The Benelux Countries are small, densely populated, and rich.

Germany is an industrial powerhouse with a rich culture. The landlocked Alpine Countries have stunning mountains.

Reviewing Vocabulary, Terms, and Places

Match each "I" statement below with the person, place, or thing that might have made the statement.

a. Berlin
b. Brussels
c. canton
d. chancellor
e. cosmopolitan city
f. Danube River
g. dike
h. navigable river
i. North Sea
j. Paris

1. "I am the capital of France and a center of business, finance, learning, and culture."
2. "I am an important waterway in the region of West-Central Europe."
3. "I am a prime minister in Germany."
4. "I am an earthen wall used to hold back water."
5. "I am a type of river that is wide and deep enough for ships to use."
6. "I am a district in Switzerland."
7. "I am a city that has many foreign influences."
8. "I am an international city and the capital of Belgium."
9. "I am a large body of water located to the north of the Benelux Countries and Germany."
10. "I was divided into two parts after World War II and am now the capital of Germany."

Comprehension and Critical Thinking

SECTION 1 *(Pages 424–427)*

11. a. **Recall** From southeast to northwest, what are the major landforms in West-Central Europe?

b. **Analyze** How have geographic features supported trade and travel across the region of West-Central Europe?

c. **Elaborate** How does West-Central Europe's mild climate serve as a valuable resource and contribute to the economy?

WEST-CENTRAL EUROPE **443**

---

12. a. Rotterdam

b. possible answers—cosmetics, wine, perfumes, fashions, film, impressionist art, Gothic cathedrals, literary classics

c. Their location in central Europe has made many cities good places for international business; their nearness to the sea and connection to major navigable rivers has helped them become centers of trade.

13. a. possible answers—1939, Nazis invade Poland; 1945, Germany defeated in World War II; 1961, Communists build Berlin Wall; 1989, Communism begins collapsing; 1990, East and West Germany reunited

b. It is a neutral country and not part of the European Union.

c. At one time Austria was the center of the powerful Habsburg Empire, which included the Netherlands, Spain, and much of Germany, Italy, and Eastern Europe.

Social Studies Skills

14. 63.7 percent

15. 26.8 percent

16. Romansh

Using the Internet

17. Go to hmhsocialstudies.com to access a rubric for this activity.

Map Activity

18. A. Paris, France
B. Northern European Plain
C. Berlin, Germany
D. Vienna, Austria
E. North Sea
F. Alps
G. Pyrenees

SECTION 2 *(Pages 428–433)*

12. a. Identify Where is the busiest seaport in the Netherlands located?

b. Summarize What are some products and cultural features for which France is famous?

c. Develop How have geographic features helped the Benelux Countries become centers of trade and international business?

SECTION 3 *(Pages 436–441)*

13. a. Recall What are three major events in German history, and when did each one occur?

b. Analyze How is Switzerland's position in European affairs unique?

c. Elaborate How has the royal Habsburg family shaped Austria's history?

Social Studies Skills

Analyzing a Circle Graph *Use the circle graph titled Languages in Switzerland in the Social Studies Skills to answer the following questions.*

14. Based on the circle graph, what percentage of the Swiss speak German?

15. What percentage of the Swiss speak French and Italian?

16. What fourth language do the Swiss speak?

Using the Internet

17. Activity: Researching Schools Imagine that your family is moving to Belgium or the Netherlands. In your new country you will be attending an international school. What kinds of classes will you have? What will your school day be like? What kinds of things might you see and do outside of school? Through your online textbook, research schools and daily life there. Then complete the online worksheet to record what you have learned. Finally, compare the schools you researched to the school you attend today.

hmhsocialstudies.com

Map Activity

18. West-Central Europe On a separate sheet of paper, match the letters on the map with their correct labels.

Alps
Berlin, Germany
North Sea
Northern European Plain
Paris, France
Pyrenees
Vienna, Austria

hmhsocialstudies.com INTERACTIVE MAP

FOCUS ON READING AND SPEAKING

19. Recognizing Word Origins Find the key term cosmopolitan in Section 2. Write the word's definition. Then use a good dictionary to research the word's origins. Explain how the word's origins relate to its definition.

20. Writing a Persuasive Speech Choose one of the issues you identified as you read the chapter. Write an opinion statement about the issue, such as "The Dutch polders should be restored to wetlands." Next, list three facts or examples that support your opinion. Use the chapter and other sources to find information. Then use the list to write your short persuasive speech. Practice delivering your speech using an assured tone of voice and a confident posture.

Focus on Reading and Speaking

19. possible answer—common to or characterized by many foreign influences; from the classical Greek *kosmopolites; kosmos* means world and *polites* means citizen; *polites* is from the classical Greek *polis*, meaning city state

RF: Focus on Reading, Recognizing Word Origins

20. Rubric Students' speeches should

• include an opinion statement about an issue

• list three facts or examples to support the opinion

• use the chapter and other sources for information

• be short and delivered in an assured tone of voice with confident posture

RF: Focus on Speaking, Presenting a Persuasive Speech

DIRECTIONS: Read questions 1 through 7 and write the letter of the best response. Then read question 8 and write your own well-constructed response.

1 The alpine mountain system includes the Alps and the
A Black Forest.
B Jura Mountains.
C Massif Central.
D Pyrenees.

2 What type of climate does *most* of West-Central Europe have?
A highland climate
B humid tropical climate
C marine west coast climate
D Mediterranean climate

3 Which three countries make up the Benelux Countries?
A Belgium, the Netherlands, and Luxembourg
B France, Belgium, and Luxembourg
C France, Germany, and Austria
D Germany, Austria, and Switzerland

4 Which French leader created a great empire only to be defeated in 1815?
A Adolf Hitler
B Charlemagne
C Napoleon
D William the Conqueror

5 What capital city in West-Central Europe was divided after World War II?
A Berlin
B Brussels
C Paris
D Vienna

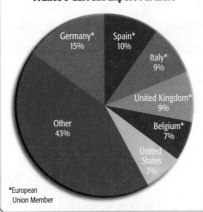

France's Current Export Partners

Germany* 15%
Spain* 10%
Italy* 9%
United Kingdom* 9%
Belgium* 7%
United States 7%
Other 43%

*European Union Member

Source: Central Intelligence Agency, *The World Factbook 2005*

6 Based on the graph above, what percentage of French goods went to France's top two export partners?
A 10%
B 15%
C 25%
D 30%

7 What is the main language spoken in both of the Alpine Countries?
A Dutch
B French
C German
D Italian

8 **Extended Response** Examine the map of Germany in Section 3. Use the map to explain how the physical geography of former East and West Germany differed. Then analyze how you think each former country's physical geography affected its economy.

WEST-CENTRAL EUROPE **445**

Reteach/Intervention Resources

Reproducible
- Guided Reading Workbook
- Differentiated Instruction Teacher Management System: Lesson Plans

Technology
- Quick Facts Transparency: West-Central Europe Visual Summary
- Differentiated Instruction Modified Worksheets and Tests CD-ROM
- Interactive Skills Tutor CD-ROM

Tips for Test Taking

I'm Stuck! Give students these tips for when they get stuck on a standardized test. If you come across a question that stumps you, don't get frustrated. First master the questions to make sure you understand what is being asked. Then work through the strategies you have already learned. If you are still stuck, circle the question and go on to others. Come back to it later. What if you still have no idea? Practice the 50/50 strategy and make an educated guess.

Answers

Standardized Test Prep

1. D
Break Down the Question This question requires students to recall factual information from Section 1.

2. C
Break Down the Question Remind students that the word *most* in this question signals that they can exclude all climate types found in only a small area of the region. This question requires students to recall factual information from Section 1.

3. A
Break Down the Question Students can use the word *Benelux* in the question to help them recall the countries in this group. Have students who miss this question review Section 2.

4. C
Break Down the Question This question requires students to recall factual information from Section 2.

5. A
Break Down the Question This question requires students to recall factual information from Section 3.

6. C
Break Down the Question This question requires students to accurately analyze the information presented in the circle graph.

7. C
Break Down the Question This question requires students to recall factual information from Section 3.

8. Extended Response Possible answer—Germany is found in the Northern European Plain, so it has good farmland and ports on the Baltic Sea and the North Sea. However, West Germany had two navigable rivers that flow to ports within its boundaries, in addition to the Rhine. East Germany had the Elbe, which flows through West Germany before reaching the sea. Thus, West Germany had an advantage for trade, which helped its economy.

Northern Europe

Overview	Instructional Resources	
CHAPTER 18 **Essential Question:** How has location shaped the development of nations in Northern Europe? 🔊 **Focus on the Essential Question Podcast**	**TOS Differentiated Instruction Teacher Management System:** • Instructional Pacing Guides • Lesson Plans for Differentiated Instruction 📑 **Guided Reading Workbook** 📑 **Resource File:** • Chapter Review • Focus on Reading: Using Context Clues–Synonyms • Focus on Writing: Writing a Letter • Social Studies Skills: Writing to Learn 📑 **Experiencing World History and Geography**	**TOS Calendar Planner** 💿 **Power Presentations with Media Gallery** 💿 **Differentiated Instruction Modified Worksheets and Tests CD-ROM** 💿 **Interactive Skills Tutor CD-ROM** 🔊 **Student Edition on Audio CD-ROM** 🔊 **The World's Music Audio Program** 📺 **Map Zone Transparency:** Northern Europe: Political 📺 **World Outline Maps: Transparencies and Activities** 📹 **Video:** Winston Churchill
Section 1: **Physical Geography** **The Big Idea:** Northern Europe is a region of unique physical features, rich resources, and diverse climates.	**TOS Differentiated Instruction Teacher Management System:** Section 1 Lesson Plan 📑 **Guided Reading Workbook:** Section 1 📑 **Resource File:** • Vocabulary Builder: Section 1 • Geography and History: Understanding Northern Europe	📺 **Daily Bellringer Transparency:** Section 1 📺 **Map Zone Transparency:** Northern Europe: Physical 📺 **Map Zone Transparency:** Satellite View: Norway's Fjords 📺 **Map Zone Transparency:** Northern Europe: Climate
Section 2: **The British Isles** **The Big Idea:** Close cultural and historical ties link the people of the British Isles today.	**TOS Differentiated Instruction Teacher Management System:** Section 2 Lesson Plan 📑 **Guided Reading Workbook:** Section 2 📑 **Resource File:** • Vocabulary Builder: Section 2 • Biography: Mary, Queen of Scots • Literature: *Romeo and Juliet* by William Shakespeare • Critical Thinking: Connecting Europe by Chunnel	📺 **Daily Bellringer Transparency:** Section 2 📺 **Map Zone Transparency:** British Isles: Political 📲 **Internet Activity:** Scottish and Irish Culture 📹 **Video:** Winston Churchill
Section 3: **Scandinavia** **The Big Idea:** Scandinavia has developed into one of the most stable and prosperous regions in Europe.	**TOS Differentiated Instruction Teacher Management System:** Section 3 Lesson Plan 📑 **Guided Reading Workbook:** Section 3 📑 **Resource File:** • Vocabulary Builder: Section 3 • Biography: Hans Christian Andersen • Primary Source: "The Scream" by Edvard Munch • Geography for Life: The Vikings Abroad	📺 **Daily Bellringer Transparency:** Section 3 📲 **Internet Activity:** Scandinavian Social Programs

CHAPTER 18 PLANNING GUIDE

Review, Assessment, Intervention

 Europe and Russia Transparencies: Northern Europe Visual Summary

 Spanish Chapter Summaries Audio CD

 Progress Assessment Support System (PASS): Chapter Test

 Differentiated Instruction Modified Worksheets CD-ROM: Modified Chapter Test

TOS **ExamView® Assessment Suite (English/Spanish)**

 Alternative Assessment Handbook

 Online Assessment Program, in the Interactive Student Edition

 PASS: Section 1 Quiz

 Online Quiz: Section 1

 Alternative Assessment Handbook

 PASS: Section 2 Quiz

 Online Quiz: Section 2

 Alternative Assessment Handbook

 PASS: Section 3 Quiz

 Online Quiz: Section 3

Alternative Assessment Handbook

Supporting Resources

HISTORY.

- Multimedia Classroom Global History Series
- Global History Teacher's Guide

Maps Globes Graphs Level F

- Student Workbook
- Teacher's Guide

Social Studies Trade Library Collections

- World Regions Trade Collection
- NCSS Middle School Trade Collection

Geography's Impact

Geography's Impact Video Program

- **Impact of Volcanoes in Iceland**

For more information or to purchase go to hmhsocialstudies.com

Power Presentations with Media Gallery

Power Presentations with Media Gallery are visual presentations of each chapter's main ideas. Presentations can be customized by including Quick Facts charts, images from the text, and video clips.

Differentiating Instruction

How do I address the needs of varied learners?
The Target Resource acts as your primary strategy for differentiated instruction.

ENGLISH-LANGUAGE LEARNERS & STRUGGLING READERS

Spanish Resources

Spanish Chapter Summaries Audio CD Program

Teacher One Stop:
- ExamView Assessment Suite, Spanish
- PuzzleView, Spanish

English-Language Learner Strategies and Activities

Additional Resources

Differentiated Instruction Teacher Management System: Lesson Plans for Differentiated Instruction

Resource File:
- Vocabulary Builder Activities
- Social Studies Skills: Writing to Learn

Quick Facts Transparencies:
- Northern Europe Visual Summary

Student Edition on Audio CD Program

Interactive Skills Tutor CD-ROM

Spanish/English Guided Reading Workbook

SPECIAL NEEDS LEARNERS

Differentiated Instruction Modified Worksheets and Tests CD-ROM

- Vocabulary Flash Cards
- Modified Vocabulary Builder Activities
- Modified Chapter Review Activity
- Modified Chapter Test

Additional Resources

Differentiated Instruction Teacher Management System: Lesson Plans for Differentiated Instruction

Guided Reading Workbook

Resource File: Social Studies Skills: Writing to Learn

Student Edition on Audio CD Program

Interactive Skills Tutor CD-ROM

Graphic Organizer Transparencies with Support for Reading and Writing

ADVANCED/GIFTED AND TALENTED STUDENTS

Resource File

The Resource File activities allow students to extend their knowledge of chapter-related places and people and to practice geography skills.

- Focus on Reading: Using Context Clues—Synonyms
- Focus on Writing: Writing a Letter
- Literature: *Romeo and Juliet* by William Shakespeare

Additional Resources

Differentiated Instruction Teacher Management System: Lesson Plans for Differentiated Instruction

World History and Geography Document-Based Questions Activities

Geography, Science, and Cultures Activities

Experiencing World History and Geography

Differentiated Activities in the Teacher's Edition

- Researching Word Origins and Meanings, p. 449
- Analyzing Neutral Countries, p. 460

Teacher One Stop™

How can I manage the lesson plans and support materials for differentiated instruction?

With the Teacher One Stop, you can easily organize and print lesson plans, planning guides, and instructional materials for all learners. The Teacher One Stop includes the following materials to help you differentiate instruction:

- **Interactive Teacher's Edition**
- **Calendar Planner and pacing guides**
- **Editable lesson plans**
- **All reproducible ancillaries in Adobe Acrobat (PDF) format**
- **ExamView Assessment Suite (English & Spanish)**
- **Transparency and video previews**

Differentiated Activities in the Teacher's Edition

- Examining British Influence on U.S. Popular Culture, p. 454

Interactive Student Edition

Complete online student edition with interactive multimedia support for chapter content assessment and reporting

- Interactive Maps and Notebook
- Standardized Test Prep
- Online Homework Practice and Research Activities
- Current Events
- Chapter-based Internet Activities
- Animated Geography Activities

Differentiated Activities in the Teacher's Edition

- Comparing and Contrasting Geographic Features, p. 449
- Writing Travel Journals, p. 459

Essential Question

Introduce the Essential Question

- Explain that although the countries of Northern Europe are located at high latitudes their climates are mild due to their locations near seas and oceans.

- Point out that the Republic of Ireland and the United Kingdom make up the British Isles. Have students discuss how their location helped them build a strong economy.

- Discuss how the cultures of Scandinavian countries are similar. Have students talk about how location affects the cultures of these countries.

Focus on Reading and Writing

Reading The Resource File provides a worksheet to help students practice using context clues–synonyms.

📖 **RF:** Focus on Reading, Using Context Clues–Synonyms

Writing The Resource File provides a worksheet to help students organize and write their letters.

📖 **RF:** Focus on Writing, Writing a Letter

Key to Differentiating Instruction

Below Level

Basic-level activities designed for all students encountering new material

At Level

Intermediate-level activities designed for average students

Above Level

Challenging activities designed for honors and gifted and talented students

Standard English Mastery

Activities designed to improve standard English usage

LS Learning Styles

446   CHAPTER 18

CHAPTER **18**

Northern Europe

Essential Question How has location shaped the development of nations in Northern Europe?

❓ **What You Will Learn...**

In this chapter you will discover Northern Europe's unique and varied physical geography. You will also study the history and culture of Northern Europe's two main regions—the British Isles and Scandinavia. Finally, you will learn about the British Isles and Scandinavia today.

SECTION 1: Physical Geography 448

The Big Idea Northern Europe is a region of unique physical features, rich resources, and diverse climates.

SECTION 2: The British Isles 452

The Big Idea Close cultural and historical ties link the people of the British Isles today.

SECTION 3: Scandinavia. 458

The Big Idea Scandinavia has developed into one of the most stable and prosperous regions in Europe.

FOCUS ON READING AND WRITING

Using Context Clues–Synonyms As you read, you may occasionally encounter a word or phrase that you do not know. When that happens, use the words and sentences around the unfamiliar word—context clues—to help you determine the word's meaning. As you read this chapter, look for words that are synonyms, or words that mean the same as the unfamiliar word. **See the lesson, Using Context Clues—Synonyms, on page 533.**

Writing a Letter Letters are a great way to stay in touch with friends and family. As you read this chapter, gather information about Northern Europe. Then imagine you are traveling through this region. Write a letter to your friends and family at home in which you describe what you have learned on your travels.

446 CHAPTER 18

Geography Fertile plains like this one in Ireland provide Northern Europe with much of its farmland.

Introduce the Chapter

At Level

Location of Capital Cities

1. Ask students to review the map of Northern Europe. Note the seven countries and the capital city of each.

2. Ask students how many of the seven capital cities are located directly on the ocean or a sea or gulf (six). Ask them why they think these capital cities are located on the water and why their location might be different than for capital cities in an area like West-Central Europe.

3. Note that three of the capitals lie at about 60° N while Reykjavik is near the Arctic Circle. Ask students if they know how this

affects the length of days and nights in the winter and summer (very long nights in the winter, very long days in the summer). Ask how they think that would affect life in these cities.

4. Note your own location in comparison to these cities and your nearness to a body of water. Explain that by the end of the chapter, students will be able to contrast life in different areas of Northern Europe with that in their own area.

LS Visual/Spatial, Verbal/Linguistic

📓 Alternative Assessment Handbook, Rubric 21: Map Reading

70°N

ARCTIC OCEAN

Arctic Circle

Tromso

Norwegian Sea

FINLAND

SWEDEN

RUSSIA

NORWAY

Bergen

Gulf of Bothnia

Oslo

Helsinki

Gulf of Finland

North Sea

Stockholm

ESTONIA

Göteborg

LATVIA

DENMARK

Baltic Sea

LITHUANIA

Copenhagen

RUSSIA

BELARUS

NETHERLANDS

GERMANY

POLAND

HISTORY Winston Churchill

↗ hmhsocialstudies.com **VIDEO**

map Zone Geography Skills

Location Much of Northern Europe is separated from the rest of the continent by the English Channel and the North and Baltic seas.

1. Identify What countries extend north of the Arctic Circle?

2. Contrast How does Northern Europe differ physically from the rest of Europe?

History The Palace of Westminster in London has been home to the British Parliament for over 600 years.

Culture Skiing and other forms of outdoor recreation are popular throughout much of Scandinavia.

447

• Chapter Preview •

Explore the Map and Pictures

Northern Europe: Political The countries of Northern Europe have many things in common. Location and the effects of the oceans and seas surrounding them cause similar climates. Each country has a strong economy, shared political views, and a similar type of government. But each country is affected by its geography in a different way and has a unique culture.

Analyzing Visuals What do the pictures tell you about life in Ireland, London, and Scandinavia? *possible answers—much of Ireland is rural, London is a modern, urban city, activities in Scandinavia are affected by the climate* What does the photo of the Palace of Westminster tell you about British government? *possible answer—it has a long history of democratic rule*

▶ Map Zone Transparency: Northern Europe: Political

Critical Thinking: Analyzing Visuals   At Level

Nickname from Geography

1. Ask students to review the photo labeled "Geography" and to locate Ireland on the map.

2. Explain that Ireland has earned a nickname that describes the color of much of its land area, as well as the type of land mass it is.

3. Give students two minutes to brainstorm Ireland's possible nickname. Listen to

students' ideas; then, share Ireland's nickname. *(the Emerald Isle)*

4. Explain that students will be learning more about the unique geography of Ireland and other areas of Northern Europe.

LS Visual/Spatial, Verbal/Linguistic

📄 Alternative Assessment Handbook, Rubric 40: Writing to Describe

Answers

Map Zone 1. *Norway, Sweden, Finland;* **2.** *Most countries are farther north than the rest of Europe; most countries are islands or peninsulas.*

447

Bellringer

If YOU lived there. . . Use the **Daily Bellringer Transparency** to help students answer the question.

▶ Daily Bellringer Transparency, Section 1

Northern Europe — Daily Bellringer Section 1

Preview Section 1

If YOU lived there …
Your family is planning to visit friends in Tromso, Norway. It is a city on the Norwegian Sea located 200 miles north of the Arctic Circle. You imagine a landscape covered in snow and ice. When you arrive, however, you discover green hills and ice-free harbors.

What might explain the mild climate?

Consider the LOCATION:
• on the North Atlantic Drift, a warm ocean current, keeps air temperatures warmer than other locations at similar latitudes
• because of northerly location, receives more direct sunlight in summer

Consider the SEASON:
• may have summers warm enough to grow plants
• may not have long winters, so ice and snow melts

Academic Vocabulary

Review with students the high-use academic term in this section.

primary main, most important (p. 450)

✍ RF: Vocabulary Builder, Section 1

Taking Notes

Have students use the graphic organizer online to take notes on the section. This activity will prepare students for the Section Assessment, in which they will complete a graphic organizer that builds on the information using the Critical Thinking Skill: Comparing and Contrasting.

SECTION 1

Physical Geography

What You Will Learn…

Main Ideas

1. The physical features of Northern Europe include low mountain ranges and jagged coastlines.
2. Northern Europe's natural resources include energy sources, soils, and seas.
3. The climates of Northern Europe range from a mild coastal climate to a freezing ice cap climate.

The Big Idea

Northern Europe is a region of unique physical features, rich resources, and diverse climates.

Key Terms and Places

British Isles, *p. 448*
Scandinavia, *p. 448*
fjord, *p. 449*
geothermal energy, *p. 450*
North Atlantic Drift, *p. 450*

hmhsocialstudies.com
TAKING NOTES

Use the graphic organizer online to take notes on the physical geography of Northern Europe.

If YOU lived there…

Your family is planning to visit friends in Tromso, Norway. It is a city on the Norwegian Sea located 200 miles north of the Arctic Circle. You imagine a landscape covered in snow and ice. When you arrive, however, you discover green hills and ice-free harbors.

What might explain the mild climate?

BUILDING BACKGROUND Although located at high latitudes, Norway and the rest of Northern Europe have surprisingly mild temperatures. All the countries of Northern Europe are located on seas and oceans. As a result, they benefit from ocean currents that bring warm water north and keep the climate reasonably warm.

Physical Features

From Ireland's gently rolling hills to Iceland's icy glaciers and fiery volcanoes, Northern Europe is a land of great variety. Because of this variety, the physical geography of Northern Europe changes greatly from one location to another.

Two regions—the British Isles and Scandinavia—make up Northern Europe. To the southwest lie the **British Isles**, a group of islands located across the English Channel from the rest of Europe. Northeast of the British Isles is **Scandinavia**, a region of islands and peninsulas in far northern Europe. The island of Iceland, to the west, is often considered part of Scandinavia.

Hills and Mountains Rough, rocky hills and low mountains cover much of Northern Europe. Rugged hills stretch across much of Iceland, northern Scotland, and Scandinavia. The jagged Kjolen (CHUH-luhn) Mountains on the Scandinavian Peninsula divide Norway from Sweden. The rocky soil and uneven terrain in these parts of Northern Europe make farming there difficult. As a result, fewer people live there than in the rest of Northern Europe.

448 CHAPTER 18

Teach the Big Idea

At Level

Physical Geography

Prep Required

Materials: atlas or maps of physical, resource, and climate maps of the U.S.

1. **Teach** Ask students the questions in the Main Idea boxes under Direct Teach.

2. **Apply** Write three headings on the board: *Physical Features, Natural Resources, Climates.* Call on students to add details under each heading that describe Northern Europe. Then ask if they can think of areas of the U.S. that have similar features.
   LS Verbal/Linguistic, Visual/Spatial

3. **Review** Ask students to list two countries in Northern Europe and two ways that the physical geography of the area affects life. Ask students to share their answers.

4. **Practice/Homework** Ask students to select one part of their local physical geography and write a few sentences on how it affects them and how it is similar to or different from one area of Northern Europe.
   LS Verbal/Linguistic
   ✍ Alternative Assessment Handbook, Rubric 37: Writing Assignments

❶ Melting glaciers created Scandinavia's jagged coastline and many fjords.

ELEVATION

Feet	Meters
13,120	4,000
6,560	2,000
1,640	500
656	200
(Sea level) 0	0 (Sea level)
Below sea level	Below sea level

ice cap

0   150   300 Miles
0   150   300 Kilometers

Projection: Azimuthal Equal-Area

map Zone
Geography Skills

Place Northern Europe is made up of many islands and peninsulas.

1. **Identify** What countries are located on islands?
2. **Contrast** How is Norway's coastline different from Finland's?

Farmland and Plains Fertile farmland and flat plains stretch across the southern parts of the British Isles and Scandinavia. Ireland's rolling, green hills provide rich farmland. Wide valleys in England and Denmark also have plenty of fertile soil.

Effects of Glaciers Slow-moving sheets of ice, or glaciers, have left their mark on Northern Europe's coastlines and lakes. As you can see on the map above, Norway's western coastline is very jagged. Millions of years ago, glaciers cut deep valleys into Norway's coastal mountains. As the glaciers melted, these valleys filled with water,

creating deep fjords. A **fjord** (fee-AWRD) is a narrow inlet of the sea set between high, rocky cliffs. Many fjords are very long and deep. Norway's Sogne (SAWNG-nuh) Fjord, for example, is over 100 miles (160 km) long and more than three-quarters of a mile (1.2 km) deep. Melting glaciers also carved thousands of lakes in Northern Europe. Sweden's Lake Vanern, along with many of the lakes in the British Isles, were carved by glaciers thousands of years ago.

READING CHECK **Summarizing** What are some physical features of Northern Europe?

NORTHERN EUROPE **449**

449

❷ **Natural Resources**

Northern Europe's natural resources include energy sources, soils, and seas.

Identify Which country has a large supply of geothermal energy? *Iceland*

Summarize Why are the seas and oceans of Northern Europe considered a natural resource? *They provide fish to the people.*

📖 **RF:** Geography and History, Understanding Northern Europe

❸ **Climates**

The climates of Northern Europe range from a mild coastal climate to a freezing ice cap climate.

Contrast How do temperatures in Northern Europe differ from those around the world in similar latitudes? *They are warmer.*

Recall What is the name of the ocean current that causes Northern Europe's mild climates? *North Atlantic Drift*

▶ Map Zone Transparency: Satellite View: Norway's Fjords

Satellite View
Norway's Fjords

Predicting Temperature Ask students to select two points on the Satellite View image. One point should be close to a fjord, the other further inland. Then ask students to predict which point would have the higher average temperatures in the winter and why. **LS** **Logical/Mathematical**

📖 Alternative Assessment Handbook, Rubric 6: Cause and Effect

Answers

Satellite View *keep temperatures mild and allow winter travel*

Reading Check *energy resources, forests and soils, seas and oceans*

Natural Resources

Natural resources have helped to make Northern Europe one of the wealthiest regions in the world. Northern Europe's primary resources are its energy resources, forests and soils, and surrounding seas.

Energy Northern Europe has a variety of energy resources. Norway and the United Kingdom benefit from oil and natural gas deposits under the North Sea. Hydroelectric energy is produced by the region's many lakes and rivers. In Iceland steam from hot springs produces **geothermal energy**, or energy from the heat of Earth's interior.

ACADEMIC VOCABULARY
primary main, most important

Satellite View

Norway's Fjords

Millions of years ago much of Norway was covered with glaciers. As the glaciers flowed slowly downhill, they carved long, winding channels, or fjords, into Norway's coastline.

As you can see in this satellite image, fjords cut many miles into Norway's interior, bringing warm waters from the North and Norwegian seas. As warm waters penetrate inland, they keep temperatures relatively mild. In fact, people have used these unfrozen fjords to travel during the winter when ice and snow made travel over land difficult.

Drawing Conclusions How do fjords benefit life in Norway?

Forests and Soils Forests and soils are two other important natural resources in Northern Europe. Large areas of timber-producing forests stretch across Finland and the Scandinavian Peninsula. Fertile soils provide rich farmland for crops, such as wheat and potatoes. Livestock like sheep and dairy cattle are also common.

Seas and Oceans The seas that surround Northern Europe are another important natural resource. For centuries, the North Sea, the Norwegian Sea, and the Atlantic Ocean have provided rich stocks of fish. Today, fishing is a key industry in Norway, Denmark, and Iceland.

READING CHECK **Summarizing** What natural resources are found in Northern Europe?

Climates

Locate Northern Europe on a map of the world. Notice that much of the region lies near the Arctic Circle. Due to the region's high latitude, you might imagine that it would be quite cold during much of the year. In reality, however, the climates in Northern Europe are remarkably mild.

Northern Europe's mild climates are a result of the **North Atlantic Drift**, an ocean current that brings warm, moist air across the Atlantic Ocean. Warm waters from this ocean current keep most of the region warmer than other locations around the globe at similar latitudes.

Much of Northern Europe has a marine west coast climate. Denmark, the British Isles, and western Norway benefit from mild summers and frequent rainfall. Snow and frosts may occur in winter but do not usually last long.

Central Norway, Sweden, and southern Finland have a humid continental climate. This area has four true seasons with cold, snowy winters and mild summers.

Cross-Discipline Activity: Science

Above Level

Understanding Geothermal Energy

Research Required

1. Divide the class into small groups. Explain that geothermal energy is an important resource in Iceland and is used in other areas of the world as well, including the U.S.

2. Have each group use the library, the Internet, or other resources to research one of the following areas: How Geothermal Energy Plants Work, How Much Geothermal Energy Is Produced Around the World, Geothermal Energy and the Environment, Geothermal Energy in the U.S. Each group should create a poster or chart that illustrates their findings.

3. When students have finished, have each group display their posters or charts, explain the information, and answer questions.
   LS **Verbal/Linguistic, Visual/Spatial, Interpersonal**

📖 Alternative Assessment Handbook, Rubrics 24: Oral Presentations; and 30: Research

Northern Europe: Climate

Climate Types
- Marine west coast
- Humid continental
- Subarctic
- Tundra
- Ice cap

❶ Skiers in Norway's Jotunheimen National Park make the most of the region's cold, snowy winters.

map zone Geography Skills

Regions The climates of Northern Europe range from mild marine west coast to freezing ice cap.

1. **Locate** What parts of Northern Europe have tundra climates?
2. **Make Inferences** What allows much of Northern Europe to have mild climates?

Far to the north are colder climates. Subarctic regions, like those in Northern Scandinavia, have long, cold winters and short summers. Iceland's tundra and ice cap climates produce extremely cold temperatures all year.

READING CHECK **Analyzing** How does the North Atlantic Drift keep climates mild?

SUMMARY AND PREVIEW Northern Europe has many different physical features, natural resources, and climates. Next, you will learn about the history and culture of the British Isles.

Section 1 Assessment

⬈ hmhsocialstudies.com
ONLINE QUIZ

Reviewing Ideas, Terms, and Places

1. **a. Describe** What are the physical features of this region?
   b. Analyze What role did glaciers play in shaping the physical geography of Northern Europe?
2. **a. Recall** What is **geothermal energy**?
   b. Make Inferences How do people in Northern Europe benefit from the surrounding seas?
3. **a. Identify** What climates exist in Northern Europe?
   b. Predict How might the climates of Northern Europe be different without the **North Atlantic Drift**?

Critical Thinking

4. **Comparing and Contrasting** Using your notes and a chart like the one below, compare and contrast the physical geography of the British Isles and Scandinavia.

	British Isles	Scandinavia
Physical Features		
Resources		
Climates		

FOCUS ON WRITING

5. **Describing the Physical Geography** Take notes on the physical features, resources, and climates of Northern Europe. In what season might you visit the region?

NORTHERN EUROPE **451**

Direct Teach

MISCONCEPTION ALERT

Temperatures in Iceland Although Iceland sounds like it might be one of the coldest countries in the world, the North Atlantic Drift keeps its capital city, Reykjavik, remarkably warm. Its average temperature in the coldest month of the year, January, is only just below freezing (-1°C or 31°F). Its average temperature in January is about the same as east coast cities in the U.S. like New York City (0°C or 32°F) and Boston, Massachusetts (-2°C or 29°F), and warmer than cities in the Midwest such as Kansas City, Missouri (-3°C or 27°F), Cleveland, Ohio (-3°C or 26°F), and Chicago, Illinois (-6°C or 22°F).

▶ Map Zone Transparency: Northern Europe: Climate

Review & Assess

Close

Briefly review the physical features, natural resources, and climates of Northern Europe.

Review

↗ Online Quiz, Section 1

Assess

SE Section 1 Assessment
PASS: Section 1 Quiz
Alternative Assessment Handbook

Reteach/Classroom Intervention

Guided Reading Workbook, Section 1
● Interactive Skills Tutor CD-ROM

Section 1 Assessment Answers

1. **a.** hills, plains, mountains, fjords
   b. created fjords and lakes
2. **a.** energy produced from the heat of Earth's interior
   b. The seas provide rich stocks of fish.
3. **a.** marine west coast, humid continental, subarctic, tundra, ice cap
   b. The climates would probably be much colder and drier.
4. British Isles: physical features—hills and plains; resources—oil and natural gas, farmland, fish; climates—marine west coast;

Scandinavia: physical features—(northern) ragged hills, mountains, and fjords, (southern) farmland and plains; resources—geothermal energy, oil and natural gas, timber, fish; climates—marine west coast, humid continental, subarctic, tundra, ice cap

5. Students may include the British Isles, fjords, geothermal energy, fishing, and the marine west coast climate.

Answers

Map Zone 1. *northern areas of Iceland, Norway, and Finland;* **2.** *The North Atlantic Drift brings warm moist air from across the Atlantic Ocean.*

Reading Check *The North Atlantic Drift brings warm moist air from across the Atlantic Ocean. Warm waters from the ocean current help keep the region warmer than other places at similar latitudes.*

Bellringer

If YOU lived there. . . Use the **Daily Bellringer Transparency** to help students answer the question.

▶ Daily Bellringer Transparency, Section 2

Academic Vocabulary

Review with students the high-use academic term in this section.

agreement a decision reached by two or more people or groups (p. 455)

📝 **RF: Vocabulary Builder, Section 2**

Taking Notes

Have students use the graphic organizer online to take notes on the section. This activity will prepare students for the Section Assessment, in which they will complete a graphic organizer that builds on the information using the Critical Thinking Skill: Summarizing.

If YOU lived there...

You have family and friends that live throughout the British Isles. On visits you have discovered that the people of England, Ireland, Scotland, and Wales share the same language, use the same type of government, and eat many of the same foods.

Why might culture in the British Isles be similar?

What You Will Learn...

Main Ideas

1. Invaders and a global empire have shaped the history of the British Isles.
2. British culture, such as government and music, has influenced much of the world.
3. Efforts to bring peace to Northern Ireland and maintain strong economies are important issues in the British Isles today.

The Big Idea

Close cultural and historical ties link the people of the British Isles today.

Key Terms and Places

constitutional monarchy, *p. 454*
Magna Carta, *p. 454*
disarm, *p. 455*
London, *p. 456*
Dublin, *p. 456*

hmhsocialstudies.com
TAKING NOTES

Use the graphic organizer online to take notes on the British Isles.

BUILDING BACKGROUND The people of the British Isles have had close ties for thousands of years. As a result, the people of England, Scotland, Ireland, and Wales share many of the same culture traits. Similar religions, languages, literary traditions, and even holidays are common throughout the British Isles.

History

Two independent countries—the Republic of Ireland and the United Kingdom—make up the British Isles. The United Kingdom is a union of four small countries: England, Scotland, Wales, and Northern Ireland. Throughout their history, the people of the British Isles have been closely linked together.

Time Line

History of the British Isles

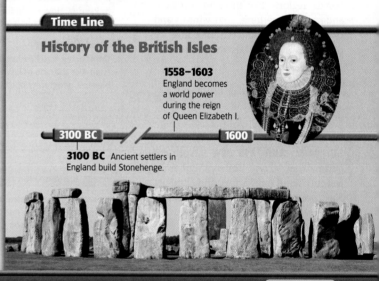

1558–1603
England becomes a world power during the reign of Queen Elizabeth I.

3100 BC   1600

3100 BC Ancient settlers in England build Stonehenge.

Teach the Big Idea

                At Level

The British Isles

1. **Teach** Ask students the questions in the Main Idea boxes under Direct Teach.

2. **Apply** Ask students to review the political map of the British Isles in this section. Then write three headings where students can see: History, Culture, British Isles Today. Ask students to provide details to go under each heading, referencing the map as they list each detail.
   🔲 **Verbal/Linguistic, Visual/Spatial**

3. **Review** Ask students to suggest the most lasting effect the British Isles have had

on the world. Then ask them to identify challenges facing the British Isles and how they might be met.

4. **Practice/Homework** Ask students to review a newspaper or magazine and make notes on stories about the British Isles or places that have been influenced by them. This might include stories about former colonies or popular culture. Have them give a short oral report on their findings.
   🔲 **Verbal/Linguistic, Visual/Spatial**

Early History

The history of the British Isles dates back thousands of years. Early settlers built Stonehenge, an ancient monument, some 5,000 years ago. Around 450 BC, the Celts (KELTS) arrived in the British Isles and settled Scotland, Wales, and Ireland. Britain was even part of the ancient Roman Empire.

In the Middle Ages a series of invaders ruled the British Isles. The Angles, Saxons, and Vikings all established small kingdoms in Britain. Finally, in 1066, the Normans from northern France conquered England and established a strong kingdom there.

Over time, England grew in strength and power. It soon overshadowed its neighbors in the British Isles. By the 1500s strong rulers like Queen Elizabeth I had turned England into a world power.

Rise of the British Empire

A strong economy and mighty navy helped England build a vast empire. Over time, England joined with Wales and Scotland to create the United Kingdom of Great Britain. Eventually, Ireland was annexed too. England also launched an overseas empire. By the 1800s Britain had colonies in the Americas, India, and Australia.

BIOGRAPHY

Sir Winston Churchill
(1874–1965)

One of Britain's greatest leaders, Sir Winston Churchill, guided the United Kingdom through the dark days of World War II. Churchill was appointed prime minister shortly after the beginning of World War II. He inspired the British to continue fighting despite Germany's defeat of much of Europe. During the Battle of Britain, Churchill gave fiery speeches. He encouraged British citizens to "never surrender." His creation of an alliance with the Soviet Union and the United States led to Germany's eventual defeat. Churchill's determination helped the Allies win the war.

Evaluating Do you think Churchill was important to British history? Why or why not?

The United Kingdom's economy soared in the 1700s and 1800s, thanks to the Industrial Revolution. Industries like iron, steel, and textiles, or cloth products, helped make the United Kingdom one of the world's richest countries.

Not everyone benefited, however. In the 1840s a severe food shortage devastated Ireland. Lack of support from the English government during the famine increased tensions between the two countries.

HISTORY

VIDEO
Winston Churchill

hmhsocialstudies.com

FOCUS ON READING
What are *textiles*? How can you tell?

Direct Teach

Main Idea

❶ **History**

Invaders and a global empire have shaped the history of the British Isles.

Recall What two countries make up the British Isles? *the Republic of Ireland and the United Kingdom*

Cause and Effect Why did the economy of the United Kingdom grow so quickly in the 1700s and 1800s? *The Industrial Revolution created strong industries like textiles, iron, and steel.*

Cause and Effect Why did tensions between the United Kingdom and Ireland increase during and after the 1840s? *Ireland experienced a famine and England did not provide needed support.*

RF: Biography, Mary, Queen of Scots

Info to Know

The Irish Potato Famine During the early 1800s, the main crop grown by Irish farmers was potatoes. When the potato crop was damaged by a disease called "late blight" in 1845, there wasn't enough food to eat. Over the next five years, about one million people died from starvation or disease.

Conditions were so bad that another one million people are estimated to have immigrated to the United States and other countries. During the famine, food was often exported to England, where people could afford it. This caused bitter feelings among many Irish people toward the British.

1730–1860
The Industrial Revolution brings great wealth to England.

1940
London is bombed during the Battle of Britain in World War II.

1700　1800　1900　2000

1858–1947
The British Empire controls India, its most valuable colony.

ANALYSIS SKILL **READING TIME LINES**

About how many years ago was Stonehenge built?

NORTHERN EUROPE **453**

Collaborative Learning

At Level

English Kings and Queens

Materials: a list of English monarchs from the Norman invasion through present day

Prep Required **Research Required**

1. Show students the list of monarchs or distribute copies to them. Explain that each monarch had strengths and weaknesses, successes and failures.

2. Explain to students that they will be researching English monarchs to get an overall feel for English history.

3. Assign one monarch to each student. Have students use the library, the Internet, or

other resources to prepare an oral report on their monarch's years of reign, wars, major changes and events, or other important details.

4. Make a list on the board and have students present their reports chronologically.

LS Verbal/Linguistic

Alternative Assessment Handbook, Rubrics 24: Oral Presentations; and 30: Research

Answers

Biography *Answers will vary, but students' opinions should be based on information in the text.*

Focus on Reading *cloth products; it is defined by the phrase "or cloth products."*

Reading Time Lines *about 5,100 years*

453

Main Idea

❷ Culture

British culture, such as government and music, has influenced much of the world.

Identify Who makes the laws in the United Kingdom? *Parliament, Britain's legislative body*

Recall Which event marked the beginning of the time when Great Britain gave up most of its colonies? *World War II*

Drawing Inferences How do you think a common ancestry helps keep the British Isles stable? *possible answer—common ancestry might strengthen national identity.*

Connect to Science

An Empire Where the Sun Never Sets At its height in the early 1900s, the British Empire had colonies around the world, including in Asia, South America, and Africa. Britain also had a strong relationship with Canada, which recognized the British monarch as head of the government. Demonstrate with a globe why people said "the sun never sets on the British Empire." Use a flashlight to represent the sun and turn the globe east to west. Point out colonies in different continents that were part of the British Empire in the early 1900s.

↗ **hmhsocialstudies.com**

Online Resources
Activity: Scottish and Irish Culture

Answers

Reading Check *Norman Conquest in 1066, world power in 1500s, Industrial Revolution in 1700s and 1800s, empire spans the globe by late 1800s, decline of empire in 1900s*

By the late 1800s the British Empire spanned the globe. Africa, Asia, Australia, and the Americas were all home to British colonies. At its height, the British Empire was the largest empire in history.

Decline of Empire

In the 1900s the British Empire began to fall apart. Both World War I and the Great Depression hurt the British economy. Rebellions in Ireland forced Britain to grant self-rule to all but the northern part of Ireland. In 1949 the Republic of Ireland gained full independence. Movements for independence also emerged in Britain's overseas colonies. After World War II, Great Britain gave up most of its colonies. The British Empire was no more.

READING CHECK **Sequencing** What major events mark the history of the British Isles?

Culture

People in different regions of the British Isles hold fast to regional traditions and customs. Here, Scots proudly display two symbols of Scottish culture—bagpipes and kilts.

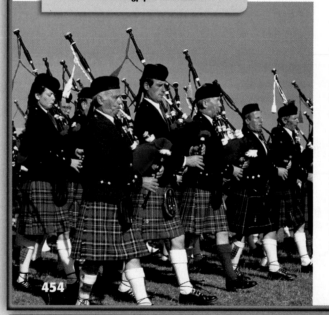

454

Culture

For years the British ruled much of the world. As a result, the government, people, and popular culture of the British Isles have influenced people all around the globe.

Government

The government of the United Kingdom is a **constitutional monarchy**, a type of democracy in which a king or queen serves as head of state but a legislature makes the laws. The English first limited the power of monarchs in the Middle Ages. A document known as **Magna Carta**, or Great Charter, limited the powers of kings. It also required everyone to obey the law. Today, a prime minister leads the British government. Most members of Britain's legislative body, known as Parliament, are elected.

The Republic of Ireland has a president as head of state. The president, who has limited powers, appoints a prime minister. Together with the Irish parliament, the prime minister runs the government.

People

For hundreds of years, the countries of the British Isles have had close ties. As a result, the countries share many culture traits. One similarity is their common heritage. Many people in the British Isles can trace their heritage to the region's early settlers, such as the Celts, Angles, and Saxons. Sports like soccer and rugby are another shared trait among the people of Britain.

Although people in the British Isles share many culture traits, each region still maintains its own unique identity. This is particularly true in Ireland and Scotland. Unlike the rest of the British Isles, most Irish are Roman Catholic. Irish Gaelic, a Celtic language, is one of the country's official languages. The people of Scotland have also maintained their unique culture.

Differentiating Instruction

At Level

Special Needs Learners

Prep Required

Materials: a collection of magazines or books focusing on aspects of popular culture such as music or fashion styles, materials for making a collage or poster

1. Ask students to name ways that British popular culture has affected culture in the United States. Examples might include popular music, fashion, or movies.

2. Provide students with magazines focusing on popular culture. Have each student prepare a

small collage or poster which displays at least three instances of British influence on the culture of the United States.

3. Have each student display a completed poster and explain what it illustrates to the class.
 LS **Visual/Spatial**

📋 Alternative Assessment Handbook, Rubric 8: Collages

It is not unusual in Scotland to see people wearing kilts and playing bagpipes on special occasions.

Immigrants from all corners of the world have settled in Britain. Many immigrants from former British colonies, such as India and Jamaica, add to the rich culture of the British Isles.

Popular Culture

British popular culture influences people all around the globe. For example, English is the language of business, education, and the Internet in many places. British music and literature are also popular. Millions of people around the globe listen to music by bands like Ireland's U2 and England's The Beatles and read works by British authors like William Shakespeare.

READING CHECK **Summarizing** What parts of British culture have spread around the world?

British Isles Today

The British Isles face some challenges. Efforts to bring peace to Northern Ireland and to maintain a powerful economy are key issues in the British Isles today.

Northern Ireland

One of the toughest problems facing the British Isles today is conflict in Northern Ireland. Disputes between the people of Northern Ireland have a long history.

In the 1500s Protestants from England and Scotland began settling in Northern Ireland. Over time, they outnumbered Irish Catholics in the area. When Ireland became a separate state, Northern Ireland's Protestant majority chose to remain part of the United Kingdom.

Since then, many Catholics in Northern Ireland believe they have not been treated fairly by Protestants. Some Catholics hope

to unite with the Republic of Ireland. For years the two sides have waged a bitter and violent struggle. In the late 1990s peace talks between the two warring sides began. An **agreement** eventually led to a cease-fire and the creation of a national assembly in Northern Ireland. However, the refusal of some groups to **disarm**, or give up all weapons, stalled the peace talks. Recently, however, hopes are once again high that peaceful relations between the groups will bring about a long-lasting peace.

hmhsocialstudies.com
ANIMATED GEOGRAPHY

British Isles: Political

Shetland Islands

⊕ National capital
● Other city

0   75   150 Miles
0   75   150 Kilometers
Projection: Azimuthal Equal-Area

ATLANTIC OCEAN

SCOTLAND

Orkney Islands

North Sea

●Edinburgh
●Glasgow

NORTHERN IRELAND
●Belfast

UNITED KINGDOM

REPUBLIC OF IRELAND

Irish Sea
●Liverpool
●Leeds
●Manchester

Dublin ⊕

●Birmingham

Cork●

WALES   ENGLAND

●London

English Channel

map zone Geography Skills

Regions The Republic of Ireland and the United Kingdom make up the British Isles.
1. Identify Which country is closer to mainland Europe?
2. Make Inferences How might the British Isles be affected by their location?

ACADEMIC VOCABULARY

agreement a decision reached by two or more people or groups

NORTHERN EUROPE **455**

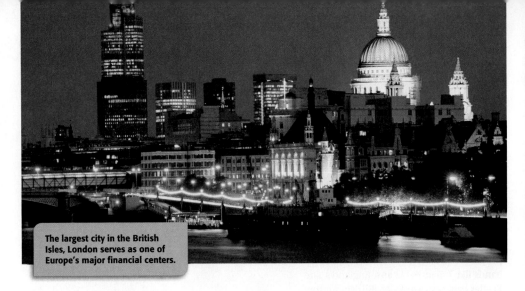

The largest city in the British Isles, London serves as one of Europe's major financial centers.

Direct Teach

Did you know...

Both London and Dublin have been settled for about 2,000 years. Dublin was probably founded by Vikings and was first mentioned in the second century by the geographer Ptolemy. In Gaelic, its name (*Dubh-linn*) means "Black Pool."

London was settled by the Romans as a communications center after they invaded England in the first century A.D. Its original name was "Londinium."

Review & Assess

Close

Briefly review the history, culture, current issues, and challenges of the Bristish Isles.

Review

 Online Quiz, Section 2

Assess

SE Section 2 Assessment

PASS: Section 2 Quiz

Alternative Assessment Handbook

Reteach/Classroom Intervention

Guided Reading Workbook, Section 2

Interactive Skills Tutor CD-ROM

The Economy

The economies of the United Kingdom and the Republic of Ireland are among Europe's strongest. **London**, the capital of the United Kingdom, is a center for world trade and industry. North Sea energy reserves have made the United Kingdom a major producer of oil and natural gas. In Ireland, computer equipment and software have become major industries, especially near **Dublin**, Ireland's capital. The economies of the United Kingdom and the Republic of Ireland also rely on service industries like banking, tourism, and insurance.

READING CHECK **Summarizing** What has been the cause of conflict in Northern Ireland?

SUMMARY AND PREVIEW You have learned about the rich history and culture of the British Isles. Next, you will learn about the countries of Scandinavia.

Section 2 Assessment

hmhsocialstudies.com
ONLINE QUIZ

Reviewing Ideas, Terms, and Places

1. **a. Identify** What peoples invaded the British Isles?
   b. Make Inferences How did the Industrial Revolution strengthen the British Empire?
2. **a. Describe** What elements of British culture are found around the world?
   b. Explain How did **Magna Carta** affect British government?
3. **a. Define** What does **disarm** mean?
   b. Analyze What are the central issues of the conflict in Northern Ireland?
   c. Elaborate Why do you think the economy of the British Isles is so strong?

Critical Thinking

4. **Summarizing** Using your notes and a graphic organizer like the one here, summarize the history and culture of the British Isles in your own words.

History

Culture

FOCUS ON WRITING

5. **Writing about the British Isles** What information about the British Isles do you think is most interesting? Take notes on what you could include in a letter to someone who has never visited the area.

456 CHAPTER 18

Section 2 Assessment Answers

1. **a.** Celts, Angles, Saxons, Vikings, Normans
   b. Industries helped make the United Kingdom one of world's richest countries.

2. **a.** literature, music, language
   b. limited the powers of kings; required everyone to obey the law

3. **a.** to give up all weapons
   b. Catholics feel they haven't been treated fairly by the Protestant majority.
   c. possible answers—stable government, resources, industries

4. history—invaders, strong empire, declining empire; culture—stable democracy, people sharing culture traits, influential popular culture; Britain's history as a strong country and world power helped make its culture influential around the world today.

5. Answers will vary but should reflect section content.

Answers

Reading Check *Catholics feel they haven't been treated fairly by the Protestant majority.*

Social Studies Skills

Chart and Graph | Critical Thinking | Geography | Study

Writing to Learn

Learn

Writing is an important tool for learning new information. When you write about what you read, you can better understand and remember information. For example, when you write a list of items you need from the grocery store, the act of writing can help you remember what to buy. Use the steps below to write to learn.

- Read the text carefully. Look for the main idea and important details.
- Think about the information you just read. Then summarize in your own words what you learned.
- Write a personal response to what you read. What do you think about the information? What questions might you have? How does this information affect you?

Practice

Use the steps you just learned to practice writing to learn. Read the paragraph below carefully, then complete a chart like the one here.

Tromso, Norway, is one of Europe's northern-most cities. Because of Earth's tilt and Tromso's location north of the Arctic Circle, the city experiences unusual conditions in both summer and winter. During the summer, the sun stays above the horizon continuously from late May to late July. In winter, residents of Tromso do not see the sun from November to January.

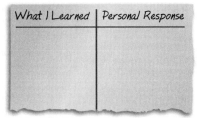

Apply

Read the information in Section 3 carefully. Then create a chart similar to the one above. In the first column, summarize the key ideas from the section in your own words. Use the second column to write your personal reaction to the information you learned.

NORTHERN EUROPE **457**

Social Studies Skills Activity: Writing to Learn

Below Level

Writing About Northern Ireland

Standard English Mastery

1. Create a What I Learned/Personal Response chart where students can see. Ask volunteers to read aloud the text under the heading Northern Ireland in Section 2.

2. Discuss with students different things they might list in each column. Assist students in identifying important details and summarizing the information in their own words using standard English. For personal responses, have students complete sentences such as *I think . . . , I believe . . . , I am unsure*

about . . . Complete the chart with students' responses. As a class, discuss any necessary corrections to the sentences to align them with standard English usage.

3. When charts are complete, ask students to record the information in their notebooks in paragraph form. Ask students if the exercise helped them better understand the information. **LS** Verbal/Linguistic

Alternative Assessment Handbook, Rubric 37: Writing Assignments

---

Social Studies Skills

Writing to Learn

Materials: a newspaper or magazine article for each student

1. Distribute copies of newspaper or magazine articles to students. Have students read their articles and complete a What I Learned/Personal Response chart.

2. Have students use their charts to write a paragraph summarizing the information. Then have them read their paragraphs to the class.

3. Discuss the topics and responses and ask students how the process of writing to learn can help them remember information.
   LS Verbal/Linguistic

   Alternative Assessment Handbook, Rubric 37: Writing Assignments

   Interactive Skills Tutor CD-ROM Lesson 14: Identify Main Ideas and Supporting Ideas

   RF: Social Studies Skills, Writing to Learn

Answers

Practice *What I Learned—Tromso, Norway, is very far north and has sunlight all the time in part of summer and no sun at all in part of winter. Personal Response—Answers will vary, but should reflect the information students learned.*

Apply *Answers will vary. Summaries should include the key ideas that the history of Scandinavia dates back to the time of the Vikings and the region today is known for its peace and prosperity. Personal responses should reflect the information students learned.*

457

Bellringer

If YOU lived there. . . Use the **Daily Bellringer Transparency** to help students answer the question.

▶ Daily Bellringer Transparency, Section 3

Northern Europe   Daily Bellringer
                                            Section 3

Review Section 2

In each of the following pairs of sentences, choose the sentence that is TRUE.

1. **a.** The British Isles have always been ruled by England.
   b. The British Isles have been ruled by many invaders in its past.

2. **a.** The United Kingdom includes England, Scotland, Wales, and the Republic of Ireland.
   b. The United Kingdom includes England, Scotland, Wales, and Northern Ireland.

3. **a.** The British Empire was the largest empire in history.
   b. The Roman Empire was the largest empire in history.

Preview Section 3

If YOU lived there ...

You live in Copenhagen, the picturesque capital of Denmark. One of your favorite walks is along the waterfront, which is lined with colorful medieval buildings. Sailing boats of all sizes are anchored here. A famous statue in the harbor shows the Little Mermaid. But your favorite place of all is the huge amusement park called Tivoli Gardens, where you can enjoy fun and good food. **What sights would you show to a visitor?**

Consider the NATURAL BEAUTY:
· boat through bays, fjords, and seas
· soak in hot springs and tour geysers
· bike around the beautiful countryside

Consider the CULTURE:
· visit castles and Viking sites
· see historic cathedrals and churches
· eat at local restaurants

Review Answers: 1. b; 2. b; 3. a

Key Terms and Places

📖 **RF:** Vocabulary Builder, Section 3

Taking Notes

Have students use the graphic organizer online to take notes on the section. This activity will prepare students for the Section Assessment, in which they will complete a graphic organizer that builds on the information using the Critical Thinking Skill: Finding Main Ideas.

Scandinavia

If **YOU** lived there...

You live in Copenhagen, the picturesque capital of Denmark. One of your favorite walks is along the waterfront, which is lined with colorful medieval buildings. Sailing boats of all sizes are anchored here. A famous statue in the harbor shows the Little Mermaid. But your favorite place of all is the huge amusement park called Tivoli Gardens, where you can enjoy fun and good food.

What sights would you show to a visitor?

> **BUILDING BACKGROUND** After a long and warlike history, the modern countries of Scandinavia are models of peace and prosperity for the rest of Europe. Their cultures are similar in several ways, but each country has its own personality.

History

Hundreds of years ago, Scandinavia was home to warlike Vikings. The **Vikings** were Scandinavian warriors who raided Europe and the Mediterranean in the early Middle Ages. Excellent sailors, the Vikings used quick and powerful longboats to attack villages along coasts or rivers. The Vikings conquered the British Isles, Finland, and parts of France, Germany, and Russia. They were some of the most feared warriors of their time.

The Vikings were also great explorers. They established the first settlements in Iceland in the 800s and in Greenland in the 900s. A short time later, Vikings led by Leif Eriksson became the first Europeans to reach North America. The ruins of a Viking colony have been found in present-day Newfoundland, off the southeast coast of Canada.

In the 1100s the Viking raids ended. Powerful Scandinavian chiefs instead concentrated on strengthening their kingdoms. During the Middle Ages three kingdoms—Norway, Sweden, and Denmark—competed for power in the region.

Denmark was the first to gain the upper hand. By the late 1300s Denmark ruled a union of all the Scandinavian kingdoms and territories. Eventually, Sweden challenged Denmark's power.

What You Will Learn...

Main Ideas

1. The history of Scandinavia dates back to the time of the Vikings.
2. Scandinavia today is known for its peaceful and prosperous countries.

The Big Idea

Scandinavia has developed into one of the most stable and prosperous regions in Europe.

Key Terms and Places

Vikings, *p. 458*
Stockholm, *p. 460*
neutral, *p. 460*
uninhabitable, *p. 461*
Oslo, *p. 461*
Helsinki, *p. 461*
geysers, *p. 462*

hmhsocialstudies.com
TAKING NOTES

Use the graphic organizer online to take notes on Scandinavia.

Teach the Big Idea

Scandinavia

1. **Teach** Ask students the questions in the Main Idea boxes under Direct Teach.

2. **Apply** Create a three-column, five-row table on the board. Label the columns: History, Similarities among Countries, and Unique Features. Label the rows with the five countries of Scandinavia. Ask students to provide details to complete the table.
   LS Verbal/Linguistic, Visual/Spatial

3. **Review** Ask students to suggest reasons why the Scandinavian countries are some of the most peaceful and prosperous countries in the world today.

4. **Practice/Homework** Have each student select one of the Scandinavian countries and write a short essay on why they would or would not want to live there.
   LS Verbal/Linguistic

In time, Sweden left the Danish-led union, taking Finland with it. Many years later, Sweden won control of Norway as well.

By the 1900s Scandinavian countries wanted their independence. Norway won its independence from Sweden in the early 1900s. Soon after, Finland became independent after centuries of foreign <u>domination</u>, or control, by Sweden and later by Russia. Iceland, then a Danish territory, declared its independence in 1944. To this day, however, Greenland remains a part of Denmark as a self-ruling territory.

READING CHECK **Analyzing** What historical ties do the countries of Scandinavia have?

FOCUS ON READING
What other word has the same meaning as *domination*? How can you tell?

Close-up

Viking Raids

The Vikings of Scandinavia launched raids on many European settlements in the early Middle Ages. Using powerful longships, Viking warriors attacked towns and villages near coasts and rivers. Vikings even sailed as far as North America in their longships.

A large woolen sail helped increase the ship's speed.

Sometimes as many as 30 oars spanned each side of a longship.

Viking longships were designed the same at each end. As a result, warriors did not have to turn the ship around to make a quick escape.

The longship's shallow design made river travel possible and allowed Viking raiders to sail their ships ashore.

ANALYSIS SKILL **ANALYZING VISUALS**
What aspects of Viking longships might have frightened Europeans who saw them approaching?

NORTHERN EUROPE **459**

Main Idea

❶ History

The history of Scandinavia dates back to the time of the Vikings.

Recall About what year did Vikings first reach North America? *around AD 1000*

Summarize Why were the Vikings feared during the Middle Ages? *They conquered the British Isles, northern France, Finland, and parts of Germany and Russia.*

Drawing Inferences How do you think Scandinavia's location helped the Vikings to become such good warriors? *They were excellent sailors because of their nearness to the sea and were able to launch attacks by boat.*

📝 RF: Geography for Life, The Vikings Abroad

Info to Know

Norse Mythology Viking myths were similar to those of early Romans and Greeks. They included stories of gods who had a variety of powers as well as weaknesses. One of the chief gods was Thor, the god of thunder. His power was symbolized by a magic hammer which he threw using iron gloves and which always returned to him. Thunder was believed to be the sound of Thor's chariot. Thursday was named after him.

About the Illustration

This illustration is an artist's conception based on available sources. However, historians are uncertain exactly what this scene looked like.

Differentiating Instruction

Above Level

Advanced/Gifted and Talented

Research Required

1. Tell students that two of the most famous Viking explorers were Leif Eriksson and his father, Erik the Red. Ask students to select one as a subject for further research. Have students choose one event to write about.

2. Ask students to write a journal entry describing the event they have chosen from the viewpoint of Erik the Red or Leif Eriksson. Ask them to imagine what thoughts and feelings their explorer might have had, and to use vivid descriptions.

3. Ask volunteers to share their journal entries with the class. 🄻 **Verbal/Linguistic**

📝 Alternative Assessment Handbook, Rubrics 15: Journals; and 30: Research

Answers

Reading Check *home to Vikings, often ruled by one country*

Focus on Reading *control; it is defined by the phrase "or control."*

Analyzing Visuals *possible answer— many oars indicating a large force, the carved head at the bow*

❷ Scandinavia Today

Scandinavia today is known for its peaceful and prosperous countries.

Identify Which is the largest and most populous country in Scandinavia? *Sweden*

Summarize What challenge will Norway's economy face over the next century? *Its oil fields are expected to run dry and it will need to replace energy sources and income from oil.*

Making Inferences How do you think Sweden's neutrality has affected its international standing? *Countries and organizations like the UN have asked their help to provide neutral observers or peacekeepers.*

📑 **RF:** Biography, Hans Christian Andersen

📑 **RF:** Primary Source, "The Scream" by Eduard Munch

Checking for Understanding

True or False Answer each statement *T* if it is true and *F* if it is false. If false, explain why.

1. The countries of Scandinavia all have strong economies. *T*

2. Most Swedes live in the northern part of the country. *F; Most Swedes live in the southern part.*

3. Denmark is one of the largest countries in Scandinavia. *F; It is the smallest country.*

Online Resources
Activity: Scandinavian Social Programs

Answers

Analyzing Visuals *pleasure boats, well dressed people enjoying leisurely walks, modern buildings*

Scandinavia Today

Today the countries of Scandinavia have much in common. Similar political views, languages, and religion unite the region. The countries of Scandinavia have large, wealthy cities, strong economies, and well-educated workers. Scandinavians enjoy some of the world's highest standards of living. Each country provides its citizens with excellent social programs and services, such as free health care. Sweden, Denmark, Greenland, Norway, Finland, and Iceland are among the world's most peaceful, stable, and prosperous nations.

Sweden

Sweden is Scandinavia's largest and most populous country. Most Swedes live in the southern part of the country in large towns and cities. In fact, more than 84 percent of Swedes live in urban areas. **Stockholm**, Sweden's capital and largest city, is located on the east coast near the Baltic Sea. Often called a floating city, Stockholm is built on 14 islands and part of the mainland.

For almost 200 years, Sweden has been a neutral country. **Neutral** means that it has chosen not to take sides in an international conflict. Sweden does, however, play an active role in the United Nations as well as the European Union.

Denmark

Denmark, once the most powerful country in Scandinavia, is also the smallest. It is Scandinavia's most densely populated country, with some 336 people per square mile (130 per square km).

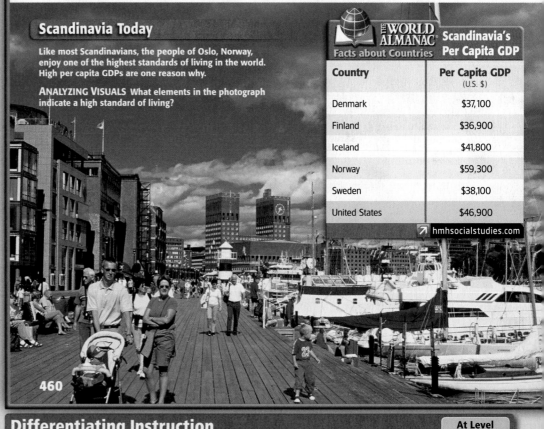

Scandinavia Today

Like most Scandinavians, the people of Oslo, Norway, enjoy one of the highest standards of living in the world. High per capita GDPs are one reason why.

ANALYZING VISUALS What elements in the photograph indicate a high standard of living?

THE WORLD ALMANAC Facts about Countries — Scandinavia's Per Capita GDP

Country	Per Capita GDP (U.S. $)
Denmark	$37,100
Finland	$36,900
Iceland	$41,800
Norway	$59,300
Sweden	$38,100
United States	$46,900

↗ hmhsocialstudies.com

460

Differentiating Instruction

At Level

English-Language Learners

1. Review the definition of the word *neutral* and discuss its meaning with students. Tell them that most cars have a gear called "neutral" which means the car does not go forward or backward. Discuss how this meaning relates to the meaning of a "neutral" country.

2. Copy the table at the right for students to see, and ask them to help fill it in. Ask them to consider the costs of defense programs and whether they think these programs improve a nation's security. Tell students that other countries such as Switzerland and Costa Rica have policies of remaining neutral.

📑 Alternative Assessment Handbook, Rubrics 7: Charts; and 16: Judging Information

Neutral Countries	
Advantages	**Disadvantages**

About 50 percent of Denmark's land is good for farming. Farm goods, especially meat and dairy products, are important Danish exports. Denmark also has modern industries, including iron, steel, textiles, and electronics industries.

Greenland

The island of Greenland is geographically part of North America. However, it is a territory of Denmark. A thick ice sheet covers about 80 percent of the island. Because of this, much of Greenland is **uninhabitable**, or not able to support human settlement. Most people live on the island's southwest coast where the climate is warmest.

Recently, a movement for complete independence from Denmark has gained popularity. However, economic problems make independence unlikely, as Greenland relies heavily on imports and economic aid from Denmark.

Norway

With one of the longest coastlines in the world, Norway takes advantage of its access to the sea. Fjords shelter Norway's many harbors. Its fishing and shipping fleets are among the largest in the world. **Oslo**, Norway's capital, is the country's leading seaport as well as its industrial center.

Norway has other valuable resources as well. Oil and natural gas provide Norway with the highest per capita GDP in Scandinavia. However, North Sea oil fields are expected to run dry over the next century. Despite strong economic ties to the rest of Europe, Norway's citizens have refused to join the European Union.

Finland

Finland is Scandinavia's easternmost country. It lies between Sweden and Russia. The capital and largest city is **Helsinki**, which is located on the southern coast.

As with other countries in the region, trade is important to Finland. Paper and other forest products are major exports. Shipbuilding and electronics are also important industries in Finland.

Iceland

Iceland is much greener than its name implies. Fertile farmland along the island's coast produces potatoes and vegetables and supports cattle and sheep.

Icelanders also make good use of their other natural resources. Fish from the rich waters of the Atlantic Ocean account for about 70 percent of Iceland's exports.

Iceland

Iceland's geysers and hot springs produce great amounts of energy. Geothermal plants like this one near the Blue Lagoon hot spring provide heat for buildings and homes throughout the country.

Direct Teach

Did you know. . .

Almost all geysers in the world are located in Iceland, New Zealand and the United States.

Old Faithful in Yellowstone National Park in the United States is famous for eruptions every 30 to 90 minutes, rising as high as 170 feet. Unfortunately, recent eruptions have not been as regular because of natural changes in the underground water system.

Review & Assess

Close

Briefly review the history of Scandinavia and the similarities and differences among Scandinavian countries.

Review

↗ Online Quiz, Section 3

Assess

SE Section 3 Assessment
📄 PASS: Section 3 Quiz
📄 Alternative Assessment Handbook

Reteach/Classroom Intervention

📄 Guided Reading Workbook, Section 3
💿 Interactive Skills Tutor CD-ROM

In addition, steam from hot springs and geysers produces geothermal energy. **Geysers** are springs that shoot hot water and steam into the air. Geothermal energy heats many of Iceland's buildings. Each year thousands of tourists flock to see Iceland's many geysers, volcanoes, and glaciers.

READING CHECK **Comparing and Contrasting** In what ways are the countries of Scandinavia similar and different?

SUMMARY AND PREVIEW Scandinavia today is a region of relative peace and stability. A common history and culture link the people of the region. Today, Scandinavia is one of the wealthiest regions in Europe and in the world. In the next chapter, you will learn about the unique geography, history, and culture of another European region—Eastern Europe.

Section 3 Assessment

hmhsocialstudies.com
ONLINE QUIZ

Reviewing Ideas, Terms, and Places

1. **a. Identify** Who were the **Vikings**?
   b. Analyze What effect did the Vikings have on Scandinavian history?
   c. Evaluate Do you think the Vikings helped or hurt the future of Scandinavia? Explain your answer.
2. **a. Define** What does the term **neutral** mean?
   b. Compare What features do the countries of Scandinavia have in common today?
   c. Elaborate In which Scandinavian country would you prefer to live? Why?

Critical Thinking

3. **Finding Main Ideas** Use your notes and this chart to identify two main ideas about Scandinavia's history and two about its culture today.

History	Today

FOCUS ON WRITING

4. **Writing about Scandinavia** Where would you travel and what would you see in Scandinavia? Take notes on the details you might include in your letter.

462 CHAPTER 18

Section 3 Assessment Answers

1. **a.** Scandinavian warriors who raided Europe in the early Middle Ages.
   b. gained power by conquering other lands, built strong kingdoms
   c. possible answers—helped by building strong kingdoms, hurt by struggling for control of each other
2. **a.** not taking sides in an international conflict
   b. common history, religion, high standard of living, large cities, excellent social programs
   c. Answers will vary but should reflect text content.

3. History—Vikings conquered countries; built kingdoms; formed independent countries; Today—similar religion, history, strong economies, unique cultures and features
4. Students may say the floating city of Stockholm, the ice sheet in Greenland, fjords in Oslo, or geysers in Iceland.

Answers

Reading Check *similar—political views, religion, high standard of living, large cities, excellent social program, strong economies; different—Denmark has a lot of farmland and is more densely populated, Greenland has little habitable land, Norway hasn't joined EU, Iceland has geysers and geothermal energy.*

Geography's Impact
video series
Review the video to answer the closing question:
How have Icelanders made good use of their island's volcanoes?

Visual Summary

Use the visual summary below to help you review the main ideas of the chapter.

QUICK FACTS

Low mountains and plentiful resources are key features of Northern Europe's physical geography.

The British Isles are known around the world for their rich history, vibrant culture, and healthy economies.

The countries of Scandinavia are among the most peaceful and prosperous in the world.

Reviewing Vocabulary, Terms, and Places

Write each word defined below, and circle each letter marked by a star. Then write the word these letters spell.

1. _ _ * _ _ _—to give up all weapons
2. _ _ _ _ _ _ _ _ *_—a decision reached by two or more people or groups
3. _ _ * _ _—a narrow inlet of the sea set between high, rocky cliffs
4. _ * _ _ _ _ _ _ _ _ _—a region in far Northern Europe that crosses the Arctic Circle
5. _ _ * _ _ _ _—warriors from Northern Europe who raided much of Europe and the Mediterranean during the early Middle Ages
6. _ _ _ _ _ * _ _ _ _ _ _ _ _ _—unable to support human settlement
7. _ _ * _ _ _ _ _ _ _ energy—energy produced by the heat of the planet's interior
8. _ _ _ * _ _—the capital of the Republic of Ireland
9. _ _ _ * _ _ _—main or most important

Comprehension and Critical Thinking

SECTION 1 *(Pages 448–451)*

10. **a. Identify** What are the major resources found in Northern Europe?

b. Analyze Explain how the North Atlantic Drift is responsible for the relatively mild climates in Northern Europe.

c. Elaborate In which region of Northern Europe would you prefer to live—the British Isles or Scandinavia? Why?

SECTION 2 *(Pages 452–456)*

11. **a. Describe** What culture traits do the people of the British Isles share in common?

b. Make Inferences Why did the people of Ireland want to break away from the British Empire?

c. Predict How might the conflict in Northern Ireland affect the future of the United Kingdom?

NORTHERN EUROPE **463**

Answers

Visual Summary

Review and Inquiry Have students use the visual summary to discuss details related to the geography of the British Isles and Scandinavia. Ask students what is pictured in each photograph and how it relates to its caption.

▶ Quick Facts Transparency: Northern Europe Visual Summary

Reviewing Vocabulary, Terms, and Places

1. disarm   6. uninhabitable
2. agreement   7. geothermal
3. fjord   8. Dublin
4. Scandinavia   9. primary
5. Vikings

Letters spell: Stockholm

Comprehension and Critical Thinking

10. **a.** energy resources, forests and soils, and seas and oceans
b. It brings warm, moist air from the Atlantic, which keeps temperatures warm and mild.
c. Answers will vary but should reflect text content.

11. **a.** ancestry, sports, language, popular culture
b. They wanted independence and control of their own affairs.
c. possible answers—If the conflict is resolved it might improve economic and social conditions. If the situation becomes more tense it may have the opposite effect.

Review and Assessment Resources

Review and Reinforce

SE Chapter Review
📖 RF: Chapter Review
▶ Quick Facts Transparency: Northern Europe Visual Summary
🔊 Spanish Chapter Summary Audio CD Program
TOS Holt McDougal PuzzleView®; Quiz Show for ExamView
💿 Quiz Game CD-ROM

Assess

SE Standardized Test Practice
📖 PASS: Chapter Test, Forms A and B
📖 Alternative Assessment Handbook
TOS ExamView Test Generator, Chapter Test
💿 Differentiated Instruction Modified Worksheets and Tests CD-ROM: Chapter Test
↗ Online Assessment Program, in the Interactive Student Edition

Reteach/Intervene

📖 Guided Reading Workbook
📖 Differentiated Instruction Teacher Management System: Lesson Plans
💿 Differentiated Instruction Modified Worksheets and Tests CD-ROM
💿 Interactive Skills Tutor CD-ROM

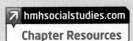
↗ hmhsocialstudies.com
Chapter Resources

Answers

12. a. Norway, Finland, Sweden, Denmark, Iceland, Greenland
b. similar—political views, religion, high standard of living, large cities, excellent social programs; different—Denmark has more farmland and is more densely populated; Greenland has little habitable land; Norway hasn't joined the European Union; Iceland has geysers and geo-thermal energy.
c. possible answers—stable democratic governments, plenty of resources

Social Studies Skills

13. possible answer—Ireland depended on the potato for food in the mid-1800s, and when the potato crop became infected with a disease, 1.5 million people died. Students' personal responses will vary.

Map Activity

14. A. Reykjavik
B. Dublin
C. London
D. English Channel
E. Scandinavian Peninsula
F. Helsinki
G. Oslo
H. Stockholm

Using the Internet

15. Go to ⌐ hmhsocialstudies.com to access a rubric for this activity.

Focus on Reading and Writing

16. wealthy

17. harsh

18. disagreement

📄 **RF:** Focus on Reading, Using Context Clues—Synonyms

19. Rubric Students' letters should
• be detailed and informative
• describe physical features
• include interesting facts about cities and cultural activities

📄 **RF:** Focus on Writing, Writing a Letter

SECTION 3 *(Pages 458–462)*

12. a. Recall What countries make up Scandinavia?
b. Compare and Contrast In what ways are the countries of Scandinavia similar and different?
c. Elaborate Why do you think Scandinavian countries today are so prosperous and stable?

Social Studies Skills

13. Writing to Learn Read the paragraph below carefully, then summarize it in your own words. Finally, write a personal response to what you learned in the paragraph.

> In the mid-1800s Ireland was devastated by a severe famine. For many Irish, the potato was a key part of their diet. When a disease infected potato crops around the country, millions were left without enough to eat. About 1.5 million Irish died as a result of the Irish Potato Famine.

Map Activity

14. Northern Europe On a separate sheet of paper, match the letters on the map with their correct labels.

Dublin	Oslo
English Channel	Reykjavik
Helsinki	Scandinavian Peninsula
London	Stockholm

⌐ **hmhsocialstudies.com** INTERACTIVE MAP

Using the Internet

15. Activity: Creating a Poster What does a medieval king have to do with modern democracy? Magna Carta was signed in 1215 by King John I of England. It established the principle that no one, including the king, is above the law. It also opened the door to a more democratic government in England. Centuries later, emerging democracies in the United States and France looked to Magna Carta for guidance. Through your online textbook, learn more about Magna Carta and its relationship with modern democracy. Then create a poster to display some of the ways this document has influenced modern governments.

⌐ **hmhsocialstudies.com**

FOCUS ON READING AND WRITING

Using Context Clues—Synonyms *Use context clues to determine the meaning of the underlined words in the sentences below.*

16. Wealthy in part because of its many natural resources, Scandinavia is one of the most affluent regions in Europe.

17. Thanks to the North Atlantic Drift, the British Isles are rarely affected by inclement, or harsh, weather.

18. Dissent, or disagreement, between Catholics and Protestants has caused years of conflict in Northern Ireland.

Writing a Letter *Use your notes from the chapter and the directions below to write a letter.*

19. Tell your friends and family members what you have seen on your travels in the British Isles and Scandinavia. You may want to organize the information by country. For example, you could start with a flight into London and end in Iceland. Include descriptions of fascinating physical features as well as any cities or cultural activities that are unusual or interesting.

DIRECTIONS: Read questions 1 through 7 and write the letter of the best response. Then read question 8 and write your own well-constructed response.

1 What group of people from Northern Europe raided Europe between 800 and 1100?

A Anglo-Saxons

B Celts

C Sami

D Vikings

2 Which of the following accounts for the relatively mild climate throughout much of Northern Europe?

A Arctic Ocean

B few mountains or hills

C North Atlantic Drift

D seasonal monsoons

3 Which Northern European city is a major European economic center?

A Dublin

B Helsinki

C London

D Stockholm

4 What important energy source does Iceland use to heat buildings?

A geothermal energy

B hydroelectric energy

C natural gas

D solar energy

5 Since the early 1900s, disputes and even violence have disrupted life in

A Finland.

B Greenland.

C Northern Ireland.

D Scotland.

Scandinavia: Population Density

6 According to the map above, which part of Scandinavia is *least* densely populated?

A Northern Scandinavia

B Southern Scandinavia

C Eastern Scandinavia

D Western Scandinavia

7 Which of the following characteristics do the countries of Scandinavia have in common?

A high standards of living

B membership in the European Union

C status as neutral nations

D high unemployment rates

8 **Extended Response Question** Use the climate map in Section 1 and the map above to write a paragraph explaining how climate might affect settlement patterns in Scandinavia.

NORTHERN EUROPE **465**

Answers

Standardized Test Prep

1. D

Break Down the Question Anglo-Saxons and Celts invaded the British Isles; Sami are a native people of Scandinavia.

2. C

Break Down the Question Answer D doesn't apply to Northern Europe. Answer B doesn't help produce a mild climate. Refer students who miss this question to Section 1.

3. C

Break Down the Question Other answers are key cities but don't serve as economic centers for all of Europe.

4. A

Break Down the Question This question requires students to recall factual information from Section 3.

5. C

Break Down the Question The other countries listed are known for peace and stability in recent years.

6. A

Break Down the Question Although many of the sparsely populated areas are located in Western Scandinavia, this part of the region also contains Scandinavia's most densely populated country.

7. A

Break Down the Question Norway has not joined the EU; Sweden is the only neutral state; and none of the countries has high unemployment.

8. Extended Response possible answer—Northern Scandinavia has long, cold winters and is too far north to support a large population. The western shores of Scandinavia are warmed by the North Atlantic Drift, which helps to make its weather milder.

Tips for Test Taking

Anticipate the Answers Give students this important tip: Before you read the answer choices, answer the question yourself. Then read the choices. If the answer you gave is among the choices listed, it is probably correct!

Chapter 19 Planning Guide

Eastern Europe

Overview	Instructional Resources	

CHAPTER 19

Essential Question: What challenges has Eastern Europe faced since the breakup of the Soviet Union?

🔊 **Focus on the Essential Question Podcast**

TOS Differentiated Instruction Teacher Management System:
- Instructional Pacing Guides
- Lesson Plans for Differentiated Instruction

Guided Reading Workbook

Resource File:
- Chapter Review
- Focus on Reading: Understanding Problems and Solutions
- Focus on Viewing: Presenting and Viewing Visual Reports
- Social Studies Skills: Analyzing Benefits and Costs

Experiencing World History and Geography

TOS Calendar Planner
- **Power Presentations with Media Gallery**
- **Differentiated Instruction Modified Worksheets and Tests CD-ROM**
- **Interactive Skills Tutor CD-ROM**
- **Student Edition on Audio CD-ROM**
- **The World's Music Audio Program**
- **World Outline Maps: Transparencies and Activities**
- **Video:** Chernobyl: Nuclear Meltdown

Section 1:

Physical Geography

The Big Idea: The physical geography of Eastern Europe varies greatly from place to place.

TOS Differentiated Instruction Teacher Management System: Section 1 Lesson Plan

Guided Reading Workbook: Section 1

Resource File:
- Vocabulary Builder: Section 1
- Geography for Life: Cities and Rivers in Eastern Europe

Daily Bellringer Transparency: Section 1

Map Zone Transparency: Eastern Europe: Physical

Internet Activity: Baltic Amber

Section 2:

Poland and the Baltic Republics

The Big Idea: The histories of Poland and the Baltic Republics, both as free states and as areas dominated by the Soviet Union, still shape life there.

TOS Differentiated Instruction Teacher Management System: Section 2 Lesson Plan

Guided Reading Workbook: Section 2

Resource File:
- Vocabulary Builder: Section 2
- Biography: Madeleine Albright

Daily Bellringer Transparency: Section 2

Map Zone Transparency: Eastern Europe under Soviet Influence, 1988

Section 3:

Inland Eastern Europe

The Big Idea: The countries of inland Eastern Europe have varied histories and cultures but face many of the same issues today.

TOS Differentiated Instruction Teacher Management System: Section 3 Lesson Plan

Guided Reading Workbook: Section 3

Resource File:
- Vocabulary Builder, Section 3
- Biography: Estée Lauder
- Geography and History: Soviet Domination of Eastern Europe
- Primary Source: The 1956 Hungarian Revolution

Daily Bellringer Transparency: Section 3

Section 4:

The Balkan Countries

The Big Idea: Life in the Balkans reflects the region's troubled past and its varied ethnic makeup.

TOS Differentiated Instruction Teacher Management System: Section 4 Lesson Plan

Guided Reading Workbook: Section 4

Resource File:
- Vocabulary Builder, Section 4
- Literature: *The Bridge on the Drina* by Ivo Andric
- Critical Thinking: Ethnic Cleansing in Bosnia
- Interdisciplinary Project: Eastern Europe's Economy

Daily Bellringer Transparency: Section 4

Map Zone Transparency: The Former Yugoslavia, 2000

Internet Activity: Conflicts in the Balkans

Review, Assessment, Intervention

- **Europe and Russia Transparencies:** Eastern Europe Visual Summary
- **Spanish Chapter Summaries Audio CD**
- **Progress Assessment Support System (PASS):** Chapter Test
- **Differentiated Instruction Modified Worksheets CD-ROM:** Modified Chapter Test
- **TOS** **ExamView® Assessment Suite (English/Spanish)**
- **Alternative Assessment Handbook**
- **Online Assessment Program,** in the Interactive Student Edition

---

- **PASS:** Section 1 Quiz
- **Online Quiz:** Section 1
- **Alternative Assessment Handbook**

- **PASS:** Section 2 Quiz
- **Online Quiz:** Section 2
- **Alternative Assessment Handbook**

- **PASS:** Section 3 Quiz
- **Online Quiz:** Section 3
- **Alternative Assessment Handbook**

- **PASS:** Section 4 Quiz
- **Online Quiz:** Section 4
- **Alternative Assessment Handbook**

Supporting Resources

HISTORY.

- Multimedia Classroom Global History Series
- Global History Series Teacher's Guide

Maps Globes Graphs Level F

- Student Workbook
- Teacher's Guide

Social Studies Trade Library Collections

- World Regions Trade Collection
- NCSS Middle School Trade Collection

Geography's Impact

Geography's Impact Video Program

- **Impact of Ethnic Conflict in Sarajevo**

For more information or to purchase go to hmhsocialstudies.com

Power Presentations with Media Gallery

Power Presentations with Media Gallery are visual presentations of each chapter's main ideas. Presentations can be customized by including Quick Facts charts, images from the text, and video clips.

Differentiating Instruction

How do I address the needs of varied learners?
The Target Resource acts as your primary strategy for differentiated instruction.

ENGLISH-LANGUAGE LEARNERS & STRUGGLING READERS

TARGET RESOURCE

Differentiated Instruction Modified Worksheets and Tests CD-ROM

- Vocabulary Flash Cards
- Modified Vocabulary Builder Activities
- Modified Chapter Review
- Modified Chapter Test

Additional Resources

Differentiated Instruction Teacher Management System: Lesson Plans for Differentiated Instruction

Resource File:
- Vocabulary Builder Activities
- Social Studies Skills: Analyzing Benefits and Costs

Quick Facts Transparencies:
- Eastern Europe Visual Summary

Spanish/English Guided Reading Workbook

Interactive Skills Tutor CD-ROM

Spanish Chapter Summaries Audio CD

Teacher One Stop:
- ExamView Assessment Suite, Spanish
- PuzzleView, Spanish

English-Language Learner Strategies and Activities

SPECIAL NEEDS LEARNERS

TARGET RESOURCE

Guided Reading Workbook

The activities in the Guided Reading Workbook engage students with questions while presenting summaries of chapter content and provide opportunities for students to practice critical thinking skills.

Additional Resources

Differentiated Instruction Teacher Management System: Lesson Plans for Differentiated Instruction

Resource File: Social Studies Skills: Analyzing Benefits and Costs

Student Edition on Audio CD Program

Interactive Skills Tutor CD-ROM

Graphic Organizer Transparencies with Support for Reading and Writing

ADVANCED/GIFTED AND TALENTED STUDENTS

TARGET RESOURCE

Differentiated Instruction Teacher Management System

Lesson Plans for Differentiated Instruction provide teachers with strategies to help plan instruction for all learners.

Additional Resources

Resource File
- Focus on Reading: Understanding Problems and Solutions
- Focus on Viewing: Presenting and Viewing Visual Reports
- Literature: *The Bridge on the Drina* by Ivo Andric

World History and Geography Document-Based Questions Activities

Geography, Science, and Cultures Activities

Experiencing World History and Geography

Teacher One Stop™

How can I manage the lesson plans and support materials for differentiated instruction?

With the Teacher One Stop, you can easily organize and print lesson plans, planning guides, and instructional materials for all learners. The Teacher One Stop includes the following materials to help you differentiate instruction:
- **Interactive Teacher's Edition**
- **Calendar Planner and pacing guides**
- **Editable lesson plans**
- **All reproducible ancillaries in Adobe Acrobat (PDF) format**
- **ExamView Assessment Suite (English & Spanish)**
- **Transparency and video previews**

Interactive Student Edition

Complete online student edition with interactive multimedia support for chapter content assessment and reporting
- Interactive Maps and Notebook
- Standardized Test Prep
- Online Homework Practice and Research Activities
- Current Events
- Chapter-based Internet Activities
- Animated Geography Activities

Essential Question

Introduce the Essential Question

- Explain that the physical features of Eastern Europe vary widely. Discuss how this creates challenges for the people who live there.

- Discuss the challenges the economies of Estonia, Latvia, Lithuania, and Poland face and why these challenges exist.

- Point out that the countries of inland Eastern Europe have mostly overcome the problems created by the Soviets. Have students discuss the challenges that still remain for these countries.

- Summarize how relations among religious and ethnic groups have caused serious challenges for people of the Balkan Countries.

Focus on Reading and Viewing

Reading The Resource File provides a worksheet to help students understand problems and solutions.

📝 **RF:** Focus on Reading, Understanding Problems and Solutions

Viewing The Resource File provides a worksheet to help students present and critique oral reports.

📝 **RF:** Focus on Viewing, Presenting and Viewing Visual Reports

Key to Differentiating Instruction

Below Level

Basic-level activities designed for all students encountering new material

At Level

Intermediate-level activities designed for average students

Above Level

Challenging activities designed for honors and gifted and talented students

Standard English Mastery

Activities designed to improve standard English usage

LS Learning Styles

CHAPTER 19

Eastern Europe

Essential Question What challenges has Eastern Europe faced since the breakup of the Soviet Union?

? What You Will Learn...

In this chapter you will learn about the countries of Eastern Europe. Once dominated by the Soviet Union, these countries have experienced major changes since the early 1990s. In some cases, those changes have been peaceful and have led to great economic success. In other places, the changes resulted in war, economic hardship, and political problems.

FOCUS ON READING AND VIEWING

Understanding Problems and Solutions Writers sometimes organize information by stating a problem and then explaining the solution taken to solve it. To understand this type of writing, you need to identify both problems and solutions. **See the lesson, Understanding Problems and Solutions, on page 534.**

Making a Presentation After you read this chapter, you will present an oral report about one Eastern European country. You will also create a poster showing important features of the country. Finally, you will view and critique your classmates' reports and posters.

466 CHAPTER 19

---

map zone

Geography Skills

Place Some of Eastern Europe's 20 countries are ancient, but others have been formed or changed more recently.
1. **Identify** What is the region's largest country?
2. **Make Inferences** Have you heard about any countries on this map in the news? What have you heard?

UNITED KINGDOM

FRANCE

ATLANTIC OCEAN

SPAIN

North Sea

⊕ National capital

| 0 | 100 | 200 Miles |
| 0 | 100 | 200 Kilometers |

Projection: Azimuthal Equal-Area

Culture Eastern Europe is home to dozens of cultures, each with its own unique customs.

Introduce the Chapter

At Level

Eastern Europe

1. Direct students' attention to the map. Note that this region is closer to Russia than Western Europe is. Ask students how proximity to a powerful neighbor might have affected the region's history and economy.

2. Tell students that the countries in this region were once either part of or greatly influenced by the Soviet Union. Point out that a map of Eastern Europe just 20 years ago looks quite different than the current map. Remind students of how the collapse of the Soviet Union affected East and West Germany. Ask students to describe what they already know about the effects of this event on Europe.

3. Point out that Communism is both an economic and political system. Have students write down three predictions about the economic or political problems the collapse of the Soviet Union and other Communist governments caused. LS **Verbal/Linguistic**

📝 Alternative Assessment Handbook, Rubric 11: Discussions

20°E

Tallinn

ESTONIA

Baltic Sea

Riga
LATVIA

LITHUANIA
Vilnius

RUSSIA

Minsk

BELARUS

RUSSIA

GERMANY

POLAND
Warsaw

50°N

Prague

CZECH REPUBLIC

SLOVAKIA
Bratislava

Kiev

UKRAINE

AUSTRIA

Budapest

HUNGARY

MOLDOVA
Chișinău

SLOVENIA
Ljubljana

Zagreb

CROATIA

ROMANIA

Bucharest

BOSNIA AND HERZEGOVINA
Belgrade

Sarajevo

SERBIA

Danube River

Black Sea

ITALY

Adriatic Sea

MONTENEGRO

Podgorica

KOSOVO
Pristina

Sofia

BULGARIA

40°E

Skopje

MACEDONIA

30°E

Tirana

ALBANIA

TURKEY

GREECE

Aegean Sea

HISTORY. Chernobyl

hmhsocialstudies.com **VIDEO**

History Buildings in cities like Prague, Czech Republic, are symbols of Eastern Europe's long history.

Geography Like the Danube River shown here, many rivers flow through the mountains and plains of Eastern Europe.

467

Chapter Preview

Explore the Map and Pictures

Eastern Europe: Political Have students examine the map and photographs. Ask them what positive and negative aspects might come from having cultures with varied customs, beliefs, and languages within a region. Then ask them what impact mountainous terrain might have on the governments and peoples of the region. Have students write one sentence about each photograph.

▶ Map Zone Transparency: Eastern Europe: Political

Analyzing Visuals Ask: What aspects of culture does the photograph of the woman suggest? *traditional dress, possibly dance or music* What landforms are shown in the Danube River picture? *mountains* Is the part of Prague in the photograph old or new? Explain. *old, both architecture and building materials of buildings suggest earlier times*

hmhsocialstudies.com
Teacher Resources

Critical Thinking: Analyzing Visuals

At Level

Exploring Eastern Europe

1. Have students examine the map and name the two largest countries in the region. Then ask if any can name the countries that once made up Czechoslovakia.

2. Then have students trace the Danube's route through the region, naming countries it passes through, the capital cities located on or near it, and the body of water it empties into.

3. Ask students what role the Danube River might play in Eastern Europe.

LS Visual/Spatial, Verbal/Linguistic

Alternative Assessment Handbook, Rubric 21: Map Reading

Answers

Map Zone 1. *Ukraine;* **2.** *Students may recall the conflicts that occurred in such places as Bosnia and Serbia in recent years. Others may know about the tourist attractions of such cities as Prague and Budapest.*

Preteach

Bellringer

If YOU lived there. . . Use the **Daily Bellringer Transparency** to help students answer the question.

▶ Daily Bellringer Transparency, Section 1

Academic Vocabulary

Review with students the high-use academic term in this section.

function use or purpose (p. 469)

📝 **RF:** Vocabulary Builder, Section 1

Taking Notes

Have students use the graphic organizer online to take notes on the section. This activity will prepare students for the Section Assessment, in which they will complete a graphic organizer that builds on the information using the Critical Thinking Skill: Categorizing.

Physical Geography

What You Will Learn...

Main Ideas

1. The physical features of Eastern Europe include wide open plains, rugged mountain ranges, and many rivers.
2. The climate and vegetation of Eastern Europe differ widely in the north and the south.

The Big Idea

The physical geography of Eastern Europe varies greatly from place to place.

Key Places

Carpathians, *p. 468*
Balkan Peninsula, *p. 469*
Danube, *p. 470*
Chernobyl, *p. 471*

📲 hmhsocialstudies.com
TAKING NOTES

Use the graphic organizer online to take notes on the physical geography of Eastern Europe.

If YOU lived there...

You are traveling on a boat down the Danube River, one of the longest in Europe. As you float downstream, you pass through dozens of towns and cities. Outside of the cities, the banks are lined with huge castles, soaring churches, and busy farms. From time to time, other boats pass you, some loaded with passengers and some with goods.

Why do you think the Danube is so busy?

> **BUILDING BACKGROUND** The physical geography of Eastern Europe varies widely from north to south. Many of the landforms you learned about in earlier chapters, including the Northern European Plain and the Alps, extend into this region.

Physical Features

Eastern Europe is a land of amazing contrasts. The northern parts of the region lie along the cold, often stormy shores of the Baltic Sea. In the south, however, are warm, sunny beaches along the Adriatic and Black seas. Jagged mountain peaks jut high into the sky in some places, while wildflowers dot the gently rolling hills of other parts of the region. These contrasts stem from the region's wide variety of landforms, water features, and climates.

Landforms

As you can see on the map, the landforms of Eastern Europe are arranged in a series of broad bands. In the north is the Northern European Plain. As you have already learned, this large plain stretches across most of Northern Europe.

South of the Northern European Plain is a low mountain range called the **Carpathians** (kahr-PAY-thee-uhnz). These rugged mountains are an extension of the Alps of West-Central Europe. They stretch in a long arc from the Alps to the Black Sea area.

468 CHAPTER 19

Teach the Big Idea

At Level

Physical Geography

1. **Teach** Ask students the questions in the Main Idea boxes under Direct Teach.

2. **Apply** Have students make a three-columned table, labeled *Baltic Region*, *Interior Plains*, and *Balkan Peninsula*. As they read the section and study the map on the next page, have them list the landforms, water features, climate, and vegetation that are associated with each region.

3. **Review** After completing the table, have students write two paragraphs identifying

the region that they think has the most favorable and least favorable physical geography. Students should support their conclusions.

4. **Practice/Homework** Have students make three suggestions for how the area with the least favorable physical geography might turn its disadvantages into assets.
   🄻🅂 **Verbal/Linguistic**

📝 **RF:** Alternative Assessment Handbook, Rubric 37: Writing Assignments

South and west of the Carpathians is another plain, the Great Hungarian Plain. As its name suggests, this fertile area is located mostly within Hungary.

South of the plain are more mountains, the Dinaric (duh-NAR-ik) Alps and Balkan Mountains. These two ranges together cover most of the **Balkan Peninsula**, one of the largest peninsulas in Europe. It extends south into the Mediterranean Sea.

Water Features

Like the rest of the continent, Eastern Europe has many bodies of water that affect how people live. To the southwest is the Adriatic Sea, an important route for transportation and trade. To the east, the Black Sea serves the same function. In the far north is the Baltic Sea. It is another important trade route, though parts of the sea freeze over in the winter.

ACADEMIC VOCABULARY

function
use or purpose

hmhsocialstudies.com **INTERACTIVE MAP**

Eastern Europe: Physical

ELEVATION

Feet	Meters
13,120	4,000
6,560	2,000
1,640	500
656	200
(Sea level) 0	0 (Sea level)
Below sea level	Below sea level

0   150   300 Miles
0   150   300 Kilometers
Projection: Azimuthal Equal-Area

1 The Carpathian Mountains run through the center of Eastern Europe.

2 Many rivers flow across the plains of Eastern Europe. The Vistula, shown here, is one of them.

map zone
Geography Skills

Place The physical features of Eastern Europe are arranged in alternating bands of rugged mountains and fertile plains.

1. **Locate** What large river flows through the southern part of the region?
2. **Interpret** Where do you think most of Eastern Europe's large cities are? Why?

EASTERN EUROPE **469**

2 Climate and Vegetation

The climate and vegetation of Eastern Europe differ widely in the north and the south.

Recall Which region has the mildest climate? *Balkan Peninsula*

Analyze Why are forests more common in the Baltic region than in the Balkan Peninsula? *Balkan Peninsula is much drier*

Cause and Effect Why do the interior plains have more varied vegetation than other parts of Eastern Europe? *variation in climate within the interior plains region, with colder, wetter climate in the north and milder, drier weather in the south*

MISCONCEPTION ALERT

Black Sea The waters of the Black Sea are not really black. The Greek name for this body of water was a word meaning inhospitable or unfriendly sea, because of its rough waters. Later, as the Greeks set up colonies along the shores of the Black Sea, they saw it as more calm and inviting, changing its name to one that meant friendly or hospitable sea. After the Turks took control of the southern shores of the sea, they changed its name once again. Turkish sailors experienced much stormy weather with rough and choppy waters, so they named this body of water the Karadeniz, or Black Sea.

↗ **hmhsocialstudies.com**
Online Resources
Activity: Baltic Amber

Answers

Analyzing Primary Sources
grasslands, colorful flowers of varied shapes, birds

Reading Check *Adriatic Sea, Baltic Sea, Black Sea, Danube River*

470

In addition to these seas, Eastern Europe has several rivers that are vital paths for transportation and trade. The longest of these rivers, the **Danube** (DAN-yoob), begins in Germany and flows east across the Great Hungarian Plain. The river winds its way through nine countries before it finally empties into the Black Sea.

BOOK
The Plains of Ukraine

One of Russia's greatest novelists, Nikolai Gogol (gaw-guhl), was actually born in what is now Ukraine. Very fond of his homeland, he frequently wrote about its great beauty. In this passage from the short story "Taras Bulba," he describes a man's passage across the wide open fields of Ukraine.

❝No plough had ever passed over the immeasurable waves of wild growth; horses alone, hidden in it as in a forest, trod it down. Nothing in nature could be finer. The whole surface resembled a golden-green ocean, upon which were sprinkled millions of different flowers. Through the tall, slender stems of the grass peeped light-blue, dark-blue, and lilac star-thistles; the yellow broom thrust up its pyramidal head; the parasol-shaped white flower of the false flax shimmered on high. A wheat-ear, brought God knows whence, was filling out to ripening. Amongst the roots of this luxuriant vegetation ran partridges with outstretched necks. The air was filled with the notes of a thousand different birds.❞

—from "Taras Bulba," by Nikolai Gogol

ANALYSIS SKILL **ANALYZING PRIMARY SOURCES**
What features does Gogol describe on the plains of Ukraine?

470 CHAPTER 19

As you might expect, the Danube is central to the Eastern European economy. Some of the region's largest cities lie on the Danube's banks. Thousands of ships travel up and down the river every year, loaded with both goods and people. In addition, dams on the western parts of the river generate much of the region's electricity. Unfortunately, the high level of activity on the Danube has left it heavily polluted.

READING CHECK **Finding Main Ideas** What are the main bodies of water in Eastern Europe?

Climate and Vegetation

Like its landforms, the climates and natural vegetation of Eastern Europe vary widely. In fact, the climates and landscapes found across Eastern Europe determine which plants will grow there.

The Baltic Coast

The shores of the Baltic Sea are the coldest location in Eastern Europe. Winters there are long, cold, and harsh. This northern part of Eastern Europe receives less rain than other areas, but fog is common. In fact, some parts of the area have as few as 30 sunny days each year. The climate allows huge forests to grow there.

The Interior Plains

The interior plains of Eastern Europe are much milder than the far north. Winters there can be very cold, but summers are generally pleasant and mild. The western parts of these plains receive much more rain than those areas farther east.

Because of this variation in climate, the plains of Eastern Europe have many types of vegetation. Huge forests cover much of the north. South of these forests are open grassy plains. In the spring, these plains erupt with colorful wildflowers.

Collaborative Learning

At Level

Getting to Know Eastern Europe

1. Organize students into three groups. Assign each group to a region: the Baltic Region, Interior Plains, or Balkan Peninsula. Make a large, physical map of Eastern Europe available.

2. Tell each group that they will present a short program to the class that describes the physical features of their area. Presentations should include pointing out the major landforms of the area on the map, giving a weather forecast for each season of the year,

suggesting what kind of outdoor clothing is appropriate for the area's climate, and describing the vegetation visitors might see walking or biking through the area.

3. Have students explain how the area is similar to and different from the other two areas of the region. **LS Intrapersonal, Visual/Spatial**

📝 Alternative Assessment Handbook, Rubrics 21: Map Reading; and 29: Presentations

Radiation Cleanup
A nuclear accident in 1986 leaked dangerous amounts of radiation into Eastern Europe's soil. Ukraine's government and scientists are still working to repair the damage.

Unfortunately, Eastern Europe's forests were greatly damaged by a terrible accident in 1986. A faulty reactor at the **Chernobyl** (chuhr-NOH-buhl) nuclear power plant in Ukraine exploded, releasing huge amounts of radiation into the air. This radiation poisoned millions of acres of forest and ruined soil across much of the region.

The Balkan Coast
Along the Adriatic Sea, the Balkan coast has a Mediterranean climate, with warm summers and mild winters. As a result, its beaches are popular tourist destinations.

Because a Mediterranean climate does not bring much rain, the Balkan coast does not have many forests. Instead, the land there is covered by shrubs and hardy trees that do not need much water.

READING CHECK **Contrasting** How do the climates and vegetation of Eastern Europe vary?

FOCUS ON READING
What problems did the Chernobyl accident cause for Eastern Europe?

SUMMARY AND PREVIEW The landforms of Eastern Europe vary widely, as do its cultures. Next you will study the cultures of the northernmost parts of the region.

Section 1 Assessment

hmhsocialstudies.com
ONLINE QUIZ

Reviewing Ideas, Terms, and Places
1. a. Identify What are the major mountain ranges of Eastern Europe?
b. Make Inferences How do you think the physical features of Eastern Europe influence where people live?
c. Elaborate Why is the **Danube** so important to the people of Eastern Europe?
2. a. Describe What is the climate of the **Balkan Peninsula** like?
b. Explain Why are there few trees in the far southern areas of Eastern Europe?
c. Predict How do you think the lingering effects of the **Chernobyl** accident affect the plant life of Eastern Europe?

Critical Thinking
3. Categorizing Draw a chart like the one shown here. In each column, identify the landforms, climates, and vegetation of each area in Eastern Europe.

	Landforms	Climates	Vegetation
Baltic coast			
Interior plains			
Balkan coast			

FOCUS ON VIEWING
4. Presenting Physical Geography Until you decide what country you will report on, take notes about all of them. Make a list of the countries of Eastern Europe and the physical features found in each.

EASTERN EUROPE **471**

Preteach

Bellringer

If YOU lived there. . . Use the **Daily Bellringer Transparency** to help students answer the question.

▶ Daily Bellringer Transparency, Section 2

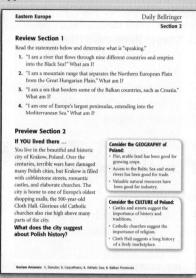

Key Terms and Places

📄 **RF:** Vocabulary Builder, Section 2

Taking Notes

Have students use the graphic organizer online to take notes on the section. This activity will prepare students for the Section Assessment, in which they will complete a graphic organizer that builds on the information using the Critical Thinking Skill: Identifying Cause and Effect.

SECTION 2

Poland and the Baltic Republics

What You Will Learn...

Main Ideas

1. History ties Poland and the Baltic Republics together.
2. The cultures of Poland and the Baltic Republics differ in language and religion but share common customs.
3. Economic growth is a major issue in the region today.

The Big Idea

The histories of Poland and the Baltic Republics, both as free states and as areas dominated by the Soviet Union, still shape life there.

Key Terms and Places

infrastructure, *p. 475*
Warsaw, *p. 475*

hmhsocialstudies.com
TAKING NOTES

Use the graphic organizer online to take notes on Poland and the Baltic Republics.

If YOU lived there...

You live in the beautiful and historic city of Krakow, Poland. Over the centuries, terrible wars have damaged many Polish cities, but Krakow is fllled with cobblestone streets, romantic castles, and elaborate churches. The city is home to one of Europe's oldest shopping malls, the 500-year-old Cloth Hall. Glorious old Catholic churches also rise high above many parts of the city.

What does the city suggest about Polish history?

BUILDING BACKGROUND Located on the Northern European Plain, Poland and the Baltic Republics are caught between east and west. As a result, the region has often been a battlefield. On the other hand, this location at a cultural crossroads has helped each country develop its own distinctive culture, traditions, and customs.

History

The area around the Baltic Sea was settled in ancient times by many different groups. In time, these groups developed into the people who live in the region today. One group became the Estonians, one became the Latvians and Lithuanians, and one became the Polish. Each of these groups had its own language and culture. Over the centuries, however, shared historical events have helped tie all these people together.

Early History

By the Middle Ages, the people of the Baltics had formed many independent kingdoms. The kingdoms of Lithuania and Poland were large and strong. Together they ruled much of Eastern and Northern Europe. The smaller kingdoms of Latvia and Estonia, on the other hand, were not strong. In fact, they were often invaded by their more powerful neighbors. These invasions continued through the 1800s.

472 CHAPTER 19

Teach the Big Idea

At Level

Poland and the Baltic Republics

1. **Teach** Ask students the questions in the Main Idea boxes under Direct Teach.

2. **Apply** Discuss the "Building Background" statement that Poland and the Baltic Republics are "caught between east and west." Have students skim the section looking for subheads, maps, and illustrations to help them understand what this sentence means. Ask: Why have these countries been forced to become involved in conflicts between more powerful nations and competing belief systems? 🆂 **Visual/Spatial**

3. **Review** Discuss whether the area is likely to become involved in conflicts between east and west in the future. Have students give reasons for their opinions.

4. **Practice/Homework** Have students pick one event from the history of Poland or a Baltic Republic and create a graphic organizer showing the causes and effects of this event. 🆂 **Visual/Spatial**

📄 Alternative Assessment Handbook, Rubrics 11: Discussions; and 13: Graphic Organizers

Eastern Europe under Soviet Influence, 1988

Extent of Soviet influence

0   100   200 Miles
0   100   200 Kilometers
Projection: Azimuthal Equal-Area

map zone
Geography Skills

Place From World War II until 1989, politics in Eastern Europe was dominated by the Soviet Union.

1. **Identify** Which modern countries were part of the Soviet Union?
2. **Name** What other countries have changed since 1988?

BIOGRAPHY

Pope John Paul II
(1920–2005)

Karol Wojtyla, later called Pope John Paul II, was born in Poland. Raised a Roman Catholic, he became a priest shortly after the Soviets took over the country. After becoming pope in 1978, he encouraged the Polish people to protest against their Communist government. Largely because of his efforts, Poland broke away from the Soviet Union in 1989.

The World Wars

Both World War I and World War II were devastating for the Baltic people. Much of the fighting in World War I took place in Poland. As a result, millions of Poles—both soldiers and civilians—died. Thousands more were killed in the Baltic countries.

World War II began when the Germans invaded Poland from the west. As the Germans pushed through Poland from the west, the army of the Soviet Union invaded Poland from the east. Once again, Poland suffered tremendously. Millions of people were killed, and property all over Poland was destroyed. Estonia, Latvia, and Lithuania also suffered. All three countries were occupied by the Soviet army.

Soviet Domination

As the map shows, the Soviet Union totally dominated Eastern Europe after World War II. Estonia, Latvia, and Lithuania became parts of the Soviet Union. Poland remained free, but the Soviets forced the Poles to accept a Communist government.

Many Eastern Europeans opposed Communist rule, and the Communist governments in the region eventually fell. Poland rejected Communism and elected new leaders in 1989. The Baltic Republics broke away from the Soviet Union in 1991 and became independent once more.

READING CHECK **Analyzing** How did the Soviet Union influence the region's history?

FOCUS ON READING

What problems were created in the Baltic region after World War II?

EASTERN EUROPE **473**

❷ Culture

The cultures of Poland and the Baltic Republics differ in language and religion but share common customs.

Explain Why are there many different languages in the Baltic countries? *because they were settled by different groups of people*

Compare How are the Baltic Republics and Poland alike? *similar foods; same crafts, such as ceramics, painting, embroidery; love of music and dance*

Contrast How have the histories of the Baltic Republics and Poland led to cultural differences? *Languages are different because countries were settled by different groups; Sweden, where most people are Lutheran, once ruled Latvia and Estonia, so most are Lutheran; Poland and Lithuania traded mostly with Roman Catholic countries, so most are Catholic.*

Linking to Today

Tallinn Each year this Estonian city attracts many tourists to its medieval Old Town, built in the 11th to 15th centuries. The town is now a UNESCO World Heritage site. Tallinn has many medieval churches and guild halls, places where craftsmen or wealthy merchants met. Another popular attraction is the Kadriorg Palace and Park, built in 1718 as a summer home for czar Peter the Great and his family. Today it serves as an art museum.

Answers

Connecting to the Arts *It takes years of practice to learn the craft and hours of work to create a single garment.*

Reading Check *similar foods, crafts, love of music and dance*

474

Culture

In some ways, the cultures of Poland and the Baltic Republics are very different from each other. For example, people in the area speak different languages and practice different religions. In other ways, however, their cultures are actually quite similar. Because the four countries lie near each other, common customs have taken root in all of them. People cook similar foods and enjoy the same types of entertainment.

Baltic Embroidery

One of the crafts for which the people of the Baltic region are best known is embroidery. This type of decorative sewing lets people create beautiful designs. They use these designs on their clothing, tablecloths, and other cloth goods.

For centuries, people in the Baltic countries—both men and women—have embroidered the clothing they wear on special occasions, such as weddings. They use many colors of thread to sew intricate patterns of flowers, hearts, and geometric designs. Because the embroidery is done by hand, it can take hours of work to create a single garment.

Drawing Conclusions Why do you think people embroider only clothing for special occasions?

Cultural Differences

The most obvious differences between the cultures of the Baltic countries are their languages and religions. Because the countries were first settled by different groups, each has its own language today. Of these languages, only Latvian and Lithuanian are similar to each other. Polish is related to the languages of countries farther south. Estonian is similar to Finnish.

Trade patterns and invasions have affected religion in the area. Poland and Lithuania traded mostly with Roman Catholic countries, and so most people there are Catholic. Latvia and Estonia, on the other hand, were ruled for a long time by Sweden. Because the Swedish are mostly Lutheran, most people in Latvia and Estonia are Lutheran as well.

Cultural Similarities

Unlike language and religion, many of the customs practiced in the Baltic countries cross national boundaries. For example, people in these countries eat many of the same types of foods. Potatoes and sausage are very popular, as is seafood.

Other shared customs tie the Baltic countries together as well. For example, people in all three countries practice many of the same crafts. Among these crafts are pottery, painting, and embroidery.

Also common to the countries of the Baltic Sea area is a love of music and dance. For centuries, people of the Baltics have been famous for their musical abilities. Frédéric Chopin (1810–1849), for example, was a famous Polish pianist and composer. Today, people throughout Poland and the Baltic Republics gather at music festivals to hear popular and traditional tunes.

READING CHECK **Comparing** How are the cultures of the Baltic countries similar?

Critical Thinking: Comparing and Contrasting ▌ At Level

Rebuilding Poland and the Baltic Republics ▌ Prep Required ▌ Research Required

1. Point out that Poland and the Baltic countries have been successful in moving from Communist economies and governments to market economies and democracy. Despite this, they still lag behind Western European nations economically. Discuss why infrastructure is so critical to economic growth.

2. Organize students into groups. Assign each group two countries: Poland or one of the Baltic Republics and one of the Western European nations of a similar size. Have

students use *The World Almanac* or an online source to compare the two countries in terms of area, population, per capita GDP, tourism, miles of railroads, number of telephones, cars, airports, and life expectancy.

3. Have each group create a poster or chart showing their data and comparing their two countries. Ask each to identify similarities and differences. ▌**LS Verbal/Linguistic, Visual/Spatial, Interpersonal**

📖 Alternative Assessment Handbook, Rubrics 9: Comparing and Contrasting; and 28: Posters

The Region Today

Estonia, Latvia, Lithuania, and Poland all still feel the effects of decades of Soviet rule. The economies of all four countries suffered because the Soviets did not build a decent infrastructure. An **infrastructure** is the set of resources, like roads, airports, and factories, that a country needs in order to support economic activities. The many factories built by the Soviets in Poland and the Baltics could not produce as many goods as those in Western Europe.

Today Poland and the Baltic Republics are working to rebuild and strengthen their economies. They are replacing the old and outdated factories built by the Soviets with new ones that take advantage of modern technology. As a result, cities like **Warsaw**, the capital of Poland, have become major industrial centers.

To further their economic growth, the countries of this region are also seeking new sources of income. One area in which they have found some success is tourism. Since the collapse of the Soviet Union in 1991, many Americans and Western Europeans have begun visiting. Polish cities like Warsaw and Krakow have long attracted tourists with their rich history and famous sites. Vilnius, Lithuania; Tallinn, Estonia; and Riga, Latvia, have also become tourist attractions. People are drawn to these cities by their fascinating cultures, cool summer climates, and historic sites.

READING CHECK **Generalizing** How has the region changed in recent years?

SUMMARY AND PREVIEW Poland and the Baltic Republics are still feeling the effects of decades of Soviet rule. In the next section, you will learn about more countries that feel the same effects.

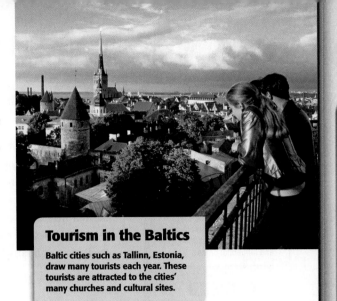

Tourism in the Baltics

Baltic cities such as Tallinn, Estonia, draw many tourists each year. These tourists are attracted to the cities' many churches and cultural sites.

Section 2 Assessment

 hmhsocialstudies.com
ONLINE QUIZ

Reviewing Ideas, Terms, and Places

1. **a. Identify** What country ran the area after World War II?
   b. Draw Conclusions How do you think the two world wars affected the people of Poland?
2. **a. Describe** How do the languages spoken in Poland and the Baltic Republics reflect the region's history?
   b. Elaborate Why do you think that people across the region practice many of the same customs?
3. **a. Recall** What is one industry that has grown in the region since the fall of the Soviet Union?
   b. Explain How did Soviet rule hurt the area's economy?

Critical Thinking

4. **Identifying Cause and Effect** Draw a chart like the one shown here. In each box on the right, explain how the event affected the cultures or economies of the region.

Event	Effect
Soviet rule	
Breakup of the Soviet Union	
Growth of tourism	

FOCUS ON VIEWING

5. **Considering Poland and the Baltics** If you were to give your report about Poland or one of the Baltic Republics, what details would you include? Write down some ideas.

EASTERN EUROPE **475**

Direct Teach

Main Idea

❸ **The Region Today**

Economic growth is a major issue in the region today.

Explain Why were the economies of Poland and the Baltic Republics hurt by Soviet rule? *The Soviet Union failed to create a strong infrastructure to support economic activities.*

Analyze Why has replacing outdated factories with new ones helped Warsaw become a major industrial center? *Factories with modern technologies are more efficient, productive, and cost effective.*

📖 RF: Biography, Madeleine Albright

Review & Assess

Close

Have students describe how Poland and the Baltic Republics changed as a result of the collapse of the Soviet Union.

Review

↗ Online Quiz, Section 2

Assess

SE Section 2 Assessment
📖 PASS: Section 2 Quiz
📖 Alternative Assessment Handbook

Reteach/Classroom Intervention

📖 Guided Reading Workbook, Section 2
💿 Interactive Skills Tutor CD-ROM

Section 2 Assessment Answers

1. **a.** the Soviet Union
   b. Many people lost family, friends, homes, property, and livelihoods.
2. **a.** Languages reflect who first settled in an area. Estonian is similar to Finnish; Polish resembles languages from farther south.
   b. They grow similar crops, have similar resources, and, as nearby countries, were influenced by each other's cultures.
3. **a.** tourism
   b. The Soviets failed to repair aging infrastructure such as roads and factories.

4. Soviet rule—weakened economies, imposition of Communist rules; Breakup—end of Communist rule, independence for Baltic Republics, increased tourism; Tourism—strengthened economies
5. possible answers: Poland—World War I and II devastation, struggling economy, strong culture; Baltic Republics—struggled to be independent of Communist rule, cultural similarities and differences, rebuilding economies

Answers

Reading Check *Infrastructure changes such as replacement of old, outdated factories with more modern ones have led to stronger economies; cities such as Warsaw have become major industrial centers; tourism has become important to the economies of many cities in the area.*

475

Bellringer

If YOU lived there. . . Use the **Daily Bellringer Transparency** to help students answer the question.

▶️ Daily Bellringer Transparency, Section 3

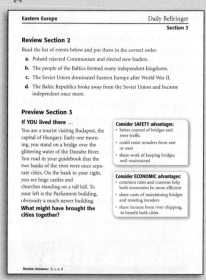

Eastern Europe   Daily Bellringer
                   Section 3

Review Section 2

Read the list of events below and put them in the correct order.

a. Poland rejected Communism and elected new leaders.
b. The people of the Baltics formed many independent kingdoms.
c. The Soviet Union dominated Eastern Europe after World War II.
d. The Baltic Republics broke away from the Soviet Union and became independent once more.

Preview Section 3

If YOU lived there ...

You are a tourist visiting Budapest, the capital of Hungary. Early one morning, you stand on a bridge over the glittering water of the Danube River. You read in your guidebook that the two banks of the river were once separate cities. On the bank to your right, you see huge castles and churches standing on a tall hill. To your left is the Parliament building, obviously a much newer building. **What might have brought the cities together?**

Consider SAFETY advantages:
• better control of bridges and river traffic
• could resist invaders from east or west
• share work of keeping bridges well-maintained

Consider ECONOMIC advantages:
• common rules and customs help both economies be more efficient
• share costs of maintaining bridges and resisting invaders
• share income from river shipping, to benefit both cities

Review Answers: b, c, a, d

Key Terms and Places

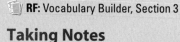

📖 **RF:** Vocabulary Builder, Section 3

Taking Notes

Have students use the graphic organizer online to take notes on the section. This activity will prepare students for the Section Assessment, in which they will complete a graphic organizer that builds on the information using the Critical Thinking Skill: Generalizing.

Inland Eastern Europe

What You Will Learn...

Main Ideas

1. The histories and cultures of inland Eastern Europe vary from country to country.
2. Most of inland Eastern Europe today has stable governments, strong economies, and influential cities.

The Big Idea

The countries of inland Eastern Europe have varied histories and cultures but face many of the same issues today.

Key Terms and Places

Prague, *p. 477*
Kiev, *p. 477*
Commonwealth of Independent States, *p. 478*
Budapest, *p. 479*

hmhsocialstudies.com
TAKING NOTES

Use the graphic organizer online to take notes on inland Eastern Europe.

If YOU lived there...

You are a tourist visiting Budapest, the capital of Hungary. Early one morning, you stand on a bridge over the glittering water of the Danube River. You read in your guidebook that the two banks of the river were once separate cities. On the bank to your right, you see huge castles and churches standing on a tall hill. To your left is the Parliament building, obviously a much newer building.

What might have brought the cities together?

BUILDING BACKGROUND The city of Budapest, like many of the cities of inland Eastern Europe, has a long, colorful history. Various parts of the city reflect wildly different eras in its past. Medieval churches, for example, stand near huge imperial fortresses and Soviet-built warehouses, all relics of the region's history.

History and Culture

Located on the Northern European and Hungarian plains, inland Eastern Europe consists of six countries. They are the Czech (CHEK) Republic, Slovakia, Hungary, Ukraine, Belarus, and Moldova. Throughout history, many different peoples ruled these countries. Each ruling group influenced the culture and customs of the area.

Czech Republic and Slovakia

The area that now includes the Czech Republic and Slovakia was once home to many small kingdoms. People called the Slavs founded these kingdoms. The Slavs were people from Asia who moved into Europe by AD 1000. Eventually, strong neighbors such as Austria conquered the Slavic kingdoms.

After World War I, the victorious Allies took land away from Austria to form a new nation, Czechoslovakia. About fifty years later, in 1993, it split into the Czech Republic and Slovakia.

Teach the Big Idea
                     At Level

Inland Eastern Europe

1. **Teach** Ask students the questions in the Main Idea boxes under Direct Teach.

2. **Apply** Remind students that the collapse of the Soviet Union brought huge changes to inland Eastern Europe. Have students locate the countries of this area on a map and speculate which of them today might have strong ties to the west and which might be more influenced by Russia. Have students discuss how these ties might affect culture, government, or the economy. ⬛ **Visual/Spatial**

3. **Review** Remind students that Hungary, the Czech Republic, and Slovakia have all recently joined the European Union. Ask students how EU membership might influence a country's relationship with the west.

4. **Practice/Homework** After completing the section, have students pick one country and write a paragraph assessing how ties to the west or Russia have helped or hurt the country. ⬛ **Verbal/Linguistic**

📖 Alternative Assessment Handbook, Rubric 42: Writing to Inform

Because of their location, these two countries have long had ties with Western Europe. As a result, Western influences are common. For example, many people in the two countries are Roman Catholic. The architecture of cities like **Prague** (PRAHG), the capital of the Czech Republic, also reflects Western influences.

Hungary

In the 900s, a group of fierce invaders called the Magyars swept into what is now Hungary. Although they were conquered by the Austrians, the Magyars continued to shape Hungarian culture. The Hungarian language is based on the language spoken by the Magyars. In fact, people in Hungary today still refer to themselves as Magyars.

Ukraine, Belarus, and Moldova

The Slavs also settled Ukraine, Belarus, and Moldova. Later other groups, including the Vikings of Scandinavia, invaded and conquered the Slavs.

A group called the Rus (RUHS) built a settlement in what is now **Kiev**, Ukraine, in the 800s. The rulers of Kiev eventually created a huge empire.

In the late 1700s, that empire became part of Russia. When the Soviet Union was formed in 1922, Ukraine and Belarus were made Soviet republics. Moldova became a republic two years later. They did not become independent until the breakup of the Soviet Union in 1991.

The long history of Russian influence in the region is reflected in the countries' cultures. For example, most people in these countries are Orthodox Christians, like the people of Russia. In addition, Ukrainian and Belarusian languages are written in the Cyrillic, or Russian, alphabet.

> **READING CHECK** Analyzing Which groups have influenced the history of the region?

The Kievan Empire

Kiev, now the capital of Ukraine, was once the capital of a large and powerful empire. At its height, the Kievan Empire stretched across much of Eastern Europe and Central Asia.

According to an old legend, the city of Kiev was built by three brothers and their sister. This monument built in the 1980s honors the city's legendary founders.

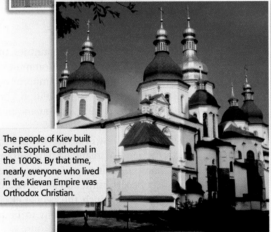

The people of Kiev built Saint Sophia Cathedral in the 1000s. By that time, nearly everyone who lived in the Kievan Empire was Orthodox Christian.

EASTERN EUROPE **477**

Direct Teach

Main Idea

❶ History and Culture

The histories and cultures of inland Eastern Europe vary from country to country.

Identify What is one way the Magyars influenced Hungarian culture? *Hungarians speak a language developed from that of the Magyars.*

Describe What events led to the creation of the Czech Republic and Slovakia? of Belarus and Moldova? *peaceful revolution in 1989 later split Czechoslovakia into the Czech Republic and Slovakia in 1993; Belarus and Moldova—breakup of Soviet Union in 1991*

Make Inferences Why were Ukraine, Belarus, and Moldova more likely to be influenced by Russian culture than by Western Europe? *located much closer to Russia than to Western Europe*

 RF: Biography, Estée Lauder

Info to Know

Velvet Revolution On November 17, 1989, tens of thousands of protesters poured onto the streets of Prague to demand an end to Communist rule in Czechoslovakia. Their protests, which lasted for six weeks, led to the fall of the Communist government. Because this successful uprising occurred without any violence, it is known as the Velvet Revolution. Four years later in 1993, the Czech Republic and Slovakia came into existence in what is known as the Velvet Divorce. Economic and power-sharing issues led to a peaceful breakup of Czechoslovakia into two separate countries.

Answers

Reading Check *Czech Republic and Slovakia—Slavs; Hungary—Magyars; Ukraine, Belarus, Moldova—Slavs, Vikings, Rus*

Differentiating Instruction

English-Language Learners

> Below Level

> Standard English Mastery

1. Write the section title where students can see. Examine the word *inland* with students. Point out that the prefix *in-* sometimes means *into* or *within*. Have students decode the word. Have students name places in their state that are inland. Direct students to the map of Eastern Europe and ask why this area is called Inland Eastern Europe.

2. Write the word *landlocked* where students can see. Note the nations that are landlocked. Have students decode this word and find these countries on the map. **LS Verbal/Linguistic**

Special Needs Learners

> Below Level

1. Pair special needs learners with high-ability students. Have each pair choose a city in this section to learn more about.

2. Have pairs create flash cards with words and images associated with that city.

3. Ask pairs to share their flashcards with the class. Have students guess what city the flashcards describe. **LS Verbal/Linguistic, Visual/Spatial**

📝 Alternative Assessment Handbook, Rubric 1: Acquiring Information

Main Idea

❷ The Region Today

Most of inland Eastern Europe today has stable governments, strong economies, and influential cities.

Identify Which countries of the region have had the most successful economic development since the collapse of the Soviet Union? *Czech Republic, Slovakia, Hungary, Ukraine*

Compare How are the governments of the countries of Eastern Europe different today than under Soviet domination? *All were Communist under Soviets. Today all are democracies except Belarus, which is a dictatorship.*

📖 **RF:** Geography and History, Soviet Domination of Eastern Europe

📖 **RF:** Primary Source, The 1956 Hungarian Revolution

Linking to Today

Belarus Aleksandr Lukashenko, often called Europe's last dictator, came to power in 1994. Two years later he disbanded the parliament, which had tried to impeach him, and held new elections won by his supporters. As the country's leader he fought privatization of state enterprises. All industries remain state-owned. Lukashenko has worked to build closer ties with Russia, which the country depends heavily on to meet its energy needs. There is little public opposition to Lukashenko's government. Many of his political opponents have disappeared, fled the country, or been put in jail.

Answers

Focus on Reading *by finding ways to cooperate on issues of mutual concern such as trade and immigration that affect former Soviet Republics*

478

Close-up
Budapest

Budapest, Hungary, is one of the largest cities of Eastern Europe. The city's two parts, Buda and Pest, are separated by the Danube River.

Once the poorer half of the city, Pest has grown quickly. Hungary's Parliament meets here.

Only a few bridges link the two halves of Budapest.

Inland Eastern Europe Today

FOCUS ON READING
How might the CIS help solve problems in this region?

All of the countries of inland Eastern Europe were either part of the Soviet Union or run by Soviet-influenced governments. Since the end of Soviet domination, the people of inland Eastern Europe have largely overcome the problems created by the Soviets. Still, a few issues remain for the region's governments and economies.

Government

During the Soviet era, the countries of inland Eastern Europe had Communist governments. Under the Communists, people had few freedoms. In addition, the Soviets were poor economic planners, and their policies caused many hardships.

Since the collapse of the Soviet Union, the governments of inland Eastern Europe have changed. Hungary, Slovakia, the Czech Republic, Ukraine, and Moldova are now republics in which the people elect their leaders. Belarus also claims to be a republic, but it is really a dictatorship.

The countries of inland Eastern Europe belong to several international alliances. One such alliance, the **Commonwealth of Independent States**, or CIS, meets to discuss issues such as trade and immigration that affect former Soviet republics. The CIS is based in Minsk, the capital of Belarus. Ukraine and Moldova are also members, as are many countries in Asia.

The Czech Republic, Slovakia, Hungary, Romania, and Bulgaria are not part of the CIS. They have sought closer ties to the West than to the former Soviet Union. As a result, all five belong to the EU.

Economy

Economic development has been a major challenge for these countries since the collapse of the Soviet Union. The Czech Republic, Slovakia, Hungary, and Ukraine have been most successful. All four are thriving industrial centers. Ukraine, with rich, productive farmlands, grows grains, potatoes, and sugar beets.

Critical Thinking: Analyzing
At Level

Breaking with the Past

1. To assess the effect of the collapse of the Soviet Union on inland Eastern Europe, have students create a two-columned chart labeled *Before* and *After*. Have them describe the governments and economic systems in these countries before and after the fall of the Soviet Union.

2. Point out that the transition from a state-controlled economy to a free market economy has not been easy. Thousands of people lost jobs as new governments shut down inefficient factories and ended many services. Ask students why they think some countries have moved more slowly towards market economies and democracy than others.

3. Have students create political cartoons expressing an opinion about how inland Eastern Europe is changing. 🅛 **Visual/Spatial**

📖 Alternative Assessment Handbook, Rubric 27, Political Cartoons

Buda, the older half of the city, contains historic castles and churches.

The Danube is a key route for moving both goods and people in Eastern Europe.

ANALYSIS SKILL **ANALYZING VISUALS**
How do you think the Danube affects daily life in Budapest?

Cities

Life in inland Eastern Europe is centered around cities, especially national capitals. In each country, the capital is both a key economic center and a cultural one.

Three cities in the region are especially important—Prague, Kiev, and **Budapest**, the capital of Hungary. They are the most prosperous cities in the region and home to influential leaders and universities. In addition, the cities are popular tourist destinations. People from all over the world visit Eastern Europe to see these cities' architectural and cultural sites.

READING CHECK **Generalizing** What are the countries of inland Eastern Europe like today?

SUMMARY AND PREVIEW Inland Eastern Europe has been successful in facing the challenges left by Soviet influence. Next, you will learn about a region that has faced more challenges, the Balkans.

Section 3 Assessment
hmhsocialstudies.com
ONLINE QUIZ

Reviewing Ideas, Terms, and Places

1. **a. Recall** In what country is **Prague** located?
   b. Sequence List the groups that ruled **Kiev** and the surrounding area in chronological order.
   c. Elaborate How has Hungary's history helped set it apart from other countries in inland Eastern Europe?
2. **a. Identify** What is the **Commonwealth of Independent States**? Which countries in this region are members?
   b. Draw Conclusions How have the economies of the region changed since the collapse of the Soviet Union?
   c. Develop Why do you think life is largely centered around cities in inland Eastern Europe?

Critical Thinking

3. **Generalizing** Draw a diagram like the one shown here. In the left oval, describe the government and economy of inland Eastern Europe under the Soviet Union. In the right oval, describe them since the Soviet Union's collapse.

Russia Today

FOCUS ON VIEWING

4. **Picturing Inland Eastern Europe** Which country sounds most interesting to you? Write down some details about it. Make a list of pictures you could use on your poster.

EASTERN EUROPE **479**

Bellringer

If YOU lived there. . . Use the **Daily Bellringer Transparency** to help students answer the question.

▶ Daily Bellringer Transparency, Section 4

Academic Vocabulary

Review with students the high-use academic term in this section.

implications consequences (p. 482)

📝 **RF:** Vocabulary Builder, Section 4

Taking Notes

Have students use the graphic organizer online to take notes on the section. This activity will prepare students for the Section Assessment, in which they will complete a graphic organizer that builds on the information using the Critical Thinking Skill: Summarizing.

The Balkan Countries

What You Will Learn...

Main Ideas

1. The history of the Balkan countries is one of conquest and conflict.
2. The cultures of the Balkan countries are shaped by the many ethnic groups who live there.
3. Civil War and weak economies are major challenges to the region today.

The Big Idea

Life in the Balkans reflects the region's troubled past and its varied ethnic makeup.

Key Terms

ethnic cleansing, *p. 482*

hmhsocialstudies.com
TAKING NOTES

Use the graphic organizer online to take notes on the Balkan countries.

If YOU lived there...

As part of your summer vacation, you are hiking across the Balkan Peninsula. As you hike through villages in the rugged mountains, you are amazed at the different churches you see. There are small Roman Catholic churches, huge Orthodox churches with onion-shaped domes, and Muslim mosques with tall minarets.

Why are there so many types of churches here?

BUILDING BACKGROUND The Balkan countries are possibly the most diverse area in Europe. In addition to practicing many religions, the people there speak many languages and have different customs. At times, the area's diversity has led to serious problems.

History

Like the rest of Eastern Europe, the Balkan Peninsula has been conquered and ruled by many different groups. The presence of these many groups continues to shape life in the area today.

Early History

By the 600s BC the ancient Greeks had founded colonies on the northern Black Sea coast. The area they settled is now part of Bulgaria and Romania. Later, the Romans conquered most of the area from the Adriatic Sea to the Danube River.

When the Roman Empire divided into west and east in the late AD 300s, the Balkan Peninsula became part of the Eastern, or Byzantine, Empire. Under Byzantine rule, many people of the Balkans became Orthodox Christians. More than 1,000 years later, Muslim Ottoman Turks conquered the Byzantine Empire. Under the Ottomans, many people became Muslims.

The Ottomans ruled the Balkan Peninsula until the 1800s. At that time, the people of the region rose up and drove the Ottomans out. They then created their own kingdoms.

Teach the Big Idea

At Level

The Balkan Countries

1. **Teach** Ask students the questions in the Main Idea boxes under Direct Teach.

2. **Apply** Write the term "shatter belt" on the board. Have students define the word *shatter* and discuss how it might apply to the Balkan Peninsula. Historians use this term to describe a region that has been splintered or shattered as it has been caught between outside forces or torn apart by cultural or political rivalries. Have students suggest reasons why the Balkan Peninsula might be called a shatter belt.

3. **Review** As students read, have them list events or cultural features that have contributed to conflict and political unrest in the region.

4. **Practice/Homework** Have students write a paragraph explaining why the term "shatter belt" does or does not apply to the region, supporting their conclusions with examples. 🔲 **Verbal/Linguistic**

   📝 Alternative Assessment Handbook, Rubric 41: Writing to Express

World War I and After

Trouble between the Balkan kingdoms and their neighbors led to World War I. In the late 1800s the Austro-Hungarian Empire, which lay north of the Balkans, took over part of the peninsula. In protest, a man from Serbia shot the heir to the Austro-Hungarian throne, sparking the war.

After World War I, the Balkans changed dramatically. Europe's leaders divided the peninsula into new countries. Among these new countries was Yugoslavia, which combined many formerly independent countries under one government.

The nation of Yugoslavia lasted until the 1990s. The country eventually broke up, however, because of conflict between ethnic and religious groups.

READING CHECK **Summarizing** How did World War I affect the Balkan Peninsula?

Culture

Culturally, the Balkans are the most diverse area of Europe. This diversity is reflected in the large number of religions practiced and languages spoken there.

Religion

Most of the people of the Balkans, like most Europeans, are Christian. However, three types of Christianity are practiced in the area. Most Balkan Christians belong to the Orthodox Church. In the western part of the peninsula, there are many Roman Catholics. In addition, many countries also have large Protestant communities.

Christianity is not the only religion in the Balkans. Because of the Ottomans' long rule, Islam is also common. In fact, Albania is the only country in Europe in which most people are Muslims.

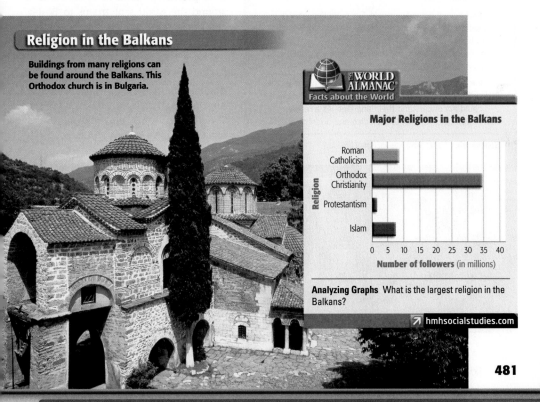

Religion in the Balkans

Buildings from many religions can be found around the Balkans. This Orthodox church is in Bulgaria.

THE WORLD ALMANAC Facts about the World

Major Religions in the Balkans

Religion (vertical axis): Roman Catholicism, Orthodox Christianity, Protestantism, Islam

Horizontal axis: Number of followers (in millions) — 0, 5, 10, 15, 20, 25, 30, 35, 40

Analyzing Graphs What is the largest religion in the Balkans?

↗ hmhsocialstudies.com

481

---

❸ The Balkans Today

Civil war and weak economies are major challenges to the region today.

Explain Where did violence occur in the Balkans after the breakup of Yugoslavia? *in all newly formed countries that had been part of Yugoslavia, except Macedonia*

Describe What ended the violence in the countries of the former Yugoslavia? *In 1995 troops from around the world came to the region of Herzegovina and Bosnia to stop the fighting.*

Predict What might be the advantages and disadvantages of having five smaller countries rather than one large one? *advantages—less conflict, more stable government; disadvantages— some countries have fewer natural and human resources, some barriers to trade, duplication of governments and services*

📄 RF: Critical Thinking, Ethnic Cleansing in Bosnia

Info to Know

The Roma Throughout their history as a nomadic people, the Roma have faced suspicion and distrust. During World War II, they were singled out along with Jews and several other groups for persecution. During the Holocaust, the Nazis killed around 400,000 Roma in the concentration camps or slave labor camps of Germany and Eastern Europe.

Answers

Reading Check *Balkan culture includes languages from many different language families. It also includes many religions such as Islam and Orthodox, Protestant, and Roman Catholic Christians.*

Focus on Culture *nomadic, roaming from place to place in horse-drawn wagons, working as blacksmiths, animal trainers, and musicians*

482

Language

People in the Balkans speak languages from three major groups. Most languages in the region belong to the Slavic family and are related to Russian. In Romania, though, people speak a language that developed from Latin. It is more closely related to French, Italian, and Spanish than to Slavic languages. In addition, some people in Romania speak Germanic languages.

Some languages of the Balkans are not related to these groups. For example, Albanian is unlike any other language in the world. In addition, a group called the Roma have a language of their own.

ACADEMIC VOCABULARY
implications consequences

READING CHECK **Drawing Conclusions** Why is Balkan culture so diverse?

FOCUS ON CULTURE

The Roma

The Roma are a nomadic people. For centuries, they have roamed from place to place in horse-drawn wagons, working as blacksmiths, animal trainers, and musicians. Although Roma live all over the world, the largest concentration of them is in southeastern Europe.

For centuries, many other Europeans did not trust the Roma. They were suspicious of the Roma's nomadic lifestyle and could not understand their language. As a result, many Roma have been subject to prejudice and discrimination.

Summarizing What is traditional Roma life like?

482 CHAPTER 19

The Balkans Today

The countries of the Balkan Peninsula, like most of Eastern Europe, were once run by Communist governments. Weak economic planning has left most of them poor and struggling to improve their economies. This area is still the poorest in Europe today.

Relations among religious and ethnic groups have had serious **implications** for the Balkans. When Yugoslavia broke apart, violence broke out among groups in some of the newly formed countries. Members of the largest religious or ethnic group in each country tried to get rid of all other groups who lived there. They threatened those who refused to leave with punishments or death. This kind of effort to remove all members of a group from a country or region is called **ethnic cleansing**.

The violence in the former Yugoslavia was so terrible that other countries stepped in to put an end to it. In 1995 countries around the world sent troops to Bosnia and Herzegovina to help bring an end to the fighting. The fighting between groups eventually ended and, in 2008, ten countries shared the Balkan Peninsula:

Albania The poorest country in Europe, Albania has struggled since the end of the Soviet period. High unemployment and crime rates have prevented the country's economy from improving.

Macedonia Once a part of Yugoslavia, Macedonia broke away in 1991. It was the first country to do so peacefully.

Slovenia Slovenia also broke from Yugoslavia in 1991. In 2004 it became the first Balkan country to join the EU.

Croatia When Croatia broke away from Yugoslavia, fighting broke out within the country. Ethnic Croats and Serbs fought over land for many years. In the end, many Serbs left Croatia, and peace was restored.

Critical Thinking: Evaluating Information   At Level

Creating a Time Line

1. Working in groups, have students create a four-part time line for the history of the Balkans: Early History, World War I, World War II and Soviet Domination, 1989 to the Present. Students can draw on information from this section and other parts of the chapter.

2. When the time lines are complete, have students list how the histories of these nations are similar. Then have them identify three events that they consider turning points in the history of the region and write two or

three sentences explaining each event. Have students share time lines and statements with the class.

3. Point out that Slovenia was the first Balkan country to join the European Union. Romania and Bulgaria joined in 2007. Have students make predictions about how EU membership for some countries might affect their economies. **LS Visual/Spatial**

📄 Alternative Assessment Handbook, Rubrics 36: Time Lines; and Rubric 41: Writing to Express

Mostar

Fighting between ethnic groups left the city of Mostar in Bosnia and Herzegovina in ruins. After the war, the people of Mostar had to rebuild their city.

ANALYZING VISUALS What does this photo suggest about life in Mostar today?

Bosnia and Herzegovina Since the end of ethnic and religious violence, peace has returned to Bosnia and Herzegovina. The people there are working to rebuild.

Serbia Serbia is the largest nation to emerge from the former Yugoslavia. Like other Balkan countries, Serbia has seen fighting among ethnic groups.

Kosovo Formerly a province of Serbia, Kosovo declared independence in 2008. Its population is mostly ethnic Albanian.

Montenegro The mountainous country of Montenegro separated peacefully from Serbia in June 2006.

Romania Romania, the largest of the Balkan states, is working to recover from years of bad government. Poor leaders have left its government and economy in ruins.

Bulgaria Since the fall of the Soviet Union, Bulgaria has changed dramatically. People there are working to develop a capitalist economy based on industry and tourism.

FOCUS ON READING

What solutions are Bulgaria's leaders seeking to their economic problems?

READING CHECK **Generalizing** What issues does the Balkan region face today?

SUMMARY AND PREVIEW The Soviet Union had a huge effect on Eastern Europe. Next, you will read about the Soviet Union and Russia.

Did you know. . .

The centuries of conflict in the Balkan Peninsula have added a new word to the English language. The term *Balkanization* is derived from the area's long history of wars and ethnic rivalries. The term means the breaking up a region into smaller and often mutually hostile political units.

↗ **hmhsocialstudies.com**

Online Resources
Activity: Conflicts in the Balkans

● **Review & Assess** ●

Close

Ask students to describe the causes of the conflicts that have troubled the Balkan Peninsula since the breakup of the Soviet Union.

Review

↗ Online Quiz, Section 4

Assess

SE Section 4 Assessment

📖 PASS: Section 4 Quiz

📖 Alternative Assessment Handbook

Reteach/Classroom Intervention

📖 Guided Reading Workbook, Section 4

💿 Interactive Skills Tutor CD-ROM

Section 4 Assessment

↗ **hmhsocialstudies.com**
ONLINE QUIZ

Reviewing Ideas, Terms, and Places

1. a. Describe What was Yugoslavia? When did it break apart?
b. Explain What role did the Balkan countries play in starting World War I?
2. a. Identify What are the four most common religions in the Balkans?
b. Analyze Why are so many different languages spoken in the Balkans?
3. a. Define What is **ethnic cleansing**?
b. Elaborate Why do you think other countries sent troops to Bosnia and Herzegovina? How has the country changed since the war ended?

Critical Thinking

4. Summarizing Draw a chart like this one. Use your notes to write a sentence about each topic listed in the left column affected life in the Balkans after the breakup of Yugoslavia.

The Balkans Today	
Soviet influence	
Ethnic diversity	
Religion	

FOCUS ON VIEWING

5. Choosing a Country Now that you have studied all of Eastern Europe, choose your topic. What information and pictures will you include?

EASTERN EUROPE **483**

Section 4 Assessment Answers

1. a. A nation in the Balkan Peninsula that was made up of what are now six separate countries—Bosnia and Herzegovina, Macedonia, Slovenia, Croatia, Serbia, and Montenegro; 1990s
b. After the Austro-Hungarian empire took over part of Balkan peninsula, a man from Serbia shot the heir to the Austro-Hungarian throne, sparking the war.
2. a. Orthodox Christianity, Roman Catholicism, Protestantism, Islam
b. People migrated from many different areas.

3. a. an effort to remove all members of a group from a country or region using violence or the threat of death
b. the violence was so terrible; five countries have been created
4. possible answers: Soviet Influence—left region poor and struggling to improve economy; Ethnic diversity—led to conflict, ethnic cleansing and intervention of other countries; Religion—religious diversity led to same problems as ethnic diversity.
5. Students should use their notes to highlight facts and details they will include in their visual reports.

Answers

Analyzing Visuals *possible answer—Mostar is successfully rebuilding. It is safe and orderly enough for tourists to return.*

Focus on Reading *a capitalist economy based on industry and tourism*

Reading Check *Many countries are struggling to recover from effects of poor economic planning, poverty, religious and ethnic conflict, and political instability.*

Case Study

Activity Cultural Geography

This case study looks at the impact of cultural geography on the Balkan region. Have students study the maps on the opposite page and explain how cultural diversity has influenced where people have settled. Point out that Macedonia was the only country that made a peaceful transition from being a part of Yugoslavia to an independent country. Ask students how they think its location and largely homogeneous ethnic makeup might have contributed to this outcome. **LS Visual/Spatial**

Alternative Assessment Handbook, Rubric 21: Map Reading

Linking to Today

War Crimes Tribunal In 2001 Serbia's leader, Slobodan Milosevic, was arrested on charges of abuse of power and corruption. He was later turned over to the UN international war crimes tribunal in the city of The Hague in the Netherlands. A year later his trial began. He was charged with war crimes in Kosovo, Croatia, and Bosnia as well as crimes against humanity and genocide. He refused to recognize the court's authority and did not enter a plea. A plea of not guilty was entered for him. His trial began in February 2002 but was delayed repeatedly because of his poor health. Milosevic was found dead in his prison cell on March 11, 2006.

The Breakup of Yugoslavia

Essential Elements

The World in Spatial Terms
Places and Regions
Physical Systems
Human Systems
Environment and Society
The Uses of Geography

Background A school playground has a limited amount of space. If many students want to use the playground at the same time, they have to work together and consider each other's feelings. Otherwise, conflict could break out.

Space on Earth is also limited. As a result, people are sometimes forced to live near people with whom they disagree. Like students on a playground, they must learn to work together to live in peace.

Yugoslavia The country of Yugoslavia was created after World War I. As a result, people from many ethnic groups—Serbs, Montenegrins, Bosnians, Croats, Slovenes, and Macedonians—lived together in one country. Each group had its own republic, or self-governed area, in the new country.

For decades, the republics of Yugoslavia worked together peacefully. People from various ethnic groups mixed within each republic. Then in 1991 Croatia, Macedonia, and Slovenia declared independence. The republic of Bosnia and Herzegovina did the same a year later. These republics were afraid Serbia wanted to take over Yugoslavia.

It appeared that they were right. Serbia's leader, Slobodan Milosevic (sloh-BOH-dahn mee-LOH-suh-vich), wanted to increase Serbia's power. He took land from other ethnic groups. He also called on Serbs who lived in other republics to vote to give Serbia more influence in the country.

Refugees Violence between ethnic groups led many people in Yugoslavia to leave their homes. The people in this photo are fleeing Bosnia to seek refuge in a safer area.

484 CHAPTER 19

Differentiating Instruction

English-Language Learners
Below Level
Standard English Mastery

Have students study the photograph above as you read the caption aloud. Write the words *refuge* and *refugee* where students can see. Have students use context clues from the caption, or a dictionary, to define the word *refuge*. Ask them to describe what is happening in the photograph. Have students suggest reasons why the people fleeing are called *refugees*. **LS Verbal/Linguistic**

Alternative Assessment Handbook, Rubric 1: Acquiring Information

Advanced/Gifted and Talented
Above Level
Research Required

Divide students into eight groups, one each for the countries of the Balkans. Have them create Nations in the News updates for each, identifying a problem the country has had since its recent independence and how it is working to solve this problem. Have students use almanacs and Internet sources to gather information, and then present their newscasts. **LS Verbal/Linguistic**

Alternative Assessment Handbook, Rubrics 35: Solving Problems; and 30: Research

The Former Yugoslavia, 2000

map zone

Yugoslavia, 1991

Zagreb
Belgrade
Sarajevo
YUGOSLAVIA
Adriatic Sea

SLOVENIA
Zagreb
CROATIA
BOSNIA AND HERZEGOVINA
Sarajevo
Belgrade
SERBIA AND MONTENEGRO
Adriatic Sea
MACEDONIA

N

Ethnic Groups
- Albanian
- Croat
- Macedonian
- Montenegrin
- Bosnian
- Serb
- Slovene
- Other or no majority

When the other republics broke away from Yugoslavia, Milosevic called on Serbs who lived there to rise up and demand that they rejoin the country. He also provided aid to Serbian military groups in these republics. In Bosnia and Herzegovina, Serbian rebels fought for three years against the Bosnian army in a destructive civil war.

Milosevic's actions caused other ethnic groups in Yugoslavia to resent the Serbs. As a result, additional violence broke out. In Croatia, for example, the army violently expelled all Serbs from their country. War raged in the area until 1995, when a peace accord was signed. As a result of that accord, Yugoslavia was dissolved. In its place were five countries that had once been Yugoslav republics.

What It Means The violent breakup of Yugoslavia has taught other countries some valuable lessons. First, it reinforced the idea that national borders are not permanent. Borders can and do change.

More importantly, however, the struggles in Yugoslavia have made some countries more aware of their people's needs. People want to feel that they have some say in their lives. When they feel as though another group is trying to take that say from them, as many in Yugoslavia felt the Serbs were doing, then trouble will often follow.

Geography for Life Activity

1. What led to the breakup of Yugoslavia?

2. Look at the maps on this page. How did the pattern of ethnic groups in Yugoslavia change between 1991 and 2000? Why do you think this is so?

3. **Investigating Ethnic Relationships** Yugoslavia is not the only country in which multiple ethnic groups lived together. Research another country in which multiple groups live together, such as Switzerland or Indonesia. How do the groups who live there live together?

EASTERN EUROPE **485**

Critical Thinking: Drawing Conclusions

At Level

Nation Building

1. Have students discuss the role of Slobodan Milosevic in the civil war that occurred in Bosnia. Have them list his actions as Serbia's leader and describe the effects of each.

2. Explain that Milosevic as well as former leaders of other Balkan countries were charged with crimes related to ethnic cleansing and tried by the United Nations International World Court located in the Netherlands. Ask students why they think these leaders were not tried in their own

countries' courts. Have students suggest types of evidence that would have helped judges to make decisions about the leaders' guilt or innocence.

3. Have students write an editorial describing one lesson they think can be learned from the violent breakup of Yugoslavia.

🔲 **Verbal/Linguistic, Interpersonal**

📝 Alternative Assessment Handbook, Rubric 41: Writing to Express

Social Studies Skills

Analyzing Benefits and Costs

Activity Analyzing Benefits and Costs

Materials: newspaper articles on local issues

Ask students to give examples of costs and benefits of decisions they make routinely such as how to spend free time or what courses, sports, or extra-curricular activities to take. Then point out that citizens and local governments make similar decisions. Make newspaper articles available that highlight local issues such as building a convention center, highway, museum, or park, creating a mass transit system, closing a military base or factory, or creating year-round public schools. Organize students into groups. Give each group a newspaper article and have them create a chart showing benefits as well as monetary and opportunity costs of decisions that the local area is in the process of making. **LS Verbal/Linguistic, Logical/Mathematical**

- Alternative Assessment Handbook, Rubric 7: Charts
- **RF:** Social Studies Skills, Analyzing Benefits and Costs
- **RF:** Teacher's Interdisciplinary Project, Eastern Europe's Economy
- Interactive Skills Tutor CD-ROM, Lesson 16: Identify Possible Solutions and Predict Consequences

---

Analyzing Benefits and Costs

Learn

Decisions can be tough to make. A seemingly simple choice can have both positive effects, or benefits, and negative effects, or costs. Before you make a decision, it can be helpful to analyze all the possible benefits and costs that will result.

One way to analyze benefits and costs is to create a chart like the one below. On one side, list all the benefits that will result from your decision. On the other side, list the costs. Not all costs involve money. You must also consider opportunity costs, or the things that you might lose as a result of your decision. For example, going to a movie might mean that you have to miss a baseball game.

Practice

The chart to the right could have been written by an official considering whether to develop a tourism industry in Croatia. Decide whether each of the numbered items listed here should be added to the benefits column or the costs column. Once you have determined that, use the chart to decide whether the benefits of tourism outweigh the costs. Write a short paragraph to support your decision.

1. Would mean that tourist areas were not available for farming or industry

2. Would improve Croatia's image to people in other parts of the world

Tourism in Dalmatia, Croatia

Benefits	Costs
■ Would create much-needed income for towns in the region	■ Would require building of hotels, airports, and roads
■ Would not require much new investment, since tourists are drawn to region's beaches and climate	■ Increase in tourism could lead to damaging of local environments
■	■
■	■

Apply

Imagine that city leaders in your area are trying to decide whether to build a new school. They cannot make a decision and have asked you to help analyze the benefits and costs of building the school. Create a chart like the one above to list those benefits and costs. Then write a brief paragraph stating whether the benefits of the plan outweigh its costs.

486 CHAPTER 19

Answers

Practice 1. *cost;* 2. *benefit; Students' paragraphs should include supporting details for their explanations of whether tourism's benefits outweigh its costs.*

Apply *Benefits—helps meet educational needs in city, makes neighborhoods nearby more attractive to families, reduces crowding at other schools, provides employment for teachers and staff; Costs—higher taxes, less money for other government services, increased traffic in area, land can't be used for other things such as parks or housing*

Social Studies Skills Activity: Analyzing Benefits and Costs

Learning the Process

Below Level

1. Reinforce students' understanding of costs and benefits by having them give examples of costs of decisions like walking or riding the bus to school, eating at home or in a restaurant, and going to a movie or doing homework. Repeat the process focusing on benefits.

2. Then pick a popular local tourist attraction or recreational facility familiar to students. Tell them to imagine that local officials are thinking of replacing it with a factory or shopping mall. Ask students to suggest possible effects of this decision. List responses where students can see without identifying them as costs or benefits.

3. Identify an area of the classroom for costs and an area for benefits. Read phrases from the board aloud to individual students. Have each student move to the cost or benefit area. Then have students decide whether costs outweigh benefits. **LS Kinesthetic, Logical/Mathematical**

- Alternative Assessment Handbook, Rubric 14: Group Activity

Chapter Review

Geography's Impact
video series
Review the video to answer the closing question:
How have the changing political borders in the Balkans affected people's lives?

Visual Summary

Use the visual summary below to help you review the main ideas of the chapter.

QUICK FACTS

Poland and the Baltics
The history of Poland and the Baltic Republics still shapes their culture, government, and economy.

Inland Eastern Europe
Once Communist, the countries of inland Eastern Europe have stable governments and strong economies.

The Balkans
Since the breakup of Yugoslavia, the Balkans have been faced with conflict and economic challenges.

Reviewing Vocabulary, Terms, and Places

Unscramble each group of letters below to spell a term that matches the given definition.

1. **arwswa**—the capital of Poland

2. **neicht glncaenis**—the effort to remove all members of a group from a country or region

3. **ebndua**—the major river that flows through Eastern Europe, one of the longest on the continent

4. **ageurp**—the capital and largest city of the Czech Republic

5. **ncimlaitpiso**—consequences

6. **laknab**—the peninsula on which much of Eastern Europe is located

7. **ufrnrtriuacste**—the set of resources, like roads and factories, that a country needs to support economic activities

8. **nrhatcapias**—a mountain range in Eastern Europe

Comprehension and Critical Thinking

SECTION 1 *(Pages 468–471)*

9. **a. Identify** Name two major bodies of water that border Eastern Europe.

   b. Explain How do the Danube and other rivers affect life for people in Eastern Europe?

   c. Evaluate If you could live in any region of Eastern Europe, where would it be? Why?

SECTION 2 *(Pages 472–475)*

10. **a. Identify** What are the three Baltic Republics? Why are they called that?

    b. Compare and Contrast What are two cultural features that Poland and the Baltic Republics have in common? What are two features that are different in those countries?

    c. Elaborate How did the collapse of the Soviet Union affect people in Poland and the Baltic Republics?

EASTERN EUROPE **487**

Answers

Visual Summary

Review and Inquiry Have students use the visual summary to write a brief paragraph summarizing the important themes depicted on the illustration.

▶ Quick Facts Transparency: Eastern Europe Visual Summary

Reviewing Vocabulary, Terms, and Places

1. Warsaw   5. implications
2. ethnic cleansing   6. Balkan
3. Danube   7. infrastructure
4. Prague   8. Carpathians

Comprehension and Critical Thinking

9. **a.** possible answers—Baltic Sea, Black Sea, Adriatic Sea
   b. important to transportation and trade, provide hydroelectric power
   c. Answers will vary, but students should provide an explanation based on information from the text.

10. **a.** Estonia, Latvia, Lithuania; all border the Baltic Sea
    b. Alike—eat same types of foods, have similar crafts, love of music and dance; Different—languages, religions
    c. Poland rejected Communism and elected new leaders. Baltic Republics broke away from the Soviet Union and regained their independence.

Review and Assessment Resources

Review and Reinforce

SE Chapter Review

📄 RF: Chapter Review

▶ Quick Facts Transparency: Eastern Europe Visual Summary

🔊 Spanish Chapter Summaries Audio CD Program

TOS Holt McDougal PuzzleView, Quiz Show for ExamView

💿 Quiz Game CD-Rom

Assess

SE Standardized Test Practice

📄 PASS: Chapter Test, Forms A and B

📄 Alternative Assessment Handbook

TOS ExamView Test Generator, Chapter Test

💿 Differentiated Instruction Modified Worksheets and Tests CD-ROM: Chapter Test

🗔 Online Assessment Program, in the Interactive Student Edition

Reteach/Intervene

📄 Guided Reading Workbook

📄 Differentiated Instruction Teacher Management System: Lesson Plans

💿 Differentiated Instruction Modified Worksheets and Tests CD-ROM

💿 Interactive Skills Tutor CD-ROM

Chapter Resources

11. a. Belarus is a dictatorship; other countries are democracies.

b. differences in natural resources, location, infrastructure, or influence of ties to Russia or the West

c. Because the Czech Republic is farther west than other Eastern European countries and borders Western Europe, it has closer ties to the West than many other inland countries.

12. a. Catholicism, Orthodox Christianity, Protestantism, Islam

b. to end the fighting among religious and ethnic groups in the former Yugoslavia

c. It may bring increased trade and tourism, improvements in the economies of the region, greater political stability, and closer ties to the West.

Map Activity

13. A. Great Hungarian Plain
B. Danube River
C. Albania
D. Kiev, Ukraine
E. Warsaw, Poland
F. Latvia

Using the Internet

14. Go to hmhsocialstudies.com to access a rubric for this activity.

Social Studies Skills

15. possible answer: Benefits—more energy, less reliance on Russia for energy, less reliance on fossil fuels, provides jobs for people building and staffing the plant; Costs—building the plant, risk of nuclear accident or other damage to environment, storage of radioactive waste; students' statements will vary but should include support for their reasoning.

---

11. a. Describe What is the government of Belarus like? What type of government do the other countries of inland Eastern Europe have?

b. Draw Conclusions Why do you think that some countries in inland Eastern Europe have stronger economies than others?

c. Elaborate How has its location influenced the culture of the Czech Republic?

SECTION 4 *(Pages 480–483)*

12. a. Identify What religions are common in the Balkan countries?

b. Explain Why did countries from around the world send troops to Kosovo?

c. Predict How do you think peace will affect life in the Balkans?

Map Activity

13. Eastern Europe On a separate sheet of paper, match the letters on the map with their correct labels.

Great Hungarian Plain	Kiev, Ukraine
Latvia	Warsaw, Poland
Albania	Danube River

hmhsocialstudies.com **INTERACTIVE MAP**

map zone

Focus on Reading and Viewing

16. Problem—need more infrastructure to support economic development; Solution—Answers will vary, but possible responses include raising taxes, reducing spending in other areas, finding foreign investors or international agencies to provide loans or funding for infrastructure improvement.

RF: Focus on Reading, Understanding Problems and Solutions

Using the Internet

14. Activity: Writing a Report For centuries the Balkans have been an arena of conflict. Through your online textbook, learn about the history and cultures of the Balkans and investigate recent conflicts there. Write a report on what you find.

hmhsocialstudies.com

Social Studies Skills

15. Analyzing Costs and Benefits Imagine that you are a government official in Ukraine. Your country cannot produce enough energy to meet its needs and has to buy energy from Russia. A company in Kiev has expressed interest in building nuclear power plants, but many people are leery of nuclear power since the Chernobyl incident. Make a list of the costs and benefits of nuclear power. Then write a statement that either supports or argues against the plan.

FOCUS ON READING AND VIEWING

16. Understanding Problems and Solutions Re-read the first paragraph under the heading The Region Today in Section 2. Then write a short paragraph that explains the main problem facing Poland and the Baltics today. End your paragraph by suggesting a solution their governments might use to address the problem.

17. Making a Presentation Write a brief report about a country in Eastern Europe and prepare a poster that illustrates your main ideas. Find pictures of major features of your chosen country and arrange them on a poster board. Write a short caption that explains what each picture is. Present your report to the class. As you discuss each main idea, point out the pictures that illustrate it on your poster. Speak clearly and keep eye contact with your audience. Then, listen as your peers present their reports and posters. Note whether they speak clearly and maintain eye contact. Do their posters illustrate the main ideas in their reports?

17. Rubric Students' reports should

- be presented in a formal voice with confident body language

- be spoken clearly and with enthusiasm

- include a poster with pictures to support the main ideas about the chosen country

RF: Focus on Viewing, Presenting and Viewing Visual Reports

Standardized Test Prep

DIRECTIONS: Read questions 1 through 7 and write the letter of the best response. Then read question 8 and write your own well-constructed response.

1 The country *most* influential in Eastern Europe after World War II was

A the United States.

B the Soviet Union.

C France.

D Germany.

2 Which of the following countries violently broke apart in the 1990s?

A Poland

B Romania

C Czechoslovakia

D Yugoslavia

3 The major river of Eastern Europe is the

A Baltic River.

B Carpathian River.

C Danube River.

D Hungarian River.

4 Which of these countries is located on the Balkan Peninsula?

A Croatia

B Poland

C Belarus

D Estonia

5 Which of these statements about religion in Eastern Europe is correct?

A Nearly everyone in the region is Muslim.

B Nearly everyone in the region is Catholic.

C Nearly everyone in the region is Orthodox Christian.

D People in the region practice many different religions.

Hungary

For those in search of the heart and soul of Europe, there's nowhere better. Hungarians, who call themselves Magyars, speak a language and revel in a culture unlike any other. Away from the cosmopolitan charms of Budapest, life in the provinces is more redolent of times past—simpler, slower, often friendlier. There are endless opportunities for those with special interests—from horse riding and cycling to bird-watching and "taking the waters" at the country's many thermal spas.

–from Lonely Planet World Guide Online

6 Read the passage above from a travel guide to Hungary. According to this passage, what do people from Hungary call themselves?

A Hungarians

B Magyars

C Budapestians

D Europeans

7 Based on the above passage, which of the following statements is true?

A Hungarian culture is similar to many others in Europe.

B There are few things to do in Hungary.

C People outside of Budapest live simpler and slower lives than people in the city.

D Hungary is the largest country in Europe.

8 **Extended Response** Life in Eastern Europe is still influenced by the Soviet era, even though the Soviet Union collapsed many years ago. Consider what you have read in this chapter and write a paragraph in which you explain how Soviet influence is still felt in the region.

Answers

Standardized Test Prep

1. B
Break Down the Question This question requires students to recall factual information from Section 2.

2. D
Break Down the Question This question requires students to recall factual information from Section 4.

3. C
Break Down the Question Students can begin by eliminating all places that they know are not rivers. Have students who miss this question review Section 1.

4. A
Break Down the Question This question requires students to recall factual information from Section 4.

5. D
Break Down the Question Remind students that *nearly everyone* means if even one area of Eastern Europe has religious diversity, then only one answer is correct. Have students who miss the question recall factual information from Sections 2, 3, and 4.

6. B
Break Down the Question This question requires students to recall the second sentence in the passage.

7. C
Break Down the Question Students should notice that the words *slower* and *simpler* are found in the passage.

8. Extended Response possible answer—Soviet influence is still felt in Eastern Europe primarily because of economic effects of poor planning and infrastructure problems that began under Soviet rule. The countries of Eastern Europe are working to replace and rebuild buildings and roads, while also increasing business opportunities. The people of Eastern Europe are learning how to function in this new environment that is less controlled and less supportive than in the Soviet era.

Reteach/Intervention Resources

Reproducible

- Guided Reading Workbook
- Differentiated Instruction Teacher Management System: Lesson Plans

Technology

- Quick Facts Transparency: Eastern Europe Visual Summary
- Differentiated Instruction Modified Worksheets and Tests CD-ROM
- Interactive Skills Tutor CD-ROM

Tips for Test Taking

Take It All In Encourage students to preview the test to get a mental map of their tasks:

- Know how many questions there are.
- Know where to stop.
- Set time checkpoints.
- Do the easy sections first; easy questions can be worth just as many points as hard ones.

Chapter 20 Planning Guide

Russia and the Caucasus

Overview	Instructional Resources	
CHAPTER 20 **Essential Question:** What cultural and geographic features help define Russia and the Caucusus? 🔊 **Focus on the Essential Question Podcast**	**TOS Differentiated Instruction Teacher Management System:** • Instructional Pacing Guides • Lesson Plans for Differentiated Instruction **Guided Reading Workbook** **Resource File:** • Chapter Review • Focus on Reading: Making Generalizations • Focus on Writing: Creating a Real Estate Ad • Social Studies Skills: Interpreting a Population Map **Experiencing World History and Geography**	**TOS Calendar Planner** **Power Presentations with Media Gallery** **Differentiated Instruction Modified Worksheets and Tests CD-ROM** **Interactive Skills Tutor CD-ROM** **Student Edition on Audio CD-ROM** **The World's Music Audio Program** **Map Zone Transparency:** Russia and the Caucasus: Political **World Outline Maps: Transparencies and Activities** **Video:** The Romanovs
Section 1: **Physical Geography** **The Big Idea:** Russia is big and cold with vast plains and forests; whereas the Caucasus countries are small, mountainous, and warmer.	**TOS Differentiated Instruction Teacher Management System:** Section 1 Lesson Plan **Guided Reading Workbook:** Section 1 **Resource File:** • Vocabulary Builder: Section 1 • Critical Thinking: A Russian Space Mystery	**Daily Bellringer Transparency:** Section 1 **Map Zone Transparency:** Russia and the Caucasus: Physical
Section 2: **History and Culture of Russia** **The Big Idea:** Strict rule, unrest, and ethnic diversity have shaped Russia's history and culture.	**TOS Differentiated Instruction Teacher Management System:** Section 2 Lesson Plan **Guided Reading Workbook:** Section 2 **Resource File:** • Vocabulary Builder: Section 2 • Biography: Catherine the Great • Literature: *War and Peace* by Leo Tolstoy • Primary Source: Russian Icon Painting • Geography and History: Serfdom in Russia, 1860	**Daily Bellringer Transparency:** Section 2 **Map Zone Transparency:** History of Russian Expansion **Map Zone Transparency:** Russia: Population **Internet Activity:** End of Communism **Internet Activity:** Treasures of Russia
Section 3: **Russia Today** **The Big Idea:** Russia is a federal republic with a growing market economy but faces tough challenges.	**TOS Differentiated Instruction Teacher Management System:** Section 3 Lesson Plan **Guided Reading Workbook:** Section 3 **Resource File:** • Vocabulary Builder: Section 3 • Interdisciplinary Project: The Russian Space Program	**Daily Bellringer Transparency:** Section 3 **Map Zone Transparency:** Russia: Culture Regions **Animated Geography:** Trans-Siberian Railroad
Section 4: **The Caucasus** **The Big Idea:** In an area long ruled by outside groups, the Caucasus republics are struggling to strengthen their economies and to deal with ethnic unrest.	**TOS Differentiated Instruction Teacher Management System:** Section 4 Lesson Plan **Guided Reading Workbook:** Section 4 **Resource File:** • Vocabulary Builder: Section 4 • Biography: Garry Kasparov	**Daily Bellringer Transparency:** Section 4 **Map Zone Transparency:** The Caucasus: Political

Chart Key:

SE Student Edition   Presentation Resource   MP3 Audio

TOS Teacher One Stop   DVD/CD-ROM   HISTORY™

 Printable Resource

Program Resources available on **TOS** and @ hmhsocialstudies.com

---

Review, Assessment, Intervention

 Europe and Russia Transparencies: Russia and the Caucasus Visual Summary

 Spanish Chapter Summaries Audio CD

Progress Assessment Support System (PASS): Chapter Test

Differentiated Instruction Modified Worksheets CD-ROM: Modified Chapter Test

TOS ExamView® Assessment Suite (English/Spanish)

Alternative Assessment Handbook

 Online Assessment Program, in the Interactive Student Edition

---

 PASS: Section 1 Quiz

 Online Quiz: Section 1

Alternative Assessment Handbook

 PASS: Section 2 Quiz

 Online Quiz: Section 2

Alternative Assessment Handbook

 PASS: Section 3 Quiz

  Online Quiz: Section 3

Alternative Assessment Handbook

  PASS: Section 4 Quiz

 Online Quiz: Section 4

Alternative Assessment Handbook

Supporting Resources

HISTORY

- Multimedia Classroom Global History Series
- Global History Teacher's Guide

Maps Globes Graphs Level F

- Student Workbook
- Teacher's Guide

Social Studies Trade Library Collections

- World Regions Trade Collection
- NCSS Middle School Trade Collection

Geography's Impact

Geography's Impact Video Program

- **Impact of Pollution**

For more information or to purchase go to **hmhsocialstudies.com**

Power Presentations with Media Gallery

Power Presentations with Media Gallery are visual presentations of each chapter's main ideas. Presentations can be customized by including Quick Facts charts, images from the text, and video clips.

Differentiating Instruction

How do I address the needs of varied learners?

The Target Resource acts as your primary strategy for differentiated instruction.

ENGLISH-LANGUAGE LEARNERS & STRUGGLING READERS

TARGET RESOURCE

Differentiated Instruction Teacher Management System

Lesson Plans for Differentiated Instruction provide teachers with strategies to help plan instruction for all learners.

Additional Resources

Resource File:
- Vocabulary Builder Activities
- Social Studies Skills: Interpreting a Population Map

Quick Facts Transparencies:
- Russia and the Caucasus Visual Summary

Student Edition on Audio CD Program

Interactive Skills Tutor CD-ROM

Spanish Chapter Summaries Audio CD Program

Teacher One Stop:
- ExamView Assessment Suite, Spanish
- PuzzleView, Spanish

English-Language Learner Strategies and Activities

Spanish/English Guided Reading Workbook

SPECIAL NEEDS LEARNERS

TARGET RESOURCE

Interactive Skills Tutor CD-ROM

The Interactive Skills Tutor CD-ROM contains lessons that provide additional practice for 20 different critical thinking skills.

Additional Resources

Differentiated Instruction Teacher Management System: Lesson Plans for Differentiated Instruction

Guided Reading Workbook

Resource File: Social Studies Skills: Interpreting a Population Map

Student Edition on Audio CD Program

Graphic Organizer Transparencies with Support for Reading and Writing

ADVANCED/GIFTED AND TALENTED STUDENTS

TARGET RESOURCE

Resource File

The Resource File activities allow students to extend their knowledge of chapter-related places and people and to practice geography skills.
- Focus on Reading: Making Generalizations
- Focus on Writing: Creating a Real Estate Ad
- Literature: *War and Peace* by Leo Tolstoy

Additional Resources

Differentiated Instruction Teacher Management System: Lesson Plans for Differentiated Instruction

World History and Geography Document-Based Questions Activities

Geography, Science, and Cultures Activities

Experiencing World History and Geography

Differentiated Activities in the Teacher's Edition

- Locating Map Labels, p. 493
- Developing a Time Line, p. 497
- Taking Notes, p. 503
- Write a Short Play, p. 507
- Reviewing Similarities and Differences, p. 509

Teacher One Stop™

How can I manage the lesson plans and support materials for differentiated instruction?

With the Teacher One Stop, you can easily organize and print lesson plans, planning guides, and instructional materials for all learners. The Teacher One Stop includes the following materials to help you differentiate instruction:

- · Interactive Teacher's Edition
- · Calendar Planner and pacing guides
- · Editable lesson plans
- · All reproducible ancillaries in Adobe Acrobat (PDF) format
- · ExamView Assessment Suite (English & Spanish)
- · Transparency and video previews

Differentiated Activities in the Teacher's Edition

- Reading a Population Map, p. 501

Interactive Student Edition

Complete online student edition with interactive multimedia support for chapter content assessment and reporting

- Interactive Maps and Notebook
- Standardized Test Prep
- Online Homework Practice and Research Activities
- Current Events
- Chapter-based Internet Activities
- Animated Geography Activities

Differentiated Activities in the Teacher's Edition

- Writing about Current Events, p. 493
- Making a Population Map, p. 501
- Write a Scene in a Play, p. 507

Essential Question

Introduce the Essential Question

- Explain that Russia and the Caucasus have varied physical features, climates, and plant life. They also have a wealth of natural resources.

- Point out that the diverse landscape of Russia may have influenced its various ethnic groups.

- Discuss why Russia is divided into several cultural regions based on features, such as population, natural resources, and economic activity.

- Have students discuss how the location of the Caucasus where Europe blends into Asia causes it to have a wide range of cultural influences.

Focus on Reading and Writing

Reading The Resource File provides a worksheet to help students practice making generalizations based on what they read.

📓 **RF:** Focus on Reading, Making Generalizations

Writing The Resource File provides a worksheet to help students plan and write a real estate ad.

📓 **RF:** Focus on Writing, Creating a Real Estate Ad

Key to Differentiating Instruction

Below Level

Basic-level activities designed for all students encountering new material

At Level

Intermediate-level activities designed for average students

Above Level

Challenging activities designed for honors and gifted and talented students

Standard English Mastery

Activities designed to improve standard English usage

LS Learning Styles

CHAPTER **20**

Russia and the Caucasus

Essential Question What cultural and geographic features help define Russia and the Caucusus?

❓ What You Will Learn...

In this chapter you will learn about the physical features, climate, and natural resources of Russia and the Caucasus. You will also study the histories and cultures of these countries. Finally, you will learn about life in each of the countries today.

FOCUS ON READING AND WRITING

Making Generalizations A generalization is a broad, general idea drawn from new information combined with what you already know. As you read this chapter, stop now and then to make a generalization. It will help you pull the pieces of information together and make sense of them. **See the lesson, Making Generalizations, on page 535.**

Creating a Real Estate Ad As you read this chapter, imagine you work for a real estate agency in Russia or the Caucasus. You are trying to sell a piece of property there. In order to sell the property, you must write an ad to be published in the newspaper and on the Internet. As you read, decide where your property would be located and what its characteristics would be.

Geography A volcano created Crater Bay in the Kuril Islands off the east coast of Russia. The islands have several active volcanoes.

Introduce the Chapter

At Level

Exploring Russia and the Caucasus

1. Talk with students about how every country, no matter what size, has its own rich history and culture. Ask them to recall information about smaller countries they studied previously.

2. Explain to students that they are going to learn about Russia and the countries of the Caucasus—Georgia, Armenia, and Azerbaijan. Discuss with students what they already know about these countries—and what they would like to learn.

3. Have students keep track of the main ideas in each section as they read. Ask them to think about what generalizations they can make based on what they learn. Remind students that generalizations are helpful learning tools, but that they need to be supported with specific details. **LS** Verbal/Linguistic

📓 Alternative Assessment Handbook, Rubric 1: Acquiring Information

Bering Strait

ARCTIC OCEAN

Barents
Sea

HISTORY The Romanovs

hmhsocialstudies.com **VIDEO**

PACIFIC
OCEAN

Ob River

Lena River

RUSSIA

Sea of
Okhotsk

Yenisey River

Angara River

Lena River

Amur River

Sakhalin
Island

Kuril Islands

Novosibirsk

Lake
Baikal

Vladivostok

Sea of
Japan
(East Sea)

JAPAN

MONGOLIA

map zone Geography Skills

Regions Russia, the world's largest country, lies north and east of the small Caucasus countries.
1. **Name** What ocean lies north of Russia?
2. **Contrast** How does the land and size of Russia differ from that of the other countries in this region?

CHINA

History The Kremlin complex houses Russia's government as well as gold-domed churches and beautiful, historical palaces.

Culture The Bolshoi Ballet in Moscow, Russia, is famous throughout the world. Above, dancers perform *Swan Lake*.

491

• Chapter Preview •

Explore the Map and Pictures

Russia and the Caucasus: Political
What can you tell about Russia and the Caucasus by looking at this map? *The location and size of the countries; Russia dominates the region; the location of rivers and other bodies of water, such as the Volga River, Don River, and Caspian Sea; the location of national capitals and major cities; Moscow is a long distance from much of Russia.*

▶ Map Zone Transparency: Russia and the Caucasus: Political

Analyzing Visuals How many seas does Russia border, and what are their names? *Seven—Sea of Japan, Sea of Okhotsk, Bering Sea, Barents Sea, Baltic Sea, Black Sea, and the Caspian Sea.* Which countries in the region do not border the Black Sea? *Azerbaijan, Armenia* What can you learn from the photograph of the Bolshoi Ballet? *Russian culture has influenced other cultures; Swan Lake is one of the world's most famous ballets.*

↗ hmhsocialstudies.com
Teacher Resources

Critical Thinking: Interpreting Maps
At Level

The Russian-Caucasus Connections

1. Explain to students that history plays a key role in the relationship between Russia and the Caucasus. After World War I, the Caucasus countries were briefly independent, then became part of the Soviet Union in the early 1920s. They regained independence when the Soviet Union broke up in 1991.

2. Ask students how they think history has influenced how people have lived in these countries. Ask students what they can learn about these countries and their relationships by studying the map.

3. Have students write six questions about Russia and the Caucasus—three which cannot be answered from the map, and three that can be. Then have students work in pairs and ask each other their questions. Ask for volunteers to share their questions and answers.

LS Verbal/Linguistic, Visual/Spatial

Alternative Assessment Handbook, Rubric 21: Map Reading

Answers

Map Zone 1. *Arctic Ocean;* **2.** *It is much larger and borders two oceans and several seas.*

492 CHAPTER 20

Preteach

Bellringer

If YOU lived there. . . Use the **Daily Bellringer Transparency** to help students answer the question.

▶ Daily Bellringer Transparency, Section 1

Key Terms and Places

RF: Vocabulary Builder, Section 1

Taking Notes

Have students use the graphic organizer online to take notes on the section. This activity will prepare students for the Section Assessment, in which they will complete a graphic organizer that builds on the information using the Critical Thinking Skill: Generalizing.

Physical Geography

What You Will Learn...

Main Ideas

1. The physical features of Russia and the Caucasus include plains, mountains, and rivers.
2. Climate and plant life change from north to south in Russia and vary in the Caucasus.
3. Russia and the Caucasus have a wealth of resources, but many are hard to access.

The Big Idea

Russia is big and cold with vast plains and forests; whereas the Caucasus countries are small, mountainous, and warmer.

Key Terms and Places

Ural Mountains, *p. 492*
Caspian Sea, *p. 492*
Caucasus Mountains, *p. 492*
Moscow, *p. 492*
Siberia, *p. 493*
Volga River, *p. 494*
taiga, *p. 495*

hmhsocialstudies.com
TAKING NOTES

Use the graphic organizer online to take notes on the physical geography of Russia and the Caucusus.

If YOU lived there...

You are making a documentary about the Trans–Siberian Railroad, a famous train that crosses the vast country of Russia. The train travels more than 5,700 miles across plains and mountains and through thick forests. As the train leaves the city of Moscow, you look out the window and see wheat fields and white birch trees.

What scenes might you include in your film?

BUILDING BACKGROUND Look at a globe, and you will see that Russia extends nearly halfway around the world. Russia is the world's largest country. It is so vast that it spans 11 time zones. While huge, much of Russia consists of flat or rolling plains.

Physical Features

Have you ever stood on two continents at once? In Russia's **Ural** (YOOHR-uhl) **Mountains**, you can. There, the continents of Europe and Asia meet. Europe lies to the west; Asia to the east. Together, Europe and Asia form the large landmass of Eurasia. On the map, you can see that a large chunk of Eurasia is the country of Russia. In fact, Russia is the world's largest country. Compared to the United States, Russia is almost twice as big.

South of Russia are three much smaller countries—Georgia, Armenia (ahr-MEE-nee-uh), and Azerbaijan (a-zuhr-by-JAHN). They lie in the Caucasus (KAW-kuh-suhs), the area between the Black Sea and the **Caspian Sea**. This area, which includes part of southern Russia, is named for the **Caucasus Mountains**.

Landforms

As the map shows, Russia's landforms vary from west to east. The Northern European Plain stretches across western, or European, Russia. This fertile plain forms Russia's heartland, where most Russians live. **Moscow**, Russia's capital, is located there.

492 CHAPTER 20

Teach the Big Idea

At Level

Physical Geography

1. **Teach** Ask students the questions in the Main Idea boxes under Direct Teach.

2. **Apply** Have each student choose a term or place that they want to learn more about from the "Key Terms and Places" list. Have students use the text to describe the term or place in a complete sentence. Then have students make posters illustrating the term or place they chose, and include their completed sentence on the poster.

3. **Review** Ask students to share their posters with the class, reading their sentence aloud.

4. **Practice/Homework** Have students write a short paragraph about the physical geography of Russia and the Caucasus, generalizing based on the posters that were shared in class.
   LS Visual/Spatial, Verbal/Linguistic

   Alternative Assessment Handbook, Rubric 28: Posters

Russia and the Caucasus: Physical

map zone Geography Skills

Regions The Caucasus Mountains separate Russia from the three Caucasus countries to the south.
1. **Locate** What part of Russia is called Siberia?
2. **Interpret** What is the land like in the Caucasus countries?

ELEVATION

Feet		Meters
13,120		4,000
6,560		2,000
1,640		500
656		200
(Sea level) 0		0 (Sea level)
Below sea level		Below sea level

0   500   1,000 Miles
0   500   1,000 Kilometers
Projection: Two-Point Equidistant

To the east, the plain rises to form the Ural Mountains. These low mountains are worn down and rounded from erosion.

The vast area between the Urals and the Pacific Ocean is **Siberia**. This area includes several landforms, shown on the map. The West Siberian Plain is a flat, marshy area. It is one of the largest plains in the world.

East of this plain is an upland called the Central Siberian Plateau. Mountain ranges run through southern and eastern Siberia.

Eastern Siberia is called the Russian Far East. This area includes the Kamchatka (kuhm-CHAHT-kuh) Peninsula and several islands. The Russian Far East is part of the Ring of Fire, the area circling the Pacific.

1 The Kamchatka Peninsula on Russia's east coast has many old and active volcanoes.

RUSSIA AND THE CAUCASUS **493**

Differentiating Instruction

Struggling Readers   Below Level

To help struggling readers, read aloud the name of each label on the map. As you do, have students locate the label. Remind students that this book has many illustrations that can help them learn. **LS Visual/Spatial**

📖 Alternative Assessment Handbook, Rubric 21: Map Reading

Advanced/Gifted and Talented   Above Level

Have students use the Internet or library resources to learn about a current event in the Caucasus region or Russia. Students should obtain information from at least three different sources. Based on their research, have students write their own news story to share with the class. **LS Verbal/Linguistic**

📖 Alternative Assessment Handbook, Rubrics 29: Presentations; and 42: Writing to Inform

---

Main Idea

❶ Physical Features

The physical features of Russia and the Caucasus include plains, mountains, and rivers.

Identify What three countries make up the Caucasus? *Georgia, Armenia, and Azerbaijan* What separates Russia from the Caucasus countries? *the Caucasus Mountains*

Describe What is Siberia like? *It is an empty land of barren plains and flat marshy areas with high mountain ranges running through the southern and eastern parts.*

Explain What is a threat to Lake Baikal? *water pollution from logging and factories*

📖 **RF:** Geography for Life, Agriculture and the Environment in the Caucasus

📖 **RF:** Critical Thinking, A Russian Space Mystery

▶ Map Zone Transparency: Russia and the Caucasus: Physical

Info to Know

Kamchatka's Volcanoes The Kamchatka Peninsula has the highest density of volcanoes in the world. Twenty-nine of Kamchatka's volcanoes are still active. This peninsula is also home to many types of wildlife, including brown bears, snow rams, sea eagles, wild salmon, gray whales, seals, and sea lions.

Answers

Map Zone 1. *the large area between the Ural Mountains and the Pacific Ocean;* **2.** *mountainous, with lowlands near the seas*

❷ Climate and Plant Life

Climate and plant life change from north to south in Russia and vary in the Caucasus.

Describe What is Russia's climate like? *short summers and long, snowy winters; milder west of the Urals, growing colder as one goes north and east*

Identify What is the taiga? *a forest of mainly evergreen trees covering about half of Russia*

Summarize How is the Caucasus' climate different from Russia's? *Russia's climate is mainly cold while the Caucasus has a wider range of climates—warm and wet along the Black Sea, and cooler in the uplands, while Azerbaijan is hot and dry.*

Activity Compare and Contrast

1. Ask students to imagine they must choose to live in either Russia or a Caucasus country.

2. Have students write a brief essay explaining where they would live, and why. Students should describe the physical features and climates that appeal to them, as well as those that don't.

3. Have students read their essays to the class. Point out that different geographical features appeal to different people. **LS Verbal/Linguistic**

📝 Alternative Assessment Handbook, Rubric 37: Writing Assignments

The Ring of Fire is known for its volcanoes and earthquakes, and the Russian Far East is no exception. It has several active volcanoes, and earthquakes can occur. In some areas, steam from within Earth breaks free to form geysers and hot springs.

South of Russia, the Caucasus countries consist largely of rugged uplands. The Caucasus Mountains cover much of Georgia and extend into Armenia and Azerbaijan.

Russia's Climate and Plant Life

In the top photo, Russians bundled up in furs hurry through the snow and cold of Moscow, the capital. In the lower photo, evergreen forest called taiga blankets a Russian plain. In the distance, the low Ural Mountains mark the division between Europe and Asia.

494 CHAPTER 20

These soaring mountains include Mount Elbrus (el-BROOS). At 18,510 feet (5,642 m), it is the highest peak in Europe. South of the mountains, a plateau covers much of Armenia. Gorges cut through this plateau, and earthquakes are common there. Lowlands lie along the Black and Caspian seas.

Bodies of Water

Some of the longest rivers in the world flow through the region of Russia and the Caucasus. One of the most important is the **Volga** (VAHL-guh) **River** in western Russia. The longest river in Europe, the Volga winds southward to the Caspian Sea. The Volga has long formed the core of Russia's river network. Canals link the Volga to the nearby Don River and to the Baltic Sea.

Even longer rivers than the Volga flow through Siberia in the Asian part of Russia. The Ob (AWB), Yenisey (yi-ni-SAY), and Lena rivers flow northward to the Arctic Ocean. Like many of Russia's rivers, they are frozen for much of the year. The ice often hinders shipping and trade and closes some of Russia's ports for part of the year.

In addition to its rivers, Russia has some 200,000 lakes. Lake Baikal (by-KAHL), in south-central Siberia, is the world's deepest lake. Although not that large in surface area, Lake Baikal is deep enough to hold all the water in all five of the Great Lakes. Because of its beauty, Lake Baikal is called the Jewel of Siberia. Logging and factories have polluted the water, but Russians are now working to clean up the lake.

In the southwest part of the region, the Black and Caspian Seas border Russia and the Caucasus. The Black Sea connects to the Mediterranean Sea and is important for trade. The Caspian Sea holds saltwater and is the world's largest inland sea.

READING CHECK Summarizing What are the major landforms in Russia and the Caucasus?

Critical Thinking: Making Generalizations

At Level

The Importance of the Volga River

1. Review with students information in the text about the Volga River. Remind students that it is the longest river in Europe.

2. Have students make a generalization about why the Volga still serves as a valuable resource today. For example, the Volga is the core of Russia's river network.

3. Have students write a short essay describing ways in which the Volga might continue to be a valuable resource in the future. For example, have students predict whether

the river will continue to be used as a transportation route, or if they think it might be valuable in other ways. **LS Verbal/Linguistic**

📝 Alternative Assessment Handbook, Rubrics 12: Drawing Conclusions; and 37: Writing Assignments

Answers

Reading Check *Nothern European Plain, Ural Mountains, West Siberian Plain, Central Siberian Plain, Kamchatka Peninsula, Caucasus Mountains*

Climate and Plant Life

Russians sometimes joke that winter lasts for 12 months and then summer begins. Russia is a cold country. The reason is its northern location partly within the Arctic Circle. In general, Russia has short summers and long, snowy winters. The climate is milder west of the Urals and grows colder and harsher as one goes north and east.

Russia's northern coast is tundra. Winters are dark and bitterly cold, and the brief summers are cool. Much of the ground is permafrost, or permanently frozen soil. Only small plants such as mosses grow.

South of the tundra is a vast forest of evergreen trees called **taiga** (TY-guh). This huge forest covers about half of Russia. In Siberia, snow covers the taiga much of the year. South of the taiga is a flat grassland called the steppe (STEP). With rich, black soil and a warmer climate, the steppe is Russia's most important farming area.

Farther south, the Caucasus countries are warmer than Russia in general. Climate in the Caucasus ranges from warm and wet along the Black Sea to cooler in the uplands to hot and dry in much of Azerbaijan.

READING CHECK Finding Main Ideas How does Russia's location affect its climate?

Natural Resources

Russia and the Caucasus have a wealth of resources. The Northern European Plain and the steppe provide fertile soil for farming. The taiga provides wood for building and paper products. Metals, such as copper and gold, and precious gems such as diamonds provide useful raw materials.

The region's main energy resources are coal, hydroelectricity, natural gas, and oil. Both Russia and Azerbaijan have large oil and gas fields. Oil also lies beneath the Caspian Sea.

The region's natural resources have been poorly managed, however. Until the early 1990s this region was part of the Soviet Union. The Soviet government put more importance on industry than on managing its resources. In Russia, many of the resources that were easy to access are gone. For example, most of the timber in western Russia has been cut down. Many remaining resources are in remote Siberia.

READING CHECK Analyzing Why are some of Russia's natural resources difficult to obtain?

SUMMARY AND PREVIEW Russia is big and cold, with vast plains and forests. The Caucasus countries are small, mountainous, and warmer. The region also has many natural resources. Next, you will read about Russia's history and culture.

FOCUS ON READING

What general idea can you draw from the text about natural resources? What facts or details support that idea?

Section 1 Assessment

hmhsocialstudies.com
ONLINE QUIZ

Reviewing Ideas, Terms, and Places

1. **a. Describe** Why are the **Ural Mountains** significant?
   b. Draw Conclusions Why might the Russian Far East be a dangerous place to live?
2. **a. Describe** What are winters like in much of Russia?
   b. Analyze How does climate affect Russia's plant life?
3. **a. Recall** What valuable resource is in the **Caspian Sea**?
   b. Make Inferences Why might resources located in remote, cold areas be difficult to use?

Critical Thinking

4. **Generalizing** Draw a chart like the one here. Use your notes and enter one general idea for each topic in the chart.

Physical Features	
Climate and Plants	
Natural Resources	

FOCUS ON WRITING

5. **Describing the Physical Geography** Now that you know the physical geography of the region, make a list of possible locations for the house or land you are selling.

RUSSIA AND THE CAUCASUS **495**

Main Idea

❸ Natural Resources

Russia and the Caucasus have a wealth of resources, but many are hard to access.

Recall What are Russia's main natural resources? *fertile soil, forests, coal, natural gas, oil, copper, gold, and diamonds*

Explain Why were resources not well managed in the Soviet Union? *The Soviet government put more importance on industry than resource management.*

Review & Assess

Close

Discuss with students the role that physical features, climate, vegetation, and natural resources play in Russia and the Caucasus.

Review

Online Quiz, Section 1

Assess

SE Section 1 Assessment
PASS: Section 1 Quiz
Alternative Assessment Handbook

Reteach/Classroom Intervention

Guided Reading Workbook, Section 1
Interactive Skills Tutor CD-ROM

Section 1 Assessment Answers

1. **a.** They separate Asia from Europe.
   b. Earthquakes are frequent, and the region has many active volcanoes.

2. **a.** long and cold
   b. In the colder climate, only mosses, wildflowers and other small plants grow. In its warmer and wetter climate, forests and mixed trees grow. In its dry, warm climate, grasses grow, and farming is possible.

3. **a.** oil deposits
   b. possible answer—These areas are difficult to get to, making transporting resources difficult and expensive.

4. possible answer: Physical Features—plains, mountains, lakes, rivers; Climate and Plants—short summers, long winters, taiga; Natural Resources—fertile soil, metals, gems, coal, hydroelectricity, natural gas, oil

5. Answers will vary, but should include locations mentioned in the text.

Answers

Reading Check (left) *Its location in the far north means it has long, cold winters and short summers.*

Focus on Reading *Russia has a wealth of natural resources, but they have not been well managed. For example, most of the timber in western Russia has been cut down.*

Reading Check (right) *Many remaining resources are in remote Siberia.*

495

Bellringer

If YOU lived there. . . Use the **Daily Bellringer Transparency** to help students answer the question.

▶ Daily Bellringer Transparency, Section 2

Academic Vocabulary

Review with students the high-use academic term in this section.

reaction a response to something (p. 498)

 RF: Vocabulary Builder, Section 2

Taking Notes

Have students use the graphic organizer online to take notes on the section. This activity will prepare students for the Section Assessment, in which they will complete a graphic organizer that builds on the information using the Critical Thinking Skill: Sequencing.

History and Culture of Russia

What You Will Learn...

Main Ideas

1. The Russian Empire grew under powerful leaders, but unrest and war led to its end.
2. The Soviet Union emerged as a Communist superpower with rigid government control.
3. Russia's history and diversity have influenced its culture.

The Big Idea

Strict rule, unrest, and ethnic diversity have shaped Russia's history and culture.

Key Terms and Places

Kiev, *p. 496*
Cyrillic, *p. 496*
czar, *p. 497*
Bolsheviks, *p. 497*
gulags, *p. 498*

hmhsocialstudies.com
TAKING NOTES

Use the graphic organizer online to take notes on the history and culture of Russia.

If YOU lived there...

It is 1992, an exciting time in your home town of Moscow. At the end of 1991 the Soviet Union fell apart. Russia became independent. You watched on TV as people pulled down the red Soviet flag and knocked down statues of former leaders. Everyone is talking about new freedoms and a new kind of government.

What new freedoms do you hope to have?

> **BUILDING BACKGROUND** The fall of the Soviet Union was not the first time Russia had experienced change. For centuries Russia was part of a great empire. Then in the early 1900s Communists overthrew the empire. The Soviet Union was born. Today it too is gone.

The Russian Empire

Russia's roots lie in the grassy, windswept plains of the steppe. For thousands of years, people from Asia moved across the steppe. These groups of people included the Slavs. As you read in the last chapter, the Slavs settled in Eastern Europe, including what is now Ukraine and western Russia.

Early History and Empire

The Slavs developed towns and began trading with people from other areas. In the AD 800s, Viking traders from Scandinavia invaded the Slavs. These Vikings were called Rus (ROOS), and the word *Russia* probably comes from their name. The Vikings shaped the first Russian state among the Slavs. This Russian state, called Kievan (KEE-e-fuhn) Rus, centered around the city of **Kiev**. This city is now the capital of Ukraine.

Over time, missionaries introduced the Orthodox Christian faith to Kiev. In addition, the missionaries introduced a form of the Greek alphabet called **Cyrillic** (suh-RI-lik). The Russians adopted this Cyrillic alphabet and still use it today.

Teach the Big Idea

At Level

History and Culture of Russia

1. **Teach** Ask students the questions in the Main Idea boxes under Direct Teach.

2. **Apply** Tell students that together you will be creating a word web. Write *History* and *Culture* where students can see, spacing the words out so that more words and phrases can be added. Ask students to suggest words and phrases that they associate with the two terms. For example, for *history* students might come up with *wars, rulers,* and *major events,* and for *culture* students might come up with *religion, traditions,* and *holidays.*

3. **Review** Ask students what details they might attach to the words that have been added to the web, such as specific dates and names of rulers. Discuss how using word webs could help them organize important information.

4. **Practice/Homework** Have students create a similar word web on another topic and add ten items to it. Ask volunteers to share their webs with the class.

LS Verbal/Linguistic

Alternative Assessment Handbook, Rubrics 1: Acquiring Information; and 13: Graphic Organizers

History of Russian Expansion

Russia, 1462–1533

Territory gained
- by 1689
- by 1725
- by 1801
- by 1945

— Russian boundary, 1993

0   250   500 Miles

0 250 500 Kilometers

Projection:
Two-Point Equidistant

map zone Geography Skills

Location The colors in the map show the growth of the Russian Empire and of the Soviet Union over time.
1. **Name** What city is located in territory gained by 1725?
2. **Interpret** When was the period of greatest expansion?

In the 1200s, fierce Mongol invaders called Tatars (TAH-ters) swept out of Central Asia and conquered Kiev. The Mongols allowed Russian princes to rule over local states. In time, Muscovy became the strongest state. Its main city was Moscow.

After about 200 years Muscovy's prince, Ivan III, seized control from the Mongols. In the 1540s his grandson, Ivan IV, crowned himself **czar** (ZAHR), or emperor. *Czar* is Russian for "caesar." As czar, Ivan IV had total power. A cruel and savage ruler, he became known as Ivan the Terrible.

In time, Muscovy developed into the country of Russia. Strong czars such as Peter the Great (1682–1725) and Catherine the Great (1762–1796) built Russia into a huge empire and a world power. This empire included many conquered peoples.

In spite of its growth, Russia remained largely a country of poor farmers, while the czars and nobles had most of the wealth. In the early 1900s Russians began demanding improvements. The czar agreed to some changes, but unrest continued to grow.

War and Revolution

In 1914 Russia entered World War I. The country suffered huge losses in the war. In addition, the Russian people experienced severe shortages of food. When the czar seemed to ignore the people's hardship, they rose up against him. He was forced to give up his throne in 1917.

Later that year the **Bolsheviks**, a radical Russian Communist group, seized power in the Russian Revolution. They then killed the czar and his family. In 1922 the Bolsheviks formed a new country, the Union of Soviet Socialist Republics (USSR), or the Soviet Union. It soon included 15 republics, the strongest of which was Russia. The first leader was Vladimir Lenin.

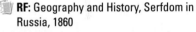

HISTORY

VIDEO
The
Romanovs

hmhsocialstudies.com

READING CHECK **Sequencing** What series of events led to the creation of the Soviet Union?

RUSSIA AND THE CAUCASUS **497**

Differentiating Instruction

Below Level

Struggling Readers

1. Have students work in pairs to draw a time line that shows the history of Russia.

2. Have students start the time line with the establishment of the first Russian state among the Slavs in the AD 800s and end with the fall of the Soviet Union in 1991.

3. Make sure students include the year of each event, and a brief description of what happened.

4. Ask students: If they could go back in time to live in Russia, what time period would they choose?

5. Have students write a two-paragraph essay explaining their choice. **LS** **Verbal/Linguistic**

Alternative Assessment Handbook, Rubrics 36: Time Lines; and 37: Writing Assignments

Main Idea

❷ The Soviet Union

The Soviet Union emerged as a Communist superpower with rigid government control.

Identify Who was the leader of Russia when it became a Communist country? *Vladimir Lenin*

Explain What is a command economy? *an economic system in which the government owns all businesses and farms and makes all economic decisions*

Describe What was the Cold War? *a period of tense rivalry between the Soviet Union and the United States, marked by an arms race between the two countries*

Info to Know

"Tear down this wall!" On June 12, 1987, President Ronald Reagan stood in front of the Berlin Wall (between democratic West Germany and communist East Germany). There, he delivered a speech that many historians say helped end the Cold War. Reagan said, "General Secretary Gorbachev, if you seek peace, if you seek prosperity for the Soviet Union and Eastern Europe, if you seek liberalization: Come here to this gate! Mr. Gorbachev, open this gate! Mr. Gorbachev, tear down this wall!"

hmhsocialstudies.com

Online Resources
Activity: End of Communism

Answers

Focus on Reading *possible answer—Command economies are not successful because there is no competition.*

Reading Check *The Cold War helped cause the Soviet Union's fall because it cost too much money when the Soviet economy was already near collapse.*

498

The Soviet Union

The Soviet Union, led by Lenin, became a Communist country. In this political system, the government owns all property and controls all aspects of life. In 1924 Lenin died. Joseph Stalin took power, ruling as a brutal and paranoid dictator.

The Soviet Union under Stalin

FOCUS ON READING
Based on the Soviet Union's economy, what generalization might you make about command economies?

Under Stalin, the Soviet Union set up a command economy. In this system, the government owns all businesses and farms and makes all decisions. People were told what to make and how much to charge. Without competition, though, efficiency and the quality of goods fell over time.

The Soviet Union strictly controlled its people as well as its economy. Stalin had anyone who spoke out against the government jailed, exiled, or killed. Millions of people were sent to **gulags**, harsh Soviet labor camps often located in Siberia.

Cold War and Collapse

ACADEMIC VOCABULARY
reaction a response to something

During World War II, the Soviet Union fought with the Allies against Germany. Millions of Soviet citizens died in the war. Stalin's **reaction** to the war was to build a buffer around the Soviet Union to protect it from invasion. To do so, he set up Communist governments in Eastern Europe.

The United States opposed communism and saw its spread as a threat to democracy. This opposition led to the Cold War, a period of tense rivalry between the Soviet Union and the United States. The two rival countries became superpowers as they competed to have superior weapons.

In part because of the high costs of weapons, the Soviet economy was near collapse by the 1980s. Mikhail Gorbachev (GAWR-buh-chawf), the Soviet leader, began making changes. He reduced government control and introduced some democracy.

Despite his actions, the Soviet republics began pushing for independence. In 1991 the Soviet Union collapsed. It broke apart into 15 independent countries, including Russia. The Soviet Union was no more.

READING CHECK **Analyzing** How did the Cold War help lead to the Soviet Union's collapse?

Culture

In the Soviet Union, the government had controlled culture just like everything else. Today, however, Russian culture is once again alive and vibrant.

People and Religion

Russia is big and diverse, with more than 140 million people. About 80 percent are ethnic Russians, or Slavs, but Russia also has many other ethnic groups. The largest are the Tatars and Ukrainians. Russia's many ethnic groups are once again taking great pride in their cultures.

Like ethnic culture, religious worship has seen a revival. The Soviet government opposed religion and closed many houses of worship. Today many have reopened, including historic Russian cathedrals with their onion-shaped domes. The main faith is Russian Orthodox Christian. Other religions include Islam, Buddhism, and other forms of Christianity.

Customs

Russian history has shaped its customs, such as holidays. Religious holidays, like Easter and Christmas, are popular. The main family holiday is New Year's Eve. To celebrate this holiday, families decorate a tree where, according to Russian folklore, Grandfather Frost and his helper the Snow Maiden leave gifts. A newer holiday is Russian Independence Day, which marks the end of the Soviet Union on June 12.

498 CHAPTER 20

Cross-Discipline Activity: English/Language Arts · **At Level**

Writing an Autobiography

Research Required

1. Review with students two of the leaders noted on this page—Vladimir Lenin and Joseph Stalin.

2. Ask students to imagine that they are one of these leaders and have been asked to write an autobiography. Give students time to research their subject. Encourage students to determine how people lived when Vladimir Lenin or Joseph Stalin were in power.

3. In their autobiographies, have students explain why, from the point of view of the leader

they've chosen, they think Communism or a command economy is good for the USSR. The autobiographies should also compare and contrast limited and unlimited government.

4. Ask volunteers to share their "autobiographies" with the class. Afterwards, discuss with students their own views of Communism and command economies. **LS Verbal/Linguistic**

📖 Alternative Assessment Handbook, Rubrics 4: Biographies; and 43: Writing to Persuade

Close-up

St. Basil's Cathedral

Colorful St. Basil's Cathedral, in Moscow's Red Square, has become a symbol of Russia. Czar Ivan IV had the cathedral built between 1555 and 1561 in honor of Russian military victories. According to legend, Ivan had the architects blinded so they could never design anything else as magnificent.

Steeply sloped towers, called tent roofs, and onion-shaped domes easily shed snow.

St. Basil's Cathedral houses nine small, separate chapels.

Onion-shaped domes, based on Byzantine designs, decorate many early Russian churches.

In 1588 a chapel was added for the tomb of St. Basil the Blessed, a popular saint in Russia. In time, his name became linked to the cathedral.

ANALYSIS SKILL ANALYZING VISUALS
Besides onion domes, what other shapes and patterns are visible on the cathedral?

RUSSIA AND THE CAUCASUS **499**

Collaborative Learning

At Level

The Making of a Cathedral

1. Divide the class into three groups.

2. Have each group research one of three aspects that makes St. Basil's Cathedral unique—the onion-shaped domes, the bright colors, and the nine separate chapels.

3. Have students work together in their groups to research the significance of their assigned aspect.

4. Have students create a presentation describing what they learned. Encourage students to use illustrations, diagrams, and graphs to help present their information.

5. Have each group choose two speakers to present their findings to the class.

LS Verbal/Linguistic, Visual/Spatial

Alternative Assessment Handbook, Rubrics 30: Research; and 24: Oral Presentations

---

Direct Teach

Close-up

St. Basil's Cathedral Review the photograph of St. Basil's Cathedral with students. Ask the following questions:

Recall What is the legend about the architects who designed the cathedral? *Czar Ivan IV—Ivan the Terrible—had them blinded so they could never design anything else as magnificent.*

Make Inferences Why do you think it would be important to design the roofs and domes so that snow will fall off easily? *because Russia has long winters with lots of snow*

Elaborate Why do you think the cathedral has become a symbol of Russia? *because the design is so unique and recognizable*

Info to Know

A War Commemorative St. Basil's Cathedral was built to commemorate Ivan the Terrible's capture of the strongholds of Kazan and Astrakhan. He named the cathedral *The Cathedral of the Intercession of the Virgin.* But the name Saint Basil comes from Basil the Blessed, who is said to have foretold a great fire in Moscow in 1547. He was also known to have opposed Ivan the Terrible's cruelty. After Ivan's death, a chapel was built for St. Basil and added to the cathedral.

↗ **hmhsocialstudies.com**
Online Resources
Activity: Treasures of Russia

Answers

Analyzing Visuals *triangles, rectangles, half-circles or arches, octagons, squares, stripes, domes arranged in a star-shape around the main spire*

499

500

Direct Teach

Main Idea

❸ Culture

Russia's history and diversity have influenced its culture.

Recall What ethnic groups besides ethnic Russians, or Slavs, live in Russia? *Tatars and Ukrainians*

Identify What is the most common religion practiced in Russia? *Russian Orthodox Christianity*

- **RF:** Primary Source, Russian Icon Painting
- **RF:** Literature, *War and Peace* by Leo Tolstoy

Review & Assess

Close

Review with students the history of the Russian Empire, the Soviet Union, and Russia today.

Review

- Online Quiz, Section 2

Assess

SE Section 2 Assessment

- PASS: Section 2 Quiz
- Alternative Assessment Handbook

Reteach/Classroom Intervention

- Guided Reading Workbook, Section 2
- Interactive Skills Tutor CD-ROM

Answers

Analyzing Primary Sources *possible answer—They might have felt they were helping to build an industry vital to the USSR.*

Reading Check *The culture was revived.*

Primary Source

Communist-era Poster

The Soviet Union used posters as propaganda. Propaganda is information designed to promote a specific cause or idea by influencing people's thoughts and beliefs. For example, Soviet posters often promoted the greatness and power of the Soviet state, its leaders, and their Communist policies.

The message of this 1924 poster reads, "Long live the Young Communist League! The young are taking over the older generation's torch!"

The color red in this poster symbolizes communism and the Russian Revolution.

ANALYSIS SKILL **ANALYZING PRIMARY SOURCES**

How do you think the poster's images and message influenced Soviet teens at the time?

The Arts and Sciences

Russia has made great contributions in the arts and sciences. In the performing arts, Russia's ballet companies are world famous for their skill. In music, Peter Tchaikovsky (chy-KAWF-skee) is Russia's most famous composer. His many works include *The Nutcracker* ballet and the *1812 Overture.*

In the material arts, Russia's Fabergé eggs are priceless. Gifts for the czars, these eggs are made of precious metals and covered with gems such as emeralds and rubies. Each egg opens to reveal a tiny surprise.

In the sciences, Russia has contributed to space research. In 1957 the Soviet Union launched Sputnik, the first artificial satellite in space. Russian scientists now help work on the International Space Station.

READING CHECK **Generalizing** How did the end of the Soviet Union affect Russian culture?

SUMMARY AND PREVIEW The history of Russia, from a great empire to a Communist superpower to a new nation, has shaped its rich culture. Next, you will read about life in Russia today.

Section 2 Assessment

hmhsocialstudies.com
ONLINE QUIZ

Reviewing Ideas, Terms, and Places

1. **a. Define** Who were the **czars**?
   b. Analyze What role did the city of **Kiev** play in Russian history?
   c. Elaborate What problems and events caused the Russian Empire to decline?
2. **a. Identify** Why are Vladimir Lenin and Joseph Stalin significant in Russian history?
   b. Evaluate Do you think life in the Soviet Union was an improvement over life in the Russian empire? Why, or why not?
3. **a. Recall** What is the main religion in Russia?
   b. Summarize How has Russian culture changed since the collapse of the Soviet Union in 1991?

Critical Thinking

4. **Sequencing** Draw a chart like the one here. Use your notes to list the order of the major events leading up to the collapse of the Soviet Union.

○ → ○ → ○ → ○

FOCUS ON WRITING

5. **Considering Russia's History and Culture** Look at the locations you listed for Section 1. For the Russian locations, make notes about historical or cultural details you could include in your ad.

500 CHAPTER 20

Section 2 Assessment Answers

1. **a.** emperors of Russia
   b. It was the central city in Kievan Rus, the first Russian state among the Slavs.
   c. slow-growing industry, poor and uneducated population, wealthy rulers who were out of touch with the people, World War I, civil unrest

2. **a.** They were the key leaders in the formation and building up of the Soviet Union.
   b. possible answer—No. The government controlled how people lived, and jailed, exiled, or killed those who spoke out against it.

3. **a.** Russian Orthodox Christianity
   b. possible answer—People have freedom to practice religion and celebrate religious and cultural holidays.

4. Possible events on students' time lines— World War II, the Cold War, economic troubles, Gorbachev's democratic reforms, Soviet Republics' push for Independence

5. Answers will vary. Students should use information from the text to add historical and cultural details to their location notes.

Social Studies Skills

Social Studies Skills

Interpreting a Population Map

Learn

Population maps give you a snapshot of the distribution of people in a region or country. Each color on a population map represents an average number of people living within a square mile or square kilometer. Sometimes symbols identify the cities with populations of a certain size. The map's legend identifies what the colors and symbols in the map mean.

Practice

❶ Based on the map below, in which region of Russia do most of the country's people live?

❷ Which two cities in Russia have the largest population?

❸ How many Russian cities have more than 1 million people?

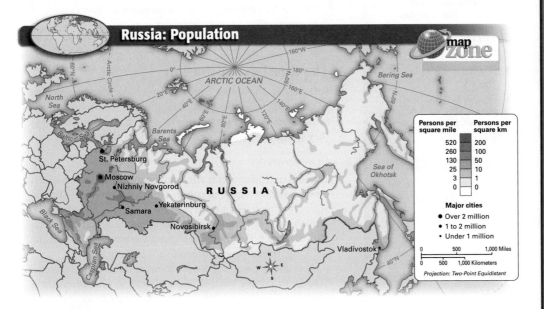

Russia: Population

Apply

Use an atlas to locate a current population map of the United States. Using the map, identify where the most and the least populated regions of the United States are. Then identify the number of U.S. cities or metropolitan areas with more than 2 million people.

501

Interpreting a Population Map

Activity Reading Population Maps

Materials: paper, drawing and coloring supplies

1. Explain to students that population maps give an overview of how many people live in a region. To understand population maps first-hand, tell the class that they will work together to make one of your school.

2. Have students start by drawing a basic map of the school, showing the location of each classroom. Then divide the class into groups, assigning each group the task of finding out the number of students in each classroom of their assigned area.

3. After students fill in the data, have them make a color key like the one on this page. Display your school's population map in your classroom where students can see it. Then ask students

• Which classroom is the most populated? Which is the least populated?

• What is the average number of students in a classroom? **LS** Visual/Spatial, Logical/Mathematical

RF: Social Studies Skills, Interpreting a Population Map

Alternative Assessment Handbook, Rubric 20: Map Creation

Interactive Skills Tutor CD-ROM, Lesson 6: Interpret Maps, Graphs, Charts, Visuals, and Political Cartoons

---

Differentiating Instruction

Special Needs Learners
Below Level

Make a copy of the population map. Help students use the color key in their textbooks to color in the same areas on their map. Have students do the same for cities, using the correct symbols. Then have students speak into a tape recorder and say one sentence about each city's population. For example, "The population of Samara is one to two million people." **LS** Visual/Spatial, Verbal/Linguistic

Alternative Assessment Handbook, Rubric 21: Map Reading

Advanced/Gifted and Talented
Above Level
Research Required

Guide students in conducting research online or at the library to find population statistics for your city or town and make their own population map. Have students create their own map key to indicate population density and other related information. Ask students to write an explanation of why population varies to go with their map. **LS** Visual/Spatial, Verbal/Linguistic

Alternative Assessment Handbook, Rubrics 30: Research; and 20: Map Creation

Answers

Practice 1. *western Russia;* **2.** *Moscow and St. Petersburg;* **3.** *six*

Apply *Answers may vary, depending on the age of the map used. According to the U.S. Census Bureau, in 2000, U.S. cities with a population of more than two million were New York City, Los Angeles, and Chicago. Note that this information refers to cities proper, not metropolitan areas.*

Bellringer

If YOU lived there. . . Use the **Daily Bellringer Transparency** to help students answer the question.

▶ Daily Bellringer Transparency, Section 3

Russia and the Caucasus	Daily Bellringer
	Section 3

Review Section 2

Read the lists of events below and put them in the correct order.

a. Czars rule Russia.
b. Bolsheviks seize power.
c. Communist government falls.
d. Stalin rules the Soviet Union.
e. World War I begins.

Preview Section 3

If YOU lived there ...
You live in St. Petersburg, a city of beautiful palaces and canals. You are looking forward to the end of school, when your family will go to their dacha, a cottage in the country. In midsummer, when the nights are long and the sun never really sets, you will go to concerts and other celebrations of the "White Nights" in your city. **What do you like about living in St. Petersburg?**

Consider the CULTURAL aspects:
• fun to live in an international city
• can enjoy wide variety of art, dance, music, and theater
• lots of historical sites to visit

Consider the NATURAL aspects:
• can enjoy rivers (with beautiful bridges and many canals)
• long summer days for more fun
• access to sea allows for recreation and travel

Review Answers: a, e, b, d, c

Academic Vocabulary

Review with students the high-use academic term in this section.

features characteristics (p. 503)

📝 **RF:** Vocabulary Builder, Section 3

Taking Notes

Have students use the graphic organizer online to take notes on the section. This activity will prepare students for the Section Assessment, in which they will complete a graphic organizer that builds on the information using the Critical Thinking Skill: Categorizing.

SECTION 3

Russia Today

What You Will Learn...

Main Ideas

1. The Russian Federation is working to develop democracy and a market economy.
2. Russia's physical geography, cities, and economy define its many culture regions.
3. Russia faces a number of serious challenges.

The Big Idea

Russia is a federal republic with a growing market economy but faces tough challenges.

Key Terms and Places

dachas, *p. 503*
St. Petersburg, *p. 504*
smelters, *p. 505*
Trans-Siberian Railroad, *p. 505*
Chechnya, *p. 506*

↗ **hmhsocialstudies.com**
TAKING NOTES

Use the graphic organizer online to take notes on Russia today.

If YOU lived there...

You live in St. Petersburg, a city of beautiful palaces and canals. You are looking forward to the end of school, when your family will go to their dacha, a cottage in the country. In midsummer, when the nights are long and the sun never really sets, you will go to concerts and other celebrations of the "White Nights" in your city.

What do you like about living in St. Petersburg?

BUILDING BACKGROUND Russians have always had a special feeling for the countryside, from the wheat fields and birch forests in the west to the endless grasslands of the steppe. But Russia's great cities are exciting, too, with many shops, museums, and events.

The Russian Federation

For decades, the Soviet Union reigned as a superpower, with Russia as its strongest republic. Then in 1991 the Soviet Union broke apart. Russia's leaders had to create a new government as they struggled to change from communism to democracy.

Government

The Russian Federation is a federal republic, a system in which power is divided between national and local governments. The voters elect a president to serve as the country's chief executive, Russia's most powerful official. The president appoints a prime minister to serve as the head of the government. A legislature, called the Federal Assembly, makes the country's laws.

Increased democracy has led to more freedom for Russians. Voters can choose from several political parties. Information flows more freely. The government no longer seeks to control every aspect of life. In addition, the move toward democracy has improved relations between Russia and Western nations.

Changing to a democratic system has been difficult, though. Problems such as government corruption, or dishonesty, have slowed the development of a free society in Russia. Time will tell whether Russia will continue to grow as a democracy.

502 CHAPTER 20

Teach the Big Idea

At Level

Russia Today

1. **Teach** Ask students the questions in the Main Idea boxes under Direct Teach.

2. **Apply** Have students create a map outlining the culture regions discussed in this section. Divide the class into six groups (one group for each region). Have them find three important facts about the region and write them in the correct area on the map.

3. **Review** Have students turn away from the map while you read a fact from the map. Have students take turns identifying the region you are referring to as you read facts.

4. **Practice/Homework** Have students write a generalization about three culture regions, based on the information on the map or from their reading. Ask volunteers to read their generalizations to the class.
   LS Verbal/Linguistic, Visual/Spatial

📝 Alternative Assessment Handbook, Rubrics 20: Map Creation; and 37: Writing Assignments

Economy

With the move to democracy, Russia also began shifting to a market economy. This type of economy is based on free trade and competition. Today the Russian government has greatly reduced its control of the economy, and most businesses and farms are now privately owned. These changes have led to economic growth. At the same time, most of Russia's wealth is now in the hands of a small number of people.

Today Russia produces and exports oil, natural gas, timber, metals, and chemicals. Heavy industry, such as machinery, is still important. However, light industry, such as clothing and electronics, has grown. Furthermore, service industries now make up the largest part of Russia's economy.

In agriculture, Russia is now a major grower and exporter of grains. Other major crops are fruits, potatoes, and sugar beets.

City and Rural Life

The changes sweeping Russia are visible in its cities. More restaurants and shopping centers are available. Stores offer a wider range of consumer goods, such as TVs. Some Russians have become wealthy and can afford luxuries. In fact, in 2005 Russia had more billionaires than any other European country. Nevertheless, the average Russian's standard of living remains low.

About 75 percent of all Russians live in cities. Most of these people live in small apartments in high-rise buildings. In rural areas, more people live in houses.

Although most Russians live in cities, they still have access to nature. Cities often have large parks and wooded areas in and around them. Many richer Russians own **dachas,** or Russian country houses, where they can garden and enjoy the fresh air.

READING CHECK **Summarizing** How has Russia changed since it became independent?

Kaliningrad

The small region of Kaliningrad—only slightly bigger than Connecticut—is more than 200 miles (320 km) from the rest of Russia. So why would Russia want this area? The reason has to do with the country's cold climate. Kaliningrad is Russia's only Baltic seaport that is free of ice all year. This important port provides Russia with year-round access to profitable European markets and trade. Railroads connect the port to Russia's major cities, as the map below shows.

Drawing Conclusions How do you think Russia's economy benefits from a Baltic seaport that is free of ice all year?

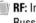

Culture Regions

You have learned that Russia is vast and diverse. For this reason, we divide Russia into several culture regions, as the map on the next page shows. These regions differ in **features** such as population, natural resources, and economic activity.

The four western culture regions make up Russia's heartland. This area is home to the vast majority of Russia's people as well as to the country's capital and largest cities. In addition, the fertile plains of Russia's heartland are the country's most productive farming area.

ACADEMIC VOCABULARY

features
characteristics

RUSSIA AND THE CAUCASUS **503**

Main Idea

❶ The Russian Federation

The Russian Federation is working to develop democracy and a market economy.

Explain What type of government does Russia have today? *The Russian Federation—Russia—is a federal republic. An elected president appoints the prime minister and a legislature called the Federal Assembly makes the Federation's laws.*

Make inferences What do you think would happen if no one paid their taxes? *There wouldn't be any money to pay for services the government usually provides such as defense, firefighting, and police.*

RF: Interdisciplinary Project, The Russian Space Program

Info to Know

Russia's Costly Delicacy The Caspian Sea produces 90 percent of the world's caviar. Caviar is salted sturgeon eggs. Russian caviar from the Caspian Sea is such a popular delicacy that it is in great demand. Many researchers worry that the Caspian Sea's sturgeon may become extinct because of overfishing—and because of increasing pollution of the sea.

Differentiating Instruction

At Level

English-Language Learners

1. Have students create a six-columned table on a blank piece of paper. At the top of each column have students write the names of each region. As students read the section, have them take notes about each region under the correct heading.

2. Have students choose a partner to compare notes with, filling in any details they missed.

3. Have students turn their paper over and create the same six columns again. This time,

under each heading, have students write three questions about the region, based on their notes.

4. Have the students work in pairs again, taking turns asking their questions and writing down the answers in complete sentences on their papers. **LS Verbal/Linguistic**

Alternative Assessment Handbook, Rubric 7: Charts

Answers

Reading Check *The shift to a more democratic government and a market economy has caused economic growth, with more consumer goods available.*

Connecting to Economics *It provides Russia with year-round access to European markets, allowing imports and exports, which is good for Russia's economy.*

Main Idea

❷ Culture Regions

Russia's physical geography, cities, and economy define its many culture regions.

Recall What Russian delicacy comes from a fishery on the Caspian Sea? *black caviar*

Contrast What are the differences between the economies of the Volga Region and the Urals Region? *The Volga Region is known as a major shipping route, for oil and gas refineries, and for black caviar. The Urals Region is known for its mining and smelters.*

Identify What is the most important industry in the Urals Region? *mining*

Make inferences Why do you think the Tatars called Siberia "Sleeping Land"? *possible answer—because it has been considered a vast, frozen wasteland, and has long, severe winters*

▶ Map Zone Transparency: Russia: Culture Regions

History Humor

What do you call it when a computer system keeps freezing? *Cyberia*

hmhsocialstudies.com INTERACTIVE MAP

Russia: Culture Regions

❶ St. Petersburg's State Hermitage Museum, once the Winter Palace of the czars, now houses priceless works of art.

❷ Moscow is Russia's capital and largest city. It is a political, cultural, and transportation center.

❸ In Siberia, a Nenets woman leads a group of decorated reindeer as part of a village festival.

The Moscow Region

Moscow is Russia's capital and largest city. The sprawling, modern city has wide boulevards and large public squares. Its many cultural attractions include the world-famous Bolshoi Ballet and Moscow Circus.

At Moscow's heart is the Kremlin, the center of Russia's government. In Russian, *kremlin* means "fortress." The Kremlin consists of several buildings surrounded by a wall and towers. The buildings include not only government offices but also palaces, museums, and gold-domed churches.

Next to the Kremlin is Red Square, an immense plaza. It is lined by many famous landmarks, such as St. Basil's Cathedral.

The Moscow region is Russia's most important economic area, and its factories produce a wide range of goods. The city is also a transportation center and links by road, rail, and plane to all parts of Russia.

The St. Petersburg Region

St. Petersburg reflects Russians' desire for Western ways. Peter the Great founded the city and styled it after those of Western Europe. For some 200 years, St. Petersburg served as Russia's capital and home to the czars. It features wide avenues, grand palaces, and numerous canals. Theaters and museums enrich the city's cultural life.

504 CHAPTER 20

Critical Thinking: Making Generalizations — At Level

A Day in the Life

Research Required

1. When discussing culture, point out to students the difference between material culture (things that a society makes or uses) and nonmaterial culture (behavior, customs, and traditions). Have students look closely at the three photographs on this page. Ask them to make one generalization about each subject that includes a material and nonmaterial aspect of culture.

2. Then have students research each subject to see if the facts confirm their generalizations.

Have them write a short summary of their research.

3. Based on the generalization they made and the facts they learned, have students pick one of the subjects to illustrate and write about in a complete paragraph.

4. Ask for volunteers to present their illustrated paragraphs to the class. 🅛🅢 **Verbal/Linguistic, Visual/Spatial**

📝 Alternative Assessment Handbook, Rubrics 3: Artwork; and 37: Writing Assignments

Culture Regions
- Moscow
- St. Petersburg
- Volga
- Urals
- Siberia
- Far East

0   300   600 Miles
0   300   600 Kilometers
*Projection:
Two-Point Equidistant*

map zone Geography Skills

Regions Russia's culture regions differ in their resources, economic activity, and other features.
1. Identify What are the six culture regions?
2. Interpret What is the major defining feature in each of the four western culture regions?

St. Petersburg's location on the Gulf of Finland has made the city a major port and trade center. This northern location also produces "White Nights," a period during summer when it never gets totally dark.

The Volga and Urals Regions

The Volga River and Ural Mountains are the third and fourth culture regions. The broad Volga is a major shipping route. Dams along its course form lakes and provide hydroelectric power. Factories in the area process oil and gas. In addition, a site on the Caspian Sea provides fish called sturgeon. The eggs of this fish are called black caviar, which is a costly delicacy, or rare and valued food.

The Ural Mountains are an important mining region and produce nearly every major mineral. **Smelters**, factories that process metal ores, process copper and iron. The Urals region is also known for gems and semiprecious stones.

Siberia

East of the Urals lies the vast expanse of Siberia. In the Tatar language, *Siberia* means "Sleeping Land." Siberian winters are long and severe. As you have read, much of the land lies frozen or buried under snow for most or all of the year. The remote region has many valuable resources, but accessing them in the harsh climate is difficult.

Siberia's main industries are lumber, mining, and oil production. Large coal deposits are mined in southwest Siberia. Rivers produce hydroelectric power. The southern steppes, where the weather is warmer, are Siberia's main farmlands.

Because of Siberia's harsh climate, jobs there pay high wages. Even so, few people choose to live in Siberia. Most towns and cities are in the western and southern parts of the region. These cities tend to follow the **Trans-Siberian Railroad**. This rail line runs from Moscow to Vladivostok on the east coast, and is the longest single rail line in the world.

The Russian Far East

Russia has a long coastline on the Pacific Ocean. There, in the Russian Far East, much land remains heavily forested. In the few cities, factories process forest and mineral resources. Farming occurs in the Amur River valley. The city of Vladivostok is a naval base and the area's main seaport. Islands off the coast provide oil, minerals, and commercial fishing.

READING CHECK **Finding Main Ideas** What areas make up Russia's culture regions?

FOCUS ON READING

Based on this description of Siberia, what generalization about human settlement can you make?

hmhsocialstudies.com
ANIMATED GEOGRAPHY
Trans-Siberian Railroad

Critical Thinking: Solving Problems

At Level

Starting a Business in Siberia

1. Review with students the information they've read about Siberia so far, including what they know about the region's climate and natural resources. Remind students that many of Siberia's rich resources are in remote, cold areas far from cities, markets, and ports.

2. Ask students to imagine they are entrepreneurs moving to Siberia to make their fortune. Have students work in pairs to write a proposal explaining which resource they would like to pursue, how they would obtain it and bring

it to market, and how they could make their business profitable. Remind students that the main source of transportation is the rail line.

3. Ask students to read their proposals to the class. Encourage them to illustrate their proposals. **LS** **Verbal/Linguistic, Visual/Spatial**

Alternative Assessment Handbook, Rubrics 35: Solving Problems; and 43: Writing to Persuade

---

Checking for Understanding

True or False Answer each statement *T* if it is true and *F* if it is false. If false, explain why.
1. Siberia's most important industries are tourism and farming. *F; Lumbering, mining, and oil production are Siberia's most important industries.*
2. Siberia's coastal areas and islands are known as the Russian Seaside. *F; They are known as the Russian Far East.*

Activity Community Service

Discuss the idea of community with your students. Talk about organizations that help people in need. Then have students develop a plan to collect money for an international service organization.

1. Break students into groups to research one of the following:
- international aid groups that do work in the Federation of Russia
- current events in the Federation of Russia that require aid
- ways to collect funds for donation (e.g., bake sales and car washes)

2. Decide as a class which aid group you want to support. Contact the aid group to determine how funds need to be sent and where. Ask if there is a way to donate toward a specific need.

3. Develop the plan(s) for collecting funds—more than one method can be chosen. Decide on a time line for the project.

4. Implement the plan when ready.
LS **Interpersonal, Kinesthetic**

Alternative Assessment Handbook, Rubric 14: Group Activity

Answers

Map Zone 1. *Moscow, St. Petersburg, Volga, Urals, Siberia, Far East;* **2.** *All are major contributors to Russia's economy.*

Focus on Reading *possible answer— People do not like to live in regions with long, severe winters because it is so difficult to survive.*

Reading Check *Moscow, St. Petersburg, Volga, Urals, Siberia, Far East*

Direct Teach

Main Idea

3 Russia's Challenges

Russia faces a number of serious challenges.

Summarize What are some of Russia's challenges as it moves forward? *Moving to a market economy has not prevented unemployment and a rising crime rate. Population is declining as well and the gap between rich and poor has widened. Russia also faces ethnic conflicts and problems with industrial pollution.*

Recall Name one area where conflict has led to fighting. *The Russian Republic of Chechnya*

Review & Assess

Close

Briefly review Russia's government, economy, culture regions, and challenges for the future.

Review

Online Quiz, Section 3

Assess

SE Section 3 Assessment

PASS: Section 3 Quiz

Alternative Assessment Handbook

Reteach/Classroom Intervention

Guided Reading Workbook, Section 3

Interactive Skills Tutor CD-ROM

Answers

Interpreting Graphs *about five million*
Reading Check *social—falling population and poor health care; economic—rising prices and unemployment, growing gap between rich and poor; political—ethnic conflicts and environmental damage*

506

THE WORLD ALMANAC
Facts about Countries

Russia's Population Decline

Interpreting Graphs Approximately how much did Russia's population decrease between 2000 and 2010?

hmhsocialstudies.com

Russia's Challenges

Although Russia has made great progress since 1991, challenges remain. First, Russia's shift to a market economy has not been without problems. For example, prices and unemployment have risen, and the gap between rich and poor has widened.

Second, Russia's population is falling, as you can see in the graph. More Russians are dying than are being born. One reason is that many Russians cannot afford good health care.

Third, the Soviet government did little to prevent pollution. As a result pollution, such as industrial chemicals, has seriously harmed Russia's environment. The government must now repair the damage.

Last, Russia faces ethnic conflicts. One of the worst is in the Russian republic of **Chechnya** (CHECH-nyah) in the Caucasus Mountains. Some people in this Muslim area want independence. Fighting and terrorism there have caused many deaths.

READING CHECK **Categorizing** What social, economic, and political challenges face Russia?

SUMMARY AND PREVIEW As you have read, Russia is a federal republic working to build a market economy. The west is Russia's heartland, but Siberia has many valuable resources. In the next section, you will read about the Caucasus.

Section 3 Assessment

hmhsocialstudies.com
ONLINE QUIZ

Reviewing Ideas, Terms, and Places

1. **a. Recall** What type of government does Russia now have?
   b. Explain How is Russia's economy changing?
2. **a. Recall** From west to east, what are Russia's major culture regions?
   b. Draw Conclusions Why do you think most Siberian towns and cities are located along the **Trans-Siberian Railroad**?
   c. Rate Which of Russia's culture regions would you most want to live in, and why?
3. **a. Identify** What are the main challenges that face Russia today?
   b. Elaborate What difficulties does **Chechnya** pose for Russia's leaders?

Critical Thinking

4. **Categorizing** Draw a concept web like the one shown. Use your notes to list facts about each Russian culture region.

Russia's Culture Regions

FOCUS ON WRITING

5. **Collecting Details about Russia Today** Based on conditions in Russia today, what location would you choose for your property? Review your notes from Section 2 and this section. Then choose one location in Russia for the property you are selling.

506 CHAPTER 20

Section 3 Assessment Answers

1. **a.** federal republic
   b. moving from a command economy to a free market economy
2. **a.** Moscow, St. Petersburg, Volga, Urals, Siberia, Russian Far East
   b. because it is the main way to transport goods and people in and out of the region
   c. Students' answers should include reasons why they would want to live in a certain Russian culture region.
3. **a.** weak economy, high unemployment, declining population, ethnic conflicts

   b. Fighting and terrorism there have caused many deaths.
4. possible answers: Moscow—Russia's largest city, industrial region; St. Petersburg—second largest city, center for trade and culture; Volga—major shipping route, heavy-machine industry; Urals—mining and manufacturing; Siberia—very large and cold, vast untapped resources; Russian Far East—seaports, oil, and minerals
5. Students' answers should reflect conditions in Russia in choosing a location for a property.

Literature

from
The Endless Steppe

by Esther Hautzig

About the Reading *In* The Endless Steppe, *an autobiographical novel, Esther Hautzig writes about her own experiences as a teenage girl. In the novel, the girl Esther is from a wealthy Jewish family in Poland. In 1941 her family is deported to a labor camp in Siberia. In the excerpt below, Esther and her family are on the train to Siberia. She is dreading their destination.*

AS YOU READ Think about what Esther feels as she watches the passing landscape. What ideas does she already have about life in Siberia?

The flatness of this land was awesome. There wasn't a hill in sight; it was an enormous, unrippled sea of parched and lifeless grass.

"Tata, why is the earth so flat here?"

"These must be steppes, Esther."

"Steppes? But steppes are in Siberia."

"This is Siberia," he said quietly.

If I had been told that I had been transported to the moon, I could not have been more stunned.

"Siberia?" My voice trembled. "But Siberia is full of snow."

"It will be," my father said. ❶

Siberia! Siberia was the end of the world, a point of no return. Siberia was for criminals and political enemies, where the punishment was unbelievably cruel, and where people died like flies. ❷ Summer or no summer—and who had ever talked about hot Siberia?—Siberia was the tundra and mountainous drifts of snow. Siberia was *wolves*.

Connecting Literature to Geography

1. **Analyzing** Russian soldiers took Esther's family from their home in Poland to work in Siberia. How do you think this fact affects Esther's feelings as she views the landscape of Siberia from the train?

2. **Drawing Inferences** Why do you think Siberia was chosen as a place of exile? What made it a punishment to live there?

507

508 CHAPTER 20

Preteach

Bellringer

If YOU lived there. . . Use the **Daily Bellringer Transparency** to help students answer the question.

📺 Daily Bellringer Transparency, Section 4

Russia and the Caucasus — Daily Bellringer, Section 4

Review Section 3

Read the statements below and determine what is "speaking."

1. "I am the Russian name for *fortress* and the center of Russia's government." What am I?
2. "I am the capital of Russia and its largest city." What am I?
3. "I am a Muslim republic in Russia, with some of my people wanting to be independent." What am I?
4. "I am a factory that processes metal ores, copper, and iron." What am I?

Preview Section 4

If YOU lived there . . .
You live in Tbilisi, the capital of the country of Georgia. Several years ago, your sister and her college friends joined the Rose Revolution, a political protest that forced a corrupt president to resign. The protestors' symbol was a red rose. Since the protest, you have become more interested in politics. **What kind of government do you want?**

Consider HONEST ELECTIONS AND LEADERS:
• want fair and free elections
• want leaders to be honest
• want stricter laws to prevent future corruption

Consider ROLE OF CITIZENS:
• want everyone to register to vote
• want everyone to vote—in every election
• want more people to communicate with leaders, to make their views known

Review Answers: 1. Kremlin; 2. Moscow; 3. Chechnya; 4. smelter

Key Places

📄 **RF:** Vocabulary Builder, Section 4

Taking Notes

Have students use the graphic organizer online to take notes on the section. This activity will prepare students for the Section Assessment, in which they will complete a graphic organizer that builds on the information using the Critical Thinking Skill: Comparing and Contrasting.

Answers

Reading Check *Persians, Greeks, Romans, Arabs, Turks, and Mongols have all ruled or invaded the area.*

508

The Caucasus

What You Will Learn...

Main Ideas

1. Many groups have ruled and influenced the Caucasus during its long history.
2. Today the Caucasus republics are working to improve their economies but struggle with ethnic unrest and conflict.

The Big Idea

In an area long ruled by outside groups, the Caucasus republics are struggling to strengthen their economies and to deal with ethnic unrest.

Key Places

Tbilisi, *p. 509*
Yerevan, *p. 509*
Baku, *p. 510*

🔗 hmhsocialstudies.com
TAKING NOTES

Use the graphic organizer online to take notes on the Caucasus.

508 CHAPTER 20

If **YOU** lived there...

You live in Tbilisi, the capital of the country of Georgia. Several years ago, your sister and her college friends joined the Rose Revolution, a political protest that forced a corrupt president to resign. The protestors' symbol was a red rose. Since the protest, you have become more interested in politics.

What kind of government do you want?

BUILDING BACKGROUND Georgia is one of three republics in the area called the Caucasus. In 1991, when the Soviet Union ended, the Caucasus republics gained independence. Since then, the republics have struggled to become democracies with market economies.

History

The Caucasus lies in the rugged Caucasus Mountains between the Black and Caspian seas. Located where Europe blends into Asia, the Caucasus reflects a range of cultural influences. At one time or another, Persians, Greeks, Romans, Arabs, Turks, and Mongols have all ruled or invaded the area. The Russians took control of much of the Caucasus in the early 1800s.

Russian control in the Caucasus did not include what is now western Armenia. The Ottoman Turks held this area. Over time, the Turks grew to distrust the Armenians, however; and in the late 1800s began abusing and killing them. During World War I (1914–1918), the Turks forced all Armenians to leave. Hundreds of thousands of Armenians died during this ethnic cleansing, or attempt to remove an ethnic group. The Turks lost World War I, though, and had to give up western Armenia.

After World War I, Armenia, Azerbaijan, and Georgia gained independence—but not for long. By the early 1920s they were part of the vast Soviet Union. Finally in 1991, when the Soviet Union fell, the Caucasus republics achieved true independence.

READING CHECK **Finding Main Ideas** Why do the countries in the Caucasus reflect a range of cultural influences?

Teach the Big Idea

At Level

The Caucasus

1. **Teach** Ask students the questions in the Main Idea boxes under Direct Teach.

2. **Apply** Have students work in groups to make posters highlighting information about the three countries that make up the Caucasus—Georgia, Armenia, and Azerbaijan. Posters should include facts about each country, as well as illustrations and maps to help inform others about the countries and the region.

3. **Review** Have each group present their posters to the class.

4. **Practice/Homework** Have students create five quiz questions based on the facts listed on the posters. Collect the questions, read them aloud, and have volunteers answer them. 🅻🆂 **Verbal/Linguistic, Visual/Spatial**

📄 Alternative Assessment Handbook, Rubrics 14: Group Activity; and 28: Posters

The snow-capped peaks of the Caucasus Mountains rise above a mountain village and the remains of a fortress built in the 900s.

The Caucasus: Political

Mount Elbrus
18,510 ft
(5,642 m)

RUSSIA

✪ National capital

0   50   100 Miles
0   50   100 Kilometers
Projection: Lambert Equal-Area

Black Sea

CAUCASUS MOUNTAINS

GEORGIA

Ingur R.

Tbilisi ✪

Kura River

ARMENIA

TURKEY

Baku ✪

AZERBAIJAN

Lake Sevan

Yerevan ✪

Aras River

Caspian Sea

IRAN

map Zone Geography Skills

Location South of western Russia, the Caucasus is located where Europe blends into Asia.
1. **Name** What two seas border the Caucasus?
2. **Contrast** Based on the map, how does Armenia differ from Azerbaijan and Georgia?

The Caucasus Today

The Caucasus may have a long history, but the Caucasus countries do not. Like other former Soviet republics, these young countries have had to create new governments and economies. Meanwhile, ethnic unrest and conflicts have slowed progress.

The Caucasus republics have similar governments. An elected president governs each nation, and an appointed prime minister runs each government. An elected parliament, or legislature, makes the laws.

Georgia

The country of Georgia lies in the Caucasus Mountains east of the Black Sea. **Tbilisi** is the capital. About 70 percent of the people are ethnic Georgians, and most belong to the Georgian Orthodox Church. The official language is Georgian, a unique language with its own alphabet. However, many other languages are also spoken.

Since 1991 Georgia has struggled with unrest and civil war. In 2003 Georgians forced out their president in the peaceful Rose Revolution. Meanwhile, ethnic groups in northern Georgia were fighting for independence. Because these groups now hold parts of northern Georgia, division and unrest continues.

Although unrest has hurt Georgia's economy, international aid is helping it improve. Georgia's economy is based on services and farming. Major crops include citrus fruits, grapes, and tea. In addition, Georgia produces steel and mines copper and manganese. Georgia is also famous for its wines. The Black Sea is a resort area, and tourism contributes to the economy, too.

Armenia

South of Georgia is the small, landlocked country of Armenia. The tiny country is slightly larger than the state of Maryland. **Yerevan** (yer-uh-VAHN) is the capital. Almost all the people are ethnic Armenian. Armenia prides itself as being the first country to adopt Christianity, and most people belong to the Armenian Orthodox Church.

RUSSIA AND THE CAUCASUS **509**

Direct Teach

Main Idea

❶ **History**

Many groups have ruled and influenced the Caucasus during its long history.

Recall Who controlled the Caucasus countries during the 1800s? *Russia controlled eastern Armenia, much of Azerbaijan, and Georgia. The Ottoman Turks ruled western Armenia.*

Identify What group of people were subject to ethnic cleansing during World War I? *The Armenians*

Explain What event allowed the countries of the Caucasus to gain full independence? *the break up of the Soviet Union in 1991*

▶ Map Zone Transparency: The Caucasus: Political

Differentiating Instruction

Below Level

Struggling Readers

1. Copy the chart shown here for students to see, omitting the answers in blue.

2. Help students fill in the graphic organizer with information from the section that shows how the countries are alike and how they are different.

3. Review the similarities and differences between the countries to conclude the activity.
LS Visual/Spatial

📄 Alternative Assessment Handbook, Rubric 13: Graphic Organizers

Georgia
Black Sea, tourism

Orthodox Christian

Armenia
mining

controlled by Soviet Union, civil unrest

Caucasus Mtns

home to Armenians

Azerbaijan
Caspian Sea, oil, Muslim

Answers

Map Zone 1. *Black Sea, Caspian Sea;*
2. *Armenia is landlocked.*

509

❸ The Caucasus Today

Today the Caucasus republics are working to improve their economies but struggle with ethnic unrest and conflict.

Recall Which Caucasus country has an economy based on oil? *Azerbaijan*

Define What is a refugee? *a person who has been forced from home by war or natural disaster*

Identify What problems and challenges has Georgia faced since independence? *ethnic unrest, with armed groups fighting for independence from Georgia holding sections of the northern part of the country*

📝 **RF: Biography: Garry Kasparov**

Close

Briefly review the history of the Caucasus region, and the differences and similarities among Georgia, Armenia, and Azerbaijan.

Review

🔲 Online Quiz, Section 4

Assess

SE Section 4 Assessment

📝 Alternative Assessment Handbook

📝 PASS: Section 4 Quiz

Reteach/Classroom Intervention

📝 Guided Reading Workbook, Section 4

💿 Interactive Skills Tutor CD-ROM

Answers

Focus on Reading *The region's countries face ethnic conflicts and economic challenges.*

Reading Check *ethnic conflict, government corruption, slow economic growth, civil war, war between countries*

Baku

Located on the Caspian Sea, the city of Baku is the capital and chief port of Azerbaijan.

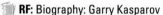

FOCUS ON READING
What general statements can you make about the Caucasus as a whole?

In the early 1990s, Armenia fought a bitter war with its neighbor Azerbaijan. The war involved an area of Azerbaijan where most people are ethnic Armenian. Armenia wanted this area to become part of its country. Although a cease-fire stopped the fighting in 1994, Armenian armed forces still control the area. The issue remained unsettled as of the early 2000s.

This conflict has greatly hurt Armenia's economy. However, international aid is helping Armenia's economy recover and expand. For example, diamond processing is now a growing industry in Armenia.

Azerbaijan

East of Armenia is Azerbaijan. In contrast to the other Caucasus republics, Azerbaijan is largely Muslim. The Azeri (uh-ZE-ree) make up 90 percent of the population.

Azerbaijan's economy is based on oil, found along and under the Caspian Sea. **Baku**, the capital, is the center of a large oil-refining industry. This industry has led to strong economic growth. Corruption is high, though; and many people are poor. In addition, Azerbaijan has many refugees as a result of its conflict with Armenia.

READING CHECK **Summarizing** What challenges do the Caucasus republics face?

SUMMARY The Caucasus republics face challenges but are working to develop democracy and build their economies.

Section 4 Assessment

🔲 **hmhsocialstudies.com**
ONLINE QUIZ

Reviewing Ideas, Terms, and Places

1. **a. Identify** Which country controlled much of the Caucasus for most of the 1800s?
   b. Identify Cause and Effect How did Turkish rule affect Armenians in the Ottoman Empire?
   c. Elaborate How has location affected the history and culture of the Caucasus area?
2. **a. Recall** How does **Baku** contribute to the economy of Azerbaijan?
   b. Compare and Contrast How is religion in Georgia and Armenia similar? How does religion in these countries differ from that in Azerbaijan?
   c. Elaborate How has the war that occurred between Armenia and Azerbaijan affected each country?

Critical Thinking

3. **Comparing and Contrasting** Draw a Venn diagram like the one here. Use your notes to identify the ways in which Georgia, Armenia, and Azerbaijan are similar and different.

Focus on Writing

4. **Collecting Details about the Caucasus** You have narrowed Russian locations to one possibility. What features do the Caucasus countries have that might be attractive to potential buyers? Identify one Caucasus location you might use in your ad.

Section 4 Assessment Answers

1. **a.** Russia
   b. Armenians were abused and killed.
   c. Many countries have ruled or invaded the region.
2. **a.** It is the country's chief port.
   b. Most people in both countries are Orthodox Christians, but most Georgians belong to the Georgian Orthodox Church while most Armenians belong to the Armenian Orthodox Church. In contrast, Azerbaijan is mostly Muslim.
   c. Armenia—economy has been hurt, occupies part of Azerbaijan; Azerbaijan—has many refugees

3. possible answers: Georgia—Black Sea, civil war; Azerbaijan—Muslims, refugees; Armenia—killed by Turks; Georgia and Azerbaijan—Caucasus Mountains; Georgia and Armenia—Orthodox Christian, mining, Azerbaijan and Armenia—at war, Armenians live there; All—ethnic conflict, democratic government, were controlled by Soviet Union

4. Locations students identify will vary, but students may mention features of the Caucasus such as the Black Sea, the diamond industry, and oil production.

Chapter Review

Geography's Impact
video series
Review the video to answer the closing question:
Why was the Soviet Union so determined to become a major industrial power?

Visual Summary

Use the visual summary below to help you review the main ideas of the chapter.

Russia is an immense, cold country with plains, mountains, and forest. The Caucasus is a small, mountainous area.

With a long history and a rich culture, Russia ranges from large modern cities to the vast plains and forests of Siberia.

The three small Caucasus republics lie between the Black and Caspian seas, and face ethnic unrest and conflict.

Reviewing Vocabulary, Terms, and Places

For each statement below, write T if it is true and F if it is false. If the statement is false, replace the boldfaced term with one that makes the sentence a true statement.

1. The **Caucasus Mountains** separate European Russia from Asian Russia.

2. Russia's capital and largest city is **St. Petersburg**.

3. The Caucasus is bordered by the Black Sea to the west and **Lake Baikal** to the east.

4. Under the rule of the **Bolsheviks**, the Russian Empire expanded in size and power.

5. Much of the country of Georgia is located in the high, rugged **Ural Mountains**.

6. Many wealthier Russians have country houses, which are called **gulags**.

7. Russia's main government buildings are located in the **Kremlin** in Moscow.

8. Russia's culture regions differ in **features** such as cities, natural resources, and economic activity.

9. **Moscow** is a major port and was once home to Russia's czars.

10. The capital city of Armenia is **Yerevan**.

Comprehension and Critical Thinking

SECTION 1 *(Pages 492–495)*

11. **a. Recall** What is Russia's most important river, and to what major bodies of water does it link?

b. Identify Cause and Effect How does Russia's location affect its climate?

c. Elaborate Why might developing the many natural resources in Siberia be difficult?

SECTION 2 *(Pages 496–500)*

12. **a. Identify** Who was Joseph Stalin?

b. Summarize How has Russia contributed to world culture?

c. Elaborate How was the end of the Soviet Union similar to the end of the Russian Empire?

RUSSIA AND THE CAUCASUS **511**

Answers

Visual Summary

Review and Inquiry Have students use the visual summary to write generalizations about Russia and the Caucasus.

 Quick Facts Transparency: Russia and the Caucasus Visual Summary

Reviewing Vocabulary, Terms, and Places

1. F; Ural Mountains
2. F; Moscow
3. F; the Caspian Sea
4. F; Czars
5. F; Caucasus Mountains
6. F; dachas
7. T
8. T
9. F; St. Petersburg
10. T

Comprehension and Critical Thinking

11. **a.** the Volga; the Caspian Sea, the Don River, and the Baltic Sea
b. Because Russia is located far north, it has a mostly cold climate.
c. They are in remote, cold areas far from cities.

12. **a.** brutal dictator of the Soviet Union
b. possible answer—Russia has world famous ballet companies and composers.
c. Economic problems and unpopular leaders contributed to the end of both regimes.

Review and Assessment Resources

Review and Reinforce

SE Chapter Review

RF: Chapter Review

Quick Facts Transparency: Russia and the Caucasus Visual Summary

Spanish Chapter Summaries Audio CD Program

TOS Holt McDougal Puzzle View, Quiz Show for ExamView

Quiz Game CD-ROM

Assess

SE Standardized Test Practice

PASS: Chapter Test, Forms A and B

Alternative Assessment Handbook

TOS ExamView Test Generator, Chapter Test

Differentiated Instruction Modified Worksheets and Tests CD-ROM: Chapter Test

Online Assessment Program, in the Interactive Student Edition

Reteach/Intervene

Guided Reading Workbook

Differentiated Instruction Teacher Management System: Lesson Plans

Differentiated Instruction Modified Worksheets and Tests CD-ROM

Interactive Skills Tutor CD-ROM

hmhsocialstudies.com
Chapter Resources

13. a. the Moscow, St. Petersburg, Volga, and Urals regions

b. Both are large urban, economic, and political centers. While Moscow reflects Russia's old values and traditions, St. Petersburg represents the country's desire for Western ideas and practices.

c. Siberia has many valuable natural resources, including timber, mining, and oil production, which could improve Russia's economy.

14. a. Tbilisi, Georgia; Yerevan, Armenia; Baku, Azerbaijan

b. They share similar histories, governments, and challenges.

c. They need to improve trade with other countries, maintain peace, and make better use of their natural resources.

Using the Internet

15. Go to [hmhsocialstudies.com] to access a rubric for this activity.

Social Studies Skills

16. Depending on the atlas used, cities in Europe with over two million people include London, Berlin, Madrid, Rome, Paris, and Bucharest.

17. Depending on the atlas used, central Europe, especially Denmark, Germany, the Netherlands, and parts of France and Italy are most populated. Spain, Portugal, Austria, and the countries along the eastern shore of the Adriatic are the least populated.

Map Activity

18. A. St. Petersburg, Russia

B. Moscow, Russia

C. Caucasus Mountains

D. Caspian Sea

E. Volga River

F. Ural Mountains

G. West Siberian Plain

H. Kamchatka Peninsula

I. Vladivostok, Russia

SECTION 3 *(Pages 502–506)*

13. a. Identify What four culture regions make up the Russian heartland?

b. Compare and Contrast How are Moscow and St. Petersburg similar and different?

c. Elaborate How might Siberia help make Russia an economic success?

SECTION 4 *(Pages 508–510)*

14. a. Recall What is the capital of each of the Caucasus republics?

b. Compare What do the three Caucasus countries have in common?

c. Elaborate What issues and challenges do the Caucasus countries need to address to improve their economies?

Using the Internet

15. Activity: Making a Map The Trans-Siberian Railroad is the longest single rail line in the world. Climb aboard in Moscow and travel all the way across Russia. Through your online textbook, research the people, places, and history along the railroad's route. Then create an illustrated map of your journey. On the map, show the train's route, indicate the places where you stopped, and include images and descriptions about what you saw.

[hmhsocialstudies.com]

Social Studies Skills

Interpreting a Population Map *Use a good atlas to find a population map of Europe. The map does not need to include Russia. Use the map to answer the following questions. Do not include the country of Russia when answering the questions.*

16. Not including the cities of Russia, how many cities or metropolitan areas in Europe have more than 2 million people?

17. Not including Russia, which regions of Europe are the most populated? Which regions of Europe are the least populated?

Map Activity

18. Russia and the Caucasus On a separate sheet of paper, match the letters on the map with their correct labels.

Caucasus Mountains   Ural Mountains

Caspian Sea   Vladivostok, Russia

Kamchatka Peninsula   Volga River

Moscow, Russia   West Siberian Plain

St. Petersburg, Russia

FOCUS ON READING AND WRITING

19. Making Generalizations Examine the information in Section 3 about the four culture regions that make up Russia's heartland. Based on the specific information about these regions, make two generalizations about western Russia.

20. Creating a Real Estate Ad Review your notes about locations in Russia and the Caucasus. Choose one location for the real estate you are selling. What are its best features? How would you describe the land and climate? What are the benefits of living there? If it is a building, what does it look like? What is nearby? Answer these questions in your real estate ad. Remember to include details that will make the property attractive to possible buyers.

Focus on Reading and Writing

19. Possible Answer Western Russia is the most populated area of Russia. Western Russia has the most diverse and successful industries in Russia.

RF: Focus on Reading, Making Generalizations

20. Rubric Students' real estate ad should

• be based on facts and not be misleading

• give details about the best features of the location chosen

• include details appealing to potential buyers

• use descriptive wording to help buyers form a clear image of the property

• use correct grammar, spelling, and punctuation

RF: Focus on Writing, Creating a Real Estate Ad

Standardized Test Prep

DIRECTIONS: Read questions 1 through 7 and write the letter of the best response. Then read question 8 and write your own well-constructed response.

1 Which word below *best* describes Russia's overall climate?

A Cold

B Dry

C Hot

D Wet

2 What is the name of the vast forest that covers much of Russia?

A Siberia

B Steppe

C Taiga

D Tundra

3 What was the name of the second Soviet leader, who ruled as a brutal dictator?

A Ivan III

B Ivan the Terrible

C Vladimir Lenin

D Joseph Stalin

4 The majority of Russians are descended from the

A Bolsheviks.

B Slavs.

C Tatars.

D Ukrainians.

5 What are the Caucasus countries?

A Armenia, Moscow, and St. Petersburg

B Azerbaijan, Georgia, and Russia

C Azerbaijan, Armenia, and Georgia

D Georgia, Moscow, and Russia

The Caucasus: Climate

6 Based on the map above, which of the following climates is found along part of the coast of the Black Sea?

A Humid subtropical

B Mediterranean

C Steppe

D Tropical Savanna

7 What year did the Soviet Union collapse and break apart into 15 independent republics?

A 1990

B 1991

C 2000

D 2001

8 **Extended Response** Examine the Section 3 map of Russia's culture regions. Based on the map, describe how the physical geography in three of the culture regions contributes to the economic activity in those regions.

Standardized Test Prep

1. A

Break Down the Question Remind students that the word *best* in this question signals that some choices may be partially true, but they should choose the answer that best describes most areas of Russia.

2. C

Break Down the Question This question requires students to recall factual information from Section 1.

3. D

Break Down the Question This question requires students to recall that Joseph Stalin became dictator after Vladimir Lenin.

4. B

Break Down the Question This question requires students to recall factual information from Section 2.

5. C

Break Down the Question This question requires students to recall factual information from Section 4.

6. A

Break Down the Question This question requires students to read the map and the key carefully.

7. B

Break Down the Question This question requires students to recall factual information from Section 3.

8. Extended Response possible answer—In the Moscow, St. Petersburg, and Volga regions, large rivers, wide plains, and closeness to seaports help industry and agriculture thrive. Being close to the rest of Europe provides a convenient market for goods.

Reteach/Intervention Resources

Reproducible

Guided Reading Workbook

Differentiated Instruction Teacher Management System: Lesson Plans

Technology

Quick Facts Transparency: Russia and the Caucasus Visual Summary

Differentiated Instruction Modified Worksheets and Tests CD-ROM

Interactive Skills Tutor CD-ROM

Tips for Test Taking

Am I Done? Offer these test-taking tips to students: After answering all the questions, check your work one more time before handing the test in. If you have time, go back and review your answers for any careless mistakes you may have made. Be sure to erase stray marks, review questions you had any trouble with, and make sure you answered all of the questions. Taking tests is not a race. Use all of your time wisely!

Preteach

Bellringer

Motivate Have students brainstorm people who have affected European or Russian history. Remind students to think beyond just listing political figures. People such as Michelangelo and Galileo are also significant figures.

Direct Teach

Prewrite

Organizing Information Remind students to organize their notes of the event in chronological order, or the order in which major parts of the event took place. Here are some tips:

- Identify the major parts of the event. This will help students to have just one main idea for each paragraph.
- Include supporting details about each major event. These details should help explain or describe what happened—as well as keep the narrative moving forward in time.
- Use vivid language to describe the person (and others) and the event itself, so the story comes alive!

Practice & Apply

Language Arts Connection

Activity **Writing Portfolios** Coordinate the following activity with your school's language arts department. If students maintain writing portfolios in their language arts class, suggest that they add this paper to them. With the permission of their teacher, they can engage in an ongoing revision of the paper as part of their language arts instruction.

Rubric

Students' papers should

- introduce the person and event.
- clearly identify the importance of the event.
- use chronological order.
- write at least one paragraph for each major part of the event.
- include facts and vivid language.
- briefly summarize the importance of the person and event in the final paragraph.
- use correct grammar, punctuation, spelling, and capitalization.

514

A Biographical Narrative

People have shaped the world. Who are the important people in history? What were the critical events in their lives? How did geography or location affect those events? These are questions we ask as we try to understand our world.

Assignment

Write a biographical narrative about a significant event in the life of a historical figure such as Queen Isabella, Martin Luther, Napoleon, or Mikhail Gorbachev.

1. Prewrite

Choose a Topic

- Choose a person who affected European or Russian history in some way.
- Choose a specific event or incident in the person's life. For example, you might choose Napoleon at the Battle of Waterloo.

TIP To choose the event, think about the person's importance or signficance. Choose an event that will help you make that point.

Gather and Organize Information

- Look for information about your topic in the library or on the Internet. Book-length biographies about the person are a good source.
- Identify the parts of the event. Organize them in chonological, or time, order. Note details about people, actions, and the location of the event.

2. Write

Use a Writer's Framework

A Writer's Framework

Introduction
- Introduce the person and the event.
- Identify the importance of the event.

Body
- Write at least one paragraph for each major part of the event. Include specific details.
- Use chronological, or time, order to organize the parts of the event.

Conclusion
- Summarize the importance of the person and event in the final paragraph.

514

3. Evaluate and Revise

Review and Improve Your Paper

- Read your first draft at least twice, and then use the questions below to evaluate your paper.
- Make the changes needed to improve your paper.

Evaluation Questions for a Biographical Narrative

1. Do you introduce the person and event and identify the importance of each?
2. Do you have one paragraph for each major part of the event?
3. Do you include specific details about people, actions, and location?
4. Do you use chronological order, the order in time, to organize the parts of the event?
5. Do you end the paper with a summary of the importance of the person and event?

4. Proofread and Publish

Give Your Explanation the Finishing Touch

- Make sure your transitional phrases—such as then, next, later, or finally—help clarify the order of the actions that took place.
- Make sure you capitalized all proper names.
- You can share your biographical narrative by reading it aloud in class or adding it to a class collection of biographies.

5. Practice and Apply

Use the steps and strategies outlined in this workshop to write your biographical narrative. Share your work with others, comparing and contrasting the importance of the people and events.

Differentiating Instruction

Struggling Readers
Below Level

Students with below level writing skills might approach this assignment in an alternate way.

- Suggest that they present a collection of "photos" to tell the story of their person. They can draw pictures or make copies of existing magazine/book illustrations, accompanied by brief captions describing each visual.

LS **Kinesthetic, Verbal/Linguistic**

Alternative Assessment Handbook, Rubrics 3: Artwork; and 40: Writing to Describe

English-Language Learners
At Level

Students with family ties to countries covered in this module may enjoy focusing on figures from those countries.

- Encourage students to use a dictionary to find descriptive words.
- When revising their papers, have students work with a partner and make any needed corrections to align them with standard English usage.

LS **Verbal/Linguistic**

Alternative Assessment Handbook, Rubric 40: Writing to Describe

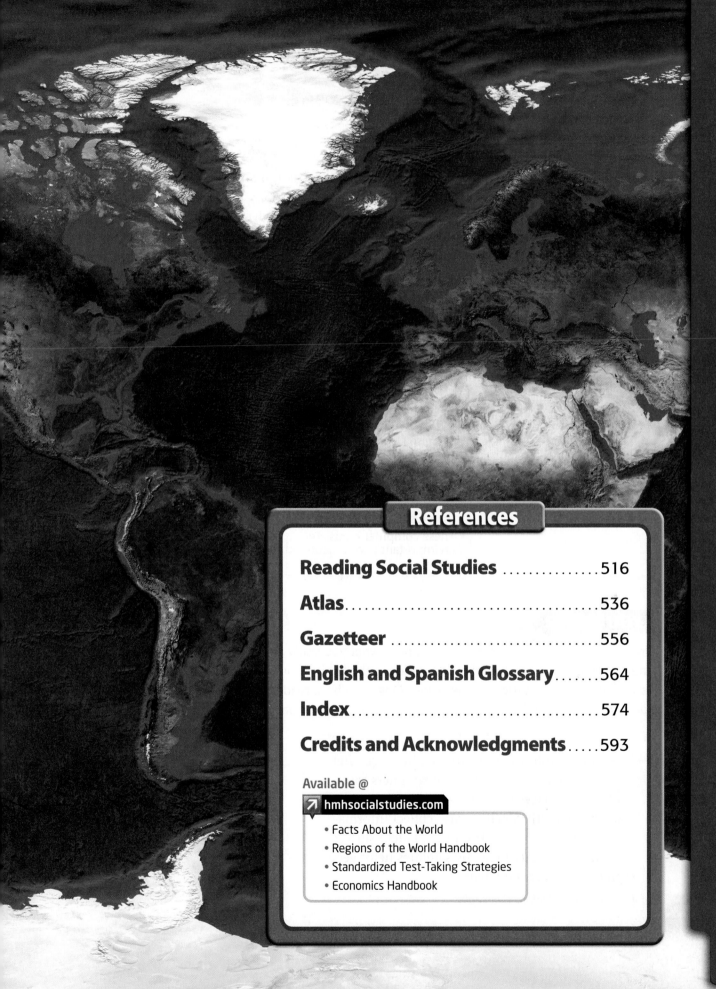

References

Available @

⌐ **hmhsocialstudies.com**

- Facts About the World
- Regions of the World Handbook
- Standardized Test-Taking Strategies
- Economics Handbook

Using Prior Knowledge

FOCUS ON READING

When you put together a puzzle, you search for pieces that are missing to complete the picture. As you read, you do the same thing when you use prior knowledge. You take what you already know about a subject and then add the information you are reading to create a full picture. The example below shows how using prior knowledge about computer mapping helped one reader fill in the pieces about how geographers use computer mapping.

In the past, maps were always drawn by hand. Many were not very accurate. Today, though, most maps are made using computers and satellite images. Through advances in mapmaking, we can make accurate maps on almost any scale, from the whole world to a single neighborhood, and keep them up to date.

From Section 3, The Branches of Geography

Computer Mapping	
What I know before reading	What else I learned
• My dad uses the computer to get a map for trips. • I can find maps on the Internet of states and countries.	• Maps have not always been very accurate. • Computers help make new kinds of maps that are more than just cities and roads. • These computer maps are an important part of geography.

YOU TRY IT!

Draw a chart like the one above. Think about what you know about satellite images and list this prior knowledge in the left column of your chart. Then read the passage below. Once you have read it, add what you learned about satellite images to the right column.

Much of the information gathered by these satellites is in the form of images. Geographers can study these images to see what an area looks like from above Earth. Satellites also collect information that we cannot see from the planet's surface. The information gathered by satellites helps geographers make accurate maps.

From Section 1, Studying Geography

Satellite Images
What I know before reading
Students' answers will vary.
What else I learned
possible answers—
• Satellite images show what an area looks like from above Earth.
• Satellite information may be things we cannot see from the planet's surface.
• Satellite images help make accurate maps.

Using Word Parts

FOCUS ON READING

Many English words are made up of several word parts: roots, prefixes, and suffixes. A root is the base of the word and carries the main meaning. A prefix is a letter or syllable added to the beginning of a root. A suffix is a letter or syllable added to the end to create new words. When you come across a new word, you can sometimes figure out the meaning by looking at its parts. Below are some common word parts and their meanings.

Common Roots		
Word Root	**Meaning**	**Sample Words**
-graph-	write, writing	autograph, biography
-vid-, -vis-	see	videotape, visible

Common Prefixes		
Prefix	**Meaning**	**Sample Words**
geo-	earth	geology
inter-	between, among	interpersonal, intercom
in-	not	ineffective
re-	again	restate, rebuild

Common Suffixes		
Suffix	**Meaning**	**Sample Words**
-ible	capable of	visible, responsible
-less	without	penniless, hopeless
-ment	result, action	commitment
-al	relating to	directional
-tion	the act or condition of	rotation, selection

YOU TRY IT!

Read the following words. First separate any prefixes or suffixes and identify the word's root. Use the chart above to define the root, the prefix, or the suffix. Then write a definition for each word.

geography	**visualize**	**movement**
seasonal	**reshaping**	**interact**
regardless	**separation**	**invisible**

Using Word Parts

Geography—geo- *means earth; the root* -graph- *means writing.* Geography *means writing about the earth.*

Seasonal—*the suffix* -al *means relating to;* seasonal *means relating to the seasons*

Regardless—*the suffix* -less *means without;* regardless *means without regard*

Visualize—*the root* -vis- *means to see;* visualize *means the act of seeing*

Reshaping—*the prefix* re- *means again;* reshaping *means to shape again*

Separation—*the suffix* -tion *means the act or condition of;* separation *means the act of separating*

Movement—*the suffix* -ment *means result;* movement *means the result of moving*

Interact—inter- *means between or among;* interact *means to act between*

Invisible—*the prefix* in- *means not;* -vis- *means to see; the suffix* -ible *means capable of;* invisible *means not capable of being seen*

Understanding Cause and Effect

FOCUS ON READING

Learning to identify causes and effects can help you understand geography. A **cause** is something that makes another thing happen. An **effect** is the result of something else that happened. A cause may have several effects, and an effect may have several causes. In addition, as you can see in the example below, causes and effects may occur in a chain. Then, each effect in turn becomes the cause for another event.

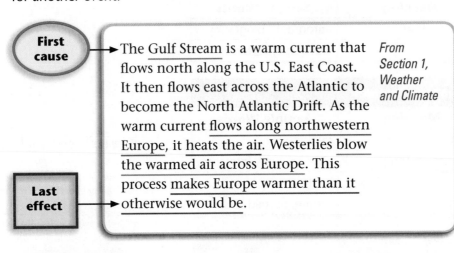

First cause

The Gulf Stream is a warm current that flows north along the U.S. East Coast. It then flows east across the Atlantic to become the North Atlantic Drift. As the warm current flows along northwestern Europe, it heats the air. Westerlies blow the warmed air across Europe. This process makes Europe warmer than it otherwise would be.

From Section 1, Weather and Climate

Last effect

Cause
Gulf Stream

Effect
Warm water flows along the coast of northwest Europe.

Effect
Warm water raises temperature of the air above.

Effect
Winds blow warm air across Europe.

Effect
Warm winds make Europe warmer.

YOU TRY IT!

Read the following sentences, and then use a graphic organizer like the one below right to analyze the cause and effects. Create as many boxes as you need to list the causes and effects.

Mountains also create wet and dry areas. . . A mountain forces wind blowing against it to rise. As it rises, the air cools and precipitation falls as rain or snow. Thus, the side of the mountain facing the wind is often green and lush. However, little moisture remains for the other side. This effect creates a rain shadow.

From Section 1, Weather and Climate

Cause → **Effect** → **Effect** → **Effect**

Understanding Cause and Effect

Cause—Mountain;
Effect—Wind blowing against the mountain rises;
Effect—Air cools as it rises up the mountainside;
Effect—Precipitation falls;
Effect—Little moisture remains for the other side of the mountain;
Effect—Rain shadow on mountainside not facing the wind

Understanding Main Ideas

FOCUS ON READING

Main ideas are like the hub of a wheel. The hub holds the wheel together, and everything circles around it. In a paragraph, the main idea holds the paragraph together and all the facts and details revolve around it. The main idea is usually stated clearly in a topic sentence, which may come at the beginning or end of a paragraph. Topic sentences always summarize the most important idea of a paragraph.

To find the main idea, ask yourself what one point is holding the paragraph together. See how the main idea in the following example holds all the details from the paragraph together.

A single country may also include more than one culture region within its borders. Mexico is one of many countries that is made up of different culture regions. People in northern Mexico and southern Mexico, for example, have different culture traits. The culture of northern Mexico tends to be more modern, while traditional culture remains strong in southern Mexico.

From Section 1, Culture

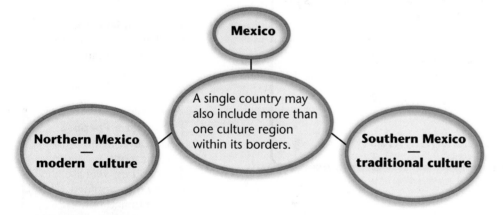

YOU TRY IT!

Read the following paragraph, and then use a graphic organizer like the one above to identify the main idea. Create as many circles as you need to list the supporting facts and details.

At the same time, the United States is influenced by global culture. Martial arts movies from Asia attract large audiences in the United States. Radio stations in the United States play music by African, Latin American, and European musicians. We even adopt many foreign words, like *sushi* and *plaza*, into English.

From Section 4, Global Connections

Understanding Main Ideas

Main Idea—The United States is influenced by global culture.

Details—martial arts movies from Asia are popular in the United States; radio stations play music by African, Latin American, and European artists; Americans adopt foreign words into English.

Setting a Purpose

FOCUS ON READING

When you go on a trip, you have a purpose or a destination in mind before you start. Maps can help you get to your destination. When you read, you should also have a purpose in mind before you start. This purpose keeps you focused and moving toward your goal of understanding. Textbooks often provide "maps" to help you set a purpose for your reading. A textbook's "map" includes a chapter's headings, pictures, and study tips. To determine a purpose for your reading, look over the headings, pictures, and study tips. Then ask yourself a question that can guide you. See how looking over the chapter's first page can help you set a purpose.

Notice Headings, Pictures or Tips
Here's a tip on what I should learn about in this chapter.

↓

Ask Questions
What do I want to learn about these three civilizations?

↓

Set a Purpose
I've never heard of these civilizations. I wonder what they were like and why they declined. I'll read to find out.

What You Will Learn...

In this chapter you will learn about the location, growth, and decline of the Maya, Aztec, and Inca civilizations in the Americas.

From Early History of the Americas

SECTION 1
The Maya **14**

SECTION 2
The Aztecs **20**

SECTION 3
The Incas **25**

YOU TRY IT!

You can also use the method described above to set a purpose for reading the main text in your book. Look at the heading for the following caption. Then write down one or two questions about what you will read. Finally, develop a purpose for reading about Tenochtitlán. State this purpose in one to two sentences.

Tenochtitlán

The Aztecs turned a swampy, uninhabited island into one of the largest and grandest cities in the world. The first Europeans to visit Tenochtitlán were amazed. At the time, the Aztec capital was about five times bigger than London.

From Section 2, The Aztecs

Question: What do I want to learn about Tenochtitlán?

Purpose: I wonder what Tenochtitlán was like and why it was so amazing. I'll read to find out.

Predicting

FOCUS ON READING

Predicting is guessing what will happen next based on what you already know. In reading about geography, you can use what you know about the place you live to help you make predictions about other countries. Predicting helps you stay involved with your reading as you see whether your prediction was right. Your mind follows these four steps when you make predictions as you read:

| Takes what you already know | → | Adds new information from your reading | → | Forms a prediction that makes sense | → | Confirms or adjusts your prediction based on what you just read |

See how you might make a prediction from the following text:

> From snowcapped mountain peaks to warm, sunny beaches, Mexico has many different climates.
>
> *From Section 1, Physical Geography*

| I know Mexico has warm weather and beaches. | → | Mexico has both mountains and beaches. | → | Maybe Mexico has some cool weather in the mountains. | → | The prediction was correct: "For example, the areas of high elevation on the Mexican Plateau can have surprisingly cool temperatures." |

YOU TRY IT!

Read the following sentences. Then use a graphic organizer like the one below to help you predict what you will learn in your reading. Check the text in Section 3 to see if your prediction was correct.

> Mexico has a democratic government. However, Mexico is not like the United States where different political parties have always competed for power.
>
> *From Section 3, Mexico Today*

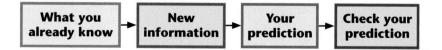

| What you already know | → | New information | → | Your prediction | → | Check your prediction |

Step 1: In a democracy, people vote for their leaders. Two main political parties compete for power in the United States.

Step 2: Mexico has a democratic government, but it is not like the United States.

Step 3: Maybe Mexico did not always have political parties or there is only one.

Step 4: The prediction was correct: "In Mexico the same political party controlled the government for 71 years."

Understanding Comparison-Contrast

FOCUS ON READING

Comparing shows how things are alike. Contrasting shows how things are different. You can understand comparison-contrast by learning to recognize clue words and points of comparison. Clue words let you know whether to look for similarities or differences. Points of comparison are the main topics that are being compared or contrasted.

> Many Caribbean islands share a similar history and culture. However, today the islands' different economies, governments, and cultural landscapes encourage many different ways of life in the Caribbean.
>
> *From Section 3, The Caribbean Islands*

Underlined words are clue words.

Highlighted words are points of comparison.

Clue Words	
Comparison	**Contrast**
share, similar, like, also, both, in addition, besides	however, while, unlike, different, but, although

YOU TRY IT!

Read the following passage to see how Haiti and the Dominican Republic are alike and different. Use a diagram like the one here to compare and contrast the two countries.

> Haiti occupies the western part of the island of Hispaniola. Haiti's capital, Port-au-Prince, is the center of the nation's limited industry. Most Haitians farm small plots. Coffee and sugarcane are among Haiti's main exports.
>
> The Dominican Republic occupies the eastern part of Hispaniola. The Dominican Republic is not a rich country. However, its economy, health care, education, and housing are more developed than Haiti's. Agriculture is the basis of the economy
>
> *From Section 3, The Caribbean Islands*

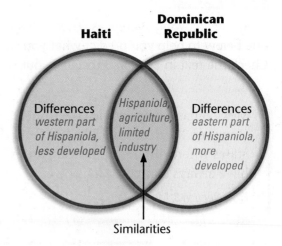

Haiti

Dominican Republic

Differences *western part of Hispaniola, less developed*

Hispaniola, agriculture, limited industry

Differences *eastern part of Hispaniola, more developed*

Similarities

Identifying Supporting Details

FOCUS ON READING

Why believe what you read? One reason is because of details that support or prove the main idea. These details might be facts, statistics, examples, or definitions. In the example below, notice what kind of proof or supporting details help you believe the main idea.

> Colombia's economy relies on several valuable resources. Rich soil, steep slopes, and tall shade trees produce world-famous Colombian coffee. Other major export crops include bananas, sugarcane, and cotton. Many farms in Colombia produce flowers that are exported around the world. In fact, 80 percent of the country's flowers are shipped to the United States.
>
> *From Section 2, Colombia*

Main Idea
Colombia's economy relies on several valuable resources.

Supporting Details			
Example	**Fact**	**Fact**	**Statistic**
Colombian coffee	Other export crops	Export flowers	80 percent shipped to U.S.

YOU TRY IT!

Read the following sentences. Then identify the supporting details in a graphic organizer like the one above.

> Caribbean South America is home to some remarkable wildlife. For example, hundreds of bird species, meat-eating fish called piranhas, and crocodiles live in or around the Orinoco River. Colombia has one of the world's highest concentrations of plant and animal species. The country's wildlife includes jaguars, ocelots, and several species of monkeys.
>
> *From Section 1, Physical Geography*

Main Idea: Caribbean South America has remarkable wildlife.

Supporting Details: Fact: hundreds of bird species, piranhas, catfish, and crocodiles in and around the Orinoco River. Fact: Colombia has one of the world's highest concentrations of plant and animal species. Example: jaguars, ocelots, and monkeys.

Using Context Clues

FOCUS ON READING

One practical way to tackle unfamiliar words you encounter is to look at the context. Reading the words and sentences surrounding the word will often help you because they give definitions, examples, or synonyms. For example, maybe you're not sure what the word *context* means. Just from reading the previous sentences, however, you probably understood that it means the "the part of a text surrounding a word or passage that makes its meaning clear." You have relied on the context to help you define the word. In reading geography, you may forget what some of the geographical terms mean. You can use context clues to figure them out. See how this process works in the example below with the word *tributary*.

The Amazon River is about 4,000 miles long. It extends from the Andes Mountains in Peru to the Atlantic Ocean. Hundreds of tributaries flow into it, draining an area that includes parts of most South American countries.

From Section 1, Physical Geography

1. Look at the surrounding words or sentences.
The passage talks about the Amazon River and what flows into it.

2. Make a guess at the word's meaning.
A tributary must be a smaller river or stream that flows into a bigger river.

3. Check your guess by inserting it into the passage.
Hundreds of smaller rivers flow into it.

YOU TRY IT!

Read the following sentences, and then use the three steps described above to help you define *hydroelectric*.

Atlantic South America also has good mineral and energy resources such as gold, silver, copper, iron, and oil. Dams on some of the region's large rivers also provide hydroelectric power.

From Section 1, Physical Geography

Step 1: The passage talks about mineral and energy resources.

Step 2: Hydroelectric power probably means a type of electricity made by using water power.

Step 3: Dams on some of the region's large rivers also provide electricity using water power.

Making Inferences

FOCUS ON READING

Sometimes reading effectively means understanding both what the writer tells you directly and what the writer doesn't tell you. When you fill in the gaps, you are making inferences, or educated guesses. Why worry about what the writer doesn't tell you? Making inferences can help you make connections with the text. It can also give you a fuller picture of the information. To make an inference, think about the text and what you know or can guess from the information. The example below shows you the process.

> At the southern tip of the continent, the Strait of Magellan links the Atlantic and Pacific oceans. A strait is a narrow body of water connecting two larger bodies of water. The large island south of the strait is Tierra del Fuego, or "land of fire."
>
> *From Section 1, Physical Geography*

1. Determine what the passage says:
The Strait of Magellan connects the Atlantic and Pacific oceans. There is an island south of it.

↓

2. Determine what you know about the topic or what you can connect to your experience.
This sounds like a shortcut to me. It would keep boats from having to sail all the way around the island.

↓

3. Make an inference.
Many ships probably use the Strait of Magellan because it is a shortcut.

YOU TRY IT!

Read the following sentences. Then use the three steps described above to make an inference about the Galápagos Islands.

> Chile and Ecuador both control large islands in the Pacific Ocean. Ecuador's volcanic Galápagos Islands have wildlife not found anywhere else in the world.
>
> *From Section 1, Physical Geography*

Step 1: The Galápagos have animals that don't live anywhere else in the world.

Step 2: People love to see and watch animals, especially different kinds.

Step 3: People probably travel to the Galapagos Islands just to see the animals.

Categorizing

FOCUS ON READING

When you sort things into groups of similar items, you are categorizing. When you read, categorizing helps you to identify the main groups of information. Then you can find and see the individual facts in each group. Notice how the information in the paragraph below has been sorted into three main groups, with details listed under each group.

> If you were traveling across the United States, you might start on the country's eastern coast. This low area, which is flat and close to sea level, is called the Atlantic Coastal Plain. As you go west, the land gradually rises higher to a region called the Piedmont. The Appalachian Mountains, which are the main mountain range in the East, rise above the Piedmont.

From Section 1, Physical Geography

Category 1:
Atlantic Coastal Plain
Details: low, flat, close to sea level

↓

Category 2:
Piedmont
Details: farther west & higher than Atlantic Coastal Plain

↓

Category 3:
Appalachian Mountains
Details: main Eastern mountain range, higher than Piedmont

YOU TRY IT!

Read the following paragraph, and then use a graphic organizer like the one above to categorize the group and details in the paragraph. Create as many boxes as you need to list the main groups.

> The eastern United States has three climate regions. In the Northeast, people live in a humid continental climate with snowy winters and warm, humid summers. Southerners, on the other hand, experience milder winters and the warm, humid summers of a humid subtropical climate. Most of Florida is warm all year.

From Section 1, Physical Geography

Category 1: Northeast; Details: snowy winters, warm summers, humid continental climate

Category 2: South; Details: milder winters, warm summers, humid subtropical climate, most of Florida warm all year

Understanding Lists

FOCUS ON READING

A to-do list can keep you focused on what you need to get done. Keeping lists while you read can keep you focused on understanding the main points of a text. In the example below, a list helps the reader identify and focus on the types of cold climates found in central and northern Canada.

> The farther north you go in Canada, the colder it gets. The coldest areas of Canada are located close to the Arctic Circle. Much of central and northern Canada has a sub-arctic climate. The far north has tundra and ice cap climates. About half of Canada lies in these extremely cold climates.
>
> *From Section 1, Physical Geography*

List of cold climates
1. subarctic
2. tundra
3. ice cap

YOU TRY IT!

Read the sentences and then list the territories that make up the Canadian North region.

> Northern Canada is extremely cold due to its location close to the Arctic Circle. The region called the Canadian North includes the Yukon Territory, the Northwest Territories, and Nunavut. These three territories cover more than a third of Canada but are home to only about 100,000 people.
>
> *From Section 3, Canada Today*

1. Yukon Territory, 2. Northwest Territories, 3. Nunavut

Re-reading

FOCUS ON READING

Have you ever hit the rewind button on the VCR or DVD player because you missed an important scene or didn't quite catch what a character said? As you rewound, you probably asked yourself such questions as, "What did he say?" or "How did she do that?" Taking a second look helped you understand what was going on.

The same idea is true for reading. When you re-read a passage, you can catch details you didn't catch the first time. As you re-read, go slowly and check your understanding by asking yourself questions. In the example below, notice the questions the reader asked. Then see how the questions were answered by re-reading the passage.

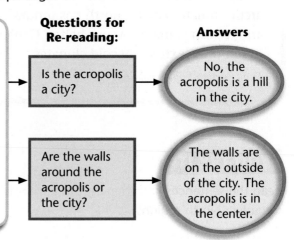

In the center of most city-states was a fortress on a hill. This hill was called the acropolis, which is Greek for "top city." In addition to the fortress, many city-states built temples and other public buildings on the acropolis. Around the acropolis was the rest of the city, including houses and markets. High walls usually surrounded the city for protection.

From Section 1, Ancient Greece

Questions for Re-reading:

Is the acropolis a city?

Are the walls around the acropolis or the city?

Answers

No, the acropolis is a hill in the city.

The walls are on the outside of the city. The acropolis is in the center.

YOU TRY IT!

Read the following passage, and then develop two questions you can answer as you re-read the passage. Write down the questions and the answers.

When historians talk about the past, they often divide it into three long periods. The first period is the ancient world, the time of the world's earliest civilizations, such as Egypt, China, Greece, and Rome. The last period historians call the modern world, the world since about 1500. Since that time, new ideas and contacts between civilizations changed the world completely. What happened between ancient and modern times? We call this period, which lasted from about 500 until about 1500, the Middle Ages.

From Section 3, The Middle Ages

Re-reading

Answers will vary.

possible responses—What are the three time periods in history? (Ancient world, Middle Ages, modern world.) About how long did the Middle Ages last? (about 1,000 years)

Understanding Chronological Order

FOCUS ON READING

History is full of fascinating events. Some of them happen quickly, while others take decades to unfold. Many events overlap. Sometimes it may be challenging to keep the sequence of events straight. One helpful strategy is to identify chronological order or the order in which events happened. Writers use dates or clue words such as *first, next, before, meanwhile,* and *then* to describe the order of events. Notice the words in the following passage that help show the sequence of events.

In **1812** Napoleon led an invasion of Russia. The invasion was a disaster. Bitterly cold weather and smart Russian tactics forced Napoleon's army to retreat. Many French soldiers died. Great Britain, Prussia, and Russia **then** joined forces and in **1814** defeated Napoleon's weakened army. He returned **a year later** with a new army, but was again defeated. The British **then** exiled him to an island, where he died in **1821**.

From Section 3, Political Change in Europe

Time Markers/Dates
1812
1814
1821

Clue Words
then
a year later

First Event:	Second Event:	Third Event:	Fourth Event:
Napoleon invades Russia.	Countries join forces and defeat Napoleon.	Napoleon returns with a new army.	Napoleon exiled to an island and dies.

YOU TRY IT!

Read the passage below. Identify the three main events the passage describes and their chronological order. List the clue words or time markers that signal the order of the events.

In 1642 England's power struggle erupted in civil war. Supporters of Parliament forced King Charles I from power. . . A new government then formed, but it was unstable. By 1660 many of the English were tired of instability. They wanted to restore the monarchy. They asked the former king's son to rule England as Charles II.

From Section 3, Political Change in Europe

Understanding Chronological Order

First Event: Civil War; King Charles forced from power; Time Marker: 1642

Second Event: New government formed; Clue Word: then

Third Event: English tired of instability; ask former king's son to rule as Charles II; Time Marker: 1660

Using Context Clues—Contrast

FOCUS ON READING

Maybe you played this game as a young child: "Which of these things is not like the others?" This same game can help you understand new words as you read. Sometimes the words or sentences around a new word will show contrast, or how the word is not like something else. These contrast clues can help you figure out the new word's meaning. Look at how the following passage indicates that *persevered* means something different from *give in*.

> The German air force repeatedly attacked British cities and military targets. Hitler hoped the British would surrender. Rather than give in, however, the British *persevered*.
>
> *From Section 2, World War II*

Contrast Clues:

1. Look for words or sentences that signal contrast.
Words that signal contrast include *however, rather than, instead of,* and *not*. In this paragraph, the words *rather than* signal the contrast clues for the unfamiliar word *persevered*.

2. Check the definition by substituting a word or phrase that fits.
Persevere likely means to keep on trying. *Rather than give in, however, the British kept on trying.*

YOU TRY IT!

Read the following paragraph, and then use the steps listed above to develop a definition for the word *compete.*

> Some people believed that creating a feeling of community in Europe would make countries less likely to go to war. Leaders like Great Britain's Winston Churchill believed the countries of Europe should cooperate rather than *compete*.
>
> *From Section 3, Europe since 1945*

New Word   **Contrasting Phrase**   **Meaning**

Using Context Clues—Contrast
1. Contrast clues—rather than
2. Compete probably means to go against each to other; Leaders like Great Britain's Winston Churchill believed the countries of Europe should cooperate rather than go against each other.

Asking Questions

FOCUS ON READING

Reading is one place where asking questions will never get you in trouble. The five W questions – who, what, when, where, and why – can help you be sure you understand the material you read. After you read a section, ask yourself the 5 Ws: **Who** was this section about? **What** did they do? **When** and **where** did they live? **Why** did they do what they did? See the example below to learn how this reading strategy can help you identify the main points of a passage.

Many Greeks were not happy under Turkish rule. They wanted to be free of foreign influences. In the early 1800s, they rose up against the Turks. The rebellion seemed likely to fail, but the Greeks received help from other European countries and drove the Turks out. After the rebellion, Greece became a monarchy.

From Section 2, Greece

The 5 Ws

Who?
Greeks

What?
Led rebellion to become independent from Turks

Where?
Greece

When?
Early 1800s

Why?
Wanted to be free of foreign influences

YOU TRY IT!

Read the following passage and answer the 5 Ws to check your understanding of it.

Italy remained divided into small states until the mid-1800s. At that time, a rise in nationalism, or strong patriotic feelings for a country, led people across Italy to fight for unification. As a result of their efforts, Italy became a unified kingdom in 1861.

From Section 3, Italy

Asking Questions

Who: Italy [or] Italians; What: fought for unification of the country; Where: Italy; When: mid-1800s; Why: strong nationalism [or] patriotic feelings

Recognizing Word Origins

FOCUS ON READING

English is a language that loves to borrow words from other languages and cultures. From the French, we took *faceon* and changed it to *fashion*. From the German, we took *strollen* and changed it to *stroll*. From the Dutch, we took *koekje* and changed it to *cookie*. Below is a list of examples of other words that come from other languages.

English Words from French	English Words from German	English Words from Latin
conquer	muffin	culture
brilliant	dollar	defeat
restaurant	rocket	general
republic	kindergarten	forces
fashion	hamburger	join
parliament	noodle	president
several	pretzel	elect
power	snorkel	control
exiled	hex	territory

YOU TRY IT!

Read the following sentences. Refer to the above word lists and make a list of the words in the passage below that originally came from other languages. After each word, list the original language.

A few years later a brilliant general named Napoleon took power. In time, he conquered much of Europe. Then in 1815 several European powers joined forces and defeated Napoleon. They exiled him and chose a new king to rule France.

France is now a republic with a parliament and an elected president. France still controls several overseas territories, such as Martinique in the West Indies.

From Section 2, France and the Benelux Countries

Recognizing Word Origins
brilliant: French
general: Latin
power: French
conquered: French
several: French
powers: French
joined: Latin
forces: Latin
defeated: Latin
exiled: French
republic: French
parliament: French
elected: Latin
president: Latin
controls: Latin
several: French
territories: Latin

Using Context Clues— Synonyms

FOCUS ON READING

You have probably discovered that geography is a subject with many new words and terms. What if you don't remember or don't know what a word means? You may be able to use context clues to determine its meaning. Context clues are words near the unfamiliar word that indicate its meaning.

One helpful context clue is the synonym—words or phrases that mean the same as the new word. Look for synonyms in the words and sentences surrounding an unfamiliar term. Synonyms can help you understand the meaning of the new word. They may come in the same sentence or in the sentence following the words they define. Notice how the following passage uses synonyms to define the word *urban*.

> Most Swedes live in the southern part of the country in large towns and cities. In fact, more than 80 percent of Swedes live in *urban* areas. Stockholm, Sweden's capital and largest city, is located on the east coast near the Baltic Sea.
>
> *From Section 3, Scandinavia*

1. Look for words or phrases that mean the same thing.
The first sentence uses the phrase large towns and cities to describe where most Swedes live.

2. Substitute the synonym for the new word to confirm its meaning.
More than 80 percent of Swedes live in large towns and cities.

YOU TRY IT!

As you read the following sentences, look for synonyms that mean the same as the italicized words. Then use a graphic organizer like the one below to define each italicized word.

> Slow-moving sheets of ice, or *glaciers*, have left their mark on Northern Europe's coastlines and lakes.
>
> As the glaciers flowed slowly downhill, they carved long, winding channels, or *fjords*, into Norway's coastline.
>
> *From Section 1, Physical Geography*

Using Context Clues—Synonyms
glaciers—slow-moving sheets of ice
fjords—long, winding channels carved into coastlines

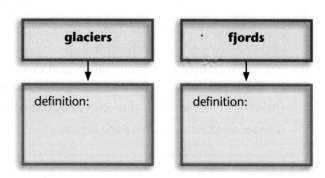

glaciers	fjords
definition:	definition:

READING SOCIAL STUDIES

Understanding Problems and Solutions

FOCUS ON READING

Throughout history, people have faced problems and found solutions to them. As a result, writers who describe historical events often structure their writing by identifying a problem and then describing its solution. The ability to identify this pattern of writing will help you understand what you read. Notice how the following passage presents one problem with a two-pronged solution.

Estonia, Latvia, Lithuania, and Poland all still suffer from decades of Soviet rule. Under the Soviets, the economies of all four countries suffered.

Today, Poland and the Baltic Republics are working to rebuild and strengthen their economies. They are replacing the old and outdated factories built by the Soviets with new ones that take advantage of modern technology.

To further their economic growth, the countries of this region are also seeking new sources of income. One area in which they have found success is tourism.

From Section 2, Poland and the Baltic Republics

Problem:
Poor economies from Soviet rule

Solution #1:
Building new factories

Solution #2:
New source of income through tourism

YOU TRY IT!

Read the following passage, and then use the process shown above to identify the problems and solutions the writer presents. Create as many boxes as you need.

Many Eastern Europeans opposed Communist rule. After years of protest, the Communist government in the region fell. Poland rejected Communism and elected new leaders in 1989. The Baltic Republics broke away from the Soviet Union in 1991 and became independent once more.

From Section 2, Poland and the Baltic Republics

Understand Problems and Solutions

Problem: Many people opposed Communist rule.

Solutions: Protesting and rejecting Communism; electing new leaders.

Making Generalizations

FOCUS ON READING

As you read about different people and cultures, you probably realize that people share some similarities. Seeing those similarities may lead you to make a generalization. A generalization is a broad, general idea drawn from new information combined with what you already know, such as your own experience. Notice how this process works with the following passage.

> Russians sometimes joke that winter lasts for 12 months and then summer begins. Russia is a cold country. The reason is its northern location partly within the Arctic Circle. In general, Russia has short summers and long, snowy winters. The climate is milder west of the Urals and grows colder and harsher as one goes north and east.
>
> *From Section 1, Physical Geography*

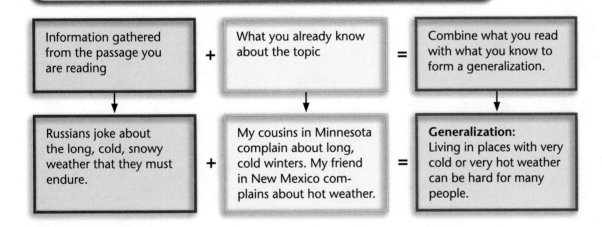

Information gathered from the passage you are reading	**+**	What you already know about the topic	**=**	Combine what you read with what you know to form a generalization.
Russians joke about the long, cold, snowy weather that they must endure.	**+**	My cousins in Minnesota complain about long, cold winters. My friend in New Mexico complains about hot weather.	**=**	**Generalization:** Living in places with very cold or very hot weather can be hard for many people.

YOU TRY IT!

Read the following passage. Using the process described above, form a general idea about holidays. Write your generalization in one sentence.

> Russian history has shaped its customs, such as holidays. Religious holidays, like Easter and Christmas, are popular. The main family holiday is New Year's Eve. To celebrate this holiday, families decorate a tree where, according to Russian folklore, Grandfather Frost and his helper the Snow Maiden leave gifts. A newer holiday is Russian Independence Day, which marks the end of the Soviet Union on June 12.
>
> *From Section 2, History and Culture of Russia*

Making Generalizations
Answers will vary.

possible answers—Celebrating holidays is important in most cultures. Many countries celebrate an Independence Day. Religious holidays are important to many families.

United States: Physical

Strait of Juan de Fuca

Puget Sound

Mount Rainier
14,410 ft
(4,392 m)

45°N

COAST RANGES

CASCADE RANGE

Columbia River

Franklin D. Roosevelt Lake

Pend Oreille River

Flathead River

Flathead Lake

Lewis Range

Bitterroot Range

Salmon River

Salmon River Mts.

Columbia Plateau

Sawtooth Mts.

Snake River

CONTINENTAL

Milk River

Missouri River

Fort Peck Lake

Yellowstone River

Lake Sakakawea

ROCKY

GREAT

Cape Mendocino

40°N

Klamath River

Goose Lake

Shasta Lake

Pyramid Lake

SIERRA NEVADA

Central Valley

Sacramento River

San Joaquin River

Lake Tahoe

GREAT BASIN

Great Salt Lake

Utah Lake

Wasatch Range

Uinta Mts.

Grand Tetons

Gannett Peak
13,804 ft
(4,207 m)

Wind River Range

Yellowstone Lake

Bighorn Mts.

Bighorn River

Powder River

Black Hills

DIVIDE

Front Range

North Platte River

Cheyenne River

White River

Niobrara River

James

Lake Oahe

MOUNTAINS

INTER

35°N

San Francisco Bay

Monterey Bay

Coast Ranges

Mount Whitney
14,494 ft
(4,419 m)

Death Valley

Mojave Desert

Colorado River

Lake Mead

Grand Canyon

Painted Desert

COLORADO

PLATEAU

Lake Powell

San Juan River

Mount Elbert
14,433 ft
(4,400 m)

Colorado River

South Platte River

Pikes Peak
14,110 ft
(4,301 m)

Republican River

Smoky Hill River

San Luis Valley

Sangre De Cristo Mts.

DIVIDE

P L A I N S

PACIFIC OCEAN

Channel Islands

Salton Sea

Imperial Valley

Gila River

Sonoran Desert

Rio Grande

CONTINENTAL

Canadian River

Pecos River

Colorado River

Amistad Reservoir

Rio Grande

Nueces River

Padre Island

Gulf of California

MEXICO

To understand the relative locations of Alaska and Hawaii, as well as the vast distances separating them from the rest of the United States, see the world map.

Kauai

Niihau

Oahu

22°N

HAWAII

Molokai

Maui

PACIFIC OCEAN

Lanai

Kahoolawe

Mauna Kea
13,796 ft
(4,206 m)

Hawaii

19°N

0   75   150 Miles

0   75   150 Kilometers

Projection: Mercator

ARCTIC OCEAN

RUSSIA

Bering Strait

Arctic Circle

BROOKS RANGE

Yukon River

Tanana River

ALASKA RANGE

Mount McKinley
20,320 ft
(6,194 m)

CANADA

St. Lawrence Island

St. Matthew Island

Nunivak Island

Kuskokwim River

Gulf of Alaska

Kodiak Island

Alexander Archipelago

55°N

Attu Island

55°N

Bering Sea

50°N

0   250   500 Miles

0   250   500 Kilometers

Projection: Albers Equal Area

PACIFIC OCEAN

ALEUTIAN ISLANDS

CANADA

Red River

Isle Royale

Mesabi Range

Lake Superior

Minnesota River

Mississippi River

Wisconsin River

Lake Michigan

Lake Huron

St. Lawrence River

St. Lawrence Seaway

St. John River

Longfellow Mts.

Penobscot River

Lake Champlain

Green Mts.

White Mts.

Connecticut River

Adirondack Mts.

Lake Ontario

Cape Cod

Hudson River

Catskill Mts.

Long Island Sound

Long Island

Lake Erie

Allegheny R.

PLATEAU

Des Moines River

Missouri River

Illinois River

Wabash River

Scioto River

Susquehanna River

Delaware River

40°N

Kansas R.

P L A I N S

Ohio River

ALLEGHENY

Monongahela R.

Potomac River

Delaware Bay

70°W

Lake of the Ozarks

River

Kanawha River

James River

ATLANTIC OCEAN

Keystone Lake

OZARK PLATEAU

White River

Lake Barkley

Cumberland Plateau

Roanoke River

Chesapeake Bay

Kentucky Lake

Cumberland River

Great Smoky Mts.

APPALACHIAN MOUNTAINS

PIEDMONT

Pamlico Sound

35°N

Cape Hatteras

ufaula Lake

Arkansas River

Ouachita Mts.

Tennessee River

BLUE RIDGE Mountains

Oconee River

Savannah River

Lake Texoma

Coosa River

Tombigbee River

Chattahoochee River

Altamaha River

Sea Islands

ELEVATION

Trinity River

Saline River

Red River

Mississippi

Pearl River

Alabama R.

P L A I N

Okefenokee Swamp

Feet | Meters
13,120 | 4,000
6,560 | 2,000
1,640 | 500
656 | 200
(Sea level) 0 | 0 (Sea level)
Below sea level | Below sea level

0 100 200 Miles
0 100 200 Kilometers

Projection: Albers Equal Area

razos River

Toledo Bend Reservoir

C O A S T A L

Chandeleur Islands

FLORIDA PENINSULA

Cape Canaveral

80°W

GULF

Mississippi Delta

N W E S

Gulf of Mexico

Lake Okeechobee

BAHAMAS

25°N

The Everglades

Straits of Florida

75°W

Cape Sable

Florida Keys

95°W 90°W 85°W

United States: Political

Strait of Juan de Fuca

Puget Sound

Seattle
Tacoma
Olympia ★
Spokane

WASHINGTON

Franklin D. Roosevelt Lake

Pend Oreille

Portland
Columbia River

★ Salem

Eugene

OREGON

Flathead Lake

Great Falls
Helena ★
MONTANA
Fort Peck Lake

Missouri River
NORTH DAKOTA
Lake Sakakawea
Bismarck

Yellowstone River

Billings

IDAHO

Boise ★
Sun Valley

Snake River

Pocatello

Yellowstone Lake

WYOMING

Cheyenne ★

Lake Oahe
SOUTH DAKOTA
Pierre ★
Rapid City

NEBRASKA
Platte River

45°N

Cape Mendocino

40°N

125°W

Goose Lake
Shasta Lake
Sacramento River

Pyramid Lake
Reno
Carson City ★
Lake Tahoe

NEVADA

Great Salt Lake
Ogden
★ Salt Lake City
Provo

Utah Lake

UTAH

Green River

Boulder
Vail
★ Denver
Aspen
COLORADO
Colorado Springs
Pueblo

Arkansas River

KANSAS

Berkeley
Oakland
San Francisco
San Francisco Bay
Sacramento ★
San Joaquin River
San Jose
Monterey Bay

Fresno

CALIFORNIA

35°N

Las Vegas

Lake Powell

Lake Mead

Colorado River

30°N

120°W

PACIFIC OCEAN

Santa Barbara
Ventura
Los Angeles
Long Beach
Anaheim
Santa Ana
San Diego
Riverside
Palm Springs
Channel Islands
Salton Sea

Flagstaff

ARIZONA

Phoenix ★

Gila River

Casa Grande
Tucson

Taos
Santa Fe ★
Albuquerque

NEW MEXICO

Las Cruces
El Paso

Gulf of California

Canadian River

OKLAHOMA
Oklahoma Cit
Amarillo
Lawto

Lubbock

Brazos River

Midland
Odessa

Abilene
Fort Wort

TEXAS

Colorado River

Pecos River

Austin

To understand the relative locations of Alaska and Hawaii, as well as the vast distances separating them from the rest of the United States, see the world map.

HAWAII

Kauai
Niihau
Oahu
Honolulu ★
Molokai
Lanai
Maui
Kahoolawe
PACIFIC OCEAN

Hilo
Hawaii

22°N

160°W
155°W
19°N

0   75   150 Miles
0   75   150 Kilometers
Projection: Mercator

ARCTIC OCEAN

RUSSIA

Bering Strait

Arctic Circle

Bering Sea

St. Lawrence Island
St. Matthew Island

Nunivak Island

Nome

Yukon River

Fairbanks

ALASKA

Anchorage
Valdez

CANADA

Skagway

Gulf of Alaska

Juneau

Kodiak Island

Alexander Archipelago

170°E
55°N
180°
50°N
170°W
160°W
150°W
55°N

0   250   500 Miles
0   250   500 Kilometers
Projection: Albers Equal Area

PACIFIC OCEAN

ALEUTIAN ISLANDS

Attu Island

Amistad Reservoir

Rio Grande

San Antonio

Corpus Christi
Laredo

Padre Island

MEXICO

CANADA

MINNESOTA
Grand Forks
Fargo
Red River
Minnesota River
Duluth
Superior
Marquette
Sault Ste. Marie
Lake Superior
MICHIGAN

WISCONSIN
Minneapolis
St. Paul
Madison
Milwaukee
Green Bay
Grand Rapids
Saginaw
Lansing
Lake Michigan
Lake Huron

Sioux Falls
Sioux City
IOWA
Cedar Rapids
Davenport
Des Moines
Rockford
Chicago
Gary
South Bend
Fort Wayne
Peoria
Mississippi River
Illinois River
Detroit
Ann Arbor
Toledo
Cleveland
Youngstown
Akron
Lake Erie

MAINE
Augusta
Portland
Lake Champlain
Burlington
Montpelier
VT
NH
Concord
Manchester
Boston
Worcester
Providence
Cape Cod
Hudson R.
Connecticut R.
Lake Ontario
Rochester
Syracuse
Albany
Springfield
MA
CT
RI
Hartford
New Haven
Buffalo
NEW YORK
Bridgeport
Jersey City
Newark
Yonkers
New York City
Long Island
Long Island Sound
40°N
70°W

PENNSYLVANIA
Susquehanna River
Allentown
Harrisburg
Philadelphia
Trenton
Camden
NJ
Atlantic City
Pittsburgh

omaha
lincoln
MISSOURI
Kansas City
Kansas City
topeka
St. Louis
East St. Louis
Jefferson City
Lake of the Ozarks
Missouri River
Springfield
ILLINOIS
INDIANA
Indianapolis
Springfield
OHIO
Columbus
Dayton
Cincinnati
WEST VIRGINIA
Charleston
Baltimore
MD
Annapolis
Washington, D.C.
DE
Dover
Delaware Bay
Chesapeake Bay
VIRGINIA
Richmond
Newport News
Norfolk
Virginia Beach
ATLANTIC OCEAN

wichita
eufaula Lake
Keystone Lake
Tulsa
Louisville
Evansville
Frankfort
Lexington
KENTUCKY
Ohio River
Lake Barkley
Kentucky Lake
Kentucky River
Mississippi River

National capital
State capitals
Other cities
0   100   200 Miles
0 100   200 Kilometers
Projection: Albers Equal Area

Cape Hatteras
35°N

Fayetteville
ARKANSAS
Little Rock
Pine Bluff
Lake Texoma
Memphis
Nashville
TENNESSEE
Chattanooga
Knoxville
Asheville
Greensboro
Durham
Raleigh
Winston-Salem
NORTH CAROLINA
Charlotte
Greenville
SOUTH CAROLINA
Columbia

dallas
waco
Shreveport
Red River
Toledo Bend Reservoir
LOUISIANA
Beaumont
Houston
MISSISSIPPI
Vicksburg
Jackson
Meridian
ALABAMA
Birmingham
Huntsville
Montgomery
Columbus
Macon
GEORGIA
Atlanta
Chattahoochee River
Savannah River
Charleston
Savannah
Sea Islands

Baton Rouge
Biloxi
New Orleans
Galveston
Chandeleur Islands
Mobile
Pensacola
Tallahassee
Gainesville
FLORIDA
Jacksonville
30°N

Gulf of Mexico
N W E S
Orlando
Tampa
St. Petersburg
Lake Okeechobee
Cape Canaveral
Fort Myers
Fort Lauderdale
Miami
Cape Sable
Florida Keys
Straits of Florida
BAHAMAS
25°N
75°W
80°W
85°W
90°W
95°W

ATLAS

ARCTIC 80°N OCEAN

Greenland

Beaufort Sea
Victoria Island
Baffin Bay
Baffin Island
Davis Strait
Iceland
Denmark Strait

Bering Strait
Mackenzie River
Great Bear Lake

Yukon River
Great Slave Lake

Hudson Bay

Bering Sea
60°N

Gulf of Alaska
Lake Winnipeg

Aleutian Islands

Vancouver Island
ROCKY MOUNTAINS
Missouri River
Great Lakes
St. Lawrence River

NORTH AMERICA
40°N

ATLANTIC OCEAN

Colorado River
Mississippi
APPALACHIAN MTS.

Strait of Gibraltar

SIERRA MADRE
Rio Grande

Gulf of Mexico
Bahamas

Tropic of Cancer

Hawaiian Islands
20°N

Greater Antilles
Caribbean Sea
Lesser Antilles

Niger

Isthmus of Panama
GUIANA HIGHLANDS

PACIFIC OCEAN

ANDES MOUNTAINS
Amazon River
SOUTH AMERICA

0° Equator

BRAZILIAN

N
W E
S

HIGHLANDS

River

20°S

ATLANTIC OCEAN

Tropic of Capricorn

Paraná

ANDES MOUNTAINS

40°S

Strait of Magellan
Falkland Islands
Tierra del Fuego
Cape Horn

60°S
160°W 140°W 120°W SOUTHERN OCEAN 60°W 40°W 20°W

Antarctic Circle

Weddell Sea

ELEVATION

Feet		Meters
13,120		4,000
6,560		2,000
1,640		500
656		200
(Sea level) 0		0 (Sea level)
Below sea level		Below sea level

Ice cap

0   500   1,000   1,500   2,000 Miles

0   1,000   2,000 Kilometers

Projection: Mollweide

ARCTIC 80°N OCEAN

North Cape
Barents Sea
Kara Sea
Laptev Sea
East Siberian Sea

EUROPE

Yenisei River
Ob River
Lena River
Kolyma River

URAL MOUNTAINS

Volga River

Baltic Sea

ALPS

Lake Baikal

60°N

KAMCHATKA PENINSULA

Sea of Okhotsk

Amur River

Black Sea

Aral Sea

Balqash Lake

Caspian Sea

ALTAY

ASIA

GOBI

Sakhalin Island

Hokkaido

40°N

Mediterranean Sea

Tigris River

Euphrates River

HIMALAYAS

Huang He (Yellow River)

Chang Jiang

Honshu

Shikoku
Kyushu

Persian Gulf

Indus River

Thar Desert

Ganges River

Yangzi River

Mekong River

East China Sea

Taiwan

SAHARA

ARABIAN PENINSULA

Nile River

Red Sea

Arabian Sea

Bay of Bengal

South China Sea

Philippine Islands

Tropic of Cancer

20°N

PACIFIC OCEAN

AFRICA

Congo River

Sri Lanka

Strait of Malacca

MALAY PENINSULA

Lake Tanganyika
Lake Victoria

Sumatra

Borneo

Celebes

New Guinea

Solomon Islands

0° Equator

Java

INDIAN OCEAN

Coral Sea

New Hebrides

Fiji Islands

Madagascar

Mozambique Channel

GREAT SANDY DESERT

New Caledonia

20°S

KALAHARI DESERT

AUSTRALIA

Tropic of Capricorn

GREAT VICTORIA DESERT

GREAT DIVIDING RANGE

Darling River

North Island

Cape of Good Hope

Tasman Sea

NEW ZEALAND

Tasmania

South Island

SOUTHERN OCEAN

20°E 40°E 60°S 120°E 140°E 160°E

ANTARCTICA

Denmark Strait

Iceland

North Cape

KJØLEN MTS.

Barents Sea

Kara Sea

0   250   500 Miles
0   250   500 Kilometers

URAL MTS.

Projection: Mollweide

60°N

North Sea

Baltic Sea

Volga River

British Isles

NORTHERN EUROPEAN PLAIN

50°N

ATLANTIC OCEAN

Bay of Biscay

Rhine River

Danube River

ALPS

Black Sea

40°N

IBERIAN PENINSULA

Strait of Gibraltar

Mediterranean Sea

Crete

World: Political

ATLAS

ARCTIC OCEAN

Greenland
(DENMARK)

ICELAN

60°N

ALASKA
(U.S.)

CANADA

Aleutian Islands

Vancouver   Winnipeg

NORTH
AMERICA

Ottawa   Montreal
Chicago   Toronto
New York City

40°N

UNITED
STATES

Washington,
D.C.

ATLANTIC
OCEAN

Rabat
Casablanca
MOROCC

Los Angeles

Houston

Bermuda
(U.K.)

Western
Sahara
(Claimed by
Morocco)

MEXICO

Tropic of Cancer

20°N

HAWAII
(U.S.)

Mexico
City

MAURITANIA

Nouakchott

CAPE VERDE   SENEGAL
Dakar
GAMBIA
GUINEA-BISSAU   GUINEA

Caracas

PACIFIC
OCEAN

0° Equator

KIRIBATI

Galápagos
Islands
(ECUADOR)

VENEZUELA GUYANA
Georgetown SURINAME
Paramaribo French Guiana
(FRANCE)

Bogotá
COLOMBIA

Quito

SIERRA
LEONE   CÔ
D'IV
LIBERIA

ECUADOR

N

W   E

S

SAMOA

American
Samoa

PERU

Lima

SOUTH
AMERICA

BRAZIL

Brasília

BOLIVIA

20°S

TONGA

La Paz

Sucre

PARAGUAY

Rio de Janeiro

São Paulo

Tropic of Capricorn

CHILE

Asunción

ATLANTIC
OCEAN

⊘ National capital

• Other city

0   500   1,000 Miles

0   500 1,000 Kilometers

Projection: Mollweide

Santiago

URUGUAY
Buenos
Aires   Montevideo

ARGENTINA

40°S

Falkland
Islands
(U.K.)

South
Georgia
(U.K.)

South Sandwich
Islands

60°S

160°W 140°W 120°W

SOUTHERN OCEAN

60°

40°W

20°W

Antarctic Circle

90°W

80°W

70°W

FLORIDA
(U.S.)

Nassau

Tropic of Cancer

60°W

0   200   400 Miles

0   200   400 Kilometers

Projection: Mercator

BAHAMAS

Havana

Turks and Caicos Is.
(U.K.)

ATLANTIC   OCEAN

20°N

Gulf of
Mexico

CUBA

Cayman Is.
(U.K.)

HAITI   DOMINICAN
Port-au-Prince REPUBLIC

Virgin Islands
(U.S. and U.K.)

1

MEXICO

BELIZE
Belmopan

JAMAICA
Kingston

Santo
Domingo

Puerto Rico
(U.S.)

2   Guadeloupe (FRANCE)

GUATEMALA
Guatemala City

HONDURAS
Tegucigalpa

Caribbean Sea

Netherlands
Antilles
(NETHERLANDS)

3

Martinique (FRANCE)

4

San Salvador
EL SALVADOR

NICARAGUA
Managua

Aruba
(NETHERLANDS)

5   6

7

Port-of-
Spain

TRINIDAD AND
TOBAGO

N

W   E

S

COSTA RICA

San José

Panama
City

PANAMA

VENEZUELA

10°N

PACIFIC   OCEAN

COLOMBIA

GUYANA

COUNTRY	CAPITAL
1 Antigua and Barbuda	St. Johns
2 St. Kitts and Nevis	Basseterre
3 Dominica	Roseau
4 St. Lucia	Castries
5 St. Vincent and the Grenadines	Kingstown
6 Barbados	Bridgetown
7 Grenada	St. George's

ARCTIC OCEAN

EUROPE

RUSSIA

Moscow

Astana

KAZAKHSTAN

ASIA

MONGOLIA
Ulaanbaatar

Harbin

60°N

GEORGIA
UZBEKISTAN
Almaty
KYRGYZSTAN
Tashkent
TURKMENISTAN
TAJIKISTAN
Ashgabat

NORTH
KOREA
Beijing
Tianjin
Pyongyang
Seoul
SOUTH
KOREA

JAPAN
Nagoya Tokyo
Yokohama
Osaka

40°N

Istanbul
Ankara ARMENIA
AZERBAIJAN
Baku

CHINA
Wuhan

Chongqing

Shanghai

Tunis
Nicosia
TURKEY
CYPRUS
SYRIA
Damascus
Beirut
IRAN
Tehran
Kabul
Islamabad

Tripoli
TUNISIA
LEBANON
Jerusalem
Baghdad
AFGHANISTAN
ISRAEL
JORDAN
Ammam
IRAQ
KUWAIT
BAHRAIN
PAKISTAN

Delhi
NEPAL
Kathmandu
BHUTAN

Guangzhou

Taipei
TAIWAN

Hong
Kong

Cairo

ERIA
EGYPT
SAUDI
ARABIA
QATAR
Riyadh
OMAN

New
Delhi
Karachi

BANGLADESH
Dhaka
Calcutta

MYANMAR
(BURMA)
LAOS
Hanoi

Northern
Mariana
(U.S.)

Tropic of Cancer
20°N

AFRICA

UNITED ARAB
EMIRATES

OMAN
Muscat

INDIA

Mumbai
(Bombay)

Chennai
(Madras)

Yangon
(Rangoon)

THAILAND
Bangkok

VIETNAM
CAMBODIA
Phnom Penh

Manila

PHILIPPINES

Guam (U.S.)

PACIFIC
OCEAN

MARSHALL
ISLANDS

NIGER
CHAD
Khartoum
ERITREA
Asmara
YEMEN
Sanaa

iamey
N'Djamena

NIGERIA
SUDAN
DJIBOUTI

Addis Ababa

SRI
LANKA
Colombo

Ho Chi
Minh City
BRUNEI

Kuala
Lumpur
MALAYSIA

PALAU

FEDERATED STATES
OF MICRONESIA

Abuja
JIN
Lagos

CENTRAL
AFRICAN
REPUBLIC
CAMEROON
ETHIOPIA

MALDIVES

Singapore
SINGAPORE

INDONESIA

NAURU
KIRIBATI

0° Equator

TORIAL
A
GABON
DEMOCRATIC
REPUBLIC
OF THE
CONGO
UGANDA
KENYA

SOMALIA

TOMÉ
ND
ICIPE
REP.
OF THE
CONGO
RWANDA
BURUNDI
Nairobi

Jakarta
Surabaya

PAPUA
NEW
GUINEA

SOLOMON
ISLANDS

TUVALU

Cabinda
(ANGOLA)
Kinshasa
TANZANIA
Dodoma
Dar es Salaam
SEYCHELLES

Luanda

INDIAN OCEAN

Port Moresby

TIMOR-LESTE

ANGOLA
MALAWI
COMOROS

VANUATU

FIJI

ZAMBIA
Lusaka
MOZAMBIQUE
MADAGASCAR
Antananarivo

New Caledonia
(FRANCE)

20°S

NAMIBIA
ZIMBABWE
Harare

MAURITIUS

AUSTRALIA

Windhoek
BOTSWANA
Gaborone
Pretoria
Réunion
(FRANCE)

Tropic of Capricorn

Johannesburg
Maputo
SWAZILAND

Bloemfontein
LESOTHO

SOUTH
AFRICA

Cape Town

Sydney
Canberra

NEW
ZEALAND

Melbourne

Tasmania

Wellington

60°S

SOUTHERN OCEAN
100°E
120°E
140°E
160°E

20°E
40°E

ANTARCTICA

Inset map (Europe)

0   250   500 Miles
0   250   500 Kilometers

Projection: Mollweide

Arctic
Circle

ICELAND
Reykjavik

SWEDEN
FINLAND
Helsinki

St. Petersburg

RUSSIA

NORWAY
Oslo
Stockholm
11

60°N

North
Sea
DENMARK
Copenhagen
10
9
Minsk
Moscow

UNITED
KINGDOM
NETHERLANDS
Amsterdam
Berlin
Warsaw
BELARUS

Dublin
IRELAND
London
BELGIUM
Brussels
GERMANY
POLAND
UKRAINE

50°N
Paris
LUXEMBOURG
1
Vienna
2
Budapest
MOLDOVA
Chis'ina'u

ATLANTIC
OCEAN
SWITZERLAND
Bern
LIECHTENSTEIN
AUSTRIA
3
HUNGARY
ROMANIA
Bucharest

FRANCE
4
5
7
MONACO
ITALY
SAN MARINO
12
BULGARIA

Corsica
(FRANCE)
Rome
Sofia
Black Sea

ANDORRA
VATICAN CITY
6
Tirane
ALBANIA

PORTUGAL
SPAIN
Madrid
Balearic
Is.
(SPAIN)
Sardinia
(ITALY)
GREECE

Lisbon

Mediterranean
Sea
Athens

Gibraltar (U.K.)
Sicily
Crete

MALTA

Country / Capital list

	COUNTRY	CAPITAL
1	Czech Republic	Prague
2	Slovakia	Bratislava
3	Slovenia	Ljubljana
4	Croatia	Zagreb
5	Bosnia and Herzegovina	Sarajevo
6	Macedonia	Skopje
7	Serbia	Belgrade
8	Montenegro	Podgorica
9	Lithuania	Vilnius
10	Latvia	Riga
11	Estonia	Tallinn
12	Kosovo	Pristina

ATLAS

North America: Physical

ASIA

ARCTIC OCEAN

North Pole

EUROPE

POLAR ICE PACK

St. Lawrence Island

Bering Sea

Nunivak Island

Kodiak Island

Gulf of Alaska

ALASKA RANGE

Mt. McKinley 20,320 ft. (6,194 m)

BROOKS RANGE

Yukon River

Bering Strait

Beaufort Sea

Banks Island

Queen Elizabeth Islands

Victoria Island

Ellesmere Island

Baffin Bay

Greenland

Cape Farewell

Denmark Strait

Davis Strait

YUKON PLATEAU

Alexander Archipelago

Queen Charlotte Islands

Vancouver Island

Great Bear Lake

Mackenzie River

Great Slave Lake

Lake Athabasca

Peace River

Athabasca River

Baffin Island

Hudson Strait

Southampton Island

Coats Island

Mansel Island

Hudson Bay

Labrador Sea

PACIFIC OCEAN

Cape Mendocino

Mount Rainier 14,410 ft (4,392 m)

CASCADE RANGE

Columbia River

Snake River

COAST RANGES

SIERRA NEVADA

CENTRAL VALLEY

DEATH VALLEY

GREAT BASIN

Great Salt Lake

COLORADO PLATEAU

Mount Whitney 14,494 ft (4,419 m)

Colorado River

Gila River

R O C K Y

G R E A T

M O U N T A I N S

Nelson River

Saskatchewan River

Lake Winnipeg

C A N A D I A N

S H I E L D

Lake Superior

Lake Michigan

Lake Huron

Lake Erie

Lake Ontario

St. Lawrence River

Anticosti Island

Prince Edward Island

Gulf of St. Lawrence

Newfoundland

Cape Breton Island

Cape Cod

Long Island

ATLANTIC OCEAN

G R E A T   P L A I N S

BLACK HILLS

Missouri River

Mississippi River

Platte River

INTERIOR PLAINS

OZARK PLATEAU

Ohio River

Cumberland R.

Tennessee River

Arkansas River

Red River

APPALACHIAN MOUNTAINS

PIEDMONT

ATLANTIC COASTAL PLAIN

Cape Hatteras

Bermuda

Rio Grande

Brazos River

SIERRA MADRE OCCIDENTAL

SIERRA MADRE ORIENTAL

Gulf of California

BAJA CALIFORNIA

Guadalupe Island

GULF COASTAL PLAIN

FLORIDA PENINSULA

Cape Canaveral

Florida Keys

Straits of Florida

Bahamas

Tropic of Cancer

Popocatépetl 17,887 ft (5,452 m)

YUCATÁN PENINSULA

Gulf of Mexico

Cuba

Greater Antilles

Jamaica

Hispaniola

Puerto Rico

Lesser Antilles

Trinidad

Caribbean Sea

SIERRA MADRE DEL SUR

Lake Nicaragua

CENTRAL AMERICA

ISTHMUS OF PANAMA

SOUTH AMERICA

0° Equator

ELEVATION

Feet		Meters
13,120		4,000
6,560		2,000
1,640		500
656		200
(Sea level) 0		0 (Sea level)
Below sea level		Below sea level

Ice cap

0   300   600 Miles

0   300   600 Kilometers

Projection: Azimuthal Equal Area

North America: Political

ASIA

ARCTIC OCEAN

+ North Pole

EUROPE

ICELAND

Greenland
(DENMARK)

Arctic Circle

Denmark Strait

Point
Barrow

St.
Lawrence
Island

Bering
Sea

Nunivak
Island

Beaufort
Sea

Banks
Island

Queen
Elizabeth
Islands

Ellesmere Island

Baffin
Bay

Cape
Farewell

ALASKA
(U.S.)

Anchorage

Gulf of
Alaska

Kodiak
Island

Victoria
Island

Great
Bear
Lake

Baffin Island

Davis Strait

Labrador
Sea

Alexander
Archipelago

Juneau

Queen
Charlotte
Islands

Great
Slave
Lake

Southampton
Island

Hudson Strait

Coats
Island

Mansel
Island

Hudson
Bay

CANADA

Newfoundland

Anticosti
Island

PACIFIC
OCEAN

Vancouver
Island

Edmonton

Calgary

Vancouver

Seattle

Portland

Winnipeg

Lake
Winnipeg

Lake
Superior

Lake
Michigan

Lake
Huron

Quebec

Montreal

Prince
Edward
Island

Gulf of
St. Lawrence

St. Pierre and
Miquelon (FRANCE)

Cape
Breton
Island

San Francisco

San
Jose

Great
Salt
Lake

Salt Lake
City

Minneapolis

Milwaukee

Chicago

Detroit

Ottawa

Toronto

Lake
Ontario

Lake Erie

Cleveland

Columbus

Boston

Cape Cod

New York City

Philadelphia

Baltimore

Washington, D.C.

ATLANTIC
OCEAN

UNITED STATES

Denver

Kansas City

Indianapolis

St. Louis

Norfolk

Los Angeles

San Diego

Tijuana

Phoenix

Memphis

Atlanta

Birmingham

Bermuda
(U.K.)

Dallas

Jacksonville

Tropic of Cancer

Austin

San
Antonio

Houston

New Orleans

Miami

BAHAMAS

Turks and Caicos
Islands (U.K.)

Monterrey

Gulf of
Mexico

Florida
Keys

Nassau

Straits of
Florida

DOMINICAN
REPUBLIC

Puerto Rico (U.S.)

San
Juan

ST. KITTS & NEVIS

ANTIGUA &
BARBUDA

Guadeloupe
(FRANCE)

MEXICO

Havana

CUBA

HAITI

Santo
Domingo

Virgin Is.
(U.S., U.K.)

DOMINICA

BARBADOS

Guadalajara

Mexico
City

Puebla

Mérida

Cayman Is.
(U.K.)

Kingston

JAMAICA

Port-au-
Prince

Martinique (FRANCE)

ST. LUCIA

ST. VINCENT AND
THE GRENADINES

GRENADA

Gulf of
California

Belmopan

BELIZE

Caribbean Sea

Netherlands
Antilles
(NETHERLANDS)

GUATEMALA

Guatemala City

San Salvador

EL SALVADOR

HONDURAS

Tegucigalpa

NICARAGUA

Managua

Aruba (NETHERLANDS)

TRINIDAD AND TOBAGO

Panama
Canal

San José

COSTA
RICA

PANAMA

Panama City

SOUTH
AMERICA

✪ National capital

● Other city

| 0 | 300 | 600 Miles |
| 0 | 300 | 600 Kilometers |

Projection: Azimuthal Equal-Area

0° Equator

ATLAS

CENTRAL
AMERICA

Caribbean Sea

Panama
Canal

Gulf
of
Panama

Malpelo
Island

Margarita
Island

Tobago

Trinidad

Orinoco River
Delta

Lake
Maracaibo

LLANOS

Meta
River

Orinoco River

Angel Falls

GUIANA

HIGHLANDS

Devil's Island

Cape Orange

ATLANTIC
OCEAN

Cauca River

Magdalena River

Mount Tolima
18,425 ft
(5,616 m)

Caquetá River

Orinoco River

Japurá
River

Rio Negro

Amazon River

Amazon
River Delta

Galápagos
Islands

Gulf of Guayaquil

Mount Chimborazo
20,561 ft
(6,267 m)

Marañón River

Amazon River

Juruá River

AMAZON

BASIN

Tapajós River

Xingu River

Tocantins River

Parnaíba River

BRAZILIAN

HIGHLANDS

PACIFIC
OCEAN

ANDES

Mount Huascarán
22,205 ft
(6,768 m)

Ucayali River

Purus River

Madeira River

MATO GROSSO

PLATEAU

Araguaia River

São Francisco River

Beni River

Mamoré River

Lake
Titicaca

Ancohuma Peak
20,958 ft
(6,388 m)

ATACAMA DESERT

Lake
Poopó

Pilcomayo River

CHACO

Paraguay River

BRAZILIAN
PLATEAU

San Félix Island

San Ambrosio
Island

Tropic of Capricorn

Salado River

Paraná River

Uruguay River

Juan Fernández
Islands

Mount Aconcagua
22,834 ft
(6,960 m)

ANDES

PAMPAS

Salado River

Rio de la Plata

ATLANTIC
OCEAN

Colorado River

ELEVATION

Feet		Meters
13,120		4,000
6,560		2,000
1,640		500
656		200
(Sea level) 0		0 (Sea level)
Below
sea level		Below
sea level

0   250   500 Miles

0   250   500 Kilometers

Projection: Azimuthal Equal Area

Gulf of San Matías

PATAGONIA

Chiloé
Island

Chonos
Archipelago

Gulf of
San Jorge

Cape Tres Puntas

Bahía
Grande

Strait of
Magellan

Tierra del
Fuego

Falkland
Islands

South
Georgia
Islands

Cape Horn

CENTRAL
AMERICA

Caribbean Sea

Barranquilla
Cartagena
Caracas
Lake
Maracaibo
VENEZUELA

Georgetown
Paramaribo
GUYANA
Cayenne
SURINAME
French
Guiana
(FRANCE)

ATLANTIC
OCEAN

Medellín
Bogotá
COLOMBIA
Cali

Malpelo
Island
(COLOMBIA)

Quito
ECUADOR
Guayaquil

0° Equator

Galápagos
Islands
(ECUADOR)

Belém

0° Equator

PERU

Trujillo

BRAZIL

Recife

Callao
Lima

PACIFIC
OCEAN

Lake
Titicaca
La Paz
Lake
Poopó
BOLIVIA
Sucre

Brasília

Salvador

Arequipa

Belo Horizonte

PARAGUAY

Asunción

Campinas
São Paulo
Rio de Janeiro
Curitiba

Tropic of Capricorn
San Ambrosio
Island
(CHILE)
San Félix Island
(CHILE)

CHILE

Pôrto Alegre

Juan Fernández
Islands
(CHILE)

Córdoba

Valparaíso
Santiago

Rosario
URUGUAY

Tropic of
Capricorn

ATLANTIC
OCEAN

Buenos Aires
Montevideo

ARGENTINA

National capital
Other city

0   250   500 Miles
0   250   500 Kilometers

Projection: Azimuthal Equal-Area

Strait of
Magellan
Falkland
Islands (U.K.)

Tierra del
Fuego

South Georgia
Island
(U.K.)

ATLAS

Europe: Physical

ELEVATION

Feet	Meters
13,120	4,000
6,560	2,000
1,640	500
656	200
(Sea level) 0	0 (Sea level)
Below sea level	Below sea level

Ice cap

0 ___ 150 ___ 300 Miles
0 ___ 150 ___ 300 Kilometers

Projection: Azimuthal Equal Area

ASIA

SOUTHWEST ASIA

AFRICA

URAL MOUNTAINS

Ural River

Pechora River

Dvina River

North Dvina River

Caspian Sea

Mt. Elbrus 18,510 ft (5,642 m)

CAUCASUS MTS.

Sea of Azov

Volga River

Don River

Dnipro River

Rybinsk Reservoir

Lake Onega

Lake Ladoga

KOLA PENINSULA

White Sea

Barents Sea

NORTHERN EUROPEAN PLAIN

CRIMEAN PENINSULA

Black Sea

Dnistro River

Dnister River

TRANSYLVANIAN ALPS

CARPATHIAN

BALKAN PENINSULA

Danube River

Sea of Marmara

Aegean Sea

Rhodes

Crete

Vistula River

Oder River

Elbe River

BALTIC PLAINS

Lake Vättern

Lake Vänern

Gulf of Finland

Gulf of Bothnia

Baltic Sea

Daugava R.

DINARIC ALPS

Adriatic Sea

APENNINES

Tiber River

Tyrrhenian Sea

Sicily

Malta

Mediterranean Sea

Corsica

Sardinia

Balearic Islands

North Cape

North Cape

ARCTIC OCEAN

KJÖLEN MOUNTAINS

Norwegian Sea

Kattegat

Skagerrak

North Sea

Shetland Islands

Orkney Islands

Faeroe Islands

Hebrides

British Isles

Irish Sea

PENNINES

Thames River

English Channel

Seine River

Loire River

Garonne River

Rhône River

Po River

ALPS

Mont Blanc 15,781 ft (4,810 m)

Lake Geneva

PYRENEES

Bay of Biscay

Cape Finisterre

ATLANTIC OCEAN

IBERIAN PENINSULA

Ebro River

Tagus River

Duero River

Guadiana River

Guadalquivir River

Strait of Gibraltar

Iceland

Arctic Circle

Rhine River

Danube River

Arctic Circle

Europe: Political

ASIA

URAL MOUNTAINS

RUSSIA

Nizhny Novgorod

Moscow ✪

SOUTHWEST ASIA

Caspian Sea

Black Sea

30°E

St. Petersburg

White Sea

Barents Sea

North Cape

FINLAND

Helsinki ✪

Gulf of Finland

ESTONIA ✪ Tallinn

LATVIA ✪ Riga

LITHUANIA ✪ Vilnius

RUSSIA

BELARUS ✪ Minsk

UKRAINE ✪ Kiev

MOLDOVA ✪ Chişinău

ROMANIA ✪ Bucharest

Belgrade

Sofia ✪ **BULGARIA**

KOSOVO ✪ Skopje

Pristina ✪ **MACEDONIA**

Tirana ✪ **ALBANIA**

GREECE ✪ Athens

Aegean Sea

Rhodes

Crete

ARCTIC OCEAN

40°E

30°E

Gulf of Bothnia

SWEDEN

Stockholm ✪

Göteborg

NORWAY

Oslo ✪

Bergen

Baltic Sea

POLAND ✪ Warsaw

Kraków ✪

SLOVAKIA ✪ Bratislava

CZECH REPUBLIC ✪ Prague

Berlin ✪

Dresden ✪

GERMANY

HUNGARY ✪ Budapest

Vienna ✪ **AUSTRIA**

SLOVENIA ✪ Ljubljana

Zagreb ✪ **CROATIA**

BOSNIA AND HERZEGOVINA ✪ Sarajevo

SERBIA

MONTENEGRO ✪ Podgorica

Adriatic Sea

DENMARK ✪ Copenhagen

Hamburg ✪

Munich ✪

SAN MARINO ✪ San Marino

ITALY ✪ Rome

Naples ✪

VATICAN CITY

Sicily

MALTA ✪ Valletta

Mediterranean Sea

ICELAND ✪ Reykjavík

Faeroe Islands (DENMARK)

Shetland Islands

SCOTLAND Edinburgh ✪

NORTHERN IRELAND Belfast ✪

IRELAND ✪ Dublin

WALES

ENGLAND ✪ London

UNITED KINGDOM

British Isles

Liverpool ✪

Channel Islands (U.K.)

English Channel

North Sea

THE NETHERLANDS ✪ Amsterdam

Cologne ✪ Bonn ✪

BELGIUM ✪ Brussels

LUXEMBOURG ✪ Luxembourg

Paris ✪

FRANCE

Lyon ✪

Lake Geneva

Bern ✪ **SWITZERLAND**

LIECHTENSTEIN ✪ Vaduz

Milan ✪

MONACO ✪ Monaco

Marseille ✪

Corsica (FRANCE)

Sardinia (ITALY)

PYRENEES

ANDORRA ✪ Andorra la Vella

Barcelona ✪

Balearic Islands (SPAIN)

Bay of Biscay

SPAIN ✪ Madrid

Valencia ✪

Seville ✪

Gibraltar (U.K.)

Strait of Gibraltar

PORTUGAL ✪ Lisbon

AFRICA

ATLANTIC OCEAN

Arctic Circle

70°N

60°N

50°N

10°W

20°W

30°W

0°

10°E

20°E

Legend

✪ National capital

● Other city

| 0 | 150 | 300 Miles |
| 0 | 150 | 300 Kilometers |

Projection: Azimuthal Equal-Area

Asia: Physical

ELEVATION

Feet	Meters
13,120	4,000
6,560	2,000
1,640	500
656	200
(Sea level) 0	0 (Sea level)
Below sea level	Below sea level

Ice cap

0 250 500 750 Kilometers
0 250 500 750 Miles

Projection: Two-Point Equidistant

EUROPE

AFRICA

AUSTRALIA

PACIFIC OCEAN

INDIAN OCEAN

Arctic Circle

North Pole

North Land

Wrangel Island

New Siberian Islands

Franz Josef Land

Novaya Zemlya

Barents Sea

Kara Sea

Aleutian Islands

KAMCHATKA PENINSULA

CENTRAL RANGE

Bering Sea

Sea of Okhotsk

KOLYMA MTS.

CHERSKIY RANGE

VERKHOYANSKIY RANGE

STANOVOY MOUNTAINS

YABLONOVY RANGE

Kuril Islands

Sakhalin Island

Hokkaido

Honshu

Shikoku

Kyushu

Sea of Japan (East Sea)

Korea Strait

Ryukyu Islands

Okinawa

Taiwan

East China Sea

Yellow Sea

NORTH CHINA PLAIN

QIN LING

GREATER KHINGAN RANGE

MONGOLIAN PLATEAU

GOBI

Huang He (Yellow River)

Chang Jiang (Yangtze) River

BOHEA HILLS

South China Sea

Hainan

Luzon Strait

Luzon

Philippines

Mindanao

Celebes Sea

Celebes

Molucca Islands

Banda Sea

Arafura Sea

MAOKE MOUNTAINS

New Guinea

Borneo

Java Sea

Java

Sumatra

Bangka

MALAY PENINSULA

Gulf of Thailand

INDOCHINA PENINSULA

Chao Phraya River

Mekong River

Red River

Gulf of Tonkin

Irrawaddy River

Andaman Sea

Andaman Islands

Nicobar Islands

Mentawai Islands

Bay of Bengal

EASTERN GHATS

WESTERN GHATS

DECCAN PLATEAU

Godavari River

Ganges River

INDO-GANGETIC PLAIN

Brahmaputra River

Sri Lanka

Maldives

Lakshadweep Islands

Socotra Island

Gulf of Aden

Red Sea

Arabian Sea

Gulf of Oman

Persian Gulf

Strait of Hormuz

RUB' AL-KHALI

AN-NAFUD

SYRIAN DESERT

SINAI PENINSULA

Mediterranean Sea

Cyprus

ANATOLIAN PLATEAU

Mount Ararat 16,945 ft (5,165 m)

Bosporus

Black Sea

CAUCASUS MTS.

Tigris River

Euphrates River

ZAGROS MTS.

GREAT SALT DESERT

Caspian Sea

URAL MOUNTAINS

WEST SIBERIAN PLAIN

Ob River

Irtysh River

Ural River

Aral Sea

Syr Darya

Amu Darya

TURAN LOWLAND

USTYURT PLATEAU

KYZYL KUM

KARA KUM

KAZAKH UPLANDS

Balqash Lake

TIAN SHAN

TARIM BASIN

TAKLIMAKAN DESERT

KUNLUN MOUNTAINS

HINDU KUSH

PLATEAU OF TIBET

Nu River

Mount Everest 29,035 ft (8,850 m)

HIMALAYAS

THAR DESERT

Indus River

Sutlej River

ALTAY MOUNTAINS

SAYAN MOUNTAINS

S I B E R I A

CENTRAL SIBERIAN PLATEAU

Lower Tunguska River

Angara River

Yenisey River

Lake Baykal

Shilka River

Amur River

Lena River

Aldan River

TAYMYR PENINSULA

Tropic of Cancer

Equator

Asia: Political

Map Labels

Oceans and Seas:
PACIFIC OCEAN, INDIAN OCEAN, Bering Sea, Sea of Okhotsk, Yellow Sea, East China Sea, South China Sea, Celebes Sea, Java Sea, Arafura Sea, Andaman Sea, Bay of Bengal, Arabian Sea, Caspian Sea, Aral Sea, Black Sea, Mediterranean Sea, Red Sea, Gulf of Aden, Persian Gulf, Barents Sea, Kara Sea, Gulf of Thailand, Luzon Strait

Continents/Regions:
EUROPE, AFRICA, AUSTRALIA, RUSSIA, CHINA, MONGOLIA, INDIA, KAZAKHSTAN, IRAN, SAUDI ARABIA

Countries:
RUSSIA, JAPAN, NORTH KOREA, SOUTH KOREA, TAIWAN, CHINA, MONGOLIA, VIETNAM, LAOS, THAILAND, CAMBODIA, MYANMAR (BURMA), PHILIPPINES, MALAYSIA, BRUNEI, INDONESIA, TIMOR-LESTE, BANGLADESH, BHUTAN, NEPAL, INDIA, SRI LANKA, MALDIVES, PAKISTAN, AFGHANISTAN, KAZAKHSTAN, UZBEKISTAN, KYRGYZSTAN, TAJIKISTAN, TURKMENISTAN, IRAN, IRAQ, KUWAIT, BAHRAIN, QATAR, UNITED ARAB EMIRATES, OMAN, YEMEN, SAUDI ARABIA, JORDAN, ISRAEL, LEBANON, SYRIA, CYPRUS, TURKEY, GEORGIA, ARMENIA, AZERBAIJAN

Cities:
Moscow, Yekaterinburg, Chelyabinsk, Omsk, Novosibirsk, Yakutsk, Irkutsk, Vladivostok, Sapporo, Tokyo, Yokohama, Kyoto, Osaka, Hiroshima, Pusan, Seoul, Pyongyang, Fushun, Harbin, Dalian, Beijing, Qingdao, Nanjing, Shanghai, Wuhan, Chongqing, Chengdu, Guangzhou, Hong Kong, Macao, Taipei, Manila, Hanoi, Vientiane, Bangkok, Phnom Penh, Ho Chi Minh City, Bandar Seri Begawan, Kuala Lumpur, Singapore, Medan, Jakarta, Bandung, Surabaya, Ujung Pandang, Dili, Mandalay, Yangon (Rangoon), Dhaka, Thimphu, Kathmandu, Delhi, New Delhi, Jaipur, Ahmadabad, Mumbai (Bombay), Bangalore, Chennai (Madras), Kolkata (Calcutta), Colombo, Male, Karachi, Lahore, Islamabad, Kabul, Ashgabat, Dushanbe, Tashkent, Bishkek, Almaty, Astana, Tehran, Shiraz, Baghdad, Mosul, Basra, Kuwait City, Manama, Doha, Abu Dhabi, Masqat (Muscat), Riyadh, Mecca, Jidda, Sanaa, Amman, Jerusalem, Tel Aviv, Beirut, Damascus, Nicosia, Ankara, Izmir, Istanbul, Tbilisi, Yerevan, Baku

Physical Features:
North Pole, Arctic Circle, Tropic of Cancer, Equator, URAL MOUNTAINS, Lake Baykal, Lake Balkhash, Ulaanbaatar, Sakhalin, Kuril Islands (RUSSIA), Ryukyu Islands (JAPAN), Aleutian Islands, Hainan (CHINA), New Guinea, Andaman Islands (INDIA), Nicobar Islands (INDIA), Lakshadweep Islands (INDIA), Socotra (YEMEN)

Legend

- ⬥ National capitals
- • Other cities

```
0   250   500   750 Miles
0   250   500   750 Kilometers
```

Projection: Two-Point Equidistant

Africa: Physical

EUROPE

SOUTHWEST ASIA

Mediterranean Sea

Azores

Madeira Islands

Strait of Gibraltar

Gulf of Sidra

Suez Canal

QATTARA DEPRESSION

Canary Islands

ATLAS MOUNTAINS

Tropic of Cancer

S A H A R A

LIBYAN DESERT

Nile River

Lake Nasser

Red Sea

Persian Gulf

Cape Blanc

EL DJOUF

AHAGGAR MOUNTAINS

AIR MTS.

TIBESTI MOUNTAINS

NUBIAN DESERT

Cape Verde Islands

Senegal R.

Niger River

S A H E L

Lake Chad

CHAD BASIN

Blue Nile

Lake Tana

Gulf of Aden

Cape Verde

S U D A N

White Nile

FOUTA DJALLON

Black Volta R.
White Volta R.

Benue River

Lake Volta

SUDAN BASIN

ETHIOPIAN HIGHLANDS

HORN OF AFRICA

SOMALI PENINSULA

Cape Palmas

Gulf of Guinea

ADAMAWA MTS.

Ubangi River

Lake Turkana

Mount Kenya 17,058 ft ▲ (5,199 m)

Equator

Cape Lopez

Congo River

CONGO BASIN

Lake Albert

Lake Edward

RIFT VALLEY

Lake Victoria

Mount Kilimanjaro 19,340 ft ▲ (5,895 m)

INDIAN OCEAN

Kasai River

Lake Kivu

SERENGETI PLAIN

MASAI STEPPE

Seychelles

Ascension

N W E S

MITUMBA MOUNTAINS

WESTERN RIFT VALLEY

EASTERN RIFT VALLEY

Lake Tanganyika

Lake Rukwa

Zanzibar

ATLANTIC OCEAN

Cuanza River

Lake Mweru

Lake Malawi (Nyasa)

Cape Delgado

Comoro Islands

Lake Kariba

Zambezi River

Madagascar

Okavango Delta

Victoria Falls

Mauritius

NAMIB DESERT

KALAHARI BASIN

Impopo River

Réunion

Tropic of Capricorn

KALAHARI DESERT

Mozambique Channel

Orange River

Vaal River

GREAT KARROO

DRAKENSBERG MOUNTAINS

Cape of Good Hope

ELEVATION

Feet	Meters
13,120	4,000
6,560	2,000
1,640	500
656	200
(Sea level) 0	0 (Sea level)
Below sea level	Below sea level

0   250   500 Miles

0   250   500 Kilometers

Projection: Azimuthal Equal-Area

ATLAS

EUROPE

SOUTHWEST ASIA

Mediterranean Sea

Strait of Gibraltar

Azores (PORTUGAL)

Madeira (PORTUGAL)

Canary Islands (SPAIN)

Casablanca · Rabat
Algiers ✪ · Tunis ✪

MOROCCO

TUNISIA · Tripoli ✪

El Aaiún

WESTERN SAHARA (Claimed by Morocco)

Tropic of Cancer

ALGERIA

LIBYA

Alexandria ·

EGYPT

Giza · Cairo ✪

Red Sea

Gulf of Aden

MAURITANIA

Nouakchott ✪

MALI

CAPE VERDE

· Praia ✪

SENEGAL

Dakar ✪

GAMBIA

Banjul ✪

Bissau ✪

GUINEA-BISSAU

GUINEA

Conakry ✪

Freetown ✪

SIERRA LEONE

Monrovia ✪

LIBERIA

Bamako ✪

BURKINA FASO

Ouagadougou ✪

NIGER

Niamey ✪

CHAD

NIGERIA

Abuja ✪

CÔTE D'IVOIRE

Yamoussoukro ✪

GHANA

Abidjan ·

Accra ✪

Lomé ✪

TOGO

BENIN

Porto-Novo ✪

Lagos ·

Lake Chad

N'Djamena ✪

Khartoum ✪

SUDAN

ERITREA

Asmara ✪

DJIBOUTI

Djibouti ✪

ETHIOPIA

Addis Ababa ✪

Gulf of Guinea

CAMEROON

Malabo ✪

Yaoundé ✪

EQUATORIAL GUINEA

SÃO TOMÉ AND PRÍNCIPE

São Tomé ✪

GABON

Libreville ✪

REPUBLIC OF THE CONGO

Brazzaville ✪

CABINDA (ANGOLA)

CENTRAL AFRICAN REPUBLIC

Bangui ✪

Kisangani ·

DEMOCRATIC REPUBLIC OF THE CONGO

Bujumbura ✪

Kinshasa ✪

UGANDA

Kampala ✪

RWANDA

Kigali ✪

BURUNDI

KENYA

Nairobi ✪

Lake Victoria

SOMALIA

· Mogadishu

0° Equator

INDIAN OCEAN

TANZANIA

Dodoma ✪

Lake Tanganyika

· Mombasa
· Pemba
Zanzibar
Dar es Salaam ✪

Lake Malawi (Nyasa)

SEYCHELLES

Victoria ✪

Luanda ✪

ATLANTIC OCEAN

St. Helena (U.K.)

ANGOLA

· Lubumbashi

ZAMBIA

Lusaka ✪

MALAWI

Lilongwe ✪

COMOROS

Moroni ✪

MOZAMBIQUE

Harare ✪

ZIMBABWE

· Bulawayo

Antananarivo ✪

MAURITIUS

Port Louis ✪

MADAGASCAR

Réunion (FRANCE)

Tropic of Capricorn

NAMIBIA

Windhoek ✪

BOTSWANA

Gaborone ✪

Pretoria ✪

Maputo ✪

Johannesburg ·

Mbabane ✪

SWAZILAND

Bloemfontein ·

Maseru ✪

LESOTHO

SOUTH AFRICA

Cape Town ·

N · W · E · S

Legend

✪ National capital

· Other city

0 — 250 — 500 Miles

0 — 250 — 500 Kilometers

Projection: Azimuthal Equal-Area

The Pacific: Political

ASIA

NORTH AMERICA

ATLAS

NORTH PACIFIC OCEAN

SOUTH PACIFIC OCEAN

AUSTRALIA

NEW ZEALAND

PAPUA NEW GUINEA

PALAU

SOLOMON ISLANDS

NAURU

TUVALU

FIJI

VANUATU

SAMOA

TONGA

KIRIBATI

MARSHALL ISLANDS

FEDERATED STATES OF MICRONESIA

MICRONESIA

MELANESIA

POLYNESIA

Tropic of Cancer

Tropic of Capricorn

0° Equator

International Date Line

Philippine Sea

South China Sea

Timor Sea

Arafura Sea

Coral Sea

Tasman Sea

Bismarck Archipelago

New Guinea

INDIAN OCEAN

Legend:
- ✪ National capital
- • Other city

Projection: Azimuthal Equal-Area

1,000 Miles
1,000 Kilometers
500
500
0
0

Cities and places:
Midway Island (U.S.)
Johnston Island (U.S.)
Hawaiian Islands
Hawaii (U.S.)
Wake Island (U.S.)
Bonin Islands (JAPAN)
Volcano Islands (JAPAN)
Northern Marianas (U.S.)
Guam (U.S.)
Agana
Truk Is.
Eniwetok I.
Kwajalein Island
Majuro
Palikir
Tarawa
Gilbert Islands
Koror
Port Moresby
Honiara
Guadalcanal I.
Espiritu Santo I.
Malekula I.
Vila
New Caledonia (FRANCE)
Loyalty Islands (FRANCE)
Noumea
Norfolk Island (AUSTRALIA)
Kermadec Islands (N.Z.)
North Island
South Island
Auckland
Wellington
Christchurch
Chatham Islands (N.Z.)
Bounty Islands (N.Z.)
Auckland Islands (NEW ZEALAND)
Kingman Reef
Palmyra Island (U.S.)
Washington Island
Fanning Island
Howland I. (U.S.)
Baker I. (U.S.)
Jarvis I.
McKean I.
Gardner
Phoenix Islands
Funafuti
Wallis & Futuna (FR.)
Suva
Tokelau (N.Z.)
American Samoa
Pago Pago
Apia
Nuku'alofa
Niue (N.Z.)
Starbuck Island
Manihiki Island
Cook Islands (NEW ZEALAND)
Rarotonga Island
Society Islands (FRANCE)
Papeete
Tahiti (FRANCE)
French Polynesia
Marquesas Islands (FRANCE)
Tuamotu Archipelago (FRANCE)
Tubuai Islands (FRANCE)
Rapa Island (FRANCE)
Pitcairn (U.K.)
Ducie Island
Easter Island (CHILE)
Christmas Island (AUSTRALIA)
Darwin
Perth
Adelaide
Melbourne
Hobart
Sydney
Canberra
Brisbane

30°N, 15°N, 0° Equator, 15°S, 30°S, 45°S
120°E, 135°E, 150°E, 165°E, 180°, 165°W, 150°W, 135°W, 120°W

The North Pole

Kara
Sea

Barents
Sea

EUROPE

Laptev
Sea

120°E

90°E

60°E

30°E

Norwegian
Sea

Arctic Circle

**ARCTIC
OCEAN**

North
Pole

0°

Greenland
Sea

ASIA

150°E

80°N

30°W

Greenland
(DENMARK)

**ATLANTIC
OCEAN**

International Date Line

70°N

POLAR ICE PACK

North
Magnetic
Pole

150°W

90°W

Baffin
Bay

60°N

60°W

Beaufort
Sea

Bering Sea

180°

120°W

90°W

**NORTH
AMERICA**

50°N

The South Pole

SOUTH
AMERICA

150°W

120°W

SOUTHERN   OCEAN

90°W

60°W

International Date Line

Antarctic Circle

Amundsen
Sea

Bellingshausen Sea

Antarctic
Peninsula

POLAR ICE PACK

**PACIFIC
OCEAN**

Ross
Sea

Marie Byrd Land

Vinson Massif
16,067 ft
(4,897 m)

Ellsworth Land

70°S

POLAR ICE PACK

Ross
Ice Shelf

Ronne
Ice Shelf

Weddell
Sea

80°S

Edith Ronne Land

Filchner
Ice Shelf

Mount Markham
over 14,275 ft
(over 4,351 m)

South
Pole

Coats
Land

150°E

30°W

Adelie
Land

ANTARCTICA

South
Magnetic
Pole

WILKES   LAND

ICE CAP

**ATLANTIC
OCEAN**

60°S

QUEEN MAUD LAND

Shackleton
Ice Shelf

American
Highland

Enderby
Land

50°S

120°E

90°E

60°E

30°E

0°

INDIAN OCEAN

SOUTHERN   OCEAN

ATLAS

ATLAS   555

Gazetteer

A

Afghanistan a landlocked country in Central Asia (p. 559)

Africa the second-largest continent; surrounded by the Atlantic Ocean, Indian Ocean, and Mediterranean Sea (p. 552)

Alabama (AL) a state in the southern United States; admitted in 1819 (pp. 538–539)

Alaska (AK) a state in northwestern North America; admitted in 1959 (pp. 538–539)

Albania a country on the Balkan Peninsula in southeastern Europe (p. 467)

Alberta a province in western Canada (p. 274)

Alps a great mountain system in central Europe (p. 401)

Amazon Basin a huge basin in the heart of South America (p. 546)

Amazon River the major river in South America (p. 546)

Amsterdam (52°N, 5°E) the capital and largest city of the Netherlands (p. 433)

Amur River a river in Asia that forms part of the Russia-China border (p. 505)

Andes a mountain range along the west coast of South America (p. 546)

Antarctica the continent around the South Pole (p. 555)

Antarctic Circle the line of latitude located at 66.5° south of the equator; parallel beyond which no sunlight shines on the June solstice (p. 555)

Apennines (A-puh-nynz) the major mountain range on the Italian Peninsula (p. 401)

Appalachian Mountains a mountain system in eastern North America (p. 248)

Arctic Circle the line of latitude located at 66.5° north of the equator; parallel beyond which no sunlight shines on the December solstice (p. 555)

Arctic Ocean the ocean north of the Arctic Circle; the world's fourth-largest ocean (p. 540)

Argentina a country in South America (p. 205)

Arizona (AZ) a state in the southwestern United States; admitted in 1912 (pp. 538–539)

Arkansas (AR) a state in the south-central United States; admitted in 1836 (pp. 538–539)

Armenia a country in the Caucasus Mountains (p. 509)

Asia the world's largest continent; located between Europe and the Pacific Ocean (p. 550)

Asia Minor a large peninsula in Southwest Asia between the Black Sea and the Mediterranean Sea, forming most of Turkey (p. 311)

Asunción (ah-soon-SYOHN) (25°N, 58°W) the capital of Paraguay (p. 205)

Atacama Desert a desert located in northern Chile near the border with Peru (p. 231)

Athens (38°N, 24°E) an ancient city and the modern capital of Greece (p. 399)

Atlanta (33°N, 84°W) capital of Georgia (p. 266)

Atlantic Ocean the ocean between the continents of North and South America and the continents of Europe and Africa; the world's second-largest ocean (pp. 540–541)

Australia the only country occupying an entire continent (also called Australia); located between the Indian Ocean and the Pacific Ocean (p. 554)

Austria a country in West-Central Europe (p. 423)

Azerbaijan (a-zuhr-by-JAHN) a country in the Caucasus Mountains (p. 509)

B

Bahamas a country and group of islands located east of Florida in the Atlantic Ocean (p. 163)

Baja California a peninsula in Mexico (p. 142)

Baku (40°N, 48°E) the capital of Azerbaijan (p. 509)

Balkan Peninsula a peninsula in Southern Europe (p. 469)

Baltic Sea a shallow arm of the Atlantic Ocean in northern Europe (p. 449)

Barbados island country in the Caribbean (p. 161)

Barcelona (41°N, 2°E) a large port city in Spain on the Mediterranean Sea (p. 416)

Basse-Terre (16°N, 62°W) the capital of St. Kitts and Nevis (p. 161)

Bavaria a state and region in southern Germany (p. 438)

Belarus a country in Eastern Europe (p. 467)

Belgium a country in West-Central Europe (p. 423)

Belgrade (45°N, 21°E) the capital of Serbia (p. 467)

Belize a country in Central America (p. 160)

Belmopan (17°N, 90°W) capital of Belize (p. 160)

Benelux a term that refers to Belgium, the Netherlands, and Luxembourg (p. 432)

Berlin (53°N, 13°E) the capital of Germany (p. 423)

Bern (47°N, 7°E) the capital of Switzerland (p. 423)

Bogotá (4°N, 72°W) capital of Colombia (p. 184)

Bolivia a country in South America (p. 227)

Bosnia and Herzegovina a country on the Balkan Peninsula (p. 467)

Boston (42°N, 71°W) the capital of Massachusetts (p. 256)

Brasília (10°S, 55°W) the capital of Brazil (p. 213)

Bratislava (48°N, 17°E) the capital of Slovakia (p. 467)

Brazil a country in South America (p. 205)

Brazilian Highlands a region of rugged, old, eroded mountains in eastern Brazil (p. 207)

British Columbia a province in Canada (p. 274)

British Isles a group of islands off the northwestern coast of Europe including Britain and Ireland (p. 449)

Brussels (51°N, 4°E) the capital of Belgium (p. 423)

Bucharest (44°N, 26°E) the capital of Romania (p. 467)

Budapest (48°N, 19°E) the capital of Hungary (p. 467)

Buenos Aires (BWAY-nuhs y-reez) (36°S, 60°W) the capital of Argentina (p. 205)

Bulgaria a country in the Balkans (p. 467)

C

Calgary (51°N, 114°W) a large city in the province of Alberta in Canada (p. 274)

California (CA) a state in the western United States; admitted in 1850 (pp. 538–539)

Canada a country in North America (p. 274)

Canadian Shield a region of ancient rock that covers more than half of Canada (p. 277)

Cancún (21°N, 87°W) a popular resort on Mexico's Caribbean coast (p. 153)

Caracas (11°N, 67°W) the capital of Venezuela (p. 185)

Caribbean Islands a group of islands in the Caribbean Sea (p. 163)

Caribbean Sea an arm of the Atlantic Ocean between North and South America (p. 161)

Carpathians (kahr-PAY-thee-uhnz) a major mountain chain in central and eastern Europe (p. 468)

Cartagena (kahr-tah-HAY-nuh) (10°N, 74°W) a coastal city in northern Colombia (p. 184)

Carthage (KAHR-thij) (37°N, 10°E) an ancient Phoenician port city in North Africa in modern Tunisia (p. 321)

Cascade Range a mountain range in western North America (p. 250)

Caspian Sea a large inland sea located between Europe and Asia (p. 490)

Caucasus Mountains a mountain system in southeastern Europe between the Black Sea and Caspian Sea (p. 492)

Cayenne (4°N, 53°W) the capital of French Guiana (p. 185)

Central America a region in North America south of Mexico (p. 162)

Central Uplands an area of hills, plateaus, and valleys in central Europe (p. 425)

Chechnya (CHECH-nyuh) a republic in Russia that is fighting a violent struggle for independence (p. 506)

Chernobyl (51°N, 30°E) a city in Ukraine; the world's worst nuclear reactor accident occurred there in 1986 (p. 471)

Chicago (42°N, 88°W) a major U.S. city and port in northeastern Illinois on Lake Michigan (p. 265)

Chile (CHEE-lay) a country in western South America (p. 227)

Chişinau (47°N, 29°E) the capital of Moldova (p. 467)

Coast Mountains a mountain range in North America along the Pacific coast (p. 277)

Colombia a country in South America (p. 184)

Colorado (CO) a state in the southwestern United States; admitted in 1876 (pp. 538–539)

Connecticut (CT) a state in the northeastern United States; admitted in 1788 and one of the original 13 colonies (pp. 538–539)

Copenhagen (56°N, 13°E) the capital of Denmark (p. 447)

Costa Rica a country in Central America (p. 160)

Croatia a country in the Balkans (p. 467)

Cuba an island country in the Caribbean Sea south of Florida (p. 161)

Cuzco (KOO-skoh) (14°S, 72°W) a city in Peru and the former capital of the Inca Empire (p. 129)

Czech Republic a country in Eastern Europe (p. 467)

D

Danube (DAN-yoob) the second-longest river in Europe; it flows from Germany east to the Black Sea (p. 425)

Delaware (DE) a state in the eastern United States; admitted in 1787 and one of the original 13 colonies (pp. 538–539)

Denmark a country in Northern Europe (p. 447)

Detroit (42°N, 83°W) a large U.S. city in Michigan (p. 539)

GAZETTEER

District of Columbia (39°N, 77°W) a federal district between Maryland and Virginia; the capital of the United States (p. 247)

Dominican Republic a country in the Caribbean (p. 161)

Dublin (53°N, 6°W) the capital of Ireland (p. 446)

Eastern Hemisphere the half of the globe between the prime meridian and 180° longitude that includes most of Africa and Europe as well as Asia, Australia, and the Indian Ocean (p. H3)

Ecuador a country in South America (p. 227)

Edinburgh (56°N, 3°W) the capital of Scotland (p. 455)

Egypt a country in North Africa on the Mediterranean Sea; home to one of the world's oldest civilizations (p. 553)

El Salvador a country in Central America (p. 160)

England a part of the United Kingdom occupying most of the island of Great Britain (p. 455)

English Channel a strait of the Atlantic Ocean between England and France (p. 426)

equator the imaginary line of latitude that circles the globe halfway between the North and South Poles (p. H2)

Estonia a Baltic country in Eastern Europe (p. 467)

Europe the continent between the Ural Mountains and the Atlantic Ocean (p. 548)

F

Finland a country in Northern Europe (p. 447)

Florence (44°N, 11°E) a city in Italy that was a major center of the Renaissance (p. 345)

Florida (FL) a state in the southeastern United States; admitted in 1845 (p. 247)

France a country in West-Central Europe (p. 423)

French Guiana (gee-A-nuh) a region of France in northern South America (p. 185)

G

Galápagos Islands a group of islands in the Pacific Ocean that are part of Ecuador (p. 229)

Georgetown (5°N, 59°W) capital of Guyana (p. 185)

Georgia (GA) a state in the southeastern United States; admitted in 1788 and one of the original 13 colonies (pp. 538–539)

Georgia a country in the Caucasus Mountains (p. 509)

Germany a country in West-Central Europe (p. 423)

Grand Banks (47°N, 52°W) a rich fishing ground near Newfoundland, Canada (p. 277)

Grand Canyon a large canyon in the southwestern United States (p. 536)

Greater Antilles an island group in the Caribbean that includes Cuba, Jamaica, Hispaniola, and Puerto Rico (p. 163)

Great Lakes a group of five large freshwater lakes in North America; they are Lake Superior, Lake Michigan, Lake Huron, Lake Erie, and Lake Ontario; the largest freshwater lake system in the world (p. 249)

Great Plains a large region of plains and grasslands in central North America (p. 249)

Greece a country in Southern Europe (p. 399)

Greenland a large island in North America controlled by Denmark that was settled by the Vikings (p. 275)

Guadalajara (21°N, 103°W) the second-largest city in Mexico (p. 141)

Guadeloupe a group of islands in the Caribbean that are part of France (p. 161)

Guatemala a country in Central America (p. 160)

Guatemala City (15°N, 91°W) the capital of Guatemala (p. 160)

Guayaquil (gwah-ah-KEEL) (2°S, 80°W) a city in Ecuador (p. 227)

Guiana Highlands (gee-YAH-nah) a large plateau region in northern South America (p. 187)

Gulf of Mexico a large gulf off the southeastern coast of North America (p. 141)

Gulf Stream a warm ocean current that flows north along the east coast of the United States (p. 52)

Guyana (gy-AH-nuh) a country in northern South America (p. 185)

H

Haiti a country in the Caribbean (p. 161)

Havana (23°N, 82°W) the capital of Cuba (p. 161)

Hawaii (HI) state in the Pacific Ocean comprised of the Hawaiian Islands; admitted in 1959 (pp. 546–547)

Helsinki (60°N, 25°E) the capital of Finland (p. 447)

Hispaniola (ees-pah-nee-O-lah) an island in the
   Caribbean (p. 163)
Holland a region in the Netherlands (p. 432)
Honduras a country in Central America (p. 160)
Hudson Bay a large bay in central Canada (p. 277)
Hungary a country in central Europe (p. 467)

Iberian Peninsula a large peninsula in Southern
   Europe; Spain and Portugal are located there
   (p. 415)
Iceland an island country in Northern Europe
   (p. 446)
Idaho (ID) a state in the northwestern United
   States; admitted in 1890 (pp. 538–539)
Illinois (IL) a state in the north-central United
   States; admitted in 1819 (pp. 538–539)
India a country in South Asia (p. 551)
Indiana (IN) a state in the north-central United
   States; admitted in 1816 (pp. 538–539)
Indian Ocean the world's third-largest ocean;
   located east of Africa, south of Asia, and west
   of Australia (p. 541)
Interior Plains a large plains region of North
   America (p. 249)
Iowa (IA) a state in the north-central United
   States; admitted in 1846 (pp. 538–539)
Iraq a country located between Iran and Saudi
   Arabia in Southwest Asia (p. 551)
Ireland a country west of Britain in the British Isles
   (p. 446)
Italy a country in Southern Europe (p. 399)

J, K

Jamaica an island country in the Caribbean
   (p. 161)
Kaliningrad (55°N, 21°E) a strategic city and port
   controlled by Russia (p. 503)
Kamchatka Peninsula a large, mountainous peninsula in eastern Russia on the Pacific Ocean
   (p. 493)
Kansas (KS) a state in the central United States;
   admitted in 1861 (pp. 538–539)
Kentucky (KY) a state in the east-central United
   States; admitted in 1792 (pp. 538–539)
Kenya a country in East Africa, south of Ethiopia
   (p. 553)

Kiev (50°N, 31°E) the capital of Ukraine (p. 467)
Kjolen Mountains a mountain range in Scandinavia along the Norway-Sweden border (p. 448)

L

Lake Baikal a huge freshwater lake in Russia; it is
   the deepest lake in the world (p. 493)
Lake Maracaibo (mah-rah-KY-boh) (10°N, 72°W)
   an oil-rich body of water in Venezuela (p. 197)
Lake Texcoco (tays-KOH-koh) an ancient lake in
   Mexico; it was the site of Tenochtitlán (p. 124)
La Paz (17°S, 65°W) the capital of Bolivia (p. 227)
Latin America a region in the Western Hemisphere;
   it includes countries where Spanish, Portuguese,
   or French culture shaped life (p. 142)
Latvia a Baltic country in Eastern Europe (p. 467)
Lesser Antilles a group of small islands in the
   Caribbean; they stretch from the Virgin Islands
   in the north to Trinidad in the south (p. 163)
Lima (10°S, 75°W) the capital of Peru (p. 227)
Lisbon (39°N, 9°W) the capital of Portugal (p. 398)
Lithuania a Baltic country in Eastern Europe
   (p. 467)
Ljubljana (46°N, 15°E) the capital of Slovenia
   (p. 467)
Llanos a plains region in South America (p. 187)
London (51°N, 1°W) the capital of England and
   the United Kingdom (p. 446)
Louisiana (LA) a state in the southeastern United
   States; admitted in 1812 (pp. 538–539)
Luxembourg a country in West-Central Europe
   (p. 423)
Luxembourg City (45°N 6°E) capital of Luxem-
   bourg (p. 423)

M

Macedonia a country on the Balkan Peninsula in
   southeastern Europe (p. 467)
Machu Picchu (MAH-choo PEEK-choo) (13°S, 73°W)
   a sacred city and fortress of the Incas (p. 131)
Madrid (40°N, 4°W) the capital of Spain (p. 398)
Magdalena River a river in Colombia (p. 184)
Maine (ME) a state in the northeastern United
   States; admitted in 1820 (pp. 538–539)
Manaus (3°S, 60°W) a major port and industrial
   city in Brazil's Amazon rain forest (p. 213)
Manitoba a province in central Canada (p. 275)

Mariana Trench the world's deepest ocean trench; located in the Pacific Ocean (p. 37)

Marseille (mar-SAY) (43°N, 5°E) a port city in France on the Mediterranean Sea (p. 423)

Martinique a group of islands in the Caribbean that are part of France (p. 175)

Maryland (MD) a state in the eastern United States; admitted in 1788 and one of the original 13 colonies (pp. 538–539)

Massachusetts (MA) a state in the northeastern United States; admitted in 1788 and one of the original 13 colonies (pp. 538–539)

Massif Central (ma-SEEF sahn-TRAHL) an upland region in south-central France (p. 425)

Mato Grosso Plateau a high plateau area in Brazil (p. 207)

Mediterranean Sea a sea surrounded by Europe, Asia, and Africa (p. 401)

Mesoamerica a region in North America; the first permanent farming settlements in the Americas developed in Mesoamerica (p. 118)

Mexican Plateau a high, mostly rugged region covering much of the interior of Mexico (p. 143)

Mexico a country in North America (p. 141)

Mexico City (23°N, 104°W) the capital of Mexico (p. 141)

Michigan (MI) a state in the north-central United States; admitted in 1837 (pp. 538–539)

Mid-Atlantic Ridge a mid-ocean ridge located in the Atlantic Ocean (p. 37)

Minnesota (MN) a state in the north-central United States; admitted in 1858 (pp. 538–539)

Mississippi (MS) a state in the southeastern United States; admitted in 1817 (pp. 538–539)

Mississippi River a major river in the central United States (p. 249)

Missouri (MO) a state in the central United States; admitted in 1821 (pp. 538–539)

Moldova a country in Eastern Europe (p. 467)

Monaco a small country in West-Central Europe (p. 423)

Montana (MT) a state in the northern United States; admitted in 1889 (pp. 538–539)

Mont Blanc (mawn BLAHN) (46°N, 7°E) a mountain peak in France; highest of the Alps (p. 426)

Monterrey (26°N, 100°W) a large city and industrial center in northern Mexico (p. 155)

Montevideo (mawn-tay-vee-DAY-oh) (35°S, 56°W) the capital of Uruguay (p. 205)

Montreal (46°N, 74°W) a major Canadian city in Quebec; founded by the French in 1642 (p. 288)

Moscow (56°N, 38°E) the capital of Russia (p. 490)

Montenegro (43°N, 19°E) a country in the Balkans (p. 171)

Mount Elbrus (el-BROOS) the highest peak of the Caucasus Mountains (p. 493)

Mount Saint Helens (46°N, 122°W) a volcano in Washington State that erupted in 1980 (p. 250)

Nassau (25°N, 77°W) the capital of the Bahamas (p. 161)

Nebraska (NE) a state in the central United States; admitted in 1867 (pp. 538–539)

Netherlands a country in West-Central Europe (p. 423)

Nevada (NV) a state in the western United States; admitted in 1864 (pp. 538–539)

New Brunswick a province in Canada (p. 275)

Newfoundland and Labrador an island province in eastern Canada (p. 275)

New Hampshire (NH) a state in the northeastern United States; admitted in 1788 and one of the original 13 colonies (pp. 538–539)

New Jersey (NJ) a state in the northeastern United States; admitted in 1787 and one of the original 13 colonies (pp. 538–539)

New Mexico (NM) a state in the southwestern United States; admitted in 1912 (pp. 538–539)

New Orleans (30°N, 90°W) a major U.S. port city located in southeastern Louisiana (p. 247)

New York (NY) a state in the northeastern United States; admitted in 1788 and one of the original 13 colonies (pp. 538–539)

New York City (41°N, 74°W) a city in the northeastern United States; the largest city in the United States (p. 539)

Nicaragua a country in Central America (p. 160)

Normandy a region in northwestern France (p. 386)

North America a continent including Canada, the United States, Mexico, Central America, and the Caribbean islands (p. 544)

North Atlantic Current a warm ocean current that flows across the Atlantic Ocean and along Western Europe (p. 52)

North Carolina (NC) a state in the southeastern United States; admitted in 1789 and one of the original 13 colonies (pp. 538–539)

North Dakota (ND) a state in the north-central United States; admitted in 1889 (pp. 538–539)

Northern European Plain a large plain across central and northern Europe (p. 425)

Northern Hemisphere the northern half of the globe, between the equator and the North Pole (p. H3)

GAZETTEER

Northern Ireland a part of the United Kingdom occupying the northeastern portion of the island of Ireland (p. 455)

North Pole (90°N) the northern point of Earth's axis (p. 555)

North Sea a shallow arm of the Atlantic Ocean in Northern Europe (p. 426)

Northwest Territories a territory in Canada (p. 274)

Norway a country in Northern Europe (p. 447)

Nova Scotia (noh-vuh SKOH-shuh) a province in eastern Canada (p. 275)

Nunavut (NOO-nah-VOOT) a territory in northern Canada created as a homeland for Canada's Inuit people (p. 275)

O

Ob River a long river in central Russia (p. 493)

Ohio (OH) a state in the north-central United States; admitted in 1803 (pp. 538–539)

Oklahoma (OK) a state in the south-central United States; admitted in 1907 (pp. 538–539)

Ontario a province in east-central Canada (p. 275)

Oregon (OR) a state in the northwestern United States; admitted in 1859 (pp. 538–539)

Orinoco River (OHR-ee-NOH-koh) a major river in Venezuela (p. 185)

Oslo (60°N, 11°E) the capital of Norway (p. 447)

Ottawa (45°N, 76°W) capital of Canada (p. 275)

P

Pacific Ocean the world's largest ocean; located between Asia and the Americas (pp. 540–541)

Palenque (pay-LENG-kay) (18°N, 92°W) an ancient Maya city in southern Mexico (p. 119)

Pampas a fertile plains region in southern South America located mainly in Argentina (p. 207)

Panama a country in Central America (p. 161)

Panama Canal (26°N, 80°W) a canal built by the United States in the early 1900s across the Isthmus of Panama (p. 172)

Panama City (8°N, 81°W) capital of Panama (p. 161)

Paraguay a country in South America (p. 205)

Paraguay River a river in South America (p. 207)

Paramaribo (6°N, 55°W) the capital of Suriname (p. 185)

Paris (46°N, 0°) the capital of France (p. 423)

Patagonia a region of dry plains and plateaus east of the Andes in southern Argentina (p. 207)

Pennsylvania (PA) a state in the eastern United States; admitted in 1787 and one of the original 13 colonies (pp. 538–539)

Peru a country in western South America (p. 227)

Podgorica (43°N, 19°E) capital of Montenegro (p. 171)

Poland a country in Eastern Europe (p. 467)

Popocatépetl (poh-poh-cah-TE-pet-uhl) (19°N, 99°W) a volcano near Mexico City (p. 143)

Po River a major river in northern Italy (p. 401)

Port-au-Prince (pohr-toh-PRINS) (19°N, 72°W) the capital of Haiti (p. 177)

Port of Spain (11°N, 61°W) the capital of Trinidad and Tobago (p. 161)

Portugal a country in Southern Europe on the Iberian Peninsula (p. 398)

Prague (50°N, 14°E) capital of the Czech Republic (p. 467)

prime meridian an imaginary line that runs through Greenwich, England, at 0° longitude (p. H2)

Prince Edward Island (46°N, 64°W) a small province in eastern Canada (p. 275)

Puerto Rico an island east of Cuba and southeast of Florida; it is a U.S. territory (p. 161)

Pyrenees (PIR-uh-neez) a high mountain range between Spain and France (p. 401)

Q, R

Quebec a province in eastern Canada (p. 275)

Quito (2°S, 78°W) the capital of Ecuador (p. 227)

Reykjavik (64°N, 22°W) the capital of Iceland (p. 446)

Rhine a major river in Europe; it begins in Switzerland and flows north to the North Sea (p. 425)

Rhode Island (RI) a state in the northeastern United States; admitted in 1790 and one of the original 13 colonies (pp. 538–539)

Riga (57°N, 24°E) the capital of Latvia (p. 467)

Ring of Fire a region that circles the Pacific Ocean; known for its earthquakes and volcanoes (p. 42)

Río Bravo the Mexican name for the river known as the Rio Grande in the United States; it forms the border between Mexico and Texas (p. 143)

Río de Janeiro (23°N, 43°W) the second-largest city in Brazil; it is a major port city and Brazil's former capital (p. 205)

Río de la Plata (REE-oh day lah PLAH-tah) a body of water in South America (p. 207)

Rocky Mountains a major mountain range in western North America (p. 249)

GAZETTEER

Romania a country in Eastern Europe (p. 467)

Rome (42°N, 13°E) the capital of Italy; it was the capital of the ancient Roman Empire (p. 399)

Ruhr a major industrial region in Germany (p. 439)

Russia a huge country that extends from Eastern Europe to the Pacific Ocean (p. 491)

S

St. Kitts and Nevis country in the Caribbean (p. 179)

St. Lawrence River a river in North America that flows from the Great Lakes to the Atlantic Ocean (p. 276)

San Andreas Fault an area at the boundary of the Pacific tectonic plate where earthquakes are common; located in California (p. 38)

San Francisco (37°N, 122°W) a major U.S. port city in Northern California (p. 246)

San Jose (10°N, 84°W) capital of Costa Rica (p. 160)

San Salvador (14°N, 89°W) the capital of El Salvador (p. 160)

Santiago (33°S, 71°W) the capital of Chile (p. 227)

Santo Domingo (19°N, 71°W) the capital of the Dominican Republic (p. 161)

São Paulo (24°S, 47°W) the largest city in Brazil and South America (p. 205)

Sarajevo (44°N, 18°E) the capital of Bosnia and Herzegovina (p. 467)

Saskatchewan a province in Canada (p. 275)

Scandinavia a region of islands and peninsulas in far northern Europe; includes the countries of Norway, Sweden, Finland, and Denmark (p. 549)

Scandinavian Peninsula a large peninsula in Northern Europe that includes Norway and Sweden (p. 449)

Scotland a part of the United Kingdom located in the northern part of Great Britain (p. 455)

Seattle (48°N, 122°W) a major U.S. port and city in Washington State (p. 246)

Serbia a country in the Balkans (p. 467)

Siberia a huge region in eastern Russia (p. 493)

Sierra Madre (SYER-rah MAH-dray) the chief mountain range in Mexico (p. 143)

Sierra Nevada a large mountain range mainly in California (p. 249)

Slovakia a country in Eastern Europe (p. 467)

Slovenia a country in Eastern Europe (p. 467)

Sofia (43°N, 23°E) the capital of Bulgaria (p. 467)

South America a continent in the Western and Southern hemispheres (p. 546)

South Carolina (SC) a state in the southeastern United States; admitted in 1788 and one of the original 13 colonies (pp. 538–539)

South Dakota (SD) a state in the north-central United States; admitted in 1889 (pp. 538–539)

Southern Hemisphere the southern half of the globe, between the equator and the South Pole (p. H3)

South Pole (90°S) the southern point of Earth's axis (p. 563)

Spain a country in Southern Europe on the Iberian Peninsula; it colonized much of the Americas (p. 398)

Sparta (37°N, 22°E) an ancient city-state in Greece (p. 315)

Stockholm (59°N, 18°E) the capital of Sweden (p. 447)

Strait of Magellan a waterway through the southern tip of South America (p. 229)

Sucre (SOO-kray) (19°S, 65°W) the capital of Bolivia (p. 227)

Suriname (soohr-uh-NAHM) a country in northern South America (p. 185)

Sweden a country in Northern Europe (p. 447)

Switzerland a country in West-Central Europe (p. 423)

T

Tallinn (59°N, 25°E) the capital of Estonia (p. 467)

Tbilisi (42°N, 45°E) the capital of Georgia (p. 509)

Tegucigalpa (15°N, 87°W) the capital of Honduras (p. 160)

Tennessee (TN) a state in the south-central United States; admitted in 1796 (pp. 538–539)

Tenochtitlán (tay-nawch-teet-LAHN) the capital of the Aztec Empire (p. 124)

Texas (TX) a state and former independent republic in the south-central United States; admitted in 1845 (pp. 538–539)

Tierra del Fuego a group of islands in southern South America (p. 229)

Tigris River a river in Southwest Asia (p. 558)

Tirana (41°N, 20°E) the capital of Albania (p. 467)

Toronto (44°N, 79°W) Canada's largest city (p. 275)

Trinidad and Tobago a country in the Caribbean just north of Venezuela (p. 161)

Tropic of Cancer the parallel 23.5° north of the equator; parallel on the globe at which the sun's most direct rays strike Earth during the June solstice (pp. 540–541)

Tropic of Capricorn the parallel at 23.5° south of the equator; parallel on the globe at which the sun's most direct rays strike Earth during the December solstice (pp. 540–541)

U

Ukraine a country in Eastern Europe (p. 467)

United Kingdom a country in the British Isles that includes England, Wales, Scotland, and Northern Ireland (p. 446)

United States of America a country in North America located between Canada and Mexico (pp. 246–247)

Ural Mountains (YOOHR-uhl) a mountain range in Russia that separates Europe and Asia (p. 492)

Uruguay a country in South America (p. 205)

Utah (UT) a state in the western United States; admitted in 1896 (pp. 538–539)

V

Valley of Mexico a large plateau region in central Mexico (p. 143)

Vancouver (49°N, 123°W) a city in western Canada just north of the U.S. border (p. 274)

Vatican City (42°N, 12°E) a small country in Rome that is the head of the Roman Catholic Church (p. 399)

Venezuela a country in South America (p. 185)

Vermont (VT) a state in the northeastern United States; admitted in 1791 (pp. 538–539)

Vienna (45°N, 12°E) the capital of Austria (p. 423)

Vilnius (55°N, 25°E) the capital of Lithuania (p. 467)

Virginia (VA) a state in the eastern United States; admitted in 1788 and one of the original 13 colonies (pp. 538–539)

Virgin Islands a group of small islands in the Caribbean (p. 161)

Volga (VAHL-guh) the longest river in Europe and Russia's most important commercial river (p. 493)

W

Wales a part of the United Kingdom located west of England on the island of Great Britain (p. 455)

Warsaw (52°N, 21°E) the capital of Poland (p. 467)

Washington (WA) a state in the northwestern United States; admitted in 1889 (pp. 546–547)

Washington, D.C. (39°N, 77°W) the capital of the United States (p. 247)

Western Hemisphere the half of the globe between 180° and the prime meridian that includes North and South America and the Pacific and Atlantic oceans (p. H3)

West Indies a group of more than 1,200 islands in the Caribbean Sea (p. 174)

West Virginia (WV) a state in the east-central United States; admitted in 1863 (pp. 538–539)

Wisconsin (WI) a state in the north-central United States; admitted in 1848 (pp. 538–539)

Wyoming (WY) a state in the northwestern United States; admitted in 1890 (pp. 538–539)

Y, Z

Yerevan (40°N, 45°E) the capital of Armenia (p. 509)

Yucatán Peninsula (yoo-kah-TAHN) a large peninsula that separates the Caribbean Sea from the Gulf of Mexico (p. 142)

Yugoslavia a former country in the Balkans that broke apart in the 1990s (p. 484)

Yukon Territory a territory in Canada (p. 274)

Zagreb (46°N, 16°E) the capital of Croatia (p. 467)

Zurich (47°N, 9°E) a city in Switzerland (p. 423)

GAZETTEER

English and Spanish Glossary

MARK	AS IN	RESPELLING	EXAMPLE
a	alphabet	a	*AL-fuh-bet
ā	Asia	ay	AY-zhuh
ä	cart, top	ah	KAHRT, TAHP
e	let, ten	e	LET, TEN
ē	even, leaf	ee	EE-vuhn, LEEF
i	it, tip, British	i	IT, TIP, BRIT-ish
ī	site, buy, Ohio	y	SYT, BY, oh-HY-oh
	iris	eye	EYE-ris
k	card	k	KAHRD
kw	quest	kw	KWEST
ō	over, rainbow	oh	OH-vuhr, RAYN-boh
ů	book, wood	ooh	BOOHK, WOOHD
ò	all, orchid	aw	AWL, AWR-kid
òi	foil, coin	oy	FOYL, KOYN
aů	out	ow	OWT
ə	cup, butter	uh	KUHP, BUHT-uhr
ü	rule, food	oo	ROOL, FOOD
yü	few	yoo	FYOO
zh	vision	zh	VIZH-uhn

*A syllable printed in small capital letters receives heavier emphasis than the other syllable(s) in a word.

Phonetic Respelling and Pronunciation Guide

Many of the key terms in this textbook have been respelled to help you pronounce them. The letter combinations used in the respelling throughout the narrative are explained in this phonetic respelling and pronunciation guide. The guide is adapted from *Merriam-Webster's Collegiate Dictionary, Eleventh Edition; Merriam-Webster's Geographical Dictionary;* and *Merriam-Webster's Biographical Dictionary.*

A

absolute location a specific description of where a place is located; absolute location is often expressed using latitude and longitude (p. 12)
  ubicación absoluta descripción específica del lugar donde se ubica un punto; con frecuencia se define en términos de latitud y longitud (pág. 12)

alliance an agreement to work together (p. 377)
  alianza acuerdo de colaboración (pág. 377)

Allies Great Britain, France, the Soviet Union, and the United States; they joined together in World War II against Germany, Italy, and Japan (p. 385)
  Aliados Gran Bretaña, Francia, la Unión Soviética y Estados Unidos; se unieron durante la Segunda Guerra Mundial contra Alemania, Italia y Japón (pág. 385)

altiplano a broad, high plateau that lies between the ridges of the Andes (p. 229)
  altiplano meseta amplia y elevada que se extiende entre las cadenas montañosas de los Andes (pág. 229)

aqueduct a human-made raised channel that carries water from distant places (p. 322)
  acueducto canal elevado hecho por el ser humano que trae agua desde lugares lejanos (pág. 322)

archipelago (ahr-kuh-PE-luh-goh) a large group of islands (p. 163)
  archipiélago grupo grande de islas (pág. 163)

arms race a competition between countries to build superior weapons (p. 390)
  carrera armamentista competencia entre países para construir armas mejores (pág. 390)

Axis Powers the name for the alliance formed by Germany, Italy, and Japan during World War II (p. 385)
  Potencias del Eje nombre de la alianza formada por Alemania, Italia y Japón durante la Segunda Guerra Mundial (pág. 385)

B

bilingual a term used to describe people who speak two languages (p. 260)
  bilingüe término utilizado para describir a las personas que hablan dos idiomas (pág. 260)

birthrate the annual number of births per 1,000 people (p. 88)
  índice de natalidad número de nacimientos por cada 1,000 personas en un año (pág. 88)

Bolsheviks a radical Russian Communist group that seized power in 1917 (p. 497)

bolcheviques grupo comunista ruso radical que obtuvo el poder en 1917 (pág. 497)

C

canton one of 26 districts in the republic of Switzerland (p. 441)

cantón uno de los 26 distritos de la república de Suiza (pág. 441)

capitalism an economic system in which individuals and private businesses run most industries (p. 368)

capitalismo sistema económico en el que los individuos y las empresas privadas controlan la mayoría de las industrias (pág. 368)

cartography the science of making maps (p. 19)

cartografía ciencia de crear mapas (pág. 19)

cash crop a crop that farmers grow mainly to sell for a profit (p. 153)

cultivo comercial cultivo que los agricultores producen principalmente para vender y obtener ganancias (pág. 153)

Catholic Reformation the effort of the late 1500s and 1600s to reform the Catholic Church from within; also called the Counter-Reformation (p. 349)

Reforma católica iniciativa para reformar la Iglesia católica desde dentro a finales del siglo XVI y en el XVII; también conocida como la Contrarreforma (pág. 349)

causeway a raised road across water or wet ground (p. 124)

carretera elevada camino construido sobre agua o terreno pantanoso (pág. 124)

chancellor a German prime minister (p. 439)

canciller primer ministro alemán (pág. 439)

circumnavigate to go all the way around (p. 355)

circunnavegar dar una vuelta completa (pág. 355)

citizen a person who has the right to take part in government (p. 319)

ciudadano persona que tiene el derecho de participar en el gobierno (pág. 319)

city-state a political unit consisting of a city and its surrounding countryside (p. 310)

cuidad estado unidad política formada por una ciudad y los campos que la rodean (pág. 310)

civil war a conflict between two or more groups within a country (p. 170)

guerra civil conflicto entre dos o más grupos dentro de un país (pág. 170)

climate a region's average weather conditions over a long period of time (p. 50)

clima condiciones del tiempo promedio de una región durante un período largo de tiempo (pág. 50)

cloud forest a moist, high-elevation tropical forest where low clouds are common (p. 164)

bosque nuboso bosque tropical de gran elevación y humedad donde los bancos de nubes son muy comunes (pág. 164)

Cold War a period of distrust between the United States and Soviet Union after World War II, when there was a tense rivalry between the two superpowers but no direct fighting (p. 388)

Guerra Fría período de desconfianza entre Estados Unidos y la Unión Soviética que siguió a la Segunda Guerra Mundial; existía una rivalidad tensa entre las dos superpotencias, pero no se llegó a la lucha directa (pág. 388)

colony a territory inhabited and controlled by people from a foreign land (p. 256)

colonia territorio habitado y controlado por personas de otro país (pág. 256)

command economy an economic system in which the central government makes all economic decisions (p. 94)

economía autoritaria sistema económico en el que el gobierno central toma todas las decisiones económicas (pág. 94)

common market a group of nations that cooperates to make trade among members easier (p. 392)

mercado común grupo de naciones que cooperan para facilitar el comercio entre los miembros (pág. 392)

commonwealth a self-governing territory associated with another country (p. 177)

mancomunidad o estado libre asociado territorio autogobernado asociado con otro país (pág. 177)

Commonwealth of Independent States (CIS) a union of former Soviet republics that meets about issues such as trade and immigration (p. 478)

Comunidad de Estados Independientes (CEI) unión de ex repúblicas soviéticas que se reúne para tratar temas como el comercio y la inmigración (pág. 478)

Communism an economic and political system in which the government owns all businesses and controls the economy (pp. 92, 380)

comunismo sistema económico y político en el que el gobierno es dueño de todos los negocios y controla la economía (págs. 92, 380)

conquistadors (kahn-KEES-tuh-dohrs) Spanish soldiers in the Americas who explored new lands, searched for gold and silver, and tried to spread Christianity (p. 128)

conquistadores soldados españoles en América que exploraron nuevas tierras, buscaron oro y plata e intentaron difundir el cristianismo (pág. 128)

constitutional monarchy a type of democracy in which a monarch serves as head of state, but a legislature makes the laws (p. 454)

monarquía constitucional tipo de democracia en la cual un monarca sirve como jefe de estado, pero una asamblea legislativa hace las leyes (pág. 454)

continent a large landmass that is part of Earth's crust; geographers identify seven continents (p. 36)

continente gran masa de tierra que forma parte de la corteza terrestre; los geógrafos identifican siete continentes (pág. 36)

continental divide an area of high ground that divides the flow of rivers towards opposite ends of a continent (p. 250)

línea divisoria de aguas zona de terreno elevado que divide el flujo de los ríos en dos direcciones, hacia los extremos opuestos de un continente (pág. 250)

cooperative an organization owned by its members and operated for their mutual benefit (p. 178)

cooperativa organización cuyos miembros son los propietarios y que es operada para beneficio de todos (pág. 178)

cordillera (kawr-duhl-YER-uh) a mountain system made up of roughly parallel ranges (p. 186)

cordillera sistema de cadenas montañosas aproximadamente paralelas entre sí (pág. 186)

cosmopolitan characterized by many foreign influences (p. 433)

cosmopolita caracterizado por muchas influencias extranjeras (pág. 433)

coup (KOO) a sudden overthrow of a government by a small group of people (p. 241)

golpe de estado derrocamiento repentino de un gobierno por parte de un grupo reducido de personas (pág. 241)

Creole an American-born descendant of Europeans (p. 236)

criollo persona de ascendencia europea y nacida en América (pág. 236)

Crusades a long series of wars between Christians and Muslims in Southwest Asia fought for control of the Holy Land; took place from 1096 to 1291 (p. 329)

cruzadas larga serie de guerras entre cristianos y musulmanes en el suroeste de Asia para conseguir el control de la Tierra Santa; tuvieron lugar entre 1096 y 1291 (pág. 329)

cultural diffusion the spread of culture traits from one region to another (p. 85)

difusión cultural difusión de rasgos culturales de una región a otra (pág. 85)

cultural diversity having a variety of cultures in the same area (p. 83)

diversidad cultural existencia de una variedad de culturas en la misma zona (pág. 83)

culture the set of beliefs, values, and practices that a group of people have in common (p. 80)

cultura conjunto de creencias, valores y costumbres compartidas por un grupo de personas (pág. 80)

culture region an area in which people have many shared culture traits (p. 82)

región cultural región en la que las personas comparten muchos rasgos culturales (pág. 82)

culture trait an activity or behavior in which people often take part (p. 81)

rasgo cultural actividad o conducta frecuente de las personas (pág. 81)

Cyrllic (suh-RIHL-ihk) a form of the Greek alphabet (p. 496)

cirílico forma del alfabeto griego (pág. 496)

czar (ZAHR) a Russian emperor (p. 497)

zar emperador ruso (pág. 497)

dachas Russian country houses (p. 503)

dachas casas de campo rusas (pág. 503)

Declaration of Independence a document written in 1776 that declared the American colonies' independence from British rule (p. 361)

Declaración de Independencia documento escrito en 1776 que declaró la independencia de las colonias de América del Norte del dominio británico (pág. 361)

Declaration of the Rights of Man and of the Citizen a document written in France in 1789 that guaranteed specific freedoms for French citizens (p. 362)

Declaración de los Derechos del Hombre y del Ciudadano documento escrito en Francia en 1789 que garantizaba libertades específicas para los ciudadanos franceses (pág. 362)

deforestation the clearing of trees (pp. 69, 209)

deforestación tala de árboles (págs. 69, 209)

democracy a form of government in which the people elect leaders and rule by majority (p. 91)

democracia sistema de gobierno en el que el pueblo elige a sus líderes y gobierna por mayoría (pág. 91)

desertification the spread of desertlike conditions (p. 65)

desertificación ampliación de condiciones desérticas (pág. 65)

developed countries countries with strong economies and a high quality of life (p. 95)

países desarrollados países con economías sólidas y una alta calidad de vida (pág. 95)

developing countries countries with less productive economies and a lower quality of life (p. 95)

países en vías de desarrollo países con economías menos productivas y una menor calidad de vida (pág. 95)

dialect a regional variety of a language (p. 176)

dialecto variedad regional de un idioma (pág. 176)

dictator a ruler who has almost absolute power (p. 383)

dictador gobernante que tiene poder casi absoluto (pág. 383)

disarm to give up all weapons (p. 455)

desarmarse renunciar a todas las armas (pág. 455)

earthquake a sudden, violent movement of Earth's crust (p. 38)
terremoto movimiento repentino y violento de la corteza terrestre (pág. 38)

ecosystem a group of plants and animals that depend on each other for survival, and the environment in which they live (p. 63)
ecosistema grupo de plantas y animales que dependen unos de otros para sobrevivir, y el ambiente en el que estos viven (pág. 63)

ecotourism the practice of using an area's natural environment to attract tourists (p. 170)
ecoturismo uso de regiones naturales para atraer turistas (pág. 170)

El Niño an ocean and weather pattern that affects the Pacific coast of the Americas; about every two to seven years, it warms normally cool ocean water and causes extreme ocean and weather events (p. 231)
El Niño patrón oceánico y del tiempo que afecta a la costa del Pacífico de las Américas; aproximadamente cada dos a siete años, calienta las aguas normalmente frías del océano, y provoca sucesos oceánicos y climatológicos extremos (pág. 231)

empire a land with different territories and peoples under a single ruler (pp. 147, 320)
imperio zona que reúne varios territorios y pueblos bajo un solo gobernante (págs. 147, 320)

English Bill of Rights a document approved in 1689 that listed rights for Parliament and the English people and drew on the principles of Magna Carta (p. 360)
Declaración de Derechos inglesa documento aprobado en 1689 que enumeraba los derechos del Parlamento y del pueblo de Inglaterra, inspirada en los principios de la Carta Magna (pág. 360)

Enlightenment a period during the 1600s and 1700s when reason was used to guide people's thoughts about society, politics, and philosophy (p. 358)
Ilustración período durante los siglos XVII y XVIII en el que la razón guiaba las ideas de las personas acerca de la sociedad, la política y la filosofía (pág. 358)

environment the land, water, climate, plants, and animals of an area; surroundings (pp. 12, 62)
ambiente la tierra, el agua, el clima, las plantas y los animales de una zona; los alrededores (págs. 12, 62)

erosion the movement of sediment from one location to another (p. 39)
erosión movimiento de sedimentos de un lugar a otro (pág. 39)

estuary a partially enclosed body of water where freshwater mixes with salty seawater (p. 207)
estuario masa de agua parcialmente rodeada de tierra en la que el agua de mar se combina con agua dulce (pág. 207)

ethnic cleansing the effort to remove all members of an ethnic group from a country or region (p. 482)
limpieza étnica esfuerzo por eliminar a todos los miembros de un grupo étnico de un país o región (pág. 482)

ethnic group a group of people who share a common culture and ancestry (p. 83)
grupo étnico grupo de personas que comparten una cultura y una ascendencia (pág. 83)

European Union (EU) an organization that promotes political and economic cooperation in Europe (p. 392)
Unión Europea (UE) organización que promueve la cooperación política y económica en Europa (pág. 392)

extinct no longer here; a species that has died out has become extinct (p. 64)
extinto que ya no existe; una especie que ha desaparecido está extinta (pág. 64)

favela (fah-VE-lah) a huge slum in Brazil (p. 213)
favela enorme barriada en Brasil (pág. 213)

feudal system the system of obligations that governed the relationships between lords and vassals in medieval Europe (p. 331)
sistema feudal sistema de obligaciones que gobernaba las relaciones entre los señores feudales y los vasallos en la Europa medieval (pág. 331)

fjord (fyawrd) a narrow inlet of the sea set between high, rocky cliffs (p. 449)
fiordo entrada estrecha del mar entre acantilados altos y rocosos (pág. 449)

fossil fuels nonrenewable resources that formed from the remains of ancient plants and animals; coal, petroleum, and natural gas are all fossil fuels (p. 69)
combustibles fósiles recursos no renovables formados a partir de restos de plantas y animales antiguos; el carbón, el petróleo y el gas natural son combustibles fósiles (pág. 69)

freshwater water that is not salty; it makes up only about 3 percent of our total water supply (p. 31)
agua dulce agua que no es salada; representa sólo alrededor del 3 por ciento de nuestro suministro total de agua (pág. 31)

front the place where two air masses of different temperatures or moisture content meet (p. 53)
frente lugar en el que se encuentran dos masas de aire con diferente temperatura o humedad (pág. 53)

gaucho (GOW-choh) an Argentine cowboy (p. 217)
  gaucho vaquero argentino (pág. 217)

geography the study of the world, its people, and the landscapes they create (p. 4)
  geografía estudio del mundo, de sus habitantes y de los paisajes creados por el ser humano (pág. 4)

geothermal energy energy produced from the heat of Earth's interior (p. 450)
  energía geotérmica energía producida a partir del calor del interior de la Tierra (pág. 450)

geyser a spring that shoots hot water and steam into the air (p. 462)
  géiser manantial que lanza agua caliente y vapor al aire (pág. 462)

glacier a large area of slow moving ice (p. 31)
  glaciar gran bloque de hielo que avanza con lentitud (pág. 31)

globalization the process in which countries are increasingly linked to each other through culture and trade (p. 97)
  globalización proceso por el cual los países se encuentran cada vez más interconectados a través de la cultura y el comercio (pág. 97)

globe a spherical, or ball-shaped, model of the entire planet (p. 8)
  globo terráqueo modelo esférico, o en forma de bola, de todo el planeta (pág. 8)

golden age a period in a society's history marked by great achievements (p. 312)
  edad dorada período de la historia de una sociedad marcado por grandes logros (pág. 312)

Gothic architecture a style of architecture in Europe known for its high pointed ceilings, tall towers, and stained glass windows (p. 330)
  arquitectura gótica estilo de arquitectura europea que se conoce por los techos altos en punta, las torres altas y los vitrales de colores (pág. 330)

Great Depression a global economic crisis that struck countries around the world in the 1930s (p. 382)
  Gran Depresión crisis económica global que afectó a países de todo el mundo en la década de 1930 (pág. 382)

gross domestic product (GDP) the value of all goods and services produced within a country in a single year (p. 95)
  producto interior bruto (PIB) valor de todos los bienes y servicios producidos en un país durante un año (pág. 95)

groundwater water found below Earth's surface (p. 32)
  agua subterránea agua que se encuentra debajo de la superficie de la Tierra (pág. 32)

guerrilla a member of an irregular military force (p. 193)
  guerrillero miembro de una fuerza militar irregular (pág. 193)

gulag a soviet labor camp (p. 498)
  gulag campo soviético de trabajos forzados (pág. 498)

habitat the place where a plant or animal lives (p. 64)
  hábitat lugar en el que vive una planta o animal (pág. 64)

hacienda (hah-see-EN-duh) a huge expanse of farm or ranch land in the Americas (p. 148)
  hacienda granja o rancho de gran tamaño en las Américas (pág. 148)

Hellenistic Greek-like; heavily influenced by Greek ideas (p. 316)
  helenístico al estilo griego; muy influenciado por las ideas de la Grecia clásica (pág. 316)

Holocaust the Nazis' effort to wipe out the Jewish people in World War II, when 6 million Jews throughout Europe were killed (p. 385)
  Holocausto intento de los nazis de eliminar al pueblo judío durante la Segunda Guerra Mundial, en el que se mató a 6 millones de judíos en toda Europa (pág. 385)

human geography the study of the world's people, communities, and landscapes (p. 18)
  geografía humana estudio de los habitantes, las comunidades y los paisajes del mundo (pág. 18)

humanism the study of history, literature, public speaking, and art that led to a new way of thinking in Europe in the late 1300s (p. 345)
  humanismo estudio de la historia, la literatura, la oratoria y el arte que produjo una nueva forma de pensar en Europa a finales del siglo XIV (pág. 345)

humanitarian aid assistance to people in distress (p. 100)
  ayuda humanitaria ayuda a personas en peligro (pág. 100)

humus (HYOO-muhs) decayed plant or animal matter; it helps soil support abundant plant life (p. 65)
  humus materia animal o vegetal descompuesta; contribuye a que crezca una gran cantidad de plantas en el suelo (pág. 65)

hydroelectric power the production of electricity from waterpower, such as from running water (p. 70)
  energía hidroeléctrica producción de electricidad generada por la energía del agua, como la del agua corriente (pág. 70)

Industrial Revolution the period of rapid growth in machine-made goods that changed the way people across Europe worked and lived; it began in Britain in the 1700s (p. 366)
  Revolución Industrial período de rápido aumento de los bienes producidos con máquinas que cambió la forma de vivir y trabajar en toda Europa; comenzó en Gran Bretaña a comienzos del siglo XVIII (pág. 366)

inflation a rise in prices that occurs when currency loses its buying power (p. 152)
inflación aumento de los precios que ocurre cuando la moneda de un país pierde poder adquisitivo (pág. 152)

informal economy a part of the economy that is based on odd jobs that people perform without government regulation through taxes (p. 219)
economía informal parte de la economía basada en trabajos pequeños que se realizan sin el pago de impuestos regulados por el gobierno (pág. 219)

infrastructure the set of resources, like roads and factories, that a country needs to support economic activities (p. 475)
infraestructura conjunto de recursos, como carreteras o fábricas, que necesita un país para sostener su actividad económica (pág. 475)

interdependence a relationship between countries in which they rely on one another for resources, goods, or services (p. 99)
interdependencia una relación entre países en que dependen unos de otros para obtener recursos, bienes, o servicios (pág. 99)

isthmus a narrow strip of land that connects two larger land areas (p. 162)
istmo franja estrecha de tierra que une dos zonas más grandes (pág. 162)

L

landform a shape on the planet's surface, such as a mountain, valley, plain, island, or peninsula (p. 35)
accidente geográfico forma de la superficie terrestre, como una montaña, un valle, una llanura, una isla o una península (pág. 35)

landlocked completely surrounded by land with no direct access to the ocean (p. 220)
sin salida al mar completamente rodeado de tierra, sin acceso directo al océano (pág. 220)

landscape all the human and physical features that make a place unique (p. 4)
paisaje todas las características humanas y físicas que hacen que un lugar sea único (pág. 4)

latitude the distance north or south of Earth's equator (p. 27)
latitud distancia hacia el norte o el sur desde el ecuador (pág. 27)

lava magma that reaches Earth's surface (p. 37)
lava magma que llega a la superficie terrestre (pág. 37)

llanero (yah-NAY-roh) Venezuelan cowboy (p. 196)
llanero vaquero venezolano (pág. 196)

M

Magna Carta a document signed in 1215 by King John of England that required the king to honor certain rights (pág. 454)
Carta Magna documento firmado por el rey Juan de Inglaterra en 1215 que exigía que el rey respetara ciertos derechos (pág. 454)

maize corn (p. 118)
maíz cereal también conocido como elote o choclo (pág. 118)

manor a large estate owned by a knight or lord (p. 332)
feudo gran finca perteneciente a un caballero o señor feudal (pág. 332)

map a flat drawing that shows all or part of Earth's surface (p. 8)
mapa representación plana que muestra total o parcialmente la superficie de la Tierra (pág. 8)

maquiladora (mah-kee-lah-DORH-ah) a U.S. or other foreign-owned factory in Mexico (p. 155)
maquiladora fábrica estadounidense o de otro país establecida en México (pág. 155)

maritime on or near the sea (p. 287)
marítimo en o cerca del mar (pág. 287)

market economy an economic system based on free trade and competition (p. 94)
economía de mercado sistema económico basado en el libre comercio y la competencia (pág. 94)

masonry stonework (p. 131)
mampostería obra de piedra (pág. 131)

Mediterranean climate the type of climate found across Southern Europe; it features warm and sunny summer days, mild evenings, and cooler, rainy winters (p. 402)
clima mediterráneo tipo de clima de todo el sur europeo; se caracteriza por días de verano cálidos y soleados, noches templadas e inviernos lluviosos y más frescos (pág. 402)

megacity a giant urban area that includes surrounding cities and suburbs (p. 212)
megaciudad zona urbana enorme que incluye los suburbios y ciudades de alrededor (pág. 212)

megalopolis a string of large cities that have grown together (p. 265)
megalópolis serie de ciudades grandes que han crecido hasta unirse (pág. 265)

Mercosur an organization that promotes trade and economic cooperation among the southern and eastern countries of South America (p. 218)
Mercosur organización que promueve el comercio y la cooperación económica entre los países del sur y el este de América del Sur (pág. 218)

mestizo (me-STEE-zoh) a person of mixed European and Indian ancestry (p. 148)
mestizo persona de origen europeo e indígena (pág. 148)

meteorology the study of weather and what causes it (p. 20)

meteorología estudio de las condiciones del tiempo y sus causas (pág. 20)

Middle Ages a period that lasted from about 500 to 1500 in Europe (p. 328)

Edad Media período que duró aproximadamente desde el año 500 hasta el 1500 en Europa (pág. 328)

migration the movement of people from one place to live in another (p. 89)

migración movimiento de personas de un lugar para ir a vivir a otro lugar (pág. 89)

mission a church outpost (p. 148)

misión asentamiento de la Iglesia (pág. 148)

monsoon a seasonal wind that brings either dry or moist air (p. 58)

monzón viento estacional que trae aire seco o húmedo (pág. 58)

nationalism a devotion and loyalty to one's country; develops among people with a common language, religion, or history (p. 376)

nacionalismo sentimiento de lealtad al país de uno; se desarrolla entre personas con un idioma, religión o historia en común (pág. 376)

nation-state a country united under a single strong government; made up of people with a common cultural background (p. 335)

nación-estado país unido bajo un solo gobierno fuerte; formado de personas con una cultura común (pág. 335)

natural resource any material in nature that people use and value (p. 68)

recurso natural todo material de la naturaleza que las personas utilizan y valoran (pág. 68)

navigable river a river that is deep and wide enough for ships to use (p. 426)

río navegable río que tiene la profundidad y el ancho necesarios para que pasen los barcos (pág. 426)

neutral not taking sides in an international conflict (p. 460)

neutral que no toma partido en un conflicto internacional (pág. 460)

newsprint cheap paper used mainly for newspapers (p. 279)

papel de prensa papel económico utilizado principalmente para imprimir periódicos (pág. 279)

New World a term used by Europeans to describe the Americas after the voyages of Christopher Columbus; the Americas were a "New World" to Europeans, who did not know they existed until Columbus's voyages (p. 355)

Nuevo Mundo término usado por los europeos para describir las Américas tras los viajes de Cristóbal Colón; las Américas eran un "Nuevo Mundo" para los europeos, que no sabían de su existencia hasta los viajes de Colón (pág. 355)

nonrenewable resource a resource that cannot be replaced naturally; coal and petroleum are examples of nonrenewable resources (p. 69)

recurso no renovable recurso que no puede reemplazarse naturalmente; el carbón y el petróleo son ejemplos de recursos no renovables (pág. 69)

North Atlantic Drift a warm ocean current that brings warm, moist air across the Atlantic Ocean to Northern Europe (p. 450)

Corriente del Atlántico Norte corriente oceánica cálida que trae aire cálido y húmedo a través del océano Atlántico al norte de Europa (pág. 450)

observatory a building from which people study the sky (p. 122)

observatorio edificio desde el cual las personas estudian el cielo (pág. 122)

ocean currents large streams of surface seawater; they move heat around Earth (p. 52)

corrientes oceánicas grandes corrientes de agua de mar que fluyen en la superficie del océano; transportan calor por toda la Tierra (pág. 52)

Orthodox Church a branch of Christianity that dates to the Byzantine Empire (p. 407)

Iglesia ortodoxa rama del cristianismo que data del Imperio bizantino (pág. 407)

parliamentary monarchy a type of government in which a king rules with the help of an elected parliament (p. 418)

monarquía parlamentaria tipo de gobierno en el que un rey gobierna con la ayuda de un parlamento electo (pág. 418)

peninsula a piece of land surrounded on three sides by water (p. 142)

península pedazo de tierra rodeado de agua por tres lados (pág. 142)

permafrost permanently frozen layers of soil (p. 61)
    permafrost capas de tierra congeladas permanentemente (pág. 61)

physical geography the study of the world's physical features—its landforms, bodies of water, climates, soils, and plants (p. 16)
    geografía física estudio de las características físicas de la Tierra: sus accidentes geográficos, sus masas de agua, sus climas, sus suelos y sus plantas (pág. 16)

pioneer an early settler; in the United States, people who settled the interior and western areas of the country were known as pioneers (p. 258)
    pionero poblador; en Estados Unidos, las personas que se establecieron en el interior y el oeste del país se llamaron pioneros (pág. 258)

plantation a large farm that grows mainly one crop (p. 257)
    plantación granja muy grande en la que se produce principalmente un solo tipo de cultivo (pág. 257)

plate tectonics a theory suggesting that Earth's surface is divided into a dozen or so slow-moving plates, or pieces of Earth's crust (p. 36)
    tectónica de placas teoría que sugiere que la superficie terrestre está dividida en unas doce placas, o fragmentos de corteza terrestre, que se mueven lentamente (pág. 36)

pope the spiritual head of the Roman Catholic Church (pp. 329, 412)
    papa jefe espiritual de la Iglesia Católica Romana (págs. 329, 412)

popular culture culture traits that are well known and widely accepted (p. 98)
    cultura popular rasgos culturales conocidos y de gran aceptación (pág. 98)

population the total number of people in a given area (p. 86)
    población número total de personas en una zona determinada (pág. 86)

population density a measure of the number of people living in an area (p. 86)
    densidad de población medida del número de personas que viven en una zona (pág. 86)

precipitation water that falls to Earth's surface as rain, snow, sleet, or hail (p. 31)
    precipitación agua que cae a la superficie de la Tierra en forma de lluvia, nieve, aguanieve o granizo (pág. 31)

prevailing winds winds that blow in the same direction over large areas of Earth (p. 51)
    vientos preponderantes vientos que soplan en la misma dirección sobre grandes zonas de la Tierra (pág. 51)

Protestant a Christian who protested against the Catholic Church (p. 349)
    protestante cristiano que protestaba en contra de la Iglesia católica (pág. 349)

province an administrative division of a country (p. 282)
    provincia división administrativa de un país (pág. 282)

pulp softened wood fibers; used to make paper (p. 279)
    pulpa fibras ablandadas de madera; usadas para hacer papel (pág. 279)

Quechua (ke-chuh-wuh) the official Inca language (p. 130)
    quechua idioma oficial de los incas (pág. 130)

referendum a recall vote (p. 198)
    referéndum voto para quitar a alguien de su cargo (pág. 198)

reforestation planting trees to replace lost forestland (p. 69)
    reforestación siembra de árboles para reemplazar los bosques que han desaparecido (pág. 69)

Reformation (re-fuhr-MAY-shuhn) a reform movement against the Roman Catholic Church that began in 1517; it resulted in the creation of Protestant churches (p. 348)
    Reforma movimiento de reforma contra la Iglesia Católica Romana que comenzó en 1517; resultó en la creación de las iglesias protestantes (pág. 348)

refugee someone who flees to another country, usually for political or economic reasons (p. 177)
    refugiado persona que escapa a otro país, generalmente por razones económicas o políticas (pág. 177)

region a part of the world that has one or more common features that distinguish it from surrounding areas (p. 6)
    región parte del mundo que tiene una o más características comunes que la distinguen de las áreas que la rodean (pág. 6)

regionalism the strong connection that people feel toward the region in which they live (p. 287)
    regionalismo gran conexión que las personas sienten con la región en la que viven (pág. 287)

Reign of Terror a bloody period of the French Revolution during which the government executed thousands of its opponents and others at the guillotine (p. 362)
    Reino del Terror período sangriento de la Revolución Francesa durante el cual el gobierno ejecutó a miles de personas, oponentes y otros, en la guillotina (pág. 362)

relative location a general description of where a place is located; a place's relative location is often expressed in relation to something else (p. 12)
    ubicación relativa descripción general de la posición de un lugar; la ubicación relativa de un lugar suele expresarse en relación con otra cosa (pág. 12)

Renaissance (REN-uh-sahns) the period of "rebirth" and creativity that followed Europe's Middle Ages (p. 344)
Renacimiento período de "volver a nacer" y creatividad que siguió a la Edad Media en Europa (pág. 344)

renewable resource a resource that Earth replaces naturally, such as water, soil, trees, plants, and animals (p. 69)
recurso renovable recurso que la Tierra reemplaza por procesos naturales, como el agua, el suelo, los árboles, las plantas y los animales (pág. 69)

republic a political system in which people elect leaders to govern them (p. 319)
república sistema politico en el que el pueblo elige a los líderes que lo gobernarán (pág. 319)

revolution the 365 ¼ day trip Earth takes around the sun each year (p. 27)
revolución viaje de 365 ¼ días que la Tierra hace alrededor del Sol cada año (pág. 27)

rotation one complete spin of Earth on its axis; each rotation takes about 24 hours (p. 26)
rotación giro completo de la Tierra sobre su propio eje; cada rotación toma 24 horas (pág. 26)

savanna an area of tall grasses and scattered trees and shrubs (p. 58)
sabana zona de pastos altos con arbustos y árboles dispersos (pág. 58)

Scientific Revolution a series of events that led to the birth of modern science; it lasted from about 1540 to 1700 (p. 351)
Revolución Científica serie de sucesos que produjeron el nacimiento de la ciencia moderna; duró desde alrededor de 1540 hasta 1700 (pág. 351)

Senate a council of rich and powerful Romans who helped run the city (p. 319)
Senado consejo de romanos ricos y poderosos que ayudaban a dirigir la ciudad (pág. 319)

slash-and-burn agriculture the practice of burning forest in order to clear land for planting (p. 153)
agricultura de tala y quema práctica de quemar los bosques para despejar el terreno y sembrar en él (pág. 153)

smelters factories that process metal ores (p. 505)
fundiciones fábricas que tratan menas de metal (pág. 505)

smog a mixture of smoke, chemicals, and fog (p. 154)
smog mezcla de humo, sustancias químicas y niebla (pág. 154)

social science a field that focuses on people and the relationships among them (p. 5)
ciencias sociales campo de estudio que se enfoca en las personas y en las relaciones entre ellas (pág. 5)

soil exhaustion the process of soil becoming infertile because it has lost nutrients needed by plants (p. 209)
agotamiento del suelo proceso por el cual el suelo se vuelve estéril porque ha perdido los nutrientes que necesitan las plantas (pág. 209)

solar energy energy from the sun (p. 26)
energía solar energía del Sol (pág. 26)

steppe a semidry grassland or prairie; steppes often border deserts (p. 59)
estepa pradera semiárida; las estepas suelen encontrarse en el límite de los desiertos (pág. 59)

strait a narrow passageway that connects two large bodies of water (p. 229)
estrecho paso angosto que une dos grandes masas de agua (pág. 229)

strike a work stoppage by a group of workers until their demands are met (p. 198)
huelga interrupción del trabajo por parte de un grupo de trabajadores hasta que se cumplan sus demandas (pág. 198)

suffragettes women who campaigned to gain the right to vote (p. 370)
sufragistas mujeres que hicieron campaña para obtener el derecho a votar (pág. 370)

superpower a strong and influential country (p. 388)
superpotencia país poderoso e influyente (pág. 388)

surface water water that is found in Earth's streams, rivers, and lakes (p. 31)
agua superficial agua que se encuentra en los arroyos, ríos y lagos de la Tierra (pág. 31)

taiga (TY-guh) a forest of mainly evergreen trees covering much of Russia (p. 495)
taiga bosque de árboles de hoja perenne principalmente que cubre gran parte de Rusia (pág. 495)

terrorism violent attacks that cause fear (p. 270)
terrorismo ataques violentos que provocan miedo (pág. 270)

textile a cloth product (p. 368)
textil producto de tela (pág. 368)

Trans-Siberian Railroad a rail line in Russia that extends about 5,800 miles (9,330 km) from Moscow to Vladivostok; it is the longest single rail line in the world (p. 505)
Ferrocarril Transiberiano línea de ferrocarril rusa de 5,800 millas (9,330 km) de largo, desde Moscú hasta Vladivostok; es la vía de ferrocarril más larga del mundo (pág. 505)

Treaty of Versailles the final peace settlement of World War I (p. 379)
Tratado de Versalles acuerdo de paz final de la Primera Guerra Mundial (pág. 379)

trench warfare a style of fighting common in World War I in which each side fights from deep ditches, or trenches, dug into the ground (p. 378)
guerra de trincheras forma de guerra comúnmente usada en la Primera Guerra Mundial, en la cual ambos bandos luchan desde profundas zanjas, o trincheras, cavadas en el suelo (pág. 378)

tributary a smaller stream or river that flows into a larger stream or river (p. 249)
tributario río o corriente más pequeña que fluye hacia un río o una corriente más grande (pág. 249)

tropics regions close to the equator (p. 29)
trópicos regiones cercanas al ecuador (pág. 29)

uninhabitable unable to support human settlement (p. 461)
inhabitable que no puede sustentar asentamientos humanos (pág. 461)

United Nations an organization of countries that promotes peace and security around the world (p. 99)
Naciones Unidas organización de países que promueve la paz y la seguridad en todo el mundo (pág. 99)

viceroy governor (p. 235)
virrey gobernador (pág. 235)

Vikings Scandinavian warriors who raided Europe in the early Middle Ages (p. 458)
vikingos guerreros escandinavos que atacaron Europa al principio de la Edad Media (pág. 458)

water cycle the movement of water from Earth's surface to the atmosphere and back (p. 33)
ciclo del agua circulación del agua desde la superficie de la Tierra hacia la atmósfera y de regreso a la Tierra (pág. 33)

water vapor water occurring in the air as an invisible gas (p. 32)
vapor de agua agua que se encuentra en el aire en estado gaseoso e invisible (pág. 32)

weather the short-term changes in the air for a given place and time (p. 50)
tiempo cambios a corto plazo en la atmósfera en un momento y lugar determinados (pág. 50)

weathering the process by which rock is broken down into smaller pieces (p. 39)
meteorización proceso de desintegración de las rocas en pedazos pequeños (pág. 39)

ENGLISH AND SPANISH GLOSSARY

Index

INDEX

INDEX

H

I

INDEX

INDEX

INDEX

Credits and Acknowledgments

For permission to reproduce copyrighted material, grateful acknowledgment is made to the following sources:

National Geographic Society: From *Geography for Life: National Geography Standards 1994.* Copyright © 1994 by National Geographic Research & Exploration. All rights reserved.

G. P. Putnam's Sons, a division of Penguin Group (USA) Inc.: From *Time Enough for Love, the Lives of Lazarus Long* by Robert Heinlein. Copyright © 1973 by Robert Heinlein. All rights reserved.

Random House Children's Books, a division of Random House, Inc.: From *The River* by Gary Paulsen. Copyright © 1991 by Gary Paulsen.

United Nations: From the *Preamble to the Charter of the United Nations.* Copyright © 1945 by United Nations.

Atheneum Books for Young Readers, an imprint of Simon & Schuster Children's Publishing Division: From *Bearstone* by Will Hobbs. Copyright ©1989 by Will Hobbs. All rights reserved.

Doubleday, a division of Random House, Inc.: From *The Diary of a Young Girl, The Definitive Edition* by Anne Frank, edited by Otto H. Frank and Mirjam Pressler, translated by Susan Massotty. Copyright © 1995 by Doubleday, a division of Random House, Inc.

HarperCollins Publishers: The Endless Steppe by Esther Hautzig. Copyright © 1968 by Esther Hautzig.

Lonely Planet: From "Hungary" from the *Lonely Planet WorldGuide Online* Web site. Copyright © 2005 by Lonely Planet. Accessed at http://www. lonelyplanet.com/worldguide/ destinations/europe/hungary/.

Estate of Erich Maria Remarque: From *All Quiet on the Western Front* by Erich Maria Remarque. Copyright 1929, 1930 by Little, Brown and Company; copyright renewed © 1957, 1958 by Erich Maria Remarque. All rights reserved. "Im Westen Nichts Neues" copyright 1928 by Ullstein A. G.; copyright renewed © 1956 by Erich Maria Remarque.

Sources used by The World Almanac® for charts and graphs:

Eruptions in the Ring of Fire: *The World Almanac and Book of Facts, 2005*; World Energy Production: Energy Information Administration of the U.S. Department of Energy; A Developed and a Developing Country: *The World Factbook, 2005*; U.S. Census Bureau; World Health Organization; Geographical Extremes: The Americas: *The World Almanac and Book of Facts, 2005*; *The World Factbook, 2005*; U.S.

Bureau of the Census; The Americas: *The World Factbook, 2005*; U.S. Bureau of the Census, International Database; United Nations Statistical Yearbook; World's Largest Cities: United Nations Population Division National Censuses; Urban Populations in the Americas: United Nations Population Division; Major Food Exports of the Americas: Food and Agriculture Organization of the United Nations; Languages of the Caribbean: Joshua Project; World's Top Oil Exporters: Energy Information Administration of the U.S. Department of Energy; Argentina's Largest Cities: National Institute of Statistics and Censuses, Argentina, 2001 Census; Languages in Pacific South America: Ethnologue: Languages of the World, 15th Edition; Population of Major U.S. Cities: U.S. Census Bureau; Canadian Ethnic Groups: The World Factbook, 2005; Geographical Extremes: Europe and Russia: *The World Almanac and Book of Facts, 2005*; *The World Factbook, 2005*; U.S. Bureau of the Census; Europe and Russia: *The World Factbook, 2005*; U.S. Bureau of the Census, International Database; United Nations Statistical Yearbook; World's Highest Per Capita GDPs: *The World Factbook, 2005*; Densely Populated Countries in Europe: *The World Factbook, 2005*; U.S. Bureau of the Census, International Database; The European Union: European Union, International Programs Center; U.S. Bureau of the Census, International Database; Per Capita GDP of Greece: *The World Factbook, 2005*; Scandinavia's Per Capita GDP: *The World Factbook, 2005*; U.S. Bureau of the Census, International Database; United Nations Statistical Yearbook; Major Religions in the Balkans: World Christian Database; Russia's Population Decline, 1980–2010: U.S. Census Bureau, International Programs Center; State Statistical Committee of Russia

Illustrations and Photo Credits

Cover: (bl), Royalty-free/Corbis; (br), Mark Segal/Getty Images

Front Matter: ii, Victoria Smith/HMH Photo; iv (bl), Anthony Cassidy/Getty Images; v (br), Martin Harvey/Corbis; v (t), Age Fotostock/SuperStock; vi (t), Getty Images; viii (t), Macduff Everton/CORBIS; ix (tr), George Hunter/Pictures Colour Library Ltd.; x (br), Ron Watts/CORBIS; x (bl), Tom Grill/Photographer's Choice/Getty Images; xi, Dave Reede/First Light/Getty Images; xii (b), Christopher Groenhout/Lonely Planet Images; xiii (b), Bettmann/Corbis; xiii (tr), The Granger Collection, New York; xiv (b), Chad Ehlers/Alamy; xv (cr), Hans Strand/Corbis; xv (t), Hans Strand/Corbis; xvi (b), AP Photo/Amel Emric; xvii (br), Kurt Scholz/SuperStock; xvii (t), Michael Yamashita/Corbis; xix NASA/Photo Researchers, Inc.; xx, Renzo Gostoli/AP/Wide World Photos; xxiv

(bl), Carl & Ann Purcell/Corbis; xxiv (br), Glen Allison/Stone/Getty Images; H12 (t), Earth Satellite Corporation/Photo Researchers, Inc.; H12 (tc), Frans Lemmens/Getty Images; H12 (c), London Aerial Photo Library/Corbis; H12 (bc), Harvey Schwartz/Index Stock Imagery/Fotosearch; H12 (b), Tom Nebbia/Corbis.

Unit 1: 1 (bc), Robert Harding/Digital Vision/Getty Images; A, Taxi/Getty Images; B (bkgd), Planetary Visions; B (cr), Frans Lemmens/Image Bank/Getty Images; B (bl), Michael Melford/Getty Images.

Chapter 1: 2 (br), M. Colonel/Photo Researchers, Inc.; 2–3 (t), Age Fotostock/SuperStock; 3 (br), Anthony Cassidy/Getty Images; 3 (bl), Digital Vision/Getty Images; 5 (b), Frans Lemmens/Getty Images; 6 (b), Kim Sayer/Corbis; 7 (br), ESA/K.Horgan/Getty Images; 7 (bl), London Aerial Photo Library/Corbis; 8 (tl), Michael Newman/PhotoEdit; 11 (br), Morton Beebe/Corbis; 11 (bc), AFP/Getty Images; 11 (tr), Miles Ertman/Masterfile; 11 (tl), David R. Frazier/Photo Researchers, Inc.; 11 (bl), Corbis; 12–13 (br), Tom Nebbia/Corbis; 15 (l), M-SAT Ltd./Science Photo Library; 15 (r), Earth Satellite Corporation/Science Photo Library; 17 (tr), Penny Tweedie/Stone/Getty Images; 17 (tl), Torleif Svensson/Corbis; 19 (b), Donna Cox and Robert Patterson/NCSA; 20 (tl), Joe Raedle/Getty Images; 21 (tr), Donna Cox and Robert Patterson/NCSA; 21 (tc), Penny Tweedie/Stone/Getty Images; 21 (tl), Frans Lemmens/Getty Images.

Chapter 2: 24 (br), Pete Saloutos/Corbis; 24–25 (t), Earth Satellite Corporation/Science Photo Library; 25 (tr), 2010 A&E Television Networks, LLC. All rights reserved; 25 (bl), George H.H. Huey/Corbis; 25 (br), Royalty-Free/Corbis; 29 (tr), Paul A. Souders/Corbis; 30–31 (b), Doug Wilson/Corbis; 31 (br), Terje Rakke/The Image Bank/Getty Images; 34 (tr), Alan Sirulnikoff/Photo Researchers, Inc.; 34 (tl), Rick Doyle/Corbis; 37 (bl), Bettmann/Corbis; 38 (cr), Yann Arthus-Bertrand/Corbis; 38 (br), Roger Cracknell 01/classic/Alamy; 39 (br), Age Fotostock/SuperStock; 40 (bl), Owaki-Kulla/Corbis; 41 (t), Age Fotostock/SuperStock; 43 (tr), Gary Braasch/Corbis; 43 (tl), David Weintraub/Photo Researchers, Inc.; 45 (tr), Galen Rowell/Corbis; 45 (tc), Rick Doyle/Corbis; 45 (tl), W.H. Mueller/Zefa Images/Corbis; 45 (tr), Roger Cracknell 01/classic/Alamy.

Chapter 3: 48 (br), Kate Thompson/National Geographic/Getty Images; 48–49 (t), Warren Faidley/WeatherStock; 49 (tr), 2010 A&E Television Networks, LLC. All rights reserved; 49 (br), Bill Ross/Corbis; 49 (bl), L. Clarke/Corbis; 53 (br), Eric Meola/Getty Images; 53 (tr), William Thomas Cain/Getty Images; 56 (tl), Age FotoStock/SuperStock; 57 (cr),

Staff Credits

The people who contributed to *Holt McDougal Social Studies: Western World* are listed below. They represent editorial, design, production, emedia, and permissions.

Melanie Baccus, Angela Beckmann, Julie Beckman-Key, Genick Blaise, Ed Blake, Jennifer Campbell, Henry Clark, Grant Davidson, Nina Degollado, Rose Degollado, Christine Devall, Michelle Dike, Lydia Doty, Chase Edmond, Mescal Evler, Susan Franques, Stephanie Friedman, Bob Fullilove, Matthew Gierhart, Bill Gillis, Ann Gorbett, Janet Harrington, Betsy Harris, Wendy Hodge, Tim Hovde, Cathy Jenevein, Carrie Jones, Kadonna Knape, Laura Lasley, Sarah Lee, Sean McCormick, Joe Melomo, Richard Metzger, Andrew Miles, Debra O'Shields, Jarred Prejean, Paul Provence, Shelly Ramos, Curtis Riker, Michael Rinella, Michelle Rimsa, Jennifer Rockwood, Carole Rollins, Beth Sample, Annette Saunders, Jenny Schaeffer, Kay Selke, Chris Smith, Jeremy Strykul, Jeannie Taylor, Terri Taylor, Joni Wackwitz, Mary Wages, Diana Holman Walker, Nadyne Wood, Robin Zaback